Street by Street

GW00360765

Enlarged areas ASHFORD, CANTERBURY, CHATHAM, DOVER, FOLKESTONE, GILLINGHAM, MAIDSTONE, MARGATE, RAMSGATE, ROCHESTER, ROYAL TUNBRIDGE WELLS, SEVENOAKS

Plus Broadstairs, Bromley, Dartford, East Grinstead, Gravesend, Herne Bay, Orpington, Tilbury, Tonbridge, Whitstable, Woolwich

2nd edition May 2005
© Automobile Association Developments Limited 2005

Original edition printed May 2001

Ordnance Survey® This product includes map data licensed from Ordnance Survey® with the permission of the Controller of Her Majesty's Stationery Office. © Crown copyright 2005. All rights reserved. Licence number 399221.

Published by AA Publishing (a trading name of Automobile Association Developments Limited, whose registered office is Southwood East, Apollo Rise, Farnborough, Hampshire, GU14 0JW. Registered number 1878835).

Mapping produced by the Cartography Department of The Automobile Association. (A02421)

A CIP Catalogue record for this book is available from the British Library.

Printed by Oriental Press in Dubai

Ref: ML103z

Key to map pages	ii–iii
Key to map symbols	iv–1
Enlarged map pages	2-23
Main map pages	24-347
Index – towns & villages	348-350
Index – streets	351-410
Index – featured places	411-422
Acknowledgements	422

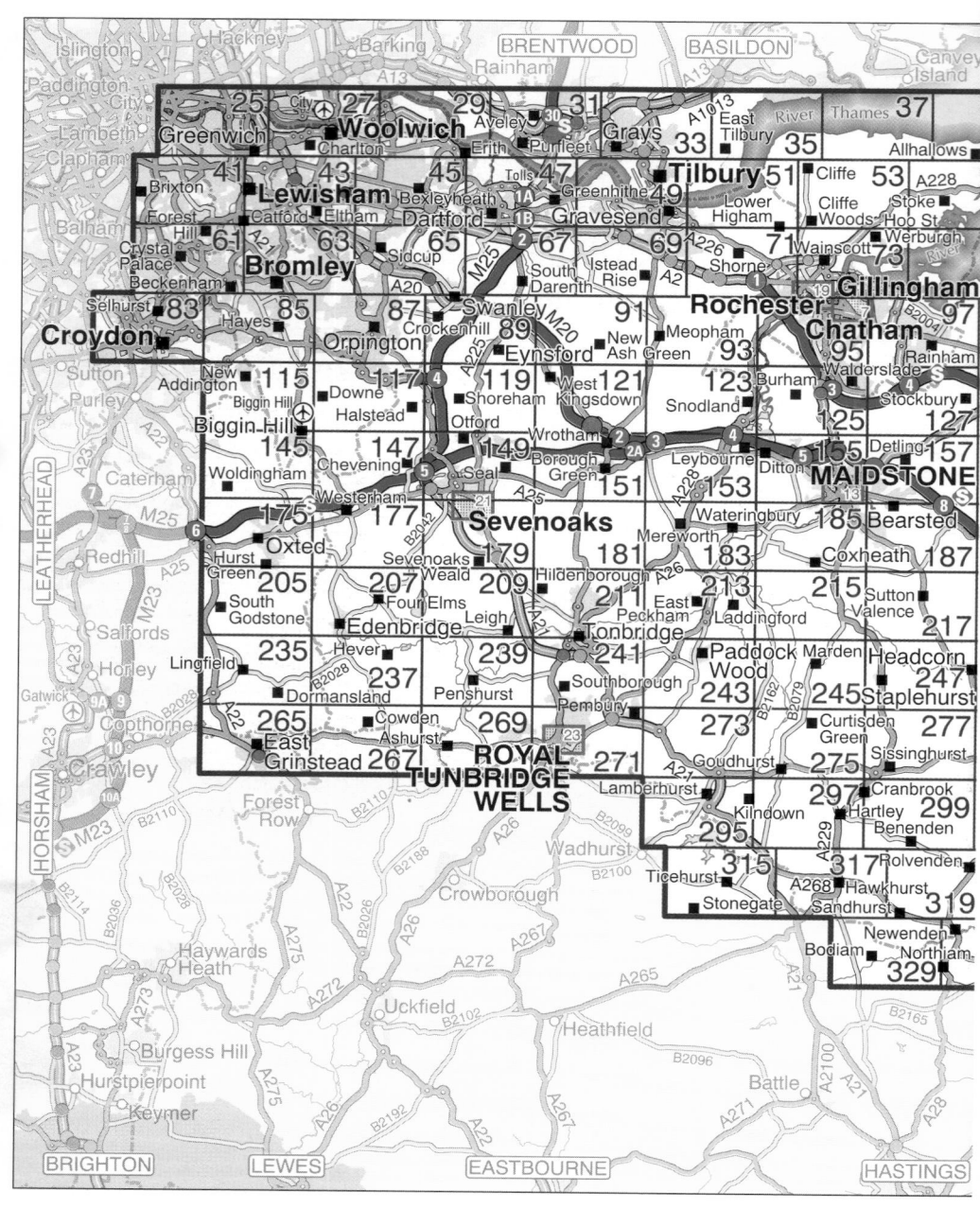

Scale of enlarged map pages 1:10,000 6.3 inches to 1 mile

0	1/4	1/2
	miles	
0	1/4	1/2
	kilometres	3/4

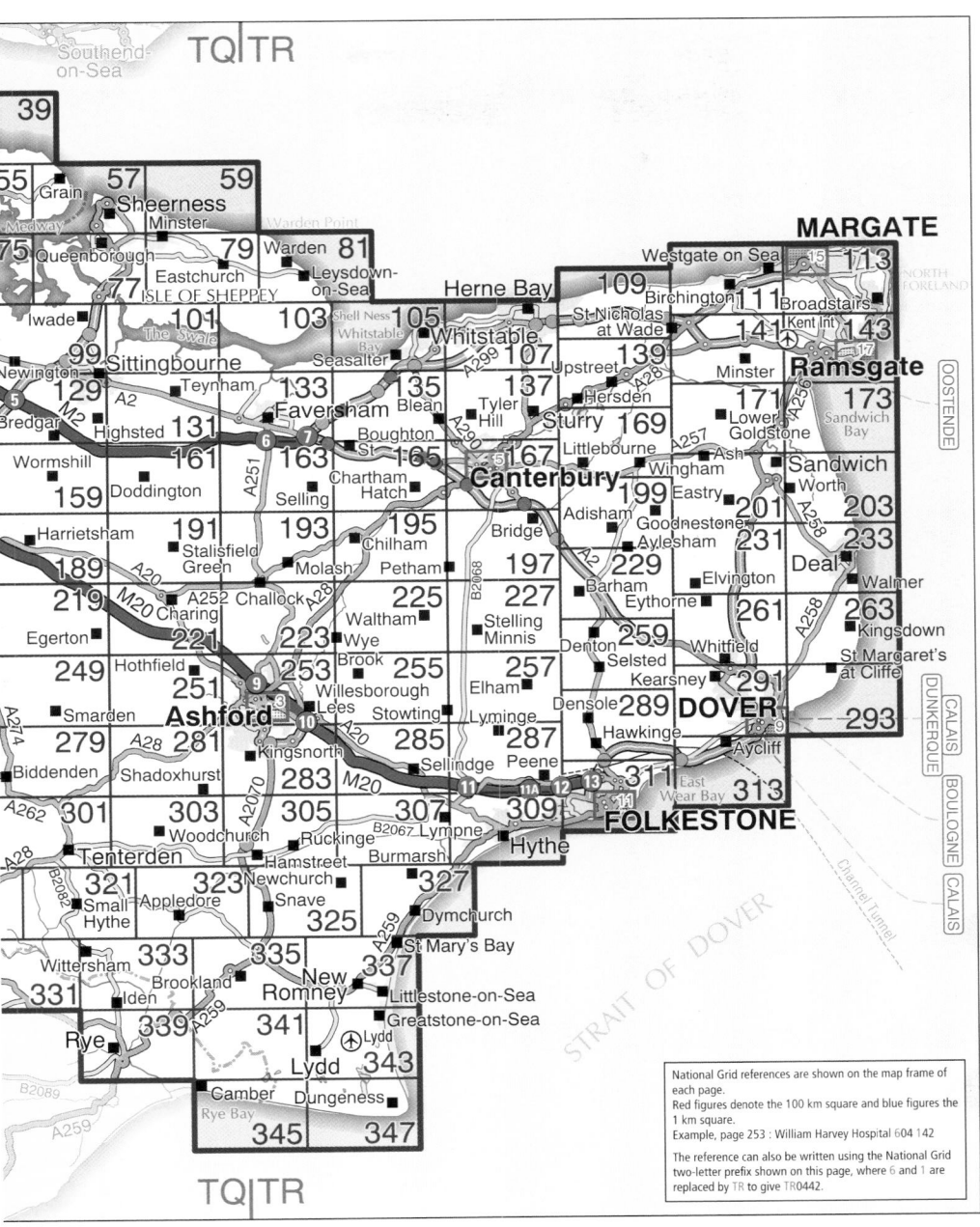

TQ|TR

Southend-on-Sea

39

55 Grain
57 Sheerness
59
Medway
Warden Point
Minster

75 Queenborough
79 Warden
81 Leysdown-on-Sea
77 Eastchurch ISLE OF SHEPPEY

Iwade
101 103 105 Herne Bay
The Swale
Shell Ness Whitstable Bay Whitstable
Seasalter
107

99 Sittingbourne
Newington
129 Teynham
133 135 137
Faversham Blean Tyler Hill
Bredgar
Highsted 131 163 165 167
A2
A251
Boughton St
Littlebourne

MARGATE

Westgate on Sea 115 113
NORTH FORELAND

109 Birchington 111 Broadstairs
St Nicholas at Wade 141 Kent Int 143

Upstreet 139 Minster 171 Ramsgate 173
Hersden 169 Lower Goldstone Sandwich Bay

OOSTENDE

Wormshill
161 Chartham Hatch
159 Doddington Selling

Canterbury 199 Eastry 201 203
Wingham Ash Sandwich
Adisham Goodnestone 231 Worth 233
Harrietsham 191 193 195 Bridge Aylesham Deal
Stalisfield Green Chilham 197 229 Elvington
189 Molash Petham Barham 259 261 263
219 A20 A252 Challock 225 227 Eythorne Walmer Kingsdown
M20 Charing Waltham Stelling Minnis Denton Whitfield St Margaret's at Cliffe
Egerton 221 223 Wye Selsted 291
249 Hothfield 253 255 257 Kearsney Dover 293
Smarden 251 Brook Elham Densole 289
279 281 Willesborough Lees Stowting 285 287 Hawkinge East Wear Bay
Biddenden Shadoxhurst Kingsnorth Sellindge Peene 311 313
A262 301 303 305 M20 307 309 Folkestone
A2070 Lympne
Tenterden Ruckinge Burmarsh Hythe
321 323 Hamstreet 327
Small Hythe Appledore Newchurch Snave 325 Dymchurch
333 335 337 St Mary's Bay
Wittersham Brookland New Romney Littlestone-on-Sea
331 Iden 341 Greatstone-on-Sea
Rye 339 Lydd
Lydd 343
Camber Dungeness
Rye Bay 345 347

STRAIT OF DOVER

Channel Tunnel

DUNKERQUE CALAIS
BOULOGNE CALAIS

TQ|TR

National Grid references are shown on the map frame of each page.
Red figures denote the 100 km square and blue figures the 1 km square.
Example, page 253 : William Harvey Hospital 604 142

The reference can also be written using the National Grid two-letter prefix shown on this page, where 6 and 1 are replaced by TR to give TR0442.

2.5 inches to 1 mile **Scale of main map pages** 1:25,000

0 1/2 miles 1 1 1/2
0 1/2 1 kilometres 1 1/2

2

Junction 9	Motorway & junction
Services	Motorway service area
	Primary road single/dual carriageway
Services	Primary road service area
	A road single/dual carriageway
	B road single/dual carriageway
	Other road single/dual carriageway
	Minor/private road, access may be restricted
← ←	One-way street
	Pedestrian area
=============	Track or footpath
	Road under construction
⊏ ⊐	Road tunnel
P	Parking
P+🚌	Park & Ride
🚌	Bus/coach station
	Railway & main railway station
	Railway & minor railway station

⊖	Underground station
⊖	Light railway & station
+++++++++	Preserved private railway
LC	Level crossing
•—•—•—•	Tramway
- - - - - -	Ferry route
··············	Airport runway
— · — · — · —	County, administrative boundary
▼▼▼▼▼▼▼▼	Mounds
47	Page continuation 1:25,000
3	Page continuation to enlarged scale 1:10,000
	River/canal, lake
	Aqueduct, lock, weir
465 ▲ Winter Hill	Peak (with height in metres)
	Beach
	Woodland
	Park
	Cemetery
	Built-up area

Featured building		Abbey, cathedral or priory	
City wall		Castle	
A&E	Hospital with 24-hour A&E department		Historic house or building
PO	Post Office	Wakehurst Place NT	National Trust property
	Public library	M	Museum or art gallery
i	Tourist Information Centre		Roman antiquity
i	Seasonal Tourist Information Centre		Ancient site, battlefield or monument
	Petrol station, 24-hour Major suppliers only		Industrial interest
†	Church/chapel		Garden
	Public toilets		Garden Centre Garden Centre Association Member
	Toilet with disabled facilities		Garden Centre Wyevale Garden Centre
PH	Public house AA recommended		Farm or animal centre
	Restaurant AA inspected		Zoological or wildlife collection
Madeira Hotel	Hotel AA inspected		Bird collection
	Theatre or performing arts centre		Nature reserve
	Cinema		Aquarium
	Golf course	V	Visitor or heritage centre
	Camping AA inspected		Country park
	Caravan site AA inspected		Cave
	Camping & caravan site AA inspected		Windmill
	Theme park		Distillery, brewery or vineyard

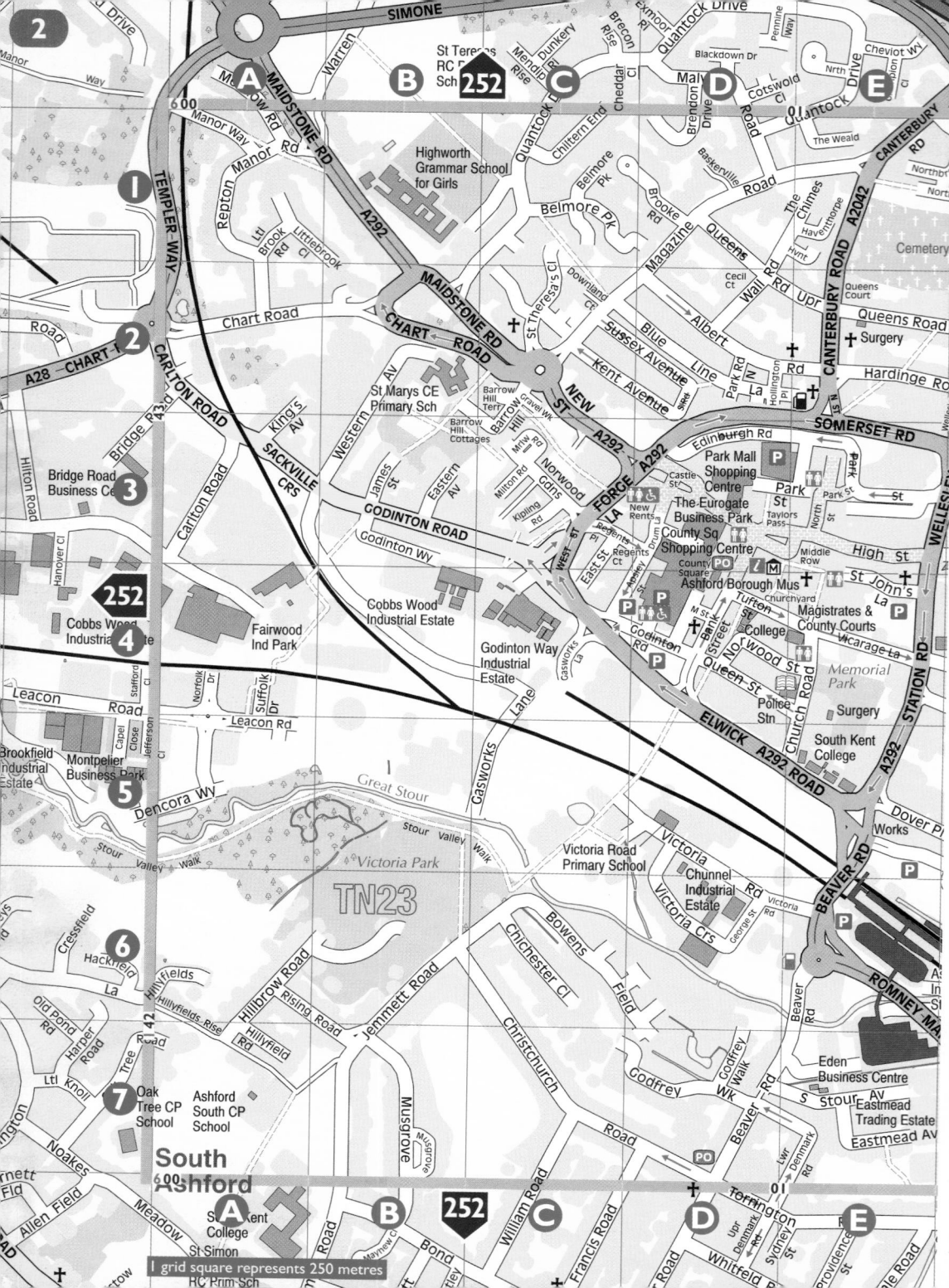

1 grid square represents 250 metres

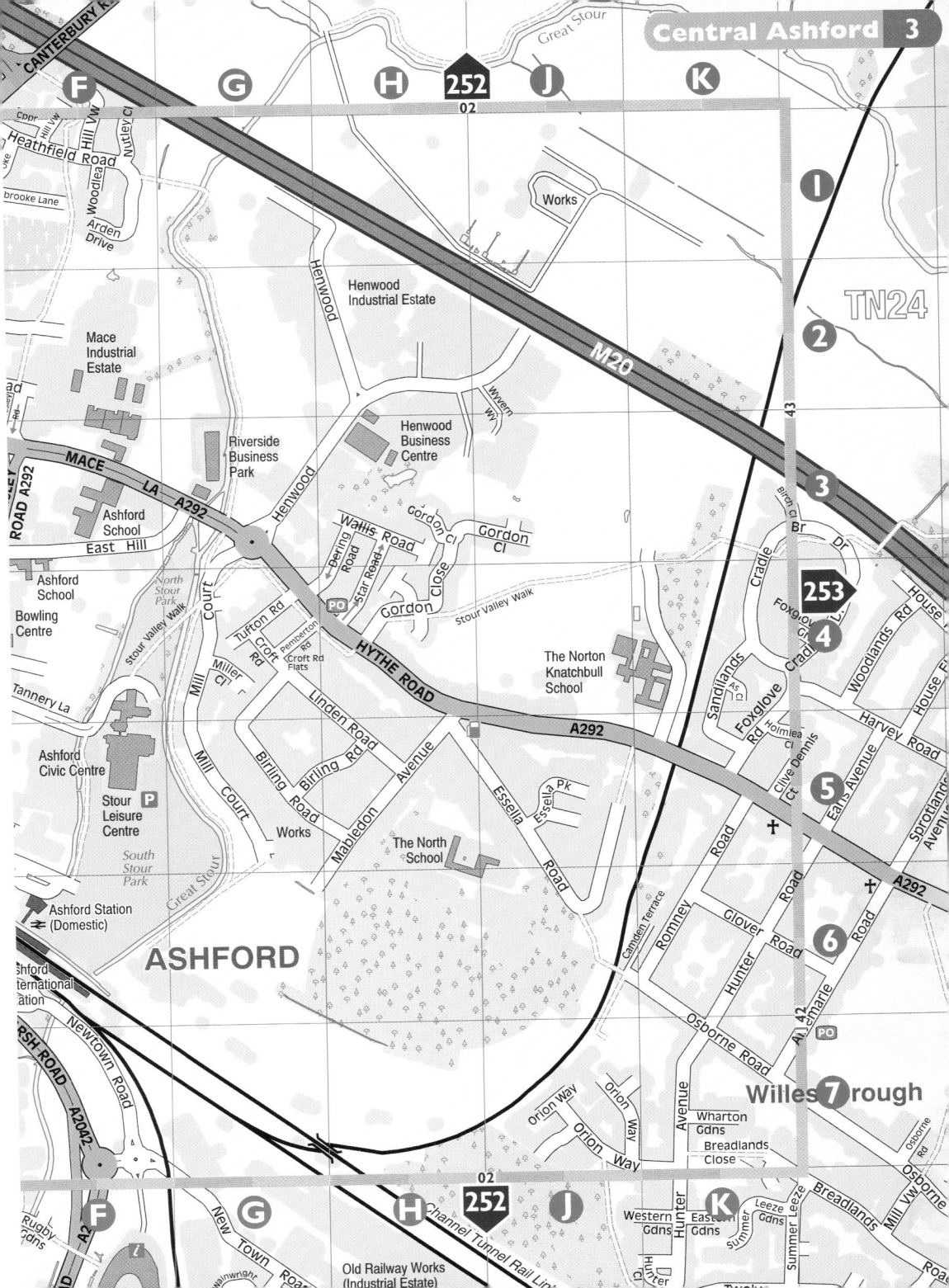

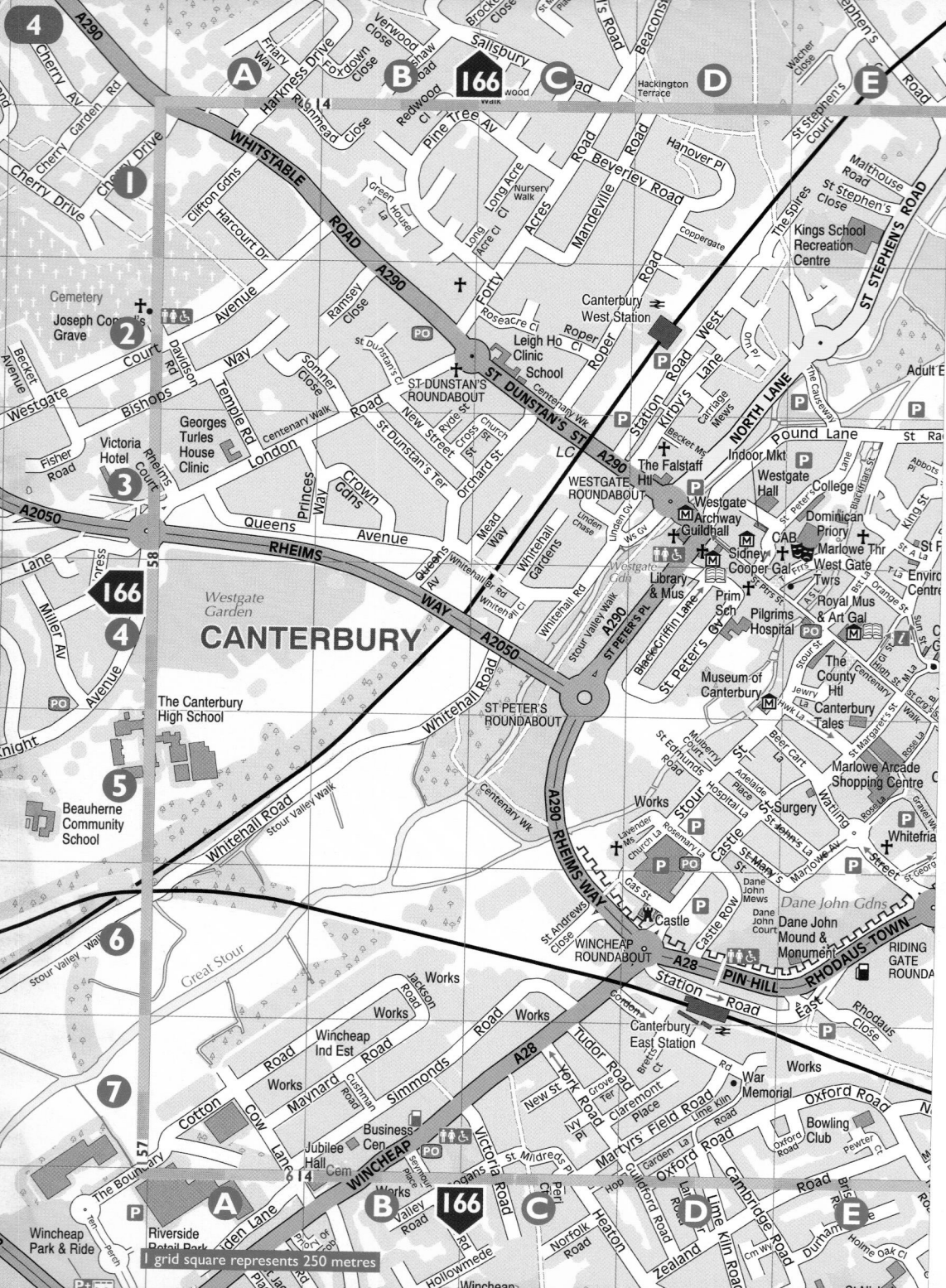

CANTERBURY

Westgate Garden

1 grid square represents 250 metres

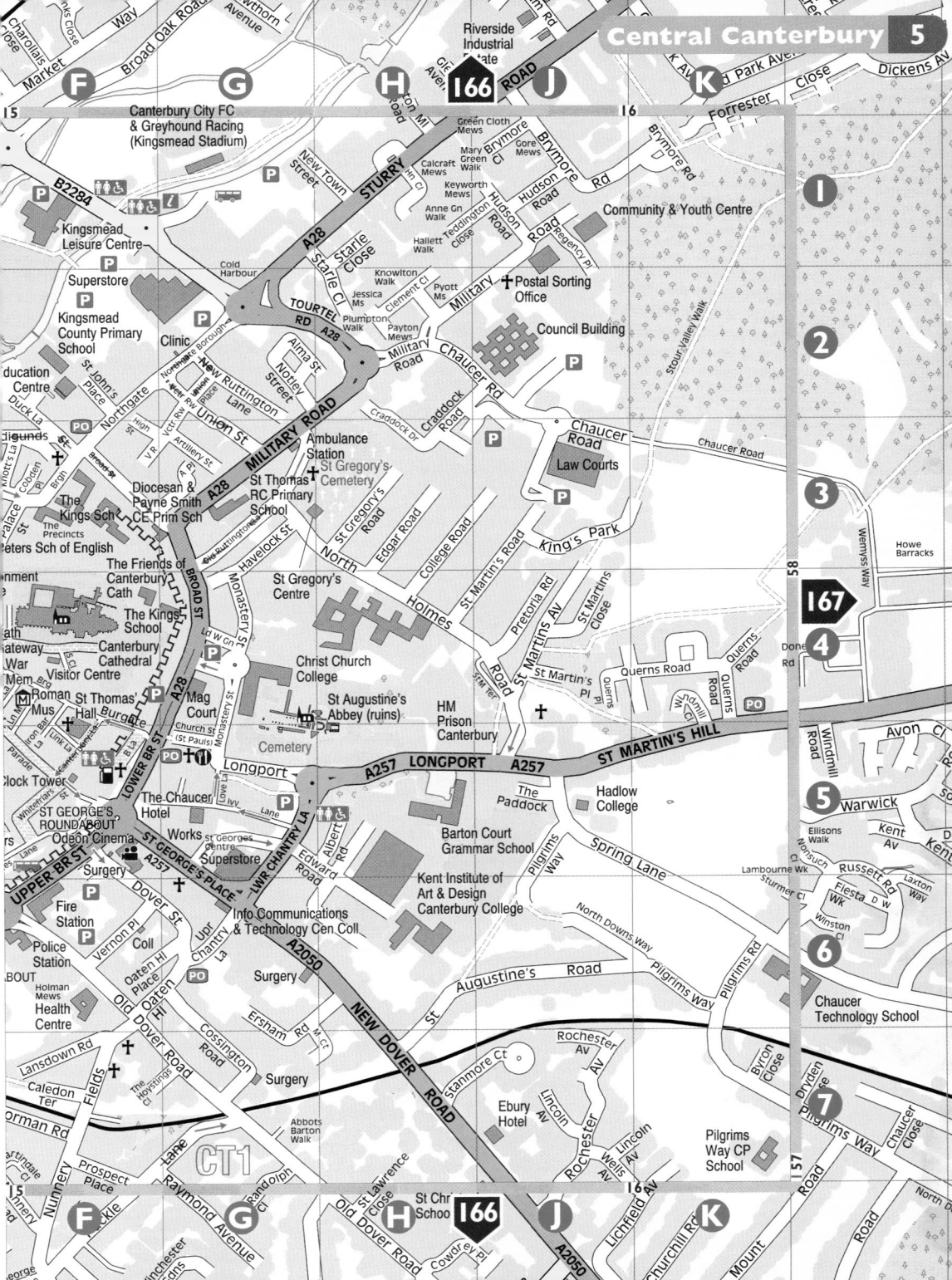

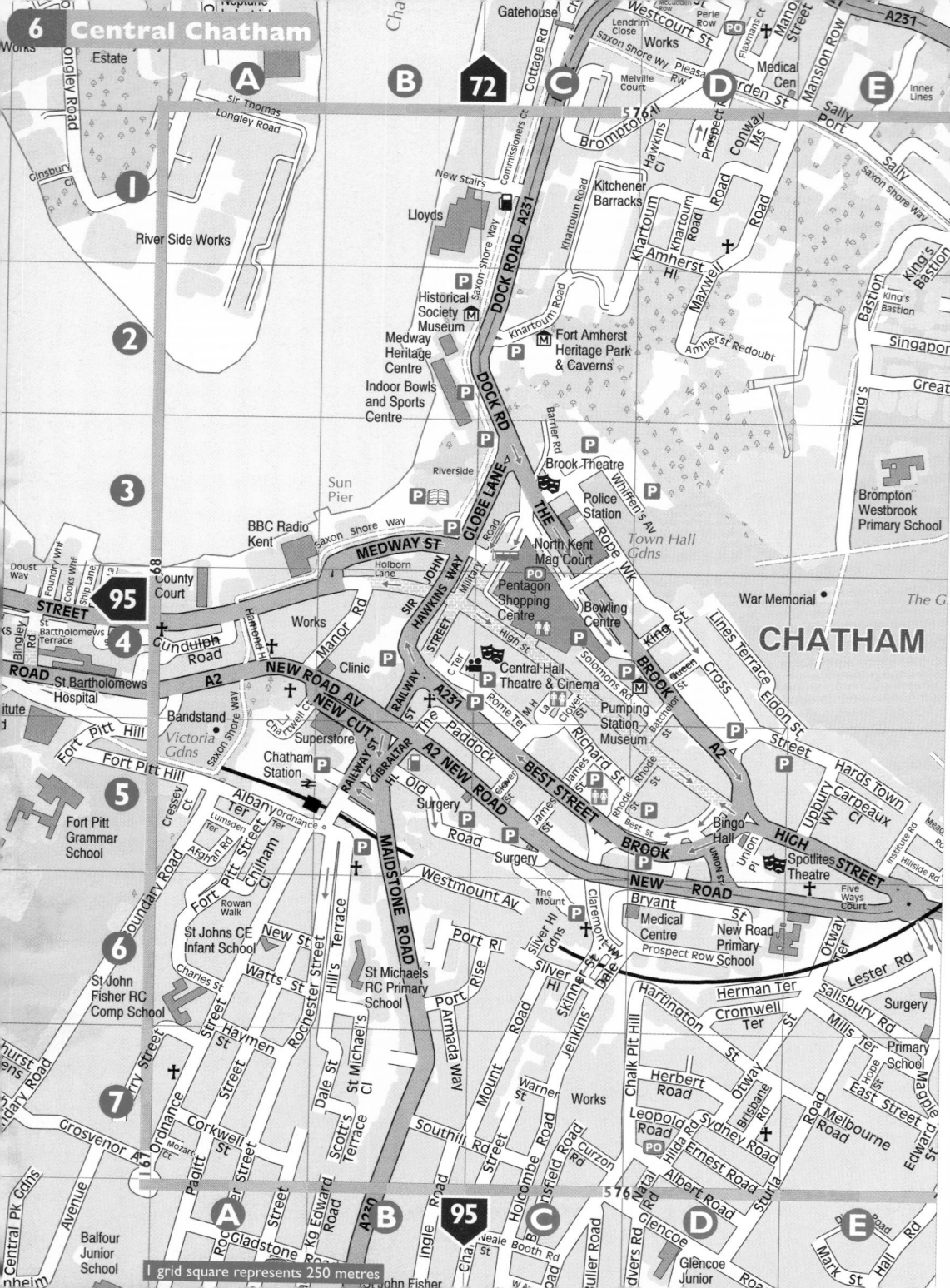

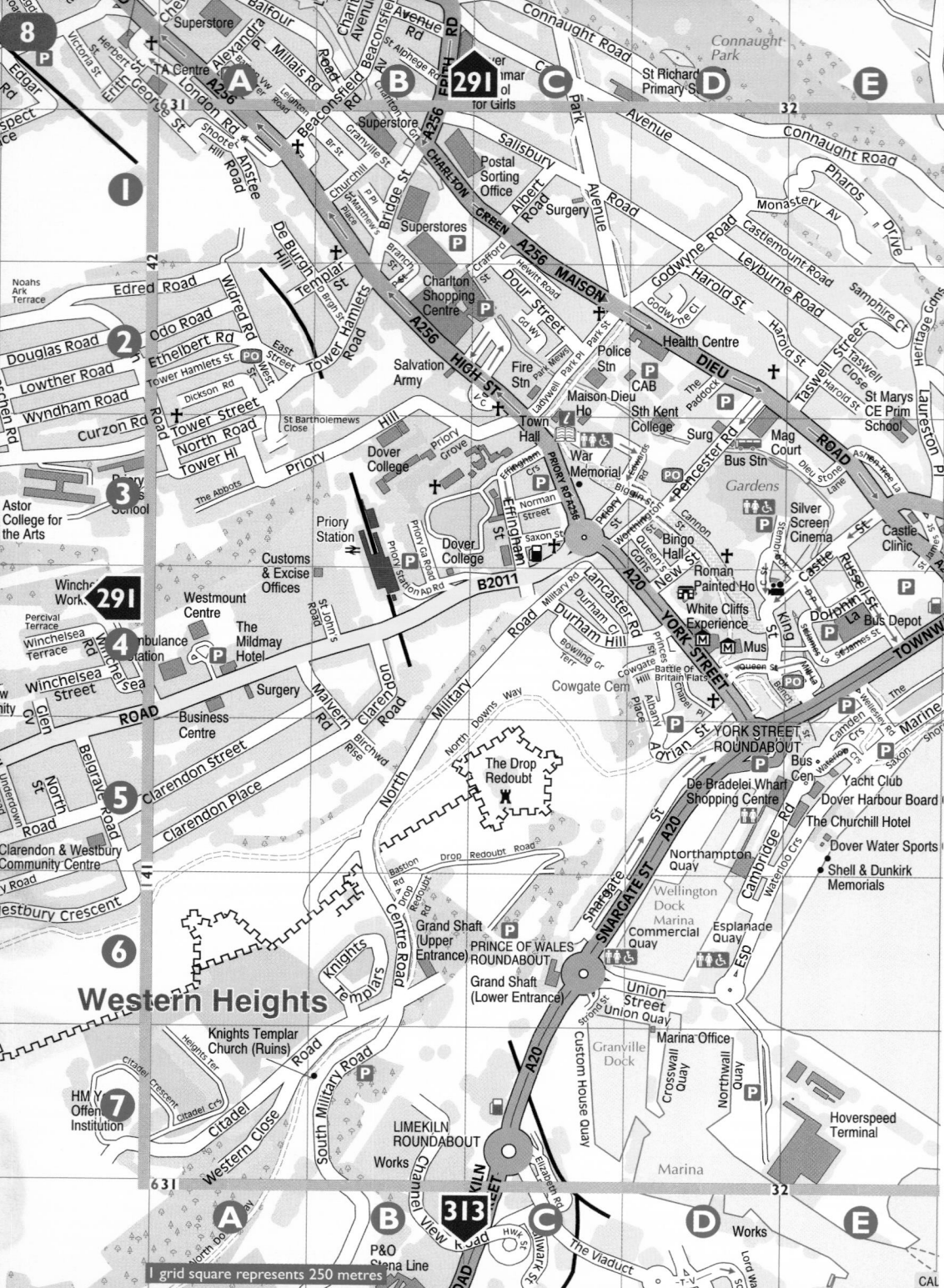

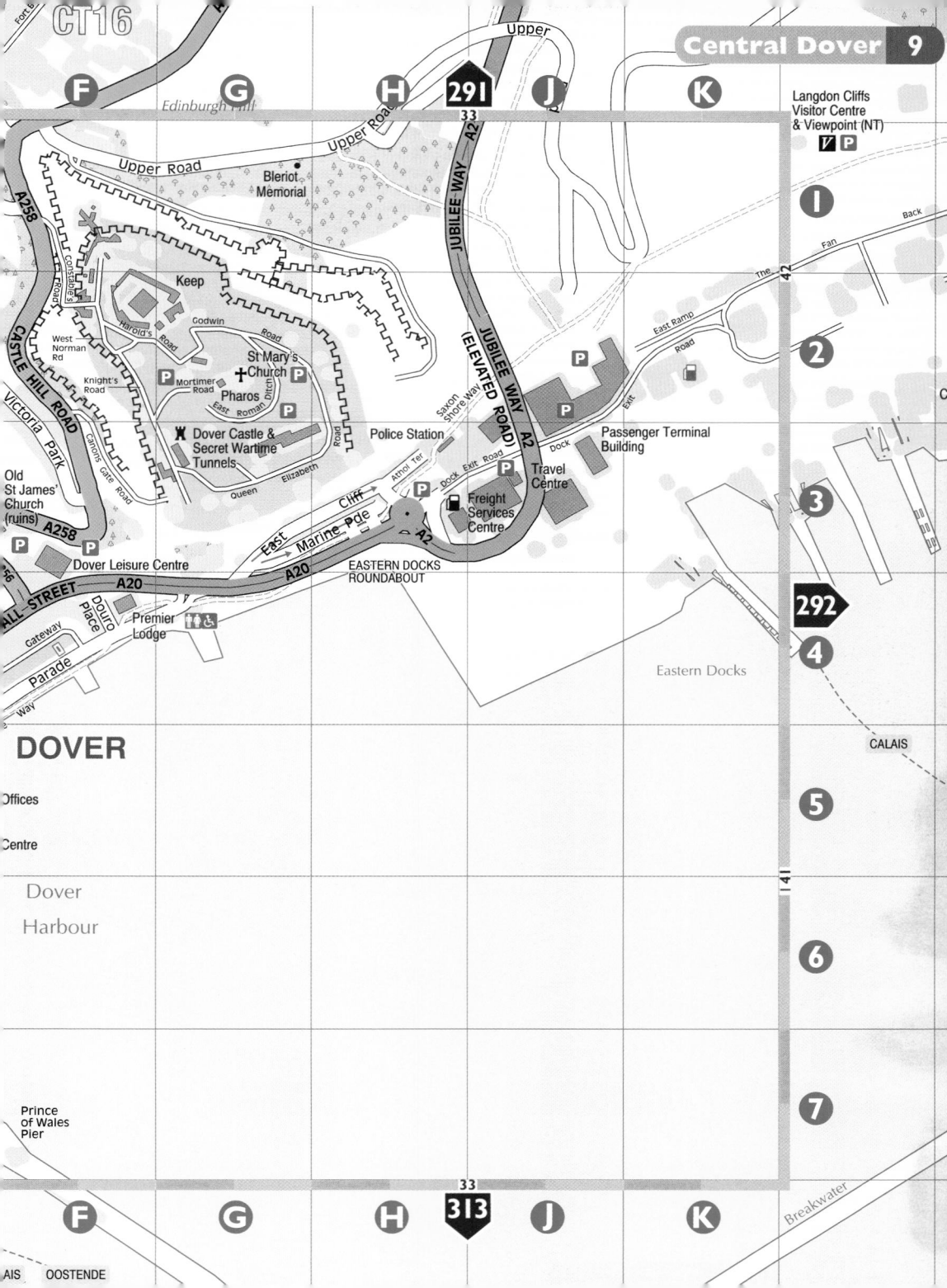

F **G** **H** 291 **J** **K**
33
Edinburgh Hill

Upper

Upper Road

Langdon Cliffs
Visitor Centre
& Viewpoint (NT)

JUBILEE WAY A2

Upper Road

Bleriot
Memorial

I

Back

A258

Fan

Keep

The

42

Constable's Road

West
Norman
Rd

Harold's Road

Godwin
Road

2

CASTLE HILL ROAD

East Ramp

Road

East
Exit

Knight's
Road

St Mary's
Church

Pharos

Mortimer
Road

Victoria Park

P

P

East Roman Ditch

Canons Gate Road

Dover Castle &
Secret Wartime
Tunnels

P

JUBILEE WAY (ELEVATED ROAD)

A2

P

P

P

Dock

Passenger Terminal
Building

3

Police Station

Saxon Shore Way

Dock

Old
St James'
Church
(ruins)

A258

Queen

Elizabeth

Road

Athol Ter

Cliff

East

Dover Leisure Centre

A20

P

Marine Pde

A20

P

P

Dock Exit Road

Travel
Centre

292

Freight
Services
Centre

EASTERN DOCKS
ROUNDABOUT

A2

4

P

P

ALL STREET

Douro
Place

Premier
Lodge

Gateway

Parade

Way

Eastern Docks

CALAIS

DOVER

Offices

5

Centre

Dover

141

Harbour

6

7

Prince
of Wales
Pier

F **G** **H** 313 **J** **K**
33
Breakwater

AIS   OOSTENDE

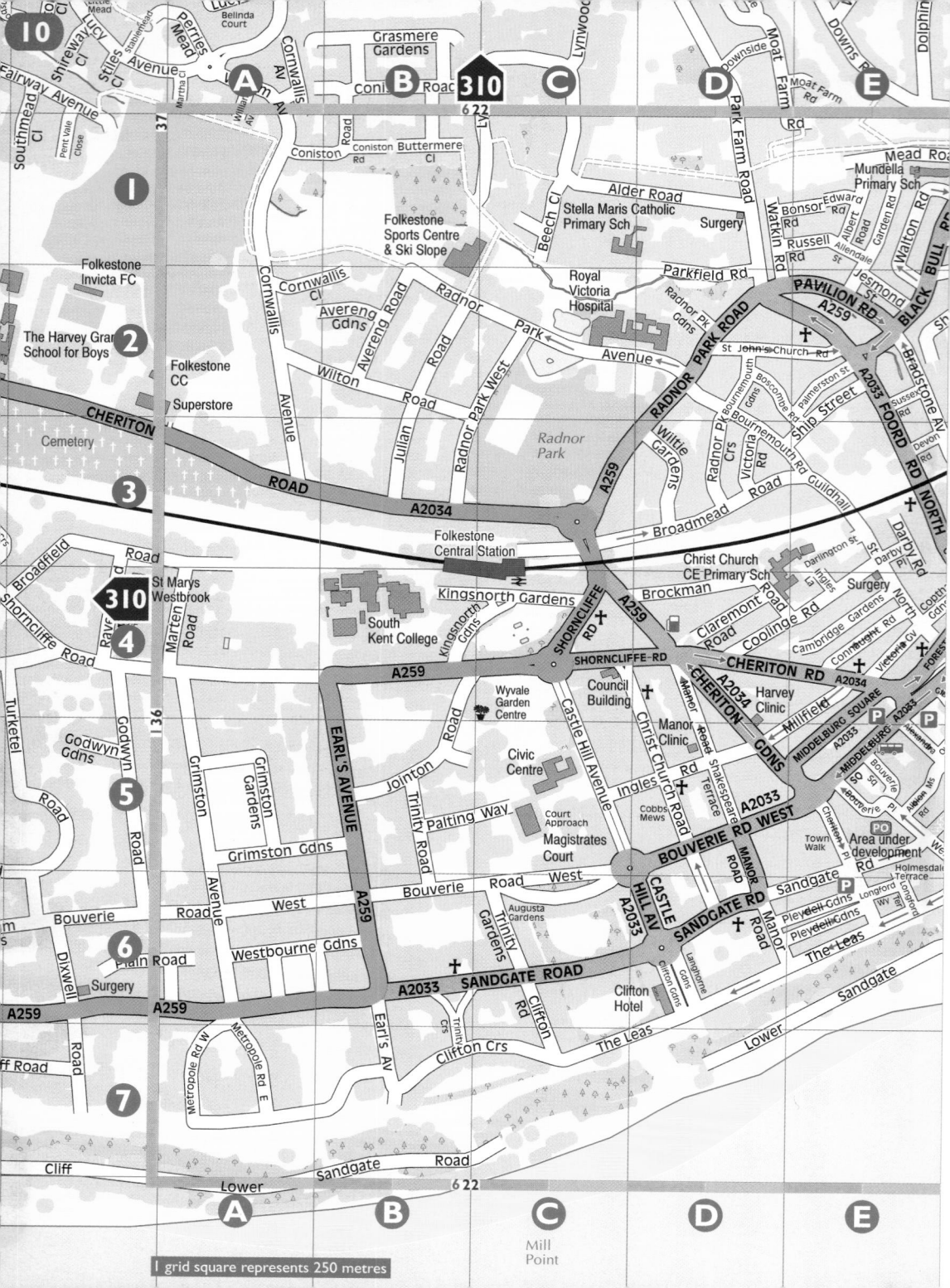

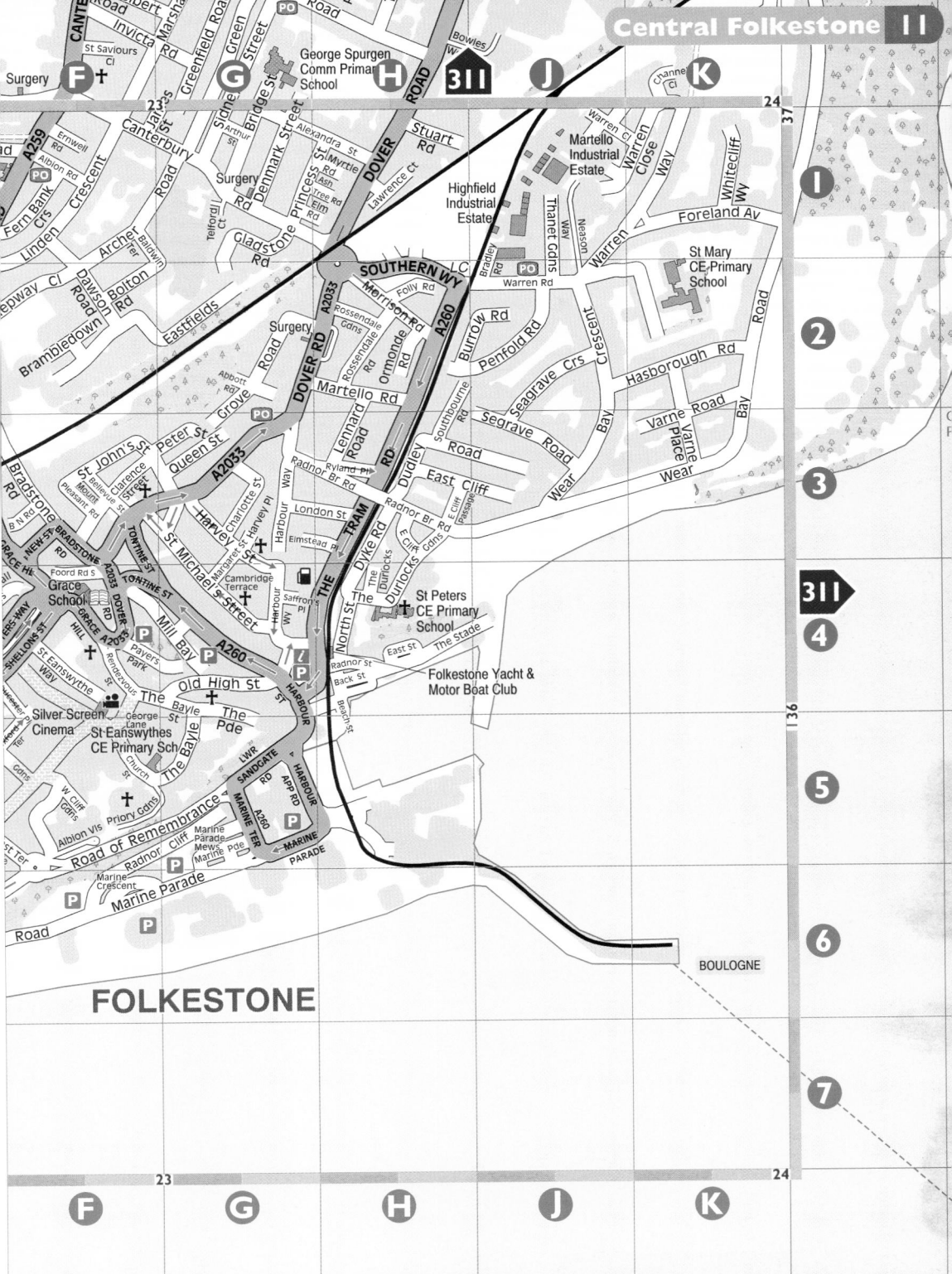

Surgery **F** +

G

George Spurgen Comm Primary School

H

311

J

K

St Saviours Cl

Invicta Rd

Telbert Road

Marshall

Greenfield Road

Green Street

Bridge Street

PO

Road

Bowles Wy

DOVER ROAD

Channel Cl

1

Ernwell Rd

A259

Albion Rd

PO

Canterbury Road

Fern Bank

Crescent

Linden

Archer Rd

Bolton Rd

Dawson Rd

Baldwin

Lane

St

Denmark Street

Sidney St

Arthur Rd

Myrtle Rd

Princes St

St Ash Tree Av

Elm Rd

Surgery

Lawrence Ct.

Alexandra St

Stuart Rd

Highfield Industrial Estate

Martello Industrial Estate

Warren Cl

Warren Close

Warren Way

Whitecliff Wy

Foreland Av

St Mary CE Primary School

2

Stepway Cl

Bramblodown

Eastfields

Gladstone Rd

Crescent

SOUTHERN WY

LC

Morrison Rd

A2033

Folly Rd

DOVER RD

A260

Rossendale Gdns

Rossendale

Ormonde Rd

Burrow Rd

Bradley Rd

Neason Way

Warren Rd

PO

Penfold Rd

Seagrave Crs

Crescent

Bay

Hasborough Rd

Bay Road

3

Abbott

Grove

PO

Martello Rd

Lennard Road

Radnor Br Rd

Ryland Pl

Southbourne Rd

Dudley Road

Segrave Road

East Cliff

Wear

Varne Road

Varne Place

Wear

311

4

Bradstone Rd

NEW ST

St John's

Peter St

Queen St

St John's

Clarence Street

Bellevue St

Mount Pleasant Rd

Harvey St

Charlotte Pl

Harvey Pl

Margaret St

London St

Radnor Br Rd

Eimstead Rd

E Cliff Passage

Cliff Gdns

Radnor Br Rd

The TRAM RD

The Durlocks

St Peters CE Primary School

The Stade

Folkestone Yacht & Motor Boat Club

5

Grace School

Foord Rd S

P

TONTINE ST

GRACE HILL

DOVER RD

A2033

TONTINE ST

Mill Bay

St Michael's Street

A260

Payers Park

P

Harbour

Saffron's Pl

Cambridge Terrace

North St

East St

Radnor St

Back St

W Cliff Gdns

Silver Screen Cinema

St Eanswythes Way

SHELLONS ST

George Lane

St Eanswythes CE Primary Sch

The Bayle

The Bayle

The Pde

HARBOUR ST

LWR SANDGATE RD

Church St

Beach St

Albion Vls

Priory Gdns

The Pde

Road of Remembrance

P

Radnor Cliff

MARINE TER

Marine Parade Mews

HARBOUR APP RD

A260

MARINE PARADE

Marine Crescent

P

P

Marine Parade

Road

6

BOULOGNE

FOLKESTONE

7

23 **F** **G** **H** **J** **K** 24

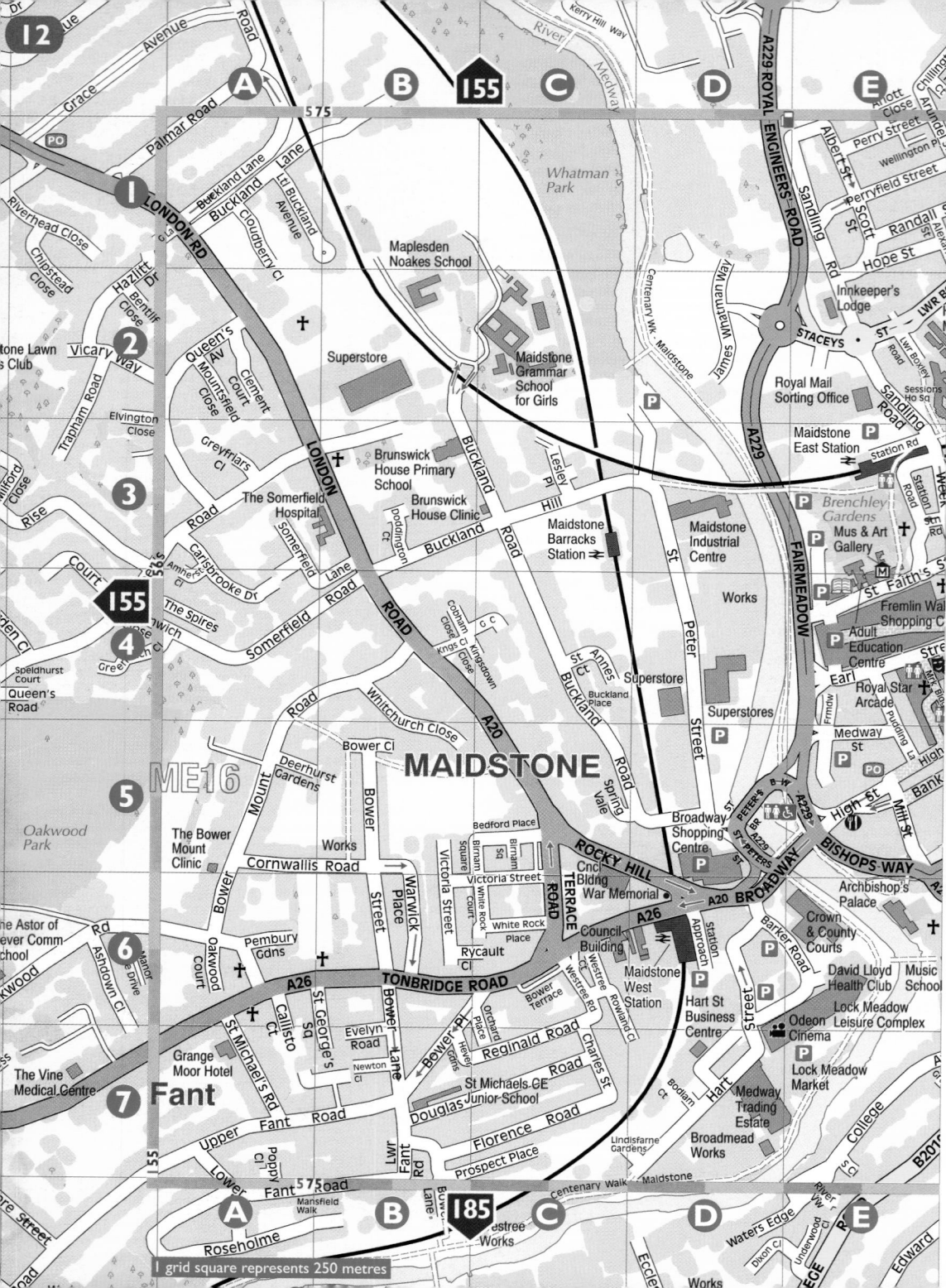

MAIDSTONE

Fant

ME16

Oakwood Park

1 grid square represents 250 metres

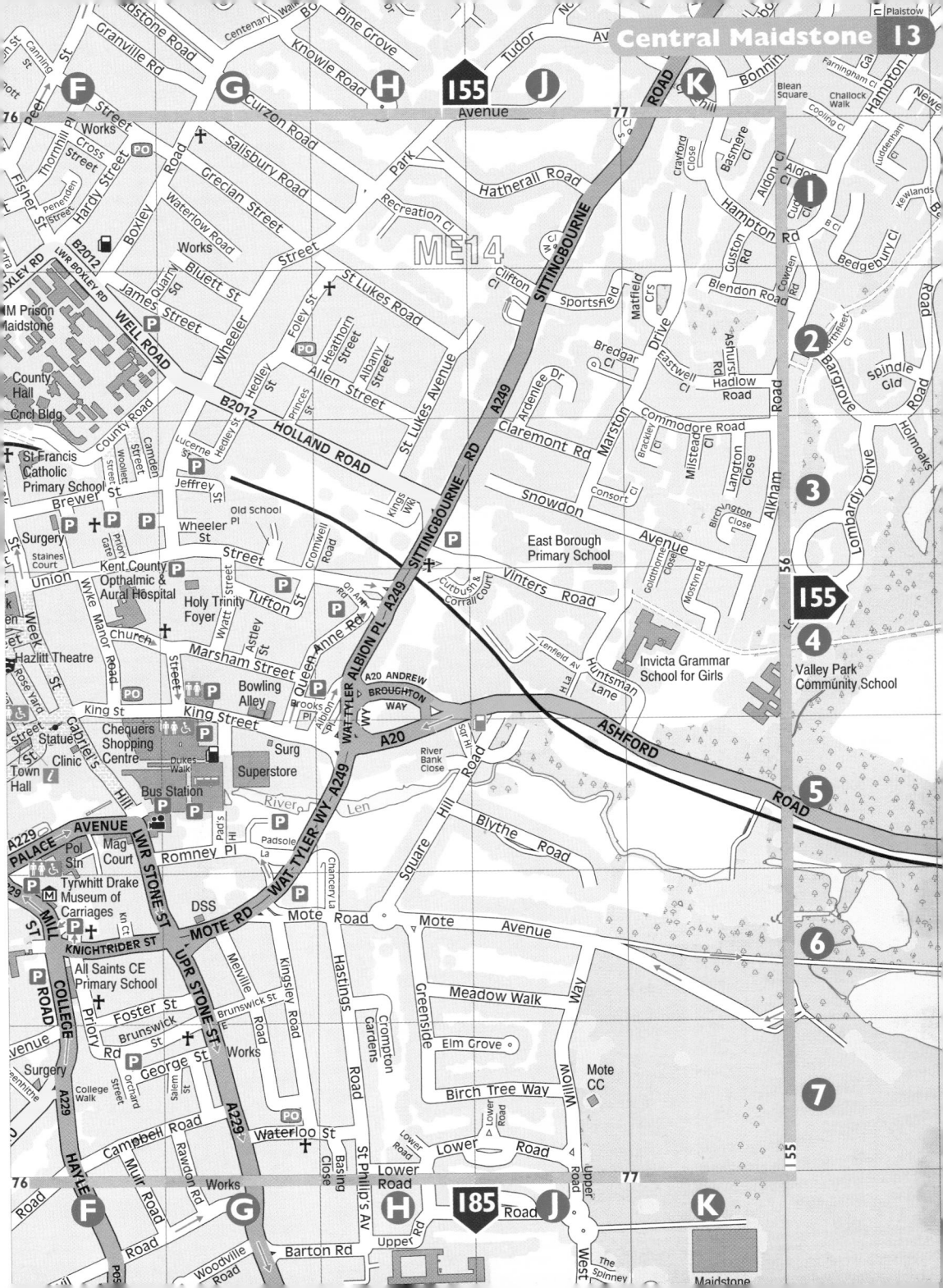

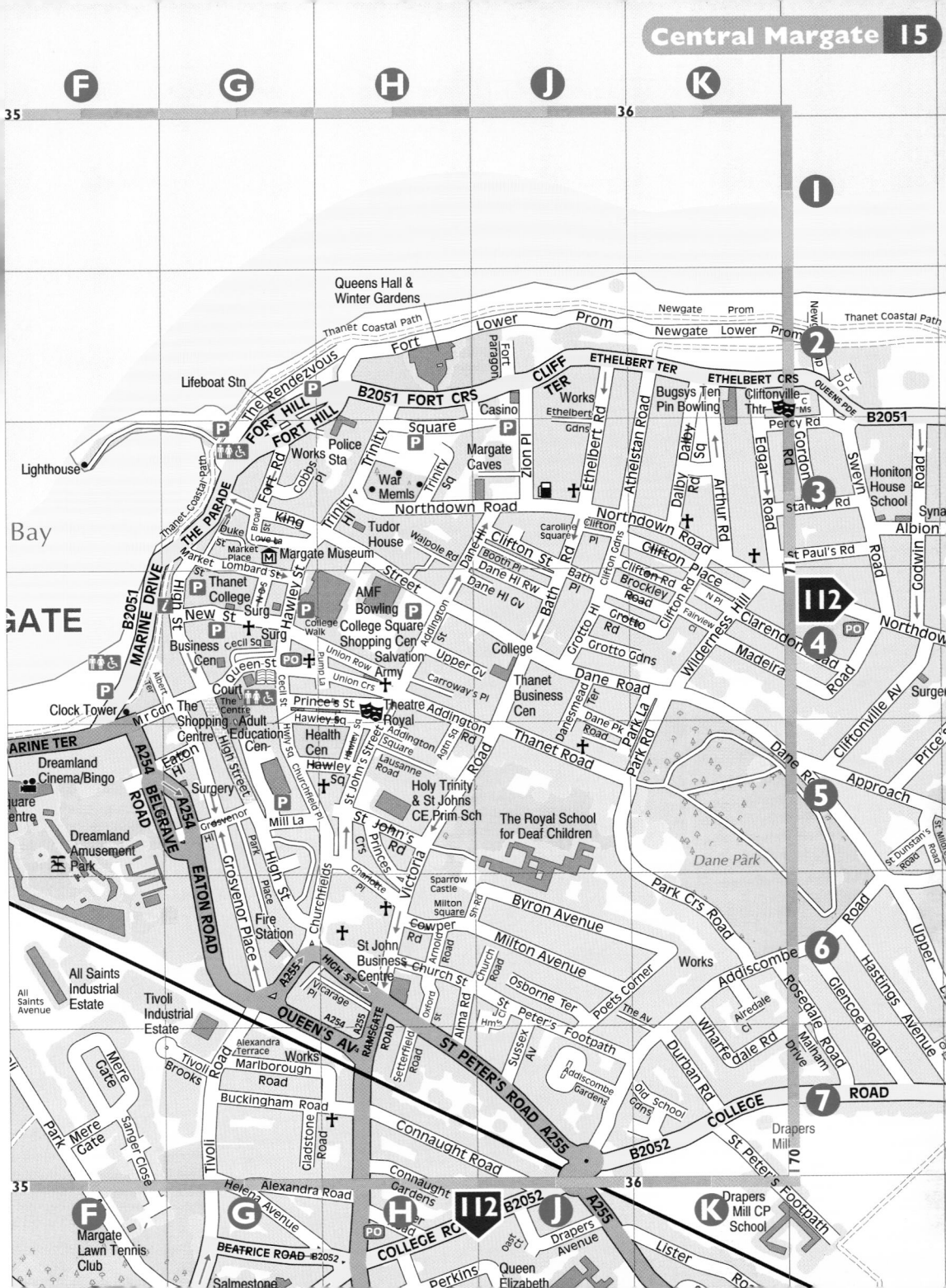

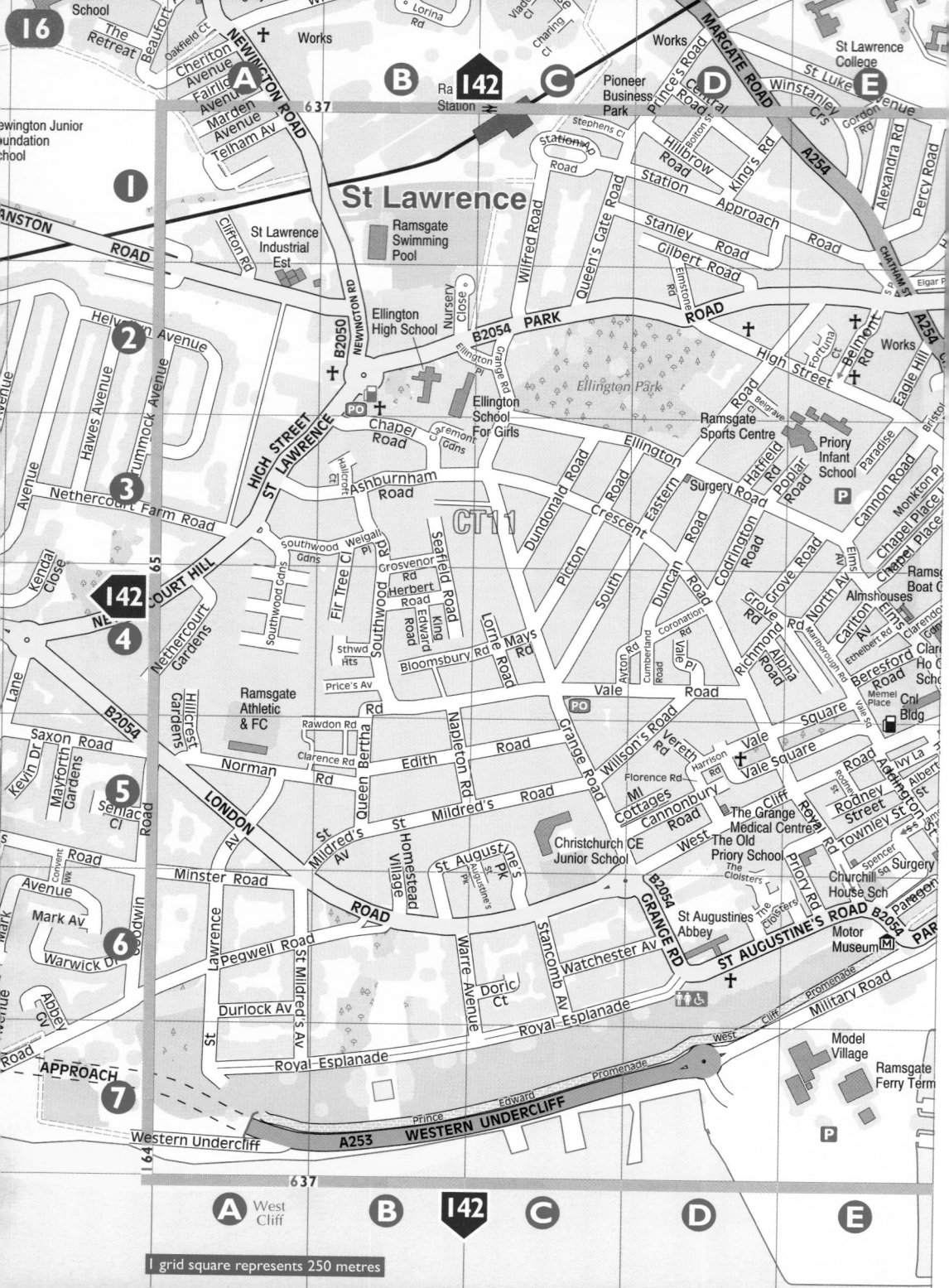

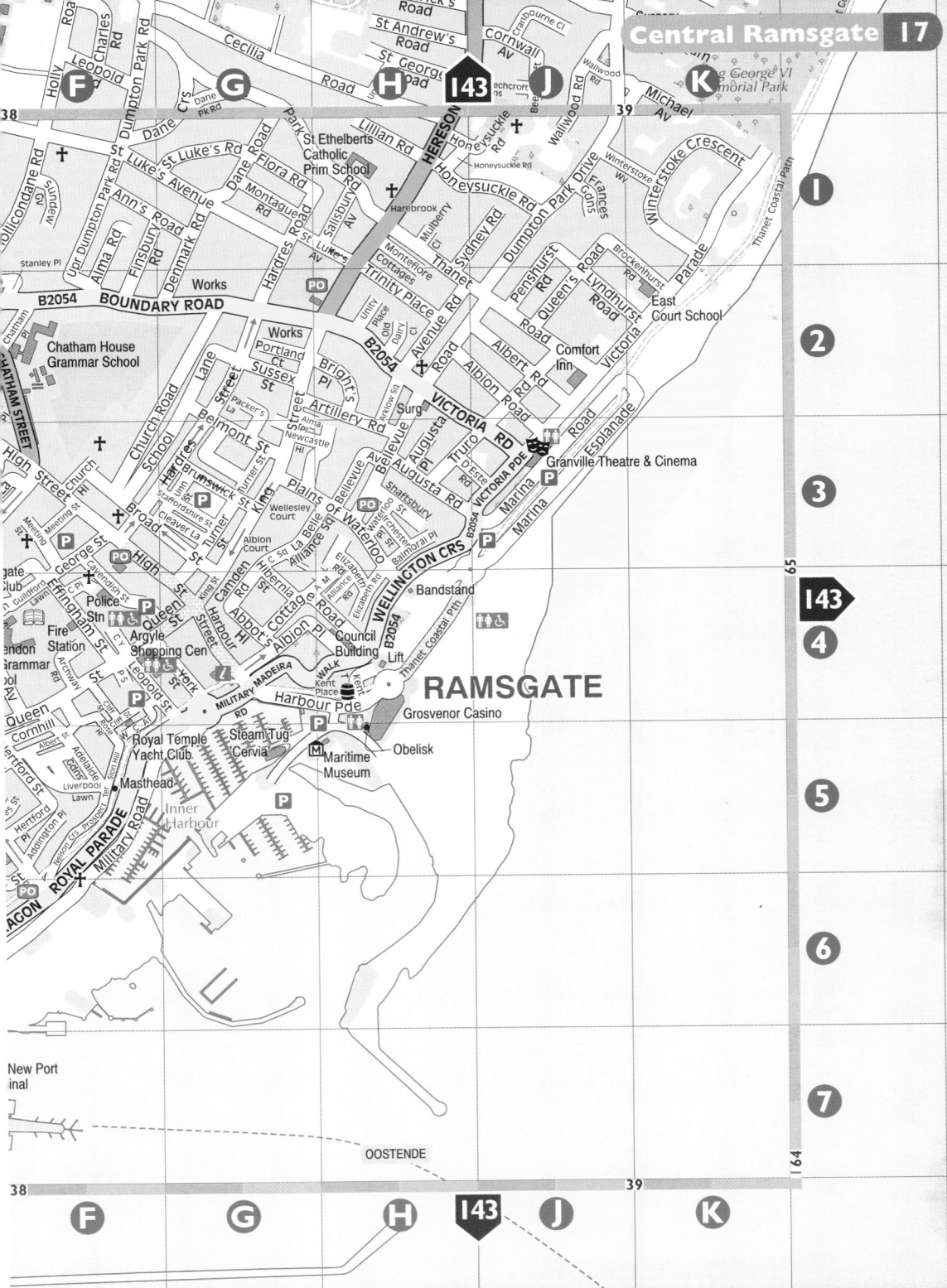

King George VI Memorial Park

Michael Av

RAMSGATE

Granville Theatre & Cinema

Grosvenor Casino

Maritime Museum

Obelisk

Steam Tug Cervia

Royal Temple Yacht Club

Masthead

Inner Harbour

New Port Terminal

OOSTENDE

143

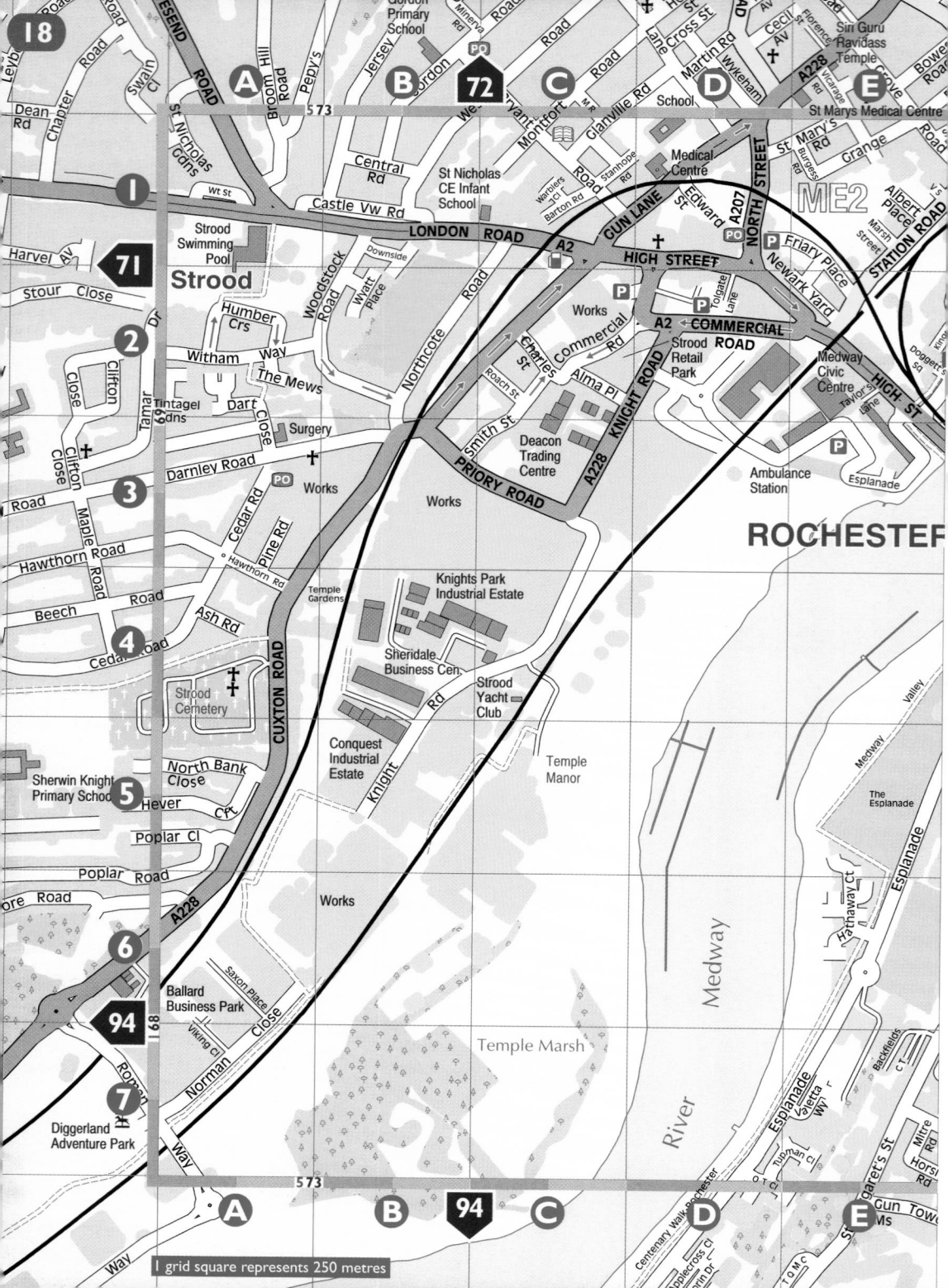

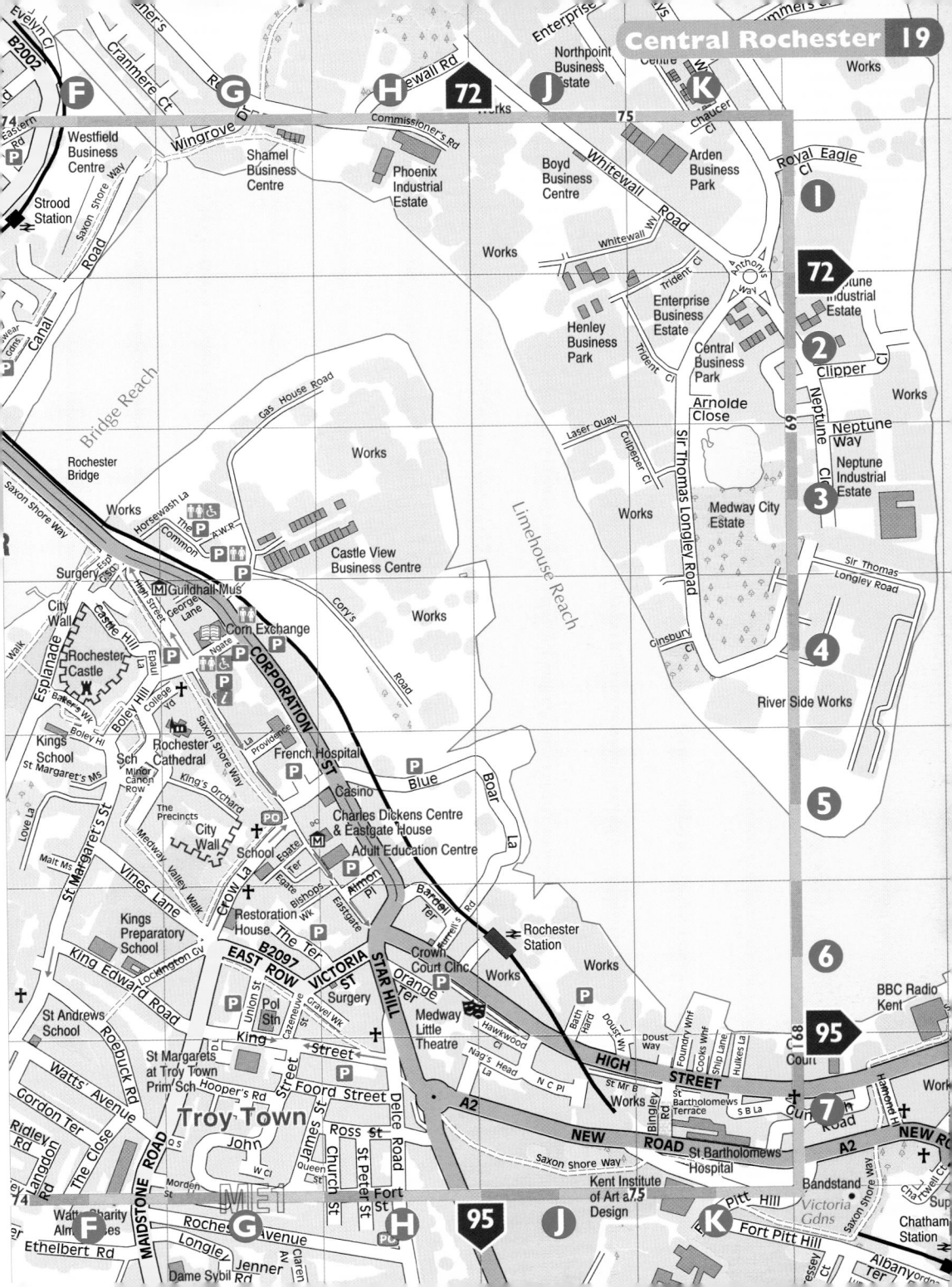

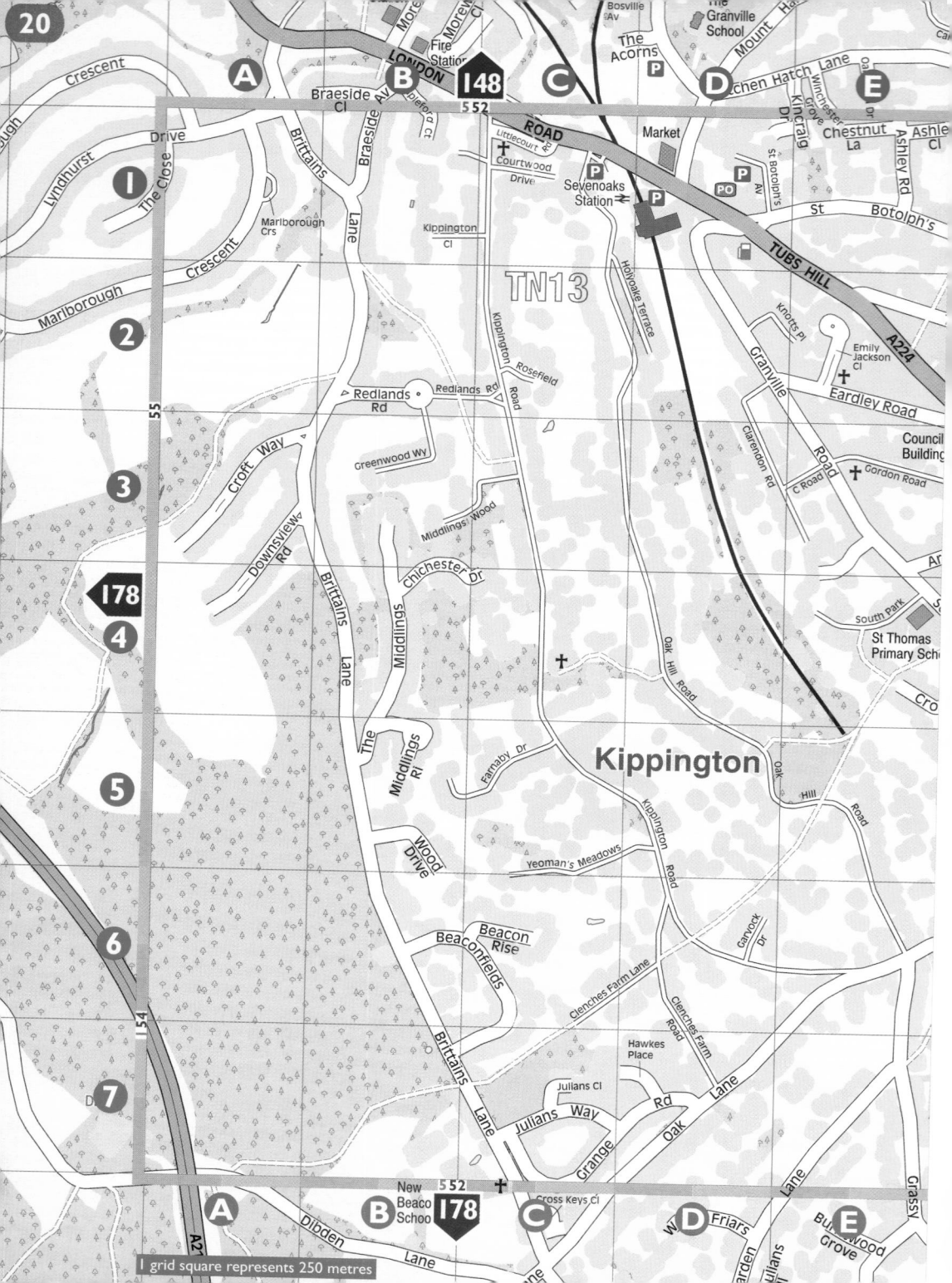

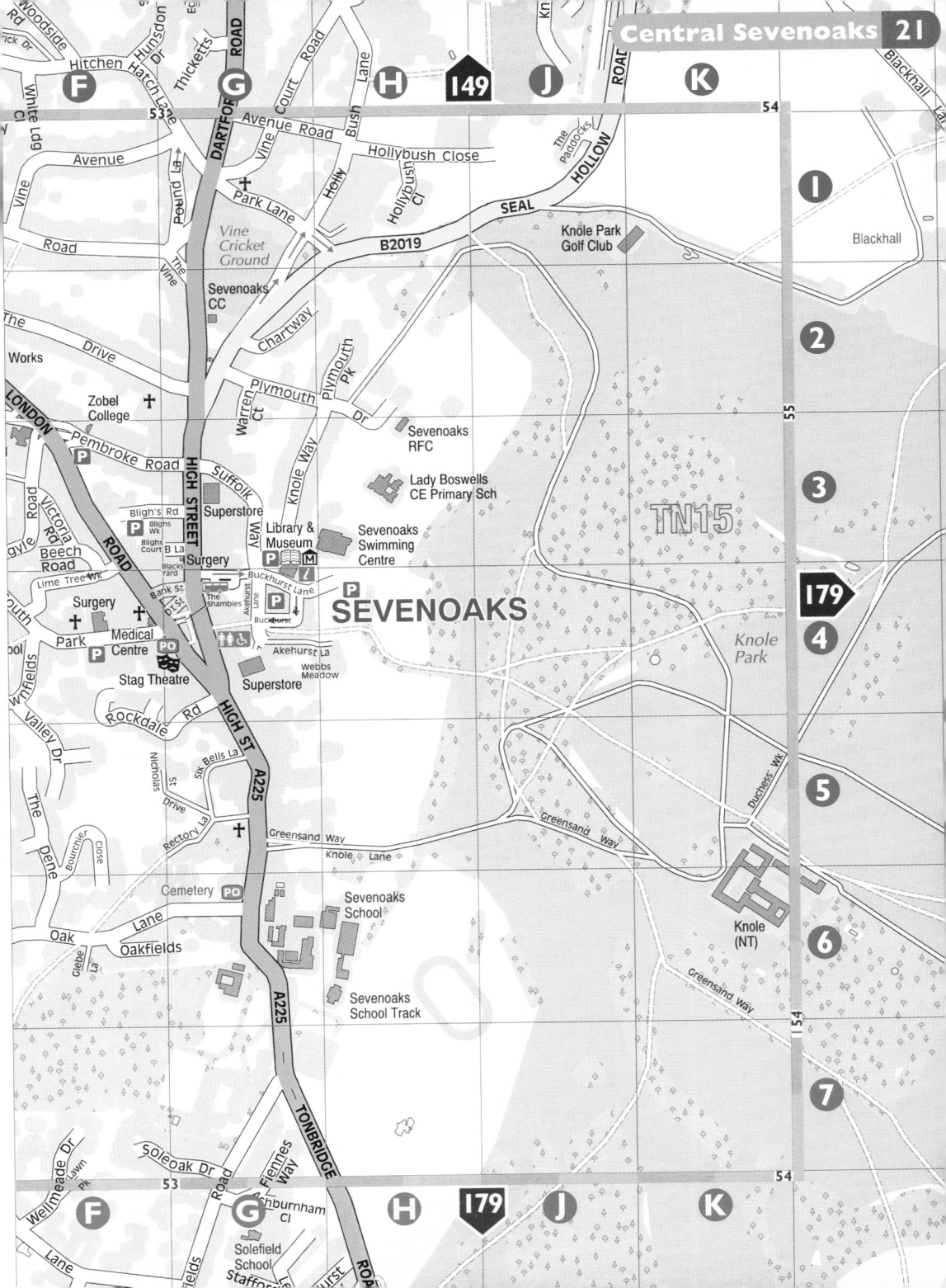

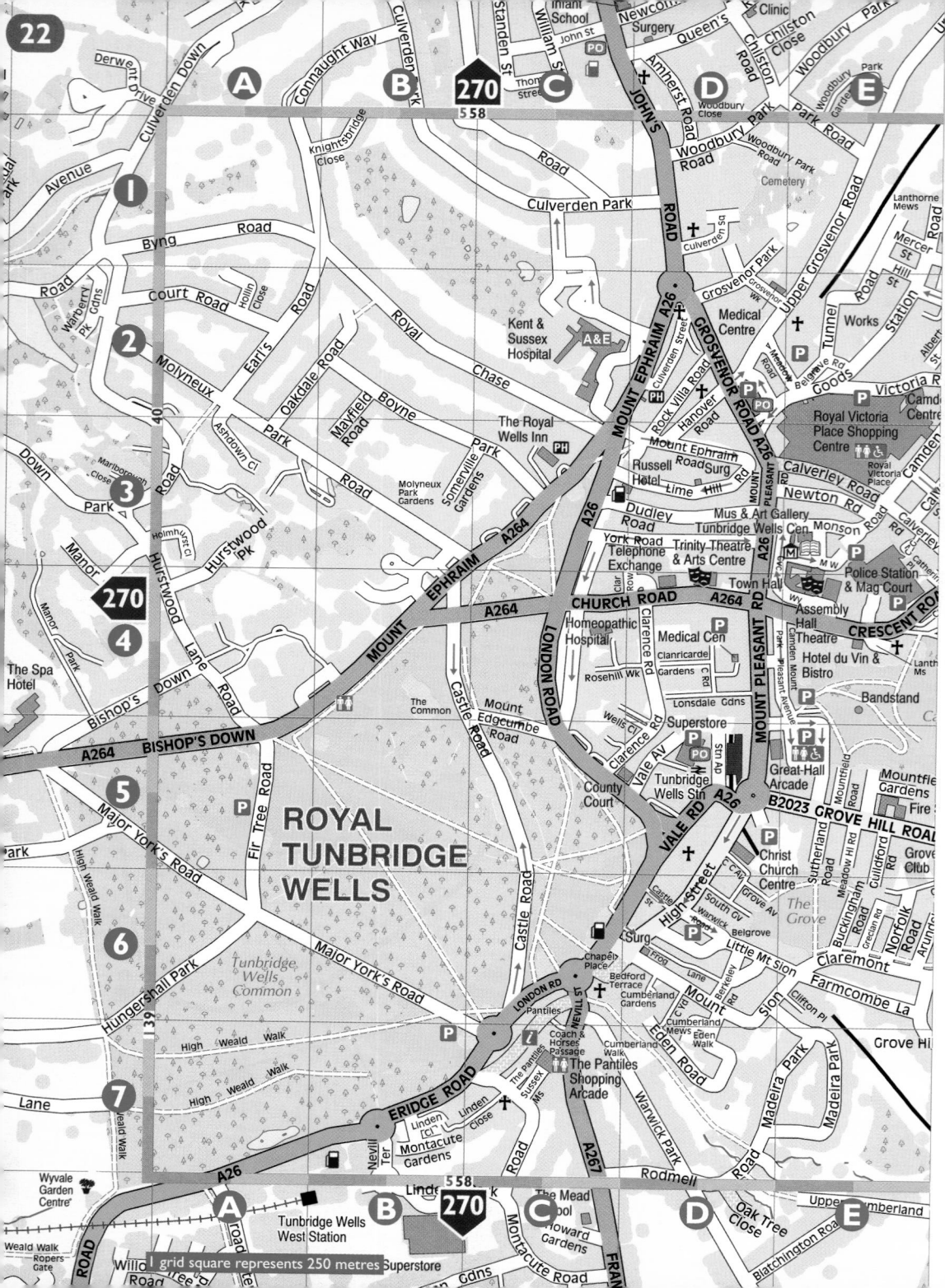

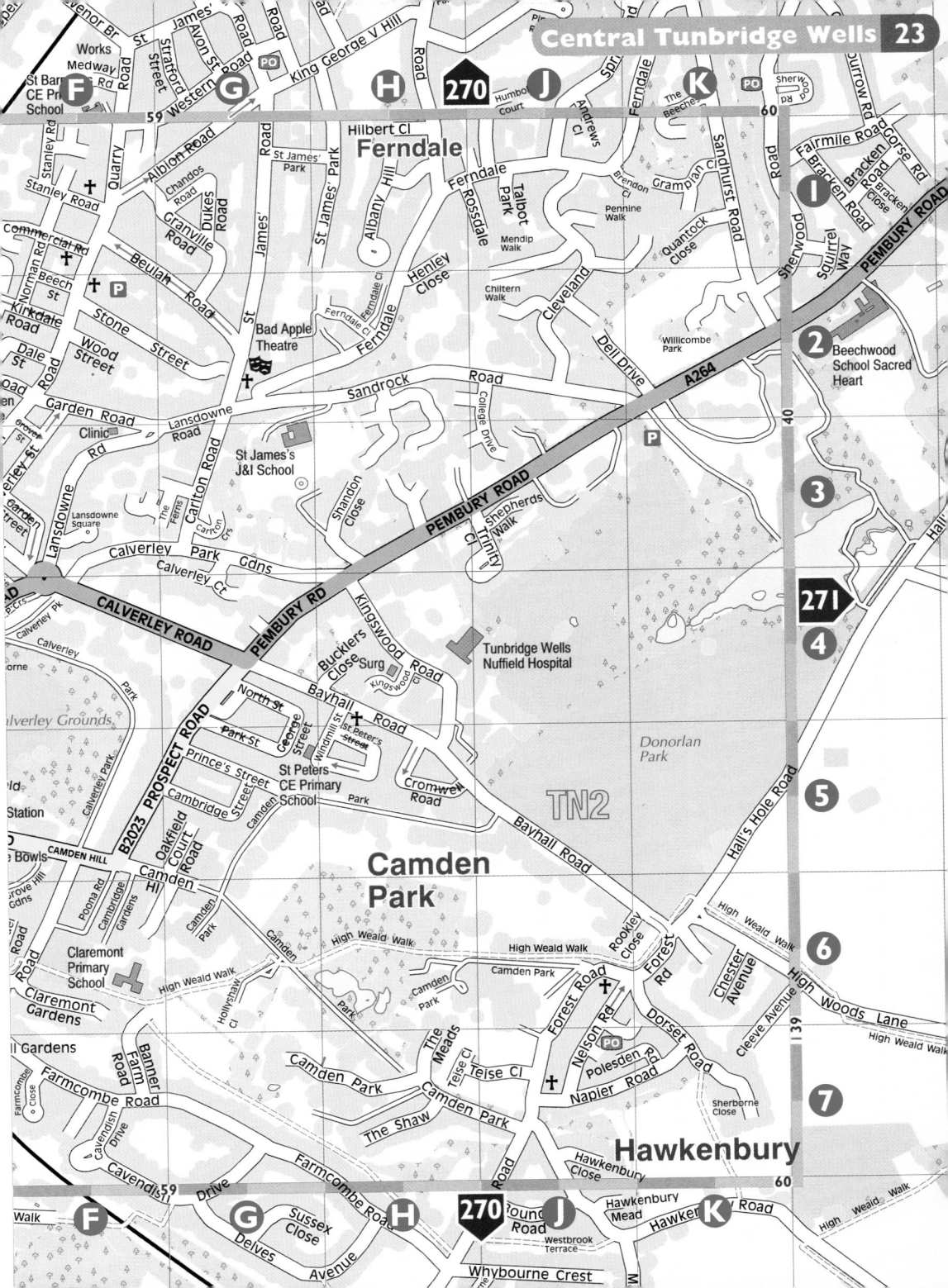

Ferndale

Hawkenbury

Camden Park

TN2

Calverley Grounds

Donorlan Park

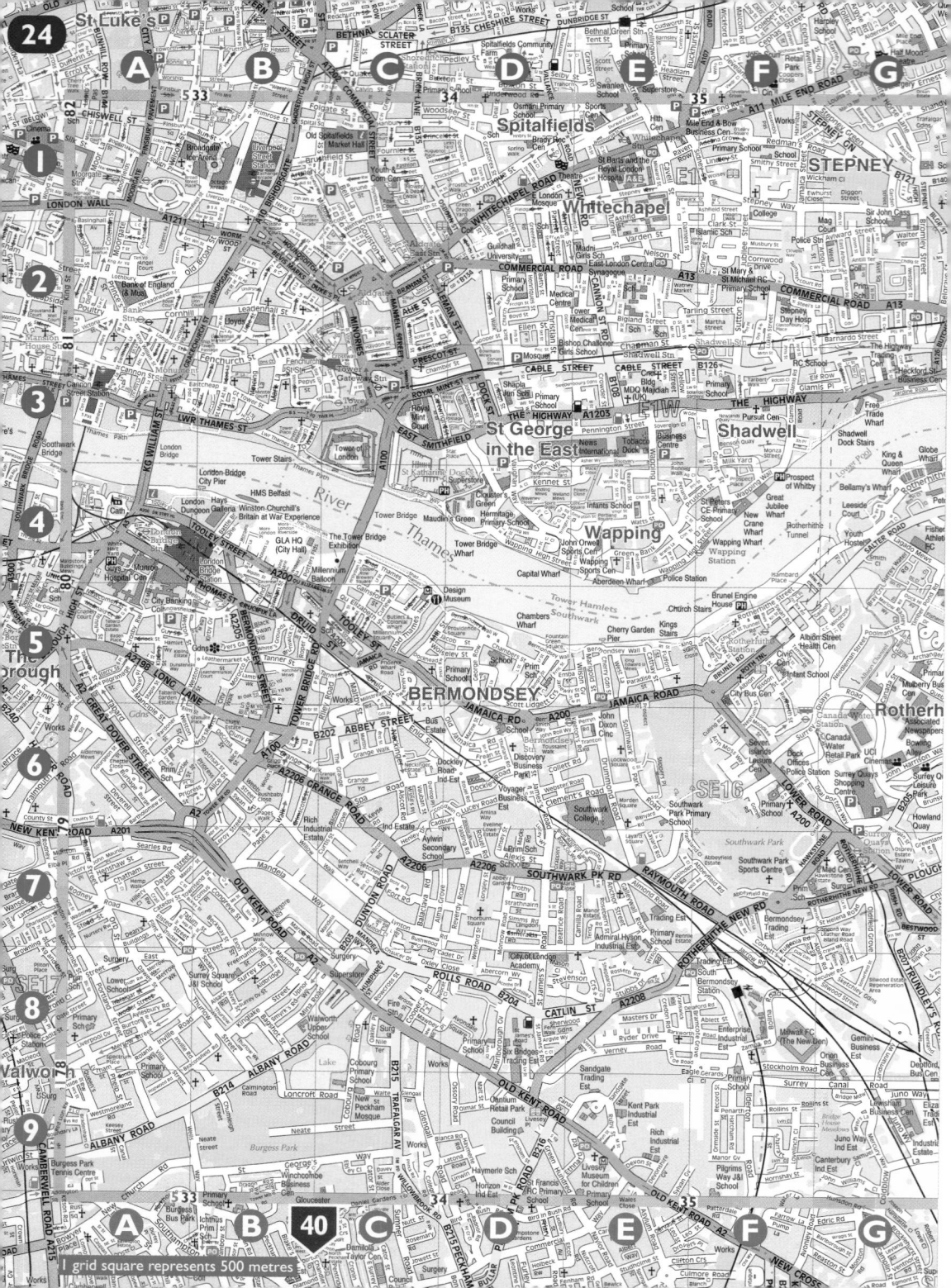

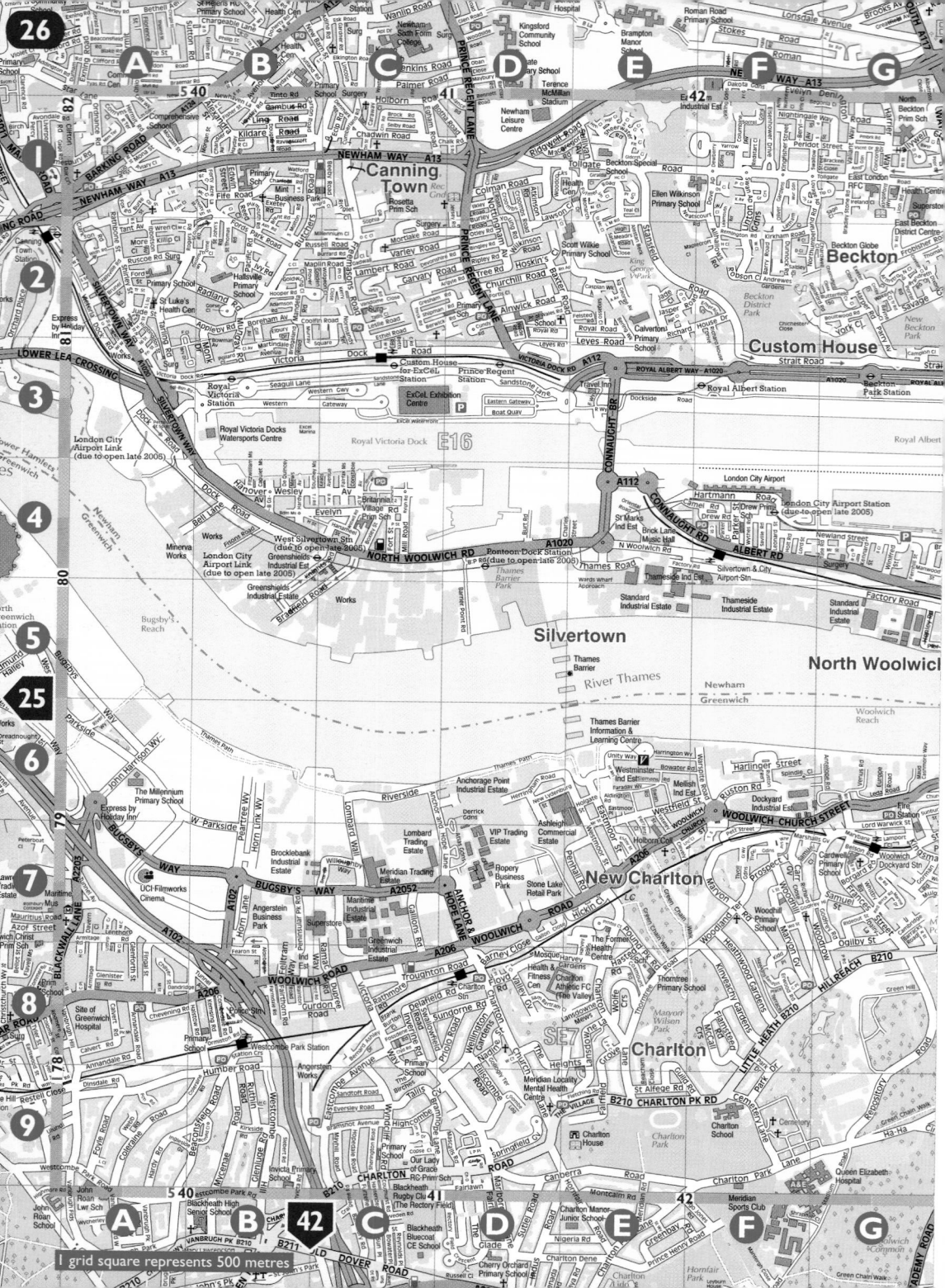

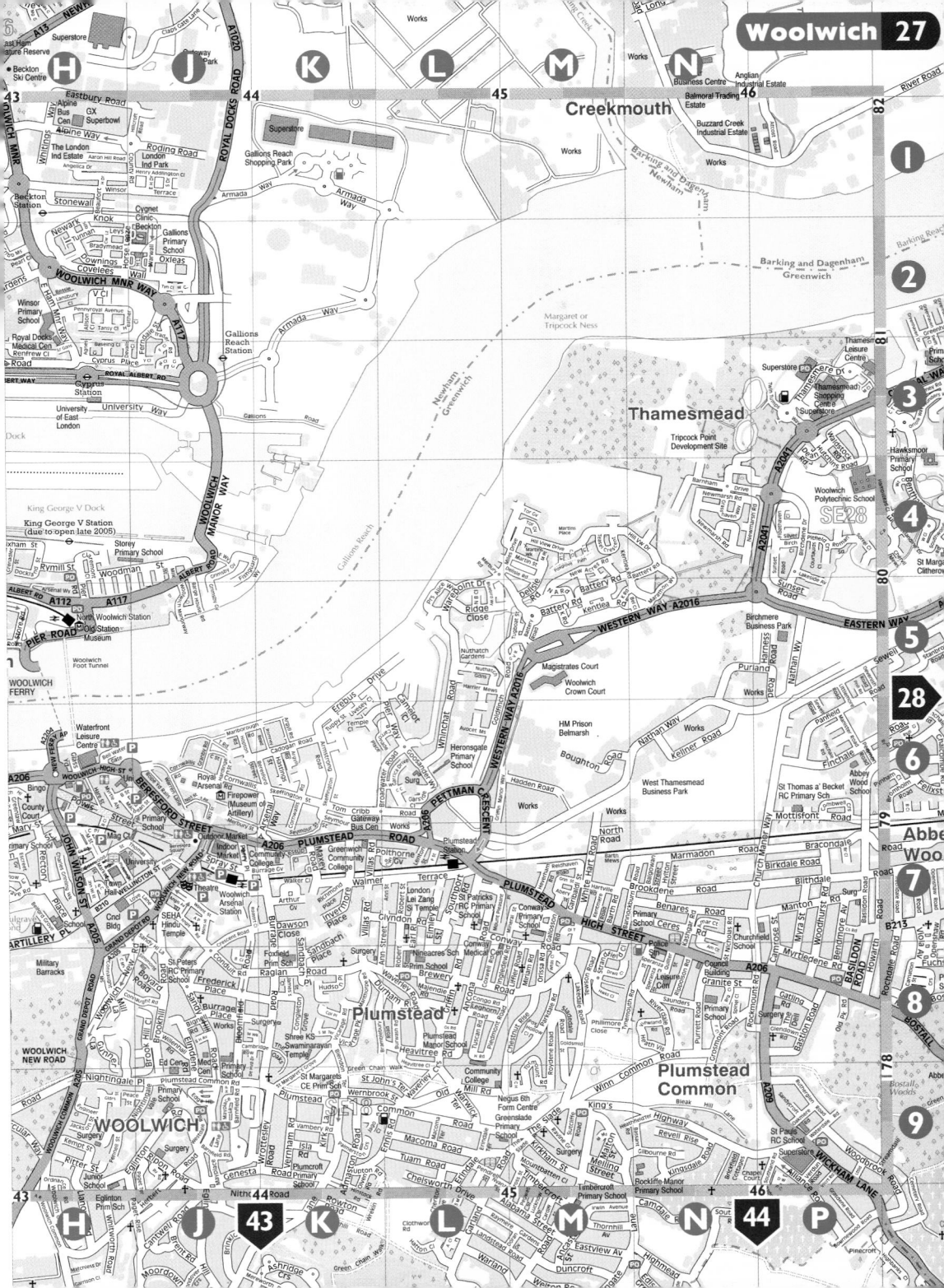

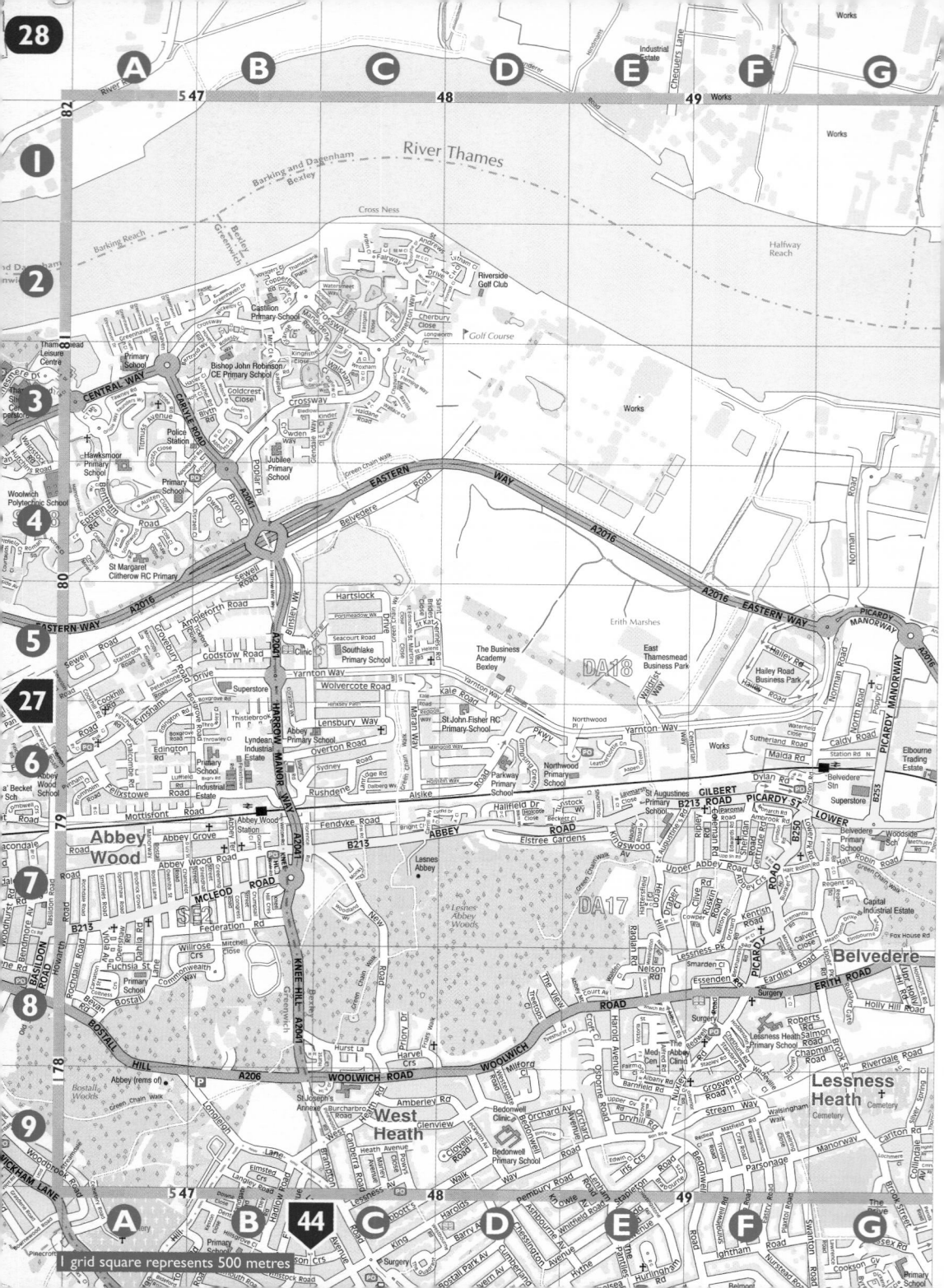

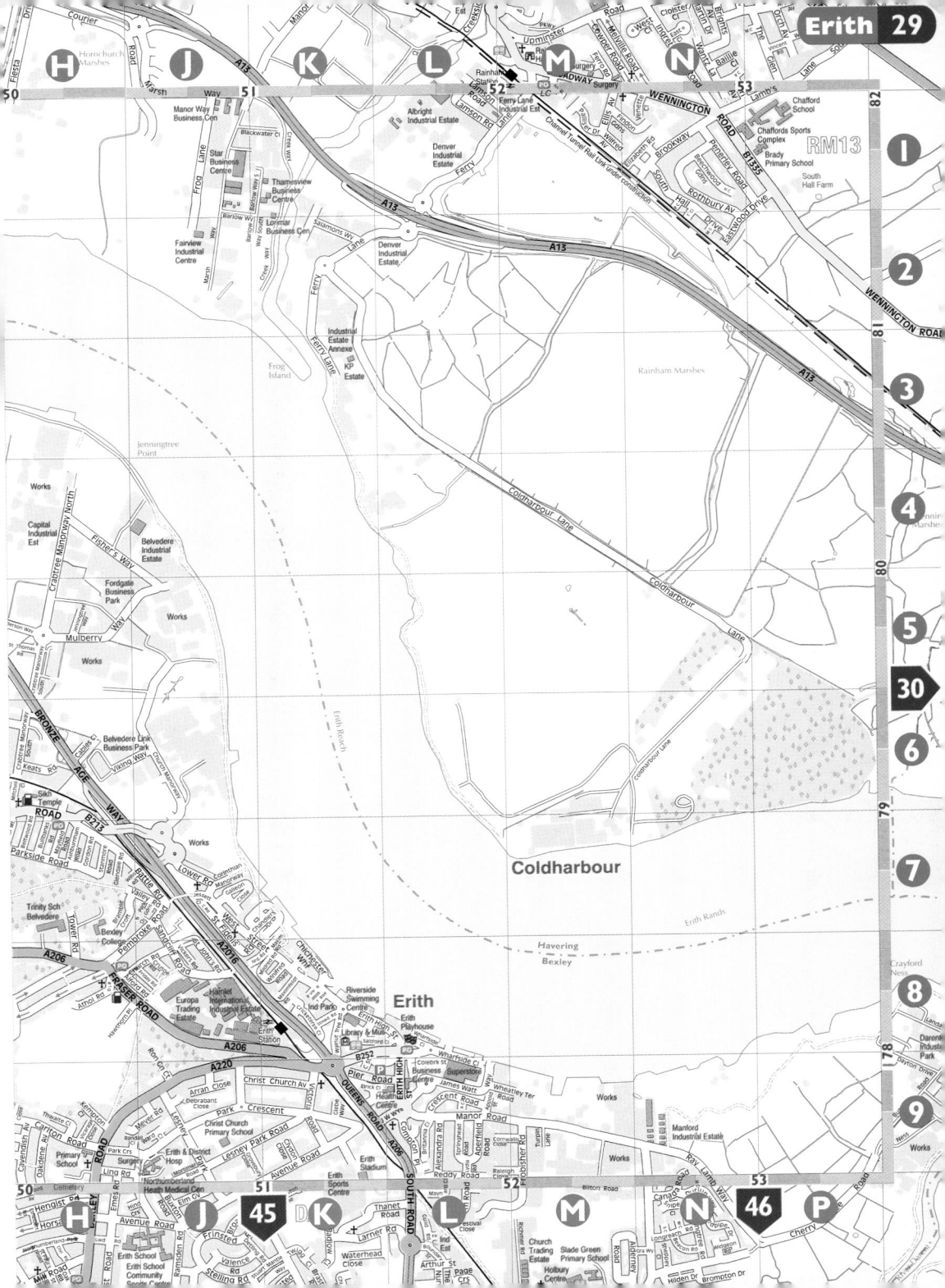

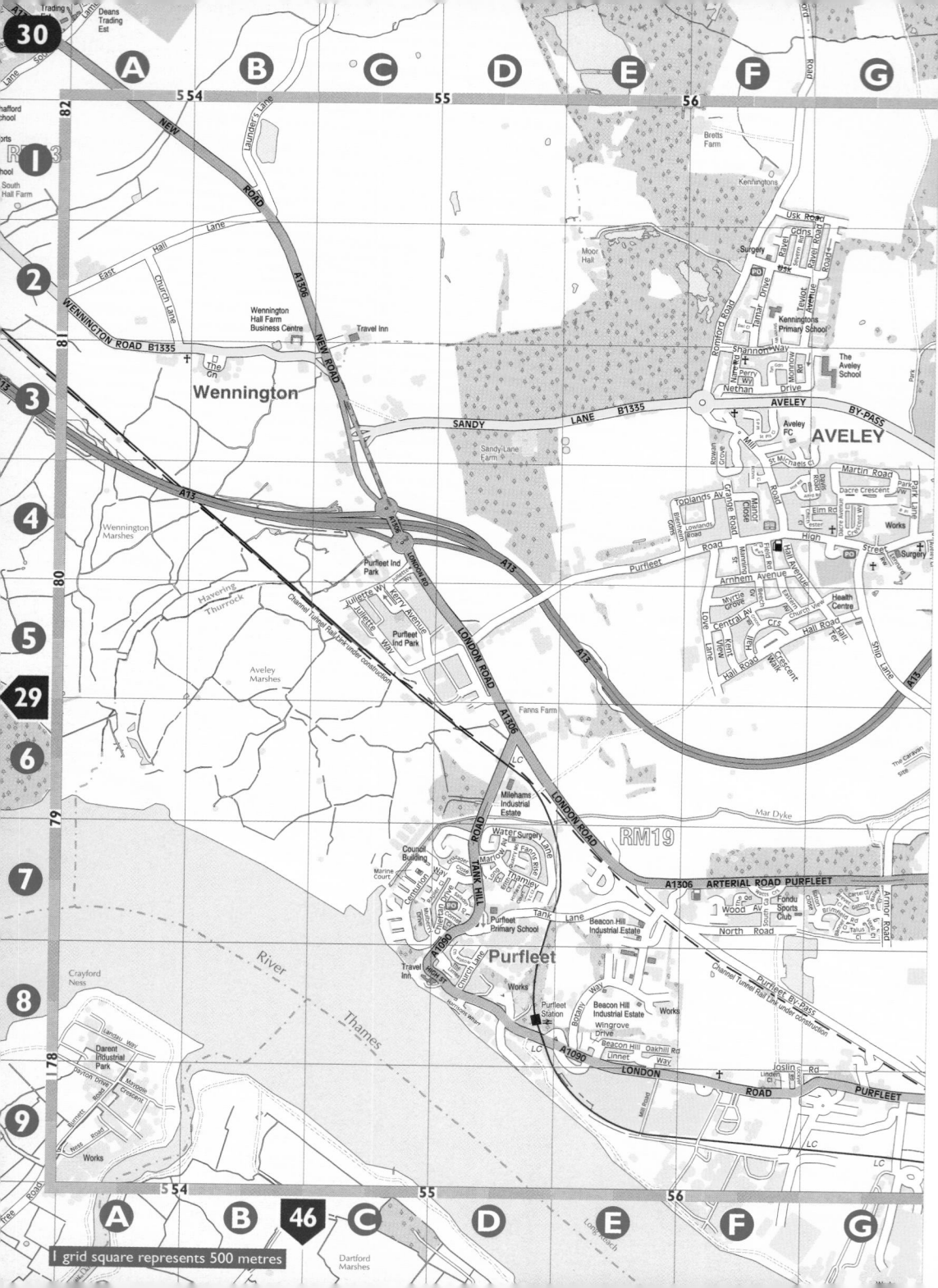

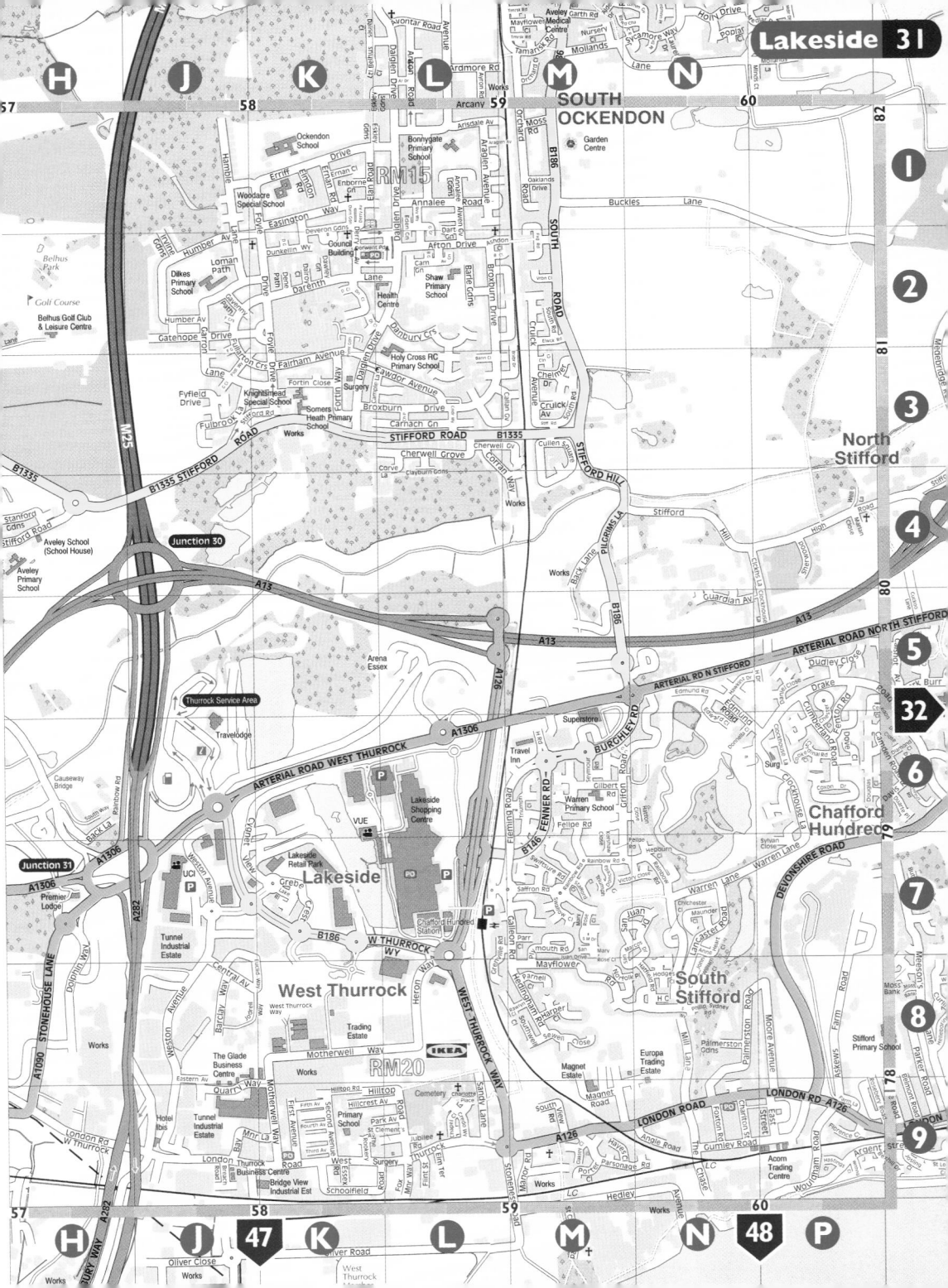

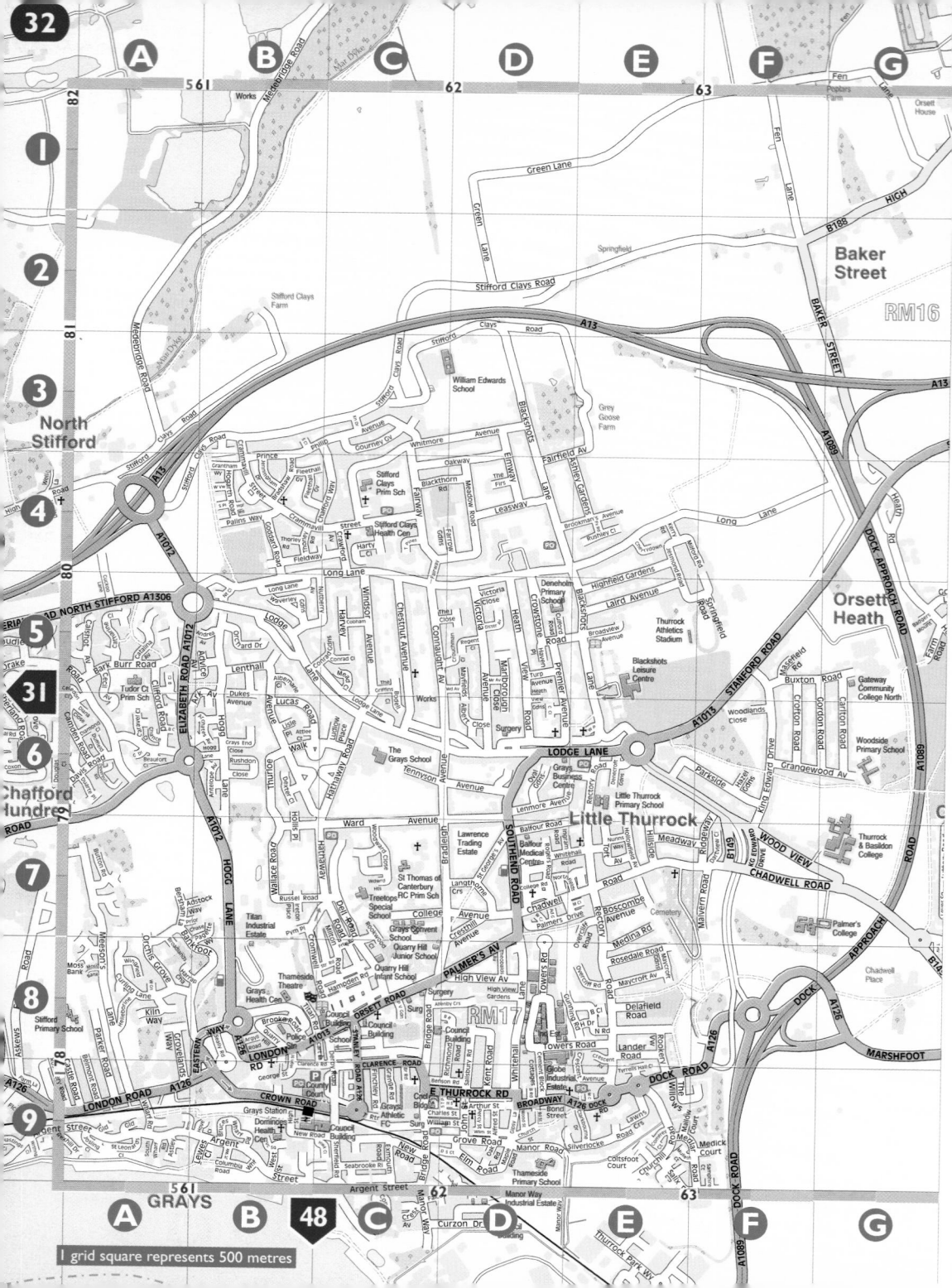

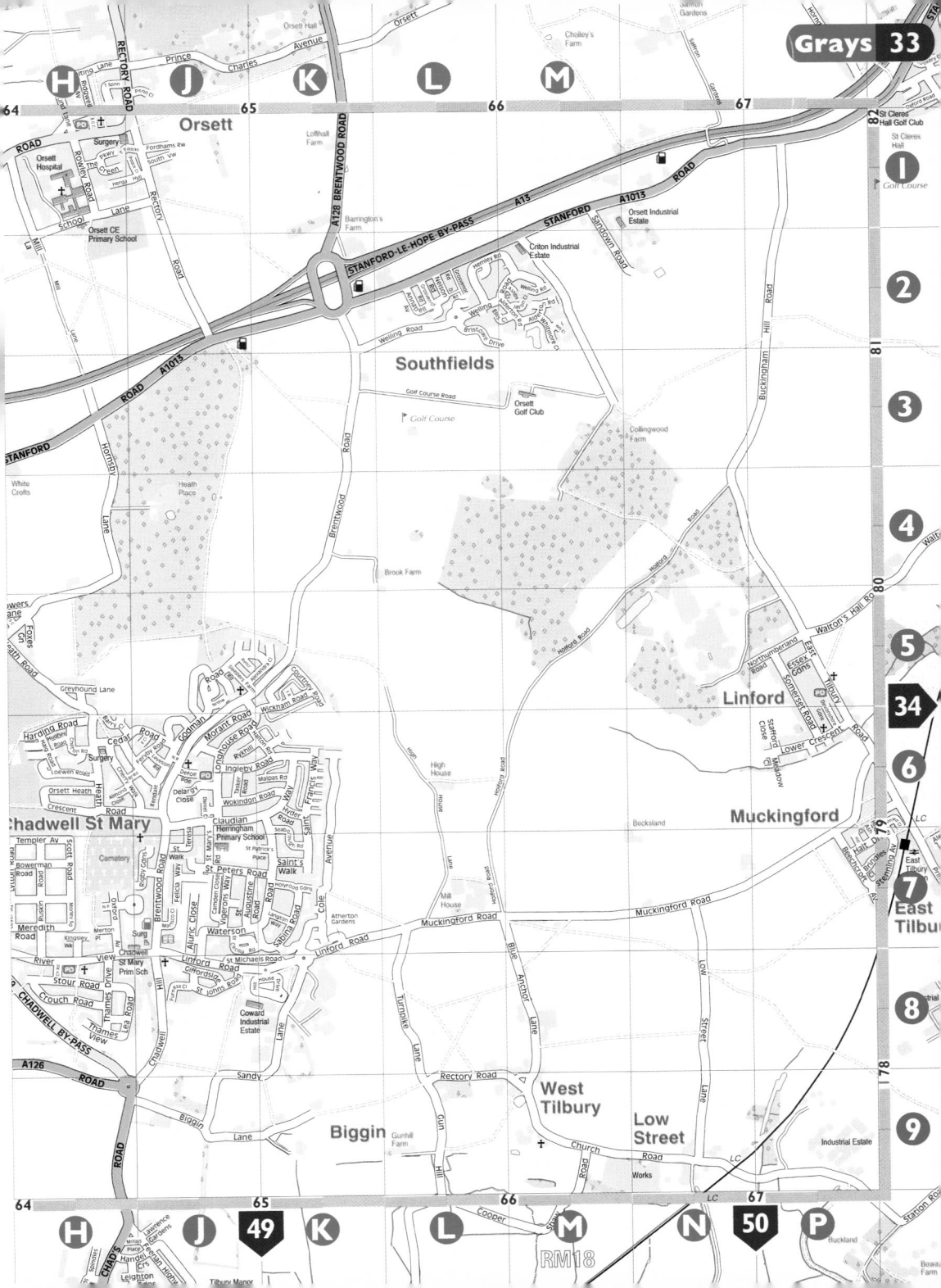

H J K L M N

71 72 73 74

82

1

2

81

3

4

80

5

36

6

79

7

8

178

9

Oil Storage Depot

Works

Works

Works

LC

LC

Works

Thames Haven

Lower Hope Point

Cliffe Fleet

Cliffe Marshes

Mead Wall

Boatrick House

71 72 73 74

H J **51** K L M N **52** P

Nature Reserve

Ryestreet Common

H J K L M

Works

Thorney Bay

Esplanade

Cineplex Movie
Starr Cinema

78 79 80 81 82

Deadman's
Point

I

2

Essex County
Medway Towns

3

4

80

5

38

West Point

6

79

St Mary's
Marshes

7

8

78

9

Swigshole

78 79 80 81

H J 53 K L M N 54 P

Shakespeare Farm Rd

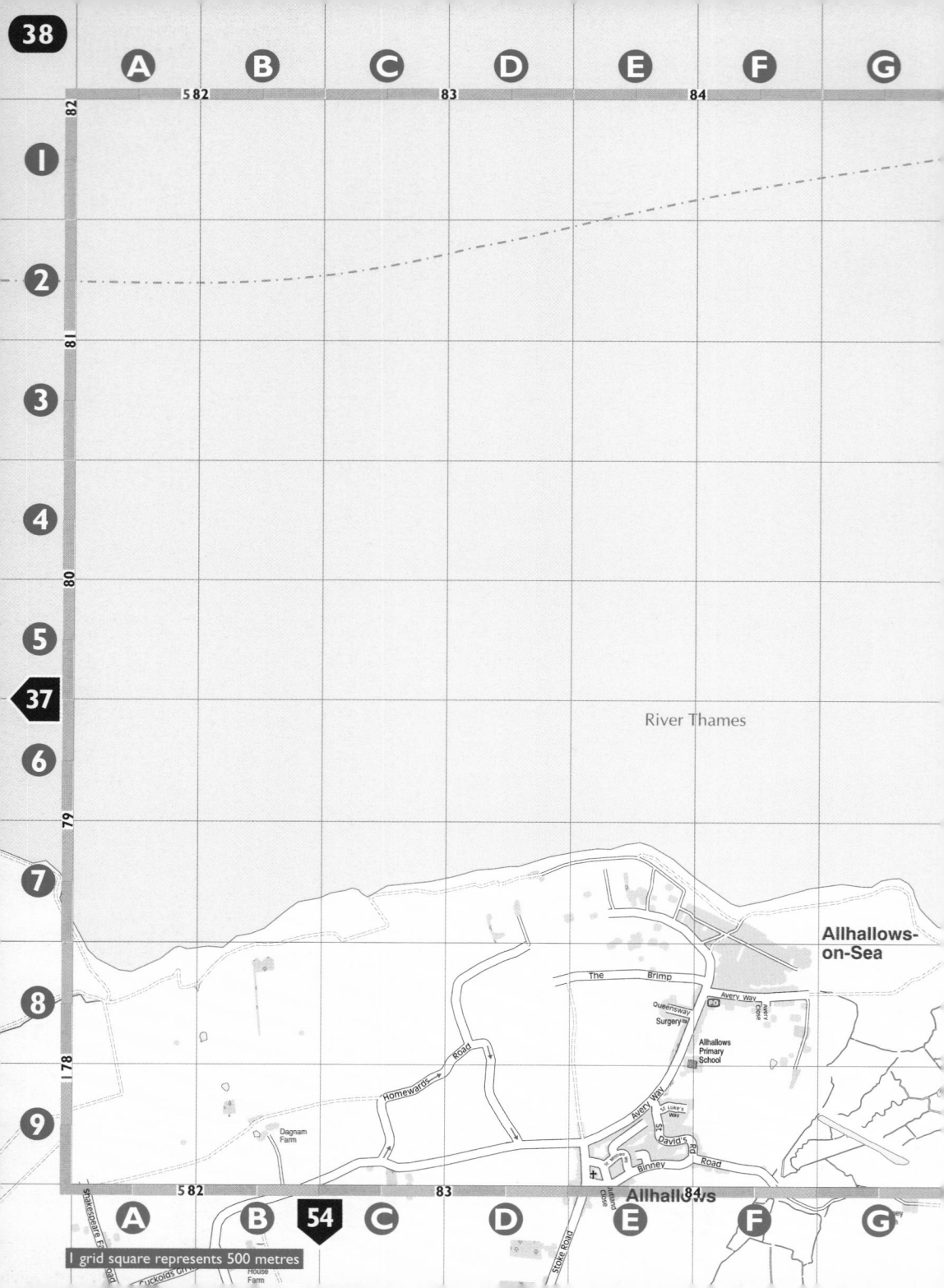

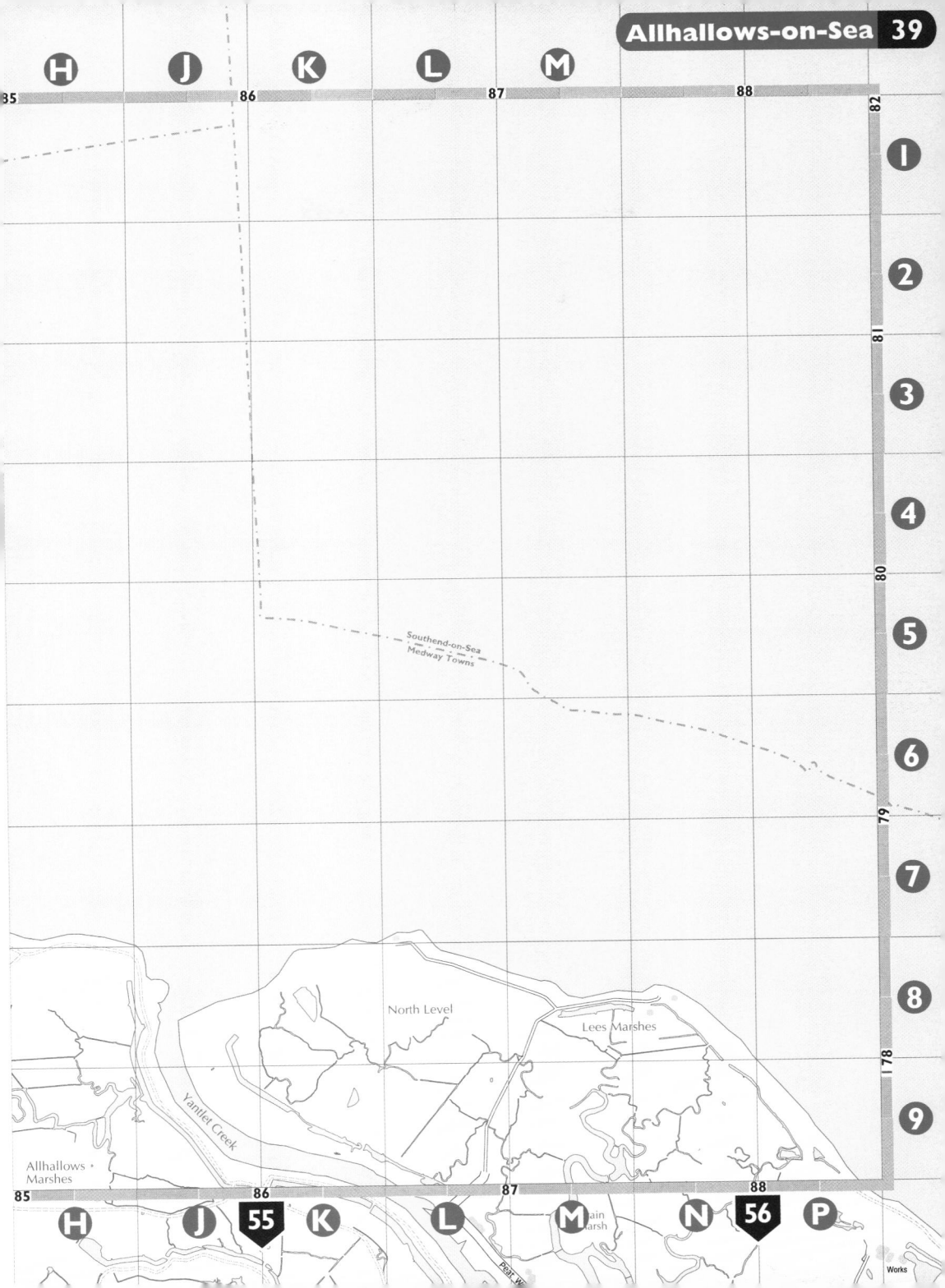

Southend-on-Sea
Medway Towns

North Level

Lees Marshes

Yantlet Creek

Allhallows
Marshes

Main Marsh

Peat W

Works

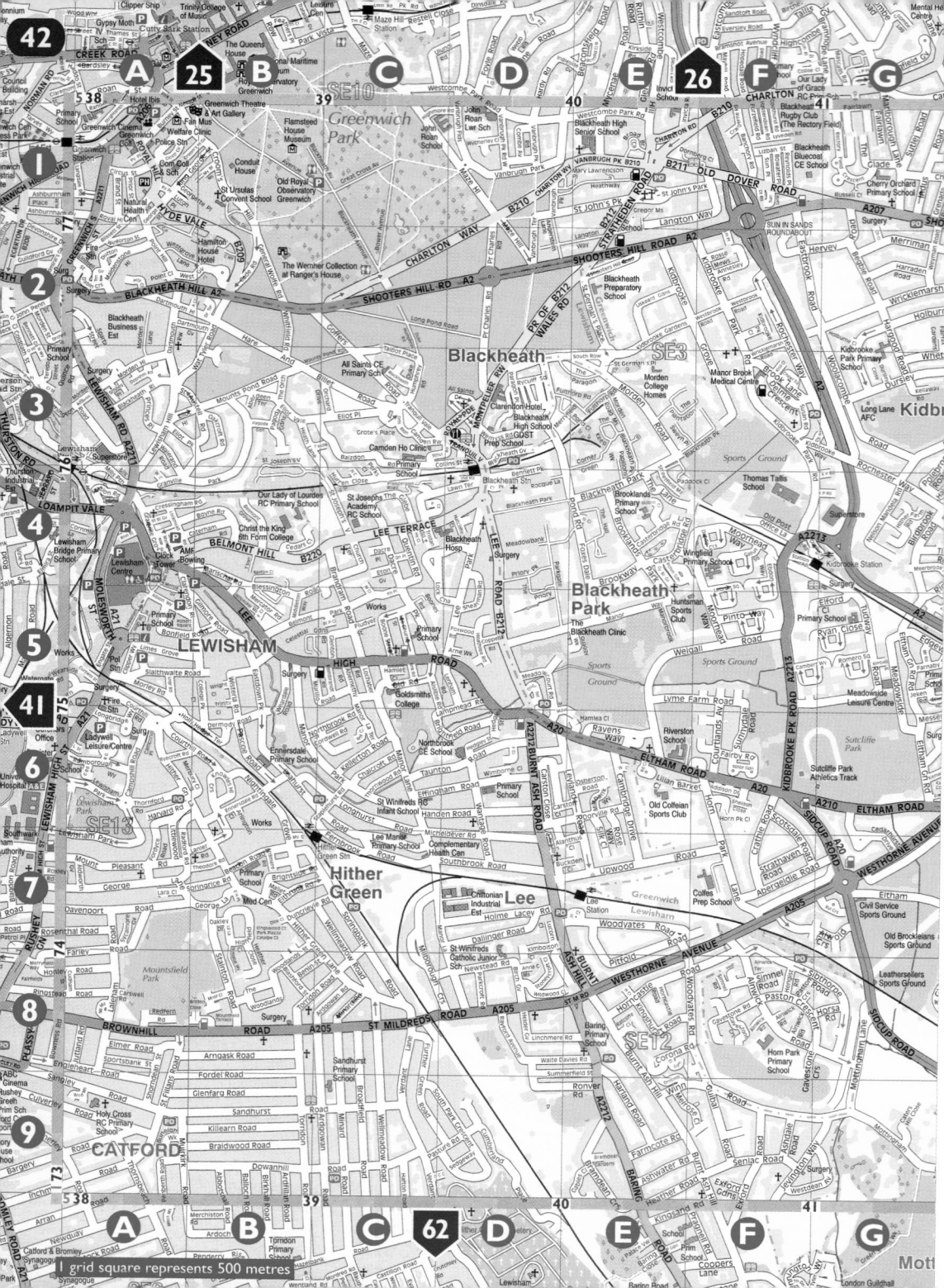

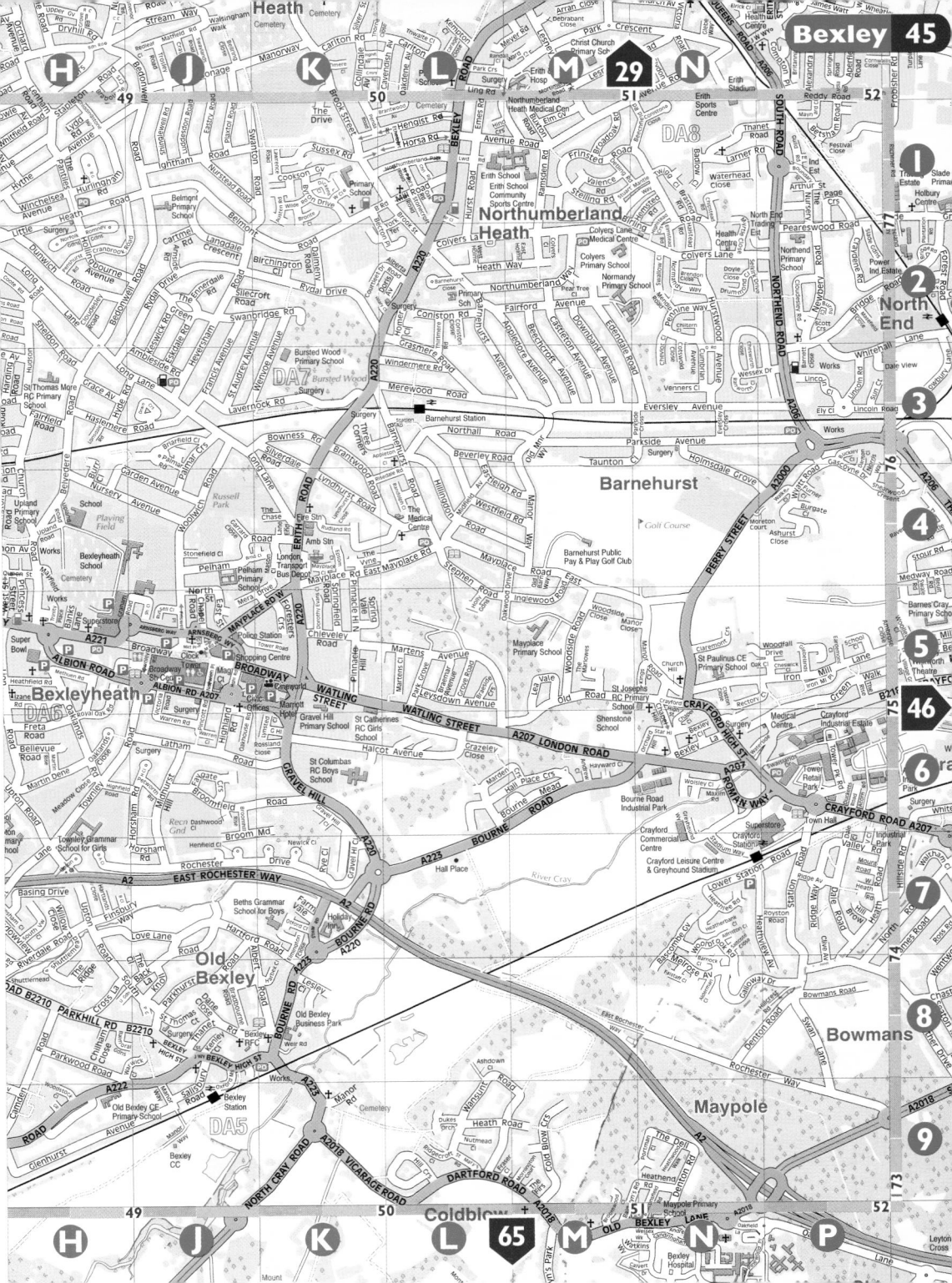

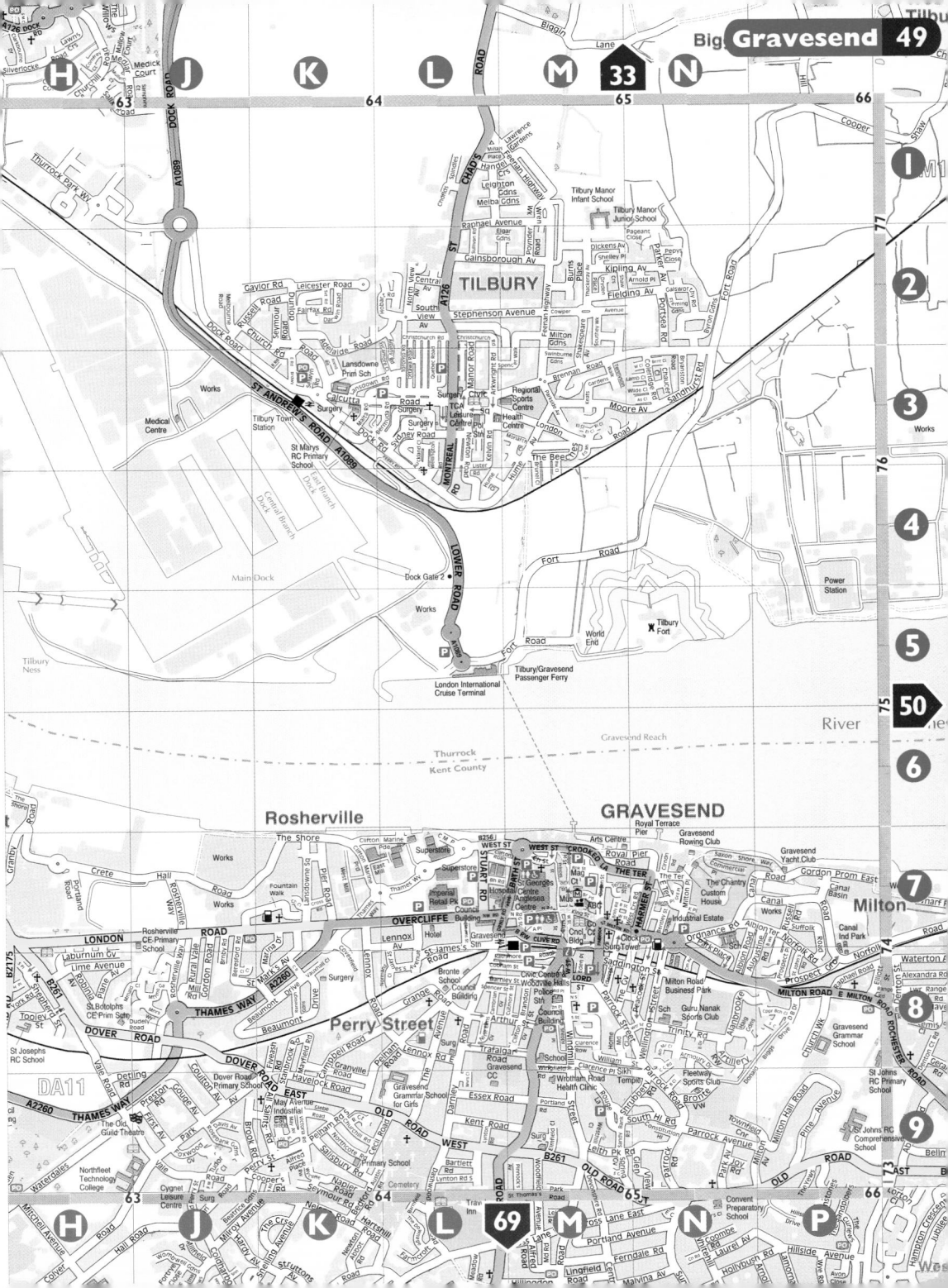

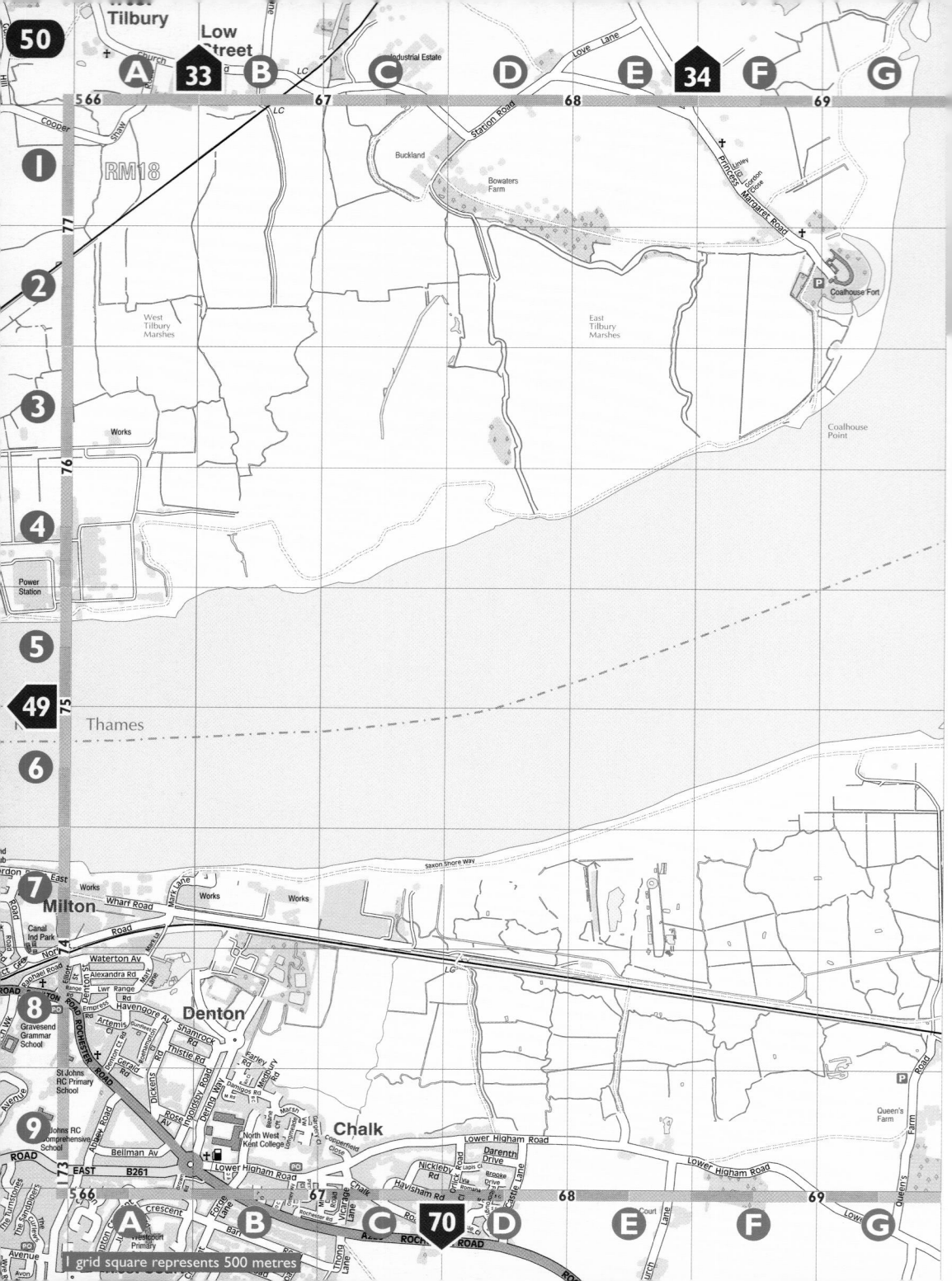

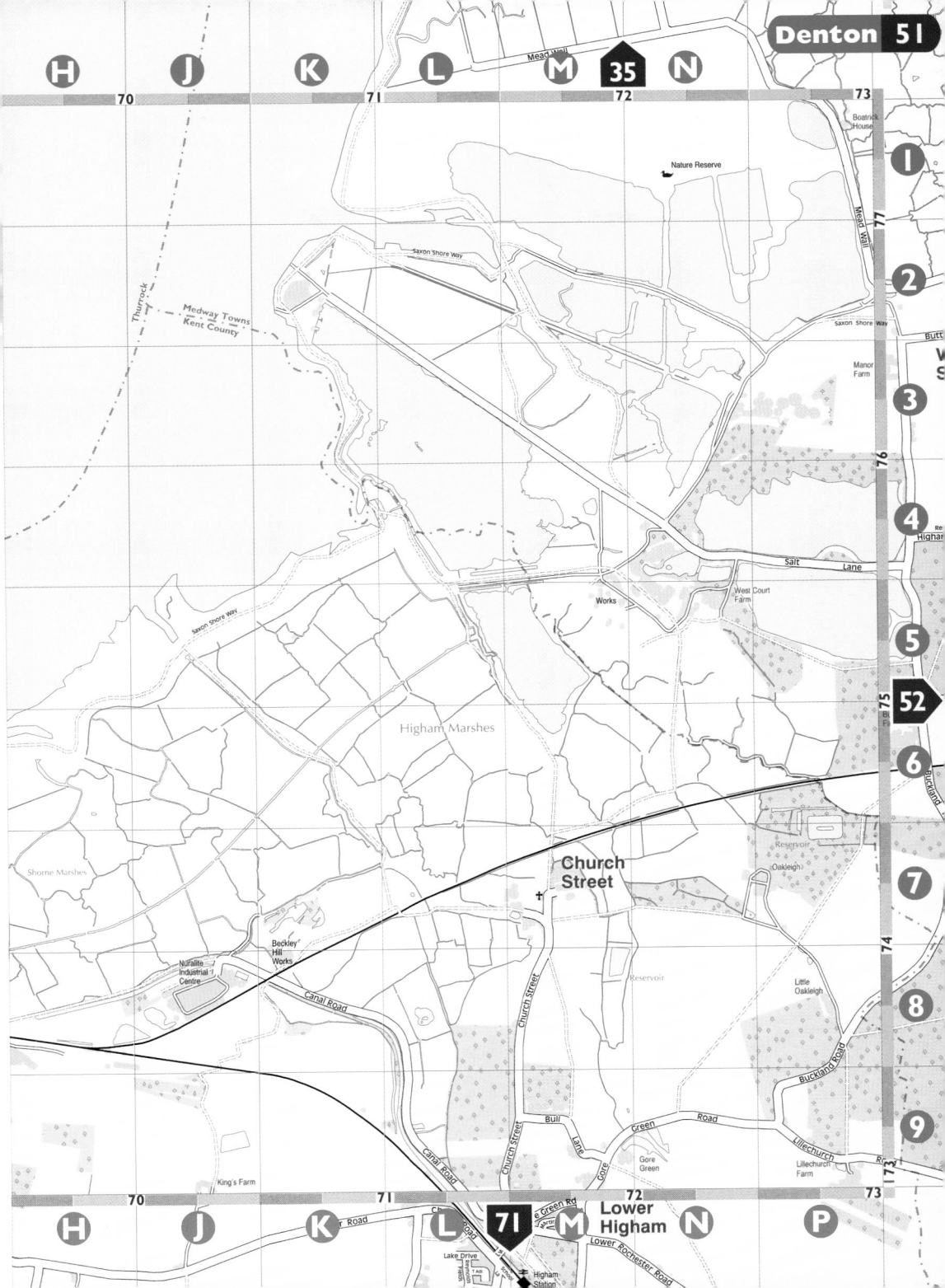

H J K L M 35 N

70 71 72 73

Boatrick House

I

Nature Reserve

Mead Wall 77

2

Saxon Shore Way

Medway Towns Kent County

Saxon Shore Way

Butt

Manor Farm

3

76

4

Re Higham

Salt Lane

5

West Court Farm

Works

75

52

Saxon Shore Way

6

Buckland

Higham Marshes

Reservoir

Oakleigh

7

Church Street

74

Shorne Marshes

Beckley Hill Works

Reservoir

Little Oakleigh

8

Nuralite Industrial Centre

Canal Road

Buckland Road

9

Bull Lane

Green Road

Lillechurch Road

A 173

Gore Green

Lillechurch Farm

King's Farm

Canal Road

Church Street

Gore Lane

H J K L M N P

70 71 72 73

H J K 71 L M N P

e Green Rd

Lower Higham

Road

Lake Drive

Lower Rochester Road

Higham Station

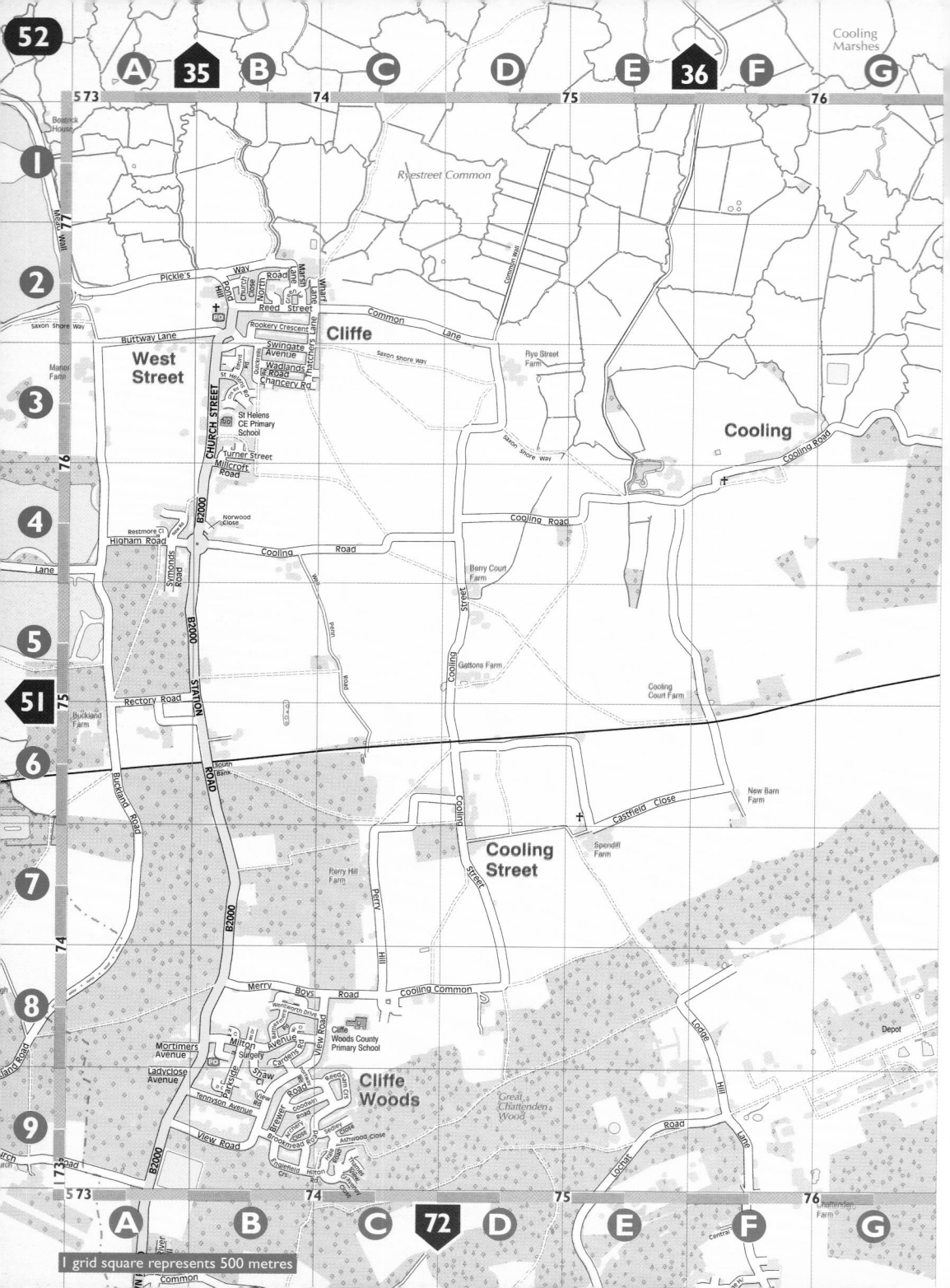

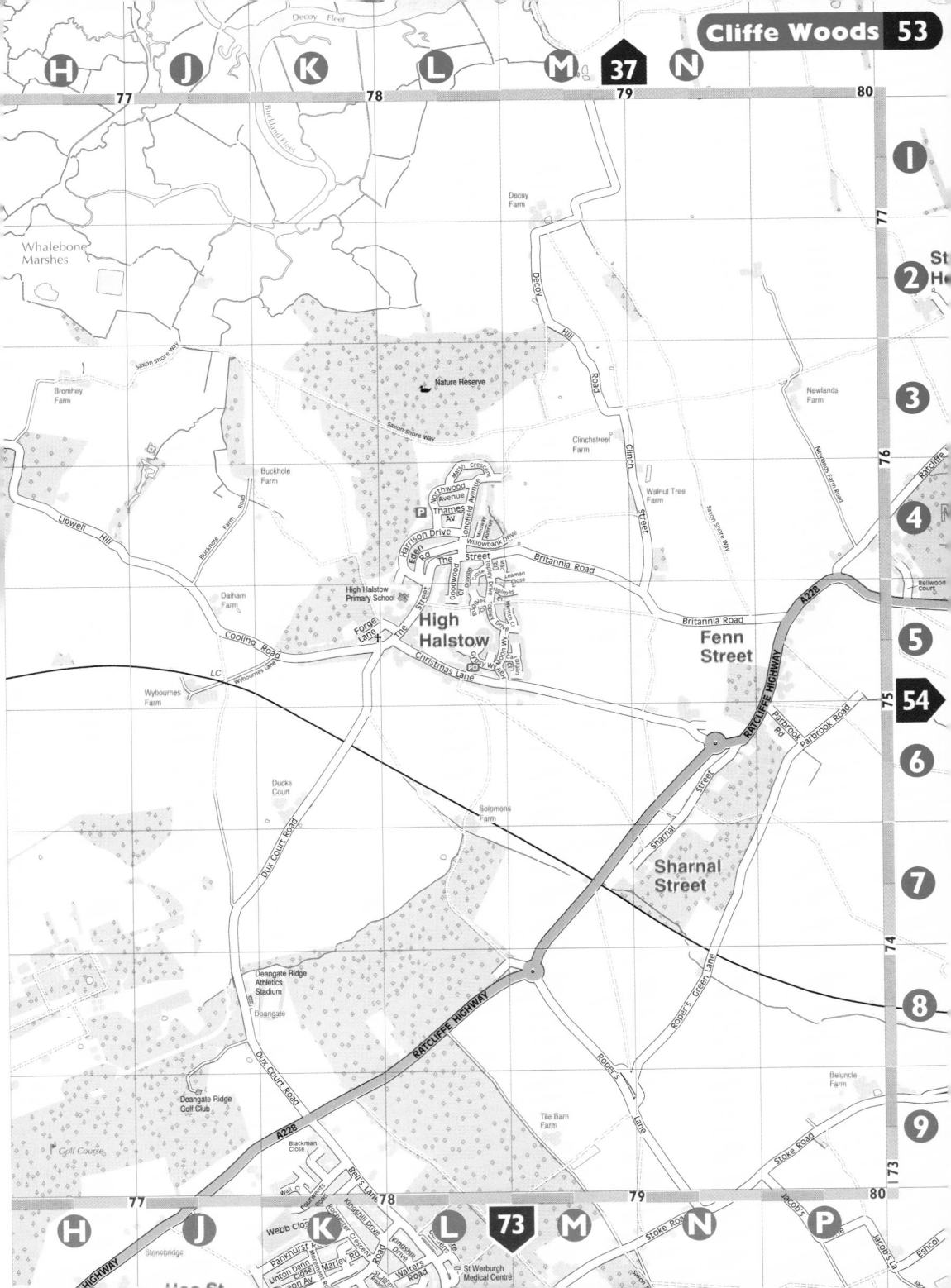

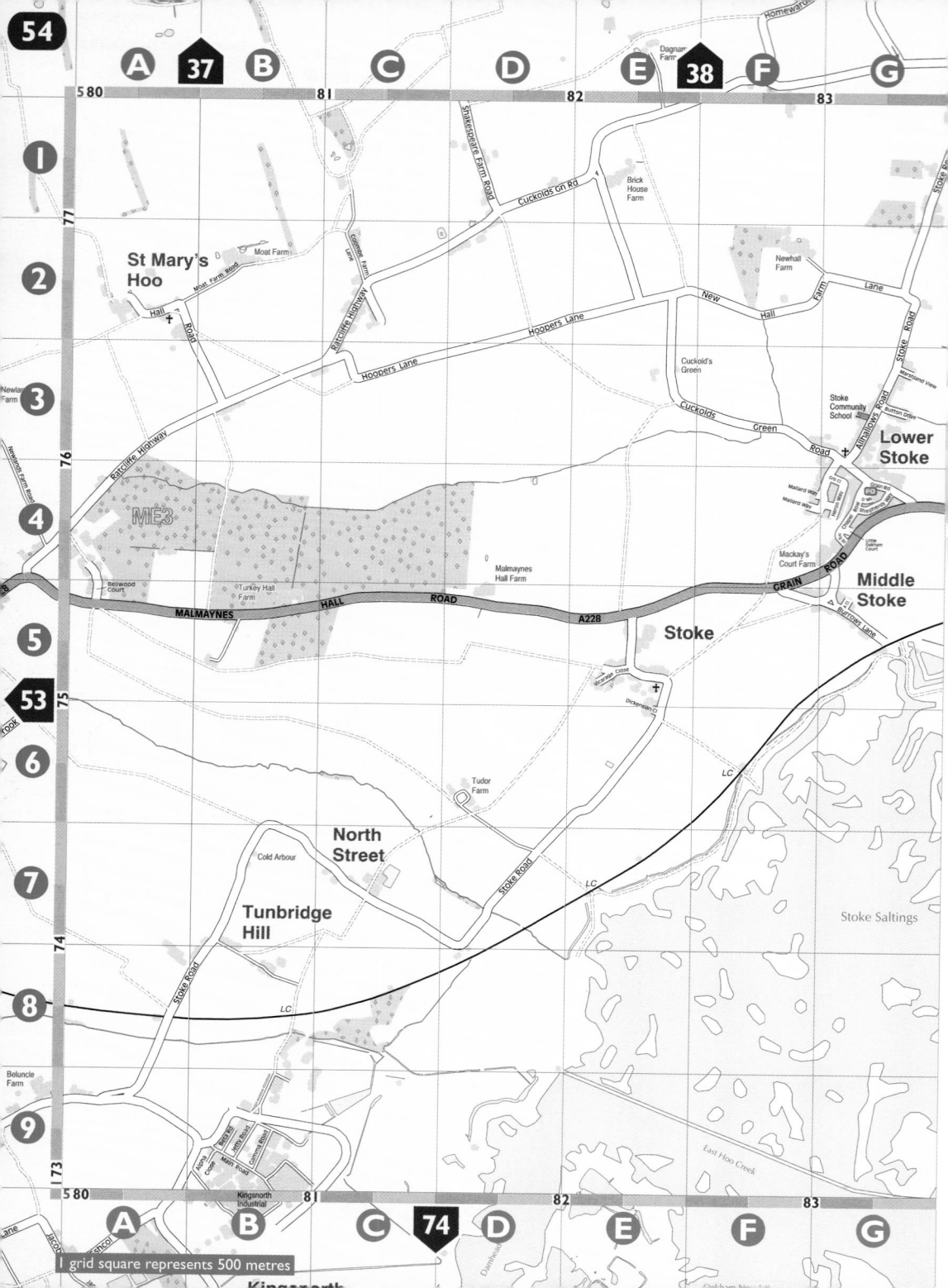

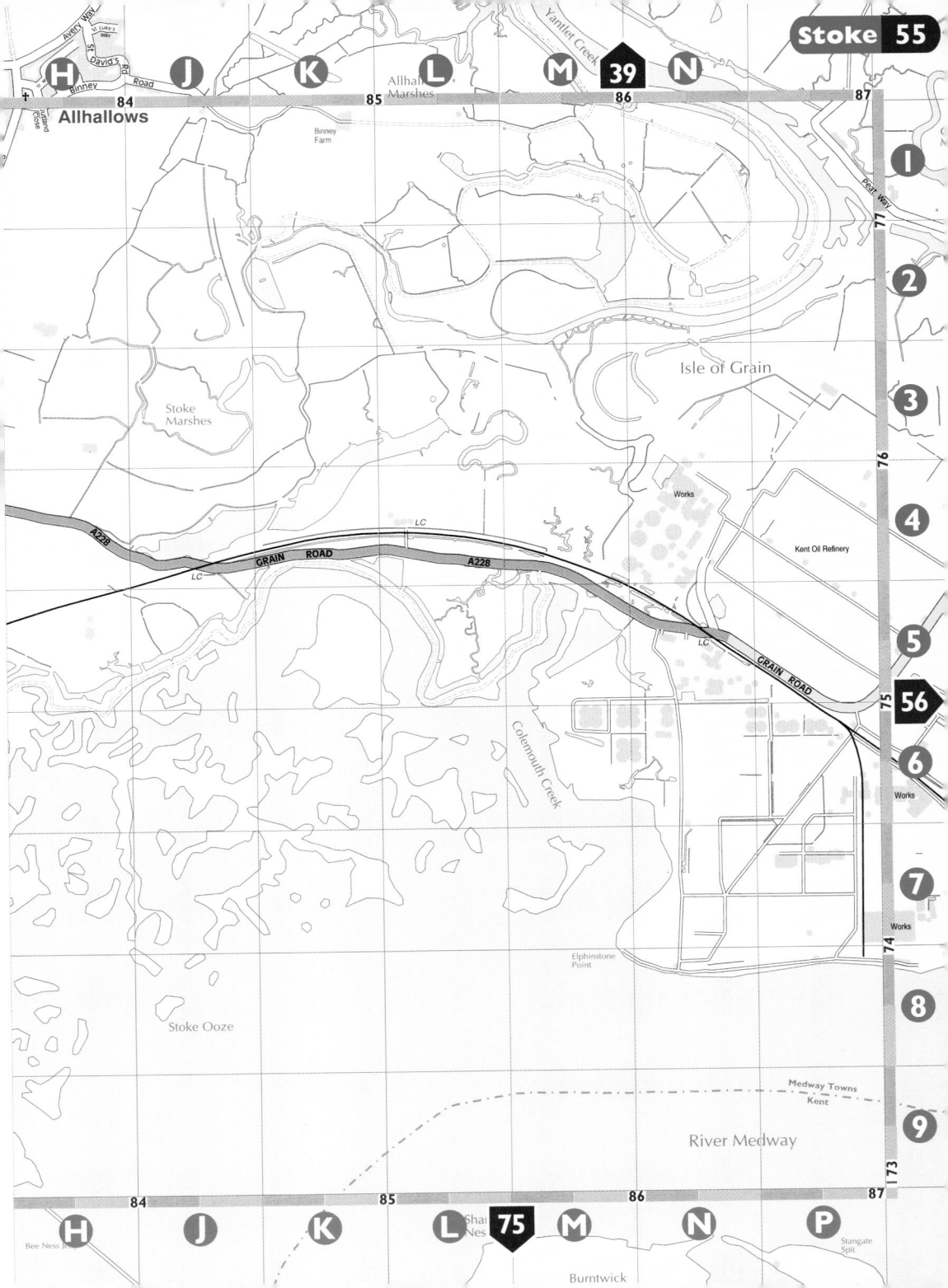

Allhallows

Isle of Grain

Binney Farm

Allhallows Marshes

Yantlet Creek

Stoke Marshes

Works

Kent Oil Refinery

A228

GRAIN ROAD

A228

LC

LC

LC

GRAIN ROAD

Colemouth Creek

Works

Works

Stoke Ooze

Elphinstone Point

Medway Towns
Kent

River Medway

Bee Ness Jty

Sharp Ness

Burntwick

Stangate Spit

Pearl Way

A   B   39   C   D   E   F   G

5 87   88   89   90

1

Grain
Marsh

Peat Way

77

West Lane

Peat Way

Rose
Court Farm

Works

2

Perry's
Farm

Pannell Road

P

HIGH STREET

St James CE
Primary School

Green Lane

Grain

B2001   Chapel

Po

Edinburgh Road

Coronation Road

Crayne
Avenue

Rivendene
Close

Surgery

Chapel Road

Port
Victoria Road

Rivendene
Close

3

GRAIN ROAD

76

B2001

4

Oil Refinery

Port Victoria Road

Grain Power Station

5

55

75

6

Works

7

Works

74

8

Medway Towns
Kent

River Medway

Towns

9

Saltpan Reach

1 73

5 87   88   89   90

A   B   C   76   D   E   F   G

Stangate
Spit

Queenborough
Spit

Deadmans
Island

West Sw

Works

1 grid square represents 500 metres

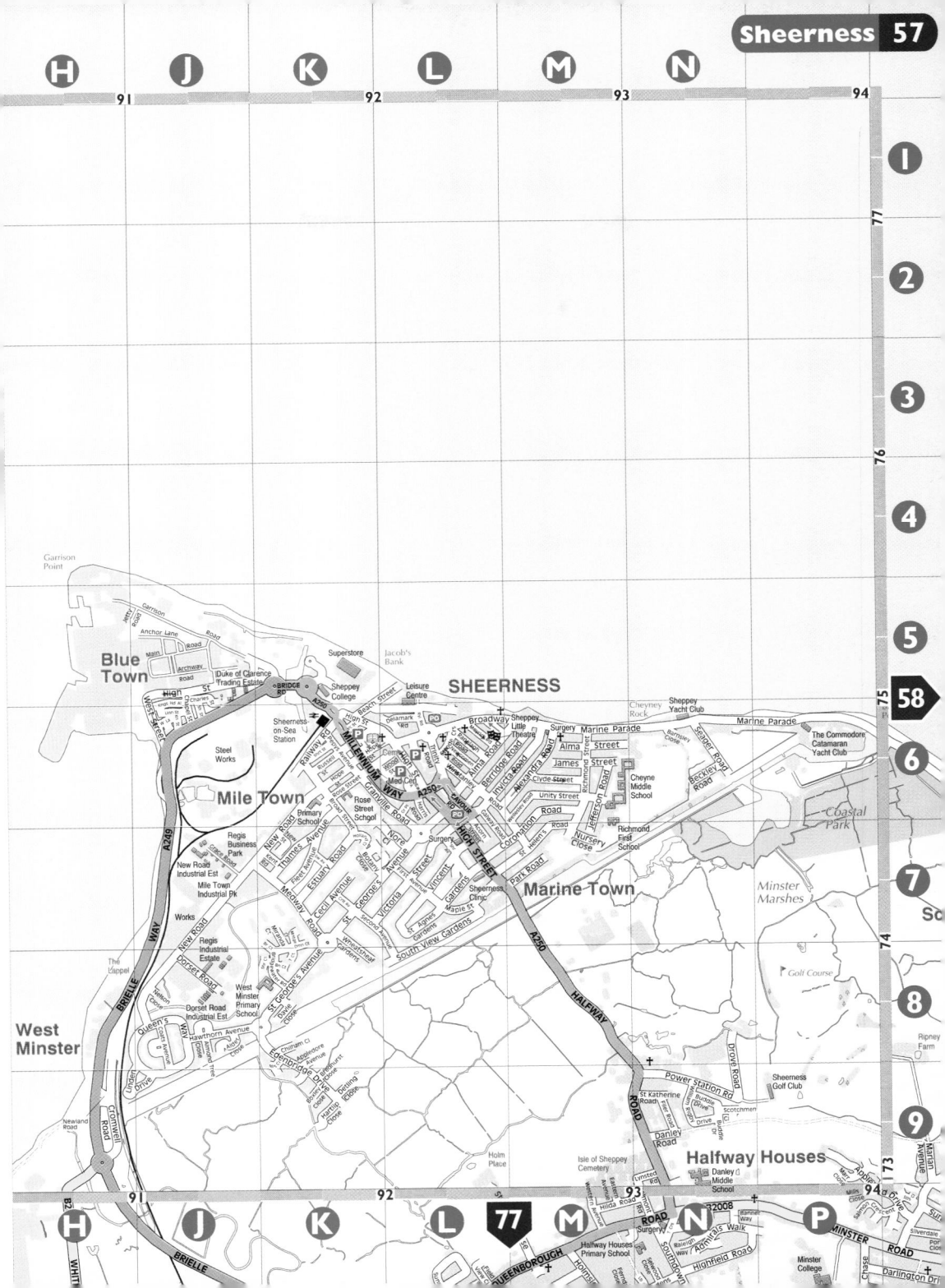

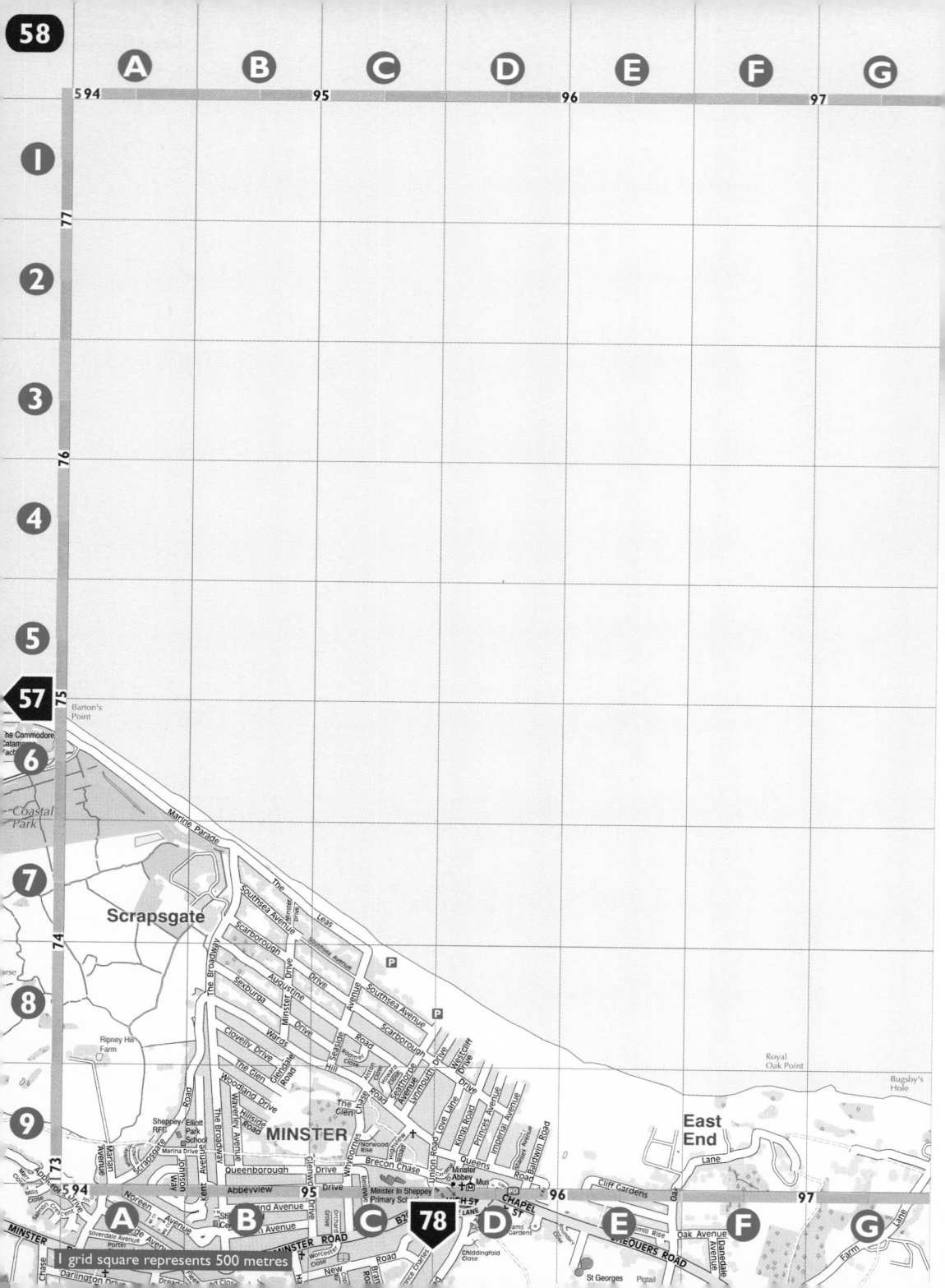

58

A B C D E F G

594 95 96 97

77

76

75

57

Barton's Point

The Commodore
Catamaran
Yacht

Coastal
Park

Marine Parade

74

Scrapsgate

The Leas

Southsea Avenue

Scarborough

Southsea Avenue

The Broadway

Augustine

Sexburga

Minster Drive

Wards

Southsea Avenue

Scarborough

Eastcliff

Ripney Hill
Farm

Clovelly Drive

The Glen

Woodland Drive

Waverley Avenue

Hillside Road

The Glen

Chase Road

Road

Westcliff Drive

Kings Road

Princes Avenue

Imperial Avenue

Baldwin Road

Royal
Oak Point

Bugsby's
Hole

73

Sheppey
RFC

Elliott
Park
School

The Broadway

MINSTER

Norwood

Brecon Chase

Union Road Love Lane

Queens
Road

Minster
Abbey

**East
End**

Lane

Marian
Avenue

Scrapsgate

Johnson Way

Kent

Queenborough

Glenwood Drive

Abbeyview

Belleview

Drive

78

HIGH ST

CHAPEL
ST

Cliff Gardens

Oak Avenue

Darnsdale Avenue

594 95 Minster In Sheppey
Primary Sc 96 97

A B C D E F G

CHEQUERS ROAD

Farm Lane

St Georges Pigtail

1 grid square represents 500 metres

79

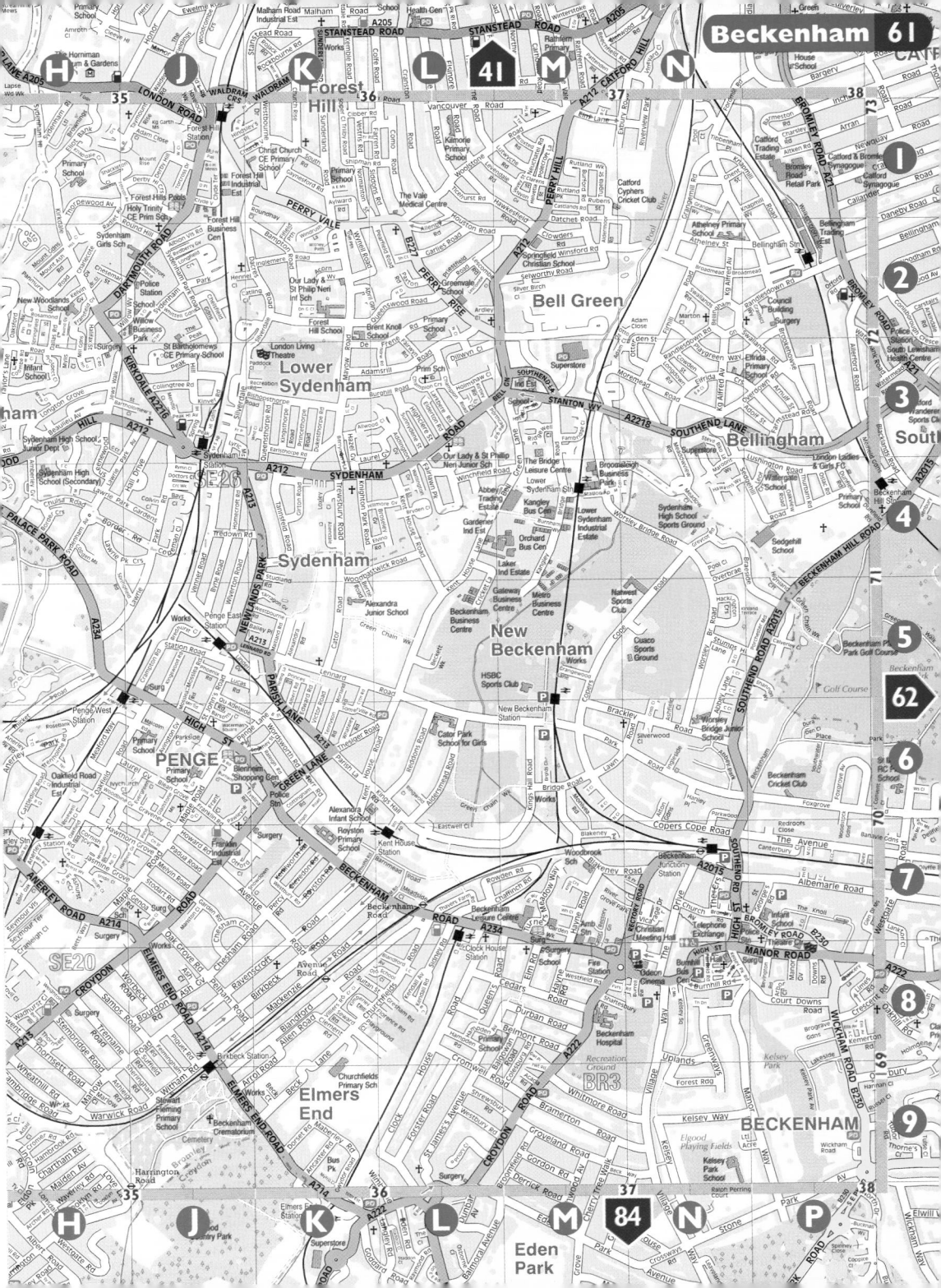

I grid square represents 500 metres

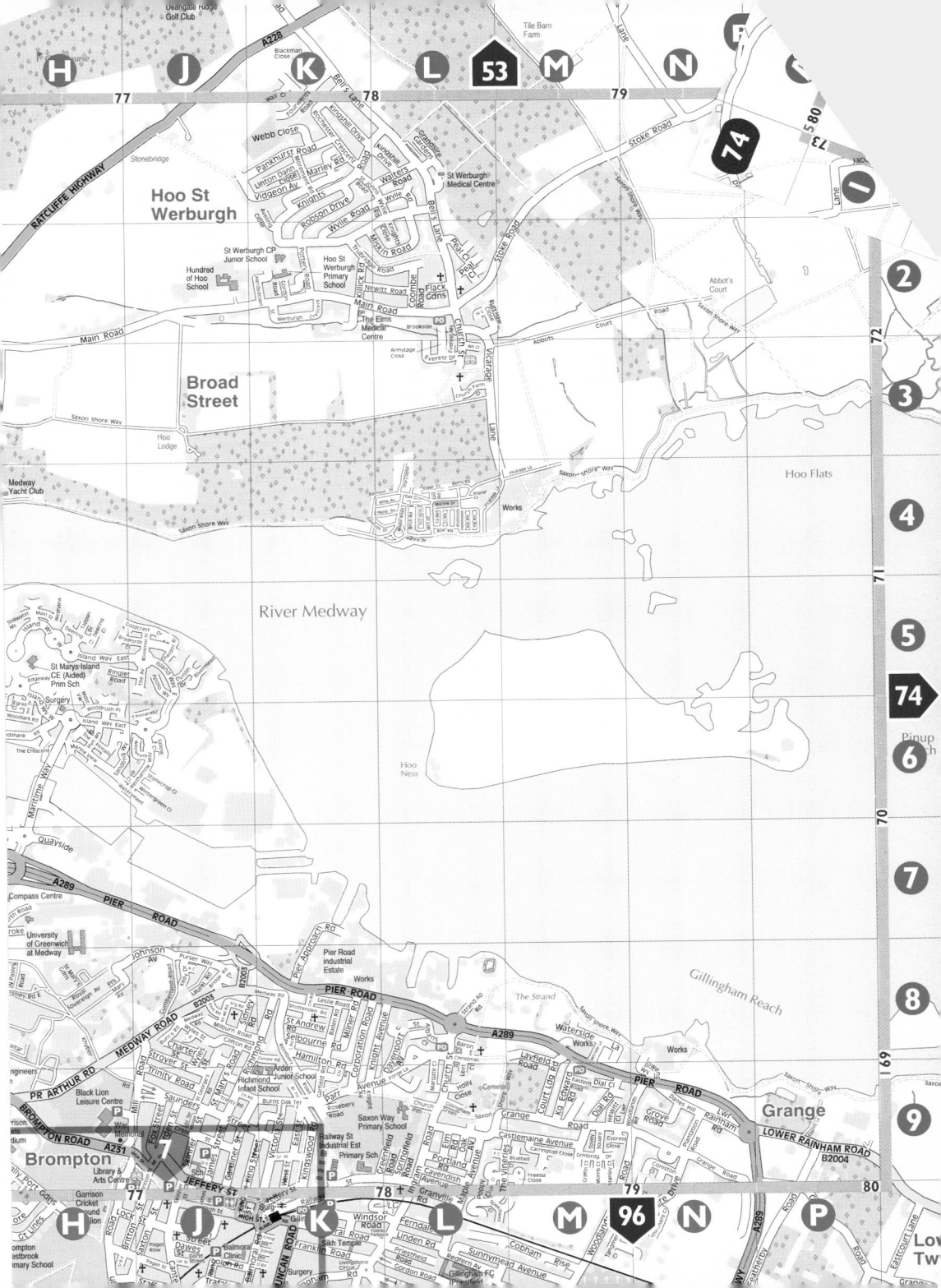

B

C

54 D

E

East Ho F

G

81

82

83

Saxon Road

Kingsnorth
Industrial
Estate

Kingsnorth

Damhead Creek

Oakham Ness Jetty

Oakham
Marsh

2

72

Kingsnorth Power Station

Slede Ooze

3

Medway

Flats

Long Reach

4

71

River

5

Damet
Fort

73

Bishop Ooze

South Yantlet Creek

6

Pinup
Reach

70

RSPB Reserve

7

Nor
Marsh

8

Bartlett Creek

169

9

Saxon Shore Way

Way

HAM ROAD
B2004

East Court
Farm

RSPB
Reserve

Motney
Hill

Works

5 80

81

82

97

83

A

Lower

B

Riverside
Country Park

C

D

RAINHAM

E

F

G

Saxon Shore Green

Shore Lane

I grid square represents 500 metres

River Medway

Kent

H J K L **55** M N

84 85 86 87 73

I

Sharp
Ness

Stangate
Spit

Bee Ness Jetty

Burntwick
Island

2

Stangate

72

Oakham
Ness

Kethole Reach

3

Sharfleet Creek

4

Bishop Spit

71

Greenborough
Marshes

Medway Towns
Kent

5

Ham Ooze

Slayhills
Marsh

76

Half Acre

6

70

7

Milfordhope
Marsh

Twinney Creek

8

Halstow Creek

69

Bayford

Shoregate Lane

9

Pool Lane

Saxon Shore Way

Ham
Green

Saxon Shore Way

84 85 86 87

H J K L M **98** N P

Wetham
Green

76

A B C 56 D E F G

5 87   88   89   90

73

I

Kent

Saltpan Reach

Queenborough
Spit

Deadmans
Island

West
Swale

Work

2

72

Stangate Creek

West
Point

3

Long
Reach

4

71

Chetney
Marshes

eenborough
arshes

5

75

Saxon Shore Way

6

70

Saxon Shore Way

Slaughterhouse
Point

7

Saxon Shore Way

The Shade

Ferry
Marshes

8

Haktow Creek

69

Chetney
Cotts

Willow Bank
Industrial
Estate

Saxon Shore Way

9

Barksore
Marshes

Bedlams Bottom

Old Ferry Road

Raspberry   Hill   Lane

5 87   88   89   90

A B C D 99 E F G

Funton Creek

ey Way

shore Way

1 grid square represents 500 metres

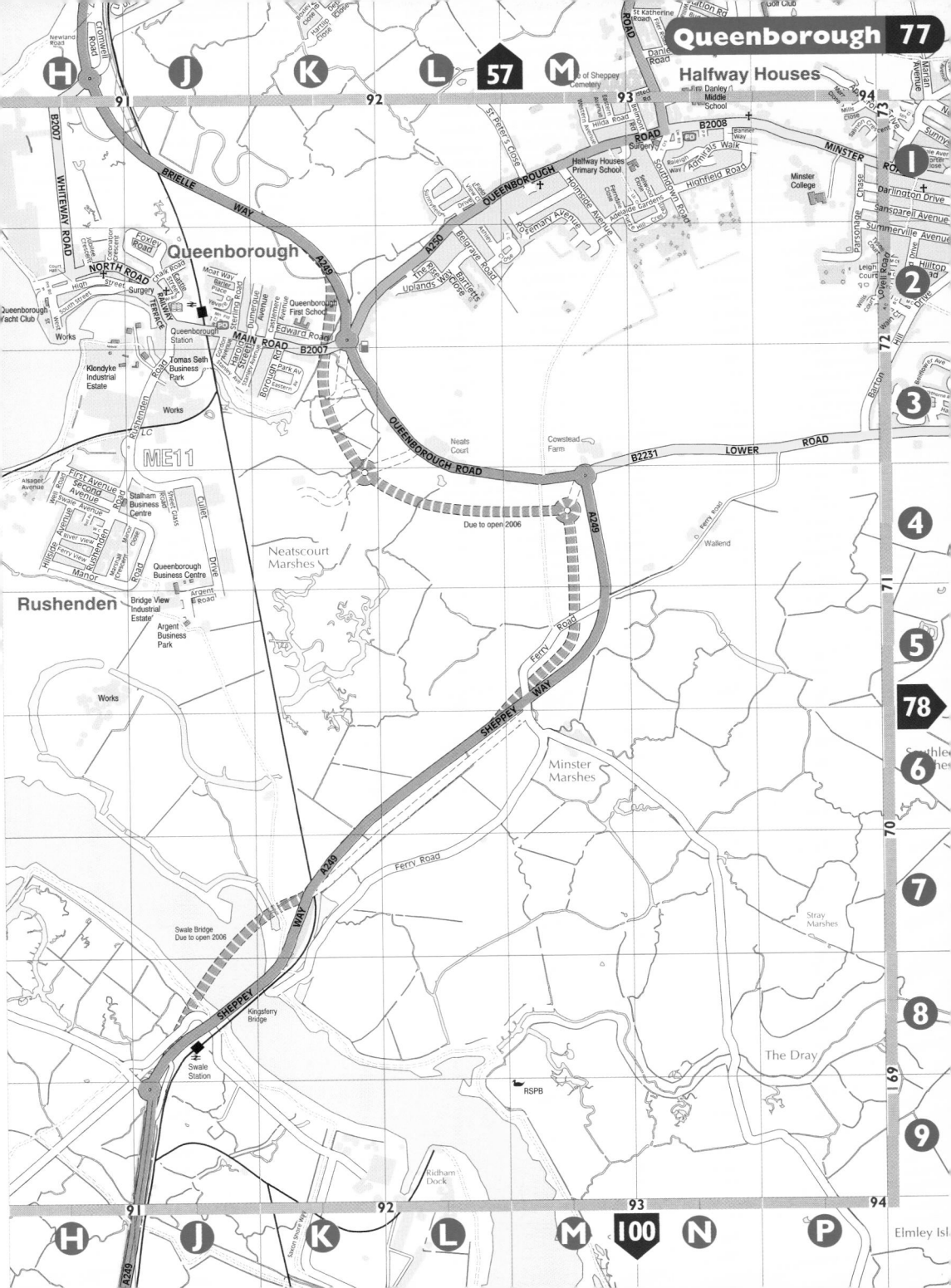

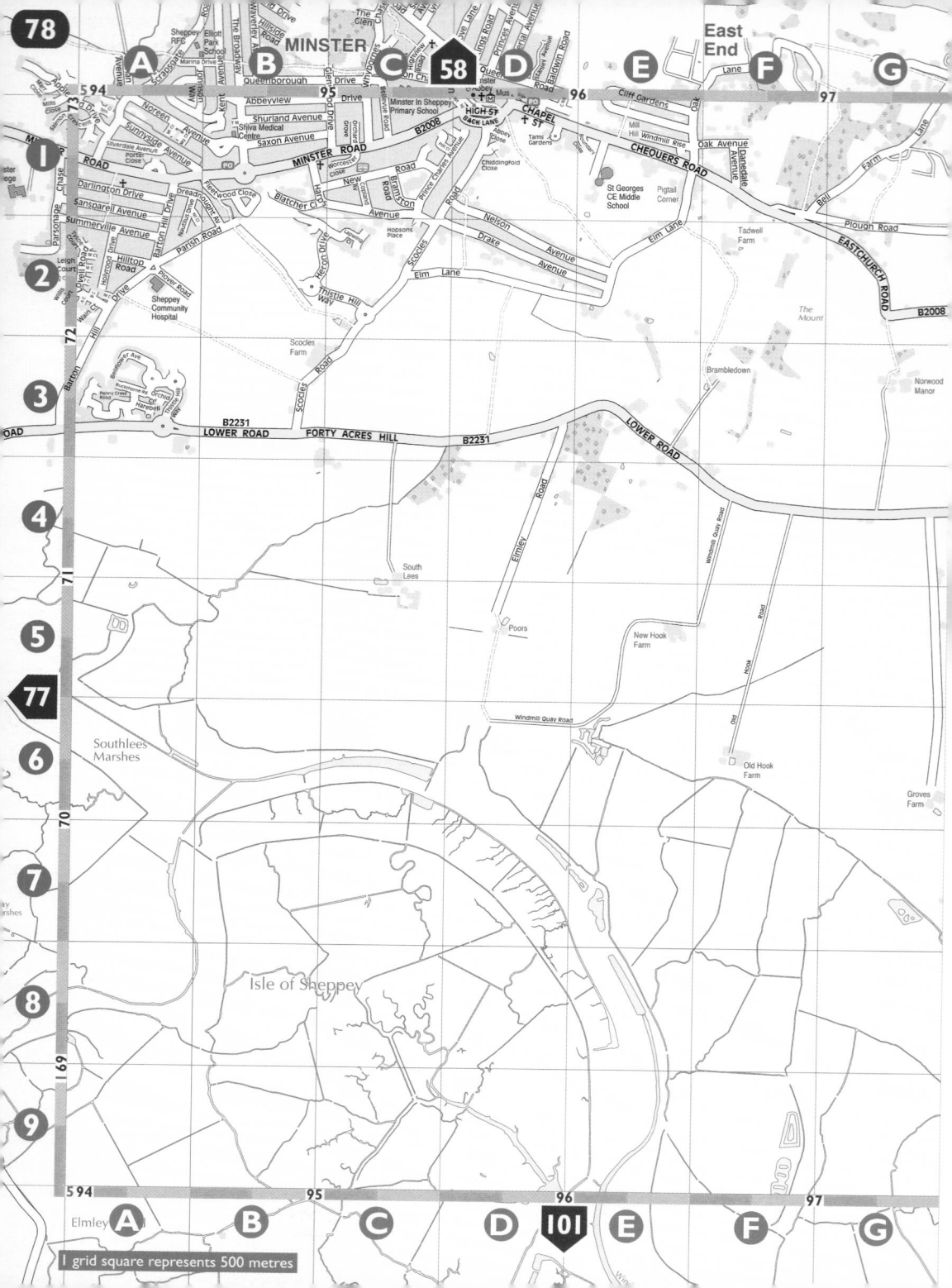

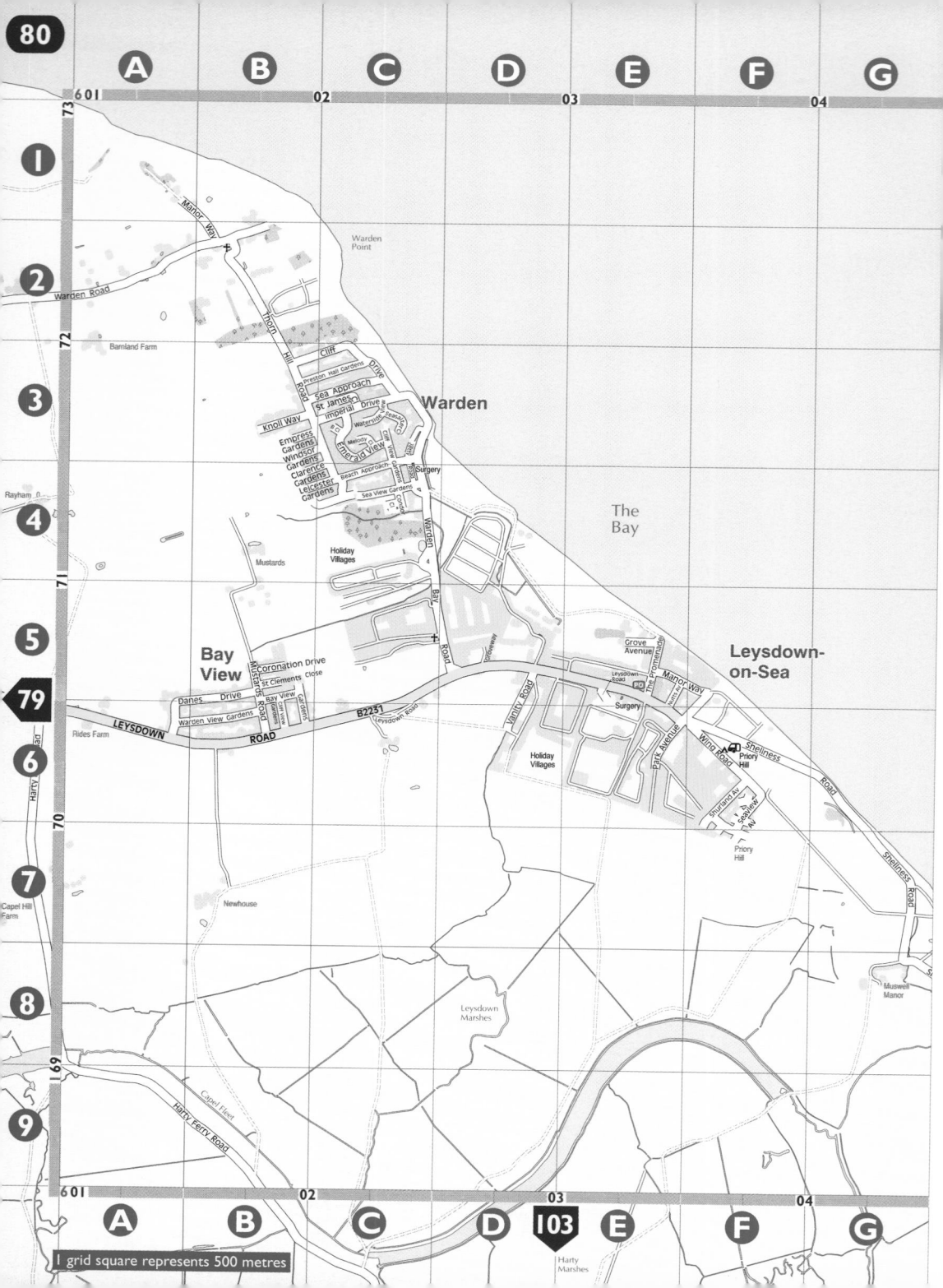

Warden 81

I grid square represents 500 metres

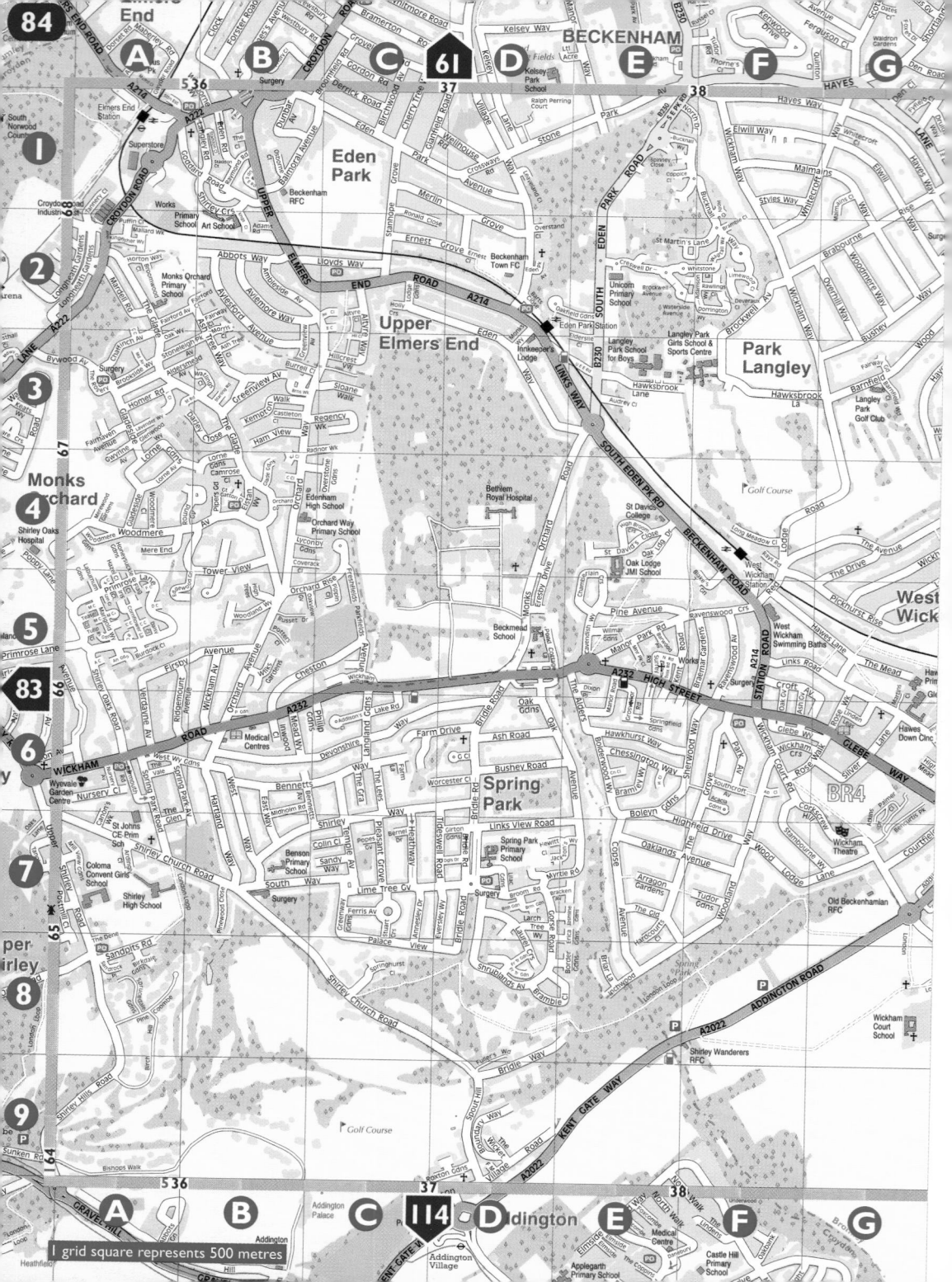

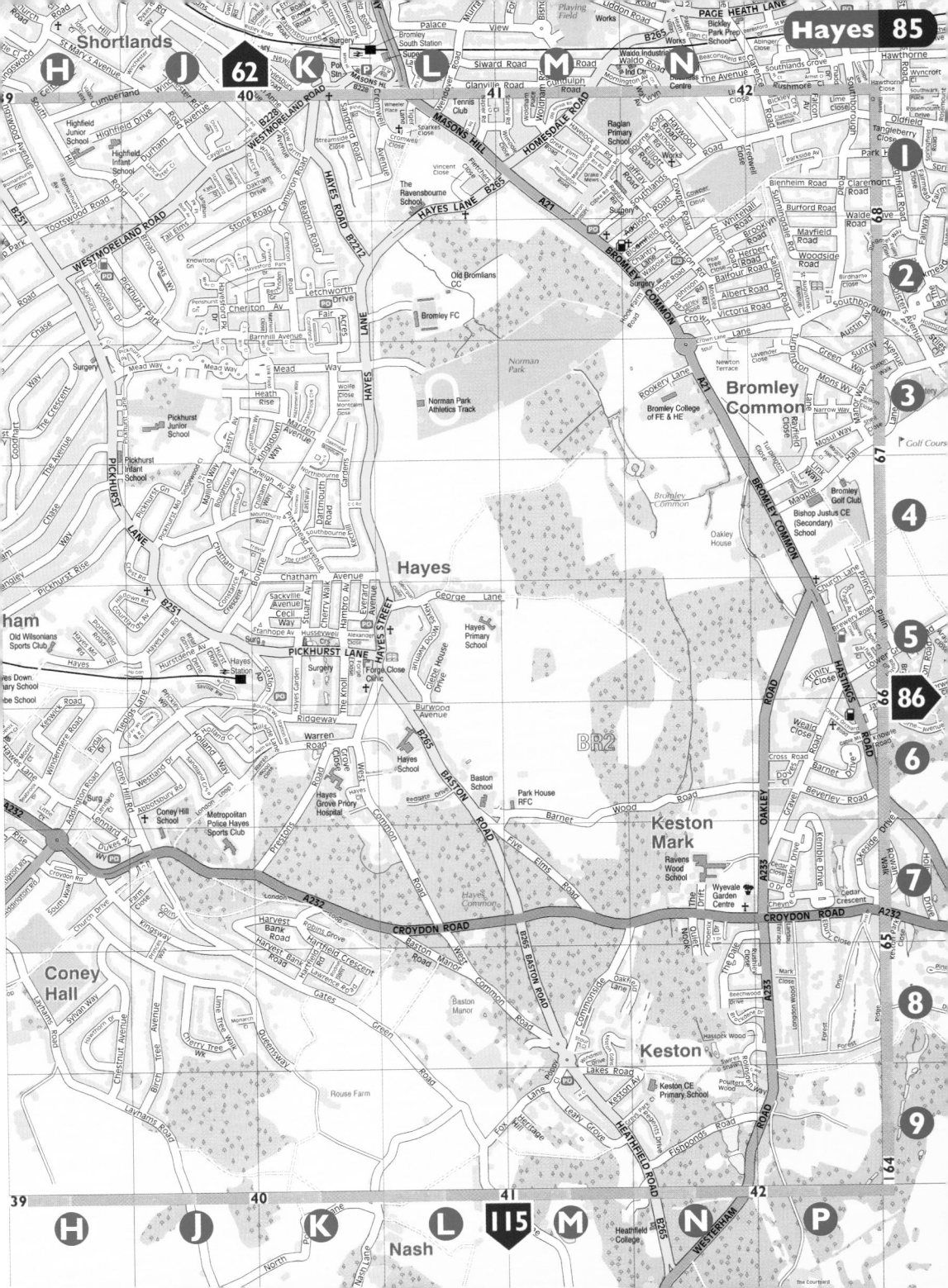

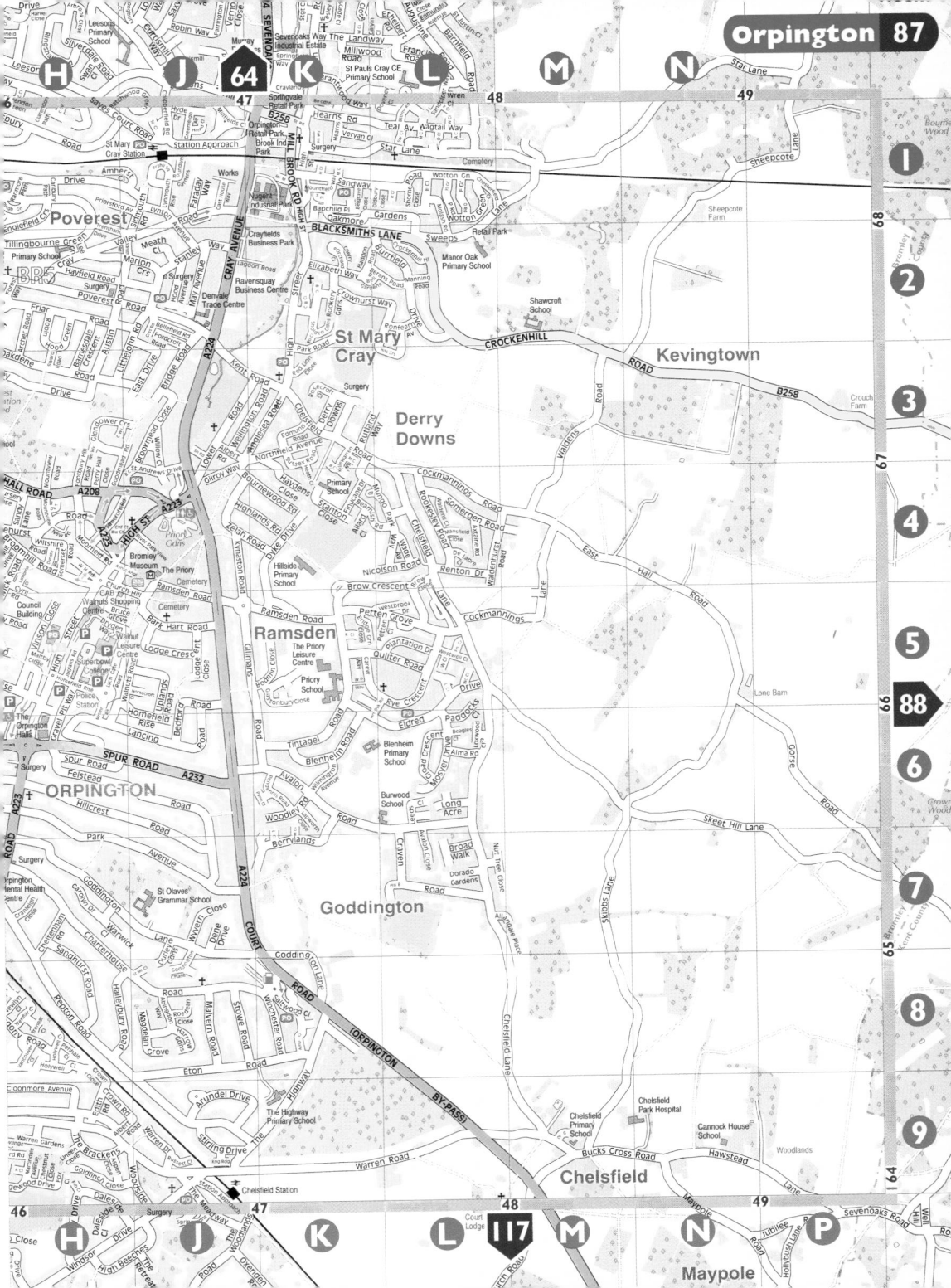

88

A   B   C   65   D   E   F   G

550

68

I

2

3

67

Crockenhill

CRAY ROAD B258   MAIN RD   Church Road

4

5

87   66

6

Road

7

65

8

Parkgate Road   Well Hill   Edmunds Road

9

164

Well Hill

550

A   B   C   118   D   E   F   G

Well Hill

Sevenoaks Road

I grid square represents 500 metres

51

BR8

A20

Wested

Hulberry

Junction 3/1

Lullingstone Roman Villa

Lullingstone Park Farm

Lullingstone Park Golf Club

Golf Course

Lullingstone Park

Beechen Wood

Darent Valley Path

Crockenhill Lane

Wested Lane

51

52

52

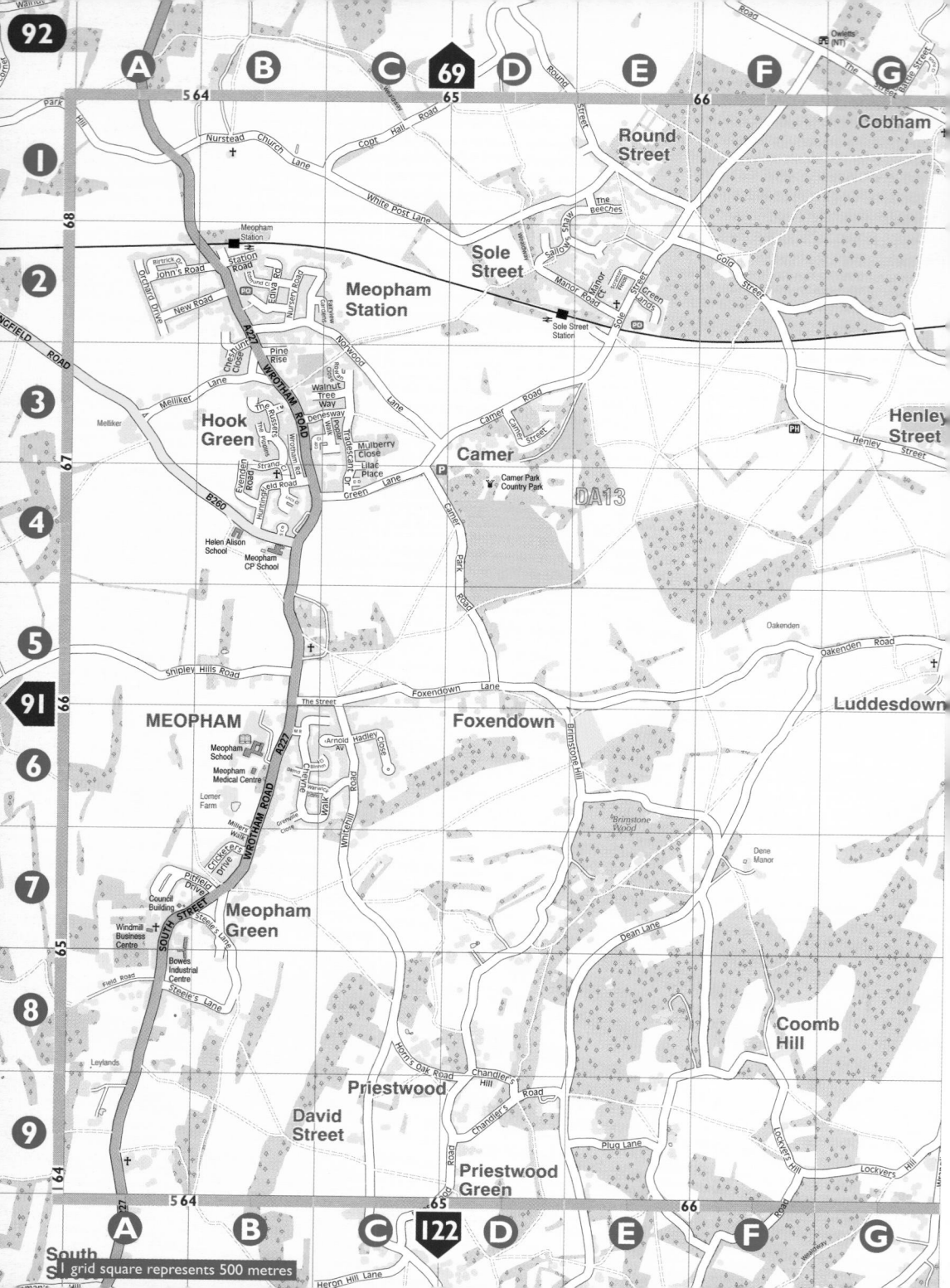

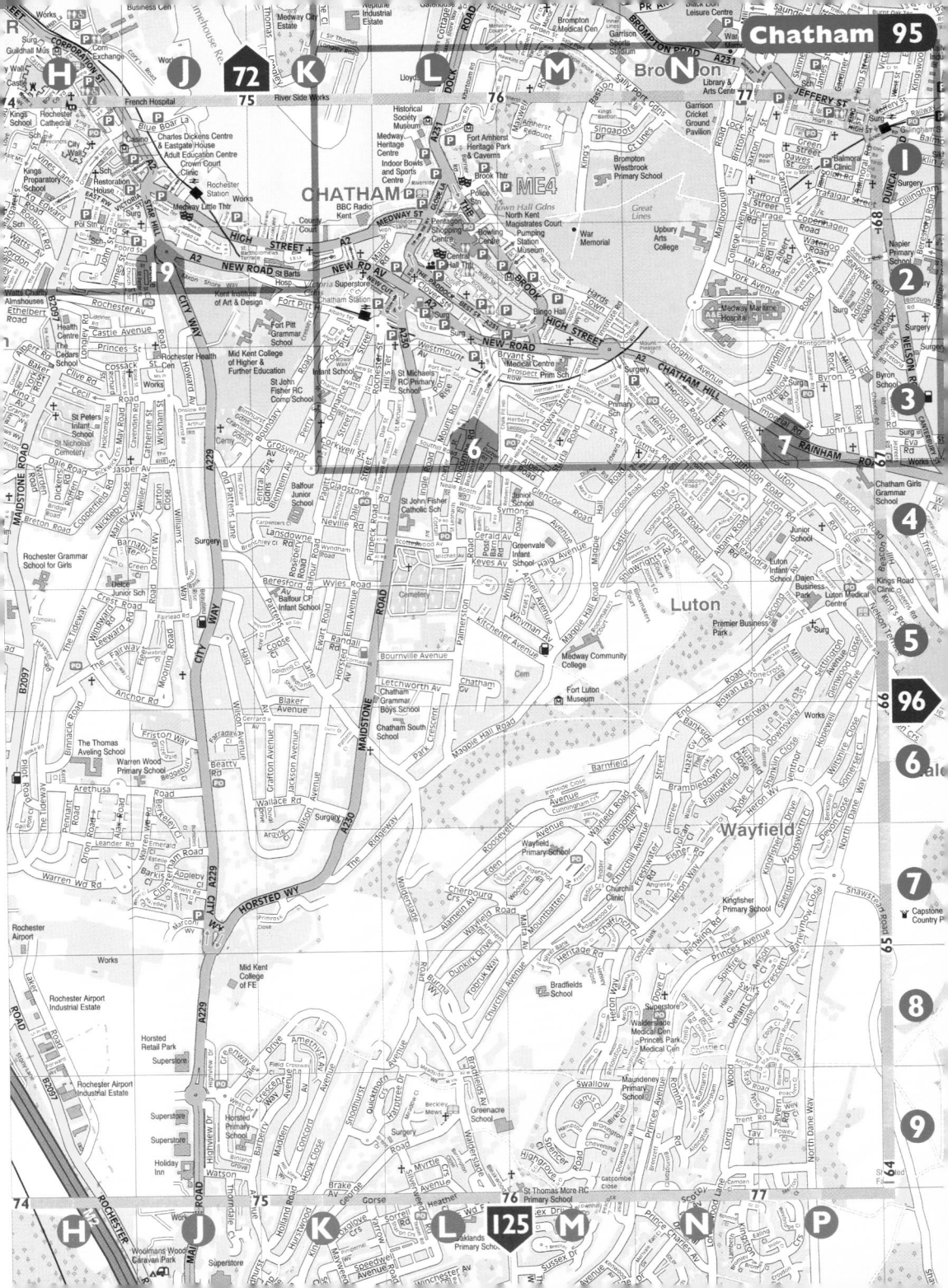

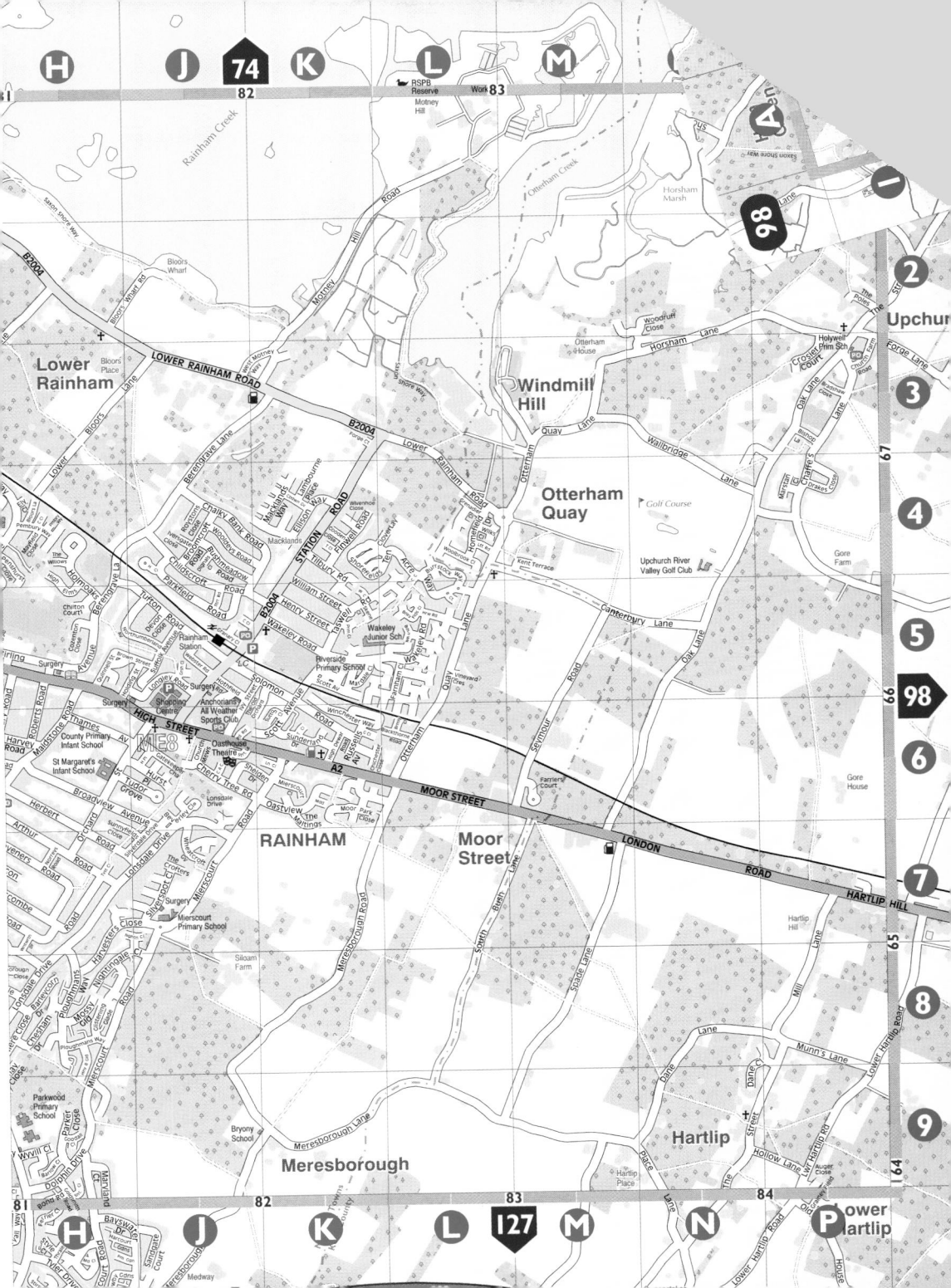

100

A   B   C   77   D   E   F   G
5 92   93   94

I

Elmley Island

Coldharbour
Marshes

68

Saxon Shore Way

2   Works

P
Kings Hill
Farm   Elmley
Marshes

3   Sharfleet Creek

67

4

The Swale

Paper
Mill   Works   The Lilies

5   Kemsley
Avenue   Down

99

Milton Creek   Saxon Shore Way

66

6   Little
Murston

Works   Tonge
Corner

7   Blacketts

65   Church Road

8   Anchor
Business
Park   Chieke's
Brickmakers   D2 Trading   Golf Course   Court
Industrial   Estate
Estate   Church
Road
Castleacre   Business
Industrial Park   Centre   Mere Court   Binny
Cotts

9   Eurolink
Industrial
Estate   East Hall
Dolphin
Sailing
Centre   The Oast
64   Eurolink   Murston   Golf Club
Industrial   Junior
Centre   School

Murston
Junior
School   Bax

A   B   93   C   130   D   E   F   G
5 92   Murston   94

All Saints Rd   Lomas Road

1 grid square represents 500 metres

H   J   **78**   K   L   M   N

95   96   97   98

1

68

2

3

67

4

Spitend Point

5

66   **102**

6

65

7

8

64

9

Great Bells

Bells

Dutchman's Island

Nature Reserve

Windmill Creek

Wellmarsh Creek

Spitend Marshes

Peg Fleet

Saxon Shore Way

Fowley Island

South Deep

Conyer Creek

swale Heritage Trail

Conyer Road

Conyer

Saxon Shore Way

The Brunswick

Teynham Level

Conyer Road

Conyer Road

Teynham Court

95   96   97   98

H   J   K   L   **131**   M   N   P

Teynham Street

St Mary

Marsh Lane

Luddenham Marshes

102

A B C **79** D E F G

5 99 600 01

I
68

Great
Bells

2

Bells Creek

3

man's

67

4

Spitend Point

Mocketts

5

101 66

The Ferry
Inn

6

Harty Ferry Road

Clavel Fleet

Harty Ferry Road

7

65

8

Nature
Reserve

Uplees

Uplees Road

Howletts

9

64

Luddenham
Marshes

A B C **132** D E F G

5 99 600 01

Poplar Hall

Court

I grid square represents 500 metres

A B C D E F G

68

67

66

103

65

Seasalter
Sailing Club

Faversham Road

Preston
Parade
Allan Road
Hodgson R
Mary's Grove
Foxdene
Road

PH

Lucerne Drive
Seasalter Cross
Ridgeway
Ladysmith
Rd
Kimberley Gr
Faversham Road

Bridge
Country
Leisure Club

64

Graveney
Marshes

Seasalter
Level

6 06 07 08

A B C **134** D E F G

1 grid square represents 500 metres

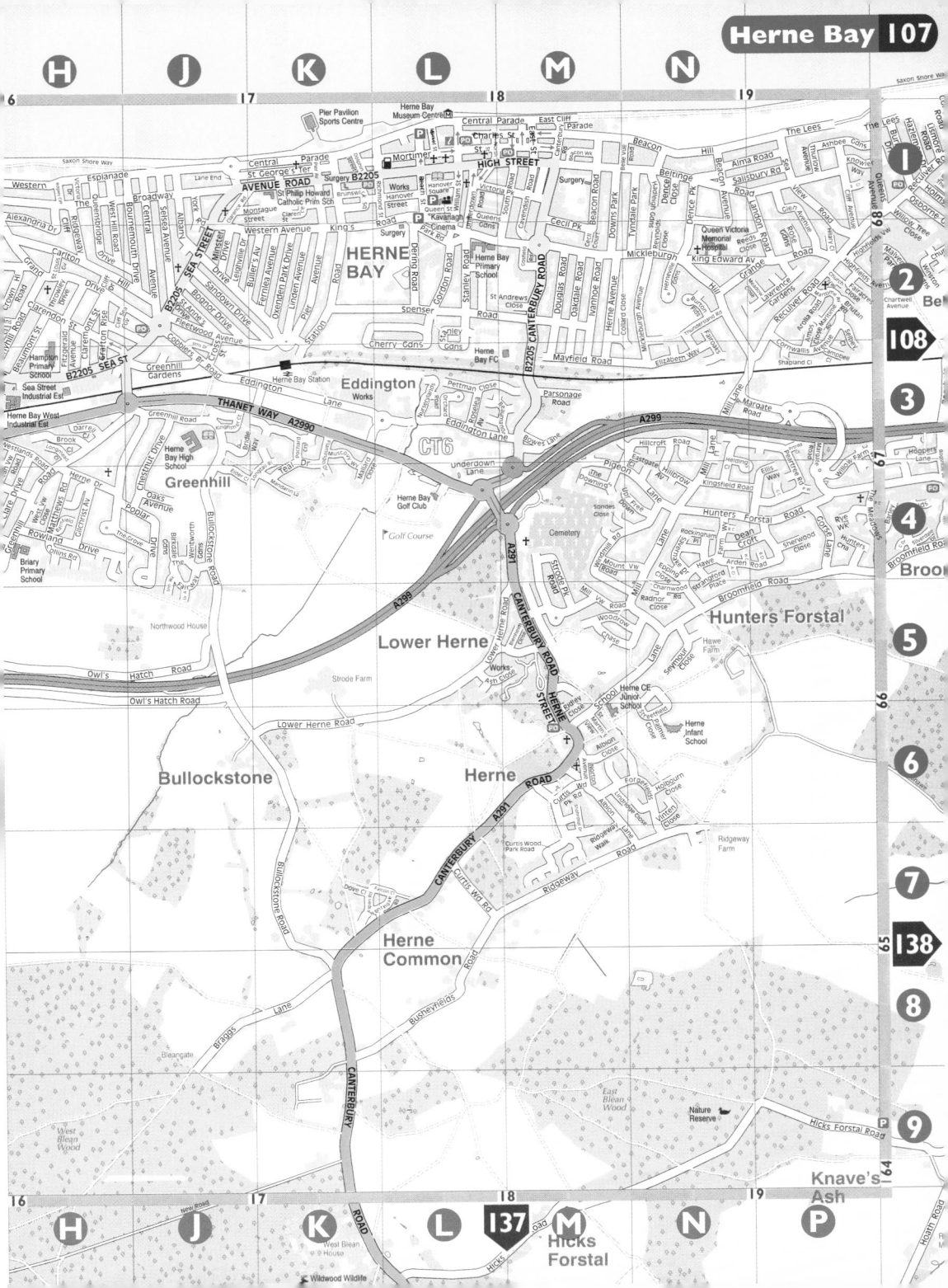

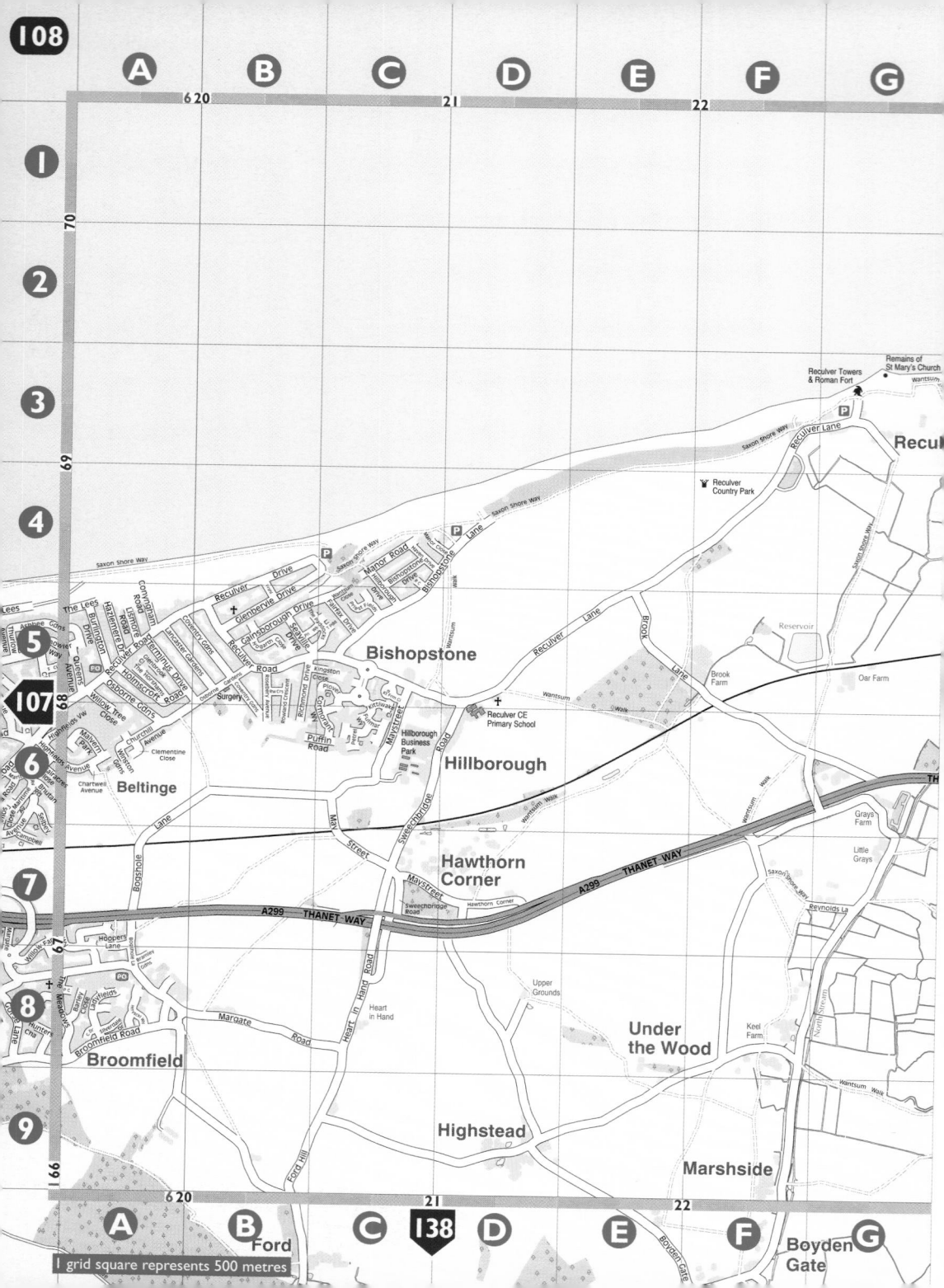

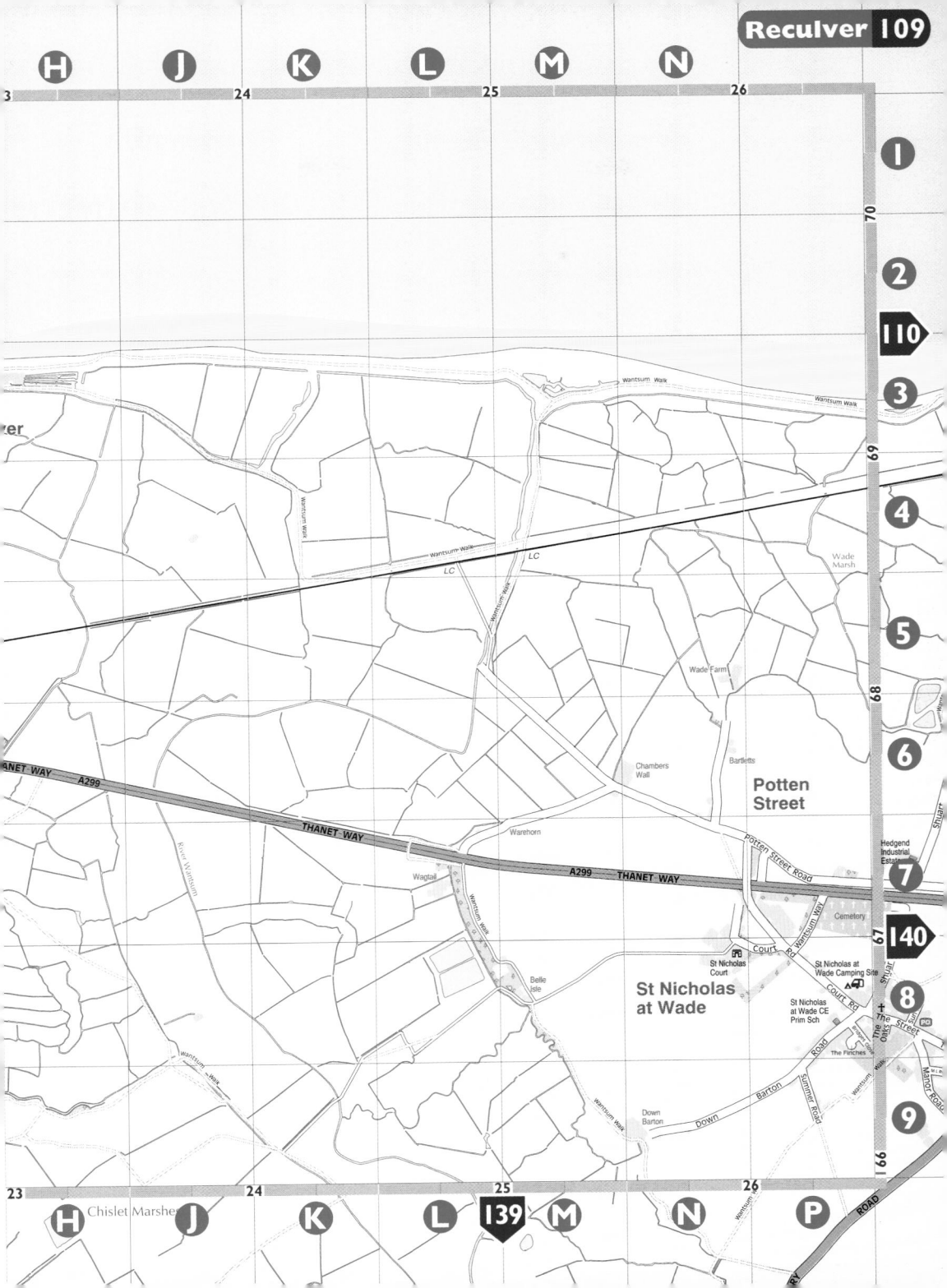

109

A B C D E F G

6 27 28 29

72

1

71

2

3

4

Grenham
Bay

70

5

Minnis Bay

Thanet Coastal Path
Cliff Road
The Parade
Harold Road
Anna Close
Green Road
Herschell
Alfred Road
Sea View Road
Beach Avenue
Grenham Road
Coulter Avenue
St Michaels Avenue
The Parade
King's Avenue
Canute Road
Minnis Road
Ingoldsby Road
Bishington-on-Sea Stn
Minnis Bay Sailing Club
Darvington Avenue
Dane Road
Wantsum Walk
Hilda Road
Pembroke Lodge
Mus & Art Gallery
Surgery
Conyer Square
London Gardens
Lincoln Gardens
Manor Drive
Essex Gardens
Devon Gardens

69

6

Plumpudding
Island

LC

LC

Wantsum Walk

7

Wade
Marsh

68

8

Shuart

Great
Brooksend
Farm

Canterbury Road Birchington

9

Shuart
Lane

Shuart
Lane

Hale

Netherhale

Brooks End

A28

Coney
Close

College Farm

Monkton
Road
Farm

A B C D E F G

6 27 28 29

CT7

Hedgend
Industrial
Estate

1 grid square represents 500 metres

Cemetery

THANET WAY

Potten Street Road

Frost

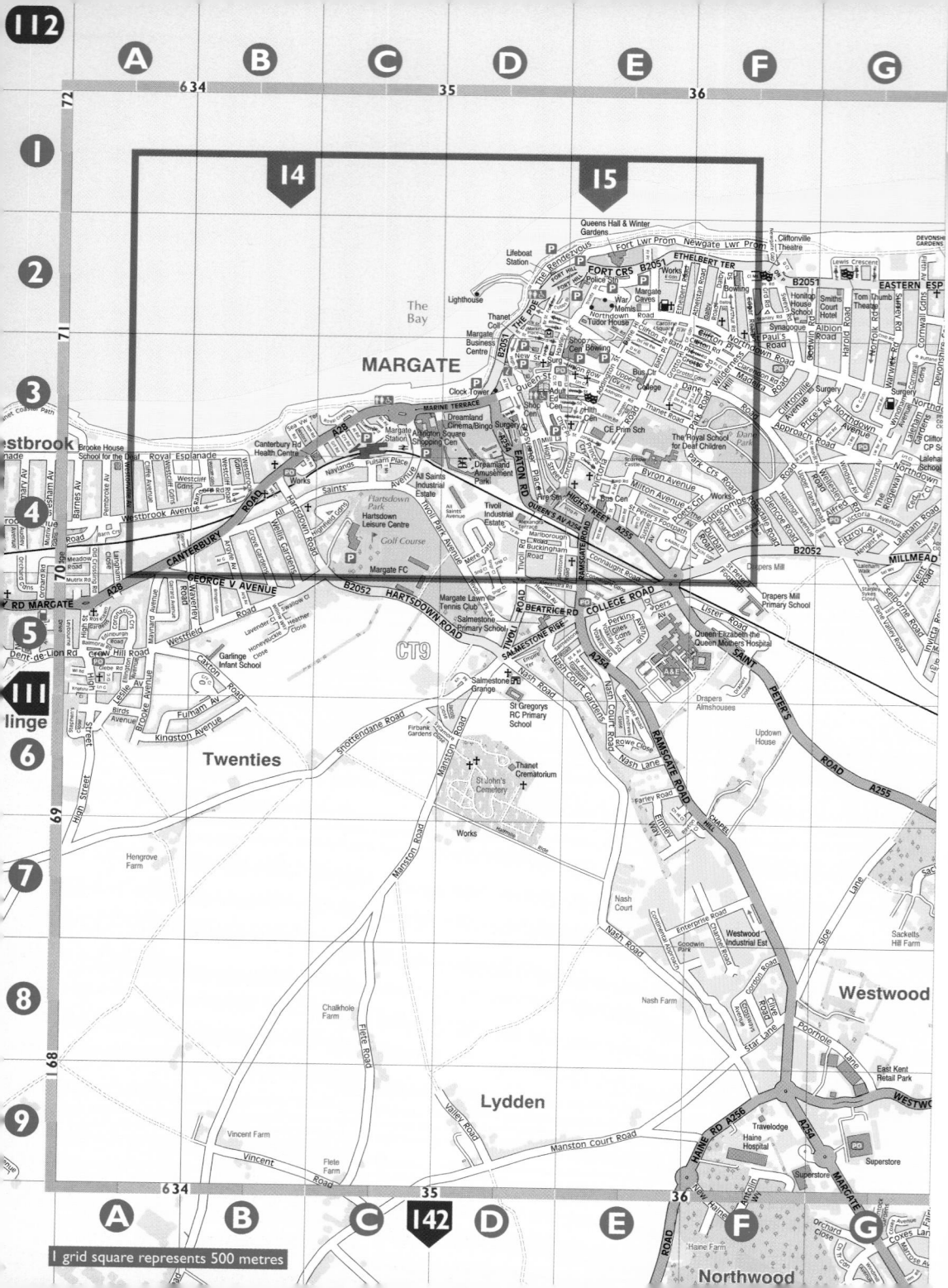

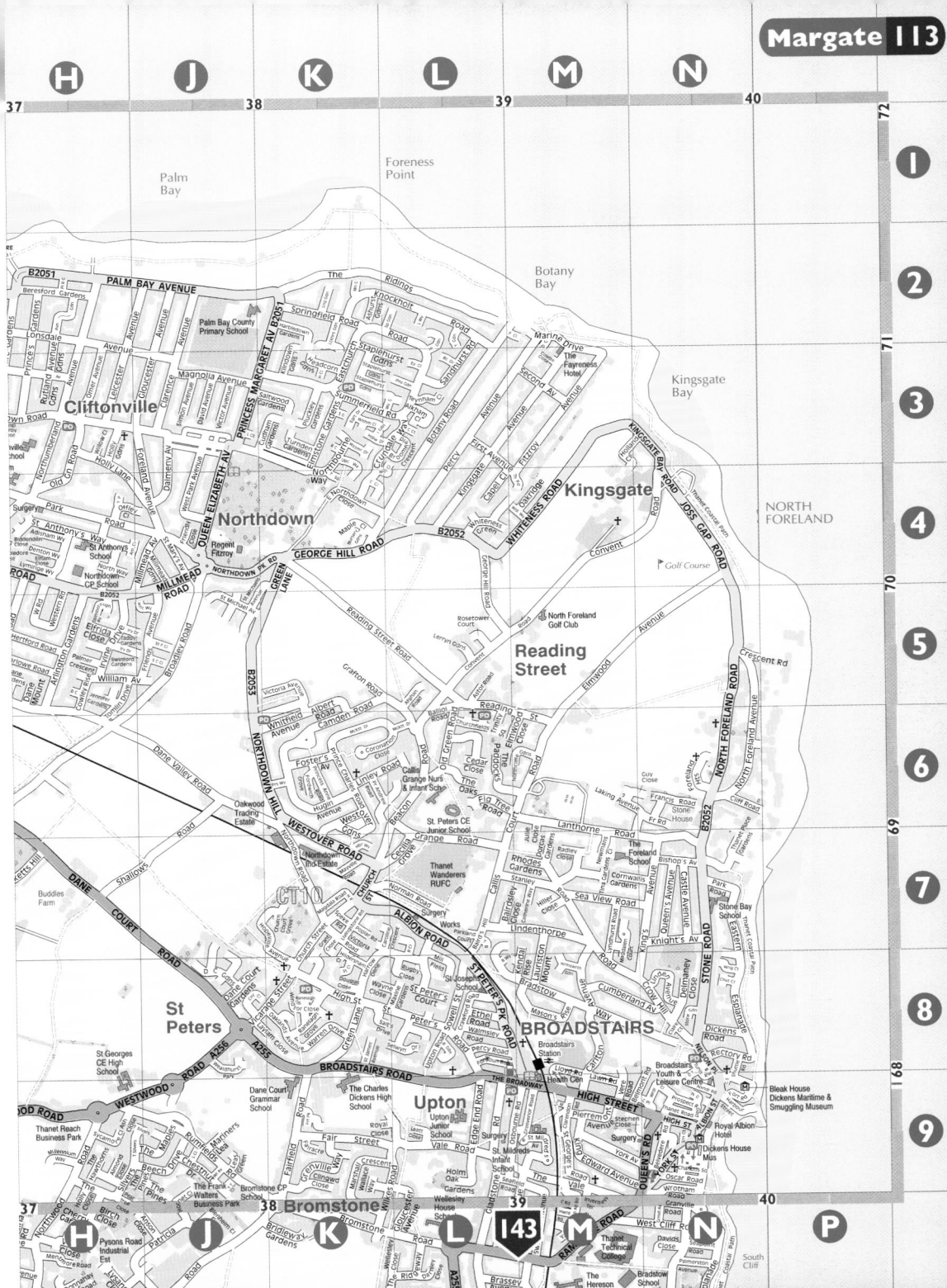

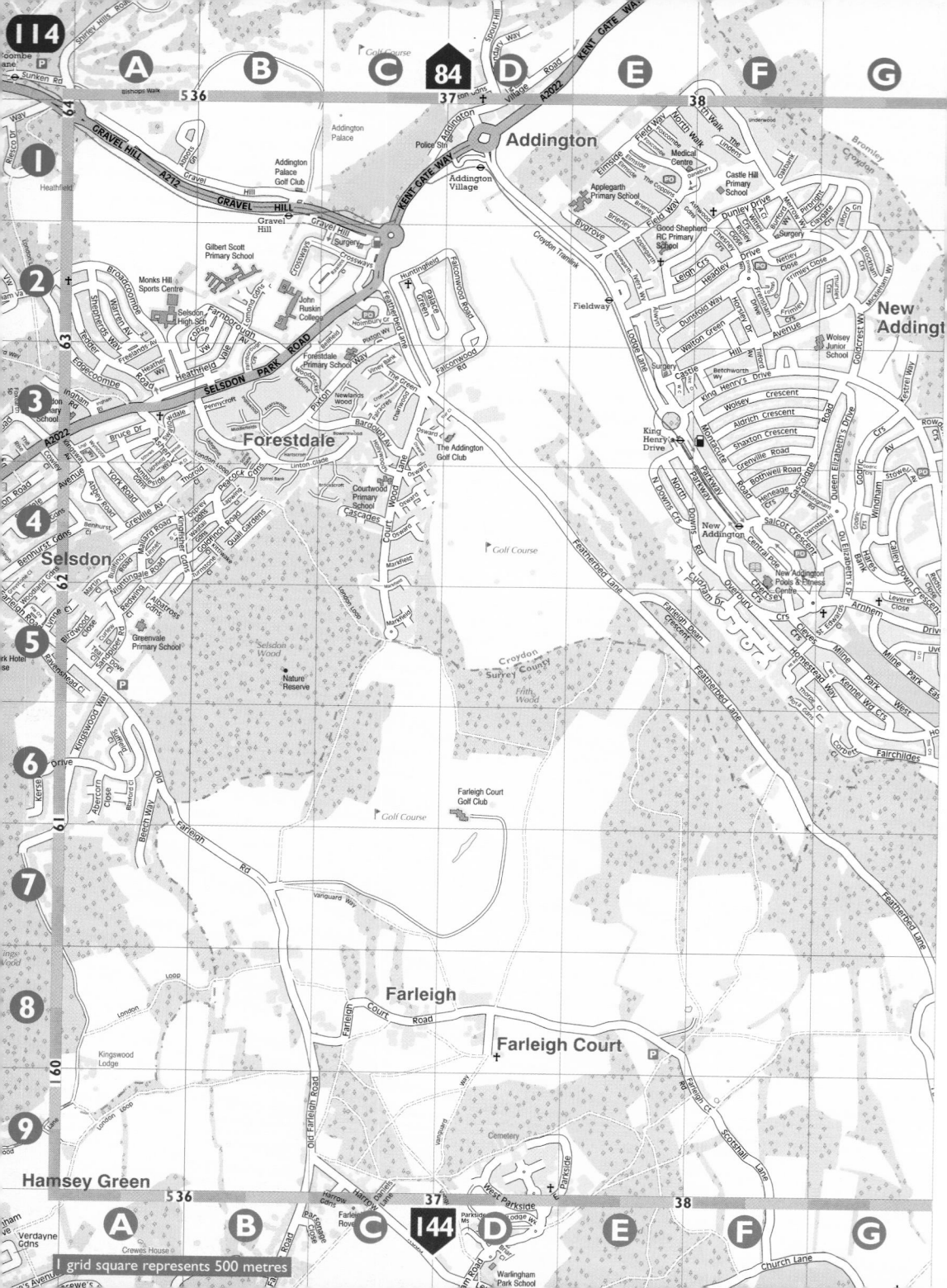

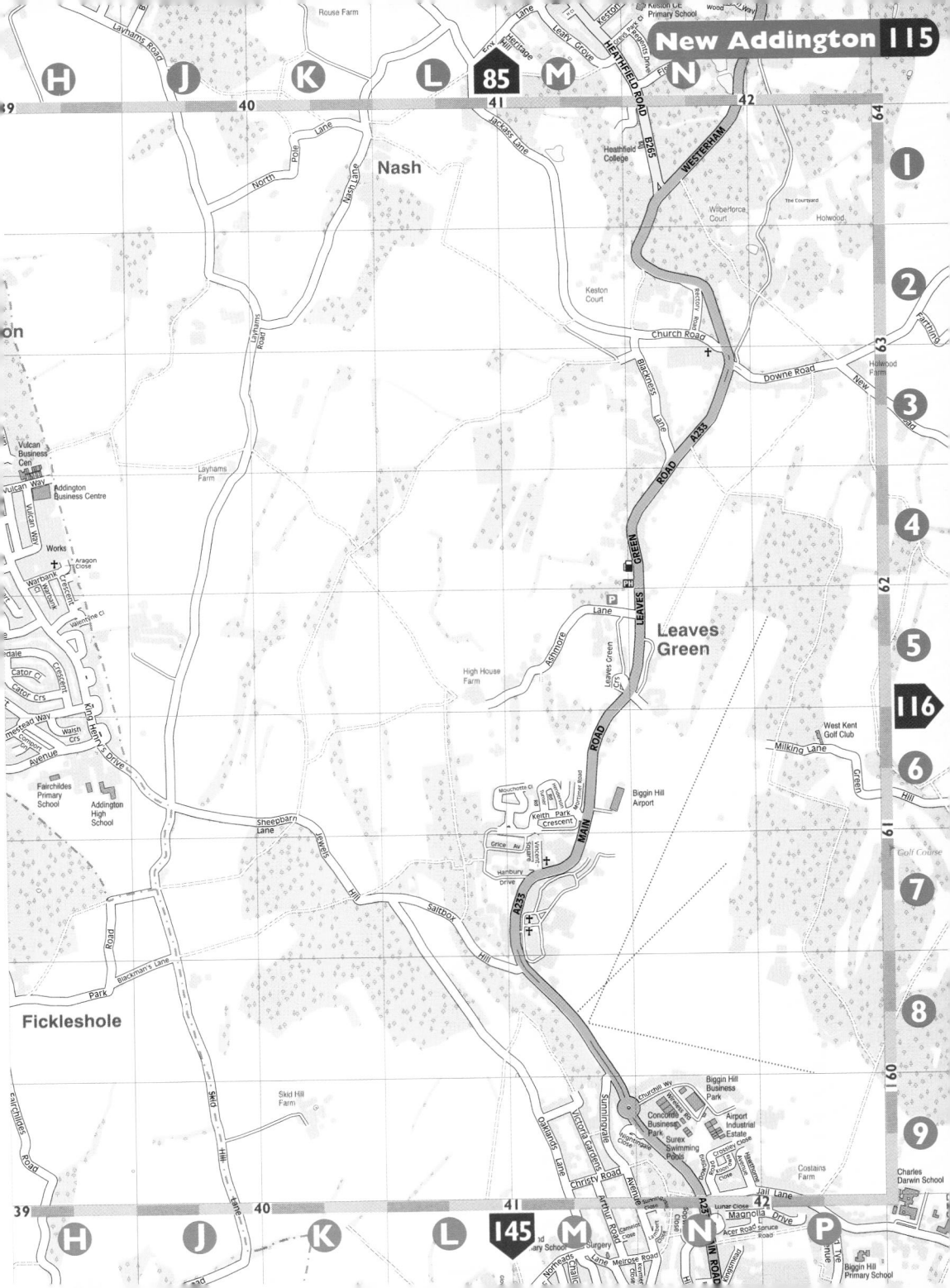

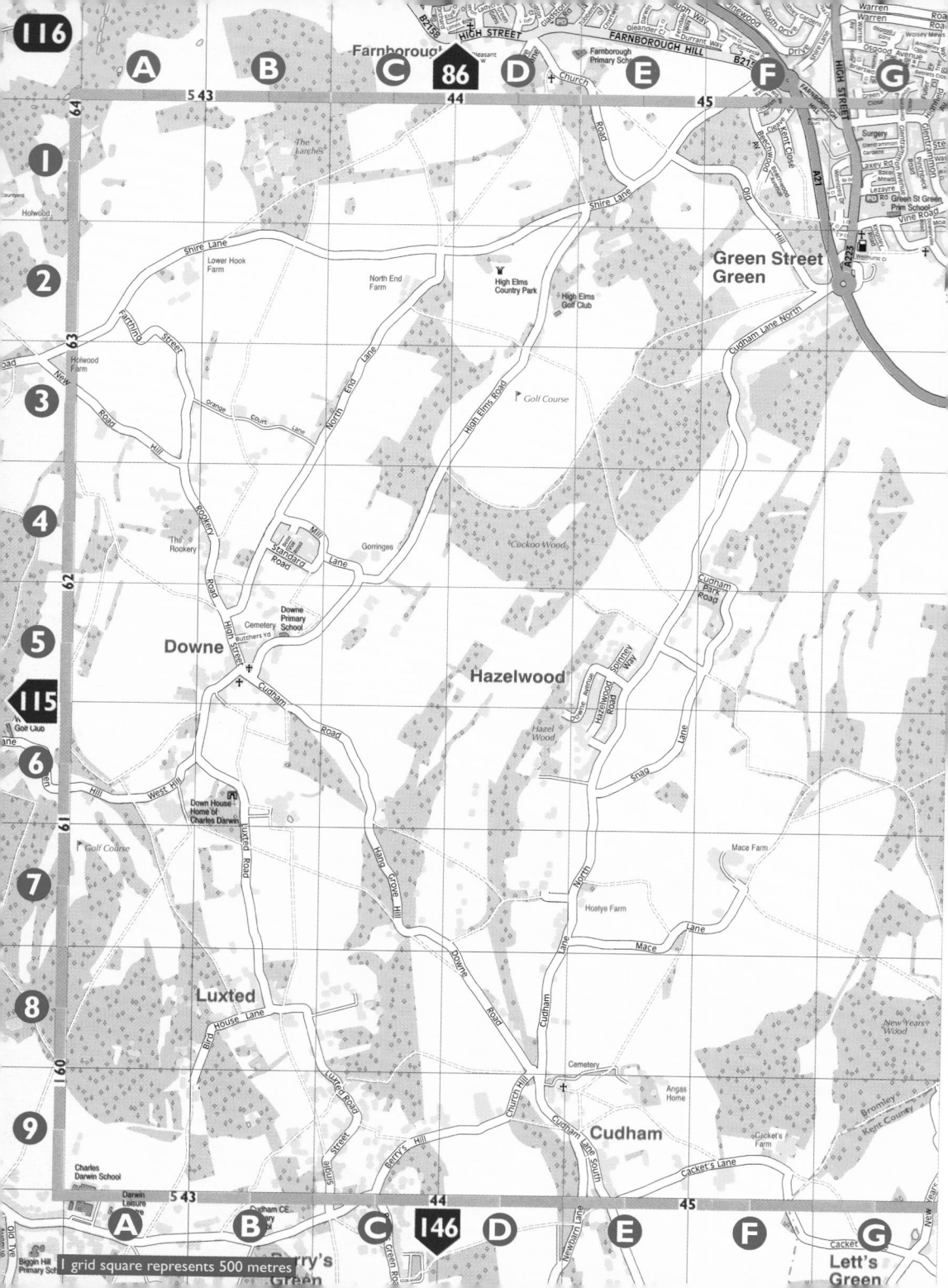

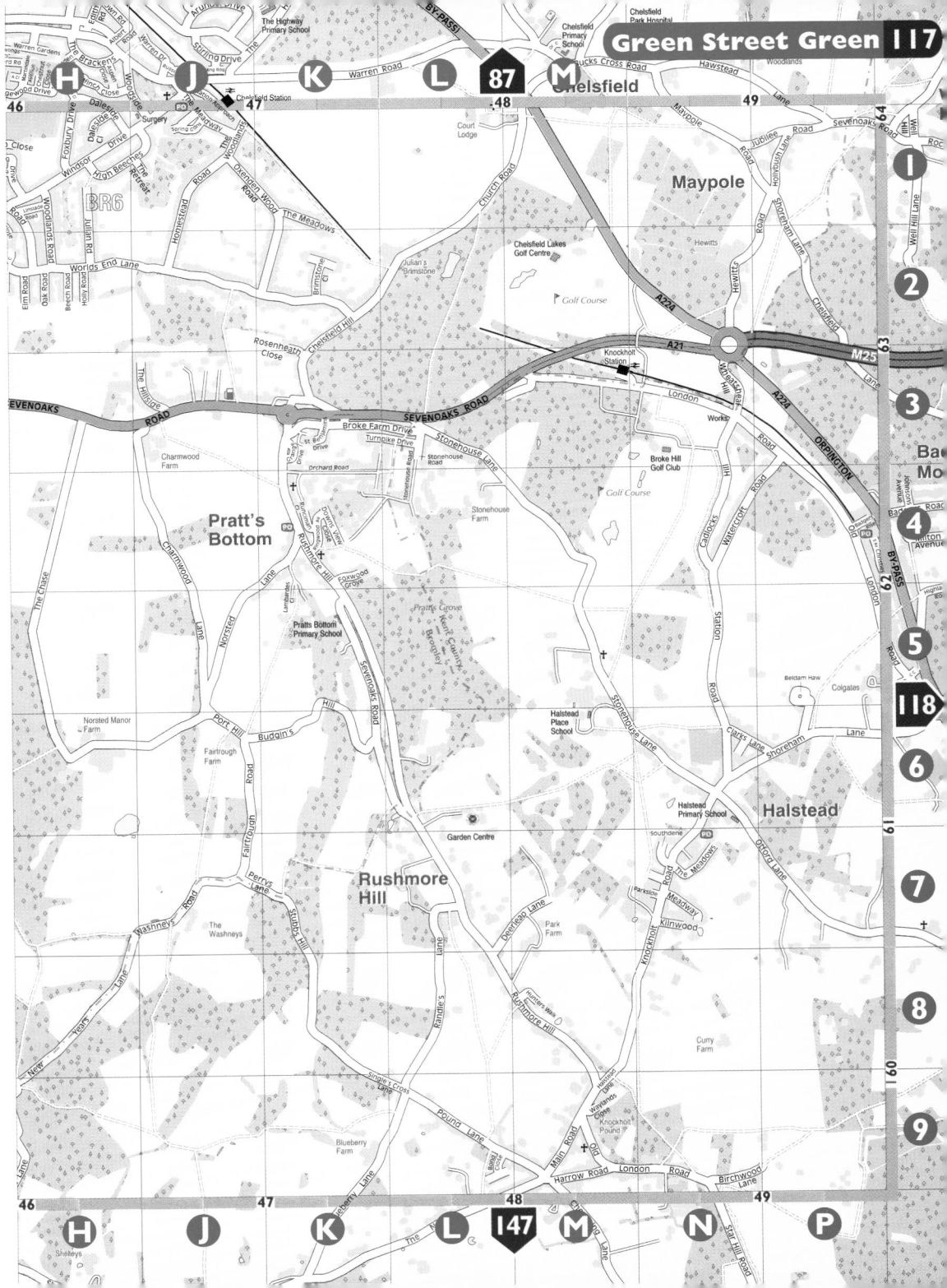

Kingsdown

Maplescomb N

H J K L 89 M

3 54 55 56 64

I

Lower Austin
Lodge

Road

Bower Park Farm

Bottsom Lane

2

The Birches

Hog Wood

Knatts Valley Road

63

Upper
Austin Lodge

Austin Lodge
Golf Club

High Castle Wood

3

Ashen Grove Road

**East
Hill**

Cherry Tree Grove

4

Golf Course

62

Bower Lane

5

Hill Road

120

**Romney
Street**

6

Dunstall Farm

Magpie Bottom

East Hill Road

Hills Lane

61

Golf Course

Eastdown

Fackenden Lane

Goodbury Road

Tinker Pot Lane

7

Highfield

Tinkerpot Rise

Woodlands

Woodlands Golf Club

Clarkes Green Road

Fernbank Farm

8

Greenhill Road

Greenhill
Wood

Rowdow Ln

Birchin Cross Rd

Birchin Cross Road

North Downs Way

Cotman's Ash Lane

60

9

SHOREHAM ROAD

Hillydeal Road

Coombe Rd

Otford Mount

Rowdow Lane

Shorehill Lane

Orford Manor

Kester

53 54 55 56

STATION ROAD

Otford

Pilgrims Way East

St Michaels Drive

Chalkways

Otford Court

Pilgrim's Way

H J K L 149 M N P

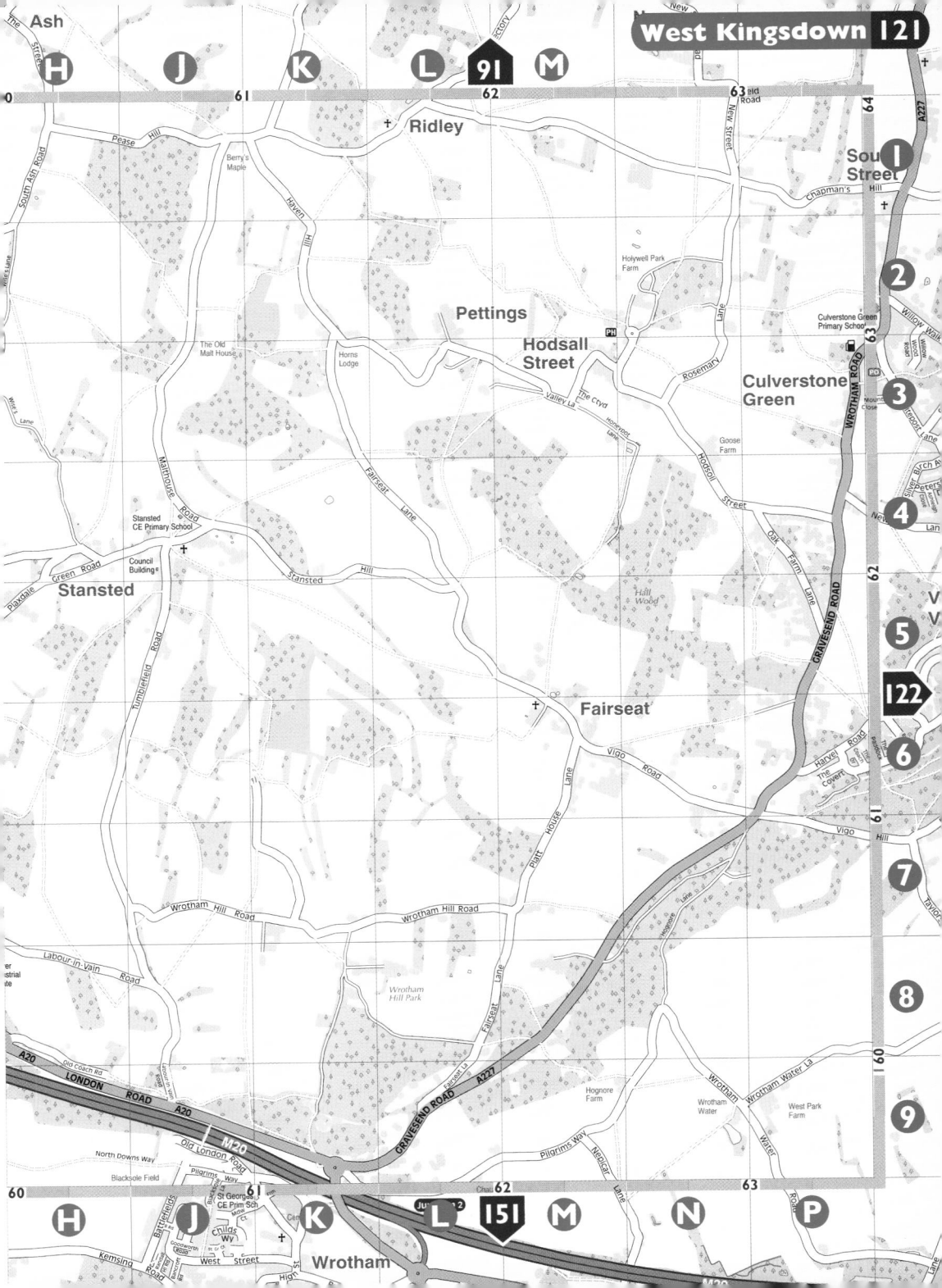

Ash

H J K L **91** M

I
Sou
Street

2

3

Culverstone
Green

4

V
V

5

122

6

7

8

9

Ridley

Pettings

Hodsall
Street

Holywell Park
Farm

Culverstone Green
Primary School

Goose
Farm

Hall
Wood

Fairseat

Vigo Road

Harvel

Vigo Hill

Stansted

Stansted
CE Primary School

Council
Building

The Old
Malt House

Horns
Lodge

Berry's
Maple

Pease Hill

South Ash Road

Malthouse Road

Fairseat Lane

Stansted Hill

Green Road

Playdale

Wrotham
Hill Park

Wrotham Hill Road

Wrotham Hill Road

Labour-in-Vain Road

Platt House Lane

Hognore
Farm

Wrotham
Water

West Park
Farm

Wrotham Water La

LONDON ROAD A20

A20

Old Coach Rd

Old London Road

M20

North Downs Way

Blacksole Field

Pilgrims Way

St George's
CE Prim Sch

GRAVESEND ROAD A227

Pilgrims Way

H J K L **151** M N P

Wrotham

Chapman's

Willow Walk

Wrotham Road

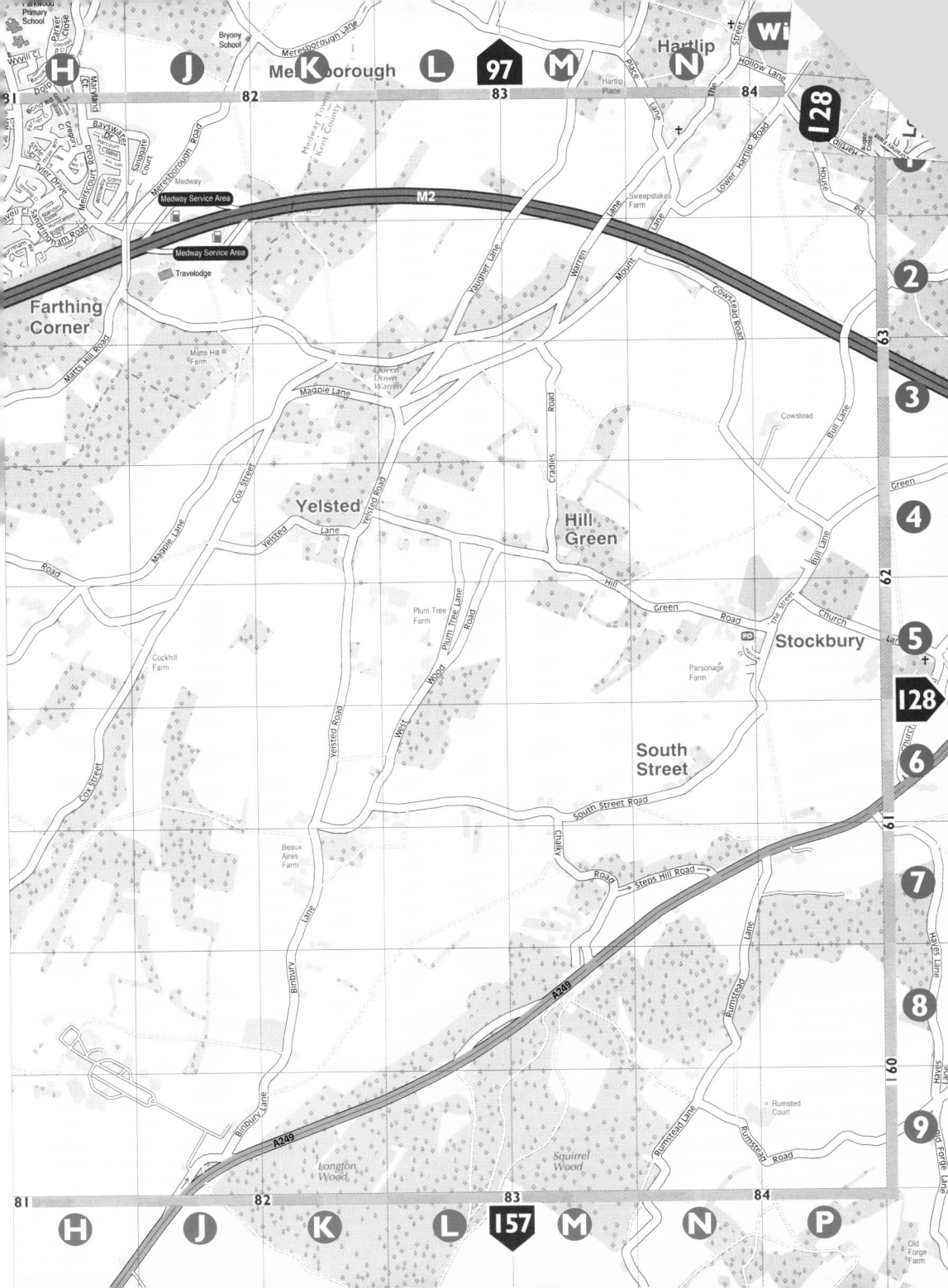

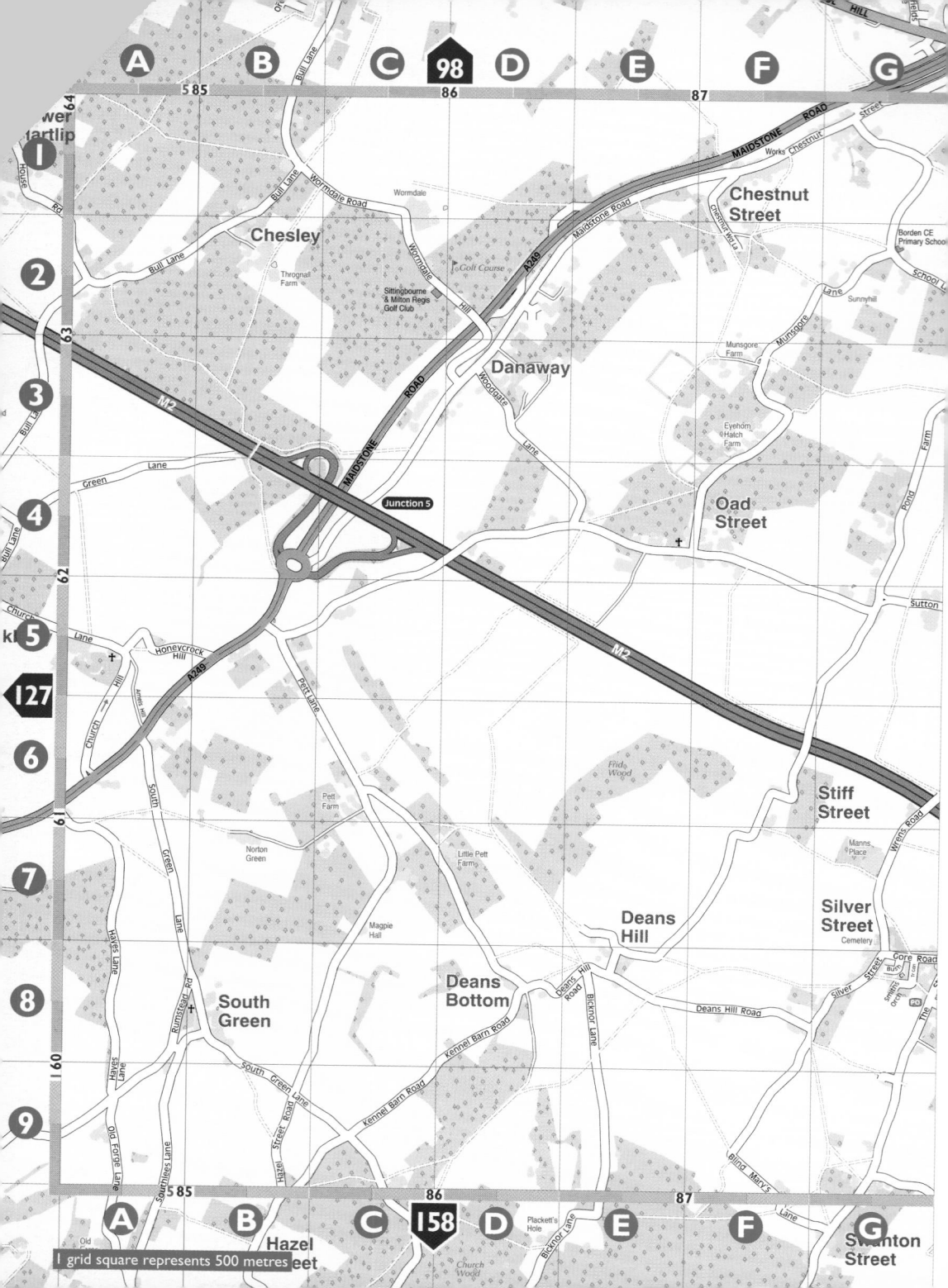

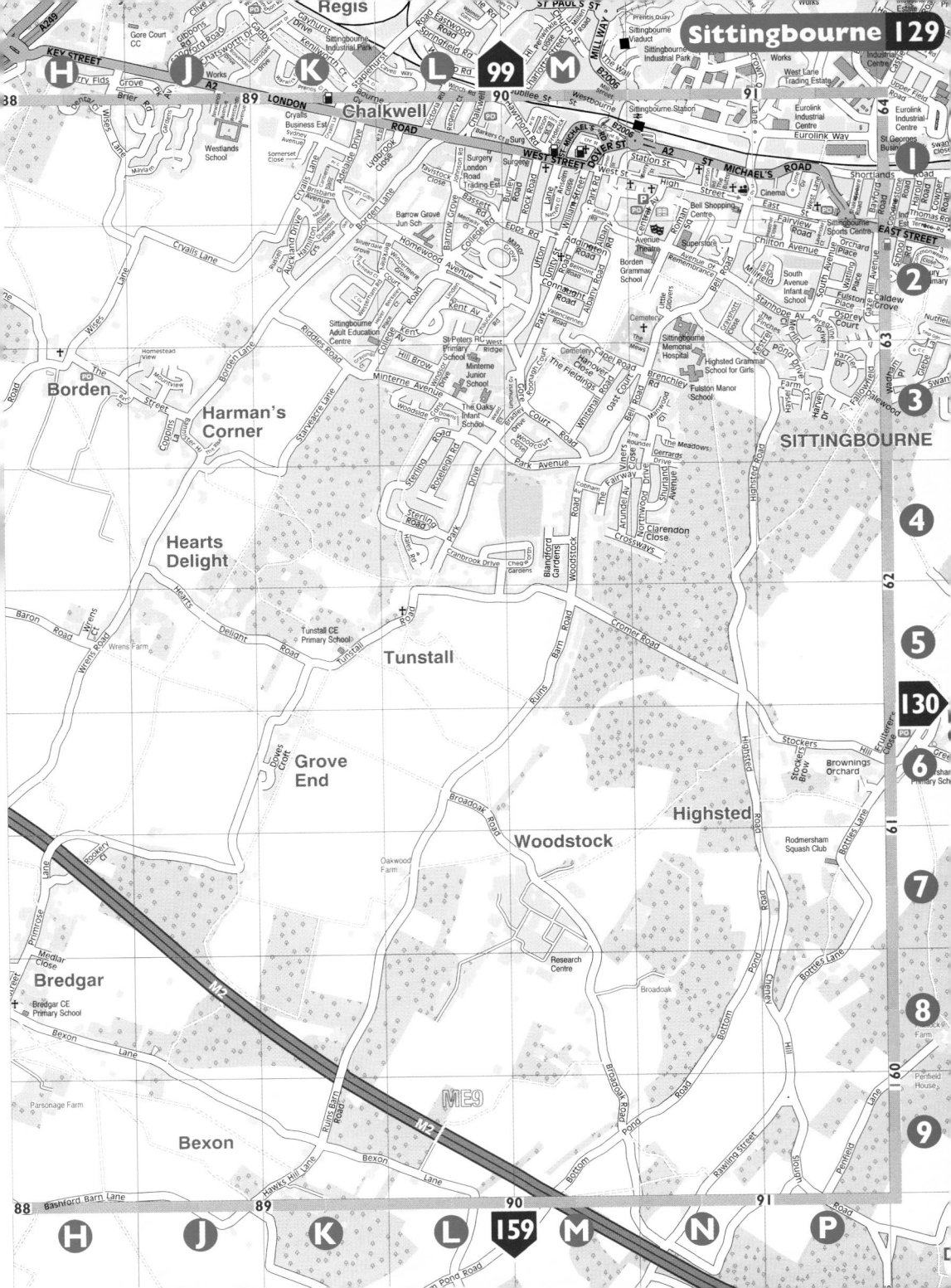

Regis

H J K L 99 M

KEY STREET

38 89 LONDON Chalkwell 90 91

ROAD

Westlands School

Somerset Close

Cryalls Lane

Borden

Harman's Corner

Sittingbourne Adult Education Centre

Homestead View

Hearts Delight

Hearts Delight Road

Wrens Farm

Wrens Ct

Baron Road

Tunstall CE Primary School

Tunstall Road

Tunstall

Dowe Croft

Grove End

Broadoak Road

Woodstock

Oakwood Farm

Bredgar

Bredgar CE Primary School

Bexon Lane

M2

ME9

Parsonage Farm

M2

Bexon

Hawks Hill Lane

88 Bashford Barn Lane 89 90 91

H J K L 159 M N P

St Paul's St

Prentis Quay

Sittingbourne Viaduct

MILL WAY

Sittingbourne Industrial Park

B2006

West Lane Trading Estate

Works

Eurolink Industrial Centre

Eurolink Way

St Georges Busin

swan Close

Sittingbourne Station

Eurolink Industrial Centre

WEST STREET

DOVER ST

ST MICHAEL'S ROAD

East Street

I

High Street

Cinema

Sittingbourne Sports Centre

Orchard Place

Chilton Avenue

2

Fairview Road

Bell Shopping Centre

Superstore

Avenue Theatre

Borden Grammar School

Stanhope Av

South Avenue Infant School

Fulston Place

Osprey Court

Caldew Grove

3

St Peters RC Primary School

Minterne Junior School

The Oaks Infant School

West Ridge

Hanover Court

The Fieldings

Capel Road

Sittingbourne Memorial Hospital

Highsted Grammar School for Girls

Fulston Manor School

SITTINGBOURNE

Minterne Avenue

Woodside

Park Avenue

Sterling Road

Cobham Rd

The Rounder

The Meadows

Gerrards

The Fairway

Arundel Av

Northwood Drive

Thurland Avenue

Clarendon Close

Crossways

4

Cranbrook Drive

Cheap Gardens

Blandford Gardens

Woodstock

Cromer Road

5

Highsted Road

Bottles Lane

6 130

Stockers

Stockers Brow

Brownings Orchard

Rodmersham Squash Club

Highsted

7

Research Centre

Broadoak

Bottom Road

Chequey Road

Hill

8

60

Penfield House

9

Rawling Street

Slough Road

Penfield Road

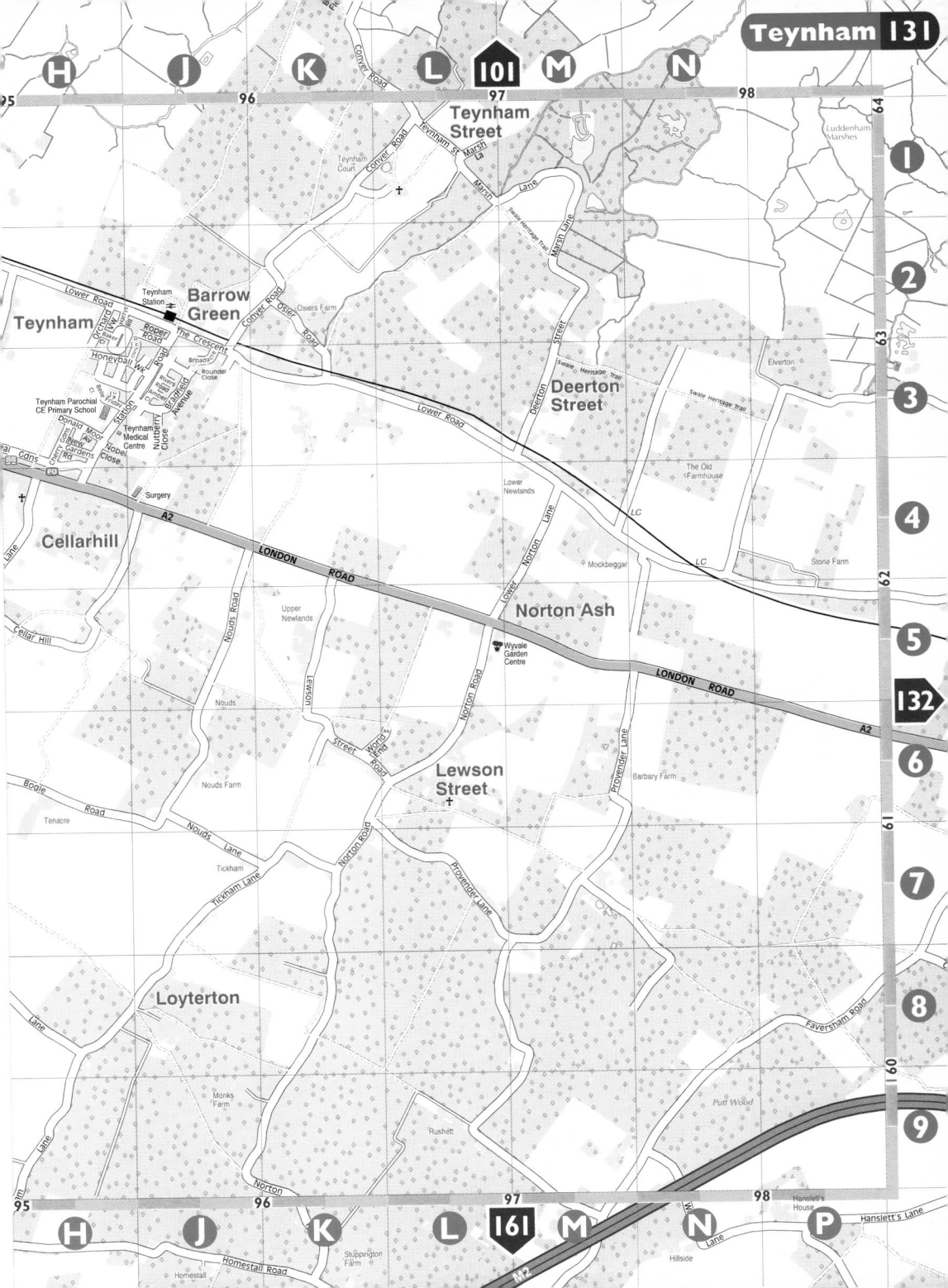

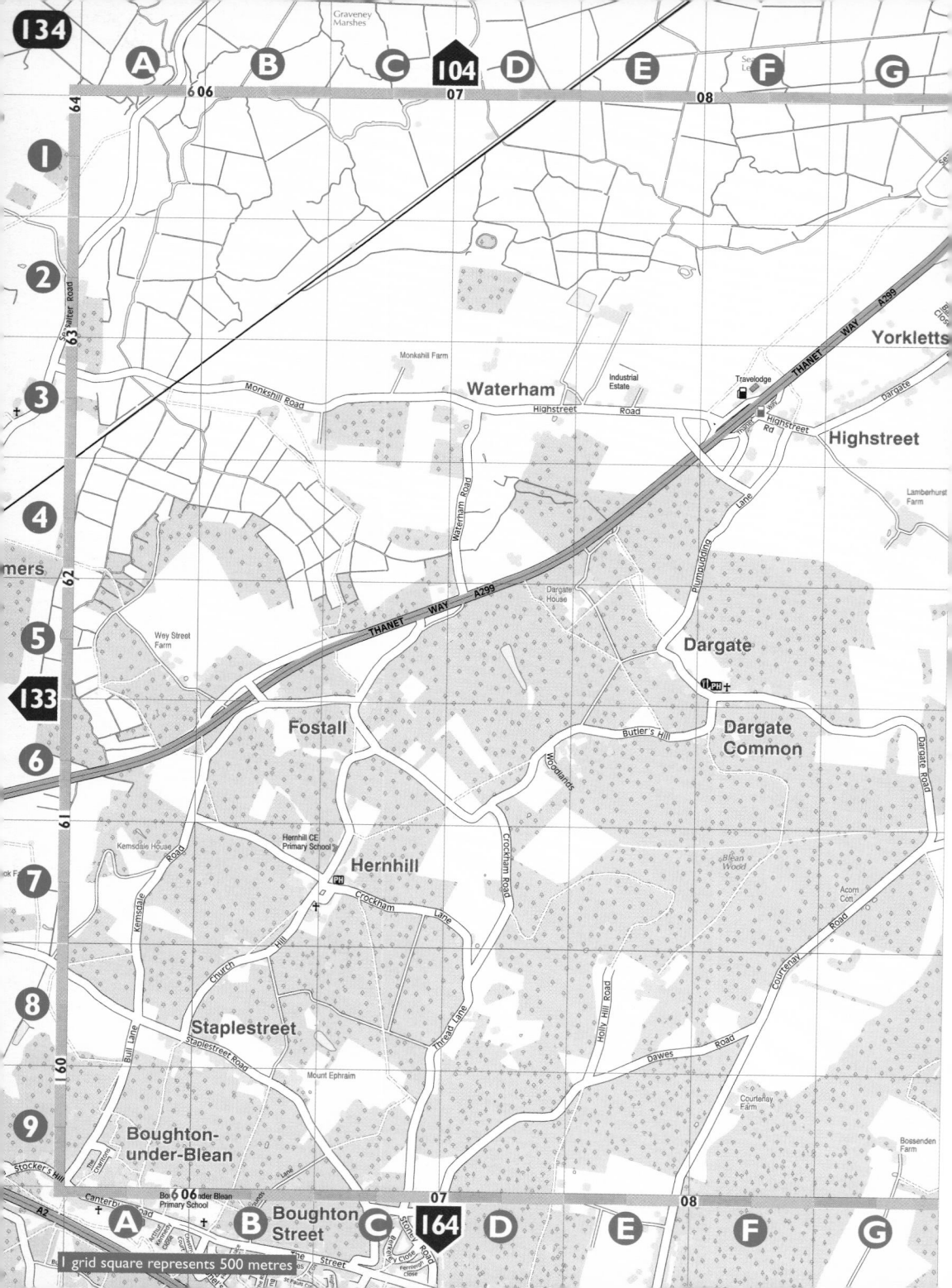

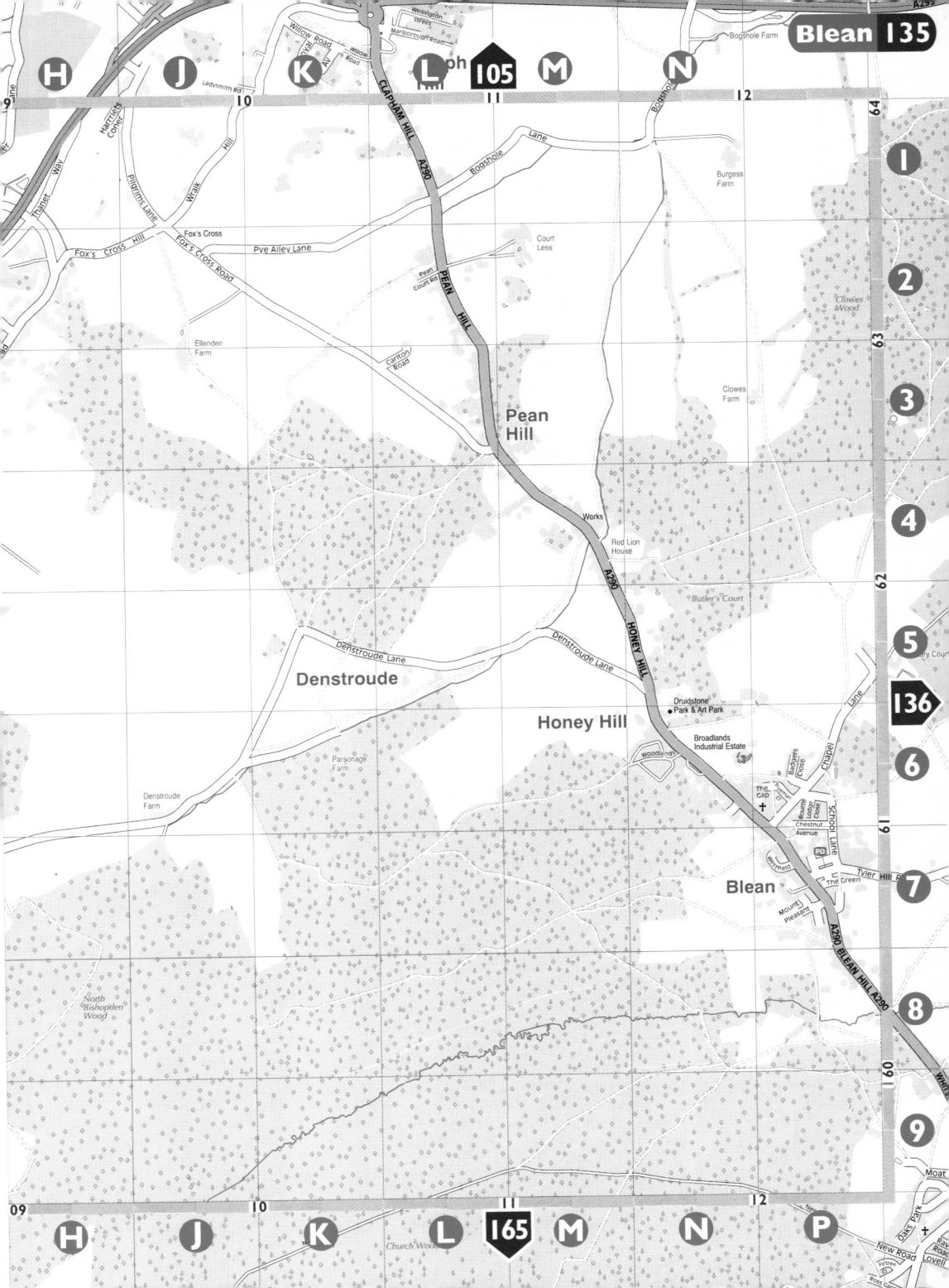

136

A   B   **106**   D   E   F   G

Radfall

613

64

I

63

2

Clowes
Wood

3

4

62

5

135

6

61

7

A290 BLEAN HILL A290

8

60

9

613

Thornden Wood

Thornden Wood Road

Radfall Road

New Road

Brambles
Farm

Mayton
Lane

Mayton Farm

Langton
Lodge

Heckinton Road

Well Court

Frog Hall

Honey
Wood

Tyler Hill Road

Hothe
Court Farm

Tyler Hill Road

Summer Lane

Park Farm
Close

Allcroft
Grange

Giles Lane

**Tyler
Hill**

CT2

Little Hall
Farm

Canterbury Hill

University of Kent
at Canterbury

Research Development
& Business Centre

Blean CP
School

Park Wd Rd

Park Wd Rd

Gulbenkian
Theatre

Cinema 3

University of
Kent Canterbury

University of
Kent Canterbury

St Stephens Hill

Downs Road

Long Meadow Way

Keynes
College

Moat Lane

WHITSTABLE ROAD

Giles Lane

A   B   **166**   D   E   F   G

Oaks Park

New Rd

Kent
College

St Edmunds
School

St Edmunds
Junior School

Archbishops
School

Moorfield

The Terr

St Stephens
Primary
School

Hales
Place

Broad
Industrial

Works

LC

613   14   15

I grid square represents 500 metres

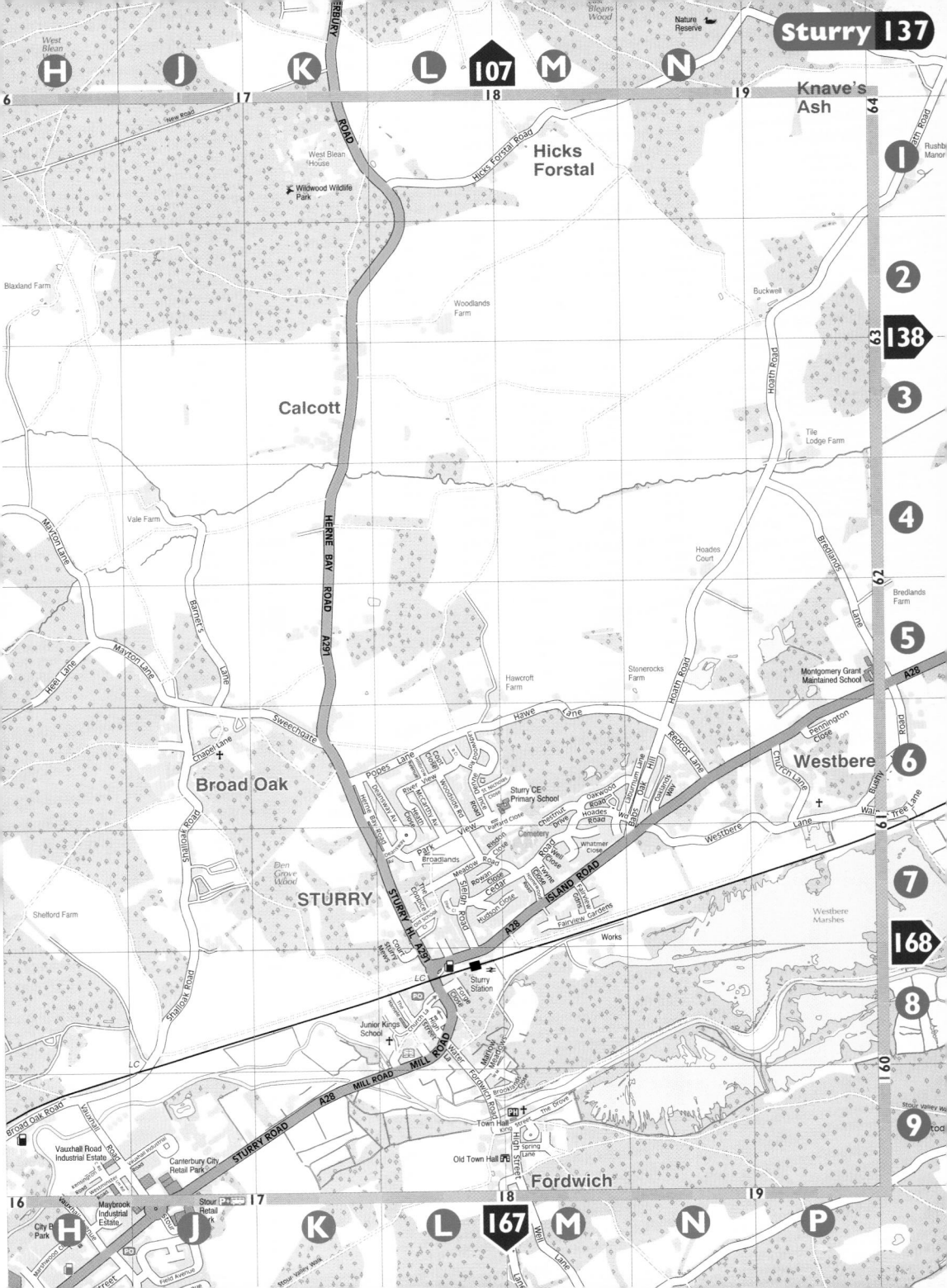

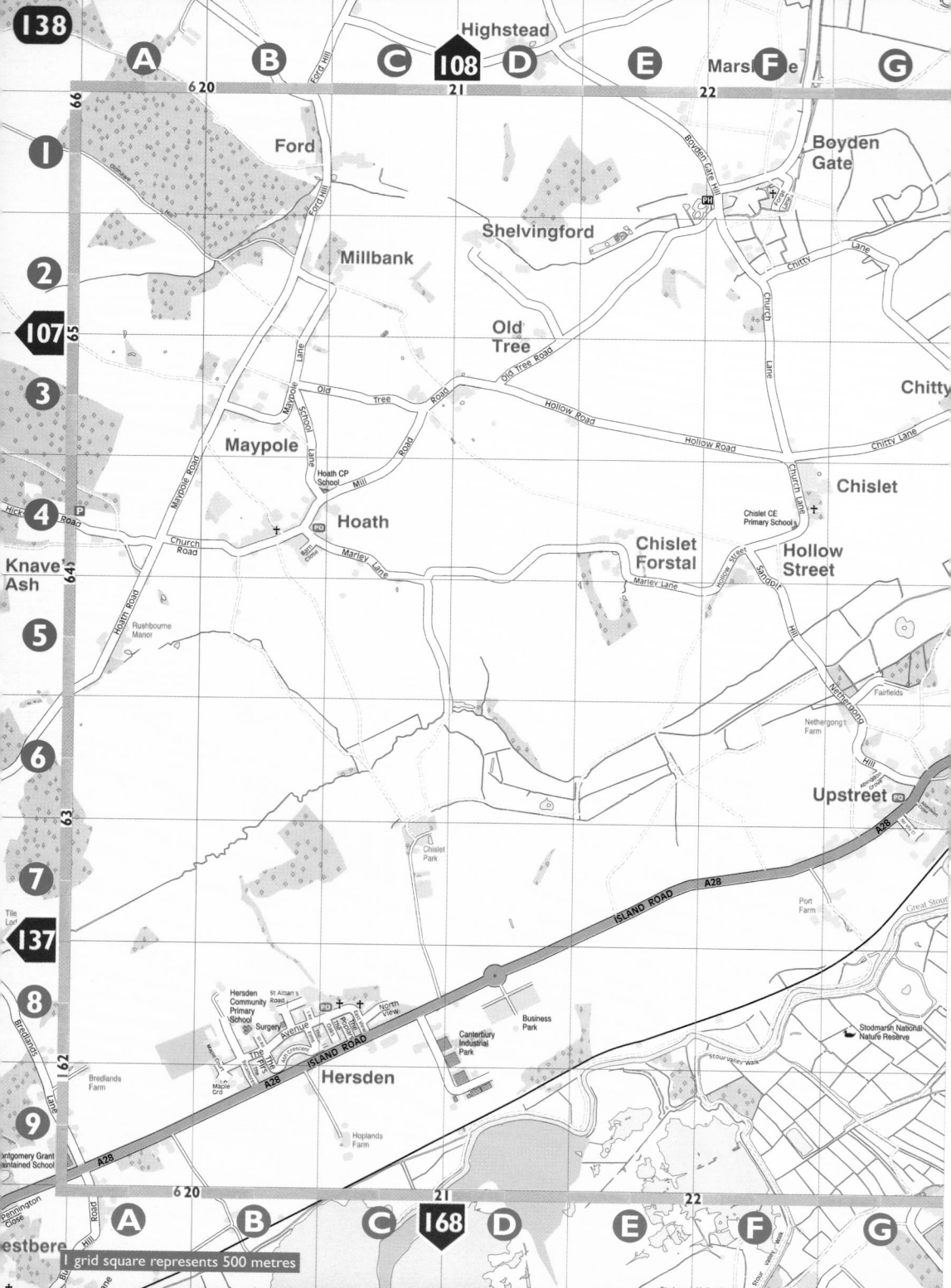

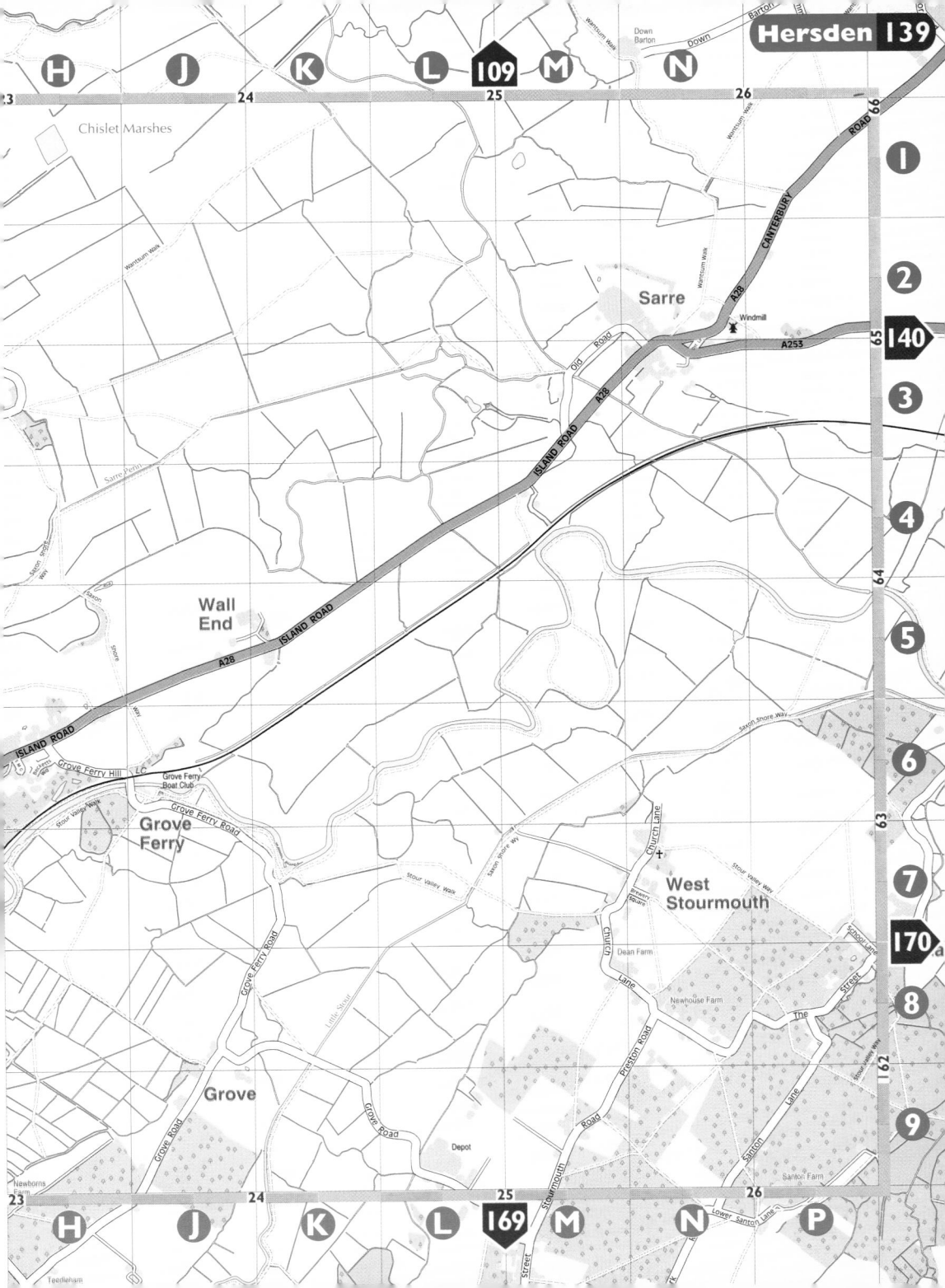

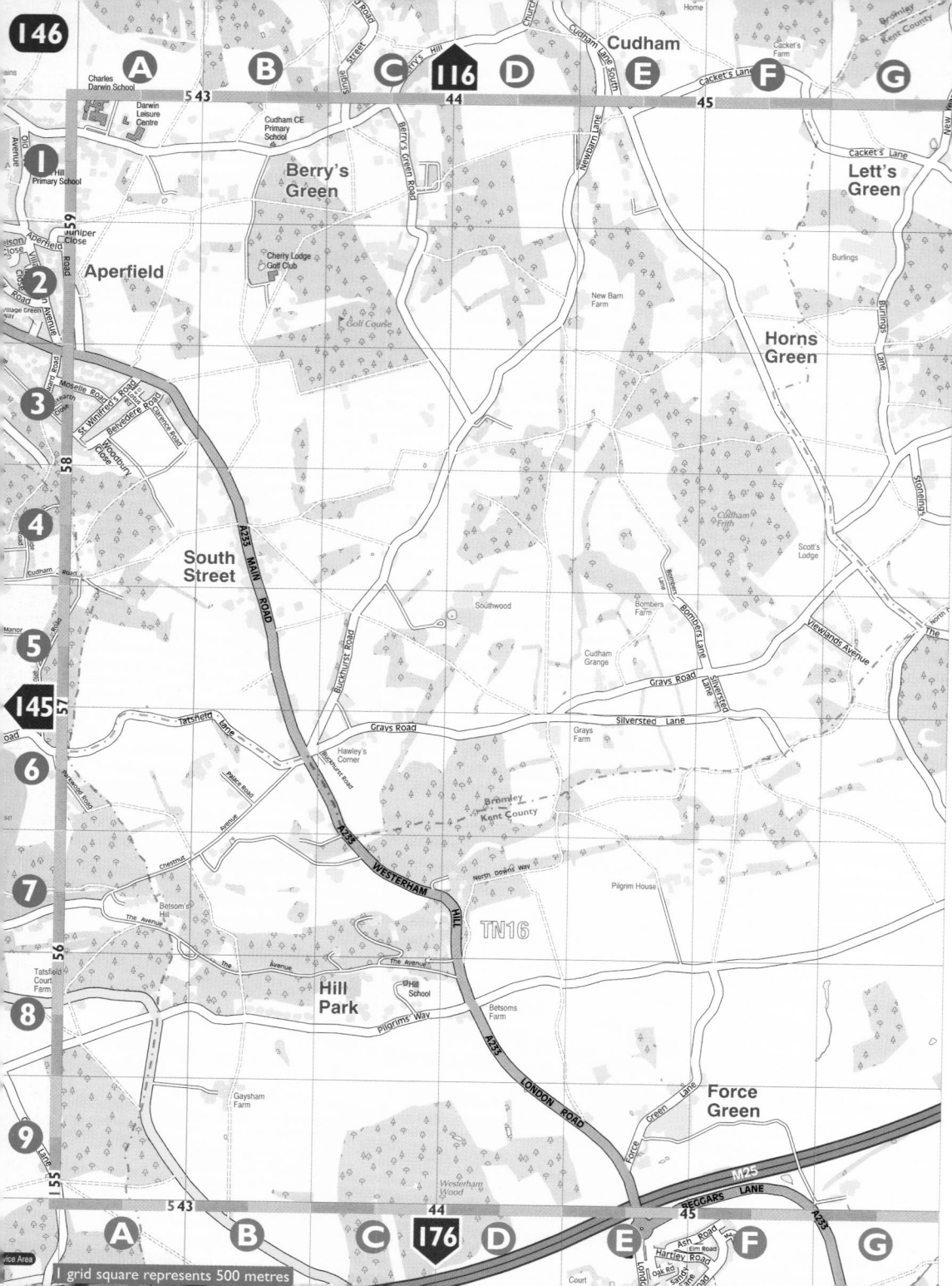

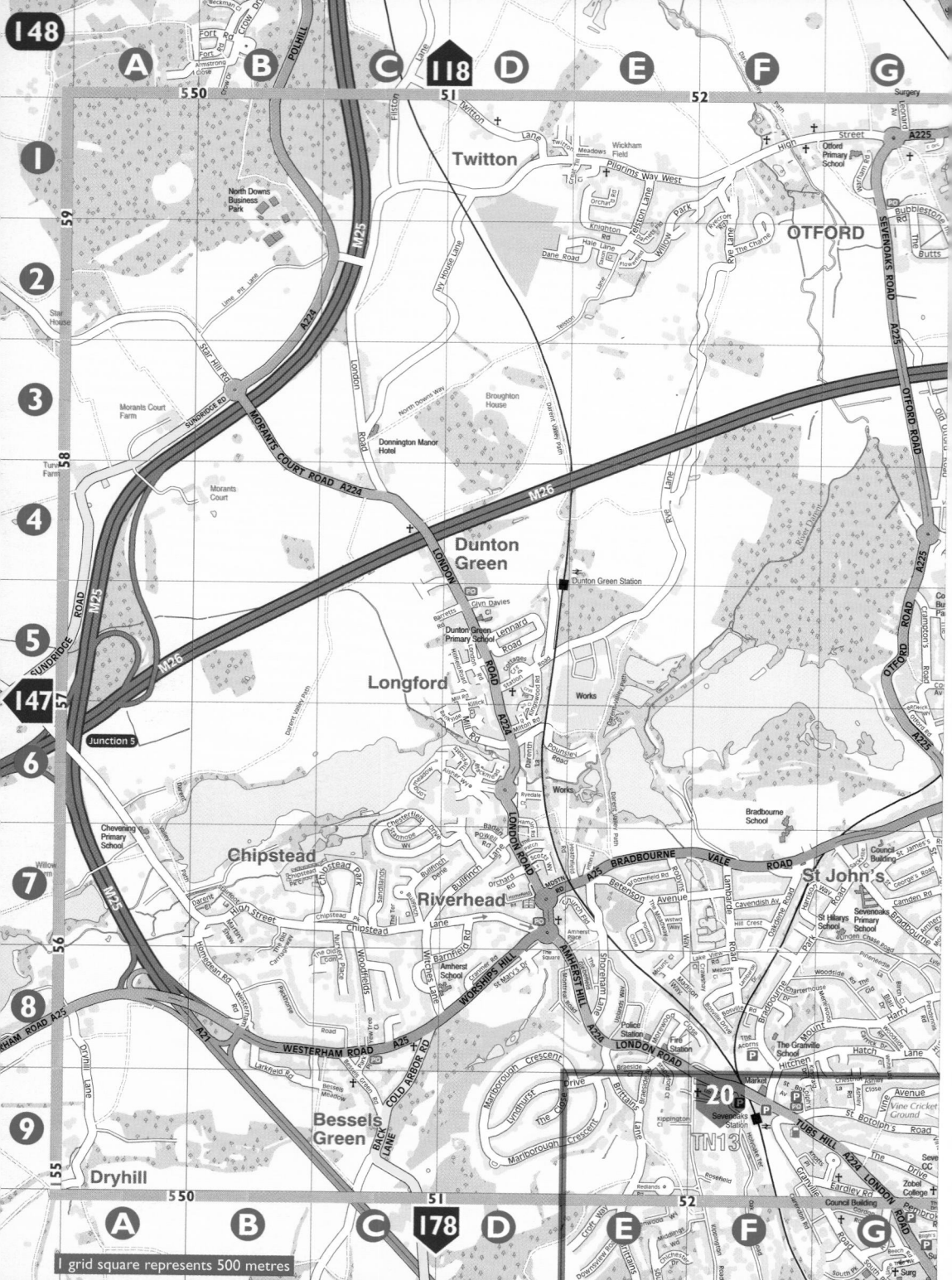

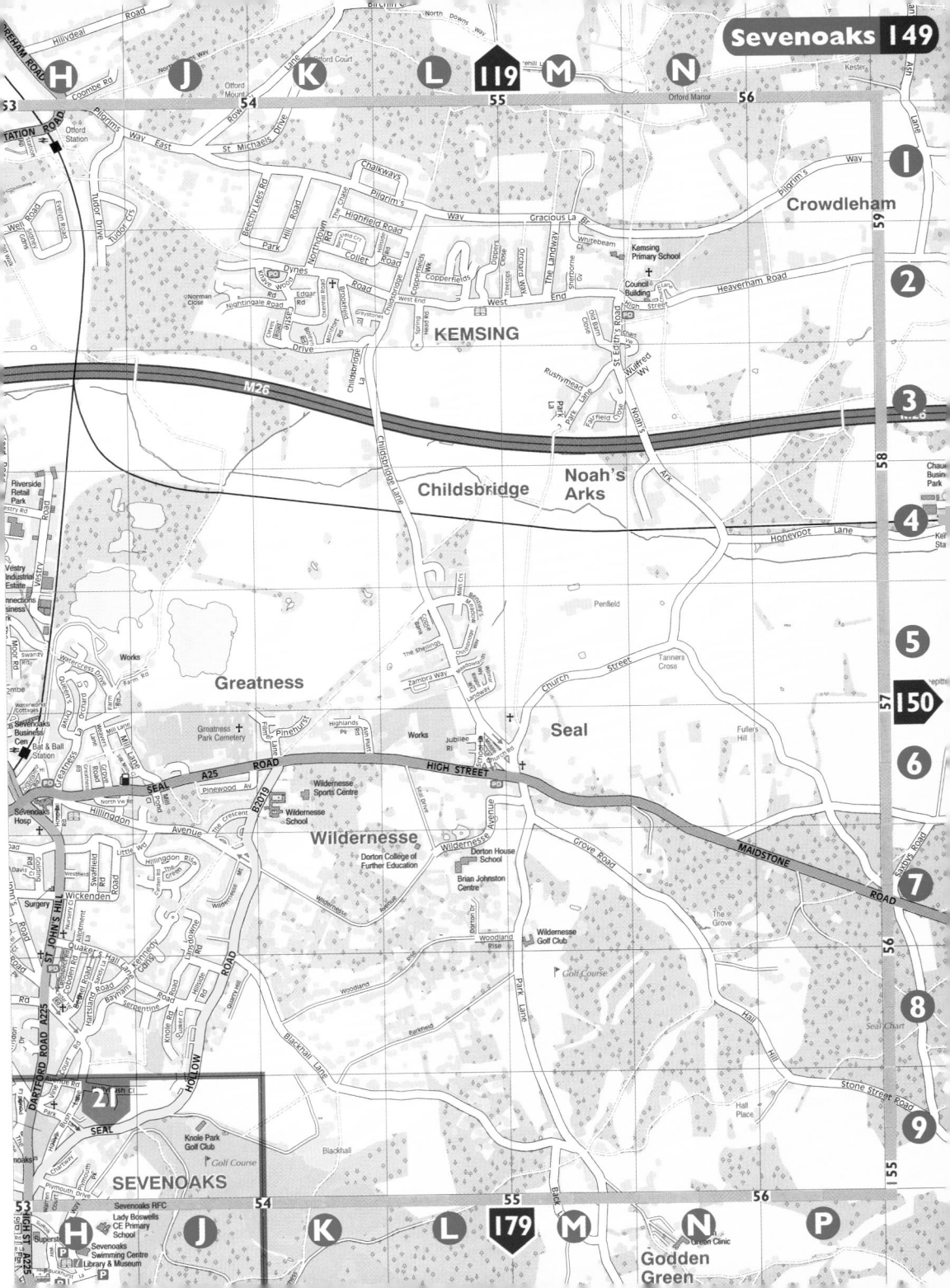

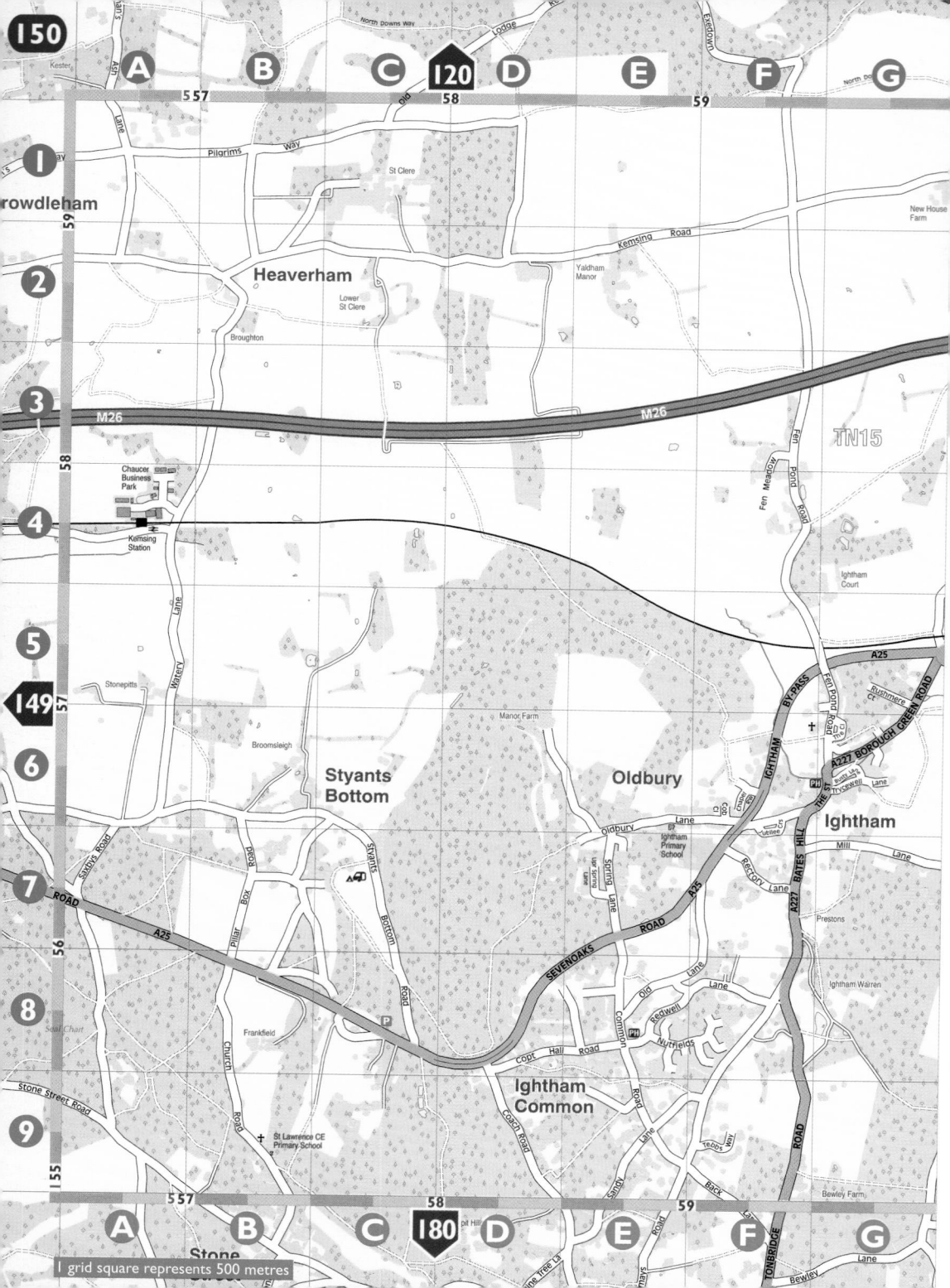

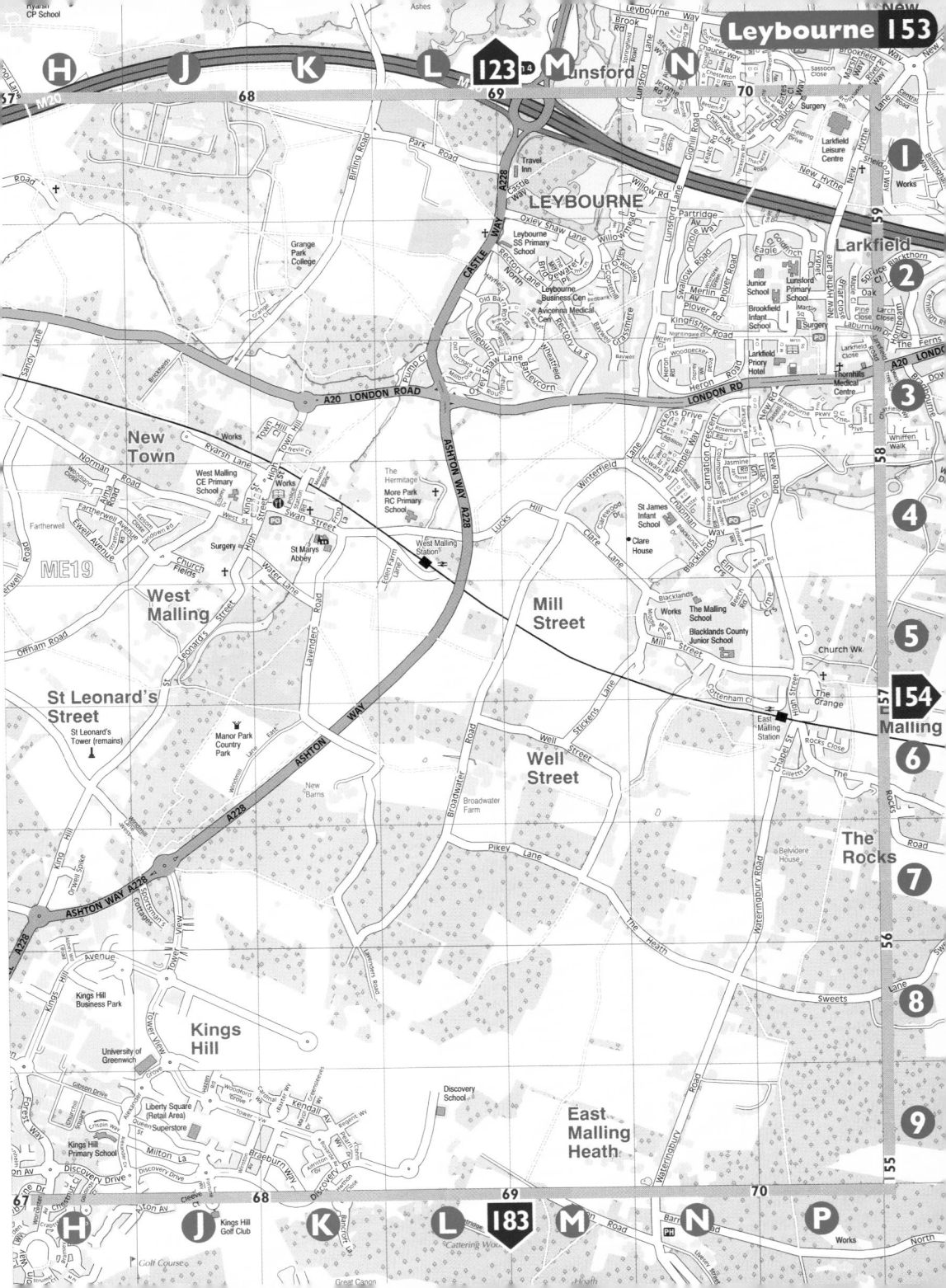

H   J   K   L   **123** 14   M   Lunsford   N   NOW

M20   68   69   70

I   Works

LEYBOURNE

Larkfield   2

Larkfield Leisure Centre

Travel Inn

Castle Hill

Grange Park College

A20 LONDON ROAD   3

London Rd

A20 LONDON ROAD

The Ferns

A228

Whiffen Walk   3

Thornhills Medical Centre

New Town

West Malling CE Primary School

Works

ME19

West Malling Station   4

West St

St Marys Abbey

Surgery

Clare House

West Malling

Church Fields

St James Infant School   4

Mill Street

Blacklands

The Malling School   5

Blacklands County Junior School

Church Wk.   5

St Leonard's Street

St Leonard's Tower (remains)

Manor Park Country Park

The Grange

East Malling Station   **154** Malling   6

ASHTON WAY   A228

New Barns

Well Street

The Rocks   7

Broadwater Farm

Belvidere House

57

56

Pikey Lane

55

Kings Hill Business Park

8

University of Greenwich

Kings Hill

Discovery School

Sweets   8

Kings Hill Primary School

Liberty Square (Retail Area) Superstore

Milton La

East Malling Heath   9

A228 ASHTON WAY

67   68   69   70   **155**

H   J   Kings Hill Golf Club   K   L   **183**   M   N   P   Works

Golf Course

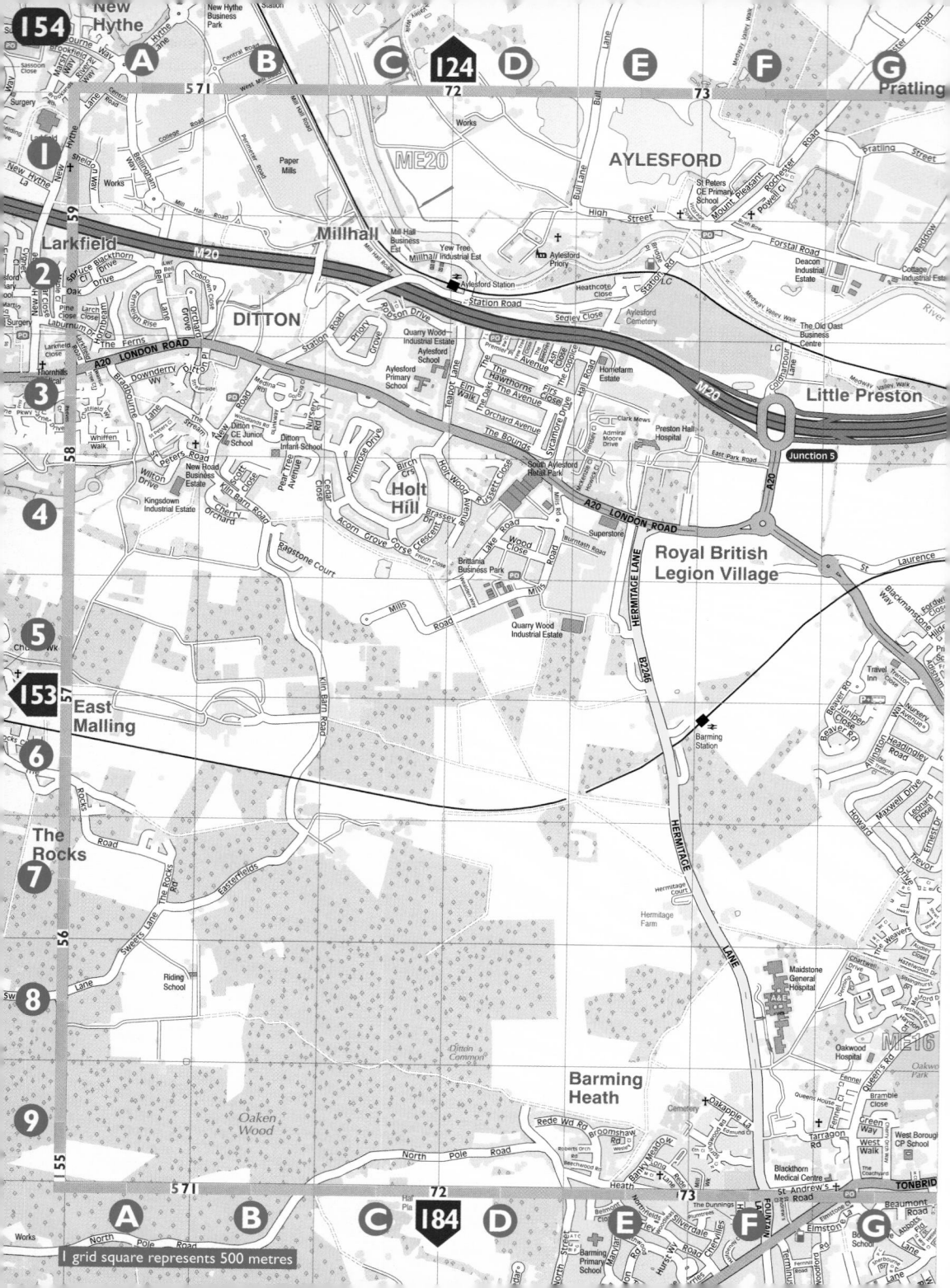

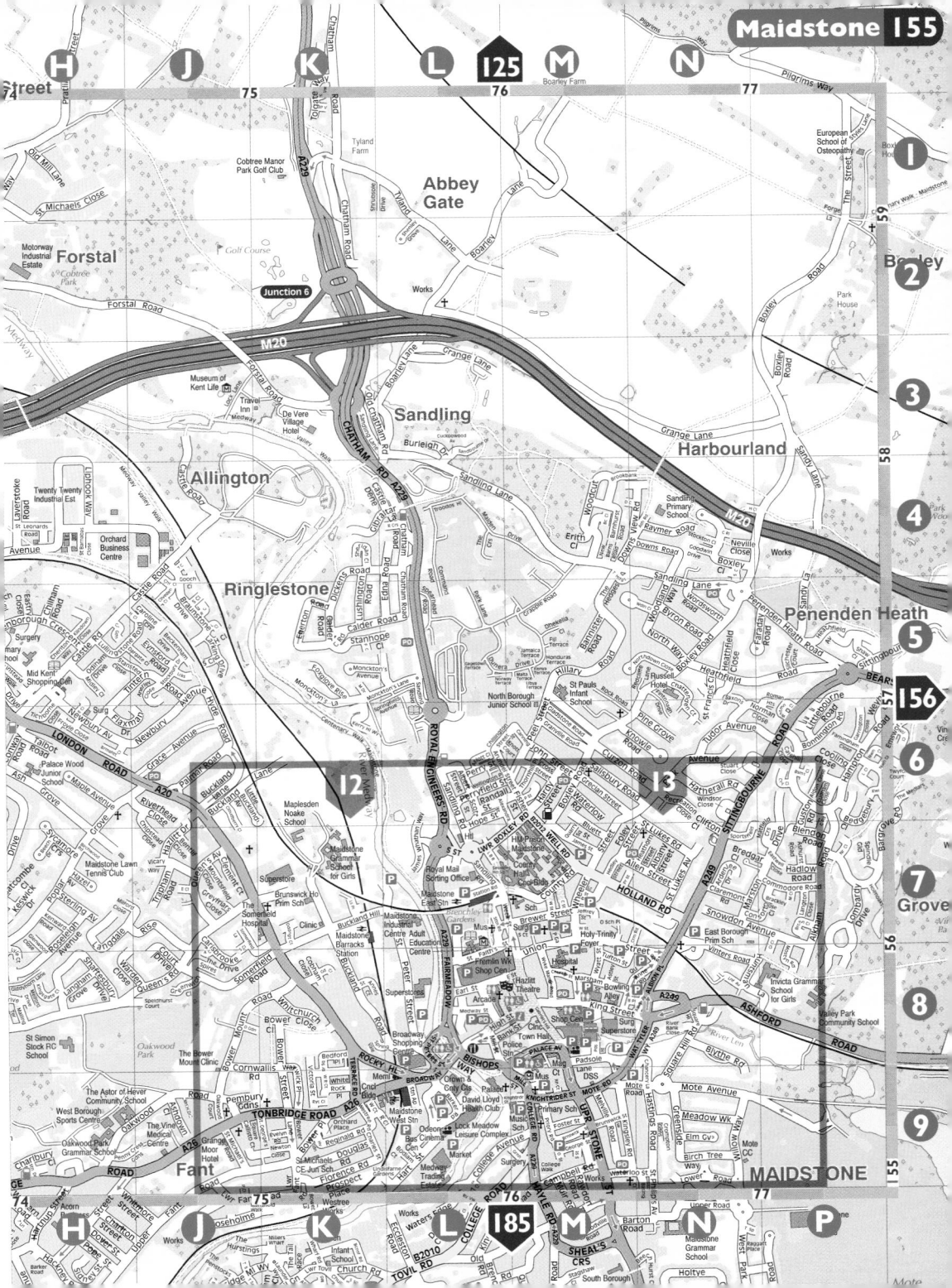

A   B   C   126   D   E   F   G

5 78   North Downs Way   79   80

European School

Boxley House

1
The Street

Forge

+ 59

2
Boxley
Park House

ME14

Pilgrims Way   North Downs Way

Broader Lane

Mount House

Kent County Showground

Detling Hill

East Court

3
Harpole

Detling CE Primary School

Pilgrims Wy   The Street   Pilgrims   Way

Detling

Thurnham

Castle Hill

58

Park Wood

Horish Wood

Hockers Close

Works

Orchard View

4

M20

Thurnham Farm

enden Heath

5
Junction 7

Newnham Court Farm

Works

Honeyhills Wood

Court Farm

155
57

BEARSTED ROAD   A249   Garden Centre

Vintners Park Crematorium

Bearsted

Golf Course

6

Works

New Cut Road

Grovewood Drive

Harrow Way

Ware Street

Birling House

Ware Street

Bearsted Golf Club

Bearsted Station

Bearsted Green Business Centre

7
Grove Green

Superstore

Surgery

Fitz William Rd

Reveril Drive

Ware Street

Works

56

St Johns CE Prim Sch

Weavering Street

Roseacre Junior School

Roseacre

The Street

8
community School

Grovewood Drive

Weavering

Birling Lane

Clarendon Close

Tower Lane

Manor Court

ROAD   A20

9

Mote Park Sailing Club

A20   ASHFORD   ROAD

Plantation Lane

The Grove

Mote House

Maidenford 79

Marriott Tudor Park Hotel & Country Club

155

5 78

Mote

Maidstone Park Infant School

BEARSTED

1 grid square represents 500 metres

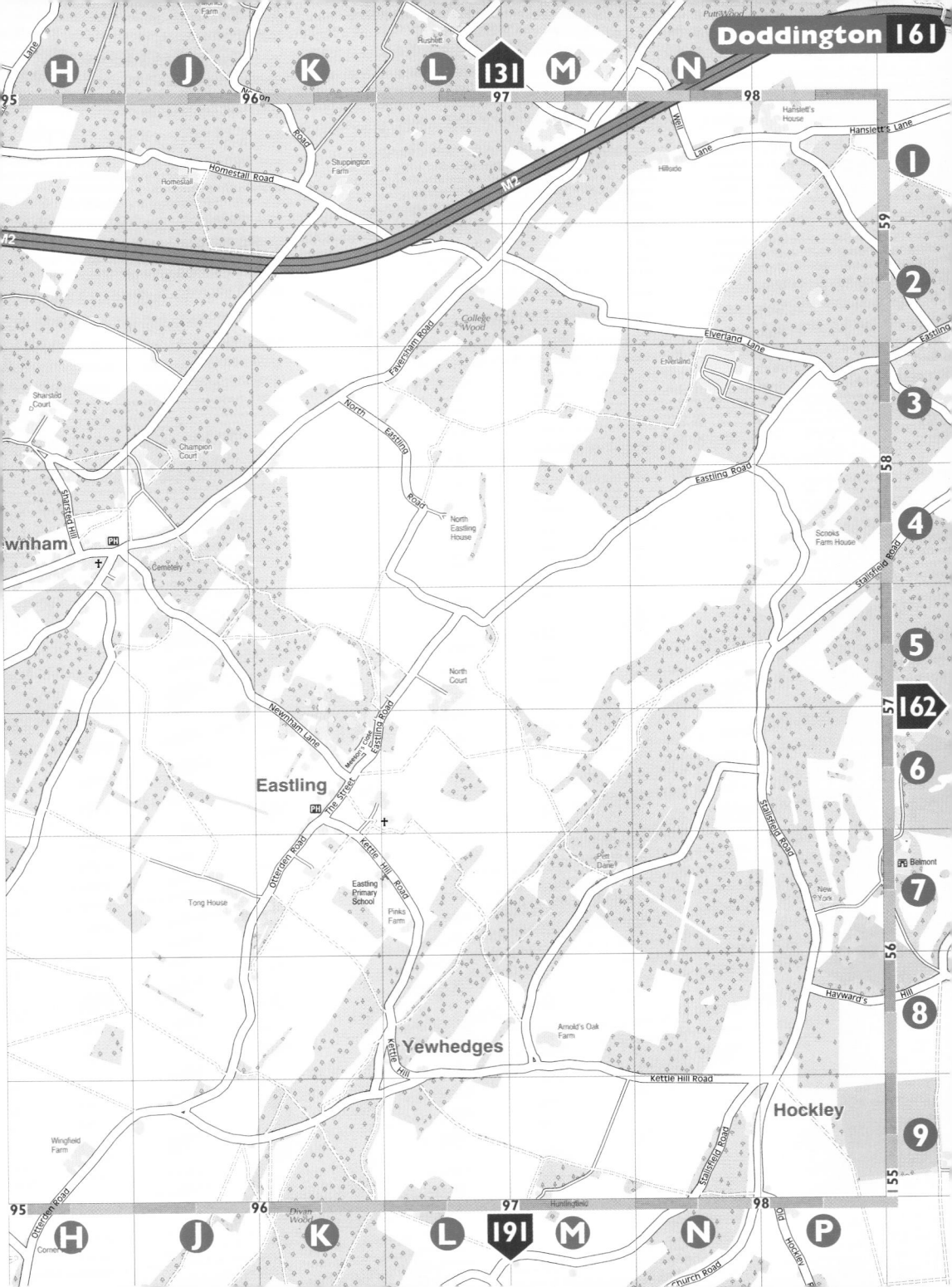

H J K L **131** M N

95 96 97 98

Putt Wood

Rushett

Well Lane

Hanslett's House

Hanslett's Lane

1

59

Homestall Road

Homestall

Stuppington Farm

M2

Hillside

Eastling

2

College Wood

Elverland Lane

Elverland

3

Faversham Road

Sharsted Court

Champion Court

North Eastling Road

North Eastling House

Eastling Road

Scrooks Farm House

Stalisfield Road

58

4

wnham

Sharsted Hill

PH

Cemetery

North Court

5

57

162

6

Newnham Lane

Eastling Road

The Street

Eastling

PH

Otterden Road

Kettle Hill Road

Eastling Primary School

Pinks Farm

Pett Dane

New York

Belmont

7

Tong House

56

Kettle Hill

Yewhedges

Arnold's Oak Farm

Hayward's Hill

8

Kettle Hill Road

Stalisfield Road

Hockley

9

Wingfield Farm

Otterden Road

55

Corner

Divan Wood

Huntingfield

Old Hockley

Church Road

95 96 97 98

H J K L **191** M N P

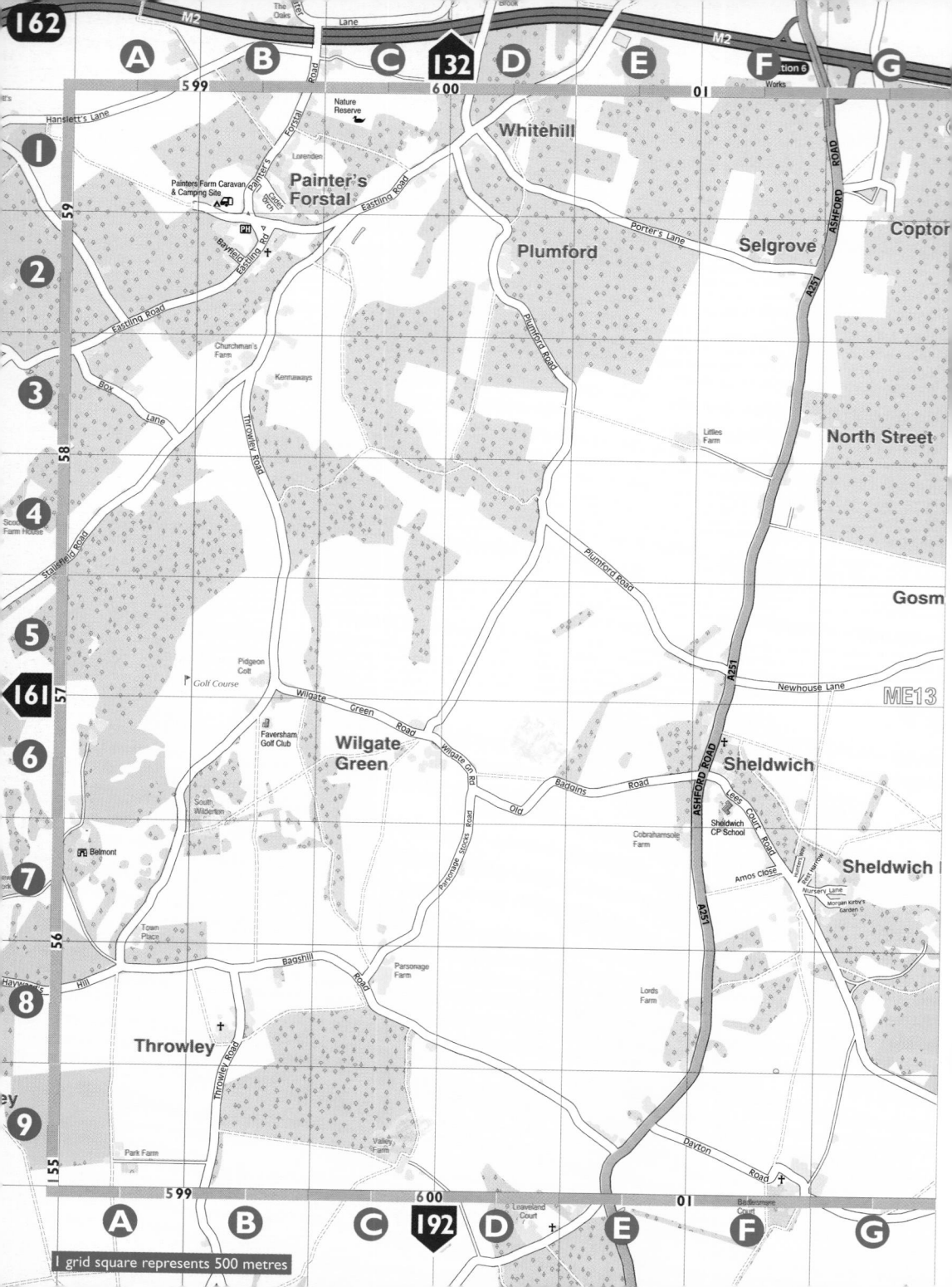

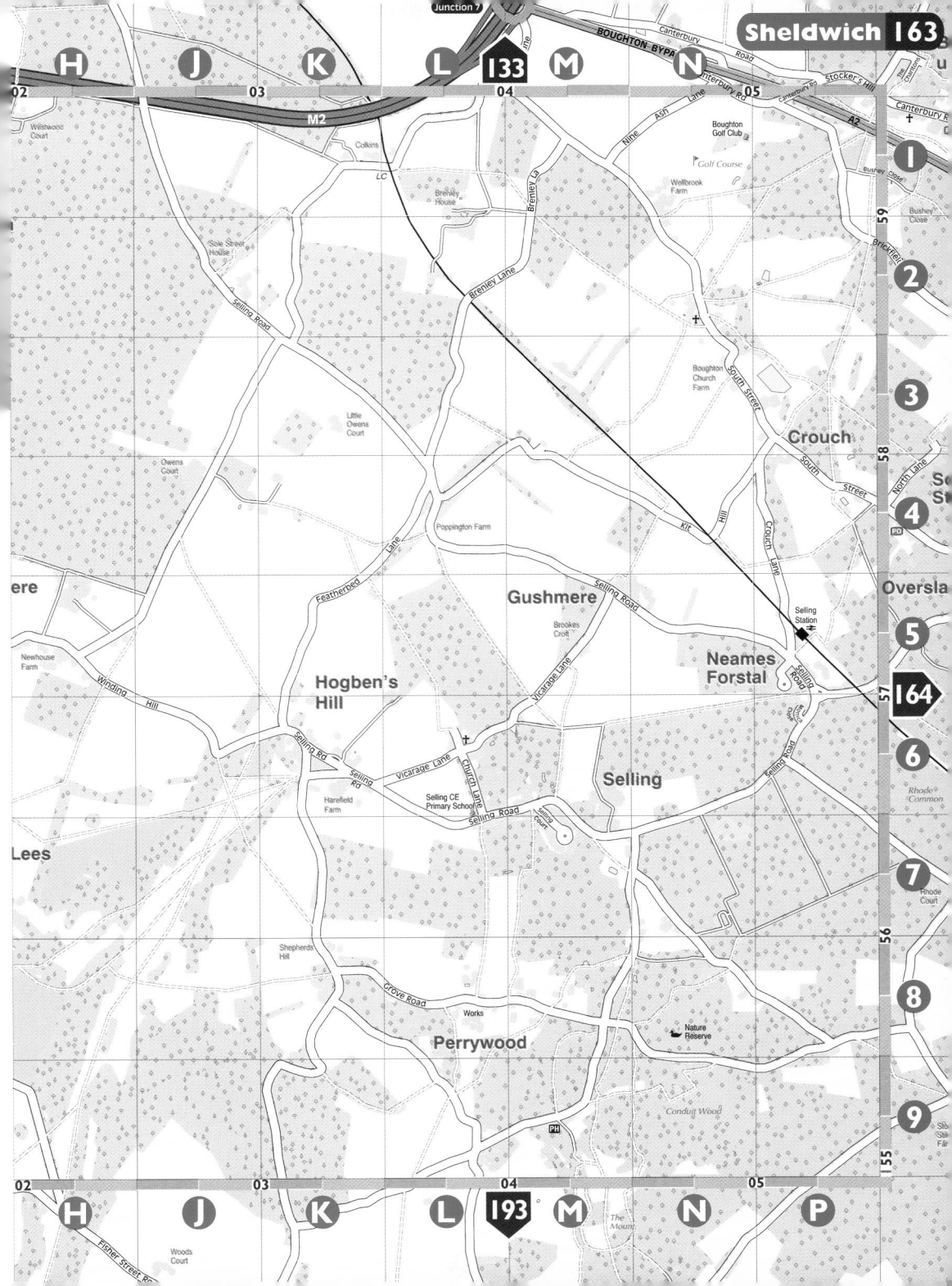

H J K L 135 M

09 10 11 12

Moat Lar

New Wood

Oaks Park

New Road

Ravens
Road/
ell Ro.

R
C

1

Church Wood

New road

59

2

Homestall
Wood

Rough Common Road

St. Michael

Cooper

Hall Place

Express by
Holiday Inn

Stumps
Farm

Roman Road

MEADOW

CRAZE
MEWS

Upper
Harbledown

3 A205

Painters Cross R

Poldhurst
Farm

A2

Roman Road

Faulkners Lane

58

Denstead
Lane

Kent College
J&I School

North Downs Way

Centenary Walk

4

Denstead
Farm

Bigbury Road

Tonford Lane

5

Primrose Hill

Petty
France

Howfield Wood

Centenary Walk Canterbury

57

166

Chartham
Hatch

Nightingale
Close

6

Than
(Cant
School of Music

Town La

Town Street

PH

New Town Street

Hatch Lane

North Downs Way

Nickle
Farm

Howfield Lane

Howfield
Farm

Thani

7

LC

Works

Stour Valley Walk

Milton
Manor
Farm

8

56

Stour Valley
Industrial Estate

ASHFORD ROAD

Cemetery

LC

Wyivale
Garden Centre

Horton

Larkeyvalley
Wood

9

ASHFORD ROAD

A28

Cockering Road

155

Riverside

LC

Chartham
Station

Works

Stour Valley Walk

Surgery

The Green

Parish Road

River Court

09 10 11 12

Shall

Street

Surgery

Boots Hill

The Hyde

H J K L 195 ha M m

N P

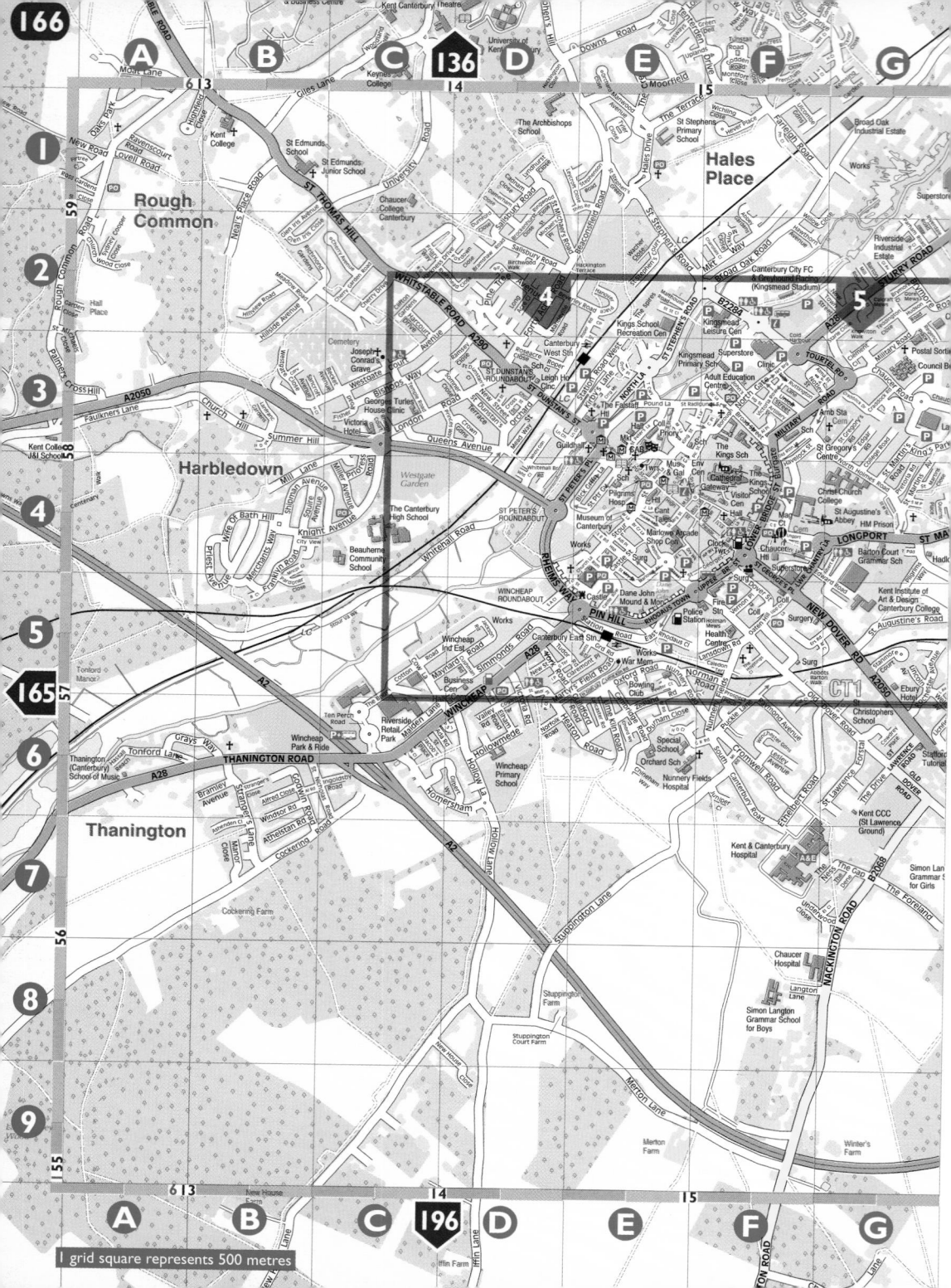

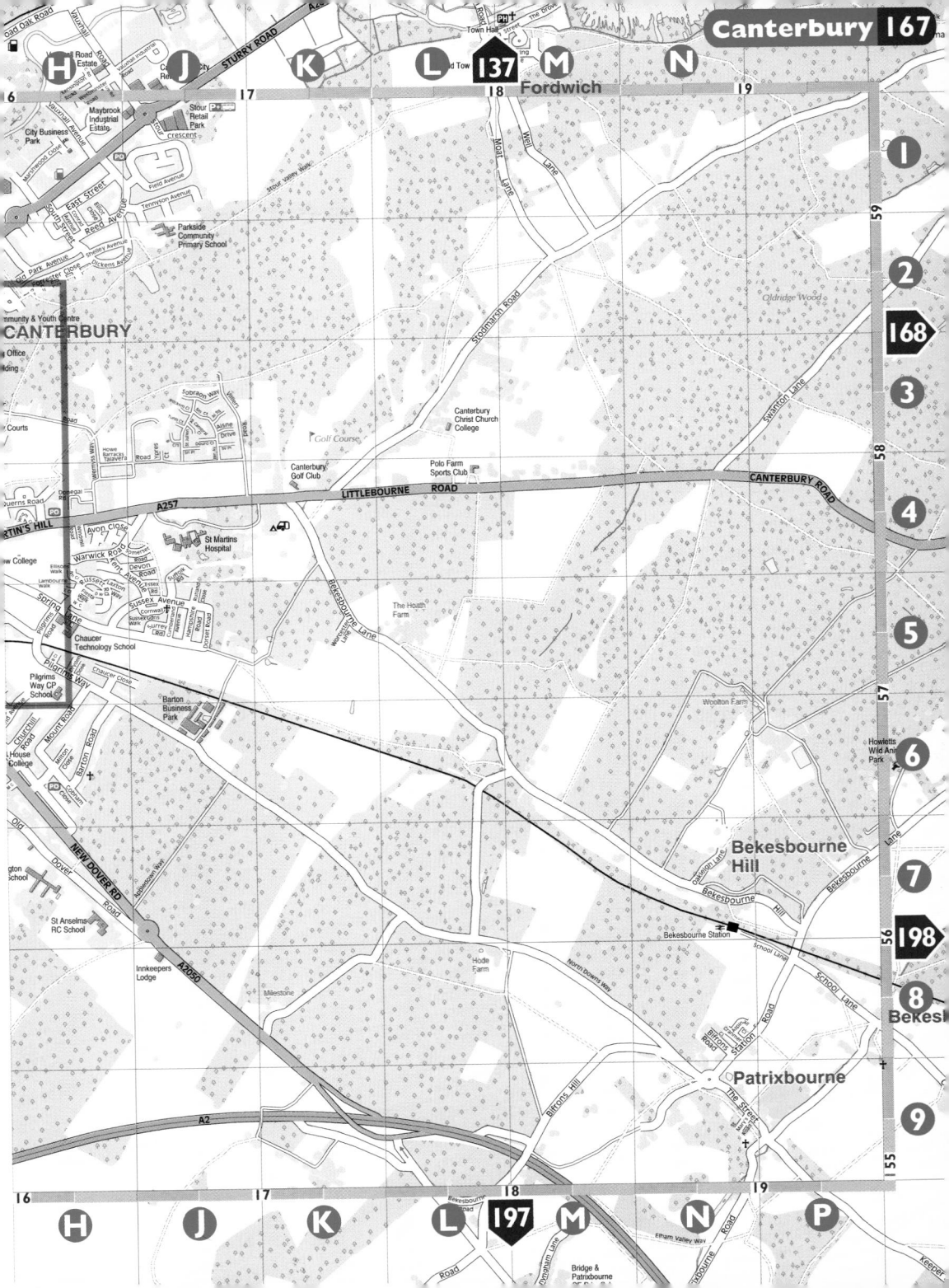

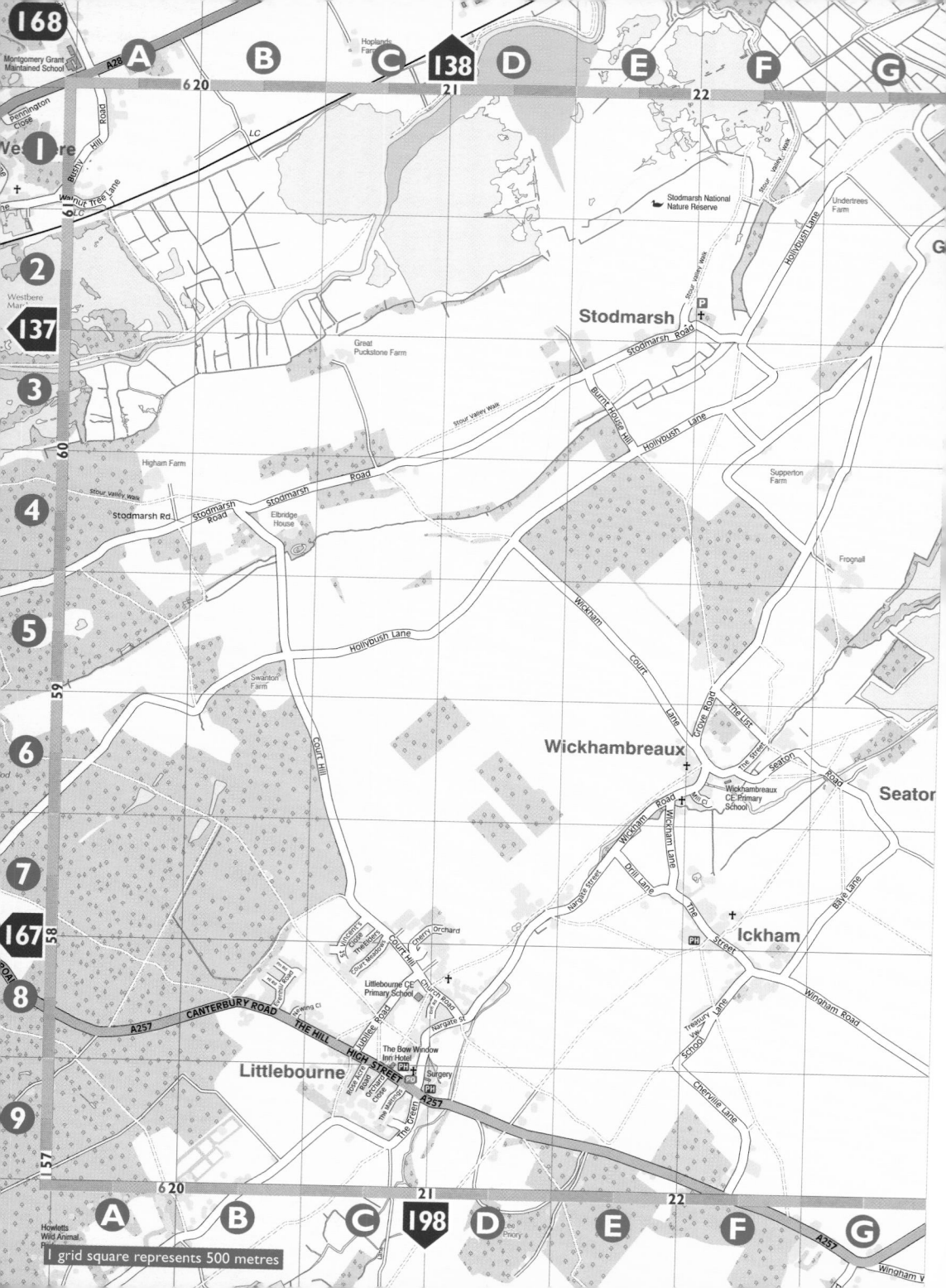

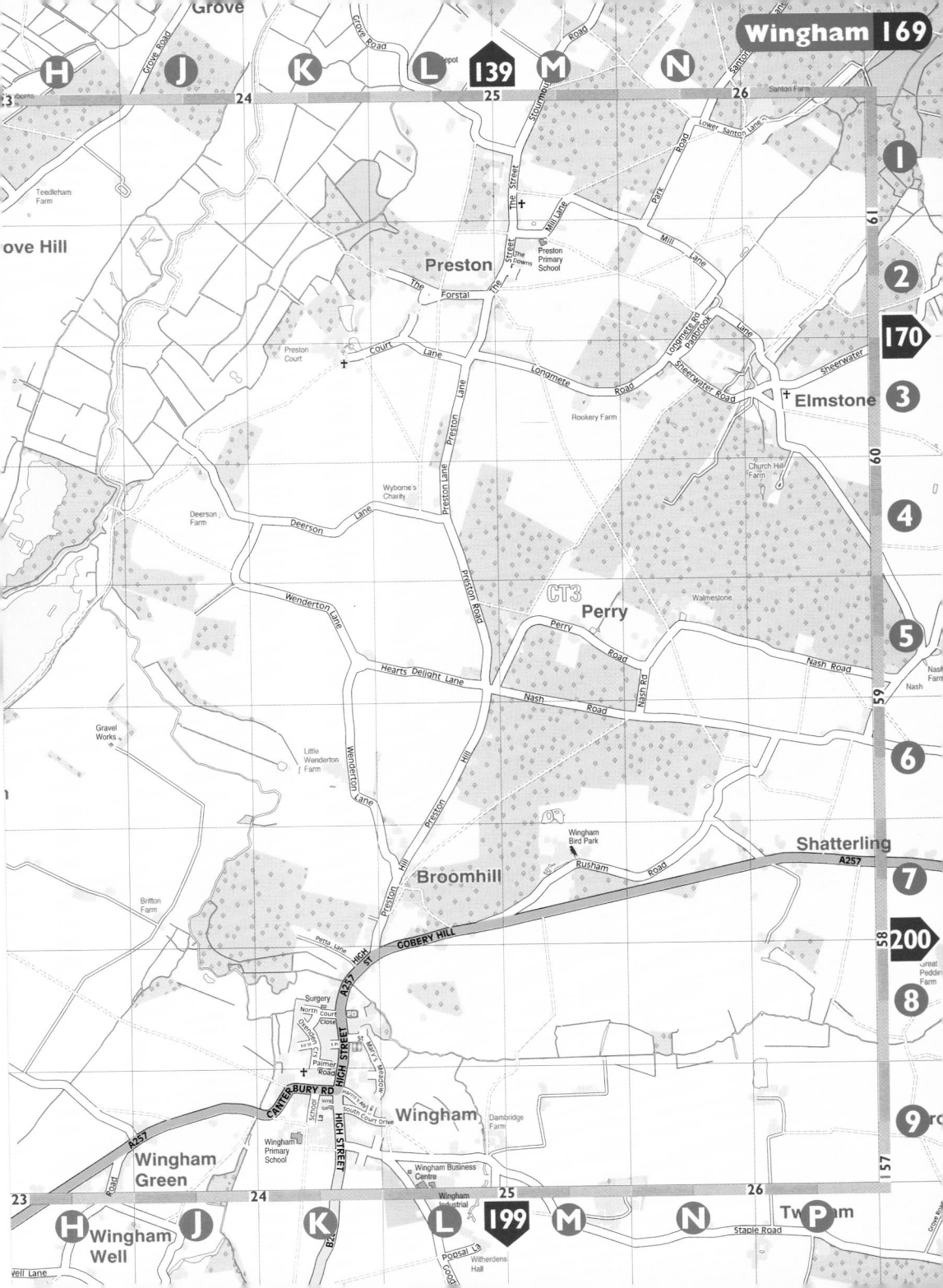

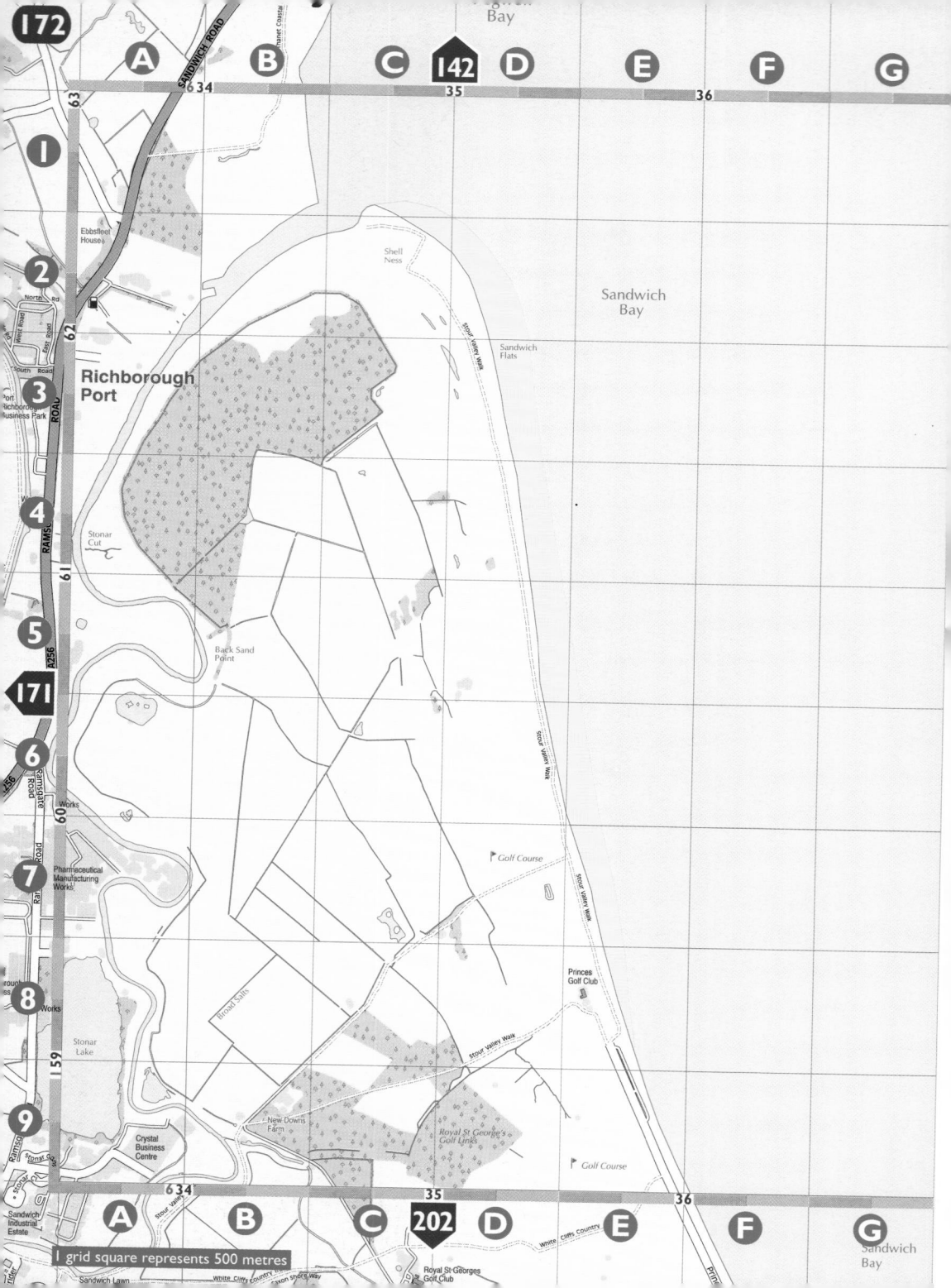

172

A B **142** C D E F G

I 63 34 35 36

Sandwich Road

Ebbsfleet House

2
North Rd
West Road
Salt Road
62
South Road
Port
Richborough Business Park

Richborough Port

3

Shell Ness

Sandwich Flats

Sandwich Bay

4
RAMS
Stonar Cut
61

Stour Valley Walk

5
A256
Back Sand Point

171

6
56
Ramsgate Road
60
Works

Stour Valley Walk

7
Pharmaceutical Manufacturing Works

Golf Course

Stour Valley Walk

8
Rail Road
Works
59
Stonar Lake

Broad Salts

Princes Golf Club

9
Ramsgate Road
Stonar Close
Crystal Business Centre

New Downs Farm

Stour Valley Walk

Royal St George's Golf Links

Golf Course

Sandwich Industrial Estate

A 634 B C **202** D E F G

Stour Valley
White Cliffs Country
Saxon Shore Way
Sandwich Bay

Sandwich Lawn
White Cliffs Country
Royal St Georges Golf Club

1 grid square represents 500 metres

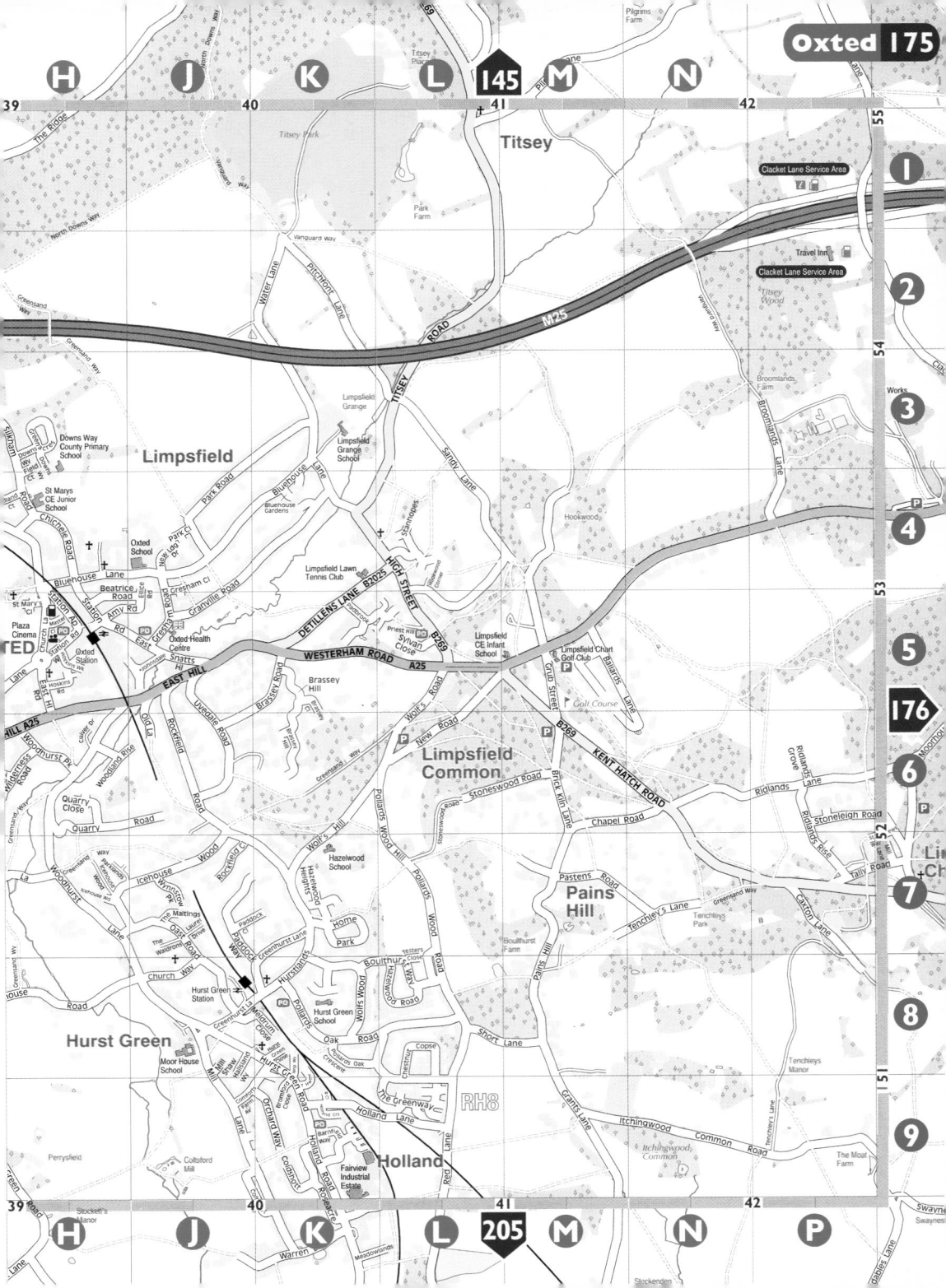

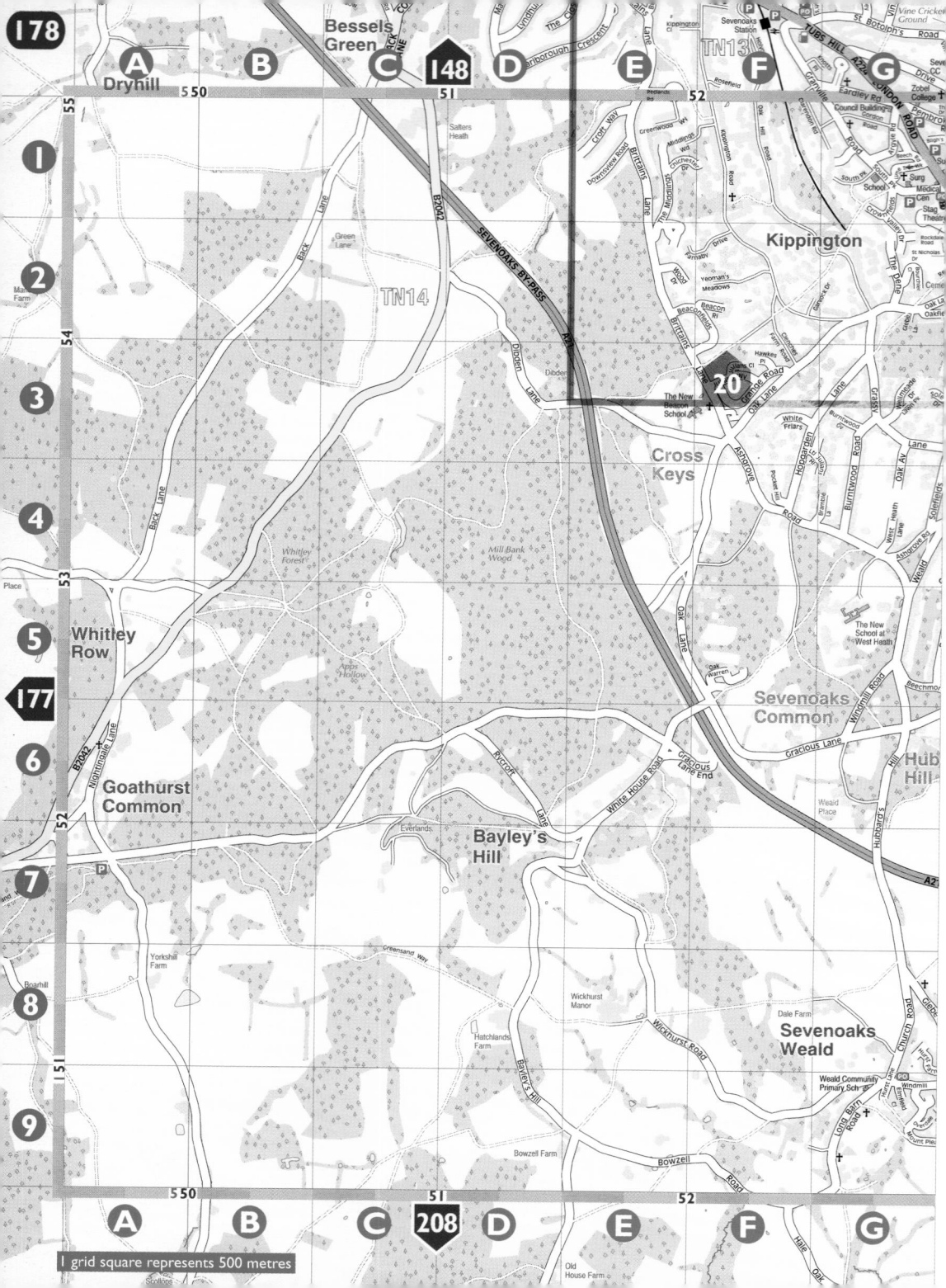

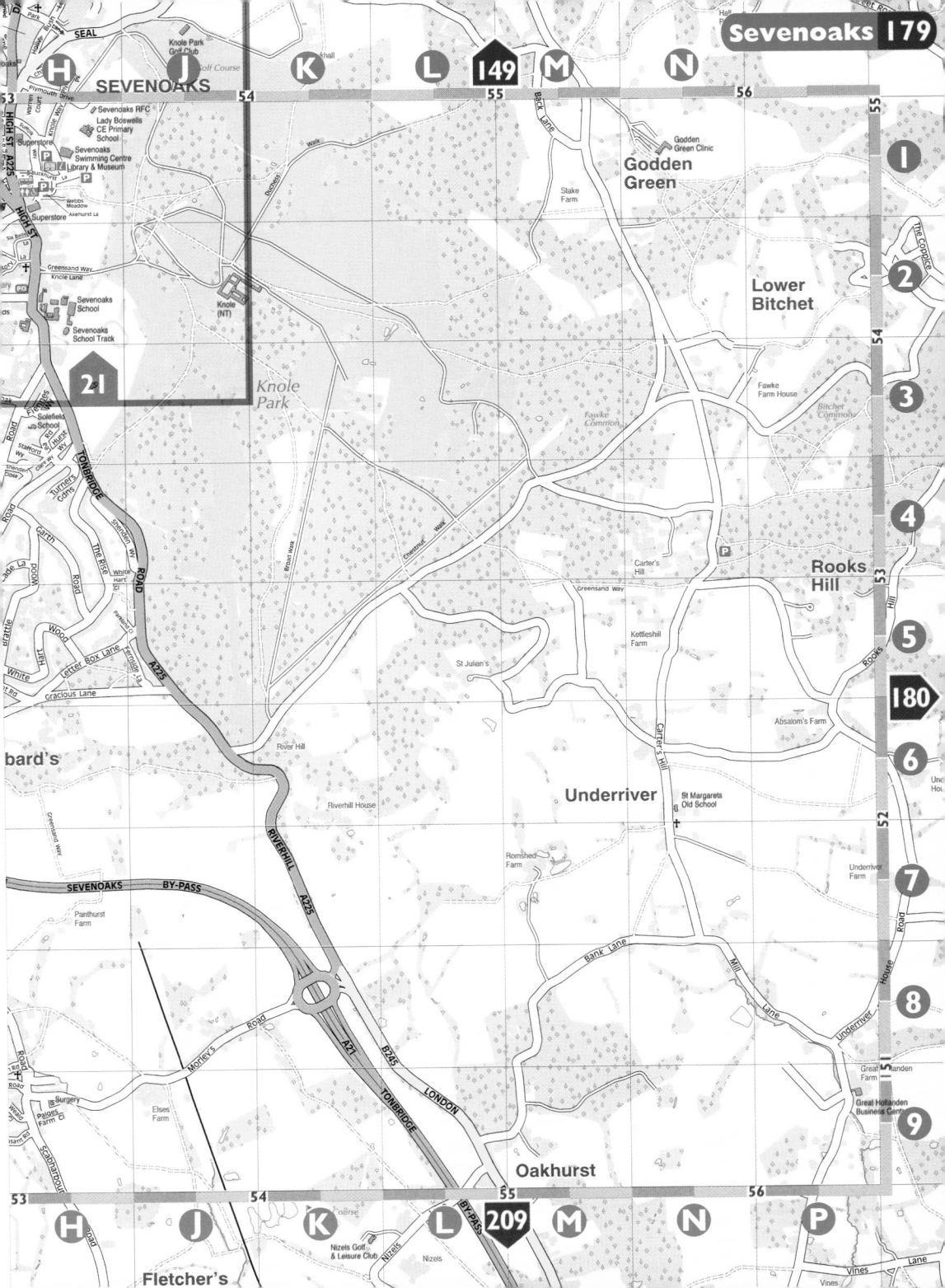

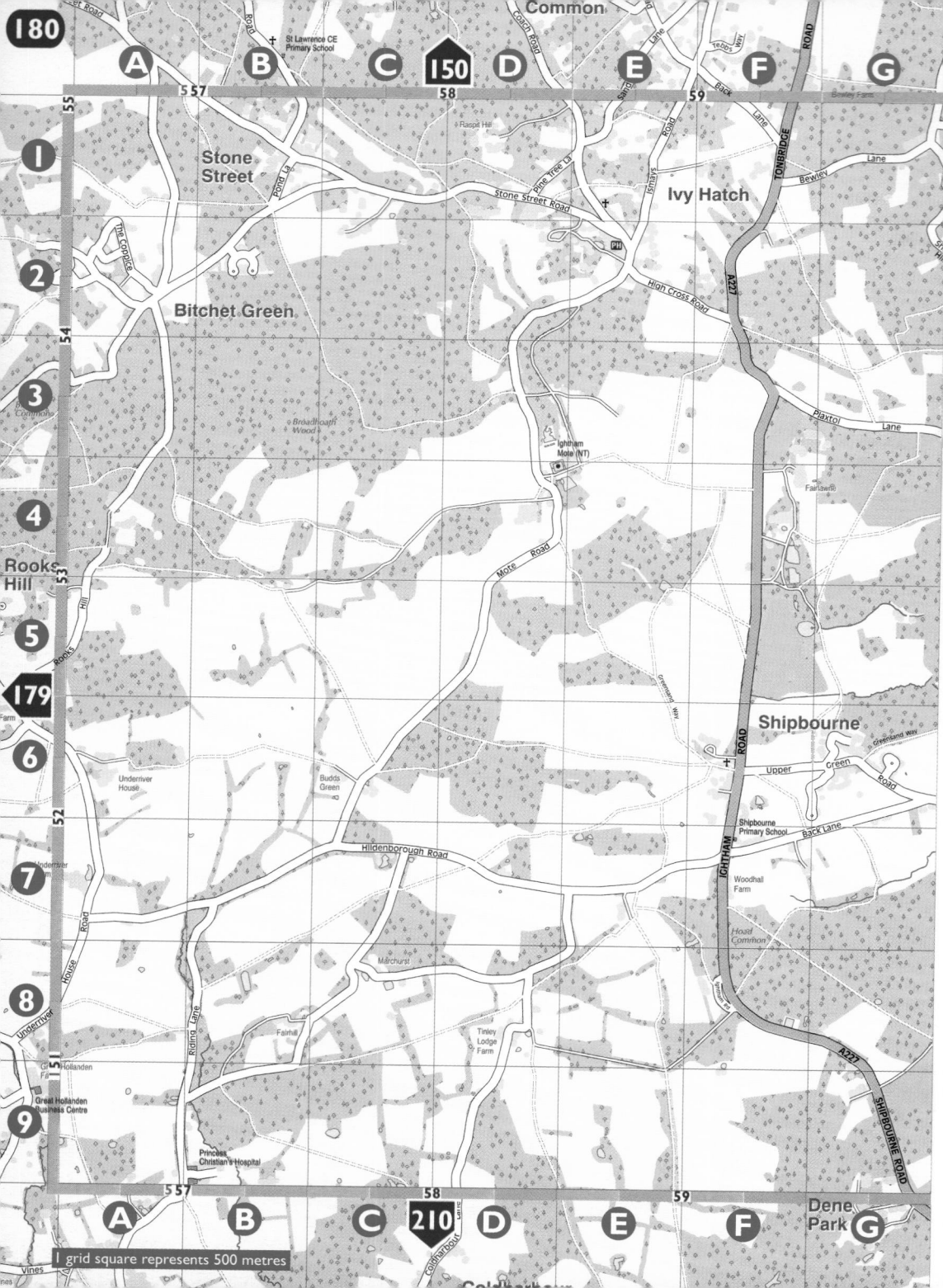

Cross

H   J   K   L   **151**   M   N

I

2

3

4

5

182

6

7

8

9

Winfield Lane

Yopps Green

Sheet Hill

Bourne Farm

Old Soar Manor (NT)

Dux Farm
Dux Lane
Long Mill Lane
Grange Hill
Dux Hill

Bourne Vale
Brook Lane
Plaxtol
St Hildas
The Street
Surgery
Plaxtol Lane
Tree Lane
Church

Plaxtol Primary School

Broadfield

The Hurst

Old Soar Road

Hurst Wood

Pepham

Gover View

Hurst Road

School Lane

Allens Lane

Allen's Farm

Roughway

Roughway Lane

Rats Castle

Gover Hill

Gover Hill

Dunk's Green

Weald Way

Gover Hill

Greensand Way

Fairlawne Home Farm

Hamptons Road

Dunk's Green Road

Greensand Way

Oxon Hoath

Reeds Lane

Claygate Lane

Puttenden Manor Farm

Hamptons

Pillar Box
PH
La

Park Road

Hamptons Road

Oxenhoath

Claygate

Hookwood House

River Bourne

Four Wents

Carpenters Lane

The Common

Common Road

TN11

Putterden Road

Mount Pleasant

Stallion's Green

Steer's Place

Steer's Place

Hope Farm

Hope Avenue

The Paddock

Hadl

H   J   K   L   **211**   M   N   P

North Frith

A227 BOURNE

TN11

High

60   61   62   63

Spar Close

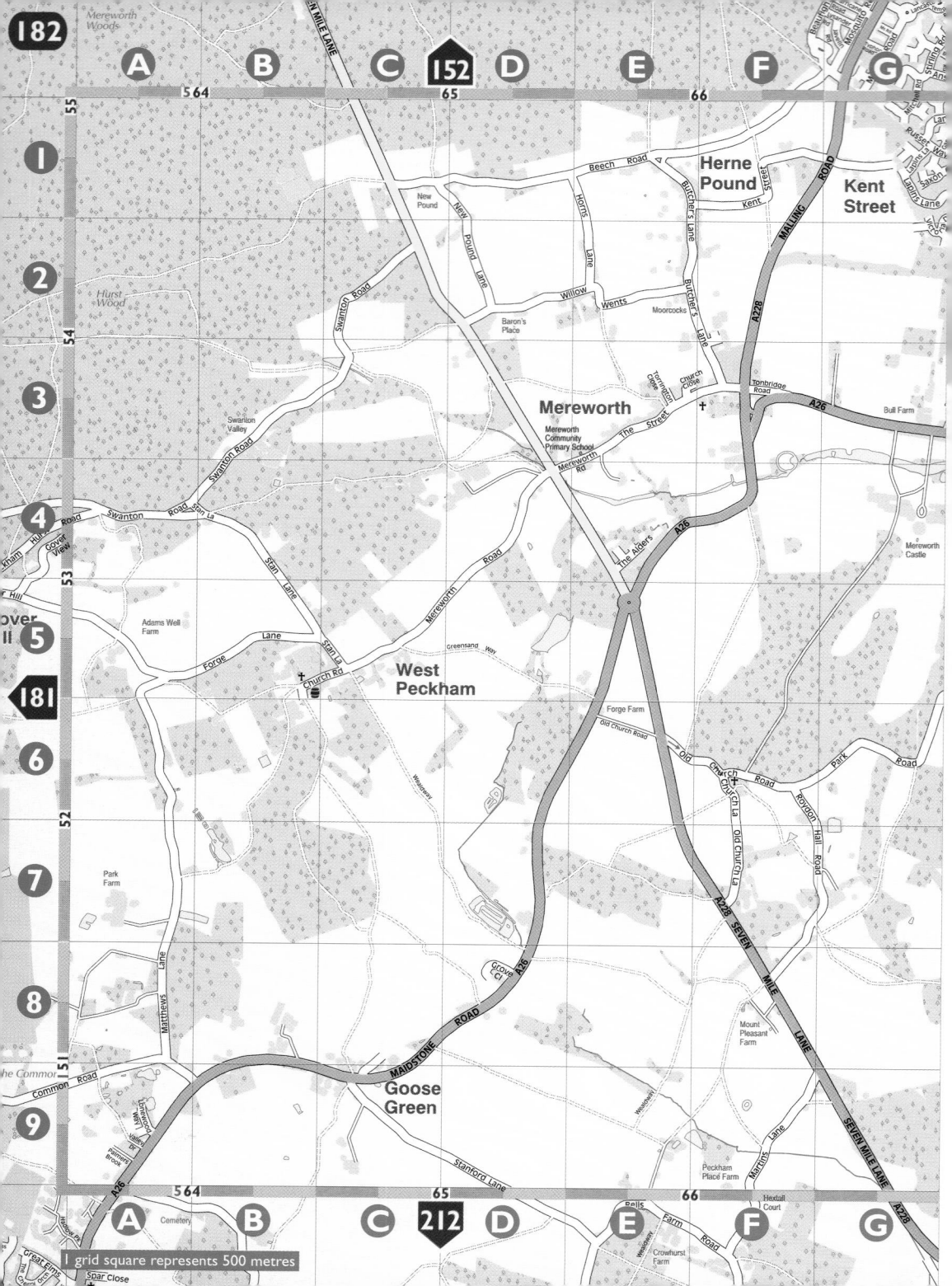

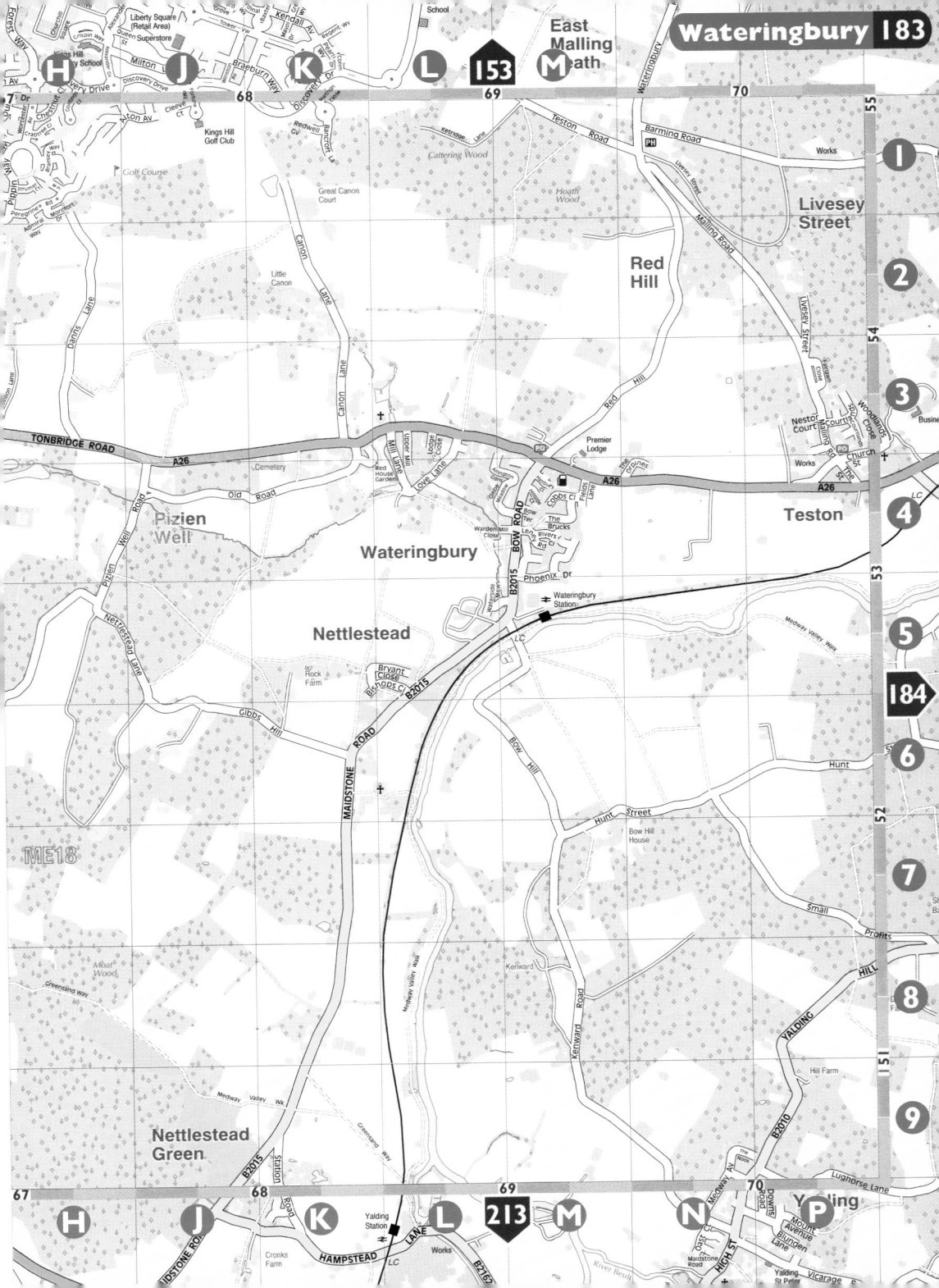

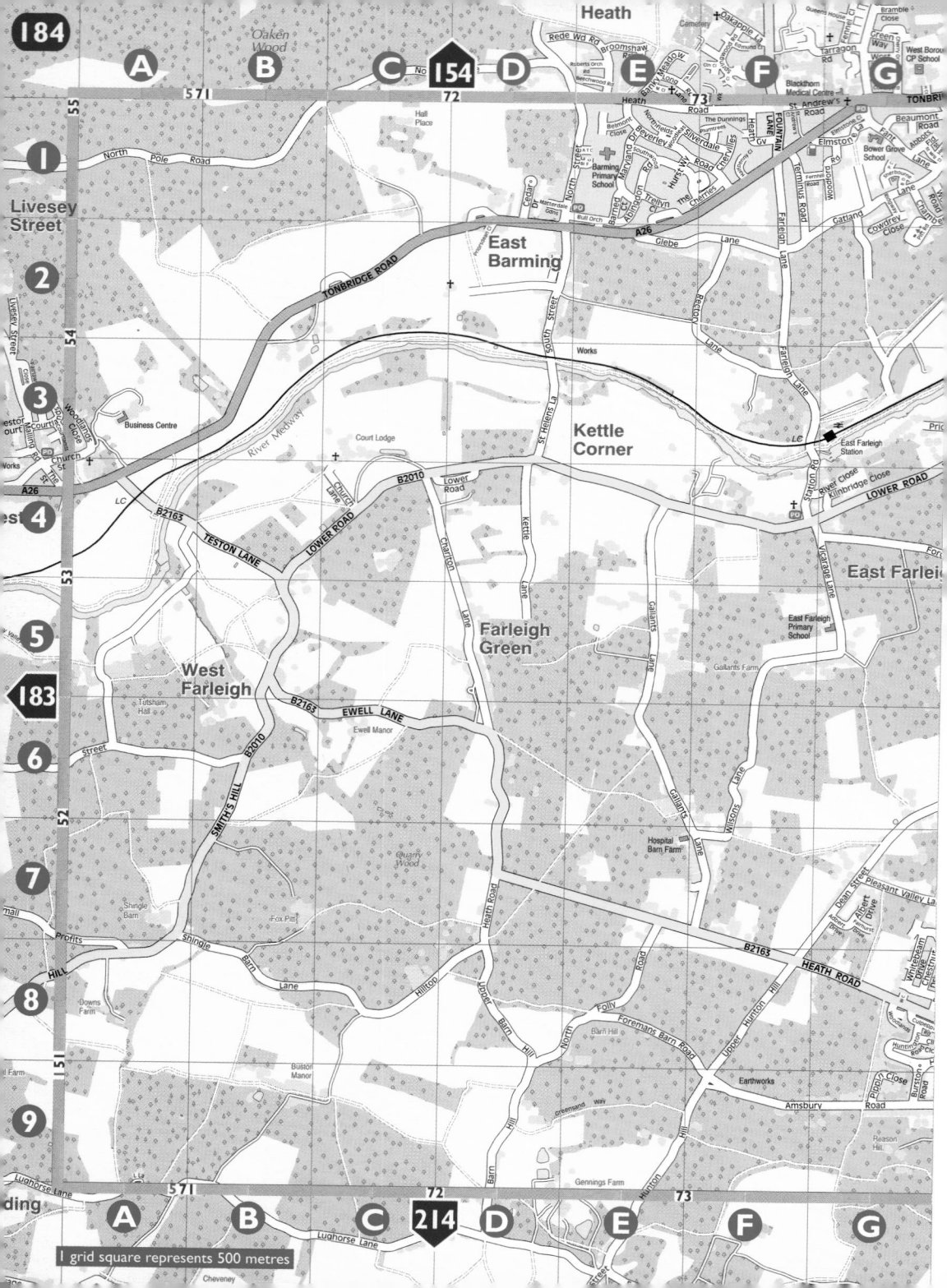

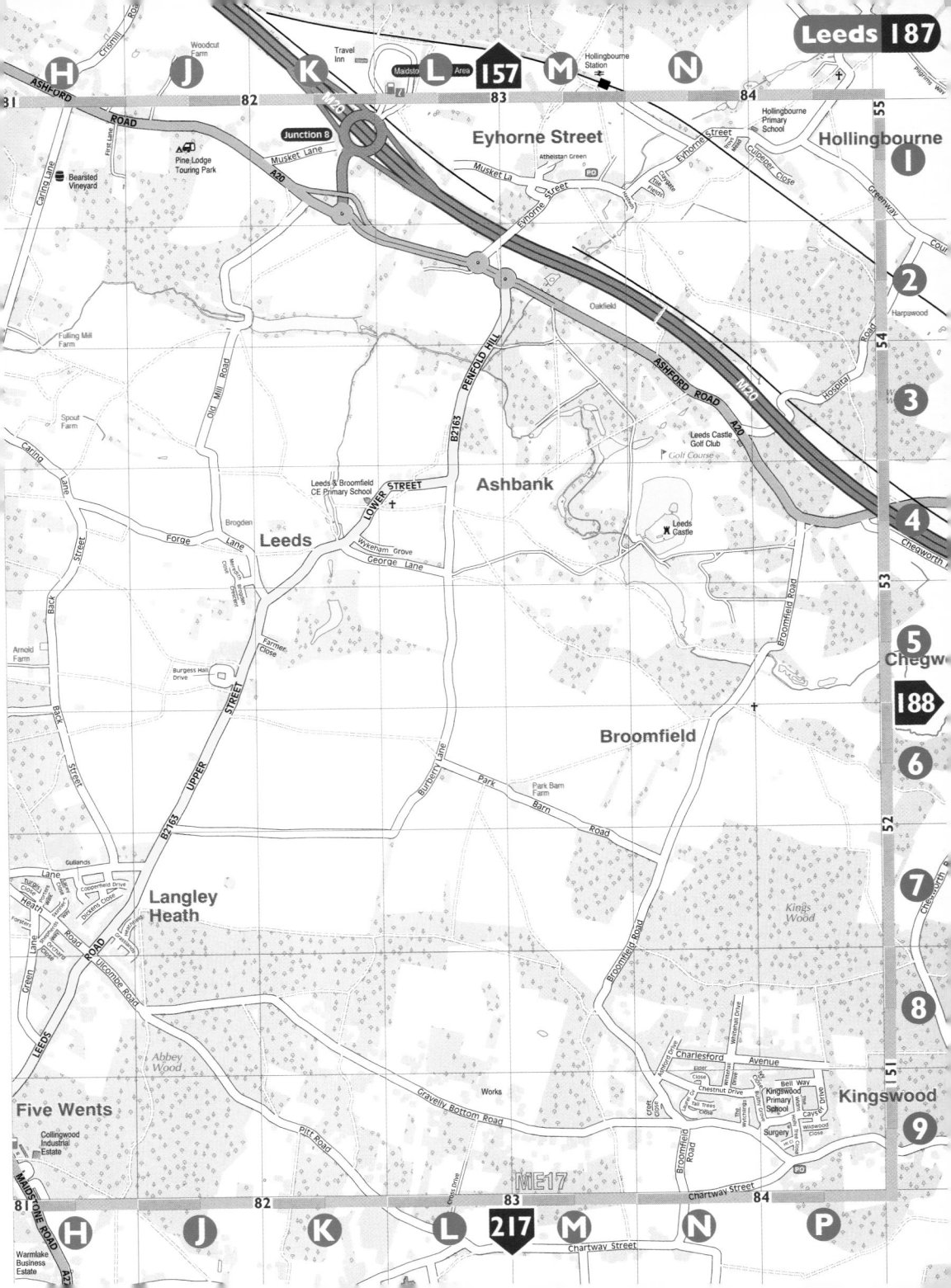

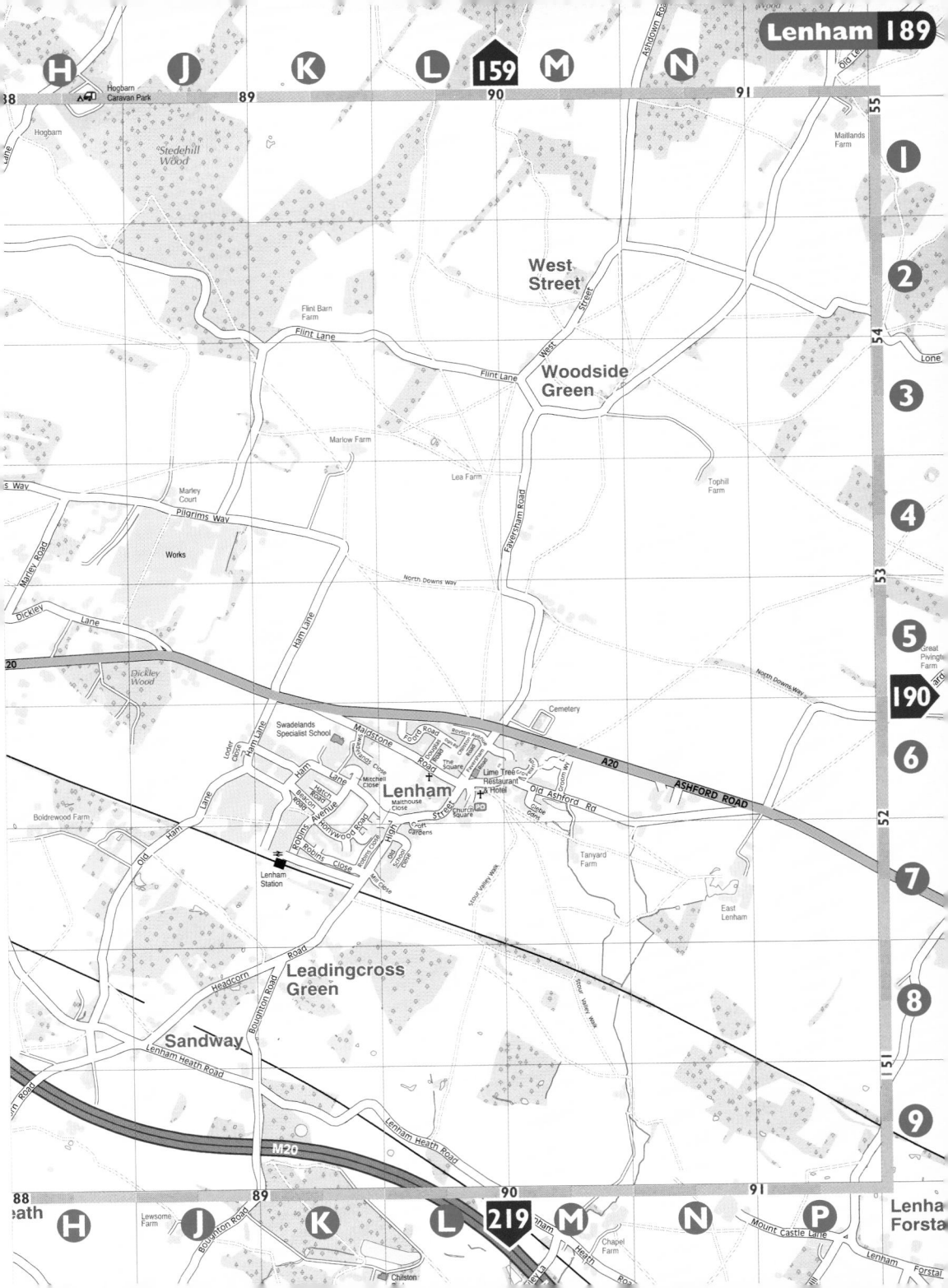

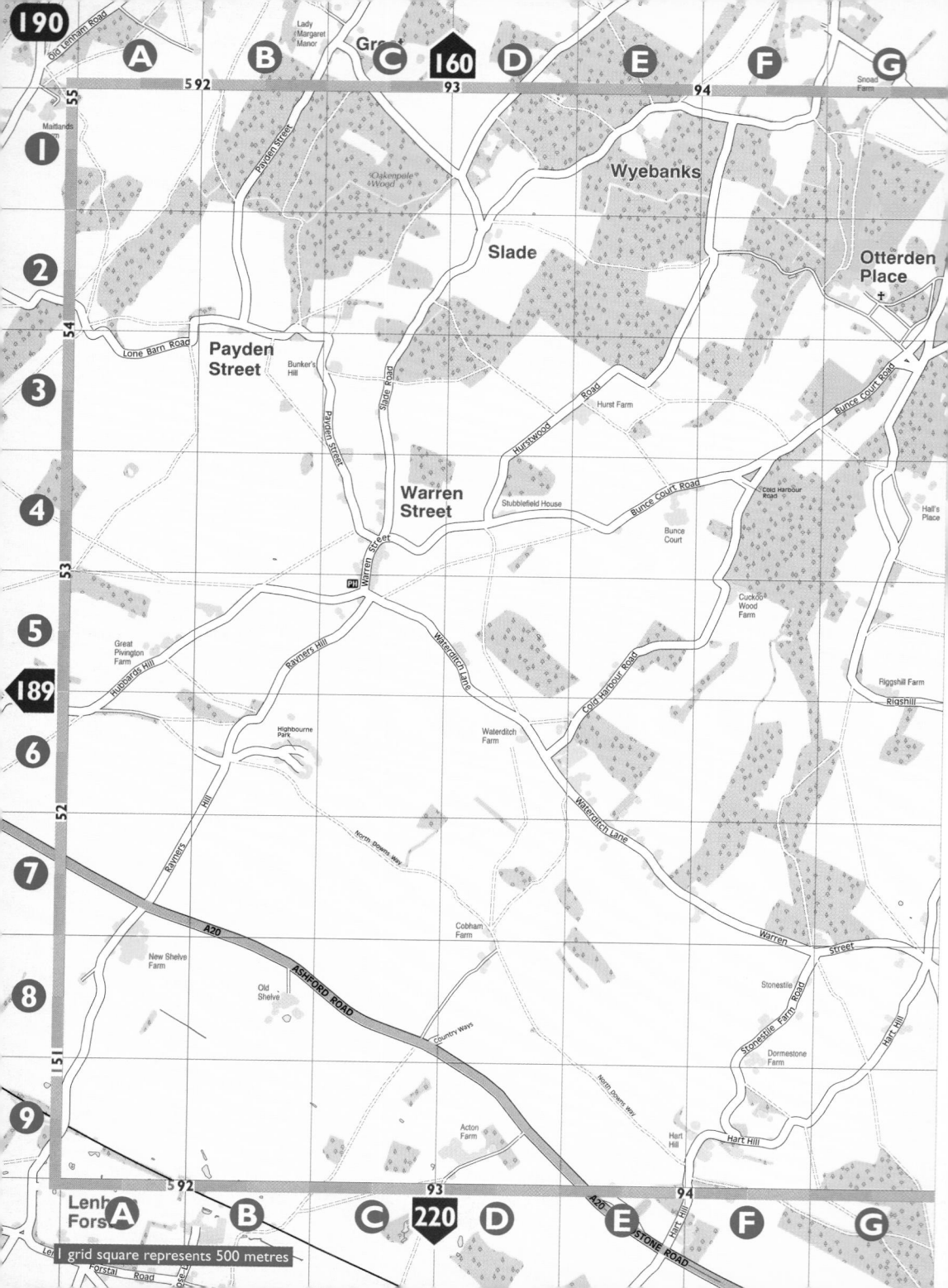

Hockley

Par

Wingfield
Farm

H

J

K

L `161` **M**

55

5

96

97

98

I

Ortenden Road

Corner House

Divan
Wood

Huntingfield

Church Road

Old Hockley Road

**Throwley
Forstal**

2

Holbeam

Holbeam Road

54

Derbies
Court

Stalisfield Road

**Tong
Green**

Pettfield Hill Road

3

Gravel Hill

**The
Valley**

Church Road

Heel Road

Cross Lane

4

53

Redborough
Farm

Woodsell

Heel
Farm

Heel Road

Almshouse Road

5

PH

Stalisfield Road

Hillside Road

School
Lane

Hillside Road

Church Road

Housefield Road

192

Shire Lane

**Stalisfield
Green**

Thornecroft Road

Rushmere
Farm

6

Road

Kennelling Road

Parsonage Farm

✝

Court
Lodge
Farm

Almshouse Road

52

Vent
House

Cornhill
Farm

Newlands
Farm

7

Bowl Road

Kenyton
Farm

Hawk's
Nest

Stalisfield Road

Almshouse Road

Monkery
Farm

8

51

Crows Hole
Farm

Faversham Road

Monkery Lane

Longbeech Wood

9

95

96

97

98

H

J

K

L

`221` **M**

N

P

Char
Hill

Bowl Road

FAVERSHAM ROAD

Stock
Lea

CANTERBURY ROAD

A252

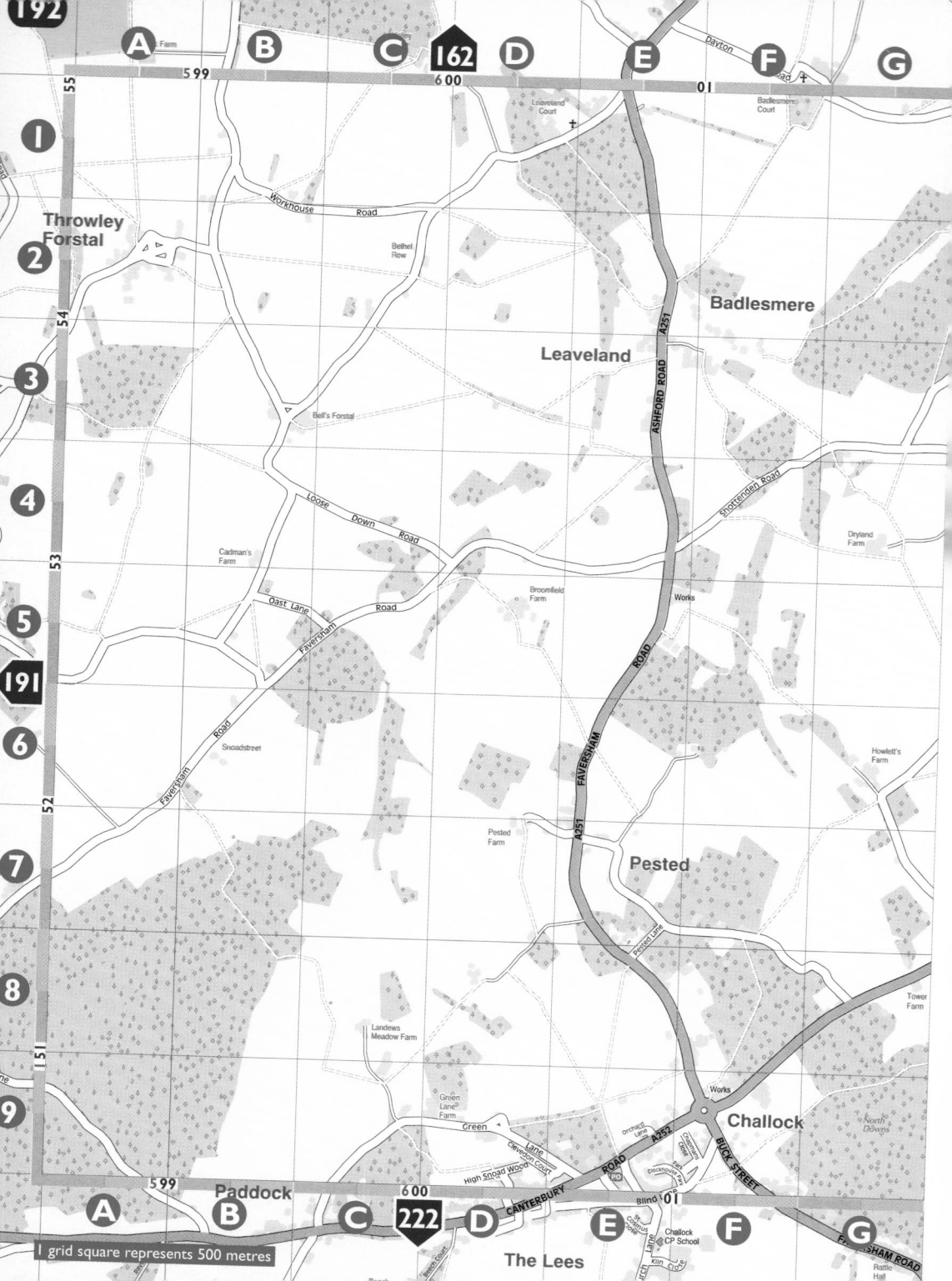

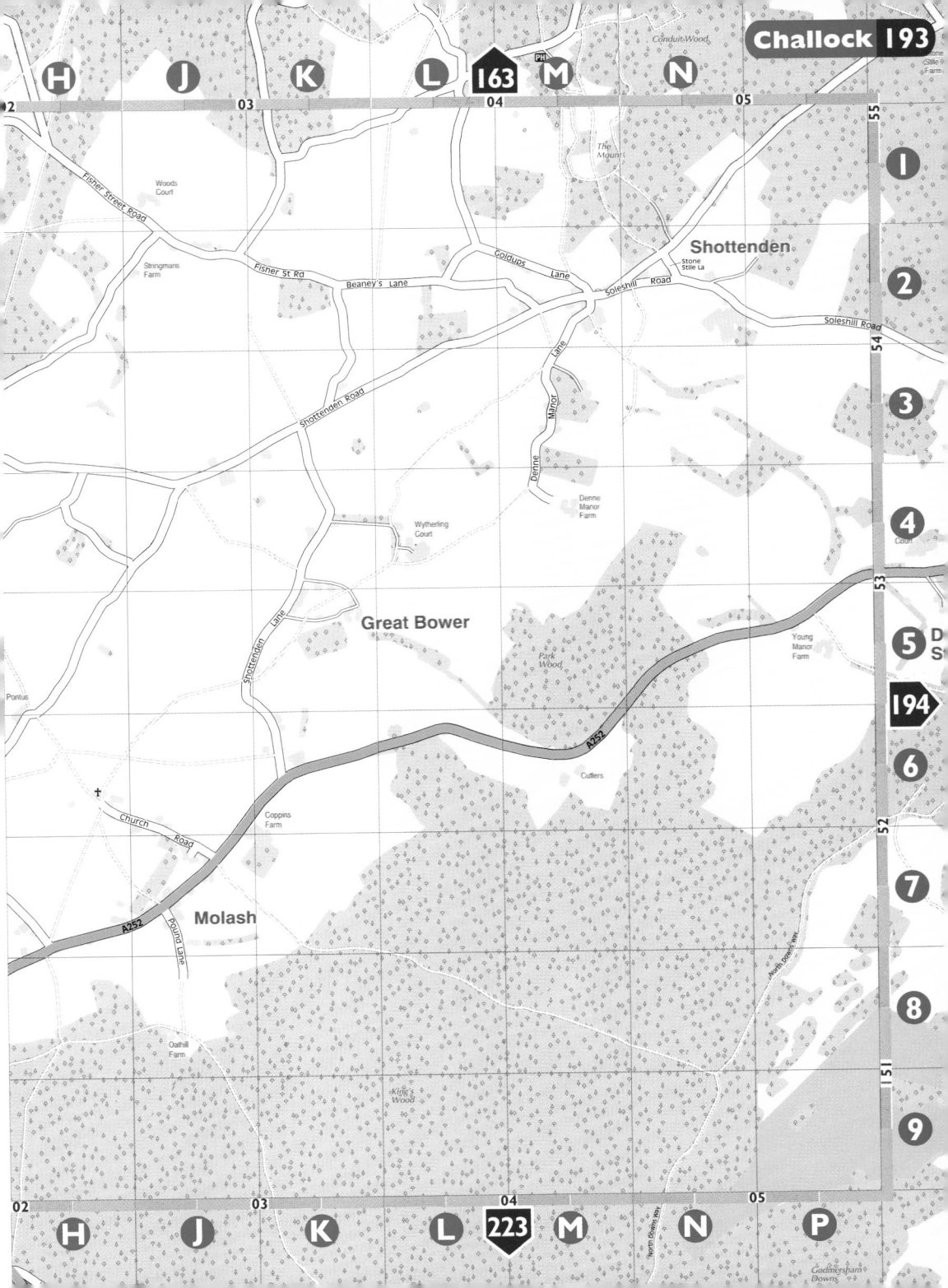

Conduit Wood

Stone Stile Farm

H **J** **K** **L** 163 PH **M** **N**

2 03 04 05

The Mount

I 55

Woods Court

Fisher Street Road

Stringmans Farm

Fisher St Rd Beaney's Lane Golduos Lane

Shottenden

2 Stone Stile La

Soleshill Road Soleshill Road 54

3

Shottenden Road

Denne Lane Manor

4 Court

Denne Manor Farm

Wytherling Court

53

Young Manor Farm

5 D S

194

Shottenden Lane

Great Bower

Park Wood

Pontius

52

6

A252

Cutlers

7

† Church Road Coppins Farm

8

A252 Pound Lane

Molash 51

North Downs Way

Oathill Farm

9

King's Wood

Godmersham Downs

2 03 04 05

H **J** **K** **L** 223 **M** **N** **P**

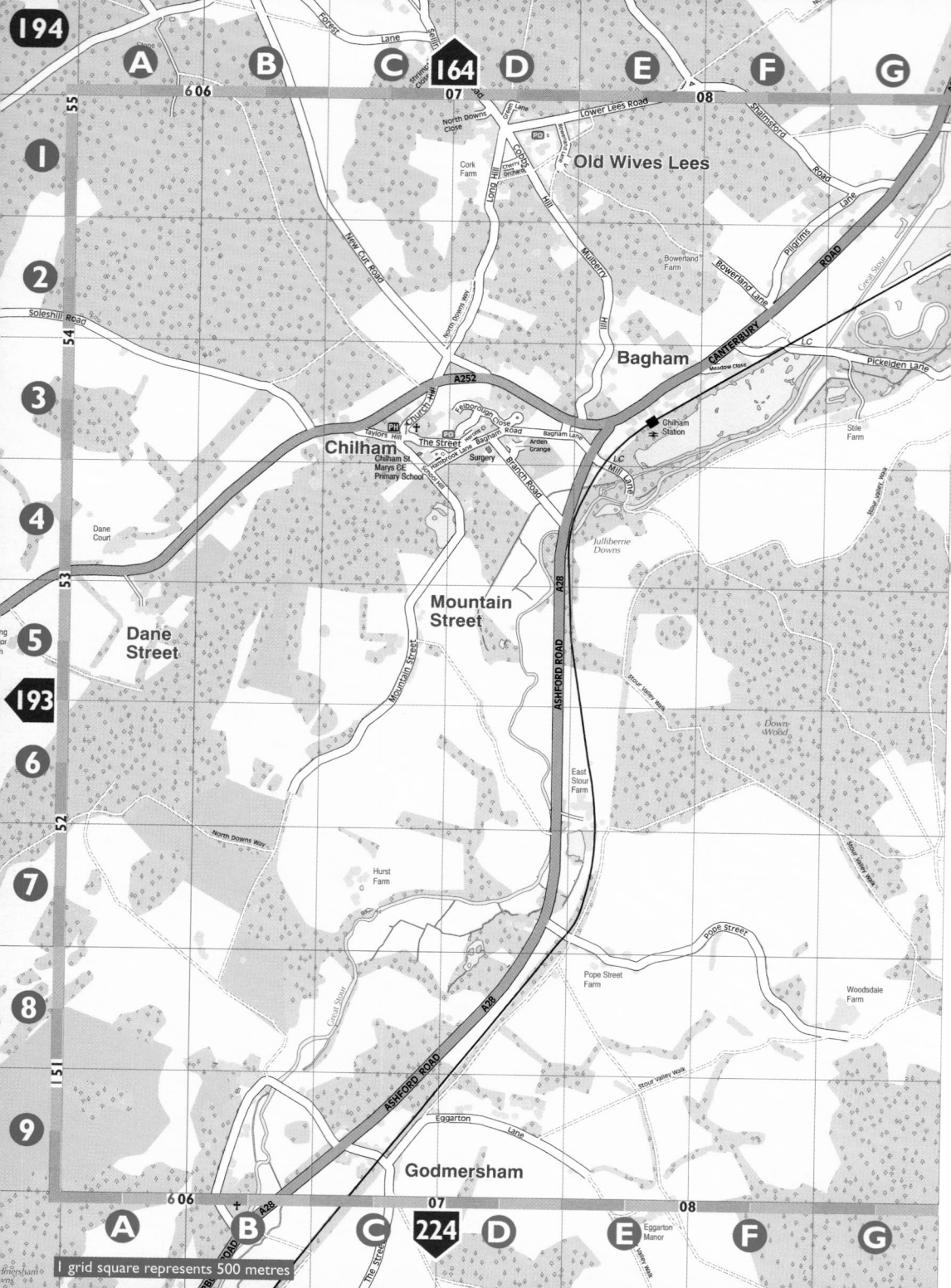

A B C **164** D E F G

6 06 07 08

I

Forest Lane
Shilling Court

North Downs Close
Cork Farm

Old Wives Lees

Lower Lees Road
E Lane
Long Hill

2

Soleshill Road
New Cut Road
Norton Downs Way
Mulberry Hill

Bowerland Farm
Bowerland Lane
Pilgrims Lane
Great Stour
Shalmsford Road

ROAD

54

Pickelden Lane

3

Church Hill
Taylors Hill
PH
Felborough Close
The Street
Horsebridge Road
Bagham
Cherry Orchard
Branch Road
A252
Bagham Lane
Arden Grange

Bagham

Meadow Close
Chilham Station
CANTERBURY
LC

Stile Farm

Chilham
Chilham St
Marys CE
Primary School
Surgery

LC
Mill Lane

4

53

Dane Court

Julliberrie Downs

Stour Valley Walk

Mountain Street

A28 ASHFORD ROAD

5

Dane Street

Mountain Street

Down Wood

6

52

7

North Downs Way
Hurst Farm

East Stour Farm

Great Stour

8

51

Pope Street
Pope Street Farm

Woodsdale Farm

Stour Valley Walk

9

ASHFORD ROAD
A28

Eggarton Lane

Godmersham

Eggarton Manor

Valley Walk

6 06 07 08

A B C **224** D E F G

1 grid square represents 500 metres

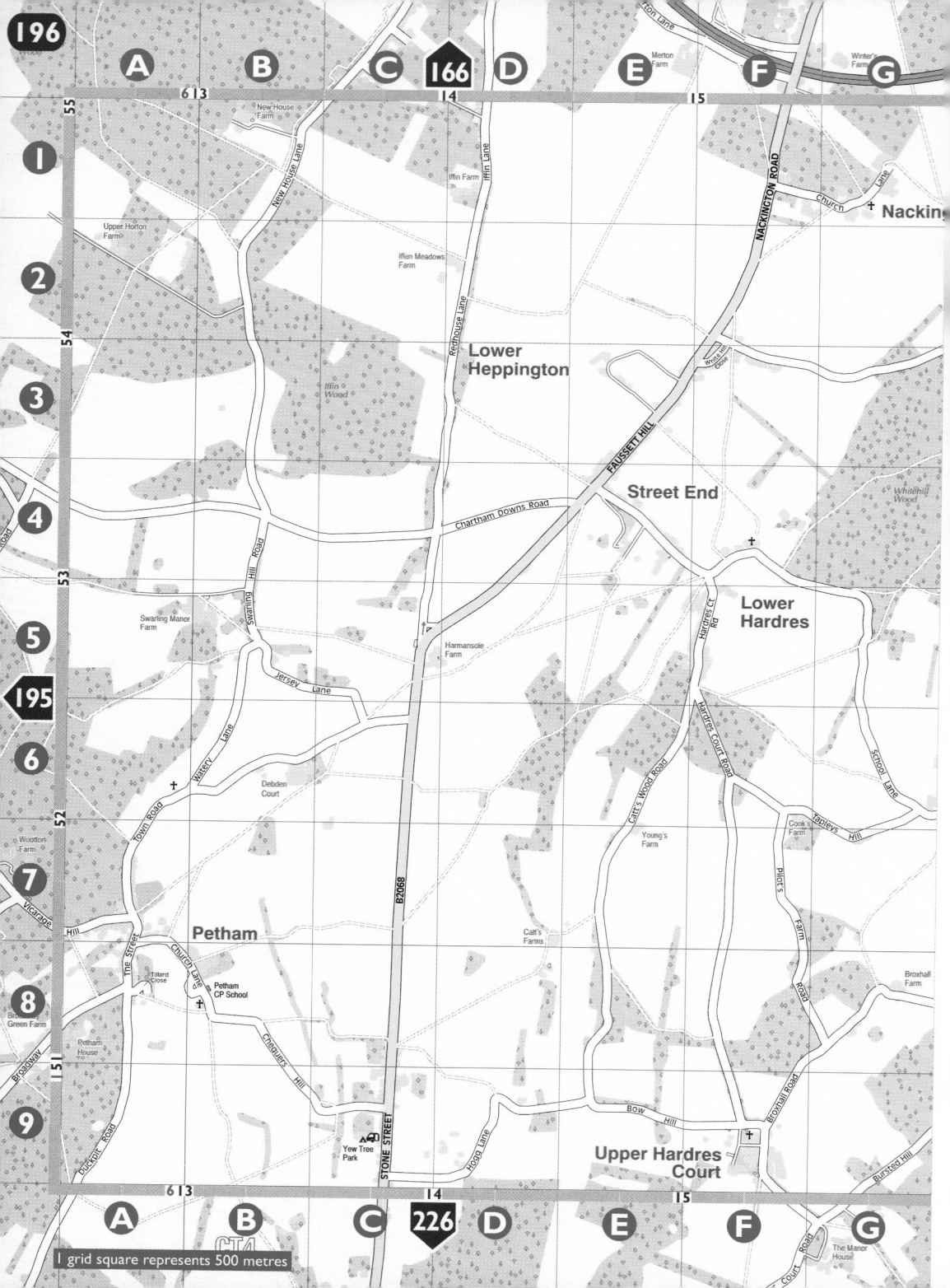

A   B   C   166   D   E   F   G

55   613   14   15

Winter's Farm

Merton Farm

I

Upper Horton Farm

New House Farm

Iffin Farm

Iffin Lane

Redhouse Lane

New House Lane

NACKINGTON ROAD

Church Lane

† Nackin

2

54

Iffen Meadows Farm

Lower Heppington

3

Iffin Wood

FAUSSETT HILL

Wratt's Hill Close

4

53

Chartham Downs Road

Street End

Hardres Ct Rd

†

Whitehill Wood

Swanling Hill Road

Swarling Manor Farm

Harmansole Farm

Lower Hardres

5

Jersey Lane

Hardres Court Road

195

School Lane

6

52

Nursery Lane

Debden Court

Calf's Wood Road

Young's Farm

Cook's Farm

Tapley's Hill

Town Road

†

Pilot's Farm

7

Wootton Farm

Vicarage Hill

Calf's Farms

8

51

Broadway

Green Farm

The Street

Church Lane

Tillard Close

Petham CP School

†

Petham House

Petham

Chequers Hill

B2068

Broxhall Farm

Broxhall Road

9

Duckpit Road

STONE STREET

Hogg Lane

Bow   Hill

Upper Hardres Court

†

Bursted Hill

Court Road

The Manor House

A   B   C   226   D   E   F   G

613   14   15

CT4

1 grid square represents 500 metres

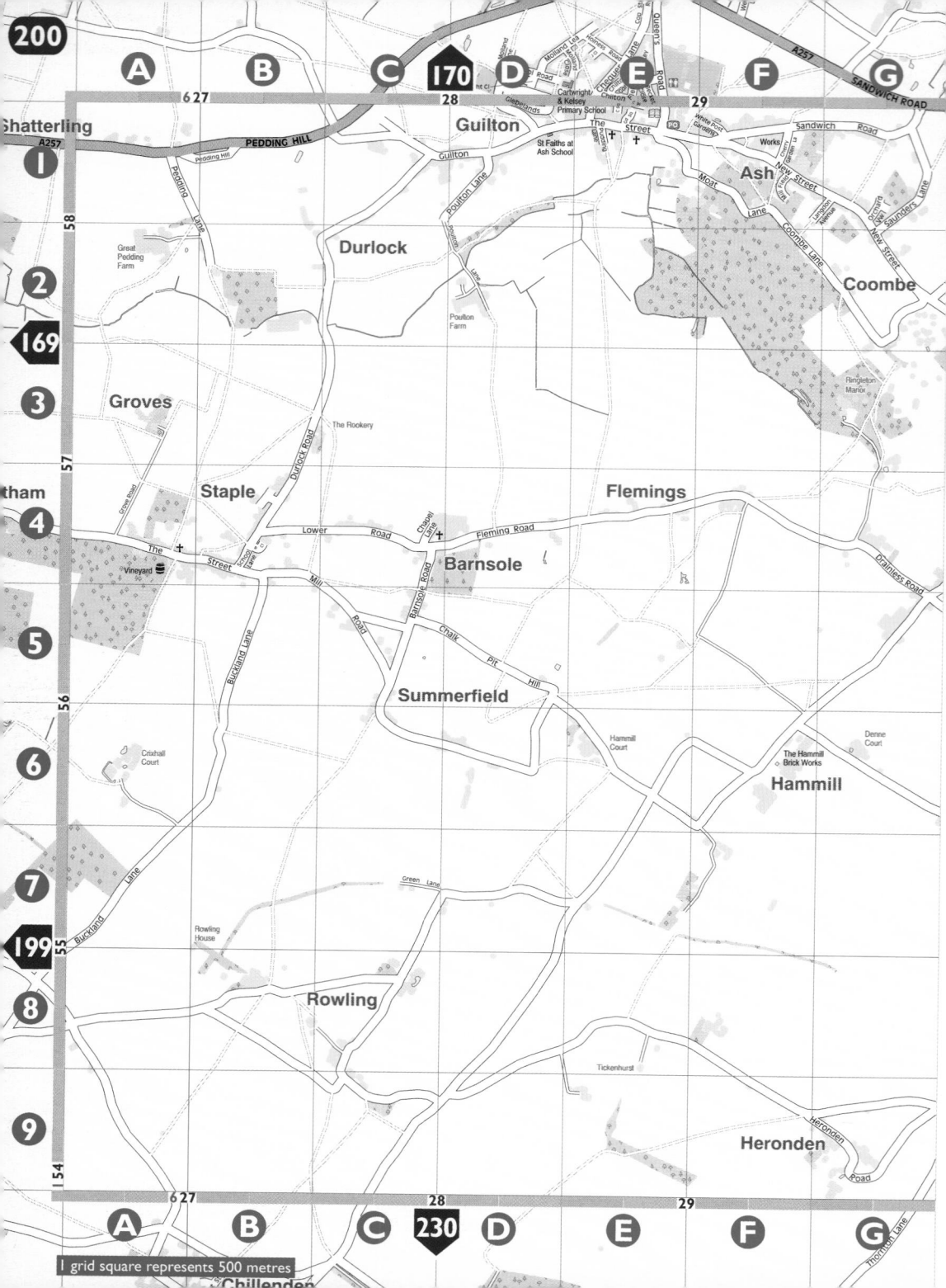

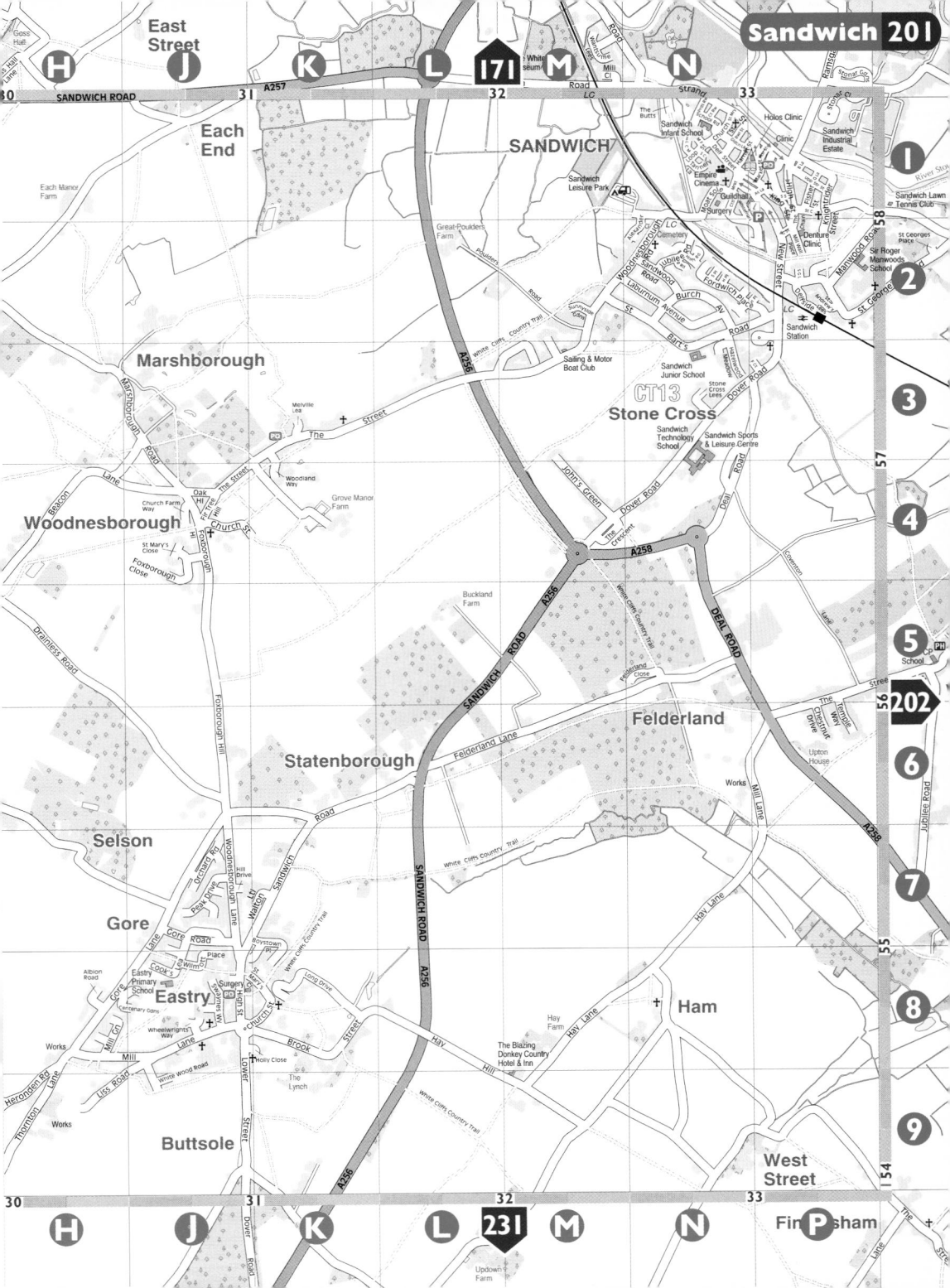

202

A **B** **C** 172 **D** **E** **F** **G**

6 34 35 36

Sandwich
Bay

1

Sandwich
Industrial

Crystal
Business
Centre

New Downs
Farm

Royal St George's
Links

Golf C

River Stour

White Cliffs Country Trail

White Cliffs Country Trail

Saxon Shore Way

Royal St Georges
Golf Club

Sandwich Lawn
Tennis Club

Knightrider Street

Denture
Clinic

St Georges
Place

58

Sir Roger
Manwoods School

Sandown Road

Toll

Princes Drive

2

St George's Road

Sandown Lane

**Sandwich
Bay Estate**

Guilford Road

King's

Avenue

North Road

Waldershare

Princes Drive

Av

Shawdon
Avenue

Francis
Avenue

Cambridge
Avenue

3

57

4

Lane

Goretop

LC

Blue
Pigeons

North Stream

5

Worth CP
School

PH

Minnis
Wk

Worth

56

Mary Bax
Stone

White Cliffs Country Trail

201

Street

Upton
Hous

6

Jubilee Road

Lydden
Valley

PH

A258

7

55

8

Hacklinge Hill

Hacklinge

Ring Wall

Sandhills

Redhouse

9

1 54

6 34 35 36

esham

A **B** A258 **C** 232 **D** **E** **F** **G**

The

ge Hi

Foulmead
Farm

1 grid square represents 500 metres

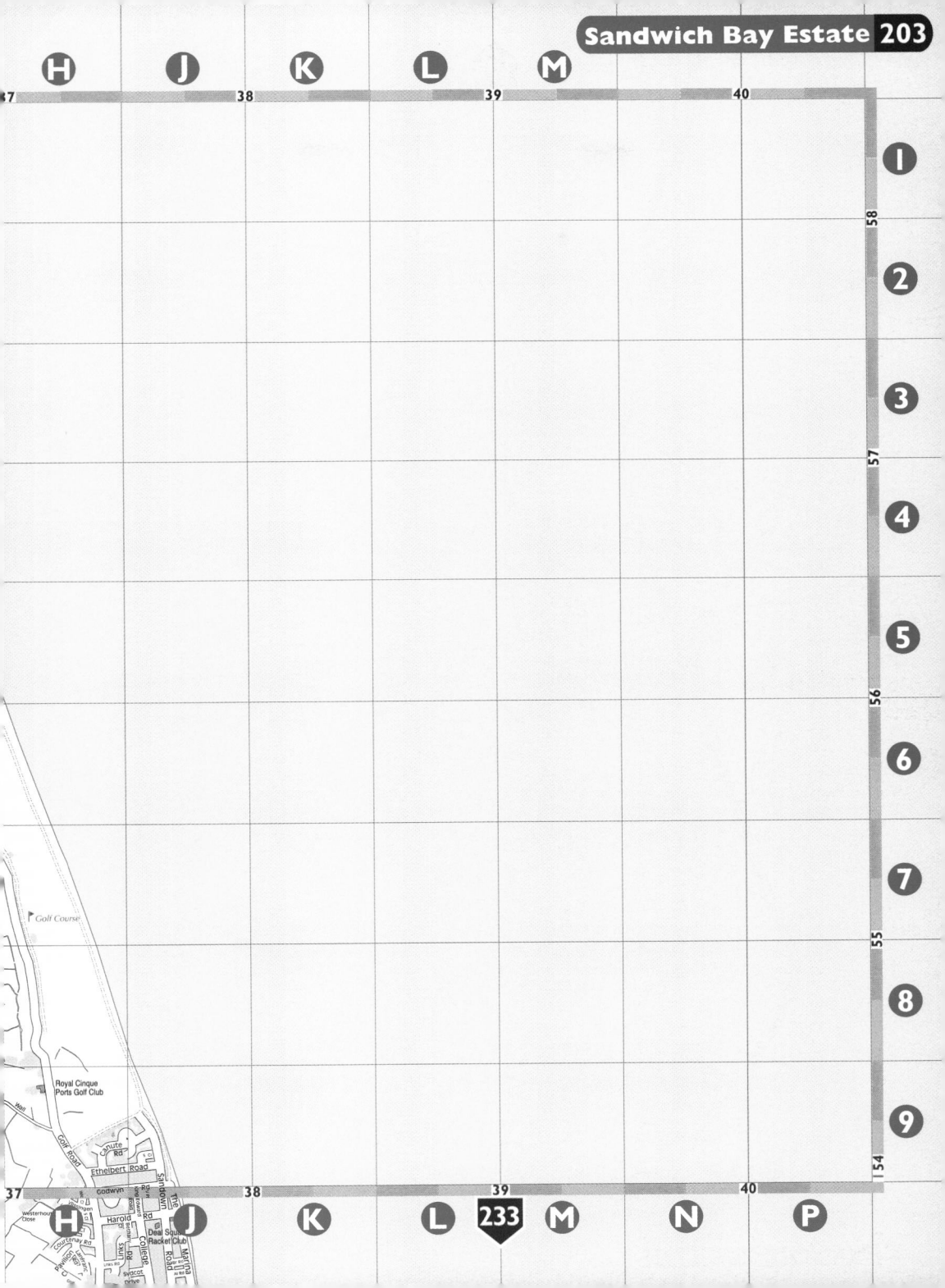

Golf Course

Royal Cinque
Ports Golf Club

Ethelbert Road

Godwyn

Harold

Deal Sandown
Racket Club

Westerhouse
Close

Courtenay Rd

233

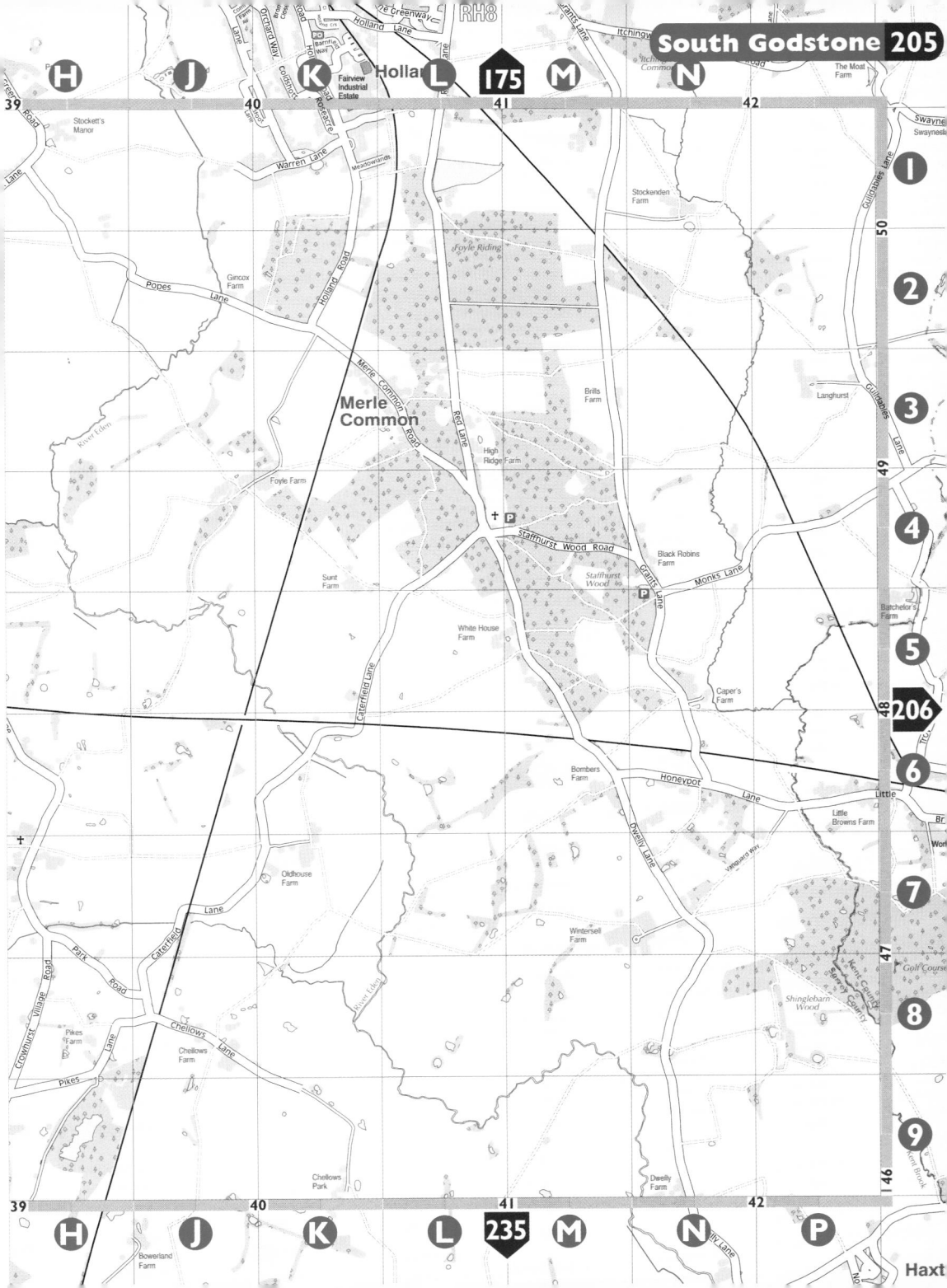

RH8

H　J　K　Holland　L　175　M　N　The Moat Farm

39　40　41　42

swayne
Swayneslea

I

Stockett's Manor

Warren Lane

Meadowlands

Stockenden Farm

50

Popes

Gincox Farm

Holland Road

Foyle Riding

2

Lane

Merle Common Road

Brills Farm

Langhurst

3

Gullidges Lane

River Eden

Merle Common

Red Lane

High Ridge Farm

49

Foyle Farm

+ P

Staffhurst Wood Road

Black Robins Farm

4

Surit Farm

Staffhurst Wood

P

Monks Lane

Batchelor's Farm

48 206

5

Caterfield Lane

White House Farm

Grants Lane

Caper's Farm

6

Little Br

Bombers Farm

Honeypot Lane

Little Browns Farm

Worl

†

Oldhouse Farm

Dwelly Lane

7

Lane

Caterfield

Wintersell Farm

47

Shinglebarn Wood

Golf Course

Surrey County

Kent Gault

8

Crownhurst Village

Park Road

Pikes Farm

Chellows Lane

Chellows Farm

9

Pikes

Chellows Park

Dwelly Farm

46

Kent Brook

39　40　41　42

H　J　K　L　235　M　N　P

Bowerland Farm

ly Lane

Haxt

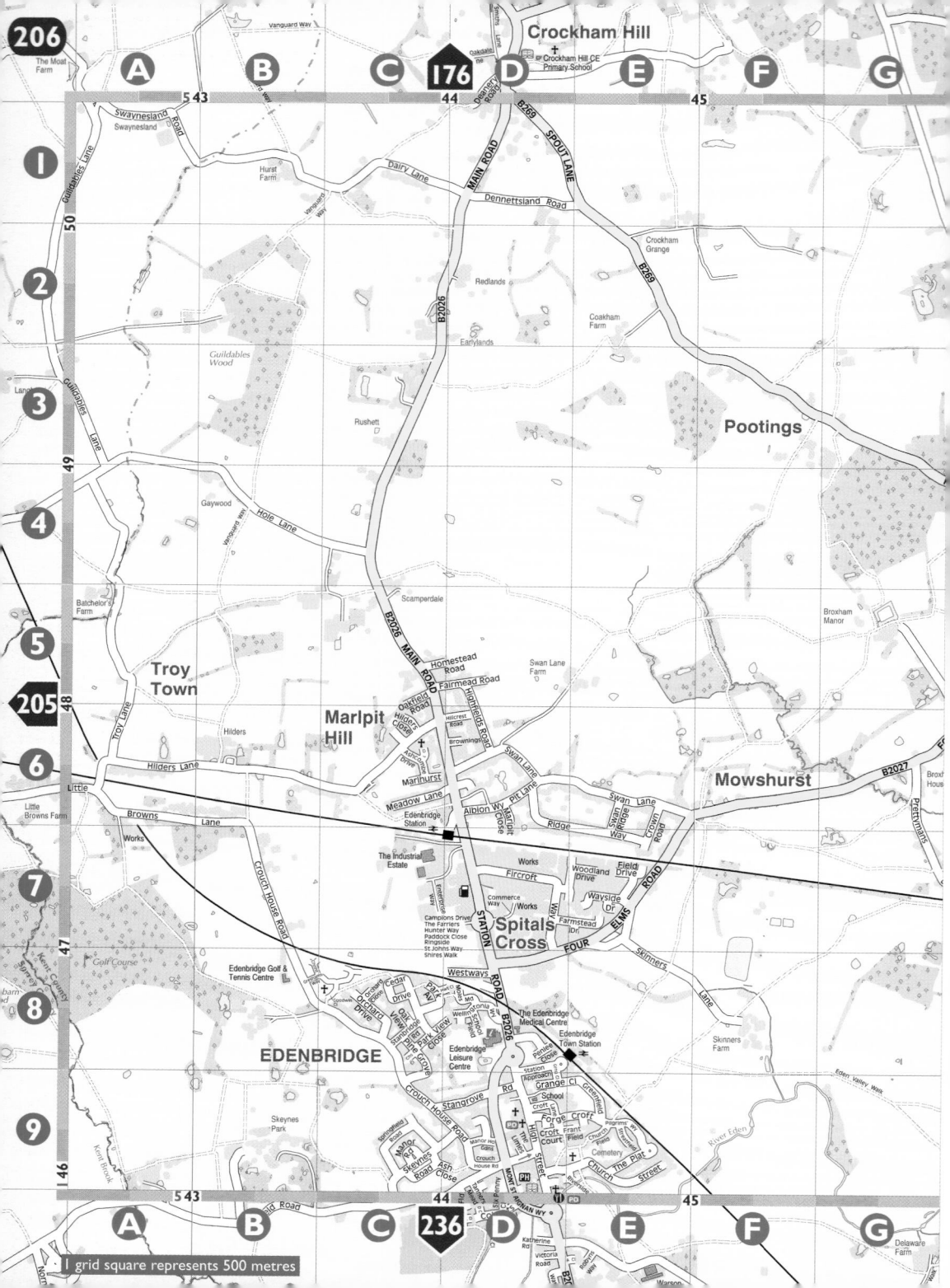

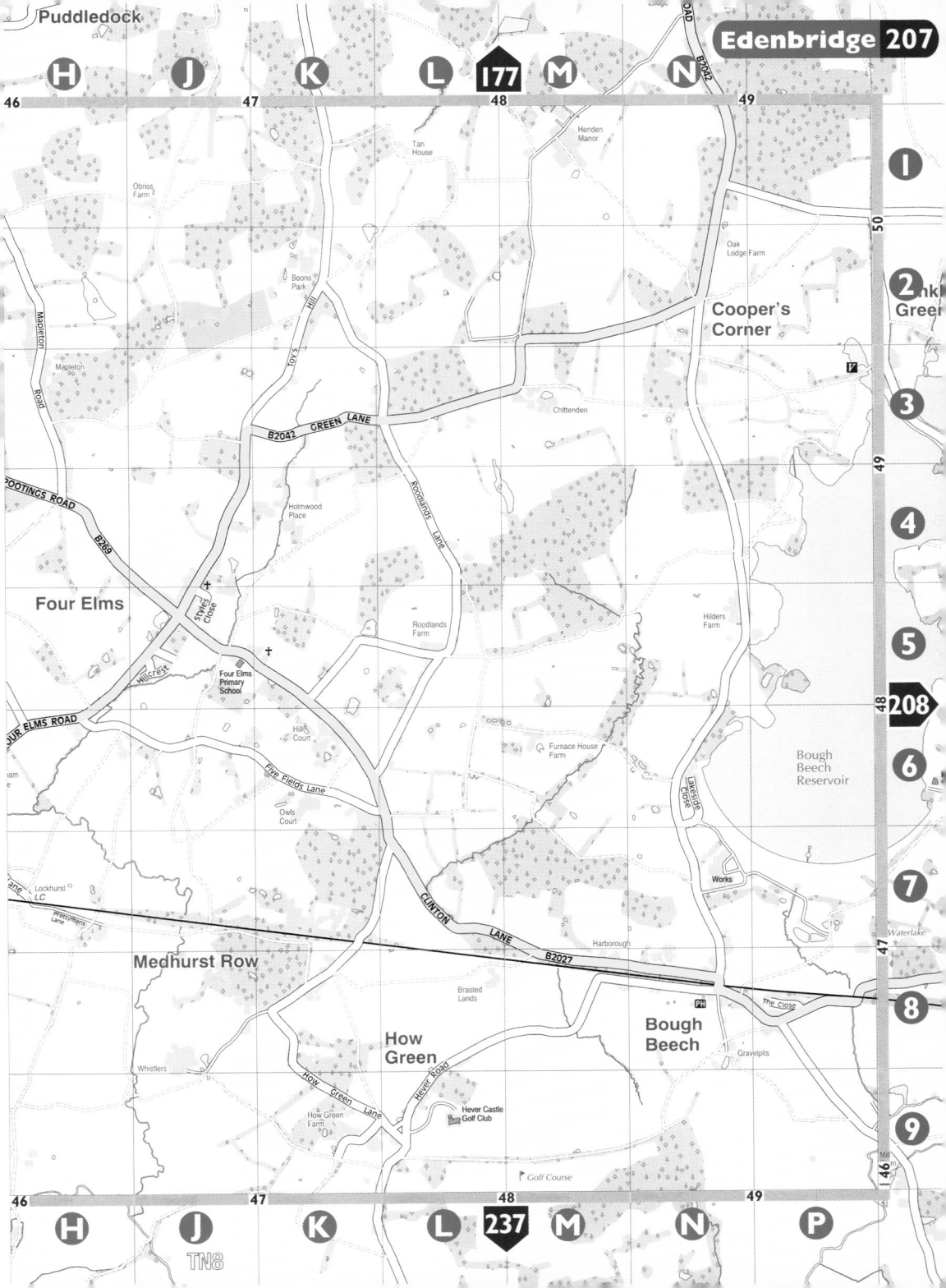

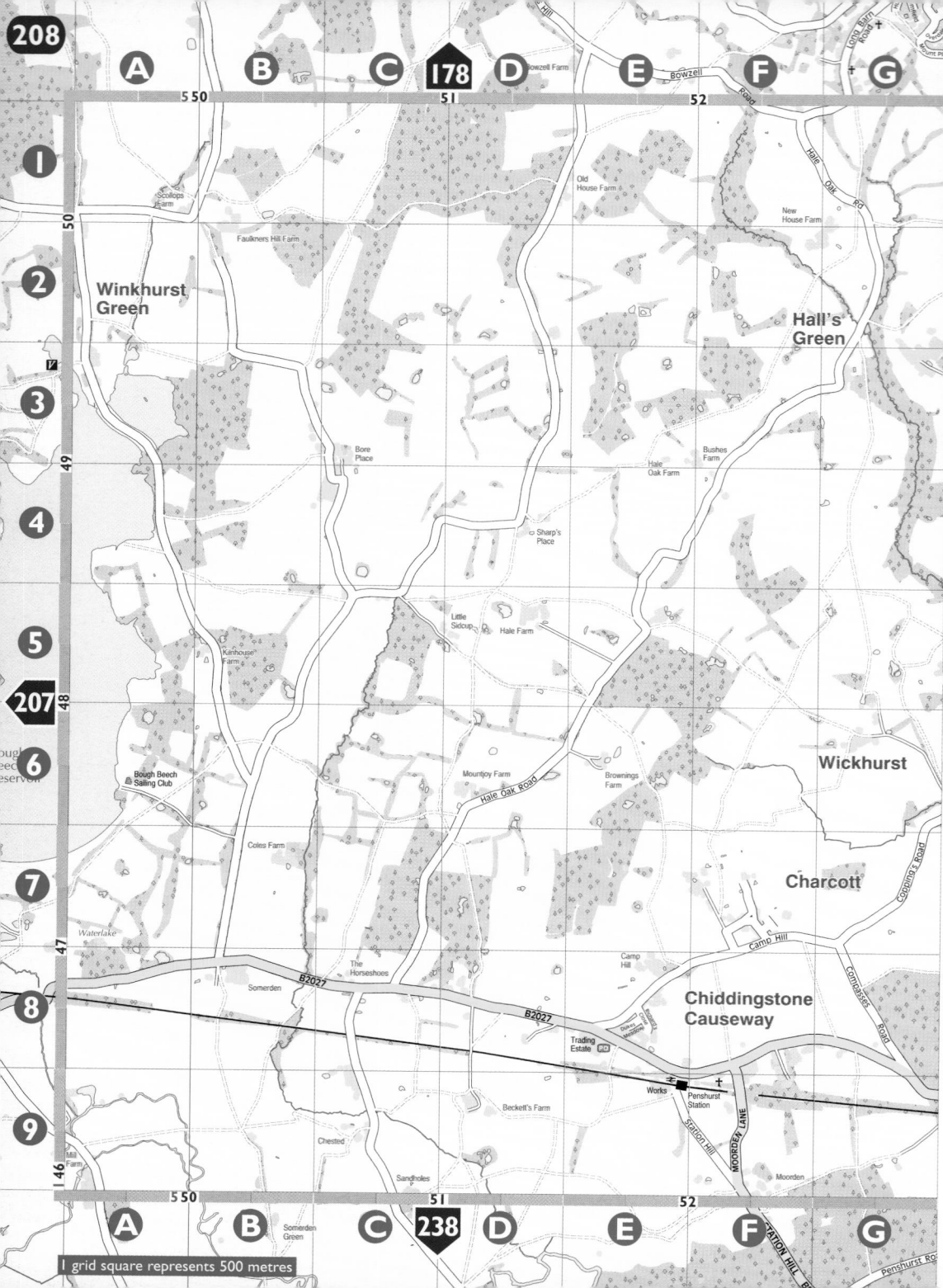

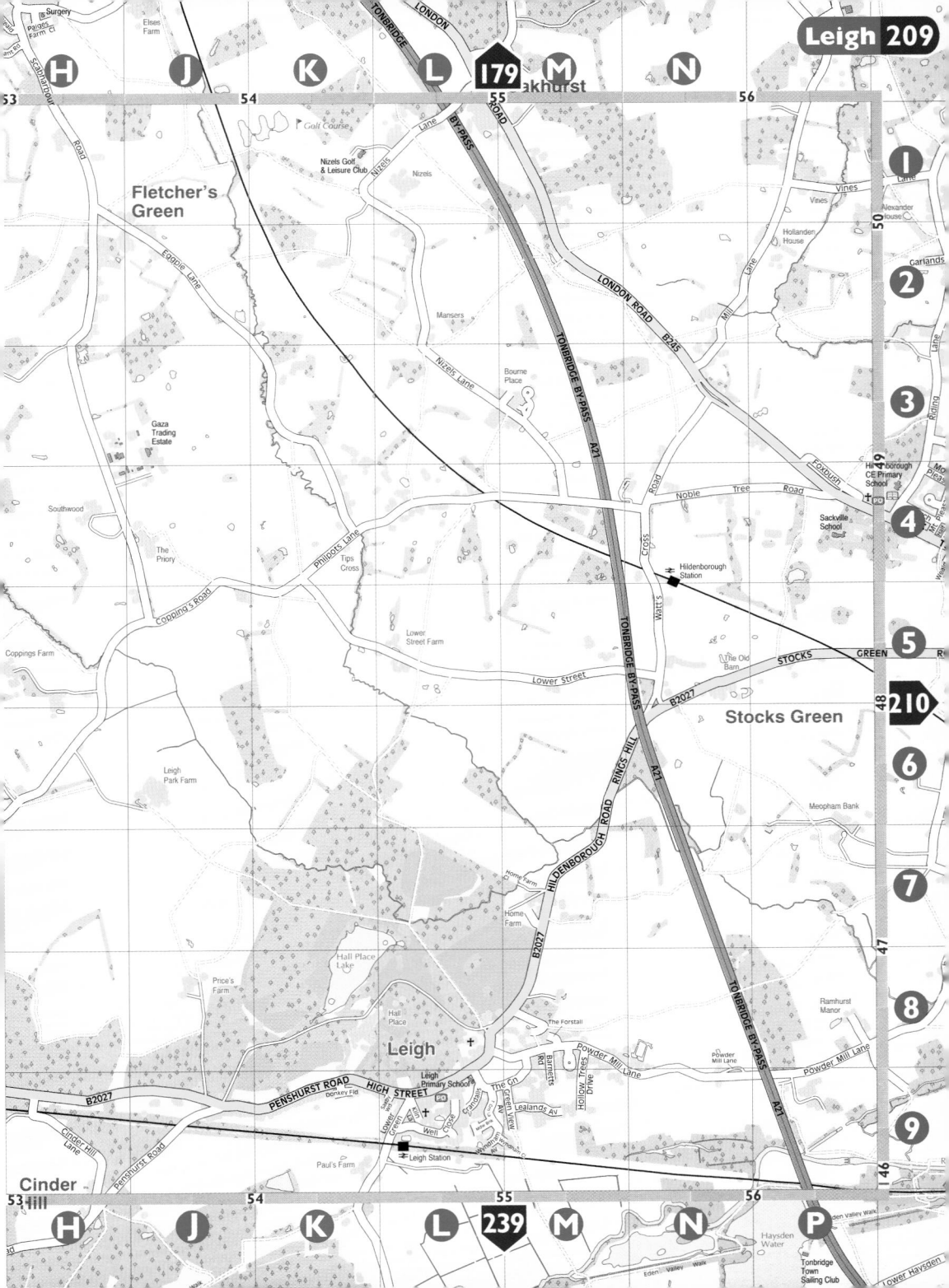

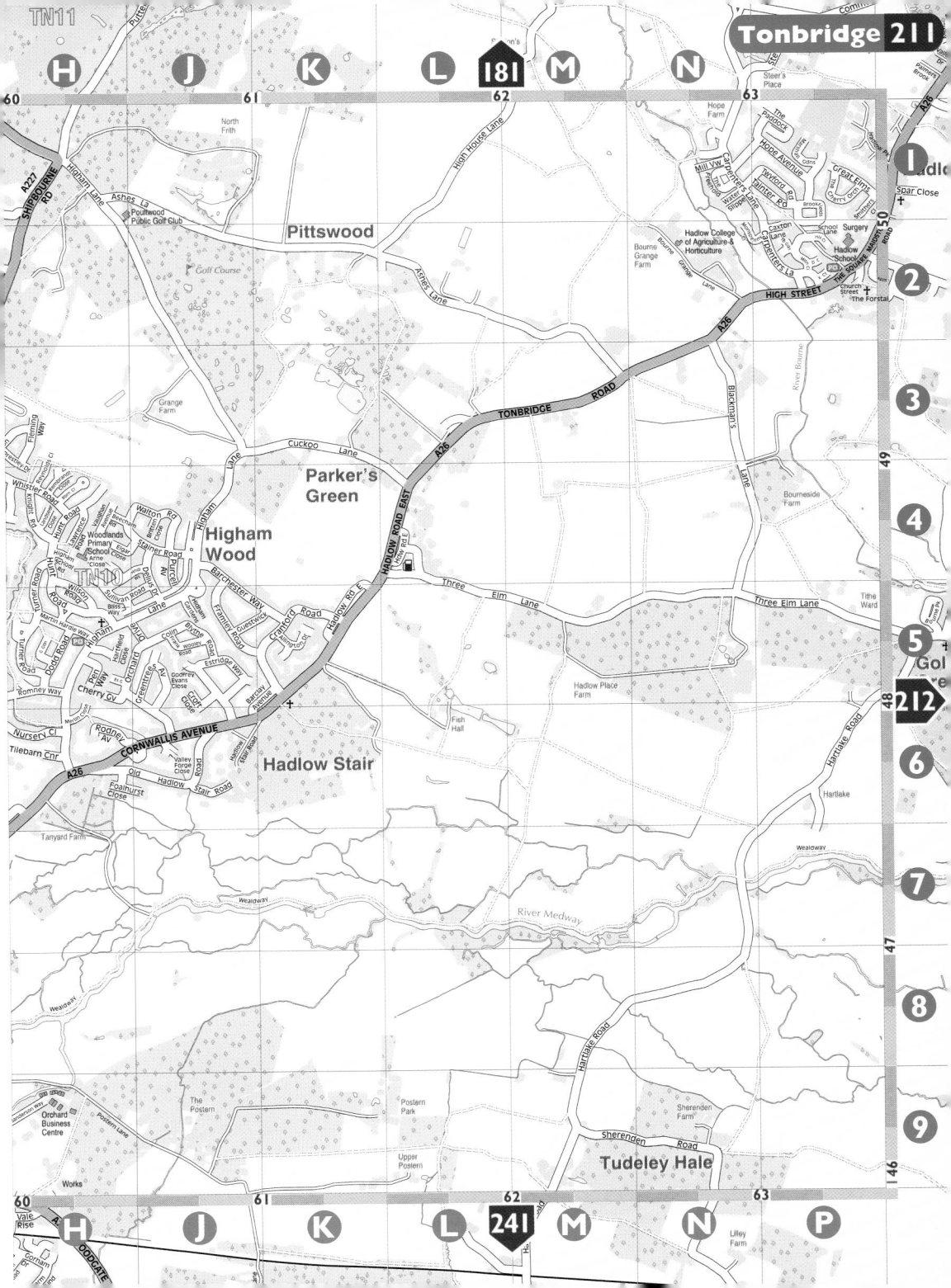

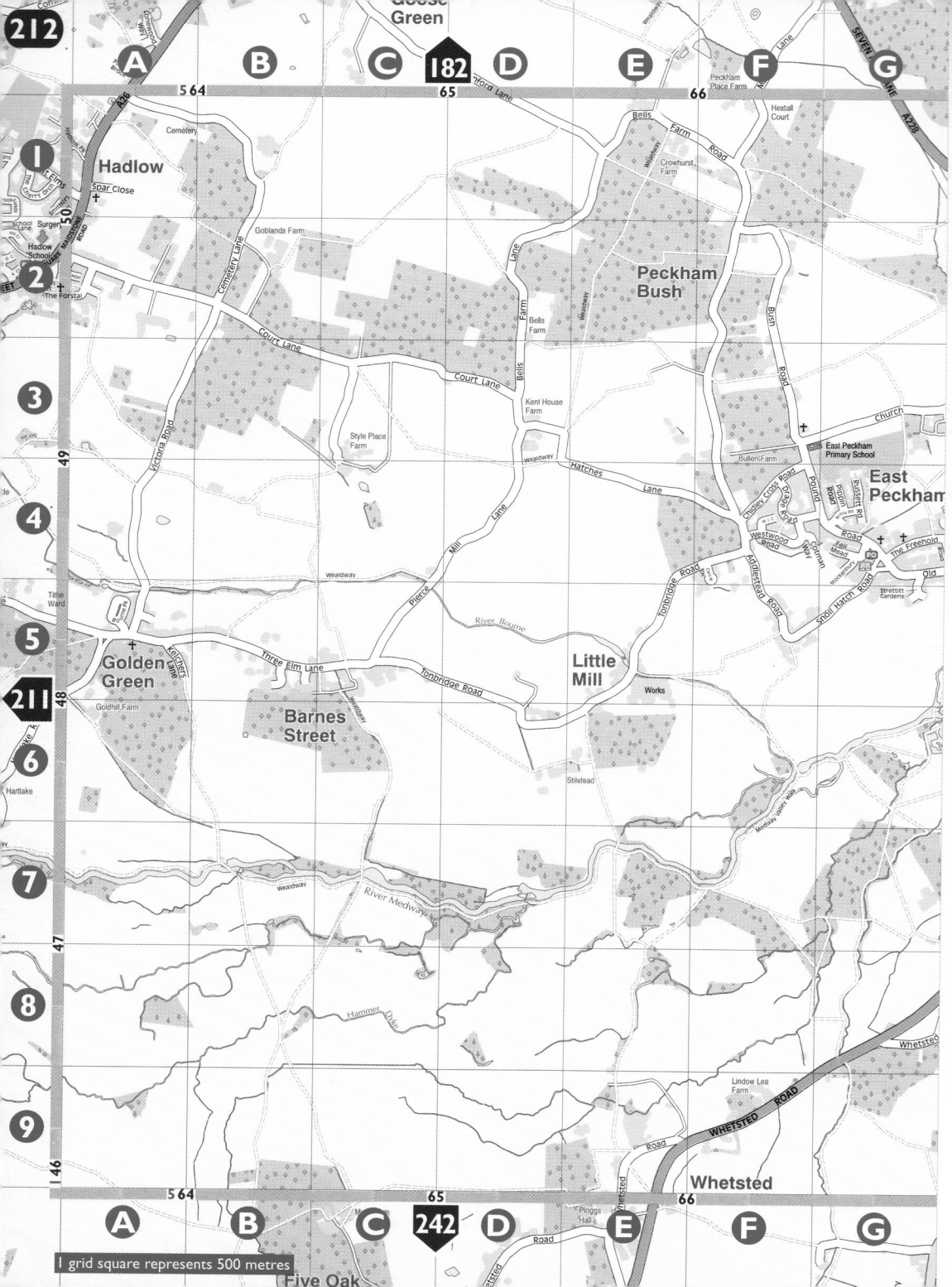

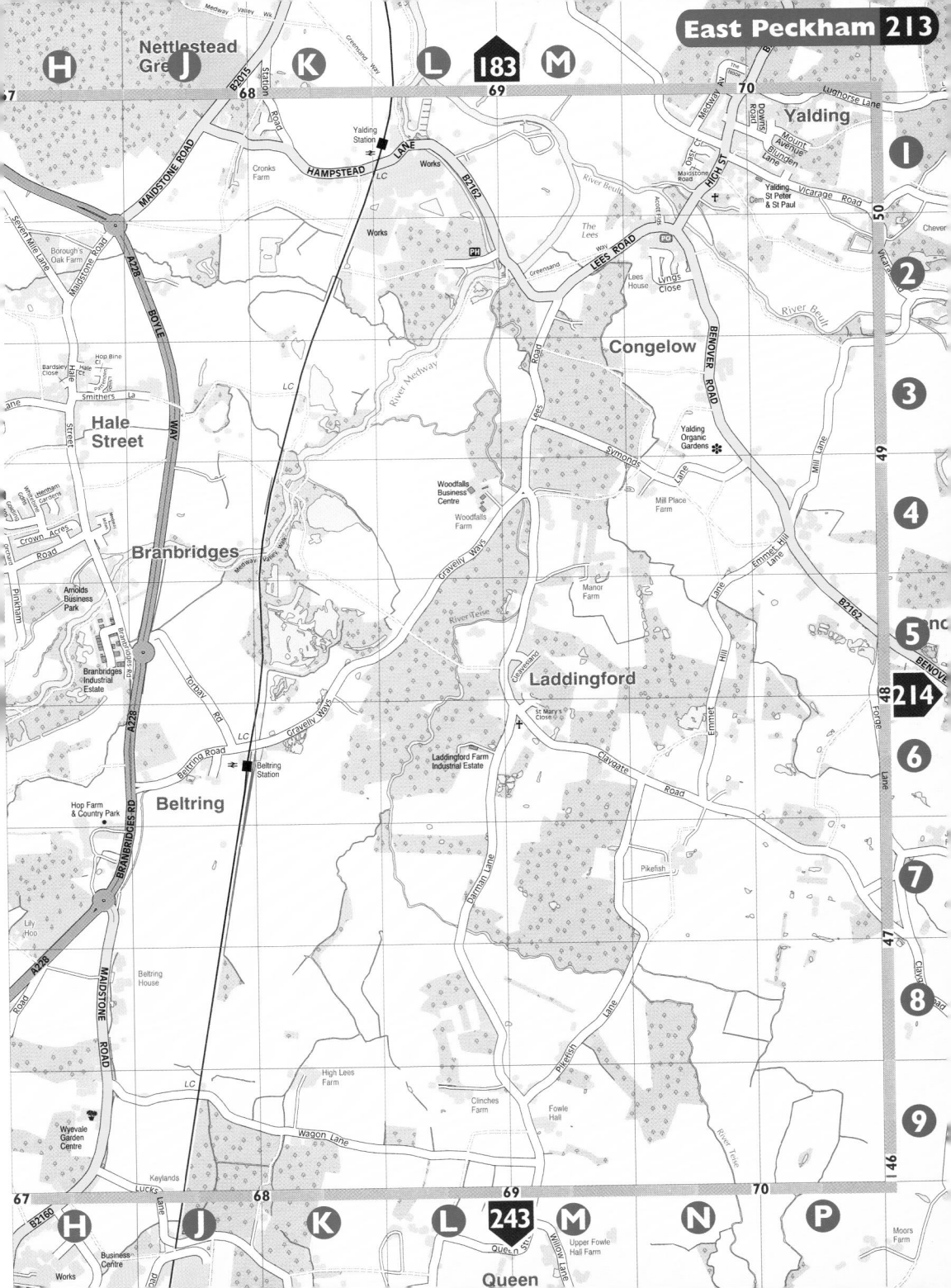

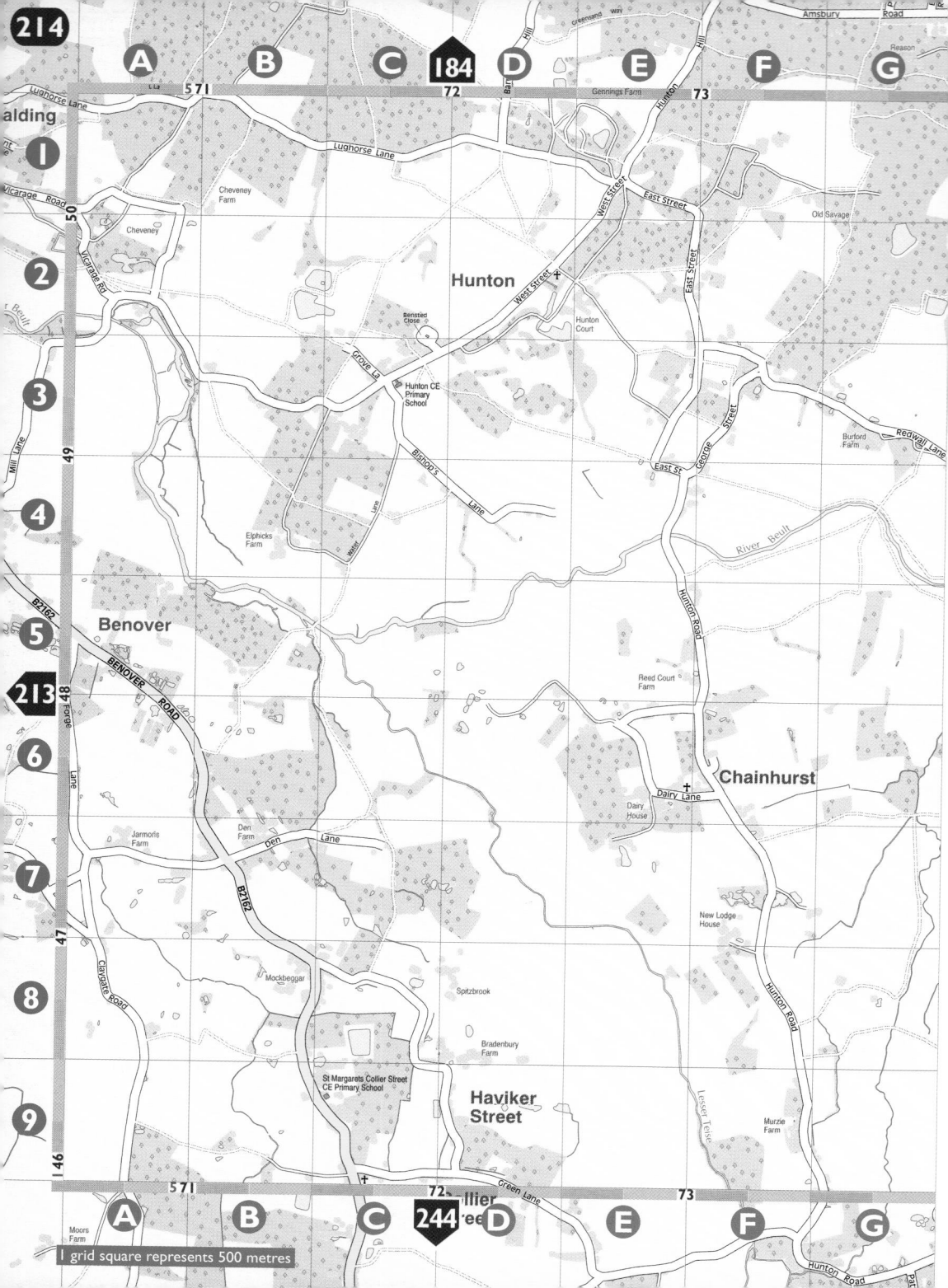

A B C **184** D E F G

72 73

alding

I

Lughorse Lane

5 71

Lughorse Lane

Vicarage Road

50

Cheveney Farm

Cheveney

Greensand Way

Amsbury Road

Reason

Gennings Farm

West Street East Street

Old Savage

2

Vicarage Rd

Hunton

West Street

Hunton Court

East Street

Bar Hill

Hunton Hill

Beristed Close

3

49

Grove La

Hunton CE Primary School

East St

George Street

Burford Farm

Redwall Lane

Mill Lane

4

Bishop's Lane

Water Lane

Elphicks Farm

River Beult

B2162

5

Benover

Hunton Road

Reed Court Farm

48

BENOVER ROAD

Forge Lane

6

Jarmons Farm

Den Farm

Den Lane

Dairy House

Dairy Lane

Chainhurst

7

47

B2162

New Lodge House

Hunton Road

Claygate Road

8

Mockbeggar

Spitzbrook

Bradenbury Farm

Lesser Teise

9

1 46

St Margarets Collier Street CE Primary School

Haviker Street

Murzie Farm

5 71

A B C **244** D E F G

72 Collier Street 73

Green Lane

Moors Farm

Hunton Road

Pit

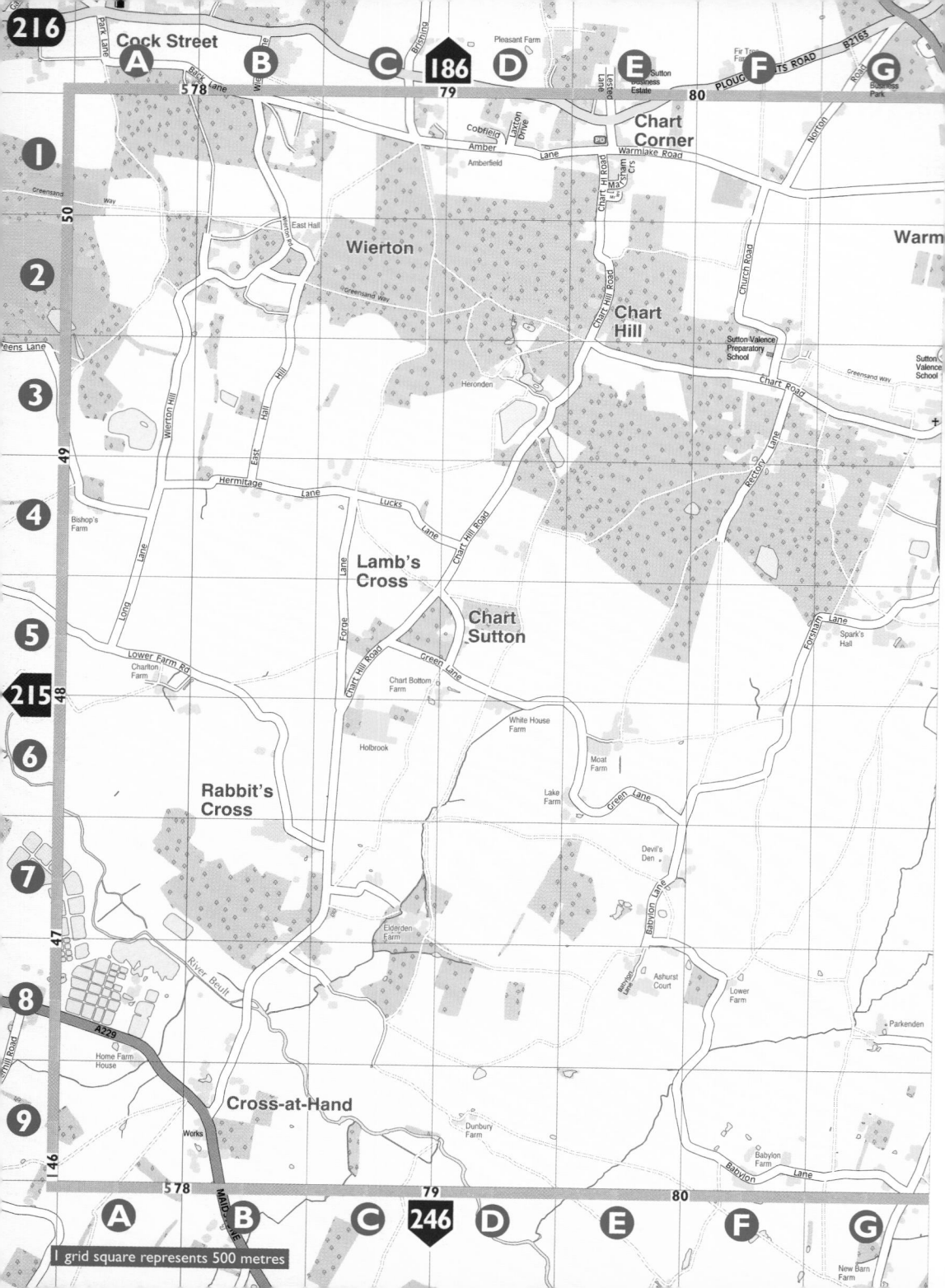

Collingwood Industrial Estate

H **J** **K** **L** **187** **M**

81 82 83 VILL 17 84

MAIDSTONE ROAD A274

Warmlake Business Estate

1

Chartway Street

Chartway Street

50

ake

Chartway Street

The Ridge Golf Club

Golf Course

Broomes Court

Greensand Way

Charlton Lane

Morry Lane

Morry House

2

A274

Cobtree Medical Centre

NORTH STREET

Sutton Valence Primary School

Sutton Valence

Church Lane

West Corner

Charlton Court

East Sutton Park

Sutton Road

3

Ulcombe

49

Ulcombe CE Primary School

Lodge

School Lane

High Street

Broad Tumblers Hill

Rectory Lane

The Plott

Castle Remains

Baker Lane

East Sutton

Pleasure House Lane

Greensand Way

Pleasure House

Boyton Court

Friday Street

Headcorn Road

4

S Bank

South Lane

Stallance

Boxton Court

Sutton Road

East Sutton Road

5

The Harbour

Heniker Lane

Brook House

Barling Farm

Brick Kiln Lane

48 **218**

6

New Barn Road

HEADCORN ROAD A274

Heniker Lane

Stickfast Lane

Crump's Lane

Stone Hall

7

Lake Farm

Jubilee Corner

Tilden Road

47

Golf Course

Sparrow Hall

8

Tong

9

Boy Court

Farthing Green

Weald of Kent Golf Club

Moatenden Farm

Hearnden Green

East Sutton Road

MAIDSTONE ROAD A274

Peckham Farm

Boy Court Lane

46

81 82 83 84

H **J** **K** **L** **247** **M** **N** **P**

Plumtree Road

Plumtree Green

Pinkhorn Farm

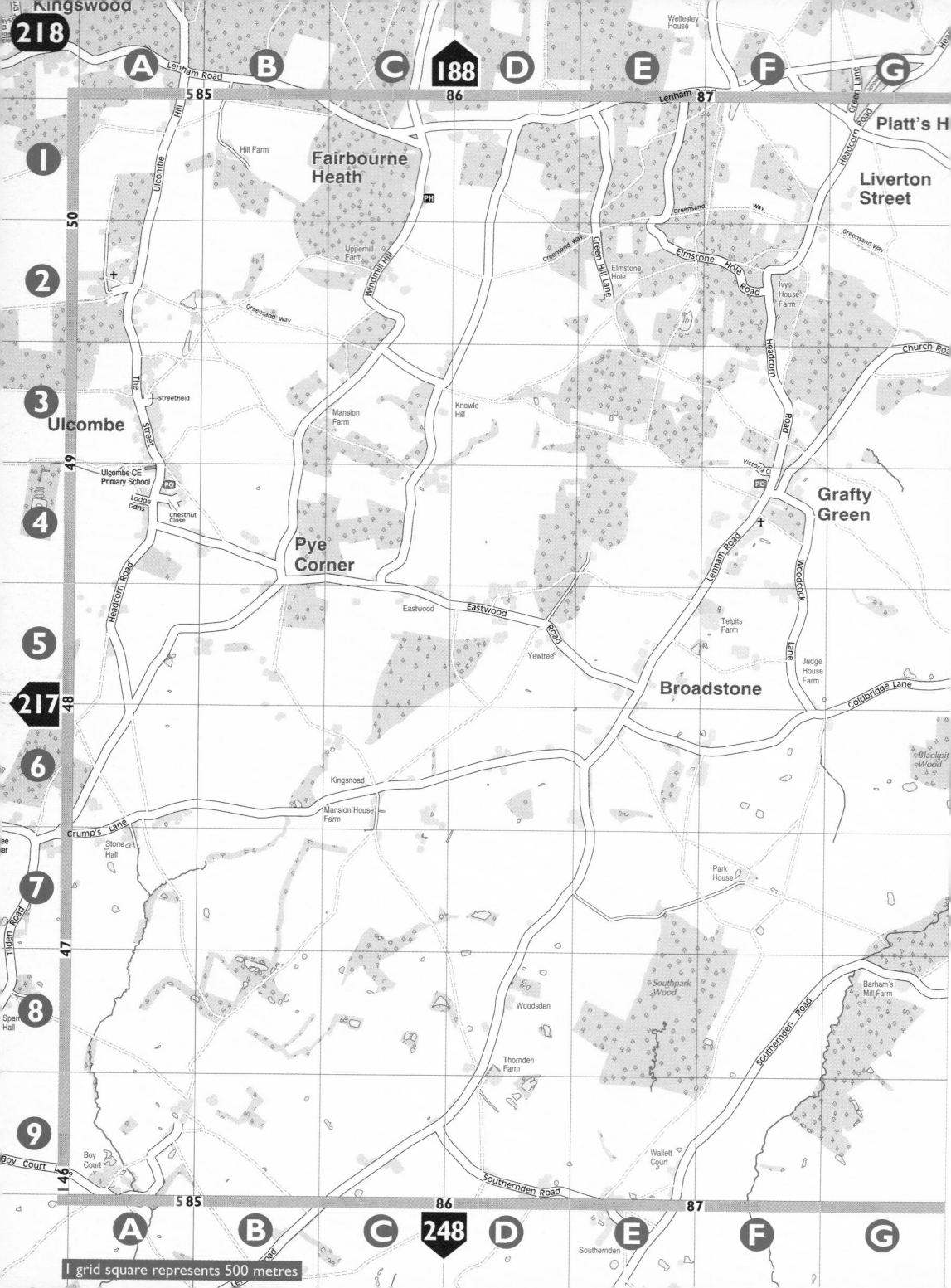

Kingswood

218

A   Lenham Road   B   C   **188**   D   E   F   G

5 85   86   Lenham Rd   87

Platt's H

1

Hill Farm

Fairbourne Heath   PH

50   Wellesley House

Liverton Street

Greenland Way

2   +   Greensand Way   Upperhill Farm   Windmill Hill   Green Hill Lane   Elmstone Hole   Greensand Way   Elmstone Hole Road   Ivye House Farm   Church Rd

Greensand Way   Headcorn Road

Greensand Way

3   The Street   Streetfield   Mansion Farm   Knowle Hill   Victoria   PO

Ulcombe

49   Ulcombe CE Primary School   PO   Grafty Green

4   Lodge Cotts   Chestnut Close   +   Woodcock Lane

Pye Corner

Headcorn Road   Eastwood   Eastwood Road   Telpits Farm   Judge House Farm

5   Yewtree   Broadstone   Coldbridge Lane

217   48   Blackpit Wood

6   Kingsnoad   Southernden Road

Mansion House Farm   Park House

Crump's Lane   Stone Hall

7   Tilden Road

47   Southpark Wood   Barham's Mill Farm

8   Spa Hall   Woodsden

Thornden Farm

9   Boy Court   Wallett Court

Boy Court   Southernden Road   Southernden

1 46

5 85   86   87

A   B   C   **248**   D   E   F   G

I grid square represents 500 metres

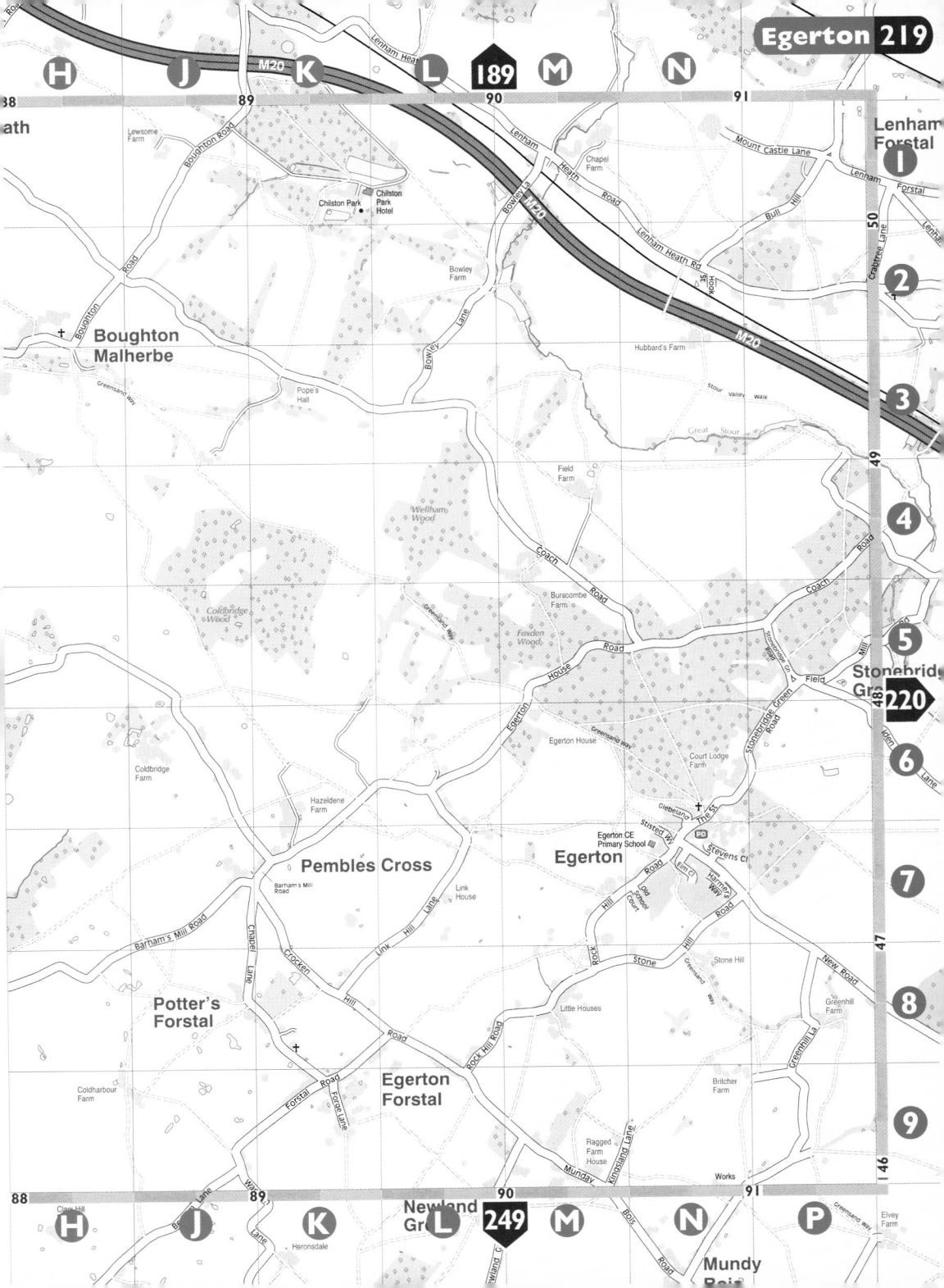

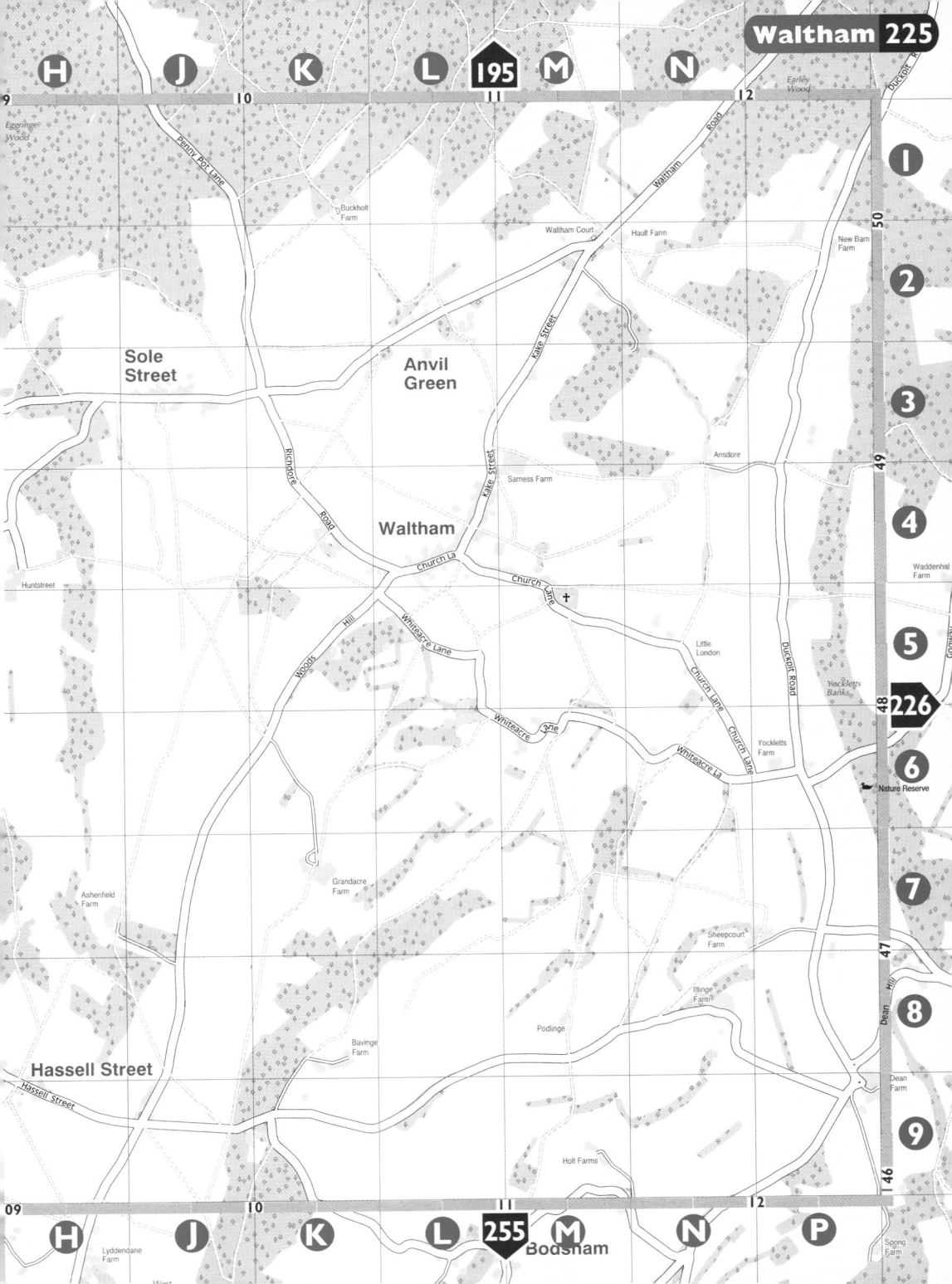

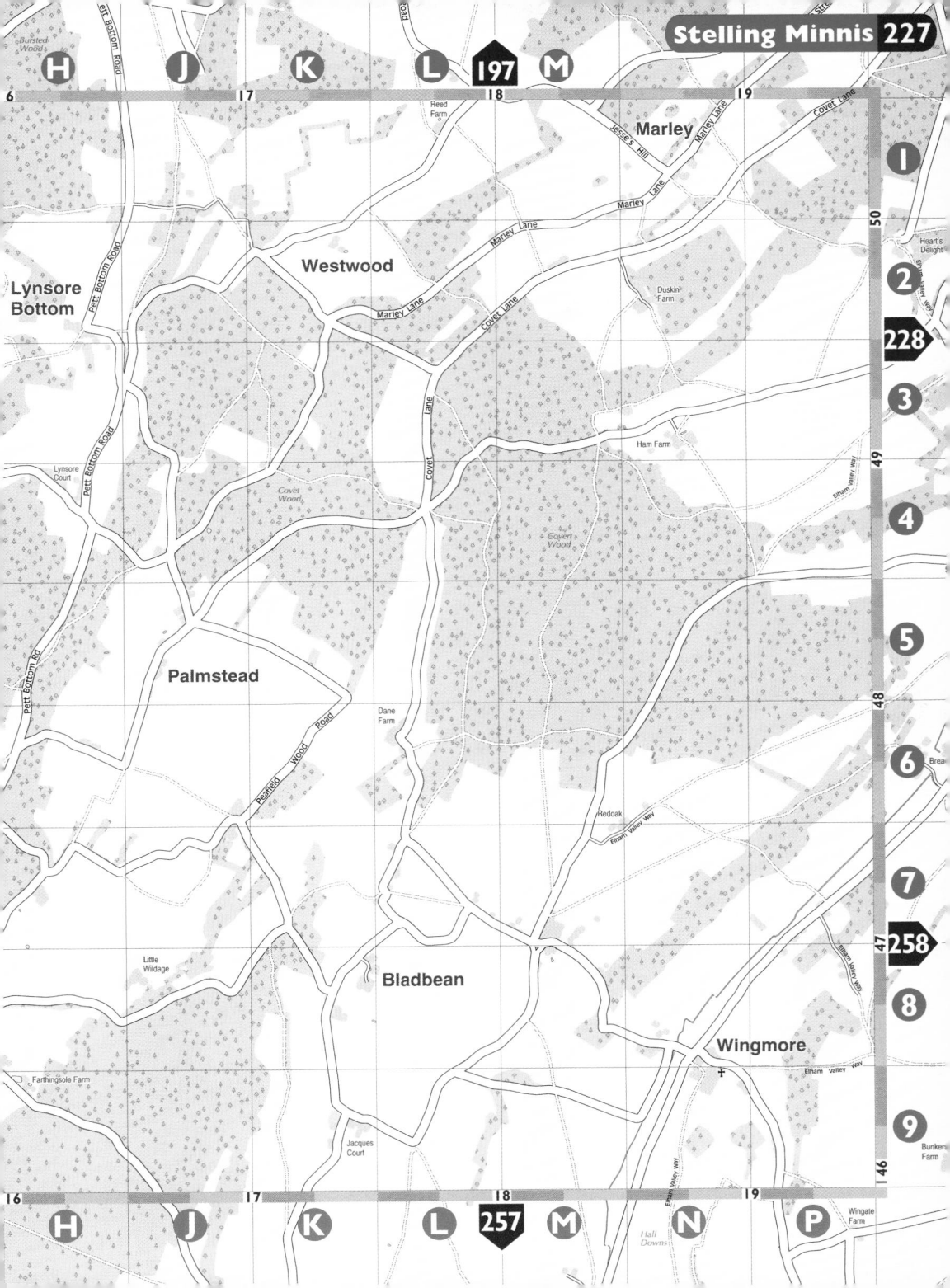

Marley

Reed Farm

Jesse's Hill

Marley Lane

Covert Lane

Westwood

Lynsore Bottom

Pett Bottom Road

Lynsore Court

Marley Lane

Covert Lane

Duskin Farm

Ham Farm

Covet Lane

Covet Wood

Covert Wood

Elham Valley Way

Palmstead

Pett Bottom Rd

Pearfield Wood Road

Dane Farm

Redoak

Elham Valley Way

Little Wildage

Bladbean

Elham Valley Way

Wingmore

Farthingsole Farm

Jacques Court

Hall Downs

Wingate Farm

Bunkers Farm

Brea

Heart's Delight

Elham Valley Way

H J K L 197 M

6   17   18   6   19

1

50

2

228

3

49

4

5

48

6 Brea

7

47 258

8

9

146

16   17   18   19

H J K L 257 M N P

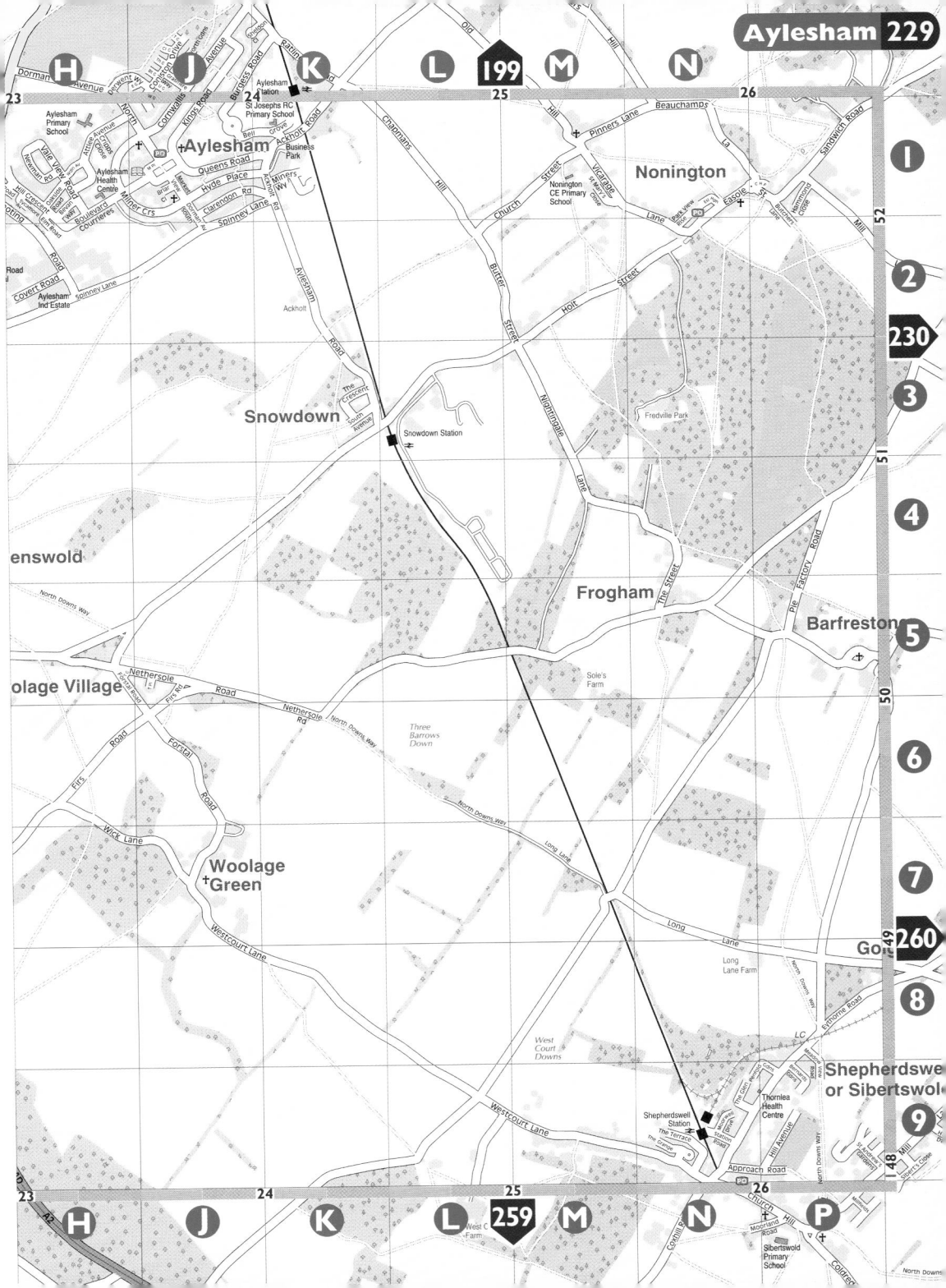

230

A   B   C   **200**   D   E   **Heronden**   F   G

627   28   29

1

Cherrygarden Lane

Chillenden
PH

Knowlton

Thornton Lane

2

199

Cherrygarden Lane

Sandwich Road

Knowlton Park

Shingleton Farm

Venson Farm

3

Sandwich Road

Thornton Lane

Thornton Farm

4

Mill Lane

5

Kittington Farm

The Downs

Dane Court

School Road

6

Pike Road

Beeches Farm

7

Works

Works

Barville Road

229

Roman Road
Sweetbriar Lane
St Johns Road
Ash Gr
Beech Drive
Cherry Gr
Adelaide
Milner Clos
Milner Road
Terrace Road

Elvington

Elmton Lane
Minting Wy
Wigmore Lane
Sandwich Rd

artlestone

8

Bartlestone Road

Elvington

9

Bartlestone Road

Lower Eythorne

Church Hill

Eythorne Elvington Primary School

Wigmore Lane

Wigmore Way

Shepherds Way

627   28   **260**   D   29

A   B   C   D   E   F   G

Eythorne Station
New Road
Green Lane
Cherry Wk
Flax Court Lane
Malmains

I grid square represents 500 metres

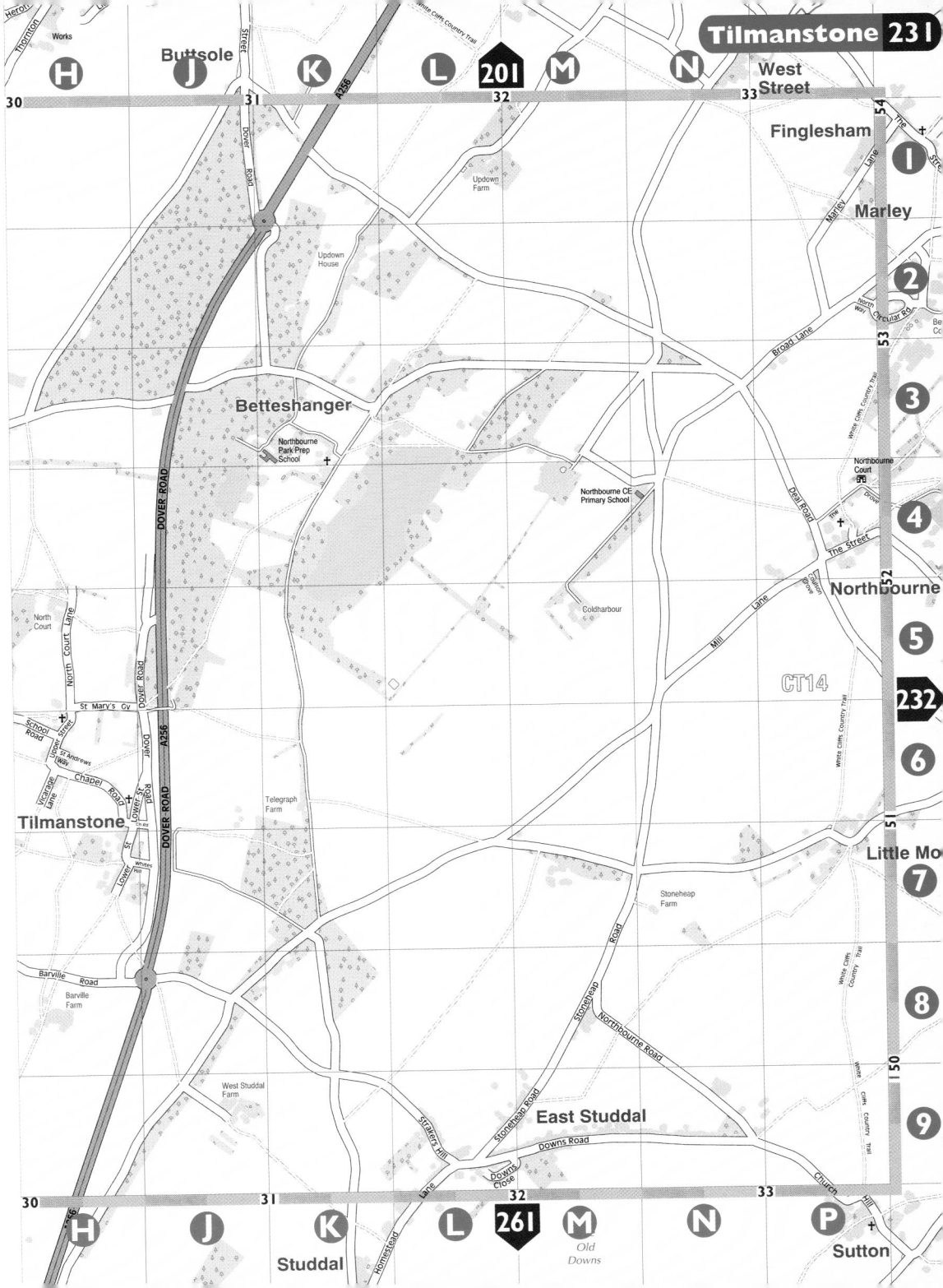

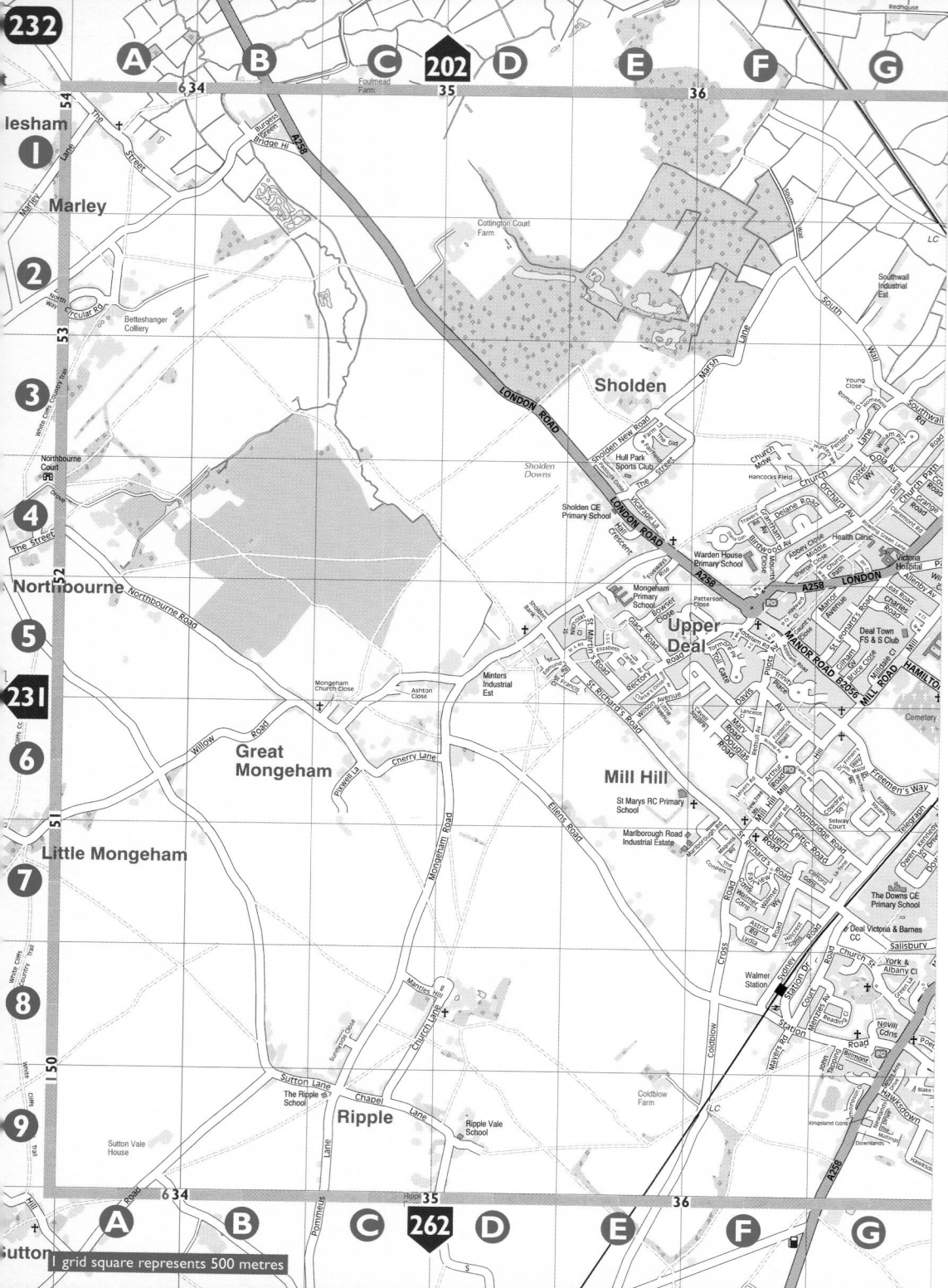

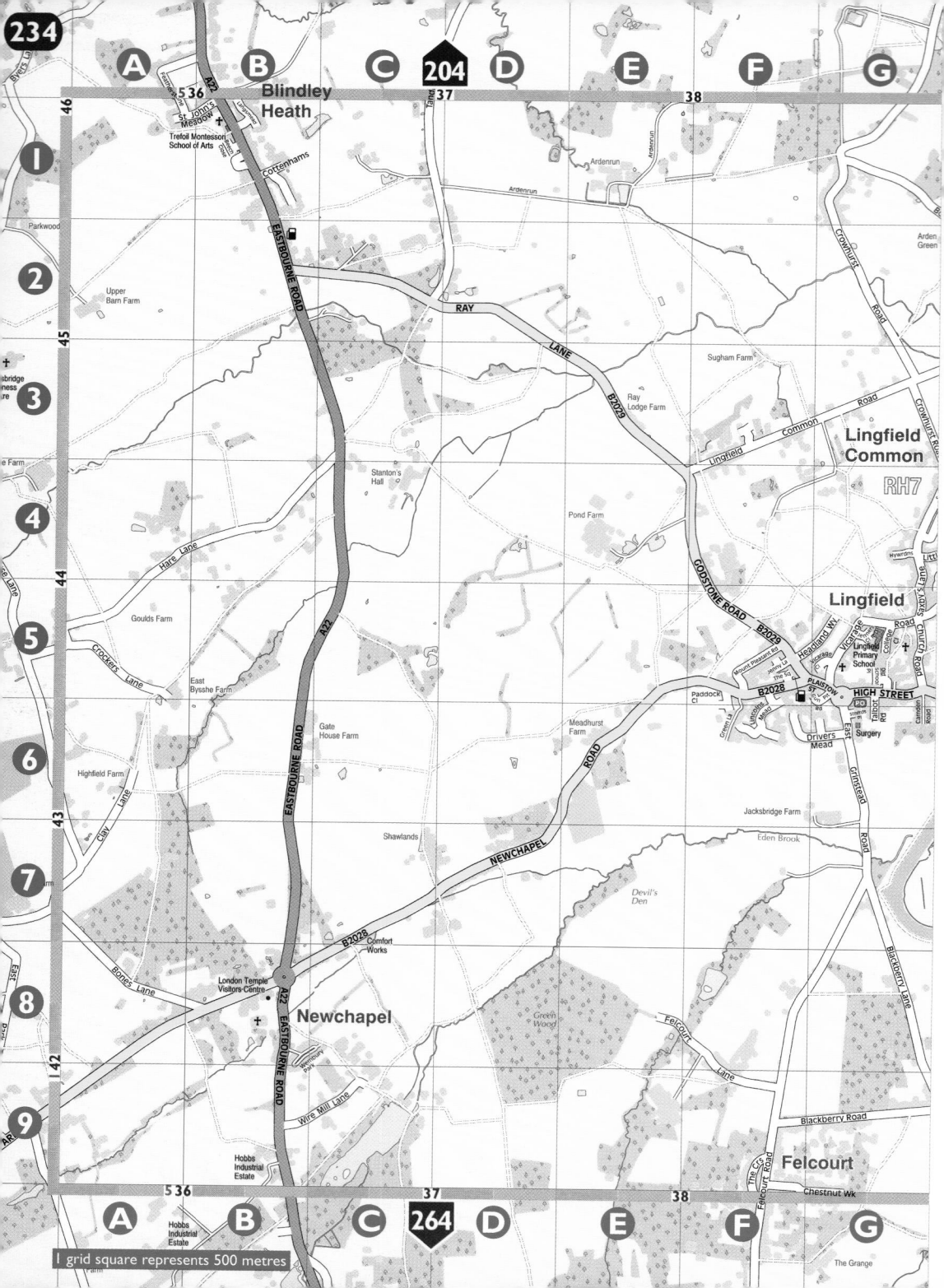

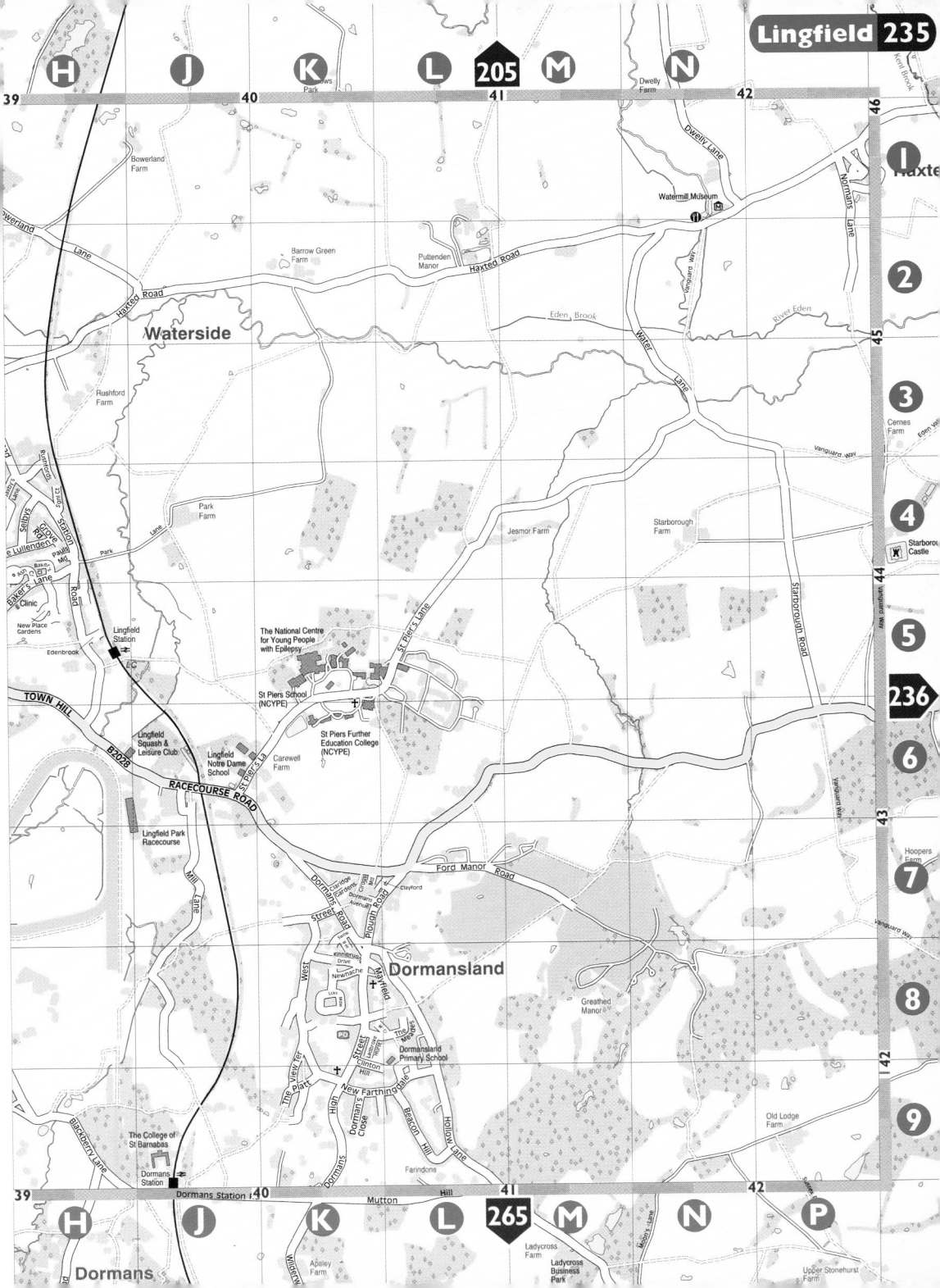

H J K L 205 M N

39 40 41 42 46

Kent Brook

I Haxte

Dwelly Farm

Dwelly Lane

Normans Lane

Bowerland Farm

Watermill Museum

2

Bowerland Lane

Haxted Road

Puttenden Manor

Barrow Green Farm

Haxted Road

Eden Brook

Water Lane

River Eden

Vanguard Way

45

Waterside

3

Cernes Farm

Eden Vale

Rushford Farm

Vanguard Way

4

Starborough Farm

Park Farm

Jesmor Farm

Starborough Castle

Park Lane

Selby's Lane

Rushfords Lane

Grove Rd

Station Road

The Lullenden

Parish MG

Bakers Lane

New Place Gardens

Baker's Lane Clinic

Edenbrook

Lingfield Station

LC

The National Centre for Young People with Epilepsy

St Piers School (NCYPE)

St Piers Lane

Starborough Road

Vanguard Way

44

5

236

6

Lingfield Squash & Leisure Club

Lingfield Notre Dame School

Carewell Farm

St Piers Further Education College (NCYPE)

TOWN HILL

B2028

St Piers La

RACECOURSE ROAD

Lingfield Park Racecourse

Mill Lane

Dormans Road

Street Road

Plough Road

Ford Manor Road

Clayford

43

Hoopers Farm

7

Vanguard Way

West Street

Ennismore Drive

Newlache

Mayfield

Dormans Avenue

Clinton Road

Dormansland

Greathed Manor

142

8

The Platt

High Street

New Farthingdale

Dormans Close

Beacon Hill

Hollow Lane

Dormansland Primary School

The View

Farindons

Old Lodge Farm

9

Blackberry Lane

The College of St Barnabas

Dormans Station

Dormans Station R

40

Mutton Hill

Hill

265

41

42

H J K L M N P

39 40 41 42

Dormans

Wildern

Apsley Farm

Dormans

Hill

Ladycross Farm

Ladycross Business Park

Moons Lane

Sussex Border Path

Upper Stonehurst Farm

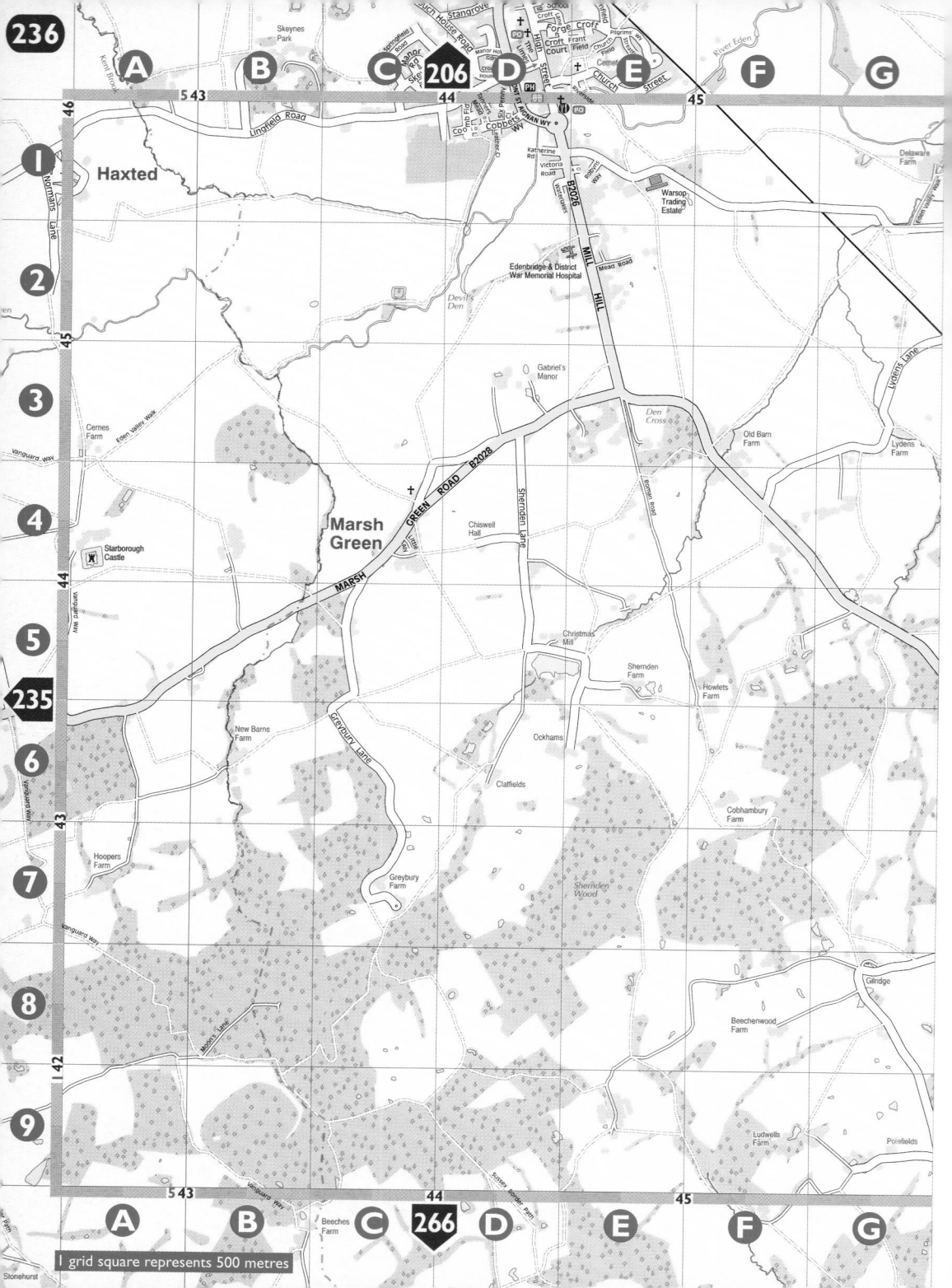

1 grid square represents 500 metres

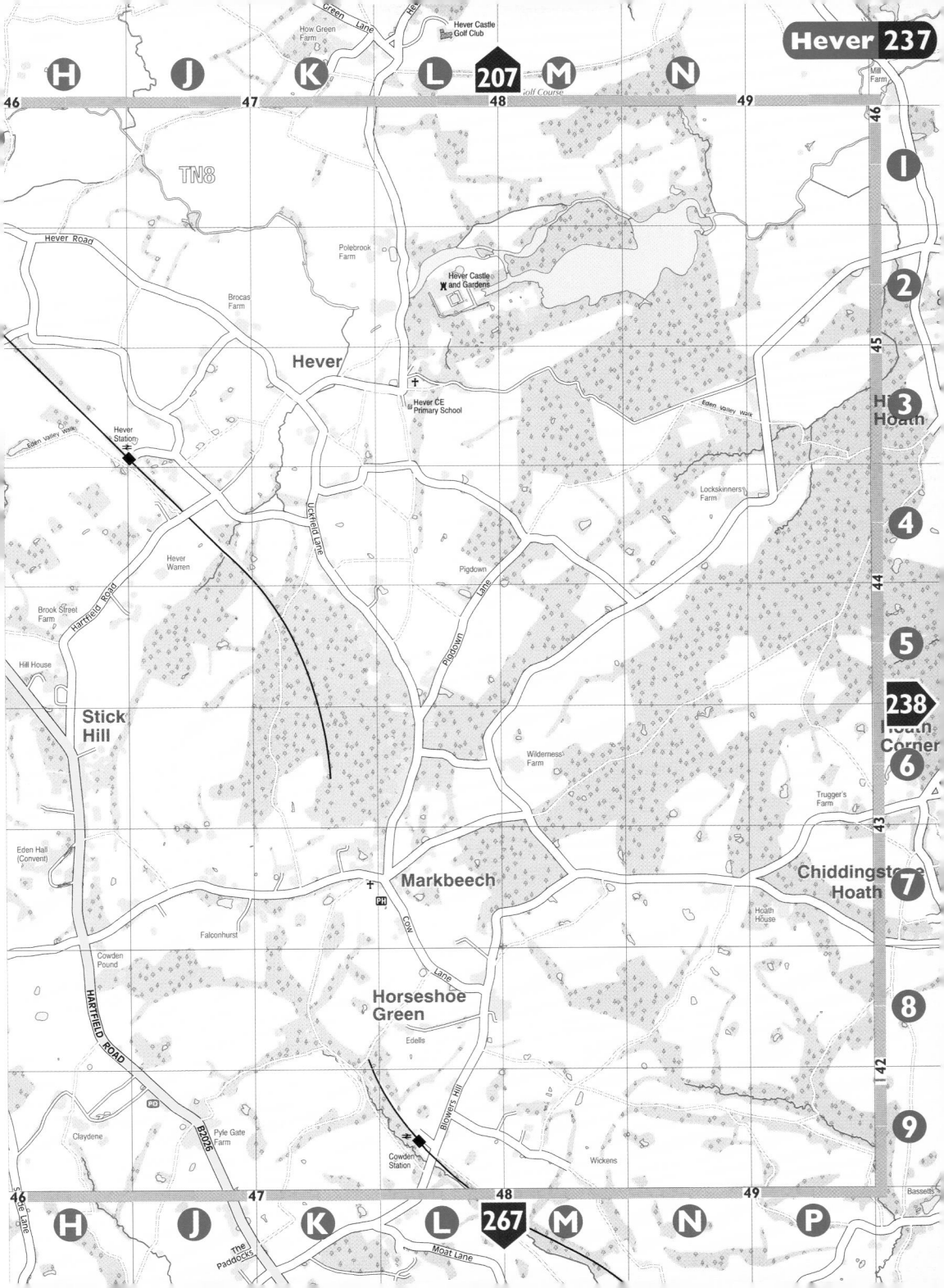

H J K L 207 M N

46 47 48 49 46

TN8

Green Lane

How Green Farm

Hever Castle Golf Club

Golf Course

Mill Farm

1

Hever Road

Polebrook Farm

Hever Castle and Gardens

2

45

Brocas Farm

Hever

Hever CE Primary School

Eden Valley Walk

H Hoath 3

Hever Station

Eden Valley Walk

Lockskinners Farm

4

Uckfield Lane

Hever Warren

Pigdown

44

Pigdown Lane

5

Brook Street Farm

Hill House

Hartfield Road

Stick Hill

238
Hoath Corner

Wilderness Farm

Trugger's Farm

6

43

Eden Hall (Convent)

Markbeech

PH

Chiddingstone Hoath 7

Cow Lane

Hoath House

Falconhurst

Cowden Pound

Horseshoe Green

Edells

8

42

HARTFIELD ROAD

Blowers Hill

PO

B2026

Claydene

Pyle Gate Farm

Cowden Station

Wickens

Bassetts

9

46 47 48 49

The Paddocks

Moat Lane

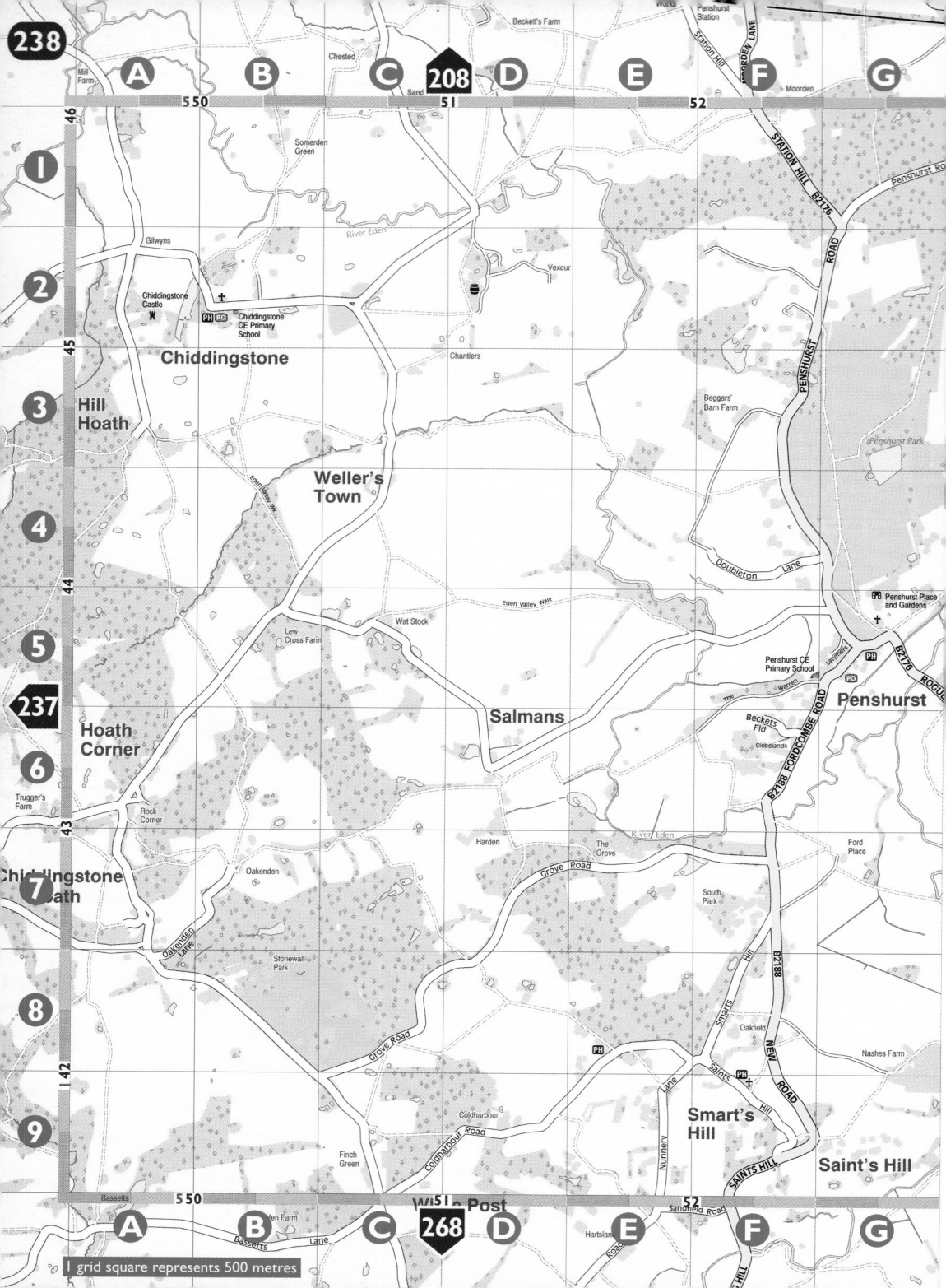

I grid square represents 500 metres

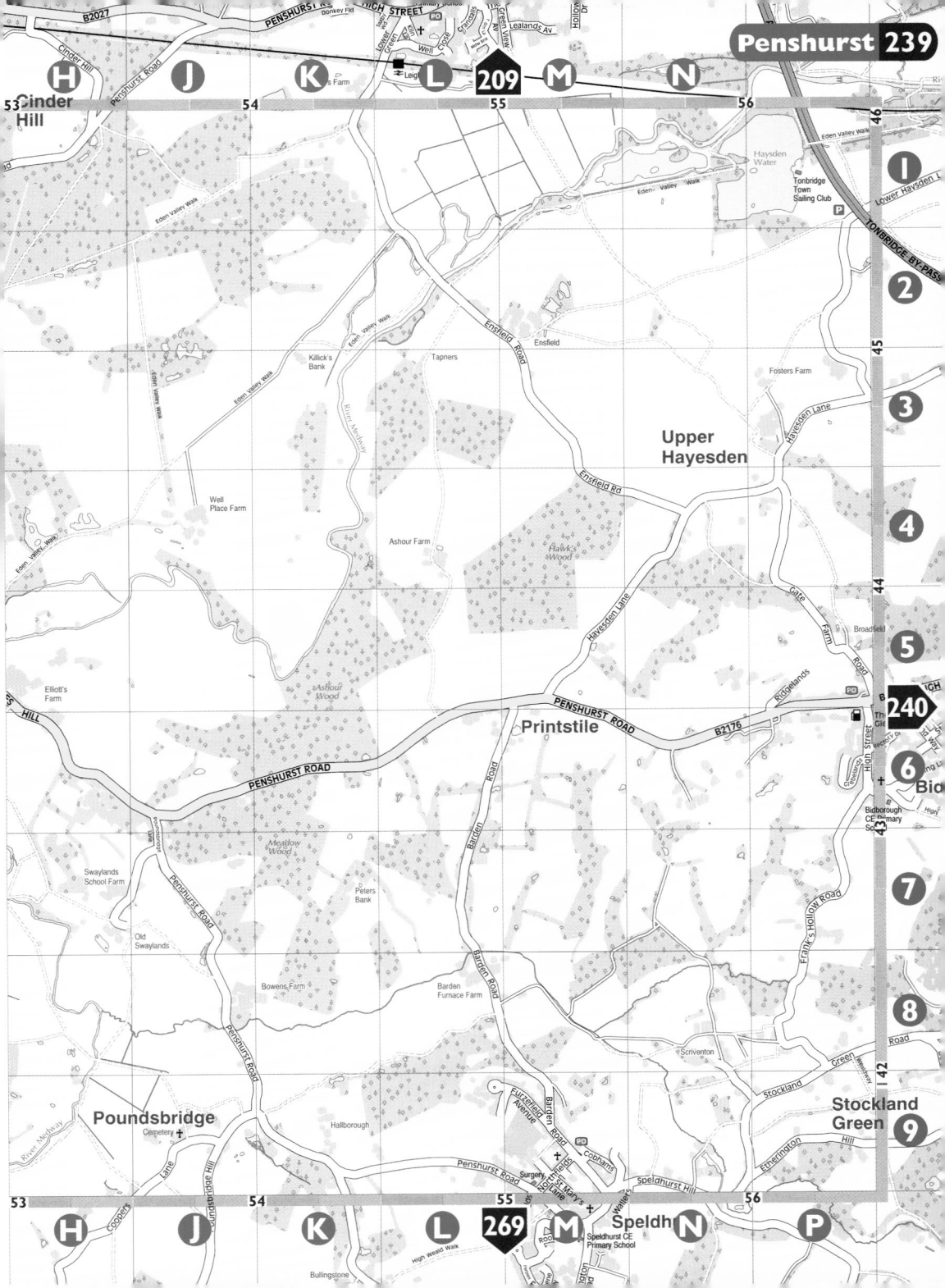

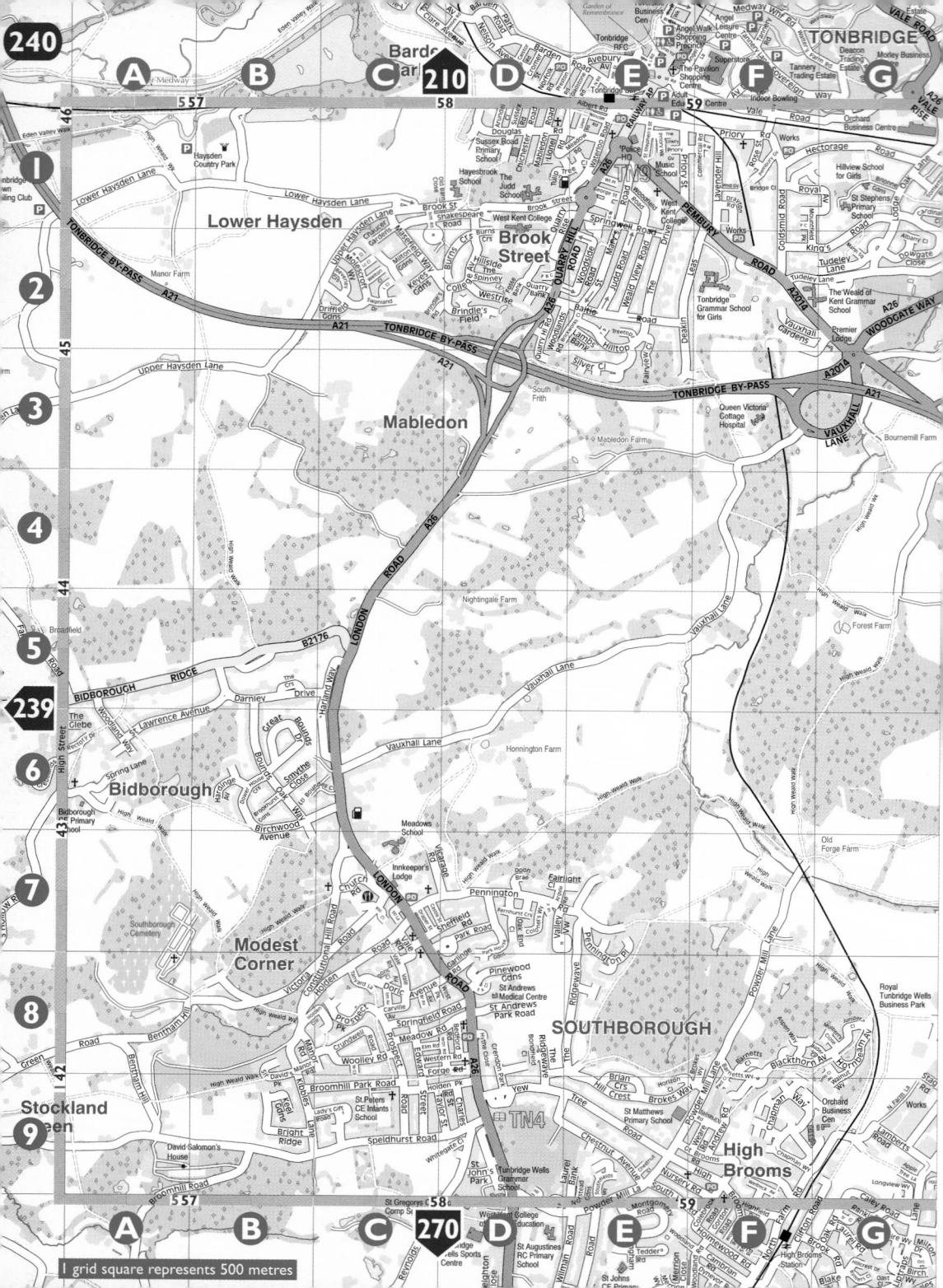

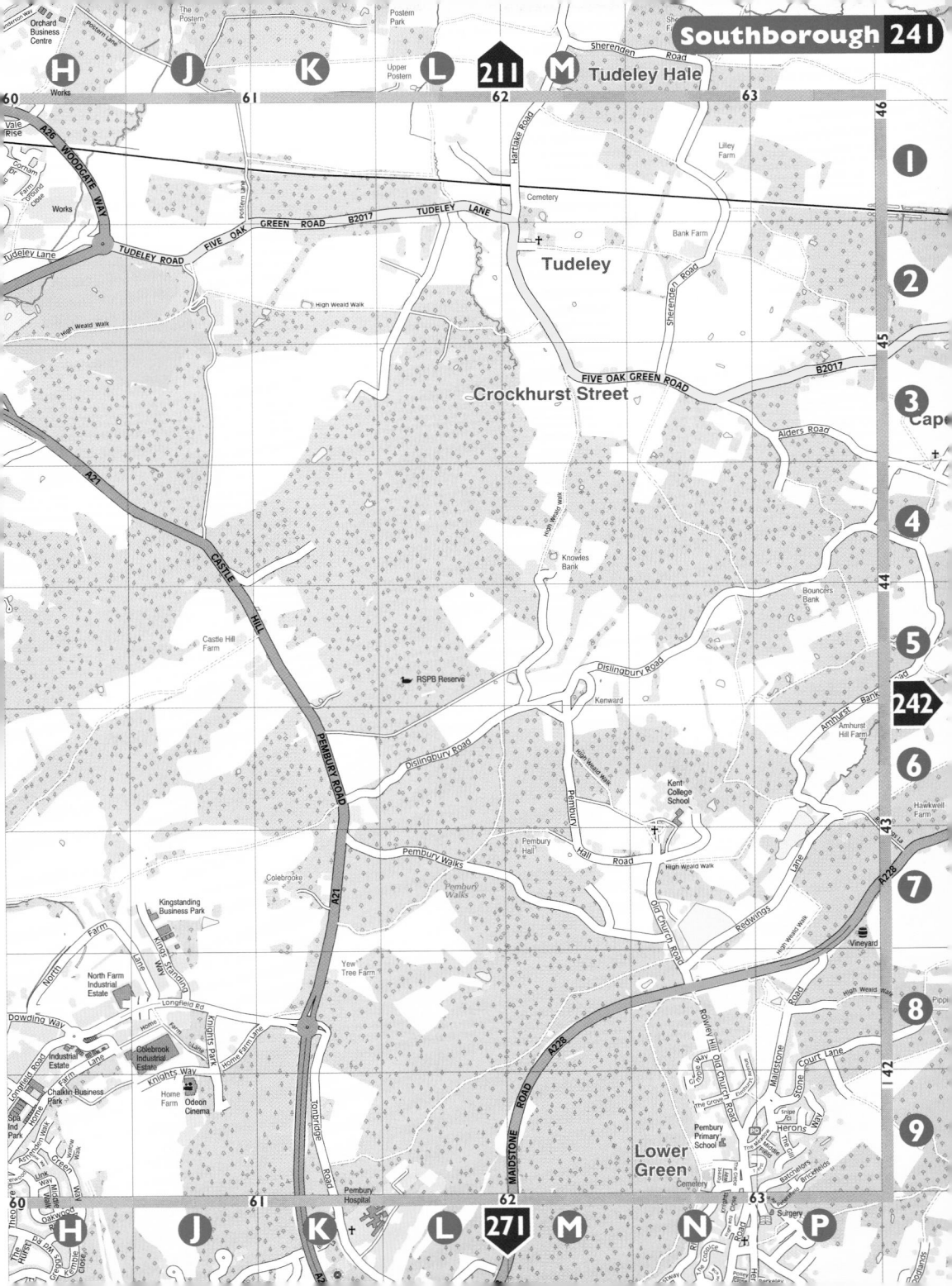

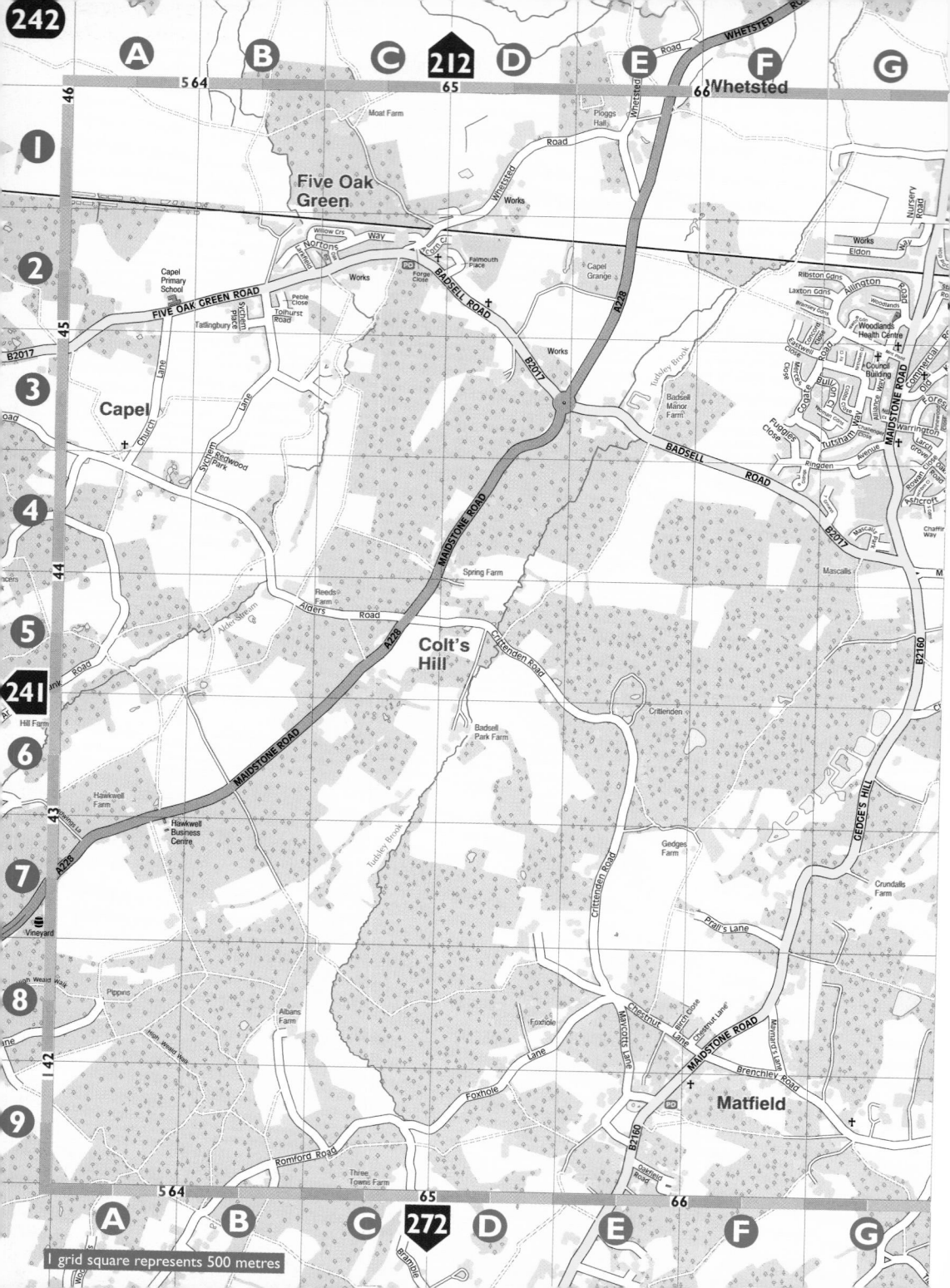

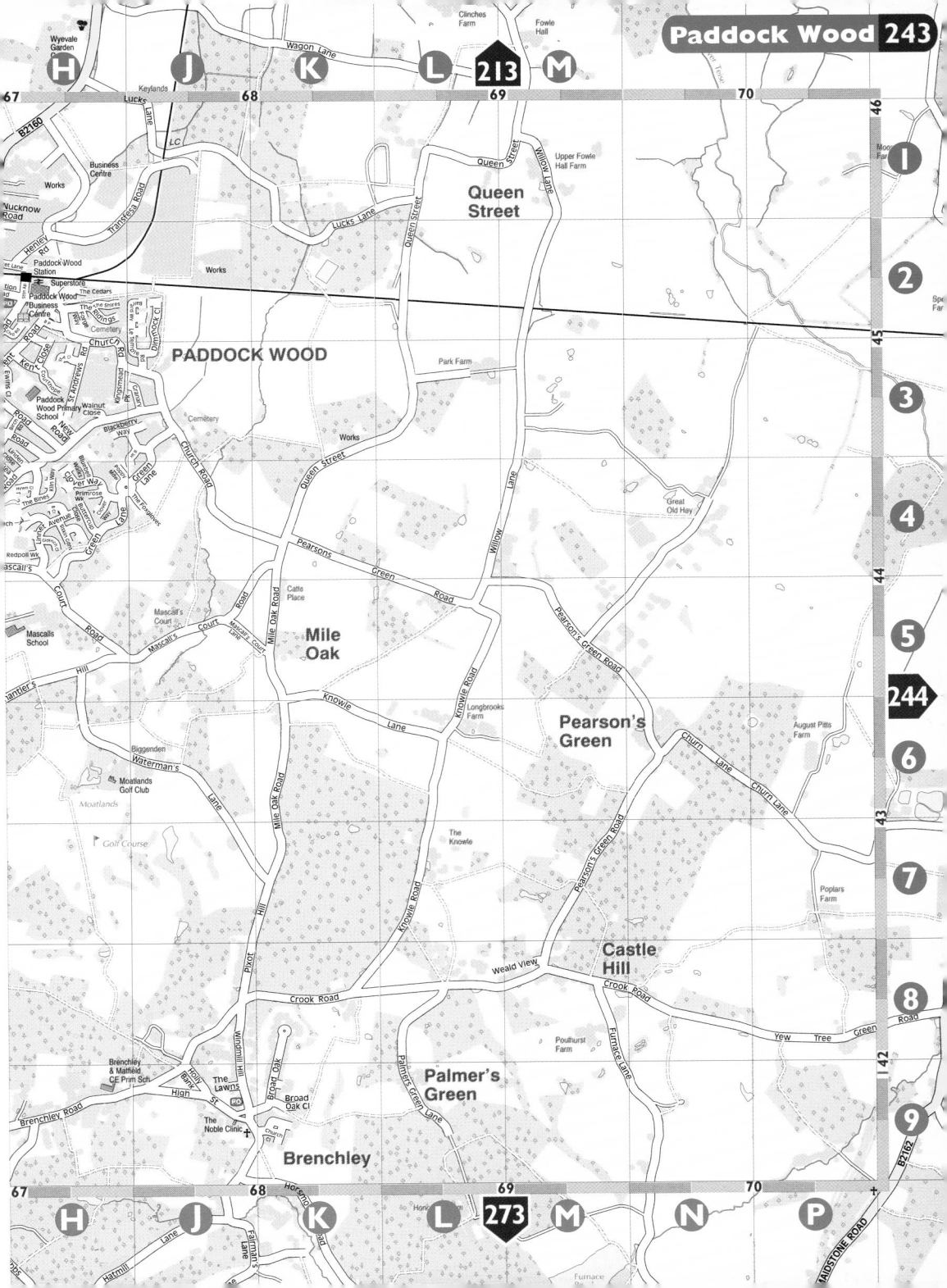

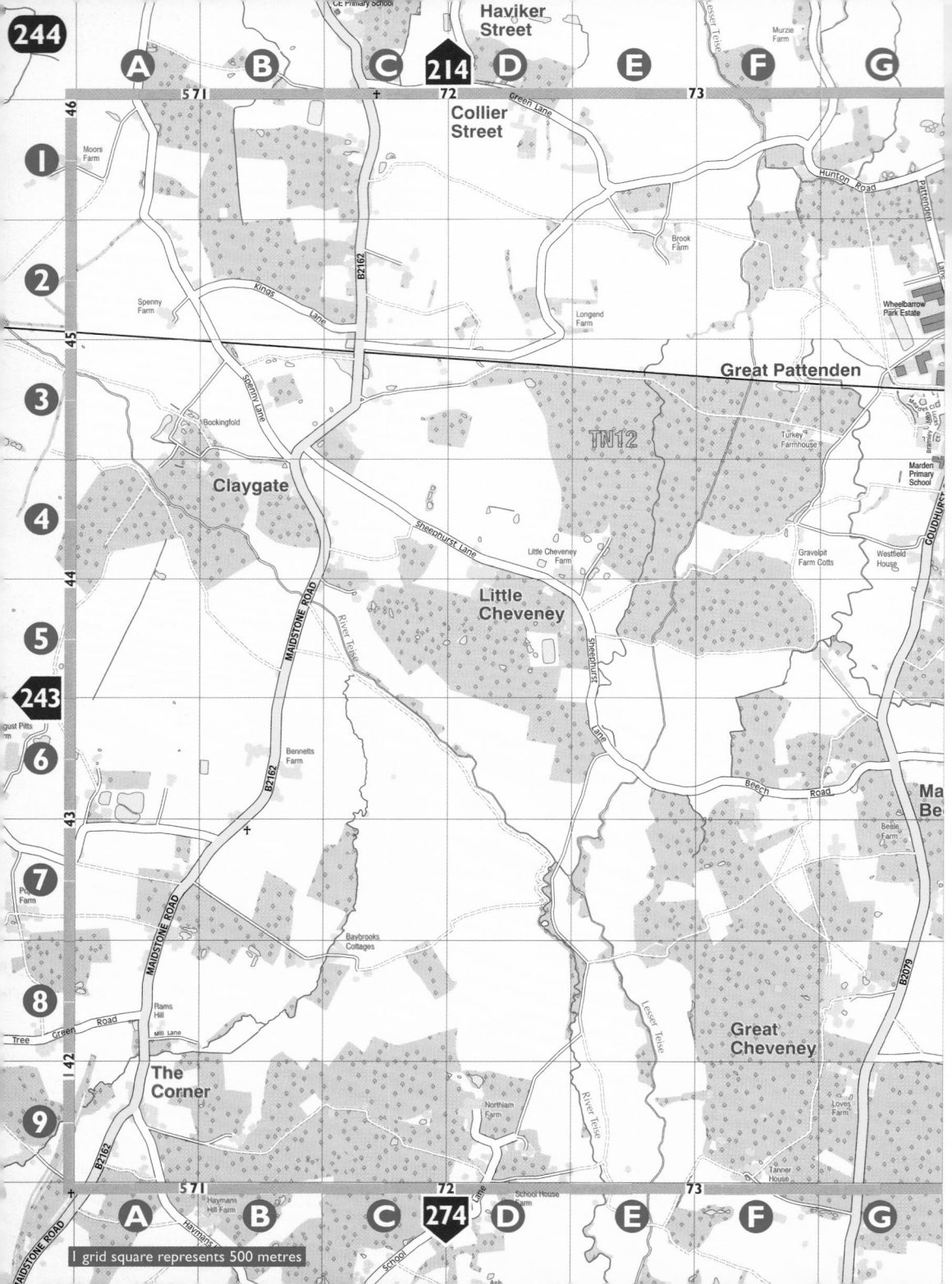

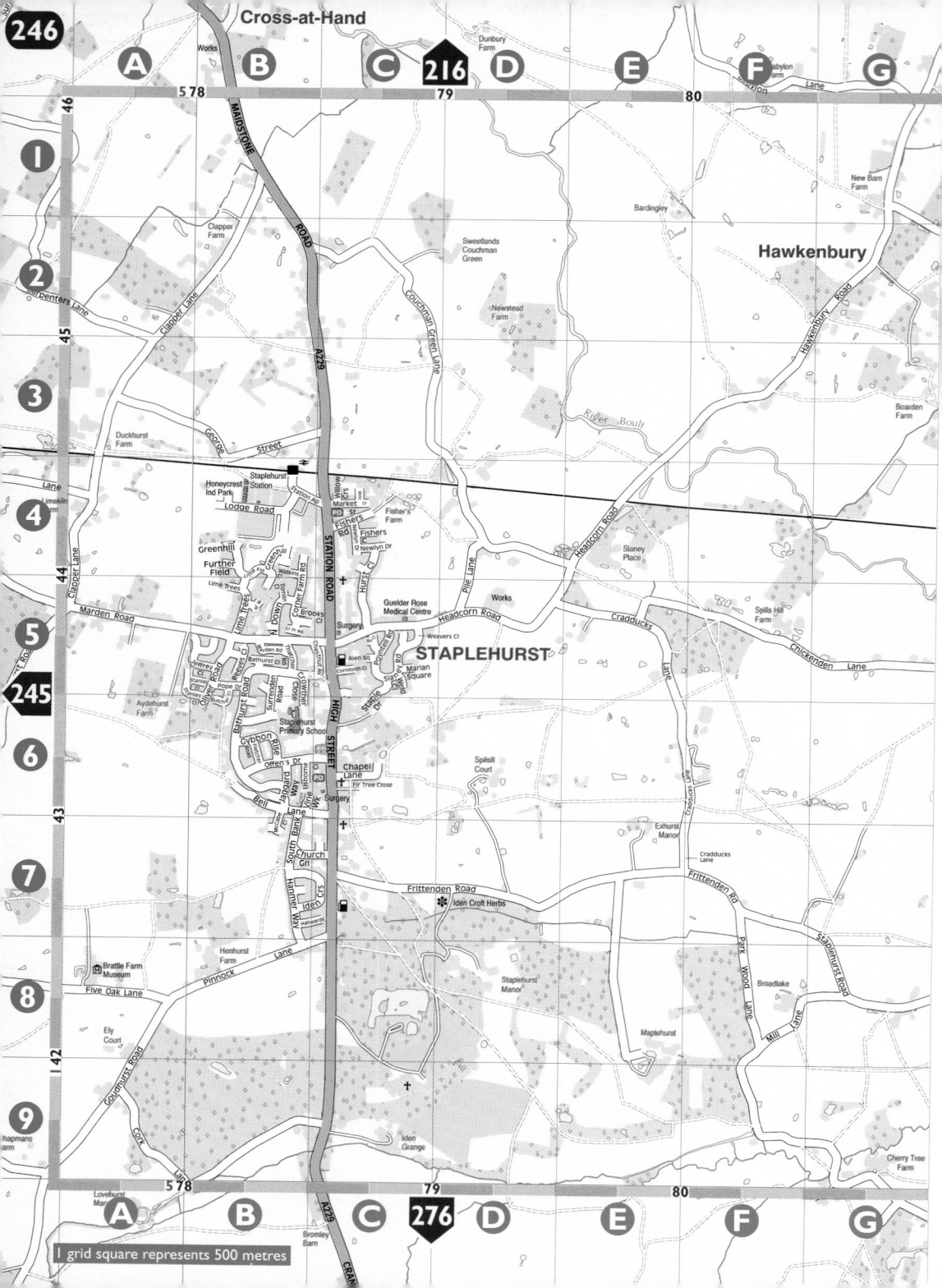

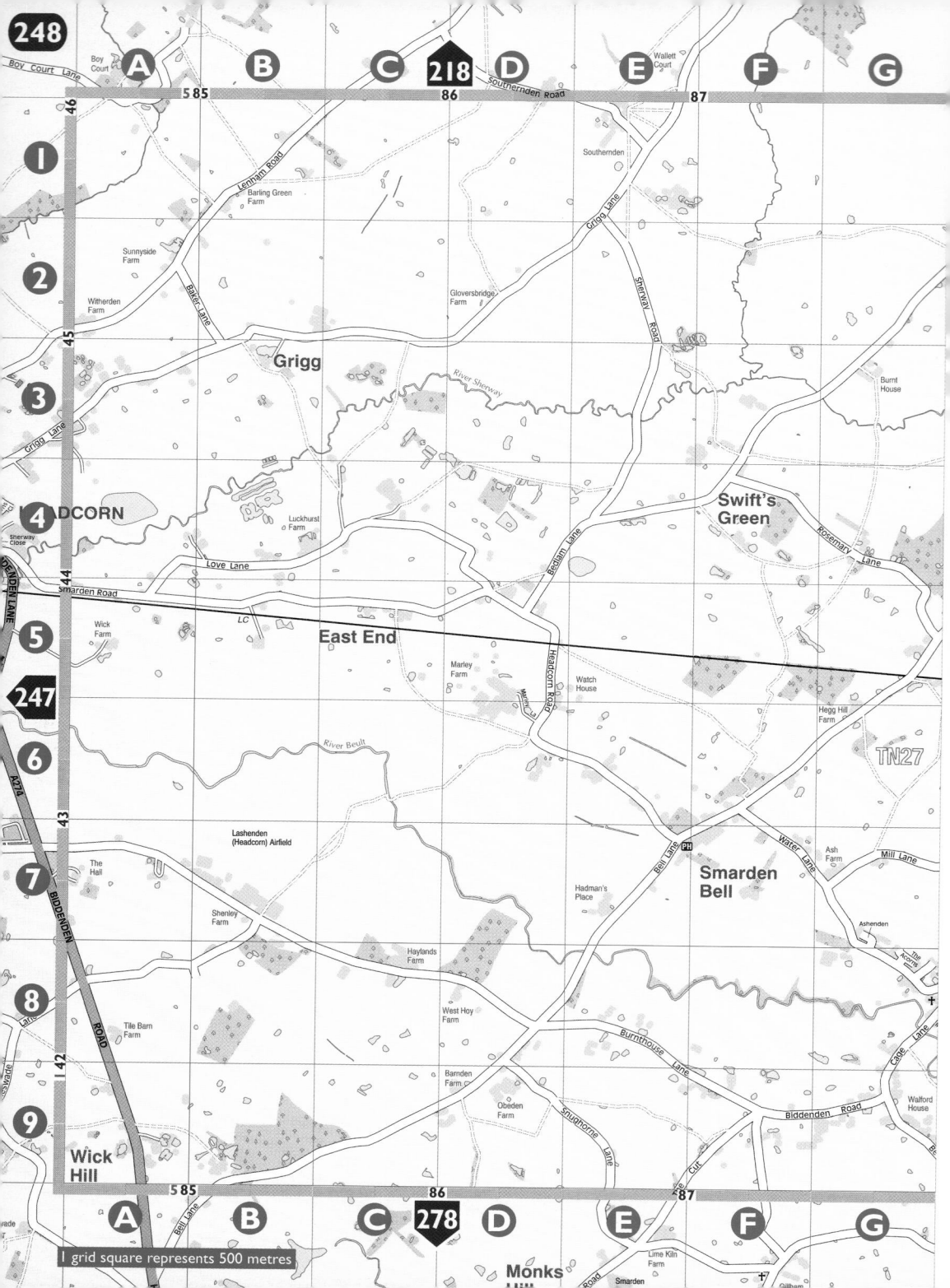

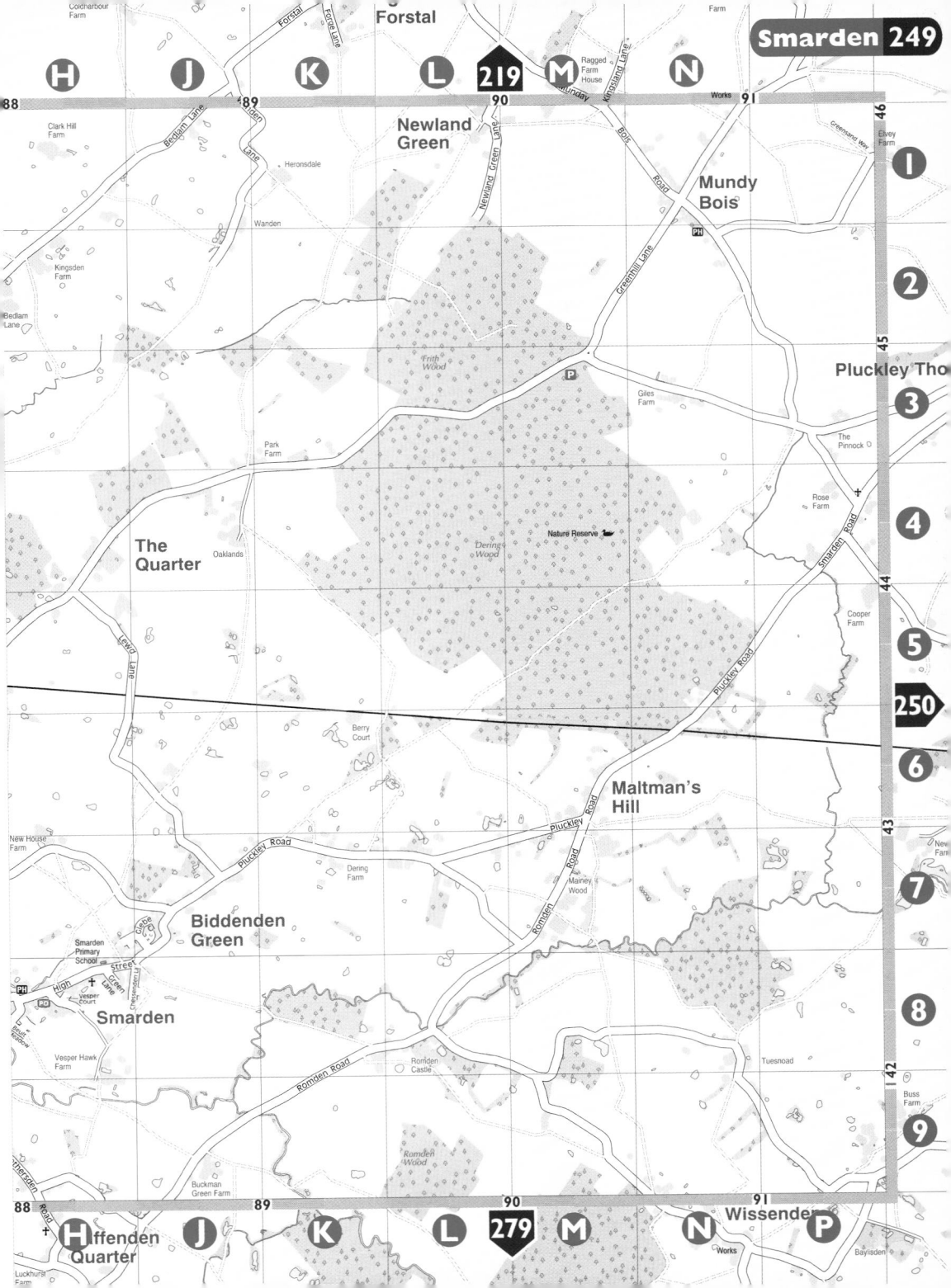

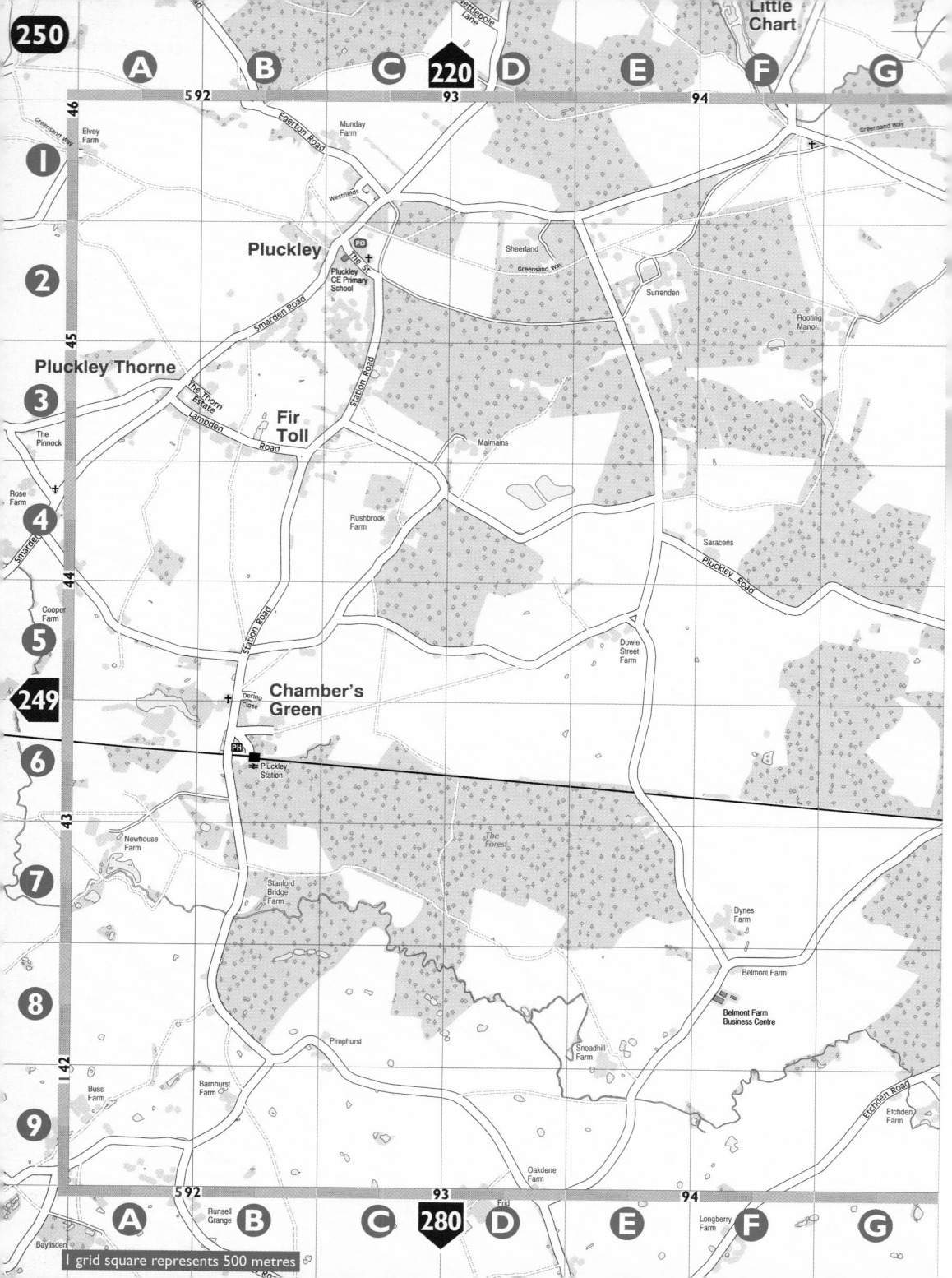

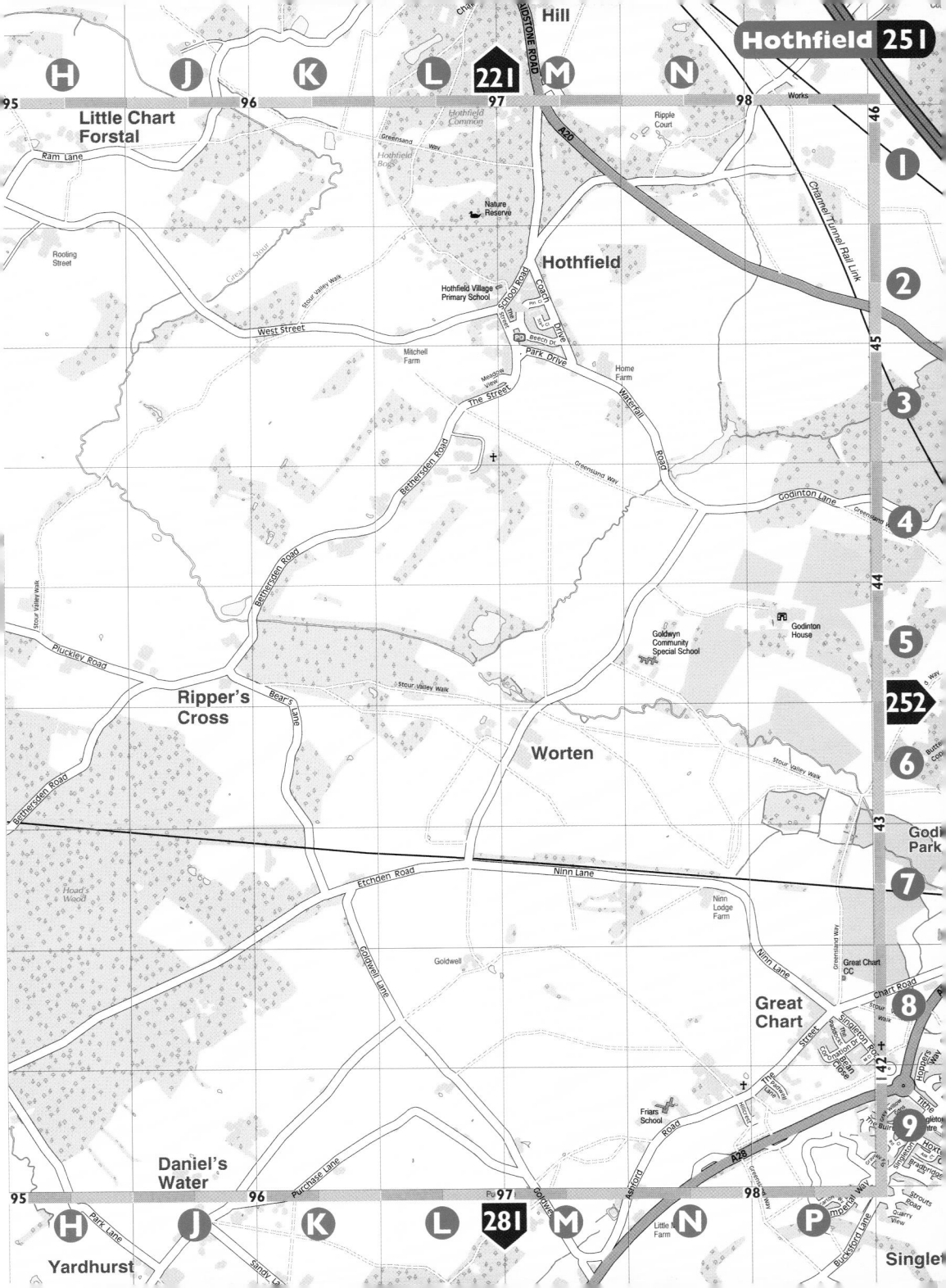

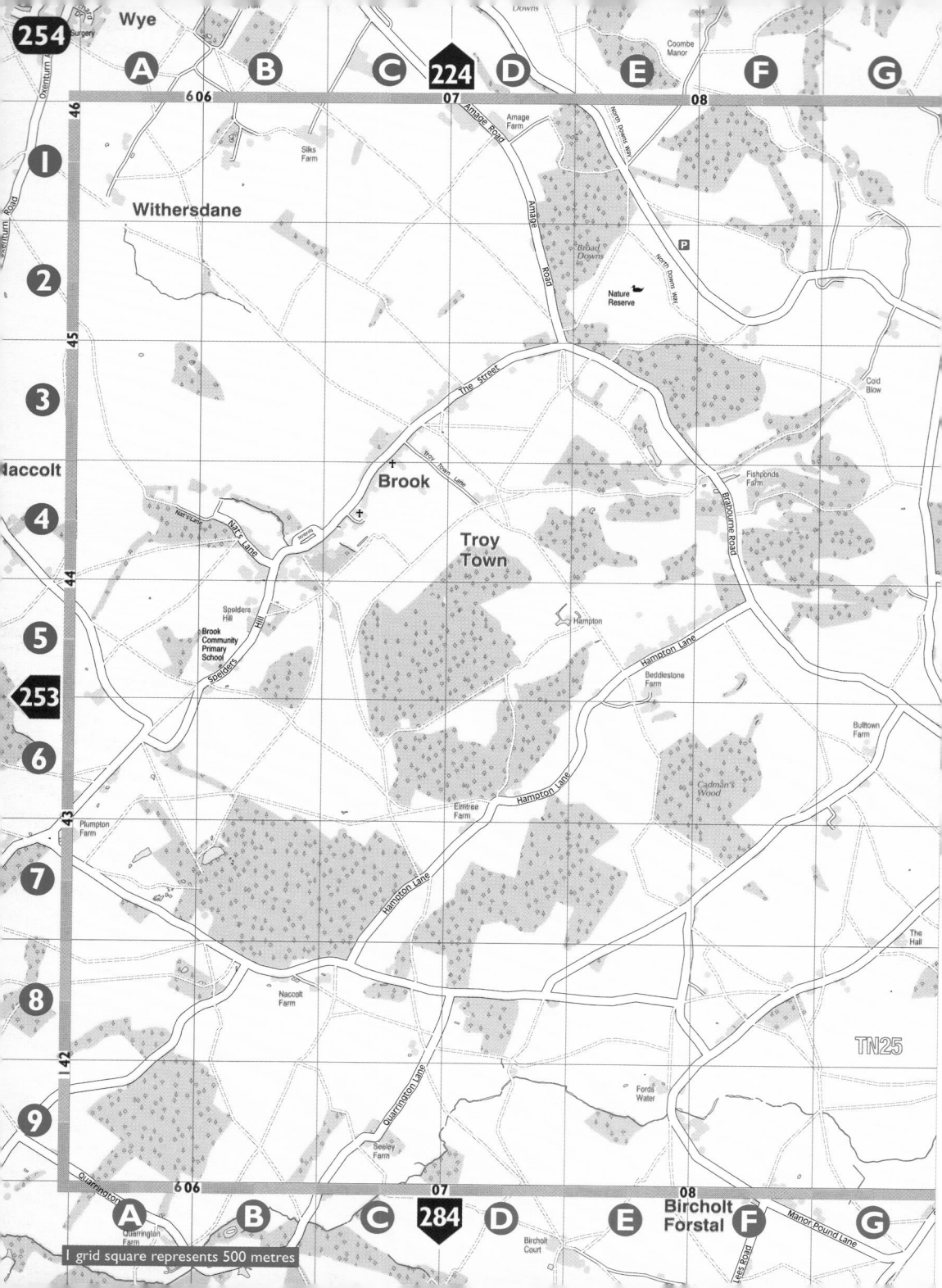

H   J   K   L   **225**   M   N

09   10   11   12

46

1

Spond
Farm

Lyddendane
Farm

Bodsham

**Hill
Street**

45

West
Down

2

Street

Hill

3

M
S

†

The Street

Evington

Elmsted

†

Hastingleigh

Tamley Lane

Crabtree
Farm

Court Lodge
†

**Whatsole
Street**

4

44

South
Hill
Farm

Kingsmill
Down

5

ml
Gre

Pett
Bottom

Dundas
Farm

**Stowting
Common**

256

North Downs Way

North Downs Way

Park
Farm

6

43

7

Stowting
Hill

Brabourne Lane

Brabourne
Coomb

North Downs Way

8

42

Stowting

Hill

Penstock
Hall

PH

The Street

Brabourne

Canterbury Road

Scot's Lane

†

Stowting CE
Primary School

9

Brabourne CE
Primary School

Canterbury   Road

Canterbury Road

Stowting

Stowting
Cou

PH

H   J   K   L   **285**   M   N   P

09   10   11   12

Fiddling Lane

North D

Way

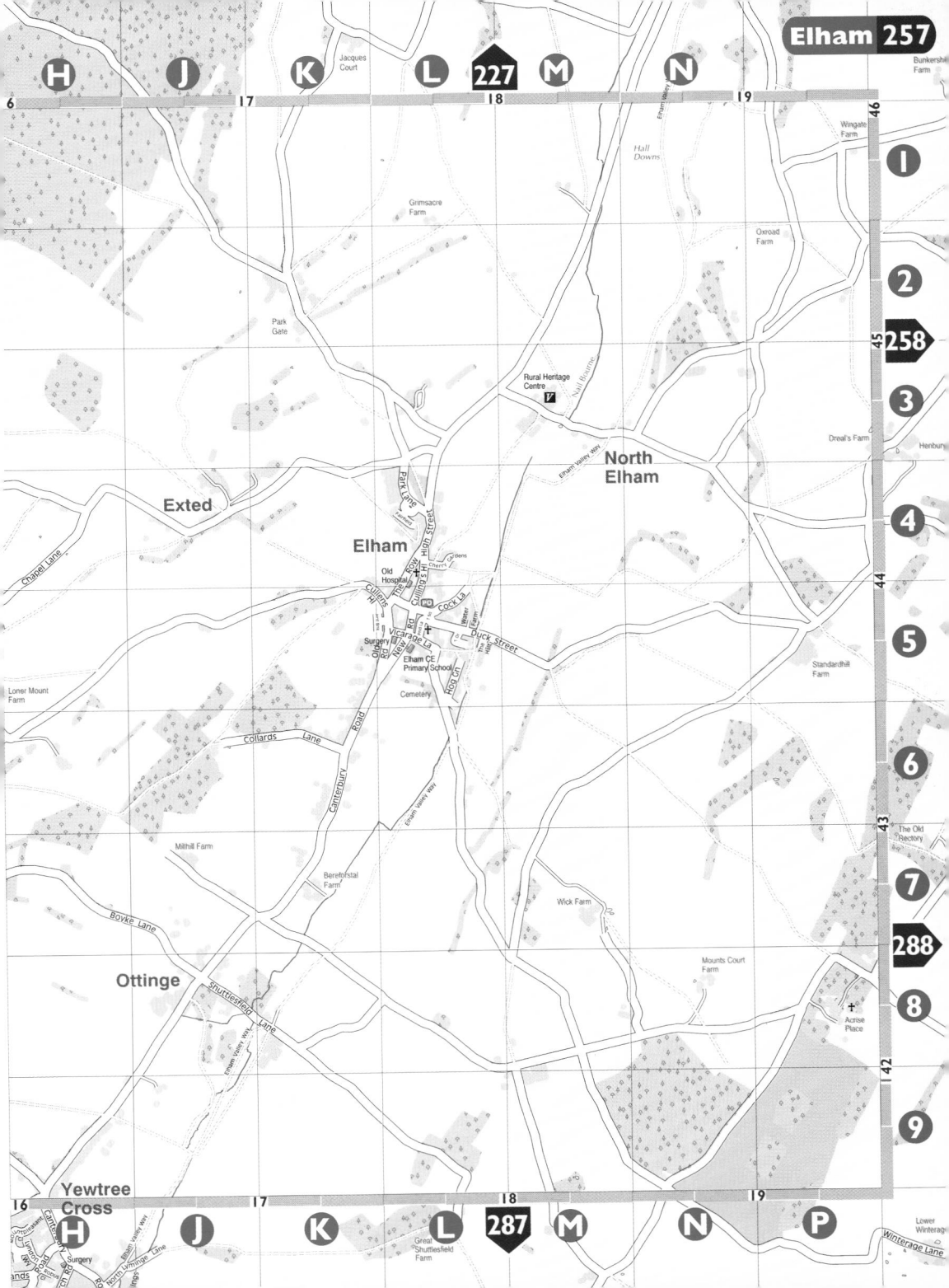

H J K L **227** M N

6 17 18 19 46

Bunkershill Farm

I 1

Wingate Farm

Hall Downs

2

Oxroad Farm

45 **258**

Grimsacre Farm

Jacques Court

Park Gate

Rural Heritage Centre

Nail Bourne

3

Dreal's Farm

Henbury

Exted

North Elham

4

44

Elham

Old Hospital

Park Lane

High Street

The Row

Culling's Rd

Cherry Gdns

Cock La.

5

Standardhill Farm

Collards Hill

Duck Street

Cullins Hill

Vicarage La.

New Rd.

Surgery Rd.

Old Rd.

Elham CE Primary School

Duck Street

6

Loner Mount Farm

Cemetery

43 The Old Rectory

Collards Lane

Canterbury Road

Elham Valley Way

Millhill Farm

Berefordstal Farm

Wick Farm

7

Boyke Lane

Mounts Court Farm

288

Ottinge

Shuttlesfield Lane

Elham Valley Way

Acrise Place

8

42

9

Yewtree Cross

16 17 18 **287** 19

H J K L M N P

Lower Winterage

Winterage Lane

Surgery

Canterbury Road

North Winterage Lane

Great Shuttlesfield Farm

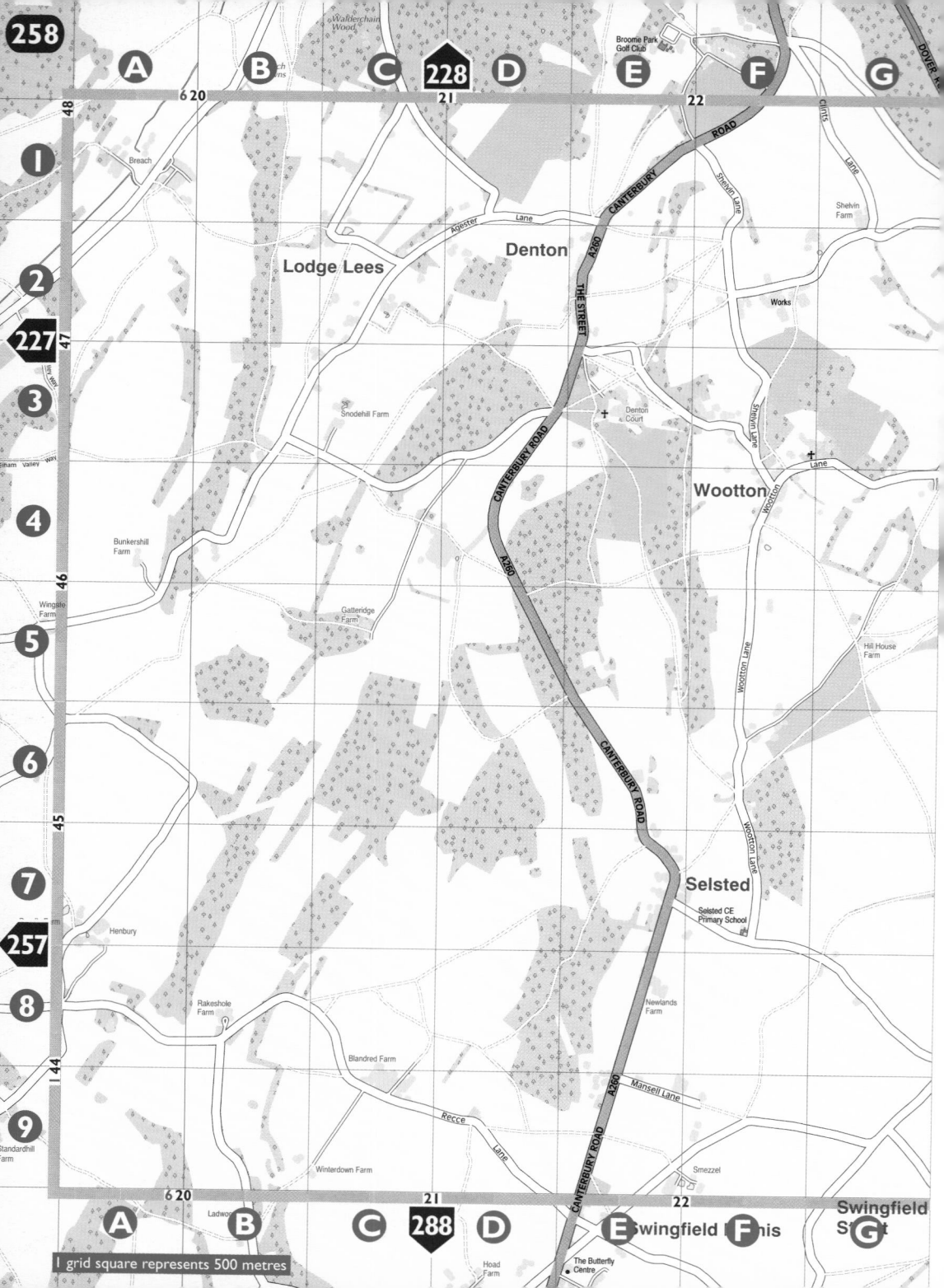

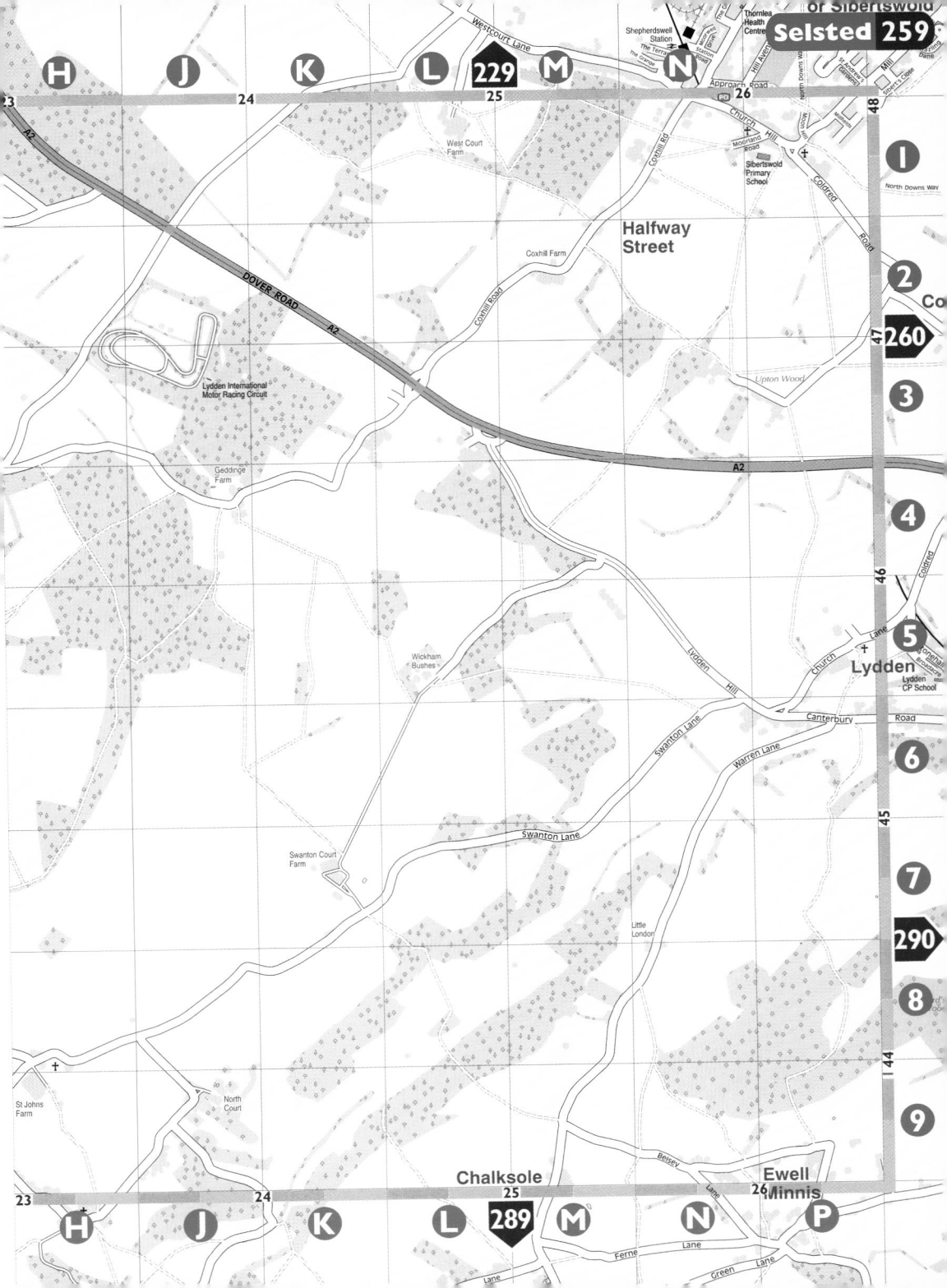

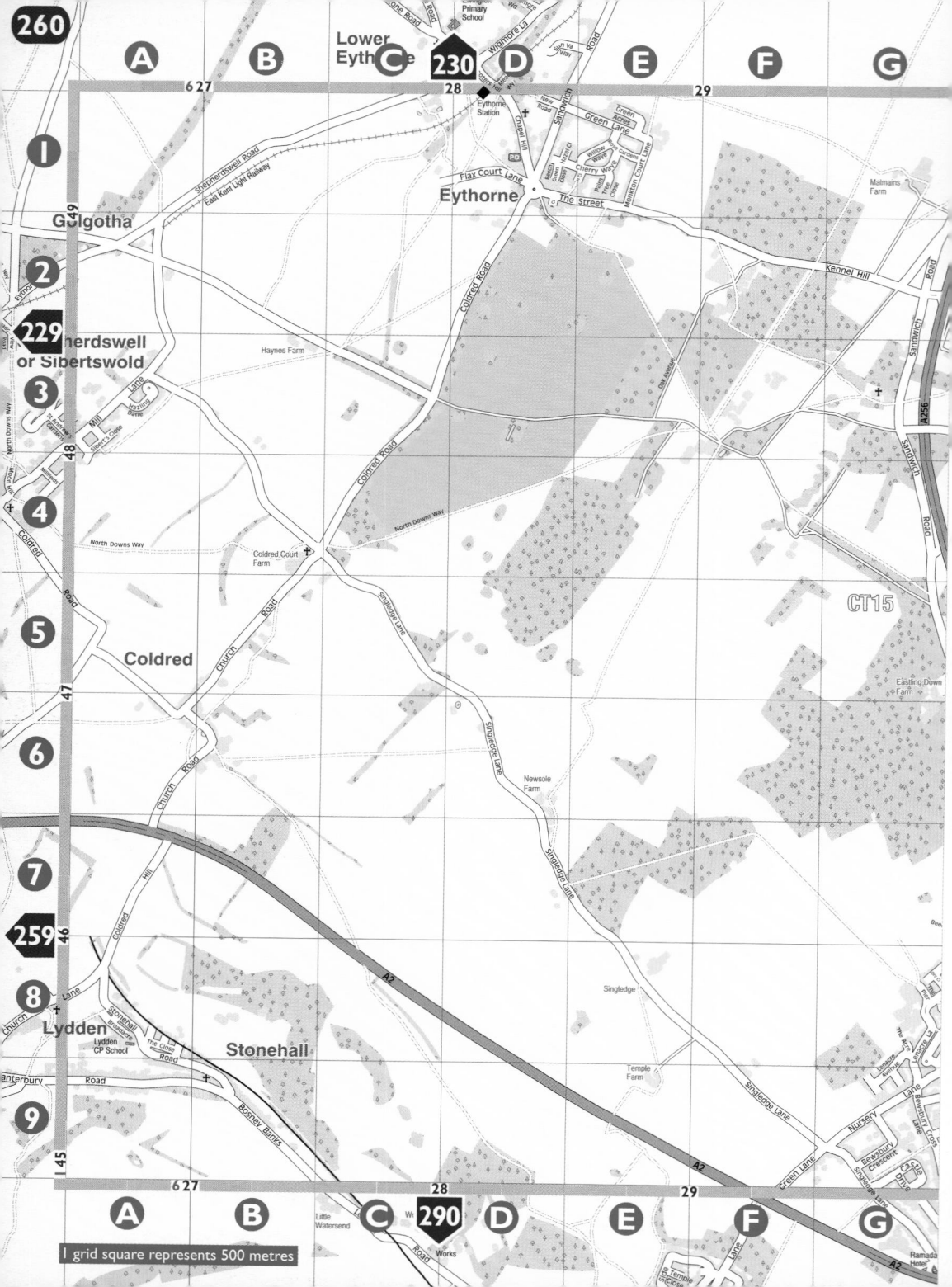

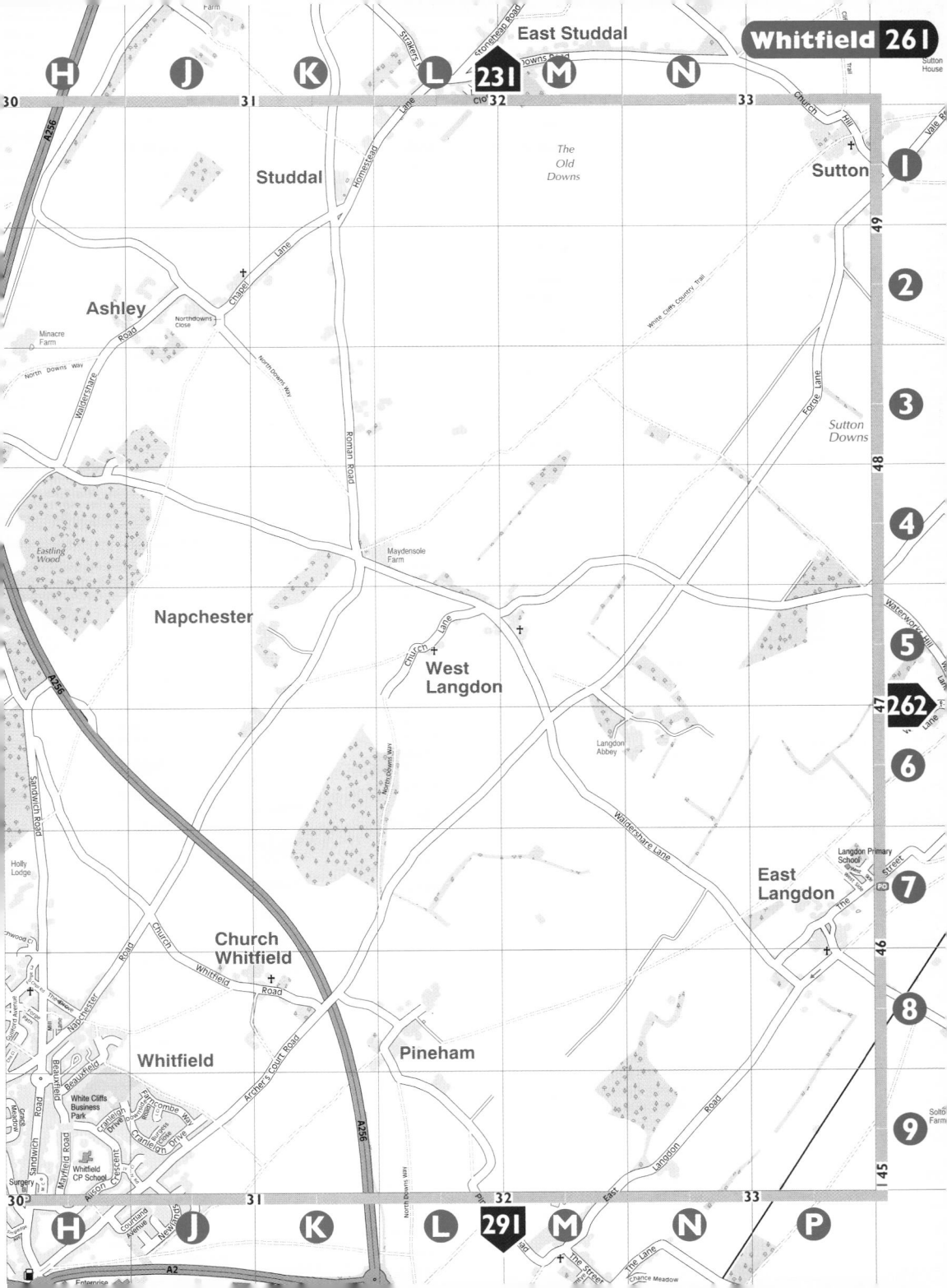

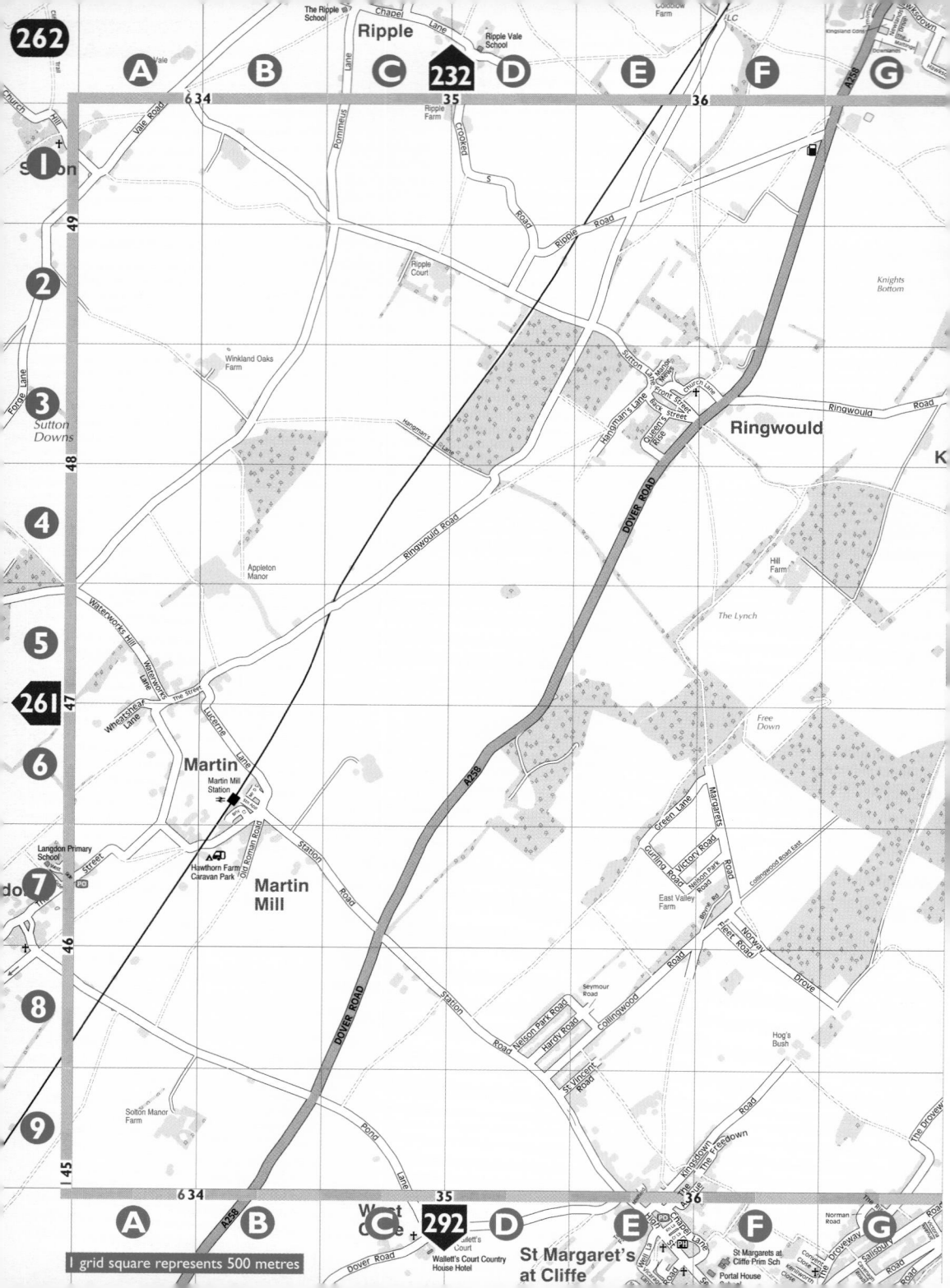

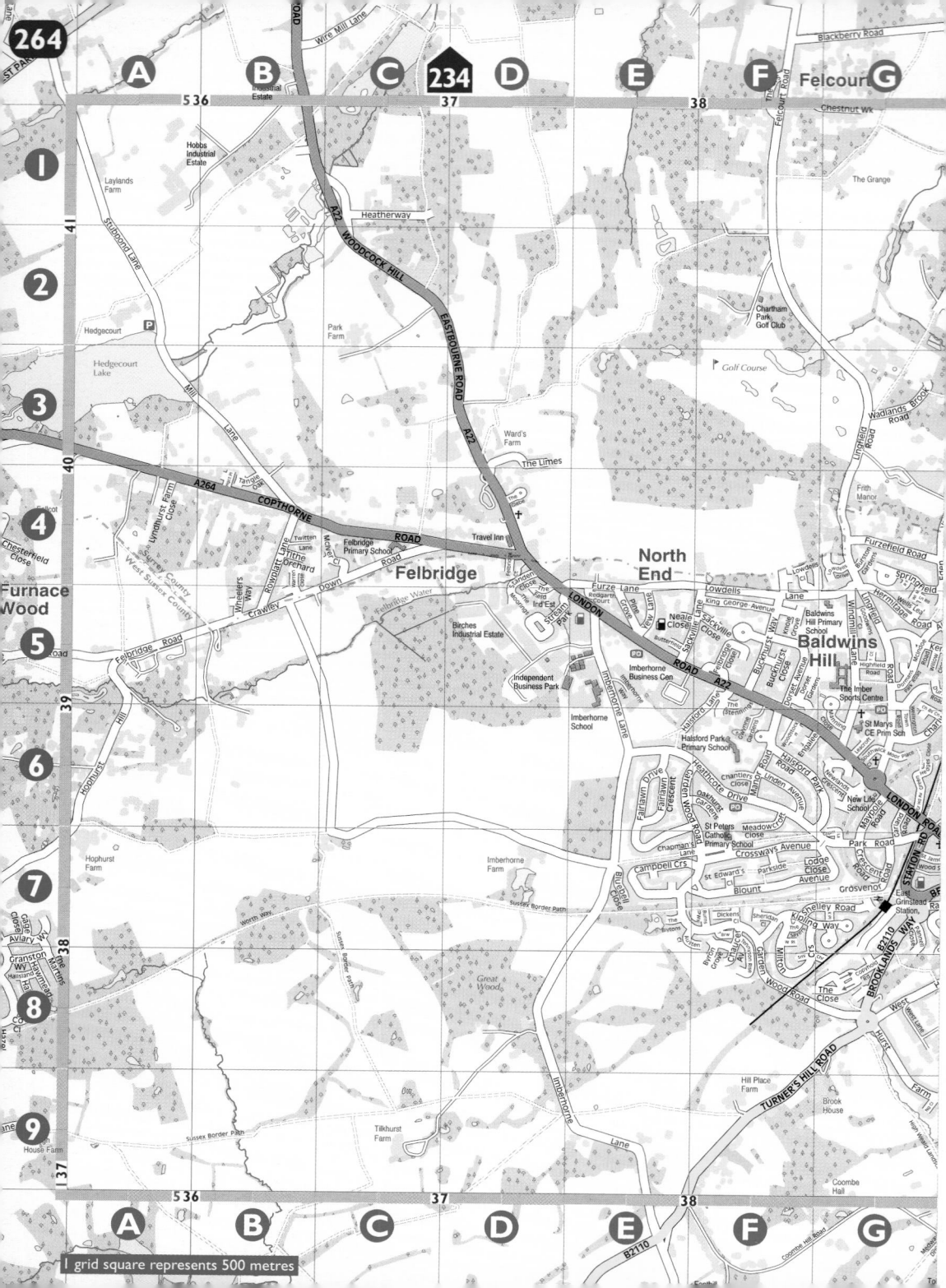

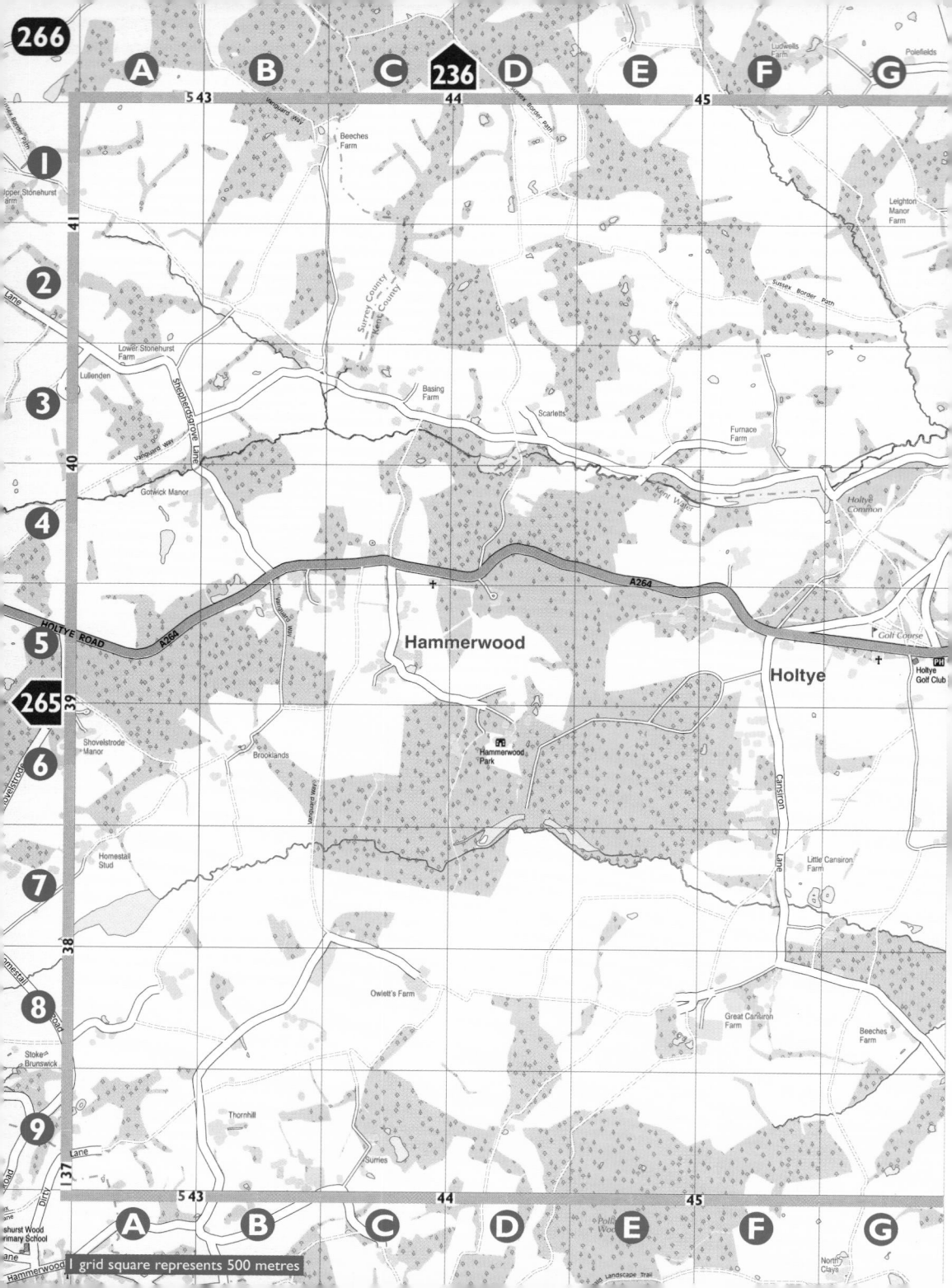

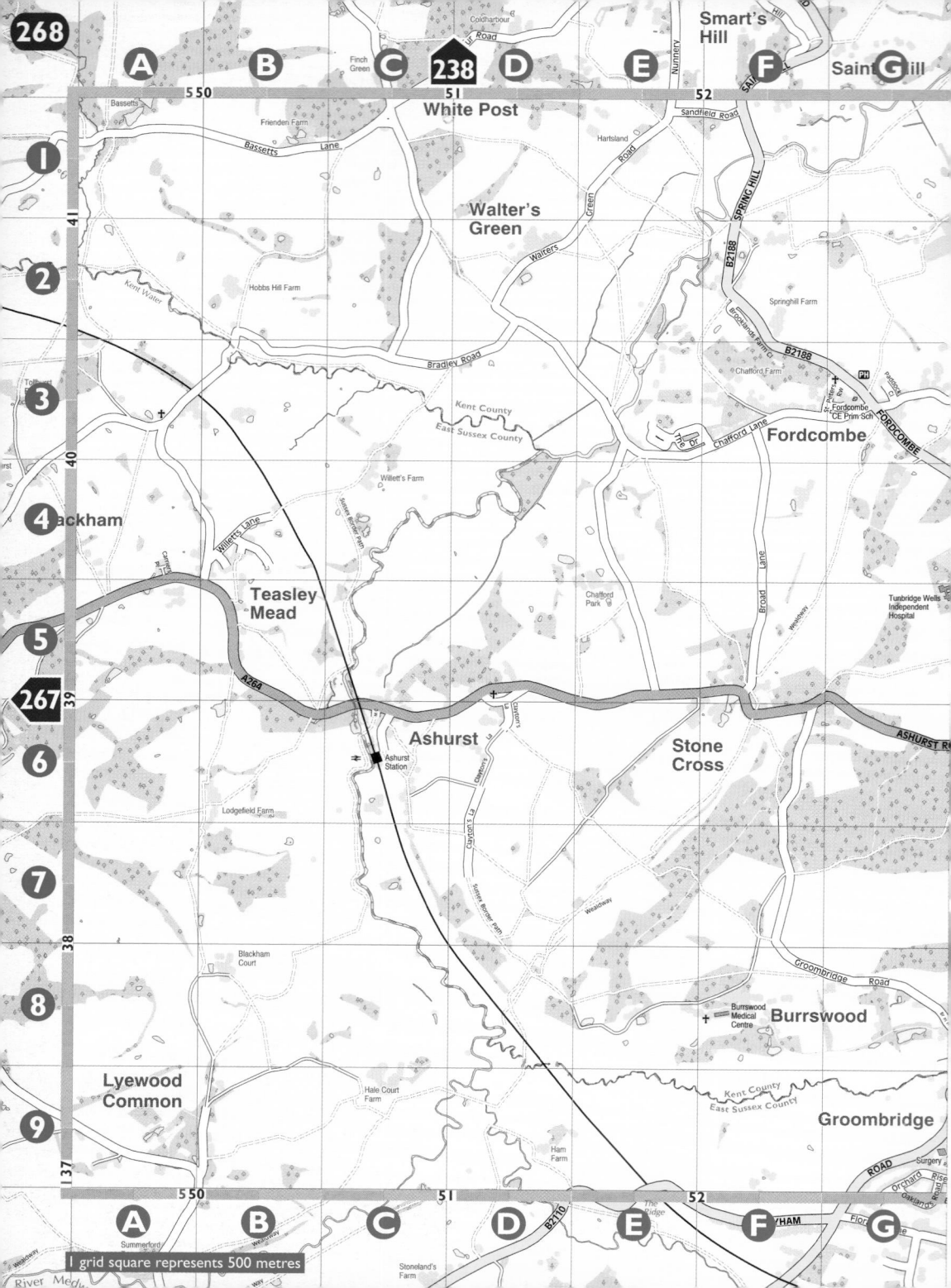

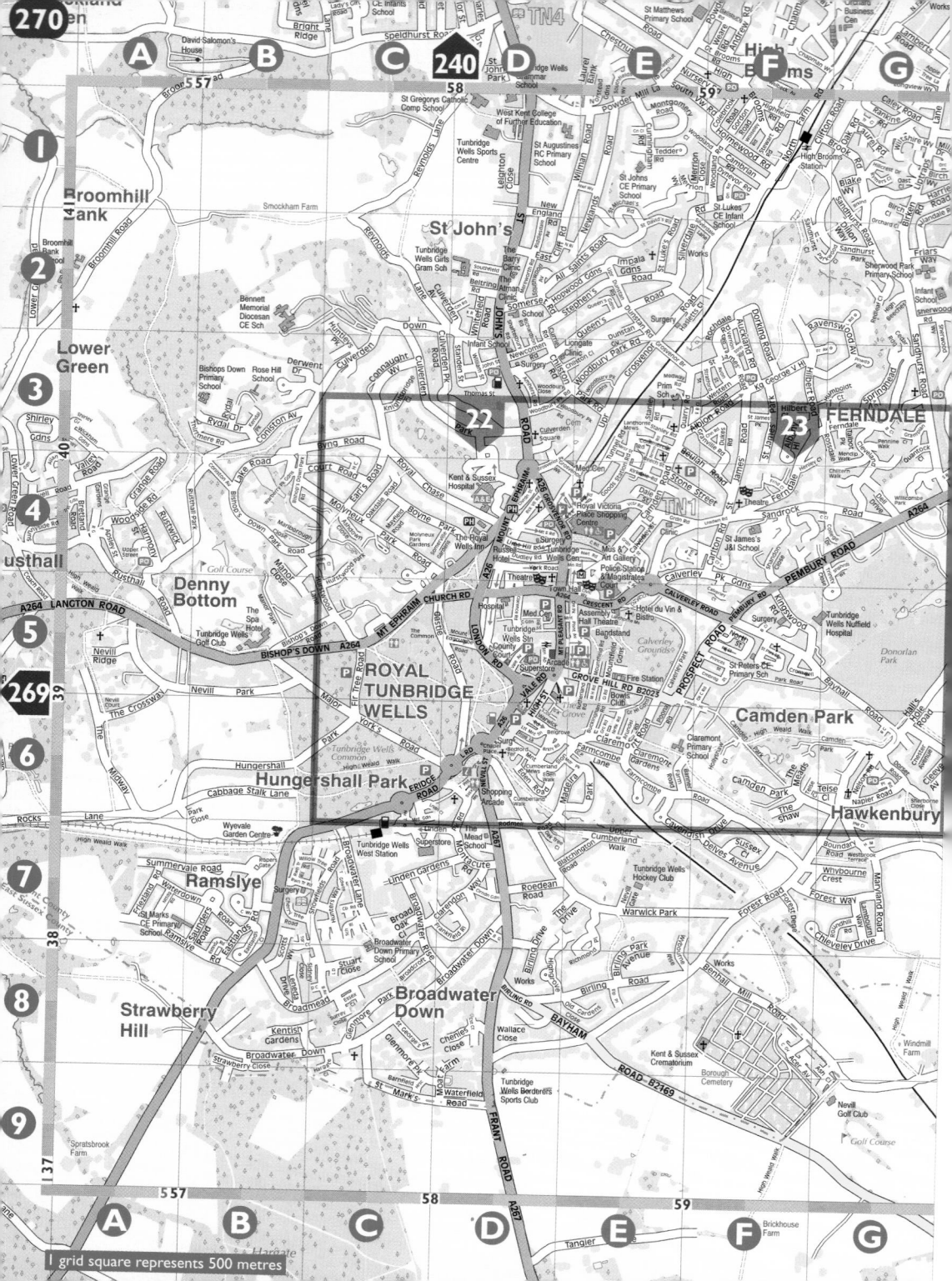

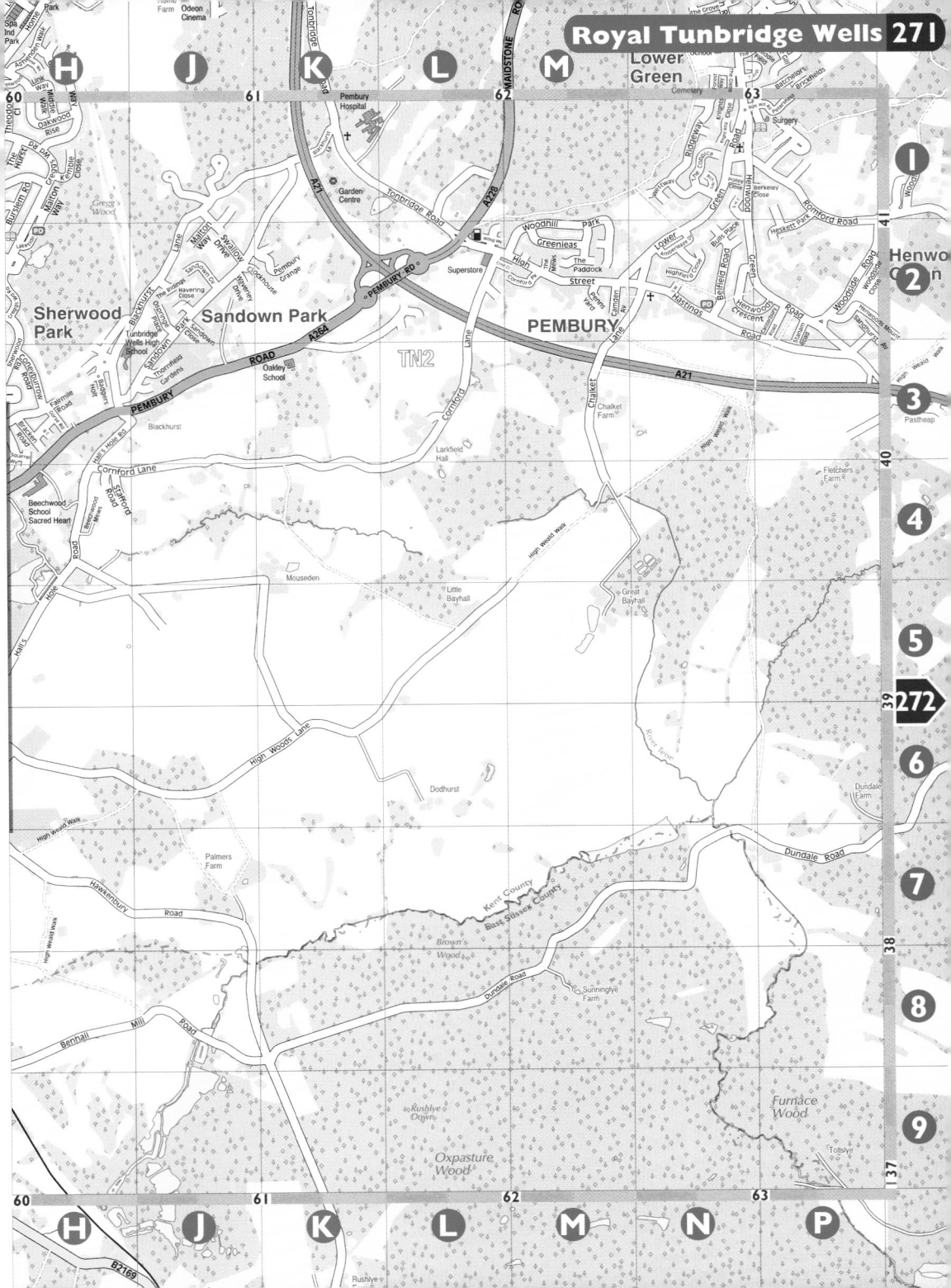

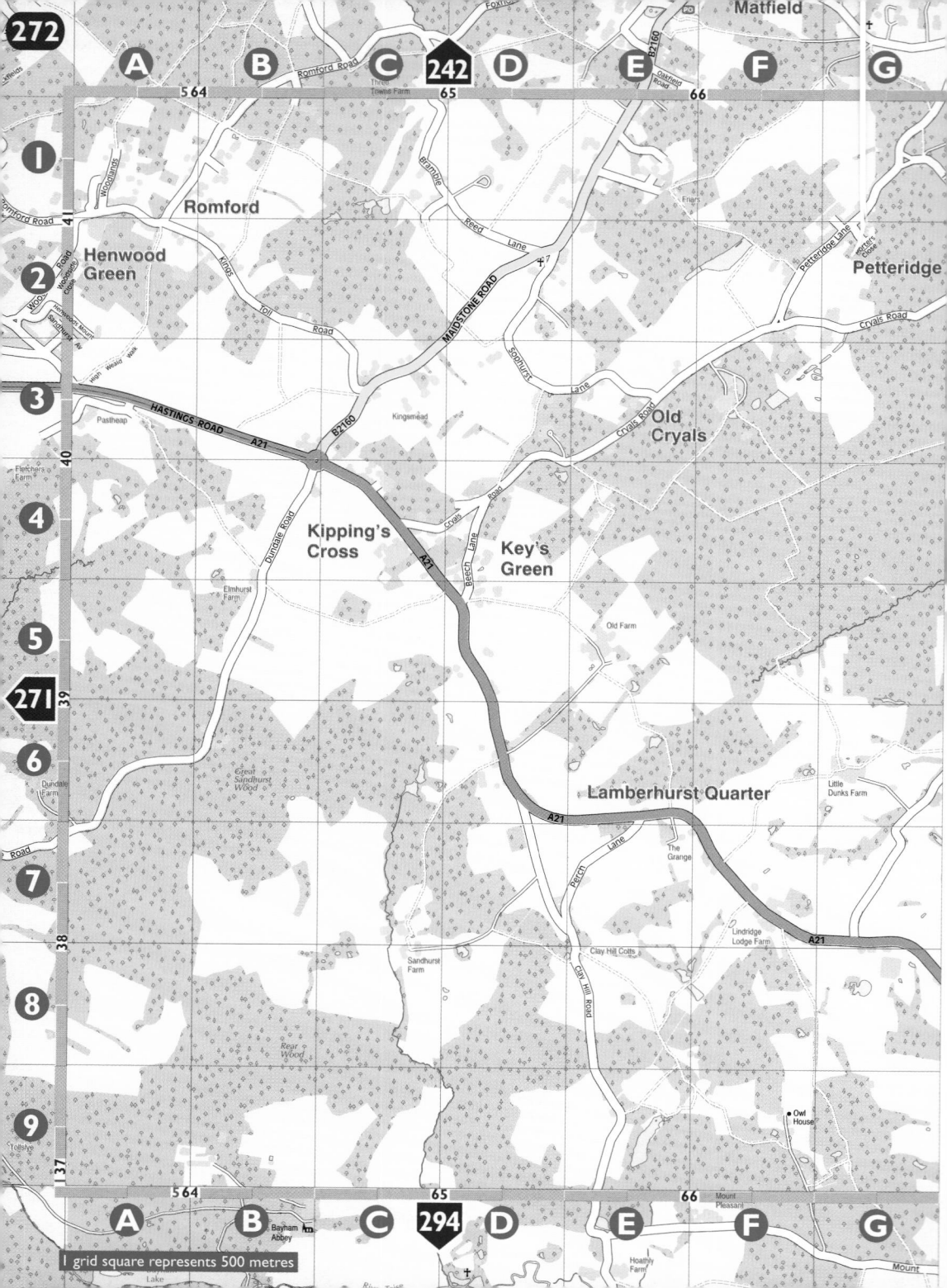

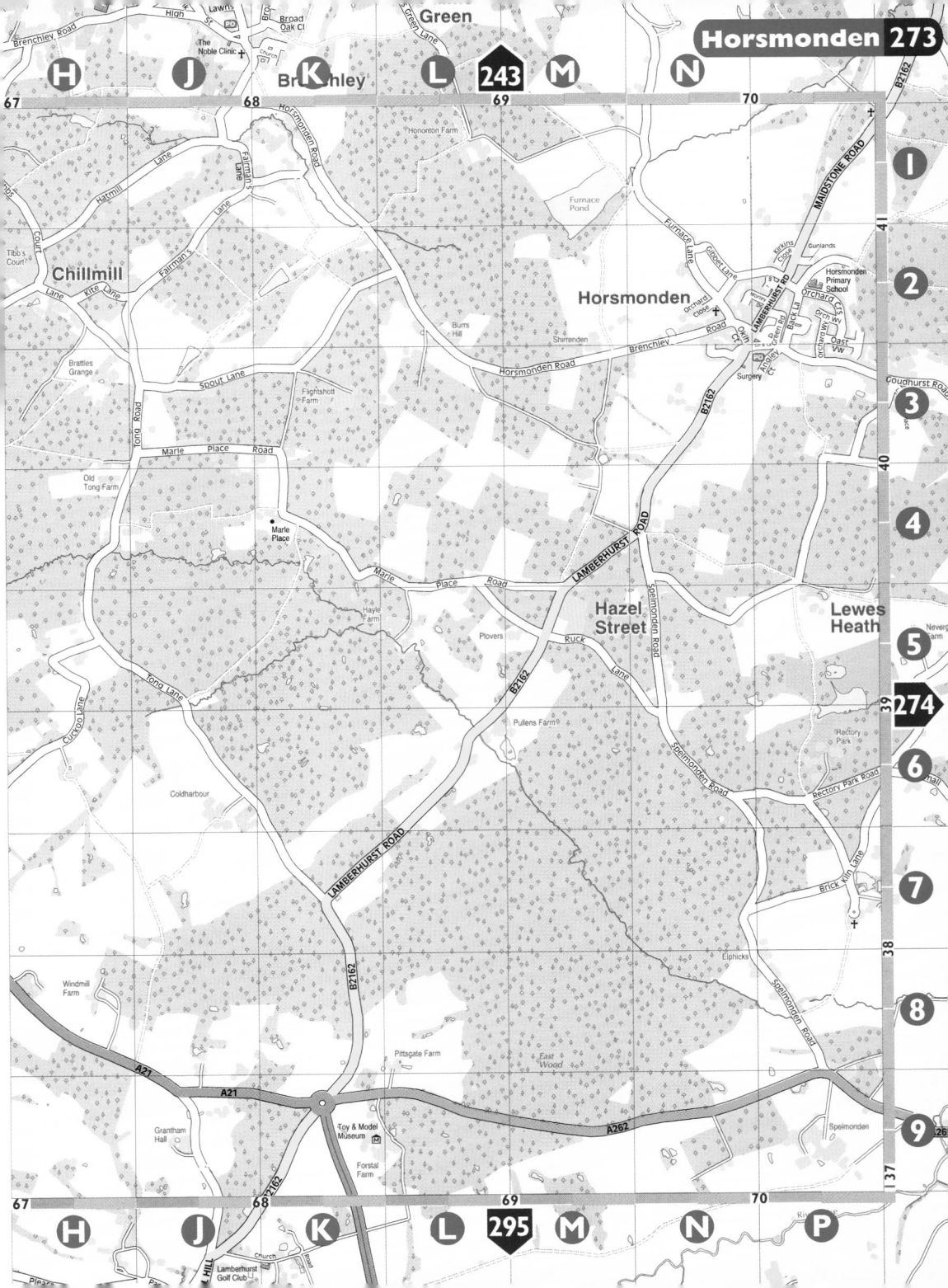

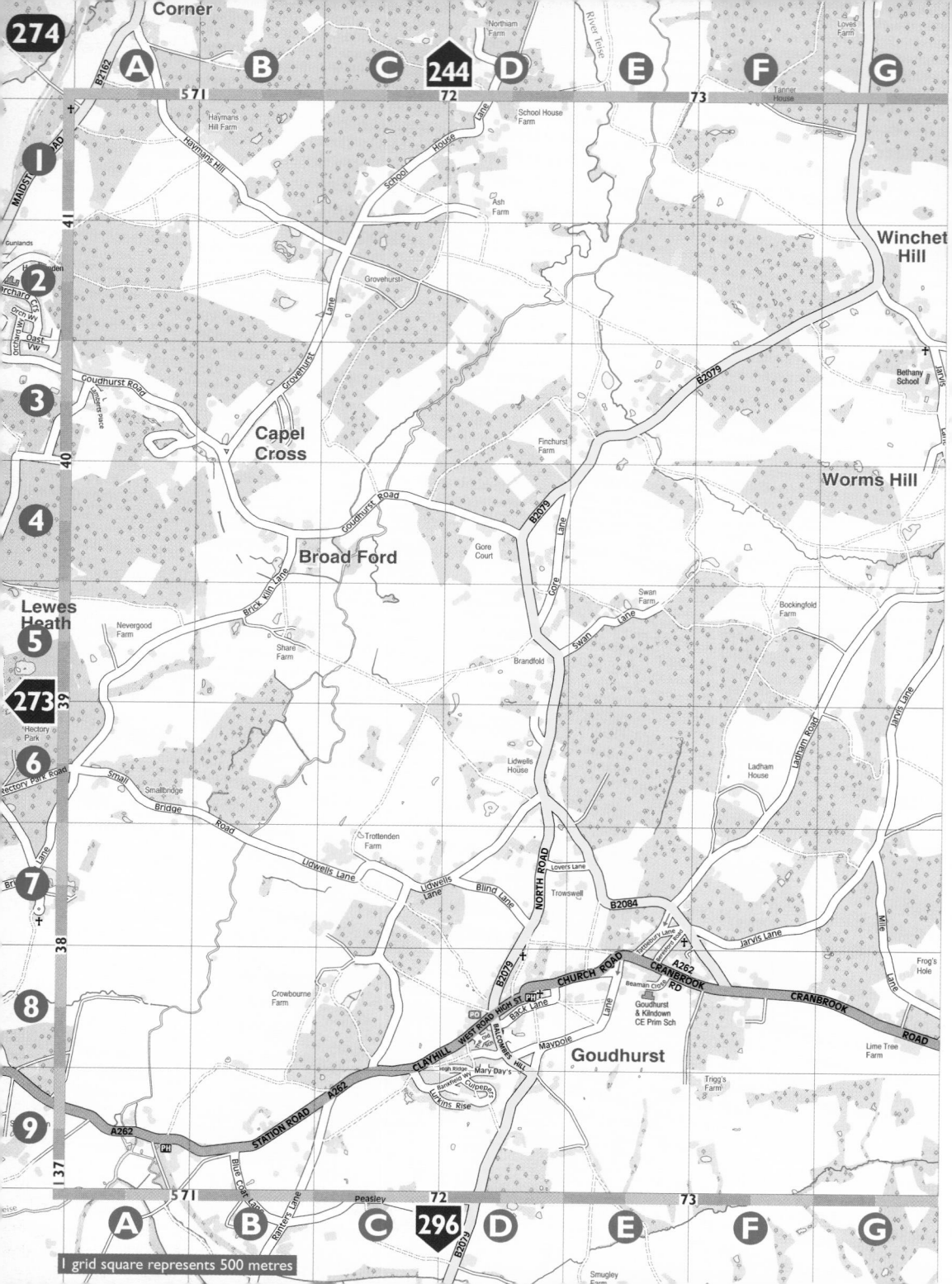

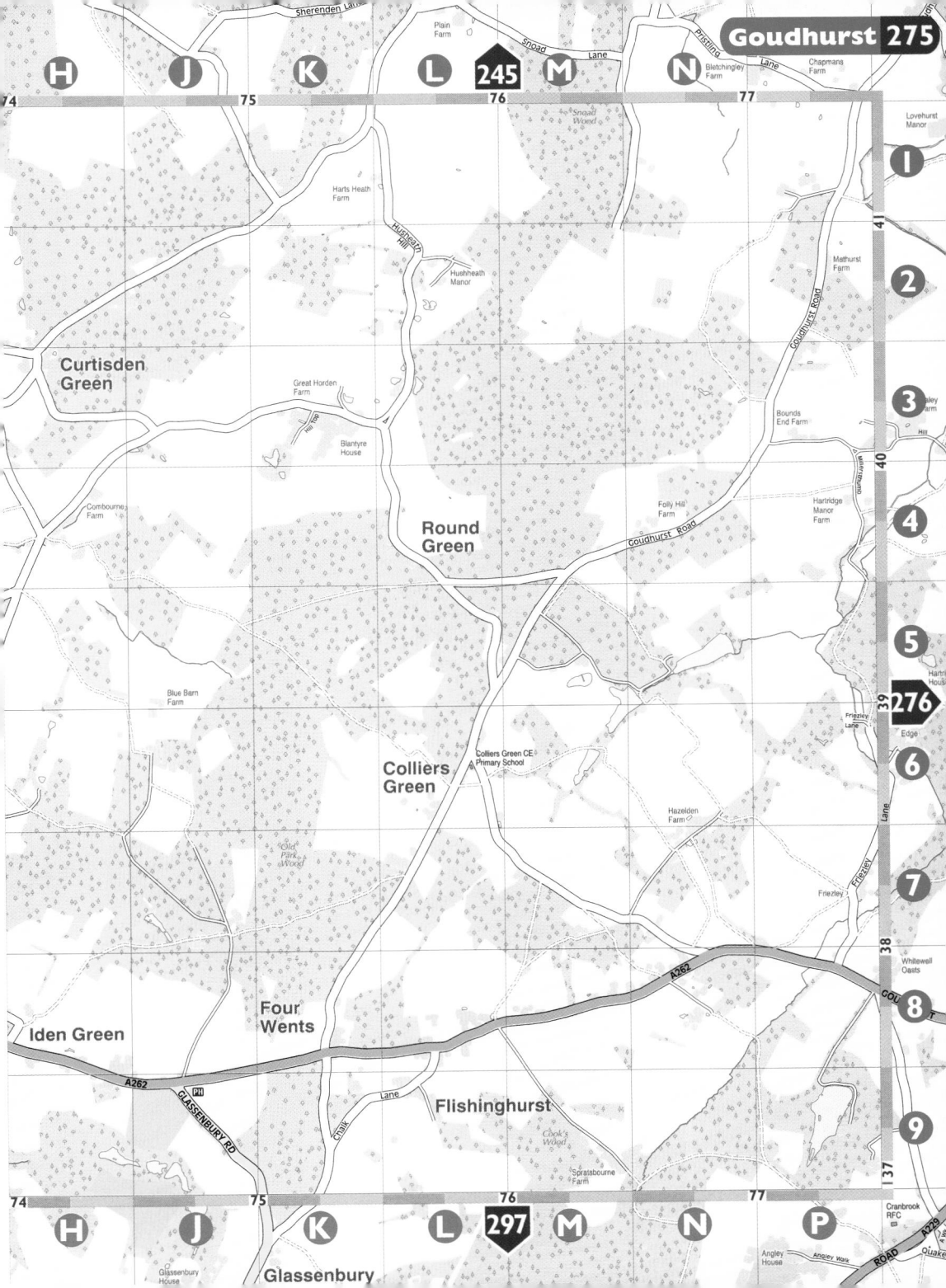

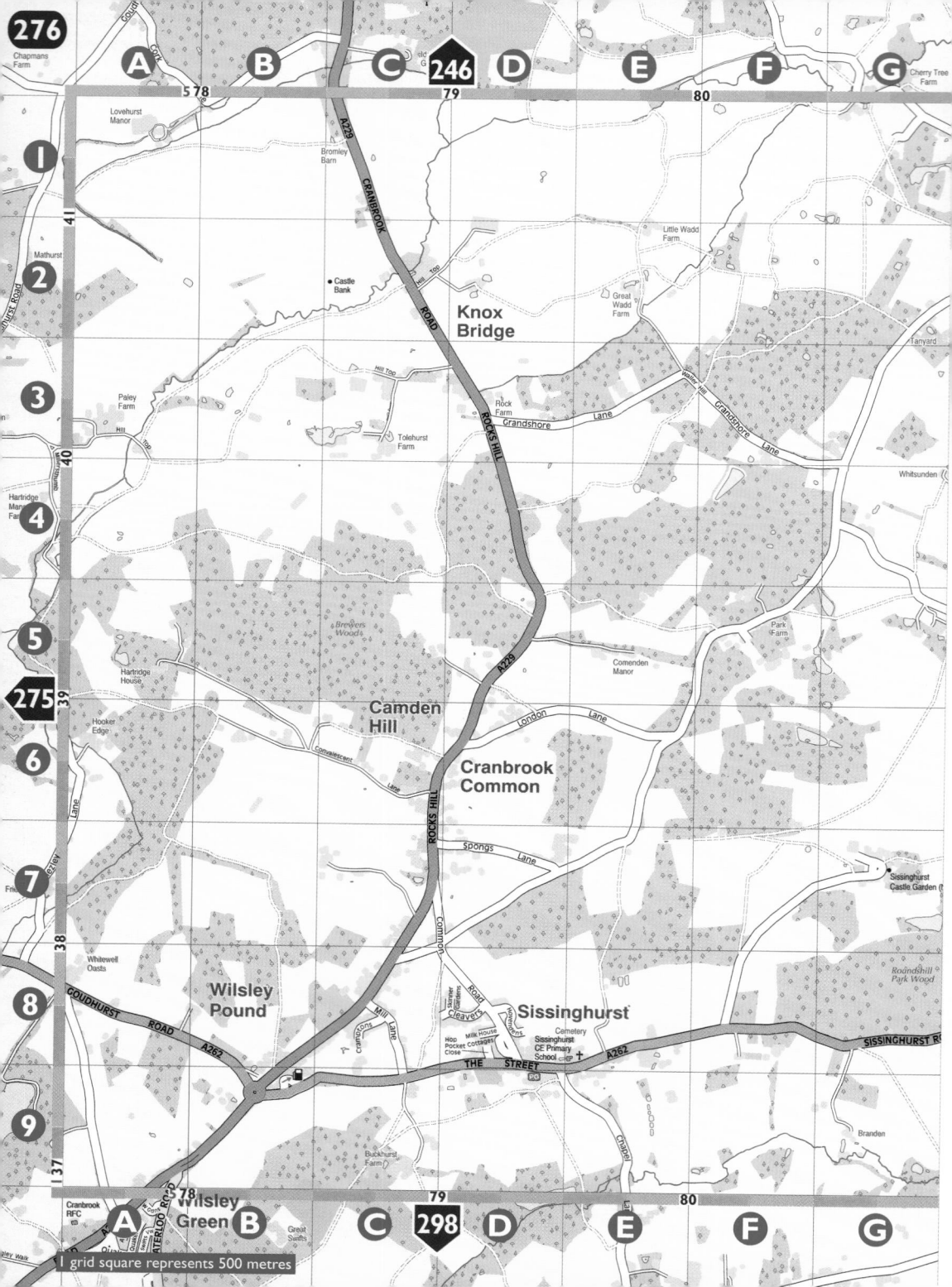

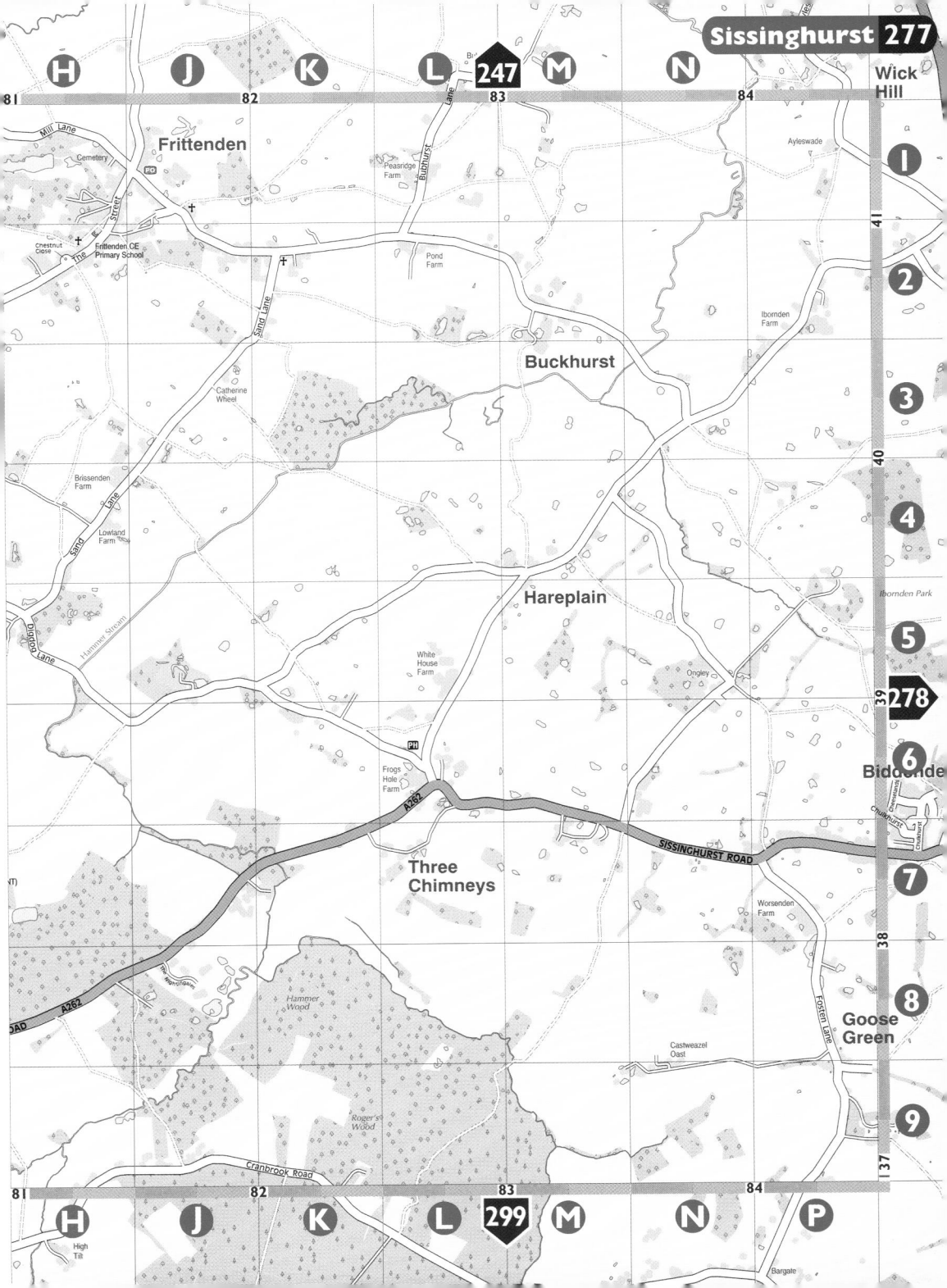

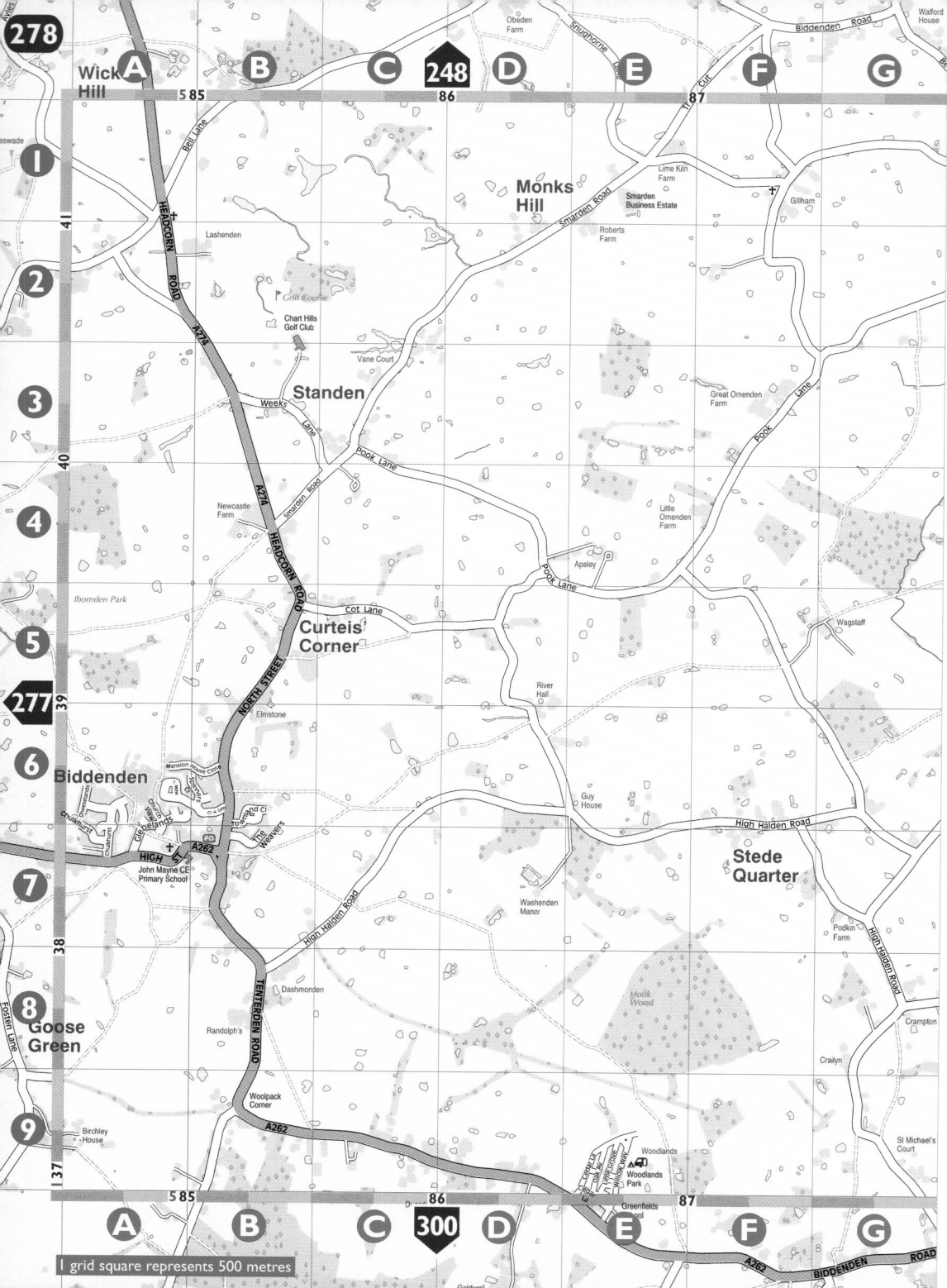

I grid square represents 500 metres

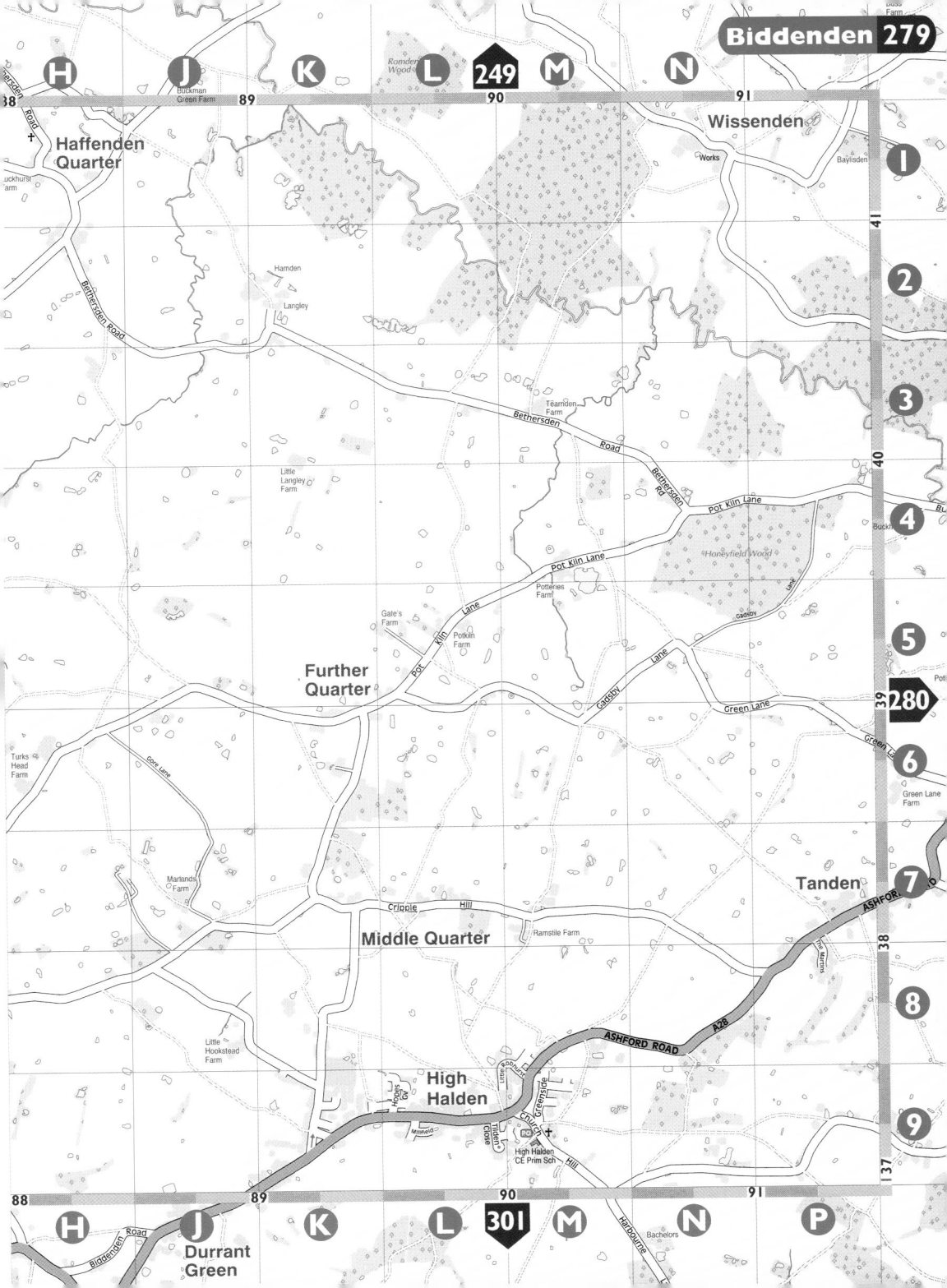

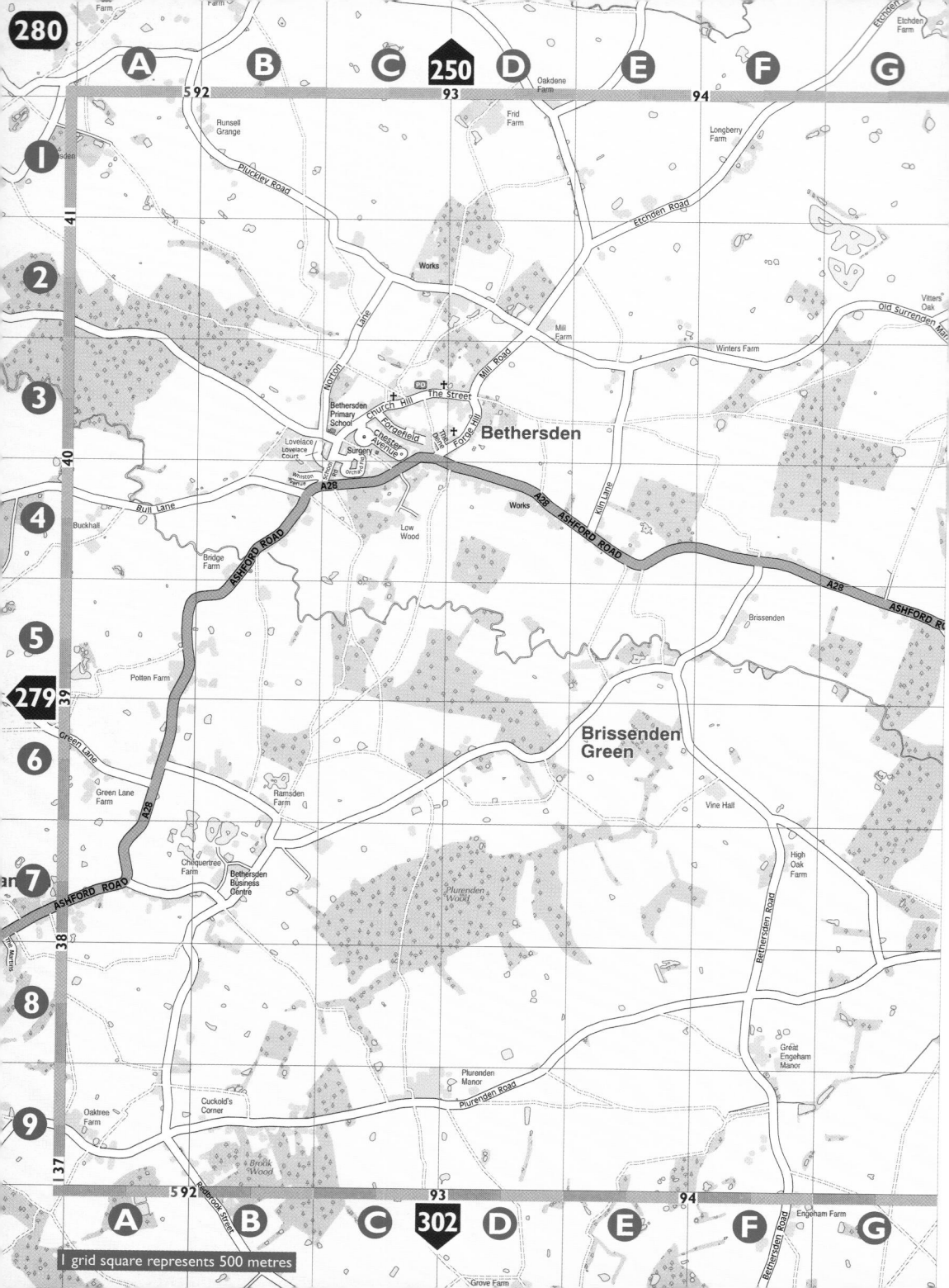

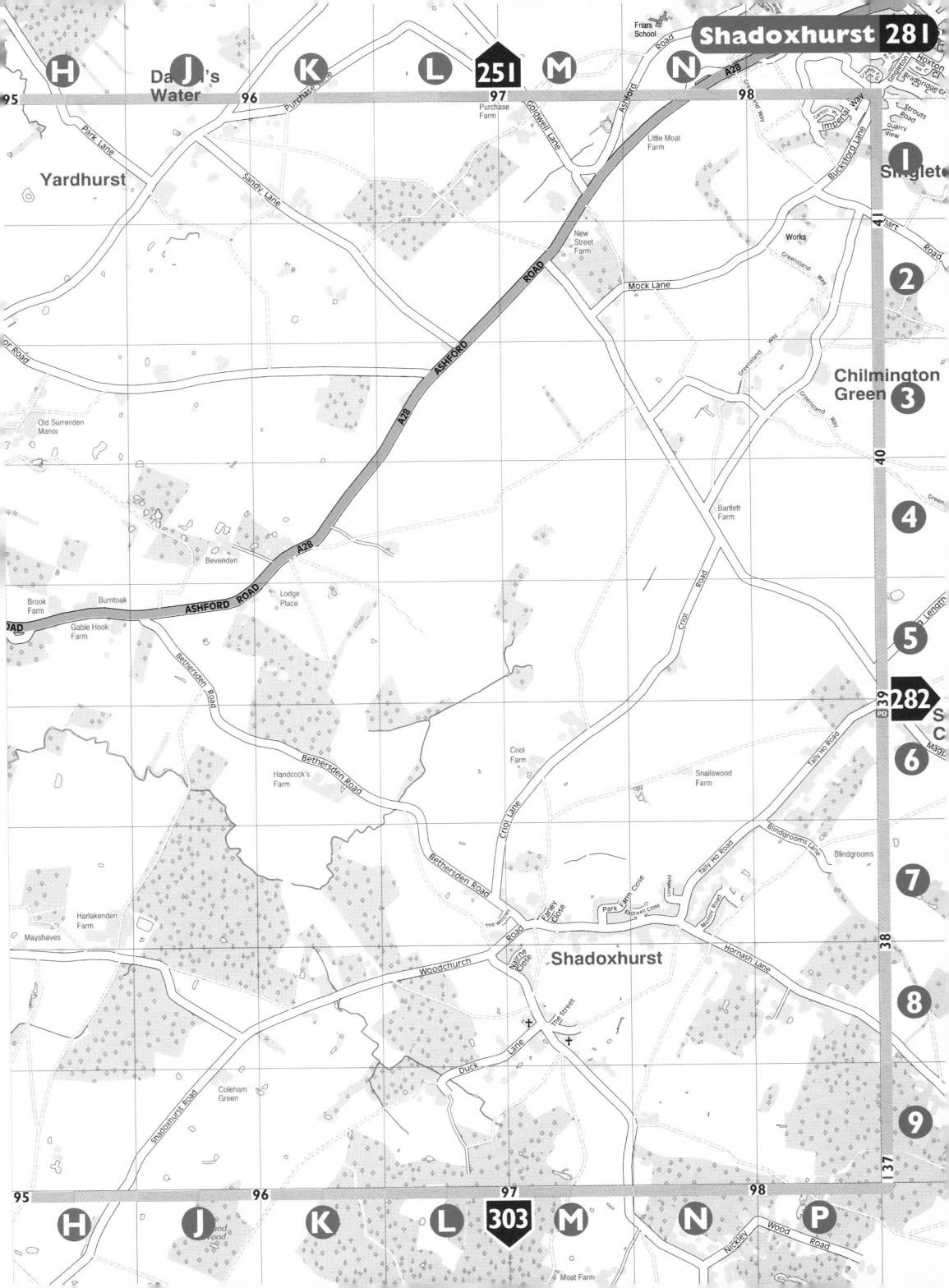

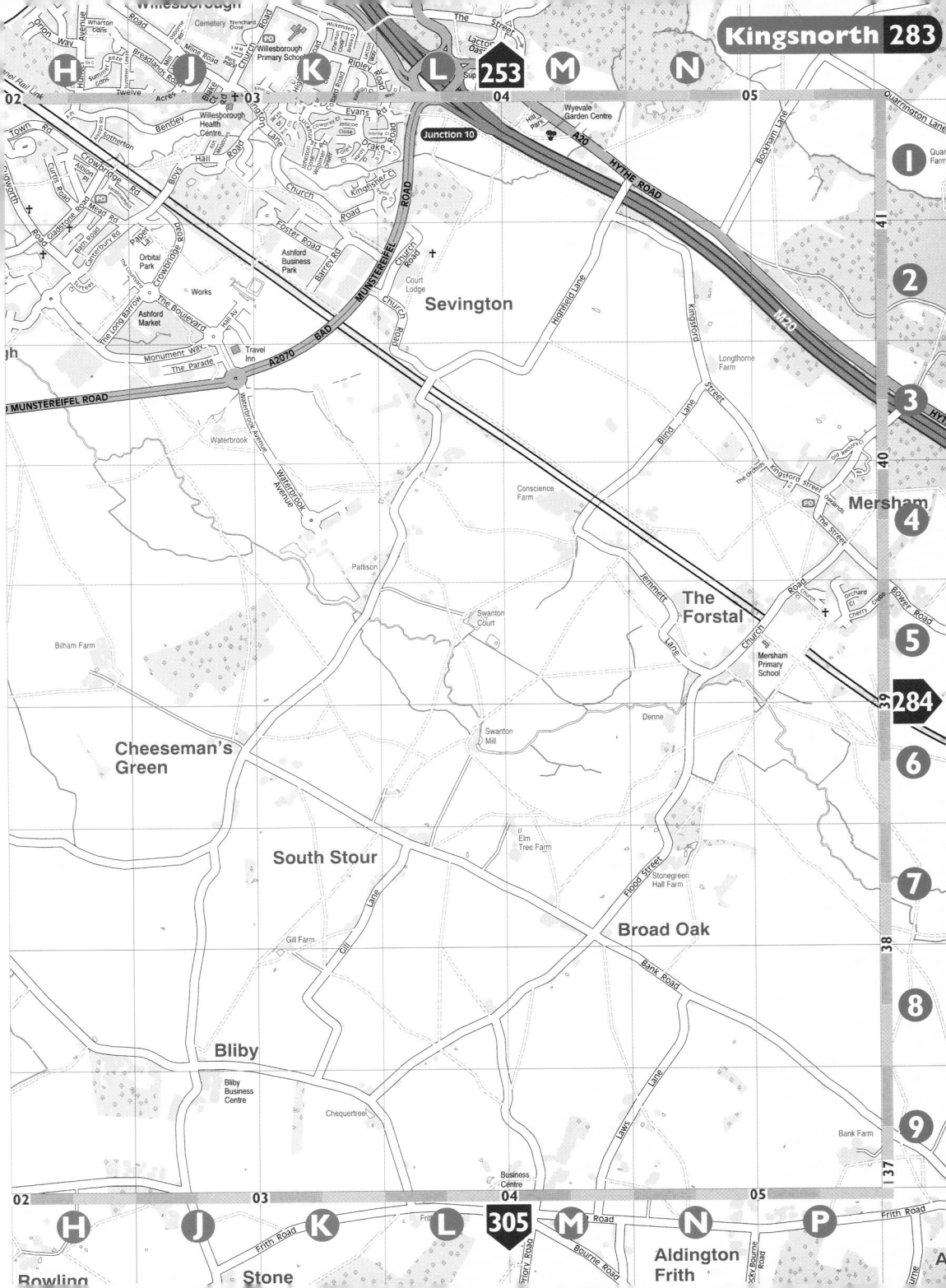

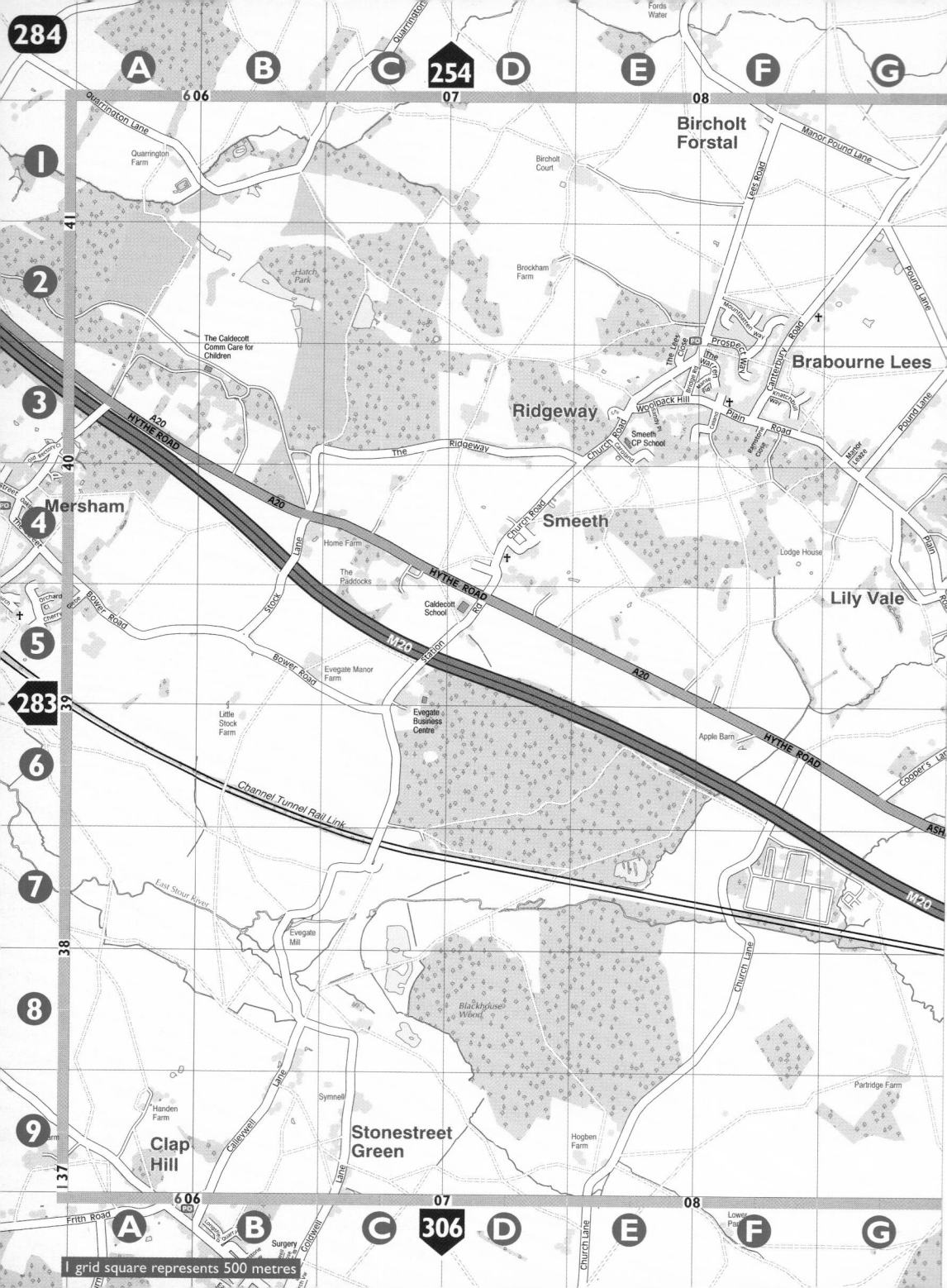

A   B   C   D   E   F   G

6 06   07   08

1
2
3
4
5

6
7
8
9

A   B   C   D   E   F   G

6 06   07   08

41
40
39
38
37

Quarrington Lane
Quarrington Farm
Quarrington
Fords Water

Bircholt Forstal
Manor Pound Lane
Lees Road
Bircholt Court
Brockham Farm
Hatch Park

Pound Lane

The Caldecott Comm Care for Children

Montgomery Way
The Lees
Close
The War Ret
Prospect
Canterbury Road
PO

Brabourne Lees

HYTHE ROAD
A20

Ridgeway
Woolpack Hill
Church Road
Smeeth CP School
Plain
Road
Manor Leas
Pound Lane

Old Stone Ct
Mersham

The Ridgeway
The Street

Home Farm
Stock Lane

Church Road
Smeeth

Lodge House

Lily Vale

Orchard
Cl
Cherry
Bower Road

HYTHE ROAD
The Paddocks
Caldecott School
Station Rd
M20

A20

Bower Road
Evegate Manor Farm
Evegate Business Centre

Apple Barn
HYTHE ROAD
Cooper's Lane

Little Stock Farm

Channel Tunnel Rail Link
ASH
M20

East Stour River
Evegate Mill

Church Lane

Blackhouse Wood

Handen Farm
Calleywell Lane
Symnell

Stonestreet Green
Hogben Farm
Partridge Farm

Clap Hill
Frith Road
PO
Surgery
Coldwell Lane
Church Lane
Lower Pas

I grid square represents 500 metres

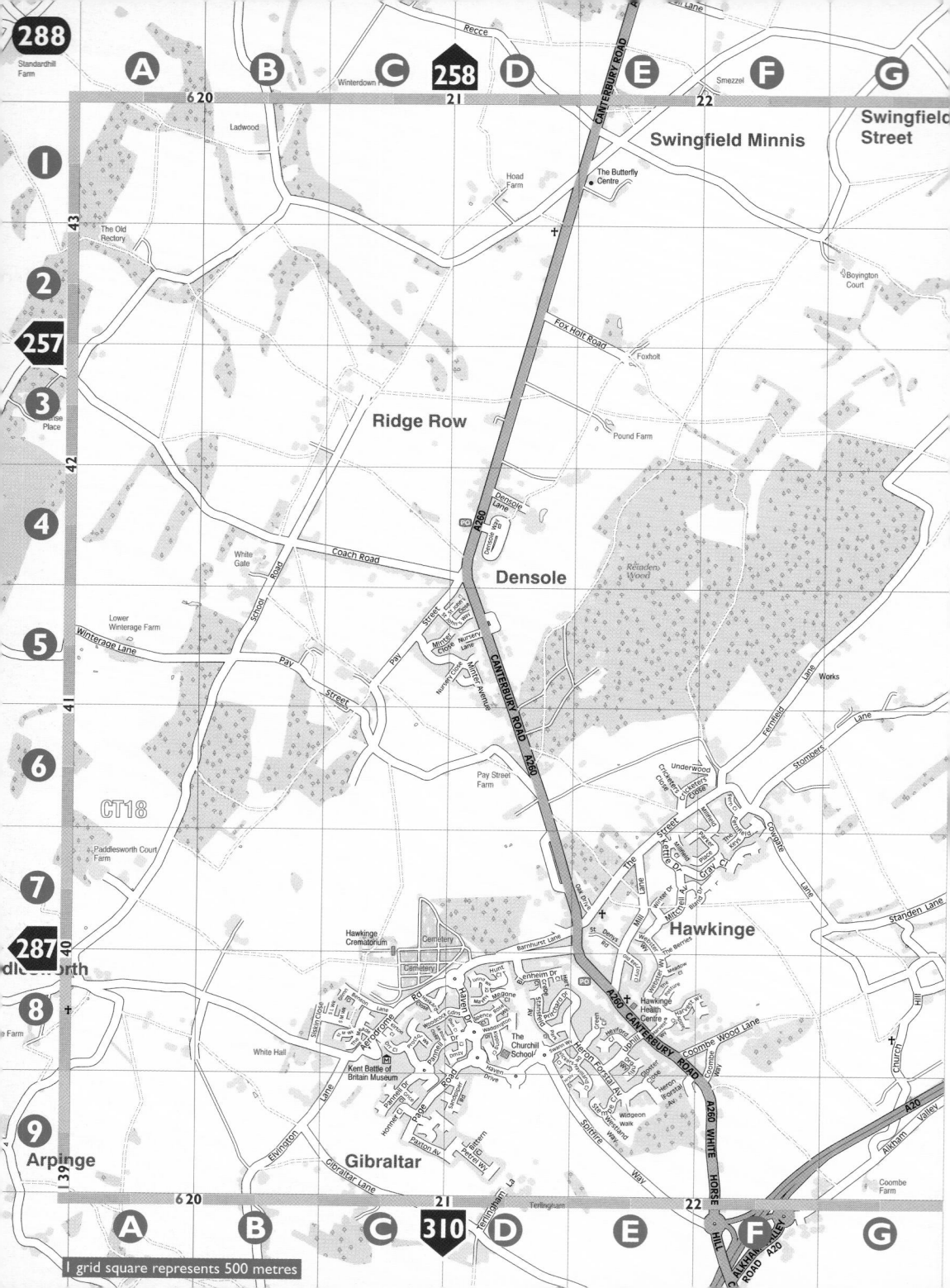

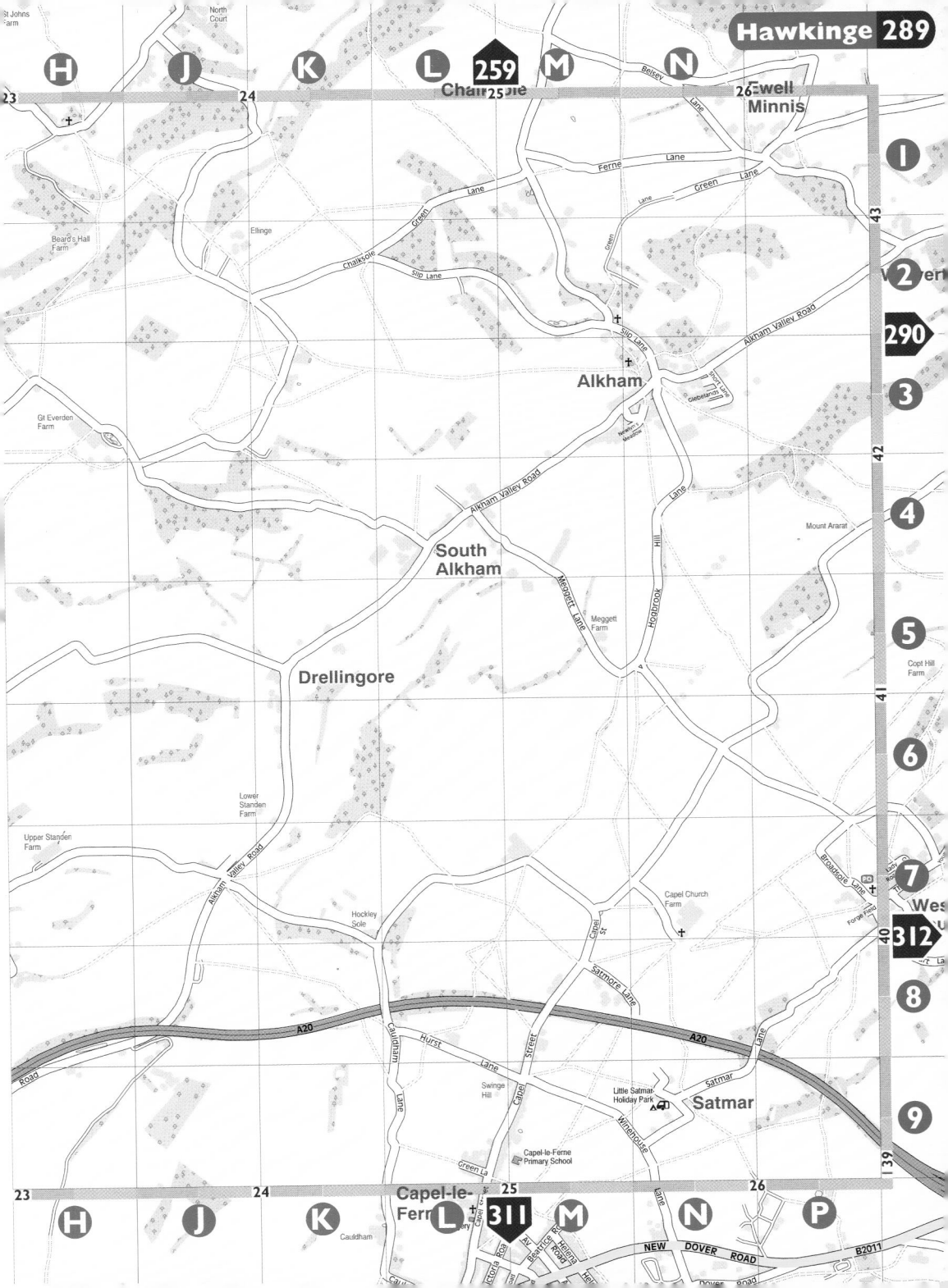

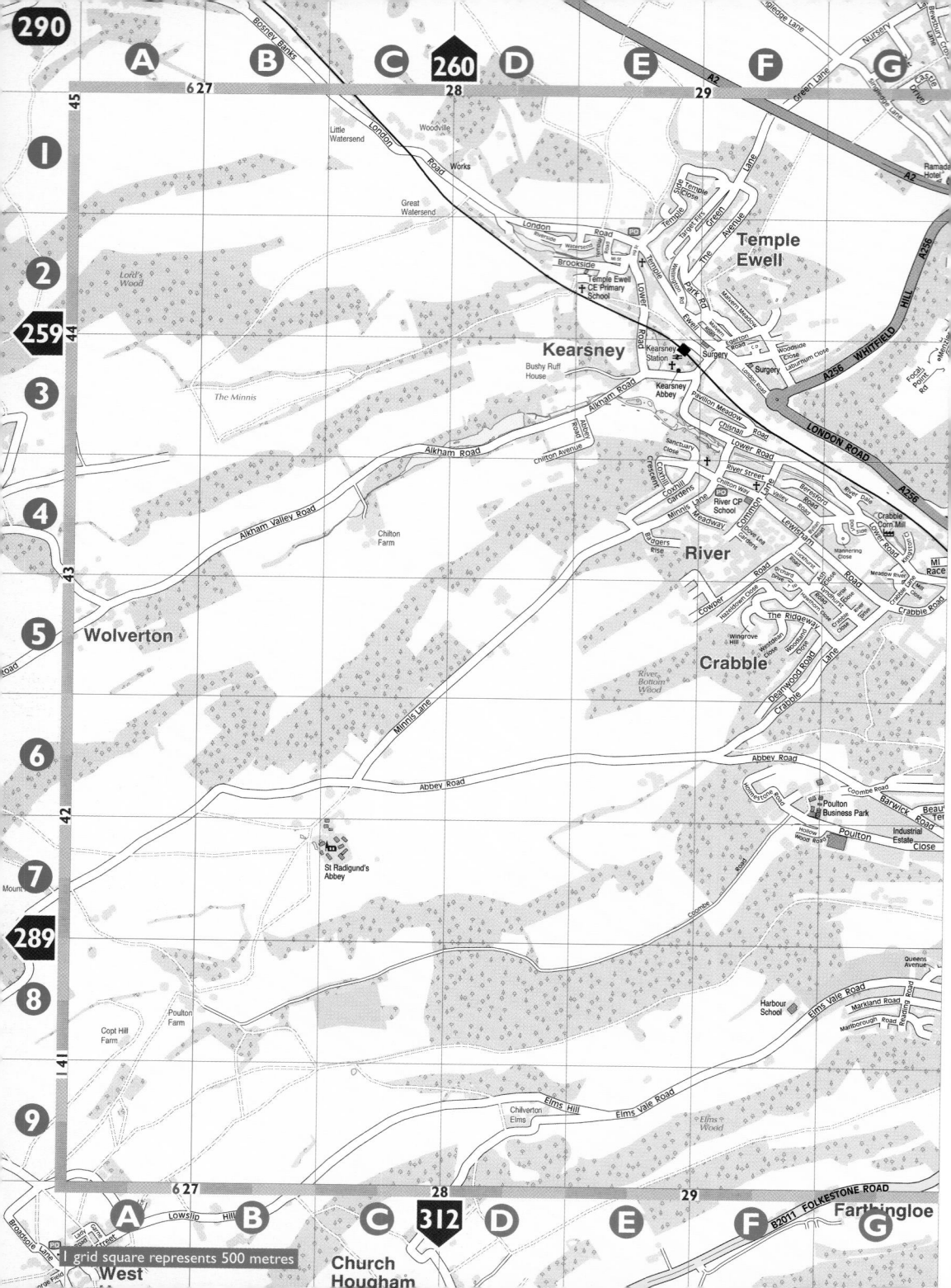

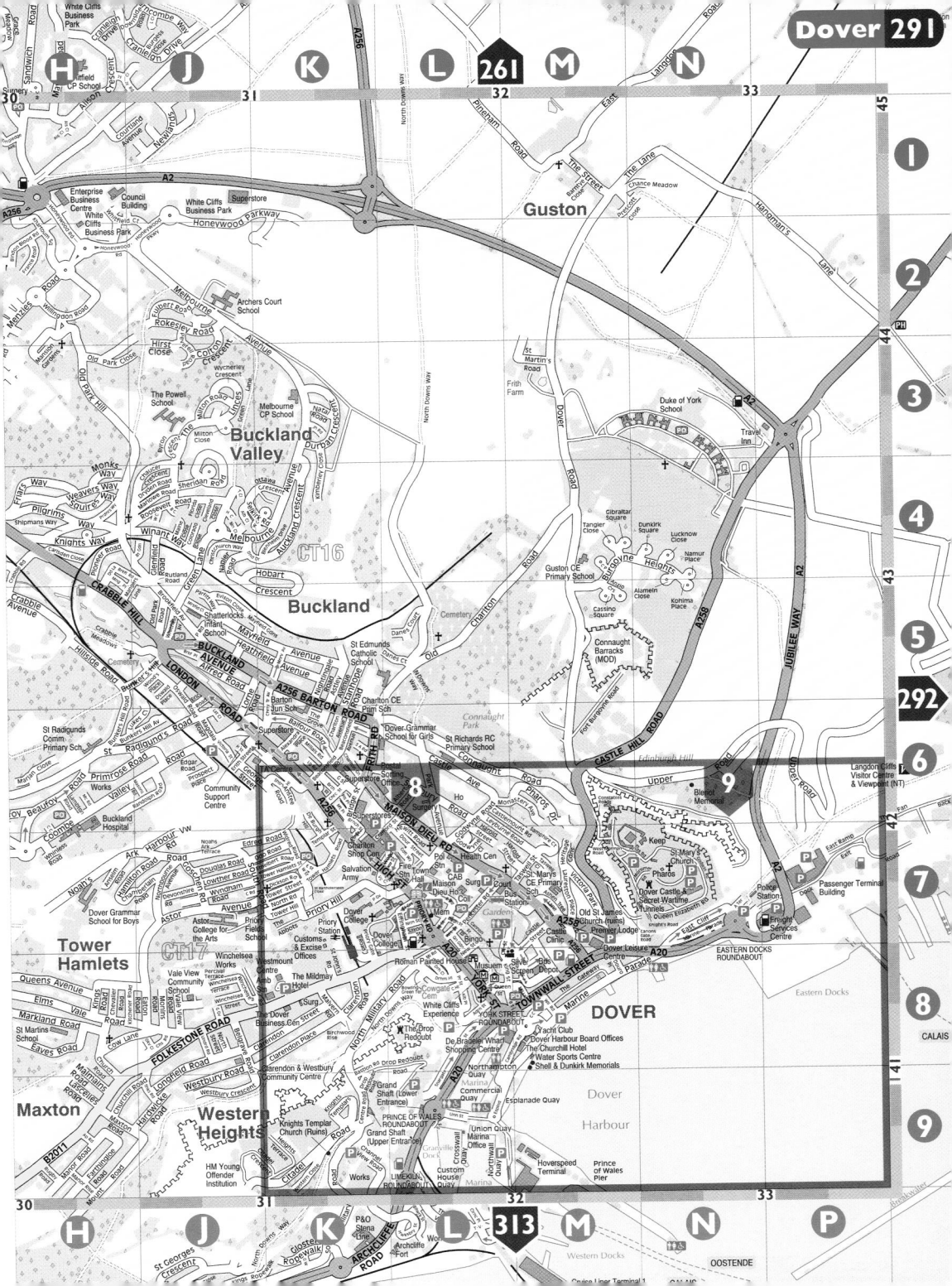

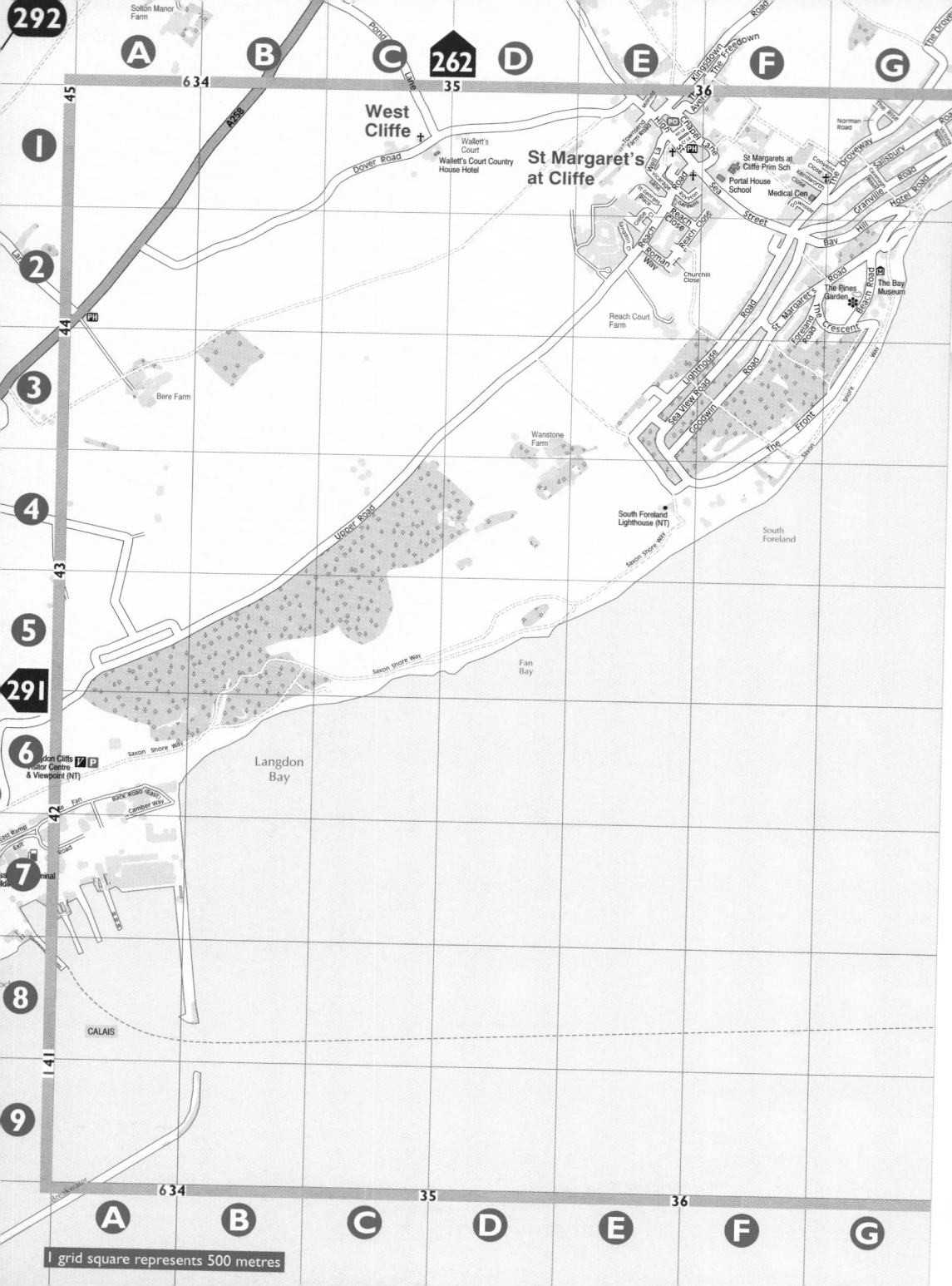

A   B   C   **262**   D   E   F   G

634   45   35   36

Solton Manor Farm

Pond Lane

West Cliffe

Wallett's Court
Wallett's Court Country
House Hotel

Dover Road

St Margaret's at Cliffe

Norman Road

Kingsdown
The Freedown

Droveway

Salisbury

Granville

Hotel Road

Bay

St Margarets at
Cliffe Prim Sch

Portal House
School

Medical Cen

Convent

West La

Sea

Street

Reach Close

Kingsdown Rd

Roman Way

Churchill Close

Reach Court Farm

The Pines Garden

The Bay Museum

Road

Beach Road

1

44

2   PH

3   Bere Farm

Wanstone Farm

Lighthouse Road

Goodwin Road

St Margaret's Road

The Crescent

Foreland Road

4

43

Upper Road

Sea View Road

The Front

South Foreland Lighthouse (NT)

South Foreland

5

Saxon Shore Way

Fan Bay

6   Langdon Cliffs
Visitor Centre
& Viewpoint (NT)

Saxon Shore Way

Langdon Bay

42   Fan

Back Road East

Camber Way

Road

Exit

7   Terminal

8

CALAIS

41

9

634   35   36

A   B   C   D   E   F   G

1 grid square represents 500 metres

St Margaret's Bay

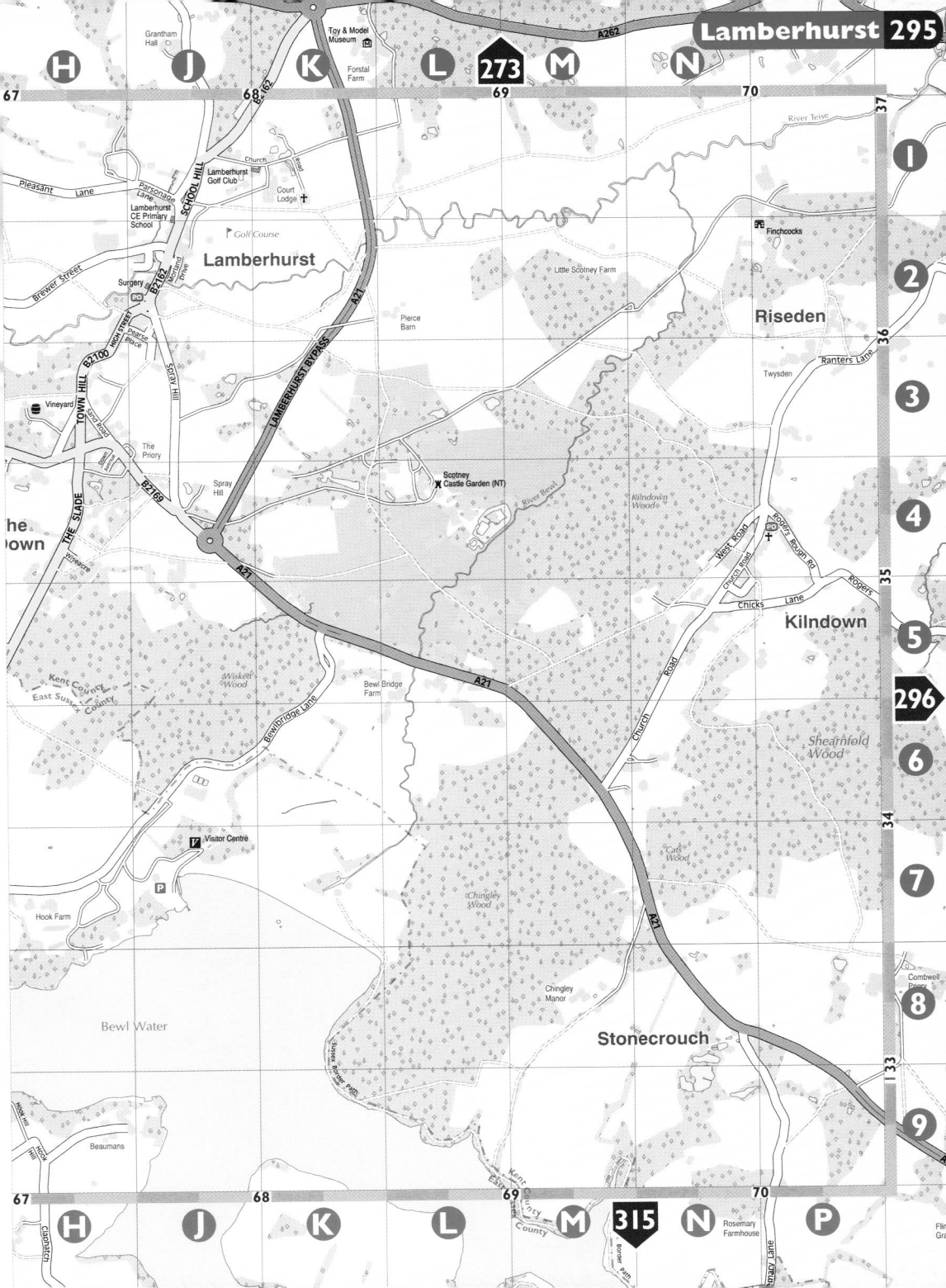

H J K L **273** M N

67 68 B2162 69 A262 70

River Teise

Grantham Hall

Toy & Model Museum

Forstal Farm

I 37

Pleasant Lane

Brewer Street

SCHOOL HILL

Parsonage Lane

Lamberhurst CE Primary School

Church

Lamberhurst Golf Club

Court Lodge

Finchcocks

2 36

Golf Course

Surgery

B2102

Lamberhurst

Pierce Barn

Little Scotney Farm

Riseden

Ranters Lane

Twysden

3

Orchard Drive

Denise Place

B2100

Vineyard

TOWN HILL

Spray Hill

The Priory

LAMBERHURST BYPASS

A21

Scotney Castle Garden (NT)

River Bewl

Kilndown Woods

4 35

The SLADE

B2169

Spray Hill

West Road

Rogers Rough Rd

Church Road

Chicks Lane

Kilndown

5

The Down

Kents County East Sussex County

Wiskett's Wood

Bewlbridge Lane

Bewl Bridge Farm

A21

Church Road

Shearnfold Wood

Rogers

296

6 34

Visitor Centre

P

Hook Farm

Chingley Wood

Cat's Wood

7

Bewl Water

Chingley Manor

Combwell Priory

8 33

Beaumans

Hook Hill

Stonecrouch

A21

9 A

67 68 69 70

H J K L M **315** N P

Kent County

Rosemary Farmhouse

Flimwell Gra

Claphatch

Sussex Border Path

Border Path

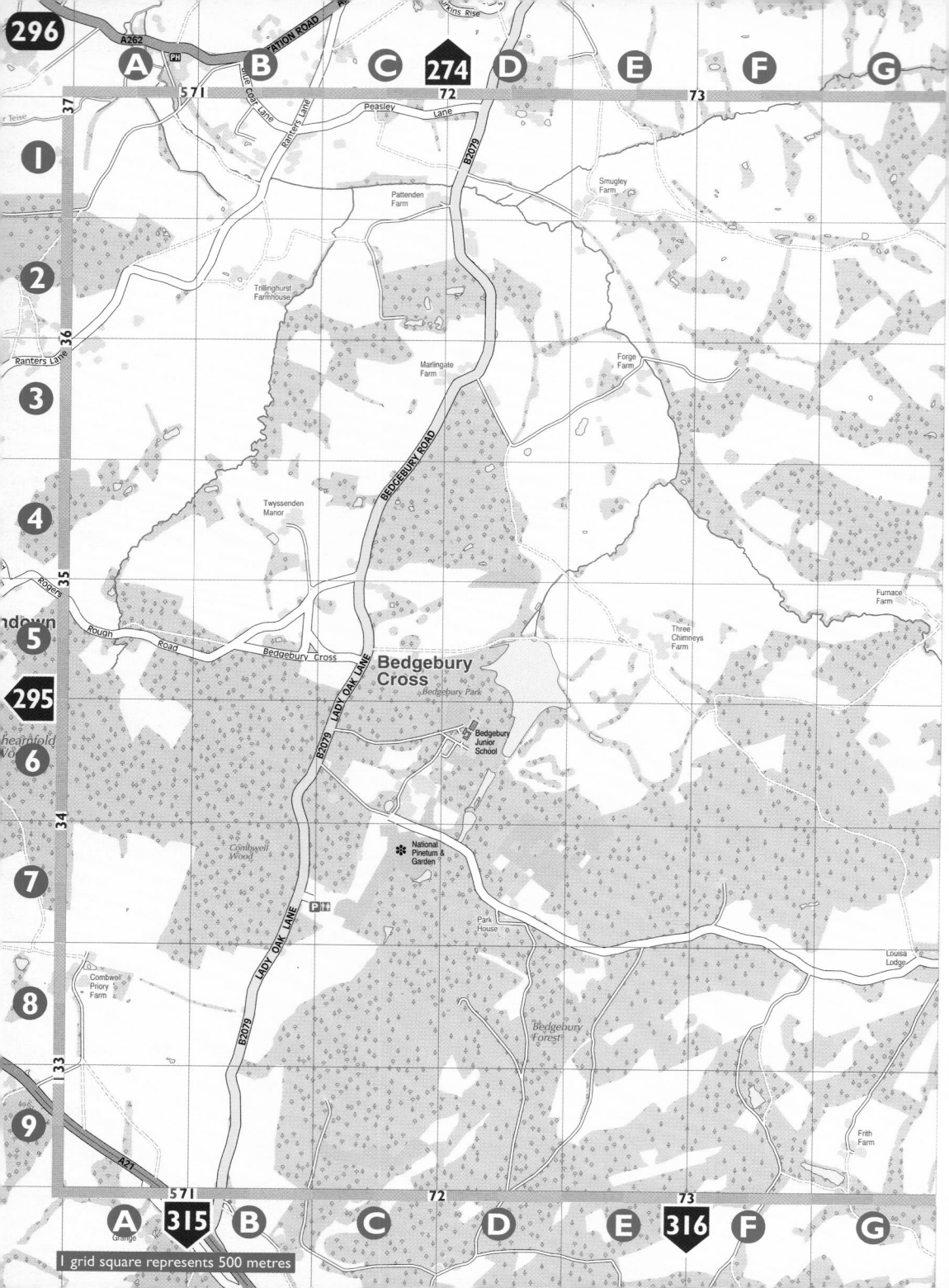

I grid square represents 500 metres

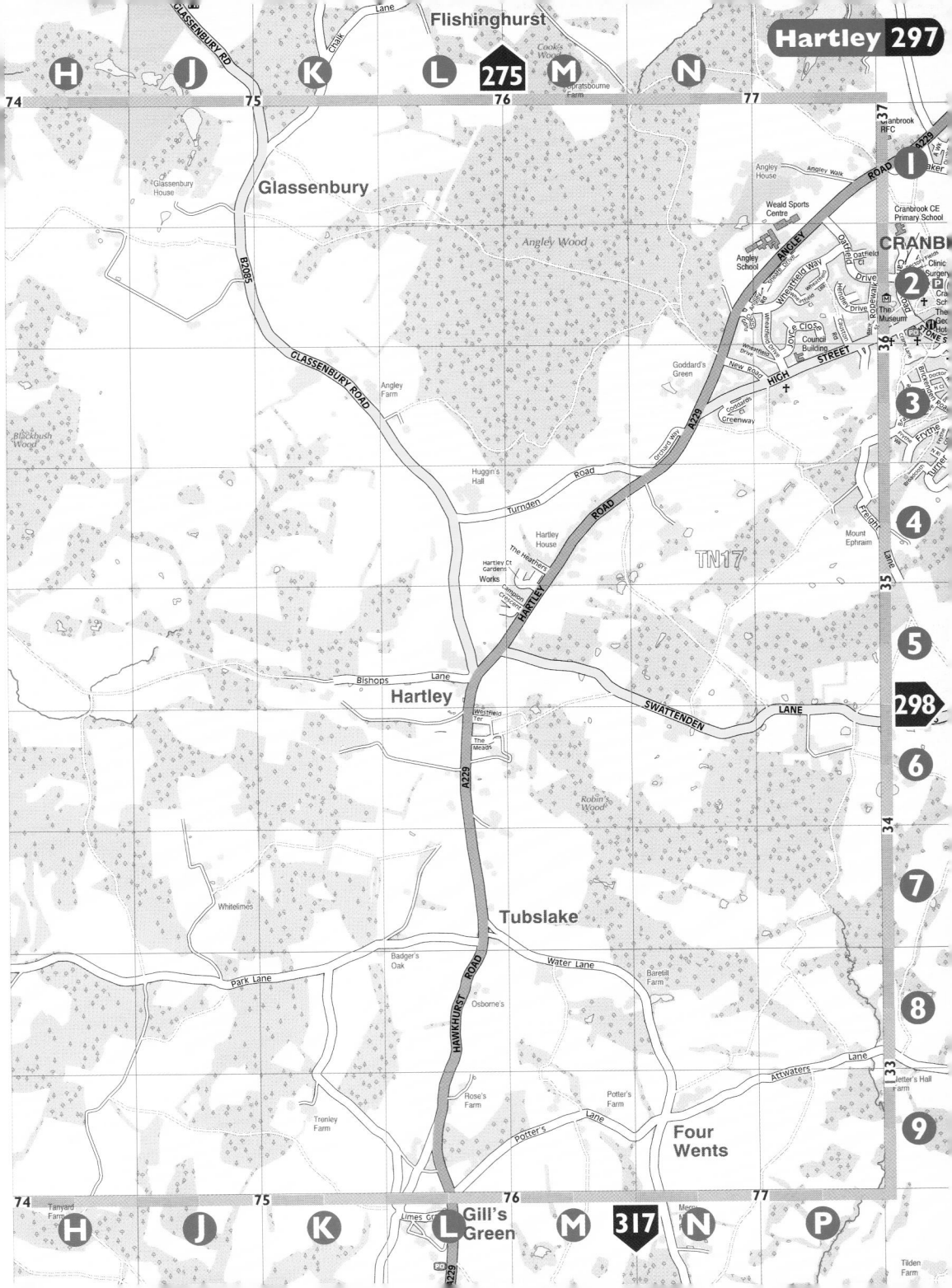

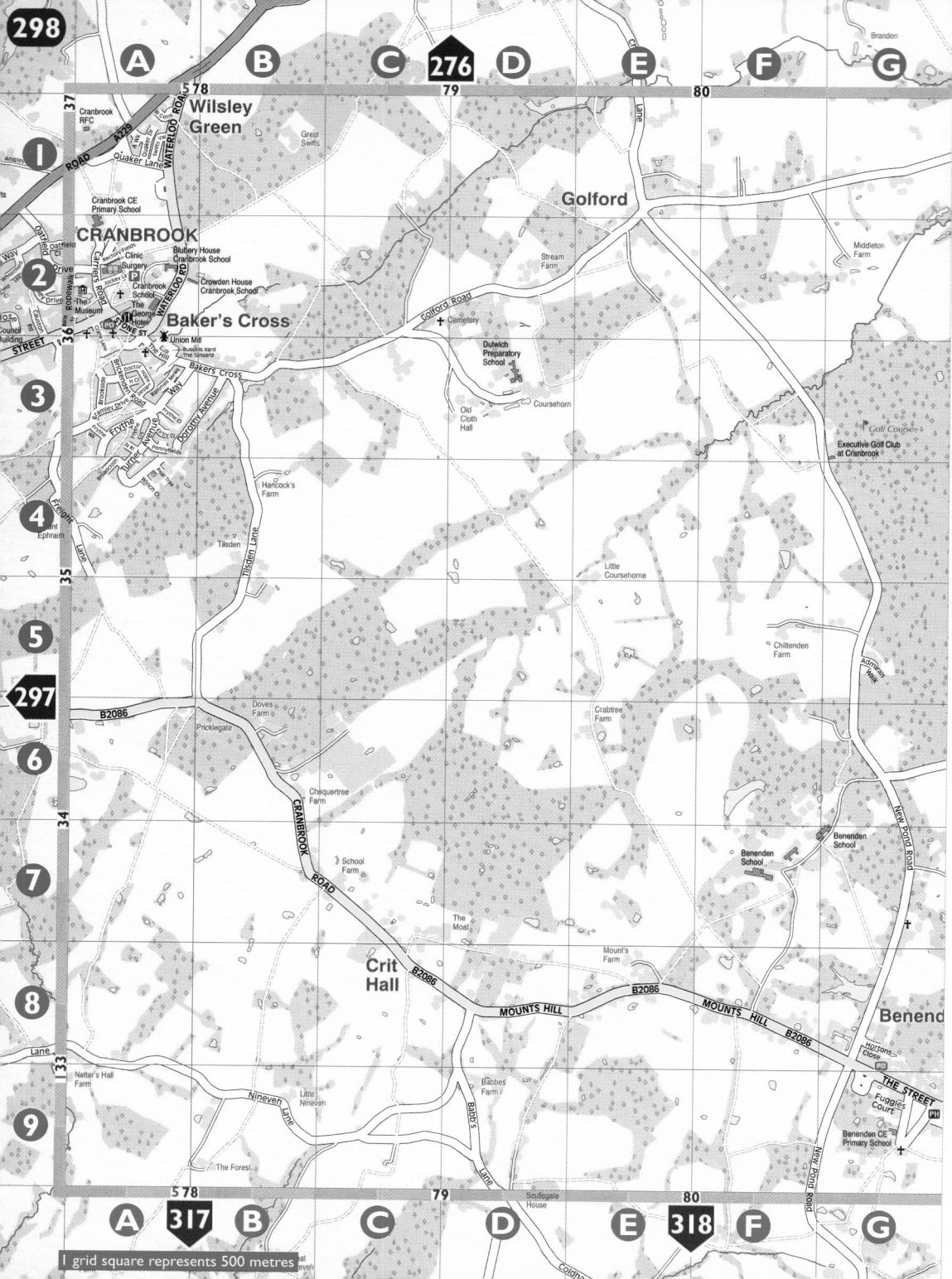

A B C **276** D E F G

79 80

I

Anglia

Cranbrook
RFC

37
Cranbrook
ROAD
Quaker Lane
578
WATERLOO ROAD
Wilsley
Green
Great
Swifts

Golford

Cranbrook CE
Primary School

CRANBROOK
2
Oatfield
Drive
Carriers Road
Bulbery House
Cranbrook School
Stream
Farm
Middleton
Farm

Clarton Rd
Crowden House
Cranbrook School

Surgery
Jockey's La
Cranbrook
School
The
George
Hotel
STONE ST
Museum
Colford Road
Cemetery

36
STREET
Baker's Cross
Union Mill
Russells Yard
The Tanyard
Dulwich
Preparatory
School

Coursehorn

3
Bakers Cross
Hancock's
Farm
Old Cloth
Hall
Golf Course

Executive Golf Club
at Cranbrook

Brackendene

Turner Avenue
Dorothy Avenue
Erryne

35
4
Mount
Ephraim
Freight
Lane
Tilsden

Tilsden Lane
Little
Coursehorne

5
Chiltenden
Farm
Admirals
Walk

297
34
B2086
Doves
Farm
Pricklegate
Crabtree
Farm
New Pond Road

6
Chequertree
Farm
Benenden
School
Benenden
School

7
CRANBROOK ROAD
School
Farm
The
Moat
Mount's
Farm

8
Crit
Hall
B2086
MOUNTS HILL
B2086
MOUNTS HILL B2086
Benend

33
Lane
Netter's Hall
Farm
Nineveh Lane
Little
Nineveh
Babbs
Farm
Hortons
Close
THE STREET
Fuggles
Court

9
Babbs Lane
Benenden CE
Primary School

The Forest
Scullsgale
House

578 79 80

I grid square represents 500 metres

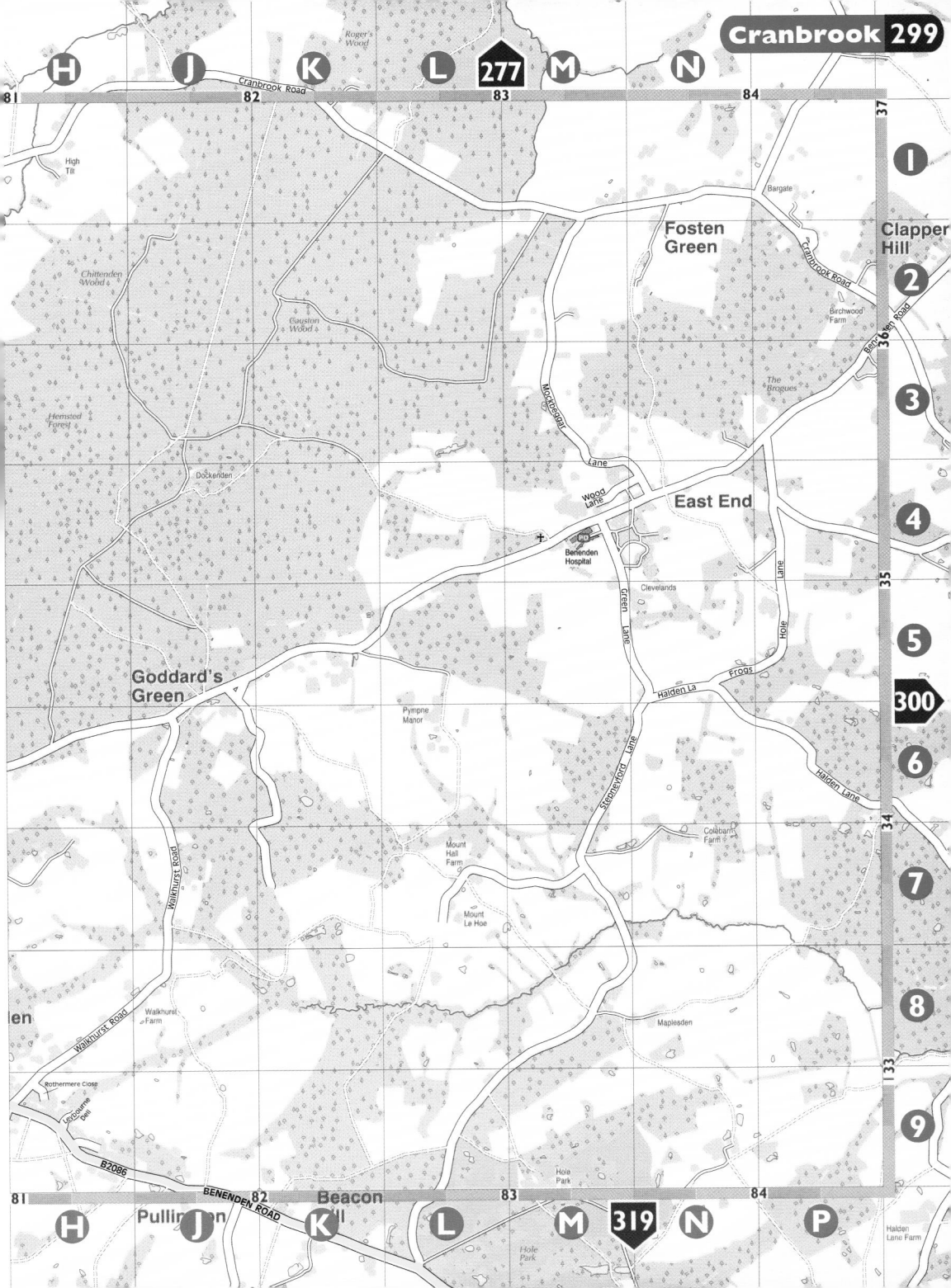

H J K L 277 M N

Cranbrook Road

81 82 83 84 37

Roger's Wood

High Tilt

I

Bargate

Fosten Green

Clapper Hill

Cranbrook Road

2

Chittenden Wood

Gauston Wood

Birchwood Farm

36

Benzen Road

The Brogues

3

Hemsted Forest

Mockbeggar Lane

4

Dockenden

Wood Lane

East End

35

Benenden Hospital

Clevelands

5

Green Lane

Hole Lane

Frogs

300

Goddard's Green

Halden La

6

Pympne Manor

Halden Lane

Stepneyford Lane

34

Coleham Farm

Mount Hall Farm

7

Walkhurst Road

Mount Le Hoe

8

Mapleden

Walkhurst Farm

133

Rothermere Close

9

Lencoine Dell

B2086

Walkhurst Road

Benenden Road

Beacon Hill

Hole Park

81 82 83 84

H J K L M 319 N P

Pullington

Beacon Road

Hole Park

Halden Lane Farm

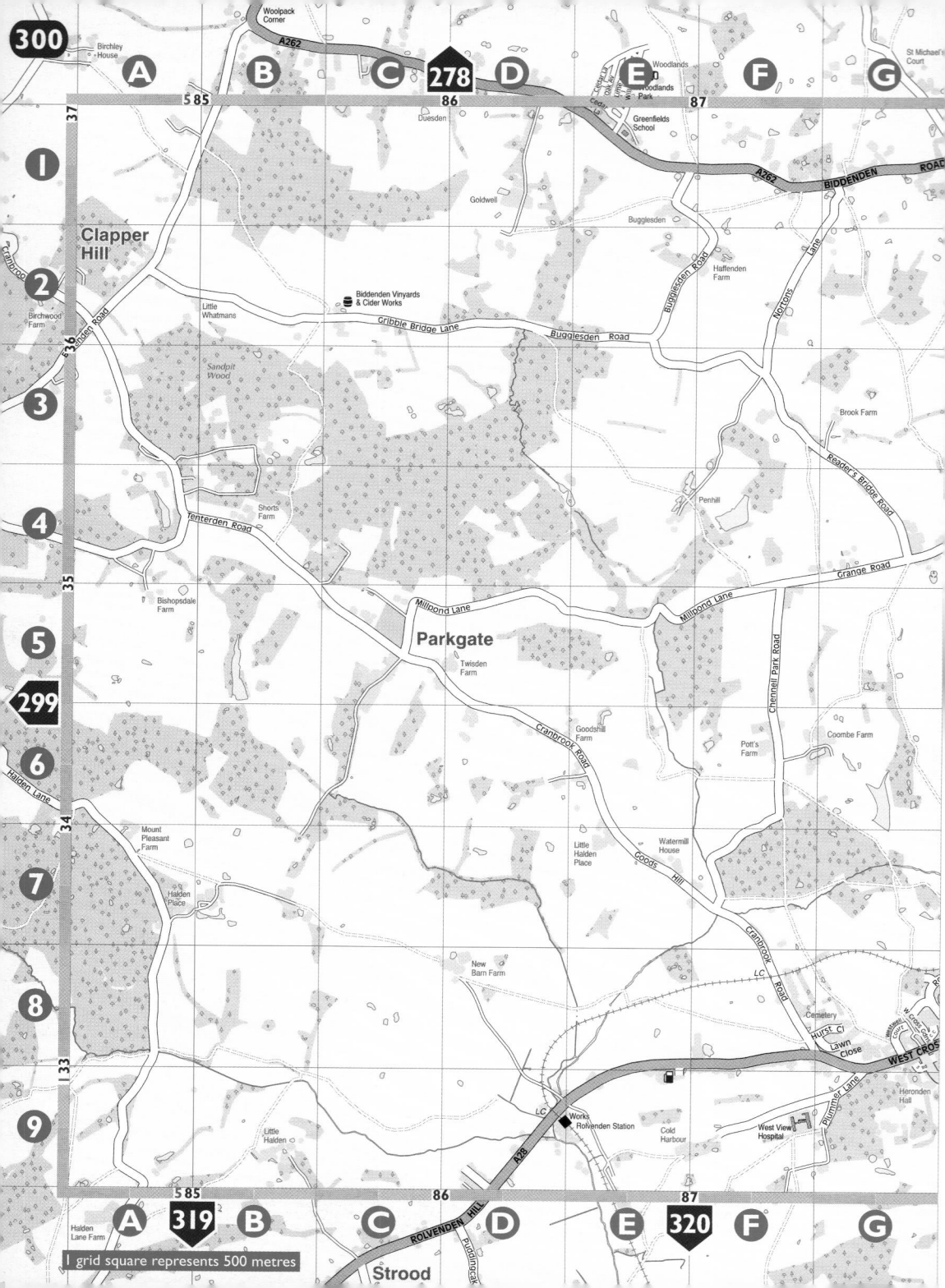

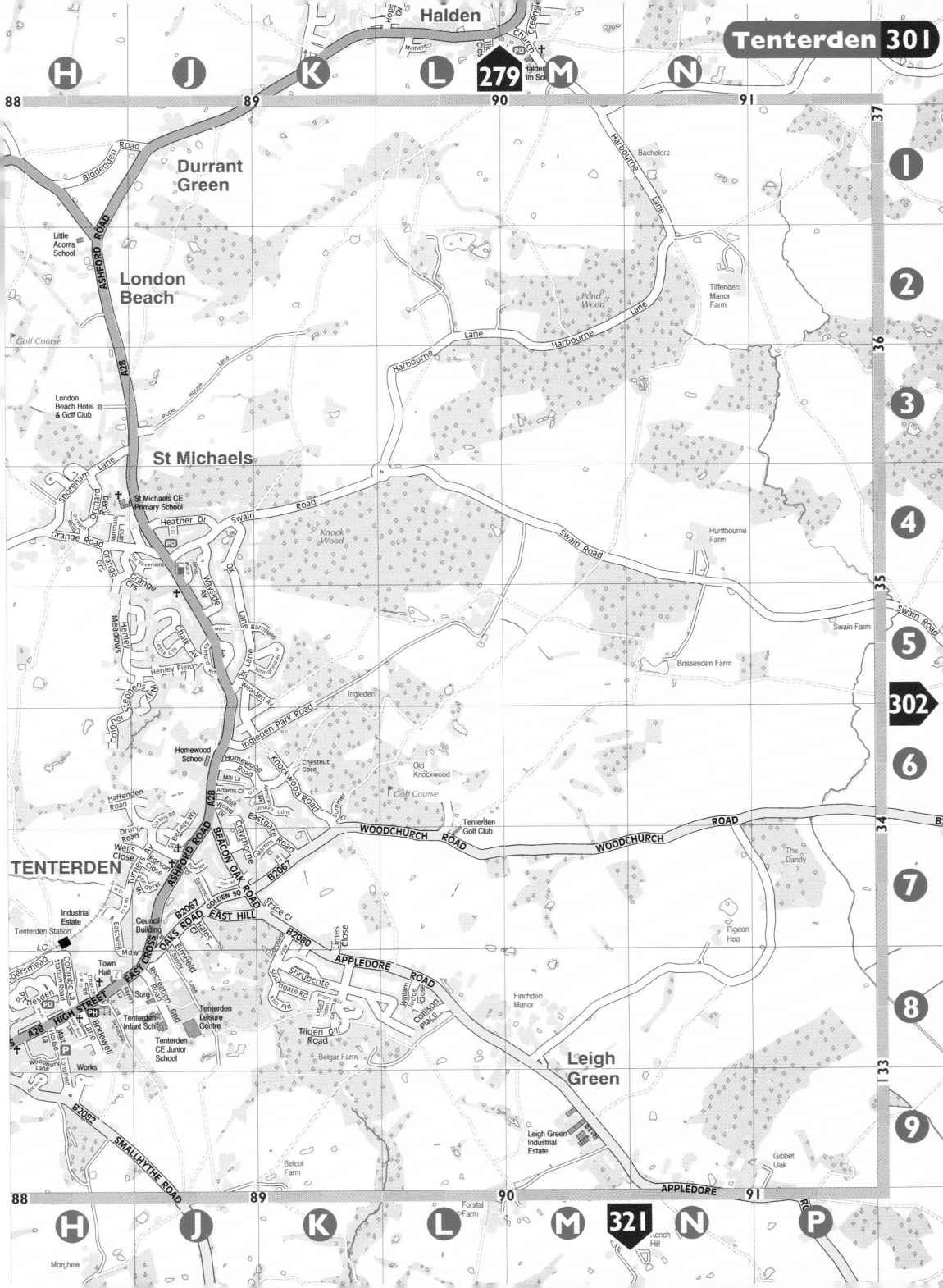

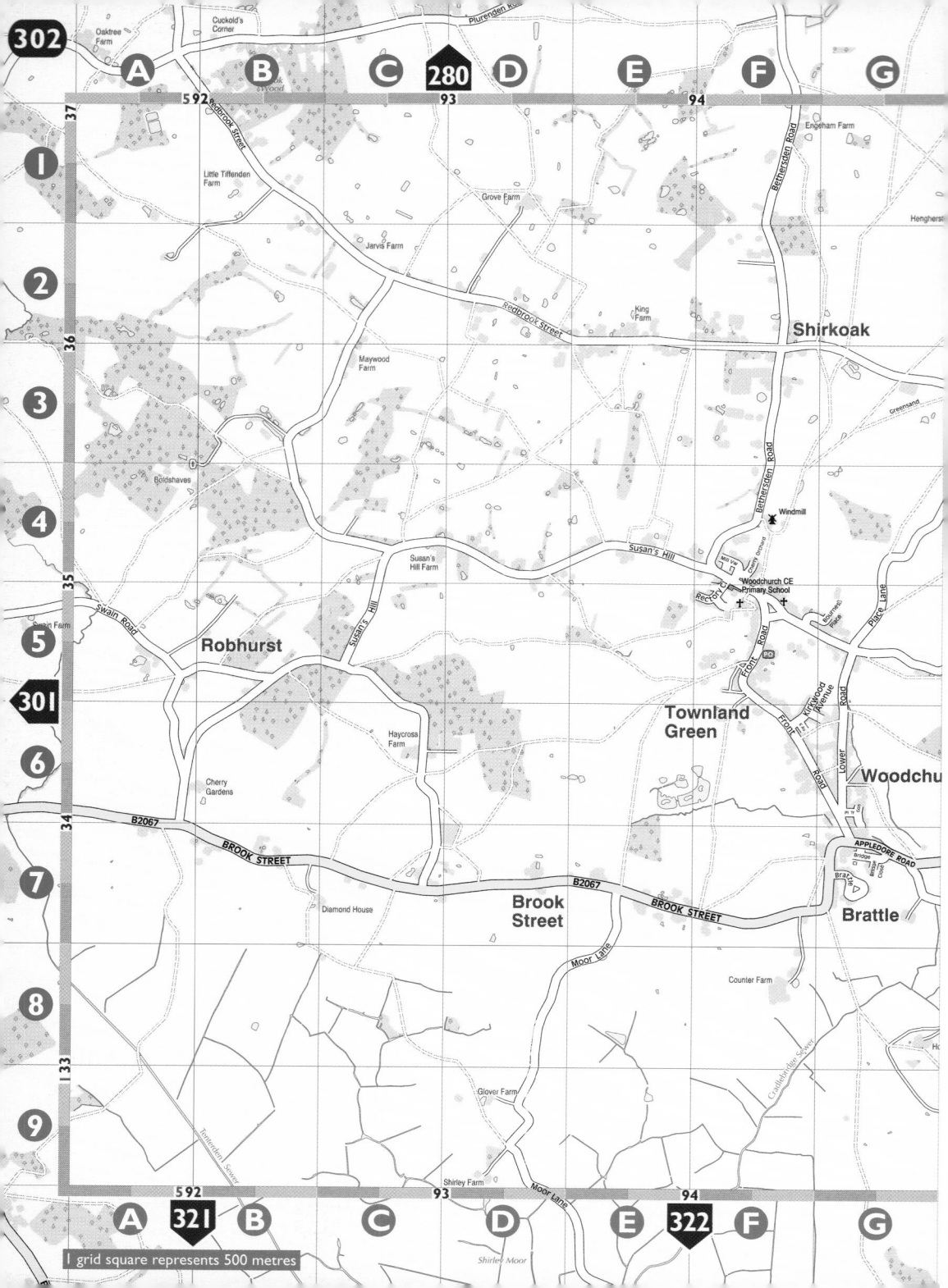

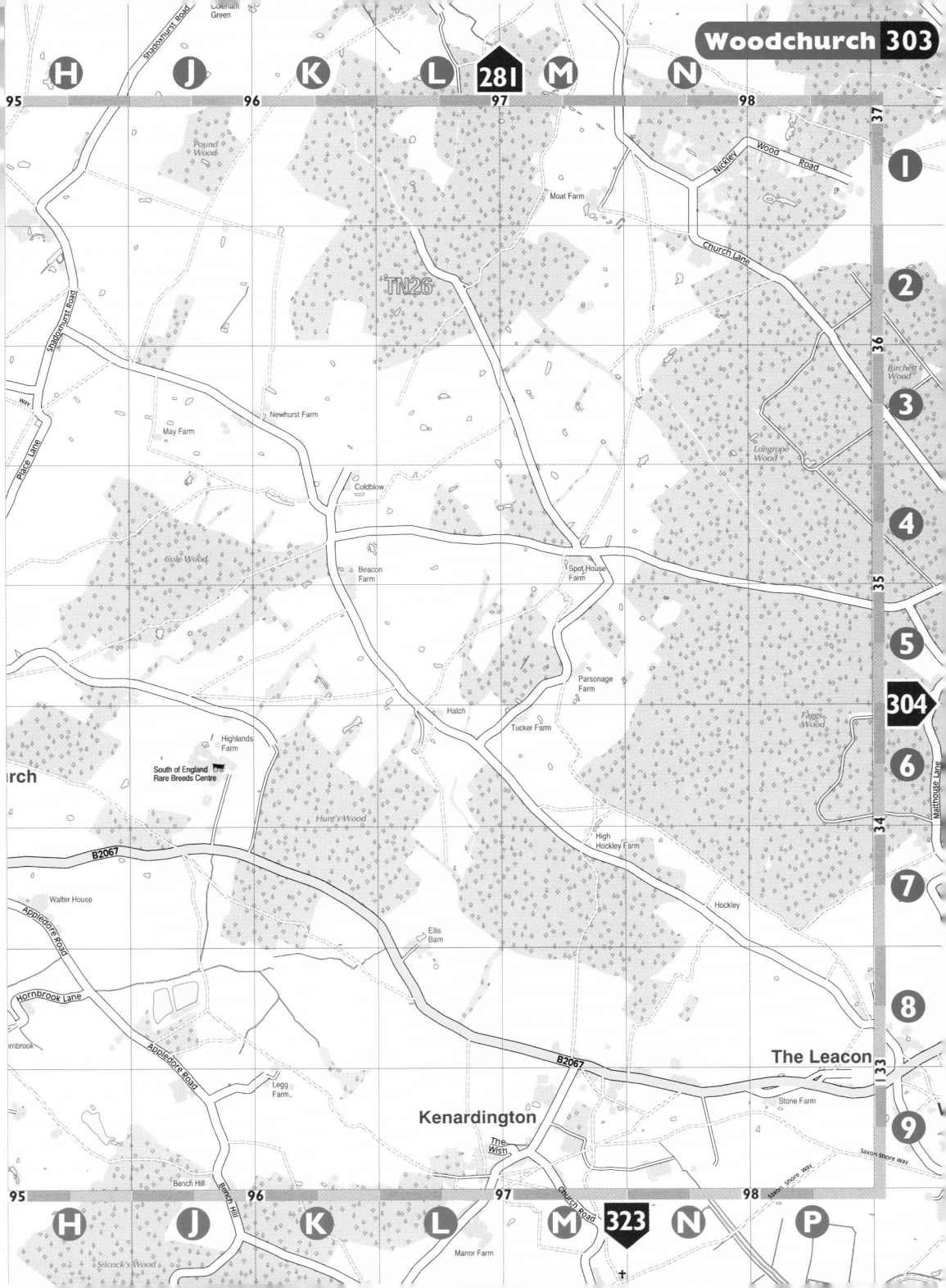

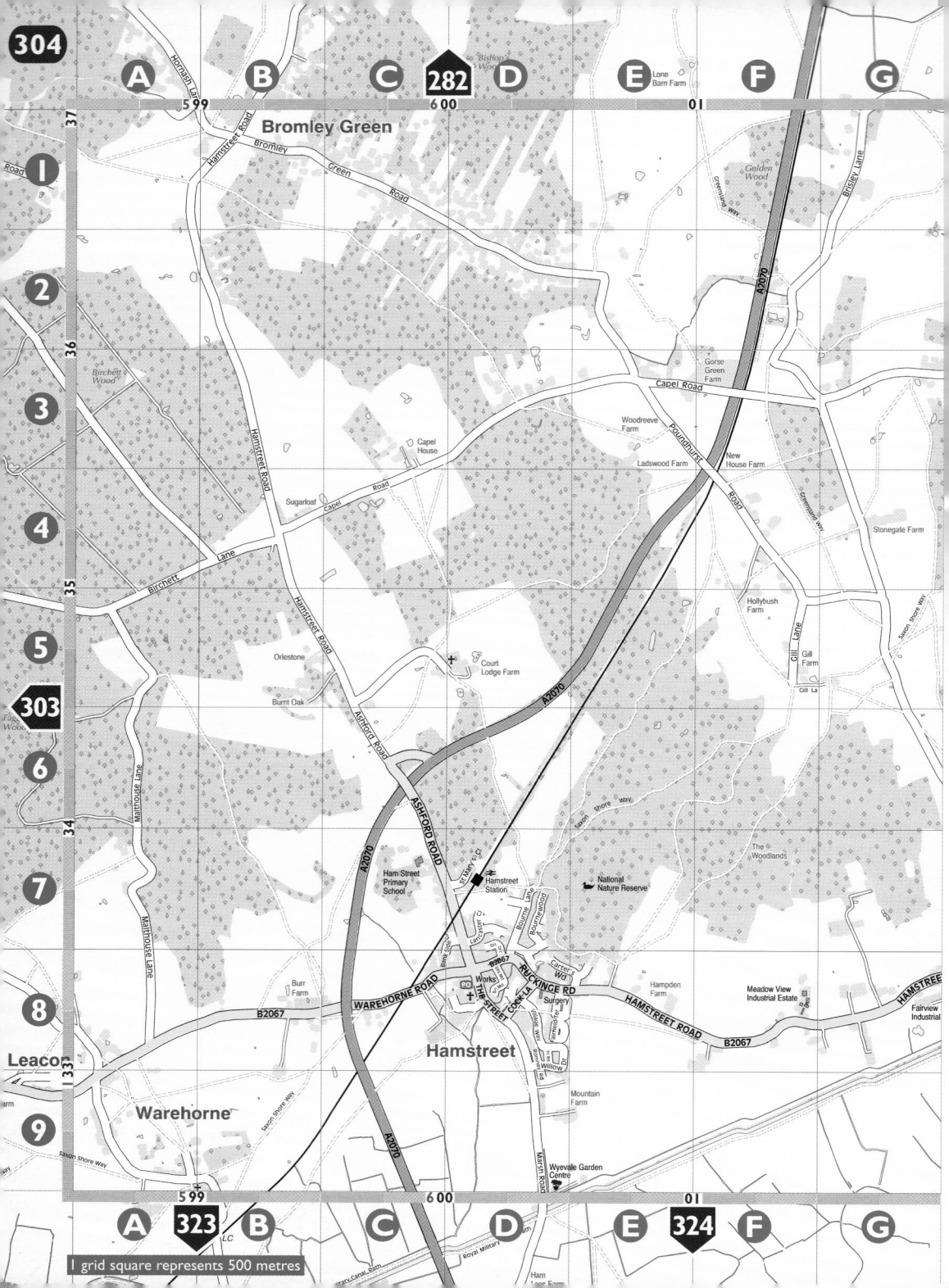

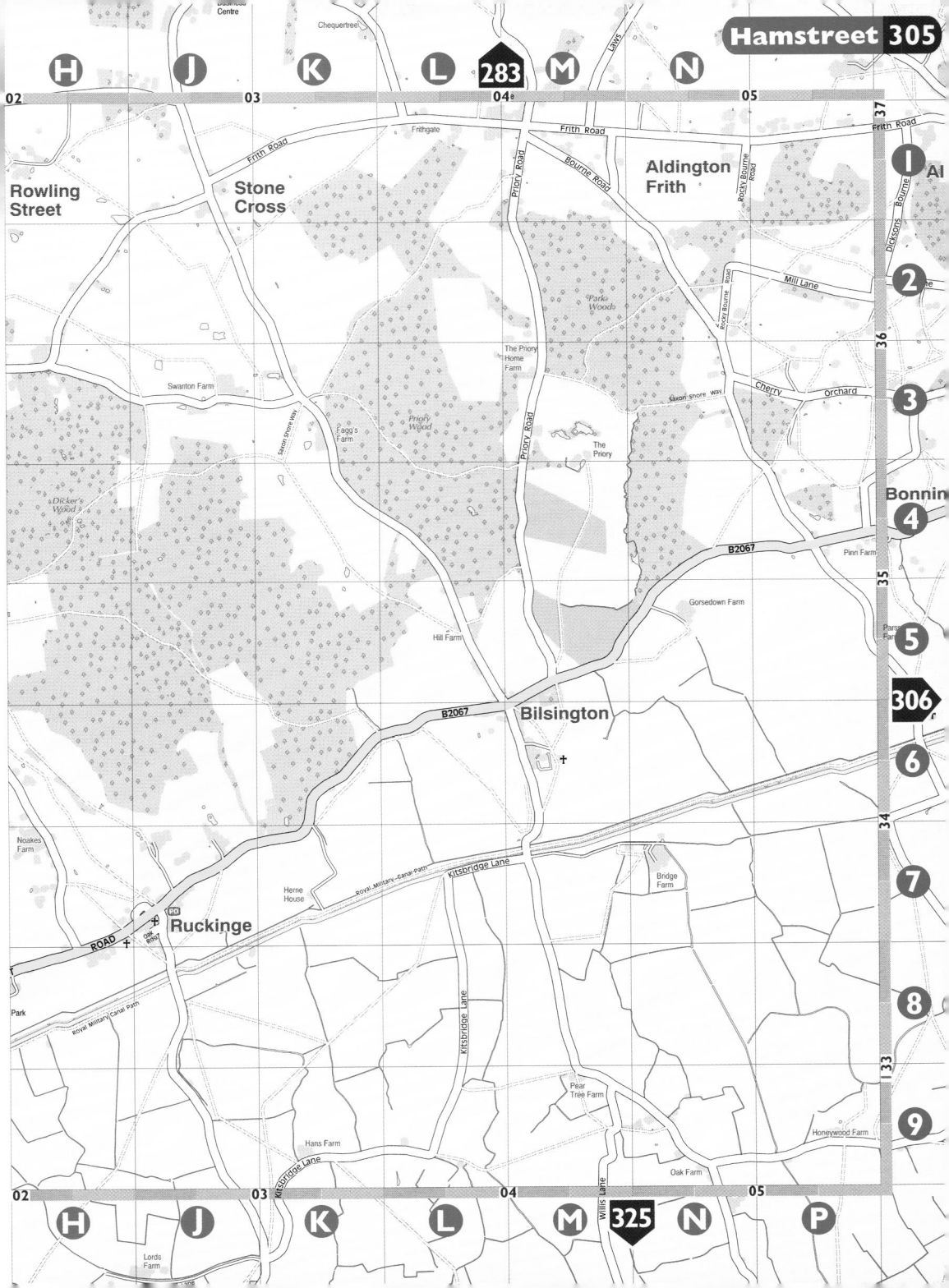

283

H J K L M N

02 03 04 05

Frithgate

Frith Road

Chequertree

Laws

Business
Centre

Frith Road

Stone
Cross

Priory Road

Bourne Road

Aldington
Frith

Rocky Bourne Road

Dicksons Bourne

Frith Road

I Al

37

Rowling
Street

Swanton Farm

Saxon Shore Way

Fagg's
Farm

Priory
Wood

Dicker's
Wood

Parks
Woods

The Priory
Home
Farm

Priory Road

Saxon Shore Way

The Priory

Rocky Bourne Road

Mill Lane

Cherry   Orchard

2

3

Bonnin

4

36

35

B2067

Pinn Farm

Gorsedown Farm

Hill Farm

B2067

Bilsington

Pars
Farm

5

306

6

Noakes
Farm

Herne
House

Royal Military Canal Path

Kitsbridge Lane

Bridge
Farm

34

7

ROAD

Ruckinge

Royal Military Canal Path

Park

Kitsbridge Lane

Kitsbridge Lane

Pear
Tree Farm

8

I33

9

Hans Farm

Kitsbridge Lane

Willis Lane

Oak Farm

Honeywood Farm

02 03 04 05

H J K L M N P

Lords
Farm

325

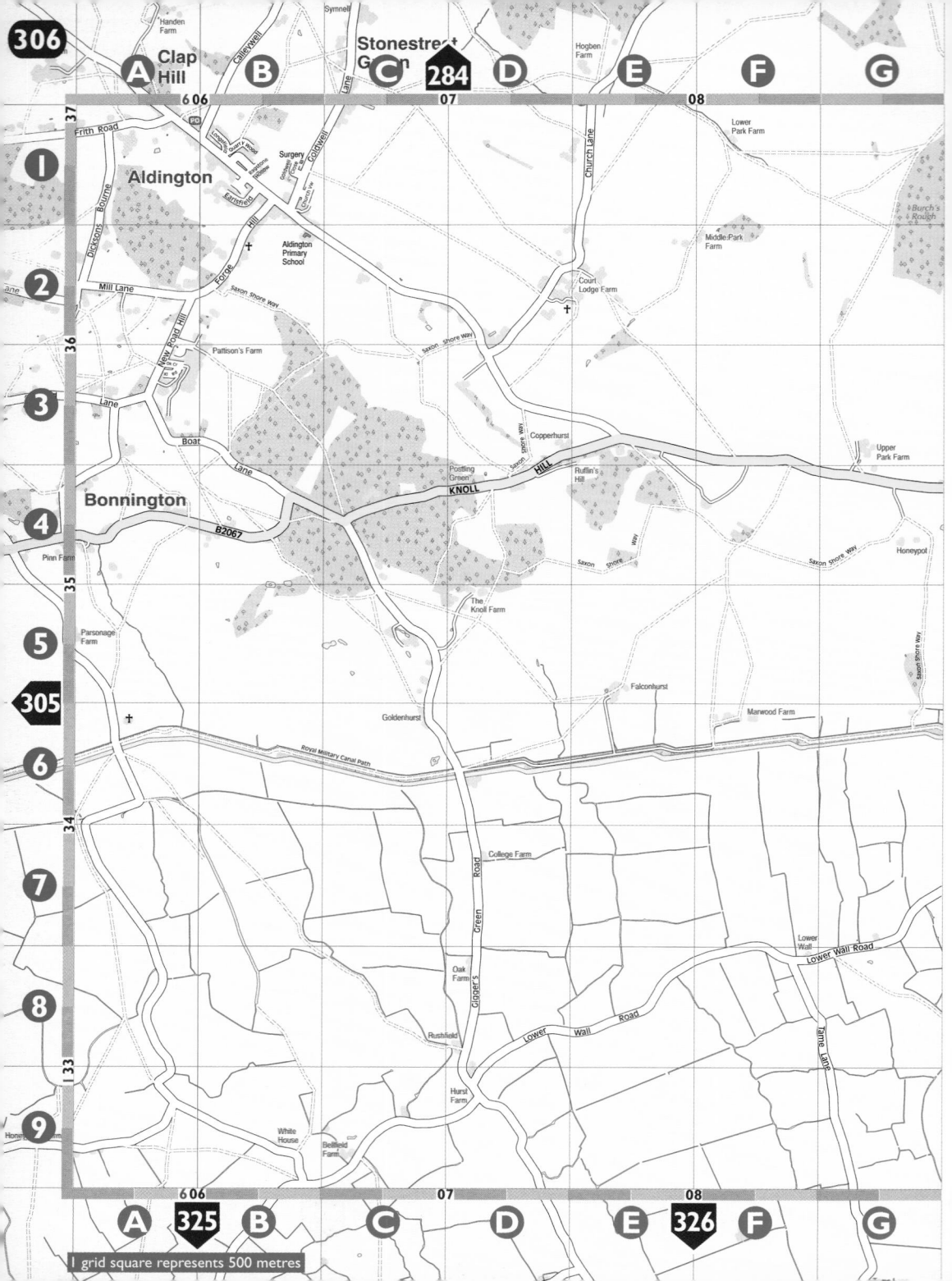

A **Clap Hill**

B

Stonestreet Green

C

D

E

F

G

6 06
07
08

I

Frith Road

Aldington

Handen Farm

Callerwell Lane

Symnell Lane

Hogben Farm

Lower Park Farm

Burch's Rough

Dicksons Bourne

Earnsfield

Surgery

Forge Hill

Coldwell

Church Lane

Middle Park Farm

2

Mill Lane

Aldington Primary School

Court Lodge Farm

3

Lane

New Road Hill

Pattison's Farm

Saxon Shore Way

Copperhurst

Upper Park Farm

Boat Lane

Postling Green

KNOLL HILL

Ruffin's Hill

4

Bonnington

B2067

Saxon Shore Way

The Knoll Farm

Saxon shore Way

Honeypot

Saxon Shore Way

Pinn Farm

5

Parsonage Farm

Falconhurst

Marwood Farm

Saxon Shore Way

6

Goldenhurst

Royal Military Canal Path

7

College Farm

8

Green Road

Oak Farm

Gigger's Road

Rushfield

Lower Wall Road

Lower Wall Road

Tame Lane

9

Honey

White House

Bellfield Farm

Hurst Farm

37

36

35

34

I 33

6 06
07
08

A

B

C

D

E

F

G

I grid square represents 500 metres

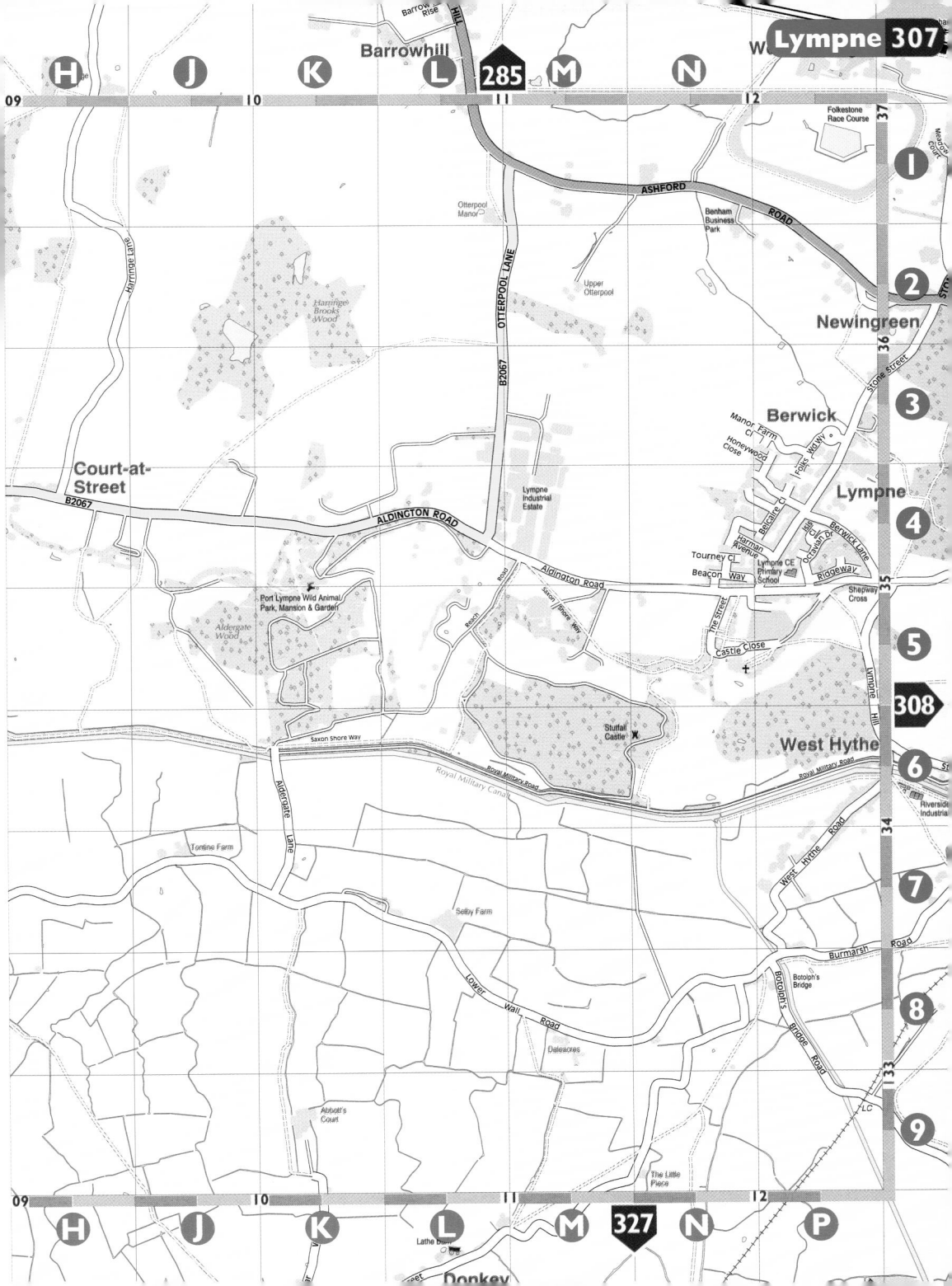

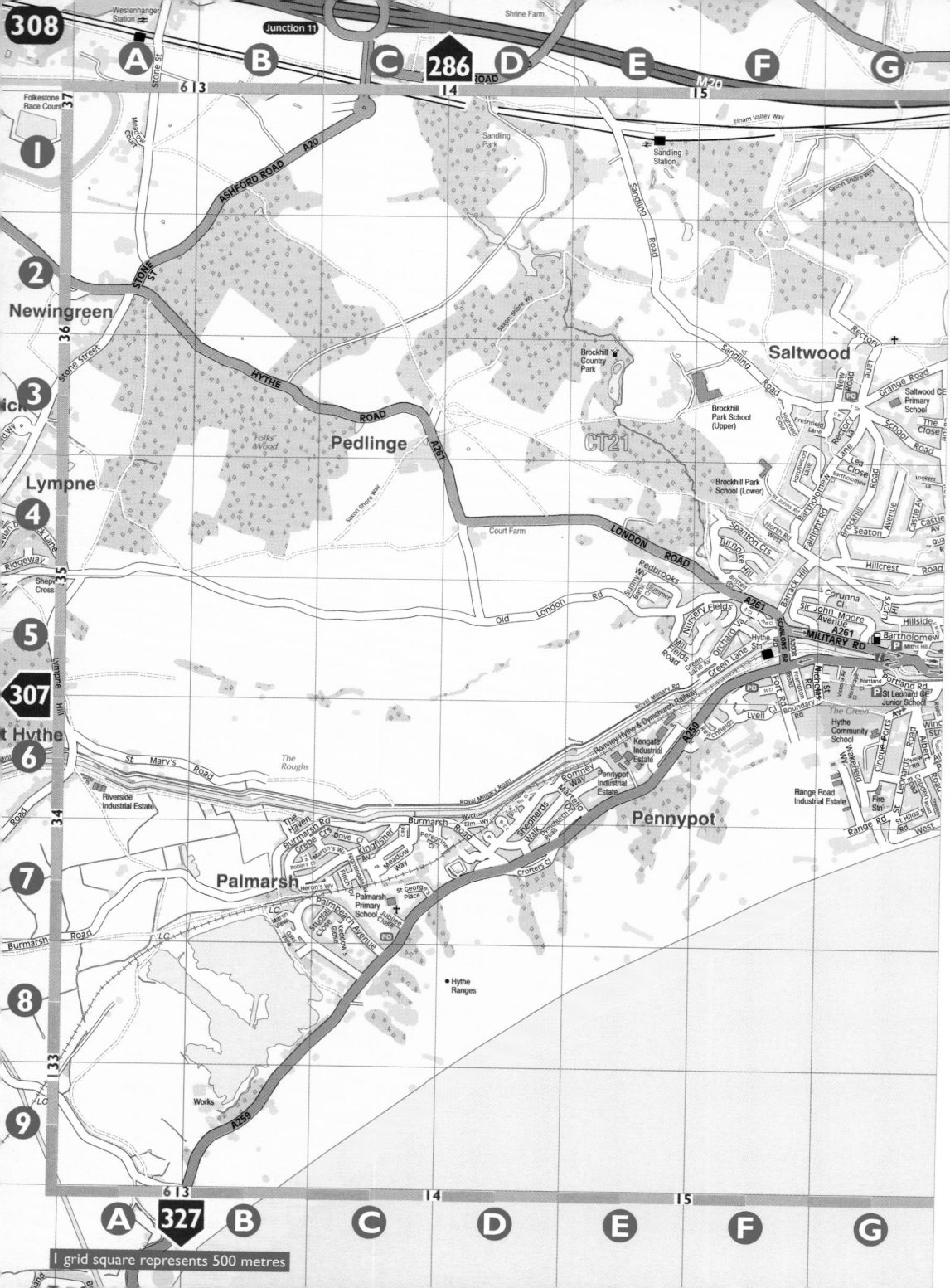

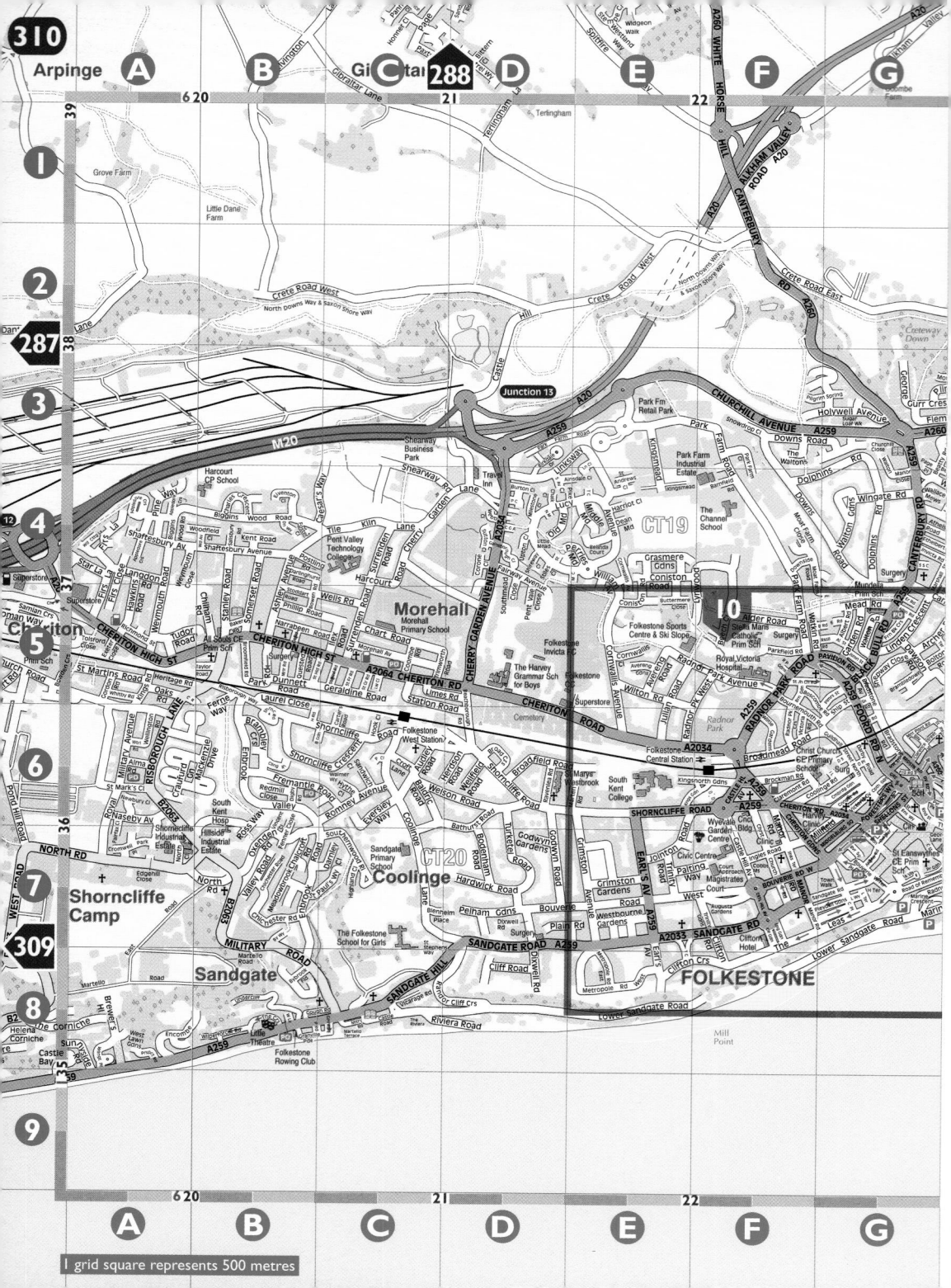

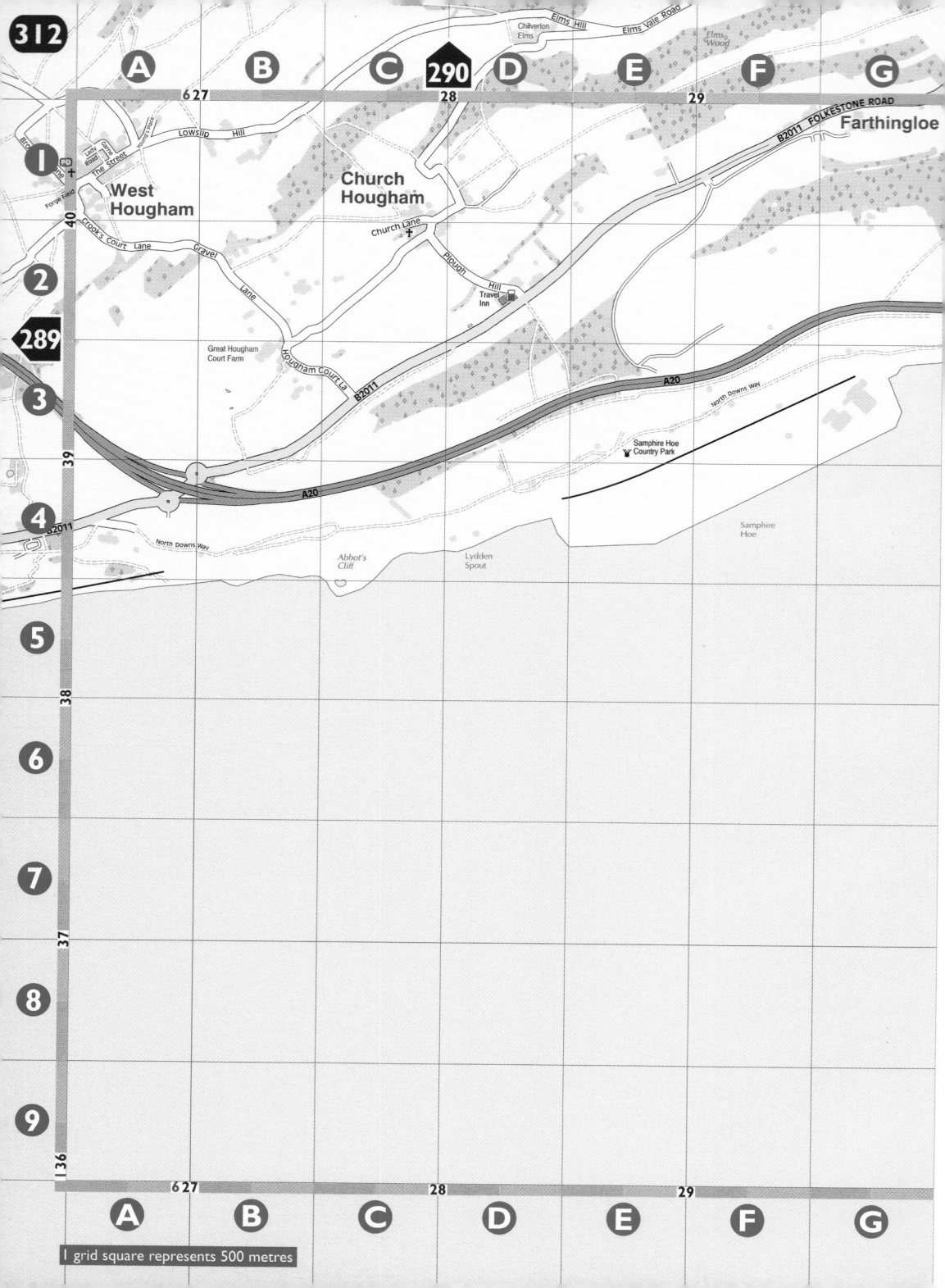

312

A B C **290** D E F G

627 28 29

B2011 FOLKESTONE ROAD

Farthingloe

Lowslip Hill

West Hougham

Church Hougham

Church Lane

1

40

2

289

3

39

4

B2011

Crook's Court Lane

Gravel Lane

Great Hougham Court Farm

Hougham Court La

B2011

Plough Hill

Travel Inn

A20

North Downs Way

Samphire Hoe Country Park

North Downs Way

A20

Abbot's Cliff

Lydden Spout

Samphire Hoe

Chilverton Elms

Elms Hill Elms Vale Road

Elms Wood

The Street

Forge Field

5

38

6

7

37

8

9

136

627 28 29

A B C D E F G

1 grid square represents 500 metres

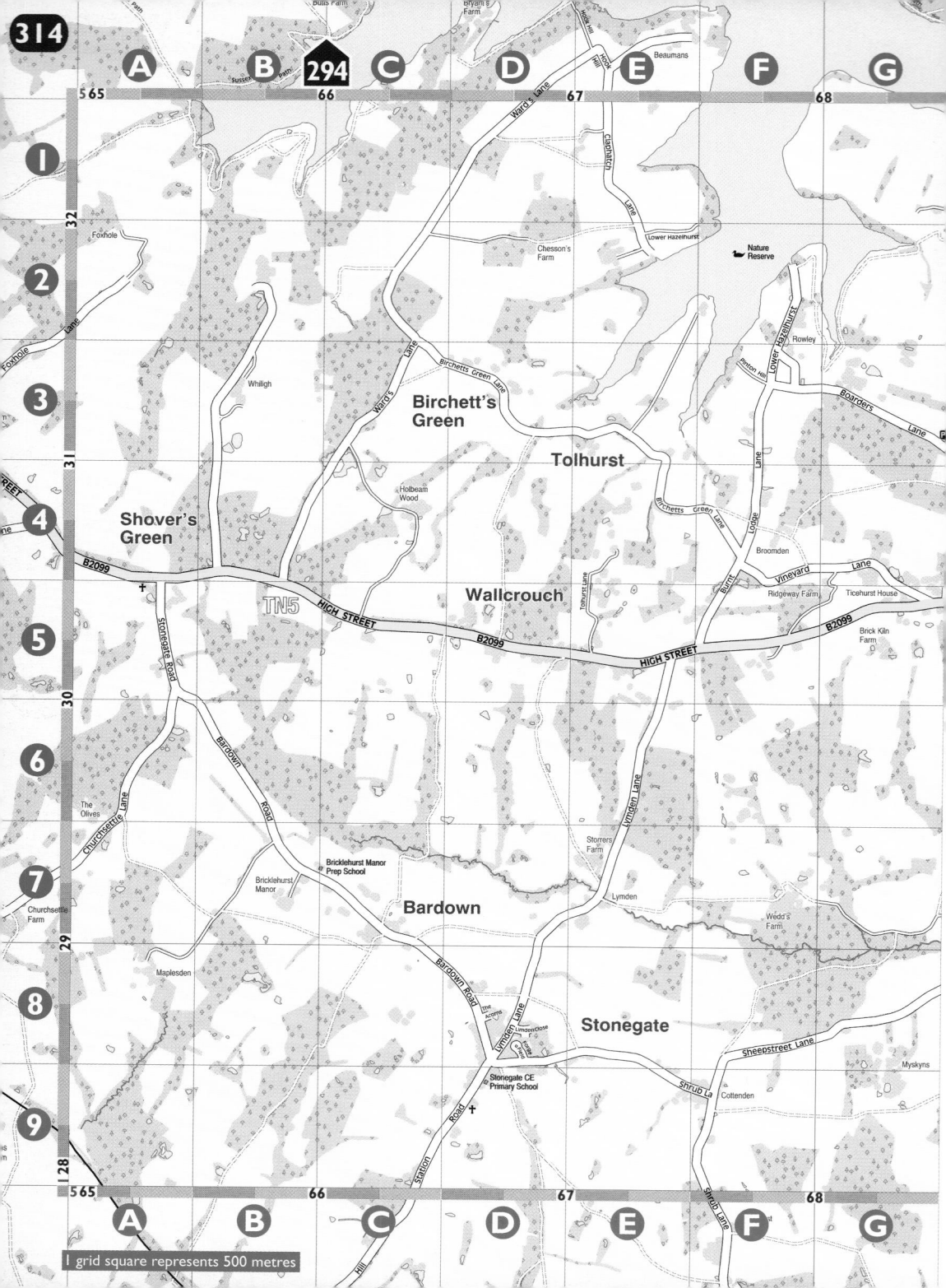

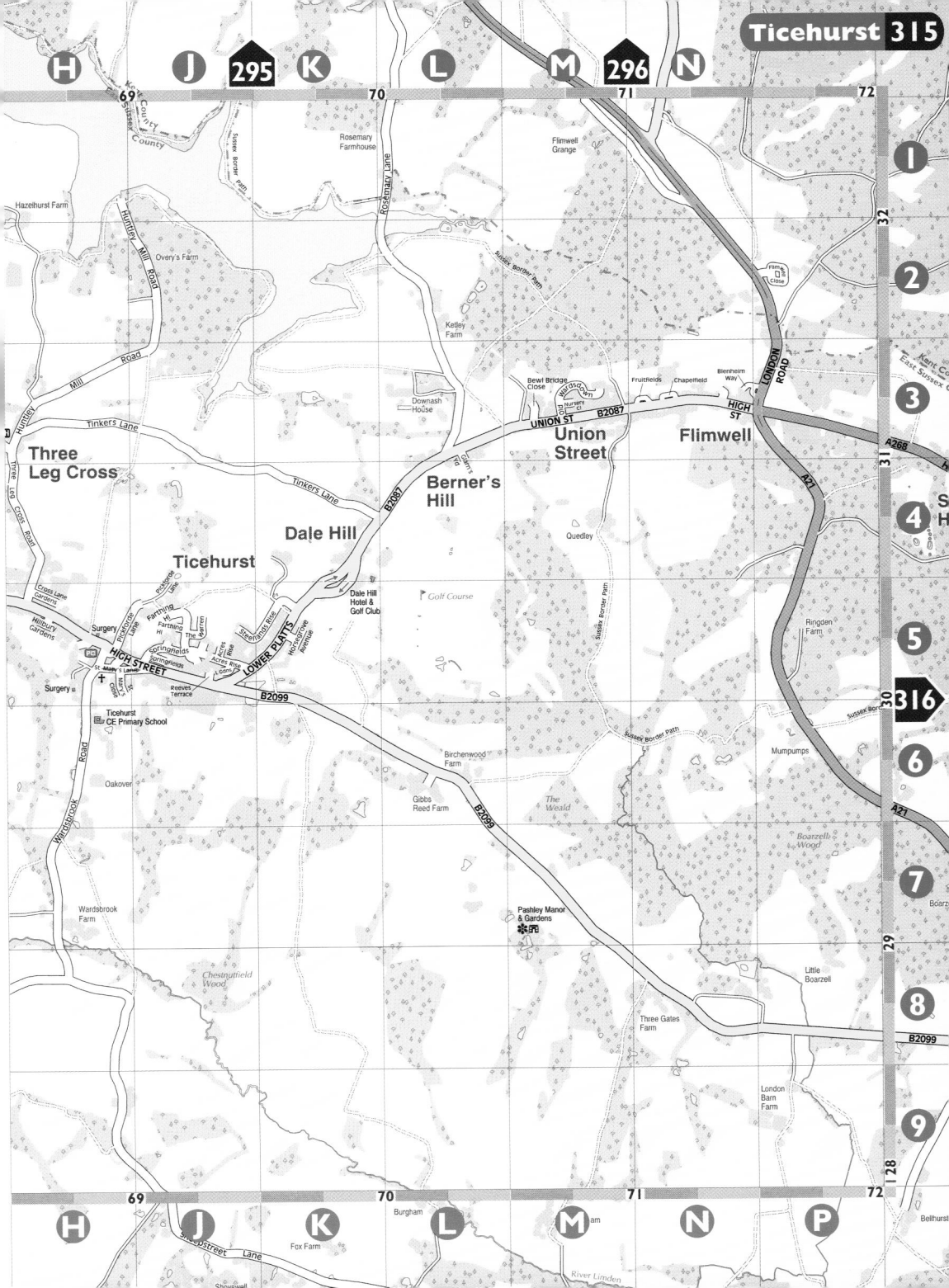

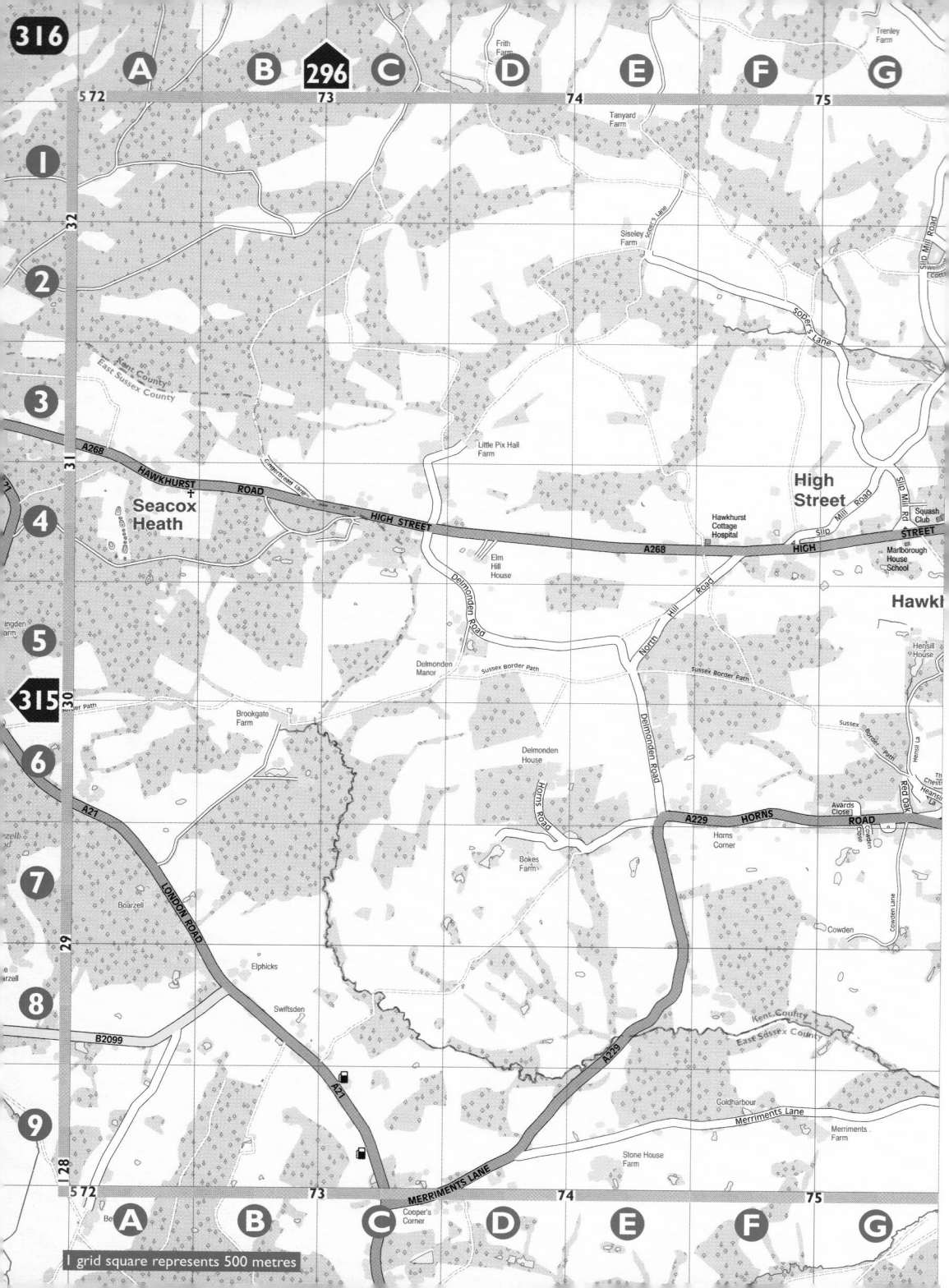

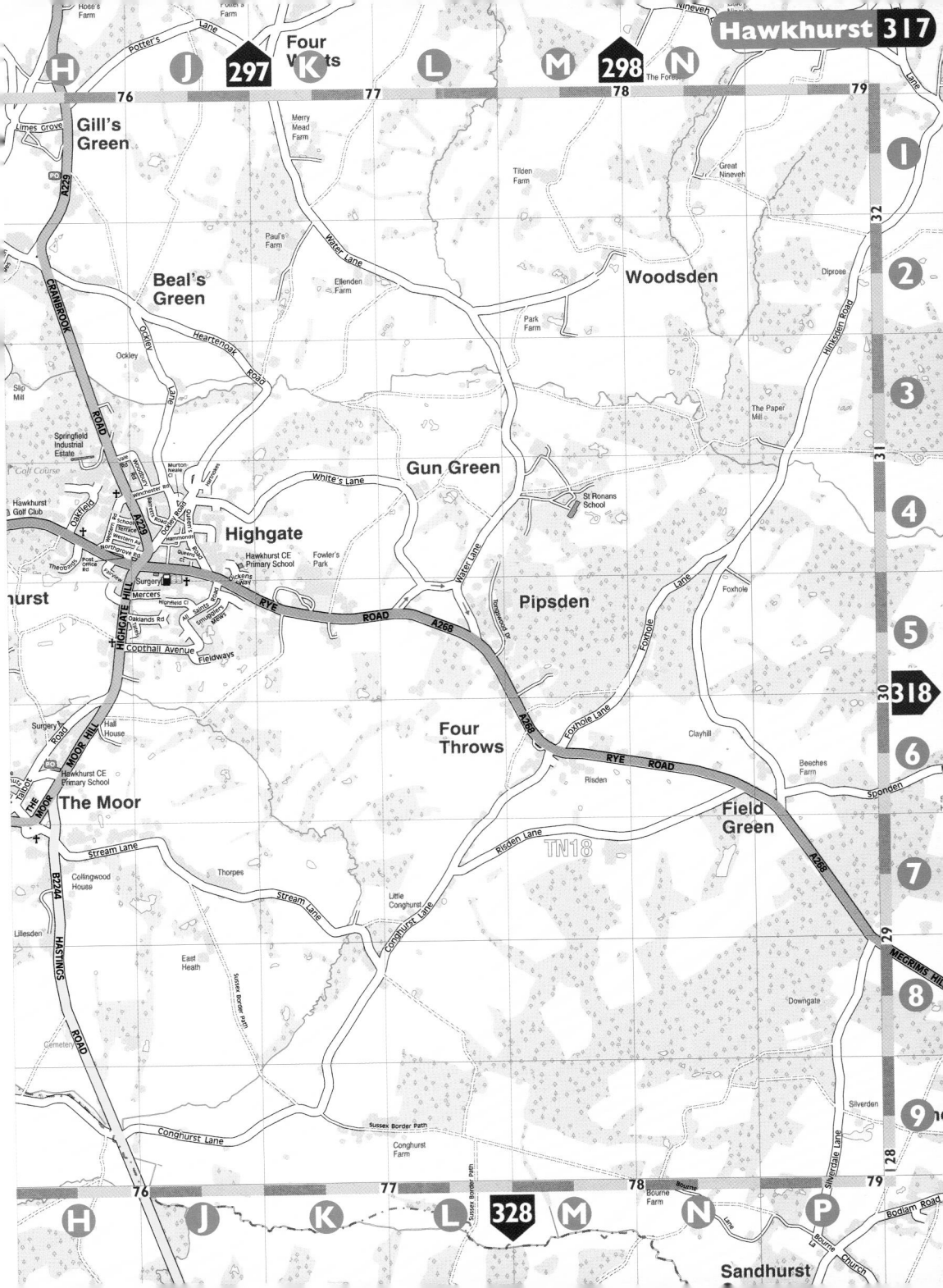

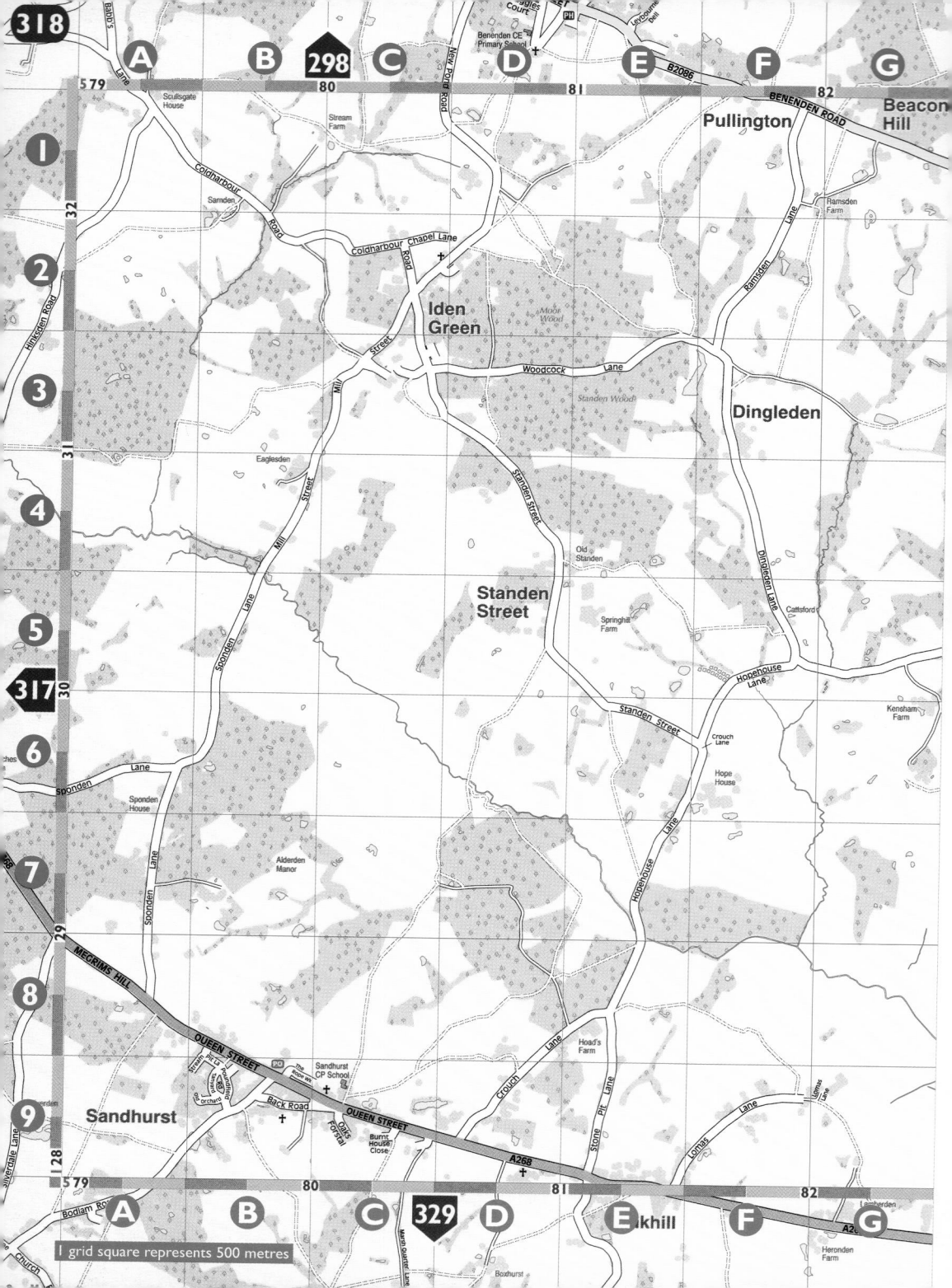

318

579 80 81 **B2086** 82

A B **298** C D E F G

I

Scullsgate
House

Coldharbour
Road

Sarnden

32

Stream
Farm

Benenden CE
Primary School

Pullington

Lanes
Court

PH

Lenchmere
Dell

**Beacon
Hill**

BENENDEN ROAD

Ramsden
Farm

2

Coldharbour Chapel Lane

Mill Street

New Pond Road

+

**Iden
Green**

Moor
Wood

Ramsden
Lane

3

31

Eaglesden

Woodcock Lane

Standen Wood

Dingleden

4

Mill Street

Spoden Lane

Standen Street

Old
Standen

Dingleden Lane

Cattsford

5

**Standen
Street**

Springhill
Farm

Hopehouse Lane

317 **30**

6

Spouden Lane

Sponden
House

standen Street

Crouch
Lane

Hope
House

Kensham
Farm

7

29

Sponden Lane

Alderden
Manor

Hopehouse Lane

MEGRIMS HILL

8

QUEEN STREET

Sandhurst
CP School

Hoad's
Farm

Stone Pit Lane

Crouch Lane

Lomas Lane

9

Sandhurst

Back Road

+
The White Hse

Oak's
Forstal

+

QUEEN STREET

Burnt
House
Close

+

A268

khill

Lamberden
Farm

Silverdale Lane

Church

Bodiam Road

128

579 80 81 82

A B C **329** D E F G

Martin Quarter Lane

Boxhurst

A2

Heronden
Farm

I grid square represents 500 metres

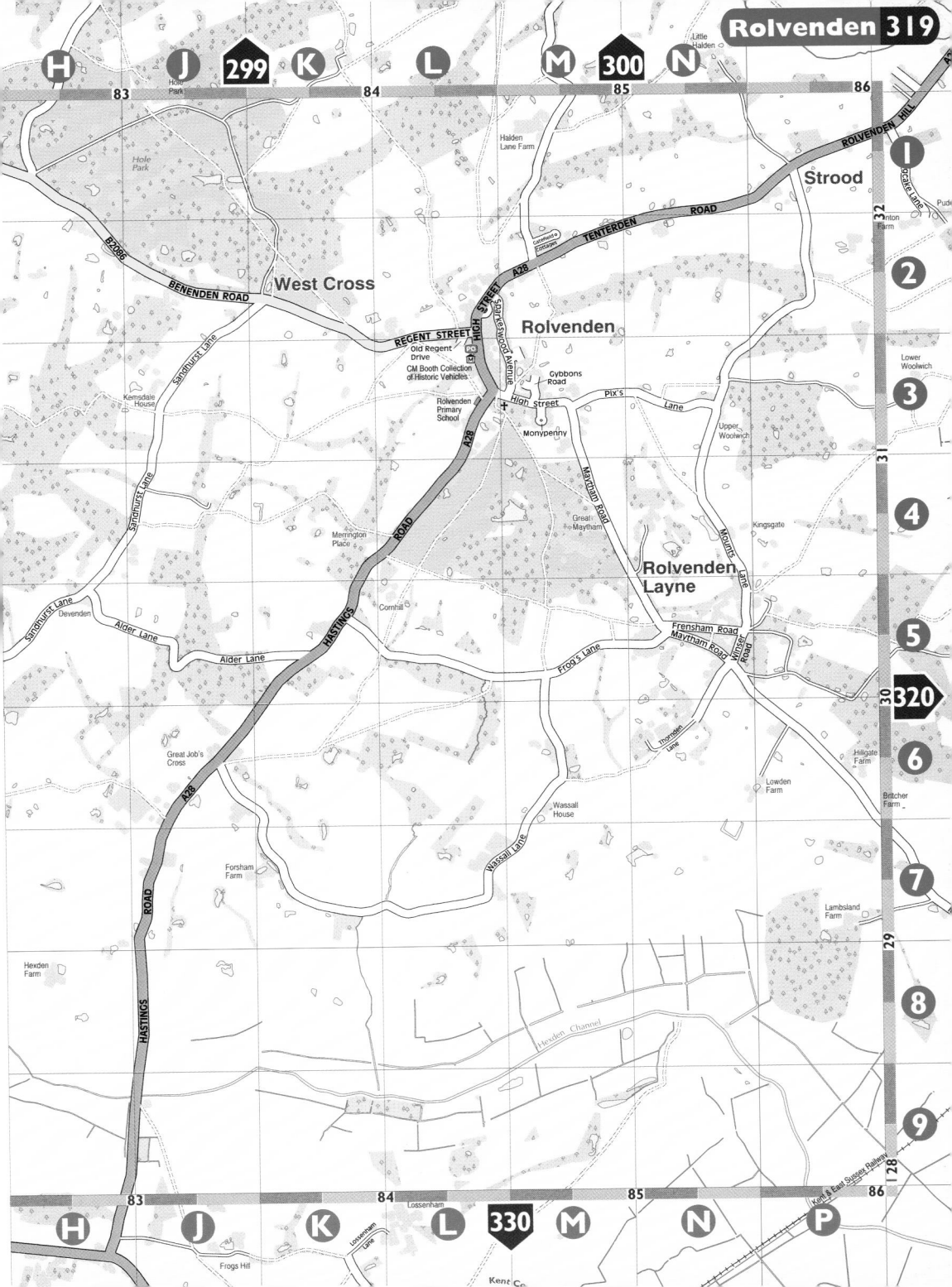

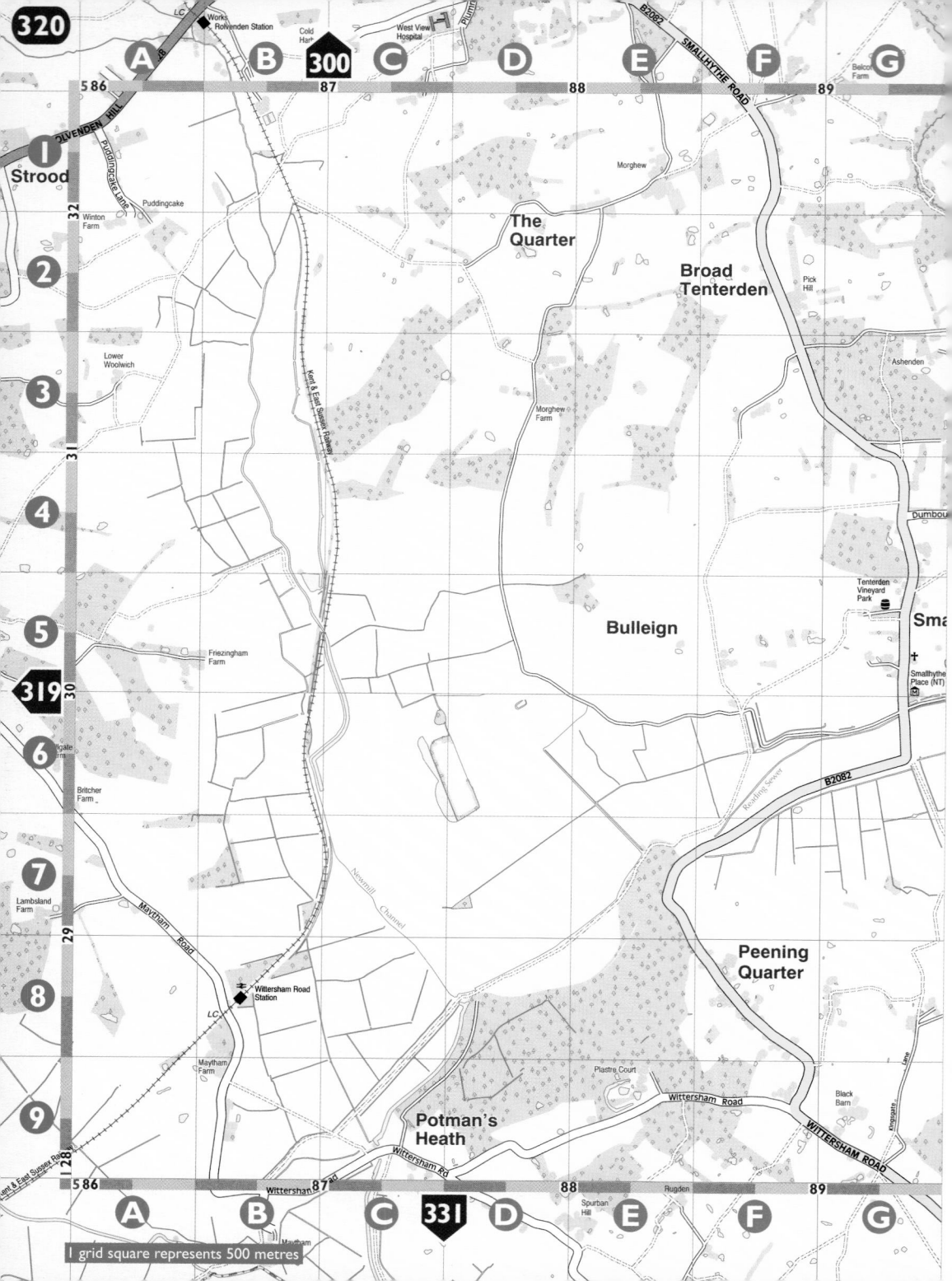

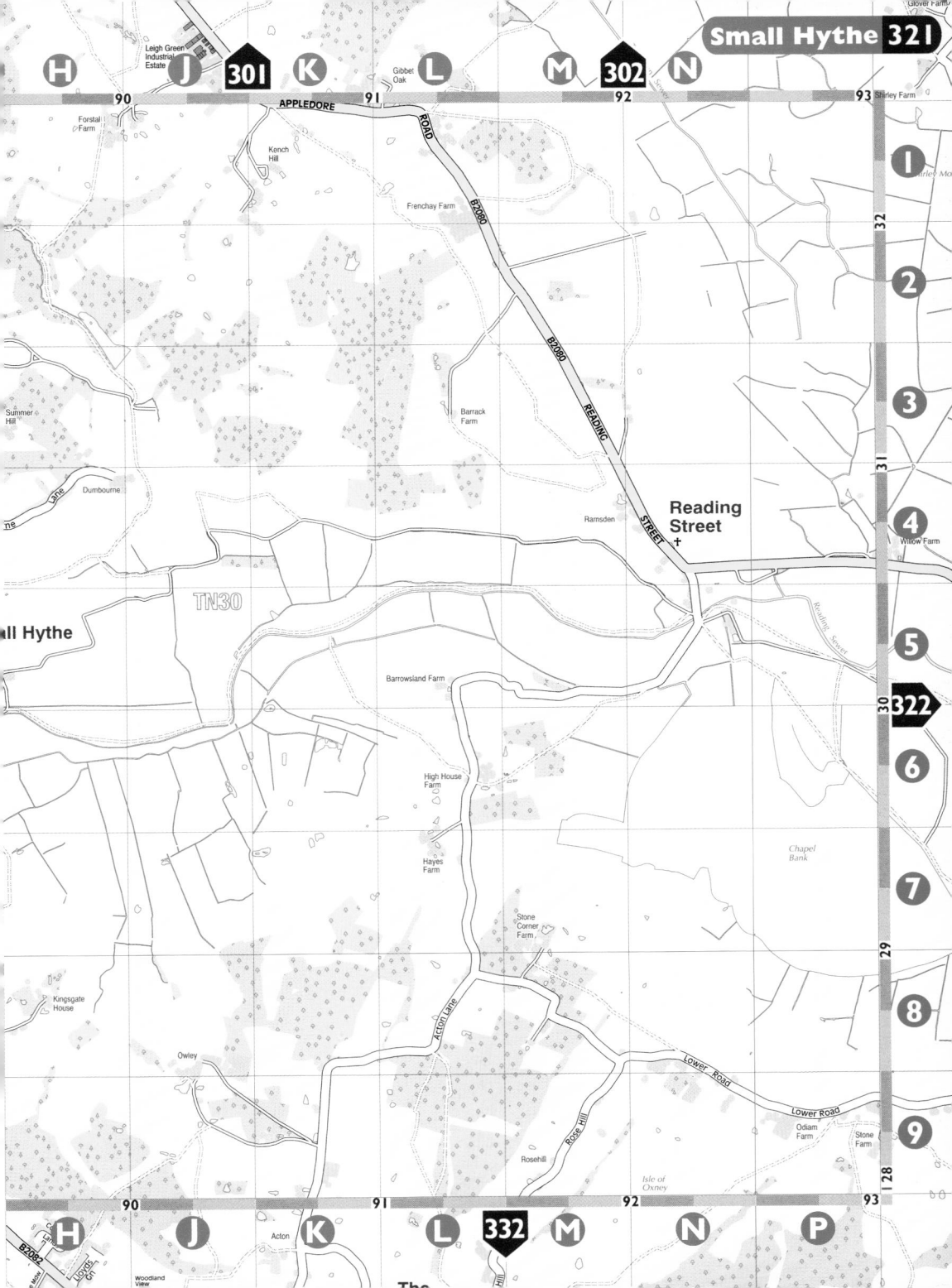

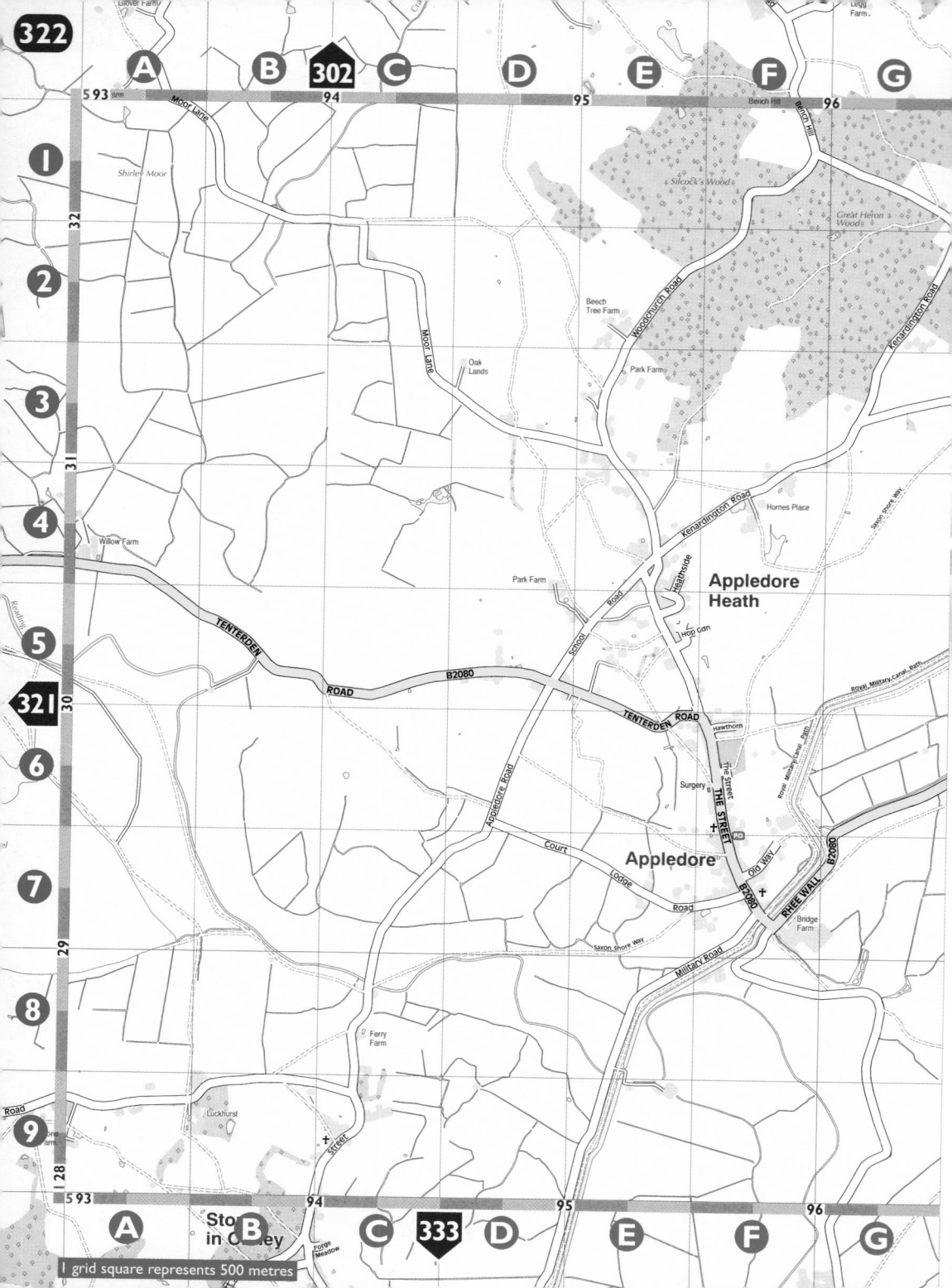

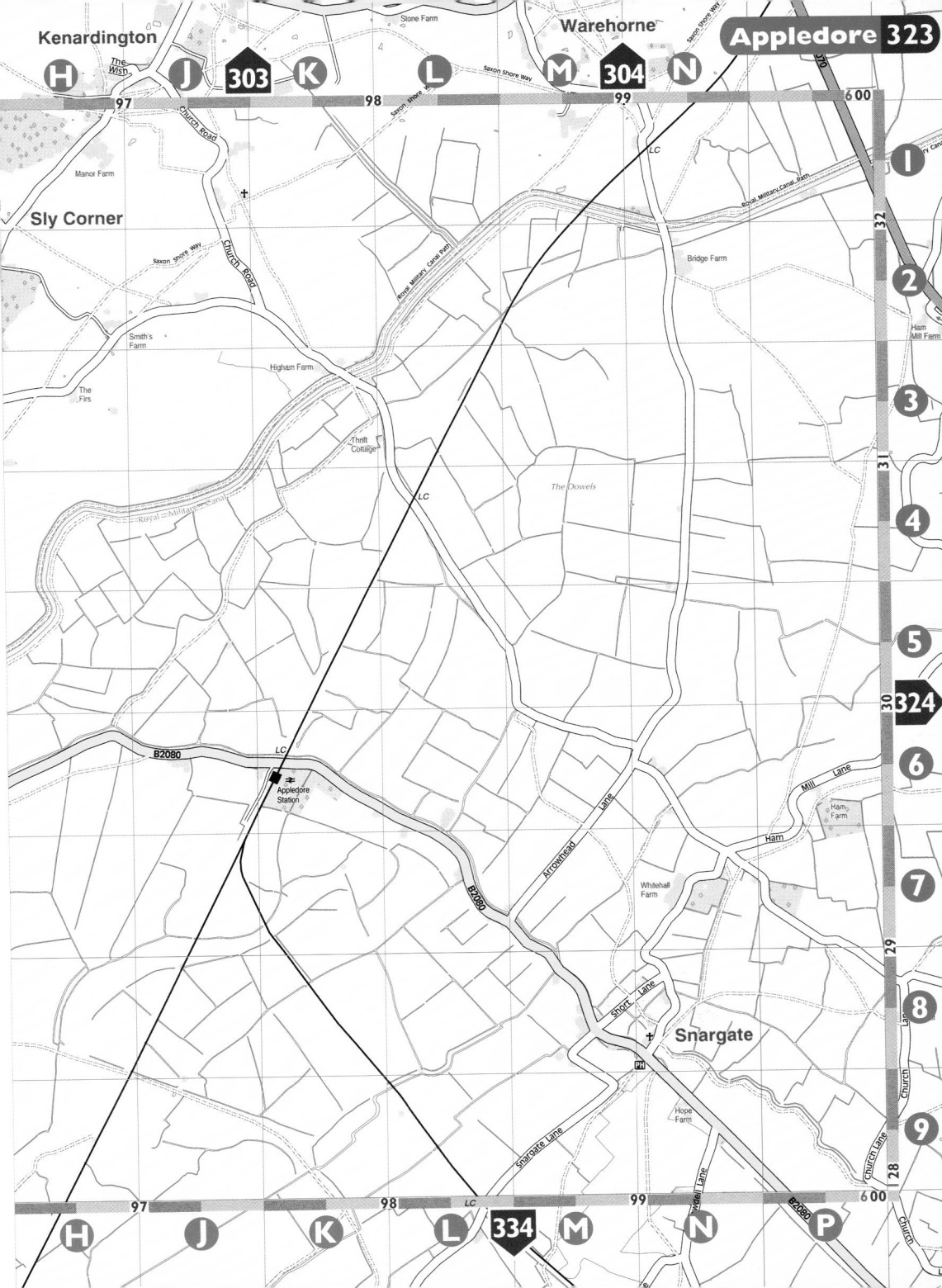

Kenardington

Warehorne

303

304

324

334

Sly Corner

Manor Farm

The Wish

Church Road

Stone Farm

Saxon Shore Way

Royal Military Canal

Royal Military Canal Path

LC

Bridge Farm

Ham Mill Farm

Smith's Farm

The Firs

Higham Farm

Thrift Cottage

LC

The Dowels

B2080

LC

Appledore Station

B2080

Arrowhead Lane

Mill Lane

Ham Farm

Whitehall Farm

Ham

Short Lane

Snargate

Church Lane

PH

Hope Farm

Snargate Lane

Tything Lane

B2080

Church

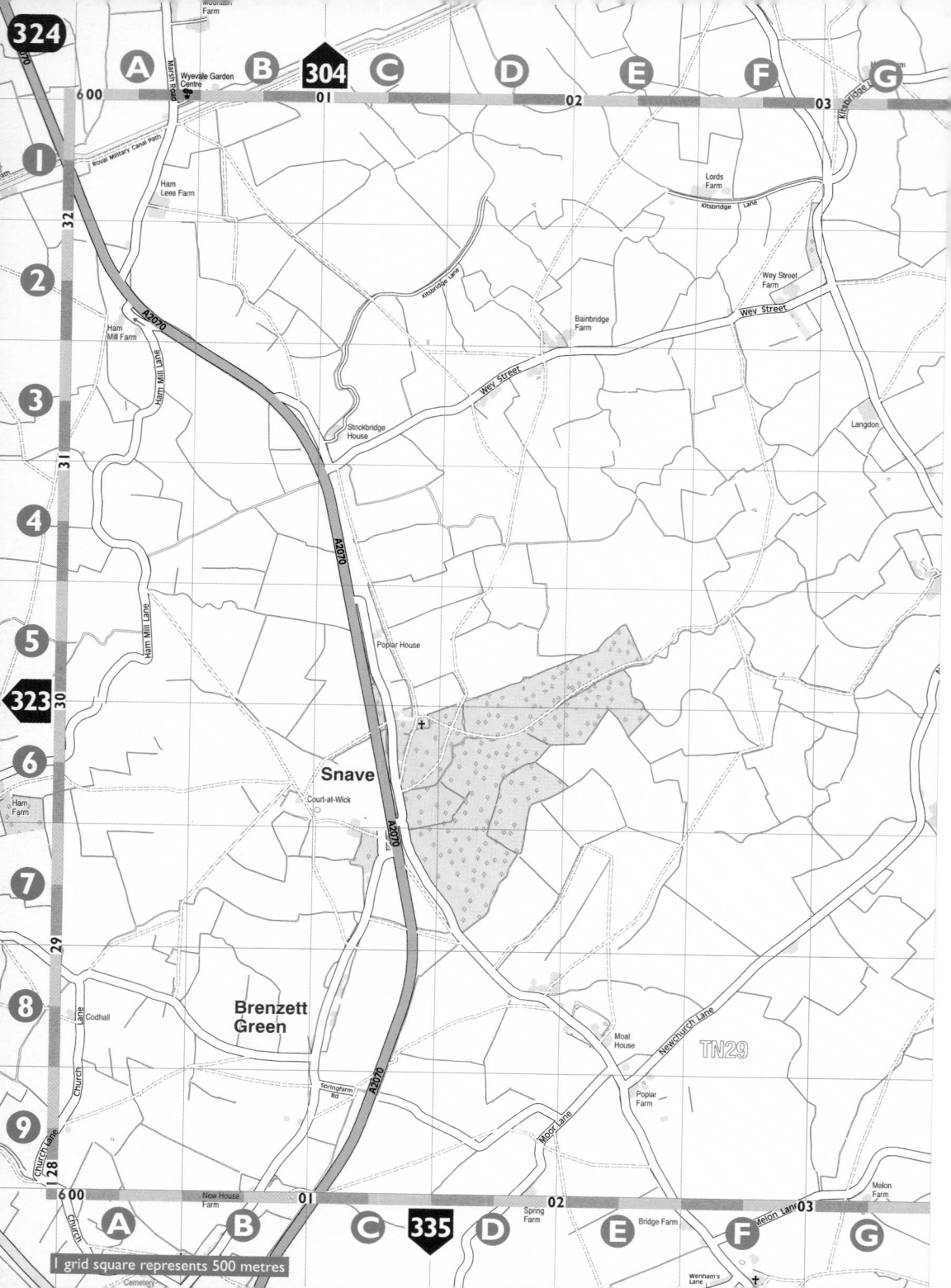

324

A
Wyevale Garden Centre
B
304
C
D
E
F
G

6 00
01
02
03
Kitsbridge Ln

Marsh Road

1
Royal Military Canal Path
Ham Lees Farm
32
Lords Farm
Kitsbridge Lane

2
A2070
Ham Mill Farm
Bainbridge Farm
Wey Street
Wey Street Farm

3
31
Stockbridge House
Wey Street
Langdon

4
A2070
Ham Mill Lane

5
Poplar House

323
30
✝

6
Snave
Ham Farm
Court-at-Wick
A2070

7
29

8
Codhall
Brenzett Green
Moat House
Newchurch Lane
TN29

Lane

9
Church Lane
28
Springfarm Rd
A2070
Poplar Farm
Melon Farm

6 00
New House Farm
01
Moor Lane
02
Spring Farm
Melon Lane 03

Church

A
B
C
335
D
E
Bridge Farm
F
G

1 grid square represents 500 metres
Wenham's Lane
Cemetery
✝

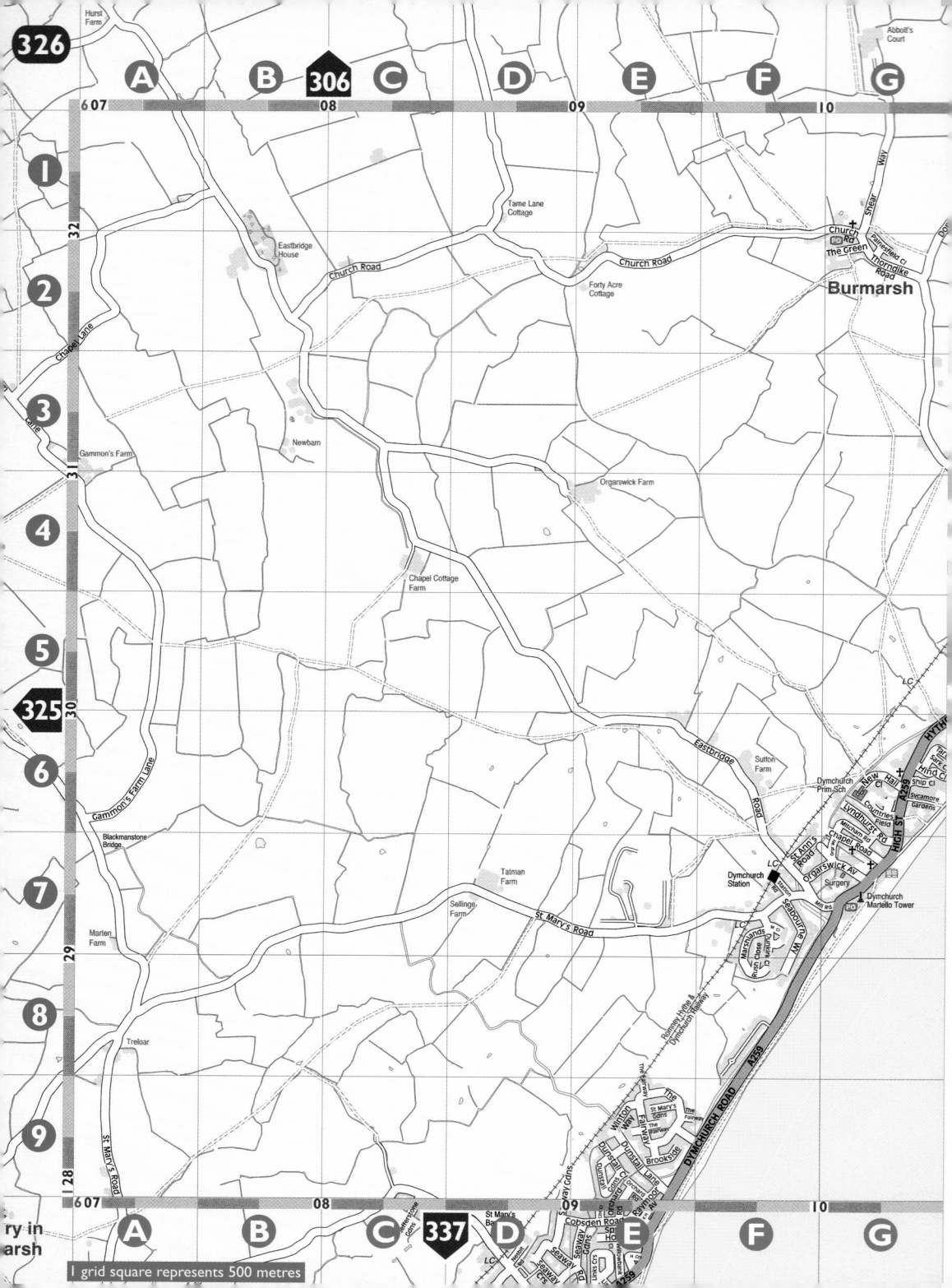

A　B　306　C　D　E　F　G

6 07　08　09　10

I

32

2

Chapel Lane

3

31

Gammon's Farm

4

5

325
30

6

Gammon's Farm Lane

Blackmanstone Bridge

7

29

Marlen Farm

8

Treloar

9

28

6 07　08　09　10

A　B　337　C　D　E　F　G

I grid square represents 500 metres

Hurst Farm

Abbott's Court

Tame Lane Cottage

Eastbridge House

Church Road

Church Road

Forty Acre Cottage

Burmarsh

Church Rd
The Green
Thorndike Road

Newbarn

Orgarswick Farm

Chapel Cottage Farm

Eastbridge Road

Sutton Farm

Dymchurch Prim Sch

Talman Farm

Sellinge Farm

St Mary's Road

Dymchurch Station

Dymchurch Martello Tower

Romney Hythe & Dymchurch Railway

St Mary's Bay

Wilton Way

Dymchurch Lane

Brookside

DYMCHURCH ROAD

A259

Copsden Road

ry in arsh

St Mary's Road

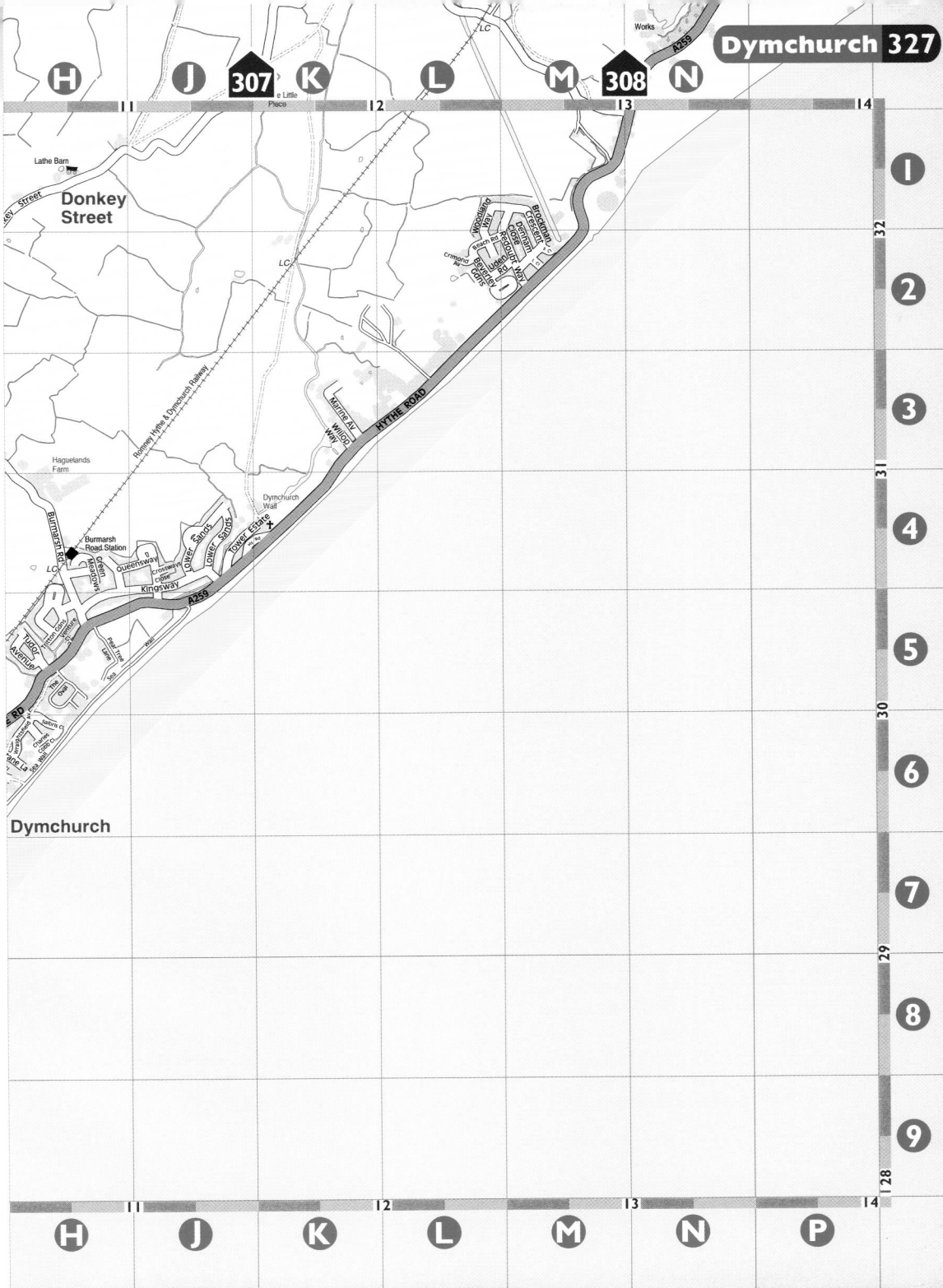

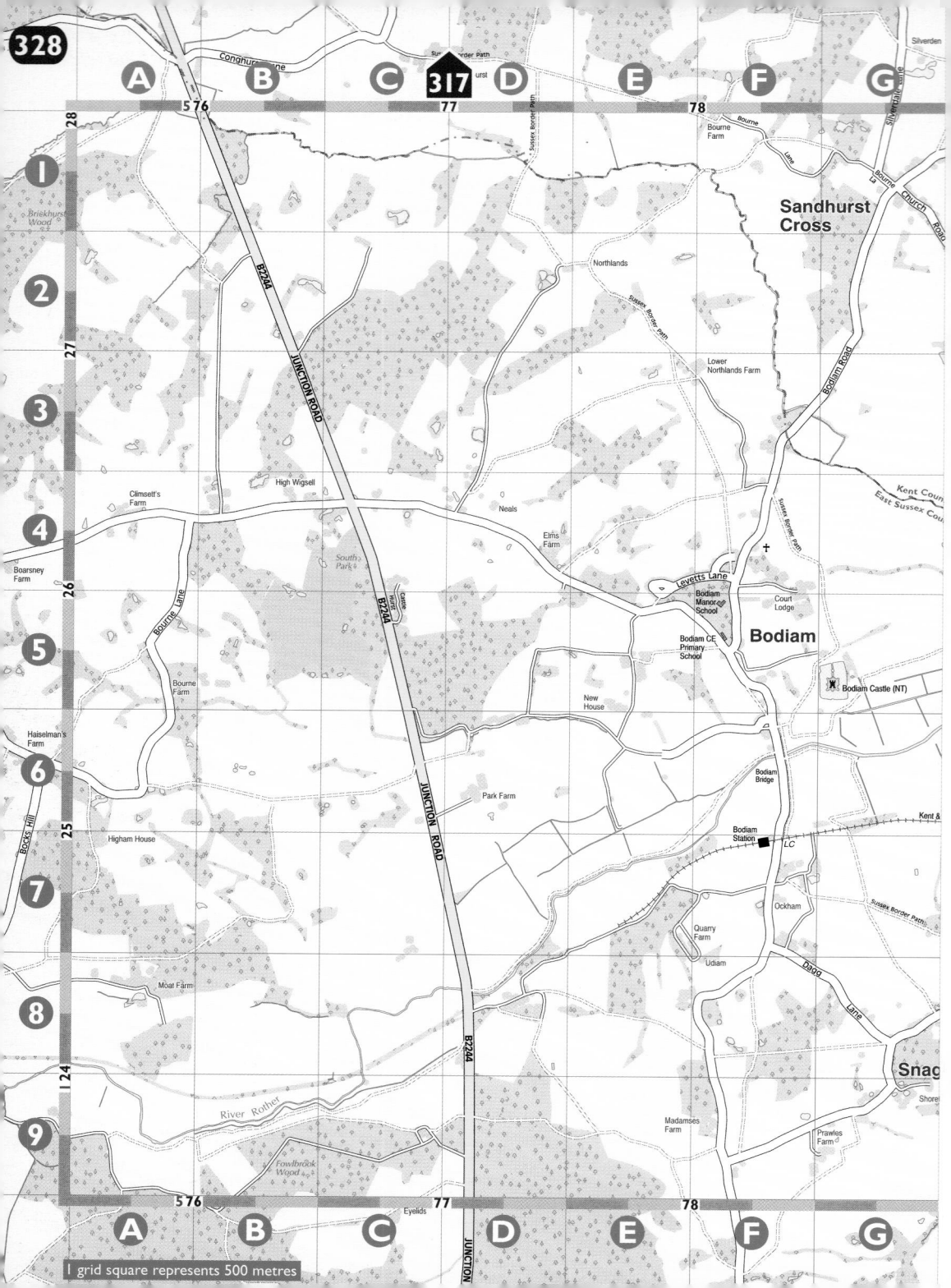

A 576 B C 317 D E F G

28

1

Brickhurst
Wood

Conghurst Lane

Sussex Border Path

Sandhurst
Cross

Bourne
Farm

Bourne

2

27

Northlands

Sussex Border Path

3

High Wigsell

Lower
Northlands Farm

4

Climsett's
Farm

Neals

Elms
Farm

JUNCTION ROAD

B2244

South
Park

Boarsney
Farm

26

Bourne Lane

Castle Road

B2244

Levetts Lane

Bodiam Manor
School

Court
Lodge

5

Bourne
Farm

Bodiam CE
Primary
School

Bodiam

Bodiam Castle (NT)

Haiselman's
Farm

New
House

6

Becks Hill

25

Higham House

JUNCTION ROAD

B2244

Park Farm

Bodiam
Bridge

Bodiam
Station   LC   Kent &

7

Ockham

Sussex Border Path

Quarry
Farm

Moat Farm

Dagg Lane

Udiam

24

8

River Rother

Snag

Shore

9

Fowlbrook
Wood

Madamses
Farm

Prawles
Farm

A 576 B C 77 Eyelids D JUNCTION E 78 F G

Silverden

Bodiam Road

Church Road

Bourne

Kent County
East Sussex County
Silverhill Lane

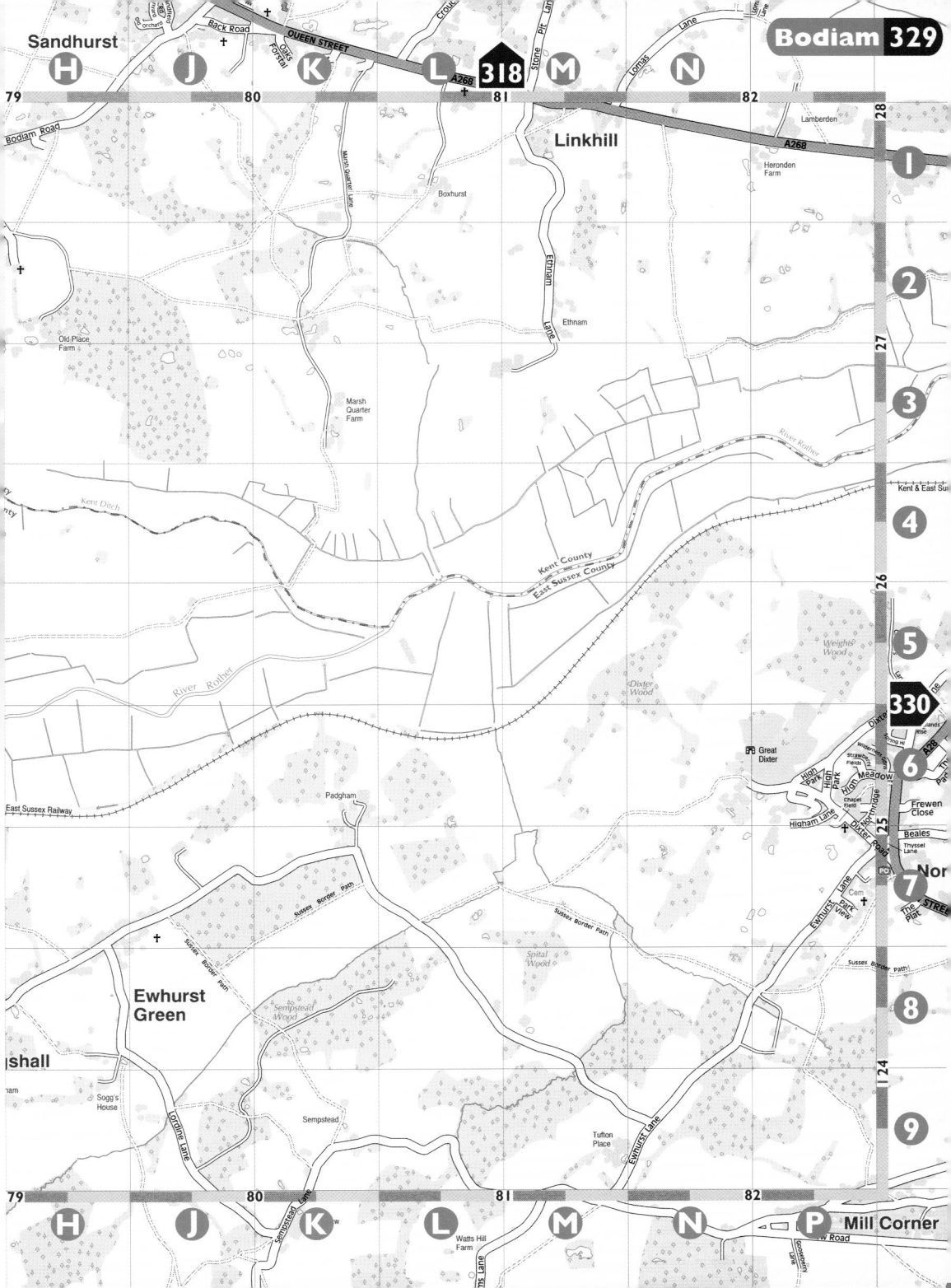

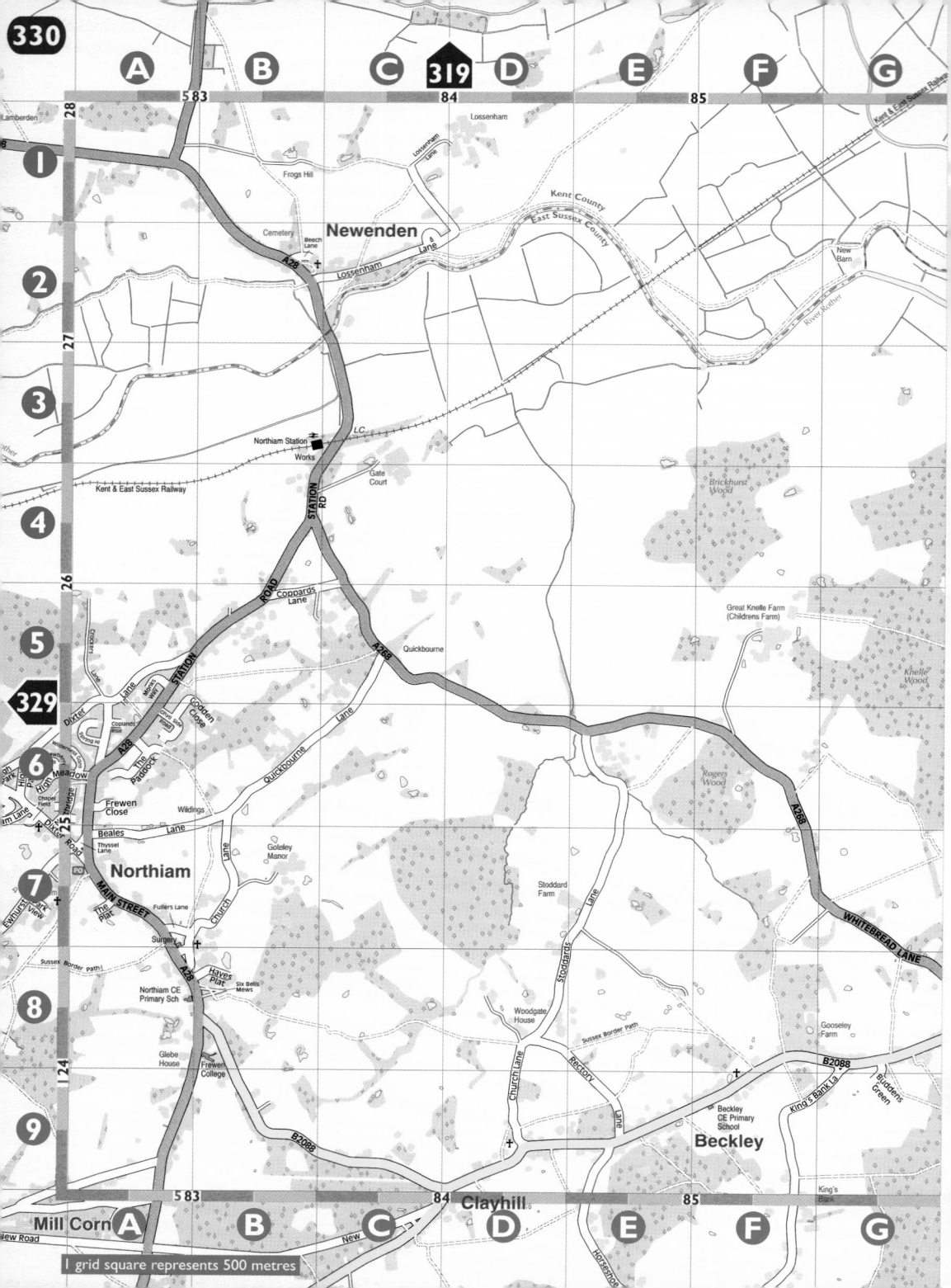

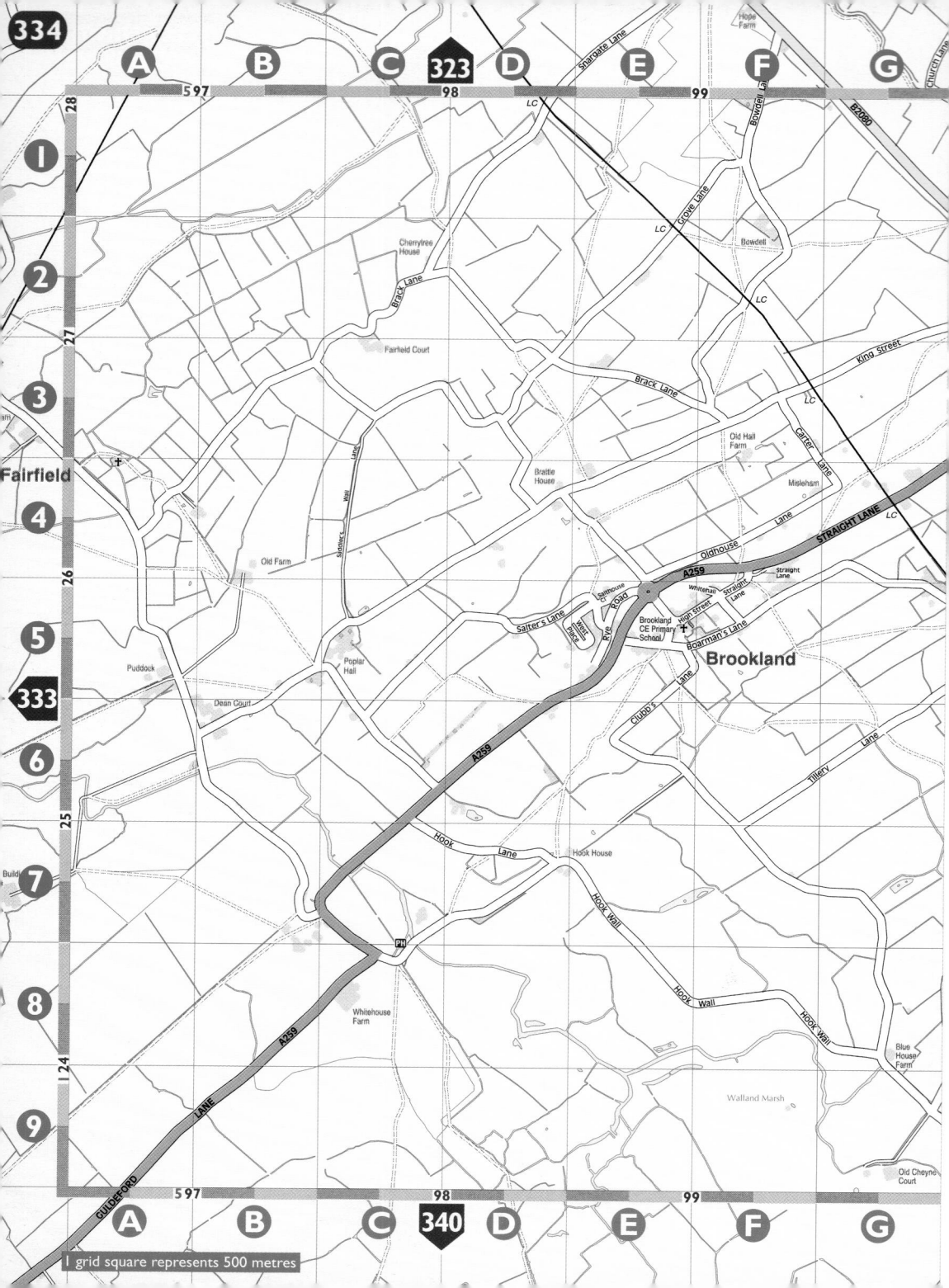

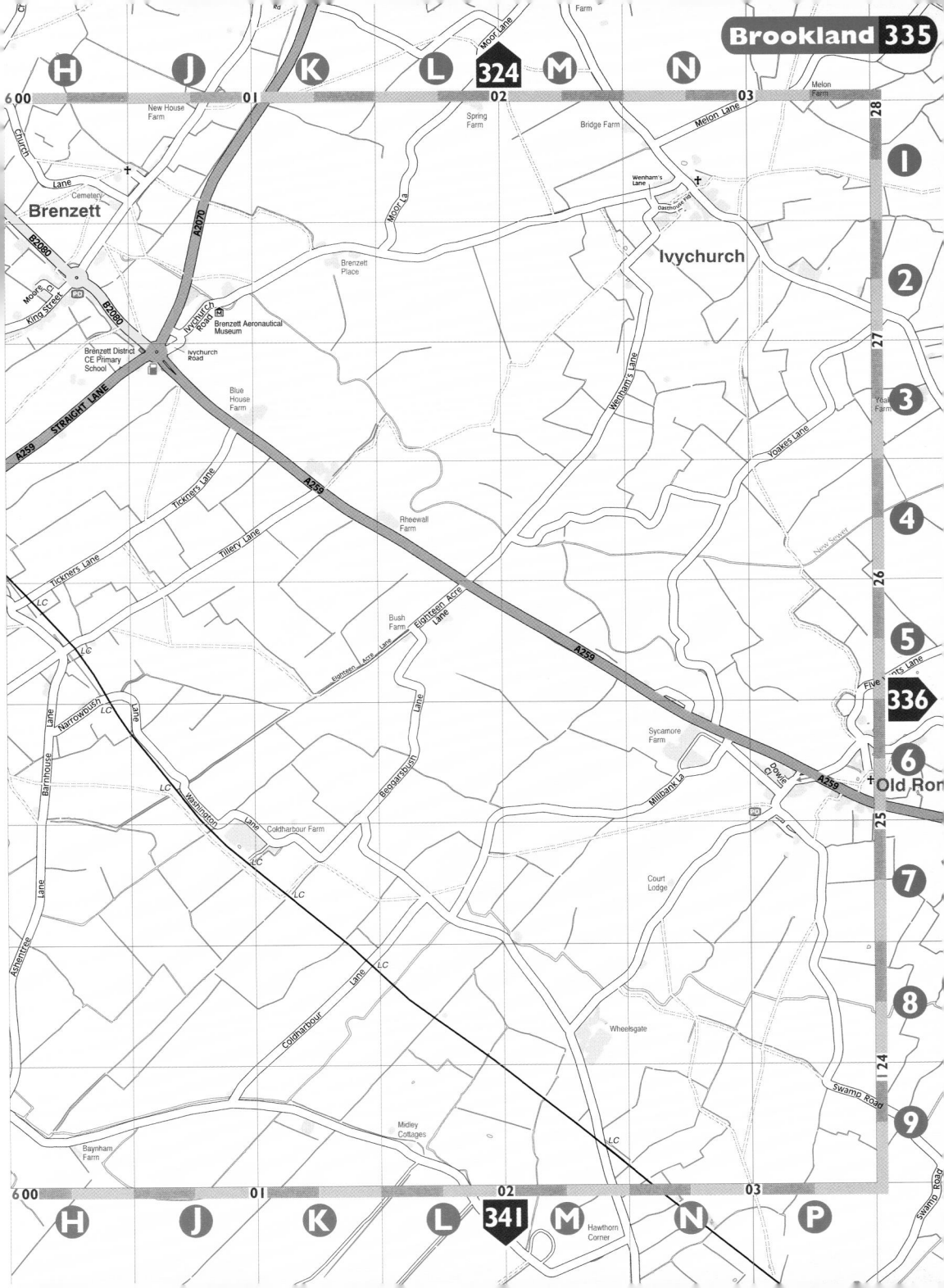

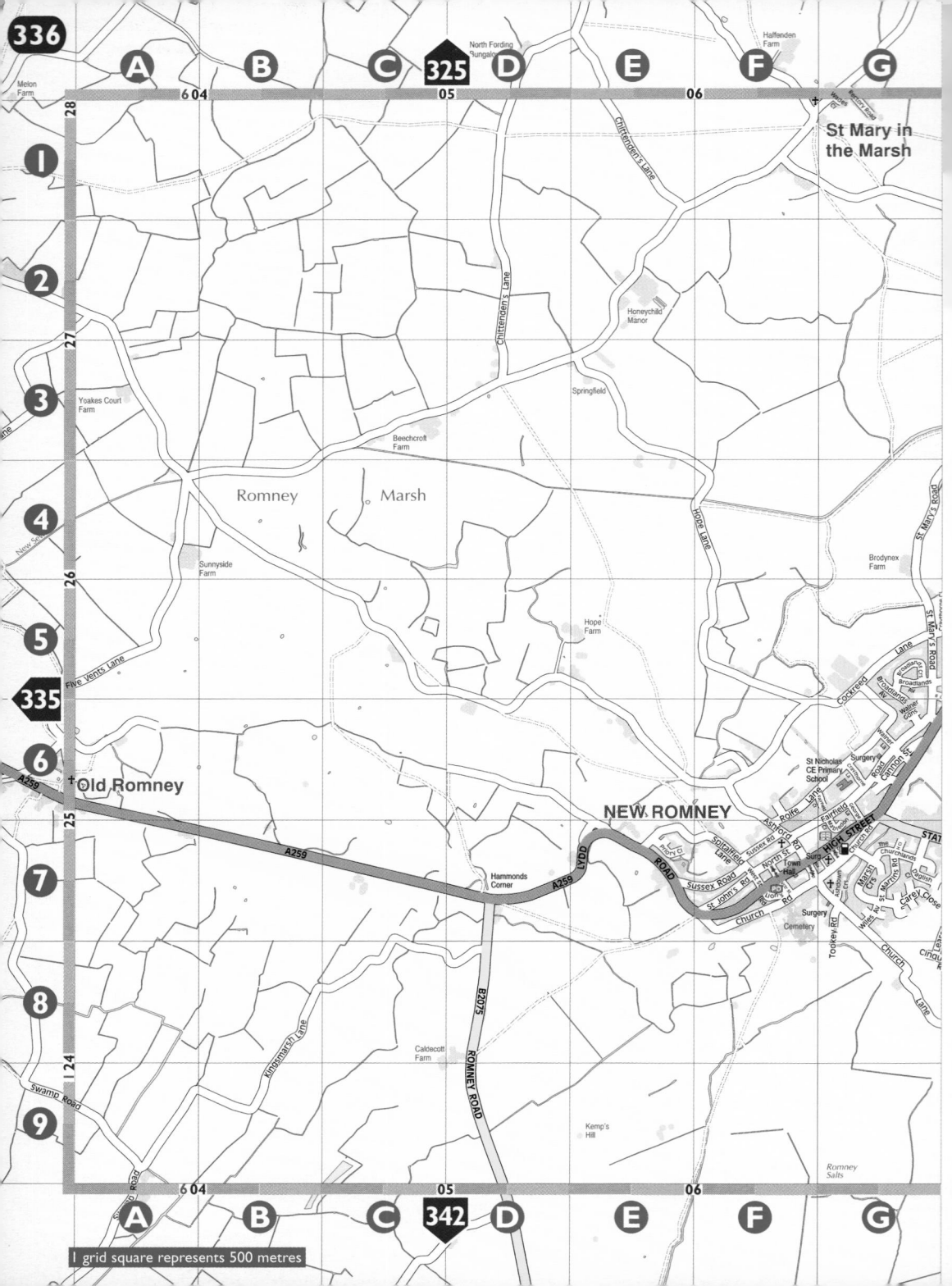

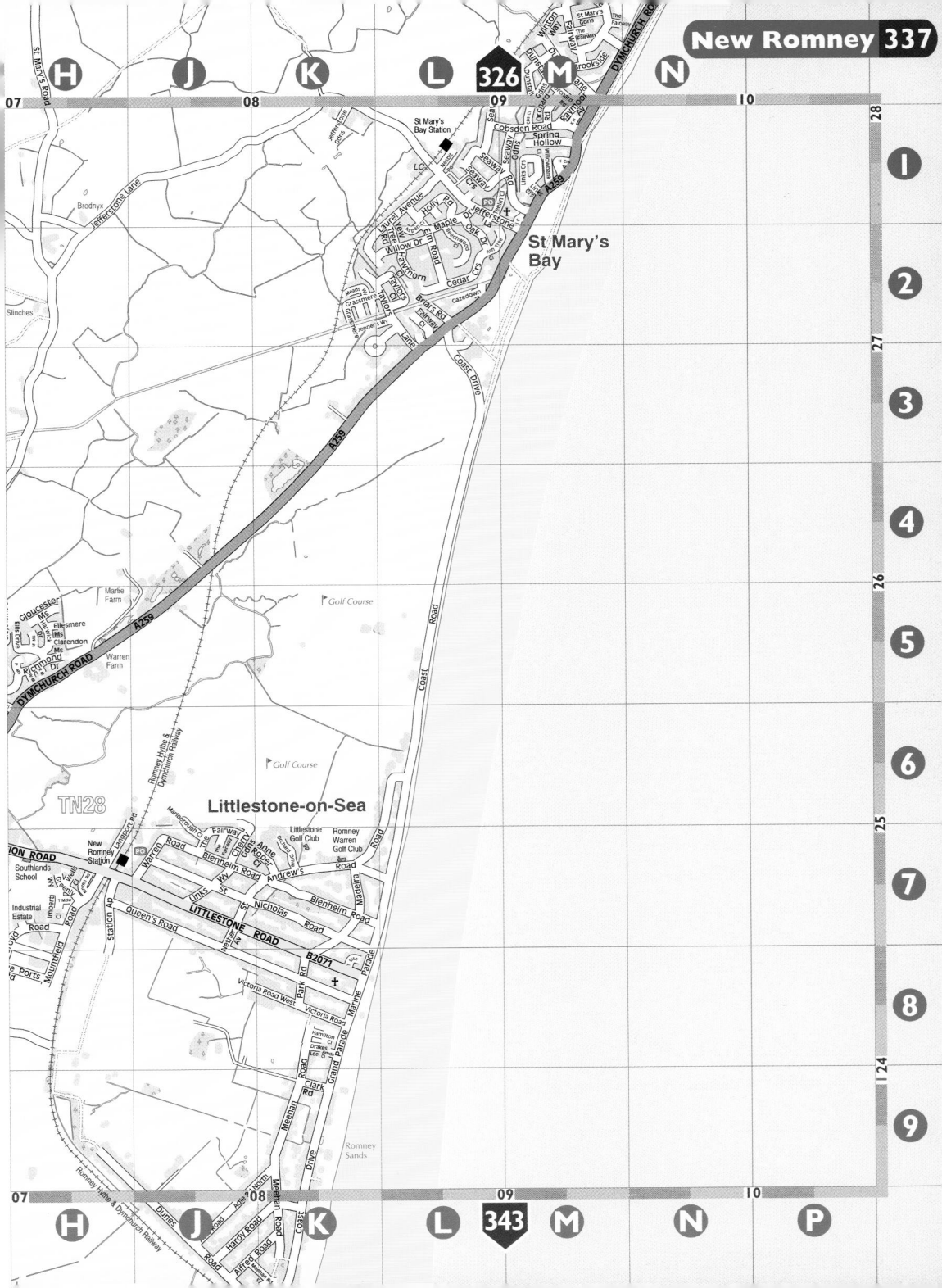

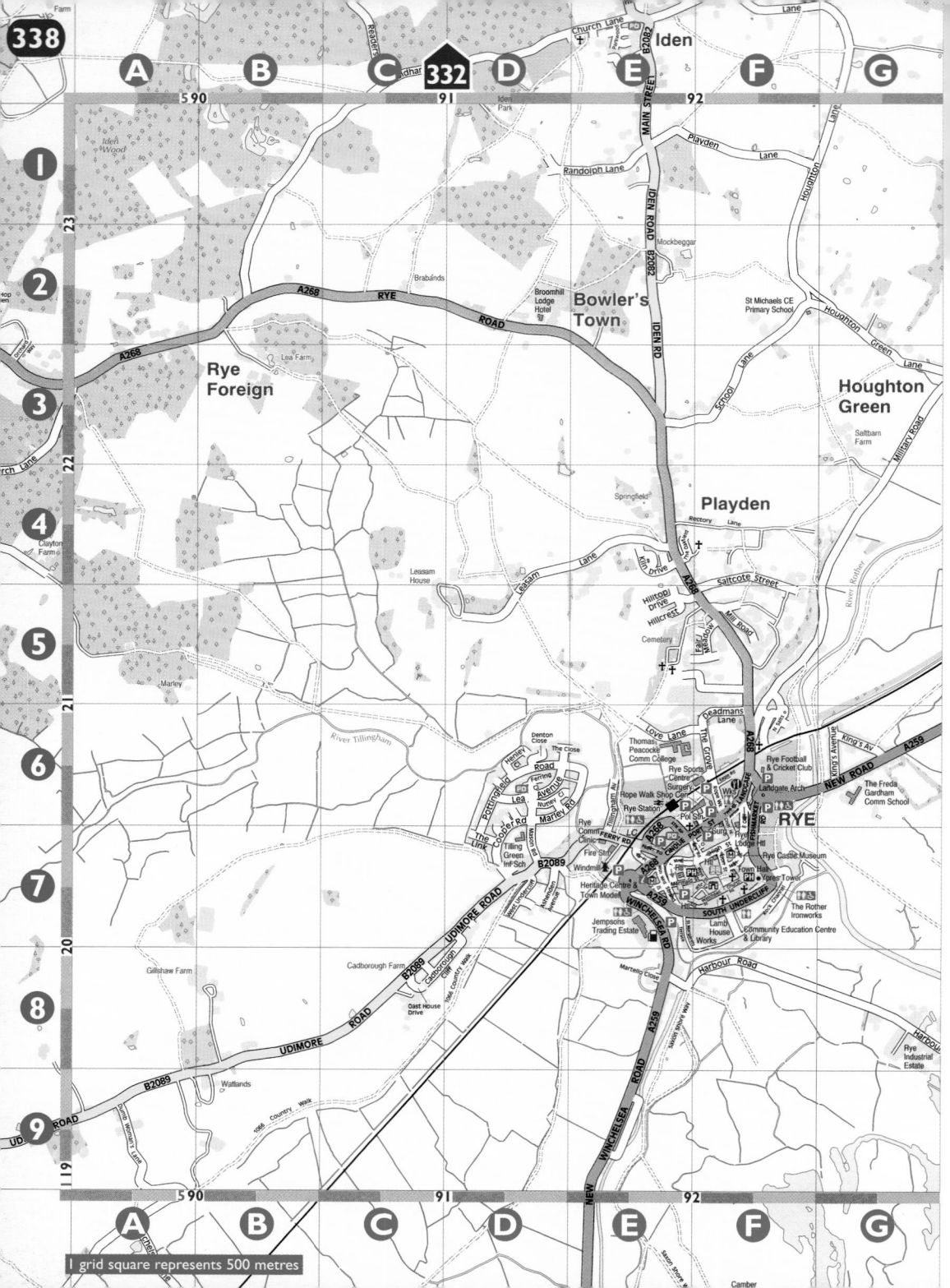

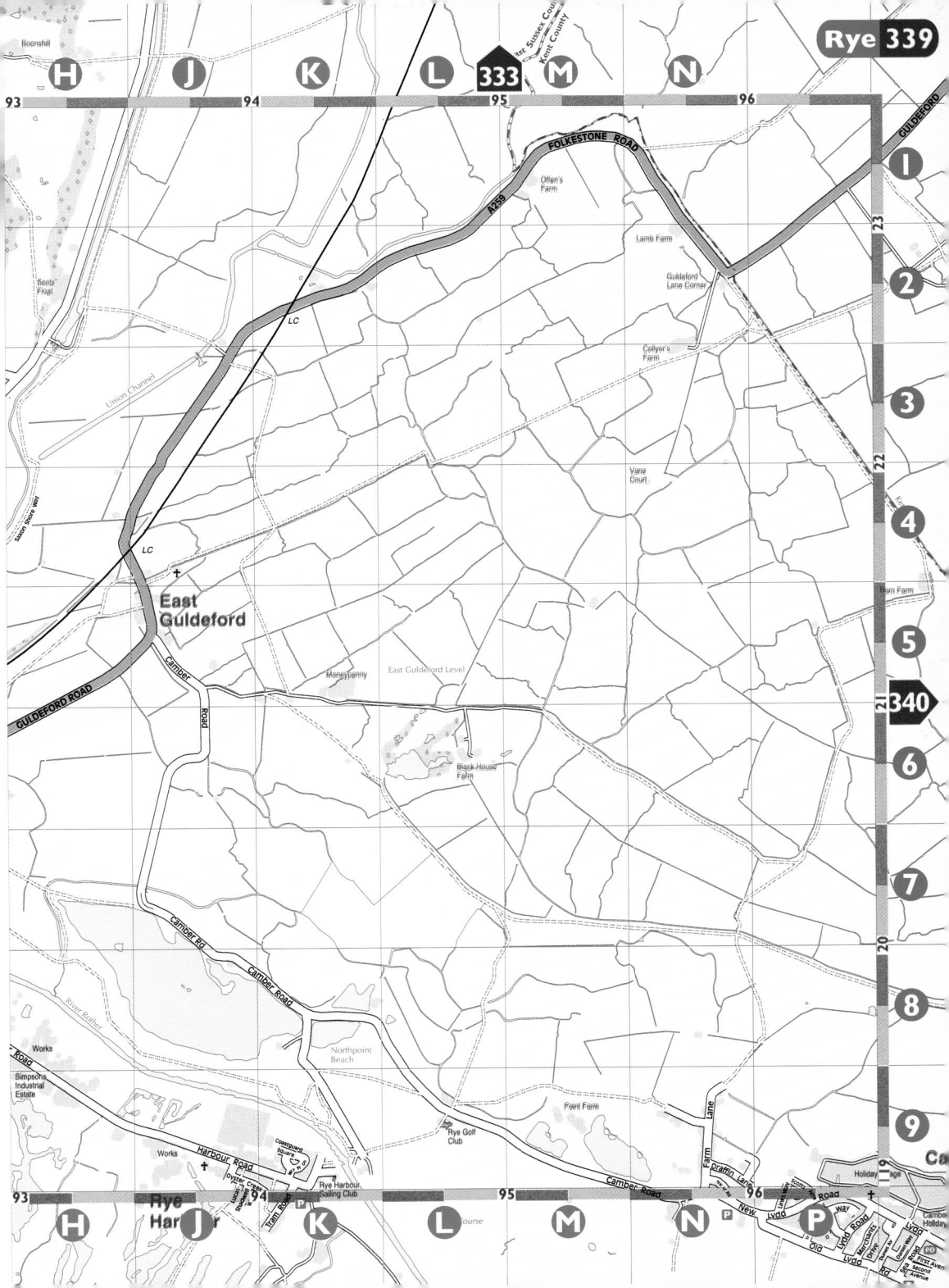

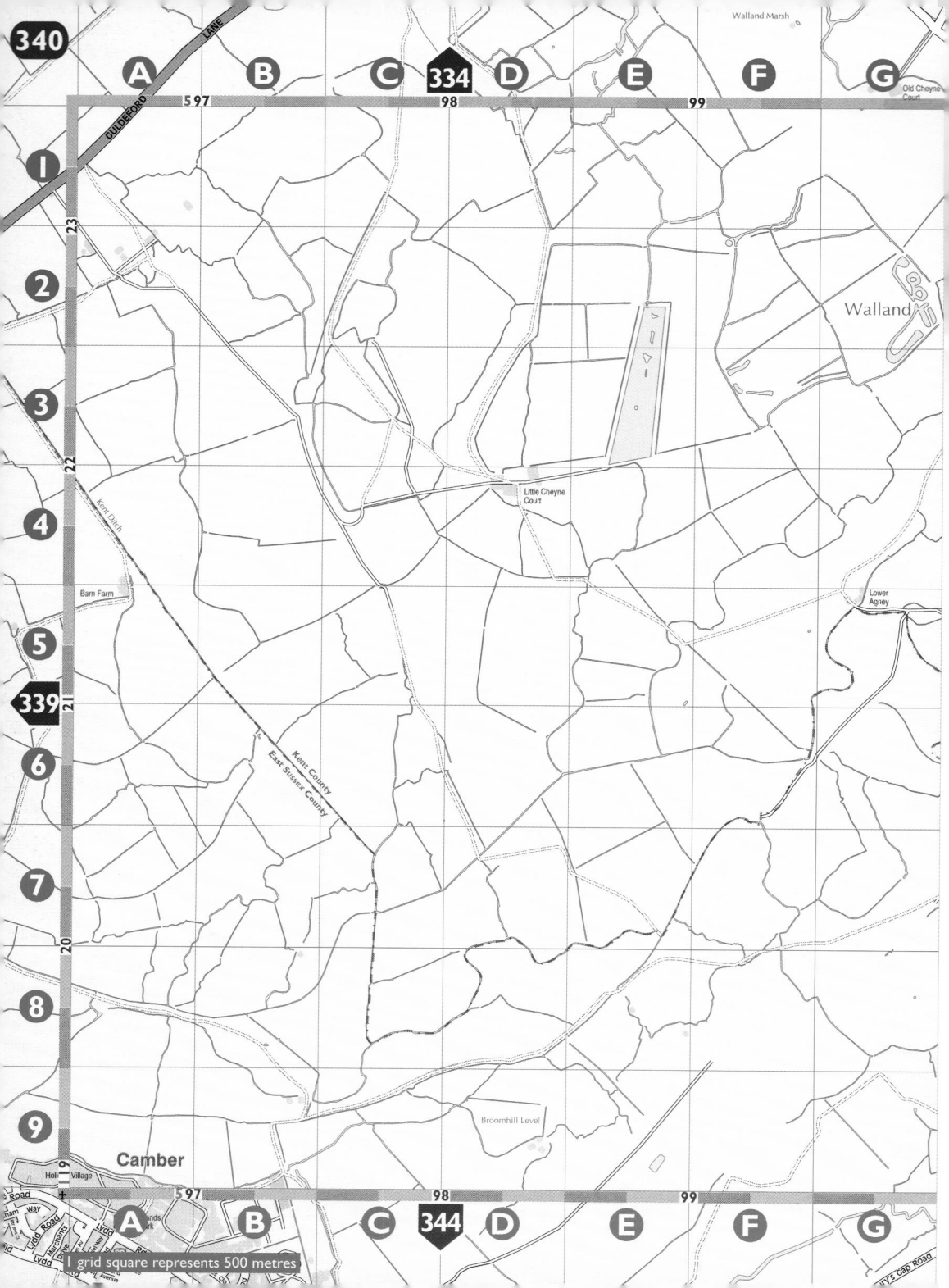

340

A   B   C **334** D   E   F   G

GULDEFORD LANE

Old Cheyne Court

Walland Marsh

1

5 97   98   99

23

2

Walland

3

22

Kent Ditch

4

Little Cheyne Court

Barn Farm

Lower Agney

5

339 21

Kent County
East Sussex County

6

7

20

8

9

Broomhill Level

Camber

Holi... Village

5 97   98   99

A   B   C **344** D   E   F   G

1 grid square represents 500 metres

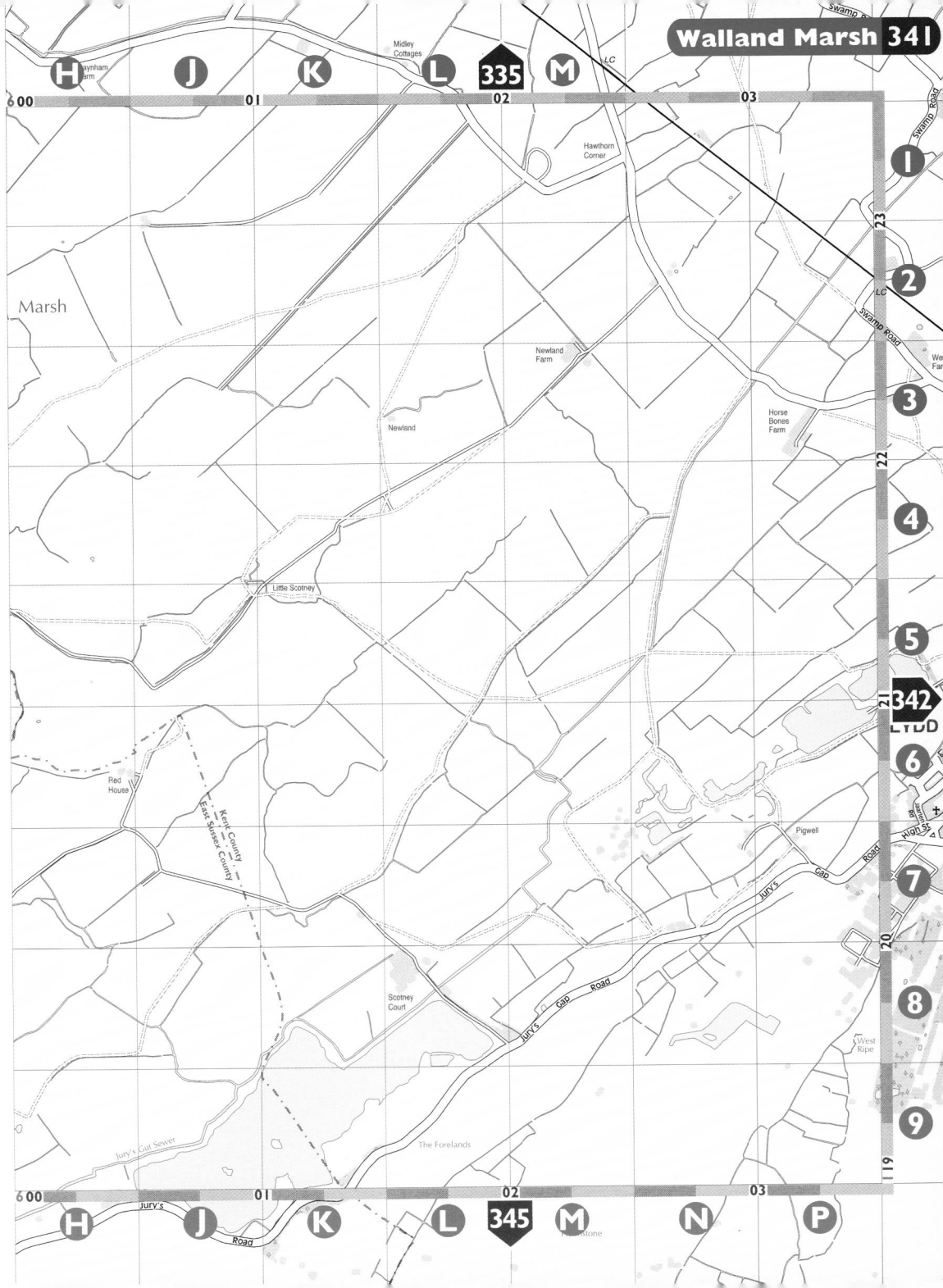

Marsh

Haynham Harm

Midley Cottages

Hawthorn Corner

Newland Farm

Newland

Horse Bones Farm

West Far

Little Scotney

Red House

Kent County
East Sussex County

Pigwell

342 LYDD

High St

Jury's Gap

Jury's Gap Road

Scotney Court

West Ripe

Jury's Gut Sewer

The Forelands

Jury's Road

335

345

Swamp Road

LC

LC

Swamp Road

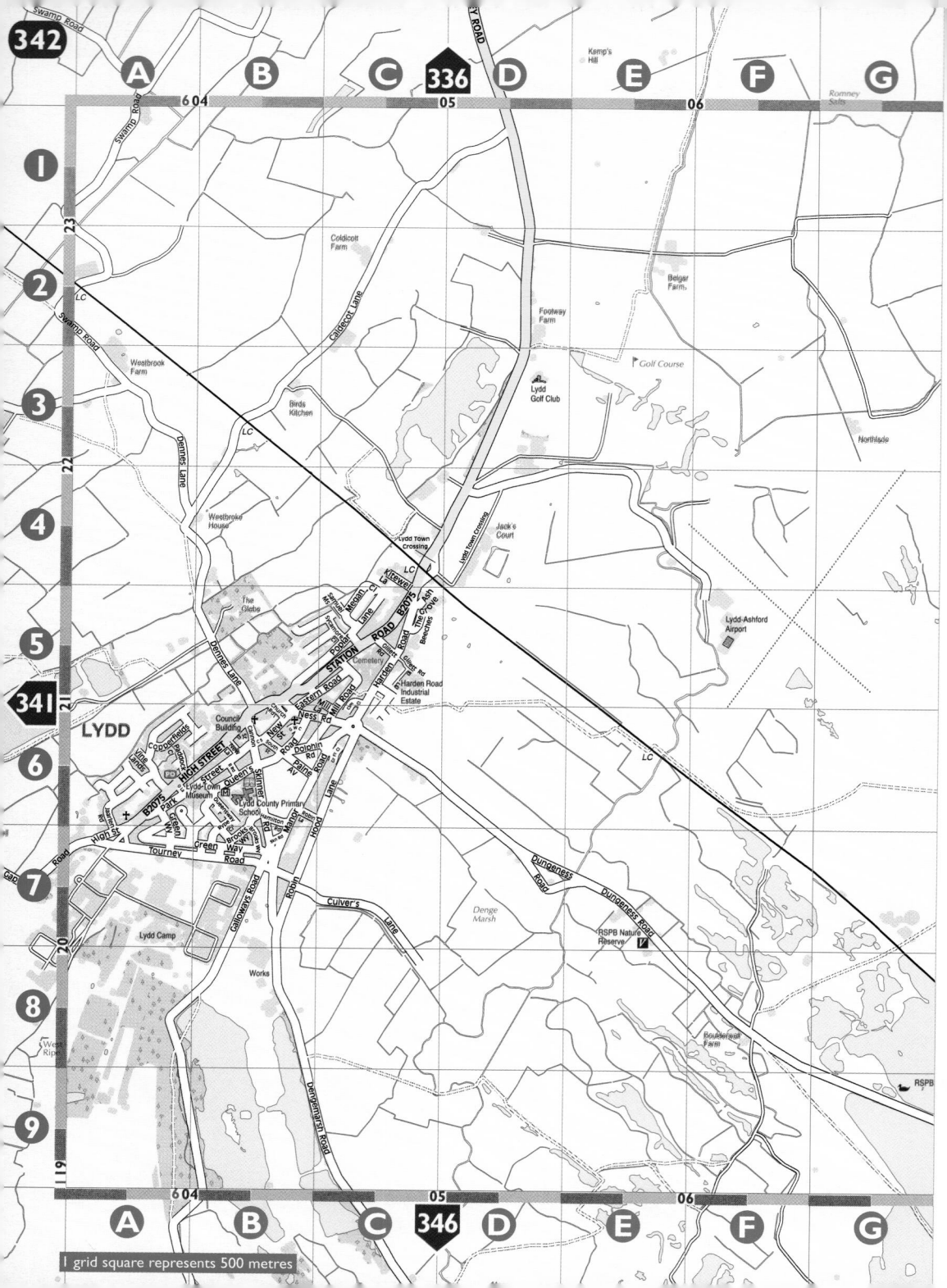

A   B   C   336   D   E   F   G

A   B   C   346   D   E   F   G

LYDD

Swamp Road

Coldicott Farm

Kemp's Hill

Belgar Farm

Romney Salts

Caldecot Lane

Dennes Lane

Westbrook Farm

Birds Kitchen

Westbrooke House

Footway Farm

Golf Course

Lydd Golf Club

Northlade

The Globe

Lydd Town Crossing

Lydd Town Crossing

Jack's Court

STATION ROAD

Lydd-Ashford Airport

Cemetery

Harden Road Industrial Estate

Council Building

Lydd Town Museum

Lydd County Primary School

HIGH STREET

Copperfields

Queen's

B2075

Park

High St

Green

Tourney Road

Green Way Road

Robin Lane

Culver's Lane

Dungeness Road

Dungeness Road

Denge Marsh

RSPB Nature Reserve

Lydd Camp

Works

Dengemarsh Road

West Ripe

Boulderwall Farm

RSPB

1 grid square represents 500 metres

A nber **B** **C** 340 **D** **E** **F** **G**

Broomhill Level

Holiday Village

Road

Glenham Way

Road

Old

I

Camber Sands Holiday Park

Lydd

Road

First Avenue

Second Avenue

The Suttons

Lydd Road

2

P

Broomhill Farm

Jury's Gap Road

Jury's Gap

Lydd Road

Broomhill Sands

3

4

5

6

7

8

9

5 97

98

99

A **B** **C** **D** **E** **F** **G**

1 grid square represents 500 metres

19

18

17

16

15

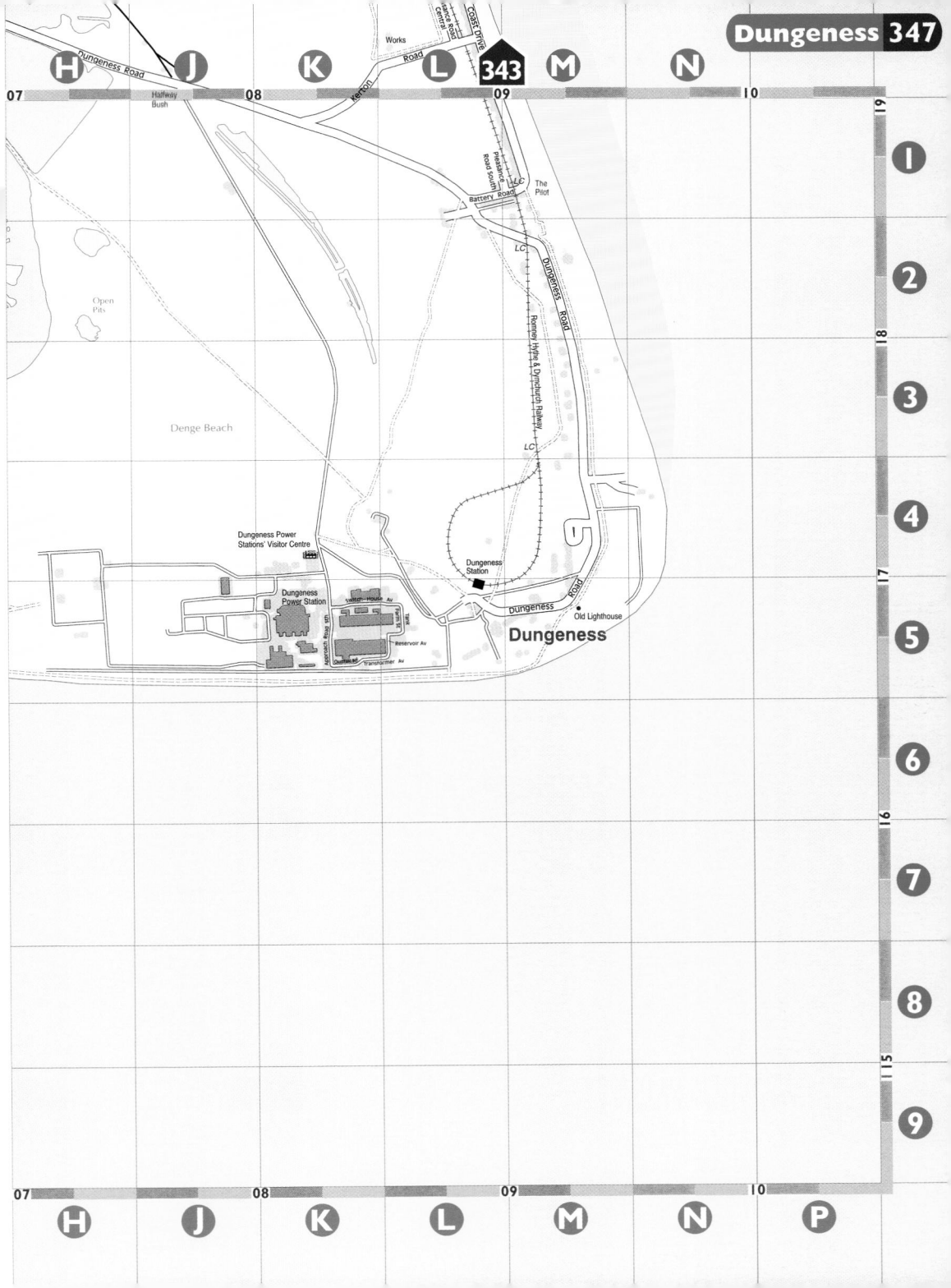

Works

Dungeness Road

Kenton Road

Halfway Bush

343

The Pilot

LC

LC

LC

LC

Romney Hythe & Dymchurch Railway

Dungeness Road

Open Pits

Denge Beach

Dungeness Power Stations' Visitor Centre

Dungeness Power Station

Switch House Av

Turbine Av

Reservoir Av

Approach Road Sth

Oudend Rd

Transformer Av

Dungeness Station

Dungeness Road

Dungeness

Old Lighthouse

H J K L M N

07 08 09 10

I

2

3

4

5

6

7

8

9

19 18 17 16 115

H J K L M N P

07 08 09 10

Coast Drive

Penzance Road South

Battery Road

Lydd Road Central

Abbey Gate 155 L1
Abbey Wood 28 A7
Acol 141 J1
Addington 114 D1
Addington 152 E2
Addiscombe 83 L4
Adisham 198 G7
Aldington 305 N1
Aldington Frith 305 N1
Alkham 289 M3
Allhallows 55 H1
Allhallows-on-Sea 38 G2
Allington 155 J4
Anerley 60 C8
Anvil Green 225 L3
Aperfield 146 A2
Appledore 322 E7
Appledore Heath 322 F4
Arpinge 287 P5
Ash 91 H9
Ash 200 T7
Ashbank 187 L4
Ashford 3 F6
Ashley 261 H1
Ashurst 268 C6
Aveley 30 C5
Avery Hill 43 N7
Aycliff 313 H1
Aylesford 154 E1
Aylesham 229 J1
Badgers Mount 118 A3
Badlesmere 192 F2
Bagham 194 E3
Baker's Cross 298 A2
Baker Street 32 G2
Baldwins Hill 264 F5
Bandonhill 82 C9
Bapchild 130 D2
Barden Park 210 C9
Bardown 314 C7
Barfrestone 229 P5
Barham 228 B5
Barming Heath 154 E9
Barnehurst 45 M4
Barnes Cray 46 B5
Barnes Street 212 B6
Barnfield 220 B6
Barnsole 200 C4
Barrow Green 131 J2
Barrowhill 285 K9
Basted 151 J8
Bayley's Hill 178 D7
Bay View 80 B5
Beacon Green 318 G1
Beal's Green 317 J2
Bean 67 P2
Bearsted 186 E1
Beckenham 61 N9
Beckley 330 F9
Beckton 26 G2
Beddington 82 D6
Bedgebury Cross 296 C5
Bekesbourne 198 A3
Bekesbourne Hill 167 N7
Bell Green 61 M2
Bellingham 61 N3
Beltinge 108 A6
Beltring 213 J6
Belvedere 28 G8
Benenden 298 G8
Benover 214 A5
Bermondsey 24 C5
Berner's Hill 315 L4
Berry's Green 146 B1
Berwick 307 P3
Bessels Green 148 C9
Bethersden 280 D3
Betsham 68 D3
Bettshanger 231 J3
Bexley 44 E5
Bexleyheath 45 H5
Bexon 129 J9
Bickley 63 J8
Bicknor 158 D2
Bidborough 240 E2
Biddenden 277 P6
Biddenden Green 249 J7
Biggin 33 K9
Biggin Hill 145 L2
Bilsington 305 M6
Bilting 223 P2
Birchett's Green 314 C3
Birchington 111 K6
Bircholt Forstal 284 E1
Birling 123 J7
Bishopsbourne 197 N5
Bishopstone 108 C5
Bitchet Green 180 A2
Blackfen 44 B7
Blackham 267 P4
Blackheath 42 D3
Blackheath Park 42 E5
Blackwall 25 N3
Blackwell 265 H6
Bladbean 227 L8
Blean 135 N7
Bliby 283 J8
Blindley Heath 204 B9
Blue Bell Hill 125 H4
Blue Town 57 H5
Bluetown 160 A5
Bobbing 99 J7
Bockhanger 252 E3
Bodiam 328 F5
Bodsham 255 M1
Bonnington 306 A4
Borden 129 H3
Borough Green 151 K4
Borstal 94 G4
Bossingham 196 C4
Bossington 98 D3
Bottom Pond 159 L2
Bough Beech 207 N8
Boughton Aluph 223 L5

Boughton Corner 223 M5
Boughton Green 185 M7
Boughton Lees 223 J7
Boughton Malherbe . 219 H2
Boughton Monchelsea 185 M8
Boughton-under-Blean 134 A9
Bow Common 25 K1
Bowler's Town 338 E2
Bowmans 245 P8
Boxley 156 A2
Boyden Gate 138 F1
Brabourne 255 K9
Brabourne Lees 284 F1
Bramling 198 G1
Branbridges 213 J4
Brasted 147 J9
Brasted Chart 177 J4
Brattle 302 C7
Breach 98 A6
Bredgar 129 H8
Bredhurst 126 E4
Brenchley 243 K9
The Brents 132 G4
Brenzett 335 H1
Brenzett Green 324 B8
Bridge 197 M2
Brissenden Green .. 280 E6
Brixton 40 A5
Broad Ford 274 B4
Broad Green 62 B4
Broadham Green 174 F8
Broad Oak 137 J6
Broad Oak 283 M7
Broadstairs 113 M8
Broadstone 218 E5
Broad Street 73 J5
Broad Street 157 L6
Broad Street 285 N5
Broad Tenterden 320 E2
Broadwater Down ... 270 C8
Brockley 41 M6
Bromley 62 F8
Bromley Common ... 85 N3
Bromley Green 304 B1
Bromley Park 62 C7
Brompton 7 F1
Bromstone 143 K1
Brook 254 C4
Brookland 334 F6
Brooks End 110 E9
Brook Street 240 D2
Brook Street 302 D7
Broomfield 108 A8
Broomfield 187 M6
Broom Hill 86 G4
Broomhill 169 L7
Broomhill Bank 269 P1
Broom Street 133 N5
Buckhurst 277 M5
Buckland 291 K5
Buckland Valley 291 J3
Bulleign 320 E5
Bullockstone 107 J6
Burham 124 E4
Burham Court 124 C4
Burmarsh 326 G2
Burrswood 268 F8
Buttsole 201 J9
Bybrook 252 F4
Cage Green 210 F6
Calcott 137 K3
Camber 340 A9
Camberwell 41 F2
Camden Hill 276 C6
Camden Park 23 H5
Camer 92 D3
Canary Wharf 25 H1
Canning Town 26 C1
Canterbury 4 A4
Capel 242 A3
Capel Cross 274 B3
Capel-le-Ferne 311 L1
Capstone 96 A7
Castle Hill 243 M8
Catford 42 A9
Cellarhill 131 H4
Chadwell St Mary ... 32 G6
Chafford Hundred ... 31 P6
Chainhurst 216 F6
Chalk 50 C9
Chalksole 259 L6
Chalkwell 129 K1
Challock 192 F9
Chamber's Green ... 250 B5
Charcott 208 F7
Charing 221 J2
Charing Heath 220 D3
Charing Hill 221 J1
Chariton 42 D4
Chart Corner 216 E1
Chartham 195 M1
Chartham Hatch 165 L6
Chart Hill 216 E2
Chart Sutton 216 E2
The Chart 177 J6
Chatham 6 D4
Chattenden 72 E2
Cheeseman's Green . 283 H6
Chegworth 188 A5
Chelsfield 87 M9
Chelsham 144 D2
Cheriton 309 P1
Chesley 128 B3
Chestfield 106 C6
Chestnut Street 128 F1
Chevening 147 N4
Chiddingstone 238 A3
Chiddingstone Causeway 208 E3
Chiddingstone Hoath . 237 P7
Childsbridge 149 L4
Chilham 194 C5
Chillenden 230 B1
Chillmill 273 H2
Chilmington Green .. 281 P3

Chilton 142 F6
Chipstead 148 B7
Chislehurst 63 N6
Chislehurst West ... 63 L5
Chislet 138 G4
Chislet Forstal 138 G3
Chitty 138 G3
Church Hougham 312 C1
Church Street 51 H7
Church Whitfield 261 J7
Cinder Hill 209 H9
Clapham Hill 105 L9
Clap Hill 284 A9
Clapper Hill 300 A2
Claret 181 J7
Claygate 244 B4
Claygate Cross 151 K9
Claypits 199 M3
Clement Street 66 D5
Cliffe 52 C2
Cliffe Woods 52 C9
Cliffs End 142 C6
Cliftonville 113 H3
Cobham 92 G1
Cock Street 185 A9
Coldblow 65 L1
Cold Harbour 98 G8
Coldharbour 29 M7
Coldharbour 210 D1
Coldred 260 A5
Colliers Green 275 L6
Collier Street 244 D1
Colt's Hill 242 C5
Comp 152 A6
Coney Hall 85 H8
Congelow 213 M3
Conyer 101 K5
Cooling 52 F3
Coolinge 310 C2
Cooling Street 52 D7
Coombe 92 F8
Coomb Hill 92 F8
Cooper's Corner 207 N2
Cooper Street 171 H7
Coppins Corner 220 F1
Cop Street 170 F7
Copton 162 G2
The Corner 244 A9
Court-at-Street 307 H4
Cousley Wood 294 D8
Cowden 267 H2
Coxheath 185 J8
Crabble 290 F5
Cranbrook 298 A2
Cranbrook Common . 276 D6
Crawford 46 A6
Creekmouth 27 M1
Crit Hall 298 C8
Crockenhill 88 B3
Crockham Hill 176 D9
Crockhurst Street .. 241 L3
Crofton 86 C9
Cross-at-Hand 216 B9
Cross Keys 178 E3
Crouch 151 L8
Crouch 163 P5
Crowdleham 149 P1
Crowhurst 204 G7
Crowhurst Lane End . 204 D5
Croydon 83 J7
Crundale 224 E5
Crystal Palace 60 G5
Cubitt Town 25 M7
Cudham 116 E9
Culmers 133 H4
Culverstone Green .. 121 P3
Curteis' Corner 278 B5
Curtisden Green 275 H3
Custom House 26 F1
Cuxton 94 B4
Dale Hill 315 K4
Danaway 128 D3
Dane Street 194 A5
Daniel's Water 251 J9
Darenth 67 J4
Dargate 134 E5
Dargate Common ... 134 F6
Dartford 46 C8
Daval Street 92 B9
Davington 132 D5
Deal 233 H4
Dean Bottom 67 P9
Deans Bottom 128 D8
Dean Hill 128 E7
Dean Street 185 J5
Deerton Street 131 M5
Dene Park 210 C1
Denny Bottom 270 A5
Densole 288 D4
Denstroude 135 K5
Denton 50 A8
Denton 258 D2
Deptford 25 J9
Derringstone 228 B7
Derry Downs 87 L3
Detling 156 E1
Dingleden 318 F3
Ditton 154 B2
Doddington 160 D5
Donkey Street 327 H1
Dormansland 235 L8
Dormans Park 265 H1
Dover 9 F3
Downe 116 A5
Downham 62 B4
The Down 294 C4
Drellingore 289 K5
Drivill 148 A9
Dulwich 60 F1
Dulwich Village 40 G8
Dumpton 143 K2
Dungate 160 A1
Dungeness 347 M5
Dunkirk 164 E2
Dunk's Green 181 K5

Dunn Street 126 D5
Dunn Street 222 B5
Dunton Green 148 D4
Durlock 141 K7
Durlock 200 C2
Durrant Green 301 J1
Dymchurch 327 H6
Each End 201 J1
East Barming 184 D2
Eastchurch 79 J4
East Dulwich 40 C6
East End 58 E9
East End 248 B5
East End 299 N4
East Farleigh 184 D8
East Grinstead 265 H6
East Guldeford 339 J5
East Hill 119 N3
East Langdon 261 P7
Eastling 161 K6
East Malling 154 A6
East Malling Heath . 153 M9
East Peckham 212 G4
Eastry 201 J9
East Stourmouth ... 170 A2
East Street 171 J9
East Studdal 231 M9
East Tilbury 34 A7
Eastwell Park 222 G7
East Wickham 44 C2
Eccles 124 F8
Eddington 107 K5
Edenbridge 206 B8
Eden Park 88 C1
Egerton 219 M7
Egerton Forstal 219 L9
Eltham 257 K4
Elmers End 61 K9
Elmstead 63 J1
Elmsted 255 N3
Elmstone 169 F8
Eltham 43 J7
Elvington 230 D8
Erith 29 L8
Errottwood 160 D1
Etchinghill 287 H5
Evington 252 C7
Ewell Minnis 259 P9
Ewhurst Green 329 J8
Exted 257 J4
Eyhorne Street 187 L1
Eynsford 89 K6
Eythorne 260 C1
Fairbourne Heath ... 218 B1
Fairfield 333 P4
Fairseat 121 M6
Falconwood 44 A5
Fant 155 J9
Farleigh 114 C8
Farleigh Court 114 D8
Farleigh Green 184 D5
Farnborough 86 C9
Farningham 89 M4
Farthing Corner 127 H2
Farthing Green 217 H9
Farthingloe 312 C1
Faversham 133 H5
Fawkham Green 90 E7
Felbridge 264 C4
Felcourt 234 F9
Felderland 201 N6
Fenn Street 53 N5
Ferndale 23 H1
Fickleshole 115 H8
Field Green 317 N6
Finglesham 231 P1
Fir Toll 250 B3
Five Oak Green 242 B1
Five Wents 187 H9
Fleet Downs 67 H1
Flemings 200 E4
Fletcher's Green 209 J1
Flimwell 315 N3
Flishinghurst 275 L9
Folkestone 11 F6
Foots Cray 64 D5
Force Green 146 F9
Ford 138 B1
Fordcombe 268 F3
Fordwich 137 M9
Forestdale 114 B3
Forest Hill 41 K9
Forstal 155 H2
The Forstal 283 N5
Fostal 134 B6
Fosten Green 299 N2
Four Elms 207 H5
Four Oaks 132 B4
Four Oaks 331 H8
Four Throws 317 L6
Four Wents 275 K8
Four Wents 297 N9
Foxbury 63 P4
Foxendown 92 D6
French Street 176 G6
Friday Street 72 C7
Frinstead 157 J3
Frinsted 159 K5
Frittenden 277 J1
Frogham 229 M5
Froghole 176 E8
Frogholt 287 K8
Further Quarter 279 K5
Gadshill 51 L5
Garlinge 111 P6
Garlinge Green 195 M5
Gibraltar 288 C9
Gill's Green 317 N1
Glassenbury 297 K1
Goathurst Common . 178 A6
Goddard's Green 299 J5
Godden Green 179 M1
Goddington 87 K7
Godinton Park 252 A7

Godmersham 194 C9
Golden Green 212 A5
Golford 298 D1
Golgotha 229 P8
Goodley Stock 176 C6
Goodnestone 133 N6
Goodnestone 199 N6
Goose Green 182 C9
Goose Green 277 P8
Gore 201 H7
Gore Street 140 B5
Gosmere 162 G5
Goudhurst 274 E8
Gover Hill 181 P5
Grafty Green 218 F4
Grain 56 E2
Grange 73 P9
Gravel Castle 228 D6
Graveney 133 N3
Gravesend 49 M6
Grays 48 D1
Great Bower 193 K5
Great Buckland 123 H1
Great Chart 251 P8
Great Cheveney 244 F8
Great Mongeham ... 232 B6
Greatness 149 J5
Great Pattenden 244 F3
Great Stonar 171 N8
Greatstone-on-Sea . 343 L9
Greenhill 107 J4
Green Hill 198 E8
Greenhithe 47 M5
Green Street Green . 67 N5
Green Street Green . 116 C2
Greenwich 25 N8
Greet 160 C9
Grigg 248 B3
Groombridge 268 F9
Grove 139 J9
Grove End 129 K6
Grove Ferry 139 J7
Grove Green 156 A7
Grove Hill 168 G2
Grove Park 62 G2
Groves 200 A3
Grubb Street 67 P7
Guilton 200 D1
Gun Green 317 L4
Gushmere 163 M5
Guston 291 M1
Hackbridge 82 A6
Hackington 202 E8
Hadlow 212 A1
Hadlow Stair 211 K6
Haffenden Quarter . 279 H1
Haine 142 E2
Hale 86 A6
Hale 110 C9
Hales Place 166 F1
Hale Street 213 H3
Halfway Houses 57 N9
Halfway Street 259 N2
Halling 94 D4
Hall's Green 208 F2
Halstead 117 P6
Ham 201 N8
Ham Green 35 K9
Ham Green 331 P4
Ham Hill 123 P7
Hammerwood 266 C5
Hammill 200 F6
Hampton 106 C9
Hamptons 181 L6
Hamstreet 304 C8
Hanging Bank 177 N8
Harbledown 166 A4
Harbourland 155 N3
The Harbour 217 H5
Harelplain 277 M5
Harman's Corner ... 129 J3
Harrietsham 188 E5
Hartley 91 J2
Hartley 297 L5
Hartley Green 91 H2
Hartlip 97 N9
Harvel 122 D2
Hassell Street 225 H8
Hastingleigh 255 J3
Haviker Street 214 D9
Hawkenbury 23 J7
Hawkenbury 246 F2
Hawkhurst 316 C5
Hawkinge 288 E7
Hawley 66 E4
Hawthorn Corner .. 107 H8
Haxted 236 A1
Hayes 85 L4
Hazel Street 158 B1
Hazel Street 273 M5
Hazelwood 116 C5
Headcorn 247 P4
Hearnden Green 217 K9
Hearts Delight 129 J4
Heath Side 65 P1
Heaverham 150 B2
Hempstead 96 B9
Hemsted 256 C9
Henhurst 70 A7
Henley Street 92 G3
Henwood Green 272 A2
Herne 107 L6
Herne Bay 107 L2
Herne Common 107 L7
Herne Hill 40 C5
Herne Pound 182 C7
Hernhill 134 C7
Heronden 200 F9
Hersden 138 C9
Hever 237 K3
Hextable 66 A6
Hickmans Green ... 164 B2
Hicks Forstal 137 M1
Higham 71 L3
Higham Wood 211 J4

Place	Page	Grid
High Brooms	240	F9
Highgate	317	J4
High Halden	279	L9
High Halstow	53	L5
Highstead	108	D9
Highsted	129	N6
Highstreet	134	C5
High Street	316	F4
Hildenborough	210	B4
Hilden Park	210	B6
Hillborough	108	D6
Hill Green	127	M4
Hill Hoath	238	A3
Hill Park	146	C8
Hill Street	255	N1
Hinxhill	253	N8
Hither Green	42	C7
Hoaden	170	A7
Hoath	138	C4
Hoath Corner	238	A6
Hockenden	65	K9
Hockley	161	P9
Hodsoll Street	121	M3
Hogben's Hill	163	K5
Holborough	123	P5
Holland	175	K9
Hollingbourne	187	P1
Hollow Street	138	F4
Hollybushes	159	P4
Holt Hill	154	C4
Hotye	266	F5
Honey Hill	135	M6
Honor Oak	41	K7
Honor Oak Park	41	L7
Hoo	140	C6
Hook Green	65	P3
Hook Green	68	D5
Hook Green	92	B3
Hook Green	294	E3
Hoo St Werburgh	73	J1
Horns Cross	47	M7
Horns Green	146	F2
Horn Street	123	M7
Horn Street	309	N3
Horsalls	188	G1
Horseshoe Green	237	K8
Horsmonden	273	M2
Horton	165	N9
Horton Kirby	90	A1
Hosey Hill	176	F4
Hothfield	251	M2
Houghton Green	321	J5
How Green	207	L8
Howt Green	99	L5
Hubbard's Hill	178	G6
Hucking	157	P9
Hulberry	88	G6
Hungershall Park	270	B6
Hunters Forstal	107	N5
Hunton	214	D2
Hurst Green	175	H8
Hythe	309	H6
Ickham	168	F7
Ide Hill	177	M7
Iden	332	E9
Iden Green	275	H8
Iden Green	318	C2
Ightham	150	G6
Ightham Common	150	D9
Isle of Dogs	25	M7
Istead Rise	69	J6
Ivychurch	335	N2
Ivy Hatch	180	E1
Iwade	70	F3
Joyden's Wood	65	P3
Jury's Gap	344	F2
Kearsney	290	D5
Kempe's Corner	223	L8
Kemsing	149	L2
Kemsley	99	N6
Kemsley Street	126	F4
Kenardington	303	L9
Kennington	253	H3
Kent Street	182	G1
Keston	85	N8
Keston Mark	85	N7
Kettle Corner	184	E3
Kevingtown	87	N3
Keycol	98	F8
Key's Green	272	D4
Key Street	99	H9
Kidbrooke	42	G3
Kilndown	295	P5
Kingsdown	130	C9
Kingsdown	262	C3
Kings Farm	89	N2
Kingsgate	113	M4
Kings Hill	153	J8
Kingsnorth	74	B1
Kingsnorth	282	D5
Kingston	197	P9
Kingswood	187	P8
Kipping's Cross	272	B4
Kippington	20	C5
Kit's Coty	125	H5
Knatts Valley	130	B4
Knave's Ash	107	P9
Knight's Hill	40	C9
Knockhall	47	P6
Knockholt	147	H2
Knockmill	120	B6
Knowlton	230	D2
Knox Bridge	276	D2
Laddingford	213	M5
Lade	343	K6
Ladywell	41	N5
Lakeside	31	K7
Lamberhurst	295	J2
Lamberhurst Quarter	272	E6
Lamb's Cross	216	C4
Lane End	67	K4
Langley	186	F7
Langley Heath	187	J7
Langton Green	269	L9
Larkfield	153	P2
The Leacon	303	P8
Leadingcross Green	189	K8
Leaveland	192	D3
Leaves Green	115	N5
Lee	66	D7
Leeds	187	K4
The Lees	222	D1
Leigh	209	L8
Leigh Green	301	M8
Lenham	189	L6
Lenham Forstal	220	A1
Lenham Heath	220	A2
Lessness Heath	28	G9
Lett's Green	146	G1
Lewes Heath	273	P5
Lewisham	42	A5
Lewson Street	131	L6
Leybourne	153	M1
Leysdown-on-Sea	80	F5
Lidsing	126	B4
Lilyvale	284	C5
Limehouse	25	H3
Limpsfield	175	J5
Limpsfield Chart	176	A7
Limpsfield Common	175	J5
Linford	33	N5
Lingfield	234	G5
Lingfield Common	234	G3
Linkhill	329	M1
Linton	215	L2
Little Bayham	294	A3
Littlebourne	168	B9
Little Chart	220	F9
Little Chart Forstal	251	H1
Little Cheveney Fm	244	D5
Little Mill	212	E5
Little Mongeham	231	P7
Little Pattenden	245	H1
Little Preston	154	F3
Littlestone-on-Sea	337	J6
Little Thurrock	32	D7
Liverton Street	218	G1
Livesey Street	183	P1
Locksbottom	86	C7
Lodge Lees	258	B2
London Beach	301	H2
Longfield	68	D9
Longfield Hill	91	N1
Longford	148	C5
Longlands	63	N2
Loose	185	L7
Loose Hill	185	L6
Lords Wood	125	P3
Lower Bitchet	179	P2
Lower Bush	93	N3
Lower Cousley Wood	294	F7
Lower Cox Street	126	C2
Lower Eythorne	230	C9
Lower Goldstone	170	G4
Lower Green	241	N9
Lower Green	269	P3
Lower Halstow	98	D3
Lower Hardres	196	F5
Lower Hartlip	127	P1
Lower Haysden	240	B1
Lower Heppington	196	D3
Lower Herne	107	L5
Lower Higham	71	N1
Lower Island	105	K5
Lower Rainham	97	H3
Lower Stoke	54	C3
Lower Sydenham	61	K3
Lower Twydall	96	F1
Lower Upnor	72	H4
Low Street	33	N9
Loyterton	131	J8
Luddesdown	92	G5
Lunsford	125	M9
Luton	205	J5
Luxted	116	B8
Lydd	342	A6
Lydden	112	D9
Lydden	259	P5
Lydd-on-Sea	343	K7
Lyewood Common	269	M5
Lymbridge Green	256	A5
Lyminge	286	G2
Lympne	307	P4
Lynsore Bottom	227	H2
Lynsted	130	F7
Mabledon	240	C3
Maidstone	12	B5
Maltman's Hill	249	M6
Manston	142	B3
Maplescombe	89	N9
Marden	245	H4
Marden Beech	244	G6
Marden Thorn	245	M7
Margate	14	E2
Marine Town	14	F3
Markbeech	237	L2
Marley	227	N1
Marley	231	P1
Marlpit Hill	206	F8
Marshborough	201	J3
Marsh Green	236	C4
Marshside	108	F3
Martin	262	A6
Martin Mill	262	B7
Matfield	242	F9
Maxted Street	256	A3
Maxton	291	H9
Maypole	45	N9
Maypole	117	N1
Maypole	138	B5
Medhurst Row	237	J3
Meopham	92	A6
Meopham Green	92	B7
Meopham Station	92	C2
Meresborough	97	K9
Mereworth	183	L6
Merle Common	205	K3
Mersham	285	H4
Middle Quarter	279	K7
Middle Stoke	54	G4
Milebush	245	K1
Mile Oak	243	K5
Mile Town	57	J6
Milstead	138	C2
Mill Hall	154	B2
Mill Hill	232	E6
Mill Street	153	M5
Millwall	25	K7
Milstead	159	M2
Milton	49	P7
Milton Regis	59	K9
Minster	58	B9
Minster	141	K6
Mockbeggar	72	A2
Modest Corner	240	B7
Molash	193	J7
Monks Hill	278	D1
Monks Orchard	83	P4
Monkton	140	E5
Moon's Green	331	M2
Moorhouse Bank	176	B4
Moorstock	285	K6
Moor Street	97	L7
The Moor	317	H6
Morehall	310	C5
Mottingham	62	G1
Mountain Street	194	C5
Mount Pleasant	141	J4
Mowshurst	206	F6
Mucking	32	A4
Muckingford	33	N6
Mundy Bois	249	N1
Murston	130	B1
Naccolt	253	P4
Nackington	196	C1
Napchester	285	H9
Nash	115	L1
Nash Street	69	K8
Neames Forstal	163	N5
Nettlestead	183	K5
Nettlestead Green	183	J9
New Addington	114	G2
New Ash Green	91	K6
New Barn	68	F8
Newbarn	286	C4
New Beckenham	61	L8
Newchapel	234	B8
New Charlton	26	E7
Newchurch	325	M3
New Cross	41	L3
New Cross Gate	41	L2
New Eltham	63	M1
Newenden	330	C2
New House	69	J1
Newingreen	307	P2
Newington	88	D2
Newington	142	F5
Newington	287	L8
Newland Green	249	L1
Newnham	160	G4
New Romney	336	E6
New Street	46	F7
New Town	93	P8
New Town	153	J5
Noah's Arks	149	P4
Noke Street	72	C5
Nonington	229	N1
Norbury	60	B8
North Cray	65	J2
Northdown	113	J4
North Elham	257	M4
North End	45	P2
North End	264	E4
Northfleet	48	G6
Northfleet Green	48	E9
North Halling	93	P7
Northiam	330	A7
North Leigh	226	B7
North Stifford	31	P3
North Street	54	C7
North Street	162	C3
Northumberland Heath	45	L1
Northwood	142	F7
North Woolwich	26	E5
Norton Ash	131	M5
Norwood New Town	60	B8
Nunhead	41	J5
Oad Street	128	F4
Oakhurst	179	M9
Oare	132	D3
Offham	152	E4
Old Bexley	65	J2
Oldbury	150	E6
Old Cryals	272	E3
Old Romney	336	A6
Old Tree	138	D2
Old Wives Lees	194	D1
Orpington	87	H8
Orsett	33	J1
Orsett Heath	32	G5
Ospringe	132	D7
Otford	130	C5
Otham	186	D4
Otham Hole	186	F5
Otterden Place	190	G2
Otterham Quay	97	M4
Ottinge	228	E9
Out Elmstead	228	A4
Overland	164	A5
Oxted	174	G5
Paddlesworth	123	L4
Paddlesworth	287	P4
Paddock	240	C3
Paddock Wood	243	J5
Pains Hill	175	M7
Painter's Forstal	162	B1
Palmarsh	308	B7
Palmer's Green	175	L9
Palmstead	227	J5
Paramour Street	170	E4
Parker's Green	211	N4
Park Farm	282	F4
Parkgate	300	C5
Park Langley	84	F3
Park Wood	126	F2
Park Wood	186	D6
Parrock Farm	69	P2
Patrixbourne	167	N9
Payden Street	190	B3
Pean Hill	135	M3
Pearson's Green	243	M6
Peckham	41	H5
Peckham Bush	212	E2
Pedling Quarter	320	F8
Pegwell	142	F7
Pell Green	294	C8
Pembles Cross	219	K7
Pembury	271	M2
Penenden Heath	155	P5
Penge	61	J6
Pennypot	308	E6
Penshurst	238	C5
Perry	169	M5
Perry Street	49	K8
Perrywood	163	L8
Pested	192	E7
Petham	196	B7
Pett Bottom	197	H6
Petteridge	272	G2
Pettings	121	L2
Petts Wood	86	E1
Pineham	261	L8
Pipsden	317	M5
Pittswood	211	K2
Pizien Well	183	J4
Plaistow	62	E5
Platt	151	M5
Platt's Heath	218	G1
Plaxtol	181	J3
Playden	338	F4
Pluckley	250	B2
Pluckley Thorne	249	P3
Plucks Gutter	140	B9
Plumford	162	D2
Plumstead	27	K8
Plumstead Common	27	L8
Plumtree Green	247	K1
Pollhill	188	C6
Pootings	237	H4
Poplar	25	K3
Postling	286	D6
Potman's Heath	320	C9
Potten Street	109	P6
Potters Corner	252	B3
Potter's Forstal	219	J3
Poundsbridge	239	H9
Poverest	87	H1
Powder Mills	210	B7
Pratling Street	124	C9
Pratt's Bottom	117	J4
Preston	132	C7
Preston	169	L2
Priestwood	92	C9
Priestwood Green	92	D9
Printstile	239	M6
Puddledock	65	M5
Puddledock	177	H9
Pullington	318	F1
Purfleet	30	D8
Pye Corner	218	B4
The Quarter	249	J4
The Quarter	320	D2
Queenborough	77	J2
Queen Street	243	L1
Rabbit's Cross	216	B6
Radfall	106	B9
Radfield	92	D2
Radnor Park	287	K7
Ram Lane	221	K8
Ramsden	87	K3
Ramsgate	17	H4
Ramslye	269	J7
Ratling	199	L8
Reading Street	113	M5
Reading Street	321	N4
Reculver	108	C3
Red Hill	183	N2
Rhodes Minnis	256	F6
Richborough Port	172	A3
Ridge Row	288	C5
Ridgeway	284	D5
Ridley	121	J2
Ringlestone	155	J5
Ringlestone	186	C2
Ringwould	262	F3
Ripper's Cross	251	J5
Ripple	232	G2
Riseden	295	P2
River	167	H7
Riverhead	148	G1
Riverview Park	70	C3
Robhurst	302	B5
Rochester	18	D3
The Rocks	153	P7
Rodmersham	130	C5
Rodmersham Green	130	A6
Rolvenden	319	M2
Rolvenden Layne	319	N4
Romford	272	A1
Rooks Hill	179	P4
Roseacre	156	D9
Rosherville	49	K6
Rotherhithe	24	G6
Rough Common	196	A4
Roughway	181	L5
Round Green	275	L4
Round Street	92	E1
Rowling	200	B8
Rowling Green	305	H1
Royal British Legion Village	154	G4
Royal Tunbridge Wells	305	J7
Ruckinge	305	L3
Rushenden	77	H5
Rushmore Hill	117	K7
Rusthall	269	P4
Ruxley	64	G5
Ryarsh	123	H9
Rye	338	F6
Rye Foreign	338	B3
St George in the East	24	D3
St Johns	41	N3
St John's	148	F7
St John's	270	C2
St Lawrence	16	B1
St Leonard's Street	153	H5
St Margaret's at Cliffe	292	D1
St Mary Cray	87	K2
St Mary in the Marsh	336	C1
St Mary's Bay	337	M2
St Mary's Hoo	54	A2
St Mary's Island	72	G5
St Michaels	301	J3
St Nicholas at Wade	109	N8
St Paul's Cray	64	C8
St Peters	113	J8
Saint's Hill	238	G9
Salmans	238	D6
Saltwood	308	F3
Sandgate	310	B8
Sandhurst	318	A9
Sandhurst Cross	328	F1
Sandling	155	L3
Sandown Park	271	J2
Sandway	218	G3
Sandwich	201	M1
Sandwich Bay Estate	202	E2
Sarre	139	N2
Satmar	289	N9
Scragged Oak	128	C1
Scrapsgate	58	A7
Seabrook	309	M5
Seacox Heath	316	A4
Seal	149	N6
Seasalter	105	H7
Seaton	168	G6
Seed	166	C6
Selgrove	162	F2
Selhurst	83	J2
Sellindge	285	K7
Selling	163	M6
Selson	201	H7
Selsted	258	E7
Sevenoaks	21	H4
Sevenoaks Common	178	F5
Sevenoaks Weald	178	F8
Sevington	283	L2
Shadoxhurst	281	M8
Shadwell	24	F3
Shalmsford Street	195	H1
Sharnal Street	55	N7
Shatterling	169	P7
Sheerness	57	J5
Sheldwich	162	F6
Sheldwich Lees	162	G7
Shelvingford	138	D2
Shepherdswell or Sibertswold	259	P9
Shepway	185	P3
Sherwood Park	271	H2
Shipbourne	180	F6
Shirkoak	302	F2
Shirley	83	P6
Sholden	232	E3
Shooters Hill	43	N2
Shoreham	118	D5
Shorncliffe Camp	310	A7
Shorne	70	G4
Shorne Ridgeway	70	F6
Shortlands	62	C9
Shottenden	193	N2
Shover's Green	314	A4
Shuttlesfield	287	M2
Sidcup	64	D3
Silver Street	128	C2
Silvertown	26	D5
Singleton	282	A1
Singlewell	69	N5
Sinkhurst Green	247	H8
Sissinghurst	276	D8
Sittingbourne	129	P3
Sixmile	256	C4
Skeete	286	C1
Slade	190	D2
Slade Green	46	A3
Sly Corner	323	H1
Small Hythe	209	G5
Smarden	249	H8
Smarden Bell	248	F7
Smart's Hill	238	E9
Smeeth	284	D4
Snagshall	328	G8
Snargate	323	N8
Snave	324	C6
Snipeshill	130	B2
Snodland	123	M4
Snowdown	229	J3
Sole Street	92	D2
Sole Street	225	J3
South Alkham	286	C1
South Ashford	2	A2
South Ashford	252	C9
Southborough	86	A3
Southborough	240	D8
South Bromley	25	L4
South Darenth	67	K7
Southend	62	A3
Southfields	33	L5
Southfleet	68	F5
South Godstone	204	C5
South Green	128	B9
South Norwood	60	D9
South Stifford	31	N8
South Stour	283	K7
South Street	105	P7
South Street	121	P1
South Street	127	N1
South Street	146	A4
South Street	164	A4
South Willesborough	282	G2

Place	Page	Ref	Place	Page	Ref
Speed Gate	90	C6	Sutton	261	P1
Speldhurst	269	M1	Sutton at Hone	66	G6
Spitalfields	24	D1	Sutton Valence	217	H3
Spitals Cross	206	D7	Swalecliffe	106	D5
Spring Park	84	D6	Swanley	65	N7
Stalisfield Green	191	J5	Swanley Village	66	A8
Standen	278	B3	Swanscombe	48	D6
Standen Street	318	D5	Swanton Street	158	C1
Stanford	286	A7	Swift's Green	248	F4
Stanhope	282	C3	Swingfield Minnis	288	E1
Stanstead	121	H5	Swingfield Street	288	G1
Staple	200	B4	Sydenham	61	K4
Staplehurst	246	C5	Tanden	279	P7
Staplestreet	134	A8	Tandridge	174	D9
Starvecrow	210	F2	Tankerton	105	P3
Statenborough	201	K6	Tatsfield	145	N5
Stede Quarter	278	F7	Teasley Mead	268	B5
Stelling Minnis	226	E8	Temple Ewell	290	F2
Stepney	24	F1	Temple Hill	46	D5
Stick Hill	237	H6	Tenterden	301	H7
Stiff Street	128	G6	Teston	183	P4
Stockbury	127	P5	Teynham	131	H2
Stocker's Head	221	L1	Teynham Street	131	L1
Stockland Green	239	P9	Thamesmead	27	L3
Stocks Green	209	N6	Thanington	166	A7
The Stocks	332	D1	Thong	70	C5
Stodmarsh	168	E2	Thornton Heath	60	B9
Stoke	54	E5	Three Chimneys	277	L7
Stone	47	M6	Three Leg Cross	315	H5
Stonebridge Green	219	P5	Throwley	162	A8
Stone Cross	201	M3	Throwley Forstal	191	P2
Stone Cross	268	E6	Thurnham	156	F4
Stone Cross	305	J1	Ticehurst	315	J4
Stonecrouch	295	M8	Tilbury	49	L2
Stonegate	314	E8	Tilmanstone	231	H6
Stonehall	260	B8	Timberden Bottom	118	D4
Stone Hill	285	H6	Titsey	175	M1
Stonehill Green	65	L5	Tolhurst	314	D4
Stone in Oxney	333	J7	Tonbridge	310	F9
Stonequarry	265	K5	Tong	217	M8
Stone Street	180	B1	Tong Corner	100	E7
Stonestreet Green	284	C9	Tong Green	191	N2
Stonewood	68	B2	Tovil	185	K2
Stowting	255	P9	Tower Hamlets	291	H7
Stowting Common	255	P5	Townland Green	302	E6
Strawberry Hill	270	A8	Toy's Hill	177	K8
Street End	196	E4	Trench Wood	210	D3
Strood	18	A2	Trottiscliffe	122	B8
Strood	319	P1	Troy Town	19	C2
Stubb's Cross	282	A6	Troy Town	206	A5
Studdal	261	K1	Troy Town	254	D4
Studd Hill	106	F3	Tubslake	297	L7
Sturry	137	K7	Tudeley	241	M2
Stryants Bottom	150	D6	Tudeley Hale	211	M9
Summerfield	200	C5	Tulse Hill	40	B9
Sundridge	62	G5	Tunbridge Hill	54	B7
Sundridge	147	N9	Tunstall	129	L5

Place	Page	Ref	Place	Page	Ref
Tutt Hill	221	M9	Weller's Town	238	B4
Twenties	112	B6	Well Hill	88	A9
Twitham	199	P1	Welling	44	D4
Twitton	148	D1	Well Street	153	M6
Twydall	96	E4	Wennington	30	B3
Tyler Hill	136	D7	Westbere	137	P6
Ulcombe	217	P3	Westbrook	111	P3
Underlining Green	215	L8	Westcliffe	292	C1
Underriver	179	M6	West Court	70	A1
Under the Wood	108	E8	West Cross	319	K2
Union Street	315	M3	West Dulwich	60	D1
Upchurch	98	A2	Wested Fm	88	D4
Upper Bush	93	N4	West End	106	F6
Upper Deal	232	E5	West End	160	C5
Upper Elmers End	84	C2	Westenhanger	285	N9
Upper Goldstone	170	F6	Westerham	176	E3
Upper Halling	93	L9	Western Heights	291	J9
Upper Harbledown	165	N3	West Farleigh	184	A5
Upper Hardres Court	196	E9	Westfield Sole	125	P6
Upper Hayesden	239	N3	Westgate on Sea	111	L4
Upper Norwood	60	D7	West Heath	28	C9
Upper Rodmersham	130	B7	West Hougham	312	A1
Upper Shirley	83	P8	West Hythe	307	P6
Upper Sydenham	60	C3	West Kingsdown	120	C2
Upper Upnor	72	E6	West Langdon	261	L5
Upstreet	138	F6	West Malling	153	J5
Upton	113	L9	Westmarsh	170	C3
The Valley	191	J3	West Minster	57	H8
Vigo Village	122	A5	West Norwood	60	C5
Waddon	82	D6	West Peckham	182	C5
Wainscott	72	C5	West Stourmouth	139	N7
Walderslade	125	L2	West Street	52	A3
Wallcrouch	314	D5	West Street	189	M2
Wall End	139	J5	West Street	201	P9
Wallington	82	A9	West Thurrock	31	K8
Walmer	233	H7	West Tilbury	33	M9
Walter's Green	268	D1	West Heath	28	C9
Waltham	225	L4	Westwell	222	B6
Wandle Park	82	F6	Westwell Leacon	221	J7
Wanshurst Green	245	M2	West Wickham	84	C5
Wapping	24	E4	Westwood	68	A6
Warden	80	C3	Westwood	112	G8
Ware	170	C5	Westwood	227	K2
Warehorne	302	A9	West Yoke	90	G7
Ware Street	156	E7	Wharram Green	98	A1
Warmlake	216	G2	Whatsole Street	255	N5
Warren Street	190	C4	Wheeelbarrow Town	256	F1
The Warren	252	C4	Whetsted	212	F9
Waterham	134	D5	Whitehill	162	D1
Wateringbury	183	K4	White Oak	65	N8
Waterman Quarter	247	N7	White Post	268	C1
Waterside	235	J2	Whitfield	261	J8
Way	141	M5	Whitley Row	178	A5
Wayfield	95	N7	Whitstable	105	L3
Weavering Street	156	C8	Wichling	160	B7
Weddington	170	E8	Wickhambreaux	168	D6
			Wick Hill	248	A9
			Wickhurst	208	G6

Place	Page	Ref
Widmore	63	H8
Wierton	216	C2
Wigmore	126	F1
Wilderness	149	K7
Wilgate Green	162	C6
Willesborough	3	K7
Willesborough Lees	253	L7
Willington	186	C2
Wilmington	66	B3
Wilsley Green	298	A1
Wilsley Pound	276	B8
Winchet Hill	274	C2
Windmill Hill	97	M3
Wingham	169	L9
Wingham Green	169	J9
Wingham Well	199	H1
Wingmore	227	N8
Winkhurst Green	208	A2
Winterbourne	164	B4
Wissenden	279	N1
Withersdane	254	A1
Wittersham	332	A2
Woldingham	144	D8
Woldingham Garden Village	144	C6
Wolverton	290	A5
Womenswold	228	G4
Woodchurch	302	C6
Woodland	286	D1
Woodlands	119	P7
Woodnesborough	201	H4
Woodsden	317	N2
Wood's Green	294	A4
Woodside	83	M3
Woodside Green	189	M3
Woodstock	129	M7
Woolage Green	229	J7
Woolage Village	228	C5
Woolwich	27	H9
Wooton	258	F4
Wormshill	159	H5
Worms Hill	274	C4
Worten	251	M6
Worth	202	A5
Wouldham	94	B9
Wrotham	151	K1
Wrotham Heath	151	P5
Wye	224	A9
Wyebanks	190	E1
Yalding	213	P1
Yardhurst	281	H1
Yeisted	127	K4
Yewhedges	161	L8
Yewtree Cross	257	H9
Yopps Green	181	N7
Yorkletts	134	G2

USING THE STREET INDEX

Street names are listed alphabetically. Each street name is followed by its postal town or area locality, the Postcode District, the page number, and the reference to the square in which the name is found.

Standard index entries are shown as follows:

Aaron Hill Rd *EHAM* E6 ....**27** H1

Street names and selected addresses not shown on the map due to scale restrictions are shown in the index with an asterisk:

Abbots Ct *HOO/HM* ME3 * **11** H5

GENERAL ABBREVIATIONS

ACC....ACCESS	CTYD....COURTYARD	HLS....HILLS	MWY....MOTORWAY
ALY....ALLEY	CUTT....CUTTINGS	HO....HOUSE	N....NORTH
AP....APPROACH	CV....COVE	HOL....HOLLOW	NE....NORTH EAST
AR....ARCADE	CYN....CANYON	HOSP....HOSPITAL	NW....NORTH WEST
ASS....ASSOCIATION	DEPT....DEPARTMENT	HRB....HARBOUR	O/P....OVERPASS
AV....AVENUE	DL....DALE	HTH....HEATH	OFF....OFFICE
BCH....BEACH	DM....DAM	HTS....HEIGHTS	ORCH....ORCHARD
BLDS....BUILDINGS	DR....DRIVE	HVN....HAVEN	OV....OVAL
BND....BEND	DRO....DROVE	HWY....HIGHWAY	PAL....PALACE
BNK....BANK	DRY....DRIVEWAY	IMP....IMPERIAL	PAS....PASSAGE
BR....BRIDGE	DWGS....DWELLINGS	IN....INLET	PAV....PAVILION
BRK....BROOK	E....EAST	IND EST....INDUSTRIAL ESTATE	PDE....PARADE
BTM....BOTTOM	EMB....EMBANKMENT	INF....INFIRMARY	PH....PUBLIC HOUSE
BUS....BUSINESS	EMBY....EMBASSY	INFO....INFORMATION	PK....PARK
BVD....BOULEVARD	ESP....ESPLANADE	INT....INTERCHANGE	PKWY....PARKWAY
BY....BYPASS	EST....ESTATE	IS....ISLAND	PL....PLACE
CATH....CATHEDRAL	EX....EXCHANGE	JCT....JUNCTION	PLN....PLAIN
CEM....CEMETERY	EXPY....EXPRESSWAY	JTY....JETTY	PLNS....PLAINS
CEN....CENTRE	EXT....EXTENSION	KG....KING	PLZ....PLAZA
CFT....CROFT	F/O....FLYOVER	KNL....KNOLL	POL....POLICE STATION
CH....CHURCH	FC....FOOTBALL CLUB	L....LAKE	PR....PRINCE
CHA....CHASE	FK....FORK	LA....LANE	PREC....PRECINCT
CHYD....CHURCHYARD	FLD....FIELD	LDG....LODGE	PREP....PREPARATORY
CIR....CIRCLE	FLDS....FIELDS	LGT....LIGHT	PRIM....PRIMARY
CIRC....CIRCUS	FLS....FALLS	LK....LOCK	PROM....PROMENADE
CL....CLOSE	FLS....FLATS	LKS....LAKES	PRS....PRINCESS
CLFS....CLIFFS	FM....FARM	LNDG....LANDING	PRT....PORT
CMP....CAMP	FT....FORT	LTL....LITTLE	PT....POINT
CNR....CORNER	FWY....FREEWAY	LWR....LOWER	PTH....PATH
CO....COUNTY	FY....FERRY	MAG....MAGISTRATE	PZ....PIAZZA
COLL....COLLEGE	GA....GATE	MAN....MANSIONS	QD....QUADRANT
COM....COMMON	GAL....GALLERY	MD....MEAD	QU....QUEEN
COMM....COMMISSION	GDN....GARDEN	MDW....MEADOWS	QY....QUAY
CON....CONVENT	GDNS....GARDENS	MEM....MEMORIAL	R....RIVER
COT....COTTAGE	GLD....GLADE	MKT....MARKET	RBT....ROUNDABOUT
COTS....COTTAGES	GLN....GLEN	MKTS....MARKETS	RD....ROAD
CP....CAPE	GN....GREEN	ML....MALL	RDG....RIDGE
CPS....COPSE	GND....GROUND	ML....MILL	REP....REPUBLIC
CR....CREEK	GRA....GRANGE	MNR....MANOR	RES....RESERVOIR
CREM....CREMATORIUM	GRG....GARAGE	MS....MEWS	RFC....RUGBY FOOTBALL CLUB
CRS....CRESCENT	GT....GREAT	MSN....MISSION	RI....RISE
CSWY....CAUSEWAY	GTWY....GATEWAY	MT....MOUNT	RP....RAMP
CT....COURT	GV....GROVE	MTN....MOUNTAIN	RW....ROW
CTRL....CENTRAL	HGR....HIGHER	MTS....MOUNTAINS	S....SOUTH
CTS....COURTS	HL....HILL	MUS....MUSEUM	SCH....SCHOOL

SE....SOUTH EAST
SER....SERVICE AREA
SH....SHORE
SHOP....SHOPPING
SKWY....SKYWAY
SMT....SUMMIT
SOC....SOCIETY
SP....SPUR
SPR....SPRING
SQ....SQUARE
ST....STREET
STN....STATION
STR....STREAM
STRD....STRAND
SW....SOUTH WEST
TDG....TRADING
TER....TERRACE
THWY....THROUGHWAY
TNL....TUNNEL
TOLL....TOLLWAY
TPK....TURNPIKE
TR....TRACK
TRL....TRAIL
TWR....TOWER
U/P....UNDERPASS
UNI....UNIVERSITY
UPR....UPPER
V....VALE
VA....VALLEY
VIA....VIADUCT
VIL....VILLA
VIS....VISTA
VLG....VILLAGE
VLS....VILLAS
VW....VIEW
W....WEST
WD....WOOD
WHF....WHARF
WK....WALK
WKS....WALKS
WLS....WELLS
WY....WAY
YD....YARD
YHA....YOUTH HOSTEL

351

POSTCODE TOWNS AND AREA ABBREVIATIONS

ABYW Abbey Wood
ASH Ashford (Kent)
BANK Bank
BARB Barbican
BARK Barking
BECK Beckenham
BELV Belvedere
BERM/RHTH Bermondsey/Rotherhithe
BFN/LL Blackfen/Longlands
BGR/WK Borough Green/West Kingsdown
BH/WHM Biggin Hill/Westerham
BKHTH/KID Blackheath/Kidbrooke
BMLY Bromley
BOW Bow
BRCH Birchington
BRDST Broadstairs
BROCKY Brockley
BRXN/ST Brixton north/Stockwell
BRXS/STRHM Brixton south/Streatham Hill
BUR/ETCH Burwash/Etchingham
BXLY Bexley
BXLYHN Bexleyheath north
BXLYHS Bexleyheath south
CAN/RD Canning Town/Royal Docks
CANST Cannon Street station
CANT Canterbury
CANTW/ST Canterbury west/Sturry
CAR Carshalton
CAT Catford
CDW/CHF Chadwell St Mary/Chafford Hundred
CHARL Charlton
CHAT Chatham
CHST Chislehurst
CITYW City of London west
CMBW Camberwell
CRAWE Crawley east
CRBK Cranbrook
CROY/NA Croydon/New Addington
CTHM Caterham
CVI Canvey Island
DAGW Dagenham west
DART Dartford
DEAL Deal
DEPT Deptford
DIT/AY Ditton/Aylesford
DUL Dulwich
DVE/WH Dover east/Whitfield
DVW Dover west
E/WMAL East & West Malling
EDEN Edenbridge
EDUL East Dulwich
EGRIN East Grinstead
EHAM East Ham
ELTH/MOT Eltham/Mottingham
ERITH Erith
ERITHM Erith Marshes
EYN Eynsford
FAV Faversham
FENCHST Fenchurch Street
FOLK Folkestone
FOLKN Folkestone north
FSTH Forest Hill
GDST Godstone
GILL Gillingham
GNWCH Greenwich
GRAYS Grays
GRH Greenhithe
GVE Gravesend east
GVW Gravesend west
HART Hartley
HAWK Hawkhurst
HAYES Hayes
HB Herne Bay
HDCN Headcorn
HDTCH Houndsditch
HNHL Herne Hill
HOO/HM Hoo St Werburgh/Higham
HRTF Hartfield
HYTHE Hythe
IOS Isle of Sheppey
KEN/WIL Kennington/Willesborough
LBTH Lambeth
LEE/GVPK Lee/Grove Park
LEW Lewisham
LING Lingfield
LOTH Lothbury
LVPST Liverpool Street
LYDD Lydd
MAID/BEAR Maidstone/Bearsted
MAID/SHEP Maidstone/Shepway
MAIDW Maidstone west
MANHO Mansion House
MARG Margate
MEO Meopham
MON Monument
MSTR Minster
MTCM Mitcham
NROM New Romney
NRWD Norwood
NWCR New Cross
OBST Old Broad Street
ORP Orpington
OXTED Oxted
PECK Peckham
PGE/AN Penge/Anerley
PLSTW Plaistow
POP/IOD Poplar/Isle of Dogs
PUR Purfleet
QBOR Queenborough
RAIN Rainham (Gt Lon)
RAM Ramsgate
RASHE Rural Ashford east
RASHW Rural Ashford west
RBTBR Robertsbridge
RCANTE Rural Canterbury east
RCANTW Rural Canterbury west
RDART Rural Dartford
RDV Rural Dover
RFOLK Rural Folkestone
RHAM Rainham (Kent)
RMAID Rural Maidstone
ROCH Rochester
RRTW Rural Royal Tunbridge Wells
RSEV Rural Sevenoaks
RSIT Rural Sittingbourne
RTON Rural Tonbridge
RTW Royal Tunbridge Wells
RTWE/PEM Royal Tunbridge Wells east/Pembury
RYE Rye
SAND/SEL Sanderstead/Selsdon
SBGH/RUST Southborough/Rusthall
SCUP Sidcup
SDTCH Shoreditch
SEV Sevenoaks
SIT Sittingbourne
SLH/COR Stanford-le-Hope/Corringham
SNOD Snodland
SNWD South Norwood
SOCK/AV South Ockendon/Aveley
STHWK Southwark
STH/RUST Southborough/Rusthall
STLK St Luke's
STMC/STPC St Mary Cray/St Paul's Cray
STPH/PW Staplehurst/Paddock Wood
STRD Strood
STRHM/NOR Streatham/Norbury
SWCH Sandwich
SWCM Swanscombe
SWLY Swanley
SYD Sydenham
TENT Tenterden
THHTH Thornton Heath
THMD Thamesmead
TIL Tilbury
TON Tonbridge
TONN Tonbridge north
TWRH Tower Hill
UPMR Upminster
VX/NE Vauxhall/Nine Elms
WADH Wadhurst
WALD Walderslade
WALW Walworth
WAP Wapping
WARL Warlingham
WBY/YAL Wateringbury/Yalding
WCHPL Whitechapel
WELL Welling
WGOS Westgate on Sea
WLGTN Wallington
WNWD West Norwood
WOOL/PLUM Woolwich/Plumstead
WSEA Winchelsea
WSTB Whitstable
WTHK West Thurrock
WWKM West Wickham

Index - streets

I Av - Alb

I

1 Av *WOOL/PLUM* SE18 27 J6

A

Aaron Hill Rd *EHAM* E6 27 H1
Abbess Cl *BRXS/STRHM* SW2 40 B9
Abbey Brewery Ct
E/WMAL ME19 * 153 K4
Abbey Cl *DEAL* CT14 232 F4
IOS ME12 78 D1
Abbey Ct *WGOS* CT8 111 L6
Abbey Crs *BELV* DA17 28 F7
Abbey Dr *BXLY* DA5 65 N1
Abbeyfield Est
BERM/RHTH SE16 24 F7
Abbeyfield Rd
BERM/RHTH SE16 24 F7
Abbey Flds *FAV* ME13 133 J5
Abbey Gdns *BERM/RHTH* SE16 24 D7
CANTW/ST CT2 166 F1
Abbey Gv *ABYW* SE2 28 A7
MSTR CT12 141 K7
RAM CT11 142 G7
Abbeyhill Rd *BFN/LL* DA15 44 E9
Abbey La *BECK* BR3 61 N6
Abbey Mt *BELV* DA17 28 E8
Abbey Pk *BECK* BR3 61 N6
Abbey Pl *DART* DA1 * 46 D6
FAV ME13 132 G5
Abbey Rd *BELV* DA17 28 C7
BXLYHS DA6 44 G5
CROY/NA CR0 82 G7
DVE/WH CT16 290 E3
FAV ME13 132 G5
GRH DA9 48 A6
GVE DA12 50 A9
RDV CT15 290 C6
RHAM ME8 96 D4
SAND/SEL CR2 114 A4
STRD ME2 71 P7
Abbey St *FAV* ME13 132 G5
STHWK SE1 24 C6
Abbey Ter *ABYW* SE2 28 B6
Abbeyview Dr *IOS* ME12 78 B1
Abbey Wy *KEN/WIL* TN24 253 K7
Abbey Wood Rd *ABYW* SE2 28 A7
E/WMAL ME19 153 H7
Abbots Barton Wk *CANT* CT1 5 G7
Abbotsbury Ms *PECK* SE15 41 J4
Abbotsbury Rd *WWKM* BR4 85 J6
Abbots Cl *STMC/STPC* BR5 86 D5
Abbots Ct *HOO/HM* ME3 * 73 N2
Abbots Court Rd
HOO/HM ME3 73 M3
Abbots Fld *MAIDW* ME16 184 C1
Abbots Gn *CROY/NA* CR0 114 A1
Abbotshade Rd
BERM/RHTH SE16 * 24 G4
Abbotshall Rd *CAT* SE6 42 B9
Abbots Hl *FAV* ME13 132 B8
RAM CT11 17 G4
Abbots La *STHWK* SE1 24 B4
Abbots Pk *BRXS/STRHM* SW2 40 A9
Abbots Pl *CANT* CT1 4 E3
Abbots Rd *FAV* ME13 133 H6
The Abbots *DVW* CT17 8 A3
Abbots Wk *RASHE* TN25 223 P8
Abbots Wy *BECK* BR3 84 B2
Abbotswell Rd *BROCKY* SE4 41 M6
Abbotswood Cl *BELV* DA17 28 D6
Abbotswood Rd *EDUL* SE22 40 E5
Abbott Dr *RSIT* ME9 * 129 L7
Abbott Rd *BGR/WK* TN15 151 J5
FOLK CT20 11 G2
POP/IOD E14 25 N2
Abbotts Cl *ROCH* ME1 94 G3
SWLY BR8 88 F1
THMD SE28 28 B3
Abbotts Rd *MTCM* CR4 82 B1
Abbott's Wk *BXLYHN* DA7 44 F1
Abchurch La *MANHO* EC4N 24 A3
Abercorn Cl *SAND/SEL* CR2 114 A6
Abercorn Wy *STHWK* SE1 24 D8
Aberdare Cl *WWKM* BR4 84 F6
Aberdeen Cl *RCANTE* CT3 138 G6
Aberdeen Rd *CROY/NA* CR0 83 H8
Aberdeen Ter *BKHTH/KID* SE3 42 B3
Aberdour St *STHWK* SE1 24 B7
Aberfeldy St *POP/IOD* E14 25 M2
Aberford Gdns
WOOL/PLUM SE18 43 J2
Abergeldie Rd *LEE/GVPK* SE12 42 F7
Abernethy Rd *LEW* SE13 42 C5
Abery St *WOOL/PLUM* SE18 27 M7
Abigail Crs *WALD* ME5 125 M4
Abingdon Cl *STHWK* SE1 * 24 C8
Abingdon Gv *RCANTE* CT3 138 G6
Abingdon Rd *MAIDW* ME16 184 E1
Abingdon Wy *ORP* BR6 87 J8
Abinger Cl *BMLY* BR1 63 J9
CROY/NA CR0 114 F1
WLGTN SM6 82 D9
Abinger Dr *NRWD* SE19 60 C6
WALD ME5 126 A3
Abinger Gv *DEPT* SE8 25 J9
Ablett St *BERM/RHTH* SE16 24 F8
Acacia Cl *DEPT* SE8 25 H7
STMC/STPC BR5 86 E2
Acacia Gdns *WWKM* BR4 84 F6
Acacia Gv *DUL* SE21 60 D1
Acacia Rd *BECK* BR3 61 M9
DART DA1 46 C9
GRH DA9 47 L7
Acacia Wy *BFN/LL* DA15 44 B9
Academy Dr *GILL* ME7 96 C6
Academy Gdns *CROY/NA* CR0 83 L5
Academy Pl *WOOL/PLUM* SE18 43 K2
Academy Rd
WOOL/PLUM SE18 43 L1
Acanthus Dr *STHWK* SE1 24 D8
Acer Av *RTWE/PEM* TN2 270 F8
Acer Rd *BH/WHM* TN16 145 N1
Achilles Cl *STHWK* SE1 24 D8
Achilles Rd *WALD* ME5 125 P3
Achilles St *NWCR* SE14 41 L1
Ackholt Rd *RCANTE* CT3 229 K1
Ackroyd Dr *BOW* E3 25 K1
Ackroyd Rd *FSTH* SE23 41 K8
Acland Cl *WOOL/PLUM* SE18 43 P1
Acland Crs *CMBW* SE5 40 D5
Acol Hl *BRCH* CT7 111 J9
Acorn Cl *ASH* TN23 282 F5
CHST BR7 63 N4
EGRIN RH19 265 H8
STPH/PW TN12 242 C2
Acorn Gdns *NRWD* SE19 60 F7
Acorn Gv *DIT/AY* ME20 154 C4
Acorn Pde *PECK* SE15 * 41 H1
Acorn Pl *MAID/SHEP* ME15 186 B5
Acorn Rd *DART* DA1 45 P6
GILL ME7 96 C2
The Acorns *HDCN* TN27 248 C8
SEV TN13 148 F8
WADH TN5 314 D8
Acorn St *IOS* ME12 57 L7
Acorn Wy *FSTH* SE23 61 K2
ORP BR6 86 C8
Acorn Wharf Rd *ROCH* ME1 19 G3
Acott Flds *WBY/YAL* ME18 213 N1
Acre Cl *ROCH* ME1 95 K5
Acre Dr *EDUL* SE22 40 G5
Acre Gv *STRD* ME2 123 P1
Acres Ri *WADH* TN5 315 J5
The Acre *DVE/WH* CT16 260 G8
Acton La *TENT* TN30 321 L8
Acton Rd *WSTB* CT5 105 L5
Acworth Pl *DART* DA1 * 46 C7
Ada Gdns *POP/IOD* E14 25 N2
Adair Cl *SNWD* SE25 61 H9
Adam Cl *CAT* SE6 61 N2
FSTH SE23 61 J1
RMAID ME17 185 J8
Adams Cl *TENT* TN30 301 J6
Adams Ct *WALD* ME5 * 95 N8
Adamson Rd *CAN/RD* E16 26 B2
Adamson Wy *BECK* BR3 84 F2
Adamsrill Rd *SYD* SE26 61 K3
Adams Rd *BECK* BR3 84 B2
Adams Sq *BXLYHS* DA6 44 G4
Adams Wy *SNWD* SE25 83 L3
Ada Rd *CANT* CT1 166 C6
CMBW SE5 40 E1
Adbert Dr *MAID/SHEP* ME15 184 G7
Addelam Cl *DEAL* CT14 232 F5
Addelam Rd *DEAL* CT14 232 F5
Adderley Gdns *ELTH/MOT* SE9 63 L3
Adderley St *POP/IOD* E14 25 M2
Addington Gv *SYD* SE26 61 L3
Addington La *E/WMAL* ME19 122 B9
Addington Pl *RAM* CT11 17 F5
Addington Rd *CROY/NA* CR0 82 F5
MARG CT9 15 H4
SIT ME10 129 M2
WWKM BR4 84 G7
Addington Sq *CMBW* SE5 40 C1
MARG CT9 15 H5
Addington St *MARG* CT9 15 H4
RAM CT11 16 E5
Addington Village Rd
CROY/NA CR0 114 C1
Addiscombe Av *CROY/NA* CR0 83 M4
Addiscombe Court Rd
CROY/NA CR0 83 K5
Addiscombe Gdns *MARG* CT9 15 J7
Addiscombe Gv *CROY/NA* CR0 83 J6
Addiscombe Rd *CROY/NA* CR0 83 K6
MARG CT9 15 K6
Addison Cl *E/WMAL* ME19 153 N3
STMC/STPC BR5 86 D3
Addison Dr *LEE/GVPK* SE12 42 F6
Addison Gdns *GRAYS* RM17 32 D7
Addison Rd *HAYES* BR2 85 N2
SNWD SE25 83 M1
Addison's Cl *CROY/NA* CR0 84 C6
Addlestead Rd
STPH/PW TN12 212 F4
Adelaide Av *BROCKY* SE4 41 N5
Adelaide Dr *SIT* ME10 129 K1
Adelaide Gdns *IOS* ME12 77 M1
RAM CT11 17 F5
Adelaide Pl *CANT* CT1 4 D5
Adelaide Rd *CHST* BR7 63 M4
GILL ME7 7 J5
RDV CT15 230 C9
TIL RM18 49 K2
The Adelaide *HOO/HM* ME3 71 L1
Adelina Gv *WCHPL* E1 24 F1
Adenmore Rd *CAT* SE6 41 N8
Adie Rd *NROM* TN28 343 J1
Adie Rd North *NROM* TN28 343 J1
Adisham Downs Rd
RCANTE CT3 198 E5
Adisham Dr *MAIDW* ME16 154 G5
Adisham Gn *SIT* ME10 99 N6
Adisham Rd *RCANTW* CT4 198 B4
RCANTW CT4 228 F4
Adisham Wy *MARG* CT9 113 H4
Adler St *WCHPL* E1 24 D1
Admaston Rd
WOOL/PLUM SE18 43 N1
Admers Wy *MEO* DA13 122 C5
Admiral Cl *STMC/STPC* BR5 87 L1
Admiral Moore Dr
DIT/AY ME20 154 E3
Admiral Pl *BERM/RHTH* SE16 25 H4
Admiral Seymour Rd
ELTH/MOT SE9 43 K5
Admiral's Ga *GNWCH* SE10 41 P2
Admiral St *DEPT* SE8 41 N2
Admirals Wk *CRBK* TN17 298 G5
GRH DA9 47 P6
HYTHE CT21 * 309 H6
IOS ME12 77 N1
TENT TN30 301 K6
Admirals Wy *POP/IOD* E14 25 L5
Admiralty Cl *FAV* ME13 132 E5
Admiralty Ms *DEAL* CT14 233 J5
Admiralty Rd *STRD* ME2 72 F6
Admiralty Ter *STRD* ME2 72 F6
Admiralty Wk *WSTB* CT5 105 H7
Admiral Wy *E/WMAL* ME19 183 H2
Adolf St *CAT* SE6 61 N3
Adolphus St *DEPT* SE8 41 M1
Adrian Ct *WGOS* CT8 * 111 M4
Adrian Ms *WGOS* CT8 * 111 N4
Adrian Sq *WGOS* CT8 111 M4
Adrian St *DVW* CT17 8 D5
Adstock Wy *GRAYS* RM17 32 A7
Advance Rd *WNWD* SE27 60 C3
Advice Av *CDW/CHF* RM16 32 B5
Adys Rd *PECK* SE15 40 F4
Aerodrome Rd *RCANTW* CT4 198 B4
RFOLK CT18 288 C8
Afghan Rd *BRDST* CT10 113 L5
CHAT ME4 6 A5
Afton Dr *SOCK/AV* RM15 31 L2
Agate Cl *CAN/RD* E16 26 E2
Agatha Cl *WAP* E1W 24 E4
Agaton Rd *ELTH/MOT* SE9 63 N1
Agester La *RCANTW* CT4 258 D2
Agnes Cl *EHAM* E6 27 H3
Agnes St *POP/IOD* E14 25 J2
Agnew Rd *FSTH* SE23 41 L8
Ailsa St *POP/IOD* E14 25 M1
Ailsworth La *RYE* TN31 * 338 F6
Ainsbrough Av *MARG* CT9 113 H5
Ainsdale Cl *FOLKN* CT19 310 D4
ORP BR6 86 E5
Ainsdale Dr *STHWK* SE1 24 D8
Ainsty St *BERM/RHTH* SE16 * 24 F5
Ainsworth Cl *CMBW* SE5 * 40 E3
Ainsworth Rd *CROY/NA* CR0 82 G5
Aintree Cl *GVE* DA12 69 M2
Aintree Rd *WALD* ME5 125 P2
Airedale Cl *MARG* CT9 15 K6
RDART DA2 47 J9
Airfield Vw *IOS* ME12 79 J7
Aisher Rd *THMD* SE28 28 B3
Aisher Wy *SEV* TN13 148 D6
Aislibie Rd *LEW* SE13 42 C5
Aisne Dr *CANT* CT1 167 J3
Aitken Rd *CAT* SE6 61 P1
Ajax Rd *ROCH* ME1 95 H7
Akabusi Cl *SNWD* SE25 83 M3
Akehurst La *BGR/WK* TN15 21 G4
Akerman Rd *CMBW* SE5 40 B2
Alabama St *WOOL/PLUM* SE18 43 P1
Alamein Av *WALD* ME5 95 L7
Alamein Cl *DVE/WH* CT16 291 N5
Alamein Gdns *RDART* DA2 47 K8
Alamein Rd *SWCM* DA10 48 B7
Alanbrooke *GVE* DA12 49 N8
Alan Cl *DART* DA1 46 C5
Alanthus Cl *LEE/GVPK* SE12 42 D7
Albacore Crs *LEW* SE13 41 P7
Alban Crs *EYN* DA4 89 M5
Albany Cl *BXLY* DA5 44 E8
TON TN9 240 C2
Albany Dr *HB* CT6 107 J1
Albany Hl *RTWE/PEM* TN2 23 H1
Albany Ms *BMLY* BR1 62 E5
Albany Pl *DVW* CT17 8 D4
Albany Rd *BELV* DA17 28 E9
BXLY DA5 44 E8
CHAT ME4 95 N4
CHST BR7 63 M4
CMBW SE5 24 A9
GILL ME7 96 A2
RFOLK CT18 311 L2
ROCH ME1 95 H3
SIT ME10 129 M2
TIL RM18 49 L2
Albany St *MAID/BEAR* ME14 13 H2
Albany Ter *CHAT* ME4 6 A5
Albatross Av *STRD* ME2 71 L9
Albatross Gdns
SAND/SEL CR2 114 A5
Albatross St *WOOL/PLUM* SE18 44 A1
Albemarle Cl *GRAYS* RM17 32 B5
Albemarle Pk *BECK* BR3 * 61 P7
Albemarle Rd *BECK* BR3 61 P7
KEN/WIL TN24 253 J9
WALD ME5 125 P3
Alberta Cl *DVE/WH* CT16 291 J4
Alberta Rd *BXLYHN* DA7 45 L2
Albert Cl *CDW/CHF* RM16 32 D6
Albert Ct *RAM* CT11 * 17 F4
WSTB CT5 * 105 L4
Albert Dr *MAID/SHEP* ME15 184 G7
Albert Gdns *WCHPL* E1 24 G2
Albert La *HYTHE* CT21 308 G6
Albert Ms *BROCKY* SE4 * 41 M5
POP/IOD E14 * 25 H3
Albert Murray Cl *GVE* DA12 49 N8
Albert Pl *STRD* ME2 18 E1
Albert Reed Gdns
MAID/SHEP ME15 185 K1
Albert Rd *BELV* DA17 28 E8
BRDST CT10 113 K6
BXLY DA5 45 J7
CAN/RD E16 26 F4
CANT CT1 5 H5
CHAT ME4 6 D7
DEAL CT14 233 H3
DVE/WH CT16 8 C1
ELTH/MOT SE9 63 J2
FOLKN CT19 10 E1
GILL ME7 7 H4
HAYES BR2 85 N2
HYTHE CT21 308 G6
KEN/WIL TN24 2 D2
MARG CT9 14 D5
ORP BR6 87 H9

PGE/AN SE20 61 K6
RAM CT11 17 J2
RDART DA2 66 C2
RFOLK CT18 311 M2
ROCH ME1 95 H3
SNWD SE25 83 N1
STMC/STPC BR5 87 J3
SWCM DA10 48 D7
TON TN9 210 E9
WARL CR6 144 B2
Albert St MAID/BEAR ME14 12 E1
RAM CT11 16 E5
RTW TN1 22 E2
WSTB CT5 105 L4
Albert Ter IOS ME12 * 78 G2
MARG CT9 15 F4
Albert Wy PECK SE15 41 H1
Albion Cl HB CT6 107 M6
Albion Ct RAM CT11 17 G3
Albion Est BERM/RHTH SE16 * 24 F5
Albion La HB CT6 107 M6
Albion Ms RAM CT11 17 H4
Albion Mews Rd FOLK CT20 10 E5
Albion Pl CANT CT1 5 G3
FAV ME13 132 F6
IOS ME12 57 L6
KEN/WIL TN24 283 H1
MAID/BEAR ME14 13 H4
MARG CT9 * 15 H3
RAM CT11 17 G4
SNWD SE25 * 60 G9
Albion Rd BRCH CT7 111 H6
BRDST CT10 113 L7
BXLYHS DA6 45 H5
DEAL CT14 233 J1
FOLKN CT19 11 F1
GVE DA12 49 N8
MARG CT9 112 F2
RAM CT11 17 H2
RTW TN1 23 F1
STPH/PW TN12 245 J4
SWCH CT13 201 H8
WALD ME5 125 N3
Albion St BERM/RHTH SE16 24 F5
BRDST CT10 113 N9
CROY/NA CR0 82 G5
Albion Ter GVE DA12 49 N7
SIT ME10 * 99 M8
Albion Vls FOLK CT20 11 F5
Albion Villas Rd FSTH SE23 61 J2
Albion Wy EDEN TN8 206 D6
LEW SE13 42 A5
Albrighton Rd EDUL SE22 40 E4
Albuhera Sq CANT CT1 167 J3
Albury Av BXLYHN DA7 44 G3
Albury Cl WALD ME5 126 A3
Albury St DEPT SE8 25 K9
Albyfield BMLY BR1 63 K9
Albyn Rd DEPT SE8 41 N2
Alcester Rd WLGTN SM6 82 A8
Aldbridge St WALW SE17 24 B8
Aldeburgh St GNWCH SE10 26 B8
Alder Cl IOS ME12 57 J8
PECK SE15 24 C9
RTWE/PEM TN2 240 F8
Aldergate La RASHE TN25 307 K6
Alderholt Wy PECK SE15 * 40 E1
Alder La CRBK TN17 319 J5
Alderman Cl DART DA1 45 N8
Aldermary Rd BMLY BR1 62 E7
Aldermoor Rd CAT SE6 61 M2
Alderney Ms STHWK SE1 24 A6
Alderney Rd ERITH DA8 46 A1
Alder Rd FOLKN CT19 10 C1
SCUP DA14 64 A2
Alders Av EGRIN RH19 264 G5
Aldersford Cl BROCKY SE4 41 K5
Aldersgrove Av ELTH/MOT SE9 62 G2
Aldershot Rd WALD ME5 95 M7
Aldershot Ter
WOOL/PLUM SE18 * 43 L1
Aldersmead Av CROY/NA CR0 84 A3
Alders Meadow TON TN9 210 C8
Aldersmead Rd BECK BR3 61 L6
Alders Rd RTON TN11 241 P3
Alders View Dr EGRIN RH19 265 H5
The Alders WBY/YAL ME18 182 E4
WWKM BR4 84 E5
Alderton Rd CDW/CHF RM16 33 M2
CROY/NA CR0 83 L4
HNHL SE24 40 C4
Alder Wy SWLY BR8 65 M8
Alderwood Rd ELTH/MOT SE9 43 P7
Aldgate FENCHST EC3M 24 B2
Aldgate Barrs WCHPL E1 * 24 C2
Aldgate High St TWRH EC3N * 24 C2
Aldington Cl WALD ME5 95 N9
Aldington La
MAID/BEAR ME14 156 G4
Aldington Rd HYTHE CT21 307 K4
MAID/BEAR ME14 156 C8
WOOL/PLUM SE18 26 E6
Aldon Cl MAID/BEAR ME14 13 K1
Aldon La E/WMAL ME19 152 C4
Aldred Rd FAV ME13 132 F7
Aldrich Crs CROY/NA CR0 114 F3
Aldridge Cl HB CT6 106 G3
Aldwick Cl CHST BR7 63 P2
Aldwick Rd CROY/NA CR0 82 E7
Aldworth Gv LEW SE13 42 A7
Alec Pemble Cl KEN/WIL TN24 253 H4
Alen Sq STPH/PW TN12 246 C5
Alers Rd BXLYHS DA6 44 F6
Alestan Beck Rd CAN/RD E16 26 E2
Alexander Cl BFN/LL DA15 44 A6
HAYES BR2 85 K5
SWCH CT13 201 N2
Alexander Ct SIT ME10 * 99 M9
Alexander Dr FAV ME13 132 E6
Alexander Evans Ms
FSTH SE23 61 K1
Alexander Gv E/WMAL ME19 153 J9
Alexander Rd BXLYHN DA7 44 F3
CHST BR7 63 M5
GRH DA9 48 A6
Alexander Ter ABYW SE2 * 28 A8
Alexandra Av GILL ME7 96 B2
WARL CR6 144 C2
Alexandra Cl CDW/CHF RM16 33 J5
SIT ME10 99 M7
SWLY BR8 65 N8
Alexandra Cottages
NWCR SE14 41 M2
Alexandra Crs BMLY BR1 62 D5
Alexandra Dr NRWD SE19 60 E4
Alexandra Gdns FOLK CT20 10 E5
Alexandra Gln WALD ME5 125 M4
Alexandra Pl CROY/NA CR0 83 K5
DVE/WH CT16 291 K6
SNWD SE25 83 J2
Alexandra Rd BH/WHM TN16 145 L4
BRCH CT7 111 H8
BRDST CT10 113 N9
CHAT ME4 95 N4
CROY/NA CR0 83 K5
DEAL CT14 233 J7
DEAL CT14 263 H3
ERITH DA8 29 L9
GVE DA12 50 A8
IOS ME12 57 M6
MARG CT9 112 D5
RAM CT11 16 E1
RFOLK CT18 311 M1
SYD SE26 61 K5
TIL RM18 49 K3
WARL CR6 144 B2
WSTB CT5 105 K6
Alexandra St CAN/RD E16 26 B1
FOLKN CT19 11 G1
MAID/BEAR ME14 12 E1
NWCR SE14 41 L1
Alexandra Ter MARG CT9 15 G7
Alexandra Wk EYN DA4 * 67 K8
Alexandra Wy TIL RM18 34 A7
Alexandria Dr HB CT6 107 H1
Alex Hughes Cl SNOD ME6 123 N7
Alexis St BERM/RHTH SE16 24 D7
Alford Gn CROY/NA CR0 114 G1
Alford Rd ERITH DA8 29 H8
Alfred Cl CANT CT1 166 B6
CHAT ME4 95 N4
RDART DA2 47 J8
Alfred Pl GVW DA11 49 K9
Alfred Rd BELV DA17 28 E8
BRCH CT7 110 E5
CANT CT1 166 B6
DVE/WH CT16 291 J5
GVW DA11 69 M1
KEN/WIL TN24 282 G1
MARG CT9 112 G4
NROM TN28 343 J1
RDART DA2 66 F3
SNWD SE25 83 M2
SOCK/AV RM15 30 F4
Alfred St GRAYS RM17 32 D9
Alfriston Av CROY/NA CR0 82 D4
Alfriston Cl DART DA1 45 N7
Alfriston Gv E/WMAL ME19 153 K9
Algernon Rd LEW SE13 41 P5
Algiers Rd LEW SE13 41 N5
Alice St STHWK SE1 24 B6
Alice Thompson Cl
LEE/GVPK SE12 62 G1
Alice Walker Cl HNHL SE24 * 40 B5
Alicia Av MARG CT9 111 P5
Alie St WCHPL E1 24 D2
Alison Cl CROY/NA CR0 84 A5
DVE/WH CT16 291 H1
EHAM E6 27 H2
Alison Crs DVE/WH CT16 291 H1
Alkerden La GRH DA9 48 A7
Alkham Cl MARG CT9 113 L3
Alkham Rd MAID/BEAR ME14 13 K3
RDV CT15 290 C3
Alkham Valley Rd RDV CT15 289 N3
RFOLK CT18 289 L4
Allan Cl STH/RUST TN4 269 P4
Allandale Pl ORP BR6 87 L7
Allandale Rd RTWE/PEM TN2 270 G2
Alland Grange La MSTR CT12 141 M3
Allan Rd WSTB CT5 104 F7
Allard Cl STMC/STPC BR5 87 K4
Allen Av WGOS CT8 111 K6
Allenby Av DEAL CT14 232 G4
Allenby Crs GRAYS RM17 32 C8
Allenby Rd BH/WHM TN16 145 P2
FSTH SE23 61 K2
MSTR CT12 142 G2
Allen Cl WALD ME5 95 P8
Allen Ct IOS ME12 78 A2
Allendale Cl CMBW SE5 40 D3
RDART DA2 68 A2
SYD SE26 61 K4
Allendale St FOLKN CT19 10 E1
Allen Fld ASH TN23 252 C9
Allen Rd BECK BR3 61 K8
CROY/NA CR0 82 E4
Allens STPH/PW TN12 * 245 J4
Allens La BGR/WK TN15 181 K4
Allen St MAID/BEAR ME14 13 G2
Allenswood Rd ELTH/MOT SE9 43 J5
Allerford Rd CAT SE6 61 P3
Alleyn Crs DUL SE21 60 D1
Alleyn Pk DUL SE21 60 D1
Alleyn Rd DUL SE21 60 D2
Allhallows La CANST EC4R 24 A3
Allhallows Rd EHAM E6 26 F2
HOO/HM ME3 54 G3
Alliance Rd RAM CT11 17 H4
WOOL/PLUM SE18 27 P9
Alliance Wy STPH/PW TN12 242 G3
Allington Dr STRD ME2 71 N7
TONN TN10 211 K5
Allington Gdns
WBY/YAL ME18 183 L4
Allington Rd ORP BR6 86 F6
RHAM ME8 96 D3
STPH/PW TN12 242 G2
Allington Wy MAIDW ME16 154 G6
Allison Av GILL ME7 96 B5
Allison Cl GNWCH SE10 42 A2
Allison Gv DUL SE21 40 E9
Allnutt Mill Cl
MAID/SHEP ME15 185 K1
Alloa Rd DEPT SE8 24 G8
Allotment La SEV TN13 149 H7
Allport Ms WCHPL E1 * 24 F1
All Saints' Av MARG CT9 14 C7
All Saints Cl SWCM DA10 48 D6
WSTB CT5 105 M5
All Saints Dr BKHTH/KID SE3 42 D3
All Saints La CANT CT1 4 E4
All Saints Ri STH/RUST TN4 * 270 D2
All Saints' Rd GVW DA11 49 K9
HAWK TN18 317 J5
SIT ME10 130 B1
STH/RUST TN4 270 D2
Allsworth Cl RSIT ME9 98 C8
Allwood Cl SYD SE26 61 K3
Alma Gv STHWK SE1 24 C7
Alma Pl CANT CT1 * 5 G2
NRWD SE19 60 F6
RAM CT11 17 G3
STRD ME2 18 C2
THHTH CR7 82 F2
Alma Rd DIT/AY ME20 * 124 E7
E/WMAL ME19 153 H4
FOLK CT20 310 A6
HB CT6 107 N1
IOS ME12 57 L6
MARG CT9 15 H7
RAM CT11 17 F2
SCUP DA14 64 C2
STMC/STPC BR5 87 L6
SWCM DA10 48 C6
Alma St CANT CT1 5 G2
IOS ME12 57 M6
The Alma GVE DA12 * 70 B3
Almond Cl BRDST CT10 113 H9
CDW/CHF RM16 33 H6
HAYES BR2 86 B4
WSTB CT5 106 C5
Almond Ct RCANTW CT4 195 M2
Almond Dr SWLY BR8 65 M9
Almond Gv GILL ME7 126 D1
Almond Rd BERM/RHTH SE16 24 E7
RDART DA2 47 J8
The Almonds
MAID/BEAR ME14 156 D8
Almond Tree Cl IOS ME12 57 J8
Almond Wy HAYES BR2 86 B4
MTCM CR4 82 C2
Almon Pl ROCH ME1 19 H6
Almshouse Rd FAV ME13 191 M8
Alnwick Rd CAN/RD E16 26 D2
LEE/GVPK SE12 42 F8
Alnwick Ter LEE/GVPK SE12 42 F8
Alpha Cl HOO/HM ME3 54 B9
Alpha Gv POP/IOD E14 25 K5
Alpha Rd BRCH CT7 111 H6
CROY/NA CR0 83 K5
NWCR SE14 41 M2
RAM CT11 16 D4
Alpha St PECK SE15 40 G3
Alpine Cl CROY/NA CR0 83 K7
Alpine Copse BMLY BR1 63 L8
Alpine Rd BERM/RHTH SE16 24 F7
Alpine Wy EHAM E6 27 H1
Alsace Rd WALW SE17 24 B8
Alsager Av QBOR ME11 77 H4
Alscot Rd BERM/RHTH SE16 24 C6
Alscot Wy STHWK SE1 24 C7
Alsike Rd BELV DA17 28 C6
Alsops Rd KEN/WIL TN24 283 H1
Alston Cl IOS ME12 58 C9
Altash Wy ELTH/MOT SE9 63 K1
Alton Av E/WMAL ME19 183 J1
Alton Cl BXLY DA5 44 G9
Alton Gdns BECK BR3 61 N6
Alton Ms GILL ME7 * 7 J5
Alton Rd CROY/NA CR0 82 F8
Alton St POP/IOD E14 25 L1
Altyre Cl BECK BR3 84 C2
Altyre Rd CROY/NA CR0 83 J6
Altyre Wy BECK BR3 84 C2
Aluric Cl CDW/CHF RM16 33 J7
Alverstone Gdns
ELTH/MOT SE9 43 M9
Alverston Gdns SNWD SE25 83 K2
Alverton St DEPT SE8 25 J8
Alvey St WALW SE17 24 B8
Alvis Av HB CT6 106 F2
Alwen Gv SOCK/AV RM15 31 L1
Alwold Crs LEE/GVPK SE12 42 G7
Alwyn Cl CROY/NA CR0 114 E2
Amage Rd RASHE TN25 254 D1
Amanda Cl WALD ME5 125 K2
Amar Ct WOOL/PLUM SE18 27 N7
Amardeep Ct
WOOL/PLUM SE18 27 N8
Amazon St WCHPL E1 24 E2
Ambassador Gdns EHAM E6 26 G1
Ambassador Sq POP/IOD E14 25 L7
Amber Cl RSIT ME9 131 J3
Amber La RMAID ME17 216 D1
Amberleaze Dr
RTWE/PEM TN2 271 N2
Amberley Cl ORP BR6 86 G9
Amberley Ct SCUP DA14 64 E4
Amberley Gv CROY/NA CR0 83 L4
SYD SE26 61 H3
Amberley Rd ABYW SE2 28 C9
Amberwood Cl WLGTN SM6 82 D9
Amblecote Cl LEE/GVPK SE12 62 F2
Amblecote Meadow
LEE/GVPK SE12 62 F2
Amblecote Mdw
LEE/GVPK SE12 * 62 F2
Amblecote Rd LEE/GVPK SE12 62 F2
Ambleside BMLY BR1 62 B5
SIT ME10 130 B2
Ambleside Av BECK BR3 84 B2
Ambleside Gdns
SAND/SEL CR2 114 A4
Ambleside Rd BXLYHN DA7 45 J3
Ambley Gn GILL ME7 96 D6
Ambley Rd GILL ME7 96 E6
Ambrook Rd BELV DA17 28 F6
Ambrose Cl DART DA1 45 P5
ORP BR6 86 G7
Ambrose Hl WALD ME5 95 P4
Ambrose St BERM/RHTH SE16 24 E7
Amels Hl RSIT ME9 128 A5
America Sq TWRH EC3N 24 C3
Amersham Gv NWCR SE14 41 M1
Amersham Rd CROY/NA CR0 83 H3
NWCR SE14 41 M2
Amersham V NWCR SE14 41 M1
Ames Av MAID/BEAR ME14 156 D8
Amesbury Rd BMLY BR1 63 H9
Ames Rd SWCM DA10 48 C7
Amethyst Av WALD ME5 95 K8
Amethyst Ct ORP BR6 116 F1
Amherst Cl MAIDW ME16 12 A3
MARG CT9 113 H4
STMC/STPC BR5 87 H1
Amherst Dr STMC/STPC BR5 86 G1
Amherst Hl GILL ME7 6 D1
SEV TN13 148 D7
Amherst Pl SEV TN13 148 E7
Amherst Redoubt GILL ME7 6 D2
Amherst Rd ROCH ME1 95 J3
SEV TN13 148 G7
STH/RUST TN4 270 D3
Amhurst Bank Rd
RTWE/PEM TN2 241 P6
Amina Wy BERM/RHTH SE16 24 D6
Amos Cl FAV ME13 162 F7
HB CT6 107 P3
Amott Rd PECK SE15 40 G4
Ampere Wy CROY/NA CR0 82 E5
Ampleforth Cl ORP BR6 87 K8
Ampleforth Rd ABYW SE2 28 A5
Amroth Cl FSTH SE23 41 H9
Amsbury Rd
MAID/SHEP ME15 184 F9
Amsterdam Rd POP/IOD E14 25 M6
Amy Rd OXTED RH8 175 H5
Amyruth Rd BROCKY SE4 41 N6
Amy Warne Cl EHAM E6 26 F1
Anatase Cl SIT ME10 99 K7
Ancaster Rd BECK BR3 61 K9
Ancaster St WOOL/PLUM SE18 44 A1
Anchorage Cl HOO/HM ME3 54 G5
Anchor Bvd DART DA1 * 47 H7
Anchor & Hope La CHARL SE7 26 D7
Anchor La IOS ME12 57 J5
Anchor Rd ROCH ME1 95 H5
Anchor St BERM/RHTH SE16 24 E7
Ancona Rd WOOL/PLUM SE18 27 L8
Ancress Cl CANTW/ST CT2 136 F9
Andace Park Gdns BMLY BR1 * 62 G7
Anderson Wy BELV DA17 28 G5
Andover Av CAN/RD E16 26 E2
Andover Rd ORP BR6 86 F5
Andrea Av CDW/CHF RM16 32 A5
Andrew Broughton Wy
MAID/BEAR ME14 13 H4
Andrew Cl DART DA1 45 M6
Andrewes Gdns EHAM E6 26 F2
Andrew Rd STH/RUST TN4 240 F9
Andrews Cl RTWE/PEM TN2 270 G3
STMC/STPC BR5 64 F9
Andrews Pl BXLY DA5 45 H9
RDART DA2 66 A3
Andrew St POP/IOD E14 25 M2
Andwell Cl ABYW SE2 28 A5
Anerley Cl MAIDW ME16 155 J5
Anerley Gv NRWD SE19 60 F6
Anerley Hl NRWD SE19 60 F5
Anerley Pk PGE/AN SE20 61 H6
Anerley Park Rd PGE/AN SE20 61 H6
Anerley Rd NRWD SE19 60 G6
PGE/AN SE20 61 H7
Anerley Station Rd
PGE/AN SE20 61 H7
Anerley V NRWD SE19 60 F6
Angel Aly WCHPL E1 24 C2
Angel Ct LOTH EC2R 24 A2
Angelica Dr EHAM E6 27 H1
Angelica Gdns CROY/NA CR0 84 A5
Angel La TON TN9 210 E9
Angell Park Gdns
BRXN/ST SW9 40 A4
Angell Rd BRXN/ST SW9 40 B4
Angell Town Est
BRXN/ST SW9 * 40 A3
Angel Ms WCHPL E1 24 E3
Angel Pas CANST EC4R 24 A3
Angerstein La BKHTH/KID SE3 42 D1
Angle Rd WTHK RM20 31 N9
Anglesea Av WOOL/PLUM SE18 27 J7
Anglesea Pl GVW DA11 49 M7
Anglesea Rd STMC/STPC BR5 87 K3
WOOL/PLUM SE18 27 J7
Anglesey Av
MAID/SHEP ME15 185 M5
Anglesey Cl WALD ME5 95 N7
Angley Ct STPH/PW TN12 273 P3
Angley Rd CRBK TN17 297 N2
Angley Wk CRBK TN17 297 P1
Angus Dr KEN/WIL TN24 252 F2
Angus St NWCR SE14 41 L1
Ankerdine Crs
WOOL/PLUM SE18 43 M2
Annabel Cl POP/IOD E14 25 L2
Annabell Av CDW/CHF RM16 33 L2
Annalee Gdns SOCK/AV RM15 31 L1
Annalee Rd SOCK/AV RM15 31 L1
Annandale Rd BFN/LL DA15 44 A8
CROY/NA CR0 83 M6
GNWCH SE10 26 A9
Anna Pk BRCH CT7 110 G5
Anne Boleyn Cl IOS ME12 79 L4
Anne Cl BRCH CT7 111 J6
Anne Compton Ms
LEE/GVPK SE12 42 D8
Anne Figg Ct ROCH ME1 * 19 G7
Anne Green Wk CANT CT1 5 H1
Anne Heart Cl WTHK RM20 31 N7
Anne of Cleves Rd DART DA1 46 D6
Anne Roper Cl NROM TN28 337 K7
Annesley Dr CROY/NA CR0 84 C7
Annesley Rd BKHTH/KID SE3 42 F2
Annetts Hall BGR/WK TN15 151 K4
Annie Rd SNOD ME6 123 N7
Ann Moss Wy
BERM/RHTH SE16 24 F6
Ann's Rd RAM CT11 17 F1
Ann St WOOL/PLUM SE18 27 L8
Annsworthy Av THHTH CR7 60 D9
Ansdell Rd PECK SE15 41 J3
Ansell Av CHAT ME4 95 M4
Anselm Cl CROY/NA CR0 83 L7
SIT ME10 129 M1
Anselm Rd DVW CT17 291 H7
Ansford Rd BMLY BR1 62 A4
Anson Av E/WMAL ME19 152 G9
Anson Cl BRDST CT10 143 H1
WALD ME5 95 P8
Anstee Rd DVW CT17 8 A1
Anstey Rd PECK SE15 40 G4
Anstridge Rd ELTH/MOT SE9 43 P7
Antelope Av CDW/CHF RM16 32 B6
Antelope Rd
WOOL/PLUM SE18 26 G6
Anthony Cl SEV TN13 148 D6
Anthony Crs WSTB CT5 105 J8
Anthony Rd SNWD SE25 83 M3
WELL DA16 44 C2
Anthony's Cl WAP E1W 24 D4
Anthonys La SWLY BR8 66 A7
Anthony St WCHPL E1 24 E2
Anthonys Wy STRD ME2 19 K2
Antill Ter WCHPL E1 24 G2
Antolin Wy MSTR CT12 142 F1
Antonius Ct ASH TN23 282 D3
Anvil Cl BRCH CT7 111 H7
Anzio Crs DVE/WH CT16 291 M5
Aperfield Rd BH/WHM TN16 145 P2
ERITH DA8 29 L9
Apex Cl BECK BR3 61 P7
Apollo Av BMLY BR1 62 F7
Apollo Wy CHAT ME4 73 J5
WOOL/PLUM SE18 27 L6
Apostle Wy THHTH CR7 60 B8
Appach Rd BRXS/STRHM SW2 40 A6
Appleby Cl ROCH ME1 95 J7
Appleby Rd CAN/RD E16 26 B2
Apple Cl RFOLK CT18 288 E8
SNOD ME6 123 N7
Apple Ct STPH/PW TN12 242 G3
Applecross Cl ROCH ME1 94 G2
Appledore Av BXLYHN DA7 45 L2
IOS ME12 57 K8
Appledore Cl HAYES BR2 85 J2
MARG CT9 112 G4
Appledore Crs BFN/LL DA15 64 A2
FOLKN CT19 310 A4
Appledore Rd RASHW TN26 302 G7
RASHW TN26 322 D6
RHAM ME8 96 D3
TENT TN30 301 K8
Appledown Wy CANT CT1 167 J7
Appleford Dr IOS ME12 57 P9
Applegarth CROY/NA CR0 114 E2
Applegarth Dr DART DA1 66 E1
Applegarth Pk WSTB CT5 * 105 H8
Applegarth Rd THMD SE28 28 A4
Apple Orch SWLY BR8 88 C1
Appleshaw Cl GVW DA11 69 L4
Appleton Cl BXLYHN DA7 45 K3
Appleton Dr RDART DA2 66 B2
Appleton Rd ELTH/MOT SE9 43 J4
Appletons RTON TN11 212 A2
Apple Tree Cl MAIDW ME16 184 E1
Appletree Cl PGE/AN SE20 61 H7
Apple Tree La
RTWE/PEM TN2 240 G9
Appold St ERITH DA8 29 L9
SDTCH EC2A 24 B1
Approach Rd DVW CT17 291 H9
MARG CT9 112 F3
RDV CT15 229 N9
WARL CR6 145 L7
Approach Rd South
LYDD TN29 347 K5
The Approach EGRIN RH19 265 K2
ORP BR6 86 G6
April Cl ORP BR6 86 G9
April Gln FSTH SE23 61 K2
April Ri WSTB CT5 105 J7
Apsley Rd SNWD SE25 83 N1
Apsley St ASH TN23 2 C4
STH/RUST TN4 270 A4
Arabin Rd BROCKY SE4 41 L5
Araglen Av SOCK/AV RM15 31 L1
Aragon Cl ASH TN23 282 B1
CROY/NA CR0 115 H4
HAYES BR2 86 A5
Arbor Cl BECK BR3 61 P8
Arbour Sq WCHPL E1 24 F2
Arbroath Rd ELTH/MOT SE9 43 J4
Arbrook Cl STMC/STPC BR5 64 C9
Arbuthnot La BXLY DA5 44 G7
Arbuthnot Rd NWCR SE14 41 K3
Arcade Chambers
ELTH/MOT SE9 * 43 L7
The Arcade ELTH/MOT SE9 * 43 L7
LVPST EC2M * 24 B1
Arcadian Av BXLY DA5 44 G7
Arcadian Cl BXLY DA5 44 G7
Arcadian Rd BXLY DA5 44 G8
Arcadia Rd MEO DA13 69 K7
Arcadia St POP/IOD E14 25 K2
Archangel St
BERM/RHTH SE16 24 G5
Archates Av CDW/CHF RM16 32 B6
Archcliffe Rd DVW CT17 313 K1
Archdale Rd EDUL SE22 40 F6
Archer Rd FOLKN CT19 11 F1
SNWD SE25 83 N1
STMC/STPC BR5 87 H3
WALD ME5 95 N8
Archer's Court Rd
DVE/WH CT16 261 J9

Archer Sq DEPT SE8 ....25 H9
Archer Wy SWLY BR8 ....55 P9
Archery Cl HOO/HM ME3 ....52 B9
Archery Rd ELTH/MOT SE9 ....43 K6
Archway Cl CROY/NA CRO * 82 D7
Archway Rd IOS ME12 ....57 J5
  RAM CT11 ....17 F4
Arcon Cl ASH TN23 ....282 D1
Arcon Rd ASH TN23 ....282 D1
Arcus Rd BMLY BR1 ....62 C5
Ardbeg Rd HNHL SE24 ....40 D7
Arden Cl THMD SE28 ....28 C2
Arden Ct CANT CT1 * 5 G6
Arden Crs POP/IOD E14 ....25 K7
Arden Dr KEN/WIL TN24 ....3 F1
Arden Gra RCANTW CT4 ....194 D3
Arden Gv ORP BR6 ....86 C8
Ardenlee Dr MAID/BEAR ME14 ....13 J3
Arden Rd FAV ME15 ....133 H6
  HB CT6 ....107 N4
Ardenrun LING RH7 ....234 D1
Arden St GILL ME7 ....7 H1
Ardent Av DEAL CT14 ....233 H5
Ardent Cl SNWD SE25 ....60 E9
Ardfern Av STRHM/NOR SW16 ....60 A9
Ardfillan Rd CAT SE6 ....42 B9
Ardgowan Rd CAT SE6 ....42 C9
Ardingly Cl CROY/NA CRO 84 A7
Ardley Cl FSTH SE23 ....61 L2
Ardlui Rd WNWD SE27 ....22 F3
Ardmere Rd LEW SE13 ....42 B7
Ardoch Rd CAT SE6 ....62 B1
Arethusa Rd GRH DA9 * 47 P5
Arethusa Rd ROCH ME1 ....95 H6
Argent Rd OBOR ME11 ....77 J5
Argent St GRAYS RM17 ....14 E7
  WTHK RM20 ....31 J9
Argent Ter WALD ME5 * 95 J5
Argent Wy SIT ME10 ....99 K8
Argles Cl GRH DA9 ....47 N6
Argyle Av MARG CT9 ....14 B7
Argyle Cl ROCH ME1 ....95 K7
Argyle Gdns MARG CT9 ....14 B8
Argyle Rd CAN/RD E16 ....26 C2
  SEV TN15 ....20 E3
  STH/RUST TN4 ....240 D7
  WSTB CT5 ....105 L5
Argyle Wy STHWK SE1 ....24 D8
Argyll Dr RAM CT11 ....143 L3
Argyll Rd GRAYS RM17 ....32 B8
  WOOL/PLUM SE18 ....27 K6
Arica Rd BROCKY SE4 ....41 L5
Ariel Cl CVE DA12 ....70 E3
Arisdale Av SOCK/AV RM15 ....31 L1
Ark Av CDW/CHF RM16 ....32 A6
Arkell Gv NRWD SE19 ....60 B6
Arkindale Rd CAT SE6 ....62 A2
Ark La DEAL CT14 ....233 H2
Arklow Rd NWCR SE14 ....25 J9
Arklow Sq NWCR SE14 ....17 H3
Arkwright Rd TIL RM18 ....49 L3
Arlingford Rd
  BRXS/STRHM SW2 ....40 A7
Arlington ASH TN23 ....252 D8
Arlington Cl BFN/LL DA15 ....44 A6
  LEW SE13 ....42 B6
Arlington Gdns MARG CT9 ....113 H5
Arlington Sq MARG CT9 ....14 E5
Armada Cl NROM TN28 ....337 K8
Armada Ct CHAT ME4 ....95 K5
Armadale Vls RAM CT11 * 16 B4
Armada St DEPT SE8 ....25 K9
Armada Wy CHAT ME4 ....6 B6
Armdale Rd IL IG1 ....27 K2
Armitage Rd GNWCH SE10 ....26 A8
Armor Rd PUR RM19 ....30 C7
Armoury Dr GVE DA12 ....49 N8
Armoury Rd DEPT SE8 ....41 P5
Armstrong Cl BMLY BR1 ....63 J9
  PEM E6 ....26 G2
  RSEV TN14 ....118 A9
Armstrong Rd
  MAID/SHEP ME15 ....185 M2
  WOOL/PLUM SE18 ....27 K6
Armstrong Sq GB CT6 ....106 F3
Armytage Cl HOO/HM ME3 ....73 L5
Arne Cl TONN TN10 ....211 H4
Arne Gv ORP BR6 ....86 C7
Arne Wk BKHTH/KID SE3 ....42 D5
Arngask Rd CAT SE6 ....42 B8
Arnhem Pl POP/IOD E14 ....25 N5
Arnhem Av SOCK/AV RM15 ....30 F4
Arnhem Dr CROY/NA CRO 114 C5
  WALD ME5 ....95 J7
Arnold Av MEO DA13 ....92 C6
Arnoldie Cl STRD ME2 ....19 K7
Arnold Est STHWK SE1 * 24 C5
Arnold Pl TIL RM18 ....49 N2
Arnold Rd GVE DA12 ....69 N1
  MARG CT9 ....15 H6
  RCANTW CT4 ....195 K1
Arnolds La RDART DA2 ....66 C5
Arnott Cl THMD SE28 ....28 B4
Arnould Av CMBW SE5 ....40 D5
Arnsberg Wy BXLYHN DA7 ....45 J3
Arnside Rd BXLYHN DA7 ....45 J2
Arnull's Rd STRHM/NOR SW16 ....60 E5
Arolla Rd HB CT6 ....107 P2
Arragon Gdns WWKM BR4 ....84 E7
Arran Cl ERITH DA8 ....29 J9
  WLGTN SM6 ....22 C1
Arran Rd CAT SE6 ....61 P1
  MAID/SHEP ME15 ....185 M5
Arrol Rd BECK BR3 ....61 J9
Arrowhead La RASHW TN26 ....323 M7
Arsenal Rd ELTH/MOT SE9 ....43 K3
Arsenal Rd DART DA1 ....46 C2
  WOOL/PLUM SE18 ....27 K7
Artemis Cl GVE DA12 ....50 A8
Arterial Rd North Stifford
  CDW/CHF RM16 ....31 N5
Arterial Rd Purfleet
  PUR RM19 ....30 F7

Arterial Rd West Thurrock
  WTHK RM20 ....31 J6
Arthurdon Rd LEW SE13 ....41 N6
Arthur Gv WOOL/PLUM SE18 ....27 K7
Arthur kennedy Cl FAV ME13 ....164 A1
Arthur Rd BH/WHM TN16 ....115 M9
  BRCH CT7 ....110 E5
  DEAL CT14 ....232 F6
  HYTHE CT21 ....309 H6
  MARG CT9 ....15 K3
  RMAID ME8 ....97 H6
  ROCH ME1 ....95 J4
Arthur Salmon Cl FAV ME13 ....132 E6
Arthur St CANST EC4R 24 A3
  ERITH DA8 ....45 P1
  FOLKN CT19 ....11 K4
  GRAYS RM17 ....32 D9
  GVW DA11 ....49 L8
  SIT ME10 ....129 M1
Artichoke Hl WAP E1W 24 E3
Artichoke Pl CMBW SE5 * 40 D2
Artillery Gdns CANT CT1 * 5 G5
Artillery Pl WOOL/PLUM SE18 ....26 G8
Artillery Rd RAM CT11 ....17 G2
Artillery Rw GVE DA12 ....49 N8
  SIT ME10 ....129 M1
Artington Cl ORP BR6 ....86 D8
Artizan St WCHPL E1 * 24 C2
Arun TIL RM18 ....34 B7
Arundel Av SIT ME10 ....129 M4
Arundel Cl BXLY DA5 ....45 H7
  CROY/NA CRO * 82 C7
  TON TN9 ....240 D1
  WALD ME5 ....126 A4
Arundel Dr ORP BR6 ....87 J9
Arundel Rd CROY/NA CRO 83 J1
  DART DA1 ....46 C5
  MARG CT9 ....112 G3
  MSTR CT12 ....142 D2
  RTW TN1 ....22 E6
Arundel St MAID/BEAR ME14 ....155 L6
Aschurch Rd CROY/NA CRO 83 L4
Ascot Cl BGR/WK TN15 ....151 L5
  WALD ME5 ....125 P3
Ascot Gdns WCOS CT8 ....111 M6
Ashbee Cl SNOD ME6 ....123 P6
Ashbee Gdns HB CT6 ....107 P1
Ashborne Cl KEN/WIL TN24 ....292 C3
Ashbourne Av BXLYHN DA7 ....44 G1
Ashbourne Gv EDUL SE22 ....40 G4
Ashbourne Ri ORP BR6 ....86 E8
Ashbourne Rd GNWCH SE10 ....41 P1
Ashburnham Retreat
  GNWCH SE10 ....25 L8
Ashburnham Rd BELV DA17 ....29 H7
  MAID/BEAR ME14 ....155 N4
  RAM CT11 ....16 B3
  TONN TN10 ....240 D4
Ashburn Ms GILL ME7 * 96 B5
Ashburton Av CROY/NA CRO 83 N5
Ashburton Cl CROY/NA CRO * 83 M5
  KEN/WIL TN24 ....3 K4
Ashburton Rd CAN/RD E16 ....26 E6
  CROY/NA CRO 83 M6
Ashbury Ct BMLY BR1 ....62 E6
Ashby Cl CDW/CHF RM16 ....33 M2
  STRD ME2 * 123 P7
Ashby Ms BROCKY SE4 ....41 M4
Ashby Rd BROCKY SE4 ....41 M3
Ashby's EDEN TN8 ....236 E1
Ashby Wk CROY/NA CRO 83 H3
Ash Cl BRDST CT10 ....113 H9
  DIT/AY ME20 ....154 D5
  DVW CT17 ....270 D4
  EDEN TN8 ....206 C9
  HB CT6 ....107 L5
  LING RH7 ....235 H4
  PGE/AN SE20 ....61 J8
  RHAM ME8 ....96 E3
  RTWE/PEM TN2 ....270 G8
  SCUP DA14 ....64 D2
  STMC/STPC BR5 ....86 E2
  SWLY BR8 ....65 L8
  WALD ME5 ....95 P3
Ash Close Wk SWCH CT13 * 201 L6
Ashcombe Dr EDEN TN8 ....206 C6
Ash Ct MSTR CT12 ....142 C8
Ash Crs HOO/HM ME3 ....71 K4
  RCANTE CT3 ....138 B8
Ashcroft Av BFN/LL DA15 ....44 D7
Ashcroft Cl BFN/LL DA15 ....44 C7
Ashcroft Rd HOO/HM ME3 ....72 B5
  STPH/PW TN11 ....242 G4
Ashdale Rd LEE/GVPK SE12 ....42 F9
Ashden Wk TONN TN10 ....210 F3
Ashdon Cl SOCK/AV RM15 ....31 L2
Ashdown Cl BECK BR3 ....61 P8
  BXLY DA5 ....45 L8
  HB CT6 ....107 N4
  MAIDW ME16 ....155 J9
  STH/RUST TN4 ....22 B1
Ashdown Crs NROM TN28 ....336 C7
Ashdown Fld RCANTW CT4 ....195 J1
Ashdown Rd RSIT ME9 ....159 N9
Ashdown Vw EGRIN RH19 ....265 H9
Ashenden HDCN TN27 ....248 G7
Ashenden Av RYE TN31 ....333 D7
Ashenden Cl CANT CT1 * 166 B7
  STRD ME2 * 72 C5
Ashenden Wk
  RTWE/PEM TN2 ....241 H9
Ashen Dr DART DA1 ....46 A7
Ashen Grove Rd
  BGR/WK TN15 ....119 N4
Ashen Tree La DVE/WH CT16 ....8 E3
Ashentree La LYDD TN29 ....335 H8
Ashen V SAND/SEL CR2 ....114 A5
Asher Reeds RRTW TN3 ....269 M4
Asher Wy WAP E1W 24 E4

Ashes La RTON TN11 ....211 H1
Ashfield Cl BECK BR3 ....61 N6
Ashfield La CHST SE9 ....63 H5
Ashfield St WCHPL E1 ....24 F1
Ashfield Yd WCHPL E1 * 24 F1
Ashford Dr RMAID ME17 ....187 N9
Ashford Rd ASH TN23 ....281 N1
  ASH TN23 ....282 D3
  FAV ME13 ....132 F8
  HB CT6 ....107 N4
  HYTHE CT21 ....308 B1
  MAID/BEAR ME14 ....13 J5
  NROM TN28 ....336 F7
  RASHE TN25 ....284 G6
  RASHW TN26 ....279 M8
  RASHW TN26 ....281 L3
  RASHW TN26 ....282 C8
  RCANTW CT4 ....165 H9
  RCANTW CT4 ....194 C9
  RMAID ME17 ....187 M1
  RMAID ME17 ....189 N6
  TENT TN30 ....301 H2
Ash Gv LYDD TN29 ....342 C5
  MAIDW ME16 ....155 H6
  PGE/AN SE20 ....61 J8
  RDV CT15 ....230 C7
  WWKM BR4 ....84 F6
Ashgrove RSEV TN14 * 117 M9
Ashgrove Rd BMLY BR1 ....62 B5
  SEV TN13 ....178 C4
Ashington Cl SIT ME10 ....99 K9
Ash keys MEO DA15 ....122 C5
Ash La BGR/WK TN15 ....120 F5
Ashlar Pl WOOL/PLUM SE18 ....27 J7
Ashleigh Cl MEO DA15 ....122 A4
Ashleigh Gdns HDCN TN27 ....247 N5
Ashleigh Rd PGE/AN SE20 ....61 H9
Ashley Av FOLKN CT19 ....310 E5
Ashley Cl IOS ME12 ....77 L2
  MSTR CT12 ....142 C2
Ashley Dr WSTB CT5 ....105 H7
Ashley Gdns CDW/CHF RM16 ....32 D4
  ORP BR6 ....86 F9
  STH/RUST TN4 ....269 P3
Ashley Av RCANTE CT3 ....229 H1
Ashley Park Cl STH/RUST TN4 ....269 P3
Ashley Rd RHAM ME8 ....96 E1
  RTON TN11 ....210 B6
  SEV TN13 ....20 E1
  THHTH CR7 ....82 C1
Ashlyn Cl CROY/NA CRO 83 N5
Ashmead Cl WALD ME5 ....125 P2
Ashmead Ga BMLY BR1 ....63 H3
Ashmead Ms DEPT SE8 * 41 N2
Ash Mdw KEN/WIL TN24 ....283 J1
Ashmead Rd DEPT SE8 ....41 N3
Ashmere Av BECK BR3 ....62 B8
Ashmore Ct BECK SE15 ....40 G1
Ashmore Gdns GVW DA11 ....69 H3
Ashmore Gv WELL DA16 ....43 P4
Ashmount La HAYES BR2 ....115 M5
Ash Platt Rd BGR/WK TN15 ....149 K6
Ashridge Crs
  WOOL/PLUM SE18 ....43 N1
Ash Rd BGR/WK TN15 ....90 G8
  BH/WHM TN16 ....176 E1
  DART DA1 ....46 D9
  GVE DA12 ....69 N3
  HART DA3 ....111 K6
  ORP BR6 ....117 H2
  RCANTE CT3 ....228 C1
  RDART DA2 ....66 F3
  STRD ME2 ....18 A4
  SWCH CT13 ....171 M9
Ashstead Dr RSIT ME9 ....130 C5
Ashton Cl DEAL CT14 ....232 C5
Ashton Ms BRDST CT10 * 113 H9
Ashton St POP/IOD E14 ....25 M5
Ashton Wy E/WMAL ME19 ....153 H7
Ash Tree Cl BGR/WK TN15 * 120 C5
  CROY/NA CRO 83 D9
Ashtree Ct BMLY BR1 ....337 L2
Ashtree Dr ORP BR6 ....86 C8
Ash Tree Dr BGR/WK TN15 ....120 C5
Ash Tree La WALD ME5 ....96 A4
Ash Tree Rd FOLKN CT19 ....11 H1
Ashurst Av CROY/NA CRO 105 K7
Ashurst Cl DART DA1 ....45 P4
  PGE/AN SE20 ....61 J8
Ashurst Gdns
  BRXS/STRHM SW2 * 40 A3
  MARG CT9 ....113 K2
Ashurst Wk CROY/NA CRO 83 N6
Ashwater Rd LEE/GVPK SE12 ....42 E9
Ashwell Cl RCANTW CT4 ....195 M2
Ashwood Gdns CROY/NA CRO 114 C1
Ashworth Av BGR/WK TN15 * 120 B2
Ashworth Cl CMBW SE5 ....40 D3
Askes Ct BXLYHS DA6 ....44 F5
Askes Ct SWCH CT13 ....201 P1
Aspdin Rd GVW DA11 ....69 H2
Aspen Cl LYDD TN29 ....337 L2
  ORP BR6 ....87 J8
  SWLY BR8 ....65 M7
Aspen Copse BMLY BR1 ....63 K8
Aspen Dr ASH TN23 ....252 A6
Aspen Gn ERITH DA18 ....28 E6
Aspen Rd HB CT6 ....107 K7
  RCANTW CT4 ....195 M2
Aspen Wy POP/IOD E14 ....25 M3
  RTWE/PEM TN2 ....240 F8
Aspian Dr RMAID ME17 ....185 J9
Aspinall Cl RCANTW CT4 ....167 N8
Aspinall Rd BROCKY SE4 ....41 K4
Aspinden Rd BERM/RHTH SE16 ....24 F7
Asquith Rd RHAM ME8 ....96 F8
Assam St WCHPL E1 * 24 D2
Assembly Pas WCHPL E1 ....24 F1

Astbury Rd PECK SE15 ....41 J2
Aster Rd HOO/HM ME3 ....73 L4
Astley GRAYS RM17 ....32 A9
Astley Av DVE/WH CT16 ....291 K5
Astley Ct DVE/WH CT16 * 291 K5
Astley St MAID/BEAR ME14 ....13 G4
Aston Cl SCUP DA14 ....64 C2
  WALD ME5 ....125 M3
Aston St WCHPL E1 ....25 H1
Astor Av DVW CT17 ....291 J7
Astor Dr DEAL CT14 ....233 H4
Astoria Wk BRXN/ST SW9 ....40 A4
Astor Rd BGR/WK TN15 ....120 B1
  BRDST CT10 ....113 L5
Astra Dr GVE DA12 ....70 A4
Astrid Rd DEAL CT14 ....233 F2
Asylum Rd PECK SE15 ....41 H1
Atcost Rd BARK IG11 ....27 P1
Athelney St CAT SE6 ....61 N2
Athelstan Gn RMAID ME17 ....187 N1
Athelstan Pl DEAL CT14 ....233 H1
Athelstan Rd CANT CT1 ....166 B7
  CHAT ME4 ....95 K4
  FAV ME15 ....132 E7
  FOLKN CT19 ....310 C4
Athelstan Wy STMC/STPC BR5 ....64 C2
Athenlay Rd PECK SE15 ....41 K6
Atherden Rd CLPT E5 ....33 K7
Atherton Gdns
  CDW/CHF RM16 ....33 K7
Athol Pl FAV ME13 ....132 D5
Athol Rd ASH TN23 ....282 C1
  ERITH DA8 ....29 H8
  WSTB CT5 ....105 M4
Athol Sq POP/IOD E14 ....25 M2
Atholl Ter DVW CT17 ....9 H3
Atkins Dr WWKM BR4 ....84 C7
Atkinson Cl ORP BR6 ....87 H9
Atkinson Rd CAN/RD E16 ....26 D1
Atkinson Wk KEN/WIL TN24 ....253 J4
Atlantic Cl SWCM DA10 ....48 C6
Atlantic Rd BRXN/ST SW9 ....40 A5
Atlas Gdns CHARL SE7 ....26 D7
Atlas Rd DART DA1 ....46 C4
Atterbury Cl BH/WHM TN16 ....176 E2
Attlee Av RCANTE CT3 ....229 H1
Attlee Cl CROY/NA CRO 60 G9
Attlee Ct GRAYS RM17 ....32 B6
Attlee Dr DART DA1 ....46 C6
Attlee Wy SIT ME10 ....99 N7
Attwaters La HAWK TN18 ....297 P9
Atwell Rd PECK SE15 * 40 C3
Auburn Cl NWCR SE14 ....41 L1
Aubyn Hl NWWD SE27 ....60 C5
Aubyn Sq SWCM DA10 ....48 C6
Auckland Crs DVE/WH CT16 ....291 K4
Auckland Dr SIT ME10 ....129 K2
Auckland Hl WNWD SE27 ....60 C5
Auckland Ri NRWD SE19 ....60 E7
Auckland Rd BGR/WK TN15 ....149 K6
  RTW TN1 ....270 C2
Aucklands Gdns NRWD SE19 ....60 E7
Aucuba Vls WELL DA16 * 44 D4
Auden Rd DIT/AY ME20 ....123 P9
Audley Av GILL ME7 ....111 P4
  MARG CT9 ....210 D3
  TON TN9 ....210 D3
Audley Cl MAIDW ME16 ....154 C7
Audley Dr CAN/RD E16 ....26 C4
Audley Ri TON TN9 ....210 C6
Audley Rd FOLK CT20 ....210 D3
Audley Wk FOLK CT20 ....210 D3
Audrey Cl BECK BR3 ....84 E5
Audrey Rd IL IG1 ....171 M9
Auger Cl RSIT ME9 ....97 P9
Augusta Cl GILL ME7 ....73 J8
Augusta Gdns FOLK CT20 ....10 C6
Augusta Pl RAM CT11 ....17 H5
Augusta Rd RAM CT11 ....17 H5
Augustus Wk ASH TN23 ....282 C5
Aurelia Gdns THHTH CR7 ....82 C2
Aurelia Rd CROY/NA CRO 82 D5
Aurellus Cl ASH TN23 ....282 D4
Austen Cl EGRIN RH19 ....264 E7
  GRH DA9 * 48 A7
  THMD SE28 ....28 A4
  TIL RM18 ....49 N3
Austen Rd ERITH DA8 ....45 L9
Austens Orch TENT TN30 * 301 H1
Austin Av HAYES BR2 ....85 P3
  HB CT6 ....106 E2
Austin Cl CAT SE6 ....42 C9
  SIT ME10 ....99 P6
  WALD ME5 ....95 N4
Austin Friars OBST EC2N 24 A2
Austin Friars Sq OBST EC2N * 24 A2
Austin Rd ASH TN23 ....282 E2
  GVW DA11 ....49 K9
  STMC/STPC BR5 ....87 H3
Austins La SWCH CT13 ....201 P1
Austral Cl BFN/LL DA15 ....64 B2
Autumn Gld
  MAID/BEAR ME14 ....126 A5
Autumn Gv BMLY BR1 ....62 F5
Avalon Cl ORP BR6 ....87 K6
Avalon Gn ORP BR6 ....87 K6
Avard Gdns ORP BR6 ....86 D8
Avards Cl HAWK TN18 ....316 G9
Avebury Av RAM CT11 ....143 M4
  TON TN9 ....210 E9
Avebury Rd ORP BR6 ....86 D2
Aveley By-Pass SOCK/AV RM15 ....30 F3
Aveley Cl ERITH DA8 ....29 L9
  SOCK/AV RM15 ....30 C4
Aveling Cl HOO/HM ME3 ....73 K1
Avenons Rd PLSTW E13 ....26 B3
Avent Wk RSIT ME9 ....130 D3
Avenue Du Puy TON TN9 ....210 F9
Avenue Gdns MARG CT9 ....113 H3

Avenue Le Puy TON TN9 ....210 F9
Avenue Ldg GRAYS RM17 * 32 C8
Avenue of Remembrance
  SIT ME10 ....129 N2
Avenue Park Rd WNWD SE27 ....60 B1
Avenue Rd BH/WHM TN16 ....145 P5
  BXLYHS DA6 ....44 G4
  ERITH DA8 ....45 L1
  PGE/AN SE20 ....107 J1
  PGE/AN SE20 ....61 J7
  RAM CT11 ....17 H2
  SEV TN13 ....21 G1
  SNWD SE25 ....60 G8
The Avenue BECK BR3 ....61 N5
  BH/WHM TN16 ....151 K4
  BH/WHM TN16 ....146 B8
  BMLY BR1 ....63 H9
  BXLY DA5 ....44 F8
  CHAT ME4 ....73 J5
  CROY/NA CRO 83 K7
  DEAL CT14 ....233 H2
  DEAL CT14 ....263 H5
  DIT/AY ME20 ....154 D3
  DVE/WH CT16 ....290 F2
  EGRIN RH19 ....265 L2
  GNWCH SE10 ....47 P5
  GRH DA9 ....47 P5
  GVW DA11 ....49 L3
  MARG CT9 ....15 J6
  ORP BR6 ....86 F5
  RCANTE CT3 ....138 B8
  RDV CT15 ....292 E1
  STMC/STPC BR5 ....64 D6
  TON TN9 ....210 E8
  WWKM BR4 ....84 G4
Averenches Rd
  MAID/BEAR ME14 ....156 C7
Avereng Gdns FOLKN CT19 ....10 A2
Avereng Rd FOLKN CT19 ....10 B2
Averil Gv STRHM/NOR SW16 ....60 B5
Averill Cl HOO/HM ME3 ....58 F8
Avern Rd E/WMAL ME19 ....185 L2
Avery Hill Rd ELTH/MOT SE9 ....43 N9
Avery La MAID/SHEP ME15 ....186 F5
Avery Wy HOO/HM ME3 ....38 F9
Avery Wy DART DA1 ....66 E1
Aviemore Cl BECK BR3 ....84 C2
Aviemore Gdns
  MAID/BEAR ME14 ....156 C8
Aviemore Wy BECK BR3 ....84 B2
Avignon Rd BROCKY SE4 ....41 K4
Avington Cl MAID/SHEP ME15 ....185 L2
Avington Wy PECK SE15 * 40 F1
Avis Sq WCHPL E1 ....24 C2
Avocet Cl STHWK SE1 ....24 C8
Avocet Ms THMD SE28 ....27 L6
Avon Cl CANT CT1 ....167 N4
  GVE DA12 ....69 P1
  TONN TN10 ....210 F5
Avondale Cl WSTB CT5 ....105 P6
Avondale Pavement
  STHWK SE1 * 24 D8
Avondale Pl HOO/HM ME3 * 54 G4
Avondale Ri PECK SE15 ....40 F4
Avondale Rd BMLY BR1 ....62 C5
  CAN/RD E16 ....25 P1
  ELTH/MOT SE9 ....43 J5
  GILL ME7 ....7 K2
  RFOLK CT18 ....311 M1
  WELL DA16 ....44 B3
Avondale Sq STHWK SE1 ....24 D8
Avon Gn SOCK/AV RM15 ....31 L2
Avonley Rd NWCR SE14 ....41 J1
Avonmouth Rd DART DA1 ....46 D6
Avon Rd BROCKY SE4 ....41 N4
Avonstowe Cl ORP BR6 ....86 D7
Avon St RTW TN1 ....270 F3
Awiscombe Rd WELL DA16 ....25 P9
Axis Ct GNWCH SE10 ....26 A8
Axminster Crs WELL DA16 ....44 C2
Axtaine Rd STMC/STPC BR5 ....87 L4
Axtane GVE DA12 ....68 D6
Axtane Cl EYN DA4 ....67 J2
Aycliffe Cl BMLY BR1 ....86 A1
Ayelands HART DA3 ....91 H6
Ayelands La HART DA3 ....91 H6
Aylesbury Rd HAYES BR2 ....62 E9
  RASHE TN25 ....252 E2
Aylesford Av BECK BR3 ....84 B2
Aylesford Crs RHAM ME8 ....96 F3
Aylesford Pl KEN/WIL TN24 ....283 H1
Aylesham Rd ORP BR6 ....86 F9
  RCANTE CT3 ....229 K2
Aylewsade La HDCN TN27 ....247 P9
Aylett Rd SNWD SE25 ....83 N1
Aylewyn Gn SIT ME10 ....99 N6
Aylton Est BERM/RHTH SE16 * 24 F5
Aylward Rd FSTH SE23 ....61 K1
Aylward St WCHPL E1 ....24 G2
Aylwin Est STHWK SE1 * 24 B6
Aynscombe Angle ORP BR6 ....87 H4
Aysgarth Rd DUL SE21 ....40 D7
Ayton Rd RAM CT11 ....18 C1
Azalea Dr SWLY BR8 ....65 J8
Azenby Rd PECK SE15 ....40 F3
Azof St GNWCH SE10 ....25 P7

B

Babbacombe Rd BMLY BR1 ....62 F7
Babb's La CRBK TN17 ....298 D9
Babs Oak Hl CANTW/ST CT2 ....137 N7
Babylon La RMAID ME17 ....216 E8
Back Church La WCHPL E1 ....24 D2
Backfields ROCH ME1 ....18 E7
Back La BGR/WK TN15 ....149 M9
  BSLY DA5 ....150 A9
  BXLY DA5 ....45 J4
  CDW/CHF RM16 ....31 M4
  CRBK TN17 ....274 D8

IOS ME12 .... 78 D1
PUR RM19 .... 31 H7
RMAID ME17 .... 186 A9
RSEV TN14 .... 179 A4
RTON TN11 .... 180 F7
SEV TN15 .... 148 C9
STPH/PW TN12 .... 273 P2
Backley Gdns SNWD SE25 .... 83 M5
Back Rd HAWK TN18 .... 310 B8
SCUP DA14 .... 64 C3
Back Rd (East) DVE/WH TN16 .... 292 A6
Back St DEAL CT14 .... 262 E3
FOLKN CT19 .... 11 H4
RMAID ME17 .... 187 H5
Bacon Gv STHWK SE1 .... 24 C5
Baddlesmere Rd WSTB CT5 .... 105 P3
Baden PI STHWK SE1 .... 24 A5
Baden Rd GILL ME7 .... 73 K8
Baden Crs WALD ME5 .... 95 M7
Bader Wk GVW DA11 .... 69 J2
Badger Rd WALD ME5 .... 125 P4
Badgers CI CANTW/ST CT2 .... 135 P6
Badgers Copse ORP BR6 .... 86 G6
Badgers Cft ELTH/MOT SE9 .... 63 L2
Badgers Holt RTWE/PEM TN2 .... 271 H5
Badgers Mt CDW/CHF RM16 .... 32 C5
Badgers Ri CDW/CHF CT14 .... 233 H9
DVW CT17 .... 290 E4
RSEV TN14 .... 117 P4
Badgers Rd RSEV TN14 .... 118 D4
Badgers Wy EGRIN RH19 .... 265 H5
Badlesmere CI ASH TN23 .... 282 B2
Badlow CI ERITH DA8 .... 45 N1
Badmans Ms CAN/RD E16 .... 26 B4
Bad Munstereifel Rd ASH TN23 .... 282 E5
Badsell Rd STPH/PW TN12 .... 242 C2
Badsworth Rd CMBW SE5 .... 40 C1
Baffin CI CHAT ME4 .... 95 L4
Bagham La RCANTW CT4 .... 194 D3
Bagham Rd RCANTW CT4 .... 194 D3
Bagley House WOOL/PLUM SE18 * 43 J1
Bagshill Rd FAV ME13 .... 162 B8
Bagshot Ct WOOL/PLUM SE18 * 43 L2
Bagshot St WALW SE17 .... 24 B8
Baildon St DEPT SE8 .... 41 M1
Bailey CI PUR RM19 .... 30 G7
Bailey Dr GILL ME7 .... 96 D6
Bailey House WOOL/PLUM SE18 * 43 J1
Bailey PI SYD SE26 .... 61 J5
Baileys Fld ASH TN23 .... 252 C8
Baillemore Ct RAM CT11 * 143 L3
Baines CI SAND/SEL CR2 .... 64 C5
Baird Gdns NRWD SE19 .... 60 E3
Baird's HI BRDST CT10 .... 113 L7
Bairdsley CI BRDST CT10 .... 113 L7
Bairdon Rd BKHTH/KID SE3 .... 42 C3
Baker CI RSIT ME9 .... 114 B1
Baker Hill CI GVW DA11 .... 69 K3
Baker La HDCN TN27 .... 248 A2
RMAID ME17 .... 217 J3
Baker Ms ORP BR6 .... 116 G1
Baker Rd FOLKN CT19 .... 310 B5
WOOL/PLUM SE18 .... 43 J1
Bakers Av ELTH/MOT SE9 .... 43 K6
Bakers CI CANTW/ST CT2 .... 166 B5
LING RH7 .... 235 H4
Bakers Cross CRBK TN17 .... 298 A3
Baker's La LING RH7 .... 235 H5
RCANTW CT4 .... 195 L1
Baker St CDW/CHF RM16 .... 32 F2
ROCH ME1 .... 95 H3
ROCH ME1 .... 124 G4
Baker's Wk ROCH ME1 .... 19 F4
Balaclava La WADH TN5 .... 294 A8
Balaclava Rd STHWK SE1 .... 24 C7
Balas Dr SIT ME10 .... 99 K8
Balcaskie Rd ELTH/MOT SE9 .... 43 K6
Balchen Rd BKHTH/KID SE3 .... 43 H5
Balchier Rd EDUL SE22 .... 61 H1
Balcomb Crs MARG CT9 .... 113 H5
Balcombe CI BXLYHS DA6 .... 44 F5
Balcombes HI CRBK TN17 .... 274 D8
Balder RI LEE/GVPK SE12 .... 62 F1
Baldric Rd FOLK CT20 .... 310 C6
Baldwin Crs CMBW SE5 .... 40 C2
Baldwin Rd IOS ME12 .... 58 D9
NROM TN28 .... 343 J3
Baldwin Ter FOLKN CT19 .... 11 F1
Baldwins Fld EGRIN RH19 * 264 F4
Baldwyn's CI BXLY DA5 .... 65 M1
Baldwyn's Rd BXLY DA5 .... 65 M1
Bale Rd WCHPL E1 .... 13 L7
Balfour Rd CHAT ME4 .... 95 K5
DEAL CT14 .... 233 J7
DVE/WH CT16 .... 291 K6
GRAYS RM17 .... 32 D7
HAYES BR2 .... 85 N2
SNWD SE25 .... 83 M1
Balfour St STHWK SE1 .... 24 A7
Balgowan Rd BECK BR3 .... 61 L9
Balgowan St WOOL/PLUM SE18 .... 27 N7
Baliol Rd WSTB CT5 .... 105 M4
Balkan Wk WAP E1W * 24 E5
Balladier Wk POP/IOD E14 .... 25 L1
Ballamore Rd BMLY BR1 .... 62 E2
Ballard CI STPH/PW TN12 .... 245 H3
Ballard Rd NROM TN28 .... 343 J3
Ballards La CROY/NA CR0 .... 82 B8
Ballater Rd SAND/SEL CR2 .... 83 L9
Ballens Rd WALD ME5 .... 125 P2
Ballina St FSTH SE23 .... 41 K8
Balliol Rd BRDST CT10 .... 113 L6
WELL DA16 .... 44 D3
Ball La KEN/WIL TN24 .... 253 H2
Balloch Rd CAT SE6 .... 42 B9
Ballow CI CMBW SE5 * 40 D1
Balmer CI RHAM ME8 .... 96 G7

Balmoral Av BECK BR3 .... 84 B1
Balmoral Gdns BXLY DA5 .... 45 H8
Balmoral PI RAM CT11 .... 17 H5
Balmoral Rd DEAL CT14 .... 263 J2
EYN DA4 .... 66 G6
GILL ME7 .... 7 K2
MARG CT9 .... 112 A5
Baltic Rd TON TN9 .... 240 E2
Baltimore PI WELL DA16 .... 44 B3
Bamford Rd BMLY BR1 .... 62 B4
Bamford Wy DEAL CT14 .... 233 H5
Bampfylde CI WLGTN SM6 .... 82 E2
Bampton Rd FSTH SE23 .... 61 K2
Banavie Gdns BECK BR3 .... 61 P7
Banbury Vls MED DA13 .... 68 D5
Banchory Rd BKHTH/KID SE3 .... 42 F1
Bancroft Gdns ORP BR6 .... 86 G5
Bancroft La E/WMAL ME19 .... 185 K1
Bancroft Rd BGR/WK TN15 .... 151 J1
Banfield Rd PECK SE15 .... 61 J2
Bangor Rd STRD ME2 .... 71 M9
Bankfields HDCN TN27 .... 247 M4
Bankfield Vls CRBK TN17 .... 274 C9
Bankfoot GRAYS RM17 .... 32 A7
Bankhurst Rd BMLY SR1 .... 62 C3
Bank House Rd CAT SE6 .... 41 M8
Bank La BGR/WK TN15 .... 179 M8
Bank Rd RASHE TN25 .... 283 N8
Bank Side RASHW TN26 .... 304 D7
Bankside CDW DA11 .... 48 C7
SEV TN13 .... 148 C6
WALD ME5 .... 95 N6
Bankside CI BH/WHM TN16 .... 145 M3
RDART DA2 .... 65 M3
Banks La BXLYHS DA6 .... 45 H5
Banks Rd ASH TN23 .... 282 D1
STRD ME2 .... 72 C7
The Banks BRDST CT10 .... 113 L7
Bank St ASH TN23 .... 2 D4
CHAT ME4 .... 7 F6
CRBK TN17 .... 297 P2
FAV ME13 .... 132 F6
GVE DA12 .... 49 M7
HYTHE CT21 .... 309 H5
MARG CT9 .... 12 E5
SEV TN13 .... 21 C4
TON TN9 .... 210 E8
Bankton Rd BRXS/STRHM SW2 .... 40 A5
Bankwell Rd LEW SE13 .... 42 C5
Banky Fields RHAM ME8 .... 97 L5
Banky Meadow MAIDW ME16 .... 154 E9
Bann CI SOCK/AV RM15 .... 31 L5
Banner CI PUR RM19 .... 30 F7
Banner Farm Rd RTWE/PEM TN2 .... 23 F7
Banner Wy IOS ME12 .... 77 N1
Banning St GNWCH SE10 .... 25 P8
STRD ME2 .... 72 A7
Bannister CI BRXS/STRHM SW2 .... 40 A9
Bannister HI RSIT ME9 .... 129 J3
Bannister Rd MAID/BEAR ME14 .... 155 M5
Bannockburn Rd WOOL/PLUM SE18 .... 27 M7
Banstead St PECK SE15 .... 41 J4
Banstead Wy WLGTN SM6 .... 82 D9
Bantry St CMBW SE5 .... 40 D1
Banwell Rd BXLY DA5 .... 44 F7
Bappard Rd BERM/RHTH SE16 .... 24 E6
Baptchild PI STMC/STPC BR5 .... 87 K1
Barberry Av WALD ME5 .... 95 J9
Barchester St POP/IOD E14 .... 25 L1
Barchester Wy TONN TN10 .... 211 J4
Barclay Av TONN TN10 .... 211 J6
Barclay Rd CROY/NA CR0 .... 83 J7
Barclay Wy WTHK RM20 .... 31 J8
Barcombe CI CHST BR7 .... 64 C9
Bardell Ter ROCH ME1 .... 19 H6
Barden Park Rd TON TN9 .... 210 D9
Barden Rd RRTW TN3 .... 239 L7
TON TN9 .... 210 D9
Barden St WOOL/PLUM SE18 .... 44 A1
Bardolph Av CROY/NA CR0 .... 114 C3
Bardown Rd WADH TN5 .... 314 B6
Bardsey PI WCHPL E1 .... 24 F1
Bardsley CI CROY/NA CR0 .... 83 L7
STPH/PW TN12 .... 213 H5
Bardsley La GNWCH SE10 .... 25 M9
Barfield EYN DA4 .... 67 H7
Barfield Rd BMLY BR1 .... 63 L9
Barfleur La DEPT SE8 .... 25 J7
Barforth Rd PECK SE15 .... 41 H4
Barfreston CI MAID/SHEP ME15 .... 185 L1
Barfrestone Rd RDV CT15 .... 230 A8
Barfrestone Wy PGE/AN SE20 .... 61 H7
Bargate CI WOOL/PLUM SE18 .... 27 N8
Bargates ASH TN23 .... 282 B2
Barge House Rd CAN/RD E16 .... 27 J3
Bargery Rd CAT SE6 .... 60 G6
Bargrove CI PGE/AN SE20 .... 60 G1
Bargrove Rd MAID/BEAR ME14 .... 156 A4
Barham CI CHST BR7 .... 63 M4
GVE DA12 .... 50 B9
HAYES BR2 .... 85 K5
MAID/SHEP ME15 .... 186 B6
Barham Rd CHST BR7 .... 63 M4
CROY/NA CR0 .... 83 H8
DART DA1 .... 46 G8
Barham's Mill Rd HDCN TN27 .... 219 K7
Baring CI LEE/GVPK SE12 .... 62 E3
Baring Rd CROY/NA CR0 .... 83 M5
LEE/GVPK SE12 .... 42 E9
Bark Burr Rd CDW/CHF RM16 .... 32 A5
Barker Rd MAIDW ME16 .... 12 C6
Barkers Ct SIT ME10 .... 129 L1
Bark Hart Rd ORP BR6 .... 86 E1
Barking Rd CAN/RD E16 .... 26 A1
POP/IOD E14 .... 25 P2

Barkis CI ROCH ME1 .... 95 J7
Barkway Dr ORP BR6 .... 86 B7
Barkworth Rd BERM/RHTH SE16 .... 24 E8
Barlborough St NWCR SE14 .... 41 K1
Barle Gdns SOCK/AV RM15 .... 31 L2
Barler PI OBOR ME11 .... 77 J2
Barley CI HB CT6 .... 108 A8
RDV CT15 .... 262 B6
Barleycorn E/WMAL ME19 .... 153 M3
Barleycorn Dr RHAM ME8 .... 97 H8
Barley Flds MAID/BEAR ME14 .... 156 A8
Barleymow CI WALD ME5 .... 95 P8
Barley Mw ASH TN23 .... 282 A3
Barling CI WALD ME5 .... 125 H4
Barlow Cl RHAM ME8 .... 97 H9
Barlow Dr BKHTH/KID SE3 .... 43 J2
Barlow St WALW SE17 .... 24 A7
Barlow Wy DAGW RM9 .... 29 J2
Barmeston Rd CAT SE6 .... 61 P1
Barming Rd E/WMAL ME19 .... 185 H4
Barmouth Rd CROY/NA CR0 .... 84 A6
Barnaby Ter ROCH ME1 .... 95 H4
Barnard CI CHST BR7 .... 63 P7
Barnardo Gdns WCHPL E1 * 24 G2
Barnardo St WCHPL E1 .... 24 G2
Barnard Rd WARL CR6 .... 144 E4
Barnberry CI ASH TN23 .... 252 B9
Barn CI RCANTE CT3 .... 138 B4
RSIT ME9 .... 129 H5
WSTB CT5 .... 134 G2
Barn Crs MARG CT9 .... 112 A4
Barncroft CI MAID/BEAR ME14 .... 156 C8
Barncroft Dr GILL ME7 .... 126 C1
Barncroft Rd MAIDW ME16 .... 184 E2
Barnehurst Av BXLYHN DA7 .... 45 L2
Barnehurst CI ERITH DA8 .... 45 L3
Barnehurst Rd BXLYHN DA7 .... 45 L3
Barn End Dr RDART DA2 .... 66 C5
Barn End La WKY BR8 .... 66 C5
Barnes Av MARG CT9 .... 112 A4
Barnes CI FAV ME13 .... 132 D5
Barnes Cray Rd DART DA1 .... 46 A5
Barnesdale Crs STMC/STPC BR5 .... 87 H5
Barnes La RMAID ME17 .... 215 J3
Barnes Sq POP/IOD E14 .... 25 H2
Barnes Ter DEPT SE8 .... 25 J8
Barnes Wk STPH/PW TN12 .... 245 J4
Barnet Dr HAYES BR2 .... 85 L7
Barnet's La CANTW/ST CT2 .... 137 J5
Barnett CI ERITH DA8 .... 45 P3
Barnett Fld ASH TN23 .... 252 C9
Barnett Rd PATTEN TN2 .... 240 F8
Barnetts Rd RYTON TN1 .... 209 M8
Barnett's Shaw OXTED RH8 .... 174 G3
Barnett Wy WCHPL E1 .... 24 F1
Barnett Wood La HAYES BR2 .... 85 M6
Barney CI CHARL SE7 .... 26 D8
Barnfield CROY/NA CR0 .... 69 L1
HB CT6 .... 107 H4
RTWE/PEM TN2 .... 270 C9
TENT TN30 .... 301 J5
WALD ME5 .... 95 M6
Barnfield Av CROY/NA CR0 .... 83 N5
MTCM CR4 .... 60 A1
Barnfield CI GRH DA9 .... 47 M7
HART DA3 .... 69 H9
SWLY BR8 .... 88 B4
Barnfield Crs BGR/WK TN15 .... 149 K2
Barnfield Gdns WOOL/PLUM SE18 * 27 J9
Barnfield Rd BELV DA17 .... 28 E9
BH/WHM TN16 .... 145 N5
HAYES BR1 .... 132 F5
FOLKN CT19 .... 11 G3
SEV TN13 .... 148 C8
STMC/STPC BR5 .... 64 F9
WOOL/PLUM SE18 .... 27 J9
Barnfield Wy OXTED RH8 .... 175 K9
Barnfield Wood CI BECK BR3 .... 84 C5
Barnfield Wood Rd BECK BR3 .... 84 C5
Barnham Dr THMD SE28 .... 27 N4
Barnham St STHWK SE1 .... 24 B5
Barn HI MAID/SHEP ME15 .... 184 D9
Barnhill Av HAYES BR2 .... 85 K2
Barn Hill La LYDD TN29 .... 335 H6
Barnhurst La RFOLK CT18 .... 288 D7
Barnhurst Rd MAID/BEAR ME14 .... 155 M4
Barn Meadow STPH/PW TN12 .... 246 B5
STRD ME2 .... 123 M1
Bammead Rd BECK BR3 .... 61 M7
Barnock CI DART DA1 .... 45 N8
Barn Platt ASH TN23 .... 252 D9
Barnsdale Av POP/IOD E14 .... 25 L7
Barnsley CI IOS ME12 .... 57 N6
Barnsole Rd GILL ME7 .... 7 J9
RCANTE CT3 .... 200 C5
Barnstaple La LEW SE13 .... 42 A5
The Barn GRAYS RM17 .... 32 C7
Barntye CI RDV CT15 .... 291 M1
Barnwell PI GILL ME7 .... 7 J5
Barnwell Rd DART DA1 .... 46 F4
HNHL SE24 .... 40 A6
Barnwood CI ROCH ME1 .... 94 C6
Baron CI GILL ME7 .... 73 L8
MAID/BEAR ME14 .... 156 C7
Barns Wk CROY/NA CR0 .... 94 M9
Barque Ms DEPT SE8 .... 25 K9
Barrack HI HYTHE CT21 .... 308 F5
Barrack Rd CHAT ME4 .... 73 H7
Barrack Rw GVW DA11 .... 49 M7
Barretts Rd HAWK TN18 .... 317 J4
SEV TN13 .... 148 C5
Barrey Rd KEN/WIL TN24 .... 283 K2
Barriedale NWCR SE14 .... 41 L2
Barrier Dr DART DA1 .... 46 B2
Barrier Point Rd CAN/RD E16 .... 26 D5
Barrier Rd CHAT ME4 .... 6 C2
Barrington CI WALD ME5 .... 95 L9

Barrington Crs BRCH CT7 .... 111 J6
Barrington Rd BRXN/ST SW9 .... 40 B4
BXLYHN DA7 .... 44 F5
Barrington Vls WOOL/PLUM SE18 * 43 L2
Barrington St NRWD SE19 * 60 E5
Barrowfields WALD ME5 .... 126 A4
Barrow Green Rd GDST RH9 .... 174 D7
Barrow Gv SIT ME10 .... 129 L2
Barrow HI ASH TN23 ....
RASHE TN25 .... 285 L8
Barrow Hill Cottages ASH TN23 .... 2 B5
Barrow Hill Rd RASHE TN25 .... 285 L9
Barrow Hill Ter RASHE TN25 .... 2 C2
Barrow La RRTW TN3 .... 269 L7
Barrow Rd CROY/NA CR0 .... 83 H3
Barrows CI BRCH CT7 .... 111 H7
Barr Rd GVE DA12 .... 70 B1
Barry Av BXLYHN DA7 .... 44 G1
Barry CI CDW/CHF RM16 .... 33 H6
ORP BR6 .... 86 F7
Barry Pde EDUL SE22 .... 40 G5
Barry Rd EDUL SE22 .... 40 G7
EHAM E6 .... 26 F2
Barset Rd PECK SE15 .... 41 J4
Barsons CI PGE/AN SE20 .... 61 H6
Barston Rd NRWD SE27 .... 60 C1
Barth Ms WOOL/PLUM SE18 .... 27 M7
Bartholomew CI HYTHE CT21 .... 308 G4
Bartholomew Gdns HYTHE CT21 * 308 F4
OBST EC2N * 24 A2
Bartholomew La HYTHE CT21 .... 308 F5
HYTHE CT21 .... 308 G5
STHWK SE1 * 24 A6
Bartholomew Wy SWLY BR8 .... 65 N9
Barth Rd WOOL/PLUM SE18 .... 27 M7
Bartlett CI POP/IOD E14 .... 25 K2
WALD ME5 .... 125 P4
Bartlett Dr WSTB CT5 .... 105 P5
Bartlett Rd BH/WHM TN16 .... 176 D2
GVW DA11 .... 69 L3
Bartletts CI IOS ME12 .... 77 L2
Bartlett St SAND/SEL CR2 .... 83 J9
Barton CI BXLYHS DA6 .... 44 G6
PECK SE15 .... 41 H4
Barton Crs EGRIN RH19 .... 265 K8
Barton Fld RFOLK CT18 .... 286 C5
Barton Hill Dr IOS ME12 .... 77 P3
Barton Mill Rd CANT CT1 .... 166 G2
Barton Rd CANT CT1 .... 167 H6
DVE/WH CT16 .... 291 K5
EYN DA4 .... 67 H7
MAID/SHEP ME15 .... 185 M1
SCUP DA14 .... 64 G5
WKY BR8 .... 18 C1
Barton View Ter DVE/WH CT16 * 291 K6
Bartram Rd BROCKY SE4 .... 41 L6
Barts CI BECK BR3 .... 84 D2
Barville Rd RDV CT15 .... 230 F8
Barward CI WOOL/PLUM SE18 .... 27 M7
Barwick Rd DVW CT17 .... 290 G6
Barwood Av WWKM BR4 .... 84 E5
Bascombe Gv DART DA1 .... 45 M6
Bascome St BRXS/STRHM SW2 .... 40 A7
Baseing CI EHAM E6 .... 27 J3
Basevi Wy DEPT SE8 .... 25 K9
Bashford Barn La RSIT ME9 .... 159 H1
Basi CI STRD ME2 .... 72 C6
Basildon Rd ABYW SE2 .... 27 P8
Basil Gdns CROY/NA CR0 .... 84 A5
Basil Ter MAID/SHEP ME15 * 185 M2
Basin Ap POP/IOD E14 .... 25 H2
Basing CI MAID/SHEP ME15 .... 13 H7
Basingdon Wy CMBW SE5 .... 40 D5
Basing Dr BXLY DA5 .... 45 H7
Basinghall Av CITYW EC2V 24 A2
Basinghall St CITYW EC2V 24 A2
Baskerville KEN/WIL TN24 .... 2 C2
Basket Gdns ELTH/MOT SE9 .... 43 J6
Basmere CI MAID/BEAR ME14 * 156 A4
Bassano St EDUL SE22 .... 40 F6
Bassant Rd WOOL/PLUM SE18 .... 27 N9
Bassett CI HYTHE CT21 .... 309 K3
Bassett Gdns RTWE/PEM TN2 .... 309 J3
Bassett La LYDD TN29 .... 335 H6
Bassett St SIT ME10 .... 129 L1
Bassetts HI LING RH7 .... 235 K7
Bassetts La EDEN TN8 .... 268 B1
Bassetts Wy ORP BR6 .... 86 C8
Basswood CI PECK SE15 .... 41 H4
Basted La BGR/WK TN15 .... 151 J7
Basted Mil BGR/WK TN15 .... 151 J7
Bastion Rd ABYW SE2 .... 27 P8
DVW CT17 .... 8 B6
Baston Manor Rd WWKM BR4 .... 85 L7
Baston Rd HAYES BR2 .... 84 G9
Bata Av TIL RM18 .... 34 A8
Batavia Rd NWCR SE14 .... 41 L1
Batchelors RTWE/PEM TN2 .... 241 P9
Batchelor St CHAT ME4 .... 6 D5
Batchwood Gn STMC/STPC BR5 .... 87 H1
Bates CI DIT/AY ME20 .... 153 P1
Bates Crs CROY/NA CR0 .... 82 F9
Bates HI BGR/WK TN15 .... 150 F7
Bate St POP/IOD E14 .... 25 J3
Bath CI PECK SE15 .... 41 J4
Bath Hard ROCH ME1 .... 19 J6
Bath House Rd CROY/NA CR0 .... 82 D5
Bath Ms KEN/WIL TN24 * 283 H2
Bath PI MARG CT9 .... 15 J4
Bath Rd DART DA1 .... 46 B8
KEN/WIL TN24 .... 283 H1
MARG CT9 .... 15 J4
Bath St GVW DA11 .... 142 G3
Bathurst CI MSTR CT12 .... 142 D5
Bathurst Rd ERITH DA8 .... 45 P5
STPH/PW TN12 .... 246 B6
Bathway WOOL/PLUM SE18 .... 27 H7

Baton CI PUR RM19 .... 30 G7
Batteries CI RSIT ME9 .... 130 C5
Battersby Rd CAT SE6 .... 62 B1
Battery Point HYTHE CT21 .... 309 N5
Battery Rd LYDD TN29 .... 347 L1
THMD SE28 .... 27 P3
Battle Bridge La STHWK SE1 .... 24 B4
Battlefields BGR/WK TN15 .... 151 J1
Battle La STPH/PW TN12 .... 215 L9
Battle of Britain Flats DVW CT17 .... 8 D4
Battle Rd ERITH DA8 .... 29 H7
Battlesmere Rd HOO/HM ME3 .... 52 B8
Battle St GVE DA12 .... 70 B9
Batts Rd GVE DA12 .... 93 H2
Batty St WCHPL E1 .... 24 E2
Baudwin Rd CAT SE6 .... 62 C1
Baugh Rd SCUP DA14 .... 64 E4
Bavent Rd EDUL SE22 .... 40 C5
Bawdale Rd EDUL SE22 .... 40 F6
Bawden CI CANTW/ST CT2 .... 136 F9
Bawtree Rd NWCR SE14 .... 41 L1
Baxendale Ct KEN/WIL TN24 .... 282 C1
Baxter Rd CAN/RD E16 .... 26 D2
Baxter Wy E/WMAL ME19 .... 153 K9
Bayeux La RCANTE CT3 .... 168 F7
Bayfield Fav ME13 .... 162 B2
Bayfield Rd ELTH/MOT SE9 .... 43 H5
Bayford Rd SIT ME10 .... 129 P1
Bayhall Rd RTWE/PEM TN2 .... 270 D8
Bay Hill RDV CT15 .... 292 F2
Bayle St FOLK CT20 .... 11 G4
The Bayle FOLK CT20 .... 11 G5
Bayley's HI RSEV TN14 .... 178 D8
Bayliss Av THMD SE28 .... 28 C3
Bayly Rd DART DA1 .... 46 G7
Bay Manor La WTHK RM20 .... 31 J9
Bayne CI EHAM E6 .... 26 G2
Baynham CI BXLY DA5 .... 45 H7
Bayswater Dr RHAM ME8 .... 127 H1
Baythorne St BOW E3 .... 25 J1
Baytree CI BFN/LL DA15 .... 44 B9
BMLY BR1 .... 63 H7
Bay View Gdns IOS ME12 .... 57 K6
Bay View Hts BRCH CT7 .... 110 E5
Bay View Rd BRDST CT10 .... 143 L2
Bayview Rd DEAL CT14 .... 263 H4
Bay Wk WSTB CT5 .... 105 L7
Baywell LEE/GVPK SE12 .... 63 H3
Bay Wk DIT/AY ME20 .... 153 M3
Bazely St POP/IOD E14 .... 25 M2
Bazes Shaw HART DA3 .... 91 J6
Beacham CI CHARL SE7 .... 26 E9
Beach Ap IOS ME12 .... 60 C4
Beach Av BRCH CT7 .... 110 C5
Beachborough Rd BMLY BR1 .... 62 A3
FOLK CT19 .... 310 D5
Beach Ct CRBK TN17 .... 298 C6
Beach House Ms MARG WGOS CT8 * 111 N4
Beach Houses MARG 14 C5
Beachmont Ct NROM TN28 .... 343 G4
Beach Ri MARG CT9 .... 111 N4
Beachmont RDV CT15 .... 292 C2
Beach St DEAL CT14 .... 233 J5
FOLKN CT19 .... 11 G4
HB CT6 .... 107 L1
IOS ME12 .... 57 K6
Beach Ter IOS ME12 .... 57 K6
The Beach DEAL CT14 .... 233 J6
Beach Wk WSTB CT5 .... 105 N5
Beacon Av HB CT6 .... 107 N1
Beacon CI RHAM ME8 .... 96 C7
Beacon Dr RDART DA2 .... 68 A2
Beaconfields SEV TN13 .... 20 B6
Beacon Ga PECK SE15 .... 41 K4
Beacon HI HB CT6 .... 107 N1
LING RH7 .... 235 L9
PUR RM19 .... 30 E8
WALD ME5 .... 96 A4
Beacon Hill La HOO/HM ME3 .... 72 F3
Beacon La SWCH CT13 .... 201 M1
Beacon Oak Rd TENT TN30 .... 301 J7
Beacon Ri CROY/NA CR0 .... 82 D7
Beacon Ri SEV TN13 .... 20 C6
Beacon Rd BRDST CT10 .... 113 L6
ERITH DA8 .... 29 H7
HB CT6 .... 107 M2
LEW SE13 .... 42 E7
RMAID ME17 .... 189 K6
WALD ME5 .... 95 P4
Beaconsfield Av CROY/NA CR0 .... 291 K6
GILL ME7 .... 96 A1
Beaconsfield CI BKHTH/KID SE3 .... 26 B9
Beaconsfield Gdns BRDST CT10 .... 113 L8
Beaconsfield Rd BKHTH/KID SE3 .... 26 B9
BMLY BR1 .... 63 H9
BXLY DA5 .... 65 N1
CANTW/ST CT2 .... 166 G2
CHAT ME4 .... 95 L4
CROY/NA CR0 .... 83 J5
DEAL CT14 .... 233 J4
DVE/WH CT16 .... 63 J2
ELTH/MOT SE9 .... 185 K1
MAID/SHEP ME15 .... 185 K1
SIT ME10 .... 130 B2
WALW SE17 .... 24 A9
The Beacons RMAID ME17 .... 189 M1
Beacon Wy HYTHE CT21 .... 307 N4
Beadles La OXTED RH8 .... 60 B3
Beadman PI NRWD SE27 .... 60 B3
Beadman St NRWD SE27 .... 60 B3
Beadnell Rd FSTH SE23 .... 41 K9
Beadon Rd HAYES BR2 .... 85 K1
Beagles CI STMC/STPC BR5 .... 87 L6
Beagles Wood Rd RTWE/PEM TN2 .... 271 N1

Beal Cl WELL DA16 44 C2
Beales La RYE TN31 330 A7
Beaman Cl CRBK TN17 274 E8
Beamish Rd STMC/STPC BR5 87 K4
Beamont Cl MSTR CT12 141 N3
The Beams MAID/SHEP ME15 186 B2
Bean Cl ASH TN23 251 P8
Beane Cft GVE DA12 50 B9
Beaney's La FAV ME13 193 K2
Bean La RDART DA2 67 N1
Bean Rd BXLYHS DA6 44 F5
GRH DA9 47 P7
Beanshaw ELTH/MOT SE9 63 L3
Beardell St NRWD SE19 60 F5
Bear's La RASHW TN26 251 K5
Bearstead Ri BROCKY SE4 41 M6
Bearstead Ter BECK BR3 * 61 N7
Bearsted Cl RHAM ME8 96 E3
Bearsted Rd
MAID/BEAR ME14 155 P5
Beaton Cl GRH DA9 47 P5
Beatrice Gdns GVW DA11 69 J1
Beatrice Hills Cl
KEN/WIL TN24 253 H4
Beatrice Ms LYDD TN29 * 343 K5
Beatrice Rd MARG CT9 112 D5
OXTED RH8 175 H4
RFOLK CT18 311 M1
STHWK SE1 24 D7
Beatty Av GILL ME7 96 C3
Beatty Cl FOLKN CT19 310 C3
Beatty Rd FOLKN CT19 310 G4
ROCH ME1 95 J6
Beauchamp Av DEAL CT14 232 F6
Beauchamp Cl KEN/WIL TN24 253 H4
Beauchamp Rd THHTH CR7 60 D7
Beauchamps La RDV CT15 229 N1
Beaufighter Rd
E/WMAL ME19 152 F9
Beaufort EHAM E6 27 H1
Beaufort Av MSTR CT12 142 G4
Beaufort Cl CDW/CHF RM16 32 A6
Beaufort Ct STRD ME2 * 6 A1
Beaufort Rd STRD ME2 71 N7
Beaufort Wk
MAID/SHEP ME15 186 B7
Beaufoy Rd DVW CT17 291 H6
Beaufoy Ter DVW CT17 290 G6
Beaulieu Av CAN/RD E16 26 C4
SYD SE26 61 H3
Beaulieu Cl CMBW SE5 40 D4
Beaulieu Ri ROCH ME1 95 J5
Beaulieu Rd TONN TN10 210 E6
Beaulieu Wk MAIDW ME16 * 155 H5
Beaumanor HB CT6 107 L3
Beaumont Davy Cl FAV ME13 132 F8
Beaumont Dr GVW DA11 49 K8
Beaumont Rd MAIDW ME16 184 G1
NRWD SE19 60 C5
STMC/STPC BR5 86 E3
Beaumont Sq WCHPL E1 24 G1
Beaumont St HB CT6 107 H3
Beaumont Ter FAV ME13 132 G7
LEW SE13 * 42 C8
Beauval Rd EDUL SE22 40 F7
Beauvoir Dr SIT ME10 99 P6
Beauworth Pk
MAID/SHEP ME15 186 B3
Beauxfield DVE/WH CT16 261 H9
Beaverbank Rd ELTH/MOT SE9 43 P9
Beaver Cl PGE/AN SE20 * 60 G6
Beaver Ct ASH TN23 282 D1
Beaver La ASH TN23 252 B7
Beaver Rd ASH TN23 2 E6
MAIDW ME16 154 G6
Beaverwood Rd CHST BR7 64 A4
Beazley Ct KEN/WIL TN24 282 G1
Bebbington Rd
WOOL/PLUM SE18 * 27 M7
Beblets Cl ORP BR6 86 G9
Beccles St POP/IOD E14 25 J2
Beck Cl LEW SE13 41 P2
Beck Ct BECK BR3 61 K9
Beckenham Dr MAIDW ME16 155 J5
Beckenham Gv HAYES BR2 62 B8
Beckenham Hill Rd BECK BR3 61 P5
Beckenham La HAYES BR2 62 C8
Beckenham Pk RHAM ME8 * 97 L3
Beckenham Place Pk
BECK BR3 61 P6
Beckenham Rd BECK BR3 61 K7
WWKM BR4 84 E4
Becket Av CANTW/ST CT2 166 C3
Becket Cl DEAL CT14 233 H1
RCANTE CT3 170 E9
SNWD SE25 83 M3
Becket Ct HDCN TN27 247 N4
Becket Ms CANTW/ST CT2 4 D3
Becket's Cl RASHE TN25 255 J3
Beckets Fld RTON TN11 238 F6
Becket St STHWK SE1 24 A6
Beckett Cl BELV DA17 28 D6
Becketts Cl ORP BR6 86 G7
Beckett St FAV ME13 132 F6
Becketts Wd RCANTE CT3 139 H6
Beckett Wk BECK BR3 61 L5
Beckett Wy EGRIN RH19 265 J8
Beckford Dr STMC/STPC BR5 86 E4
Beckford Rd CROY/NA CR0 83 L3
Beck La BECK BR3 61 K9
Beckley Cl GVE DA12 70 D1
Beckley Ms WALD ME5 95 L9
Beckley Pl RASHE TN25 286 A8
Beckley Rd IOS ME12 57 N6
Beckman Cl RSEV TN14 118 B9
Beck River Pk BECK BR3 61 M7
Becksbourne Cl
MAID/BEAR ME14 155 M4
Becks Rd SCUP DA14 64 C2
Beck Wy BECK BR3 61 M9
Beckway St WALW SE17 24 B7
Beckwith Gn FOLK CT20 * 310 B6
Beckwith Rd HNHL SE24 40 D7
Beckworth Pl MAIDW ME16 * 154 G9
Becondale Rd NRWD SE19 60 E4
Becton Pl ERITH DA8 45 K1
Bedale St STHWK SE1 24 A4
Beddington Farm Rd
CROY/NA CR0 82 D5
Beddington Gn
STMC/STPC BR5 64 B7
Beddington Gv WLGTN SM6 82 C9
Beddington La MTCM CR4 82 B2
Beddington Rd
STMC/STPC BR5 64 A7
Beddington Ter
CROY/NA CR0 * 82 E4
Beddlestead La WARL CR6 145 J3
Beddow Wy DIT/AY ME20 154 C2
Bedens Rd SCUP DA14 64 G5
Bedford Av RHAM ME8 96 G5
Bedford Pk CROY/NA CR0 83 H5
Bedford Pl CROY/NA CR0 83 J5
MAIDW ME16 12 B5
Bedford Rd BFN/LL DA15 64 A2
DART DA1 46 G8
GRAYS RM17 * 32 C8
GVW DA11 69 K1
ORP BR6 87 J6
STH/RUST TN4 240 D8
Bedford Sq MSTR CT12 * 142 G2
Bedford Ter RTW TN1 22 C6
Bedford Wy BRCH CT7 140 A3
Bedgebury Cl
MAID/BEAR ME14 155 P6
ROCH ME1 95 J6
Bedgebury Cross CRBK TN17 296 B5
Bedgebury Rd CRBK TN17 296 C4
ELTH/MOT SE9 43 H5
Bedingfield Wy RFOLK CT18 286 G1
Bedivere Rd BMLY BR1 62 E2
Bedlam Court La MSTR CT12 141 K7
Bedlam La HDCN TN27 248 D4
Bedlington Sq FAV ME13 * 132 G6
Bedlow Wy CROY/NA CR0 82 E8
Bedonwell Rd BXLYHN DA7 45 H2
Bedser Cl THHTH CR7 60 C9
Bedson Wk RHAM ME8 97 L5
Bedwardine Rd NRWD SE19 60 E6
Bedwell Rd BELV DA17 28 F8
Bedwin Cl ROCH ME1 95 J7
Beeby Rd CAN/RD E16 26 C1
Beecham Rd TONN TN10 211 H4
Beech Av BFN/LL DA15 44 C8
BH/WHM TN16 145 N4
RCANTW CT4 195 M2
SWLY BR8 88 E1
Beech Cl DEPT SE8 25 J9
EGRIN RH19 * 264 G6
FAV ME13 132 E6
FOLKN CT19 10 C1
LING RH7 234 B1
Beech Copse BMLY BR1 63 K8
SAND/SEL CR2 83 K9
Beech Ct ELTH/MOT SE9 * 43 J7
RASHE TN25 222 D1
Beechcroft CHST BR7 63 L6
WSTB CT5 106 C5
Beechcroft Av BXLYHN DA7 45 M2
TIL RM18 33 P7
Beechcroft Cl ORP BR6 86 E8
Beechcroft Gdns RAM CT11 143 L4
Beechcroft Rd ORP BR6 86 E8
Beech Dell HAYES BR2 86 A8
Beech Dr BRDST CT10 113 H9
MAIDW ME16 155 H7
RASHW TN26 251 M2
RDV CT15 230 C7
Beechen Bank Rd WALD ME5 125 M4
Beechenlea La SWLY BR8 88 F1
Beechen Pl FSTH SE23 61 J1
Beeches Cl PGE/AN SE20 61 J7
The Beeches DIT/AY ME20 154 D3
HART DA3 68 G8
LYDD TN29 342 C5
MEO DA13 92 E1
SWLY BR8 65 P6
TIL RM18 49 M3
WALD ME5 125 M1
Beech Farm Rd WARL CR6 144 C5
Beech Flds EGRIN RH19 265 J5
Beechfield Rd BMLY BR1 62 G8
CAT SE6 41 M9
ERITH DA8 45 N1
Beech Green Cl RDV CT15 260 D1
Beech Green La HRTF TN7 267 N8
Beech Gv HOO/HM ME3 71 K4
MSTR CT12 142 B7
MTCM CR4 82 C2
SOCK/AV RM15 30 F5
Beech Hl RCANTW CT4 197 N3
Beechhill Rd ELTH/MOT SE9 43 L6
Beech House Rd CROY/NA CR0 83 J7
Beech Hurst RTWE/PEM TN2 271 N1
Beech Hurst Cl
MAID/SHEP ME15 185 N1
Beeching Rd WALD ME5 125 N2
Beechings Gn RHAM ME8 96 F3
Beechings Wy RHAM ME8 96 D2
Beeching Wy EGRIN RH19 264 G7
Beechin Wood La
BGR/WK TN15 151 M7
Beechlands Cl HART DA3 91 K2
Beech La HAWK TN18 330 B2
STPH/PW TN12 272 D5
Beechmont Cl BMLY BR1 62 C4
Beechmont Ri TONN TN10 210 E4
Beechmont Rd SEV TN13 178 G5
Beechmore Dr WALD ME5 125 M3
Beecholme Dr KEN/WIL TN24 252 F4
Beech Rd BH/WHM TN16 145 M2
DART DA1 46 D9
E/WMAL ME19 153 N5
HOO/HM ME3 73 L4
ORP BR6 117 H2
SEV TN13 21 F3
STPH/PW TN12 244 F6
STRD ME2 71 P9
WBY/YAL ME18 182 E1
Beech St RTW TN1 23 F2
Beech Vw STPH/PW TN12 * 212 G4
Beech Wk DART DA1 46 A5
Beechway BXLY DA5 44 F7
Beech Wy SAND/SEL CR2 114 A7
Beechwood Av DEAL CT14 233 H4
ORP BR6 116 F1
SIT ME10 99 M8
THHTH CR7 82 G1
WALD ME5 96 A4
Beechwood Cl DVE/WH CT16 260 G7
LYDD TN29 337 L2
Beechwood Ct DEAL CT14 * 233 H4
Beechwood Crs BXLYHN DA7 44 F4
Beechwood Dr HAYES BR2 85 N8
MEO DA13 122 B5
Beechwood Gdns MEO DA13 122 B4
RAIN RM13 29 N1
Beechwood La WARL CR6 144 A4
Beechwood Ms
RTWE/PEM TN2 271 H4
Beechwood Ri CHST BR7 63 M3
Beechwood Rd MAIDW ME16 154 E9
Beechy Lees Rd RSEV TN14 149 J2
Beecroft Cl CANTW/ST CT2 136 F9
Beecroft La BROCKY SE4 41 L6
Beecroft Ms BROCKY SE4 41 L6
Beecroft Rd BROCKY SE4 41 L6
Beehive Pl BRXN/ST SW9 40 A4
Beeken Dene ORP BR6 86 D8
Beer Cart La CANT CT1 4 D5
Beesfield La EYN DA4 89 M5
Begbie Rd BKHTH/KID SE3 42 G2
Beggarsbush La LYDD TN29 335 L6
Beggars La BH/WHM TN16 176 E1
Begonia Av RHAM ME8 96 F4
Begonia Cl EHAM E6 26 F1
Beke Rd RHAM ME8 126 G1
Bekesbourne Hl RCANTW CT4 167 N7
Bekesbourne La RCANTE CT3 167 K5
Bekesbourne Rd
RCANTW CT4 197 L1
Bekesbourne St
POP/IOD E14 * 25 H2
Belcaire Cl HYTHE CT21 307 P4
Belcroft Cl BMLY BR1 62 D6
Beldam Haw RSEV TN14 117 P5
Belfast Rd SNWD SE25 83 N1
Belfield Rd RTWE/PEM TN2 271 N2
Belford Gv WOOL/PLUM SE18 27 H7
Belfort Rd PECK SE15 41 J3
Belfry Cl BERM/RHTH SE16 * 24 E8
Belgrave Cl RAM CT11 16 D2
STMC/STPC BR5 87 K1
Belgrave Rd DVW CT17 291 J8
IOS ME12 77 L2
MARG CT9 15 F5
RTW TN1 22 E2
SNWD SE25 83 L1
Belgrave St DIT/AY ME20 124 E7
WCHPL E1 24 G2
Belgravia Gdns BMLY BR1 62 C5
Belgrove RTW TN1 22 D6
Belinda Ct FOLKN CT19 310 E4
Belinda Rd BRXN/ST SW9 40 B4
Bellamaine Cl THMD SE28 27 N5
Bellamy Cl POP/IOD E14 25 K5
Bell Chapel Cl ASH TN23 282 F4
Bell Cl GRH DA9 47 M6
Bell Crs ROCH ME1 124 E5
Bell-Davies Dr MSTR CT12 141 P3
Bellefield Rd STMC/STPC BR5 87 J2
Belle Friday Cl RSIT ME9 131 H3
Bellegrove Cl WELL DA16 44 B3
Bellegrove Rd WELL DA16 44 A3
Bellenden Rd PECK SE15 40 F3
Bellevue Av RAM CT11 17 H3
Bellevue Pk THHTH CR7 60 C9
Belle Vue Rd HB CT6 107 N1
ORP BR6 116 B4
Bellevue Rd BXLYHS DA6 45 H6
IOS ME12 58 C9
RAM CT11 17 H3
WSTB CT5 105 N6
Bellevue St FOLK CT20 11 F3
Bell Farm Gdns MAIDW ME16 184 E1
Bell Farm La IOS ME12 78 F1
Bellfield CROY/NA CR0 114 C3
Bellflower Av IOS ME12 78 A3
Bell Gdns STMC/STPC BR5 87 K2
Bell Gn CAT SE6 61 L3
Bell Green La SYD SE26 61 M4
Bell Gv RCANTE CT3 229 J1
Bellgrove Ct WALD ME5 125 M5
Bell Hammer EGRIN RH19 265 H8
Bellingham Gn CAT SE6 61 N2
Bellingham Rd CAT SE6 62 A2
Bellingham Wy DIT/AY ME20 154 A1
Bell La CAN/RD E16 26 B4
DIT/AY ME20 154 A2
HDCN TN27 278 A1
MAID/BEAR ME14 125 M6
MAID/BEAR ME14 156 D7
ROCH ME1 124 E5
STPH/PW TN12 246 B6
SWCH CT13 201 P1
WCHPL E1 24 C1
Bellman Av GVE DA12 50 A9
Bellmeadow
MAID/SHEP ME15 186 B5
Bell Meadow NRWD SE19 60 E3
Bello Cl BRXS/STRHM SW2 40 B9
Bellot St GNWCH SE10 25 P8
Bell Pde WWKM BR4 * 84 F6
Bellring Cl BELV DA17 28 F9
Bell Rd MAID/SHEP ME15 186 C6
SIT ME10 129 M3
Bells Farm La RTON TN11 212 D3
Bells Farm Rd STPH/PW TN12 212 E1
Bell's La HOO/HM ME3 53 K9
TENT TN30 301 H8
Bell St WOOL/PLUM SE18 43 J2
Bell Water Ga
WOOL/PLUM SE18 27 H6
Bell Wy RMAID ME17 187 P9
Bellwood Ct HOO/HM ME3 54 A5
Bellwood Rd PECK SE15 41 K5
Bell Yard Ms STHWK SE1 24 B5
Belmont DEAL CT14 232 G8
Belmont Av WELL DA16 44 A3
Belmont Cl MAIDW ME16 184 E1
Belmont Gv LEW SE13 42 B4
Belmont Hl LEW SE13 42 B4
Belmont La CHST BR7 63 N4
Belmont Pde CHST BR7 * 63 M4
Belmont Pk LEW SE13 42 B5
Belmont Park Cl LEW SE13 42 C5
Belmont Pl ASH TN23 282 F1
KEN/WIL TN24 252 G9
Belmont Rd BECK BR3 61 L8
BRDST CT10 113 M9
CHST BR7 63 M4
ERITH DA8 45 K1
FAV ME13 132 F7
GILL ME7 7 H4
GRAYS RM17 32 A8
IOS ME12 77 N1
KEN/WIL TN24 252 G3
RAM CT11 16 E2
SIT ME10 129 M2
SNWD SE25 83 N2
WGOS CT8 111 N5
WLGTN SM6 82 B9
WSTB CT5 105 L5
Belmont St RAM CT11 17 G2
Belmont Vls BRDST CT10 * 113 K7
Belmore Pk KEN/WIL TN24 2 C1
Belnor Av RSIT ME9 98 F5
Belsey La RDV CT15 259 N9
Belson Rd WOOL/PLUM SE18 26 G7
Beltana Dr GVE DA12 70 A3
Beltinge Rd HB CT6 107 N1
Belton Cl WSTB CT5 105 M6
Belton Rd SCUP DA14 64 C3
Belton Wy BOW E3 25 K1
Beltring Rd STH/RUST TN4 270 D2
STPH/PW TN12 213 J6
Beltwood Rd BELV DA17 29 H7
Beluncle Halt HOO/HM ME3 * 54 A8
Belvedere Cl FAV ME13 132 F5
GVE DA12 49 N9
Belvedere Ct BELV DA17 28 E6
Belvedere Ms PECK SE15 41 J4
Belvedere Rd BH/WHM TN16 146 A3
BRDST CT10 113 N9
BXLYHN DA7 45 H4
FAV ME13 132 G5
NRWD SE19 60 F6
THMD SE28 28 C4
Belvoir Rd EDUL SE22 40 G8
Benacre Rd WSTB CT5 105 L8
Benares Rd WOOL/PLUM SE18 27 N7
Benbow St DEPT SE8 25 K9
Benbury Cl BMLY BR1 62 A4
Benchfield Cl EGRIN RH19 265 L8
Bench Hl TENT TN30 303 J9
Bench St DVE/WH CT16 8 D4
Bencurtis Pk WWKM BR4 84 G7
Benden Cl STPH/PW TN12 246 C5
Bendmore Av ABYW SE2 27 P8
Bendon Wy RHAM ME8 96 G6
Benedict Cl ORP BR6 86 F7
STRD ME2 124 A1
Benenden Gn HAYES BR2 85 K2
Benenden Rd CRBK TN17 318 F1
HDCN TN27 299 P3
STRD ME2 72 C5
Bengal Rd MSTR CT12 142 F3
Benhall Mill Rd
RTWE/PEM TN2 270 F8
Benhill Rd CMBW SE5 40 D1
Benhurst Cl SAND/SEL CR2 114 A4
Benhurst La
STRHM/NOR SW16 60 A4
Benin St LEW SE13 42 B8
Ben Jonson Rd WCHPL E1 24 G1
Benledi St POP/IOD E14 25 N2
Bennells Av WSTB CT5 106 A4
Bennett Cl WELL DA16 44 C3
Bennett Gv LEW SE13 41 P2
Bennett Pk BKHTH/KID SE3 42 D4
Bennett Rd BRXN/ST SW9 40 A3
Bennetts Av BGR/WK TN15 120 F6
CROY/NA CR0 84 B6
Bennetts Copse CHST BR7 63 J5
Bennetts Wy CROY/NA CR0 84 B6
Bennett Wy RDART DA2 67 K3
Benover Rd WBY/YAL ME18 213 N2
Bensham Cl THHTH CR7 83 H1
Bensham Gv THHTH CR7 60 C8
Bensham La THHTH CR7 82 G1
Bensham Manor Rd
THHTH CR7 83 H1
Ben Smith Wy
BERM/RHTH SE16 24 D6
Benson La RFOLK CT18 288 C8
Benson Quay WAP E1W 24 F3
Benson Rd CROY/NA CR0 82 F7
FSTH SE23 41 J9
GRAYS RM17 32 C9
Bensted ASH TN23 282 C3
Bensted Cl MAID/SHEP ME15 214 C2
Bensted Gv FAV ME13 132 D6
Bentham Hl RRTW TN3 240 A8
Bentham Rd THMD SE28 28 A4
Ben Tillet Cl CAN/RD E16 * 26 G4
Bentley Av HB CT6 106 G2
Bentley Cl DIT/AY ME20 154 E3
HART DA3 68 G9
WALD ME5 126 A3
Bentley Rd KEN/WIL TN24 283 J1
Bentley's Meadow
BGR/WK TN15 149 L5
Bentley St GVE DA12 49 N7
Bentlif Cl MAIDW ME16 155 J7
Benton's La WNWD SE27 60 C3
Benton's Ri WNWD SE27 60 D4
Benwick Cl BERM/RHTH SE16 24 E7
Berber Pde
WOOL/PLUM SE18 * 43 J1
Berber Rd STRD ME2 72 B7
Bercta Rd ELTH/MOT SE9 63 N1
Berengrave La RHAM ME8 97 H5
Berens Rd STMC/STPC BR5 87 K2
Berens Wy CHST BR7 86 G1
Beresford Av CHAT ME4 95 K4
Beresford Ct BRCH CT7 * 110 G5
Beresford Dr BMLY BR1 63 H9
Beresford Gap BRCH CT7 110 G5
Beresford Gdns MARG CT9 113 H2
Beresford Rd CRBK TN17 274 E8
DIT/AY ME20 125 H6
DVW CT17 290 F4
GILL ME7 7 K4
GVW DA11 49 J8
RAM CT11 16 E4
WSTB CT5 105 L5
Beresfords Hl RMAID ME17 185 N7
Beresford Sq
WOOL/PLUM SE18 27 J7
Beresford St
WOOL/PLUM SE18 27 K6
Bere St WAP E1W 24 G3
Berger Cl STMC/STPC BR5 86 E3
Bergland Pk STRD ME2 * 72 D7
Bering Wk CAN/RD E16 26 E2
Berkeley Av BXLYHN DA7 44 F2
Berkeley Cl FAV ME13 164 C1
FOLKN CT19 * 310 D4
ORP BR6 86 F4
ROCH ME1 95 J6
RTWE/PEM TN2 271 P1
Berkeley Ct SIT ME10 129 L2
WLGTN SM6 82 B7
Berkeley Crs DART DA1 46 F9
Berkeley Mt CHAT ME4 * 6 B5
Berkeley Pl RTW TN1 * 22 D6
Berkeley Rd BRCH CT7 110 G5
RTW TN1 22 D6
The Berkeleys SNWD SE25 * 83 M1
Berkeley Ter TIL RM18 * 49 L1
Berkhampstead Rd BELV DA17 28 F8
Berkley Rd GVE DA12 49 M7
Berkley Rw GVE DA12 * 49 M7
Berkshire Cl WALD ME5 95 P6
Berkshire Wy MTCM CR4 82 D1
Bermondsey St STHWK SE1 24 B5
Bermondsey Wall East
BERM/RHTH SE16 24 E5
Bermondsey Wall West
BERM/RHTH SE16 24 D5
Bermuda Rd TIL RM18 49 L3
Bernal Cl THMD SE28 28 C3
Bernard Ashley Dr CHARL SE7 26 C8
Bernard Cassidy St
CAN/RD E16 * 26 A1
Bernard Rd WLGTN SM6 82 A9
Bernards Gdns RDV CT15 229 P9
Bernard St GVE DA12 49 M7
Bernel Dr CROY/NA CR0 84 C7
Berne Rd THHTH CR7 82 G2
Berner Ter WCHPL E1 * 24 D2
Berney Rd CROY/NA CR0 83 J4
Berridge Rd IOS ME12 57 L6
NRWD SE19 60 D4
The Berries RFOLK CT18 288 E8
Berryfield Cl BMLY BR1 63 J7
Berryhill ELTH/MOT SE9 43 M5
Berryhill Gdns ELTH/MOT SE9 43 M5
Berrylands HART DA3 91 K3
ORP BR6 87 K7
Berry La DUL SE21 60 D3
Berryman's La SYD SE26 61 K3
Berry Rd HOO/HM ME3 73 L4
Berry's Green Rd
BH/WHM TN16 146 C1
Berry's Hl BH/WHM TN16 116 C9
Berry St SIT ME10 129 N1
Bersham La CDW/CHF RM16 32 A7
Berthon St DEPT SE8 41 N1
Bertie Rd SYD SE26 61 K5
Bertrand St LEW SE13 41 P4
Bertrand Wy THMD SE28 28 A3
Bert Rd THHTH CR7 83 H2
Berwick Crs BFN/LL DA15 44 A7
Berwick La HYTHE CT21 307 P4
Berwick Rd CAN/RD E16 26 C2
WELL DA16 44 D2
Berwick Wy RSEV TN14 148 G6
STRD ME2 72 D6
Berwyn Gv MAID/SHEP ME15 185 M5
Berwyn Rd HNHL SE24 40 B9
Beryl Av EHAM E6 26 F1
Besant Placee PECK SE15 40 F4
Bessels Green Rd SEV TN13 148 C8
Bessels Meadow SEV TN13 148 C9
Bessemer Rd CMBW SE5 40 C3
Bessie Lansbury Cl EHAM E6 27 H2
Besson St NWCR SE14 41 J2
Best La CANT CT1 4 E4
Best St CHAT ME4 6 C5
Best Ter SWLY BR8 * 88 B2
Bestwood St DEPT SE8 24 G7
Beta Rd HOO/HM ME3 54 B9
Betchley Cl EGRIN RH19 265 H5
Betchworth Wy
CROY/NA CR0 114 F3
Betenson Av SEV TN13 148 E7
Bethany Cl DEAL CT14 233 H1
Bethel Rd SEV TN13 149 H8
WELL DA16 44 E4
Bethersden Cl BECK BR3 61 M6
Bethersden Rd HDCN TN27 248 C9
RASHW TN26 251 H6
RASHW TN26 279 N4
RASHW TN26 302 F4
Bethwin Rd CMBW SE5 40 B1
Betjeman Cl DIT/AY ME20 153 N1
Betony Cl CROY/NA CR0 84 A5
Betsham Rd ERITH DA8 45 P1
MAID/SHEP ME15 186 C5
MEO DA13 68 C4
SWCM DA10 48 C8
Betterton Dr SCUP DA14 64 G1
Bettescombe Rd RHAM ME8 96 G7
Betts Cl BECK BR3 61 L8

Betts Rd *CAN/RD* E16 ....26 C2
Betts St *WCHPL* E1 ....24 E3
Beulah Av *THHTH* CR7 ....60 C8
Beulah Crs *THHTH* CR7 ....60 C8
Beulah Hl *NRWD* SE19 ....20 C5
Beulah Rd *RTW* TN1 ....23 F1
    THHTH CR7 ....60 C9
Beulah Wk *CTHM* CR3 ....144 B5
Beult Meadow *HDCN* TN27 .....247 J6
Beult Rd *DART* DA1 ....46 A4
Bevan Ct *CROY/NA* CRO 72 E9
Bevan Pl *SWLY* BR8 ....88 C1
Bevan Rd *ABYW* SE2 ....28 A8
Bevans Cl *CRH* DA9 ....48 A7
Bevan Wy *RCANTE* CT5 ....229 H1
Beverley Av *BFN/LL* DA15 ....44 B8
Beverley Cl *CDW/CHF* RM16 * 33 L2
    RHAM ME8 ....97 J6
Beverley Ct *BROCKY* SE4 ....49 M4
Beverley Crs *TON* TN9 ....240 C2
Beverley Gdns *LYDD* TN29 ......327 L2
Beverley Rd *BXLYHN* DA7 ....45 L3
    CANTW/ST CT2 ....4 C1
    HAYES BR2 ....85 P6
    MAIDW ME16 ....184 E1
    MTCM CR4 ....82 C1
    PGE/AN SE20 ....50 C1
Beverley Wy *MSTR* CT12 ....143 H3
Beverly Cl *BRCH* CT7 * 111 J5
Beverstone Rd *THHTH* CR7 ......82 F1
Bevill Cl *SNWD* SE25 ....60 C9
Bevin Cl *BERM/RHTH* SE16 .....25 H4
Bevington Rd *BECK* BR3 ....61 P8
Bevington St
    BERM/RHTH SE16 ....24 D5
Bevis Cl *RDART* DA2 ....47 J8
Bevis Marks *HDTC* EC3A 24 A4
Bewick Ms *PECK* SE15 ....41 H1
Bewl Bridge Cl *WADH* TN5 .....315 N5
Bewlbridge La *RRTW* TN3 ....295 K6
Bewley La *BGR/WK* TN15 ....180 F1
Bewley St *WCHPL* E1 ....24 E3
Bewlys Rd *WNWD* SE27 ....60 B4
Bewsbury Crs *CDW/WH* CT16 ...260 C9
Bewsbury Cross La
    DVE/WH CT16 ....260 C9
Bexhill Dr *GRAYS* RM17 ....31 P9
Bexhill Rd *BROCKY* SE4 ....41 M7
Bexley Cl *DART* DA1 ....45 N6
Bexley High St *BXLY* DA5 ....45 N6
Bexley La *DART* DA1 ....45 N6
    SCUP DA14 ....64 C1
Bexley Rd *ELTH/MOT* SE9 ....43 L7
    ERITH DA8 ....45 L1
Bexon La *RSIT* ME9 ....129 H8
Bhutan Rd *HB* CT6 ....107 P2
Bianca Rd *PECK* SE15 ....24 C9
Bibury Cl *PECK* SE15 ....24 B9
Bickles Yd *STHWK* SE1 ....24 B5
Bickley Crs *BMLY* BR1 ....85 P7
Bickley Park Rd *BMLY* BR1 ......65 K9
Bickley Rd *BMLY* BR1 ....65 H8
Bickmore Wy *TON* TN9 ....210 F7
Bicknell Rd *CMBW* SE5 ....40 C4
Bicknor Cl *CANTW/ST* CT2 .....156 A5
Bicknor La *RSIT* ME9 ....130 D1
Bicknor Rd *MAID/SHEP* ME15 ..186 C7
    ORP BR6 ....86 F4
Bidborough Cl *HAYES* BR2 ......85 J2
Bidborough Rdg
    STH/RUST TN4 ....240 A5
Biddenden Cl
    MAID/SHEP ME15 ....156 C9
    MARG CT9 ....113 H4
Biddenden La *HDCN* TN27 .....247 P4
Biddenden Rd *HDCN* TN27 .....247 P4
    RASHW TN26 ....301 H1
Biddenden Wy *ELTH/MOT* SE9 ...63 L3
    MEO DA13 ....69 P4
Bidder St *CAN/RD* E16 ....25 P1
Bideford Rd *BMLY* BR1 ....62 D2
    WELL DA16 ....44 D1
Bidwell St *PECK* SE15 * 41 H2
Bifrons Hl *RCANTW* CT4 ....167 M9
Bifrons Rd *RCANTW* CT4 ....167 N8
Bigbury Rd *CANTW/ST* CT2 ....165 M5
Biggins St ....
Biggin Hl *NRWD* SE19 ....39 J9
Biggin La *GRAYS* RM17 ....33 J9
Biggin St *DVE/WH* CT16 ....8 B3
Biggins Wood Rd *FOLKN* CT19 ..310 B4
Biggin Wy *NRWD* SE19 ....39 H9
Bigginwood Rd
    STRHM/NOR SW16 ....60 B6
Bigland St *WCHPL* E1 ....24 E2
Bignell Rd *WOOL/PLUM* SE18 ...27 J8
Bilberry Cl *RMAID/BEAR* ME14 ..156 B7
Billet Hl *BGR/WK* TN15 ....90 F8
Bill Hamling Cl *ELTH/MOT* SE9 ..63 K1
Billingford Cl *BROCKY* SE4 ......41 K5
Billings *HART* DA3 ....91 J3
Billington Gdns
    KEN/WIL TN24 ....253 H5
Billington Rd *NWCR* SE14 * 41 K1
Billiter Sq *FENCHST* EC3M 24 B2
Billson St *POP/IOD* E14 ....25 M7
Bill Street Rd *STRD* ME2 ....72 C7
Bilsington Cl *WALD* ME5 ....95 N9
Bilton Rd *ERITH* DA8 ....46 A1
Binbury La *MAID/BEAR* ME14 ...127 K8
Bindon Blood Rd
    DVE/WH CT16 ....291 H2
The Bines *STPH/PW* TN12 ......243 H4
Binfield Cl *SAND/SEL* CR2 ....83 J3
Bingley Cl *SNOD* ME6 ....123 N5
Bingley Rd *CAN/RD* E16 ....26 C3
    ROCH ME1 ....19 K7
Binnacle Rd *ROCH* ME1 ....95 H6
Binney Rd *HOO/HM* ME3 ....38 E9

Binnie Cl *BRDST* CT10 ....143 L2
Binsey Wk *ABYW* SE2 ....28 C3
Birbetts Rd *ELTH/MOT* SE9 ......63 K1
Birchanger Rd *SNWD* SE25 ......83 M2
Birch Cl *BRDST* CT10 ....143 H1
    CAN/RD E16 ....26 C4
    EYN DA4 ....89 J7
    HART DA3 ....68 G8
    KEN/WIL TN24 ....10 C5
    RTON TN11 ....210 A6
    SEV TN13 ....270 C1
    SEV TN13 ....148 G8
    STPH/PW TN12 ....242 EB
Birch Ct *RAM* CT11 * 16 D1
    RCANTW CT4 ....228 C7
Birch Crs *DIT/AY* ME20 ....154 C4
Birchdene Dr *THMD* SE28 ....27 P4
Birch Dr *WALD* ME5 ....126 A4
Birchen La *BANK* EC3V 24 A7
The Birches *CHARL* SE7 ....26 C9
    CMBW SE5 * 41 H7
    ORP BR6 ....86 B8
    SWLY BR8 ....65 N8
    TON TN9 ....240 E2
Birchett La *RASHW* TN26 ....304 A5
Birchetts Av *RRTW* TN3 ....269 K5
Birchetts Green La
    WADH TN5 ....314 C3
Birchfield Cl
    MAID/SHEP ME15 ....185 N5
Birchfields *WALD* ME5 ....125M2
Birchfield St *POP/IOD* E14 ....25 K3
Birch Gv *GILL* ME7 ....96 D9
    LEE/GVPK SE12 ....42 D8
    WELL DA16 ....44 C5
Birch Hl *CROY/NA* CRO 84 A9
Birch Hill Ct *BRCH* CT7 ....111 J6
Birchin Cross Rd *RSEV* TN14 ..119 K9
Birchington Cl *BXLYHN* DA7 .....45 K2
    MAID/BEAR ME14 ....13 K3
Birch Md *HAYES* BR2 ....86 B6
Bircholt Forstal
    RASHE TN25 * 284 F1
Bircholt Rd *MAID/SHEP* ME15 ..186 C7
Birch Pl *GRH* DA9 ....47 L7
Birch Rd *HOO/HM* ME3 ....73 L4
    STPH/PW TN12 ....243 H3
    WSTB CT5 ....39 G9
Birch Rw *HAYES* BR2 ....86 B4
Birch Tree Av *WWKM* BR4 ....85 J9
Birch Tree Wy *CROY/NA* CRO 61 N4
Birch Vls *FOLK* CT20 * 310 A8
Birchway *BGR/WK* TN15 ....120 C5
Birch Wy *RTWE/PEM* TN2 ....270 G1
    WARL CR6 ....85 M9
Birchwood Av *BECK* BR3 ....84 C1
    SCUP DA14 ....64 D2
    STH/RUST TN4 ....240 B6
Birchwood Dr *RDART* DA2 ....65 N3
Birchwood La *RSEV* TN14 ......117 N9
Birchwood Park Av *SWLY* BR8 ..65 N9
Birchwood Ri *DVE* CT17 * 8 B5
Birchwood Rd *MAIDW* ME16 ...155 H7
    RDART DA2 ....65 L6
    STMC/STPC BR5 ....86 E1
    SWLY BR8 * 65 L7
Birchwood Wk
    CANTW/ST CT2 ....166 D2
Birdbrook Rd *BKHTH/KID* SE3 ..42 C4
Birdham Cl *BMLY* BR1 ....85 P2
Bird House La *ORP* BR6 ....116 B8
Birdhurst Av *SAND/SEL* CR2 ....83 K9
Birdhurst Gdns *SAND/SEL* CR2 ..83 K9
Birdhurst Ri *SAND/SEL* CR2 .....83 K9
Bird in Bush Rd *PECK* SE15 .....40 G1
Bird-in-Hand La *BMLY* BR1 ......63 H8
Bird-in-Hand Ms *FSTH* SE23 ....61 J1
Bird-in-Hand Pas *FSTH* SE23 * ..61 J1
Bird in Hand St *RRTW* TN3 ....268 C8
Birds Av *MARG* CT9 ....112 A6
Birdwood Av *DEAL* CT14 ....232 F4
Birkbeck Hl *DUL* SE21 ....60 B1
Birkbeck Pl *DUL* SE21 ....60 B1
Birkbeck Rd *BECK* BR3 ....61 K8
    SCUP DA14 ....64 C3
Birkdale Cl *BERM/RHTH* SE16 * ..24 E8
Birkdale Dr *FOLKN* CT19 ....310 D4
Birkdale Gdns *CROY/NA* CRO 84 A8
    HB CT6 ....107 J4
Birkdale Rd *ABYW* SE2 ....28 B7
Birken Rd *RTWE/PEM* TN2 .....270 G2
Birkhall Cl *WALD* ME5 ....95 M9
Birkhall Rd *CAT* SE6 ....42 B9
Birkhall Rd *MAID/BEAR* ME14 ..156 D8
    RHAM ME8 ....96 C5
Birling Cl *MAID/BEAR* ME14 ...156 CA
Birling Dr *RTWE/PEM* TN2 .....270 D8
Birling Hl *MEO* DA13 ....123 H4
Birling Pk *E/WMAL* ME19 ....123 K8
Birling Park Av
    RTWE/PEM TN2 ....270 E8
Birling Rd *E/WMAL* ME19 ......123 H9
    ERITH DA8 ....45M1
    KEN/WIL TN24 ....3 C5
    RTWE/PEM TN2 ....270 E8
Birling Road Rookery Hl
    SNOD ME6 ....123 N6
Birnam Sq *MAIDW* ME16 ....12 C5
Birtrick Dr *MEO* DA15 ....92 A2
Biscoe Wy *LEW* SE13 * 42 D3
Bisenden Rd *CROY/NA* CRO 83 K6
Bishop Butt Cl *ORP* BR6 ....86 C7
Bishop Ct *SIT* ME10 * 99M9
Bishopden Ct
    CANTW/ST CT2 * 136 B9
Bishop Jenner Ct
    RCANTE CT5 * 169M2
Bishop La *RSIT* ME9 ....97 P3

Bishops Av *BMLY* BR1 ....62 C9
    BRDST CT10 ....113 N7
Bishops Cl *ELTH/MOT* SE9 ......63 N1
    WBY/YAL ME18 ....183 K5
Bishops Ct *GRH* DA9 ....47 M6
Bishop's Down
    STH/RUST TN4 ....270 B5
Bishop's Down Park Rd
    STH/RUST TN4 ....270 B4
Bishop's Down Rd
    STH/RUST TN4 ....270 B5
Bishopsgate *LVPST* EC2M 24 B1
Bishopsgate Ar *LVPST* EC2M * ..24 B1
Bishops Gn *ASH* TN23 ....282 A1
    BMLY BR1 * 62 G7
Bishops La *CRBK* TN17 ....297 K5
    MAID/SHEP ME15 ....214 C3
Bishops Md *CMBW* SE5 * 40 C1
Bishops Ms *TON* TN9 ....240 A4
Bishops Oak Ride *TONN* TN10 ..210 F4
Bishops Rd *CROY/NA* CRO 82 G4
Bishops Ter
    MAID/SHEP ME15 * 12 C5
Bishopsthorpe Rd *SYD* SE26 ....61 J7
Bishopstone Dr *HB* CT6 ....108 C4
Bishopstone La *HB* CT6 ....108 C5
Bishops Wk *CHST* BR7 ....64 A9
    CROY/NA CRO 84 A9
    ROCH ME1 ....19 C6
Bishops Wy *CANTW/ST* CT2 ...166 C3
    MAID/SHEP ME15 ....12 E5
Bishopswood *ASH* TN23 ....282 F5
Bittern Cl *RFOLK* CT18 ....288 D9
Blackberry Fld
    STMC/STPC BR5 ....64 C7
Blackberry La *LING* RH7 ....234 G7
Blackberry Rd *EGRIN* RH19 ....234 F9
Blackberry Wy
    STPH/PW TN12 ....243 H3
    WSTB CT5 ....106 A6
Blackbrook La *HAYES* BR2 ......86 B2
Black Bull Rd *FOLKN* CT19 .....10 C2
Blackburn Rd *HB* CT6 ....106 C4
Blackdown Ter
    WOOL/PLUM SE18 * 43 K2
Black Eagle Cl *BH/WHM* TN16 ..176 C5
    BH/WHM TN16 ....177 J5
Blacketts Rd *RDIT* ME9 ....100 E8
Blackfen Pde *BFN/LL* DA15 * 44 C7
Blackfen Rd *BFN/LL* DA15 ....44 B6
Blackfriars St *CANT* CT1 ....4 E5
Black Griffin La *CANT* CT1 ....4 D3
Blackhall La *BGR/WK* TN15 ....149 K8
Blackheath Av *GNWCH* SE10 ....42 C1
Blackheath Gv *BKHTH/KID* SE3 ..42 D3
Blackheath Hl *GNWCH* SE10 ....42 A2
Blackheath Ri *LEW* SE13 ....42 A2
Blackheath Rd *GNWCH* SE10 ....41 P2
Blackheath V *BKHTH/KID* SE3 ..42 D3
Black Horse Ct *STHWK* SE1 .....24 A6
Blackhorse La *CROY/NA* CRO 83 M4
Black Horse Ms
    BGR/WK TN15 ....151 K5
Blackhorse Rd *DEPT* SE8 ....25 H9
Black Horse Rd *SCUP* DA14 .....64 C3
Blackhouse Ri *HYTHE* CT21 ....309 J4
Blackhouse Rd *HYTHE* CT21 ....309 J4
Blackhurst La *RTWE/PEM* TN2 ..271 K1
Blacklands *E/WMAL* ME19 .....153 N5
Blacklands Dr *E/WMAL* ME19 ..153 N4
Blacklands Rd *CAT* SE6 ....62 A3
Blackman Cl *HOO/HM* ME3 .....53 K9
Blackmans Cl *DART* DA1 ....46 C9
Blackman's La *RTON* TN11 .....211 N3
    WARL CR6 ....115 H8
Blackmanstone Br
    LYDD TN29 ....326 A7
Blackmanstone Wy
    DIT/AY ME20 ....154 C5
Black Mill La *HDCN* TN27 ......247 L4
Blackmore Rd *GRAYS* RM17 .....32 D8
Blackness La *HAYES* BR2 ....85 J6
Blackpool Rd *PECK* SE15 ....41 H3
Black Robin La *RCANTW* CT4 ..228 B3
Black Rock Gdns *GILL* ME7 ....126 E1
Blacksheath La *CDW/CHF* RM16 ..32 D5
Blacksmith Dr
    MAID/BEAR ME14 ....156 A7
Blacksmiths La
    STMC/STPC BR5 ....87 K2
Blacksole La *BGR/WK* TN15 ....151 J1
Black Sole Rd *BGR/WK* TN15 ..151 J1
Black Swan Yd *STHWK* SE1 .....24 A6
Blacks Yd *SEV* TN13 ....21 F5
Blackthorn Av
    RTWE/PEM TN2 ....240 F8
    WALD ME5 ....125M2
Blackthorn Cl *BGR/WK* TN15 ..148 A8
Blackthorn Dr *DIT/AY* ME20 ...154 A2
Blackthorne Av *CROY/NA* CRO ..83 M6
Blackthorne Rd *RHAM* ME8 .....97 K6
Blackthorn Gv *BXLYHN* DA7 ....44 G4
Blackthorn Rd
    BH/WHM TN16 ....145 P1
    CDW/CHF RM16 ....32 C4
Blacktree Ms *BRXN/ST* SW9 * ..40 A4
Blackwall La *GNWCH* SE10 ......25 M6
Blackwall Ms *KEN/WIL* TN24 ..253 M4
Blackwall North
    KEN/WIL TN24 ....253 K7
Blackwall South
    KEN/WIL TN24 ....253 K7
Blackwall Tunnel Ap
    POP/IOD E14 ....25M3
Blackwall Tunnel Northern Ap
    POP/IOD E14 ....25 N3
Blackwall Wy *POP/IOD* E14 .....25 N5
Blackwater Cl *RAIN* RM13 ......29 J1
Blackwater St *EDUL* SE22 ......40 F6
Blackwell Farm Rd
    EGRIN RH19 ....265 J5

Blackwell Hollow *EGRIN* RH19 ..265 J6
Blackwell Rd *EGRIN* RH19 ......265 J6
Bladindon Dr *BXLY* DA5 ....44 F8
Blagdon Rd *LEW* SE13 ....41 P7
Blair Cl *BFN/LL* DA15 ....44 B6
Blair Dr *SEV* TN13 ....148 G8
Blair St *POP/IOD* E14 ....25 M7
Blake Cl *DEAL* CT14 ....232 C9
    WELL DA16 ....43 M4
Blake Gdns *DART* DA1 ....46 F5
Blake Rd *CROY/NA* CRO 83 K6
Blakemore Rd *THHTH* CR7 ......82 C2
Blakemore Wy *BELV* DA17 ....28 D6
Blakeney Cl *BECK* BR3 ....61 M7
Blakeney Ct *MAID/BEAR* ME14 ..156 E8
Blakeney Rd *BECK* BR3 ....61 M7
Blaker Av *ROCH* ME1 ....95 K5
Blaker Ct *CHARL* SE7 * 42 C1
Blakes Av *MAID/BEAR* ME14 ....13 C1
Blake's Gn *WWKM* BR4 ....84 F4
Blakes Rd *PECK* SE15 ....40 E1
Blake Wy *RTWE/PEM* TN2 .....270 G1
Blanchard Cl *ELTH/MOT* SE9 ....63 J2
Blanch Cl *PECK* SE15 ....41 J1
Blanchedowne *CMBW* SE5 ......60 D5
Blanchmans Rd *WARL* CR6 ....144 B5
Bland Dr *RFOLK* CT18 ....288 E7
Blandfield Rd
    STRHM/NOR SW16 ....59 M8
Blandford Av *BECK* BR3 ....61 L8
Blandford Cl *CROY/NA* CRO 82 D7
Blandford Gdns *SIT* ME10 .....129M4
Blandford Rd *BECK* BR3 ....61 L8
Bland St *ELTH/MOT* SE9 ....43 H7
Blanmerle Rd *ELTH/MOT* SE9 ...43 M9
Blann Cl *ELTH/MOT* SE9 ....43 H7
Blashford St *LEW* SE13 ....62 B8
Blatcher Cl *IOS* ME12 ....78 B1
Blatchford Cl *E/WMAL* ME19 ..153 N3
Blatchington Rd *RTW* TN1 .....270 D7
Blaxland Cl *FAV* ME15 ....132 E4
Bleak Hill La *WOOL/PLUM* SE18 ..27 N9
Bleak Rd *LYDD* TN29 ....342 B6
Bleakwood Rd *WALD* ME5 ....95 L8
Blean Cl *HB* CT6 ....107 N2
Blean Hl *CANTW/ST* CT2 ....135 P6
Blean Rd *RHAM* ME8 ....96 F5
Blean Sq *MAID/BEAR* ME14 ....155 P6
Blean View Rd *HB* CT6 ....106 C4
Bledlow Cl *THMD* SE28 ....28 B3
Blendon Dr *BXLY* DA5 ....44 F7
Blendon Rd *BXLY* DA5 ....44 E7
    MAID/BEAR ME14 ....13 K2
Blendon Ter *WOOL/PLUM* SE18 ..27 K8
Blendworth Wy *PECK* SE15 .....40 E1
Blenheim Av *CANT* CT1 ....167 J3
    CHAT ME4 ....95 H4
    FAV ME15 * 133 H8
Blenheim Cl *BRDST* CT10 ......143 J1
    DART DA1 ....46 C7
    EGRIN RH19 ....265 K5
    HB CT6 ....107 M5
    MAID/SHEP ME15 ....156 C9
Blenheim Ct *BFN/LL* DA15 ......64 B5
Blenheim Dr *DVE/WH* CT16 ....291 K4
    RFOLK CT18 ....288 D8
    WELL DA16 ....44 A4
Blenheim Gv *GVE* DA12 ....49 NB
Blenheim Pl *FOLK* CT20 ....310 C7
Blenheim Rd *BFN/LL* DA15 ......44 E9
    DART DA1 ....46 C7
    DEAL CT14 ....233 J4
    E/WMAL ME19 ....152 C9
    HAYES BR2 ....85 P1
    NROM TN28 ....337 K7
    ORP BR6 ....86 E9
    PGE/AN SE20 ....61 J6
Blenheim Wy *WADH* TN5 ......315 N5
Blessington Cl *LEW* SE13 ....42 E5
Bletchingly Cl *THHTH* CR7 ......82 C1
Bligh Rd *GVW* DA12 ....49 L7
Bligh's Cl *SEV* TN13 ....21 F3
Bligh's Rd *SEV* TN13 ....21 F3
Blighs Wk *SEV* TN13 ....21 F3
Bligh Wy *STRD* ME2 ....71 L9
Blindgrooms La *RASHW* TN26 ..281 P7
Blindhouse La *RASHE* TN25 ....285 F5
Blind La *CRBK* TN17 ....274 D7
    GILL ME7 ....126 D4
    RASHE TN25 ....222 E1
    RASHE TN25 ....283 N5
Bloers La *LING* RH7 * 234 E3
Blind Mary's La *RSIT* ME9 .....128 F9
Blissett St *GNWCH* SE10 ....42 A2
Bliss Wy *TONN* TN10 ....211 H5
Blithdale Rd *ABYW* SE2 ....27 P7
Blockhouse Rd *GRAYS* RM17 ....32 D9
Blockmakers Ct *CHAT* ME4 ......95 H5
Bloomfield St *LVPST* EC2M 24 A1
Bloomfield Rd *HAYES* BR2 ......85 N2
    WOOL/PLUM SE18 ....27 J8
Bloom Gv *WNWD* SE27 ....60 B2
Bloomsbury Rd *NRWD* SE19 ....60 D4
Bloomsbury Rd *RAIN* RM13 .....16 B4
Bloomsbury Wk
    MAID/BEAR ME14 ....13 C4
Bloomsbury Wy
    KEN/WIL TN24 ....252 E3
Bloors La *RHAM* ME8 ....96 A5
Bloors Wharf Rd *RHAM* ME8 ....97 H1
Blossom Cl *SAND/SEL* CR2 ......83 L9
Blossom St *WCHPL* E1 ....24 B1
Blount Av *EGRIN* RH19 ....264 F7
Blount St *POP/IOD* E14 ....25 H2
Blowers Grove Wd *GILL* ME7 ..126 E3
Blowers Hl *EDEN* TN8 ....237 C9
Bloxam Gdns *ELTH/MOT* SE9 ...43 J6
Bloxworth Cl *WLGTN* SM6 ......82 B7
Blucher Rd *CMBW* SE5 ....40 C1
Blue Anchor La
    BERM/RHTH SE16 ....24 D7
    TIL RM18 ....33 M7

Blue Anchor Yd *WCHPL* E1 .....24 D3
Bluebell Cl *ASH* TN23 ....282 F3
    EGRIN RH19 ....264 F7
    GILL ME7 ....73M9
    SNOD ME6 ....80 F5
    SYD SE26 ....60 F5
    WLGTN SM6 ....82 A5
Bluebell Rd *ASH* TN23 ....282 F5
Bluebell Wk *RSEV/PW* TN12 ...243 H3
Blueberry La *RSEV* TN14 ....147 K1
Bluebird Wy *THMD* SE28 ....27 L7
Blue Boar La *ROCH* ME1 ....19 H5
Blue Coat La *CRBK* TN17 ......274 B9
Bluehouse Gdns *OXTED* RH8 ..175 K4
Blue House La *HYTHE* CT21 ....286 C9
Bluehouse La *OXTED* RH8 ......175 H4
Blue Line La *KEN/WIL* TN24 .....3 C4
Blue Lion Pl *STHWK* SE1 ....24 Bc
Blue Riband Est
    CROY/NA CRO * 82 G6
Bluett St *MAID/BEAR* ME14 .....13 C1
Bluewater River Pway *GRH* DA9 ..47 M9
Blunden La *WBY/YAL* ME18 ....213 P1
Blunt Rd *CROY/NA* CRO 83 J9
Blunts Rd *ELTH/MOT* SE9 ....43 L6
Blyth Cl *CAT* SE6 ....41 M8
Blythe Cl *HYTHE* CT21 * 309 J5
Blythe Cl *FSTH* SE23 ....41 M8
    STMC/STPC BR5 ....64 B7
Blythe Hill La *CAT* SE6 ....41 M8
Blythe Hill Pl *FSTH* SE23 * 41 L8
Blythe Rd *MAID/SHEP* ME15 ....13 J5
Blythe V *CAT* SE6 ....41 M9
Blythe Rd *BMLY* BR1 ....62 D7
    THMD SE28 ....28 B5
Blyth's Whf *POP/IOD* E14 * 25 H5
The Blytons *EGRIN* RH19 ....264 E7
Boakes Meadow *RSEV* TN14 ...118 E5
Boarders La *WADH* TN5 ....314 C3
Boardwalk Pl *POP/IOD* E14 ......25M4
Boarley La *MAID/BEAR* ME14 ...155 L3
Boarman's La *LYDD* TN29 .....334 E5
Boatemah Wk *BRXN/ST* SW9 ....40 A5
Boathouse Wk *PECK* SE15 ......40 F1
Boat La *RASHE* TN25 ....306 A3
Boat Lifter Wy
    BERM/RHTH SE16 ....25 H7
Boat Quay *CAN/RD* E16 ....26 D3
Bob Amor Cl *FAV* ME15 ....133 H6
Bobbing Hl *RSIT* ME9 ....99 H9
Bobbin Lodge Hl
    RCANTW CT4 ....195 J2
Bob Marley Wy *BRXN/ST* SW9 ..40 A5
Bockhanger La
    KEN/WIL TN24 ....252 F3
Bockingford La
    MAID/SHEP ME15 ....185 K3
Bodell Cl *CDW/CHF* RM16 ....32 C5
Bodenham Rd *FOLK* CT20 .....310 D7
Bodiam Br *RBTBR* TN32 ....328 F6
Bodiam Cl *RHAM* ME8 ....96 F4
Bodiam Ct *MAID/BEAR* ME14 ...12 D7
Bodiam Rd *MAID/BEAR* ME14 ...13 C1
Bodkins Cl *RMAID* ME17 ....186 A6
Bodle Av *SWCM* DA10 ....48 C7
Bodmin Cl *STMC/STPC* BR5 .....87 K5
Bodmin St
    MAID/SHEP ME15 ....156 E9
Bofors House
    WOOL/PLUM SE18 * 43 J1
Bogle Rd *RSIT* ME9 ....131 H6
Bognor Dr *HB* CT6 ....107 J2
Bognor Rd *WELL* DA16 ....44 E2
Bogshole La *HB* CT6 ....108 A7
    WSTB CT5 ....135 L1
Bohn Rd *WCHPL* E1 ....25 H1
Bolden St *DEPT* SE8 ....41 P3
Bolderwood Wy *WWKM* BR4 ....84 E6
Boley Hl *ROCH* ME1 ....19 F4
Boleyn Av *MARG* CT9 ....111 P4
Boleyn Cl *CDW/CHF* RM16 ....32 A6
Boleyn Ct *CANT* CT1 * 5 H5
Boleyn Gdns *WWKM* BR4 ....84 E6
Boleyn Rd *BGR/WK* TN15 ......149 K2
Boleyn Wy *SWCM* DA10 ....48 C8
Bolina Rd *BERM/RHTH* SE16 ....24 G8
Bolner Cl *WALD* ME5 ....125 L3
Bolton Gdns *BMLY* BR1 ....62 D5
Bolton La *ASH* TN23 ....282 D6
Bond Rd *ASH* TN23 ....252 D9
    RHAM ME8 ....127 H1
    WARL CR6 ....144 A3
Bond St *GRAYS* RM17 ....32 D9
Boneashe La *BGR/WK* TN15 ....151 H6
Bone Mill La *GDST* RH9 ....204 B1
Boneta Rd *WOOL/PLUM* SE18 ..26 G6
Bonetta Ct *IOS* ME12 ....57 K8
Bonfield Rd *LEW* SE13 ....42 C5
Bonflower La *RMAID* ME17 ....215 H5
Bonham Dr *SIT* ME10 ....99 P9
Bonita Ms *BROCKY* SE4 ....41 K4
Bonner Wk *CDW/CHF* RM16 * ...32 A6
Bonney Wy *SWLY* BR8 ....65 M6
Bonnington Rd
    MAID/BEAR ME14 ....155 P6
Bonny Bush Hl *RCANTW* CT4 ..228 A1
Bonsor Rd *FOLKN* CT19 ....10 D1
Bonsor St *CMBW* SE5 ....40 E1
Bonville Rd *BMLY* BR1 ....62 D4
Boones Rd *LEW* SE13 ....42 C5
Boone St *LEW* SE13 ....42 C5

Boord St GNWCH SE10 .....25 P6
Boormans Ms
  WBY/YAL ME18 * 183 M4
Bootham CI STRD ME24 .....94 C2
Booth CI THMD SE28 .....28 J4
Booth PI MARG CT9 .....15 J3
Booth Rd CHAT ME4 .....95 J4
  CROY/NA CRO * 82 C6
Borden La RSIT ME9 .....129 J3
Border Crs SYD SE26 .....23 P3
Border Ct EGRIN RH19 .....265 J4
Border Gdns CROY/NA CRO 84 E8
Border Rd SYD SE26 .....61 H4
Bordyke TON TN9 .....210 F8
Boreham Av CAN/RD ME15 .....26 B2
Boresisle TENT TN30 * 301 J5
Borgard House
  WOOL/PLUM SE18 * 43 J1
Borgard Rd WOOL/PLUM SE18 .....26 D7
Borkwood Pk ORP BR6 .....86 G8
Borkwood Wy ORP BR6 .....86 F8
Borland CI GRH DA9 .....47 N6
Borland Rd PECK SE15 .....61 J5
Bornefields ASH TN23 .....282 D1
Borough CANT CT1 .....5 F3
Borough Green Rd
  BGR/WK TN15 .....150 C6
Borough High St STHWK SE1 .....24 A4
Borough HI CROY/NA CRO 82 C7
Borough Rd BH/WHM TN16 .....145 N6
  GILL ME7 .....7 J3
  OBOR ME1 .....77 K3
Borrowdale Av RAM CT11 .....142 F5
Borstal HI WSTB CT5 .....105 K6
Borstal Rd ROCH ME1 .....94 G3
Borstal St ROCH ME1 .....94 F4
Borthwick St DEPT SE8 .....25 K8
Bosbury Rd CAT SE6 .....62 K2
Boscobel CI BRH BR1 .....63 K8
Boscombe Av GRAYS RM17 .....32 E7
Boscombe Rd FOLK CT19 .....10 D2
Bosney Banks RDV CT15 .....260 E8
Bossingham Rd RCANTW CT4 .....226 C5
Bossington Rd RCANTE CT3 .....198 G6
Boss St STHWK SE1 .....24 C5
Bostall Heath ABYW SE2 * 28 B8
Bostall HI ABYW SE2 .....28 A8
Bostall Ln ABYW SE2 .....28 A8
Bostall Manorway ABYW SE2 .....28 A7
Bostall Park Av BXLYHN DA7 .....44 G1
Boston CI DVE/WH CT16 .....291 J3
Boston Gdns RHAM ME8 .....96 F5
Boston Rd CROY/NA CRO 82 C5
  WALD ME5 .....125 N3
Bosville Dr SEV TN13 .....148 F8
Bosville Rd SEV TN13 .....148 E7
Boswell CI STMC/STPC BR5 .....87 K3
Boswell Rd THHTH CR7 .....83 H1
Botany TON TN9 .....210 F9
Botany Bay La CHST BR7 .....63 M8
Botany La IOS ME12 .....57 K7
Botany Rd BRDST CT10 .....113 L3
Botany Ter PUR RM19 .....30 D8
Botany Wy PUR RM19 .....30 E8
Botha Rd PLSTW E13 .....26 C1
Bothwell CI CAN/RD E16 .....26 B1
Bothwell Rd CROY/NA CRO 114 C4
Botolph Aly MON EC3R * 24 A4
Botolph La MON EC3R 24 B5
Botolph's Br HYTHE CT21 .....307 P8
Botolph's Bridge Rd
  HYTHE CT21 .....307 P8
Botsom La BGR/WK TN15 .....119 P1
Bottlescrew HI RMAID ME17 .....185 N7
Bottles La RSIT ME9 .....129 P8
Bottom Pond Rd RSIT ME9 .....159 J3
Bott Rd RDART DA2 .....66 F5
Boucher Dr GVW DA11 .....69 K2
Boughton Av BRDST CT10 .....143 M5
  HAYES BR2 .....85 J4
Boughton La FAV ME13 .....164 D2
Boughton La
  MAID/SHEP ME15 .....185 N4
Boughton Pde
  MAID/SHEP ME15 * 185 M4
Boughton Rd RMAID ME17 .....189 J8
  THMD SE28 .....27 M6
Boulcott St WCHPL E1 .....24 C2
Boulevard Courrieres
  RCANTE CT3 .....229 H2
The Boulevard CANT CT1 * 166 C6
Boulogne Rd CROY/NA CRO 83 H3
Boulthurst Wy OXTED RH8 .....175 K8
Boultwood Rd EHAM E6 .....26 G2
Boundary CI IOS ME12 .....78 E1
Boundary CI CANT CT1 * 166 B6
Boundary Rd BFN/LL DA15 .....44 A6
  DEAL CT14 .....263 J2
  HYTHE CT21 .....308 F6
  RAM CT11 .....17 F2
  ROCH ME1 .....95 K3
  RTWE/PEM TN2 .....270 C7
Boundary St ERITH DA8 .....45 P1
The Boundary CANT CT1 .....166 C6
  RRTW TN3 .....269 N5
Boundary Wy CROY/NA CRO 84 D9
Boundfield Rd CAT SE6 .....62 D1
Bounds La FAV ME13 .....164 B1
Bounds Oak Wy
  STH/RUST TN4 .....240 B6
The Bounds DIT/AY ME20 .....154 D3
Bourchier CI SEV TN13 .....21 F5
Bourdon Rd PGE/AN SE20 .....61 J8
Bourg-de-Peage Av
  EGRIN RH19 .....265 K7
Bournbrook Rd
  BKHTH/KID SE3 .....43 H4
Bourne CI TON TN9 .....210 G7
Bourne Grange La
  RTON TN11 .....211 N2
Bourne Gv SIT ME10 .....99 K9
Bourne La BGR/WK TN15 .....181 J1
  HAWK TN18 .....328 C1
  RASHW TN26 .....304 D7
RBTBR TN32 .....328 A5
  TON TN9 .....210 F7
Bourne Lodge CI
  CANTW/ST CT2 .....135 P6
Bourne Md BXLY DA5 .....45 L6
Bournemouth CI PECK SE15 .....40 G3
Bournemouth Dr HB CT6 .....107 J1
Bournemouth Gdns
  FOLKN CT19 .....10 D3
Bournemouth Rd FOLKN CT19 .....10 D2
  PECK SE15 .....40 G3
Bourne Pde BXLY DA5 * 45 K8
Bourne Pk Rd RTON TN11 .....212 A5
Bourne Park Rd RCANTW CT4 .....197 N4
Bourne Place Ctyd
  RTON TN11 * 209 M3
Bourne Place Mdw
  RTON TN11 * 209 M3
Bourne Rd BXLY DA5 .....45 L7
  GVE DA12 .....70 B1
  HAYES BR2 .....85 N1
  RASHE TN25 .....305 M1
Bournes CI CANTW/ST CT2 .....137 L6
Bourneside Gdns CAT SE6 .....62 A1
Bourneside Ter
  RMAID ME17 * 187 N1
Bournes PI RASHW TN26 .....302 C5
Bourne St CROY/NA CRO 82 C6
Bourne V BGR/WK TN15 .....181 K3
  HAYES BR2 .....85 K5
Bourne Wy HAYES BR2 .....85 K6
  SWLY BR8 .....65 L9
Bournewood RASHW TN26 .....304 D7
Bournewood CI
  MAID/SHEP ME15 .....186 C2
Bournewood Rd
  STMC/STPC BR5 .....87 J4
  WOOL/PLUM SE18 .....44 C1
Bournville Av CHAT ME4 .....95 L5
Bournville Rd CAT SE6 .....41 N8
Bousfield Rd NWCR SE14 .....41 K3
Boutique Hall LEW SE13 * 42 A5
Bouverie Rd FOLK CT20 .....10 E5
Bouverie Rd West FOLK CT20 .....10 B6
Bouverie Sq FOLK CT20 .....10 D5
Bovarde Av E/WMAL ME19 .....155 K9
Boveney Rd FSTH SE23 .....41 K8
Bovill Rd FSTH SE23 .....41 K8
Bow Arrow La DART DA1 .....46 C7
  RDART DA2 .....47 H7
Bowater PI BKHTH/KID SE3 .....42 F1
Bowater Rd WOOL/PLUM SE18 .....26 E6
Bowdell La LYDD TN29 .....334 F1
Bowden Crs FOLK CT20 .....309 P1
Bowditch DEPT SE8 .....25 J8
Bowen Dr DUL SE21 .....60 E2
Bowen Rd DOV CT17 .....310 B5
  STH/RUST TN4 .....269 N3
Bowens Fld ASH TN23 .....2 C6
Bowen St POP/IOD E14 .....25 L2
Bowenswood CROY/NA CRO 114 C3
Bowen Wd CROY/NA CRO * 114 C3
Bower Av GNWCH SE10 .....42 C2
Bower CI MAIDW ME16 .....12 B5
Bowerland La LING RH7 .....234 C1
  RCANTW CT4 .....194 D1
Bower La EYN DA4 .....89 K7
  MAIDW ME16 .....12 B6
Bowerman Av NWCR SE14 .....25 H9
Bower Mount Rd
  MAIDW ME16 .....12 A6
Bower PI MAIDW ME16 .....12 B7
Bower Rd RASHE TN25 .....284 A5
  SWLY BR8 .....66 A6
Bowers Av GVW DA11 .....69 K3
Bowers Rd RSEV TN14 .....118 E5
Bower St MAIDW ME16 .....12 B5
  WCHPL E1 .....24 C2
Bower Ter MAIDW ME16 .....12 C6
Bowes Av MARG CT9 .....111 P4
Bowes CI BFN/LL DA15 .....44 D7
Bowesden La GVE DA12 .....71 P8
Bowes La HB CT6 .....107 M3
Bowes Rd STRD ME2 .....52 F1
Bowes Vls DEAL CT14 * 201 M6
Bowes Wd DART DA1 .....91 J7
Bowford Av BXLYHN DA7 .....44 C2
Bow HI RCANTW CT4 .....196 E9
Bowhill CI BRXN/ST SW9 .....40 A1
Bowland CI HB CT6 .....107 P4
Bowles Well Gdns
  FOLKN CT19 .....311 J4
Bowles Wells Gdns
  FOLKN CT19 .....311 J4
Bowley CI NRWD SE19 * 60 F5
Bowley La NRWD SE19 .....60 F4
  RMAID ME17 .....219 L3
Bowley St POP/IOD E14 .....25 J3
Bowl Yd Rd RASHE TN25 .....255 J5
Bowling Green La DEAL CT14 .....232 G4
Bowling Green PI STHWK SE1 * 24 A5
Bowling Green Rw
  WOOL/PLUM SE18 * 26 C7
Bowling Green Ter DVW CT17 * 8 C4
Bowling St SWCH CT13 .....201 N1
Bowl Rd HDCN TN27 .....191 H8
Bowls PI STPH/PW TN12 .....243 H2
Bowman Av CAN/RD E16 .....26 B3
Bowman CI MAID ME15 .....95 P9
Bowmans Lea FSTH SE23 .....41 J8
Bowman's Meadow
  WLGTN SM6 .....82 A7
Bowmans Ms WCHPL E1 .....24 C3
Bowmans Rd DART DA1 .....45 P8
Bowmead ELTH/MOT SE9 .....63 K1
Bown CI TIL RM18 .....49 M3
Bowness Rd BXLYHN DA7 .....45 K3
  CAT SE6 .....41 P8
Bow Rd WBY/YAL ME18 .....183 M4
Bowser CI DEAL CT14 .....232 E5
Bow Ter WBY/YAL ME18 .....183 M4
Bowyer CI EHAM E6 .....26 G1
Bowyer PI CMBW SE5 .....40 C1
Bowyer Rd WSTB CT5 .....104 C7
Bowyer St CMBW SE5 .....40 C1
Bowzell Rd RSEV TN14 .....178 E9
Boxall Rd DUL SE21 .....40 E7
Boxford CI SAND/SEL CR2 .....114 A6
Boxgrove Rd ABYW SE2 .....28 B6
Box La FAV ME13 .....162 A3
Boxley Ash TN23 .....252 C9
Boxley CI IOS ME12 .....57 K9
  MAID/BEAR ME14 .....155 N4
Boxley Rd MAID/BEAR ME14 .....13 J1
  WALD ME5 .....125 N4
Boxley St CAN/RD E16 .....26 C4
Boxted La RSIT ME9 .....98 B5
Boxwood Wy WARL CR6 .....144 A2
Boyard Rd WOOL/PLUM SE18 .....27 J8
Boyces HI RSIT ME9 .....98 B8
Boy Court La HDCN TN27 .....217 P9
Boyden Gate HI RCANTE CT3 .....138 E1
Boyes La RCANTE CT3 .....199 N5
Boyke La RCANTW CT4 .....257 H7
Boyland Rd BMLY BR1 .....62 D4
Boyle Wy STPH/PW TN12 .....213 J2
Boyne Pk STH/RUST TN4 .....269 M4
Boyne Rd LEW SE13 .....42 B4
  RDV CT15 .....262 F7
Boys Hall Rd RASHE TN24 .....283 J1
Boystown PI SWCH CT13 .....201 J7
Boyton Court Rd
  RMAID ME17 .....217 K5
Brabazon PI IOS ME12 .....79 J7
Brabazon St POP/IOD E14 .....25 L2
Brabner CI FOLKN CT19 .....311 H3
Braddick CI DUL SE21 .....60 E2
Brabourne Av CHAT ME4 .....96 F2
Brabourne CI CANTW/ST CT2 .....136 F9
  NRWD SE19 .....60 E4
Brabourne Crs BXLYHN DA7 .....28 F9
Brabourne Gdns FOLK CT20 .....310 B6
Brabourne La RASHE TN25 .....255 H8
Brabourne Rd RASHE TN25 .....254 F4
Brabourn Gv PECK SE15 .....41 J3
Bracewood Gdns
  CROY/NA CRO 83 L7
Bracken Av CROY/NA CRO 84 D7
Bracken CI EHAM E6 .....26 G1
  KEN/WIL TN24 .....252 F3
  RTWE/PEM TN2 .....271 H3
Bracken HI WALD ME5 .....125 M4
Bracken Hill CI BMLY BR1 .....62 D7
Bracken Hill La BMLY BR1 .....62 D7
Bracken Lea WALD ME5 .....125 M4
Bracken Rd RTWE/PEM TN2 .....271 H3
The Brackens ORP BR6 .....87 H9
Bracken Wk TONN TN10 .....210 E4
Brack La LYDD TN29 .....334 C2
Brackley CI MAID/BEAR ME14 .....13 K3
Brackley Rd BECK BR3 .....61 M6
Bracklyn Av EGRIN RH19 * 265 K2
Brackondale Av MEO DA13 .....96 K7
Brackwood CI RHAM ME8 .....96 K9
Bracondale Rd ABYW SE2 .....28 C3
Bradbourne Park Rd
  SEV TN13 .....148 F8
Bradbourne Pkwy
  DIT/AY ME20 .....153 P5
Bradbourne Rd BXLY DA5 .....45 J8
  SEV TN13 .....148 G7
Bradbourne Vale Rd
  SEV TN13 .....148 E7
Bradbridge Gn ASH TN23 .....252 A9
Braddick CI MAID/SHEP ME15 .....185 L6
Braddyll St GNWCH SE10 .....25 P6
Bradenham Av WALG DA16 .....44 A9
Bradenham CI WALW SE17 .....24 A9
Bradfield Av RSIT ME9 .....131 J3
Bradfield Rd CAN/RD E16 .....26 B5
  KEN/WIL TN24 .....252 E4
Bradfields Av WALD ME5 .....95 L8
Bradfields Av West WALD ME5 .....95 L9
Bradford CI HAYES BR2 .....85 N9
  SYD SE26 .....61 H3
Bradfords CI CHAT ME4 .....79 N5
Bradgate St TON TN9 .....210 E9
Bradgate Rd CAT SE6 .....41 P7
Brading Rd CROY/NA CRO 82 E3
Bradleigh Av GRAYS RM17 .....32 D7
Bradley Dr SIT ME10 .....129 M3
Bradley Rd FOLKN CT19 .....11 J2
  NRSTP CT12 .....143 H3
  NRWD SE19 .....60 C5
  RRTW TN3 .....268 C3
  STRD ME2 .....53 M9
Bradley Stone Rd EHAM E6 .....26 G2
Bradshaw CI BRST VB3 .....97 P3
Bradshaw Rd CDW/CHF RM16 .....32 B4
Bradshaws CI SNWD SE25 .....46 C1
Bradstone New Rd
  FOLKN CT19 .....11 F3
Bradstone Rd FOLK CT20 .....11 F3
Bradstow Wy BRDST CT10 .....113 M8
Bradymead EHAM E6 .....27 H2
Brady Rd RFOLK CT18 .....286 F2
Braeburn Wy E/WMAL ME19 .....153 H4
Braemar Av BXLYHN DA7 .....45 L5
  THHTH CR7 .....60 B9
Braemar Gdns BFN/LL DA15 .....63 P2
  WWKM BR4 .....84 C9
Braeside BECK BR3 .....61 N4
Braeside Av SEV TN13 .....20 B1
Braeside CI SEV TN13 .....148 E8
Braeside Crs BXLYHN DA7 .....45 L5
The Braes HOO/HM ME3 .....71 L4
Braesyde CI BELV DA17 .....28 H8
Brafferton Rd CROY/NA CRO 83 H8
Braggs La HB CT6 .....107 J8
Braham St WCHPL E1 .....24 C2
Braidwood Rd CAT SE6 .....42 B9
Brailsford Rd
  BRXS/STRHM SW2 .....40 A7
Brake Av WALD ME5 .....95 K9
Brakefield Rd MEO DA13 .....148 F5
Brakes PI BGR/WK TN15 .....120 B1
Bramber Wy WARL CR6 .....144 C1
Bramble Av RDART DA2 .....68 A2
Bramble Bank MEO DA13 .....122 A6
Bramble CI BECK BR3 .....84 F7
  CROY/NA CRO 84 D8
  MAIDW ME16 .....27 L8
Bramblebury Rd
  WOOL/PLUM SE18 .....27 L8
Bramble Cft ERITH DA8 .....29 H7
Brambledown FOLKN CT19 .....11 F2
Brambledown Rd
  HART DA3 .....91 J1
  WALD ME5 .....95 L6
Brambledown CI HAYES BR2 .....85 N5
Bramblefield CI HART DA3 .....68 C9
Bramblefield La SIT ME10 .....99 M5
Bramblefields CI HB CT6 .....107 N4
Bramblehill Rd FAV ME13 .....132 F5
Bramblehurst La RASHE TN25 .....223 N7
Bramble Reed La
  STPH/PW TN12 .....272 C1
Brambletree Crs ROCH ME1 .....94 C4
Brambletree Wharf ROCH ME1 * 94 D4
Bramble Wk
  RTWE/PEM TN2 .....270 C1
Bramcote Gv
  BERM/RHTH SE16 .....24 F8
Bramdean Crs LEE/GVPK SE12 .....42 E9
Bramdean Gdns
  LEE/GVPK SE12 .....42 E9
Bramerton Rd BECK BR3 .....61 H9
Bramhope La CHARL SE7 .....26 C9
Bramley Av CANT CT1 .....166 B6
Bramley CI IOS ME12 .....79 K4
  MEO DA13 .....69 K6
  ORP BR6 .....86 G5
  RHAM ME8 .....97 L6
  SAND/SEL CR2 .....82 G9
  SWLY BR8 .....88 D1
Bramley Crs STPH/PW TN12 .....244 G3
Bramley Dr
  MAID/SHEP ME15 .....156 C9
Bramley Gdns ASH TN23 .....282 D2
  DVE/WH CT16 .....260 C9
  HB CT6 .....108 A8
  RMAID ME17 .....185 J8
  STPH/PW TN12 .....242 F2
Bramley HI SAND/SEL CR2 .....83 H9
Bramley Hyrst SAND/SEL CR2 * 83 H9
Bramley PI DART DA1 .....46 B4
Bramley RI STRD ME2 .....71 N7
Bramley Rd SNOD ME6 .....123 P5
  STPH/PW TN12 .....212 G4
Bramleys HDCN TN27 .....247 N4
Bramley Wy E/WMAL ME19 .....183 H1
  IOS ME12 .....79 K4
  WWKM BR4 .....84 E6
Bramling Rd RCANTW CT4 .....154 E8
Brampton Bank RTON TN11 .....241 P3
Brampton Rd BXLYHN DA7 .....45 J3
  CROY/NA CRO 83 L4
Bramshot Av CHARL SE7 .....26 D6
Bramshott CI MAIDW ME16 .....155 H6
Bramston Rd MEO DA13 .....78 C1
Branbourne Rd RMAID ME17 .....213 H5
Branch Rd POP/IOD E14 .....25 J3
  RCANTW CT4 .....194 D1
Brandon Ms BARB EC2Y * 24 A1
Brandon Rd DART DA1 .....46 G8
  MSTR CT12 .....142 F3
Brandon St GVE DA12 .....13 J3
  WALW SE17 .....49 M8
Brandram Ms LEW SE13 * 42 C3
Brandram Rd LEW SE13 .....42 C4
Brandreth Rd EHAM E6 .....26 G2
The Brandries WLGTN SM6 .....82 C7
Brands Hatch Pk HART DA3 * 90 D7
Brands Hatch Rd
  BGR/WK TN15 .....90 D9
Brangbourne Rd BMLY BR1 .....62 A1
Branscombe St LEW SE13 .....41 P4
Bransell CI SWLY BR8 .....87 P3
Bransgore CI RHAM ME8 .....96 G7
Branston Crs STMC/STPC BR5 .....86 E5
Branton Rd GRH DA9 .....47 P6
Brantwood Av ERITH DA8 .....45 L1
Brantwood Rd BXLYHN DA7 .....45 M1
  HNHL SE24 .....40 G6
Brantwood Wy
  STMC/STPC BR5 .....64 E9
Brasenose Rd GILL ME7 .....96 B3
Brasier CI IOS ME12 .....78 A2
Brassey Av BRDST CT10 .....143 L1
Brassey CI OXTED RH8 .....175 K5
Brassey Dr DIT/AY ME20 .....153 C4
Brassey HI OXTED RH8 .....175 K5
Brassey Rd OXTED RH8 .....175 K5
Brasted CI BXLYHN DA7 .....45 J3
  SYD SE26 .....61 J3
Brasted Ct STRD ME2 .....72 A6
Brasted HI RSEV TN14 .....147 K7
Brasted Hill Rd
  BH/WHM TN16 .....147 K7
Brasted La RSEV TN14 .....147 H4
Brasted Rd BH/WHM TN16 .....176 C7
  ERITH DA8 .....45 N1
Brattle RASHW TN26 .....302 C7
Brattle Wd SEV TN13 .....179 H5
Braundton Av BFN/LL DA15 .....44 B9
Braunstone Dr MAIDW ME16 .....155 J5
Braxfield Rd BROCKY SE4 .....41 L5
Brayard's Rd PECK SE15 .....41 H5
Braybrooke Gdns NRWD SE19 .....60 E6
Bray Crs BERM/RHTH SE16 .....24 G5
Bray Dr CAN/RD E16 .....26 A3
Brayford Sq WCHPL E1 * 24 F2
Bray Gdns MAID/SHEP ME15 .....185 L6
Braywood Rd ELTH/MOT SE9 .....43 P5
Breach La RSIT ME9 .....98 A6
Breach Rd WTHK RM20 .....31 J9
Breadlands CI KEN/WIL TN24 .....3 K7
Breadlands Rd KEN/WIL TN24 .....253 J9
Breakneck HI GRH DA9 .....47 P6
Breakspears Dr
  STMC/STPC BR5 .....64 C7
Breakspears Ms BROCKY SE4 .....41 N3
Breakspears Rd BROCKY SE4 .....41 M3
Brecon Cha IOS ME12 .....58 C9
Brecon CI MTCM CR4 .....82 D1
Brecon RI ELTH/MOT SE9 .....252 E5
Brecon Sq MSTR CT12 .....142 F3
Bredgar CI ASH TN23 .....282 B2
  MAID/BEAR ME14 .....13 J2
Bredgar Rd RHAM ME8 .....96 D2
Bredhurst CI IOS ME12 .....57 K9
  PGE/AN SE20 .....61 J5
Bredhurst Rd RHAM ME8 .....96 E4
Bredon La RHAM ME8 .....96 E4
  SIT ME10 .....129 N3
  STMC/STPC BR5 .....64 A7
  STPH/PW TN12 .....242 F8
  STPH/PW TN12 .....273 N3
Brendon SCUP DA14 * 64 B6
Brendon Av WAP E1W * 24 D7
Brendon CI ERITH DA8 .....45 N2
  RTWE/PEM TN2 .....23 J1
Brendon Dr CRBK TN17 .....298 A3
Brendon Rd CHST ME7 .....63 P1
Brenley Gdns ELTH/MOT SE9 .....133 M9
Brenley La RH RM18 .....49 M3
Brennan Rd TIL RM18 .....49 M3
Brent CI BXLY DA5 .....44 G9
  RDART DA2 .....47 H7
  WALD ME5 .....95 K9
Brentfield Rd DART DA1 .....46 G7
Brent HI FAV ME13 .....132 F5
Brentlands Dr DART DA1 .....46 G9
Brent La DART DA1 .....46 G8
Brenton St POP/IOD E14 .....25 H2
Brent Rd CAN/RD E16 .....26 B2
  SAND/SEL CR2 .....114 B7
  WOOL/PLUM SE18 .....43 M1
The Brent DART DA1 .....47 H8
  TONN TN10 .....210 F4
Brent Wy DART DA1 .....47 H7
Brentwood ASH TN23 .....282 C3
Brentwood CI ELTH/MOT SE9 .....43 N9
Brentwood Rd
  CDW/CHF RM16 .....33 J7
Brenzett CI WALD ME5 .....125 N3
Bretland Rd STH/RUST TN4 .....270 A4
Breton Rd ROCH ME1 .....95 H4
Brettell St WALW SE17 .....24 A8
Bretts Ct CANT CT1 .....4 D7
Brevet CI PUR RM19 .....30 G7
Brewer Rd HOO/HM ME3 .....52 B9
Brewers Fld RDART DA2 .....66 C5
Brewers HI FOLK CT20 .....310 A8
Brewers PI RCANTE CT3 * 170 F1
Brewers Rd GVE DA12 .....70 E7
Brewer St DEAL CT14 .....233 J5
  MAID/BEAR ME14 .....13 F5
  RRTW TN3 .....295 H2
Brewery La RCANTW CT4 .....197 M2
  SEV TN13 .....21 G3
Brewery Rd HAYES BR2 .....85 P5
  SIT ME10 .....59 N8
  WOOL/PLUM SE18 .....27 L8
Brewery Sq RCANTE CT3 .....139 N7
  STHWK SE1 * 24 C4
Brewhouse La RASHE TN25 .....223 J6
  WAP E1W 24 E5
Brewhouse Rd
  WOOL/PLUM SE18 .....26 D7
Brewhouse Wk
  BERM/RHTH SE16 .....25 H4
Brewood Sq WAP E1W * 49 M7
Brian Crs STH/RUST TN4 .....240 E9
Briant St NWCR SE14 .....41 J2
Briar CI DIT/AY ME20 .....153 P2
  DVW CT17 .....290 C5
  KEN/WIL TN24 .....252 F3
  RASHE TN25 * 223 N7
  RCANTE CT3 .....229 J1
  WARL CR6 .....144 D1
Briar Dr HOO/HM ME3 .....71 K4
Briarfield CI BXLYHN DA7 .....45 J3
Briar Flds MAID/BEAR ME14 .....156 B7
Briarfield Rd HARB SE3 .....33 N3
Briar Gdns HAYES BR2 .....85 L8
Briar La CROY/NA CRO 84 E8
Briar Rd BXLY DA5 .....65 M2
Briars Rd LYDD TN29 .....337 L2
The Briars BGR/WK TN15 .....120 A1
  CHST TN5 .....105 K8
Briars Wy HART DA3 .....91 N5
Briarswood Wy ORP BR6 .....86 G9
Briar Wk TONN TN10 .....210 F4
Briary Ct MARG CT9 .....111 N5
Briary Ct SCUP DA14 .....64 D4

Briary Gdns BMLY BR1 .....62 F4
Brice Av RCANTW CT4 .....195 K1
Brice Rd HOO/HM ME3 .....71 K4
Brice Ct GRAYS RM17 * 32 B9
Brickenden Rd CRBK TN17 .....298 A3
Brickfield Cottages
  WOOL/PLUM SE18 .....44 B1
Brickfield Farm HART DA3 .....68 E9
Brickfield Farm Gdns ORP BR6...86 D8
Brickfield La FAV ME13 .....163 P2
Brickfield Rd RCANTW CT4 .....228 C7
  THHTH CR7 .....60 B7
Brickfields E/WMAL ME19 .....153 J5
  RTWE/PEM TN2 .....241 P9
Brick Field Vw STRD ME2 .....72 C6
Brick Kiln La OXTED RH8 .....175 M6
  RMAID ME17 .....217 N5
Stpk/Homp TN1 .....273 P7
Brickwood Cl SYD SE26 .....61 H2
Brickwood Rd CROY/NA CRO 83 K6
Brickworks Cl TON TN9 .....240 D2
Brideale Cl PECK SE15 * 24 C9
Bridewain St STHWK SE1 .....24 C6
Bridewell La TENT TN30 .....301 H8
Bridewell Pk WSTB CT5 .....105 P5
Bridge Ap WSTB CT5 .....105 P5
The Bridge Ap WSTB CT5 .....
Bridge Cl GRH DA9 .....47 K4
Bridge St GRAYS RM17 * .....
  HYTHE CT21 .....308 F5
  RASHW TN26 .....302 C7
  TON TN9 .....240 F1
Bridge Ct GRAYS RM17 * 32 C9
Bridge Down RCANTW CT4 .....197 N3
Bridgefield Rd WSTB CT5 .....106 A3
Bridgeford Wy RCANTW CT4 ...197 M2
Bridge Hl DEAL CT14 .....232 D1
  RCANTW CT4 .....198 C1
Bridge House SIT ME10 * 129 P1
Bridge House Quay
  POP/IOD E14 .....25 M4
Bridgeland Rd CAN/RD E16 .....26 B3
Bridgelands Cl BECK BR3 .....61 M6
Bridgemans Ct HYTHE CT21 * ..308 C3
Bridge Mdw NWCR SE14 .....24 C9
Bridge Mill Wy
  MAID/SHEP ME15 .....185 J1
Bridgen Rd BXLY DA5 .....45 J6
Bridge Pl CROY/NA CRO 83 J5
  DIT/AY ME20 .....154 E2
Bridgeport Pl WAP E1W * 24 D4
Bridge Rd ASH TN23 .....252 C7
  BECK BR3 .....61 M6
  BXLYHN DA7 .....45 G4
  DEAL CT14 .....233 J2
  ERITH DA8 .....45 P2
  FAV ME13 .....132 F5
  GILL ME7 .....73 J8
  GRAYS RM17 .....32 C9
  IOS ME12 .....57 K5
  MARG CT9 .....3 J7
  RASHE TN25 .....284 E5
  RCANTW CT4 .....197 K2
  ROCH ME1 .....95 H4
  STMC/STPC BR5 .....87 J3
  WLGTN SM6 .....83 A9
Bridge Rw CROY/NA CRO * 83 J5
Bridges Cl BRCH CT7 .....109 P8
Bridges Dr DART DA1 .....47 H6
Bridgeside DEAL CT14 .....233 H3
Bridges La CROY/NA CRO 82 D8
Bridge St DVE/WH CT16 .....8 B1
  FOLKN CT19 .....11 D4
  MAID/SHEP ME15 .....185 L6
  RASHE TN25 .....223 N8
Bridge Ter LEW SE13 * 42 B5
Bridgetown Cl NRWD SE19 .....60 A2
Bridge Vw GRH DA9 .....47 P5
Bridgewater Cl CHST BR7 .....64 A9
Bridgewater Pl
  E/WMAL ME19 .....153 M2
Bridgewater Rd IOS ME12 .....57 K8
Bridgewood Cl PGE/AN SE20....61 M1
Bridle Pth CROY/NA CRO 82 D7
Bridle Rd CROY/NA CRO 84 D6
Bridle Wy CROY/NA CRO 84 D9
  HB CT6 .....107 J3
  ORP BR6 .....86 D8
Bridleway Gdns BRDST CT10 ...143 J5
Bridleway La ASH TN23 .....282 E4
The Bridle Wy WLGTN SM6 .....82 B8
Bridlington Cl BH/WHM TN16 ...145 L4
Bridport Rd THHTH CR7 .....60 A9
Brief St CMBW SE5 .....40 E2
Brielle Wy IOS ME12 .....57 J7
Brier Cl WALD ME5 .....95 P6
Brierley CROY/NA CRO 114 E1
Brierley Cl SNWD SE25 .....83 M1
Brier Rd SIT ME10 .....99 H9
Brigade St BKHTH/KID SE3 * ...42 D3
Bright Cl BELV DA17 .....
Brightfield Rd LEW SE13 .....42 C6
Brightlands GVW SN11 .....205 J5
Brightling Rd BROCKY SE4 .....41 N7
Brightlingsea Pl POP/IOD E14 ...25 J5
Bright Rdg RTON TN11 .....
Bright Rd CHAT ME4 .....95 N4
Brightside Rd LEW SE13 .....42 E7
Bright's Pl RAM CT11 .....17 H2
Bright St POP/IOD E14 .....25 L2
Brightwell Cl CROY/NA CRO 82 F5
Brig Ms DEPT SE8 .....25 K9
Brigstock Rd BELV DA17 .....
  THHTH CR7 .....82 C2
Brimfield Rd PUR RM19 .....30 C7
Brimpsfield Cl ABYW SE2 .....28 A6
The Brimp HOO/HM ME3 .....38 E8
Brimstone Cl ORP BR6 .....117 K2
Brimstone Hl EME CT4 .....92 D6
Brindle Ga BFN/LL DA15 .....44 A9
Brindle Gv RAM CT11 .....143 L5
Brindles TIL RM18 .....33 P7
Brindle's Fld TON TN9 .....240 D2

Brindle Wy WALD ME5 .....125 P4
Brindley Cl BXLYHN DA7 .....45 J4
Brindley St NWCR SE14 .....41 M2
Brindley Wy BMLY BR1 .....62 E4
Brinklow Cl ABYW SE2 .....27 P7
Brinklow Crs
  WOOL/PLUM SE18 .....43 M1
Brinsley St WCHPL E1 * 24 E2
Brintone Gdns TON TN9 .....240 G1
Brion Pl POP/IOD E14 .....25 M1
Brisbane Av SIT ME10 .....129 K1
Brisbane Dr MSTR CT12 .....142 F3
Brisbane Rd E/WMAL ME19 .....6 D7
Brisbane St CMBW SE5 .....40 D1
Briset Rd ELTH/MOT SE9 .....43 H4
Brishing Cl MAID/SHEP ME15...186 B6
Brishing La RMAID ME17 .....186 A8
Brishing Rd RMAID ME17 .....186 B7
Brisley La RASHE TN25 .....304 C1
Brissenden La NROM TN28 .....336 C5
  STRD ME2 .....72 C4
Bristol Cl STRD ME2 .....94 C1
Bristol Pl RAM CT11 .....16 E3
Bristol Rd RAM CT11 .....16 E3
  GVE DA12 .....69 P7
Bristowe Dr CDW/CHF RM16 ....33 L2
Bristow Rd BXLYHN DA7 .....44 G2
  CROY/NA CRO 82 D8
  NRWD SE19 .....60 E4
Britannia Av WSTB CT5 .....105 J7
Britannia Cl ERITH DA8 .....29 L9
  SIT ME10 .....99 M7
  STRD ME2 .....123 P1
Britannia Dr GVE DA12 .....70 B4
Britannia Ga CAN/RD E16 .....26 B4
Britannia La ASH TN23 .....282 D3
Britannia Rd DEAL CT14 .....233 J1
  HOO/HM ME3 .....53 N5
  WCHPL E1 .....25 K7
Briton Ct IOS ME12 .....57 K7
Briton Rd FAV ME13 .....132 F6
Brittains La SEV TN13 .....20 A1
Britten Cl HYTHE CT21 .....308 F4
  TONN TN16 .....211 J4
Brittenden Pde ORP BR6 * 116 C1
Britton Cl LEW SE13 .....42 B8
Britton St GILL ME7 .....7 H2
Brixham Rd WELL DA16 .....44 F2
Brixton St CAN/RD E16 .....26 C6
Brixton Ov BRXN/ST SW9 .....40 A5
Brixton Rd BRXN/ST SW9 .....40 A4
Brixton Station Rd
  BRXN/ST SW9 .....40 A4
Brixton Water La
  BRXS/STRHM SW2 .....40 A6
Broadacre RDV CT15 .....260 A8
Broad Bridge Cl
  BKHTH/KID SE3 .....42 E1
Broadcloth CRBK TN17 .....298 A4
Broadcoombe SAND/SEL CR2 ..114 A2
Broadcroft RTWE/PEM TN2 .....270 C8
Broadcroft Rd STMC/STPC BR5...87 J3
Broad Ditch Rd MEO DA13 .....68 C6
Broadeaves Cl SAND/SEL CR2 ..114 C2
Broader La MAID/BEAR ME14 ..156 E2
Broadfield Crs FOLK CT20 .....13 K9
Broadfield Rd CAT SE6 .....42 C9
  FOLK CT20 .....310 D6
  MAID/SHEP ME15 .....185 M3
Broad Green Av CROY/NA CRO ..82 G4
Broad Gv RTWE/PEM TN2 .....270 D7
Broadham Green Rd
  OXTED RH8 .....174 C9
Broadham Pl OXTED RH8 .....174 C8
Broadlands Dr CHST BR7 .....63 K4
Broadheath BGR/WK TN15 * ...180 B2
Broadhope Rd SLH/COR SS17 ....34 D4
Broadhurst Dr KEN/WIL TN24 ..252 C2
Broadland La MAID/BEAR ME14...156 E2
Broadfield Crs FOLK CT20 * 13 K9
Broadlands Av NROM TN28 .....336 C5
Broadlands Crs NROM TN28 ....336 C5
Broadlands Dr WALD ME5 .....125 P1
Broadlands Rd BMLY BR1 .....62 D3
Broad La DEAL CT14 .....231 P3
  RDART DA2 .....
  RRTW TN3 .....268 F5
Broad Lawn ELTH/MOT SE9 .....43 J1
Broadley Av BRCH CT7 .....110 C8
Broadley Rd MARG CT9 .....113 J5
Broadmead ASH TN23 .....282 B2
  CAT SE6 .....61 N2
  RTWE/PEM TN2 .....270 B8
Broadmead Av
  RTWE/PEM TN2 .....270 C8
Broadmead Rd FOLKN CT19.....10 D3
Broadoak E/WMAL ME19 * 12 A6
Broadoak La FAV ME13 .....163 N6
Broad Oak STPH/PW TN12 .....243 K9
Broadoak Av
  MAID/SHEP ME15 .....185 M3
Broadoak Cl RDART DA2 .....66 C5
Broad Oak La RTWE/PEM TN2 ...270 C7
Broad Oak Rd CANTW/ST CT2 ..137 H9
  STMC/STPC BR5 .....64 C9
  STPH/PW TN12 .....243 K9
Broad Oaks Wy HAYES BR2 .....85 J2
Broad Rd SWCM DA10 .....48 C7
Broadsole La RDV CT15 .....289 P7
Broadstairs Rd BRDST CT10 ....143 J4
Broad St CANT CT1 .....5 C4
  DEAL CT14 .....233 J3
  IOS ME12 .....56 F5
  MARC CT9 .....15 C3
  RAM CT11 .....17 J4
  RASHE TN25 .....285 M3
Broad Street Hl RMAID ME17 ..157 N5
Broad Street Rd LVPST EC2M ...24 A1
Broadview FOLK CT20 .....309 P1
Broadview Av CDW/CHF RM16 ...32 E5

RHAM ME8 .....97 H6
Broad Wk BGR/WK TN15 .....179 K4
  BKHTH/KID SE3 .....42 C5
  ORP BR6 .....87 L7
  WOOL/PLUM SE18 .....43 K3
Broadwater Down
  RTWE/PEM TN2 .....270 C8
Broadwater Forest La
  RRTW TN3 .....269 P9
Broadwater Gdns ORP BR6 .....86 C8
Broadwater La
  RTWE/PEM TN2 .....270 C7
Broadwater Ri
  RTWE/PEM TN2 .....270 C7
Broadwater Rd
  E/WMAL ME19 .....153 L6
  WOOL/PLUM SE18 .....27 L6
The Broadway BRDST CT10 .....113 L9
  HB CT6 .....107 H1
  IOS ME12 .....57 J8
  RTON TN11 * 211 P2
Broadwood GVW SN11 .....69 M4
Broadwood Rd HOO/HM ME3....72 F5
Brockdene Dr HAYES BR2 .....85 N8
Brockenhurst Av
  RTWE/PEM TN2 * 185 N2
Brockenhurst Cl
  CANTW/ST CT2 .....166 D2
  RAM CT11 .....96 F7
Brockenhurst Dr
  SLH/COR SS17 .....34 B1
Brockenhurst Rd
  CROY/NA CRO 83 N4
  RAM CT11 .....114 G2
Brockett Rd CDW/CHF RM16.....33 H5
Brock Gun Crs CROY/NA CRO ...114 C2
Brockhill Rd HYTHE CT21 .....308 C4
Brockill Crs BROCKY SE4 .....41 L5
Brocklebank Rd CHARL SE7 .....26 C7
Brocklehurst St NWCR SE14 .....41 K1
Brocklesby Rd SNWD SE25.....83 N1
Brockley Cross BROCKY SE4 .....41 L4
Brockley Gv BROCKY SE4 .....41 M7
Brockley Hall Rd BROCKY SE4 ..41 L7
Brockley Ms BROCKY SE4 .....41 L6
Brockley Pk FSTH SE23 .....41 L8
Brockley Ri FSTH SE23 .....41 L8
Brockley Rd BROCKY SE4 .....41 M4
  MARC CT9 .....15 J4
Brockley Vw FSTH SE23 .....41 L8
Brockman Crs LYDD TN29 .....327 M1
Brockman Ri BMLY BR1 .....62 B3
Brockman's Cl MSTR CT12 .....141 J5
Brock Rd PLSTW E13 .....26 C3
Brockway Gdns WSTB CT5 * .....
Brockwell Av BECK BR3 .....84 F2
Brockwell Park Gdns
  HNHL SE24 .....40 B8
Brodie St STHWK SE1 .....24 C8
Brodlove La WAP E1W 24 G3
Brodrick Gv ABYW SE2 .....28 A7
Brogdale Pl FAV ME13 .....132 E5
Brogdale Rd FAV ME13 .....132 E8
Brogden Crs RMAID ME17 .....187 J8
Brograve Gdns BECK BR3 .....61 P2
Broke Farm Dr ORP BR6 .....117 K3
Brokes Wy STH/RUST TN4 .....240 F8
Bromar Rd CMBW SE5 .....40 E4
Bromehead St WCHPL E1 .....24 F2
Brome Rd ELTH/MOT SE9 .....43 K4
Bromford Cl OXTED RH8 .....175 K9
Bromhedge ELTH/MOT SE9 .....63 K2
Bromholm Rd ABYW SE2 .....28 B4
Bromley Av BMLY BR1 .....62 A4
Bromley Cl WALD ME5 .....125 N1
Bromley Common HAYES BR2 ...85 J4
Bromley Crs HAYES BR2 .....62 D9
Bromley Gdns HAYES BR2 .....62 D8
Bromley Green Rd
  RASHW TN26 .....304 D1
Bromley Hall Rd POP/IOD E14 ..25 M1
Bromley Hl BMLY BR1 .....61 P3
Bromley La CHST BR7 .....63 N6
Bromley Rd BECK BR3 .....61 P4
  CAT SE6 .....61 P2
  CHST BR7 .....63 N6
Bromley St WCHPL E1 .....24 G1
Brompton Farm Rd STRD ME2 ...71 P6
Brompton Hl CHAT ME4 .....
Brompton La STRD ME2 .....72 A7
Brompton Rd GILL ME7 .....7 F1
Brompton Ter
  WOOL/PLUM SE18 * 43 L2
Bromstone Rd BRDST CT10 ....143 K1
Bronington Cl WALD ME5 .....95 M9
Bronte Cl DIT/AY ME20 .....155 N1
  ERITH DA8 .....45 M1
Bronte Gv DART DA1 .....46 F5
The Brontes STPH/PW TN12 * ..264 G7
Bronte Vw GVE DA12 .....49 N9
Bronze Ga BVEL DA17 .....29 H6
Bronze St DEPT SE8 .....41 K5
Brook CHAT ME4 .....6 D5
Brookbank MAID/BEAR ME14....155 M4
Brookbank Rd LEW SE13 .....41 N4
Brook Cl EGRIN RH19 .....265 L7

HB CT6 .....107 H3
  RTWE/PEM TN2 .....309 H4
Brook Ct BGR/BR3 * .....
Brookdale Rd BXLY DA5 .....44 G7
  CAT SE6 .....41 P8
Brookdene Rd
  WOOL/PLUM SE18 .....27 M7
Brooke Av MARG CT9 .....112 A6
Brooke Dr GVE DA12 .....50 D9
Brooke End OXTED RH8 * 175 K9
Brookehowse Rd CAT SE6 .....61 P2
Brookend Rd BFN/LL DA15 .....44 A9
Brooker Cl POP/IOD E14 .....25 J1
  RMAID ME17 .....186 A6
Brookes Pl RSIT ME9 .....98 C8
Brookfield Av CAT SE6 .....
Brookfield Cl DVE/WH CT16 ....291 J5
Brookfield Pl DVE/WH CT16 ....291 J5
Brookfield Rd ASH TN23 .....252 B8
  DVE/WH CT16 .....291 H4
Brookfields RTON TN11 .....211 N4
Brook Hl OXTED RH8 .....174 F6
Brook Hill Cl
  WOOL/PLUM SE18 .....27 J8
Brookhill Rd
  WOOL/PLUM SE18 .....27 J8
Brookhurst Gdns
  STH/RUST TN4 .....240 B6
Brooklands DART DA1 .....46 E9
  HDCN TN27 .....247 M3
  RTWE/PEM TN2 .....185 N2
Brooklands Av BERM/RHTH SE16...24 F5
Brooklands Cl CANTW/ST CT2 ..137 L9
Brooklands Farm Cl
  RRTW TN3 .....268 F2
Brooklands Pk BKHTH/KID SE3...42 A2
Brooklands Rd DIT/AY ME20 ...153 P1
Brook La BGR/WK TN15 .....181 K3
  BKHTH/KID SE3 .....42 C5
  BMLY BR1 .....62 E5
  HB CT6 .....108 E5
  MSTR CT12 .....141 N8
  RASHE TN25 .....285 M6
  SNOD ME6 .....123 P7
  TON TN9 .....210 G8
Brooklands Wy EGRIN RH19 ....264 G8
Brooklyn Av SNWD SE25 .....83 N1
Brooklyn Gv SNWD SE25 .....83 N1
Brooklyn Paddock GILL ME7 ....73 K9
Brooklyn Rd HAYES BR2 .....85 N2
  SNWD SE25 .....83 N1
Brooklyn Vls
  STPH/PW TN12 * 245 H4
Brookman's Av
  CDW/CHF RM16 .....32 D4
Brookmead MTCM CR4 .....82 E5
  RTON TN11 .....210 B6
Brookmead Cl ORP BR6 .....87 J4
Brookmead Rd CROY/NA CRO ...82 B3
  HOO/HM ME3 .....52 B9
Brookmill Rd DEPT SE8 .....41 L3
Brook Rd DIT/AY ME20 .....123 M9
  FAV ME13 .....132 F5
  LEW SE13 .....41 J9
  RTWE/PEM TN2 .....270 F1
  STMC/STPC BR5 .....87 H1
  THHTH CR7 .....83 H1
  WSTB CT5 .....106 B3
Brooks Cl STPH/PW TN12 .....246 B5
Brookscroft CROY/NA CRO 114 C4
Brookside CRBK TN17 .....298 A3
  DVE/WH CT16 .....
  GDST RH9 .....204 A5
  HOO/HM ME3 .....73 J2
  LYDD TN29 .....326 E9
  ORP BR6 .....86 G4
  STPH/PW TN12 * 243 J4
Brookside Av
  MAID/SHEP ME15 .....185 K1
Brookside CVE DA12 .....49 P7
Brookside Pl MAID/BEAR ME14..13 C4
Brook St CHST BR7 .....
  ERITH DA8 .....45 L1
  RASHW TN26 .....302 B7
  SNOD ME6 .....124 A5
  SWCH CT13 .....201 K8
Brooks Wy LYDD TN29 .....342 B7
The Brook CHAT ME4 .....6 D4
Brookway BKHTH/KID SE3 .....42 E4
  RAIN RM13 .....29 N1
Broom Av STMC/STPC BR5 .....87 J1
Broom Bank WARL CR6 .....144 F4
Broome Cl HAYES BR2 .....85 P3
Broomcroft Rd RHAM ME8 .....97 J4
Broome Pl SOCK/AV RM15 .....30 C4
Broomes Ct RMAID ME17 .....217 K2
Broome Wy CMBW SE5 .....40 D2
Broomfield KEN/WIL TN24 * ...253 L9
Broomfield Crs MARG CT9 .....113 L3
Broomfield Ga STMC/STPC BR5...106 C9
Broomfield Rd BECK BR3 .....84 B1
  BXLYHS DA6 .....45 J6
  FAV ME13 .....132 F4
  FOLKN CT19 .....310 B5
  HB CT6 .....107 N5
  RMAID ME17 .....187 N9
  SEV TN13 .....148 C7
  SWCM DA10 .....48 E8
Broomfields HART DA3 .....91 H2
Broomhill Rd BXLYHS DA6 .....45 J6
  DART DA1 .....46 B7
  ORP BR6 .....87 H4
  RRTW TN3 .....270 A2

Broom Hill Rd STRD ME2 .....71 P7
Broomhills MEO DA13 .....68 C3
Broomlands La OXTED RH8 .....175 P5
Broom La RRTW TN5 .....269 L7
Broom Md BXLYHS DA6 .....45 J7
Broom Pk RRTW TN5 .....269 K5
Broom Rd CROY/NA CRO 100 B9
Broomshaw Rd MAIDW ME16 ...154 E9
Broomwood Cl BXLY DA5 .....65 M1
  CROY/NA CRO 84 A2
Broomwood Rd
  STMC/STPC BR5 .....64 D8
Broseley Gv SYD SE26 .....61 L4
Broster Gdns SNWD SE25 .....60 F9
Broughton Cl ASH TN23 * 252 B6
Broughton Dr BRXN/ST SW9 ....40 A5
Broughton Rd ORP BR6 .....86 E6
  THHTH CR7 .....
Brow Cl STMC/STPC BR5 .....87 L4
Brow Crs STMC/STPC BR5 .....87 K5
Browndens Rd STRD ME2 .....123 M1
Brownelow Copse WALD ME5 ..125 M4
Brownfield St POP/IOD E14 .....25 M2
Brownhill Cl WALD ME5 .....125 M1
Brownhill Rd CAT SE6 .....42 A8
Browning Cl DIT/AY ME20 .....123 N9
  WELL DA16 .....44 A2
Browning Rd DART DA1 .....46 F5
Browning Wy FOLKN CT19 .....311 H4
The Brownings EDEN TN8 .....206 D6
Brownings Orch RSIT ME9 .....129 P6
Brownspring Dr
  ELTH/MOT SE9 .....63 M3
Brown St RHAM ME8 .....97 H5
Browne Rd EGRIN RH19 .....265 H4
Broxbourne Rd ORP BR6 .....86 G5
Broxburn Dr SOCK/AV RM15 ....31 K3
Broxhall Rd RCANTW CT4 .....196 F9
Broxholm Rd WNWD SE27 .....60 A2
Broxted Rd CAT SE6 .....61 M1
Bruce Cl DEAL CT14 .....44 D2
  WELL DA16 .....
Bruce Gv ORP BR6 .....87 H5
Bruce Rd SNWD SE25 .....83 J1
Bruces Wharf Rd GRAYS RM17 ...32 B2
The Brucks WBY/YAL ME18 .....183 M4
Bruford Ct DEPT SE8 .....25 K9
Brundell Ter RCANTW CT4 * 195 K1
Brunel CHAT ME4 * 72 B2
Brunel Cl NRWD SE19 .....60 F5
  TIL RM18 .....49 M3
Brunel House
  WOOL/PLUM SE18 * 43 J1
Brunel Rd BERM/RHTH SE16 ....24 F5
Brunel St CAN/RD E16 .....26 A2
Brunel Wy CHAT ME4 .....72 C7
Brune St WCHPL E1 .....24 C1
Brunswick Cl BXLYHS DA6 .....44 F5
Brunswick Ct STHWK SE1 .....24 B5
Brunswick Fld RSIT ME9 .....101 K9
Brunswick Gdns
  DVE/WH CT16 .....291 J4
Brunswick Pk CMBW SE5 .....40 D2
Brunswick Pl NRWD SE19 .....60 G6
Brunswick Quay
  BERM/RHTH SE16 .....24 G6
Brunswick Rd ASH TN23 .....252 C7
  BRCH CT7 .....111 H8
  BXLYHS DA6 .....44 F5
Brunswick Sq
  MAID/SHEP ME15 .....13 F7
  RAM CT11 .....17 G3
Brunswick St East
  MAID/SHEP ME15 .....13 G6
Brunswick St West CT14 * 252 C5
  RTW TN1 .....22 C6
Brunswick Vls CMBW SE5 * 40 D2
Brunswick Wk CVE DA12 .....49 P7
Brunton Pl POP/IOD E14 .....25 H2
Brushfield St WCHPL E1 .....24 B1
Brushwood Cl POP/IOD E14 .....25 L1
Bruton Cl CHST BR7 * 63 K6
Bryan Rd BERM/RHTH SE16 .....25 J5
Bryanston Rd TIL RM18 .....49 N3
Bryant Cl WBY/YAL ME18 .....183 L5
Bryant Rd STRD ME2 .....72 A7
Bryden Cl SYD SE26 .....61 L4
Brymore Cl CANT CT1 .....5 J1
Brymore Rd CANT CT1 .....5 K1
Bryony Dr ASH TN23 .....282 F5
Bubblestone Rd RSEV TN14 ....148 C1
Bubhurst La CRBK TN17 .....277 L1
Buchanan Cl SOCK/AV RM15 ...31 G1
Buchan Rd PECK SE15 .....41 J4
Buckden Cl LEE/GVPK SE12 .....42 D7
Buckham Thorns Rd
  BH/WHM TN16 .....176 D2
Buckhole Farm Rd
  HOO/HM ME3 .....53 J4
Buckhurst Av BGR/WK TN15 ....21 C4
Buckhurst Cl EGRIN RH19 .....264 F5
Buckhurst Dr MARG CT9 .....113 L3
Buckhurst Rd BH/WHM TN16 ..146 C6
Buckhurst Wy EGRIN RH19 ....264 F5
Buckingham Av THHTH CR7 .....60 A7
  WELL DA16 .....44 A5
Buckingham
  STMC/STPC BR5 .....86 F4
Buckingham Dr CHST BR7 .....63 M4
  EGRIN RH19 .....
Buckingham Gdns THHTH CR7 ..60 A8
Buckingham Hill Rd
  CDW/CHF RM16 .....33 P3
Buckingham La FSTH SE23 .....41 N8
Buckingham Rd
  BRDST CT10 .....113 N9
  GILL ME7 * 96 A1

GVW DA11 ....49 H8
MARG CT9 ....15 C2
MTCM CR4 ....88 D2
RTW TN1 ....22 E6
WSTB CT5 ....106 A4

Buckingham Rw
MAID/SHEP ME15 ....186 B4
Buckland Av *DVE/WH* CT16 ....291 J5
Buckland Cl *MAID* ME16 ....125 M5
Buckland Hl *MAIDW* ME16 ....12 E5
Buckland La *MAIDW* ME16 ....12 A1
RCANTE CT3 ....200 A7
Buckland Pl *MAIDW* ME16 ....12 C4
Buckland Rd *HOO/HM* ME3 ....9 P9
MAIDW ME16 ....12 E3
MEO DA13 ....93 H7
ORP BR6 ....87M9
Buckleigh Wy *NRWD* SE19 ......60 F7
Bucklersbury *MANHO* EC4N ...24 A2
Bucklers Cl *IOS* ME12 ....80 C3
RTWE/PEM TN2 ....23 H4
Buckles La *SOCK/AV* RM15 ...31M1
Buckle St *WCHPL* E1 ....24 C2
Buckley Cl *DART* DA1 ....45 P5
Bucknall Wy *BECK* BR3 ....84 F5
Bucks Cross Rd *DVW* DA11 ......69 K2
ORP BR6 ....87M9
Bucksford La *ASH* TN23 ....252 A9
ASH TN23 ....281 P5
Buckstone Cl *FSTH* SE23 ....41 J7
Buck St *RASHE* TN25 ....192 F9

Buckters Rents
BERM/RHTH SE16 ....25 H4
Buckthorne Rd *BROCKY* SE4 ....41 L7
IOS ME12 ....78 A3
Buddens Gn *RYE* TN31 ....330 C9
Buddle Dr *IOS* ME12 ....57 N9
Budd's La *TENT* TN30 ....332 B3
Budgin's Hl *ORP* BR6 ....117 J6
Budleigh Crs *WELL* DA16 ....44 E2
Buenos Ayres *MARG* CT9 ....14 D5
Buffs Av *FOLK* CT20 ....309 N1
Bugglesden Rd *HDCN* TN27 ....300 E2
Bug Hl *WARL* CR6 ....144 A5
Bugsbys Wy *GNWCH* SE10 ....25 P5
Builders Sq *RCANTE* CT3 ....168 D8
Buiganak Rd *THHTH* CR7 ....83 H1
Bullace Rw *CMBW* SE5 ....40 D2
Bull Aly *WELL* DA16 ....44 C8
Bull Cl *PECK* SE15 ....40 G1
Bullbanks Rd *BELV* DA17 ....29 H7
Bull Cl *CDW/CHF* RM16 ....32 A5
Bulldog Rd *WALD* ME5 ....125 N3
Bulleid Pl *ASH* TN23 ....282 C1
THHTH CR7 ....84 B1
Buller's Av *HB* CT6 ....107 K2
Bullers Cl *SCUP* DA14 ....64 C4
Bullers Wood Dr *CHST* BR7 ......63 J7
Bull Fids *SNOD* ME6 ....123 P5
Bullfinch Cl *STPH/PW* TN12 ...148 C7
STPH/PW TN12 ....243 H4
Bullfinch Dene *SEV* TN13 ....98 C3
Bullfinch La *SEV* TN13 ....148 D7
Bullfinch Rd *SAND/SEL* CR2 ...114 A4
Bull Hl *RMAID* ME17 ....269 L1
Bullingstone La *RRTW* TN5 .....269 L1
Bullion Cl *STPH/PW* TN12 ......242 F5
Bullivant Cl *DEN* DA9 ....47 N6
Bullivant St *POP/IOD* E14 .....25M3
Bull La *BGR/WK* TN15 ....151 K1
CHST BR7 ....63 P6
DIT/AY ME20 ....13 L4
FAV ME13 ....134 A8
HOO/HM ME3 ....51M9
RASHW TN26 ....280 A4
RSIT ME9 ....127 P4
Bulls Av *BKHTH/KID* SE3 ....42 C3
Bull Orch *MAIDW* ME16 ....108 A1
Bull Rd *E/WMAL* ME19 ....123 K8
Bullrush Cl *CROY/NA* CR0 ....83 K3
Bulls Pl *RTWE/PEM* TN2 ....271 N2
Bullwark St *DVW* CT17 ....313 L1
Bull Yd *GVE* DA12 * 49M7
PECK SE15 ....2 D5
The Bull Yd *ASH* TN23 * 2 D3
Bulrush Cl *WALD* ME5 ....125 L2
The Bulrushes *ASH* TN23 ......251 P9
Bulwark Rd *DEAL* CT14 ....233 J2
Bumbles Cl *ROCH* ME1 ....95 J6
Bunce Court Rd *FAV* ME13 ....190 E4
Bungalow Rd *SNWD* SE25 ....83 K1
The Bungalows *SWCH* CT13 * ..201 J5
WTHK RM20 * 31 K9
The Bungalow *BRDST* CT10 * ..112 C2
Bunkers Hl *DVW* CT17 ....291 H5
Bunkers Hill Av *DVW* CT17 ....291 H6
Bunkers Hill Rd *DVW* CT17 ....291 H6

Bunkley Meadow
MAID ME16 * 304 D8
Bunkley Ter *RASHW* TN26 * ...304 D8
Bunny Hl *GVE* DA12 * 70 G5
Bunters Hill Rd *HOO/HM* ME3 ..72 A2
Bunton St *WOOL/PLUM* SE18 ..27 H6
Burbage Cl *STHWK* SE1 ....18 B6
Burbage La *RMAID* ME17 ....187 L6
Burberry La *RMAID* ME17 ....28 C9
Burcham St *POP/IOD* E14 ....25 L2
Burcharbro Rd *ABYW* SE2 ....28 C9
Burchall Rd *SWCH* CT13 ....201 N2
Burchell Rd *PECK* SE15 ....41 K6
Burdens *HDCN* TN27 ....247 N4
Burdett Av *GVE* DA12 ....70 C3
Burdett Cl *SCUP* DA14 ....64 G4
Burdett Rd *CROY/NA* CR0 ....83 J3
POP/IOD E14 ....25 L2
STH/RUST TN4 ....269 N4
Burdock Cl *CROY/NA* CR0 ....84 A5
Bure *TIL* RM18 ....34 B6
Burford Rd *BMLY* BR1 ....85 P1
CAT SE6 ....64 B3
Burford Wy *CROY/NA* CR0 .....114 F2
Burgate *CANT* CT1 ....5 F4
Burgate Cl *DART* DA1 ....45 P4

Burgate La *CANT* CT1 ....5 F5
Burgess Cl *DVE/WH* CT16 ....261 J9
MSTR CT12 ....141 K5
Burgess Gn *DEAL* CT14 ....232 B1
Burgess Hall Dr *RMAID* ME17 .187 J5
Burghfield Rd *MEO* DA15 ....69 K6
Burghill Rd *SYD* SE26 ....61 K5
Burghley Rd *CDW/CHF* RM16 ..31M6
Burgoyne Cl *GNWCH* SE10 ....41 P2
Burgoyne Barracks *FOLK* CT20 *.309 P3
Burgoyne Hts *DVE/WH* CT16 ...291M5
Burgoyne Rd *ROCH* ME1 * 94 D7
Burial Ground La
MAID/SHEP ME15 ....185 K2
Burkeston Cl *SIT* ME10 ....99 P6
Burke St *CAN/RD* E16 ....26 A2
Burleigh Av *BFN/LL* DA15 ....45 M8
Burleigh Cl *STRD* ME2 * 93 N1
Burleigh Dr *MAID/BEAR* ME14 .155 L3
Burleigh Rd *HDCN* TN27 ....221 H5
Burleigh Wk *CAT* SE6 ....42 A9
Burley Rd *CAN/RD* E16 ....26 D2
Burlings La
ORP BR6 ....86 C6
Burlington Dr *HB* CT6 ....108 A5
Burlington Gdns *MARG* CT9 ....112 B5
Burlington House
DVE/WH CT16 * 8 E4
Burlington Rd *THHTH* CR7 ....60 C8
Burma Crs *CANT* CT1 ....167 J3
Burma La *RDART* DA2 ....47 J8
Burmarsh Cl *WALD* ME5 ....95 N9
Burmarsh Rd *LYDD* TN29 ....327 H4
Burma Ter *NRWD* SE19 ....60 E4
Burma Wy *WALD* ME5 ....95 L8
Burnan Rd *WGW* DA11 ....49 J8
Burnan Rd *WSTB* CT5 ....106 B4
Burnell Av *WELL* DA16 ....44 C8
Burnell Wk *STHWK* SE1 * 24 C8
Burnett Rd *ERITH* DA8 ....30 A9
Burney St *GNWCH* SE10 ....41 P2
Burnham Cl *WALD* ME5 * 95 M2
Burns Av *BFN/LL* DA15 ....44 D7
Burns Cl *ERITH* DA8 ....45 P2
WELL DA16 ....44 B2
Burns Crs *TON* TN9 ....240 D2
Burnside Cl *BERM/RHTH* SE16 ..24 C4
Burns Pl *TIL* RM18 ....49M2
Burn's Rd *GILL* ME7 ....73 J8
MAIDW ME16 ....185 H1
Burnt Ash Hl *LEE/GVPK* SE12 ..42 E8
Burnt Ash La *BMLY* BR1 ....62 F4
Burntash Rd *DIT/AY* ME20 .....154 D4
Burnt House La *HAWK* TN18 ...318 C9
STRD ME2 ....72 C5
Burnt House Hl *RCANTE* CT3 ..168 E5
Burnthouse La *HDCN* TN27 ....248 E8
Burnt House La *RDART* DA2 .....66 C5
RRTW TN3 ....269 L3
Burnt Lodge La *WADH* TN5 ....314 F5
Burnt Oak La *BFN/LL* DA15 ......44 C7
Burnt Oak Ter *GILL* ME7 ....73 K9
Burnt Oast Rd *FAV* ME13 ....164 B1
Burntwick Dr *RSIT* ME9 ....98 C3
Burntwood Gv *SEV* TN13 ....178 G3
Burntwood Rd *SEV* TN13 ....178 G4
Burntwood Vw *NRWD* SE19 * ...60 F4
Buross St *WCHPL* E1 ....24 E2
Burrage Gv *WOOL/PLUM* SE18 ..27 J7
Burrage Pl *WOOL/PLUM* SE18 ...27 J8
Burrage Rd *WOOL/PLUM* SE18 ..27 K7
Burrard Rd *CAN/RD* E16 ....26 B2
Burr Bank Ter *RDART* DA2 * 45 H4
Burr Cl *BXLYHN* DA7 ....45 H4
WAP E1W * 24 D4
Burrell Cl *CROY/NA* CR0 ....84 B5
Burrell Rw *BECK* BR3 ....61 N8
Burrels Whf *POP/IOD* E14 ....25 L8
Burrfield Dr *STMC/STPC* BR5 ...87 L2
Burrow Rd *EDUL* SE22 ....40 E5
FOLKN CT19 ....11 H2
Burrows La *HOO/HM* ME3 ....54 C5
The Burrs *SIT* ME10 ....129 N2
Bursdon Cl *BFN/LL* DA15 ....64 B1
Bursill Crs *MSTR* CT12 ....142 C5
Burslem Rd *RTWE/PEM* TN2 ...271 H2
Burslem St *WCHPL* E1 * 24 E2
Bursted Hl *RCANTW* CT4 ....196 C9
Burston Gdns *EGRIN* RH19 ....264 C4
Burston Rd *RMAID* ME17 ....184 D9
Burton Cl *FOLKN* CT19 ....310 D4
HOO/HM ME3 ....51M9
THHTH CR7 ....60 D9
Burton Flds *HB* CT6 ....107 N2
Burton Gv *WALW* SE17 ....24 A8
Burton La *BRXN/ST* SW9 * 40 A3
Burton Rd *BRXN/ST* SW9 ....40 A4
KEN/WIL TN24 ....252 C5
Burt Rd *CAN/RD* E16 ....26 D4
Burtwell La *WNWD* SE27 ....60 D5
Burwash Cl *STMC/STPC* BR5 ....87 K2

Burwash Rd *WOOL/PLUM* SE18 ..27 L8
Burwell Cl *WCHPL* E1 * 24 E2
Burwood Av *HAYES* BR2 ....85 L6
Bury Av *BERM/RHTH* SE16 ....24 C4
Bury Ct *HDTCH* EC3A 24 B2
Bury St *HDTCH* EC3A 24 B2
Busbridge Rd
MAID/SHEP ME15 ....185 K6
SNOD ME6 ....123M6
Bush Av *MSTR* CT12 ....142 C3
Bushbaby Cl *STHWK* SE1 ....24 B6
Bush Cl *RSIT* ME9 ....128 C8
Bushell Wy *CHST* BR7 ....63 K1
Bushey Av *STMC/STPC* BR5 ......86 E4
Bushey Cl *FAV* ME13 ....163 P1
Bushey Cft *OXTED* RH8 ....174 F6
Bushey Flds *HB* CT6 ....107 L8
Bushey Hill Rd *CMBW* SE5 ......40 F2
Bushey Lees *BFN/LL* DA15 * 44 B7
Bushey Rd *CROY/NA* CR0 ....84 D6
Bushey Wy *BECK* BR3 ....84 G3
Bush House
WOOL/PLUM SE18 * 43 J1
Bush La *CANST* EC4R 24 A3
Bushmeadow Rd *RHAM* ME8 .....97 J4
Bushmoor Crs
WOOL/PLUM SE18 ....43M1
Bush Rd *BERM/RHTH* SE16 ....25 H2
STPH/PW TN12 ....212 F2
STRD ME2 ....93 N3
STRD ME2 ....94 A4
Bush Rw *DIT/AY* ME20 ....154 F2
Bushwood Dr *STHWK* SE1 ....24 C7
Bushy Gill *RMAID* ME17 ....269M5
Bushy Gv *RMAID* ME17 ....179 H4
Bushy Hill Rd *CANTW/ST* CT2 ..137 P6
Bushy Royds *KEN/WIL* TN24 ...250 C2
Busty La *BGR/WK* TN15 ....150 C6
Butcher Cl *STPH/PW* TN12 .....246 B6
Butcherfield La *HRTF* TN7 ......267 H9
Butcher Rw *POP/IOD* E14 ....25 M3
Butchers La *BGR/WK* TN15 ....90 C6
RDV CT15 ....289 P1
WDY/WAL ME18 ....182 E2
Butchers Rd *CAN/RD* E16 ....26 E2
Butchery Gn *STPL/WR* TN12 ....220 A4
Butchery La *CANT* CT1 * 4 E3
The Butchery *SWCH* CT13 * 201 P1
Bushy Dene *BR* 154 E6
Butlers Hl *FAV* ME13 ....134 E6
Butlers Pl *HART* DA3 ....91 H7
Buttell Cl *GRAYS* RM17 ....32 E8
Buttercup Cl *STPH/PW* TN12 ..243 H4
Butterfield Dr *ECRIN* RH19 ....264 E5
Butterfield Cl
BERM/RHTH SE16 * 24 G6
Butterfield House
WOOL/PLUM SE18 * 43 J1
Butterfield Sq *EHAM* E6 ....26 G2
Butterfly Av *DART* DA1 ....66 F2
Butterfly La *ELTH/MOT* SE9 ....43M7
Butterfly Wk *CMBW* SE5 * 40 D1
Butterly Av *DART* DA1 ....66 F1
Buttermere Cl *FOLKN* CT19 .....10 B1
GILL ME7 ....96 C1
STHWK SE1 ....24 C7
Buttermere Gdns
RCANTE CT3 ....199 J9
Buttermere Rd
STMC/STPC BR5 ....87 L1
Butternut Copse *ASH* TN23 ...252 A6
Butterside Rd *ASH* TN23 ....282 F4
Butter St *RDV* CT15 ....229 L2
Butt Field Rd *ASH* TN23 ....252 B9
Butt Green La *RMAID* ME17 ....215 L4
Butt Haw Cl *HOO/HM* ME3 ....73 L2
Buttmarsh Cl
WOOL/PLUM SE18 ....27 J8
Button Dr *HOO/HM* ME3 ....54 G5
Button La *MAID/SHEP* ME15 ...186 E1
Button Rd *CDW/CHF* RM16 ......32 A7
Button St *SWLY* BR8 ....89 H1
Butts La *SLH/COR* SS17 ....294 D8
The Butts *RSEV* TN14 ....148 G2
SIT ME10 ....129 N1
SNOD ME6 ....101 N1
Buttway La *HOO/HM* ME3 ....52 A2
Buxted Rd *EDUL* SE22 ....40 E5
Buxton Cl *MAID/CHEP* ME15 ...186 A9
WALD ME5 ....95 M1
Buxton Rd *CDW/CHF* RM16 ......32 C5
ERITH DA8 ....45M1
MSTR CT12 ....142 C2
Bybrook Ct *KEN/WIL* TN24 .....252 F5
Bybrook Fld *FOLK* CT20 ....310 B8
Bybrook Rd *KEN/WIL* TN24 ....252 F4
Bybrook Wy *FOLK* CT20 ....310 B7
Bychurch Pl
MAID/SHEP ME15 * 13 C7
Bycliffe Ms *GVW* DA11 * 49 K8
Bycliffe Ter *GVW* DA11 * 49 K8
Bycroft St *PGE/AN* SE20 ....61 K6
Byefield Cl *BERM/RHTH* SE16 ..25 H5
Byelands Cl *BERM/RHTH* SE16 .25 H5
Bygrove *CROY/NA* CR0 ....114 E1
Bygrove St *POP/IOD* E14 ....25 L2
Byland Cl *ABYW* SE2 ....28 A6
Byllan Rd *DVW* CT17 ....290 F4
Byne Rd *SYD* SE26 ....61 K5
Byng Rd *STH/RUST* TN4 ....270 B5
Byng St *POP/IOD* E14 ....25 K5
Bynon Av *BXLYHN* DA7 ....44 C4
Byrneside *RTON* TN11 ....210 B6
Byron Cl *MARG* CT9 ....15 J6

Byron Cl *CANT* CT1 ....5 K7
PGE/AN SE20 * 61 H9
SYD SE26 * 61 J3
THMD SE28 ....28 B7
Byron Crs *DVE/WH* CT16 ....291 J3
Byron Dr *ERITH* DA8 ....45 K1
Byron Gdns *TIL* RM18 ....49 N3
Byron Gv *EGRIN* RH19 ....264 F8
Byron Rd *DART* DA1 ....47 H5
GILL ME7 ....7 H6
Byron St *POP/IOD* E14 ....25M2
Bysing Wood Rd *FAV* ME13 ....132 B5
Bythorne Ct *RHAM* ME8 ....97 L3
Byward St *MON* EC3R 24 B3
Bywater Pl *BERM/RHTH* SE16 ..25 H4
Bywood Av *CROY/NA* CR0 ....83 P3

C

Cabbage Stalk La
STH/RUST TN4 ....270 B6
Cabborns Crs *SLH/COR* SS17 ...34 C1
Cable Pl *GNWCH* SE10 ....42 A2
Cable Cl *BELV* DA17 ....29 H4
Cable St *WCHPL* E1 ....24 E3
Cabot Sq *POP/IOD* E14 ....25 K4
Cacket's La *RSEV* TN14 ....116 E9
Cactus Cl *CMBW* SE5 * 40 E5
Cadborough Cliff *RYE* TN31 ...338 C8
Cadbury Wy *BERM/RHTH* SE16 .24 C8
Cade La *SEV* TN13 ....179 H4
Cade Rd *ASH* TN23 ....282 D1
GNWCH SE10 ....42 B2
Cadet Dr *STHWK* SE1 ....24 C9
Cadet Pl *GNWCH* SE10 ....25 P8
Cadlocks Hl *RSEV* TN14 ....117 N4
Cadman Cl *BRXN/ST* SW9 ....40 B1
Cadnam Cl *CANTW/ST* CT2 .....166 D1
Cadogan Av *RDART* DA2 ....47 K8
Cadogan Gdns *RTW* TN1 ....22 E3
Cadogan Rd *WOOL/PLUM* SE18 .27 N8
Caerleon Cl *SCUP* DA14 ....64 E4
Caernarvon Dr
MAID/SHEP ME15 ....185 L1
Caesar Av *ASH* TN23 ....282 C4
Caesar's Wy *FOLKN* CT19 ....310 B4
Cage Green Rd *TON* TN9 ....240 D1
Cage La *HDCN* TN27 ....248 C8
Cagney Cl *HOO/HM* ME3 ....72 C4
Cahir St *POP/IOD* E14 ....25 L7
Cairndale Cl *BMLY* BR1 ....62 D6
Cairns Cl *DART* DA1 ....46 C4
Cairo New Rd *CROY/NA* CR0 ....82 C6
Caistor Rd *TON* TN9 ....210 D9
Caithness Gdns *BFN/LL* DA15 ..44 B7
Calais Cl *CANTW/ST* CT2 ....136 C7
Calais St *CMBW* SE5 ....40 C1
Calcraft Ms *CANT* CT1 * 5 K7
Calcroft Av *GRH* DA9 ....48 A5
Calcutta Rd *TIL* RM18 ....49 K3
Caldecote Cl *RHAM* ME8 ....97 L5
Caldecot La *LYDD* TN29 ....342 C2
Caldecot Rd *CMBW* SE5 ....40 C3
Calder Rd *MAID/BEAR* ME14 ...155 K5
Calderwood Gdns
HAYES BR2 * 99 M5
Calderwood St
WOOL/PLUM SE18 ....27 H7
Caldew Av *RHAM* ME8 ....96 F5
Caldew Gv *SIT* ME10 ....129 H4
Caldy Rd *BELV* DA17 ....28 G6
Caledonian Wharf Rd
POP/IOD E14 ....25 N7
Caledon Ter *CANT* CT1 * 5 N7
Calehill Cl *MAID/BEAR* ME14 ..155 L6
Caley Rd *RTWE/PEM* TN2 ....240 C9
Calfstock La *EYN* DA4 ....89 K1
Calgary Crs *FOLKN* CT19 ....311 H3
Calgary Ter *DVE/WH* CT16 * 291 J4
Caling Cft *HART* DA3 ....91 J5
Caliph Cl *GVE* DA12 ....70 D2
Callander Rd *CAT* SE6 ....64 B3
Callander Rdshe *TN25* 284 F5
Callan Gv *SOCK/AV* RM15 ....31M5
Callaways La *RSIT* ME9 ....98 C8
Calley Down Crs
CROY/NA CR0 ....114 G4
Callewall La *RASHE* TN25 ....284 B9
Callingham Cl *POP/IOD* E14 .....25 J1
Callis Court Rd *BRDST* CT10 ...113 L7
Callista Ct *MAIDW* ME16 ....34 B9
Calmington Rd *CMBW* SE5 ......24 B9
Calmont Rd *BMLY* BR1 ....62 B5
Calshot Av *CDW/CHF* RM16 ......32 A5
Calton Av *DUL* SE21 ....40 G6
Calverden Rd *MSTR* CT12 ....142 F5
Calverley Cl *BECK* BR3 ....61 N6
Calverley Ct *RTW* TN1 * 23 F5
Calverley Ms *RTW* TN1 * 23 F5
Calverley Park Crs *RTW* TN1 ...22 E4
Calverley Park Gdns *RTW* TN1 .22 E3
Calverley Rd *RTW* TN1 ....22 E3
Calverley St *RTW* TN1 ....22 E2
Calvert Cl *BELV* DA17 ....29 H4
SCUP DA14 ....65 L3
Calvert Dr *BXLY* DA5 ....65M1
Calvert Rd *GNWCH* SE10 ....26 C8
Calvin Cl *STMC/STPC* BR5 ....64 F9
Calydon Rd *CHARL* SE7 ....26 C9
Calypso Crs *PECK* SE15 ....40 F1
Calypso Wy *BERM/RHTH* SE16 ..25 J6
Campbell Crs *EGRIN* RH19 .....264 E7
Camber Rd *RYE* TN31 ....339 J6
Camber Wy *BKHTH/KID* SE3 ....42 F5
Camber Wy *DVE/WH* CT16 ......292 A6
Camberwell Church St
CMBW SE5 ....40 D2
Camberwell Glebe *CMBW* SE5 ..40 D2
Camberwell Gn *CMBW* SE5 ......40 D2

Camberwell Gv *CMBW* SE5 ......40 D2
Camberwell La *RSEV* TN14 .....177 N7
Camberwell New Rd
CMBW SE5 ....40 B1
Camberwell Station Rd
CMBW SE5 ....40 C2
Camborne Rd *CROY/NA* CR0 ....83 M4
SCUP DA14 ....64 E2
WELL DA16 ....44 A3
Cambourne Av *WGOS* CT8 ....111 L5
Cambrai Ct *CANT* CT1 ....167 J3
Cambray Rd *ORP* BR6 ....86 F1
Cambria Av *MEO* DA13 ....94 E4
Cambria Crs *GVE* DA12 ....70 A3
Cambria Rd *CMBW* SE5 ....40 C4
Cambrian Gv *GVW* DA11 ....49 J8
Cambrian Rd *STH/RUST* TN4 ..270 F1
Cambria Rd *CMBW* SE5 ....40 C4
Cambridge Av *SWCH* CT13 .....202 F4
WELL DA16 ....44 B5
Cambridge Barracks Rd
WOOL/PLUM SE18 ....26 G7
Cambridge Cl *BRCH* CT7 ....111 J6
Cambridge Crs
MAID/SHEP ME15 ....186 A4
Cambridge Dr *LEE/GVPK* SE12 ..42 E3
Cambridge Gdns
CDW/CHF RM16 ....33 H7
FOLK CT20 ....10 L4
RTWE/PEM TN2 ....23 H6
Cambridge Gn *ELTH/MOT* SE9 ..43M9
Cambridge Gv *PGE/AN* SE20 * ..61 H7
Cambridge Rd *BMLY* BR1 ....62 E6
CANT CT1 ....4 D7
DEAL CT14 ....233 J6
DVW CT17 ....8 D6
FAV ME13 ....132 E7
PGE/AN SE20 ....60 G9
RHAM ME8 ....96 F8
SCUP DA14 ....64 A3
SIT ME10 ....129 M1
STRD ME2 ....72 A7
Cambridge Rw *WOOL/PLUM* SE18 .27 J8
Cambridge St *RTWE/PEM* TN2 ..23 G5
FOLK CT20 ....11 C4
MARG CT9 ....112 C4
Cambridge Wy *CANT* CT1 ....166 E6
Cambus Rd *CAN/RD* E16 ....26 B1
Camdale Rd *WOOL/PLUM* SE18 .44 B1
Camden Av *RTWE/PEM* TN2 ....271M2
Camden Cl *CDW/CHF* RM16 ......33 J7
CHST BR7 ....63 L4
GVW DA11 ....48 G9
WALD ME5 ....95 N9
Camden Crs *DVE/WH* CT16 ....8 E5
Camden Gdns *THHTH* CR7 ....60 B9
Camden Gn *CHST* BR7 ....63M5
Camden Hl *RTW* TN1 ....23 F5
Camden Hill Rd *NRWD* SE19 ....60 F5
Camdenhurst St *POP/IOD* E14 .25 K2
Camden Pk *RTW* TN1 ....22 E4
Camden Park Rd *CHST* BR7 ......63 K6
Camden Rd *BRDST* CT10 ....113 K6
BXLY DA5 ....45 H9
CDW/CHF RM16 ....31 P6
GILL ME7 ....73 H1
LING RH7 ....234 G6
RAM CT11 ....17 G4
RTW TN1 ....22 E3
SEV TN13 ....148 G7
Camden Rw *BKHTH/KID* SE3 ....42 C3
Camden Sq *RAM* CT11 ....17 G3
Camden St *MAID/BEAR* ME14 ..13 F3
Camden Ter *KEN/WIL* TN24 ......3 K2
Camden Wy *CHST* BR7 ....63 K6
Camelot Cl *BH/WHM* TN16 .....145M1
WOOL/PLUM SE18 ....27 L5
Camel Rd *CAN/RD* E16 ....26 F4
Cameron Cl *BXLY* DA5 ....65M6
WALD ME5 ....95 N6
Cameron Rd *STRHM/NOR* SW16 .60 A2
Cameron Rd *CAT* SE6 ....61M1
CROY/NA CR0 ....60 D5
HAYES BR2 ....85 K2
Cameron Ter *LEE/GVPK* SE12 * ..42 F2
Camer Park Rd *MEO* DA13 ....92 C4
Camer Rd *MEO* DA13 ....92 D3
Camilla Rd *BERM/RHTH* SE16 ..24 F7
Camille Cl *SNWD* SE25 ....61 J8
Camomile St *LVPST* EC2M 24 B2
Campana Rd *FUL/PGN* SW6 ....24 C4
Campbell Crs *EGRIN* RH19 .....264 E7
Campbell Rd *CROY/NA* CR0 ......83 K9
DEAL CT14 ....233 J6
GVW DA11 ....49 K9
MAID/SHEP ME15 ....186 A4
STH/RUST TN4 ....270 D2
Campden Crs *CRBK* TN17 ......297 L5
Camperdown St *WCHPL* E1 ....24 D2
Campfield Rd *ELTH/MOT* SE9 ...43 H8
Camp Hl *RTON* TN11 ....208 F7
Campion Cl *EHAM* E6 ....26 G3
GVW DA11 ....69 J3
SAND/SEL CR2 ....113 K6
WALD ME5 ....125 K2
Campion Crs *CRBK* TN17 ....297 L5
Campion Pl *THMD* SE28 ....28 A4
Campions Dr *EDEN* TN8 ....201 K4
Campion La *SOCK/AV* RM15 .....31 K5
Campleshon Rd *RHAM* ME8 ......96 G7
Campshill Pl *LEW* SE13 ....41 A4
Campshill Rd *LEW* SE13 ....42 A4
Campus Wy *GILL* ME7 ....96 C9

Camp Wy MAID/SHEP ME15.....185 P4
Camrose Av ERITH DA8 .....28 G9
Camrose Cl CROY/NA CR0 .....28 B4
Camrose St SE17 .....27 P8
Canada Cl RFOLK CT18 .....309 P1
Canada Farm Rd EYN DA4 .....90 E2
Canada Rd DEAL CT14 .....233 H5
  ERITH DA8 .....46 B1
Canada Square POP/IOD E14 ....25 L4
Canada St BERM/RHTH SE16 ....24 C5
  GILL ME7 .....96 B2
Canal Ap DEPT SE8 .....25 H9
Canal Basin GVE DA12 .....49 P7
Canal Gv PECK SE15 .....24 D9
Canal Rd GVE DA12 .....49 N7
  HOO/HM ME3 .....51 K8
  STRD ME2 .....19 F7
Canal St CMBW SE5 .....24 A9
Canal Wk CROY/NA CR0 .....83 K3
Canberra Gdns SIT ME10 ....129 K1
Canberra Rd ABYW SE2 .....28 C9
  CHARL SE7 .....26 D9
Canbury Ms SYD SE26 .....60 C2
Canbury Pth STMC/STPC BR5 ....87 L1
Cancell Rd BRXN/ST SW9 .....40 A2
Cander Wy SOCK/AV RM15 ....31 L3
Canham Rd SNWD SE25 .....60 E9
Canning Cross CMBW SE5 ....40 D3
Canning Rd CROY/NA CR0 .....83 L6
Canning St MAID/BEAR ME14 ..159 N6
Cannonbury Rd RAM CT11 ....16 D5
Cannon Dr POP/IOD E14 .....25 L3
Cannongate Av HYTHE CT21 ...309 J4
Cannongate Cl HYTHE CT21 ...309 H4
Cannongate Gdns
  HYTHE CT21 ....309 H4
Cannongate Rd HYTHE CT21 ..309 J4
Cannon La WBY/YAL ME18 ....185 K2
Cannon Pl CHARL SE7 .....26 F8
Cannon Rd BXLYHN DA7 .....44 C2
  RAM CT11 .....16 E3
Cannon St DEAL CT14 .....233 H2
  DVE/WH CT16 .....8 B2
  LYDD TN29 .....342 H6
  MANHO EC4N 24 A3
  NROM TN28 .....336 G6
Cannon Street Rd WCHPL E1 ..24 E2
Canon Beck Rd
  BERM/RHTH SE16 .....24 C5
Canonbie Rd FSTH SE23 .....41 J8
Canon Cl RCANTE CT3 .....94 C4
Canon Gn RCANTE CT3 * 169 K9
Canon La WBY/YAL ME18 ....185 K2
Canon Murnane Rd
  STHWK SE1 * 24 C6
Canon Rd BMLY BR1 .....62 G9
Canons Gate Rd DVE/WH CT16 ...9 F5
Canon's Wk CROY/NA CR0 ....84 A7
Canon Woods Wy
  KEN/WIL TN24 .....253 J3
Cansiron La EDEN TN8 .....266 F6
Cantelope Ms EGRIN RH19 * ..265 J7
Cantelupe Rd EGRIN RH19 ....265 J7
Canterbury Av BFN/LL DA15 ...64 E1
Canterbury Cl BECK BR3 .....51 P7
  BRDST CT10 .....113 J8
  CMBW SE5 * 40 C3
  DART DA1 .....46 G8
  RHAM ME8 .....96 *
Canterbury Crs BRXN/ST SW9 ...40 A4
  TONN TN9 .....210 C5
Canterbury Gdns WNWD SE27 ..60 B2
Canterbury Hl CANTW/ST CT2 .136 D8
Canterbury La CANT CT1 .....5 F5
  RHAM ME8 .....97 M5
Canterbury Rd BRCH CT7 ....139 N2
  CROY/NA CR0 .....82 E4
  FAV ME13 .....133 J8
  FAV ME13 .....163 P1
  FOLKN CT19 .....11 F1
  GVE DA12 .....49 J7
  HB CT6 .....107 L7
  KEN/WIL TN24 .....2 E2
  KEN/WIL TN24 .....252 G5
  RASHE TN25 .....221 M1
  RASHE TN25 .....222 D1
  RASHE TN25 .....284 F5
  RCANTE CT3 .....167 P4
  RCANTE CT3 .....169 K9
  RCANTW CT4 .....194 F5
  RCANTW CT4 .....224 B2
  RCANTW CT4 .....258 E1
  RDV CT15 .....259 P6
  RFOLK CT18 .....287 H1
  RFOLK CT18 .....288 E8
  RTWE/PEM TN2 .....11 *
  SIT ME10 .....130 A2
  WSTB CT5 .....105 L6
Canterbury Rd Birchington
  BRCH CT7 .....110 F9
Canterbury Rd East
  RAM CT11 .....142 E5
Canterbury Rd Margate
  MARC CT9 .....111 P5
Canterbury Rd West
  MSTR CT12 .....142 C5
Canterbury St Westgate
  WGOS CT8 .....111 L5
Canterbury St GILL ME7 .....7 H3
  GILL ME7 .....7 K7
Canterbury Wy DART DA1 ....47 J5
  WTHK RM20 .....47 L2
Cantley Gdns NRWD SE19 ....60 F9
Canton St POP/IOD E14 .....25 M3
Cantwell Rd WOOL/PLUM SE18 ..43 M1
Canute Rd BRCH CT7 .....110 E5
  DEAL CT14 .....203 H9
  FAV ME13 .....133 P7
Capel Av WLGTN SM6 .....82 E9
Capel Cl ASH TN23 .....252 C8
  BRDST CT10 .....113 L4
  HAYES BR2 .....85 P5

RHAM ME8 .....96 F9
Capel Court Pk RFOLK CT18 * .311 N1
Capel Cl RMAID ME17 .....185 H8
Capel Pl RDART DA2 .....66 C3
Capel Rd FAV ME13 * 132 E6
  RASHW TN26 .....304 C4
  RCANTW CT4 .....195 N7
  SIT ME10 .....129 M3
Capel St RFOLK CT18 .....311 L2
Capri Rd CROY/NA CR0 .....83 L4
Capstan Ct GRH DA9 .....47 J5
Capstan Rd DEPT SE8 .....25 J7
Capstan Rw DEAL CT14 .....233 J2
Capstan Sq POP/IOD E14 ....25 M5
Capstan Wy BERM/RHTH SE16 ..25 H4
Capstone Rd BMLY BR1 .....62 D3
  WALD ME5 .....95 P5
Capulet Ms WOOL/PLUM SE18 ..26 B4
Caracas St GNWCH SE10 .....25 P8
The Caravan Site
  SOCK/AV RM15 .....30 C6
Caravel Cl CDW/CHF RM16 ...32 A6
Caravel Ms DEPT SE8 * 25 K9
Caraway Cl PLSTW E13 .....26 C1
Caraway Pth WLGTN SM6 * ...82 A7
Carberry Rd NRWD SE19 ....60 C5
Carbis Rd POP/IOD E14 .....25 M6
Cardale St POP/IOD E14 ....25 M6
Carden Rd PECK SE15 .....41 H4
Cardens Rd HOO/HM ME3 ....52 B8
Cardiff St WOOL/PLUM SE18 ..44 A1
Cardigan Cl HOO/HM ME3 ...53 M5
Cardigan Pl BKHTH/KID SE3 * ..42 B3
Cardinal Bourne St
  STHWK SE1 * 24 A6
Cardinal Cl CHST BR7 .....63 P7
  IOS ME12 .....58 D9
  TON TN9 .....240 G1
Cardinal Rd CDW/CHF RM16 ...31 P6
Cardinal Wk E/WMAL ME19 ...153 J9
Cardine Cl SIT ME10 .....99 M7
Cardine Ms PECK SE15 .....41 H1
Carew Rd THHTH CR7 .....60 B9
Carew St CMBW SE5 .....40 C3
Carew Wy STMC/STPC BR5 ....87 K5
Carey Cl NROM TN28 .....336 G7
Carey's Fld SEV TN13 .....148 D5
The Carfax SYD SE26 * 61 J2
Cargreen Rd SNWD SE25 ....83 L1
Carholme Rd FSTH SE23 ....41 P6
Caring La RMAID ME17 .....186 G5
Caring Rd RMAID ME17 .....186 G2
Carisbrooke Av BXLY DA5 ....44 F9
Carisbrooke Dr MAIDW ME16 ..12 A3
Carisbrooke Gdns PECK SE15 * ..40 F1
Carisbrooke Rd HAYES BR2 ...76 B1
  MTCM CR4 .....82 D1
  STRD ME2 .....71 N7
Carleton Pl EYN DA4 .....89 P1
Carleton Rd DART DA1 .....46 G8
Carlisle Av TWRH EC3N 24 C3
Carlisle Rd DART DA1 .....46 G7
Carlsden Cl DVE/WH CT16 ...291 H4
Carlton Av BRDST CT10 ....113 M8
  GILL ME7 .....96 B2
  GRH DA9 .....47 L7
  IOS ME12 .....57 K7
  RAM CT11 .....16 E4
Carlton Crs RTW TN1 .....23 G5
Carlton Gdns
  MAID/SHEP ME15 .....185 N3
Carlton Gn SCUP DA14 * 64 B3
Carlton Gv PECK SE15 .....41 H2
Carlton Hl HB CT6 .....107 H2
Carlton Ldg RTW TN1 * 23 G3
Carlton Pde SEV TN13 * 148 A1
Carlton Ri WGOS CT8 .....111 K5
Carlton Rd ASH TN23 .....2 A3
  CDW/CHF RM16 .....32 G5
  DEAL CT14 .....263 H2
  ERITH DA8 .....46 B1
  RTW TN1 .....23 G5
  SCUP DA14 .....64 B4
  WELL DA16 .....44 D4
  WSTB CT5 .....135 L5
Carlton Rd East WGOS CT8 ....111 L5
Carlton Rd West WGOS CT8 ...111 K5
Carlton Ter SYD SE26 * 61 J2
Carlyle Av BMLY BR1 .....63 H9
Carlyle Rd CROY/NA CR0 ....83 M6
  THMD SE28 .....28 A3
Carlys Cl BECK BR3 .....61 K8
Carmel Cl RCANTW CT4 * 195 J1
Carmelite Wy HART DA3 .....91 J2
Carmen St POP/IOD E14 .....25 L2
Carmichael Rd SNWD SE25 ...83 M2
Carnach Gn SOCK/AV RM15 ...31 L3
Carnac St WNWD SE27 .....60 E1
Carnation Crs E/WMAL ME19 .153 P4
Carnation Rd STRD ME2 .....71 M8
Carnation St ABYW SE2 .....28 A8
Carnbrook Rd BKHTH/KID SE3 ..42 B4
Carnecke Gdns ELTH/MOT SE9 ..43 J6
Caroland Cl RASHE TN25 ....284 E3
Carolina Rd THHTH CR7 .....60 B8
Caroline Cl CROY/NA CR0 ....83 K3
  WSTB CT5 .....105 J8
Caroline Crs BRDST CT10 ....113 K7
  MAIDW ME16 .....155 J5
Caroline Gdns PECK SE15 * ..41 H1
Caroline Sq MARC CT9 .....3 H3
Caroline St WCHPL E1 .....24 G2
Carolyn Dr ORP BR6 .....87 H7
Carpeaux Cl CHAT ME4 .....6 E5
Carpenters Cl ROCH ME1 .....95 K4
Carpenters La RTON TN11 ....181 N8
  STPH/PW TN12 * 225 P2
Carpinus Cl WALD ME5 .....125 N4
Carr Gv WOOL/PLUM SE18 ...26 F7
Carriage Ms CANTW/ST CT2 ...4 D3

The Carriageway RSEV TN14 ..147 L9
Carrick Dr SEV TN15 .....148 G8
Carrick Ms DEPT SE8 .....25 K9
Carriers Pl RRTW TN5 .....268 A4
Carriers Rd CRBK TN17 .....298 A2
Carrill Wy BELV DA17 .....28 C7
Carrington Cl CROY/NA CR0 ...84 B4
  GILL ME7 .....73 M9
Carrington Rd DART DA1 ....46 F7
Carroll Cl STRD ME2 .....123 P1
Carroll Gdns SIT ME10 .....153 N1
Carronade Pl
  WOOL/PLUM SE18 .....27 L6
Carron Cl POP/IOD E14 .....25 L2
Carroway's Pk HART DA3 ....15 H4
Carr St POP/IOD E14 .....25 H2
Carsington Gdns DART DA1 ...66 D1
Carson Rd CAN/RD E16 .....26 B1
  DUL SE21 .....60 D1
Carstairs Rd CAT SE6 .....62 A2
Carston Cl LEE/GVPK SE12 ...42 D6
Carswell Rd CAT SE6 .....42 A8
Cartel Cl PUR RM19 .....30 G7
Carter Av BGR/WK TN15 * ...120 B2
Carter Wy DEPT SE8 .....25 H7
Carter La FLST/FETLN EC4A ...334 F5
Carter's Hl BGR/WK TN15 ...179 N6
Carters Hill La MEO DA13 ...122 A3
Carter Rd FOLK CT20 .....310 C6
Carter's Wd RASHW TN26 ...304 D8
Lar La GRAYS RM17 .....32 C8
Cartmel Rd BXLYHN DA7 ....45 J2
Carton Cl ROCH ME1 .....95 J4
Cartwright Cl RCANTE CT3 ...170 D9
Cartwright St TWRH EC3N ...24 C3
Carver Dr RSIT ME9 .....129 L7
Carver Rd HNHL SE24 .....40 C7
Carville Av STH/RUST TN4 ...240 C8
Carvoran Wy RHAM ME8 ....98 D4
Cascade Cl STMC/STPC BR5 ..64 E9
Cascades CROY/NA CR0 ....114 C4
Casella Rd NWCR SE14 .....41 K1
Casewick Rd WNWD SE27 ....60 B4
Casino Av HNHL SE24 .....40 C3
Caslocke St FAV ME13 .....132 F6
Caspian St CMBW SE5 .....40 D1
Caspian La CAN/RD E16 .....26 E2
Caspian Wy SWCM DA10 ....48 C6
Cassilda Rd ABYW SE2 .....28 A3
Cassino Sq DVE/WH CT16 ..291 H5
Cassland Rd THHTH CR7 ....83 J1
Casslee Rd CAT SE6 .....41 M8
Casson St WCHPL E1 .....24 D1
Casterbridge Rd
  BKHTH/KID SE3 .....42 E4
Castfield Cl HOO/HM ME3 ...52 E6
Castile Rd WOOL/PLUM SE18 ..27 H7
Castillon Rd CAT SE6 .....62 C1
Castlands Rd CAT SE6 .....61 M7
Castle Av BRDST CT10 ....113 N7
  DVE/WH CT16 .....291 L6
  HYTHE CT21 .....308 C4
Castle Bay FOLK CT20 ....309 P4
Castle Cl HAYES BR2 .....62 B9
  CROY/NA CR0 .....307 N5
Castlecombe Rd
  ELTH/MOT SE9 .....63 J4
Castle Ct BANK EC3V * 24 A2
  SEV TN13 .....61 L3
Castle Dene
  MAID/BEAR ME14 .....155 K4
Castledine Rd PGE/AN SE20 ...61 H6
Castle Dr BGR/WK TN15 ....149 K2
Castle Farm Rd RSEV TN14 ..198 C2
Castle Fld TON TN9 * 210 E8
Castlefields MEO DA13 .....69 K7
Castleford Av ELTH/MOT SE9 ..43 M9
Castle Hl FOLKN CT19 ....310 D3
  HART DA3 .....91 M3
  MAID/BEAR ME14 .....156 C4
  ROCH ME1 .....19 F4
  RTON TN11 .....241 J4
Castle Hl Av CROY/NA CR0 ..114 E3
Castle Hill Ct ROCH ME1 * 19 F4
Castle Hill Rd DVE/WH CT16 ...9 F2
Castle La GVE DA12 .....70 D1
Castlemaine Av GILL ME7 ....73 J9
  SAND/SEL CR2 .....86 A6
Castle Mayne Av BRCH CT7 ..141 N1
Castle Md CMBW SE5 * 40 C1
Castlemere Av QBOR ME11 ....77 K2
Castle Ms CDAL CT14 * 232 G5
Castlemount Rd DVE/WH CT16 ..9 F3
Castle Rd CHAT ME4 .....95 M4
  EYN DA4 .....118 C1
  FOLK CT20 .....310 C8
  GRAYS RM17 .....31 P1
  HYTHE CT21 .....308 G3
  MAIDW ME16 .....155 J4
  SIT ME10 .....100 A9
  STH/RUST TN4 .....22 B4
  SWCM DA10 .....48 D7
  TON TN9 .....210 F8
Castle Rough La SIT ME10 ...99 N6
Castle Rw CANT CT1 .....4 D6
Castle St ASH TN23 .....2 D5
  CANT CT1 .....4 D5
  DVE/WH CT16 .....8 E4
  GRH DA9 .....47 M8
  OBOR ME11 .....77 J2
  ROCH ME1 .....124 B1
  RTW TN1 .....22 D6
  STH/RUST TN4 .....240 C7
  STRD ME2 .....19 E2
  SWCM DA10 .....48 D7
  TON TN9 .....210 F8
Castle Ter RTON TN11 * 211 P2

Castleton Av BXLYHN DA7 ....45 M2
Castleton Cl CROY/NA CR0 ...84 B3
Castleton Rd ELTH/MOT SE9 ..63 H3
  MTCM CR4 .....82 C1
Castle Vw RTON TN11 * 211 P2
Castle View Wl STRD ME2 ....19 F4
Castle Wy DIT/AY ME20 ....123 M8
  E/WMAL ME19 .....153 M1
Castlewood Dr ELTH/MOT SE9 ..43 K3
Castor La POP/IOD E14 .....25 L5
Catalina Av CDW/CHF RM16 ...32 A6
Catalpa Ct LEW SE13 .....63 J2
Caterfield La LINC RH7 .....205 J8
Caterham Rd LEW SE13 .....42 A4
Catesby St WALW SE17 .....24 A7
Catford Broadway CAT SE6 ....41 P9
Catford Hl CAT SE6 .....41 M9
Catford Island CAT SE6 * 41 P8
Catharine Cl CDW/CHF RM16 ..32 A5
Cathay St BERM/RHTH SE16 ..24 E5
Cathcart Dr ORP BR6 .....66 F6
Cathedral St STHWK SE1 * ...24 A4
Catherine Cl MAIDW ME16 ...154 F9
Catherine Gv GNWCH SE10 ...41 P2
Catherine St RTW TN1 .....22 E3
Catherine St ROCH ME1 ....95 J3
Catherine Wy BRDST CT10 ..113 M7
Catherine Wheel Aly
  LVPST EC2M 24 B1
Catkin Cl WALD ME5 .....125 L4
Catling Cl FSTH SE23 .....61 J4
Catlin St BERM/RHTH SE16 ...24 D8
Catlyn Cl E/WMAL ME19 ....153 P4
Cator Cl CROY/NA CR0 ....115 H5
Cator Crs CROY/NA CR0 ....115 H5
Cator La BECK BR3 .....61 M8
Cator Rd SYD SE26 .....61 K5
Cator St PECK SE15 .....24 C9
Catsole Hl RCANTE CT3 ....199 N5
Catterick Rd WALD ME5 ....126 A3
Cattistock Rd ELTH/MOT SE9 ..63 J4
Cattle Market SWCH CT13 ...201 N1
Catt's Hl TENT TN30 .....333 J1
Catts Pl STPH/PW TN12 * ...243 K5
Cattsgood La RCANTW CT4 ..196 E6
Cauldham Cl RFOLK CT18 ...311 H1
Cauldham La RFOLK CT18 ..289 L8
Caulfield Rd PECK SE15 .....41 H3
Causeway Br RDV CT15 ....292 G1
The Causeway CANTW/ST CT2 ..4 E2
Cavalier Wy EGRIN RH19 ....265 J9
Cave Hl MAID/SHEP ME15 ...185 L2
Cave La RCANTE CT3 .....199 N4
Cavell Crs DART DA1 .....46 G5
Cavell Sq DEAL CT14 * 233 H2
Cavell St WCHPL E1 .....24 E1
Cavell Wy SIT ME10 .....99 L9
Cavenagh Rd RDV CT15 ....292 G1
Cavendish Av BFN/LL DA15 ...44 C8
  ERITH DA8 .....29 H9
  GILL ME7 .....73 L9
  SEV TN13 .....148 F7
  WELL DA16 .....44 B4
Cavendish Cl TONN TN9 ....210 G5
Cavendish Dr RTWE/PEM TN2 ..23 F7
Cavendish Rd CROY/NA CR0 ...82 C5
  HB CT6 .....107 M2
  ROCH ME1 .....95 J3
Cavendish Sq HART DA3 ....68 B9
Cavendish St IS N1 .....17 F3
Cavendish Wy
  MAID/SHEP ME15 .....156 D9
  WWKM BR4 .....84 E5
Caversham Cl RHAM ME8 ....97 J5
Cavour Rd FAV ME13 .....132 F6
Cawdor Av SOCK/AV RM15 ...31 K1
Cawnpore St NRWD SE19 ....60 E4
Caxton Cl HART DA3 .....91 J1
  RTON TN11 * 210 C2
Caxton Rd MARC CT9 .....112 B5
The Caxtons CMBW SE5 * 40 B1
Caxton St North CAN/RD E16 ..26 A2
Caygill Cl HAYES BR2 * 84 B4
Cayser Dr MAID/SHEP ME15 ..187 P9
Caysers Cft STPH/PW TN12 ..212 F4
Cazenovre St ROCH ME1 ....19 G7
Cecil Av CDW/CHF RM16 ....32 A5
  RHAM ME8 .....96 D4
  STRD ME2 .....72 B7
Cecil Ct HB CT6 * 107 M2
  KEN/WIL TN24 .....2 D2
Cecilia Gv BRDST CT10 ....113 L7
Cecil Pk HB CT6 .....107 M2
Cecil Rd CROY/NA CR0 .....82 G4
  DEAL CT14 .....263 J1
  GVW DA11 .....49 K9
  ROCH ME1 .....95 H3
Cecil Sq MARC CT9 .....3 G4
Cecil St WALW SE17 .....15 G4
Cecil Wy HAYES BR2 .....85 K5
Cedar Av BFN/LL DA15 .....64 B2
  GVE DA12 .....69 N3
Cedar Cl ASH TN23 .....2 A5
  BRDST CT10 .....113 L6
  DIT/AY ME20 .....154 C4
  DUL SE21 .....60 D1
  HAYES BR2 .....85 P7
  MARC CT9 .....112 G4
  MEO DA13 .....113 K8
  SIT ME10 .....130 A3
  SWLY BR8 .....65 P3
  WARL CR6 .....144 B3
Cedar Copse BMLY BR1 .....63 K8
Cedar Crs HAYES BR2 .....85 P7

LYDD TN29 .....337 L2
TONN TN9 .....210 F3
Cedar Dr EDEN TN8 .....206 C8
  EYN DA4 .....118 B1
Cedar Gdns RSIT ME9 * 127 P5
Cedar Gv BXLY DA5 .....44 F7
  GILL ME7 .....96 D3
Cedarhurst BMLY BR1 * 62 C6
Cedarhurst Dr ELTH/MOT SE9 ..42 G6
Cedar La HDCN TN27 .....278 E9
Cedar Mt ELTH/MOT SE9 ....43 H9
Cedar Pl CHARL SE7 .....26 D9
Cedar Rdg BTRM/PEM TN2 ..270 G2
Cedar Rd BMLY BR1 .....62 G8
  CANTW/ST CT2 .....137 L7
  CDW/CHF RM16 .....33 H6
  CROY/NA CR0 .....83 K6
  DART DA1 .....46 D7
  ERITH DA8 .....46 A2
  STRD ME2 .....18 A3
Cedars Cl LEW SE13 .....42 B4
Cedars Rd BECK BR3 .....61 L8
  CROY/NA CR0 .....82 D7
The Cedars SIT ME10 .....100 B9
  STPH/PW TN12 .....243 H2
Cedar Ter DVE/WH CT16 * ...291 J2
  FAV ME13 * 132 D9
Cedar Terrace Rd SEV TN13 .149 H8
Cedar Tree Gv WNWD SE27 ...60 B4
Cedarview CANTW/ST CT2 ...166 B3
Cedric Rd ELTH/MOT SE9 ....63 M2
Cel Vis DEAL CT14 * 202 A6
Celandine Cl POP/IOD E14 * ...25 K1
Celandine Dr THMD SE28 ....28 A4
Celedon Cl CDW/CHF RM16 ...31 P5
Celestial Gdns LEW SE13 ....42 B5
Celestine Cl WALD ME5 ....125 N4
Celia Av ASH TN23 .....120 B2
Cellar Hl RSIT ME9 .....131 H5
Celt Cl SIT ME10 .....99 N6
Celtic Av HAYES BR2 .....62 C9
Celtic Rd DEAL CT14 .....232 F7
Celtic St POP/IOD E14 .....25 L1
Cement Block Cottages
  GRAYS RM17 * 32 D8
Cemetery La CHARL SE7 ....26 F9
  KEN/WIL TN24 .....252 F5
  RTON TN11 .....212 B2
Cemetery Rd ABYW SE2 ....28 A9
  SNOD ME6 .....123 N4
Centenary Gdns SWCH CT13 .201 H8
Centenary Wk CANTW/ST CT2 ..4 A3
Centenary Walk-Canterbury
  RCANTW CT4 .....165 M6
Centenary Walk-Maidstone
  DIT/AY ME20 .....124 F7
  MAID/BEAR ME14 .....124 F7
Centenary Walk-Rochester
  ROCH ME1 .....94 F3
Central Av GVE DA12 .....69 M1
  HB CT6 .....107 J1
  SIT ME10 .....129 N2
  SOCK/AV RM15 .....30 F5
  TIL RM18 .....49 L2
  WELL DA16 .....44 B4
  WLGTN SM6 .....82 D9
Central Hl NRWD SE19 .....60 C4
Central Ldg BGR/WK TN15 * .121 F7
Central Pde CROY/NA CR0 ..114 F4
  HB CT6 .....107 K1
  PGE/AN SE20 * 61 K6
  RFOLK CT18 * 67 H6
Central Park Gdns ROCH ME1 ..95 K4
Central Pl SNWD SE25 * 83 M1
Central Rd DART DA1 .....46 E6
  DIT/AY ME20 .....124 A9
  RAM CT11 .....143 J4
  STRD ME2 .....18 B1
Central St FSBYE EC1V 17 F3
  HOO/HM ME3 .....72 F1
Central Wy OXTED RH8 ....174 G3
  THMD SE28 .....28 A3
The Centre MARC CT9 .....15 G4
Centurion Wy ERITHM DA18 ..28 E6
Centurion Cl GILL ME7 .....96 C5
Centurion Ct WLGTN SM6 * ...82 C4
Centurion Sq
  WOOL/PLUM SE18 .....43 J1
Centurion Wk ASH TN23 ....282 E4
Centurion Wy PUR RM19 ....30 C7
Century Rd FAV ME13 .....133 H6
  RHAM ME8 .....96 G6
Ceres Rd WOOL/PLUM SE18 ...43 J1
Cerise Rd PECK SE15 .....40 G2
Cerne Rd GVE DA12 .....70 A3
Cervia Wy GVE DA12 .....70 A3
Chada Av GILL ME7 .....96 B3
Chadbourn St POP/IOD E14 ...25 L1
Chadd Dr BMLY BR1 .....63 J9
Chadfields TIL RM18 .....49 L1
Chadwell By-Pass GRAYS RM17 ..33 H8
Chadwell Hl CDW/CHF RM16 ..33 J8
Chadwell Rd GRAYS RM17 ...32 D7
Chadwick Cl GVW DA11 .....69 J1
Chadwick Rd PECK SE15 ....40 F3
Chadwick Wy THMD SE28 ....28 C1
Chaffes La RSIT ME9 .....97 P4
Chaffes Ter RSIT ME9 * 97 P4
Chaffinch Av CROY/NA CR0 ...84 A3
Chaffinch Cl CROY/NA CR0 ...84 A2
Chaffinch Cl ORP BR6 .....95 M7
Chaffinch Dr ASH TN23 ....282 F5
Chaffinch Rd BECK BR3 .....61 L7
Chaffinch Wy STPH/PW TN12 .242 G4
Chafford La RRTW TN3 .....268 F3
Chafford Wy CDW/CHF RM16 ..32 B8
The Chain SWCH CT13 .....201 P2

Chalcombe Rd *ABYW* SE2 ....28 A6
Chalcroft Rd *FOLK* CT20 ....310 B7
LEW SE13 ....42 C6
Chalet CI *RDART* DA2 ....65 M5
Chalfont Dr *HB* CT6 ....108 A8
RHAM ME8 ....96 G8
Chalfont Rd *SNWD* SE25 ....48 F9
Chalford Rd *DUL* SE21 ....60 D3
Chalgrove Ms *STRD* ME2 * 93 P9
Chalice Wy *GRH* DA9 ....47 L6
Chalk Av *TENT* TN30 ....301 J5
Chalk CI *FOLKN* CT19 ....310 D4
Chalk Ct *GRAYS* RM17 * 32 B9
Chalkenden Av *RHAM* ME8 ....96 D4
Chalkenden CI *PGE/AN* SE20 ....61 H6
Chalket La *RTWE/PEM* TN2 ....271 M5
Chalk HI *RAM* CT11 ....142 E6
Chalk Hill Rd *DEAL* CT14 ....263 H5
Chalk La *CRBK* TN17 ....275 K9
Chalk Pit Av *STMC/STPC* BR5 ....64 E9
Chalk Pit HI *CHAT* ME4 ....6 D7
RCANTE CT3 ....200 C5
Chalkpit HI *RCANTW* CT4 ....198 A4
Chalkpit La *EGRIN* RH8 ....174 F3
Chalkpit Wd *OXTED* RH8 ....174 G5
Chalk Rd *GVE* DA12 ....50 C9
HOO/HM ME3 ....71 L1
PLSTW E13 ....26 C1
OBOR ME11 ....77 J2
Chalksole Green La *RDV* CT15 .....289 K2
Chalkstone CI *SIT* ME10 ....129 H5
Chalkways *RSEV* TN14 ....149 K1
Chalkwell Rd *SIT* ME10 ....129 L1
Chalky Bank *GVW* DA11 ....69 L5
Chalky Bank Rd *RHAM* ME8 ....97 J4
Chalky Rd *RSIT* ME9 ....127 M7
Challenge CI *GVE* DA12 ....70 E3
Challenger CI *SIT* ME10 ....99 M7
STPH/PW TN12 ....242 G3
Challin St *PGE/AN* SE20 ....61 J7
Chalmers Wy *RHAM* ME8 ....96 D2
Chalsey Rd *BROCKY* SE4 ....41 M5
Chaltons Av *MAIDW* ME16...184 G1
chamberlain CI
WOOL/PLUM SE18 ....27 L6
Chamberlain Ct *RHAM* ME8 ....96 E9
Chamberlain La *EGRIN* RH19 ....174 A5
Chamberlain Dr *HB* CT6 ....106 G2
Chamberlain Rd *CHAT* ME4 ....95 N4
DVW CT17 ....291 H7
Chambers CI *GRH* DA9 ....47 N6
Chambers St
BERM/RHTH SE16 ....24 D5
Chambers Crs *SYD* SE26 ....61 L3
Champion Gv *CMBW* SE5 ....40 D4
Champion HI *CMBW* SE5 ....40 D5
Champion Pk *CMBW* SE5 ....40 D4
Champion Sq *SNWD* SE26 ....61 L3
Champness CI *WNWD* SE27 ....60 G5
Chance CI *CDW/CHF* RM16 ....32 A6
Chancel CI *MEO* DA13..........120 B2
Chancellor Gv *DUL* SE21 ....60 D4
Chancelot Rd *ABYW* SE2 ....28 A7
Chance Meadow *RDV* CT15 ....291 N1
Chancery La *BECK* BR3 ....61 P8
MAID/SHEP ME15 ....13 H5
Chanctonbury Cha *WSTB* CT5 ......105 H8
Chanctonbury CI
ELTH/MOT SE9 ....63 M2
Chandler Av *CAN/RD* E16 ....26 B1
Chandlers Ct *LEE/GVPK* SE12 * 62 F1
Chandlers Dr *ERITH* DA8 ....29 J7
Chandler's HI *MEO* DA13...........92 D9
Chandlers Ms *POP/IOD* E14 ....25 K5
Chandler's Rd *MEO* DA13...........92 D9
Chandler St *WAP* E1W 24 E4
Chandler Wy *PECK* SE15 ....40 F1
Chandos Av *RTW* TN1 ....23 C1
Chandos Sq *BRDST* CT10 ....11 N9
Chandos Ter *RAM* CT11 * 17 F2
Chanlock Pth *SOCK/AV* RM15 ....31 L3
Channel CI *FOLKN* CT19 ....311 J4
Channel Lea *DEAL* CT14 ....233 H8
Channel View Ct *RAM* CT11 * 17 J3
Channel View Rd *DVW* CT17 ....3 B7
Channon Rd *LYDD* TN29 ....343 J5
Chantlers CI *EGRIN* RH19 ....264 F6
Chantler's HI *STPH/PW* TN12 ......242 G6
Chantlers Md *EDEN* TN8 ....267 H5
Chantry Av *HART* DA3 ....91 H5
Chantry Ct *CANT* CT1 * 4 E5
Chantry La *HAYES* BR2 ....85 N2
Chantry Rd *STPH/PW* TN12 ....245 H4
Chantry Rd *STPH/PW* TN12 ....245 H4
Chapel CI *DART* DA1 ....45 N6
E/WMAL KT3 ....122 G8
WTHK RM20 ....31 L9
Chapel Ct *STRHM* SE1 ....24 A5
WOOL/PLUM SE18 ....27 N9
Chapel Farm Rd
ELTH/MOT SE9 ....63 K2
Chapel Fld *RYE* TN31 ....329 P6
Chapelfield *WADH* TN5 ....315 N5
Chapel HI *DART* DA1 ....40 A9
RBRCH ME9 ....112 F6
RDV CT15 ....260 D1
Chapel Hill Rd *MARG* CT9 ....112 E6
Chapel House St *POP/IOD* E14 .....25 L8
Chapel La *CANTW/ST* CT2 ....135 P6
CANTW/ST CT2 ....170 C1
CRBK TN17 ....276 E9
CRBK TN17 ....318 C2
DEAL CT14 ....232 C9
GILL ME7 ....126 D1
HDCN TN27 ....181 J9
LYDD TN29 ....325 P5
MAID/BEAR ME14 ....156 D7
RCANTE CT3 ....200 C4

RCANTW CT4 ....257 H4
RDV CT15 ....261 J2
RDV CT15 ....292 E1
STPH/PW TN12 ....246 C6
STRD ME2 ....123 K1
Chapel Pk *SIT* ME10 * 100 B3
Chapel PI *DVW* CT17 ....8 D4
RAM CT11 ....16 E4
STH/RUST TN4 ....22 C6
Chapel Place La *RAM* CT11 ....16 C5
Chapel Rd *BXLYHN* DA7 ....45 J5
DEAL CT14 ....231 H6
DVE/WH CT16 ....261 H8
HOO/HM ME3 ....56 D3
LYDD TN29 ....326 C6
OXTED RH8 ....175 M6
RAM CT11 ....16 B3
RASHW TN26 ....221 L9
RMAID ME17 ....217 H5
SNOD ME6 ....72 A3
WARL CR6 ....144 A3
WNWD SE27 ....60 E3
Chapel Rw *BGR/WK* TN15 ....150 F6
HOO/HM ME3 ....54 G4
Chapel St *DEAL* CT14 ....233 J5
E/WMAL ME19 ....122 G9
E/WMAL ME19 ....155 P6
FAV ME13 ....132 C7
HYTHE CT21 ....308 G5
IOS ME12 ....57 J5
IOS ME12 ....78 D1
The Chapel *MAIDW* ME16 * 154 C9
Chapel Wd *HART* DA3 ....91 H6
Chapel Wood Rd *HART* DA3 ....91 H6
Chaplin CI *HOO/HM* ME3 ....72 C4
Chaplin Dr *HDCN* TN27 ....247 N4
Chapman Av
MAID/SHEP ME15 ....186 C2
CROY/NA CRO 82 F5
Chapmans CI *RASHE* TN25 ....192 F9
Chapman's HI *BGR/WK* TN15 ....121 P1
RCANTE CT3 ....229 L1
Chapman's La *EGRIN* RH19 ....264 E7
STMC/STPC BR5 ....64 F8
SWLY BR8 ....65 J8
Chapmans Rd *RSEV* TN14 ....147 M9
Chapman St *WCHPL* E1 ....24 E3
Chapman Wy *E/WMAL* ME19 ....153 N4
RTWE/PEM TN2 ....240 F9
Chappell Wy *SIT* ME10 ....99 L8
Chapter Rd *STHD* ME9 ....71 P8
Chardwell CI *EHAM* E6 ....26 F2
Charford Rd *CAN/RD* E16 ....26 B1
Charing Ct *MSTR* CT12 ....143 H4
ORP BR6 ....86 G8
Charing Crs *WGOS* CT8 ....111 L6
Charing Heath Rd
HDCN TN27 ....220 E2
Charing HI *HDCN* TN27 ....221 K1
Charing Rd *RHAM* ME8 ....96 F3
Charlot Wy *STRD* ME2 ....94 D5
Charlbury CI *MAIDW* ME16 ....155 H9
Charldane Rd *ELTH/MOT* SE9 ....63 M2
Charlecote Gv *SYD* SE26 ....61 H2
Charles CI *SCUP* DA14 ....64 A8
SNOD ME6 ....123 P5
Charles Cobb CI *LYDD* TN29 ......337 L6
Charles Cobb Gdns
CROY/NA CRO 82 F9
Charles Coveney Rd
PECK SE15 * 40 F2
Charles Crs *FOLKN* CT19 ....310 B4
Charles Dickens Av *STRD* ME2 ....71 L5
Charles Dickens Ter
PGE/AN SE20 * 61 J6
Charles Drayson Ct
FAV ME13 * 133 H6
Charles Dr *STRD* ME2 ....94 A3
Charlesfield *ELTH/MOT* SE9 ....62 G2
Charles Flemwell Ms
CAN/RD E16 * 26 B4
Charlesford Av *RMAID* ME17 ......187 N1
Charles Grinling Wk
WOOL/PLUM SE18 ....27 H7
Charles Haller St
BRXS/STRHM SW2 ....40 A8
Charles Rd *DEAL* CT14 ....232 G5
RAM CT11 ....143 K4
RSEV TN14 ....118 A4
Charles St *CAN/RD* E16 ....26 D4
CHAT ME4 ....6 A6
CROY/NA CRO 83 H7
GRAYS RM17.........................13 P9
GRH DA9 ....47 M6
HB CT6 ....107 L1
IOS ME12 ....57 J5
MAIDW ME16 ....12 C7
STH/RUST TN4 ....240 D9
STRD ME2 ....71 M1
Charlesworth Dr *BRCH* CT7 ....111 J6
Charleville Circ *SYD* SE26 ....60 G4
Charleville Rd *ERITH* DA8 ....45 L1
Charlock CI *MAIDW* ME16 ....155 J4
Charlotte CI *BXLYHS* DA6 ....44 G6
WALD ME5 ....95 N8
Charlotte Dr *RHAM* ME8 ....96 F5
Charlotte Ms *CANT* CT1 * 4 C6
Charlotte Pde *FSTH* SE23 * 61 L1
Charlotte Park Av *BMLY* BR1 ......63 J9
Charlotte PI *MARG* CT9 * 11 J3
WTHK RM20 ....31 L9
Charlotte Sq *MARG* CT9 * 15 H5
Charlotte St *FOLK* CT20 ....11 L3
SIT ME10 ....99 M9
Charlton Av *DVE/WH* CT16 * 8 B2
Charlton Av *DVE/WH* CT16 ....291 K6
Charlton Centre High St
DVE/WH CT16 * 8 B2
Charlton Church La *CHARL* SE7 ....26 D8
Charlton CI *KEN/WIL* TN24 ....253 K9
Charlton Dene *CHARL* SE7 ....42 G1
Charlton Gn *DVE/WH* CT16........8 B1

Charlton La *CHARL* SE7 ....26 E8
MAID/SHEP ME15 ....188 F4
RMAID ME17 ....217 M2
Charlton Park La *CHARL* SE7 ......43 H1
Charlton Park Rd *CHARL* SE7 ......26 E9
Charlton Rd *BKHTH/KID* SE3 ....26 C9
The Charltons *MAIDW* ME16 ....134 A9
Charlton St *MAIDW* ME16.........185 L1
WTHK RM20 ....31 N9
Charlton's Wy *STH/RUST* TN4 .....270 D7
Charlton Wy *BKHTH/KID* SE3 ....42 D1
Charlwood *CROY/NA* CRO...........114 C3
Charlwoods PI *EGRIN* RH19 ....265 H5
Charlwoods Rd *EGRIN* RH19 ......264 G6
Charminster *ASH* TN23 ....282 B2
Charminster Rd
ELTH/MOT SE9 ....63 H5
Charmouth Rd *WELL* DA16..........44 G2
Charnwood La *ORP* BR6 ....117 J4
The Charne *RSEV* TN14 ....148 F2
Charnock *SWLY* BR8 ....88 D1
Charnwood *WSTB* CT5 ....106 C5
Charnwood Gdns
POP/IOD E14 * 25 K7
Charnwood Rd *HB* CT6 ....107 N5
SNWD SE25 ....83 J2
Charollais CI *CANTW/ST* CT2 .....166 F2
Charrington Rd *CAN/RD* CRO 82 C6
Charsley Rd *CAT* SE6 ....61 P1
Chart CI *KEN/WIL* TN24 ....253 P3
WTHK RM20 ....31 K9
Chart Ct *CROY/NA* CRO 132 E6
FAV ME13 * 151 N9
HAYES BR2 ....84 A7
Charter Dr *BXLY* DA5 ....44 G8
Charterhouse Dr *SEV* TN13 ....148 F8
Charterhouse Rd *ORP* BR6 ....87 H7
Charters CI *NRWD* SE19 ....60 F8
Charter St *CHAT* ME4 ....95 L4
GILL ME7 ....73 J8
Chartham Downs Rd
RCANTW CT4 ....196 D4
Chartham Gv *WNWD* SE27 ....60 A2
Chartham Rd *SNWD* SE25 ....61 H9
Chartham Ter *RAM* CT11 * 16 D6
Chart Hill Rd *RMAID* ME17 ....216 D4
Chart Hills CI *THMD* SE28 ....28 D2
Chart La *BH/WHM* TN16 ....177 K1
Charton CI *BELV* DA17............28 E9
Chart PI *RHAM* ME8 ....126 F2
Chart Rd *ASH* TN23 ....2 B2
ASH TN23 ....252 A8
FOLKN CT19 ....310 C5
RMAID ME17 ....216 F3
Chart Vw *BGR/WK* TN15 ....149 M2
Chartway *SEV* TN13 ....21 C2
Chartway St *RMAID* ME17 ....217 J1
Chartwell Av *HB* CT6 ....108 A6
Chartwell CI *CHST* BR7 ....63 P1
CROY/NA CRO 83 J5
STRD ME2 ....94 A4
Chartwell Ct *CHAT* ME4 * 6 A5
Chartwell Dr *MAIDW* ME16 ....154 C8
ORP BR6 ....86 E9
Chartwell Gv *SIT* ME10 ....129 K2
Chartwell Wy *PGE/AN* SE20 ....61 H7
Charwood *STRHM/NOR* SW16 * 60 A3
Chaseley St *POP/IOD* E14 * 25 J2
Chasemore Gdns
CROY/NA CRO 82 F9
Chase Sq *GVE* DA12 * 49 M7
The Chase *BGR/WK* TN15 ....149 K1
BMLY BR1 ....62 F9
BXLYHN DA7 ....45 K4
ORP BR6 ....117 H5
RAM CT11 * 143 L3
RHAM ME8 ....96 D4
ROCH ME1 ....95 J4
TONN TN10 ....210 F5
WLGTN SM6 ....82 D9
WTHK RM20 ....31 N9
Chastilian Rd *DART* DA1 ....44 A8
Chater CI *DEAL* CT14 ....233 H5
Chatfield Rd *CROY/NA* CRO 82 G5
Chatfield Wy *DIT/AY* ME20.......153 A5
Chatham Av *HAYES* BR2 ....85 K4
Chatham Gv *CHAT* ME4 ....95 L5
Chatham HI *CHAT* ME4 ....7 F6
Chatham Hill Rd *RSEV* TN14 .....149 H6
Chatham PI *RAM* CT11 * 17 F2
Chatham Rd *DIT/AY* ME20 ....125 J5
MAID/BEAR ME14 ....155 K1
Chatham St *RAM* CT11 ....16 E2
WALW SE17 ....24 A7
Chatsworth Av *BFN/LL* DA15.......64 C4
BMLY BR1 ....62 F4
Chatsworth CI *WWKM* BR4 ....85 K9
Chatsworth Dr *SIT* ME10 ....99 J9
STRD ME2 ....72 B6
Chatsworth Rd *CROY/NA* CRO 83 J8
DART DA1 ....46 C6
GILL ME7 ....73 J9
Chatsworth Wy *WNWD* SE27 ....60 C1
Chaucer Av *EGRIN* RH19 ....264 F8
WSTB CT5 ....106 C6
Chaucer CI *CANT* CT1 ....167 H5
STRD ME2 ....94 A3
TIL RM18 ....19 K1
Chaucer Crs *DVE/WH* CT16...291 J4
Chaucer Dr *STHWK* SE1 ....24 C8
Chaucer Gdns *TON* TN9 ....240 C2
Chaucer Gn *CROY/NA* CRO 83 N6
Chaucer Ms *CANTW/ST* CT2 ....165 N5
Chaucer Pk *DART* DA1 ....46 F8
Chaucer Rd *BFN/LL* DA15 ....64 A3
BRDST CT10 ....143 M1
CANT CT1 ....5 K3
GVE ME7 ....73 J8
GVW DA11 ....69 H2
HNHL SE24 ....40 B6
RDV CT15 ....230 C8
SIT ME10 ....129 L2

WELL DA16 ....44 B2
Chaucer Wy *DART* DA1 ....46 D5
RDART DA2 ....123 N9
Chaundrye CI *ELTH/MOT* SE9.......63 M4
Chauntler Rd *CAN/RD* E16 ....26 C2
Chave Rd *DART* DA1 ....66 E2
Cheam St *PECK* SE15 * 41 H4
Cheddar CI *KEN/WIL* TN24 ....252 E5
Cheeselands *HDCN* TN27 ....256 A6
Cheesmans CI *CHAT* ME12 ....141 K7
Chegwell Dr *WALD* ME5 ....125 N1
Chegworth Gdns *SIT* ME10 ....129 M4
Chegworth Rd *RMAID* ME17 ....188 D4
Cheldoc Ri *CHAT* ME4 ....73 J5
Chelford Rd *BMLY* BR1 ....62 B4
Cheliows La *LING* RH7 ....205 J8
Chelmar Rd *CHAT* ME4 ....7 F5
Chelmer Dr *SOCK/AV* RM15 ....31 M3
Chelmer Rd *RCANTE* CT3 ....33 H8
Chelmsford CI *EHAM* E6 ....26 C2
Chelmsford Rd *STRD* ME2 ....71 M9
Chelsea Rd *CANT* CT1 ....137 H9
Chelsfield Gdns *SYD* SE26.......61 L2
Chelsfield HI *ORP* BR6 ....117 K5
Chelsfield La *RSEV* TN14 ....118 E3
STMC/STPC BR5 ....87 L4
WALD ME5 ....125 M4
Chelsfield Rd *STMC/STPC* BR5 ....87 K4
Chelsham Court Rd
WARL CR6 ....144 C3
Chelsworth Dr
WOOL/PLUM SE18 ....27 J3
Cheltenham CI *GVE* DA12 ....69 N4
MAID/SHEP ME15 ....186 C5
Cheltenham Rd *ORP* BR6 ....87 H2
PECK SE15 ....41 J5
Cheney CI *RHAM* ME8 ....96 C9
Cheney HI *RSIT* ME9 ....129 PB
Cheney Rd *FAV* ME13 ....133 J6
Chenies CI *RTWE/PEM* TN2 ....270 D8
The Chenies *ORP* BR6 ....86 F5
RDART DA2 ....65 N3
Chennell Park Rd *TENT* TN30 ....300 F6
Chepstow Ri *CROY/NA* CRO 83 K7
Chepstow Rd *CROY/NA* CRO 83 K7
Chequer La *RCANTE* CT3 ....199 N7
Chequer Rd *EGRIN* RH19 * 265 J1
STMC/STPC BR5 ....86 C1
WALD ME5 ....125 M4
Chequers St *STRD* ME2 ....72 A6
Chequers Orch *RCANTW* CT4 * 196 D4
Chequers Pk *RASHE* TN25 ....223 P9
Chequers Rd *IOS* ME12 ....78 E1
Cherbourg Crs *WALD* ME5 ....95 L7
Cherbury CI *THMD* SE28 ....28 G6
Cheriton Av *HAYES* BR2 ....85 J2
MSTR CT12 ....142 C4
Cheriton Court Rd *FOLK* CT20 ...309 P2
Cheriton Dr *WOOL/PLUM* SE18 .....43 P1
Cheriton Gdns *FOLK* CT20 ....10 C4
Cheriton High St *FOLKN* CT19 ...310 B5
RFOLK CT18 ....309 N1
Cheriton Int *FOLKN* CT19 ....309 P1
Cheriton PI *DEAL* CT14 * 233 J5
FOLK CT20 ....10 C5
Cheriton Rd *DEAL* CT14..........233 J6
FOLK CT20 ....10 D4
FOLKN CT19 ....310 A5
RHAM ME8 ....96 G7
Cheriton Wy *MAIDW* ME16.........155 H5
The Cherries *MAIDW* ME16 ....184 E1
Cherry Amber CI *RHAM* ME8 ....97 J6
Cherry Av *CANTW/ST* CT2 ....166 C2
SWLY BR8 ....65 M9
Cherrybrook Rd *FOLK* CT20 ......310 A5
Cherry CI *BRXS/STRHM* SW2 * 40 A8
SIT ME10 ....99 L8
Cherrycroft Ri *ORP* BR6 ....86 D8
Cherrydown *CDW/CHF* RM16 ....32 E4
Cherrydown Rd *SCUP* DA14.........64 H1
Cherry Dr *CANTW/ST* CT2 ....166 C2
Cherry Fids *SIT* ME10 ....99 H9
Cherry Garden Av
FOLKN CT19 ....310 D4
Cherry Garden Crs
RASHE TN25 ....224 A8
Cherry Garden La
FOLKN CT19 ....310 C4
RASHE TN25 ....224 A8
RCANTE CT3 ....200 F1
Cherrygarden La *RCANTE* CT3 ....199 P7
RDV CT15 ....230 A2
Cherry Garden Rd
CANTW/ST CT2 ....166 C2
Cherry Gdns *BRDST* CT10 ....143 H1
HB CT6 ....107 K3
NROM TN28 ....357 J7
RCANTW CT4 ....194 D1
RSIT ME9 ....131 H3
Cherry Garden St
BERM/RHTH SE16 ....24 E5
Cherry Glebe *RASHE* TN25 ......283 P5
Cherry Gv *RDV* CT15 ....261 P1
TONN TN10 ....211 H5
Cherry Hill CI *RSIT* ME9 * 98 D8
Cherry Hill Gdns *CROY/NA* CRO ...82 D9
Cherry La *DEAL* CT14 ....232 C6
Cherry Orch *CHARL* SE7 ....26 D9
DIT/AY ME20 ....154 B4
RASHW TN26 ....168 D2
RCANTE CT3 ....194 D1
TENT TN30 ....301 H9
WSTB CT5 ....106 B6
Cherry Orchard CI
STMC/STPC BR5 ....87 K2
Cherry Orchard Gdns
CROY/NA CRO 83 J5
Cherry Orchard La
RASHE TN25 ....305 J5
Cherry Orchard Rd
CROY/NA CRO 83 J5
HAYES BR2 ....85 P6
The Cherry Orch *RTON* TN11 .....211 P1

Cherry Orchard Wy
WWKM BR4 ....154 C9
Cherry Rd *HOO/HM* ME3 ....73 L4
Cherry Tree Av *DVE/WH* CT16 ....291 K6
Cherry Tree CI *RHAM* ME9 ....131 J3
Cherry Tree Ct *CHARL* SE7 ....26 D9
Cherry Tree Gdns *MSTR* CT12 ...142 C2
Cherry Tree Gv *BGR/WK* TN15....119 N4
Cherry Tree La *RDART* DA2 ....65 P2
Cherry Tree Rd *ERITH* DA8 ....46 C1
HDCN TN27 ....220 D3
RAM CT11 ....16 A6
RTWE/PEM TN2 ....270 B7
Cherry Trees *HART* DA3 ....91 J3
Cherry Tree Ter *STHWK* SE1 * 24 B5
Cherry Wk *BECK* BR3 ....84 C1
WWKM BR4 ....85 J8
Cherry Wy *CDW/CHF* RM16 ....35 H6
HAYES BR2 ....85 K5
Cherry Waye *RDV* CT15 ....260 D1
Cherrywood Ri *RASHE* TN25 .....252 C5
Cherrywood Ri *RASHE* TN25 .....252 C5
Chertsey Crs *CROY/NA* CRO 114 A9
Cherville La *RCANTE* CT3 ....168 F9
Chervilles *MAIDW* ME16 ....184 F1
Chervil Ms *THMD* SE28 ....28 A4
Cherwell CI *TONN* TN10 ....210 E6
Cherwell Gv *SOCK/AV* RM15 ....31 L5
Cheseman St *SYD* SE26............61 H2
Chesfield CI *RTON* TN11 * 212 A2
Chesham Av *HAYES* BR2 ....86 C5
Chesham Crs *PGE/AN* SE20 ....61 J7
Chesham Rd *RHAM* ME8 ....97 H8
Chesham Rd *PGE/AN* SE20 ....61 J8
WARL CR6 ....144 D1
Cheshire Rd
MAID/SHEP ME15 ....186 B1
Chesnut Av *MEO* DA13...........92 B3
Cheshunt Rd *BELV* DA17 ....28 F8
Chesney Crs *CROY/NA* CRO 114 F2
Chesnut Av North *WCHPL* E1 .....24 C3
Chessenden La *HDCN* TN27 ....249 H8
Chessington Av *BXLYHN* DA7 .....44 G1
Chessington Wy *WWKM* BR4 ....85 K9
Chester Av *RASHW* TN26 ....280 C3
Chester CI *CDW/CHF* RM16 ....31 P6
STRD ME2 ....71 M9
Chesterfield CI
STMC/STPC BR5 ....87 L1
SEV TN13 ....148 C7
Chesterfield Dr *DART* DA1 ....46 B6
Chesterfield Gdns
GNWCH SE10 ....42 B1
Chesterfield Dr *EDUL* SE22 ......40 F3
Chesterfield Wy *PECK* SE15 ......41 J1
Chester Rd *BFN/LL* DA15 ....44 A6
GILL ME7 ....96 A4
WGOS CT8 ....111 L6
Chesterton CI *EGRIN* RH19 .....265 J9
Chesterton Rd *DIT/AY* ME20......123 N9
HOO/HM ME3 ....52 B3
Chestfield CI *RHAM* ME8 ....97 H4
Chestfield Rd *WSTB* CT5 ....106 B7
Chestnut Av *BH/WHM* TN16 ....135 P7
CANTW/ST CT2 ....165 K7
CDW/CHF RM16 ....32 C5
GRH DA9 ....47 N8
STH/RUST TN4 ....240 E9
WALD ME5 ....125 M7
WWKM BR4 ....85 H9
Chestnut CI *ASH* TN23 ....252 B6
BFN/LL DA15 ....64 C1
CAT SE6 ....62 A3
CRBK TN17 ....277 K2
DVE/WH CT16 ....261 H8
E/WMAL ME19 ....183 H1
EDEN TN8 ....206 C8
EGRIN RH19 ....265 K7
HYTHE CT21 ....308 D7
NWCR SE14 ....41 M2
ORP BR6 ....87 H9
RCANTW CT4 ....195 N2
RMAID ME17 ....218 A4
RMAID ME17 ....187 N9
STRHM/NOR SW16 ....60 A3
TENT TN30 ....301 K6
Chestnut Copse *OXTED* RH8 ......175 J3
Chestnut Ct *FAV* ME13 ....164 A1
RTWE/PEM TN2 ....270 D8
Chestnut Dr *BXLYHN* DA7 ....45 H4
BXLYHN DA7 ....44 F4
CANTW/ST CT2 ....137 M7
DEAL CT14 ....201 P6
HB CT6 ....107 J4
RMAID ME17 ....184 G8
RMAID ME17 ....187 N9
Chestnut Gv *MTCM* CR4 ....82 C2
RDART DA2 ....65 M4
Chestnut La *ASH* TN23 ....282 F4
MEO DA13 ....122 C5
SEV TN13 ....148 C8
STPH/PW TN12 ....242 F8
Chestnut Mnr *WLGTN* SM6 ....82 E8
Chestnut Ri *SEV* TN13 ....148 C7
Chestnut Ri *WOOL/PLUM* SE18 ....27 M8
Chestnut Rd *DART* DA1 ....46 A4
DVW CT17 ....291 J8
STRD ME2 ....94 A3
WNWD SE27 ....60 B2
Chestnuts *RASHE* TN25 ....283 M3
The Chestnuts *BECK* BR3 * 61 J3
E/WMAL ME19 ....152 D1
HAWK TN18 ....316 C6
RASHE TN25 * 284 E3
Chestnut St *RSIT* ME9 ....128 F1
Chestnut Ter *HYTHE* CT21 * 308 F6
Chestnut Wk *BGR/WK* TN15 ....119 L4
EGRIN RH19 ....265 K7
TON TN9 ....210 C6
Chestnut Wood La *RSIT* ME9 ....128 F1
Cheston Av *CROY/NA* CRO 84 B5
Cheswick CI *DART* DA1 ....45 P5

Chesworth Cl *ERITH* DA8 ....45 N2
Chetney Cl *STRD* ME2 ....71 L8
Chetney Vw *RSIT* ME9....................99 L2
Chettle Cl *STHWK* SE1 ....24 A6
Chevalier Rd *DVW* CT17 ....291 H8
Cheval St *POP/IOD* E14 ....25 K6
Cheveney Wk *HAYES* BR2............62 E9
Chevening La *RSEV* TN14 ....147 M1
Chevening Rd *GNWCH* SE10......26 A8
   NRWD SE19 ....60 D6
   RSEV TN14 ....99 L5
The Chevenings *SCUP* DA14 ......64 D2
Cheviot Cl *BXLYHN* DA7 ....45 N3
   TON TN9 ....210 F6
Cheviot Ct *BRDST* CT10 ....113 N8
Cheviot Gdns
   MAID/SHEP ME15 ....186 D2
Cheviot Rd *WNWD* SE27 ....60 B4
Cheviot Wy *KEN/WIL* TN24........252 F5
Chevron Cl *CAN/RD* E16 ....26 B2
Cheyne Cl *HAYES* BR2 ....85 P7
   SIT ME10 ....99 N6
Cheyne Rd *IOS* ME12 ....79 K4
Cheyne Wk *CROY/NA* CR0 ....3 J6
   MEO DA15 ....92 B6
Chicago Av *GILL* ME7 ....96 B1
Chichele Gdns *CROY/NA* CR0 .....83 K8
Chichele Rd *OXTED* RH8 ....175 H4
Chichester Cl *ASH* TN23 ....2 C6
   BKHTH/KID SE3 ....42 C1
   CDW/CHF RM16 ....31 N7
   EHAM E6.......................................26 F2
   RHAM ME8 ....97 K6
   WGOS CT8 ....50 F4
Chichester Dr *SEV* TN13 ....20 B4
Chichester Ri *DVA* DA12 ....69 P3
Chichester Rd *CROY/NA* CR0 .....83 K7
   FOLK CT20 ....310 B7
   IOS ME12 ....47 M6
   MSTR CT12 ....142 C5
   TON TN9 ....240 D1
Chichester Wy *POP/IOD* E14 .....25 N7
Chichester Whf *ERITH* DA8 ....29 K8
Chickenden La
   STPH/PW TN12 ....246 F5
Chickfield Gdns *WALD* ME5 ....95 P4
Chicksand St *WCHPL* E1 ....24 D1
Chicks La *CRBK* TN17 ....295 N5
Chiddingfold Cl *IOS* ME12 ....78 D1
Chiddingstone Av
   BXLYHN DA7 ....28 E9
Chiddingstone Cl
   MAID/SHEP ME15 ....186 C5
Chidley Cross Rd
   STPH/PW TN12 ....212 F4
Chieftain Cl *GILL* ME7 ....96 E5
Chieftan Dr *PUR* RM19 ....30 D7
Chieveley Dr *RTWE/PEM* TN2 ...270 F7
Chieveley Pde *BXLYHN* DA7 * 45 K4
Chieveley Rd *BXLYHN* DA7 ....45 K4
Chiffinch Gdns *DVW* DA11 ....69 J2
Chigwell Hl *WAP* E1W 24 E3
Childeric Rd *NWCR* SE14 ....41 L1
Childers St *DEPT* SE8 ....25 H9
Childsbridge La
   BGR/WK TN15 ....149 L2
Childsbridge Wy
   BGR/WK TN15 ....149 L5
Childs Crs *SWCM* DA10 ....48 B7
Childscroft Rd *RHAM* ME8 ....97 J4
Childs La *NRWD* SE19 * 60 E5
Childs Wy *BGR/WK* TN15 ....151 J1
Chilham Av *WGOS* CT8 ....111 L6
Chilham Cl *BXLY* DA5....................45 H8
   CHAT ME4 ....63 J5
   IOS ME12 ....57 K8
Chilham Rd *ELTH/MOT* SE9 ....63 J5
   FOLKN CT19 ....310 B5
   MAIDW ME16 ....155 H5
   RHAM ME8 ....97 J4
Chilham Wy *HAYES* BR2 ....85 K4
Chillington St
   MAID/BEAR ME14 ....155 L6
Chilliwack Rd *HOO/HM* ME3 ......72 F2
Chilston Cl *STH/RUST* TN4 ....270 D3
Chilston Rd *RMAID* ME17 ....189 L6
   STH/RUST TN4 ....270 B7
Chiltern Av *RHAM* ME8 ....97 H5
Chiltern Dr *HOO/HM* ME3 ....71 M4
Chiltern Fld *RCANTE* CT3 ....170 E9
Chiltern Gdns *RCANTE* CT3 ....170 E9
Chiltern Gv *DVE* CT2 ....24 G7
Chiltern La *RAM* CT11 ....142 F6
Chiltern Pl *RCANTE* CT3 ....170 E9
Chiltern Rd *CDW/CHF* RM16 .....33 H6
Chiltern Sq *RCANTE* CT3 ....200 E1
Chiltern Wy *DVW* CT17 ....290 F4
Chilver St *GNWCH* SE10 ....26 A8
The Chimes *KEN/WIL* TN24 ....2 D1
China Hall Ms
   BERM/RHTH SE16 ....24 F7
Chinbrook Crs
   LEE/GVPK SE12 ....62 F2
Chinbrook Rd *ELTH/MOT* SE9 ....62 G2
Chineham Wy *CANT* CT1.............66 E6
Chingley Cl *BMLY* BR1 ....62 C5
Chipka St *POP/IOD* E14 ....25 M5
Chipley St *NWCR* SE14 ....25 H9
Chipman's Wy *MSTR* CT12 ....140 F5
Chippendale Cl *WALD* ME5 ....125 L4
Chippendayle Dr
   RMAID ME17 ....188 E5

Chipperfield Rd
   STMC/STPC BR5.........................64 D9
Chipstead Av *THHTH* CR7 ....82 G1
Chipstead Cl *MAID/SHEP* ME16..155 J6
   NRWD SE19 ....60 F6
Chipstead La *SEV* TN13 ....148 C7
Chipstead Pk *SEV* TN13 ....148 C7
Chipstead Park Cl *SEV* TN13 ....148 B7
Chipstead Rd *ERITH* DA8 ....45 N1
   RHAM ME8 ....60 D4
Chisholm Rd *CROY/NA* CR0 ....83 K6
Chislehurst Cl
   MAID/SHEP ME15 ....186 C5
Chislehurst High St *CHST* BR7 ....63 M5
Chislehurst Rd *BMLY* BR1 ....63 J8
   ORP BR6 ....86 C4
   SCUP DA14 ....64 C4
   STMC/STPC BR5.........................86 F1
Chislet Cl *BECK* BR3 ....61 N6
Chislet Ct *HB* CT6 * 107 K1
Chislett Cl *RANTE* TN25 ....285 M6
Chisnall Rd *DVW* CT17 ....290 F5
Chiswell Sq *BKHTH/KID* SE3 ......42 F3
Chiswell St *CMBW* SE5 * 40 D1
   STLK EC1Y 24 A1
Chiswick Cl *CROY/NA* CR0 ....82 E7
Chittenden's La *LYDD* TN29 ....336 D5
Chitty La *RCANTE* CT3 ....138 G3
Chorleywood Crs
   STMC/STPC BR5.........................64 B8
Choumert Gv *PECK* SE15 ....40 G5
Choumert Rd *PECK* SE15 ....40 F5
Chrismill La *MAID/BEAR* ME14...157 J8
Chrisp St *POP/IOD* E14 ....25 L2
Christ Church Av *ERITH* DA8 ....29 J9
   RTW TN1 ....22 D5
Christ Church Rd *FOLK* CT20 .....10 D4
   GVE DA12 ....49 N9
Christchurch Rd *ASH* TN23 ....2 C3
   BECK BR3 * 61 N8
   BFN/LL DA15 ....64 B3
   DART DA1 ....46 C8
   TIL RM18 ....49 J2
Christchurch Wy
   DVE/WH CT16 ....291 J4
   SNWD SE19 ....25 P8
Christian Flds
   STRHM/NOR SW16 ....60 A6
Christian Fields Av *GVE* DA12 .....49 P8
Christian St *WCHPL* E1 ....24 D2
Christie Dr *DIT/AY* ME20 ....123 N9
   SNWD SE25 ....83 M2
Christies *EGRIN* RH19 ....264 G8
Christies Av *RSEV* TN14 ....117 P4
Christmas La *HOO/HM* ME3 ....53 L5
Christmas St *GILL* ME7 ....73 L8
Christopher Bushell Wy
   KEN/WIL TN24 ....2 B7
Christopher Cl *BFN/LL* DA15 ......44 B6
Christopher Rd *EGRIN* RH19 .....265 H7
Christy Rd *BH/WHM* TN16 ....115 M9
Chrysler Av *HB* CT6 ....106 F2
Chryssell Rd *BRXN/ST* SW9.......40 A1
Chubworthy St *NWCR* SE14 ....25 H9
Chudleigh Rd *BROCKY* SE4 ....41 M6
Chudleigh St *WCHPL* E1 ....24 G2
Chulkhurst *HDCN* TN27 ....277 P6
Chulsa Rd *SYD* SE26 ....61 H4
Chumleigh Gdns *CMBW* SE5 * 24 B9
Chumleigh St *CMBW* SE5 ....24 B9
Church Ap *DUL* SE21 ....60 D2
   NROM TN28 ....336 F7
Church Av *BECK* BR3 ....61 N7
   SCUP DA14 ....64 C4
Churchbury Rd *ELTH/MOT* SE9 ..43 H8
Church Cliff *DEAL* CT14 ....263 J2
Church Court Gv *BRDST* CT10 ..113 K7
Church Crs *RMAID* ME17 ....188 G5
Churchdown *BMLY* BR1 ....62 C3
Church Dr *WWKM* BR4 ....85 H7
Church Farm Cl *HOO/HM* ME3 ....73 L3
Church Farm Rd *FAVT* ME13 ......97 P5
Church Farm Wy *SWCH* CT15 ...201 J4
Church Fld *DART* DA1 ....26 D1
   EDEN TN8 ....206 E9
   RASHE TN25 ....286 A7
   SEV TN13 ....148 E7
   SNOD ME16 ....124 A4
Churchfield Pl *MARC* CT9 ....15 G5
Churchfield Rd *WELL* DA16 ....44 C4
Churchfields *BRDST* CT10 ....113 L6
Church Flds *E/WMAL* ME19 ....153 J4
Churchfields *GNWCH* SE10 ....26 A8
Churchfields Rd *BECK* BR3 ....61 K8
Churchfields Ter *ROCH* ME1 ....18 E7
Churchfield Wy *RASHE* TN25 ....223 P8
Church Gn *BRXN/ST* SW9 * 40 A3
Church Gn *DEAL* CT14 ....157 P9
   STPH/PW TN12 ....245 H3
   STPH/PW TN12 ....246 B7
   STRD ME2 ....72 C7
Church Gv *LEW* SE13 ....41 P5
Church Hts *HYTHE* CT21 * 309 H5
Church Hl *ASH* TN23 ....41 K9
   BGR/WK TN15 ....181 H5
   BH/WHM TN16 ....145 N7
   CANTW/ST CT2 ....166 B5
   DART DA1 ....45 N5
   DART DA1 ....66 D2
   DVE/WH CT16 * 290 E2
   FAV ME13 ....134 B8
   GRH DA9 ....47 L3
   HDCN TN27 ....220 B2
   ORP BR6 ....67 H3
   RASHW TN26 ....279 M9
   RASHW TN25 ....280 C3
   RCANTW CT4 ....194 C3

RDV CT15 ....230 C9
RDV CT15 ....231 P9
RDV CT15 ....259 N1
RFOLK CT18 ....288 G8
RMAID ME17 ....185 N9
RSEV TN14 ....116 D9
RSIT ME9 ....128 A6
RSIT ME9 ....160 E5
TENT TN30 ....333 J2
WALD ME5 ....95 P4
WOOL/PLUM SE18 ....26 C6
Church Hollow *PUR* RM19 ....30 D8
Church Hyde
   WOOL/PLUM SE18 ....27 M9
Churchill Av *DEAL* CT14 ....233 H7
   FOLKN CT19 ....310 F3
   HB CT6 ....108 A6
   WALD ME5 ....95 L8
Churchill Cl *DART* DA1 ....310 G3
   FOLKN CT19 ....310 G3
   RCANTW CT4 ....197 L2
Churchill Crs *RDV* CT15 ....255 P5
   RDV CT15 ....292 E2
Churchill House Hts
   DVE/WH CT16 * 291 J4
Churchill Pl *POP/IOD* E14 ....25 L4
Churchill Rd *CAN/RD* E16 ....26 D7
   CANT CT1 ....167 H6
   DVW CT17 ....291 H9
   EYN DA4 ....89 P1
   GRAYS RM17..............................32 E9
   GVW DA11 ....49 K9
   IOS ME12 ....78 D1
Churchill Sq *E/WMAL* ME19 ....153 H9
Churchill Vw *CANTW/ST* CT2 ....8 B1
Churchill Wy *BH/WHM* TN16 .....115 N9
   BMLY BR1 ....62 E8
The Churchlands *NROM* TN28 ...336 C7
Churchland Vls *NROM* TN28 * 336 G7
Church La *BGR/WK* TN15 ....149 N2
   CANT CT1 ....4 D5
   CANTW/ST CT2 ....137 L8
   CHAT ME4 ....72 F9
   CHST BR7 ....63 N7
   DEAL CT14 ....232 C8
   DEAL CT14 ....262 E3
   EGRIN RH19 ....265 J7
   E/WMAL ME19 ....122 B8
   FAV ME13 ....163 L6
   CDST RH9 ....174 A8
   GVE DA12 ....70 E2
   HAYES BR2 ....85 P5
   LYDD TN29 ....323 P9
   MAID/SHEP ME15 ....134 C4
   NROM TN28 ....336 D9
   OXTED RH8 ....174 G6
   PUR RM19 ....30 D8
   RAIN RM13 ....30 A3
   RASHE TN25 ....222 E2
   RASHE TN25 ....223 K5
   RASHE TN25 ....285 N4
   RASHW TN26 ....286 A2
   RASHW TN26 ....303 N2
   RCANTE CT3 ....138 F2
   RCANTE CT3 ....138 F4
   RCANTE CT3 ....139 N7
   RCANTE CT3 ....198 G6
   RCANTW CT4 ....196 A8
   RCANTW CT4 ....196 F1
   RCANTW CT4 ....225 M4
   RCANTW CT4 ....228 A3
   RCANTW CT4 ....228 C5
   RCANTW CT4 ....228 C5
   RDV CT15 ....259 P5
   RDV CT15 ....261 L5
   RDV CT15 ....312 C2
   RMAID ME17 ....188 F5
   RMAID ME17 ....217 L2
   RSIT ME9 ....98 C8
   RSIT ME9 ....127 P5
   RTON TN11 ....242 A3
   RYE TN31 ....330 B7
   RYE TN31 ....330 D9
   RYE TN31 ....332 G9
   STPH/PW TN12 ....210 D3
   TON TN9 ....210 F8
   WARL CR6 ....144 A2
   WARL CR6 ....144 F1
   WBY/YAL ME18 ....182 F6
   WSTB CT5 ....105 H8
Churchley Rd *SYD* SE26 ....61 H3
Church Manor Wy *ABYW* SE2 .....27 P7
Church Manorway *ERITH* DA8......29 K6
Church Mdw *CMBW* SE5 * 40 C1
Church Meadow
   STPH/PW TN12 * 273 P1
Church Mdw *DEAL* CT14 ....232 F3
Church Ms *MAID/BEAR* ME14 .....97 J6
Church Paddock Ct
   WLGTN SM6 ....82 C7
Church Pth *DEAL* CT14 ....232 G4
   GILL ME7 ....73 J9
   GRH DA9 ....47 M7
   GVW DA11 ....48 C7
Church Rd *FSTH* SE23 ....61 L9
Church Rd *ASH* TN23 ....41 K9
   BGR/WK TN15 ....120 B2
   BGR/WK TN15 ....149 L6
   BGR/WK TN15 ....150 B8
   BH/WHM TN16 ....145 N2
   BH/WHM TN16 ....147 J9
   BXLYHN DA7 ....45 J7
   CRBK TN17 ....274 D8
   CRBK TN17 ....295 N6
   CROY/NA CR0............................83 H8
   DEAL CT14 ....157 J8
   DVW CT17 ....291 H8
   E/WMAL ME19 ....152 F3
   ERITH DA8 ....29 H8
   EYN DA4 ....66 G5

FAV ME13 ....132 E2
FAV ME13 ....132 G6
FAV ME13 ....191 L5
FOLK CT20 ....10 B5
GRH DA9 ....47 L6
GVE DA12 ....69 N5
HART DA3 ....91 J2
HAWK TN18 ....328 C1
HAYES BR2 ....62 C9
HAYES BR2 ....115 N2
HYTHE CT21 ....309 H5
IOS ME12 ....79 K5
KEN/WIL TN24 ....253 H5
KEN/WIL TN24 ....253 J9
LING RH7 ....283 L2
LING RH7 ....234 C5
LYDD TN29 ....326 C2
LYDD TN29 ....326 G1
LYDD TN29 ....342 B5
MAID/BEAR ME14 ....157 N5
MAID/SHEP ME15 ....185 K1
MAID/SHEP ME15 ....186 C3
MARC CT9 ....15 J6
MEO DA13 ....69 N7
NROM TN28 ....336 C7
NRWD SE19 ....86 D9
ORP BR6 ....117 L1
RAM CT11 ....17 F5
RASHE TN25 ....283 N5
RASHE TN25 ....284 E5
RASHW TN26 ....303 M9
RCANTE CT3 ....138 A4
RCANTE CT3 ....168 C8
RCANTW CT4 ....164 B3
RDV CT15 ....260 B5
RFOLK CT18 ....287 H1
RMAID ME17 ....188 F6
RMAID ME17 ....216 F2
RTW TN1 ....22 D4
RTW TN1 ....295 J1
RSEV TN14 ....178 G8
RSEV TN14 ....100 E7
RSIT ME9 ....130 D1
RTON TN11 ....210 A4
SCUP DA14 ....64 C4
SIT ME10 ....100 A9
STH/RUST TN4 ....240 C7
STPH/PW TN12 ....243 J3
SWCM DA10 ....48 B5
SWLY BR8 ....66 D7
SWLY BR8 ....88 C4
TENT TN30 ....301 H8
TIL RM18 ....33 H9
TIL RM18 ....49 J2
WARL CR6 ....144 A2
WBY/YAL ME18 ....182 B5
WELL DA16 ....44 D5
WSTB CT5 ....82 B7
Church Row *CHST* BR7 ....63 N6
Churchsettle La *WADH* TN5 ....314 A1
Churchside *MED* DA13 ....122 B5
Church Sq *BH/WHM* TN16 ....113 N9
   RMAID ME17 ....189 L6
   RYE TN31 ....338 F7
Church St *BGR/WK* TN15 ....149 M5
   CANTW/ST CT2 ....113 K8
   CANTW/ST CT2 ....6 D5
   CHAT ME4 * 63 H9
   CROY/NA CR0............................82 C7
   DEAL CT14 ....232 G7
   DVE/WH CT16 ....8 D4
   EDEN TN8 ....206 E9
   EDEN TN8 ....267 J8
   FAV ME13 ....132 C5
   FOLK CT20 ....11 F5
   GILL ME7 ....73 L9
   GRAYS RM17 ....32 D8
   GVW DA11 ....49 M7
   HOO/HM ME3 ....51 J9
   HOO/HM ME3 ....52 B4
   HOO/HM ME3 ....73 L2
   MAID/BEAR ME14 ....13 F4
   MAID/SHEP ME15 ....157 N5
   MAID/SHEP ME15 ....185 L6
   MARC CT9 ....15 H6
   MEO DA13 ....68 E4
   MSTR CT12 ....141 K7
   RASHE TN25 ....223 P8
   RDV CT15 ....258 D5
   RMAID ME17 ....185 N8
   ROCH ME1 ....19 H7
   ROCH ME1 ....124 D5
   RSIT ME9 ....118 E5
   RSIT ME9 ....160 A8
   SWCH CT15 ....201 J4
   SWCH CT15 ....201 J8
   TON TN9 ....210 B7
   TON TN9 ....210 F8
   WBY/YAL ME18 ....183 P4
   WSTB CT5 ....105 N5
Church St (St Pauls)
   CANT CT1 ....5 G5
Church Ter *BGR/WK* TN15 * 149 L6
   LEW SE13 ....42 C4
   WALD ME5 ....95 P4
Church V *FSTH* SE23 ....61 L9
Church Vw *HB* CT6 ....107 P2
   HDCN TN27 ....220 B2
   LYDD TN29 ....325 L3
   RASHE TN25 ....306 B1
   SOCK/AV RM15 ....30 F5
Church Wk *DART* DA1 ....66 D2
   E/WMAL ME19 ....153 J2
   GVE DA12 ....49 P8
   HDCN TN27 ....247 M4
   RCANTW CT4 ....257 L5
Church Wy *OXTED* RH8 ....175 J8

Church Whitfield Rd
   RDV CT15 ....261 J7
Church Wood Cl
   CANTW/ST CT2 ....166 A2
Churchwood Dr *WSTB* CT5 ....106 C5
Churchyard *ASH* TN23 ....2 D4
Churn La *STPH/PW* TN12 ....243 N6
Churston Cl
   BRXS/STRHM SW2 * 40 B9
Chute Cl *RHAM* ME8 ....126 C1
Chyngton Cl *BFN/LL* DA15 ....64 B2
Cibber Rd *FSTH* SE23 ....61 K1
Cicely Rd *PECK* SE15 ....40 G2
Cinder Hill *DEAL* CT14 ....70 A3
Cinderford Wy *BMLY* BR1 ....62 C5
Cinder Hill La *RTON* TN11 ....209 H9
Cinder Hill Wd
   STPH/PW TN12 ....242 D8
Cinnabar Cl *WALD* ME5 * 125 M4
Cinnabar Dr *SIT* ME10 ....100 A8
Cinnamon Ct *CROY/NA* CR0 * 82 D4
   PECK SE15 ....40 F1
Cinnamon St *WAP* E1W 24 C4
Cinque Ports Av *HYTHE* CT21 ...308 G6
Cinque Ports Rd *NROM* TN28 ....336 C8
Cinque Ports St *RYE* TN31 ....338 E7
Cintra Pk *NRWD* SE19 ....60 F6
Circular Rd *DEAL* CT14 ....231 P2
Circular Wy *WOOL/PLUM* SE18 ...26 G9
Cirrus Pl *LYPST* EC2M 24 A1
Cirrus Sq *GNWCH* SE10 ....49 H2
Cirrus Crs *GVE* DA12 ....70 A4
Citadel Crs *DVW* CT17 ....8 A7
Citadel Rd *DVW* CT17 ....8 A7
Citroen Cl *HB* CT6 ....106 G2
Citron Ter *PECK* SE15 * 41 J4
City Vw *CANTW/ST* CT2 ....166 B4
City Wk *STHWK* SE1 ....24 B6
City Wy *ROCH* ME1 ....95 J2
Civic Sq *TIL* RM18 ....49 L3
Civic Wy *RTW* TN1 ....43 J6
Clacket La *BH/WHM* TN16 ....145 P9
Clack St *BERM/RHTH* SE16 ....24 F5
Claire Cswy *GRH* DA9 * 47 L5
Claire Ct *BRDST* CT10 ....113 N8
Claire Pl *POP/IOD* E14 ....25 K6
Clancy Gdns *CRBK* TN17 ....297 N2
Clandon Rd *WALD* ME5 ....126 A4
Clandon St *DEPT* SE8 ....41 N3
Clanricarde Gdns *RTW* TN1 ....22 D4
Clanricarde Rd *RTW* TN1 ....22 D4
Clanwilliam Rd *DEAL* CT14 ....233 J4
Clapham Hl *WSTB* CT5 ....105 L9
Claphatch La *WADH* TN5 ....314 E1
Clapper La *STPH/PW* TN12 ....246 A5
Clare Av *TON* TN9 ....210 C9
Clare Cswy *GRH* DA9 ....47 L5
Clare Cnr *BRDST* CT10 * 43 M8
Clare Ct *CTHM* CR3 ....144 D8
Clare Cres *RTW* TN1 ....43 J6
Clare La *E/WMAL* ME19 ....153 M4
Claremont Cl *CAN/RD* E16 ....27 H4
   CDW/CHF RM16 ....32 D6
   ORP BR6 ....86 B8
Claremont Crs *DART* DA1 ....45 N5
Claremont Gdns *RAM* CT11 ....16 E3
   RTW TN1 ....43 J6
Claremont Pl *CANT* CT1 ....4 C7
   CRBK TN17 ....318 C2
Claremont Rd *BMLY* BR1 ....85 P1
   CROY/NA CR0............................83 M5
   DEAL CT14 ....263 H2
   FOLK CT20 ....10 D4
   MAID/BEAR ME14 ....13 J3
   RTW TN1 ....22 E6
Claremont St *GNWCH* SE10 ....25 L9
   HB CT6 ....107 H3
Claremont Vls *CMBW* SE5 * 40 D1
Claremont Wy *CHAT* ME4 ....6 C6
Clare Rd *HAYES* BR2 ....85 P1
   MARC CT9 ....113 J5
Clarence Ct *MAID/BEAR* ME14 ..156 B8
Clarence Crs *SCUP* DA14 ....64 D2
Clarence Dr *EGRIN* RH19 ....265 J4
Clarence Gdns *IOS* ME12 ....80 B4
Clarence Pl *DEAL* CT14 ....232 G7
   DVW CT17 ....313 L1
   GVE DA12 ....49 M8
Clarence Rd *BH/WHM* TN16 ......146 A3
   BMLY BR1 ....63 J9
   BXLYHS DA6 ....44 G5
   CHAT ME4 ....95 N4
   CROY/NA CR0............................83 J4
   DEAL CT14 ....233 J6
   DEPT SE8 ....25 J3
   ELTH/MOT SE9 ....63 J1
   GRAYS RM17..............................32 E9
   HB CT6 ....107 J1
   RAM CT11 ....16 A5
   RFOLK CT18 ....311 L2
   RTW TN1 ....22 D4
   SIT ME10 ....64 D2
   WLGTN SM6 ....82 B4
Clarence Rw *GVE* DA12 ....49 M8
   RTW TN1 ....22 D4
Clarence St *FOLK* CT20 ....11 F3
   HB CT6 ....107 K1
Clarendon Cl
   MAID/BEAR ME14 ....156 D8
   SIT ME10 ....129 N4
   STMC/STPC BR5.........................64 C9
Clarendon Dr *STRD* ME2 ....72 A6
Clarendon Gdns *RAM* CT11 ....16 E4
   RDART DA2 ....47 K9
   RTWE/PEM TN2 ....270 C7
Clarendon Gn *STMC/STPC* BR5 ..64 C9
Clarendon Gv *STMC/STPC* BR5 ..87 H1
Clarendon Ms *BRDST* CT10 ....113 M9
   NROM TN28 ....337 H5
Clarendon Pth
   STMC/STPC BR5.........................87 H1
Clarendon Pl *DVW* CT17 ....8 A5

MAID/SHEP ME15 * 13 G5
RDART DA2 65 M4
SEV TN13 * 20 D3
Clarendon Ri LEW SE13 42 A4
Clarendon Rd BRDST CT10 113 M9
CROY/NA CR0 82 G6
DVW CT17 8 B5
GVE DA12 49 N7
MARG CT9 15 K4
RCANTE CT3 229 J1
SEV TN13 20 D3
WLGTN SM6 82 B9
Clarendon St DVW CT17 291 J8
HB CT6 107 H2
Clarendon Wy CHST BR7 64 B9
RTWE/PEM TN2 270 C7
Clarens St CAT SE6 61 M1
Clare Rd NWCR SE14 41 M3
WSTB CT5 105 M4
Claret Gdns SNWD SE25 83 K1
Clareville Rd STMC/STPC BR5 86 D6
Clare Wy BXLYHN DA7 44 G2
SEV TN13 179 H4
Clarewood Dr E/WMAL ME19 153 M4
Claribel Rd BRXN/ST SW9 40 B3
Claridge Cl GILL ME7 126 C1
Claridge Gdns LING RH7 235 K7
Claridge Ms HYTHE CT21 * 309 H5
Claridges Md LING RH7 235 K7
Clarkbourne Dr GRAYS RM17 32 E9
Clark Cl ERITH DA8 46 A2
Clarke Crs KEN/WIL TN24 253 J5
Clarke's Cl DEAL CT14 232 E5
Clarkes Green Rd
BGR/WK TN15 119 M8
Clark Ms DIT/AY ME20 154 E3
Clark Rd NROM TN28 337 K9
Clarks La RSEV TN14 117 N6
WARL CR6 145 L8
Clarkson Rd CAN/RD E16 26 A2
Clark St WCHPL E1 24 F2
Claston Cl DART DA1 45 N5
Claude Rd PECK SE15 41 H3
Claude St POP/IOD E14 25 K7
Claudian Wy CDW/CHF RM16 33 J6
Claudius Gv ASH TN23 282 C3
Clavadal Rd STPH/PW TN12 243 H2
Clavell Cl RHAM ME8 126 G2
Clavell St GNWCH SE10 25 M9
Clave St WAP E1W 24 F4
Claxfield Rd RSIT ME9 130 F6
Claybank Gv LEW SE13 41 P4
Claybridge Rd LEE/GVPK SE12 62 G3
Clayburn Gdns SOCK/AV RM15 31 L4
Claydon Dr CROY/NA CR0 82 D8
Claydown Ms
WOOL/PLUM SE18 27 H8
Clayfarm Rd ELTH/MOT SE9 63 N1
Clayford LING RH7 235 L7
Claygate ASH TN23 282 B3
MAID/SHEP ME15 186 A2
RMAID ME17 187 N1
Claygate Crs CROY/NA CR0 114 F1
Claygate Cross BGR/WK TN15 151 K9
Claygate La RTON TN11 181 J6
Claygate Rd STPH/PW TN12 214 A8
WBY/YAL ME18 213 M6
Clayhill CRBK TN17 274 C9
Clayhill Crs ELTH/MOT SE9 63 H3
Clay Hill Rd RRTW TN3 272 E8
Claylands Pl BRXN/ST SW9 40 A1
Clay La LING RH7 234 A7
Clays Cl EGRIN RH19 265 H8
Clayton Cl EHAM E6 26 G2
Clayton Croft Rd RDART DA2 66 A1
Clayton Dr DEPT SE8 25 H8
Clayton Ms GNWCH SE10 42 B2
Clayton Rd PECK SE15 40 G2
Clayton's La RRTW TN3 268 D7
Claytonville Ter BELV DA17 * 29 H5
Clay Wood Cl ORP BR6 86 F4
Claywood La RDART DA2 68 B2
Clayworth Cl BFN/LL DA15 44 D7
Cleanthus Cl
WOOL/PLUM SE18 43 M2
Cleanthus Rd
WOOL/PLUM SE18 43 M2
Clearbrook Wy WCHPL E1 24 F2
Clearmount Dr HDCN TN27 221 H2
Clearway BGR/WK TN15 152 B3
Cleave Av ORP BR6 116 F1
Cleaverholme Cl SNWD SE25 83 N3
Cleaver La RAM CT11 17 F3
Cleave Rd GILL ME7 96 B4
Cleavers CRBK TN17 276 D8
Cleavesland WBY/YAL ME18 213 M5
Cleeve Av RTWE/PEM TN2 23 K7
Cleeve Ct E/WMAL ME19 183 J1
Cleeve Hl FSTH SE23 41 H9
Cleeve Park Gdns SCUP DA14 64 D1
Clegg St WAP E1W 24 E4
Clematis Av RHAM ME8 96 E9
Clemence St POP/IOD E14 25 J1
Clement Cl CANT CT1 5 H2
SIT ME10 99 M6
Clement Ct MAIDW ME16 12 A2
Clementine Cl HB CT6 108 A6
Clement Rd BECK BR3 61 K8
Clements Av CAN/RD E16 26 B3
Clement's La MANHO EC4N 24 A3
Clements Rd BERM/RHTH SE16 24 D6
MSTR CT12 143 H2
Clement St SWLY BR8 66 D5
Clenches Farm La SEV TN13 20 C6
Clenches Farm Rd SEV TN13 20 D6
Clendon Wy WOOL/PLUM SE18 27 L7
Clerke Dr SIT ME10 99 P6
Clerks Fld HDCN TN27 247 M4
Clermont Cl GILL ME7 126 D1
Clevedon Ct RASHE TN25 192 D9
Clevedon Rd PGE/AN SE20 61 K7
Cleveland RTWE/PEM TN2 23 J2
Cleveland Cl DVE/WH CT16 291 J4
Cleveland Rd GILL ME7 73 K9
WELL DA16 44 B3
Clevely Cl CHARL SE7 26 E7
Cleve Rd SCUP DA14 64 F2
Cleves Crs CROY/NA CR0 114 F5
Cleves Rd BGR/WK TN15 149 K2
Cleves Wy ASH TN23 252 B9
Clewson Ri MAID/BEAR ME14 155 N4
Cliff Av HB CT6 107 P1
Cliff Cl HYTHE CT21 309 J4
Cliff Dr HB CT6 107 H2
IOS ME12 80 C3
Cliffe Av MARG CT9 14 A6
Cliffe Rd DEAL CT14 263 J2
SAND/SEL CR2 83 J9
STRD ME2 72 B7
Cliff Fld WGOS CT8 111 K5
Cliff Gdns IOS ME12 58 E9
Cliff Hl RMAID ME17 185 P7
Cliff Hill Rd RMAID ME17 185 P7
Clifford Av CHST BR7 63 K5
WLGTN SM6 82 B8
Clifford Dr BRXN/ST SW9 40 B5
Clifford Gdns DEAL CT14 232 F7
Clifford Rd CDW/CHF RM16 32 A5
SNWD SE25 83 M1
WSTB CT5 105 N6
Cliff Reach GRH DA9 47 L7
Cliff Rd BRCH CT7 110 F5
BRDST CT10 113 N6
FOLK CT20 310 D8
HYTHE CT21 309 L4
WSTB CT5 105 N3
Cliff Sea Gv HB CT6 107 H2
Cliffs End Gv MSTR CT12 142 C7
Cliffs End Rd MSTR CT12 142 C7
Cliffside Dr BRDST CT10 143 M3
Cliff St RAM CT11 17 F5
Cliff Ter DEPT SE8 41 N3
MARG CT9 15 J2
Clifftown Gdns HB CT6 106 G2
Cliff View Gdns IOS ME12 80 B5
Cliffview Rd LEW SE13 41 N4
Cliff View Rd MSTR CT12 142 C6
Cliff Wk CAN/RD E16 26 A1
Clifton Cl MAID/BEAR ME14 13 J2
ORP BR6 86 D9
STRD ME2 71 P8
Clifton Ct BECK BR3 * 61 P7
Clifton Crs FOLK CT20 10 B7
PECK SE15 41 H1
Clifton Gdns CANTW/ST CT2 4 A1
FOLK CT20 10 D6
MARG CT9 15 J4
Clifton Gv GVW DA11 49 M8
Clifton Lawn RAM CT11 * 16 E6
Clifton Marine Pde GVW DA11 49 L7
Clifton Ms SNWD SE25 83 K1
Clifton Pl BERM/RHTH SE16 24 F5
MARG CT9 15 K3
RTW TN1 22 E6
Clifton Ri NWCR SE14 41 L1
Clifton Rd CAN/RD E16 25 P1
FOLK CT20 10 C6
GILL ME7 73 J8
GVW DA11 49 L7
MARG CT9 15 K4
RAM CT11 16 A1
RTWE/PEM TN2 270 F1
SCUP DA14 64 A3
SNWD SE25 83 K1
WELL DA16 44 E4
WLGTN SM6 82 A9
WSTB CT5 105 L6
Clifton St MARG CT9 15 J3
SDTCH EC2A 24 B1
Cliftonville Av MARG CT9 112 F3
MSTR CT12 142 G3
Clifton Wy PECK SE15 41 J1
Clinch St HOO/HM ME3 53 M3
Clink St STHWK SE1 24 A4
Clinton Av STRD ME2 71 M7
WELL DA16 44 C5
Clinton Cl RMAID ME17 184 G8
Clinton Hl LING RH7 235 K8
Clinton La EDEN TN8 207 L7
Clinton Ter DEPT SE8 * 25 K9
Clints La RCANTW CT4 228 F9
Clipper Bvd GRH DA9 47 L5
Clipper Bvd West GRH DA9 47 K4
Clipper Cl BERM/RHTH SE16 24 G5
STRD ME2 72 E8
Clipper Ct STRD ME2 * 72 E8
Clipper Crs GVE DA12 70 B3
Clipper Wy LEW SE13 42 A5
Clive Av DART DA1 45 P7
Cliveden Cl MAIDW ME16 155 J5
Clive Dennis Ct KEN/WIL TN24 3 K5
Clive Rd BELV DA17 28 F7
DUL SE21 60 D2
GVW DA11 49 M7
MARG CT9 112 F8
MSTR CT12 142 C6
ROCH ME1 95 H3
SIT ME10 99 J9
Clockhouse ASH TN23 252 B8
RTWE/PEM TN2 271 J2
Clockhouse La CDW/CHF RM16 31 N4
Clockhouse Pk RASHE TN25 192 E9
Clock House Rd BECK BR3 61 L9
Clock Tower Ms THMD SE28 28 A3
Cloister Gdns SNWD SE25 83 N3
Cloisterham Rd ROCH ME1 95 J7
Cloisters SIT ME10 * 129 M1
Cloisters Av HAYES BR2 86 A2
The Cloisters RAM CT11 16 D6
Cloonmore Av ORP BR6 86 G9
The Close ASH TN23 282 B1
BECK BR3 84 B1
BGR/WK TN15 150 G6
BGR/WK TN15 151 K4
BH/WHM TN16 * 146 C1
BXLY DA5 45 J9
CANTW/ST CT2 136 F9
CDW/CHF RM16 32 C5
E/WMAL ME19 123 J8
EDEN TN8 207 P8
EGRIN RH19 264 G8
FAV ME13 132 F7
FOLKN CT19 311 H3
HART DA3 68 F8
HYTHE CT21 308 G3
RASHE TN25 223 P9
RCANTW CT4 * 197 L2
RDART DA2 66 C2
RDV CT15 260 A8
ROCH ME1 19 F7
RYE TN31 338 D6
SCUP DA14 64 D4
SEV TN13 148 D9
SNWD SE25 * 83 M3
STMC/STPC BR5 86 F3
Cloth Hall Gdns HDCN TN27 278 B6
Clothier St HDTCH EC3A 24 B2
Clothworkers Rd
WOOL/PLUM SE18 43 P1
Cloudberry Cl MAIDW ME16 12 A1
Cloudesley Cl ROCH ME1 94 G5
Cloudesley Rd BXLYHN DA7 45 H2
ERITH DA8 45 P2
Clouston Cl WLGTN SM6 82 D9
Clove Crs POP/IOD E14 25 M3
Clovelly Dr IOS ME12 58 B8
Clovelly Rd BXLYHN DA7 28 D9
WSTB CT5 105 L7
Clovelly Wy ORP BR6 86 G3
WCHPL E1 24 F2
Clover Bank Vw WALD ME5 95 N8
Cloverdale Gdns BFN/LL DA15 44 B7
Clover Lay RHAM ME8 97 L4
Clover Ri WSTB CT5 106 A5
Clover Rd HOO/HM ME3 73 L4
The Clovers GVW DA11 69 J3
Clover St CHAT ME4 6 C5
Clover Ter MAID/SHEP ME15 * 186 A3
Clover Wy STPH/PW TN12 243 H4
Clowders Rd CAT SE6 61 M2
Clowes Ct CANTW/ST CT2 * 136 B9
Cloysters Gn WAP E1W * 24 D4
Clubb's La LYDD TN29 334 E6
Club Gardens Rd HAYES BR2 85 K4
Cluny Est STHWK SE1 24 B6
Cluny Pl STHWK SE1 24 B6
Cluny Rd FAV ME13 133 J6
Clutton St POP/IOD E14 25 L1
Clyde TIL RM18 34 B7
Clyde Rd CROY/NA CR0 83 L6
TONN TN10 210 F5
WLGTN SM6 82 B9
Clyde St CANT CT1 * 5 G2
DEPT SE8 25 J9
IOS ME12 57 M6
Clyde Ter FSTH SE23 61 J1
Clyde V FSTH SE23 61 J1
Clydon Cl ERITH DA8 29 K9
Clynton Wy ASH TN23 282 D1
Coach Dr RASHW TN26 251 M2
The Coach Dr MEO DA13 121 P6
Coach & Horses Pas
RTWE/PEM TN2 22 C7
Coach House Ms FSTH SE23 41 J7
NWCR SE14 * 41 K2
Coach Rd BGR/WK TN15 150 D9
HDCN TN27 219 M4
RFOLK CT18 288 C4
STH/RUST TN4 269 P5
The Coachyard MAIDW ME16 154 G9
Coalpit La RSIT ME9 159 P6
Coal Post Cl ORP BR6 116 G2
Coast Dr LYDD TN29 337 L3
Coastguard Sq RYE TN31 339 K9
Coast Rd NROM TN28 337 L5
Coates Hill Rd BMLY BR1 63 L8
Coats Av IOS ME12 57 J8
Cobay Cl HYTHE CT21 309 J5
Cobb Cl STRD ME2 71 M7
Cobbets Wy EDEN TN8 236 D1
Cobbett Cl E/WMAL ME19 153 N4
Cobbett Rd ELTH/MOT SE9 43 J4
Cobbett's Ride
RTWE/PEM TN2 270 C7
Cobblers Bridge Rd HB CT6 107 J2
Cobblestone Pl CROY/NA CR0 83 H5
Cobblestones GILL ME7 96 C9
Cobbs Cl STPH/PW TN12 242 G3
WBY/YAL ME18 183 M4
Cobbs Hl RCANTW CT4 194 D1
Cobbs Ms FOLK CT20 10 D5
Cobbs Pl MARG CT9 15 G3
Cobb St WCHPL E1 24 C2
Cob Cl BGR/WK TN15 150 F6
Cobden Ms SYD SE26 61 H4
Cobden Pl CANT CT1 5 F3
Cobden Rd CHAT ME4 95 N4
HYTHE CT21 308 G6
ORP BR6 86 E8
SEV TN13 149 H8
SNWD SE25 83 M2
Cobdown Cl DIT/AY ME20 154 A2
Cobdown Gv RHAM ME8 97 K4
Cob Dr GVE DA12 70 G4
Cobfield RMAID ME17 216 D1
Cobham CDW/CHF RM16 32 C5
Cobham Av SIT ME10 129 M4
Cobhambury Rd GVE DA12 93 H1
Cobham Cha FAV ME13 132 E5
Cobham Cl BFN/LL DA15 44 D7
CANT CT1 167 H6
GRH DA9 47 P7
HAYES BR2 85 P4
MAIDW ME16 12 B4
STRD ME2 71 N8
Cobham Dr E/WMAL ME19 153 K9
Cobham Pl BXLYHS DA6 44 F6
Cobham Ri GILL ME7 96 B1
Cobhams RRTW TN3 239 M9
Cobham St GVW DA11 49 L8
Cobham Ter GRH DA9 * 47 P6
GVW DA11 * 49 K9
Cobland Rd LEE/GVPK SE12 62 G3
Cobourg Rd CMBW SE5 24 C9
Cobsden Cl LYDD TN29 337 M1
Cobsden Rd LYDD TN29 337 L1
Cobtree Cl WALD ME5 95 P6
Cobtree Rd RMAID ME17 185 H8
Cockerhurst Rd RSEV TN14 118 D3
Cockering Rd RCANTW CT4 195 L2
Cock La RASHW TN26 304 D8
RCANTW CT4 257 L5
Cockmannings La
STMC/STPC BR5 87 L5
Cockmannings Rd
STMC/STPC BR5 87 L4
Cockreed La NROM TN28 336 G6
Cocksett Av ORP BR6 116 F1
Cocksure La SCUP DA14 65 J3
Codling Cl WAP E1W 24 D4
Codrington Crs GVE DA12 69 N4
Codrington Gdns GVE DA12 69 P4
Codrington Hl FSTH SE23 41 L8
Codrington Rd RAM CT11 16 D4
Coe Av SNWD SE25 83 M3
Coffey St DEPT SE8 41 N1
Cogans Ter CANT CT1 166 D6
Cogate Rd STPH/PW TN12 242 F3
Coinston Av RAM CT11 142 F5
Cokers La DUL SE21 40 C9
Coke St WCHPL E1 24 D2
Colburn Rd BRDST CT10 143 M3
Colby Rd NRWD SE19 60 E4
Colchester Cl WALD ME5 95 L7
Colchester St WCHPL E1 24 C2
Cold Arbor Rd SEV TN13 148 C9
Coldbath St LEW SE13 41 P3
Coldblow DEAL CT14 232 F8
Cold Blow Crs BXLY DA5 45 M9
Coldblow La
MAID/BEAR ME14 157 K3
NWCR SE14 41 K1
Coldbridge La RMAID ME17 218 G5
Cold Harbour CANT CT1 5 G1
Coldharbour POP/IOD E14 25 M4
Coldharbour Crest
ELTH/MOT SE9 * 63 L2
Cold Harbour La RSIT ME9 98 G8
Coldharbour La BRXN/ST SW9 40 A5
DIT/AY ME20 154 F3
LYDD TN29 335 K8
MAID/BEAR ME14 157 L3
RAIN RM13 29 M4
RASHE TN25 224 A8
RCANTW CT4 197 P4
RTON TN11 210 B4
RYE TN31 332 C9
SIT ME10 99 N5
Coldharbour Pl CMBW SE5 40 C3
Coldharbour Rd CRBK TN17 318 A1
CROY/NA CR0 82 F9
GVW DA11 69 J1
Cold Harbour Rd
RMAID ME17 190 E6
Coldharbour Rd RTON TN11 238 C9
Coldharbour Wy CROY/NA CR0 82 F9
Coldred Hl RDV CT15 260 A8
Coldred Rd MAID/SHEP ME15 186 C7
RDV CT15 259 P1
Coldrum La E/WMAL ME19 122 D8
Coldshott OXTED RH8 175 K9
Coldswood Rd MSTR CT12 142 D2
Cole Av CDW/CHF RM16 33 K7
Colebrook Ri HAYES BR2 62 C8
Colebrook Rd STH/RUST TN4 270 F1
Colebrook St ERITH DA8 29 L9
Coleby Pth CMBW SE5 * 40 D1
Cole Cl THMD SE28 28 A4
Colegate Dr
MAID/BEAR ME14 156 F8
Colegates Cl FAV ME13 132 D3
Colegates Ct FAV ME13 132 E3
Colegates Rd FAV ME13 132 D3
Colegrove Rd PECK SE15 24 C9
Coleman Cl SNWD SE25 60 G8
Coleman Crs MSTR CT12 143 H3
Coleman Dr SIT ME10 99 N5
Coleman Rd BELV DA17 28 F6
CMBW SE5 40 E1
Colemans Cl LYDD TN29 342 C6
Colemans Heath
ELTH/MOT SE9 63 L2
Coleman's Stairs Rd
BRCH CT7 111 H5
Coleman St LOTH EC2R 24 A2
Coleman's Yd RAM CT11 17 F4
Colenso Vls STPH/PW TN12 * 245 H3
Colepits Wood Rd
ELTH/MOT SE9 43 P6
Coleraine Rd BKHTH/KID SE3 26 B9
Coleridge Cl DIT/AY ME20 123 P9
Coleridge Gdns RCANTE CT3 199 J9
Coleridge Rd CROY/NA CR0 83 P4
DART DA1 46 G5
TIL RM18 49 N3
Coleridge Wy ORP BR6 87 H3
Cole Rd FAV ME13 133 H6
Colesburg Rd BECK BR3 61 M9
Coleshall Cl MAID/SHEP ME15 186 C5
Coles La BH/WHM TN16 147 K8
Cole Ter RMAID ME17 * 189 K6
Colets Orch RSEV TN14 148 G1
Colette Cl BRDST CT10 113 M3
Coleville Crs LYDD TN29 343 K5
Colewood Dr STRD ME2 71 K7
Colewood Rd WSTB CT5 106 D3
Colfe & Hatcliffe Glebe
LEW SE13 * 41 P6
Colfe Rd FSTH SE23 41 L9
Colfe Wy SIT ME10 99 P6
Colin Blythe Rd TONN TN10 211 J5
Colin Chapman Wy HART DA3 90 C7
Colin Cl CROY/NA CR0 84 C7
RDART DA2 47 H7
WWKM BR4 85 J7
Colin's Wy HYTHE CT21 309 M4
Collard Cl HB CT6 107 N2
Collard Rd KEN/WIL TN24 283 K1
Collards Cl MSTR CT12 140 D5
Collards La RCANTW CT4 257 J6
College Ap GNWCH SE10 25 M9
College Av GILL ME7 7 G4
GRAYS RM17 32 C7
MAID/SHEP ME15 12 E7
TON TN9 240 D2
College Cl EGRIN RH19 265 J7
LING RH7 234 G5
College Ct MAID/SHEP ME15 * 13 F7
College Dr RTWE/PEM TN2 23 J2
College East WCHPL E1 * 24 C1
College Gn NRWD SE19 60 E6
College La EGRIN RH19 265 J7
College Park Cl LEW SE13 42 B5
College Pl GRH DA9 48 A5
College Rd BMLY BR1 62 E7
CANT CT1 5 H4
CHAT ME4 72 G8
CROY/NA CR0 83 J6
DEAL CT14 233 J1
DIT/AY ME20 154 A1
DUL SE21 40 E8
GRAYS RM17 32 D7
GVW DA11 48 F6
MAID/SHEP ME15 13 F6
MAID/SHEP ME15 185 L1
MARG CT9 15 K7
RAM CT11 143 K3
SIT ME10 129 L3
SWLY BR8 65 N6
College Rw DVW CT17 * 291 J8
The College ROCH ME1 * 19 G5
College Vw ELTH/MOT SE9 43 H9
College Wk MAID/SHEP ME15 13 F7
MARG CT9 15 G4
College Wy RCANTE CT3 169 K9
College Yd ROCH ME1 19 F4
Coller Crs RDART DA2 67 L4
Collet Rd BGR/WK TN15 149 K2
Collett Rd BERM/RHTH SE16 24 D6
Collet Wk RHAM ME8 126 G1
Collie Dr ASH TN23 282 B3
Collier Cl EHAM E6 27 J3
Colliers Water La THHTH CR7 82 F2
Colliers Wd HAYES BR2 85 N9
Collindale Av BFN/LL DA15 44 C9
ERITH DA8 28 G9
Collingbourne ASH TN23 282 B2
Collington Cl GVW DA11 49 J8
Collington St GNWCH SE10 * 25 N8
Collington Ter
MAID/SHEP ME15 186 C7
Collingtree Rd SYD SE26 61 J3
Colling Wood Cl PGE/AN SE20 61 H7
Collingwood Cl BRDST CT10 113 K9
EGRIN RH19 265 J9
WGOS CT8 111 L6
Collingwood Ri FOLK CT20 310 B6
Collingwood Rd DIT/AY ME20 125 H6
RDV CT15 262 E8
WSTB CT5 105 K5
Collingwood Rd East
RDV CT15 262 F7
Collins Rd HB CT6 107 H4
Collins St BKHTH/KID SE3 42 C3
Collison Pl TENT TN30 301 L8
Colls St STRD ME2 72 A7
Coll's Rd PECK SE15 41 J2
Collyer Av CROY/NA CR0 82 D8
Collyer Pl PECK SE15 40 G2
Collyer Rd CROY/NA CR0 82 D8
Colman Pde
MAID/BEAR ME14 * 13 F4
Colman Rd CAN/RD E16 26 D1
Colmore Ms PECK SE15 41 H2
Colne TIL RM18 34 B6
Colne Cl SOCK/AV RM15 31 M3
Colne Rd TONN TN10 210 E5
Colney Rd DART DA1 46 F7
Colombo Sq MSTR CT12 142 F3
Colomb St GNWCH SE10 25 P8
Colonel's La FAV ME13 164 B1
Colonel Stephens Wy
TENT TN30 301 H6
Colonel's Wy STH/RUST TN4 240 D7
The Colonnade DEPT SE8 * 25 J7
Colorado Cl DVE/WH CT16 291 J4
Colson Dr RSIT ME9 99 L3
Colson Rd CROY/NA CR0 83 J6
Coltness Crs ABYW SE2 28 A8
Colton Crs DVE/WH CT16 291 J3
Coltsfoot Ct GRAYS RM17 32 E9
Coltsfoot Dr
MAID/BEAR ME14 156 C8
Coltsfoot La OXTED RH8 175 J9
Colts Hill Pl STPH/PW TN12 * 242 C4
Coltstead HART DA3 91 H7
Columbia Av WSTB CT5 105 J7
Columbia Wharf Rd
GRAYS RM17 32 B9
Columbine Av EHAM E6 26 F1
Columbine Cl E/WMAL ME19 153 N3
STRD ME2 71 N8
WSTB CT5 105 K8
Columbine Rd
E/WMAL ME19 153 N3
STRD ME2 71 N8
Columbine Wy LEW SE13 * 42 A3
Columbus Av MSTR CT12 141 L3
Colveiw Ct ELTH/MOT SE9 43 H9
Colvin Cl SYD SE26 61 J4
Colvin Rd THHTH CR7 82 F2
Colwell Rd EDUL SE22 40 F6
Colworth Rd CROY/NA CR0 83 M5
Colyer Cl ELTH/MOT SE9 63 M1
Colyer Rd GVW DA11 69 H1
Colyers Cl ERITH DA8 45 M2
Colyers La ERITH DA8 45 L2
Colyton Cl WELL DA16 44 F2
Colyton La STRHM/NOR SW16 60 A4
Colyton Rd EDUL SE22 41 H6
Combe Av BKHTH/KID SE3 42 D1
Combe Bank Dr RSEV TN14 147 M8
Combedale Rd GNWCH SE10 26 B8
Comber Gv CMBW SE5 40 C1
Combeside WOOL/PLUM SE18 44 B1

Combwell Crs ABYW SE2 ....27 P6
Comerford Rd BROCKY SE4 ....41 L5
Comet Cl PUR RM19 ....30 D7
Comet Pl DEPT SE8 ....41 N1
Comet St DEPT SE8 ....41 N1
Comforts Farm Av OXTED RH8 ....175 J9
Comfrey Ct GRAYS RM17 ....32 E9
Command Rd MAID/BEAR ME14 ....155 L4
Commerce Wy CROY/NA CR0 ....82 E7
EDEN TN8 ....206 D7
Commercial Pl GVE DA12 ....49 N7
Commercial Quay DVW CT17 ....8 D6
Commercial Rd POP/IOD E14 ....25 H2
RTW TN1 ....23 F1
STPH/PW TN12 ....242 G3
STRD ME2 ....18 D2
TONN TN9 ....241 J9
WCHPL E1 ....24 C2
Commercial Wy PECK SE15 ....40 C1
Commerell Pl GNWCH SE10 ....26 A8
Commerell St GNWCH SE10 ....25 P8
Commissioners Ct CHAT ME4 ....6 C1
Commissioner's St STRD ME2 ....72 D7
Commodore Rd MAID/BEAR ME14 ....13 K2
Commodore St WCHPL E1 ....24 G1
Common La DVW CT17 ....290 F4
MAID ME3 ....52 C2
RDART DA2 ....66 A1
Common Rd BGR/WK TN15 ....150 E8
CRBK TN17 ....276 C7
HOO/HM ME3 ....72 B5
ROCH ME1 ....124 C3
RTON TN11 ....181 P9
Commonside HAYES BR2 ....85 M8
Commonside East MTCM CR4 ....82 C2
The Common ROCH ME1 ....19 G3
STH/RUST TN4 ....269 M4
Common Vw STH/RUST TN4 ....269 P5
Common Wall HOO/HM ME3 ....52 D2
Commonwealth Cl SIT ME10 ....130 A2
Commonwealth Wy ABYW SE2 ....28 A8
Commonwealth Wy MEO DA13 ....122 C5
Communications Pk STRD ME2 * 18 B5
Como Rd FSTH SE23 ....61 L1
Compass Cl ROCH ME1 ....95 H5
Compasses Rd RTON TN11 ....208 G8
The Compasses HOO/HM ME3 * 52 B2
Comp La BGR/WK TN15 ....151 M6
E/WMAL ME15 ....152 B5
Comport Gn CROY/NA CR0 ....115 H6
Compton Cl WALD ME5 ....126 A3
Compton Pl ERITH DA8 ....29 L9
Compton Rd CROY/NA CR0 ....83 N5
Comus Pl WALW SE17 ....24 M7
Comyns Cl CAN/RD E16 ....26 A1
Comyns Rd WCHPL E1 ....24 D3
Concord Av WALD ME5 ....95 K9
Concord Cl RTWE/PEM TN2 * 23 H2
STPH/PW TN12 ....242 F5
Concorde Dr EHAM E6 ....26 C1
Conder St POP/IOD E14 ....25 P7
Condor Cl IOS ME12 ....80 C4
Condover Crs WOOL/PLUM SE18 ....43 M1
Conduit Hl RYE TN31 ....338 F6
Conduit La SAND/SEL CR2 ....83 M9
Conduit Rd WOOL/PLUM SE18 ....27 J8
Conduit St FAV ME13 * 132 C5
Coney Banks FAV ME13 * 133 M5
Coneyburrow Rd RTWE/PEM TN2 ....271 H3
Coney Hall Pde WWKM BR4 ....85 H7
Coney Hill Rd WWKM BR4 ....85 H6
Conference Rd ABYW SE2 ....28 B7
Conghurst La HAWK TN18 ....317 J9
Congleton Gv WOOL/PLUM SE18 ....27 K8
Congo St WOOL/PLUM SE18 ....27 L8
Congress Rd ABYW SE2 ....28 B7
Congreve Rd ELTH/MOT SE9 ....43 K4
Congreve St WALW SE17 ....24 B7
Conifer Av HART DA3 ....91 H5
Conifer Cl ORP BR6 ....86 E8
Conifer Dr MEO DA13 ....122 A5
WALD ME5 ....126 A4
Conker Cl ASH TN23 ....282 F5
Conley St GNWCH SE10 * 25 P8
Connaught Av CDW/CHF RM16 ....32 C5
Connaught Br CAN/RD E16 ....26 E4
Connaught Cl MAID/SHEP ME15 ....186 C7
Connaught Gdns MARG CT9 ....15 H7
Connaught Ms WALD ME5 ....95 H4
Connaught Rd CAN/RD E16 ....26 E4
CHAT ME4 ....95 N4
DVW/CT16 ....291 L6
FOLK CT20 ....10 E4
GILL ME7 ....7 K2
MARG CT9 ....15 H7
SIT ME10 ....129 M2
WOOL/PLUM SE18 ....27 H8

Connaught Wy STH/RUST TN4 ....270 C3
Conrad Av CANT CT1 ....167 H1
Conrad Cl CDW/CHF RM16 ....32 C5
RHAM ME8 ....115 J5
Consort Cl MAID/BEAR ME14 ....13 J3
Consort Rd PECK SE15 ....41 H5
Constable Av CAN/RD E16 ....26 C4
Constable Rd BRCH CT7 ....111 L5
GVW DA11 ....69 J2
TONN TN10 * 211 H5
Constable's Rd DVE/WH CT16 ....8 F1
Constable Wk DUL SE21 ....60 F2
Constance Crs HAYES BR2 ....85 J5
Constance Rd CROY/NA CR0 ....82 C4
Constance St CAN/RD E16 ....26 F4
Constantine Rd ASH TN23 ....282 C5
Constitution Hill Rd STH/RUST TN4 ....240 B8
Constitution Rl CHAT ME4 ....95 N4
GVE DA12 ....49 N9
SNOD ME6 ....123 N5
Constitution Ri WOOL/PLUM SE18 ....43 L2
Constitution Rd WALD ME5 ....7 C7
Consul Gdns SWLY BR8 * 66 A6
Contessa Cl ORP BR6 ....86 F9
Convalescent La CRBK TN17 ....276 B6
Convent Cl BECK BR3 ....62 A6
RDV CT15 ....292 F1
Convent Hl NRWD SE19 ....60 C5
Convent Rd BRDST CT10 ....113 M4
Conway Cl BRCH CT7 ....110 H6
SNOD ME6 ....71 N6
Conway Gdns GRAYS RM17 ....48 F1
MTCM CR4 ....82 C1
Conway Ms GILL ME7 ....6 D1
Conway Rd MAIDW ME16 ....155 H6
WOOL/PLUM SE18 ....27 L7
Conyerd Rd BGR/WK TN15 ....151 J5
Conyer Rd RSIT ME9 ....101 K8
Conyngham La MSTR CT12 ....142 G2
Conyngham La RCANTW CT4 ....197 M1
Conyngham Rd HB CT6 ....108 A4
MSTR CT12 ....141 K7
Cooden Cl BMLY BR1 ....62 H1
RHAM ME8 ....97 K4
Cook Cl GRH DA9 ....47 P5
MAID ME5 ....95 P8
Cooke Cl CDW/CHF RM16 ....31 P6
Cookham Dene Cl CHST BR7 ....63 P7
Cookham Hl ROCH ME1 ....94 F4
Cookham Rd SWLY BR8 ....65 M1
Cookham Wood Rd ROCH ME1 ....94 C6
Cookhill Rd ABYW SE2 ....28 A5
Cooks La SIT ME10 ....99 M8
Cook's Lea SWCH CT13 ....201 J8
Cookson Gv ERITH DA8 ....45 K1
Cooks Whf ROCH ME1 ....19 K7
Coolfin Rd CAN/RD E16 ....26 C6
Cooling Cl MAID/BEAR ME14 ....155 P6
Cooling Common HOO/HM ME3 ....52 C8
Coolinge La FOLK CT20 ....310 C6
Coolinge Rd FOLK CT20 ....10 C6
Cooling Rd HOO/HM ME3 ....52 D6
HOO/HM ME3 ....53 J5
STRD ME2 ....72 B5
Cooling St HOO/HM ME3 ....52 D6
Coombe Av DVW CT17 ....83 K8
RSEV TN14 ....148 C5
Coombe Cl DVW CT17 ....291 H6
SNOD ME6 ....123 P6
WALD ME5 ....125 N2
Coombe Dr SIT ME10 ....130 B1
Coombe Farm La HOO/HM ME3 ....54 C2
Coombe Lands TENT TN30 ....332 A1
Coombe La CROY/NA CR0 ....83 N9
RCANTE CT3 ....200 F1
TENT TN30 ....301 H8
Coombe Lea BMLY BR1 ....62 B1
Coombe Ldg CHARL SE7 ....26 D9
Coombe Rd FOLKN CT19 ....310 C5
GVE DA11 ....69 L9
HOO/HM ME3 ....73 L2
MAID/SHEP ME15 ....185 L1
RDV CT15 ....290 E7
RSEV TN14 ....119 H9
SAND/SEL CR2 ....83 K8
SYD SE26 ....61 J5
Coombe Vw CROY/NA CR0 ....82 D4
Coombe Valley Rd DVW CT17 ....291 H7
Coombe Wy RFOLK CT18 ....309 K8
Coombe Wood La RFOLK CT18 ....288 E8
Coomb Fld EDEN TN8 ....236 D1
Coombefield Dr RDART DA2 ....67 K3
Coombs Ct RYE TN31 ....331 H8
Cooper Cl GRH DA9 ....47 L6
Cooper Rd CROY/NA CR0 ....82 F9
RYE TN31 ....338 D7
SNOD ME6 ....123 N7
WALD ME5 ....125 M2
Coopers Cl EYN DA4 ....67 J7
Cooper Shaw Rd TIL RM18 ....49 P7
Coopers La LEE/GVPK SE12 ....62 F1
RASHE TN25 ....264 G6
RRTW TN3 ....269 H2
Coopers Ms BECK BR3 ....61 N8
Cooper's Rd GVW DA11 ....49 J9
STHWK SE1 ....24 C8
Coopers Rw TWRH EC3N 24 C3
Cooper St CAN/RD E16 ....26 A1
Cooper Street Dro RCANTE CT3 ....171 J6
Cooper's Yd NRWD SE19 ....60 E5
Coote Rd BXLYHN DA7 ....45 H2
Cooting La RCANTE CT3 ....198 C8
Cooting Rd RCANTE CT3 ....228 C1
Copeland Rd PECK SE15 ....40 C3
Copeman Cl SYD SE26 ....61 J1
Copenhagen Pl POP/IOD E14 ....25 J2

Copenhagen Rd GILL ME7 ....7 H3
Copers Cope Rd BECK BR3 ....61 N7
Cope St BERM/RHTH SE16 ....24 G7
Copinger Cl CANTW/ST CT2 ....136 F9
Copland Av IOS ME12 ....78 C1
Coplands Ri RYE TN31 ....330 A6
Copleston Rd PECK SE15 ....40 E4
Copley Dene BMLY BR1 ....63 H7
Copperda La RYE TN31 ....330 D5
Coppelia Rd BKHTH/KID SE3 ....42 C5
Copperas St DEPT SE8 ....25 L9
Copper Beech Cl GVE DA12 ....49 P8
STMC/STPC BR5 ....87 K2
Copperfield Rd STRD ME2 ....71 L5
Copperfield Dr RMAID ME17 ....187 H7
Copperfield Rd BGR/WK ME15 ....95 H4
THMD SE28 ....28 E3
Copperfields BGR/WK TN15 ....149 L2
LYDD TN29 ....342 A6
The Copperfields ROCH ME1 * 18 D7
Copperfields Wk BGR/WK TN15 ....149 L2
Copperfield Wy CHST BR7 ....63 N5
Coppergate CANTW/ST CT2 ....4 D1
GILL ME7 ....96 C9
Coppergate Cl BMLY BR1 ....62 F7
Copperhouse La GILL ME7 ....73 P9
Copperhouse Rd STRD ME2 ....71 L8
Copperpenny Dr GILL ME7 ....126 E2
Copper Tree Ct MAID/SHEP ME15 ....185 M6
Copperwood KEN/WIL TN24 * 252 F5
Coppice Cl BECK BR3 ....84 E1
Coppice Ct GILL ME7 ....126 E1
Coppice Gv WALD ME5 ....125 P5
The Coppice BGR/WK TN15 ....180 A2
BXLY DA5 ....137 L7
CANTW/ST CT2 ....137 L2
DIT/AY ME20 ....154 D3
RHAM ME8 ....122 C5
RTWE/PEM TN2 ....271 N1
Coppice Side HART DA3 ....68 D9
The Copse ASH TN23 ....252 B6
HOO/HM ME3 ....73 L4
Copse Vw SAND/SEL CR2 ....116 A5
Copsewood Cl BFN/LL DA15 ....44 A7
Copse Av WWKM BR4 ....84 E7
Cop Street Rd RCANTE CT3 ....170 E9
Copt Cl CANTW/ST CT2 ....137 L6
Coptefield Dr BELV DA17 ....28 C6
Copthall HAWK TN18 * 330 C2
Copthall Av HAWK TN18 ....317 H5
LOTH EC2R 24 A2
Copthall Gdns FOLK CT20 ....10 E4
Copt Hall Rd BGR/WK TN15 ....150 D8
MEO DA13 ....92 C1
Copthorne Av HAYES BR2 ....86 A6
Copthorne Rd EGRIN RH19 ....264 B4
Copyhold Rd EGRIN RH19 ....264 C8
Coralline Wk ABYW SE2 ....28 B5
Corbet Pl WCHPL E1 ....24 C1
Corbett Cl CROY/NA CR0 ....116 C6
Corbett's La BERM/RHTH SE16 ....24 F7
Corbylands Rd BFN/LL DA15 ....44 A9
Cordelia Cl HNHL SE24 ....40 B5
Cordelia Crs ROCH ME1 ....94 F4
Cordelia St POP/IOD E14 ....25 N2
Cordingham Rd WSTB CT5 ....105 H8
Cording St POP/IOD E14 ....25 L1
Cordwell Rd LEW SE13 ....42 B6
Corelli Rd BKHTH/KID SE3 ....43 J2
Carlander Av POP/IOD E14 ....25 N2
Corinthian Manorway ERITH DA8 ....29 J7
Corinthian Rd ERITH DA8 ....29 J7
Cork La STPH/PW TN12 ....246 F9
Cork St BERM ME5 ....185 M6
Corkscrew Hl WWKM BR4 ....84 F6
Cork Sq WAP E1W 24 G4
Cork St DIT/AY ME20 ....124 E7
Corkwell St CHAT ME4 ....6 A7
Cormont Rd CMBW SE5 ....40 B2
Cormorant Cl STRD ME2 ....71 L8
Cormorant Wy HB CT6 ....106 F2
Cornbrook Rd HYTHE CT21 ....308 C7
Cornelis Dr MSTR CT12 ....141 J7
Cornell Cl SCUP DA14 ....64 C5
Corner Farm Rd STPH/PW TN12 ....246 B5
Corner Rd ASH TN23 ....282 E3
Corner Gn BKHTH/KID SE3 ....42 E5
Corner House Buildings HYTHE CT21 * 308 C5
Cornes Cl KEN/WIL TN24 ....253 K8
Cornfield Wy TONN TN10 ....210 C4
Cornflower Cl MAID/BEAR ME14 ....156 B8
Cornflower La EDUL SE22 ....41 H7
RTWE/PEM TN2 ....271 N1
Cornford La RTWE/PEM TN2 ....271 H4
Cornford Pk RTWE/PEM TN2 ....271 M2
Cornford Rd BRCH CT7 ....111 H7
Cornforth Cl STPH/PW TN12 ....246 C5

Cornforth Dr RSIT ME9 * 129 L7
Cornhill BANK EC3V 24 A2
RAM CT11 ....17 F5
The Cornhill FOLK CT20 ....309 P4
Cornish Gv PGE/AN SE20 ....61 H7
Corn Mill Dr ORP BR6 ....86 G4
Cornmill La LEW SE13 ....41 P4
Cornwall Av RAM CT11 ....143 L4
WELL DA16 ....44 A4
Cornwall Cl MAID/SHEP ME15 ....186 B4
Cornwall Crs ROCH ME1 ....124 B1
Cornwall Dr STMC/STPC BR5 ....64 E6
Cornwall Gdns CANT CT1 ....167 J3
EGRIN RH19 ....265 J8
MARG CT9 ....112 G5
SNWD SE25 * 83 L1
Cornwallis Av BFN/LL DA15 ....63 P1
CHAT ME4 ....95 K5
FOLKN CT19 ....10 A2
GILL ME7 ....96 C2
HB CT6 ....107 P3
RCANTE CT3 ....229 J1
RMAID ME17 ....215 K2
TONN TN10 ....211 H6
Cornwallis Cir WSTB CT5 ....105 K5
Cornwallis Cl ERITH DA8 ....29 L9
FOLKN CT19 ....10 A2
KEN/WIL TN24 ....283 L1
Cornwallis Rd MAIDW ME16 ....12 A5
WOOL/PLUM SE18 ....27 K7
Cornwallis Wk ELTH/MOT SE9 ....43 K4
Cornwall Rd CROY/NA CR0 ....82 G5
DART DA1 ....46 F4
DEAL CT14 ....233 H6
GILL ME7 * 7 G4
HB CT6 ....106 G4
ROCH ME1 ....95 H3
Cornwall St WCHPL E1 * 24 G5
Cornwell Av GVE DA12 ....49 N8
Cornwood Dr WCHPL E1 ....24 F2
Corona Rd LEE/GVPK SE12 ....42 E8
Coronation Av TIL RM18 ....34 B7
Coronation Cl BRDST CT10 ....113 K6
BXLY DA5 ....45 H9
Coronation Crs MARG CT9 ....112 A5
OBOR ME11 ....77 H2
Coronation Dr ASH TN23 ....251 P8
IOS ME12 ....80 B5
Coronation Rd EGRIN RH19 ....265 H9
HOO/HM ME3 ....52 F7
IOS ME12 ....57 L7
RAM CT11 ....16 D4
WALD ME5 ....95 P4
Coronation St LYDD TN29 ....342 B6
Corone Cl FOLKN CT19 ....310 D4
Corporation Rd GILL ME7 ....73 K9
Corporation St ROCH ME1 ....19 G4
Corral Cl WALD ME5 ....96 A4
Corran Gn MAID/SHEP ME15 ....185 M3
Corran Wy SOCK/AV RM15 ....31 L3
Correnden Rd RTON TN11 ....210 D7
Cortland Cl SIT ME10 ....99 M8
Cortland Ms SIT ME10 ....99 M8
Corunna Cl HYTHE CT21 ....308 G5
Corunna Pl DVE/WH CT16 ....291 M4
Corve La SOCK/AV RM15 ....31 L3
Cory's Rd ROCH ME1 ....19 H4
Cosbycote Av HNHL SE24 ....40 C6
Cosedge Crs CROY/NA CR0 ....82 F9
Cossack St ROCH ME1 ....95 H5
Cossall Wk PECK SE15 ....41 H2
Cossington Rd CANT CT1 ....5 G5
SYD SE26 ....61 K6
Costa St PECK SE15 ....40 G3
Costells Meadow BH/WHM TN16 ....176 G2
Cotall St POP/IOD E14 ....25 K2
Cotelands CROY/NA CR0 ....83 K7
Cotland Rd THMTH CR7 ....83 H1
Cot La HDCN TN27 ....278 C5
Cotleigh Av BXLY DA5 ....64 F1
Cotmandene Crs STMC/STPC BR5 ....64 D8
Cotman's Ash La BGR/WK TN15 ....120 A9
Cotman Wy STPH/PW TN12 ....212 F4
Coton Rd WELL DA16 ....44 C4
Cotswold Cl BXLYHN DA7 ....45 N2
KEN/WIL TN24 ....252 E5
Cotswold Gdns MAID/SHEP ME15 ....186 D2
Cotswold Ri ORP BR6 ....86 G3
Cotswold Rd GVW DA11 ....69 J2
Cotswold Wy WNWD SE27 ....60 B3
Cottage Av HAYES BR2 ....85 P5
Cottage Field Cl SCUP DA14 ....44 G9
Cottage Gn CMBW SE5 ....40 D1
Cottage Rd CHAT ME4 ....72 F9
RAM CT11 ....17 G4
Cottage Rw SWCH CT13 ....201 N1
Cottages Crs SEV TN13 ....148 D5
Cottage St POP/IOD E14 ....25 M2
Cottall Av CANT ME4 ....95 L4
Cottenham Cl E/WMAL ME19 ....153 N5
Cottenhams LING RH7 ....234 B1
Cottesbrook St NWCR SE14 ....41 L1
Cottesmore Rd PGE/AN SE20 ....61 K6
Cottington St POP/IOD E14 ....142 E7
Cottongrass Cl CROY/NA CR0 ....84 A5
Cotton Hl BMLY BR1 ....62 B5
Cotton La GRH DA9 ....47 K6
Cotton Rd CANT CT1 ....4 A7
Cotton St POP/IOD E14 ....25 M3
Couchman Green La STPH/PW TN12 ....246 C2
Coulgate St BROCKY SE4 ....41 L4
Coulman St GILL ME7 ....96 A1
Coulson Gv DEAL CT14 ....233 H4
Coulter Rd ASH TN23 ....282 B5
HB CT6 ....106 C4
Coulters Cl MAID/BEAR ME14 ....156 A8
Coulton Av GVW DA11 ....49 J8

Coultrip Cl IOS ME12 ....79 H2
Council Av GVW DA11 ....48 G7
Councillor St CMBW SE5 ....40 C1
Counter St STHWK SE1 * 24 B8
Countries Fld LYDD TN29 ....326 G6
Country Ways HDCN TN27 ....190 D6
County Ga DART DA1 ....63 N2
County Gv CMBW SE5 ....40 C2
E/WMAL ME15 ....153 J4
County Rd EHAM E6 ....27 J1
MAID/BEAR ME14 ....13 F3
THHTH CR7 ....60 B8
County Sq ASH TN23 ....2 D3
County St STHWK SE1 * 24 A9
Coupland Pl WOOL/PLUM SE18 ....27 K8
The Course ELTH/MOT SE9 ....63 L2
Court Ap FOLK CT20 ....10 C5
Courtaulds Ct THMD SE28 ....27 P4
Court Cl ABYW DA12 ....28 J8
Court Cl ECRIN RH19 ....265 J7
Court Crs EGRIN RH19 ....265 K7
SWLY BR8 ....88 D1
Court Downs Rd BECK BR3 ....61 P8
Court Dr CROY/NA CR0 ....82 E8
MAIDW ME16 ....155 J7
Courtenay Dr BECK BR3 ....62 B8
CDW/CHF RM16 ....32 C2
Courtenay Rd CANTW/ST CT2 ....134 F3
DEAL CT14 ....233 H1
MAID/SHEP ME15 ....186 E2
PGE/AN SE20 ....61 K6
Courteney Rd RHAM ME8 ....96 E6
Courtenwell RRTW TN3 * 269 K4
Court Farm Rd ELTH/MOT SE9 ....63 H1
Courtfield Av WALD ME5 ....125 N3
Courtfield Ri WWKM BR4 ....84 G7
Court Hall OBOR ME11 ....77 H2
Court Hl RCANTE CT3 ....168 C7
Courthill Rd LEW SE13 ....42 A6
Courthope STPH/PW TN12 ....229 P1
Court House Farm RDV CT15 ....229 P1
Courtland Av DVE/WH CT16 ....291 H1
Courtland Dr DVE/WH CT16 ....290 F3
Courtland Gv THMD SE28 ....28 C3
Courtlands DEAL CT14 ....263 J2
RTON TN11 ....182 D7
WBY/YAL ME18 ....183 P3
Courtlands Av HAYES BR2 ....85 H5
LEE/GVPK SE12 ....42 F6
Courtlands Cl MSTR CT12 ....142 C7
Courtlands Wy WGOS CT8 ....114 M4
Court La DUL SE21 ....40 F8
MAID/BEAR ME14 ....126 F8
RCANTE CT3 ....169 K3
RTON TN11 ....212 B2
Court Lane Gdns DUL SE21 ....40 E8
Courtlet Dr BXLYHN DA7 ....45 K2
Court Lodge Farm ME18 * 183 M4
Court Lodge Rd GILL ME7 ....73 M9
RASHW TN26 ....322 D7
Courtmead Cl HNHL SE24 ....40 C7
Court Meadow RHAM ME8 ....96 E4
Court Mdw RCANTE CT3 ....168 C8
Court Mt BRCH CT7 * 111 H7
Courtney Cl NRWD SE19 ....60 E5
Courtney Rd CDW/CHF RM16 ....33 C1
CROY/NA CR0 ....82 F7
Courtrai Rd BRCH CT7 ....109 P8
DEAL CT14 ....232 F8
ELTH/MOT SE9 ....43 J1
RDART DA2 ....67 L4
ROCH ME1 ....124 C4
SIT ME10 ....99 M7
SNWD SE25 ....60 F8
STH/RUST TN4 ....270 B4
Court Rd (Orpington By-Pass) ORP BR6 ....87 J7
Courtside SYD SE26 * 61 J2
The Courts MAID CT9 ....111 P4
Court St BMLY BR1 ....62 E8
FAV ME13 ....132 C6
WCHPL E1 ....24 E1
The Court WARL CR6 ....144 B3
Court Tree Dr IOS ME12 ....79 H2
Courtwood Dr SEV TN13 ....20 C1
Court Wood La CROY/NA CR0 ....114 C4
Courtwood Vls RDV CT15 * 259 N1
Court Wurtin Beaver La ASH TN23 ....282 D1
Court Yd ELTH/MOT SE9 ....43 K8
The Courtyard BH/WHM TN16 * 176 G2
BRG/WK TN15 ....121 M3
EGRIN RH19 ....265 L7
GILL ME7 * 96 C9
KEN/WIL TN24 ....283 H2
RCANTE CT3 * 143 G6
Cousin La CANST EC4R 24 A3
Cousley Wood Rd WADH TN5 ....294 B9
Couthurst Rd BKHTH/KID SE3 ....26 C9
Couts Av GVE DA12 ....70 C3
Coveleees Wall EHAM E6 ....27 H2
Coventon La DEAL CT14 ....201 P4
Coventry Cl EHAM E6 ....26 G2
STRD ME2 ....71 M9
Coventry Gdns HB CT6 ....108 B5
Coventry Rd RSWND SE25 ....83 M1
TONN TN10 ....210 C5
Coverack Cl CROY/NA CR0 ....84 B4
Coverdale Av MAID/SHEP ME15 ....186 A5
Coupland Pl WOOL/PLUM SE18 ....95 N7
Coverdale Gdns CROY/NA CR0 ....83 L7
Coverley Cl WCHPL E1 * 24 D1
Covert Rd RCANTE CT3 ....229 N2
The Covert MEO DA13 ....121 P6
ORP BR6 ....86 F5
WALD ME5 ....125 M4
Covesfield GVW DA11 ....49 K7
Covet La RCANTW CT4 ....227 L4

Covet Wood Cl
 STMC/STPC BR5.................................86 C3
Covey Hall Rd SNOD ME6......................123 P5
Covington Gdns
 STRHM/NOR SW16.............................60 B6
Covington Wy
 STRHM/NOR SW16.............................60 B6
Cowbeck Cl RHAM ME8...........................96 C8
Cowden Cl HAWK TN18.........................316 C6
Cowden La HAWK TN18.........................316 G7
Cowden Ms EDEN TN8..........................267 H5
Cowden Rd MAID/BEAR ME14....155 P7
 ORP BR6...86 C4
Cowden St CAT SE6................................61 N3
Cowdray Rd DEAL CT14........................232 F6
Cowdray Sq DEAL CT14..........................232 C6
Cowdrey Cl KEN/WIL TN24.................283 K1
 MAIDW ME16..184 G2
 ROCH ME1...94 C4
Cowdrey Ct DART DA1.............................46 B8
Cowdrey Pl CANT CT1...........................166 C6
Cowdrey Hl DVW CT17.............................8 C4
Cowgate La ROLF CT18........................288 F6
Cow La CANT CT1......................................4 A7
 DVW CT17...291 H8
 EDEN TN8...237 L7
Cow Leaze EHAM E6..................................27 H2
Cowley Av GRH DA9...............................47 M6
Cowley Ri MARG CT9.............................113 H5
Cowley Rd BRXN/ST SW9.......................40 A2
Cowper Av TIL RM18............................49 M2
Cowper Cl BELV DA17.............................85 N1
 DEAL CT14..232 G4
 DVW CT17...290 F5
 GILL ME7..7 K6
 HAYES BR2..85 N1
 MARG CT9..115 J3
 SIT ME10..130 A1
Cowstead Rd RSIT ME9.......................127 N2
Coxes Av MSTR CT12............................142 C1
Coxes La MSTR CT12............................142 C1
Coxett Hl FAV ME15..............................132 A8
Cox Gdns RHAM ME8...............................96 D4
Coxhill Crs DVW CT17...........................290 E4
Coxhill Gdns DVW CT17......................290 E4
Coxhill Rd RDV CT15............................259 L2
Coxmount Rd CHARL SE7.....................26 E8
Coxon Dr CDW/CHF RM16...................31 P6
Cox's Cl SNOD ME6...............................123 N5
Coxson Wy STHWK SE1...........................24 C5
Cox St MAID/BEAR ME14....................126 F9
Coxwell Rd NRWD SE19........................60 D6
 WOOL/PLUM SE18................................27 L8
Cozenton Cl RHAM ME8..........................97 H5
Crabble Av DVW CT17...........................291 M3
Crabble Cl DVW CT17............................290 G5
Crabble Hl DVW CT17............................290 G5
Crabble La DVW CT17............................290 G5
Crabble Mdw DVW CT17.......................291 H5
Crabble Rd DVW CT17...........................291 H5
Crabbs Croft Cl ORP BR6......................86 D9
Crab Hl BECK BR3...................................62 B6
Crabtree Cl E/WMAL ME19...................185 H1
Crabtree La RMAID ME17.....................220 L2
Crabtree Manorway North
 BELV DA17..29 H5
Crabtree Manorway South
 BELV DA17..29 H6
Crabtree Rd RHAM ME8...........................96 C6
Craddock Dr CANT CT1............................5 H2
Craddock Rd CANT CT1..........................5 H3
Craddock Wy STPH/PW TN12...........246 E5
Cradle Bridge Dr
 KEN/WIL TN24..3 K4
Cradles Rd HAYES BR2..........................127 M4
Cradley Rd ELTH/MOT SE9....................43 P9
Crafford St DVW/WH CT16......................8 C2
Craigen Av CROY/NA CRO.....................63 N5
Craigerne Rd BKHTH/KID SE3............43 M3
Craigholm WOOL/PLUM SE18..............43 L3
Craigton Rd ELTH/MOT SE9...................43 K5
Crail Rw WALW SE17..............................24 A7
Crammavill St CDW/CHF RM16.............32 B4
Crampton Rd PGE/AN SE20...................61 J5
Cramptons CRBK TN17.........................276 C8
Crampton's Rd RSEV TN14...................148 C5
Cranborne Av
 MAID/SHEP ME15.............................185 N3
Cranbourne Cl RAM CT11....................143 L2
Cranbrook Cl HAYES BR2......................85 K3
Cranbrook Rd
 MAIDW ME16..186 C4
 MARG CT9...113 K4
 ....96 F3
Cranbrook Dr SIT ME10........................129 L4
Cranbrook Rd BXLYHN DA7.................74 A8
 CRBK TN17..274 F8
 CRBK TN17..298 B6
 DEPT SE8..41 N3
 HAWK TN18...317 H2
 HDCN TN27..314 B9
 STPH/PW TN12.....................................276 C1
 TENT TN30...300 F7
 THHTH CR7...60 C8
Crandalls RTON TN11.............................209 L9
Crandon Wk EYN DA4 *...........................67 L8
Crane La CRBK TN17..............................298 G6
Crane Md BERM/RHTH SE16................24 C8
Crane St PECK SE15..................................40 F2
Cranfield Rd BROCKY SE4...................41 M4
Cranford Cl RHAM ME8............................96 C5
Cranford Rd DART DA1...........................46 E9
 TONN TN10..211 K5
Cranford St WAP E1W.............................24 C3
Cranleigh Cl BXLY DA5 *.......................45 K7
 ORP BR6..87 H7
 PGE/AN SE20..61 H8
Cranleigh Dr DVE/WH CT16...............261 H4
 SWLY BR8...88 D1
Cranleigh Gdns MAIDW ME16............155 H5
 ROCH ME1...95 J3
 SNWD SE25..60 E9
 WSTB ST5...105 M6

Cranley Rd PLSTW E13...........................26 C1
Cranmer Cl RCANTW CT4....................167 N8
 WARL CR6...144 B2
Cranmer Ct MAID/SHEP ME15..........185 N3
Cranmere Ct STRD ME2..........................72 C7
Cranmer Gdns WARL CR6...................144 B2
Cranmer Rd BRXN/ST SW9...................40 A1
 CROY/NA CRO..82 C7
 SEV TN13..148 D8
Cranmore Rd BMLY BR1...........................62 C2
 CHST BR7...63 K4
Cranston Rd EGRIN RH19.....................265 J6
 FSTH SE23..41 L9
Cranswick Rd
 BERM/RHTH SE16.................................24 E8
Crantock Rd CAT SE6...............................62 A1
Cranwell Rd STH/RUST TN4...............269 P4
Cranworth Gdns BRXN/ST SW9............40 A2
Crathie Rd LEE/GVPK SE12...................42 F7
Craufurd Gn FOLK CT20......................310 A6
Craven Cl MAID ME13............................112 B5
Craven Rd CROY/NA CRO.......................83 N5
 ORP BR6...87 L7
Crawford Av CDW/CHF RM16..............32 C4
Crawford Gdns MARG CT9...................112 C3
Crawford Rd BRDST CT10.....................113 L8
 CMBW SE5..63 N6
Crawfords SWLY BR8................................65 N6
Crawford Wy EGRIN RH19..................265 J6
Crawley Down Rd EGRIN RH19........264 B5
Crawshay Cl SEV TN13..........................148 F8
Crawthew Gv EDUL SE22.......................40 F5
Cray Av STMC/STPC BR5.........................87 J2
Craybrooke Rd SCUP DA14..................68 D4
Crayburne MED DA13..............................68 D4
Craybury End ELTH/MOT SE9...............63 N1
Cray Cl DART DA1.....................................46 A6
Crayden Rd ERITH DA8...........................45 P2
Crayford Cl MAID/BEAR ME14..............13 K1
Crayford High St DART DA1...................45 N6
Crayford Rd DART DA1............................45 P6
Crayford Wy DART DA1...........................46 A5
Craylands STMC/STPC BR5....................64 E9
Craylands La SWCM DA10.....................48 C7
Craylands Sq SWCM DA10....................48 B6
Crayleigh Ter SCUP DA14 *....................64 E5
Cray Rd BELV DA17..................................28 F9
 SCUP DA14...64 E5
 SWLY BR8...88 B3
Crays Pde STMC/STPC BR5 *................64 E8
Craythorne TENT TN30.........................301 J6
Craythorne Cl HYTHE CT21.................309 N5
 NROM TN28..337 H5
Craythorne La NROM TN28.................336 C6
Cray Valley Rd
 STMC/STPC BR5.....................................87 H2
Creasy Est STHWK SE1 *........................24 B6
Crebor St EDUL SE22.................................40 G7
Credenhall Dr HAYES BR2......................86 A5
Credon Rd BERM/RHTH SE16...............24 E4
Credo Wy WTHK RM20...........................31 L9
Creechurch La HDTCH EC3A.................24 B2
Creechurch Pl HDTCH EC3A *...............24 B2
Creek Rd DEPT SE8..................................41 N1
Creekside DEPT SE8..................................41 P1
The Creek GVW DA11..............................29 K1
Creek Wy RAIN RM13...............................29 K1
Creeland Gv CAT SE6.............................41 M9
Cremer La RCANTW CT4.......................195 K1
Cremer Pl HAV HA1................................132 D5
Cremers Rd SIT ME10...........................100 A9
Cremorne Rd GVW DA11.........................49 K8
Crendon Pk STH/RUST TN4................240 D8
Crescent TWRH ECN *..............................24 C3
Crescent Av GNWCH SE10....................25 M9
Crescent Av GRAYS RM17 *....................32 E8
Crescent Dr STMC/STPC BR5................85 LB
Crescent Gdns SWLY BR8........................65 LB
Crescent Rd BECK BR3...........................61 N7
 BFN/LL DA15...64 B2
 BMLY BR1...62 E6
 BRCH CT7...85 K9
 BRDST CT10..113 N5
 EGRIN RH19..264 C7
 ERITH DA8..29 L9
 FAV ME13..112 B5
 MARG CT9...16 C3
 RAM CT11...16 C3
 RTW TN1...15 F5
 SOCK/AV RM15.......................................30 F5
 WOOL/PLUM SE18..................................27 J8
The Crescent BECK BR3...........................61 N7
 BGR/WK TN15..151 K4
 BXLY DA5..45 J5
 CANTW/ST CT2.....................................166 E1
 CHAT ME4...73 H6
 CTHM CR3..101 P3
 EGRIN RH19..234 F9
 FAV ME13..164 B1
 FOLK CT20...310 B8
 GRH DA9...48 A7
 GVW DA11..69 K1
 HART DA3...68 C9
 IOS ME12..77 N1
 MAID/BEAR ME14................................155 L4
 RCANTW CT4...195 L2
 RDV CT15...229 K5
 RDV CT15...260 D1
 RDV CT15...292 F2
 RSIT ME9..131 J2
 SCUP DA14...64 B3
 SEV TN13...149 J7
 SIT ME10...99 N5
 SNWD SE25..60 E9
 STH/RUST TN4......................................240 B5
 SWCH CT13..201 M4
 TON TN9...210 E8
 WWKM BR4...49 K1
Crescent Wk SOCK/AV RM15...............30 F5
Crescent Wy BROCKY SE4.....................41 N4
 ORP BR6..86 G9
 SOCK/AV RM15.......................................30 G4
 WALD ME5..95 J9
Crescent Wood Rd SYD SE26...............60 G2

Cressey Ct CHAT ME4................................6 A5
Cressfield ASH TN23..............................252 C8
Cressingham Rd LEW SE13....................42 A4
Cress Wy FAV ME13................................132 D6
Cresswell Pk BKHTH/KID SE3................43 J4
Cresswell Rd SNWD SE25.....................83 M1
Cressy Houses WCHPL E1 *..................24 F1
Cressy Pl WCHPL E1.................................24 F1
Crest Av GRAYS RM17............................32 D8
Crest Rd HAYES BR2.................................48 F1
 ROCH ME1...95 H5
Crest View Dr STMC/STPC BR5...........86 C2
Crestway WALD ME5..............................95 N6
Creswell Dr BECK BR3..............................61 N5
Crete Hall Rd GVW DA11.........................49 H7
Crete Rd East RFOLK CT18..................310 F2
Crete Rd West FOLKN CT19................310 B2
Creteway Cl FOLKN CT19 *..................311 H3
Crève Coeur Cl
 MAID/BEAR ME14................................156 D7
Crewe's La WARL CR6.............................144 A1
Crews St POP/IOD E14.............................25 K7
Crewys Rd PECK SE15............................41 H5
Crichton Av WLGTN SM6......................62 D9
Cricket Cl EGRIN RH19........................265 H5
Cricketers Cl ERITH DA8........................29 K8
 RFOLK CT18..288 E6
 RMAID ME17...188 E5
 SIT ME10...99 N6
Cricketers Dr MEO DA13........................92 B7
Cricketers Wk SYD SE26..........................61 J5
Cricket Ground Rd CHST BR7................63 M7
Cricket La BECK BR3...............................61 L5
Criol La AROD TN29...............................327 L2
Crimscott St STHWK SE1 *....................24 B6
Crinan Ct BRDST CT10 *........................143 L3
Criol La RASHW TN26...........................281 L7
Criol Rd RASHW TN26............................281 L7
Cripple Hl RASHW TN26........................271 P2
Cripple St MAID/SHEP ME15.............185 M4
Cripps Cl RCANTE CT3..........................229 H1
Cripps' La RDV CT15................................292 E1
Crismill Rd MAID/BEAR ME14............157 H9
Crispe Cl RHAM ME8.............................126 C1
Crispe Park Cl BRCH CT7......................111 J6
Crispe Rd BRCH CT7...............................141 H1
Crispin Cl FAV ME13................................132 C5
Crispin Ct RMAID ME17.......................185 H6
Crispin Crs CROY/NA CRO.....................82 C7
Crispin Rd MAID ME13...........................71 N7
Crispin St WCHPL E1................................24 C1
Crispin Wy E/WMAL ME19...................153 H9
Crittenden Rd STPH/PW TN12...........242 D5
Crockenhill Wy MEO DA13.....................69 J7
Crockenhill La SWLY BR8......................88 F4
Crockenhill Rd HDCN TN27.................219 K8
Crockenhill Rd
 STMC/STPC BR5.....................................87 L3
Crockers La LING RH7..........................234 A5
 RYE TN31..118 A3
Crockham La FAV ME13.........................134 C7
Crockham Rd FAV ME13........................134 D7
Crockham Wy ELTH/MOT SE9...............63 N3
Crockshard Hl RCANTE CT3.................199 L5
Crockshard La RCANTE CT3................199 L5
Crocus Cl CROY/NA CRO.........................64 A5
Crofs Av WWKM BR4..............................84 F5
Croft Av BELV DA17..................................28 E8
 CHST BR7...63 K4
 RMAID ME17..187 N9
 SWLY BR8...65 L9
 WALD ME5...125 P4
Croft Cl BH/WHM TN16........................176 C2
 BMLY BR1...62 E5
 CHST BR7...63 J1
 KEN/WIL TN24...3 G4
 STRHM/NOR SW16...............................60 A6
Croft Rd Flats KEN/WIL TN24................3 G4
Croftside MEO DA13..............................122 B5
Croft's Pl BRDST CT10..........................113 N9
Crofts St WCHPL E1.................................24 C3
Crofts St DEPT SE8....................................25 H7
 WCHPL E1...24 C3
The Croft E/WMAL ME19......................153 M2
 SWLY BR8..65 L9
Croft Wy BFN/LL DA15...........................64 A2
 SEV TN13...20 A3
Croftwood ASH TN23............................282 A2
Croham Park Av
 SAND/SEL CR2.......................................83 L9
Croham Rd SAND/SEL CR2...................83 K9
Croindene Ct CRS ME12 *......................78 A1
Crombie Rd BFN/LL DA15......................43 P9
Cromer Rd SIT ME10..............................129 M5
 SNWD SE25..60 F9
 STRD ME2..72 B7
Cromer St STON TN9..............................210 D9
Cromford Cl ORP BR6.............................86 F7
Cromlix Cl CHST BR7...............................63 M8
Crompton Gdns
 MAID/SHEP ME15.................................13 H6
Cromwell Av HAYES BR2........................62 F9
Cromwell Cl HAYES BR2.........................85 L1

Cromwell Park Pl FOLK CT20...........310 A7
Cromwell Pl EGRIN RH19.....................265 J9
Cromwell Rd BECK BR3..........................61 LB
 BRXN/ST SW9...40 B2
 CANT CT1...166 F6
 CANT CT1...166 F6
 GRAVS RM17..32 B7
 IOS ME12...57 H9
 MAID/BEAR ME14.................................13 G3
 RTWE/PEM TN2.....................................23 H5
 WSTB CT5...105 L5
Cromwell Ter CHAT ME4..........................6 D6
Cronin Cl DIT/AV ME20.........................123 N9
Cronin St PECK SE15................................40 F1
Crooked La GVE DA12.............................49 M7
Crooked S Cl SEV TN13...........................20 C7
Crooked St DEAL CT14..........................262 D1
Crookenden Pl
 RCANTW CT4...228 C7
Crooke Rd DEPT SE8................................25 H8
Crook Log BXLYHN DA7..........................44 F4
Crook Rd STPH/PW TN12.....................243 K8
Crook's Court La RDV CT15..................312 A2
Crookston Rd ELTH/MOT SE9...............43 M4
Croombs Rd CAN/RD E16......................26 D1
Croom's Hl GNWCH SE10......................42 B1
Croom's Hill Gv GNWCH SE10............42 A1
Crosby Rw STHWK SE1 *........................24 A4
Crosier Cl WOOL/PLUM SE18...............43 J2
Crosier Ct RSIT ME9.................................97 P3
Crosley Cl BH/WHM TN16...................115 N9
Crosmead ELTH/MOT SE9....................43 J3
Cross Bnk BRCH CT7.............................111 H5
 CMBW SE5..40 E3
 CROY/NA CRO..83 J5
 DEAL CT14...232 F8
 GVW DA11..49 K7
 HAYES BR2..85 P6
 RDART DA2..66 F3
 SCUP DA14...64 B5
 STMC/STPC BR5.....................................87 J2
Cross Stile ASH TN23............................252 B9
Cross St CANTW/ST CT2..........................4 B3
 CHAT ME4...73 L5
 ERITH DA8...29 K9
 HB CT6..107 J3
 MAID/BEAR ME14.................................13 J8
 STRD ME2..72 B7
Crosswaite Av HNHL SE24.....................40 G5
Crosswall TWRH ECN..............................24 C3
Crosswall Quay DVW CT17......................8 D7
Cross Wy ROCH ME1................................94 G2
Crossways STMC/STPC BR5...................86 E1
 THMD SE28..37 K3
 WALD ME5..95 K8
Crossways BH/WHM TN16....................145 M5
 CANTW/ST CT2.....................................136 B2
 SAND/SEL CR2...83 L8
 SIT ME10...114 C2
 SIT ME10...129 M4
Crossways Av EGRIN RH19..................264 F7
 MARG CT9...112 F8
Crossways Bvd GRH DA9.........................47 J7
Crossways Cl LYDD TN29......................335 H4
Crossways Rd BECK BR3........................84 D1
The Crossway KEN/WIL TN24 *...............2 D2
 STH/RUST TN4......................................270 A6
Crothall Hvn KEN/WIL TN24 *................2 D2
Crouch Cl BECK BR3................................61 N5
Crouch Cft ELTH/MOT SE9.....................63 N3
Crouch Hill Ct RSIT ME9........................98 D3
Crouch House Rd EDEN TN8................206 B7
Crouch La BGR/WK TN15......................151 L7
 FAV ME13..134 B9
 HAWK TN18..318 D9
Crouchmann Cl CDW/CHF RM16........32 D5
Crouchmans Cl SYD SE26.......................60 F2
Crouch Rd GRAYS RM17.........................33 H8
Crowborough Cl WARL CR6.................144 B9
Crowborough Dr WARL CR6...............144 B3
Crowbridge Rd
 KEN/WIL TN24..283 J2
Crowden Wy THMD SE28......................28 B3
Crowder St WCHPL E1 *...........................24 D3
Crow Dr RSEV TN14................................118 B9
Crow Hl BRDST CT10............................113 N8
Crowhurst La BH/WHM TN16.............116 A4
The Croft RCANTW CT4........................257 L5
Crowhurst Cl BRXN/ST SW9..................40 A3
Crowhurst La BGR/WK TN15...............90 E9
 BGR/WK TN15.......................................204 C5
 LING RH7...204 A4
Crowhurst Rd BGR/WK TN15..............151 K4
 LING RH7...234 C3
Crowhurst Village Rd
 LING RH7...205 H8
Crowhurst Wy
 STMC/STPC BR5.....................................87 K2
Crowland Rd THHTH CR7 *....................83 J1
Crow La ROCH ME1...................................19 G6
Crowley Crs CROY/NA CRO...................82 F9
Crown Acres STPH/PW TN12...............213 H4
Crown Cl ORP BR6...................................87 H9
Crown Di NRWD SE19............................60 C5
Crownfield Rd ASH TN23.......................252 C9
Crownfields
 MAID/BEAR ME14................................156 B8
 SEV TN13..20 E4

Crown Gdns CANTW/ST CT2..................4 B3
Crown Gn GVE DA12................................70 G4
Crown Hl CROY/NA CRO *.....................83 H6
Crown Hill Rd HB CT6...........................107 H2
Crown La CHST BR7..................................63 N7
 GVE DA12...82 N2
 HAYES BR2...85 N2
 RCANTW CT4..226 D8
 STRHM/NOR SW16................................60 A4
Crown Lane Gdns
 WNWD SE27 *...60 A4
Crown Lane Sp HAYES BR2....................85 N3
Crown Quay La SIT ME10........................99 N9
Crown Rd EDEN TN8..............................206 E7
 GRAYS RM17..32 B9
 ORP BR6..87 H9
 RSEV TN14...118 E4
 SIT ME10..99 M9
Crownstone Rd
 BRXS/STRHM SW2.................................40 A6
 SNWD SE25..40 C1
 GILL ME7...7 K1
Crown Whf STRD ME2 *............................19 K1
Crown Woods Wy
 ELTH/MOT SE9.......................................43 P6
Crows Camp Rd RCANTW CT4....197 L7
Crowstone Rd CDW/CHF RM16.........32 D5
Crowther Cl STPH/PW TN12...............246 B5
Crowther Rd SNWD SE25.....................83 M1
Crowton Cl SNOD ME6..........................124 A5
Croxley Cl STMC/STPC BR5....................64 D8
Croxley Gn STMC/STPC BR5..................64 D8
Croxted Cl DUL SE21................................40 C8
Croxted Rd DUL SE21...............................60 D1
Croyde Cl ELTH/MOT SE9........................43 P9
Croydon Cl WALD ME5..........................125 P1
The Croydon F/O
 CROY/NA CRO..82 G5
Croydon Gv CROY/NA CRO....................82 G5
Croydon Rd BH/WHM TN16................176 C5
 CROY/NA CRO...82 D8
 CROY/NA CRO...84 A2
 MTCM CR4..62 B8
 PGE/AN SE20..61 H8
 WARL CR6...144 G2
 WLGTN SM6...62 A8
 WWKM BR4...85 H7
Crucifix La STHWK SE1...........................24 B5
Cruden Rd GVE DA12..............................70 B2
Cruick Av SOCK/AV RM15.....................31 N5
Crumpsall St ABYW SE2..........................28 B7
Crump's La RMAID ME17......................217 P7
Crundale Cl ASH TN23..........................282 C2
Crundale Rd RHAM ME8..........................96 F5
Crundale Wy MARG CT9.......................113 K3
Crundwell Rd STH/RUST TN4.............240 C8
Crusader Cl GILL ME7..............................96 D6
 PUR RM19..30 D7
Crusader Gdns CROY/NA CRO.............83 K7
Crusoe Rd ERITH DA8...............................29 J8
Crutched Friars TWRH ECN...................24 C3
Crutches La STRD ME2.............................71 K7
Crutchley Rd CAT SE6...............................61 P1
Cryalls La RSIT ME9...............................129 J2
Cryals Rd STPH/PW TN12.....................272 E3
Cryol Rd ASH TN23.................................282 C1
Crystal Palace NRWD SE19 *.................60 G6
Crystal Palace Pde
 NRWD SE19...60 F5
Crystal Palace Park Rd
 SYD SE26..60 G4
Crystal Palace Rd EDUL SE22...............40 F7
Crystal Ter NRWD SE19..........................60 D5
Cuba St POP/IOD E14..............................25 K5
Cubitt St CROY/NA CRO..........................82 E9
Cuckolds Green Rd
 HOO/HM ME3...54 D1
Cuckoo La ASH TN23..............................282 B1
 CDW/CHF RM16......................................32 A5
 HYTHE CT21..286 E6
 RTON TN11...211 K3
 STPH/PW TN12.....................................273 H6
Cuckoowood Av
 MAID/BEAR ME14................................155 L3
Cudham Dr MAID/BEAR ME14...........155 P6
Cudham Gdns MARG CT9.....................113 K3
Cudham La North RSEV TN14...........116 D8
Cudham La South RSEV TN14...........116 F4
Cudham Park Rd RSEV TN14..............116 F4
Cudham Rd BH/WHM TN16................145 P4
 ORP BR6...116 B5
Cudham St CAT SE6.................................41 N4
Cudworth Rd KEN/WIL TN24.............282 G1
Cuff Crs ELTH/MOT SE9..........................43 J7
Cugley Rd RDART DA2.............................47 J8
Culcroft HART DA3....................................91 J1
Culford Rd CDW/CHF RM16................32 D5
Cullens Hl RCANTW CT4......................257 K5
Cullen Sp SOCK/AV RM15...................31 M3
Cullet Dr OBOR ME11...............................77 J4
Culling Rd BERM/RHTH SE16............24 F6
Culmers La RCANTW CT4.....................257 L5
Culloden Cl STHWK SE1 *........................24 D9
Culloden St POP/IOD E14.....................25 M2
Cullum St FENCHST EC3M....................24 B3
Culmers La RSIT ME9 *............................133 P4
Culmore Rd PECK SE15...........................41 H1
Culpeper Cl RMAID ME17....................187 N1
 ....19 J3
Culpepers CRBK TN17...........................274 D9
Culpepper Cl CANTW/ST CT2.............136 F9
Culpepper Rd RHAM ME8....................126 C1
 RMAID ME17...184 C8
Culverden Down
 STH/RUST TN4......................................270 C3
Culverden Park Rd
 STH/RUST TN4......................................270 C2
Culverden Sq RTW TN1............................22 D1
Culverden St RTW TN1............................22 D2
Culver Dr OXTED RH8.............................175 H6
Culverley Rd CAT SE6...............................61 P1
Culver's La LYDD TN29..........................342 C7

Culverstone Cl HAYES BR2 * 85 J3
Culvey Cl HART DA3 .....91 H2
Cumberland Av BRDST CT10 ..113 M8
　CANT CT1 .....167 J5
　GVE DA12 .....49 N8
　MAID/SHEP ME15 .....186 A3
　WELL DA16 .....98 C3
Cumberland Dr BXLYHN DA7 .....44 C1
　DART DA1 .....46 F8
　RSIT ME9 .....98 C3
Cumberland Gdns RTW TN1 .....22 C6
Cumberland Ms RTW TN1 .....22 C6
Cumberland Pl CAT SE6 .....42 D9
Cumberland Rd
　CDW/CHF RM16 .....31 P5
　GILL ME7 .....73 J8
　HAYES BR2 .....85 H1
　MARG CT9 .....112 C2
　PLSTW SE13 .....26 C1
　RAM CT11 .....16 D4
　SNWD SE25 .....83 N3
Cumberland Ter
　PCE/AN SE20 * 61 H6
Cumberland Wk RTW TN1 .....22 D7
Cumberland Yd RTW TN1 .....22 D6
Cumberlow Av SNWD SE25 .....60 D8
Cumbrian Av BXLYHN DA7 .....45 N3
Cundy Rd CAN/RD E16 .....26 D2
Cunningham Cl
　STH/RUST TN4 .....270 E1
　WWKM BR4 .....95 M6
Cunningham Crs BRCH CT7 .....110 F5
　WALD ME5 .....95 M6
Cunningham Rd
　STH/RUST TN4 .....270 E1
Cupola Cl BMLY BR1 .....62 F4
Curates Wk DART DA1 .....66 D2
Curlew Av RSIT ME9 .....98 D3
Curlew Cl SAND/SEL CR2 .....114 A5
　THMD SE28 .....28 C3
Curlew Crs STRD ME2 .....71 L9
Curlew St STHWK SE1 * 24 C5
Curlinge Ct RAM CT11 .....142 F6
Curling La GRAYS RM17 .....32 K8
Curness St LEW SE13 .....42 A5
Curnick's La WNWD SE27 .....60 C3
Curran Av BFN/LL DA15 .....44 B6
Currie Rd STH/RUST TN4 .....270 D2
Curteis Rd TENT TN30 .....301 J7
Curtis La RCANTW CT4 .....226 C6
Curtismill Cl STMC/STPC BR5 ..64 D9
Curtis Rd KEN/WIL TN24 .....283 H1
Curtis St STHWK SE1 .....24 C7
Curtis Wy RTW TN13 * 132 F6
　STHWK SE1 * 24 C7
Curtis Wood Park Rd HB CT6 ..107 N7
Curtis Wood Rd HB CT6 .....107 L7
Curzon Cl DEAL CT14 .....233 H6
　ORP BR6 .....86 B8
Curzon Dr GRAYS RM17 .....48 C1
Curzon Rd CHAT ME4 .....6 C7
　DVW CT17 .....291 J7
　MAID/BEAR ME14 .....155 M6
　THHTH CR7 .....82 F3
Cushman Rd CANT CT1 .....4 E7
Custom House Quay
　DVW CT17 .....8 C6
Custom House Reach
　BERM/RHTH SE16 .....25 J6
Cutbush Cl RMAID ME17 .....188 E5
Cutbush & Corrall Ct
　MAID/BEAR ME14 .....84 C2
Cutcombe Rd CMBW SE5 .....40 C3
Cuthbert Gdns SNWD SE25 .....60 B9
Cuthbert Rd CROY/NA CR0 .....82 C6
　WGOS CT8 .....111 M5
Cutlers Gardens Ar WCHPL E1 ..24 F3
Cutler St HDTCH EC3A 24 F2
Cutmore St GVW DA11 .....49 M8
Cutter Cl STRD ME2 .....72 F4
Cutter Ridge Rd MEO DA13 .....93 H5
The Cut HDCN TN17 .....278 C1
The Cuttings MSTR CT12 .....143 H5
Cutty Sark Ct GRH DA9 * 9 K2
Cuxton Cl BXLYHS DA6 .....44 C6
Cuxton Rd MAID/SHEP ME15 ..186 C6
　STRD ME2 .....18 A5
Cyclamen Rd SWLY BR8 .....88 C1
Cygnet Cl DITRY MED00 * 42 A3
Cygnet Rd WALD ME5 .....125 P5
Cygnet Vw WTHK RM20 .....31 J6
Cygnet Wy ASH TN23 .....252 C8
Cylinder Rd HYTHE CT21 .....308 C5
Cypress Av ASH TN23 .....73 L4
　HOO/HM ME3 .....73 L4
Cypress Cl GILL ME7 .....73 M9
　WSTB CT5 .....105 K7
Cypress Ct GILL ME7 .....73 M9
Cypress Gdns RDV CT15 .....280 D7
　RTWE/PEM TN2 .....270 F8
Cypress Rd SNWD SE25 .....60 E8
　STRD ME2 .....72 F4
Cypress Tree Cl BFN/LL DA15 ..44 B9
Cyprus Pl BHAM E6 .....26 L5
　RYE TN31 .....338 E7
Cyprus Rd FAV ME13 .....133 H6
Cyrena Rd EDUL SE22 .....40 L7
Cyril Rd BXLYHN DA7 .....44 C3
　ORP BR6 .....87 H4
Czar St DEPT SE8 .....25 K9

D

Dabbling Cl ERITH DA8 * 46 B1
Dabin Crs GNWCH SE10 .....42 A2
Dacca St DEPT SE8 .....25 J9
Dacre Av SOCK/AV RM15 .....30 G4
Dacre Gdns LEW SE13 * 42 C5

Dacre Pk LEW SE13 .....42 C4
Dacre Rd CROY/NA CR0 .....82 D4
Dacres Est FSTH SE23 * 61 K2
Dacres Rd FSTH SE23 .....61 K2
Daerwood Cl HAYES BR2 .....86 A5
Daffodil Cl CROY/NA CR0 .....82 D5
Daffodil Rd STRD ME2 .....71 N8
Dagg La RBTBR TN32 .....328 F8
Daglish Cl NROM TN28 .....336 C7
Dagmar Rd CHAT ME4 .....95 N4
　CMBW SE5 .....40 E2
　SNWD SE25 .....83 J2
Dagnall Pk SNWD SE25 .....83 K2
Dagnall Rd SNWD SE25 .....83 K2
Dagonet Rd BMLY BR1 .....62 E2
Dahlia Dr SWLY BR8 .....65 PB
Dahlia Gdns MTCM CR4 .....32 C1
Dahlia Rd ABYW SE2 .....28 A8
Daiglen Dr SOCK/AV RM15 .....31 K3
Daimler Av HB CT6 .....106 C5
Dainford Cl BMLY BR1 .....62 B4
Dairsie Rd ELTH/MOT SE9 .....43 L4
Dairy Cl BMLY BR1 * 62 F6
　EYN DA4 .....67 H6
　THHTH CR7 .....60 C8
Dairy La EDEN TN8 .....206 C1
　STPH/PW TN12 * 214 E6
Daisy Cl CROY/NA CR0 .....84 A5
Daisy Pl WCHPL E1 .....25 H1
The Dakins EGRIN RH19 .....265 H8
Dalberg Rd BRXS/STRHM SW2 ..40 A6
Dalberg Wy ABYW SE2 .....28 C6
Dalby Rd MARG CT9 .....15 K3
Dalby Sq MARG CT9 .....15 K3
Dale Cl BKTH/KID SE3 .....42 E4
　DART DA1 .....45 P7
　SOCK/AV RM15 .....31 K2
Dale Ct WALD ME5 .....125 M3
Dale Park Rd NRWD SE19 .....60 C7
Dale Rd CDW/CHF RM16 .....31 N3
　MEO DA13 .....68 E5
　ROCH ME1 .....95 H5
　SWLY BR8 .....65 L9
Daleside Cl ORP BR6 .....87 H9
Dale St CHM ME4 .....117 H1
Dale Vw ERITH DA8 .....46 A3
The Dale HAYES BR2 .....85 N8
Dale Vw KEN/WIL TN24 .....252 F2
Dalewood SIT ME10 .....129 P5
Dale Wood Rd ORP BR6 .....86 F4
Dalison Ct STRD ME2 .....124 A1
Dalkeith Rd DUL SE21 .....40 C9
Dallas-Brett Crs FOLKN CT19 ..311 H5
Dallas Rd SYD SE26 .....61 K6
Dallaway Gdns EGRIN RH19 ..265 H7
Dallinger Rd BRCH CT7 .....110 C5
　LEE/GVPK SE12 .....42 D7
Dalmally Rd CROY/NA CR0 .....83 L4
Dalmain Rd FSTH SE23 .....61 K9
Dalmeny Av CROY/NA CR0 .....83 L4
　STRHM/NOR SW16 .....60 A8
Dalmeny Cl ALP/SUD HA0 * 45 K2
Dalmeny Ter HYTHE CT21 * ..308 F5
Dalmore Rd DUL SE21 .....60 C1
Dalroy Cl SOCK/AV RM15 .....31 K2
Dalrymple Rd BROCKY SE4 .....41 L5
Dalton Cl ORP BR6 .....86 B8
Dalton Rd SWLY BR8 .....88 B6
Dalton St GILL ME7 .....7 J1
　WNWD SE27 .....60 B1
Dalwood St CMBW SE5 .....40 F2
Damerham Cl CANTW/ST CT2 ..166 D1
Damien Cl CHAT ME4 .....95 M4
Damien St WCHPL E1 .....24 E1
Damigos Rd GVE DA12 .....50 B9
Damon Cl SCUP DA14 .....64 F2
Damsel Ct BERM/RHTH SE16 * ..24 D7
Damson Dr HOO/HM ME3 .....73 K4
Danbury Crs SOCK/AV RM15 .....31 L2
Danbury Ms CAR SM5 .....62 A5
Danby St PECK SE15 .....40 F4
Dando Crs BKHTH/KID SE3 .....42 F4
Dandridge Cl GNWCH SE10 .....26 A8
Dan Er MAI ME13 .....132 D5
Danebury CROY/NA CR0 .....114 E1
Danebury Rd GVE DA12 .....49 J7
　WALD ME5 .....97 N9
Dane Ct RMAID ME17 .....185 H9
Dane Court Gdns BRDST CT10 ..113 J8
Danecourt Gdns CROY/NA CR0 ..83 L7
Dane Court Rd BRDST CT10 ..113 K7
Dane Crs RAM CT11 .....17 F1
Danecroft Rd HNHL SE24 .....40 C5
Danedale Av IOS ME12 .....78 F1
Dane End Rd WGOS CT8 .....111 L5
Dane Gdns MARG CT9 .....112 C5
Dane Hl MARG CT9 .....15 H4
Dane Hill Gv MARG CT9 .....15 H4
Dane Hill Rw MARG CT9 .....15 J3
Danehurst WGOS CT8 .....111 M4
Dane John Ct CANT CT1 .....4 D6
Dane John Ms CANT CT1 .....4 D6
Dane La RSIT ME9 .....97 N9
Danemore TENT TN30 .....301 J7
Danemore La GDST RH9 .....204 B8
Dane Mt MARG CT9 .....113 H5
Dane Park Rd MARG CT9 .....15 J4
　RAM CT11 .....143 K4
Dane Park Vis MARG CT9 * 15 J4
Dane Rd BRCH CT7 .....110 D6
　MARG CT9 .....15 J4
　RAM CT11 .....17 G1
　SEV TN13 .....148 D2
　WARL CR6 .....144 A2
Danes Cl GVW DA11 .....68 G2

Danescombe LEE/GVPK SE12 .....42 E9
Danes Ct DVE/WH CT16 .....291 L5
Danes Dr IOS ME12 .....80 M2
Danes Hl GILL ME7 .....73 N9
Danesmead Ter MARG CT9 .....15 J5
Daneswood Av CAT SE6 .....42 A7
Dane Valley Rd BRDST CT10 ..113 J6
　MARG CT9 .....112 G5
Danesleigh Gdns IOS ME12 .....40 D7
Daniel Bolt Cl POP/IOD E14 .....25 L1
Daniel Cl CDW/CHF RM16 .....31 P5
　CDW/CHF RM16 .....31 P5
Daniel Gdns PECK SE15 .....40 F1
Daniel Wy CROY/NA CR0 .....82 D5
Daniels Ct WSTB CT5 .....105 K5
Daniels La WARL CR6 .....144 C1
Daniel's Rd PECK SE15 .....41 J3
Daniel Wy RYE TN31 .....344 A1
Danley Rd IOS ME12 .....57 N9
Danns La WBY/YAL ME18 .....183 H3
Dansington Rd WELL DA16 .....44 D4
Danson Crs WELL DA16 .....44 D4
Danson La WELL DA16 .....44 D4
Danson Md WELL DA16 .....44 D4
Danson Rd BXLYHS DA6 .....44 A5
Danson Wy BFN/LL DA15 .....44 B5
Danson Wy RHAM ME8 .....96 G5
Danton La RFOLK CT18 .....237 P7
Danvers Rd TON TN9 .....210 E9
Daplyn St WCHPL E1 .....24 D1
Darby Gdns HOO/HM ME3 .....71 K4
Darby Pl FOLK CT20 .....10 E3
Darby Rd FOLK CT20 .....10 E3
D'Arcy Av WLGTN SM6 .....82 B8
D'Arcy Pl HAYES BR2 .....85 K1
Darent Cl SEV TN13 .....148 B7
Darenth Av TON TN10 .....210 C5
Darenth Ct DVE DA12 .....132 C9
Darenth Gdns BH/WHM TN16 ..176 E2
Darenth Hl RDART DA2 .....67 H4
Darenth La SEV TN13 .....148 D6
　SOCK/AV RM15 .....31 K2
Darenth Park Av RDART DA2 ...67 L1
Darenth Pl RDART DA2 * 67 H4
Darenth Ri WALD ME5 .....125 N2
Darenth Rd DART DA1 .....66 G1
　WELL DA16 .....44 C1
Darenth Rd South RDART DA2 ..67 H5
Darenth Wy SEV TN14 .....118 F5
Darenth Wood Rd RDART DA2 ..47 L9
Darent Rd EYN DA4 .....67 H7
Darent Valley Pth DART DA1 ...46 D2
　EYN DA4 .....89 N2
　RSEV TN14 .....118 F9
　SEV TN13 .....148 B6
Darfield Rd BROCKY SE4 .....41 M6
Dargate Cl MAIDW ME16 .....155 H5
　NRWD SE19 .....60 D9
Dargate Rd WSTB CT5 .....134 C5
Dargets Rd WALD ME5 .....125 M2
Dark Hl FAV ME13 .....132 E5
Darland Av GILL ME7 .....96 B4
Darley Cl CROY/NA CR0 .....83 H6
Darlinghurst Rd FOLKN CT19 ..310 B4
Darling Rd BROCKY SE4 .....41 N6
Darlington Rd IOS ME12 .....77 P1
Darlington Rd WNWD SE27 .....60 B4
Darlington St FOLK CT20 .....10 E3
Darlton Cl DART DA1 .....45 M4
Darman La STPH/PW TN12 .....213 L7
Darnets Fld RSEV TN14 .....148 E2
Darnley Cl BRDST CT10 .....143 L1
　FOLK CT20 .....310 C2
Darnley Dr STH/RUST TN4 .....240 B5
Darnley Rd GRAYS RM17 .....32 C9
　GVW DA11 .....49 L2
　STRD ME2 .....71 M9
Darns Hl SWLY BR8 .....87 N6
Darracott Cl DEAL CT14 .....232 G4
Darrell Cl HB CT6 .....107 H3
Darren Gdns BRDST CT10 .....143 L2
Darrick Wood Rd ORP BR6 .....86 E6
Dart Cl STRD ME2 .....72 F3
Dartford Rd BXLY DA5 .....45 L9
　DART DA1 .....46 A7
　EYN DA4 .....89 M2
　SEV TN13 .....21 G1
Dart Gn SOCK/AV RM15 .....31 L2
Dartmoor Wk POP/IOD E14 * ...25 K7
Dartmouth Hl GNWCH SE10 .....42 A2
Dartmouth Pl FSTH SE23 .....61 J1
Dartmouth Rd HAYES BR2 .....85 K4
　SYD SE26 .....61 J3
Dartmouth Rw GNWCH SE10 .....42 A3
Dartmouth Ter GNWCH SE10 ...42 B3
Dartnell Rd CROY/NA CR0 .....83 L4
Dartview Cl GRAYS RM17 .....32 F7
Darwin Cl ORP BR6 .....86 F9
Darwin Ct ROCH ME1 * 19 H6
Darwin Dr TONN TN10 .....210 G4
Darwin Rd FOLK CT20 .....110 G5
　TIL RM18 .....49 K2
　WELL DA16 .....44 A7
Darwin St WALW SE17 .....24 A7
Daryngton Av BRCH CT7 .....110 D6
Dashmonden Cl STRD ME2 .....72 C5
Dashwood Cl BXLYHS DA6 .....45 J6
Dashwood Rd GVW DA11 .....49 L9
Dassett Rd WNWD SE27 .....60 B5
Datchelor Pl CMBW SE5 * 40 D2
Datchet Rd CAT SE6 .....61 M2
Davenant St WCHPL E1 .....24 D1
Davenport Av GILL ME7 .....73 L9
Davenport Rd LEW SE13 .....41 P7
　SCUP DA14 .....64 J1
Davern Cl GNWCH SE10 .....26 A7
Davey St PECK SE15 .....24 C9
David Av MARG CT9 .....113 J3
Davids Cl BRDST CT10 .....143 N1
Davidson Rd CANTW/ST CT2 .....4 A2

　CROY/NA CR0 .....83 K5
David's Rd FSTH SE23 .....61 J9
Davie Cl IOS ME12 .....57 K8
Davies Cl SNWD SE25 .....83 L3
Davington Hl FAV ME13 .....132 F5
Davis Av DEAL CT14 .....232 F5
Davis Cl SEV TN15 .....149 H7
Davis Rd CDW/CHF RM16 .....32 A6
　SOCK/AV RM15 .....30 G4
Davy's Pl GVE DA12 .....70 A5
Davy Ct BH/WHM TN16 .....145 M2
Dawes Cl GRH DA9 .....47 H6
Dawes Rd CANTW/ST CT2 .....134 E8
Dawes St GILL ME7 .....7 H2
　WALW SE17 .....24 A8
Dawley Gn SOCK/AV RM15 .....31 K2
Dawn Rd IOS ME12 .....71 N1
Dawson Av STMC/STPC BR5 .....64 D8
Dawson Gdns BRDST CT10 .....27 K7
Dawson Dr SWLY BR8 .....65 N6
Dawsons Rw FAV ME13 * 132 D7
Dawson's Rd PECK SE15 .....41 J2
Days La BFN/LL DA15 .....44 A8
Daytona Wy HB CT6 .....106 F2
Dayton Dr ERITH DA8 .....30 A9
Dayton Gv PECK SE15 .....41 J2
Dayton Rd FAV ME13 .....162 B9
Deacon Ct STRD ME2 * 71 N7
Deacon Cl LING RH7 .....234 F5
Deacons Leas ORP BR6 .....86 E8
Deadmans La RYE TN31 .....338 F6
Deakin Leas TON TN9 .....240 C2
Deakins Ter ORP BR6 .....87 H4
Deal Castle Rd DEAL CT14 .....233 J4
Deal Porters Wy
　BERM/RHTH SE16 .....24 F6
Deal Rd DEAL CT14 .....231 D4
　SWCH CT13 .....201 N5
Deals Ctwy DEPT SE8 .....41 P2
The Deals RYE TN31 .....338 E7
Deal St WCHPL E1 .....24 D1
Deal Wk BRXN/ST SW9 .....40 A1
Dean Crl HB CT6 .....107 N4
Deancross St WCHPL E1 .....24 E2
Deane Cl WSTB CT5 .....105 M7
Deanery Rd EDEN TN8 .....206 D1
Deanfield Gdns
　CROY/NA CR0 .....83 J8
Dean Hl RCANTW CT4 .....226 A6
Dean La MEO DA13 .....92 E7
Dean Rd CROY/NA CR0 .....83 J8
　GVW DA11 .....68 F3
　HYTHE CT21 .....309 H5
　RASHW TN26 .....280 C5
　SEV TN13 .....68 C9
Dene Wk HART DA3 .....68 C9
Dene Wy RRTW TN3 .....269 M1
Dengemarsh Rd LYDD TN29 ..342 B9
Dengrove Pk
　CANTW/ST CT2 * 137 J7
Denham Cl LYDD TN29 .....327 M1
Denham Rd RSIT ME9 .....98 C7
Denison Ms HOO/HM ME3 .....54 G4
Deniston Av BXLY DA5 .....44 F9
Denleigh Gdns TONN TN10 .....214 B7
Denman Rd PECK SE15 .....40 F2
Denmark Hl HNHL SE24 .....40 D5
Denmark Rd BMLY BR1 .....62 C2
　CMBW SE5 .....40 C2
　RAM CT11 .....17 G2
　SNWD SE25 .....61 L1
Denmark St FOLKN CT19 .....11 G1
　PLSTW SE13 .....26 C1
Denmark Ter ASH TN23 * 2 E7
Denmead Rd CROY/NA CR0 .....82 G5
Dene Manor La
　RCANTW CT4 .....193 M4
Dennes La LYDD TN29 .....342 A3
Dennes Mill Cl RASHE TN25 ..225 N8
Denness Rd ASH TN23 .....282 E1
Dennett Rd CROY/NA CR0 .....82 G5
Dennett's Gv NWCR SE14 .....41 K3
Dennettsland Rd EDEN TN8 ...206 D1
Dennett's Rd NWCR SE14 .....41 J2
Denning Av CROY/NA CR0 .....82 F9
Denning Cl MAIDW ME16 .....154 G8
Dennis Rd GVW DA11 .....49 J8
Dennis Wy FOLKN CT19 .....310 B4
Den Rd HAYES BR2 .....62 B9
Densole La BECK BR3 .....61 L7
Densole La RFOLK CT18 .....288 D4
Densole Wy RFOLK CT18 .....288 C4
Densted Ct CANTW/ST CT2 * ..136 B9
Denstead La RCANTW CT4 .....165 J4
Denstroude La
　CANTW/ST CT2 .....135 K5
Dental Cl SIT ME10 .....129 H1
Dental St HYTHE CT21 .....309 H5
Dent Cl SOCK/AV RM15 .....31 K2
Dent-de-Lion Ct MARG CT9 ...111 P5
Dent-de-Lion Rd MARG CT9 ...111 P5

Delisle Rd THMD SE28 .....27 M5
Delius Dr TONN TN10 .....211 J4
Dell Cl WLGTN SM6 .....82 D8
Dell Dr RTWE/PEM TN2 .....23 J2
Dellfield Cl BECK BR3 .....62 A7
Dellow St WCHPL E1 .....24 E3
Dell Rd GRAYS RM17 .....32 F7
The Dell ABYW SE2 .....27 P8
　BECK BR3 .....61 N6
　BXLY DA5 .....45 N9
　ECRIN RH19 .....265 L7
　GRH DA9 .....47 F6
　NRWD SE19 .....60 D3
Delmaney Cl BRDST CT10 .....113 N8
Delme Crs BKHTH/KID SE3 .....42 F5
Delmey Cl CROY/NA CR0 .....83 L7
Delmonden Rd HAWK TN18 .....316 D4
Deloraine St DEPT SE8 .....41 N2
De Lucy Rd ERITH DA8 .....29 H8
De Lucy St ABYW SE2 .....28 A7
Delves Av RTWE/PEM TN2 .....270 F7
De Mere Cl RHAM ME8 .....96 G8
Demesne Rd WLGTN SM6 .....82 D8
Demozay Cl RFOLK CT18 .....288 D8
Denbeigh Dr TONN TN10 .....210 G4
Denberry Dr SCUP DA14 .....64 D2
Denbigh Av RHAM ME8 .....96 G5
Denbigh Cl CHST BR7 .....63 K5
　RHAM ME8 .....99 M7
Denbigh Pl ASH TN23 * 252 E9
Denbigh Rd MSTR CT12 .....142 F5
　STH/RUST TN4 .....270 F1
Dence Cl HB CT6 .....107 N1
Dence Pk HB CT6 .....107 N2
Den Cl BECK BR3 .....84 C1
Dencora Wy ASH TN23 .....2 A5
Dene Av BFN/LL DA15 .....44 D8
Dene Cl BROCKY SE4 .....41 L4
　HAYES BR2 .....85 J5
　RDART DA2 .....66 G3
Denecroft Gdns GRAYS RM17 ..32 E6
Dene Dr HART DA3 .....68 F8
　ORP BR6 .....87 J2
Dene Farm La RCANTE CT3 .....199 K3
Dene Holm Rd GVW DA11 .....49 J1
Dene Lodge Cl BGR/WK TN15 ..151 J5
Dene Pth SOCK/AV RM15 .....31 K2
Dene Rd DART DA1 .....46 F8
Deneway RDV CT15 .....280 A2
The Dene CANT CT1 .....166 C7
　CROY/NA CR0 .....84 A8
　HYTHE CT21 .....309 H5
Denton Court Rd GVE DA12 .....50 A9
Denton Rd BXLY DA5 .....45 M9
　WELL DA16 .....44 E1
Denton St GVE DA12 .....50 A9
Denton Ter BXLY DA5 * 45 M9
Denton Wy MARG CT9 .....113 H4
Denton Whf GVE DA12 * 50 B7
Denver Ct ORP BR6 .....86 F5
Denver Rd DART DA1 .....46 A8
Depot Cl CHAT ME4 .....6 C4
Depot St CMBW SE5 .....24 B8
Deptford Br GNWCH SE10 .....41 N2
Deptford Broadway DEPT SE8 ..41 N2
Deptford Church St DEPT SE8 ..41 N1
Deptford Gn DEPT SE8 .....25 K9
Deptford High St DEPT SE8 ...25 K9
Deptford Whf DEPT SE8 .....25 J7
De Quincey Ms CAN/RD E16 .....26 B8
Derby Cl RTON TN11 .....210 B4
　SIT ME10 .....99 L8
Derby Hl FSTH SE23 .....61 J1

Derby Hill Crs *FSTH* SE23 ....61 J1
Derby Rd *CROY/NA* CR0 ....82 C6
   MAID/SHEP ME15 ....185 P3
   WALD ME5 ....84 B4
Derby Road Br *GRAYS* RM17 ....32 C8
Derek Av *WLGTN* SM6 ....82 A7
Derek Walcott Cl *HNHL* SE24 * 40 B6
Derifall Cl *EHAM* E6 ....26 C1
Dering Cl *HDCN* TN27 ....250 B5
Dering Rd *CROY/NA* CR0 ....83 H8
   HB CT6 ....107 J2
   KEN/WIL TN24 ....3 H4
   RCANTW CT4 ....197 L2
Dering Wy *GVE* DA12 ....50 B9
Deringwood Dr
   MAID/SHEP ME15 ....186 C2
Dermody Gdns *LEW* SE13 * 42 B6
Dermody Rd *LEW* SE13 ....42 B6
Dernier Rd *TON* TN9 ....210 F6
Deronda Rd *BRXS/STRHM* SW2 ....40 B9
Derrick Gdns *CHARL* SE7 ....26 D6
Derrick Rd *BECK* BR3 ....61 M9
Derringstone HI *RCANTW* CT4 ....228 C8
Derringstone St *RCANTW* CT4 ....228 C7
Derry Av *SOCK/AV* RM15 ....31 K1
Derry Downs *STMC/STPC* BR5 ....87 K3
Derry Rd *CROY/NA* CR0 ....82 D6
Derville Rd *LYDD* TN29 ....343 K5
Derwent Av *RAM* CT11 ....142 F5
Derwent Cl *DART* DA1 ....46 B9
Derwent Dr *BXLYHN* DA7 ....45 J3
Derwent Dr *STH/RUST* TN4 ....270 B3
   STMC/STPC BR5 ....86 E4
Derwent Pde *EDUL* SE22 * 61 H1
Derwent Pde *SOCK/AV* RM15 ....31 K2
Derwent Rd *POE/AN* SE20 ....60 G8
   TONN TN10 ....210 F5
Derwent St *GNWCH* SE10 ....25 P8
Derwent Wy *RCANTW* CT3 ....169 J3
   RHAM ME8 ....96 C6
Desenfans Rd *DUL* SE21 ....40 E7
Desmond Crs *MAID/SHEP* ME15 * 133 K8
Desmond St *NWCR* SE14 ....25 H9
Desmond Tutu Dr *FSTH* SE23 ....41 L4
D'Este Rd *RAM* CT11 ....17 H3
Detillens La *OXTED* RH8 ....175 K5
Detling Cl *BRDST* CT10 ....143 M5
   RHAM ME8 ....57 K9
Detling HI *MAID/BEAR* ME14 ....156 D3
Detling Rd *BMLY* BR1 ....62 E4
   ERITH DA8 ....45 M1
   GVW DA11 ....49 H9
Devalls Cl *EHAM* E6 ....27 H3
Devema Cl *CHST* BR7 ....63 L7
Devenish Rd *ABYW* SE2 ....27 P5
Deveraux Cl *BECK* BR3 ....84 F2
Deverell St *STHWK* SE1 ....24 A6
Devereux Rd *CDW/CHF* RH16 ....32 A6
Devon Av *CHST* BR7 ....63 J6
Devon Cl *RHAM* ME8 ....97 J5
   WALD ME5 ....95 P7
Devon Gdns *DART* CT14 ....110 G7
Devonport St *WCHPL* E1 ....24 F2
Devon Rd *CANT* CT1 ....167 J4
   EYN DA4 ....67 H7
   FOLKN CT19 ....10 E3
   MAID/SHEP ME15 ....185 P2
Devonshire Av *DART* DA1 ....46 B7
Devonshire Cl
   RTWE/PEM TN2 ....270 C8
Devonshire Dr *GNWCH* SE10 ....41 P2
Devonshire Gdns *MARG* CT9 ....112 G3
   SLH/COR SS17 ....33 P6
Devonshire Gr *PECK* SE15 ....24 E9
Devonshire Rd *BXLYHS* DA6 ....44 G5
   CAN/RD E16 ....26 B5
   CDW/CHF RH16 ....31 P7
   CROY/NA CR0 ....83 J4
   DVW CT17 ....291 J7
   ELTH/MOT SE9 ....43 J1
   FSTH SE23 ....41 K8
   GILL NE2 ....73 J8
   GVW DA11 ....49 M9
   ORP BR6 ....87 H4
Devonshire Rw *LVPST* EC2M 24 B1
Devonshire Sq *HAYES* BR2 ....85 L1
   LVPST EC2M 24 B2
Devonshire Ter *BRDST* CT10 ....113 N9
   EDUL SE22 * 40 C5
Devons Rd *BOW* E3 ....25 K1
Devon St *PECK* SE15 ....24 E9
Dewar St *PECK* SE15 ....40 G4
Dewberry Gdns *EHAM* E6 ....26 F1
Dewberry St *POP/IOD* E14 ....25 M2
Dewbury Cl *CHAT* ME4 ....73 H6
Dewlands Av *RDART* DA2 ....47 H8
Dewsbury Gdns *RAM* CT11 ....142 B6
   RASHE TN25 ....252 F1
Dexter Dr *EGRIN* RH19 ....265 H8
D'Eynsford Rd *CMBW* SE5 ....40 D2
Dhekelia Cl *MAID/BEAR* ME14 ....155 M5
Dial Cl *GILL* ME7 ....72 D3
Dial Rd *GILL* ME7 ....73 M9
Diameter Rd *STMC/STPC* BR5 ....86 C4
Diamond Cl *CDW/CHF* RH16 ....32 A6
Diamond Ct *IOS* ME12 ....57 K8
Diamond Rd *WALD* CT5 ....100 NE
Diamond St *PECK* SE15 ....40 E1
Diamond Vis *NROM* TN28 * 336 E7
Diana Cl *CDW/CHF* RH16 ....32 A6
   DEPT SE8 ....41 L9
   SCUP DA14 ....64 D7
Diana Gdns *DEAL* CT14 ....232 F4
Diana Rd *CHAT* ME4 ....95 M4
Dianthus Cl *ABYW* SE2 * 28 A8
Dibden La *SEV* TN14 ....178 D3
Dibdin Rd *DEAL* CT14 ....233 J2

Dickens Av *CANT* CT1 ....167 H2
   DART DA1 ....46 C5
   TIL RM18 ....49 M2
Dickens Cl *EGRIN* RH19 ....264 F7
   ERITH DA8 ....45 K1
   RAM CT11 ....91 H2
   RMAID ME17 ....187 H7
Dickens Dr *CHST* BR7 ....63 N5
   RHAM ME9 ....153 N3
Dickens Est
   BERM/RHTH SE16 * 24 C6
Dickensian Cl *HOO/HM* ME3 ....54 E5
Dickenson's La *SNWD* SE25 ....83 M3
Dickenson's Pl *SNWD* SE25 ....83 M3
Dickens Rd *BRDST* CT10 ....113 N8
   GVE DA12 ....50 A9
   MAID/BEAR ME14 ....155 J5
   ROCH ME1 ....95 H4
Dickens Wk *HOO/HM* ME3 * 52 F4
Dickens Wood Cl *NRWD* SE19 ....60 B6
Dickley La *RMAID* ME17 ....189 H5
Dickson House
   WOOL/PLUM SE18 * 43 J1
Dickson Rd *ELTH/MOT* SE9 ....8 A3
   ELTH/MOT SE9 ....43 H1
Dicksons Bourne *RASHE* TN25 ....306 A2
Dieu Stone La *DVE/WH* CT16 ....8 E3
Digby Pl *CROY/NA* CR0 ....83 L6
Digby Rd *FOLK* CT20 ....310 B6
Digdoga La *CRBK* TN17 ....277 H5
Diggon St *WCHPL* E1 ....24 G1
Dignals Cl *RHAM* ME8 ....97 J4
Dilhorne Cl *LEE/GVPK* SE12 ....62 F2
Diligent Dr *SIT* ME10 ....99 N7
Dillon Wy *RTWE/PEM* TN2 ....270 C2
Dillwyn Cl *SYD* SE26 ....61 L3
Dilly Fields Wd *HOO/HM* ME3 ....72 A4
Dillywood La *HOO/HM* ME3 ....71 N5
Dilnot La *BRCH* CT7 ....141 J1
Dimmock Cl *STPH/PW* TN12 ....243 J5
Dingleden La *CRBK* TN17 ....318 F4
Dingle Gdns *POP/IOD* E14 * 25 K3
Dingwall Av *CROY/NA* CR0 ....83 H6
Dingwall Rd *CROY/NA* CR0 ....83 J6
Dinsdale Gdns *BKHTH/KID* SE3 ....26 A3
Dinsdale Rd *BKHTH/KID* SE3 ....26 A9
Dippers Cl *BGR/WK* TN15 ....149 L2
Discovery Dr *E/WMAL* ME19 ....153 J9
Discovery Rd
   MAID/SHEP ME15 ....186 D1
Discovery Wk *CANT* CT1 ....167 H5
   WAP E1W 24 E3
Disraeli Rd *RTON* TN11 ....241 L6
Disraeli Cl *MAID/SHEP* ME15 ....186 B6
   THMD SE28 ....27 P7
Ditchburn St *POP/IOD* E14 ....25 M3
Dittisham Rd *ELTH/MOT* SE9 ....63 J3
Ditton Court Cl
   DIT/AY ME20 * 154 A3
Dittoncroft Cl *SAND/SEL* CR2 ....83 K8
Ditton Pl *DIT/AY* ME20 * 154 A3
   PGE/AN SE20 * 61 H7
Ditton Rd *BXLYHS* DA6 ....44 F6
Divis Cl *EHAM* E6 ....26 C2
   MAID/SHEP ME15 ....185 L1
Dixon Pl *WWKM* BR4 ....84 E5
Dixon Rd *NWCR* SE14 ....41 L2
   SNWD SE25 ....83 G6
Dixter La *RYE* TN31 ....329 P6
Dixter Rd *RYE* TN31 ....329 P6
Dixwell Cl *RHAM* ME8 ....96 G9
Dixwell Rd *FOLK* CT20 ....310 D8
Dobbie Cl *SIT* ME10 ....99 M8
Dobell Rd *ELTH/MOT* SE9 ....43 K6
Dobson Rd *GVE* DA12 ....70 A4
Dock Approach Rd
   GRAYS RM17 ....32 F8
Dockers Tanner Rd
   POP/IOD E14 ....25 K7
Dock Exit Rd *DVE/WH* CT16 ....9 J3
Dockhead *STHWK* SE1 ....24 C5
Dock Head Rd *CHAT* ME4 ....72 G6
Dock Hill Av *BERM/RHTH* SE16 ....24 G4
Dockland St *CAN/RD* E16 ....27 H4
Dockley Rd *BERM/RHTH* SE16 ....24 C6
Dock Rd *CAN/RD* E16 ....26 B4
   CHAT ME4 ....6 C1
   CHAT ME4 ....72 G8
   GRAYS RM17 ....32 E9
Dockside Rd *CAN/RD* E16 ....26 E3
Dock St *WCHPL* E1 ....24 D2
Doctor Hope's Rd *CRBK* TN17 ....298 A3
Doctors Cl *SYD* SE26 ....61 J4
Dodbrooke Rd *WNWD* SE27 ....60 A2
Doddington La *MAIDW* ME16 ....12 B3
Doddington Rd *RHAM* ME8 ....96 B6
Dodd Rd *TONN* TN10 ....211 H5
Dodd's La *DVE/WH* CT16 ....291 H4
Dod St *POP/IOD* E14 ....25 J2
Doebury Wk
   WOOL/PLUM SE18 ....27 P9
Doggerel Acre *WSTB* CT5 * 105 N7
Doggets Cl *EDEN* TN8 ....236 D1
Doggett Rd *CAT* SE6 ....41 N8
Doggetts Rw *HOO/HM* ME3 ....52 D8
Doggett's Sq *STRD* ME2 * 18 E2
Dog Kennel HI *EDUL* SE22 ....40 E4
Dog Kennel La *RFOLK* CT18 ....286 F2
Dogwood Cl *GVW* DA11 ....69 H1
   WALD ME5 ....126 A4
Dola Av *DEAL* CT14 ....232 G5
Dolben Ct *DEPT* SE8 * 25 J7
Dolphin Cl *BRDST* CT10 ....113 M3
   THMD SE28 ....28 B2
Dolphin Dr *RHAM* ME8 ....97 H9
Dolphin La *DVE/WH* CT16 ....8 E4
   POP/IOD E14 ....25 L3
Dolphin Pas *DVE/WH* CT16 ....8 E4
Dolphin Rd *FOLKN* CT19 ....310 C4
Dolphin St *DEAL* CT14 ....233 J2
   HB CT6 ....107 K1

Dolphin Wy *WTHK* RM20 ....31 H8
Dombey Cl *HOO/HM* ME3 ....71 L4
   ROCH ME1 * 95 H5
Dome Hill Pk *SYD* SE26 ....60 F5
Domett Cl *CMBW* SE5 ....40 D5
Dominion Rd *CROY/NA* CR0 ....83 L4
Dominion St *LVPST* EC2M 24 A1
Domneva Rd *MSTR* CT12 ....141 J6
   WCOS CT8 ....111 L5
Domonic Dr *ELTH/MOT* SE9 ....63 M2
Donald Biggs Dr *GVE* DA12 ....49 M9
Donald Moor Av *RSIT* ME9 ....131 H5
Donald Rd *CROY/NA* CR0 ....82 E3
Donaldson Rd
   WOOL/PLUM SE18 ....43 L2
Doncaster Cl
   MAID/SHEP ME15 ....186 C5
Doncella Cl *CDW/CHF* RH16 ....31 M7
Donegal Rd *CANT* CT1 ....5 K4
Donemowe Dr *SIT* ME10 ....99 N6
Donet Cl *RHAM* ME8 ....96 F9
Dongola Rd *STRD* ME2 ....72 A5
   WCHPL E1 ....25 H1
Donkey Aly *EDUL* SE22 ....40 G8
Donkey Fld *RTON* TN11 ....209 K9
Donkey La *EYN* DA4 ....89 H6
   RCANTE CT3 ....198 F7
Donkey St *LYDD* TN29 ....326 G2
Donnahay Rd *MSTR* CT12 ....143 H1
Donnella Cl *CDW/CHF* RH16 ....31 N6
Donne Pl *MTCM* CR4 ....82 A1
Don Phelan Cl *CMBW* SE5 ....40 D2
Don Brae *STH/RUST* TN4 ....240 D7
Dorado Gdns *ORP* BR6 ....87 L7
Doran Av *E/WMAL* ME19 ....44 A1
Dora St *POP/IOD* E14 ....25 J2
Dorchester Av *BXLY* DA5 ....44 F9
Dorchester Cl *DART* DA1 ....46 F8
   HOO/HM ME3 ....52 B9
   STMC/STPC BR5 ....64 D6
Dorchester Ct *HNHL* SE24 ....40 C6
Dorchester Rd *GVE* DA12 ....69 P2
Dorcis Av *BXLYHN* DA7 ....44 G3
Doric Av *STH/RUST* TN4 ....240 C8
Doric Cl *STH/RUST* TN4 ....240 D7
   RCANTE CT3 ....116 C6
Doris Vis *SWCH* CT13 * 201 P1
Dorking Cl *DEPT* SE8 ....25 J9
Dorking Rd *RTW* TN1 ....270 F2
Dorman Av North
   RCANTE CT3 ....199 H9
Dorman Av South
   RCANTE CT3 ....229 J1
Dormans Av *LING* RH7 ....235 K7
Dormans Cl *LING* RH7 ....235 K9
Dormans High St *LING* RH7 ....265 K1
Dormans Park Rd
   EGRIN RH19 ....264 C5
   EGRIN RH19 ....265 H2
Dormans Rd *LING* RH7 ....235 K7
Dormans Station Rd
   LING RH7 ....265 J1
Dormers Dr *MEO* DA13 ....57 N4
Dornberg Cl *BKHTH/KID* SE3 ....42 E1
Dornberg Rd *BKHTH/KID* SE3 * 42 F1
Dornden Gdns *WALD* ME5 ....125 N3
Dorney Ri *STMC/STPC* BR5 ....86 C1
Dornton Rd *SAND/SEL* CR2 ....83 K9
Dorothy Av *CRBK* TN17 ....298 A3
Dorothy Dr *RSIT* ME9 ....131 P7
Dorothy Evans Cl *BXLYHN* DA7 ....45 N5
Dorrington Wy *BECK* BR3 ....84 F2
Dorrit Wy *CHST* BR7 ....63 N5
   ROCH ME1 ....95 J4
Dorset Av *EGRIN* RH19 ....264 F5
   WELL DA16 ....44 A5
Dorset Crs *WSTB* CT5 ....105 J7
Dorset Dr *WSTB* CT5 ....105 J7
Dorset Rd *BRCH* CT7 ....110 G6
   DEAL CT14 ....233 H7
   EGRIN RH19 ....264 F5
   STRHM/NOR SW16 ....82 B2
Dorville Rd *LEE/GVPK* SE12 ....42 E6
Dothill Rd *WOOL/PLUM* SE18 ....43 M1
Dotterel Cl *WALD* ME5 ....126 A4
Doubleday Dr *RSIT* ME9 ....130 C5
Doubleton La *RTON* TN11 ....238 F4
Douglas Av *HYTHE* CT21 ....309 H5
   THHTH CR7 ....105 M5
Douglas Cl *BRDST* CT10 ....113 K8
   CDW/CHF RH16 ....31 P6
Douglas Dr *CROY/NA* CR0 ....84 D7
Douglas Pth *POP/IOD* E14 ....25 M8
Douglas Pl *POP/IOD* E14 * 25 M8
Douglas Rd *CAN/RD* E16 ....26 B1
   DEAL CT14 ....233 K6
   DVW CT17 ....291 J7
   HB CT6 ....107 M2
   MAIDW ME16 ....11 L3
   MEO DA13 ....189 L6
   TON TN9 ....44 D2
   WELL DA16 ....44 D2
Douglas Wy *NWCR* SE14 ....41 M1
Doug Siddons Ct *GRAYS* RM17 ....32 D9
Dour Cl *DVE/WH* CT16 ....9 J4
Douro Pl *DVE/WH* CT16 ....9 F4
Dour Side *DVW* CT17 ....290 C4
Dour St *DVE/WH* CT16 ....8 C2
Dout Wy *ROCH* ME1 ....19 K7
Douthwaite Sq *WAP* E1W 24 E4
Dove Ap *EHAM* E6 ....26 F1

Dove Cl *ASH* TN23 ....282 F5
Dove Cl *HOO/HM* ME3 ....31 P6
   HB CT6 ....107 K7
   HYTHE CT21 ....308 C7
   SAND/SEL CR2 ....114 A5
   WALD ME5 ....95 N8
   WSTB CT5 ....105 K7
Dove Ct *LOTH* EC2R * 24 A2
Dovedale Brch CT7 ....111 J6
Dovedale Cl *WELL* DA16 ....44 C2
Dovedale Ct *BRCH* CT7 ....111 J6
   KEN/WIL TN24 * 2 C7
Dovedale Rd *EDUL* SE22 ....41 H6
   RDART DA2 ....47 J9
Dove Lea Gdns *DART* CT17 ....290 F4
Doveney Cl *STMC/STPC* BR5 ....87 K7
Dover Cl *STH/RUST* TN4 ....82 F1
Dovercourt Rd *EDUL* SE22 ....40 E7
Dover Hl *TONN* TN10 ....311 H3
Dover Patrol *BKHTH/KID* SE3 ....42 F5
Dover Pl *ASH* TN23 ....231 L5
   DEAL CT14 ....231 J5
   DEAL CT14 ....262 E4
   FOLK CT20 ....11 F4
   LYDD TN29 ....344 B8
   NRWD SE19 ....60 D5
   RCANTW CT4 ....197 P5
   RDV CT15 ....262 C8
   RDV CT15 ....291 M3
   SWCH CT13 ....201 N5
   SWCH CT13 ....231 J1
   WOOL/PLUM SE18 ....43 M3
Dover Rd East *GVW* DA11 ....49 J8
Dover Rd *CANT* CT1 ....5 F6
   SIT ME10 ....129 M1
Doves Cl *HAYES* BR2 ....85 P6
Doves Cft *RSIT* ME9 ....129 K6
Doveton Rd *SAND/SEL* CR2 ....83 J9
Dowanhill Rd *CAT* SE6 ....42 B9
Dowding Rd *BH/WHM* TN16 ....115 N9
Dowding Wy *RTWE/PEM* TN2 ....241 H6
Dower House Crs
   STH/RUST TN4 ....240 B6
Dowgate Cl *TON* TN9 ....240 C2
Dowgate Hl *CANST* EC4R 24 A2
Dowlas St *CMBW* SE5 ....40 E1
Dowle Cl *LYDD* TN29 ....335 P6
Dowlerville Rd *ORP* BR6 ....116 C1
Dowling Cl *SNOD* ME6 ....123 M6
The Downage *GVW* DA11 ....69 L1
Down Av *RRTW* TN3 ....295 H4
Downbank Av *BXLYHN* DA7 ....45 M2
Down Barton Rd *BRCH* CT7 ....109 N9
Down Ct *ASH* TN23 ....282 B5
Down Court Rd *RSIT* ME9 ....160 A5
Downderry Rd *BMLY* BR1 ....62 B7
Downderry Wy *DIT/AY* ME20 ....154 A3
Downe Av *RSEV* TN14 ....116 D6
Downe Cl *WELL* DA16 ....44 E1
Downend *WOOL/PLUM* SE18 ....43 M1
Downer Ct *ROCH* ME1 ....95 K6
Downe Rd *HAYES* BR2 ....115 P5
   RSEV TN14 ....116 D6
Downham Wy *BMLY* BR1 ....62 C4
Downhill Cl *DVE/WH* CT16 * 290 E1
The Downings *EHAM* E6 ....27 H2
The Downings *HB* CT6 ....107 M4
Downland Cl *KEN/WIL* TN24 ....2 C2
Downlands *DEAL* CT14 ....232 C9
   RMAID ME17 ....188 C5
Downland Wk *MAID/SHEP* ME15 ....95 M9
Downleys Cl *ELTH/MOT* SE9 ....43 J4
Downman Rd *ELTH/MOT* SE9 ....43 K4
Downs Av *DART* DA1 ....46 B3
   WSTB CT5 ....105 M5
Downs Bridge Rd *BECK* BR3 ....62 B7
Downsend Cl *HDCN* TN27 ....221 H2
   HDCN TN27 ....247 P4
   MAID/BEAR ME14 ....155 M4
   RDV CT15 ....231 J9
   RFOLK CT18 ....288 D8
   SIT ME10 ....100 B6
Downs HI *BECK* BR3 ....62 B7
Downside Rd *BECK* BR3 * 61 N7
   FOLKN CT19 ....310 F4
   RCANTW CT4 ....198 B4
   RDV CT15 ....292 F1
   STRD ME2 ....18 B3
Downside *DVE/WH* CT16 ....261 H9
Downs Pk *HB* CT6 ....107 M2
Downs Rd *BECK* BR3 ....61 P8
   CANTW/ST CT2 ....136 E9
   DEAL CT14 ....232 C9
   FOLKN CT19 ....310 F5
   MAID/BEAR ME14 ....155 M4
   MEO DA13 ....69 H4
   RAM CT11 ....142 F6
   RDV CT15 ....231 M9
   THHTH CR7 ....82 C4
   WBY/YAL ME18 ....213 P1
The Downs *RAM* CT11 * 16 C6
   RCANTE CT3 ....169 M2
   RCANTW CT4 ....195 L2
Downs Vw *HART* DA3 ....91 H1
Downs Vw *ROCH* ME1 ....124 C4
Downsview Cl *SWLY* BR8 ....65 P9
Downsview Gdns *NRWD* SE19 ....60 A4
Downs View Rd
   MAID/BEAR ME14 ....155 M4
Downsview Rd *NRWD* SE19 ....60 A5
   SEV TN13 ....20 A4
Downsway *HDCN* TN27 ....221 H2
   OXTED RH8 ....285 K7
   RASHE TN25 ....285 K7
Downsway *ORP* BR6 ....86 F9
Downs Wd *MEO* DA13 ....122 A5
Downtown Rd
   BERM/RHTH SE16 ....25 H5

Dowson Cl *CMBW* SE5 * 40 D5
Doyle Cl *ERITH* DA8 ....45 N2
Draffin La *RYE* TN31 ....333 N9
Drage Rd *STPH/PW* TN12 ....212 F4
Dragonfly Wy *RFOLK* CT18 ....288 E8
Dragon Rd *PECK* SE15 ....24 B9
Dragoon Cl *DEPT* SE8 ....25 J8
Drainless Rd *SWCH* CT13 ....200 C4
Drake Cl *DEAL* CT14 ....233 H5
Drake Dr *BERM/RHTH* SE16 ....24 G5
Drake Crs *THMD* SE28 ....28 B2
Drakefeild Rd *NWCR* SE14 ....41 K3
Drake Ms *HAYES* BR2 ....85 M1
Drake Rd *BROCKY* SE4 ....41 M4
   CDW/CHF RH16 ....31 P5
   CROY/NA CR0 ....82 E4
   KEN/WIL TN24 ....283 K1
Drake's Av *STRD* ME2 ....71 P7
Drakes La *MROM* TN28 ....337 K9
Drakes Lee *NROM* TN28 ....337 K9
Draper Cl *BELV* DA17 ....28 E7
Drapers Av *MARG* CT9 ....112 C5
Drapers Cl *MARG* CT9 ....112 F5
Draper St *STH/RUST* TN4 ....240 C7
Drappers Wy
   BERM/RHTH SE16 ....24 D7
Draven Cl *HAYES* BR2 ....85 J4
Drawbridge Cl
   MAID/SHEP ME15 ....186 B3
Drawell Cl *WOOL/PLUM* SE18 ....27 M8
Dray Corner Rd *HDCN* TN27 ....247 J2
Draycott Cl *CMBW* SE5 ....40 D1
Dray Ct *RTON* TN11 ....211 P2
Drayton Av *ORP* BR6 ....86 E1
Drayton Cl *HOO/HM* ME3 ....53 L5
Drayton Rd *CROY/NA* CR0 ....82 C6
   TON TN9 ....240 F1
Dreadnought Av *IOS* ME12 ....78 A1
Dreadnought St *GNWCH* SE10 ....25 P6
Dressington Av *BROCKY* SE4 ....41 N7
Drewery Ct *BKHTH/KID* SE3 * 42 C4
Drewery Dr *RHAM* ME8 ....96 F9
Drew La *DEAL* CT14 ....233 H5
Drew Rd *CAN/RD* E16 ....26 D4
Driffield Gdns *STH/RUST* TN4 ....240 B2
The Drift *HAYES* BR2 ....85 N7
Drill La *RCANTE* CT3 ....168 E7
Drivers Rd *MAID* LING RH7 ....234 F6
The Drive *BECK* BR3 ....61 N8
   BXLY DA5 ....45 H1
   CANT CT1 ....166 C6
   CHST BR7 ....64 B7
   ERITH DA8 ....45 K1
   GVE DA12 ....69 P3
   HART DA3 ....91 H7
   ORP BR6 ....86 G6
   RRTW TN3 ....268 E3
   RTWE/PEM TN2 ....270 D7
   SCUP DA14 ....64 D2
   SEV TN13 ....83 J1
   TON TN9 ....240 E2
   WSTB CT5 ....106 C6
   WWKM BR4 ....84 C4
Droitwich Cl *SYD* SE26 ....60 G2
Drop Redoubt Rd *DVE/WH* CT17 ....8 B6
Drove Rd *IOS* ME12 ....57 N8
Drovers Pl *PECK* SE15 ....41 H1
Drovers Rd *SAND/SEL* CR2 ....83 J9
The Drove *CANTW/ST* CT2 ....137 M9
   DEAL CT14 ....261 H3
   DVE/WH CT16 ....261 H3
   WSTB CT5 ....106 C6
The Drove Wy *MEO* DA13 ....69 J6
The Droveway *RDV* CT15 ....292 C1
Druce Rd *DUL* SE21 ....40 E7
Drudgeon Wy *RDART* DA2 ....67 P2
Druid St *STHWK* SE1 ....24 C5
Druids Wy *HAYES* BR2 ....84 C1
Drum La *ASH* TN23 ....2 D3
Drum Major Dr *DEAL* CT14 ....232 C6
Drummond Cl *ERITH* DA8 ....45 N2
Drummond Rd
   BERM/RHTH SE16 ....24 C6
   CROY/NA CR0 ....83 H6
Drum St *WCHPL* E1 ....24 C2
Drury Crs *CROY/NA* CR0 ....82 D6
Drury Rd *TENT* TN30 ....301 H7
Dry Bank Ct *TONN* TN10 ....210 E6
Drybeck Av *RAM* CT11 ....142 E5
Dryden Cl *CANT* CT1 ....167 H5
Dryden Pl *TIL* RM18 ....49 M2
Dryden Rd *DVE/WH* CT16 ....291 J4
   WOOL/PLUM SE18 ....43 B2
Dryden Wy *ORP* BR6 ....87 H5
Dryhill La *SEV* TN14 ....148 A8
Dry Hill Park Crs *TONN* TN10 ....210 E7
Dry Hill Park Rd *TONN* TN10 ....210 E7
Dryhill Rd *BELV* DA17 ....28 F5
Dry Hill Rd *TONN* TN10 ....210 E7
Dryland Av *ORP* BR6 ....86 G8
Dryland Rd *BGR/WK* TN15 ....151 J6
Drywall *SIT* ME10 * 100 A8
   SNOD ME6 ....123 N5
Duarte Pl *CDW/CHF* RH16 ....32 A6
Ducard St *DEPT* SE8 ....71 N7
Duchess of Kent Ct
   DIT/AY ME20 * 154 D3
Duchess of Kent Dr
   CANT CT1 ....125 J1
Duchess' Wk *BGR/WK* TN15 ....21 K5
Ducketts Rd *DART* DA1 ....45 P6
Duckett St *WCHPL* E1 ....24 G1
Duck La *CANT* CT1 * 5 F2
   RASHW TN26 ....281 L9
Duckpit Rd *RCANTW* CT4 ....225 P5
Duck St *RCANTW* CT4 ....257 L5
Duckworth Cl *KEN/WIL* TN24 ....4 A2
Duddington Cl *ELTH/MOT* SE9 ....63 H3
Dudely Rd *DEAL* CT14 ....49 H8
Dudley Av *WCOS* CT8 ....111 K5
Dudley Cl *CDW/CHF* RH16 ....31 P5
Dudley Rd *FOLKN* CT19 ....11 H3

KEN/WIL TN24 ....253 H4
RTW TN31 ....22 C5
Dudrich Ms EDUL SE22 ....40 F6
Dudsbury Rd DART DA1 ....40 B7
Duffield Cl CDW/CHF RM16 ....32 A6
Duff St POP/IOD E14 ....25 L2
Dufrey Pl CMBW SE5 * 40 D1
Duggan Dr CHST BR7 ....63 J5
Duke Humphrey Rd
    BKHTH/KID SE3 ....42 C3
Dukes Av CDW/CHF RM16 ....32 B6
Dukes Hl CTHM CR3 ....304 A5
Dukes Meadow RASHW TN26 ....304 D8
    RTON TN31 ....208 E8
Dukes Orch BXLY DA5 ....45 L9
Duke's Pl HDTCH EC3A 24 B2
Dukes Rd RTW TN1 ....23 G1
Dukesthorpe Rd SYD SE26 ....61 K3
Duke St DEAL CT14 ....233 J2
    MARG CT9 ....15 G3
Duke Street Hl STHWK SE1 ....24 A4
Dukes Wk MAID/SHEP ME15 ....13 G5
Dukes Wy WWKM BR4 ....85 H7
Dukeswood WSTB CT5 ....106 C9
Dully Rd RSIT ME9 ....130 C9
Dulverton Rd ELTH/MOT SE9 ....63 N1
Dulwich Common DUL SE21 ....40 D9
The Dulwich Oaks DUL SE21 * 60 F2
Dulwich Rd HNHL SE24 ....40 G6
Dulwich Village DUL SE21 ....40 D7
Dulwich Wood Av NRWD SE19 ....60 E4
Dulwich Wood Pk NRWD SE19 ....60 E3
Dumborne La TENT TN30 ....320 G4
Dumbreck Rd ELTH/MOT SE9 ....43 L5
Dumb Woman's La RYE TN31 ....338 A9
Dumergue Av OBOR ME11 ....77 K2
Dumpton Gap Rd
    BRDST CT10 ....143 M2
Dumpton La RAM CT11 ....143 K3
Dumpton Park Dr RAM CT11 ....17 J1
Dumpton Park Rd RAM CT11 ....17 F1
Dunbar Cl BECK BR3 ....84 B1
    STRHM/NOR SW16 ....60 A8
Dunblane Rd ELTH/MOT SE9 ....43 J4
Duncan Cl WSTB CT5 ....105 L3
Duncan Rd BRCH CT7 ....110 F5
Duncan Rd GILL ME7 ....7 K3
    RAM CT11 ....16 D4
    WSTB CT5 ....105 L7
Dunch St WCHPL E1 ....24 E2
Duncombe Rd EDUL SE22 ....41 L8
Duncrievie Rd LEW SE13 ....42 B7
Duncroft WOOL/PLUM SE18 ....44 A1
Dundalk Rd BROCKY SE4 ....41 L4
Dundas Rd PECK SE15 ....41 J5
Dundee Rd SNWD SE25 ....83 N2
Dundee St WAP E1W 24 E4
Dundonald Cl ELTH/MOT SE9 * 63 J3
Dundonald Cl EHAM E6 ....26 F2
Dundonald Rd RAM CT11 ....16 C3
Dunedin Cl SIT ME10 ....129 K2
Dunedin Rd MSTR CT12 ....142 E3
Dunfield Gdns CAT SE6 ....60 C5
Dunelm St WCHPL E1 ....24 E2
Dunera Dr MAID/BEAR ME14 ....155 L5
Dunes Av RTN TN31 ....344 A1
Dunes Rd NROM TN28 ....343 J1
Dunfield Rd CAT SE6 ....61 P4
Dungeness Rd LYDD TN29 ....347 N5
    LYDD TN29 ....347 M5
Dunheved Cl THHTH CR7 ....82 F3
Dunheved Rd North
    THHTH CR7 ....82 F3
Dunheved Rd South
    THHTH CR7 ....82 F3
Dunheved Rd West
    THHTH CR7 ....82 F3
Dunkeld Rd SNWD SE25 ....83 J1
Dunkellin Gv SOCK/AV RM15 ....31 K2
Dunkellin Wy SOCK/AV RM15 ....31 K2
Dunkery Ri KEN/WIL TN24 ....252 E5
Dunkery Rd ELTH/MOT SE9 ....63 H3
Dunkin Rd DART DA1 ....46 C6
Dunkirk Dr WALD ME5 ....95 L8
Dunkirk Rd FAV ME13 ....164 B5
Dunkirk Rd North FAV ME13 ....164 C5
Dunkirk Rd South FAV ME13 ....164 C5
Dunkirk Sq RDV CT15 ....291 N4
Dunk's Green Rd RTON TN11 ....181 K6
Dunley Dr CROY/NA CRO 114 F1
Dunlin Dr CHAT ME4 ....73 J5
Dunlop Rd TIL RM18 ....49 K2
Dunnett Rd FOLKN CT19 ....310 B5
Dunning Cl SOCK/AV RM15 ....31 K1
Dunning's Rd ROCH ME1 ....19 G7
The Dunnings MAIDW ME16 ....184 F1
Dunning's Rd EGRIN RH19 ....265 H9
Dunnock Rd EHAM E6 ....26 F2
    RASHE TN25 ....252 E2
Dunn Street Rd GILL ME7 ....126 D5
Dunoon Ct RAM CT11 * 143 L3
Dunoon Gdns FSTH SE23 ....41 K8
Dunsfold Wy CROY/NA CRO 114 D8
Dunstall Cl LYDD TN29 ....326 F3
Dunstall Gdns LYDD TN29 ....326 E9
Dunstall La LYDD TN29 ....326 E9
Dunstall Welling Est
    WELL DA16 ....44 D3
Dunstan Av WGOS CT8 ....111 L6
Dunstan Gap
    STMC/STPC BR5 * 86 E3
Dunstan Gv STH/RUST TN4 ....270 F8
Dunstan Houses WCHPL E1 * 24 F1
Dunstan Rd STH/RUST TN4 ....270 E2
Dunstan's Gv EDUL SE22 ....61 J1
Dunstan's Rd EDUL SE22 ....40 G8
Dunster Ct MON EC3R 24 B3

Dunster Ter
    MAID/SHEP ME15 * 186 B5
Dunsterville Wy STHWK SE1 ....24 A5
Dunton Rd STHWK SE1 ....24 C7
Dunvegan Rd ELTH/MOT SE9 ....43 H5
Dunwich Rd BXLYHN DA7 ....45 H2
Duppas Av CROY/NA CRO 82 G8
Duppas Hill La CROY/NA CRO 82 F8
Duppas Hill Ter CROY/NA CRO 82 G7
Duppas Rd CROY/NA CRO 82 F8
Dupree Rd CHARL SE7 ....26 C8
Dura Den Cl BECK BR3 ....61 P6
Durant Rd SWLY BR8 ....66 A5
Durban Crs DVE/WH CT16 ....291 L5
Durban Rd BECK BR3 ....61 M8
    MARG CT9 ....15 K7
    WNWD SE27 ....60 C3
Durfey Pl CMBW SE5 * 40 D1
Durham Av HAYES BR2 ....83 M4
Durham Cl CANT CT1 ....166 E6
    DVW CT17 ....8 C4
    MAID/SHEP ME15 ....186 A2
Durham Hl BMLY BR1 ....62 D3
    DVW CT17 ....8 C4
Durham Ri WOOL/PLUM SE18 ....27 K8
Durham Rd BXLYHN DA7 ....85 K1
    RHAM ME8 ....96 F7
    SCUP DA14 ....64 D4
Durham Rd WCHPL E1 ....24 C1
Durham Ter PGE/AN SE20 * 61 H6
Durlin St HAYES BR2 ....46 B1
Durkins Rd EGRIN RH19 ....264 C5
Durley Gdns ORP BR6 ....87 J8
Durlock Rd MSTR CT12 ....141 K7
Durlock Av RAM CT11 ....16 A6
Durlock Rd RCANTE CT3 ....200 B4
The Durlocks FOLKN CT19 ....11 H4
Durndale La GVW DA11 ....69 K3
Durnford Cl CANTW/ST CT2 ....166 D2
Durning Rd NRWD SE19 ....60 D4
Durrant Wy ORP BR6 ....86 E9
    SWCM DA10 ....48 C8
Durrell Gdns WALD ME5 ....95 P5
Dursley Cl BKHTH/KID SE3 ....42 G3
Dursley Gdns BKHTH/KID SE3 ....43 H2
Dursley Rd BKHTH/KID SE3 ....42 G3
Durward St WCHPL E1 ....24 E1
Duthie St POP/IOD E14 ....25 M3
Dutton St GNWCH SE10 ....42 A2
Duval Dr ROCH ME1 ....95 K6
Dux Court Rd HOO/HM ME3 ....53 J8
Dux Hl BGR/WK TN15 ....181 J3
Dux La BGR/WK TN15 ....181 J2
Dwelly La LING RH7 ....205 M6
Dyke St STMC/STPC BR5 ....87 K4
Dyke Rd FOLKN CT19 ....11 H4
Dykes Wy HAYES BR2 ....82 D9
Dykewood Cl BXLY DA5 ....65 M2
Dylan Rd BELV DA17 ....29 H8
Dylways CMBW SE5 ....40 D5
Dymchurch Cl ORP BR6 ....86 F8
Dymchurch Rd HYTHE CT21 ....308 D7
    NROM TN28 ....337 H5
Dyneley Rd LEE/GVPK SE12 ....62 F3
Dynes Rd BGR/WK TN15 ....149 K2
Dynevor Rd STH/RUST TN4 ....270 F1
Dyngley Cl SIT ME10 ....99 M7

E

Eadred Wy SIT ME10 ....99 P5
Eagle Cl BERM/RHTH SE16 ....24 E8
    DIT/AY ME20 ....153 P2
Eagle Hl NRWD SE19 ....60 D5
    RAM CT11 ....16 C2
Eagle Rd RTW TN31 ....338 F6
Eagles Cl SIT ME10 ....130 B1
Eagles Dr BH/WHM TN16 ....145 N3
Eaglesfield Rd
    WOOL/PLUM SE18 ....43 M2
Eagles Rd GRN DA9 ....47 P5
Eaglestone Cl BGR/WK TN15 ....151 K4
Eagle Wy GVW DA11 ....48 E6
Ealdham Sq ELTH/MOT SE9 ....42 G5
Ealham Cl CANT CT1 ....166 C7
    KEN/WIL TN24 ....253 K9
Ealing Cl WALD ME5 ....125 N1
Eardemont Cl DART DA1 ....45 P5
Eardley Rd BELV DA17 ....28 F8
    SEV TN13 ....20 E2
Earl Cl WALD ME5 ....125 N1
Earl El WOOL/PLUM SE18 ....27 L8
Earl Rd GVW DA11 ....69 J1
Earl's Av FOLK CT20 ....10 B6
    KEN/WIL TN24 ....253 J8
Earlsfield Rd RASHE TN25 ....306 D1
Earlsfield Rd ELTH/MOT SE9 ....309 J5
Earlshall Rd ELTH/MOT SE9 ....43 K5
Earlsmead Crs MSTR CT12 ....142 B7
Earl's Rd STH/RUST TN4 ....22 A2
Earlsthorpe Rd SYD SE26 ....61 K3
Earl's St MAID/BEAR ME14 ....12 E4
    SDTCH EC2A 24 B1
Earlswood Av THHTH CR7 ....82 F2
Earlswood St GNWCH SE10 ....25 P8
Earlsworth Rd KEN/WIL TN24 ....282 C2
Easington Wy SOCK/AV RM15 ....31 K1
Easole Hts RDV CT15 ....229 N1
Eason Vis STPH/PW TN12 * 245 J3
East Arbour St WCHPL E1 ....24 G2
East Av CROY/NA CRO 82 E9
Eastbourne Rd EGRIN RH19 ....264 C2
    GDST RH9 ....204 C5
Eastbridge Rd LYDD TN29 ....326 E6
Eastbrook Pl DVE/WH CT16 * 8 E3
Eastbrook Rd BKHTH/KID SE3 ....270 L5
Eastbury Rd STMC/STPC BR5 ....86 E5
Eastchase FENCHST ECSM 24 A1
Eastchurch Rd IOS ME12 ....79 G2
    MARG CT9 ....113 K3
East Cliff DVE/WH CT16 ....9 G3

FOLKN CT19 ....11 H3
    RYE TN31 ....338 F7
East Cliff Gdns FOLKN CT19 ....11 H3
East Cliff Pde HB CT6 ....107 M1
East Cliff Pas FOLKN CT19 ....11 H3
East Cliff Rd STH/RUST TN4 ....270 D2
Eastcombe Av CHARL SE7 ....26 C9
Eastcote ORP BR6 ....86 G5
Eastcote Rd WELL DA16 ....43 P5
Eastcourt La EGRIN RH19 * 265 J6
    MAID/SHEP ME15 * 185 M2
Eastcourt Dr RHAM ME8 ....96 E5
Eastcourt La RHAM ME8 ....96 E4
East Cross TENT TN30 ....301 H8
Eastdown Pk LEW SE13 ....42 B5
East Dr STMC/STPC BR5 ....87 J3
East Dulwich Gv EDUL SE22 ....40 F7
East Dulwich Rd EDUL SE22 ....40 G5
Easterfields E/WMAL ME19 ....154 B7
Eastern Av ASH TN23 ....2 B3
    IOS ME12 ....57 M9
    QBOR ME11 ....77 K3
    SOCK/AV RM15 ....30 F5
    WTHK RM20 ....31 J8
Eastern Docks Rbt
    DVE/WH CT16 ....9 H5
Eastern Esp BRDST CT10 ....113 N7
    MARG CT9 ....112 G2
Eastern Gdns KEN/WIL TN24 ....253 H9
Eastern Gtwy CAN/RD E16 ....26 D3
Eastern Rd BROCKY SE4 ....41 N5
    GILL ME7 ....73 H9
    LYDD TN29 ....342 B6
Eastern Vw BH/WHM TN16 ....145 M2
Eastern Wy GRAYS RM17 ....32 B9
    TENT TN30 ....301 J6
Easter Wy GDST RH9 ....204 C5
East Ferry Rd POP/IOD E14 ....25 M6
Eastfield Gdns THHTH CR7 ....83 H6
Eastfield Rd BRCH CT7 ....111 H6
Eastfields FOLKN CT19 ....11 G2
Eastfield St POP/IOD E14 ....25 H1
Eastgate ROCH ME1 ....19 H6
Eastgate Cl HB CT6 ....107 N3
    THMD SE28 ....28 C2
Eastgate Ct ROCH ME1 ....19 G5
Eastgate Rd TENT TN30 ....301 J8
East Gn SIT ME10 ....99 M9
East Grinstead Rd LING RH7 ....234 C6
East Hall Hl RMAID ME17 ....216 B4
East Hall La RAIN TN13 ....100 B9
    SIT ME10 ....100 B9
East Hall Rd STMC/STPC BR5 ....87 M4
East Ham Manor Wy EHAM E6 ....27 H2
East Harbour 3 F5
    BH/WHM TN16 ....145 L3
    DART DA1 ....46 D3
    EGRIN RH19 ....265 H2
    EYN DA4 ....67 K7
    OXTED RH8 ....175 J5
East Hill Dr DART DA1 ....46 D3
East Hill Rd BGR/WK TN15 ....119 N6
    OXTED RH8 ....175 H5
East Holme ERITH DA8 ....45 M2
East India Dock Rd
    POP/IOD E14 ....25 K2
East India Wy CROY/NA CRO 83 L5
East Kent Av GVW DA11 ....69 H6
Eastlake Rd CMBW SE5 ....40 B3
Eastlands Cl OXTED RH8 ....174 C3
    STH/RUST TN4 ....270 E8
Eastlands Crs EDUL SE22 ....40 F7
Eastlands Wy OXTED RH8 ....174 G3
East La BERM/RHTH SE16 ....24 D5
    IOS ME12 ....57 J6
East Langdon Rd RDV CT15 ....291 M1
Eastleigh Rd BXLYHN DA7 ....45 M1
Eastling Cl RHAM ME8 ....96 C3
Eastling Rd FAV ME13 ....161 K6
East Lodge Rd ASH TN23 ....252 B6
Eastmead Av RAM CT11 ....142 C6
Eastmead Cl BMLY BR1 ....63 H4
Eastmearn Rd DUL SE21 ....60 C1
East Ml GVW DA11 ....49 K7
East Milton Rd GVW DA11 ....49 P8
Eastmoor Pl WOOL/PLUM SE18 ....26 G6
Eastmoor St CHARL SE7 ....26 E7
East Mountain La
    RASHE TN25 ....255 J2
East Mount St WCHPL E1 * 24 E1
East Park La CROY/NA CRO 82 G5
East Parkside WARL CR6 ....144 D1
East Pi WNWD SE27 ....60 C3
East Rd DVE/WH CT16 ....291 J6
    CAN/RD E16 ....5 H3
    DVW CT17 ....291 J6
    MSTR CT12 ....17 J5
East Rochester Wy
    BFN/LL DA15 ....44 A6
    DART DA1 ....45 M8
East Roman Ditch
    DVE/WH CT16 ....9 G2
East Rw ROCH ME1 ....19 J5
Eastry Av HAYES BR2 ....83 N3
Eastry Cl ASH TN23 ....282 C2
Eastry Ms MSTR CT12 * 201 J8
Eastry Rd ERITH DA8 ....116 N6
East Smithfield TWRH EC3N 24 C5
East St ASH TN23 ....2 E3
    BMLY BR1 ....62 B8
    BXLYHN DA7 ....45 M2
    CANT CT1 ....167 H1
    CHAT ME4 ....6 A2
    DVW CT17 ....8 A2

E/WMAL ME19 ....152 E2
    FAV ME13 ....132 C6
    FOLKN CT19 ....11 H4
    GILL ME7 ....7 K1
    SIT ME10 ....130 A1
    MAID/SHEP ME15 ....214 E2
    RMAID ME17 ....188 F6
    RYE TN31 ....338 F7
    SIT ME10 ....129 P2
    SNWD SE25 ....124 A5
    TON TN9 ....210 F8
East St (North) E/WMAL ME19 ....152 E1
East Surrey Gv PECK SE15 ....40 F1
East Sutton Rd HDCN TN27 ....217 K9
    MAID ME17 ....217 J3
East Ter WCHPL E1 ....44 A9
    GVE DA12 ....13 M6
East Thurrock Rd GRAYS RM17 ....32 C9
East Tilbury Rd SLH/COR SS17 ....33 P5
East Vw LYDD TN29 * 334 E5
    RCANTE CT3 ....138 C2
Eastview Av WOOL/PLUM SE18 ....44 A1
East Vls RCANTW CT4 ....164 C9
East Wy CROY/NA CRO 84 B6
Eastway HAYES BR2 ....85 K4
    WLGTN SM6 ....82 B8
East Weald Dr TENT TN30 ....301 J6
East Tenter St WCHPL E1 ....24 D2
Eastwell Cl BECK BR3 ....84 A8
    MAID/BEAR ME14 ....13 K2
    RASHW TN26 ....281 M7
    STPH/PW TN12 ....242 F2
Eastwell Mdw TENT TN30 ....301 H7
Eastwood Dr RAIN TN13 ....29 N2
Eastwood Rd RMAID ME17 ....218 D5
    SIT ME10 ....99 J3
Eaton Dr BRXN/ST SW9 ....40 B5
Eaton Dr BXLY DA5 ....46 A5
Eaton Rd MARG CT17 ....291 J8
    MARG CT9 ....15 G5
    SCUP DA14 ....64 F1
Eaves Rd DVW CT17 ....291 H8
Ebbsfleet La MSTR CT12 ....141 P9
Ebdon Wy BKHTH/KID SE3 ....42 B4
Ebley Cl PECK SE15 ....24 G9
Ebsworth St FSTH SE23 ....41 K8
Ebury Cl HAYES BR2 ....85 P3
Ecclesbourne Rd THHTH CR7 ....83 H2
Ecclesbourne Rw DIT/AY ME20 ....124 E7
Eccleston Cl ORP BR6 * 86 E5
Eccleston Rd
    MAID/SHEP ME15 ....185 N5
Echo Pl MAID/SHEP ME15 ....186 C5
Echo Ct GVE DA12 ....69 N1
Eclipse Dr SIT ME10 ....99 M6
Eclipse Rd PLSTW E13 ....26 C2
Ector Rd CAT SE6 ....62 C1
Eddington Cl
    MAID/SHEP ME15 ....185 N5
Eddy Rd CHAT ME4 ....107 J3
Eddystone Rd BROCKY SE4 ....41 N6
Eden Av WALD ME5 ....95 L7
Edenbridge Rd
    BERM/RHTH SE16 * 24 E8
    STMC/STPC BR5 ....87 L1
Edenbridge Dr IOS ME12 ....57 K8
Edenbridge Rd EDEN TN8 ....201 K6
Edenbrook LING RH7 ....235 H5
Eden Cl BXLY DA5 ....65 M5
Edendale Rd BXLYHN DA7 ....45 M2
Eden Farm La E/WMAL ME19 ....153 L5
Edenfield BRCH CT7 ....111 J6
Eden Gn SOCK/AV RM15 ....31 L1
Eden Park Av BECK BR3 ....84 D2
Eden Pde GVE DA12 ....49 M8
Eden Rd BECK BR3 ....84 D1
    BXLY DA5 ....65 L3
    CROY/NA CRO 83 J8
    HOO/HM ME3 ....53 L4
    RTW TN1 ....22 D7
    WNWD SE27 ....60 C1
    WSTB CT5 ....105 H7
Eden V EGRIN RH19 ....265 H4
    EGRIN RH19 ....265 H5
Eden Valley Wk EDEN TN8 ....236 A3
    RTON TN11 ....239 K2
Eden Wy BECK BR3 ....84 D3
    WARL CR6 ....144 B3
Edgar Cl SWLY BR8 ....65 P9
Edgar Rd BGR/WK TN15 ....149 K2
    BH/WHM TN16 ....145 N6
    CANT CT1 ....5 H3
    DVW CT17 ....291 J6
    MSTR CT12 ....15 K3
Edgeborough Wy BMLY BR1 ....63 H7
Edgebury CHST BR7 ....63 M5
Edgecombe SAND/SEL CR2 ....114 A3
Edge End Rd BRDST CT10 ....113 L9
Edgefield Cl DART DA1 ....46 C6
Edgehill Cl FOLK CT20 ....310 A4
Edgehill Gdns MEO DA13 ....69 K7
Edgehill Rd CHST BR7 ....63 N2
Edgeler Ct SNOD ME6 ....123 N6
Edgepoint Cl WNWD SE27 * 60 C3
Edgeway CHAT ME4 ....73 H5
Edgewood Dr ORP BR6 ....86 C9
Edgewood Gn CROY/NA CRO 84 A5
Edgeworth Rd
    ELTH/MOT SE9 ....42 G5
Edgington Wy SCUP DA14 ....64 E6
Edinburgh Ms TIL RM18 ....49 M3
Edinburgh Rd CHAT ME4 ....95 P4
    GILL ME7 ....7 J3
    HOO/HM ME3 ....56 C3
    KEN/WIL TN24 ....2 B5
    MARG CT9 ....112 A5

Edinburgh Sq
    MAID/SHEP ME15 ....185 P5
Edinburgh Wy EGRIN RH19 ....265 J6
Edington Rd ABYW SE2 ....28 A6
Edison Gv WOOL/PLUM SE18 ....44 B1
Edison Rd HAYES BR2 ....62 E8
    WELL DA16 ....44 B2
Edith Cavell Wy
    WOOL/PLUM SE18 ....43 J2
Edith Nesbit Wk
    ELTH/MOT SE9 ....43 J5
Edith Rd FAV ME13 ....132 F7
    ORP BR6 ....87 H9
    RAM CT11 ....16 B5
    SNWD SE25 ....83 J2
    WGOS CT8 ....111 N4
Ediva Rd MEO DA13 ....92 B2
Edmanson Av MARG CT9 ....111 P4
Edmund Cl MAIDW ME16 ....154 F9
    MEO DA13 ....92 B2
Edmund Halley Wy
    GNWCH SE10 ....25 P5
Edmund Hurst Dr EHAM E6 ....27 J1
Edmund Rd CDW/CHF RM16 ....31 N5
    STMC/STPC BR5 ....87 K3
    WELL DA16 ....44 C3
Edmunds Av STMC/STPC BR5 ....64 F9
Edmund St CMBW SE5 ....40 D2
    RCANTE CT3 ....169 K8
Edna Rd MAID/BEAR ME14 ....155 L5
Edred Rd DVW CT17 ....291 J7
Edric Rd NWCR SE14 ....41 L1
Edridge Rd CROY/NA CRO 83 H7
Edward Cl CDW/CHF RM16 ....31 N5
    CAN/RD E16 ....26 B1
Edward Ct CHAT ME4 ....6 E7
    WALD ME5 ....95 P5
Edward Dr BRCH CT7 ....111 J6
Edward Mann Cl West
    WCHPL E1 * 24 G2
Edward Mann Cl East
    WCHPL E1 * 24 G2
Edward Pl DEPT SE8 ....25 J9
Edward Rd BH/WHM TN16 ....145 P5
    BMLY BR1 ....62 C5
    CANT CT1 ....5 G5
    CHST BR7 ....63 M4
    CROY/NA CRO 83 K4
    DEAL CT14 ....233 P1
    FOLKN CT19 ....10 E1
    PGE/AN SE20 ....61 K6
    QBOR ME11 ....77 K2
Edwards Cl RHAM ME8 ....96 F9
Edwards Cl ES EYN DA4 ....89 K7
Edwards Gdns SWLY BR8 ....87 P1
Edwards Rd BELV DA17 ....28 F7
    DVE/WH CT16 ....8 D3
Edward St CHAT ME4 ....6 E7
    DEPT SE8 ....25 J9
    NWCR SE14 ....41 L1
    STH/RUST TN4 ....269 N4
    STRD SE8 ....18 D1
Edward Tyler Rd
    LEE/GVPK SE12 ....62 F1
Edward Wk E/WMAL ME19 ....153 N4
Edwina Av IOS ME12 ....58 A9
Edwin Hall Pl LEW SE13 ....42 B7
Edwin Petty Pl RDART DA2 * 47 J8
Edwin Rd RDART DA2 ....66 E6
    RHAM ME8 ....96 F6
Edwin St CAN/RD E16 ....26 B1
    DART DA1 ....49 M8
Edyngham Cl SIT ME10 ....99 P6
Effingham Crs DVW CT17 ....8 C3
Effingham Rd CROY/NA CRO 82 E4
    LEW SE13 ....42 C6
Effingham St DVW CT17 ....8 C3
    RAM CT11 ....17 F4
Effra Pde BRXS/STRHM SW2 ....40 A6
Effra Rd BRXS/STRHM SW2 ....40 A6
Egbert Rd BRCH CT7 ....110 E5
    FAV ME13 ....132 E7
    MSTR CT12 ....141 J6
    WGOS CT8 ....111 M4
Egerton Av SWLY BR8 ....65 P7
Egerton Cl DART DA1 ....46 B9
Egerton Dr GNWCH SE10 ....41 P2
    MARG CT9 ....113 K3
Egerton House Rd
    HDCN TN27 ....219 M6
Egerton Rd DVE/WH CT16 ....290 F5
    HDCN TN27 ....220 A8
    MAID/BEAR ME14 ....155 K5
    SNWD SE25 ....83 H3
Egerton Vls CROY/NA CRO * 311 H4
Eggarton La RCANTW CT4 ....194 C9
Eggpie La RTON TN11 ....209 J2
Eggringe ASH TN23 ....252 B8
Egham Rd PLSTW E13 ....26 C1
Eglantine La EYN DA4 ....89 N3
Eglinton Hl WOOL/PLUM SE18 ....27 J9
Eglinton Rd SWCM DA10 ....48 D7
    WOOL/PLUM SE18 ....27 H9
Eglise Rd WARL CR6 ....144 B2
Egmont St NWCR SE14 ....41 K1
Egremont Rd
    MAID/SHEP ME15 ....186 C1
    WNWD SE27 ....60 A2
Egret Cl CHAT ME4 ....73 H5
Eider Cl HB CT6 ....107 J4
Eighteen Acre La LYDD TN29 ....335 L5
Eighteenth Rd MTCM CR4 ....324 F7
Eileen Rd SNWD SE25 ....83 J2
Eisenhower Dr EHAM E6 ....26 F1
Elaine Av STRD SE8 ....71 N8
Elam Cl CMBW SE5 ....40 B3
Elam St CMBW SE5 ....40 B3
Eland Rd CROY/NA CRO 82 G5
Eland Rd SWCM DA10 ....31 K1
Elberon Av CROY/NA CRO 82 B3
Elborough St SNWD SE25 ....83 M2
Elbury Dr CAN/RD E16 ....26 B2
Elcot Av PECK SE15 ....25 J1
Elder Cl BFN/LL DA15 ....44 B9

HOO/HM ME3 ....73 L4
RMAID ME17 ....187 N9
Elder Ct RHAM ME8 ....96 E8
Elder Oak Cl PGE/AN SE20 ....61 H7
Elder Rd WNWD SE27 ....60 E3
Elderslie Cl BECK BR3 ....84 D3
Elderslie Rd ELTH/MOT SE9 ....43 L5
The Elders RCANTE CT3 ....168 C8
Elder St WCHPL E1 ....24 C1
Elderton Rd SYD SE26 ....61 L3
Eldon Av CROY/NA CRO 2 A5
Eldon Pk SNWD SE25 ....83 N1
Eldon Pl BRDST CT10 * 113 N9
Eldon St CHAT ME4 ....6 D4
LVPST EC2M * 24 A1
Eldon Wy STPH/PW TN12 ....242 G2
Eldred Dr STMC/STPC BR5 ....87 L6
Eleanor Dr SIT ME10 ....99 N6
Electric Av BRXN/ST SW9 ....42 G5
Electric La BRXN/ST SW9 * 40 A5
Elephant La BERM/RHTH SE16 ...24 F5
Elfindale Rd HNHL SE24 ....40 C6
Elford Cl BKHTH/KID SE3 ....42 G5
Elford Rd HOO/HM ME3 ....52 B3
Elfrida Ct MARG CT9 ....115 H5
Elfrida Crs CAT SE6 ....61 N3
Elf Rw WAP E1W 24 F5
Elgal Cl ORP BR6 ....86 C9
Elgar Cl DEPT SE8 ....41 N1
TONN 211 H4
Elgar Gdns TIL RM18 ....49 J2
Elgar Pl RAM CT11 ....16 E2
Elgar St BERM/RHTH SE16 ....25 H5
Elgin Rd CROY/NA CRO 83 J6
MARG CT9 ....3 H4
RHAM ME8 ....96 E4
Elham Cl BMLY BR1 ....63 H6
MARG CT9 ....3 H4
RHAM ME8 ....96 L4
Elham Rd CANT CT1 ....166 D6
Elham Valley Wy HYTHE CT21 ...308 F1
RCANTW CT4 ....197 N1
RFOLK CT18 ....287 H1
Elham Wy BRDST CT10 ....143 M2
Elibank Rd ELTH/MOT SE9 ....43 L5
Elim Est STHWK SE1 * 24 A6
Elim Est STHWK SE1 ....24 A6
Eliot Bank FSTH SE23 ....61 H1
Eliot Hi LEW SE13 ....42 A3
Eliot Pk LEW SE13 ....42 A3
Eliot Pl BKHTH/KID SE3 ....42 E3
Eliot Rd DART DA1 ....47 H6
Eliot V BKHTH/KID SE3 ....42 B3
Elizabeth Carter Av
DEAL CT14 ....232 E5
Elizabeth Cl TIL RM18 ....49 J2
Elizabeth Crs EGRIN RH19 ....265 J5
Elizabeth Ct RHAM ME8 ....96 F5
Elizabeth Dr RFOLK CT18 ....311 L1
Elizabeth Gdns HYTHE CT21 ....308 G6
Elizabeth Kemp Ct
MSTR CT12 ....143 H5
Elizabeth Pl EYN DA4 * 29 K1
Elizabeth Rd CDW/CHF RM16 ......32 A6
DVW CT17 ....8 C7
RAIN RM13 ....29 N1
RAM CT11 ....17 H3
Elizabeth Smith Ct
E/WMAL ME19 * 153 N5
Elizabeth Sq BERM/RHTH SE16 ...25 H3
Elizabeth St GRH DA9 ....65 J7
Elizabeth Wy HB CT6 ....107 N3
NRWD SE19 ....60 D6
STMC/STPC BR5 ....87 K2
Elland Rd PECK SE15 ....41 K4
Ellen Av RAM CT11 ....143 K5
Ellenborough Rd SCUP DA14 ......64 F5
Ellen Cl BMLY BR1 ....64 C3
Ellenden Rd CANTW/ST CT2 * ...136 B9
Eliens Rd DEAL CT14 ....232 D6
Ellen St WCHPL E1 ....24 D2
Ellenswood Cl
MAID/SHEP ME15 ....186 D2
Ellerdale St LEW SE13 ....41 P5
Ellerman Rd TIL RM18 ....49 K3
Ellery Rd NRWD SE19 ....60 D6
Ellery St PECK SE15 ....41 H3
Ellesmere Av BECK BR3 ....61 P8
Ellesmere Ms NROM ME8 ....337 H5
Ellesmere St POP/IOD E14 ....25 L2
Ellice Rd OXTED RH8 ....175 J5
Ellingham Leas
MAID/SHEP ME15 ....185 P3
Ellingham Wy ASH TN23 ....282 D3
Ellington Av MARG CT9 ....112 A5
Ellington Pl RAM CT11 ....16 C3
Ellington Rd RAM CT11 ....16 C3
Elliott Cl CANT CT1 ....167 H1
Elliott Pl FAV ME13 ....132 G6
Elliott Rd BRXN/ST SW9 ....42 B1
HAYES BR2 ....85 N1
THHTH CR7 ....82 C1
Elliotts La BW/WHM TN16 ....147 K9
Elliott's Rd FAV ME13 * 132 G6
Elliott St GVE DA12 ....13 M5
Ellis Av RAIN RM13 ....29 M1
Ellis Cl CDW/CHF RM16 ....33 L2
ELTH/MOT SE9 ....63 P6
Elliscombe Ms CHARL SE7 * 26 D9
Elliscombe Rd CHARL SE7 ....26 C9
Ellison Cl WSTB CT5 ....106 B5
Ellison Rd BFN/LL DA15 ....43 P9
Ellis La MEO DA13 ....54 F2
Ellison Wk RHAM ME8 ....96 F1
Ellison Wy SWLY BR8 ....80 A2
Ellis Rd WSTB CT5 ....105 P3
Ellis Waterton Cl SWLY BR8 ....80 E1
Ellis Wy DART DA1 ....66 F1
Elm Av CHAT ME4 ....6 D7
HOO/HM ME3 ....95 K5
Elmbank Dr RHAM ME8 ....96 F5
Elmbourne Dr BELV DA17 ....28 C7
Elmbrook Gdns ELTH/MOT SE9 ...43 L4
Elm Cl DART DA1 ....46 C9
HDCN TN27 ....219 N7
HOO/HM ME3 ....71 L4

WARL CR6 ....144 A2
Elm Ct GILL ME7 * 126 B2
HYTHE CT21 * 308 D6
Elmcourt Rd WNWD SE27 ....60 E1
Elm Crs E/WMAL ME19 ....153 N4
Elmcroft Av BFN/LL DA15 ....44 B8
Elmcroft Rd ORP BR6 ....87 H4
Elmdene Cl BECK BR3 ....84 C2
Elmdene Rd WOOL/PLUM SE18 ...27 J8
Elmdon Rd SOCK/AV RM15 ....31 K7
Elm Dr EGRIN RH19 ....265 K7
SWLY BR8 ....65 M8
Elmer Rd CAT SE6 ....42 A8
Elmers End Rd BECK BR3 ....61 J9
Elmerside Rd BECK BR3 ....84 B1
Elmers Rd CROY/NA CRO 83 M4
Elmfield RHAM ME8 ....96 D3
TENT TN30 ....301 J7
Elmfield Cl GVW DA11 ....49 M9
RSEV TN14 ....178 G9
Elmfield Ct RMAID ME17 * 185 H8
Elmfield Pk BMLY BR1 ....62 E9
Elmfield Rd BMLY BR1 ....62 E9
Elm Gdns HYTHE CT21 ....309 K5
MTCM CR4 ....62 G3
Elm Gv ERITH DA8 ....45 M1
MAID/SHEP ME15 ....13 H7
MSTR CT12 ....142 C3
ORP BR6 ....86 G5
PECK SE15 ....41 J4
SIT ME10 ....210 C6
SIT ME10 ....130 A1
WGOS CT8 ....111 M5
Elmgrove Rd CROY/NA CRO 83 N4
Elmhurst BELV DA17 ....28 D9
Elmhurst Av RTWE/PEM TN2 .....241 N9
Elmhurst Ct RASHE TN25 ....252 B5
Elmhurst Gdns ROCH ME1 ....95 J3
Elmhurst Rd ELTH/MOT SE9 ....63 J1
Elmington Cl BXLY DA5 ....45 K8
Elmington Est CMBW SE5 ....40 D1
Elmington Rd CMBW SE5 ....40 D1
Elmira St LEW SE13 ....41 P4
Elm La CAT SE6 ....61 M1
IOS ME12 ....78 C2
Elmlea Dr HAYES BR2 ....63 K5
Elmleigh Rd RCANTE CT3 ....168 D8
Elmley Rd IOS ME12 ....78 F2
Elmley St WOOL/PLUM SE18 ....27 L7
Elmley Wy MARG CT9 ....112 E6
Elm Pde SCUP DA14 * 64 F5
Elm Park Rd SNWD SE25 ....60 F9
Elm Rd BECK BR3 ....61 M8
BH/WHM TN16 ....176 F1
DART DA1 ....46 D9
ERITH DA8 ....45 M1
FOLKN CT19 ....11 L1
GRAYS RM17 ....32 D9
GRH DA9 ....47 L7
GVE DA12 ....69 N2
HOO/HM ME3 ....73 L4
LYDD TN29 ....337 L2
ORP BR6 ....117 H2
RCANTE CT3 ....229 H1
SCUP DA14 ....64 C3
SOCK/AV RM15 ....30 M4
STH/RUST TN4 ....240 C8
THHTH CR7 ....85 H1
WARL CR6 ....144 A2

Eltham Gn ELTH/MOT SE9 ....42 G6
Eltham Green Rd
ELTH/MOT SE9 ....42 G6
Eltham High St ELTH/MOT SE9 ....43 K7
Eltham Hl ELTH/MOT SE9 ....43 H6
Eltham Palace Rd
ELTH/MOT SE9 ....42 G7
Eltham Park Gdns
ELTH/MOT SE9 ....43 L5
Elthiruda Rd LEW SE15 ....42 B7
Elventon Cl FOLKN CT19 ....310 B4
Elverland La FAV ME15 ....161 N2
Elverson Ms DEPT SE8 ....41 M1
Elverson Rd DEPT SE8 ....41 P3
Elvington La MAIDW ME16 ....155 J1
Elvington La HAYES BR2 ....85 J2
Elvington La RFOLK CT18 ....288 D9
Elvino Rd SYD SE26 ....61 K4
Elwick Rd ASH TN23 ....2 D4
SOCK/AV RM15 ....31 M2
Elwill Wy BECK BR3 ....84 C1
MEO DA13 ....69 K7
Elwyn Gdns LEE/GVPK SE12 ....42 E8
Ely Ct ERITH DA8 ....45 J4
RHAM ME8 ....97 H4
Ely Ct RTW TN1 * 22 E3
Ely Gdns TON TN9 ....210 C6
Ely Rd CROY/NA CRO 83 J2
Elysian Av STMC/STPC BR5 ....86 F5
Embassy Cl GILL ME7 * 5 J5
Embassy Ct SCUP DA14 ....64 D2
Emba St BERM/RHTH SE16 ....24 D5
Ember Cl STMC/STPC BR5 ....86 D4
Embleton Rd LEW SE13 ....41 P5
Emerald Cl CAN/RD E16 ....26 F1
ROCH ME1 ....95 K4
Emerald Vw IOS ME12 ....80 C3
Emersons Av SWLY BR8 ....65 P6
Emerton Cl BXLYHS DA6 ....45 L5
Emes Rd ERITH DA8 ....45 L1
Emily Jackson Cl SEV TN13 ....20 E2
Emily Rd WALD ME5 ....95 N8
Emily St CAN/RD E16 ....26 A2
Emmerson Gdns WSTB CT5 ....106 B3
Emmet Hill La WBY/YAL ME18 ...213 N6
Emmett Hill La
WBY/YAL ME18 ....213 N5
Emmetts Rd BH/WHM TN16 ......177 K6
Empire Ter MARG CT9 ....112 D5
Empire Wharf Rd
POP/IOD E14 ....25 N7
Empress Dr CHST BR7 ....63 M5
Empress Gdns IOS ME12 ....80 B3
Empress Rd GVE DA12 ....50 A6
Emsworth Gv
MAID/BEAR ME14 ....156 A6
Enborne Gn SOCK/AV RM15 ....31 K1
Enbrook Rd FOLK CT20 ....310 B7
Enbrook Va FOLK CT20 ....310 B6
Encombe FOLK CT20 ....310 A8
Endeavour Pk
BGR/WK TN15 * 152 B3
Endeavour Wy CROY/NA CRO 82 D4
Enderby St GNWCH SE10 ....25 P8
Endwell Rd BROCKY SE4 ....41 L4
Enfield Rd DEAL CT14 ....233 J2
Engadine Cl CROY/NA CRO 3 L7
Engalee EGRIN RH19 ....264 F6
Engate St LEW SE13 ....42 A5
Engineer Cl WOOL/PLUM SE18 ...27 H9
Englefield Cl CROY/NA CRO 3 H1
Englefield Crs STMC/STPC BR5 ...86 G1
Englefield Pth STMC/STPC BR5 ...87 H1
Engleheart Rd CAT SE6 ....42 A8
Enid St STHWK SE1 ....24 B6
Enmore Av SNWD SE25 ....83 M2
Enmore Rd SNWD SE25 ....83 M2
Ennerdale FAV ME13 ....133 H7
Ennerdale Gdns RCANTE CT3 ....199 J9
Ennerdale Rd BXLYHN DA7 ....45 J2
Ennersdale Rd LEW SE13 ....42 A6
Ennis Rd WOOL/PLUM SE18 ....27 L9
Ensfield Rd RTON TN11 ....239 L2
Enslin Rd ELTH/MOT SE9 ....43 L7
Enterprise Cl CROY/NA CRO 82 F5
Enterprise Rd
MAID/SHEP ME15 ....185 M2
Enterprise Wy EDEN TN8 ....206 G1
Enterprise Wy DEPT SE8 * 25 J7
Enticott Cl WSTB CT5 ....105 P5
Epaul La ROCH ME1 ....6 B5
Epping Cl HB CT6 ....107 N4
POP/IOD E14 ....25 K7
Epple Bay Av BRCH CT7 ....111 H5
Epple Bay Rd BRCH CT7 ....111 H5
Epple Rd BRCH CT7 * 111 J5
Epps Rd SIT ME10 ....129 M2
Epsom Cl BXLYHN DA7 ....45 N4
E/WMAL ME19 ....153 J4
MAID/SHEP ME15 ....186 C5
Epsom Rd CROY/NA CRO 83 H4
Epsom Rd THMD SE28 ....28 A4
Erebus Dr WOOL/PLUM SE18 .....27 K6
Eresby Dr BECK BR3 ....84 D5
Erica Gdns CROY/NA CRO 84 E8
Eric Rd DVW CT17 ....291 J5
Eridge Green Cl
STMC/STPC BR5 ....87 K5
Erin Cl BMLY BR1 ....62 D5
Erindale WOOL/PLUM SE18 ....27 L9
Erindale Ter WOOL/PLUM SE18 ...27 L9
Erith Cl PUR RM19 ....30 D7
Erith High St ERITH DA8 ....29 M1
Erith Rd BELV DA17 ....45 J1
BXLYHN DA7 ....45 K4
ERITH DA8 ....45 M4
Erlanger Rd NWCR SE14 ....41 L3
Ermine Rd LEW SE13 ....41 P5
Ermington Rd ELTH/MOT SE9 .....63 N1

Ernan Cl SOCK/AV RM15 ....31 K1
Ernan Rd SOCK/AV RM15 ....31 K1
Ernest Av WNWD SE27 ....60 B3
Ernest Cl BECK BR3 ....84 D2
Ernest Dr MAIDW ME16 ....154 C2
Ernest Gv BECK BR3 ....84 C2
Erriff Dr SOCK/AV RM15 ....31 K1
Errington Cl CDW/CHF RM16 ......33 L8
Ersham Rd CANT CT1 ....5 C6
Erskine Park Rd
STH/RUST TN4 ....269 N4
Erskine Rd MEO DA13 ....122 C5
Erwood Rd CHARL SE7 ....26 F8
Esam Wy STRHM/NOR SW16 ......60 A4
Escreet Gv WOOL/PLUM SE18 ....27 H7
Eshcol Rd HOO/HM ME3 ....74 A1
Esher Cl BXLY DA5 ....44 E6
Eskdale Av RAM CT11 ....142 F5
Eskdale Cl RDART DA2 ....67 J1
Eskdale Rd BXLYHN DA7 ....45 J3
Eskley Gdns SOCK/AV RM15 ......31 L1
Eskmont Rdg NRWD SE19 ....60 E6
Esmeralda Rd STHWK SE1 ....24 D7
Esmonde Dr MSTR CT12 ....141 N2
Esplanade DVW CT17 * 8 D6
ROCH ME1 ....18 E6
Esplanade Quay WSTB CT17 ....18 D5
The Esplanade ROCH ME1 ....18 E5
Essella Pk KEN/WIL TN24 ....3 J5
Essella Rd KEN/WIL TN24 ....3 J5
Essenden Rd ASH TN23 ....282 D1
Essetford Rd ASH TN23 ....282 D1
Essex Cl RTWE/PEM TN2 ....270 C8
Essex Gdns BRXS/STRHM SW2 ...60 A2
Essex Rd RTWE/PEM TN2 ....270 C8
SLH/COR SS17 ....33 P5
Essex Gv NRWD SE19 ....60 D5
Essex Rd CANT CT1 ....167 J5
DART DA1 * 49 L9
GVW DA11 ....49 J9
HART DA3 ....68 B8
MAID/SHEP ME15 ....186 B5
STRD ME2 * 31 K9
WGOS CT8 ....111 N5
WTHK RM20 ....31 K9
Essex St WSTB CT5 ....105 L6
Essian St WCHPL E1 ....25 H1
Estcots Dr EGRIN RH19 ....265 K7
Estcourt Rd SNWD SE25 ....84 B1
Estelle Ct FOLKN CT19 ....95 J7
Esther Ct SIT ME10 ....99 M6
Estoria Cl BRXS/STRHM SW2 ......40 A3
Estridge Wy TONN TN9 ....211 J5
Estuary Rd IOS ME12 ....80 C3
Estuary Wy WSTB CT5 ....106 D4
Etchden Rd RASHW TN26 ....280 E2
Etfield Gv SCUP DA14 ....64 D4
Ethelbert Cl HAYES BR2 ....62 E8
Ethelbert Crs MARG CT9 ....15 J2
Ethelbert Gdns MARG CT9 ....15 J2
Ethelbert Rd BMLY BR1 ....62 E9
BRCH CT7 ....110 E5
CANT CT1 ....166 F7
DEAL CT14 ....203 H9
DVW CT17 ....8 D7
ERITH DA8 ....45 L1
FAV ME13 ....132 E7
FOLKN CT19 ....310 G4
RAM CT11 ....16 E4
RDART DA2 ....67 H1
STMC/STPC BR5 ....64 F9
Ethelbert Sq WGOS CT8 ....111 M4
Ethelbert Ter MARG CT9 ....15 J2
Etherington Hl RRTW TN3 ....239 P9
Etherow St EDUL SE22 ....40 C7
Ethnam La HAWK TN18 ....329 M2
Ethnard Rd PECK SE15 ....24 E9
Ethronvi Rd BXLYHN DA7 ....45 J4
Eton Cl WALD ME5 ....125 L1
Eton Gv LEW SE13 ....42 C4
Eton Rd ORP BR6 ....87 J8
Eton Wy DART DA1 ....46 C5
Etta St DEPT SE8 ....41 L5
Ettrick St POP/IOD E14 ....25 M2
Euclid Wy WTHK RM20 ....31 J7
Eugenia Rd BERM/RHTH SE16 ....25 H8
Eurolink Wy SIT ME10 ....129 J1
Europa Pk WTHK RM20 * 31 M9
Europe Pl WOOL/PLUM SE18 ......26 G6
Eustace Pl WOOL/PLUM SE18 .....26 G6
Euston Rd CROY/NA CRO 82 F5
Evandale Rd BRXN/ST SW9 ....42 B8
Evans Cl GRH DA9 ....47 P6
Evans Rd CAT SE6 ....62 C1
Eva Rd GILL ME7 ....7 K7
Evelina Rd PECK SE15 ....41 J4
SNWD SE25 ....61 J6
Eveline Lowe Est
BERM/RHTH SE16 ....24 D6
Evelyn Cl STRD ME2 ....72 C7
Evelyn Est DEPT SE8 ....25 H9
Evelyn Rd CAN/RD E16 ....26 F3
MAIDW ME16 ....154 B7
RSEV TN14 ....149 H1
Evelyn St DEPT SE8 ....25 H8
Evelyn Wy WLCTN SM6 ....82 D8
Evenden Rd MEO DA13 ....122 C5
Evenhill Rd RCANTE CT3 ....168 B9
Everard Av HAYES BR2 ....85 K5
Everard Wy FAV ME13 ....132 E5
Everest Cl GVW DA11 ....69 J2

Everest Dr HOO/HM ME3 ....73 L3
Everest La STRD ME2 ....72 B6
Everest Ms HOO/HM ME3 ....73 L3
Everest Pl POP/IOD E14 ....25 M1
SWLY BR8 ....88 C1
Everest Rd ELTH/MOT SE9 ....43 J6
Everglade BH/WHM TN16 ....146 D8
Everglade Cl HART DA3 ....91 J1
Evergreen Cl E/WMAL ME19 ......153 M2
GILL ME7 ....96 D9
HOO/HM ME3 ....73 L4
PGE/AN SE20 ....61 J6
Eversfield La 99 L2
Eversley Av BXLYHN DA7 ....45 N3
Eversley Cl MAIDW ME16 ....155 H6
Eversley Cross BXLYHN DA7 ....45 N3
Eversley Rd CHARL SE7 ....26 C9
HYTHE CT21 ....308 G6
NRWD SE19 ....60 D6
Eversley Wy CROY/NA CRO 84 D7
FOLK CT20 ....310 C6
Everthorpe Rd PECK SE15 ....40 F4
Everton Rd CROY/NA CRO 83 M5
Evesham Rd GVE DA12 ....69 P1
Evesham Wk BRXN/ST SW9 ....40 A3
Evison Cl DVE/WH CT16 ....291 J5
Evry Rd SCUP DA14 ....64 E5
Ewart Rd CHAT ME4 ....45 K8
Ewe Cl HOLWY N7 ....99 L2
Ewehurst La RRTW TN3 ....269 J2
Ewell Av E/WMAL ME19 ....153 H4
Ewell La MAID/SHEP ME15 ....184 C6
Ewelme Rd FSTH SE23 ....41 J9
Ewen Crs BRXS/STRHM SW2 ......40 A3
Ewhurst Cl WCHPL E1 ....24 F1
Ewhurst La RYE TN31 ....329 N9
Ewhurst Rd BROCKY SE4 ....41 N7
Ewins Cl STPH/PW TN12 ....243 H5
Exbury Rd CAT SE6 ....61 M3
Excel Marina CAN/RD E16 ....26 B3
Excel Waterfront CAN/RD E16 .....26 C3
Exchange Ar LVPST EC2M 24 B1
Exchange Sq SDTCH EC2A * 24 B1
Exchange St DEAL CT14 ....233 J2
Exedown Rd BGR/WK TN15 ....120 F9
Exeter Cl EHAM E6 ....26 C2
FOLK CT20 ....310 A5
TON TN9 ....210 G6
Exeter Rd CAN/RD E16 ....26 B4
CROY/NA CRO 83 K4
GVE DA12 ....69 P2
WELL DA16 ....44 B5
Exeter Wy NWCR SE14 ....41 M1
Exford Gdns LEE/GVPK SE12 ......62 F1
Exford Rd LEE/GVPK SE12 ....62 F1
Exmoor Ri KEN/WIL TN24 ....252 E5
Exmouth Rd GILL ME7 ....73 J8
GRAYS RM17 ....32 C9
WELL DA16 ....44 E2
Exmouth St WCHPL E1 ....25 H1
Exton St WAD ME5 ....125 P3
Exton Gdns MAID/BEAR ME14 ...156 C7
Eynhorne St RMAID ME17 ....187 M2
Eylewood Rd WNWD SE27 ....60 C4
Eynella Rd DUL SE21 ....60 F8
Eynsford Cl MARG CT9 ....113 L3
STMC/STPC BR5 ....86 D4
Eynsford Ri EYN DA4 ....89 J8
Eynsford Rd EYN DA4 ....89 J8
GRH DA9 ....48 A6
MAIDW ME16 ....155 J5
SWLY BR8 ....88 D5
Eynsham Dr ABYW SE2 ....28 A6
Eynswood Dr SCUP DA14 ....64 D4
Eythorne Cl KEN/WIL TN24 ....252 G4
Eythorne Rd BRXN/ST SW9 ....40 A2
RDV CT15 ....229 P8

F

The Facade FSTH SE23 * 61 J1
Fackenden La BGR/WK TN15 ......119 M7
Factory La CROY/NA CRO 82 F6
Factory Pl POP/IOD E14 ....25 M8
Factory Rd CAN/RD E16 ....26 E4
GVW DA11 ....48 C7
Faesten Wy BXLY DA5 ....65 N2
Fagus Cl WALD ME5 ....125 N4
Fairacre BRDST CT10 ....113 K9
Fairacres CROY/NA CRO 114 C3
Fair Acres HAYES BR2 ....85 K2
Fairacres Cl HB CT6 ....107 P2
Fairbank Av ORP BR6 ....86 F6
Fairbourne La RMAID ME17 ....188 D6
Fairby Hl HART DA3 ....91 H2
Fairby La HART DA3 ....91 H3
Fairby Rd LEE/GVPK SE12 ....42 F6
Fairchildes Av CROY/NA CRO 114 G6
Fairchildes Rd WARL CR6 ....114 G9
Fairclough St WCHPL E1 ....24 D2
Fairfax Cl FOLK CT20 ....310 A4
RHAM ME8 ....96 G8
Fairfax Dr HB CT6 ....108 C5
Fairfax Gdns BKHTH/KID SE3 .....42 C2
Fairfax Ms CAN/RD E16 ....26 B4
Fairfax Rd GRAYS RM17 ....32 C8
TIL RM18 ....49 K2
Fairfield DEAL CT14 ....232 E6
GVE DA12 ....70 A4
RCANTW CT4 ....257 L4
Fairfield Av CDW/CHF RM16 ....33 H6
RTWE/PEM TN2 ....270 F3
Fairfield Cl BFN/LL DA15 ....44 B7
BGR/WK TN15 ....149 M5
NROM TN28 ....337 J5
Fairfield Crs TON TN9 ....240 F1
Fairfield Gv CHARL SE7 ....26 E9
Fairfield Pk BRDST CT10 ....113 K9
Fairfield Pth CROY/NA CRO 83 J7

Fairfield Rd BECK BR3...........61 N8
  BGR/WK TN15.......151 J4
  BMLY BR1.......62 E6
  BRDST CT10.......113 K9
  BXLYHN DA7.......45 H5
  CROY/NA CR0.......85 J7
  EGRIN RH19.......265 J8
  MSTR CT12.......141 J5
  NROM TN28.......336 G7
  RAM CT11.......143 K5
  STMC/STPC SE6.......86 E4
Fairfields CAT SE6.......41 P8
Fairfield Ter RASHW TN26.......304 D8
Fairfield Wy RTON TN11.......210 B5
Fairford Av BXLYHN DA7.......45 L2
  CROY/NA CR0.......
Fairford Cl CROY/NA CR0.......84 A2
Fairgreen Rd THHTH CR7.......82 G2
Fairham Av SOCK/AV RM15.......31 K3
Fairhaven Av CROY/NA CR0.......84 A3
Fairholme Rd CROY/NA CR0.......82 F4
Fairhurst Dr RASH/SHEP ME15 ..184 G7
Fairlands Av THHTH CR7.......82 E1
  WSTB CT5.......106 C5
Fairlawn CHARL SE7.......42 C1
Fairlawn Av BXLYHN DA7.......44 F3
Fairlawn Cl IWBY/YAL ME18 ..183 P5
Fairlawn Crs EGRIN RH19.......264 E6
Fairlawn Ct THART *.......42 C1
Fairlawn Dr EGRIN RH19.......264 E6
Fairlawn Pk SYD SE26.......61 L4
Fairlawn Rd MSTR CT12.......142 C1
Fairlead Rd ROCH ME1.......95 J5
Fairleas SIT ME10.......130 A3
Fairlie Gdns FSTH SE23.......41 J8
Fairlight Av MSTR CT12.......142 C4
Fairlight Cl STH/RUST TN4.......240 D7
Fairlight Cross HART DA3.......68 G3
Fairlight Rd THART TN18.......308 F4
Fairlight Ter NROM TN28 *.......336 G7
Fairman's La STPH/PW TN12....273 J2
Fairmead BXLY BR1.......86 A1
Fairmead Cl BMLY BR1.......86 A1
Fairmead Rd BGR/BEAR ME14...12 E4
Fair Meadow RYE TN31.......338 F5
Fairmead Rd CROY/NA CR0.......82 F4
  EDEN TN8.......
Fairmile Rd RTWE/PEM TN2....271 H5
Fairmont Cl BELV DA17.......28 E8
Fairoak Cl STMC/STPC BR5.....86 C4
Fairoak Dr ELTH/MOT SE9.......43 P6
Fairoaks HB CT6.......107 N2
Fairseat La BGR/WK TN15.......121 K4
Fair St BRDST CT10.......113 K9
  STHWK SE1.......24 C5
Fairthorn Rd CHARL SE7.......26 B8
Fairtrough Rd ORP BR6.......117 J7
Fairview ERITH DA8.......45 P1
  HART DA3 *.......90 E7
  HAWK TN18.......317 H4
  RSIT ME9 *.......98 D4
Fairview Av MSTR CT12.......142 C4
Fairview Cha SLH/COR SS17 ....34 B1
Fairview Cl MARG CT9.......15 K4
  RTON TN11.......240 E3
  SYD SE26 *.......61 L4
Fairview Dr HOO/HM ME3.......71 K3
  ORP BR6.......88 E8
Fairview Gdns CANTW/ST CT2...137 N7
  DEAL CT14.......232 F7
  MEO DA13.......92 C2
Fairview La RRTW TN3 *.......269 N8
Fairview Rd MEO DA13.......69 H6
  RDV CT15.......181 N9
  SIT ME10.......129 P2
Fairwater Av WELL DA16.......44 C4
Fairway BXLYHS DA6.......44 G6
  CDW/CHF RM16.......32 C5
  STMC/STPC BR5.......86 E3
Fairway Av FOLKN CT19.......310 D4
Fairway Cl CROY/NA CR0.......84 B2
  LYDD TN29.......337 L2
  ROCH ME1.......95 H5
Fairway Crs GRAVE SE25.......
Fairway Dr RDART DA2.......47 H8
  THMD SE28.......28 C2
Fairway Gdns BECK BR3.......
The Fairway FAV ME13.......132 D7
  STH/RUST TN4.......270 D1
The Fairway BMLY BR1.......86 A2
  DEAL CT14.......
  GVW DA11.......69 L1
  HB CT6.......107 J4
  HYTHE CT21.......309 H6
  LYDD TN29.......326 E9
  NROM TN28.......337 J7
  ROCH ME1.......95 H5
  SIT ME10.......
Fairwyn Rd SYD SE26.......61 L3
Falcon Av BMLY BR1.......63 J9
  GRAVS RM17.......
Falcon Cl DART DA1.......46 F6
  HB CT6.......107 K7
Falcon Gdns IOS ME12.......58 D9
Falcon Ms GVW DA11.......49 J9
Falcons Cl BH/WHM TN16.......145 N2
Falcon Wy ASH TN23.......282 B1
Falconwood Av WELL DA16......43 J5
Falconwood Pde WELL DA16.....44 B5
Falconwood Rd
  CROY/NA CR0.......114 D2
Falkland Pk Av SNWD SE25......60 E9
Falkland Pl WALD ME5.......125 K4
Fallow Ct STHWK SE1 *.......24 D8
Fallowfield RDART DA2.......67 P2
  SIT ME10.......129 P3
  WALD ME5.......95 N6
Fallowfield Cl
  MAID/BEAR ME14.......156 B8
Falmouth Cl LEE/GVPK SE12 ....42 D6
Falmouth Pl STPH/PW TN12 ....242 D2
Falstaff Cl DART DA1.......45 N8
Fambridge Ct SYD SE26.......61 M5
Fanconi Rd WALD ME5.......125 N2
Fane Wy RHAM ME8.......126 G1

Fanns Ri PUR RM19.......30 D7
Fanshawe Rd
  CDW/CHF RM16 *.......33 H6
Fans La RSIT ME9.......99 L2
Fantail Cl THMD SE28.......28 B2
The Fan DVE/WH CT16.......9 K2
Fant La MAIDW ME16.......184 G1
Faraday Av SCUP DA14.......64 D1
Faraday Ride TONN TN10.......210 G3
Faraday Rd MAID/BEAR ME14...155 P5
  WELL DA16.......44 C4
Faraday Wy STMC/STPC BR5....87 J1
  WOOL/PLUM SE18.......26 E6
Faringdon Av HAYES BR2.......86 C5
Farjeon Rd BKHTH/KID SE3 .....43 H2
Farleigh Av HAYES BR2.......85 J4
Farleigh Court Rd
  CROY/NA CR0.......82 E6
  WARL CR6.......114 C8
Farleigh Dean Crs
  CROY/NA CR0.......114 E5
Farleigh Hl MAID/SHEP ME15 ..185 L2
Farleigh La MAIDW ME16.......184 F1
Farleigh La CANTW/ST CT2 ....166 F4
  WARL CR6.......144 B2
Farley Cl RASHW TN26.......281 M7
  WALD ME5.......126 A5
Farleycroft BH/WHM TN16 .....176 C2
Farley La BH/WHM TN16.......176 C6
Farley Nursery
  BH/WHM TN16.......176 D3
Farley Pk OXTED RH8.......174 C6
Farley Pl SNWD SE25.......83 M1
Farley Rd HART SE6.......42 C1
  GVE DA12.......50 B8
  MARG CT9.......112 E6
Farlow Cl GVW DA11.......69 K2
Farm Av SWLY BR8.......65 L9
Farm Cl ASH TN23.......282 B1
  EGRIN RH19.......265 L8
  WWKM BR4.......
Farmcombe Cl RTW TN1.......23 F7
Farmcombe La RTW TN1.......22 E6
Farmcombe Rd RTW TN1.......23 F7
Farmcote Rd LEE/GVPK SE12 ...42 E9
Farm Crs SIT ME10.......129 P5
Farmcroft GVW DA11.......69 L1
Farmdale ROCH ME1.......94 E4
Farmdale Av ROCH ME1.......94 E4
Farmdale Rd GNWCH SE10.......26 B8
Farm Dr CROY/NA CR0.......84 C6
Farm Ct HYTHE CT21.......309 J4
  RMAID ME17.......187 K5
Farmers Rd CMBW SE5.......40 B1
Farmfield Rd BMLY BR1.......62 C4
Farm Ground Cl TON TN9.......241 H1
Farm Hall Av STRD ME2.......71 P6
Farm Holt HART DA3.......91 J5
Farmhouse Cl RCANTW CT4 * ..228 C7
Farm House Cl WSTB CT5.......105 N6
Farmland Wk CHST BR7.......63 M4
Farm La CROY/NA CR0.......84 C6
  DEAL CT14.......232 E5
  RTON TN11.......210 D6
  RYE TN31.......339 N9
  WTHK RM20.......31 P9
Farm Pl DART DA1.......46 A5
Farm Rd CDW/CHF RM16.......32 G5
  RASHW TN26.......304 D8
  RSEV TN14.......149 H5
  TIL RM18.......34 B7
  WALD ME5.......125 K2
  WARL CR6.......144 B4
Farmstead Dr EDEN TN8.......206 E7
Farmstead Rd CAT SE6.......61 P3
Farm V BXLY DA5.......45 J6
Farnaby Dr SEV TN13.......20 C5
Farnaby Rd BMLY BR1.......62 C7
  ELTH/MOT SE9.......42 G5
Farnborough Av
  SAND/SEL CR2.......114 B2
Farnborough Cl
  MAIDW ME16 *.......185 H1
Farnborough Common
  ORP BR6.......86 A7
Farnborough Crs HAYES BR2 ...85 J5
  SAND/SEL CR2.......114 B5
Farnborough Hl ORP BR6.......116 A1
Farnborough Wy ORP BR6.......116 F1
  PECK SE15 *.......40 E1
Farncombe St
  BERM/RHTH SE16.......24 D5
Farncombe Wy
  DVE/WH CT16.......261 J9
Farne Cl MAID/SHEP ME15....185 M5
Farnham Beeches RRTW TN3...269 M4
Farnham Ct RHAM ME8.......97 L5
Farnham La RRTW TN3.......269 M4
Farnham Pl RTW TN1.......23 G3
Farnham Rd WELL DA16.......44 E3
Farningham Cl
  MAID/BEAR ME14.......156 B8
Farningham Hill Rd SWLY BR8...89 H2
Farnley Rd THHTH CR7.......83 J1
Farnol Rd DART DA1.......46 G6
Farol Cl BMLY BR1.......63 L8
Farquhar Rd NRWD SE19.......60 F4
Farquharson Rd CROY/NA CR0...2 C3
Farraday Cl ROCH ME1.......95 J6
Farrance Cl RTW TN1 *.......23 F5
Farrance St POP/IOD E14.......25 K2
Farrant Cl ORP BR6.......117 K2
Farrar Rd BRCH CT7.......111 H7
Farren Rd FSTH SE23.......61 L1
The Farriers ASH TN23.......282 E4
Farrier Cl BMLY BR1.......63 H9
  MAID/BEAR ME14.......156 A7
  RASHE TN25.......252 C4
Farriers Cl GVE DA12.......50 B9
Farriers Ct RHAM ME8.......97 M6
Farrier St DEAL CT14.......233 J2
Farrington Av STMC/STPC BR5...63 P9
Farrington Pl CHST BR7.......

Farrins Rents
  BERM/RHTH SE16.......25 H1
Farrow Gdns CDW/CHF RM16 ...32 C4
Farrow La NWCR SE14.......41 J1
Farrow Pl BERM/RHTH SE16.....25 H1
Fartherwell Av
  E/WMAL ME19.......153 H4
Fartherwell Rd
  E/WMAL ME19.......
Farthing Aly STHWK SE1 *.......24 D5
Farthingfield BGR/WK TN15.....151 K1
Farthing HI WADH TN5.......315 J5
Farthingloe Rd DVW CT17.......291 H9
Farthings Ct CANTW/ST CT2 *..136 B9
Farthing Rd SCUP DA14.......86 C6
Farwig La BMLY BR1.......62 E7
Fashion St WCHPL E1.......24 C1
Fashoda Rd HAYES BR2.......85 N1
Fauchon's Cl
  MAID/BEAR ME14.......156 C9
Fauchon's La
  MAID/BEAR ME14.......156 C9
Faulkners La CANTW/ST CT2 ...166 A3
Faulkner St NWCR SE14.......41 J2
Faussett Hl RCANTW CT4.......166 E4
Faustina Gn ASH TN25.......282 C4
Faversham Reach FAV ME13 ...132 G3
Faversham Rd BECK BR3.......61 M8
  CAT SE6.......41 M8
  FAV ME13.......131 P8
  HDCN TN27.......192 G5
  RASHE TN27.......223 H7
  RASHE TN25.......252 F1
  RCANTW CT14.......199 N7
  RMAID ME17.......189 L6
  RSIT ME9.......160 C6
  RSIT ME9.......161 L3
  WSTB CT5.......104 D8
Favourite Rd WSTB CT5.......105 H8
Fawcett Cl STRHM/NOR SW16...61 H1
Fawcett Rd CROY/NA CR0.......82 C7
Fawe St POP/IOD E14.......25 L1
Fawkes Av DART DA1.......66 F1
Fawkham Av HART DA3.......90 G7
Fawkham Green Rd HART DA3...90 F7
Fawkham Rd BGR/WK TN15......90 D7
  HART DA3.......90 C7
Fawley Cl MAID/BEAR ME14 ...155 K5
Fawnbrake Av HNHL SE24.......40 B6
Faygate Crs BXLYHS DA6.......45 J6
Faygate La GDST RH9.......202 D5
Faymore Gdns SOCK/AV RM15..31 K3
Fearon St GNWCH SE10.......26 D8
Feather Bd CROY/NA CR0.......83 K5
  FAV ME13.......163 K5
  RSIT ME9.......99 M4
Featherby Rd RHAM ME8.......96 D3
Feathers Pl GNWCH SE10.......25 N9
Featherstone Av FSTH SE23 ....61 H1
Feenan Hwy TIL RM18.......34 B9
Felborough Cl RCANTW CT4 ...194 D3
Felbridge Av EGRIN RH19.......264 F5
  STRHM/NOR SW16.......60 A5
Felbridge Cl EGRIN RH19.......264 D4
Felbridge Pl EGRIN RH19.......264 D4
Felcourt La LING RH7.......234 E8
Felcourt Rd EDEN TN8.......206 G1
The Feld EGRIN RH19.......264 D5
Felday Rd LEW SE13.......41 P7
Felderland Cl DEAL CT14.......201 M5
  RMAID ME17.......186 B6
Felderland Rd RMAID ME17.....186 B6
Felderland La SWCH CT13.......201 L6
Felderland Rd RMAID ME17......186 B6
Feldspar Cl SIT ME10.......99 L8
  WALD ME5.......
Felhampton Rd ELTH/MOT SE9..63 H2
Felicia Wy CDW/CHF RM16.......33 J7
Felipe Rd CDW/CHF RM16.......31 M7
Felix Pl BRXS/STRHM SW2.......40 B4
Felixstowe Rd ABYW SE2.......28 B6
Fellbrigg Rd EDUL SE22.......40 F6
Fell Md STPH/PW TN12.......212 C4
Fellmongers Yd CROY/NA CR0 ...83 H7
Fellowes Wy RTON TN11.......210 B5
Fell Rd CROY/NA CR0.......83 H7
Felmingham Rd PGE/AN SE20...61 M3
Felold Rd WOOL/PLUM SE18.....27 N8
Felstead Rd ORP BR6.......87 H6
Felsted Rd CAN/RD E16.......26 G6
Felton Cl ORP BR6.......86 F3
Felton Lea SCUP DA14.......64 D5
Fenchurch Av FENCHST EC3M...24 B2
Fenchurch Buildings
  FENCHST EC3M.......24 B2
Fenchurch Pl FENCHST EC3M ...24 B3
Fenchurch St FENCHST EC3M ...24 B3
Fendall St STHWK SE1 *.......24 B6
Fendt Cl CAN/RD E16.......26 E2
Fendyke Rd ABYW SE2.......28 A7
Fen Gv BFN/LL DA15.......44 B7
Fen Meadow RPCK SE15.......40 G1
Fenn Cl BMLY BR1.......62 G5
Fennel Cl CROY/NA CR0.......84 D6
  MAIDW ME16.......154 G9
  ROCH ME1.......94 G3
Fennell St WOOL/PLUM SE18....27 H9
Fenner Rd CDW/CHF RM16.......31 M6
Fenning St STHWK SE1 *.......24 B5
Fen Pond Rd BGR/WK TN15.....150 F3
Fen St CAN/RD E16.......26 D3
Fens Wy SWLY BR8.......65 K5
Fenton Cl CHST BR7.......63 K4
Fenton Ct DEAL CT14.......232 G5

Fenton Rd CDW/CHF RM16.......31 P6
Fenwick Gv PECK SE15.......40 C4
Fenwick Rd PECK SE15.......40 C4
Ferbies RRTW TN3.......269 H1
Ferdinand Ter RRTW TN3 *......269 K3
Ferguson Av GVE DA12.......69 N5
Ferguson Cl BECK BR3.......62 A9
  HYTHE CT21.......309 G5
Fern Av MTCM CR4.......82 C1
Fernbank EYN DA4 *.......89 L6
Fernbank Av WALD ME5.......125 K4
Fernbank Crs FOLKN CT19......311 H5
Fernbrook Rd LEW SE13.......42 C7
Fern Cl ERITH DA8.......46 B2
  RFOLK CT18.......288 F6
  WARL CR6.......144 B5
  WSTB CT5.......106 B5
Ferndale BMLY BR1.......62 G8
  RTWE/PEM TN2.......23 H2
Ferndale Cl BXLYHN DA7.......45 H2
  IOS ME12.......57 M1
  RTWE/PEM TN2.......23 H2
Ferndale Ct BRCH CT7.......111 H7
Ferndale Point
  RTWE/PEM TN2 *.......23 H2
Ferndale Rd GILL ME7.......96 B1
  GVE DA12.......69 M1
  SNWD SE25.......83 N2
Ferndale St EHAM E6.......27 J5
Ferndale Wy ORP BR6.......86 E8
Ferndell Av BXLY DA5.......65 M2
Ferndene Rd HNHL SE24.......40 B6
Fern Down MEO DA13.......122 C5
Fern Dr ORP BR6.......86 E5
Ferndown Cl GILL ME7.......96 D9
Ferne RDV CT15.......289 M1
Ferne Wy FOLK CT20.......310 B6
Fernfield RFOLK CT18.......288 F6
Fernham Rd THHTH CR7.......83 H1
Fernheath Wy RDART DA2.......65 M4
Fernhill Rd MAIDW ME16.......184 F1
Fernhill St CAN/RD E16.......26 C4
Fernholme Rd PECK SE15.......41 K6
Fernhurst TOWN TN10.......210 F5
Fernhurst Rd CROY/NA CR0.....83 M4
Fernlea Av HB CT6.......107 K2
Fernleigh Cl CROY/NA CR0.......82 F8
  FAV ME13.......164 C1
Fernleigh Ri SEV TN13.......179 H5
Fernside Av SEV TN13.......179 H5
The Ferns BGR/WK TN15.......151 K1
Fern Wk STHWK SE1 *.......24 D8
Fernwood Cl BMLY BR1.......62 G8
Ferranti Ct WOOL/PLUM SE18 ...26 F6
Ferrers Av WLCTN SM6.......82 G2
Ferrey Ms BRXN/ST SW9 ....40 A5
Ferrier Cl RHAM ME8.......127 H1
Ferring Cl RYE TN31.......338 C6
Ferrings DUL SE21.......60 E1
Ferris Av CROY/NA CR0.......84 C7
Ferris Rd EDUL SE22.......40 F3
Ferry La RAIN RM13.......29 L1
  ROCH ME1.......124 B1
Ferry Rd IOS ME12.......77 L7
Ferry Sq OBOR ME11.......77 H4
  RYE TN31.......338 E7
  STRD ME2.......123 P1
  TIL RM18.......49 L3
Ferry St POP/IOD E14.......25 M8
Ferry vw OBOR ME11.......77 H4
Festival Av HART DA3.......69 H9
Festival Cl BXLY DA5.......44 F9
  ERITH DA8.......45 P1
Festoon Wy CAN/RD E16.......26 C5
Ffinch Cl DIT/AY ME20.......154 C4
Ffinch St DEPT SE8.......41 N1
Fiddlers Ct GRH DA9.......49 P5
Fiddling La RASHE TN25.......285 M1
Field Av CANT CT1.......167 J1
Field Cl BMLY BR1.......62 G8
  WALD ME5.......
Field Ct OXTED RH8.......175 H4
Field Dr BRCH CT7.......206 E7
Field End KEN/WIL TN24.......253 J4
Fieldfare Rd THMD SE28.......28 B3
Fieldgate St WCHPL E1.......24 D1
Fielding Av TIL RM18.......49 M2
Fielding Dr DIT/AY ME20.......153 P1
Field La TON TN9.......241 H2
The Fieldings FSTH SE23.......41 J9
  SIT ME10.......129 M3
Fielding St FAV ME13 *.......132 C7
Field Mill Rd HDCN TN27.......219 P5
Field Rd BGR/WK TN15.......91 P9
  MEO DA13.......92 A8
  SOCK/AV RM15.......30 F4
Fieldside Cl ORP BR6.......86 B6
Fields La WBY/YAL ME18.......183 M4
Field Vw ASH TN23.......282 D4
  WSTB CT5.......105 J7
Field View Cl IOS ME12.......77 L1
Fieldway CROY/NA CR0.......114 C2
Fieldway CDW/CHF RM16.......32 C5
  STMC/STPC BR5.......86 E5
Fieldways HAWK TN18.......317 G5
Fieldworks Rd CHAT ME4.......72 C8
Fiennes Wy SEV TN13.......179 H3
Fiesta Wk CANT CT1.......167 H5
Fife Rd CAN/RD E16.......26 E1
  IOS ME12.......106 C4
Fifield Pth FSTH SE23.......61 K2
Fifth Av MARG CT9.......112 G2
  WTHK RM20.......31 K9
Fig Tree Rd BRDST CT10.......113 L6
Fig Tree Wk RDV CT15 *.......260 D1

Fiji Ter MAID/BEAR ME14.......155 M5
Filborough Wy GVE DA12.......50 D9
Filer Rd IOS ME12.......57 N9
Filey Cl BH/WHM TN16.......145 L4
Filmer La RSEV TN14.......149 K6
Filmer Rd RCANTW CT4.......199 L2
Filston La RSEV TN14.......148 C1
Finchale Rd ABYW SE2.......27 P6
Finch Av WNWD SE27.......60 D3
The Finches BRCH CT7.......109 P8
  SIT ME10.......129 P2
Finch Gr FN/FH CT1 *.......308 C7
Finch La BANK EC3V.......24 A2
Finchley Cl DART DA1.......46 C7
Finchley Rd GRAYS RM17.......32 C9
Finch Ms PECK SE15.......233 H5
  PECK SE15 *.......
Findhorn St POP/IOD E14.......25 M2
Findlay Cl RHAM ME8.......96 G9
Findon Gdns RAIN RM13.......29 M1
Fingal St GNWCH SE10.......26 D8
Finglesham Ct
  MAID/SHEP ME15.......185 P3
Finland Cl BROCKY SE4.......41 L6
Finland St BERM/RHTH SE16 ....25 H6
Finlay Cl FAV ME13.......132 B2
Finn Farm Ct ASH TN23.......282 C7
Finsbury Av LVPST EC2M.......24 A1
Finsbury Circ LVPST EC2M.......24 A1
Finsbury Pavement
  SDTCH EC2A.......24 A1
Finsbury Rd RAM CT11.......17 F2
Finsbury Sq SDTCH EC2A.......24 A1
Finsbury St BARB EC2Y.......24 A1
Finsbury Wy BXLY DA5.......45 H7
Fintonagh Dr MAID HE24.......40 C5
Finucane Dr STMC/STPC BR5...87 K4
Finwell Rd RHAM ME8.......97 K4
Firbank Cl CAN/RD E16.......26 E1
Firbanks Gdns MARG CT9.......112 C6
Firbank Rd PECK SE15.......41 K5
Firbanks WSTB CT5.......105 N6
Fir Ct KEN/WIL TN24.......253 J8
Fircroft Wy EDEN TN8.......206 D7
Fir Dene ORP BR6.......86 A7
Firecrest Cl HART DA3.......68 F9
Firethorn Cl GILL ME7.......73 F7
Firhill Rd CAT SE6.......61 N2
Firmin Av RMAID ME17.......186 A6
Firmingers Rd ORP BR6.......88 G3
Firmin Rd DART DA1.......46 A4
Firsby Av CROY/NA CR0.......84 A5
Firs Cl DIT/AY ME20.......154 D3
  FOLKN CT19.......310 A5
Firside Gv BFN/LL DA15.......43 K8
Firs La FOLKN CT19.......310 A5
Firs Rd RCANTW CT4.......229 J5
First Av BRDST CT10.......113 J4
  BXLYHN DA7.......44 E1
  CHAT ME4.......96 B4
  GILL ME7.......96 C4
  GVW DA11.......49 J9
  IOS ME12.......57 L7
  IOS ME12.......79 L2
  MARG CT9.......112 G2
  OBOR ME11.......77 H4
  WTHK RM20.......31 K9
The Firs BXLY DA5.......45 M9
  CDW/CHF RM16.......32 D4
  ORP BR6 *.......117 P1
  RCANTE CT3.......138 B8
First La MAID/SHEP ME15.......187 H1
First St WRTH TN3.......269 L5
Firtree Cl CANTW/ST CT2.......165 F1
Fir Tree Cl ORP BR6.......116 B4
  RAM CT11.......16 B4
  RTON TN11 *.......210 B5
  STPH/PW TN12.......246 C8
Fir Tree Gdns CROY/NA CR0.....84 D8
Fir Tree Gv GILL ME7.......126 A4
Fir Tree HI SWCH CT13.......201 J4
Fir Tree Rd STH/RUST TN4.......22 A5
Fir Trees Cl BERM/RHTH SE16 ...25 H4
Fisher Cl CROY/NA CR0.......83 L5
  HYTHE CT21.......309 J6
Fishermans Dr
  BERM/RHTH SE16.......25 H3
Fishermen's Hl GVW DA11.......48 F6
Fisher Rd CANTW/ST CT2.......166 C3
  WALD ME5.......95 N7
Fishers Ct STPH/PW TN12......246 C4
Fishers Rd NWCR SE14.......41 K2
Fishers Rd STPH/PW TN12......246 C4
Fisher St CAN/RD E16.......26 E1
  SWCH CT13.......201 P1
Fisher Street Rd FAV ME13 ....193 H1
Fisher's Wy BELV DA17.......29 H4
Fishguard Wy CAN/RD E16.......27 J4
Fishmarket Rd RYE TN31.......338 F7
Fishmonger's La
  DVE/WH CT16.......8 E4
Fishponds Rd HAYES BR2.......85 N9
Fish Street HI MON EC5R.......24 A3
Fisons Rd CAN/RD E16.......26 E4
Fitzgerald Av KFB CT6.......107 H3
Fitzjames Av CROY/NA CR0.....83 M6
Fitzmary Av MARG CT9.......111 P4
Fitzroy Av BRDST CT10.......113 M3
  MARG CT9.......112 C4
  MSTR CT12.......142 C2
Fitzroy Gdns NRWD SE19.......60 E6
Fitzroy Rd WSTB CT5.......105 N3
Fitzwalter Ct DVE/WH CT16 * ..291 J3
Fitzwilliam Ms CAN/RD E16......26 B4
Fitzwilliam Rd
  MAID/BEAR ME14.......156 C7
Fiveacre Cl THHTH CR7.......82 F3

Fiveash Rd *GVW* DA11 ....49 K8
Five Bells La *ROCH* ME1 * 19 J7
Five Elms Rd *HAYES* BR2 ....85 M7
Five Fields La *EDEN* TN8 ....207 K6
Five Oak Green Rd *TON* TN9 ......241 J2
Five Oak La *STPH/PW* TN12 .....245 M8
Five Oak Rd *BMLY* BR1 ....62 E2
Five Vents La *LYDD* TN29 ....335 F5
Fiveways Cnr *ELTH/MOT* SE9 ....65 M1
Five Ways Ct *CHAT* ME4 ....6 E6
Fiveways Ri *DEAL* CT14 ....232 E4
Fiveways Rd *BRXN/ST* SW9 ......60 A3
Five Wents *SWLY* BR8 ....66 A8
Five Wents Vls
  STPH/PW TN12 * 242 E8
Flack Gdns *HOO/HM* ME3 ....73 L2
Flag Cl *CROY/NA* CRO 84 A5
Flamborough Cl
  BH/WHM TN16 ....145 L4
Flamborough St *POP/IOD* E14 ...25 H2
Flamborough Wk
  POP/IOD E14 * 25 H2
Flamingo Cl *MAID* ME5 ....95 M7
Flamingo Dr *HB* CT6 ....107 K3
Flamsteed Rd *CHARL* SE7 ....26 F8
Flanders Cl *SIT* ME10 ....99 N5
Flanders Fld *RASHE* TN25 ....283 P4
Flank St *WCHPL* E1 ....24 D5
Flavell Ms *GNWCH* SE10 ....25 P8
Flax Court La *RDV* CT15 ....260 D1
Flaxman Dr *MAIDW* ME16 ....155 H6
Flaxman Rd *CMBW* SE5 ....40 B3
Flaxmans Ct *GILL* ME7 ....72 C9
Flaxmere Rd *RH/RUST* TN4 ....240 D7
Flaxpond Rd *ASH* TN23 ....282 C1
Flaxton Rd *WOOL/PLUM* SE18 ...43 P2
Fleet Av *IOS* ME12 ....57 K7
  RDART DA2 ....47 J9
Fleetdale Pde *RDART* DA2 * 47 J9
Fleethall Gv *CDW/CHF* RH16 ....32 B4
Fleet Rd *GVW* DA11 ....68 C2
  RDART DA2 ....47 J9
  RDV CT15 ....262 F7
  ROCH ME1 ....5 J5
Fleets La *CANTW/ST* CT2 ....136 C6
Fleet Ter *CAT* SE6 * 42 A8
Fleetwood Av *HB* CT6 ....107 J2
Fleetwood Cl *CAN/RD* E16 ....26 E1
  CROY/NA CRO 4 J6
  IOS ME12 ....78 B1
Fleming Cl *CROY/NA* CRO 82 F9
Fleming Gdns *TIL* RM18 ....49 N2
  RCANTE CT3 ....200 D4
Fleming Wy *FOLKN* CT19 ....310 C3
  THMD SE28 ....28 C3
  TONN TN9 ....211 H3
Fletcher Cl *EHAM* E6 ....27 J3
Fletcher Rd *STPH/PW* TN12 ....246 B6
Fletchers Cl *HAYES* BR2 ....85 L1
Fletcher St *WCHPL* E1 ....24 C5
Fletching Rd *CHARL* SE7 ....26 E9
Flete Rd *MARG* CT9 ....112 C8
Flimwell *ASH* TN23 ....282 A2
Flimwell Cl *BMLY* BR1 ....62 C4
Flint Cl *ORP* BR6 ....116 C2
  SIT ME10 ....99 M6
Flint Down Cl
  STMC/STPC BR5 ....64 C7
Flint Gn *MAID* ME5 ....95 L4
Flint La *RMAID* ME17 ....189 L3
Flintmill Crs *BKHTH/KID* SE3 ....43 J3
Flinton St *WALW* SE17 ....24 B8
Flint St *WALW* SE17 ....24 A7
  WADH TN5 ....31 L9
Floathaven Cl *THMD* SE28 ....27 P4
The Floats *SEV* TN13 ....148 D6
Flockton St *BERM/RHTH* SE16 ..24 D5
Flodden Rd *CMBW* SE5 ....40 C2
Flood Hatch
  MAID/SHEP ME15 ....185 J1
Flood La *FAV* ME13 ....132 F6
Flood St *RASHE* TN25 ....283 M7
Flora Cl *POP/IOD* E14 ....25 L2
Flora Gdns *CROY/NA* CRO 114 F5
Flora Rd *RAM* CT11 ....18 F3
Flora St *BELV* DA17 ....28 E8
Florence Av *WSTB* CT5 ....105 H7
Florence Cl *WTHK* RM20 ....31 P9
Florence Rd *ABYW* SE2 ....28 B6
  BECK BR3 ....61 K8
  BMLY BR1 ....62 E7
  MAIDW ME16 ....41 M2
  NWCR SE14 ....41 M2
  RAM CT11 ....16 C5
Florence St *STRD* ME2 ....72 B7
Florence Ter *NWCR* SE14 ....41 M2
Florence Wy *WALD* ME5 ....125 L4
Florida Rd *THHTH* CR7 ....60 B7
Florin Dr *ROCH* ME1 ....94 C2
Flower & Dean Wk *WCHPL* E1 ..24 C1
Flowerfield *RSEV* TN14 ....148 E2
Flowerhill Wy *MEO* DA13 ....186 A6
Flower La *GDST* RH9 ....174 A5
Floyd Rd *CHARL* SE7 ....26 D8
Fludyer St *LEW* SE13 ....42 C5
Flume End *MAIDW* ME16 ....185 J1
The Flyers Wy *BH/WHM* TN16 ..176 E2
Flying Horse La
  DVE/WH CT16 * 8 E4
Foads Hl *MSTR* CT12 ....142 C6
Foads La *MSTR* CT12 ....142 C7
Foalhurst Cl *TONN* TN10 ....211 H6
Foarden Point Rd *DVE/WH* CT16 * 8 E4
Foley Cl *KEN/WIL* TN24 ....283 K1
Foley Ct *MAIDW* ME16 ....145 N3
Foley St *MAID/BEAR* ME14 ....13 C2
Folgate St *WCHPL* E1 ....24 B1
Folkestone Rd *DVW* CT17 ....291 J8
  RDV CT15 ....270 F2
  RYE TN31 ....339 H1
Folks Wood Wy *HYTHE* CT21 ...307 P4
Follett St *POP/IOD* E14 ....25 M2
Folly Rd *FOLK* CT20 ....11 H2

Folly Wall *POP/IOD* E14 ....25 M5
Fonblanque Rd *IOS* ME12 * 57 L6
Fontwell Cl *MAID/SHEP* ME15 ..186 C5
Fontwell Dr *HAYES* BR2 ....86 B2
Foord Cl *RDART* DA2 ....47 J9
Foord Rd *RMAID* ME17 ....189 L6
Foord Rd North *FOLKN* CT19 .....10 E2
Foord Rd South *FOLK* CT20 ......11 F4
Foord St *ROCH* ME1 ....19 C7
Footbury Hill Rd *ORP* BR6 ....87 H4
Foots Cray High St *SCUP* DA14 ..64 F5
Foots Cray La *BXLY* DA5 ....65 J2
Footscray Rd *ELTH/MOT* SE9 ....43 L7
Forbes Rd *FAV* ME13 ....132 F7
Forbes St *WCHPL* E1 ....24 D2
Force Green La
  BH/WHM TN16 ....146 E9
Ford Cl *HB* CT6 ....106 C2
  RCANTW CT4 ....197 L2
  THHTH CR7 ....82 C5
Fordcombe Cl
  MAID/SHEP ME15 ....186 C4
Fordcombe Rd *RRTW* TN3 ....268 C3
  RTON TN11 ....238 F6
Fordcroft Rd *STMC/STPC* BR5 ...27 L7
Forde Av *BMLY* BR1 ....62 C9
Fordel Rd *CAT* SE6 ....42 B9
Fordhams Rw *CDW/CHF* RM16 ...3 J1
Fordham St *WCHPL* E1 ....24 D2
Ford Hl *ROCH* ME1 ....138 B2
Fordingbridge Cl
  MAIDW ME16 ....154 G7
Ford La *BGR/WK* TN15 ....113 J2
  E/WMAL ME19 ....122 B9
Ford Manor Rd *LING* RH7 ....235 L7
Fordmill Rd *CAT* SE6 ....61 N1
Fordoun Rd *BRDST* CT10 ....113 L8
Ford Rd *GVW* DA11 ....68 E6
Fords Park Rd *CAN/RD* E16 ....26 B2
Ford Sq *WCHPL* E1 ....24 E1
Ford St *CAN/RD* E16 ....26 A2
Ford Wy *ASH* TN23 ....252 C8
Fordwich Cl *MAIDW* ME16 ......154 G5
  ORP BR6 ....86 C4
Fordwich Dr *HOO/HM* ME3 ....73 L3
Fordwich Gv *BRDST* CT10 ....113 K6
Fordwich Pl *SWCH* CT13 ....201 N2
Fordwich Rd *CANTW/ST* CT2 ..137 L9
Fordyce Rd *LEW* SE13 ....42 A7
Foreland Av *FOLKN* CT19 ....113 J5
  MARG CT9 ....113 J3
Foreland Ct *RAM* CT11 * 16 D6
Foreland Hts *BRDST* CT10 ....113 N6
Foreland Rd *RDV* CT15 ....292 F5
Foreland Sq *DEAL* CT14 ....232 C6
Foreland St *WOOL/PLUM* SE18 ..27 L7
The Foreland *CANT* CT1 ....166 C7
Foremans Barn Rd
  MAID/SHEP ME15 ....184 E8
Foreness Cl *MARG* CT9 ....113 M2
Forest Meadow *ASH* TN23 ......282 D4
Forest Av *ASH* TN23 ....252 B5
Forest Cl *CHST* BR7 ....63 J7
Forestdale Rd *MAID* ME5 ....125 M5
Forest Dene *RTWE/PEM* TN2 ...270 F7
Forest Dr *HAYES* BR2 ....85 P8
  WALD ME5 ....125 L3
Forester Rd *PECK* SE15 ....41 H5
Foresters Cl *MAID* ME5 ....125 L3
Foresters Crs *BXLYHN* DA7 ......45 K5
Foresters Wy *FOLK* CT20 ....10 D4
Forest Gv *TONN* TN10 ....210 F5
Forest Hl *MAID* ME5 ....185 L2
Forest Hill Rd *EDUL* SE22 ....41 H7
Forestholme Cl *FSTH* SE23 ....61 L3
  SYD SE26 ....61 N5
Fore St *BARB* EC2Y 24 A1
Forest Ridg *BECK* BR3 ....61 N9
  HAYES BR2 ....85 P8
Forest Rd *ERITH* DA8 ....46 A2
  RTWE/PEM TN2 ....23 H6
  STPH/PW TN12 ....242 C5
Forest Wy *BFN/LL* DA15 ....43 P8
  E/WMAL ME19 ....153 H9
  RTWE/PEM TN2 ....241 N9
  RTWE/PEM TN2 ....270 F7
  STMC/STPC BR5 ....27 J6
Forge Cl *CANTW/ST* CT2 ....137 L8
  FAV ME13 * 132 C7
  HAYES BR2 ....85 K5
  RASHE TN25 ....285 L8
  RDV CT15 ....260 D1
  STPH/PW TN12 ....242 C5
Forge Ct *RHAM* ME8 ....97 K3
Forgefield *BH/WHM* TN16 ....145 N1
Forge Fld *RDV* CT15 ....289 P7
  WADH TN5 ....314 D8
Forgefields *HB* CT6 ....107 M6
Forge Hl *RASHE* TN25 ....306 B2
  RASHW TN26 ....280 D3
Forge La *ASH* TN23 ....120 D4
  BGR/WK TN15 ....261 H8
  DVE/WH CT16 ....261 H8
  EYN DA4 ....89 P1
  GILL ME7 ....73 L9
  GILL ME7 ....126 D4
  GVE DA12 ....70 B1
  HDCN TN27 ....219 K9
  HDCN TN27 ....247 N4
  HOO/HM ME3 ....53 K5
  HOO/HM ME3 ....53 J1
  MAID/BEAR ME14 ....155 P1
  MAID/SHEP ME15 ....184 C4
  RCANTE CT3 ....138 F1
  RDV CT15 ....261 P5
  RMAID ME17 ....187 J4
  RMAID ME17 ....188 B3
  RSIT ME9 ....98 A3
  WBY/YAL ME18 ....182 B5
  WBY/YAL ME18 ....213 P6
Forge Meadow *RMAID* ME17 ...188 E5
  TENT TN30 ....333 K1

Forge Mdw *HDCN* TN27 ....247 N4
Forge Meads *TENT* TN30 ....332 B2
Forge Ms *CROY/NA* CRO 84 D9
Forge Pth *DVE/WH* CT16 ....261 H8
Forge Pl *GVE* DA12 * 50 B9
Forge Rd *SIT* ME10 ....99 M8
  SOCK/AV RM15 ....31 K2
Forge Wy *SEV* TN14 ....118 E5
  STPH/PW TN12 ....243 H7
Formby Rd *STRD* ME2 ....93 P8
Formunt Cl *CAN/RD* E16 ....26 A1
The Forrens *CANT* CT1 * 5 F5
Forrester Cl *CANT* CT1 ....5 K1
Forrester Pth *SYD* SE26 ....61 J3
Forson Cl *TENT* TN30 ....301 J7
Forstal Cl *HAYES* BR2 ....62 E9
Forstall *RRTW* TN3 ....269 M4
Forstal La *RMAID* ME17 ....185 J7
The Forstall *RTON* TN11 ....209 M8
Forstal Rd *DIT/AY* ME20 ....156 F2
  HDCN TN27 ....219 K9
  RCANTW CT4 ....229 J6
  RTON TN11 ....211 P2
  RTWE/PEM TN2 ....23 J6
The Forstal *RASHE* TN25 ....223 P8
  RCANTE CT3 ....169 L2
  RTON TN11 ....211 P2
Forstal Vls *HDCN* TN27 * 219 K9
Forster Rd *BECK* BR3 ....61 L9
Forsters *RMAID* ME17 ....187 H7
Forsyte Crs *NRWD* SE19 ....60 E7
Forsyth Cl *E/WMAL* ME19 ....153 P3
Fort Bridgewood *ROCH* ME1 * ...94 C7
Fort Burgoyne Rd
  DVE/WH CT16 ....291 M6
Fort Cl *LYDD* TN29 ....343 K6
Fort Crs *MARG* CT9 ....15 H2
Fort Hl *MARG* CT9 ....15 G3
Fortin Cl *SOCK/AV* RM15 ....31 K3
Fortin Wy *SOCK/AV* RM15 ....31 K3
Fortis Cl *CAN/RD* E16 ....26 D2
Fort Lower Prom *MARG* CT9 ....15 H2
Fort Paragon *MARG* CT9 ....15 J2
Fort Pitt Hl *ROCH* ME1 ....95 K2
Fort Pitt St *CHAT* ME4 ....6 A6
Fort Rd *BRDST* CT10 ....113 N9
  HYTHE CT21 ....308 F5
  MARG CT9 ....15 G3
  RSEV TN14 ....180 A3
  STHWK SE1 ....24 C7
  TIL RM18 ....49 M5
Fortrose Cl *POP/IOD* E14 ....25 N3
Fortrye Cl *GVW* DA11 ....69 J1
Fort St *CAN/RD* E16 ....26 D5
  ROCH ME1 ....6 A4
  WCHPL E1 ....24 B1
Fortuna Cl *RAM* CT11 ....16 D8
Fortune Pl *STHWK* SE1 ....24 C8
Fortune Wy *E/WMAL* ME19 ......153 J9
Forty Acre La *CAN/RD* E16 ....26 B1
Forty Acres Hl *IOS* ME12 ....78 B3
Forward Wy *ROCH* ME1 ....95 H8
Fosbury Av *MEO* DA13 ....88 C3
Fossdene Rd *CHARL* SE7 ....26 D9
Fosse Bank *TON* TN9 ....240 D2
Fosse Bank Cl *TON* TN9 ....240 D2
Fosse Rd *TON* TN9 ....240 D2
Fossil Rd *LEW* SE13 ....41 N4
Fossington Rd *BELV* DA17 ....28 C7
Fostall Gn *ASH* TN23 ....282 C1
Fostall Rd *FAV* ME13 ....132 F4
Fosten La *HDCN* TN27 ....277 P8
Foster Clarke Dr
  MAID/SHEP ME15 ....186 A6
Foster Cl *FOLKN* CT19 ....310 B4
Foster Ct *SWCH* CT15 * 5 P3
Foster Rd *KEN/WIL* TN24 ....283 K4
Foster's Av *BRDST* CT10 ....113 K6
Foster's Cl *CHST* BR7 ....63 K4
Foster's Ct *SWCH* CT13 ....201 P3
Foster St *MAID/SHEP* ME15 .....13 F6
Foster Wy *DEAL* CT14 ....232 C6
Fostington Rd *KEN/WIL* TN24 ...252 D5
Fougeres Wy *KEN/WIL* TN24 ....252 D5
Foulds Cl *RHAM* ME8 ....126 E1
Foulsham Rd *THHTH* CR7 ....60 C6
Founders Gdns *NRWD* SE19 ......60 C6
Foundry La *BERM/RHTH* SE16 ...25 H4
Foundry Whf *ROCH* ME1 ....19 K7
Foundry Dr *NRWD* SE19 ....60 E5
Fountain Green Sq
  BERM/RHTH SE16 ....24 D5
Fountain La *MAIDW* ME16 ....184 F1
Fountain Pl *BRXN/ST* SW9 ....40 A2
Fountain Rd *STRD* ME2 ....71 M8
  THHTH CR7 ....60 C8
Fountains Cl *KEN/WIL* TN24 .....253 K8
Fountain St *SIT* ME10 ....129 M1
Fountain Wk *CDW/CHF* DA11 ....49 K7
Four Elms Hl *HOO/HM* ME3 ....72 F3
Four Elms Rd *EDEN* TN8 ....206 E6
Four Horseshoes Pk
  FAV ME13 * 133 N4
Fournier St *WCHPL* E1 ....24 C1
Four Oaks Rd *STPH/PW* TN12 ..247 H2
Fourth Av *GILL* ME7 ....52 G6
  IOS ME12 ....79 M1
  WTHK RM20 ....31 K9
Fourwents Rd *HOO/HM* ME3 .....73 K1
Fowey Cl *WALD* ME5 ....95 P9
  WAP E1W * 24 F4
Fowler Cl *RHAM* ME8 ....126 F2
  SCUP DA14 ....64 C4
Foxberry Rd *BROCKY* SE4 ....41 L5
Foxborough Hl *SWCH* CT13 ......201 J4
Foxborough Hl *SWCH* CT13 ......201 J4
Foxborough La *MTCM* CT4 ....141 K6
Foxburrow Cl *RHAM* ME8 ....96 C9
Foxbury Av *CHST* BR7 ....63 P5
Foxbury Cl *BMLY* BR1 ....62 F5
  ORP BR6 ....87 H9

Foxbury Dr *ORP* BR6 ....117 H1
Foxbury Rd *BMLY* BR1 ....62 F5
Foxbush *RTON* TN11 ....209 P4
Fox Cl *CAN/RD* E16 ....26 E1
  ORP BR6 ....87 H9
RFOLK CT18 ....288 C1
Foxcombe *CROY/NA* CRO 114 E1
Foxcroft Rd *WOOL/PLUM* SE18 ...43 M2
Foxden Dr *MAID/SHEP* ME15 ...186 C2
Foxdene Rd *WSTB* CT5 ....104 G8
Foxdown Cl *CANTW/ST* CT2 ....166 A6
Foxearth Cl *BH/WHM* TN16 .....145 P3
Foxendown La *MEO* DA13 ....92 C5
Foxes Cn *CDW/CHF* RM16 ....33 H5
Foxfield Rd *ORP* BR6 ....86 E6
Foxglove Cl *BRN/LL* DA15 ....44 C7
Foxglove Crs *WALD* ME5 ....125 K1
Foxglove Gn *KEN/WIL* TN24 ....3 K9
Foxglove Ri
  MAID/BEAR ME14 ....155 K5
Foxglove Rd *KEN/WIL* TN24 ....3 K5
  SOCK/AV RM15 ....31 M2
Foxglove Rw *STRD* ME2 * 93 N9
The Foxgloves
  MAID/BEAR ME14 ....243 J4
Foxgrove *SIT* ME10 ....99 M7
Foxgrove Av *BECK* BR3 ....61 P6
Foxgrove Rd *BECK* BR3 ....61 P6
  WSTB CT5 ....105 P4
Fox Hill Gdns *NRWD* SE19 ....60 F6
Foxhills *RDV* CT15 ....270 F2
Foxhole La *HAWK* TN18 ....317 N5
  STPH/PW TN12 ....242 D9
Foxhole Rd *ELTH/MOT* SE9 ....43 J6
Fox Hollow Cl
  WOOL/PLUM SE18 ....27 M8
Fox Hollow Dr *BXLYHN* DA7 .....44 F4
Fox Holt Rd *RDV* CT15 ....288 D2
Foxholme Cl *CHST* BR7 ....63 L5
Fox House Rd *BELV* DA17 ....28 F8
Fox La *HAYES* BR2 ....85 L9
Fox Lea *BGR/WK* TN15 ....151 J5
Foxley Rd *CMBW* SE5 ....40 C2
  WRY RCANTW CT4 ....228 C6
Foxwell St *BROCKY* SE4 ....41 L4
Foxwood Gv *GVW* DA11 ....49 J9
Foxwood Rd *BKHTH/KID* SE3 ....43 J5
  ORP BR6 ....117 M5
Foyle Dr *SOCK/AV* RM15 ....31 K2
Foyle Rd *BKHTH/KID* SE3 ....43 J1
Framley Rd *TONN* TN10 ....211 J5
Framlingham Crs
  ELTH/MOT SE9 ....63 J3
Frampton Rd *HYTHE* CT21 ......308 F5
Framptons Rd *LEW* SE15 ....41 N8
France Rd *DVE/WH* CT16 ....291 H2
Frances Gdns *RAM* CT11 ....17 J1
  SOCK/AV RM15 ....31 J2
Frances St *WOOL/PLUM* SE18 ...26 F7
Francis Av *BXLYHN* DA7 ....45 J3
  SWCH CT13 ....202 F3
Francis Dr *WALD* ME5 ....125 M3
Francis La *MAID/SHEP* ME15 ...186 C6
Francis Ms *LEE/GVPK* SE12 * 42 G7
Francis St *BRDST* CT10 ....113 N6
  BRDST CT10 ....113 N6
  CROY/NA CRO 84 C6
  DART DA1 ....46 D6
  RTON TN11 ....210 A4
  STMC/STPC BR5 ....64 F9
Frankapps Cl *RSIT* ME9 ....98 C8
Frank Burton Cl *CHARL* SE7 ......26 C8
Frank Dixon Cl *DUL* SE21 ....40 E8
Frank Dixon Wy *DUL* SE21 ....40 E8
Frank Edinger Cl
  KEN/WIL TN24 ....252 G5
Frankfield Ri *RTWE/PEM* TN2 ...270 C7
Frankfurt Rd *HNHL* SE24 ....40 C6
Frankham St *DEPT* SE8 ....41 N1
Frankland Cl *BERM/RHTH* SE16 ...24 E6
Franklin Dr *MAID/BEAR* ME14 ...156 A8
Franklin Rd *BXLY* DA5 ....65 N1
  BXLYHN DA7 ....45 J1
  GVE DA12 ....7 K5
  PCE/AN SE20 ....61 J8
Franklin Wy *CROY/NA* CRO 82 D5
Franklyn Rd *CANTW/ST* CT2 ...166 B5
Franks Cl *RHAM* ME8 ....96 B5
Frank's Hollow Rd *RRTW* TN3 ..239 P8
Franks La *EYN* DA4 ....89 N2
Franks Wood Av
  STMC/STPC BR5 ....27 L6
Frank Woolley Rd
  KEN/WIL TN24 ....211 J5
Fransfield Gv *SYD* SE26 ....61 H2
Frant Cl *PGE/AN* SE20 ....61 J6
Frant Fld *EDEN* TN8 ....206 E9
Frant Rd *RTWE/PEM* TN2 ....270 D9
  THHTH CR7 ....60 C8
Fraser Cl *BXLY* DA5 ....45 J3
Fraser Rd *ERITH* DA8 ....29 H8
Frean St *BERM/RHTH* SE16 ......24 D6
Freathy La *RASHE* TN25 ....252 F1
Freda Cl *BRDST* CT10 ....143 L5
Freda Corbett Cl *PECK* SE15 ......40 G1
Frederick Crs *BRXN/ST* SW9 .....40 B1

Frederick Gdns *CROY/NA* CRO ...82 G3
Frederick Pl *WOOL/PLUM* SE18 ..27 J8
Frederick Rd *RTN* CT14 ....232 F6
  GILL ME7 ....7 H5
Frederick's Pl *LOTH* EC2R 24 A2
Frederick Sq *BERM/RHTH* SE16 ...25 H5
Frederick St *KEN/WIL* TN24 .....129 M1
Frederick's Pl *LOTH* EC2R 24 A2
The Freedown *RDV* CT15 ....262 F9
Free Heath Rd *RRTW* TN3 ....294 D4
The Freehold *RTON* TN11 ....211 N1
  STPH/PW TN12 ....212 G4
Freelands Av *SAND/SEL* CR2 ...114 A3
Freelands Gv *BMLY* BR1 ....62 F7
Freelands Rd *BMLY* BR1 ....62 F7
  SNOD ME6 ....123 M5
Freeland Wy *ERITH* DA8 ....46 A2
Freeman Gdns *CHAT* ME5 ....95 L5
Freeman Rd *GVE* DA12 ....70 A2
Freeman's Rd *MSTR* CT12 ....141 J6
Freeman's St *WALW* SE17 ....24 B8
Freeman Wy
  MAID/SHEP ME15 ....186 B4
Freemasons Rd *CAN/RD* E16 ....26 C2
  CROY/NA CRO 83 K5
Freemen's Wy *DEAL* CT14 ....232 G6
Freesia Cl *GILL* ME7 ....89 L2
  ORP BR6 ....86 G9
Freethorpe Cl *NRWD* SE19 ....60 E7
Freight La *CRBK* TN17 ....297 P4
Freightmaster Est
  RAIN RM13 * 29 M7
Fremantle Rd *BELV* DA17 ....28 F7
  FOLK CT20 ....310 B6
Fremlin Cl *STH/RUST* TN4 ....269 N4
Fremlins Rd
  MAID/BEAR ME14 ....156 F8
Frencham Ct *CANTW/ST* CT2 ...136 F9
Frendsbury Rd *BROCKY* SE4 .....41 L5
Frensham Cl *SIT* ME10 ....130 A1
Frensham Dr *CROY/NA* CRO 114 F2
Frensham Rd *BFN/LL* DA15 ....63 P5
  CRBK TN17 ....319 N5
Frensham St *PECK* SE15 ....24 D9
Frensham Wk *MAID* ME5 ....125 L4
Freshfield Cl *LEW* SE13 ....42 B5
Freshfield La *HYTHE* CT21 ....308 F5
Freshfields *CROY/NA* CRO 84 C4
Freshland Rd *MAIDW* ME16 .....154 G8
Freshlands *HB* CT6 ....108 B5
Freshwater Cl *HB* CT6 ....106 G3
Freshwater Rd *WALD* ME5 ....95 H7
Freshwood Cl *BECK* BR3 ....61 P6
Freta Rd *BXLYHS* DA6 ....45 H6
Frewen Cl *RYE* TN31 ....330 A6
Friar Ms *WNWD* SE27 ....60 B2
Friars Av *WALD* ME5 ....125 L3
Friars Cl *WSTB* CT5 ....105 N5
Friars Ms *ELTH/MOT* SE9 ....43 L6
The Friars *CANT* CT1 * 4 D4
  HOO/HM ME3 * 53 M4
Friars Wk *ABYW* SE2 ....28 C8
Friars Wy *DVE/WH* CT16 ....291 H4
  RTWE/PEM TN2 ....270 C2
Friarswood *CROY/NA* CRO 114 B5
Friars Wd *CROY/NA* CRO 114 B5
Friary Ct *STPH/PW* TN12 * 40 C1
Friary Pl *STRD* ME2 ....18 D1
Friary Rd *PECK* SE15 ....40 G1
Friary St *RMAID* ME17 ....217 L3
Friendly Cl *MARG* CT9 ....113 J4
Friendly Pl *LEW* SE13 ....41 N2
Friendly Street Ms *DEPT* SE8 ....41 N3
Friendly St *DEPT* SE8 ....113 J5
Friends' Rd *CROY/NA* CRO 83 J7
Friern Rd *EDUL* SE22 ....40 G7
Friesian Wy *KEN/WIL* TN24 .....252 F2
Friezland Rd *STH/RUST* TN4 ....270 A7
Friezley La *CRBK* TN17 ....275 P7
Frimley Av *GILL* ME7 ....25 K9
Frimley Cl *CROY/NA* CRO 114 F2
Frimley Ct *SCUP* DA14 ....64 E4
Frimley Crs *CROY/NA* CRO 114 F2
Frinstead Ho *STRD* ME2 ....72 C6
Frinsbury Rd *KEN/WIL* TN24 ......3 M7
Frinstead Gv *STMC/STPC* BR5 ...87 L1
Frinstead Wk *MAIDW* ME16 .....154 G5
Frinsted Cl *RHAM* ME8 ....45 M1
  RSIT ME9 ....159 M3
Frinton Rd *SCUP* DA14 ....64 G3
Friston Wy *ROCH* ME1 ....95 J6
Friswell Pl *BXLYHN* DA7 ....45 J5
Frith Pk *EGRIN* RH19 ....265 H6
Frith Rd *CROY/NA* CRO 82 G5
  DVE/WH CT16 ....291 K6
  RASHE TN25 ....305 J1
Frithwood Cl
  MAID/SHEP ME15 ....186 C2
Frittenden Cl *ASH* TN23 ....282 B2
Frittenden Rd *STPH/PW* TN12 ..246 C7
  STRD ME2 ....72 C6
Frobisher Cl *SIT* ME10 ....99 M7
Frobisher Gdns *ROCH* ME1 ....95 H4
Frobisher Rd *EHAM* E6 ....28 B1
  ERITH DA8 ....46 A1
Frobisher Wy *GRH* DA9 ....48 A4
  GVE DA12 ....70 A4
Frog La *DAGW* RM9 * 29 J1
  E/WMAL ME19 ....153 K4
  RCANTW CT4 ....197 N5
  RTW TN1 ....22 D6
Frogley Rd *EDUL* SE22 ....40 G7
Frognal Av *SCUP* DA14 ....64 C5
Frognal Cl *SCUP* DA14 ....64 C5
Frognal Gdns *RSIT* ME9 ....130 G3
Frognal La *RSIT* ME9 ....130 G3

Frognal Pl SCUP DA14......64 D4
Frogs Hole La CRBK TN17......299 N5
Frog's La CRBK TN17......319 M5
Froissart Rd ELTH/MOT SE9......43 J6
Frome TIL RM18......34 B7
Front Brents FAV ME13......132 C5
Frontfield Rd RASHW TN26......302 F6
Front St DEAL CT14......242 N7
The Front RDV CT15......292 F3
Frost Crs WALD ME5......95 M7
Frostic Wk WCHPL E1......24 D1
Frostland La RASHW TN26......325 J4
Frovle Cl MAIDW ME16......15 H6
Fruiterer's Cl RSIT ME9......129 P6
Fruitfields WADH TN5......315 N5
Fry Cl HOO/HM ME3......56 C2
Frying Pan Aly WCHPL E1 *......24 B1
Fryston Av CROY/NA CR0......83 M6
Frythe Cl CRBK TN17......298 A3
Frythe Crs CRBK TN17......298 A3
Frythe Wk CRBK TN17......298 A3
Frythe Wy CRBK TN17......298 A3
Fuchsia St ABYW SE2......6 B6
Fuggles Cl STPH/PW TN12......242 F3
Fuggles Ct CRBK TN17......298 A3
Fulbert Dr MAID/BEAR ME14......156 C7
Fulbert Rd DVE/WH CT16......291 J2
Fulbourne St WCHPL E1......24 E1
Fulbrook La SOCK/AV RM15......31 J5
Fulford St BERM/RHTH SE16......24 E5
Fulham Av MARG CT9......112 A6
Fullarton Crs SOCK/AV RM15......31 L2
Fuller Cl ORP BR6......85 J8
Fullers Cl MAID/BEAR ME14......156 D8
Fullers Hi RYE TN31......176 E2
Fullers La RYE TN31......330 A7
Fuller's Wd CROY/NA CR0......84 B7
Fullerton Rd CROY/NA CR0......83 N8
Fulmar Dr EGRIN RH19......265 K5
Fulmar Rd STRD ME2......94 C1
Fulmar Wy HB CT6......108 C6
Fulmer Rd CAN/RD E16......26 E1
Fulsam Pl MARG CT9......14 D6
Fulston Pl SIT ME10......129 P2
Fulthorp Rd BKHTH/KID SE3......42 E5
Fulwich Rd DART DA1......46 F7
Furfield Cl MAID/SHEP ME15......186 B6
Furley Rd PECK SE15......45 H6
Furlong Cl WLGTN SM6......82 A5
Furnace Av RRTW TN3......294 C4
Furnace La RRTW TN3......294 E3
...RRTW TN3......295 J4
...STPH/PW TN12......243 M8
Furneaux Av WNWD SE27......60 B8
Furner Cl DART DA1......45 H4
Furness Cl CDW/CHF RM16......33 J8
Furnival Ct RTWE/PEM TN2 *......270 C8
Furrell's Rd ROCH ME1......19 H6
Furtherfield Cl CROY/NA CR0......83 J2
Further Field STPH/PW TN12......246 E4
Further Green Rd CAT SE6......42 C8
Furzefield Cha EGRIN RH19......265 H2
Furzefield Cl CHST BR7......63 M5
Furzefield Rd BKHTH/KID SE3......26 C9
...EGRIN RH19......264 G4
Furze Hill Crs IOS ME12......77 M1
Furzehill Sq STMC/STPC BR5......87 J1
Furze La EGRIN RH19......265 J5
Furze Rd THHTH CR7......60 C9
Furze St BOW E3 *......25 K1
Fusedale Wy SOCK/AV RM15......31 J3
Fusilier Av FOLK CT20......309 N2
Future Ct STRD ME2 *......72 E7
Fyfe Wy BMLY BR1......62 A3
Fyfield Cl BECK BR3......84 C1
Fyfield Dr SOCK/AV RM15......31 J3
Fyfield Rd BRXN/ST SW9......40 A4

G

Gabion Av PUR RM19......30 C7
Gable Cl DART DA1......46 C6
Gable Ct SYD SE26......61 H5
Gable Ms HAYES BR2......85 P6
Gables Cl CMBW SE5......40 E2
...LEE/GVPK SE12......42 E9
The Gables GRAYS RM17 *......32 A7
...HART DA3......
...NRWD SE19 *......60 E7
Gabriel Gdns GVE DA12......70 A4
Gabriel's HI MAID/BEAR ME14......155 K4
Gabrielspring Rd EYN DA4......90 A6
Gabriel Spring Rd (East)
...EYN DA4......90 B6
Gabriel St FSTH SE23......41 K8
Gadby Rd SIT ME10......99 K9
Gadsby La RASHW TN26......279 N5
Gads Hill Rd HOO/HM ME3 *......71 K4
Gadwall Cl CAN/RD E16......26 C7
Gage Rd CAN/RD E16......25 P1
Gagetown Ter
...MAID/BEAR ME14......155 L5
Gain Hl STPH/PW TN12 *......214 A8
Gainsborough Av DART DA1......46 C5
...MARG CT9......113 H5
...TIL RM18......49 L2
Gainsborough Cl BECK BR3......61 N6
CRTG19......310 D4
...RHAM ME8......96 G8
SIT ME10......99 J9
Gainsborough Dr GVW DA11......69 H2
...HB CT6......108 B5
...MAID/BEAR ME16 *......154 C8
Gainsborough Gdns
...TOWN TN15......211 H5
Gainsborough Ms DUL SE21......40 C9
...SYD SE26 *......61 H2
Gainsborough Sq BXLYHN DA7......44 F4
Gainsford St STHWK SE1......24 C5
Gairloch Rd CMBW SE5......40 E3

Gaitskell Rd ELTH/MOT SE9......43 N9
Galahad Av RDART ME2......71 N9
Galahad Rd BMLY BR1......62 E2
Galatea Sq PECK SE15......41 H4
Galbraith St POP/IOD E14......25 M6
Galena Cl SIT ME10......99 K8
Gale St BOW E3......25 K1
Galey Gn SOCK/AV RM15......31 L1
Gallants La MAID/SHEP ME15......184 E5
Galleon Bvd CRH DA9......47 K5
Galleon Cl BERM/RHTH SE16......26 H5
...ERITH DA8......29 J7
...ROCH ME1......95 H6
Galleon Rd CDW/CHF RM16......35 L7
Galleon Wy STRD ME2......72 F4
Galley Rd DUL SE21......40 D9
Galley St RSIT ME9 *......129 L7
Galley Hill Rd SWLY BR8......
Galleywall Rd
...BERM/RHTH SE16......24 E7
Galliard St SWCH CT13......201 P2
Gallions Rd CAN/RD E16......27 J5
...CHARL SE7......26 C7
Gallions View Rd THMD SE28......27 M5
Gallon Cl CHARL SE7......26 D7
The Gallops MEO DA13......122 A6
Gallosson Rd
...WOOL/PLUM SE18......27 M7
Galloway Dr DART DA1......45 N8
...RASHE TN25......252 F1
Galloway Pth CROY/NA CR0......83 J8
Galloways Rd LYDD TN29......342 B7
Gallus Sq BKHTH/KID SE3......42 F4
Gallwey Av BRCH CT7......110 F6
Galpin's Rd THHTH CR7......82 D1
Galsworthy Av POP/IOD E14......25 H2
Galsworthy Cl THMD SE28......27 H6
Galsworthy Crs
...BKHTH/KID SE3......42 G2
Galsworthy Rd TIL RM18......49 N2
Galway Cl BERM/RHTH SE16 *......24 E8
Galway Rd IOS ME12......57 L6
Gamma Rd HOO/HM ME3......54 B9
Gammon's Farm La
...LYDD TN29......325 N2
Gandolfi St PECK SE15 *......24 B9
Gandy's La RMAID ME17......185 P9
Gange Ms FAV ME13 *......132 G6
Gangers Hi GDST RH9......174 C5
Gann Rd WSTB CT5......105 N4
The Gap CANT CT1......166 C7
...CANTW/ST CT2......135 P6
Garden Av BXLYHN DA7......45 H4
Garden Cl CANTW/ST CT2......165 P2
...EGRIN RH19......265 J9
...LEE/GVPK SE12......62 F2
...MAID/SHEP ME15......186 B4
...SEV TN13......149 J7
Garden Ct ROCH ME1......94 B9
Gardeners Quay SWCH CT13 *......201 P1
Gardeners Rd CROY/NA CR0......82 G5
Garden House La EGRIN RH19......265 J9
Garden La STRD ME2......72 B6
Garden La BMLY BR1......62 F5
Garden of England Pk
...RMAID ME17......188 C4
Garden Pl KEN/WIL TN24......253 H5
...RDART DA2......66 D2
Garden Rd BMLY BR1......62 F5
...FOLKN CT19......10 E1
...PGE/AN SE20......61 J7
...RTW TN1......23 F2
...SEV TN13......149 J7
...TON TN9......210 G8
Garden Rw CVW DA11......69 K2
The Gardens BECK BR3......62 A8
...EDUL SE22......40 G5
...RMAID ME17 *......185 H8
Garden St GILL ME7......7 G2
...RTW TN1......23 F3
...WCHPL E1......24 G1
Garden Wk BECK BR3......61 M7
Garden Wy KEN/WIL TN24......182 G1
Garden Wood Rd EGRIN RH19......264 F7
...STMC/STPC BR5......64 E8
Gardiner House
...WOOL/PLUM SE18 *......43 J1
Gardiner's HI RYE TN31......332 E7
Gardyne Ms TON TN9......240 E1
Gareth Gv BMLY BR1......62 E3
Garfield Pl FAV ME13......132 C6
Garfield Rd GILL ME7......73 K9
...MARG CT9......14 D5
Garford St POP/IOD E14......25 L6
Garganey Wk THMD SE28......28 B3
Gargery Cl GVE DA12......50 B9
Garibaldi St WOOL/PLUM SE18......27 M7
Garland Ct EGRIN RH19 *......264 C7
Garland Rd EGRIN RH19......264 C7
...WOOL/PLUM SE18......43 M1
Garlands RTTW TN3......210 A2
Garlies Rd FSTH SE23......61 L2
Garlinge Green Rd
...RCANTW T14......195 M5
Garlinge Rd STH/RUST TN4......240 D8
Garner Dr E/WMAL ME19......153 P5
Garnet Rd THHTH CR7......83 H1
Garnet St WAP E1W......24 F5
Garnett Cl ELTH/MOT SE9......43 K4
Garnett St FSTH SE23......61 P1
Garrard Av MARG CT9......112 E6
Garrard Cl BXLYHN DA7......45 J4
...CHST BR7......63 M4
Garratt Cl CROY/NA CR0......82 D8
Garrick Crs CROY/NA CR0......83 K6
Garrick Dr WOOL/PLUM SE18......27 L6
Garrick St CVW DA11......69 K2
Garrington Cl
...CROY/NA CR0......155 P6
Garrison Cl WOOL/PLUM SE18......43 L1
Garrison Rd IOS ME12......57 J5
Garrolds Cl SWLY BR8......65 M8

Garron La SOCK/AV RM15......31 J2
Garrow HART DA3......68 F9
Garside Cl WOOL/PLUM SE18......27 L6
Garsington Ms BROCKY SE4......41 M4
Garthorne Rd FSTH SE23......41 K8
Garth Av SEV TN13......179 H4
Garton Wy ASH TN23......281 P1
Garvary Rd CAN/RD E16......26 D2
Garvock Dr SEV TN13......00 D6
Gascoigne Rd CROY/NA CR0......114 F4
Gascoyne Cl
...MAID/SHEP ME15......186 E1
Gascoyne Dr DART DA1......45 N4
Gaselee St POP/IOD E14......25 M5
Gas House Rd ROCH ME1......19 G2
Gas Rd SIT ME10......99 N9
Casson Rd SWCM DA10......48 C7
Casson Rd SNOD ME6......123 M5
Gas St CANT CT1......4 C4
Gasworks La ASH TN25......2 A5
Gataker St BERM/RHTH SE16......24 E6
Gatcombe Cl MAIDW ME16......154 G7
...WALD ME5......95 M9
Gateacre Rd WSTB CT5......105 H8
Gate Farm Rd RRTW TN3......239 P5
Gatefield Cottages
...CRBK TN17......319 M2
Gatehope Dr SOCK/AV RM15......31 J2
Gatekeeper Cha RHAM ME8......97 J6
Gates Green Rd WWKM BR4......85 K8
Gatestone Rd NRWD SE19......60 E5
Gateway Pde CAT SE6 *......70 B3
Gatland La MAIDW ME16......184 G1
Gatling Rd ABYW SE2......43 P6
Gatonby St PECK SE15......40 F2
Gattons Wy SCUP DA14......65 H3
Gatwick Rd GVE DA12......69 M1
Gault Cl MAID/SHEP ME15......186 D1
Gaunt's Cl DEAL CT14......232 F5
Gautrey Rd PECK SE15......41 K3
Gavel St WALW SE17 *......24 A7
Gavenny Pth SOCK/AV RM15......31 J2
Gaverick St POP/IOD E14......25 L9
Gavestone Crs LEE/GVPK SE12......42 F9
Gavestone Rd LEE/GVPK SE12......42 F9
Gayhurst Cl RHAM ME8......96 G8
Gayhurst St SIT ME10......99 K9
Gaylor Rd TIL RM18......49 J2
Gaynesford Rd FSTH SE23......61 K1
Gazedown LYDD TN29......337 L2
Gaze Hill Av RSIT ME9......129 P2
Gazelle Gld GVE DA12......70 B4
Gean Cl WALD ME5......125 M4
Gedges HI BXLYHN DA7......45 H6
Gedge's HI STPH/PW TN12......242 G7
Gedling Pl STHWK SE1......24 C6
Geldart Rd PECK SE15......41 H1
Gellatly Rd PECK SE15......41 J3
General Wolfe Rd
...GNWCH SE10......42 B2
Genesta Av WSTB CT5......105 J7
Genesta Cl SIT ME10......99 M7
Genesta Gld GVE DA12......70 C4
Genesta Rd WOOL/PLUM SE18......43 L8
Geneva Av RHAM ME8......96 D4
Geneva Dr BRXN/ST SW9......40 A5
Geneva Rd THHTH CR7......83 H2
Genoa Rd PGE/AN SE20......61 J7
Gentian Cl MAID/BEAR ME14......156 B7
Geoffrey Cl CMBW SE5......40 E2
Geoffrey Rd BROCKY SE4......41 M4
George Beard Rd DEPT SE8......25 J7
George Groves Rd
...PGE/AN SE20......60 G7
George Gurr Crs FOLKN CT19......310 D9
George Hill Rd BRDST CT10......113 L4
George Inn Yd STHWK SE1......24 A4
George La FOLK CT20......11 F5
...HAYES BR2......85 L5
...LEW SE13......63 H1
...NROM TN28......336 G6
...RMAID ME17......187 K4
...ROCH ME1......19 G4
George Pk MARG CT9......14 A7
George Parris Ct IOS ME12 *......78 C1
George Roche Rd CANT CT1......166 F6
George Rw BERM/RHTH SE16......24 D6
George's Cl DEAL CT14......105 H7
George St ASH TN23......2 D6
...CROY/NA CR0......26 A2
...DEAL CT14......233 J2
...DVW CT17......291 J6
...GRAYS RM17......32 B9
...MAID/SHEP ME15......13 F7
...RAM CT11......17 F4
...RTWE/PEM TN2......23 G5
...SIT ME10......130 A2
...STPH/PW TN12......246 B3
...TON TN9......240 L1
...WADH TN5......317 L5
George Summers Cl STRD ME2......72 E7
Georgetown Cl NRWD SE19......60 D4
Georgette Pl GNWCH SE10......42 A1
George V Av MARG CT9......112 A5
George Williams Wy
...KEN/WIL TN24......253 H5
George Wood Cl LYDD TN29......342 B6
George Yd BANK EC3V......24 A2
Georgian Cl HAYES BR2......85 L5
Georgian Dr RMAID ME17......185 J8
Georgia Rd THHTH CR7......60 A8
Geraint Rd BMLY BR1......62 E2
Gerald Av CHAT ME4......95 K4
Geraldine Rd FOLKN CT19......310 C5
Gerald Rd GVE DA12......50 A8
Gerards Cl BERM/RHTH SE16......24 E8
Gerda Rd ELTH/MOT SE9......63 M1
Gerdview Dr RDART DA2......66 C5
Gerrard Av ROCH ME1......95 H2
Gerrards St IOS ME12......
Gertrude Rd BELV DA17......28 F7

Gervase St PECK SE15......41 H1
Ghent St CAT SE6......61 N1
Ghyll Side Rd RYE TN31......330 A6
Giant Arches Rd HNHL SE24......60 F3
Gibbet La STPH/PW TN12......273 N2
Gibbetts RRTW TN3......269 L5
Gibbon Rd PECK SE15......41 J3
Gibbons Rd SIT ME10......99 J9
Gibbs Av NRWD SE19......60 D4
Gibbs Brook La OXTED RH8......204 G1
Gibbs Cl NRWD SE19 *......60 D4
Gibbs HI HDCN TN27......247 P4
...WBY/VAL ME18......183 J6
Gibbs Sq NRWD SE19 *......60 D4
Gibraltar Av GILL ME7......60 C5
Gibraltar HI CHAT ME4......6 B5
Gibraltar La MAID/BEAR ME14......155 K4
...RFOLK CT18......288 C9
Gibraltar Sq RDV CT15......291 M4
Gibson Cl GVW DA11......69 K2
Gibson Dr E/WMAL ME19......152 C8
Gibson's HI STRHM/NOR SW16......60 E6
Gibson St GNWCH SE10......25 P8
Giddyhorn La MAIDW ME16......155 H8
Gideon Cl BELV DA17......28 G7
Giffards Cl EGRIN RH19......265 J7
Giffin St DEPT SE8......41 N1
Gifford Cl GILL ME7......96 F7
Giffordside CHAT ME4......33 J8
Gigger's Green Rd
...RASHE TN25......306 D8
Giggs HI STMC/STPC BR5......64 C8
Gighill Rd CHT AV ME20......153 N1
Gilbert Cl GILL ME7......96 D6
...SWCM DA10......48 D7
...WOOL/PLUM SE18......43 K2
Gilbert Rd BELV DA17......28 F6
...BMLY BR1......62 E6
...CDW/CHF RM16......31 N6
...RAM CT11......17 L3
Gilbert Rw CVW DA11 *......69 K1
Gilbert St CANT CT1......166 C6
Gilbourne Rd
...WOOL/PLUM SE18......27 N9
Gilchrist Av HB CT6......107 H4
Gildenhill Rd SWLY BR8......66 C6
Gildersome St
...WOOL/PLUM SE18......27 H9
Giles Coppice NRWD SE19......60 F3
Giles Gdns MARG CT9......112 E5
Giles La CANTW/ST CT2......166 B1
Giles Young Ct SIT ME10 *......99 M9
Gilford Rd DEAL CT14......233 H4
Gilham Gv DEAL CT14......232 G5
Gilkes Crs DUL SE21......40 F3
Gilkes Pl DUL SE21......40 F3
Gill Av CAN/RD E16......26 B2
...STRD ME2......72 D4
Gill Crs GVW DA11......69 K2
Gillett Rd LYDD TN29......342 C5
...THHTH CR7......83 J1
Gilletts La EWMAL ME19......153 P6
Gillian St LEW SE13......41 P6
Gillies Rd GCR/WK TN15......90 B9
Gillingham Gn GILL ME7......7 L3
Gillingham Rd GILL ME7......7 J4
Gillison Wk BERM/RHTH SE16 *......24 D6
Gill La RASHE TN25......283 K8
...RASHW TN26......304 F5
Gilman Cl RFOLK CT18......288 C8
Gilmans Rd CROY/NA CR0......87 J5
Gills Ct STRD ME2 *......67 L7
Gill's Rd EYN DA4......67 J7
The Gill RTWE/PEM TN2......241 P9
Gilmore Rd LEW SE13......41 Q2
Gilroy Wy STMC/STPC BR5......87 J4
Gilsland Rd THHTH CR7......83 J1
Gilton Rd CAT SE6......62 C2
Gimble Wy RTWE/PEM TN2......241 N9
Gingerbread La HAWK TN18......316 E5
Ginsbury Cl STRD ME2......19 K4
Gipps Cross La RRTW TN3......269 L5
Gipsy HI NRWD SE19......60 E4
Gipsy La GRAYS RM17......32 D9
Gipsy Rd WELL DA16......44 E3
...WNWD SE27......60 E5
Gipsy Road Gdns WNWD SE27......60 C3
Giralda Cl CAN/RD E16......26 E1
Giraud Dr FAV ME13......132 E5
Giraud St POP/IOD E14......25 L2
Girton Gdns CROY/NA CR0......84 D7
Girton Rd SYD SE26......61 L4
Gisbourne Cl WLGTN SM6......82 C7
Gittens Cl BMLY BR1......62 D3
Glack Rd DEAL CT14......232 E5
Gladeside CROY/NA CR0......83 M6
The Glades EGRIN RH19......265 L7
...GVE DA12......69 M3
The Glade BMLY BR1......63 H8
...CHARL SE7......26 A7
...CROY/NA CR0......84 A2
...DEAL CT14......232 E5
...SEV TN13......179 H3
...WALD ME5......125 M3
...WWKM BR4......84 E1
Gladiator St FSTH SE23......41 L7
Gladstone Dr SIT ME10......130 B2
Gladstone Ms WNWD SE27 *......60 J6
...CHAT ME4......95 K4
...CROY/NA CR0......26 A3
...DEAL CT14......233 J2
...FOLKN CT19......11 C1
...KEN/WIL TN24......253 H4
...MAID/SHEP ME15......155 M6
...PGE/AN SE20......61 J7
Gladstone Ter WNWD SE27 *......60 C3

Gladwell Rd BMLY BR1......62 E5
Gladwyn Cl RHAM ME8......126 C1
Glaisher St DEPT SE8......25 L9
Glamford Rd STRD ME2......72 D3
Glamis Cl MAID/ME5......95 M9
Glamis Pl WAP E1W......24 F3
Glamis Rd WAP E1W......24 F3
Glanfield Rd BECK BR3......84 C1
Glanville Rd GILL ME7......96 A1
...HAYES BR2......62 F9
...STRD ME2......18 C1
Glarn's Yd WADH TN5......315 L3
Glasbrook Rd ELTH/MOT SE9......43 H8
Glassenbury Rd CRBK TN17......275 J9
Glasshouse Flds WAP E1W......24 G3
Glassmill La HAYES BR2......62 D8
Glass Yd WOOL/PLUM SE18......27 H6
Glastonbury Cl
...STMC/STPC BR5......87 K5
Glastonbury Pk WCHPL E1......24 F2
Glaucus St BOW E3......25 L1
Glazebrook Cl DUL SE21......60 D1
Gleaming Wood Dr
...MAID/BEAR ME14......126 A5
Gleaners Cl MAID/BEAR ME14......156 D8
Gleanings Ms ROCH ME1 *......19 F6
Gleave Cl EGRIN RH19......265 K6
Glebe Cl HDCN TN27......249 J7
...RDV CT15......292 E2
Glebe Cl BKHTH/KID SE3 *......42 C4
The Glebefield SEV TN15......148 E8
Glebe Gdns MARG CT9......112 A5
...RMAID ME17......189 M6
Glebe House Dr HAYES BR2......85 L5
Glebeland HDCN TN27......219 H6
Glebelands DART DA1......45 P5
...RCANTE CT3......170 D9
...RDV CT15......289 N3
...RTW TN1......239 F6
...RTON TN11......238 C6
Glebelands Cl CMBW SE5 *......40 F1
Glebe La MAIDW ME16......184 E2
...SEV TN15......211 J3
...SIT ME10......130 A3
Glebe Meadow
...WBY/VAL ME18......183 L4
Glebe Pl EYN DA4......89 P1
Glebe Rd BMLY BR1......62 E7
...GILL ME7......96 B3
...GVW DA11......69 K3
...MARG CT9......112 A5
...RSEV TN14......178 G8
...WARL ME7......144 A2
The Glebe BKHTH/KID SE3......42 C4
...CHST BR7......63 M7
...EGRIN RH19......221 H3
...HDCN TN27......221 H3
...RTWE/PEM TN2......240 A6
...STH/RUST TN4......240 A6
Glebe Wy ERITH DA8......29 K9
...KEN/WIL TN24......252 G2
...WSTB CT5......105 L6
...WWKM BR4......84 G6
Gleeson Dr ORP BR6......86 G9
Glenafric Av POP/IOD E14......25 M7
Glenalvon Wy
...WOOL/PLUM SE18......27 P1
Glen Av HB CT6......107 P1
Glenbarr Cl ELTH/MOT SE9......43 N4
Glenbervie Dr HB CT6......108 B5
Glenbow Rd BMLY BR1......62 C5
Glenbrook Gv SIT ME10......99 M7
Glencairne Cl CAN/RD E16......26 E1
Glencoe Rd CHAT ME4......95 M4
...MARG CT9......112 F4
Glendale Cl
...BERM/RHTH SE16 *......24 EB
...ORP BR6......86 E5
Glendale Rd MAID/SHEP ME15......185 L2
Glendale Wy THMD SE28......28 B4
Glendower Crs ORP BR6......87 H3
Glendown Rd ABYW SE2......27 P8
Glendye Wy EGRIN RH19......265 K8
Gleneagles Cl
...BERM/RHTH SE16 *......24 EB
...ORP BR6......86 E5
Gleneagles Dr
...MAID/SHEP ME15......185 L2
Glemsk est ELTH/MOT SE9......43 L5
Glenfarg Rd CAT SE6......62 C1
Glenfield Rd DVE/WH CT16......291 J4
Glenfinlas Wy CMBW SE5......40 B1
Glengall Br POP/IOD E14......25 L6
Glengall Gv POP/IOD E14......25 L6
Glengall Ter PECK SE15......24 C9
Glen Gdns CROY/NA CR0......82 G7
Glengarnock Av POP/IOD E14......25 N7
Glengarry Rd EDUL SE22......40 G5
Glen Gv DVW CT17......291 J8
Glenhead Cl ELTH/MOT SE9......43 M4
Glenhouse Rd ELTH/MOT SE9......43 M4
Glenhurst Av BXLY DA5......45 H9
Glenhurst Rd NRWD SE19......60 C6
Glen Iris Av CANTW/ST CT2......166 B2
Glen Iris Cl CANTW/ST CT2......166 B2
Glenister Rd GNWCH SE10......26 A8
Glenlea Rd ELTH/MOT SE9......43 L5
Glenluce Rd BKHTH/KID SE3......42 F4
Glenluge Rd BKHTH/KID SE3......42 B9
Glenlyon Rd ELTH/MOT SE9......43 L6
Glenmore Pk RTWE/PEM TN2......270 C8
Glenmore Rd WELL DA16......44 B3
Glennie Rd WNWD SE27......60 C4
Glen Rd DEAL CT14......263 H1
Glenrosa Gdns GVE DA12......70 B4
Glensdale Rd BROCKY SE4......41 M4

Glenshiel Rd ELTH/MOT SE9........43 L6
Glenside WSTB CT5.................105 P6
Glenside Av CANT CT1..............166 G2
Glen Ter POP/IOD E14..............25 M5
The Glen CROY/NA CRO..............84 A7
 HAYES BR2........................62 C8
 IOS ME12.........................58 C9
 ORP BR6..........................86 A7
 RDV CT15........................229 N9
Glenthorne Av CROY/NA CRO.........83 P5
Glenton Rd LEW SE15...............24 D3
Glentrammon Av ORP BR6...........116 G1
Glentrammon Cl ORP BR6...........116 G1
Glentrammon Gdns ORP BR6.........116 G1
Glentrammon Rd ORP BR6...........116 G1
Glenure Rd ELTH/MOT SE9...........43 L6
Glenview ABYW SE2.................28 C9
Glen Vw GVE DA12..................49 N9
Glen View Rd BMLY BR1.............63 H8
Glenville Gv DEPT SE8.............41 H1
Glen Vue EGRIN RH19..............265 H7
Glenwood TENT TN30...............301 J4
Glenwood Cl GILL ME7..............96 C7
 MAIDW ME16......................155 H7
 TENT TN30.......................301 J4
 WALD ME5.........................95 P5
Glenwood Dr IOS ME12..............58 B9
Glenwood Rd CAT SE6...............41 M9
Glenwood Wy NRWD SE19 *...........60 F7
Glenwood Wy CROY/NA CRO...........84 A3
Glenworth Av POP/IOD E14..........25 N7
Glimpsing Gn ERITHM DA18..........28 D6
Glistening Gld RHAM RM17..........97 H8
Cload Crs STMC/STPC BR5...........87 L6
Globe La CHAT ME4..................6 B5
Globe Pond Rd
 BERM/RHTH SE16...................25 H4
Globe St STHWK SE1................24 A5
Gloster Cl ASH TN23..............288 E9
Gloster Ropewalk DVW CT17........313 K1
Gloster Ter FOLK CT20 *..........310 A9
Gloster Wy DVW CT17..............313 K1
Gloucester Av BFN/LL DA15.........64 A1
 BRDST CT10......................143 L1
 CDW/CHF RM16.....................32 D5
 MARC CT9........................113 J3
 TIL RM18.........................44 B6
 WELL DA16........................44 B6
Gloucester Circ GNWCH SE10........42 A1
Gloucester Cl RHAM ME8...........113 H6
Gloucester Crs NROM 24 D3
 MTCM CR4 *.......................82 D2
Gloucester Ms NROM TN28..........337 H5
Gloucester Pde BFN/LL DA15 *......44 C6
Gloucester Pl FOLK CT20..........10 E4
Gloucester Rd BELV DA17...........28 E8
 CROY/NA CRO
 DART DA1.........................46 B7
 GVE DA12.........................69 N5
 MAID/SHEP ME15..................186 A3
 WADH TN5.........................
 WSTB CT5........................105 N4
Glover Cl ABYW SE2................28 B7
 SIT ME10.........................99 N5
Glover Rd KEN/WIL TN24.............3 K6
Glovers Crs SIT ME10 *...........129 N2
Gixonia Rd MEO DA15...............68 F5
Glyn Cl SNWD SE25.................60 B6
Glyn Davies Cl SEV TN13..........148 D5
Glyndebourne Pk ORP BR6...........86 C7
Glynde Rd BXLYHN DA7..............44 G4
Glynde St BROCKY SE4..............41 M7
Clyndon Rd WOOL/PLUM SE18.........27 K7
Glyn Dr SCUP DA14.................64 D3
Goad Av WALD ME5.................125 N2
Goat Lees La KEN/WIL TN24........252 C2
Goatsfield Rd BH/WHM TN16........145 M5
Gobery HI RCANTE C13.............169 L8
Godalming Av WLGTN SM6............82 D9
Godalming Rd POP/IOD E14..........25 L1
Goddard Rd BECK BR3...............84 A1
 CDW/CHF RM16.....................32 B2
Goddards Cl CRBK TN17............297 N5
Godden Cl RYE TN31...............330 A5
Godden Rd CANTW/ST CT2...........136 F9
 SNOD ME6........................123 N5
Godden Wy RHAM ME8................96 D2
Goddings Dr ROCH ME1..............94 F3
Coddington La ORP BR6.............87 J8
Coddington Rd STRD ME2............72 B7
 RMAID RM17......................188 D4
Coddington Rd STRD ME2............72 B7
Godfrey Evans Cl TONW TN10.......211 J5
Godfrey Gdns RCANTW C14..........195 N2
Godfrey HI WOOL/PLUM SE18.........26 F7
Godfrey Wk WOOL/PLUM SE18.........26 C7
Godfrey Wk ASH TN23...............2 D7
Godinton La ASH TN26............251 P4
Godinton Rd ASH TN23..............2 A6
Godinton Wy ASH TN23..............2 B3
Godman Rd CDW/CHF RM16............33 J6
 PECK SE15........................41 H3
Godric Crs CROY/NA CRO...........114 D4
Godson Rd CROY/NA CRO.............82 F7
Godstone Rd GDST RH9.............174 E7
 LING RH7........................234 F4
Gdstow Rd WOOL/PLUM SE2...........28 B5
Godwin Cl SIT ME10................99 N5
Godwin Rd CANT CT1...............166 B6
 DVE/WH CT16......................
 HAYES BR2........................62 C9
 MARG CT9........................112 F3
Godwyn Cl DVE/WH CT16 *...........8 D7
Godwyne Cl DVE/WH CT16 *..........8 D7
Godwyne Rd DVE/WH CT16............8 D2
Godwyn Gdns FOLK CT20...........310 D7
Godwyn Rd DEAL CT14..............233 H1
 FOLK CT20.......................310 D7
Coffers Rd BKHTH/KID SE3..........42 L5
Gogway RCANTW CT4................226 A5
Goldel Cl WLGTN SM6...............82 C8
Goldace GRAYS RM17................32 A9
Goldcrest Cl CAN/RD E16...........26 E1
 THMD SE28........................28 B3

Goldcrest Dr CHAT ME4.............73 J5
Goldcrest Wy CROY/NA CRO.........114 C3
Golden Acre La WGOS CT8..........111 L6
Golden Cl WGOS CT8...............111 L6
Golden Hl WSTB CT5...............105 J7
Golden Hind Pl DEPT SE8 *.........25 J7
Golden Plover Cl CAN/RD E16.......26 B2
Golden Sq TENT TN30..............301 J7
Golden St DEAL CT14..............233 J2
Golden Wood Cl WALD ME5..........126 A5
Goldfinch Cl DIT/AY ME20.........153 P2
 FAV ME13........................132 F4
 HB CT6..........................107 P4
 ORP BR6..........................87 H3
 STPH/PW TN12....................243 H4
Goldfinch Rd SAND/SEL CR2........114 B4
 THMD SE28........................27 L6
Gold HI RASHE TN25...............222 A7
Gold HI East RASHE TN25..........222 A7
Gold HI West RASHE TN25..........222 A6
Golding Gdns STPH/PW TN12........213 H4
Golding Rd SEV TN13..............149 H7
Goldings STPH/PW TN12............242 F4
Goldings Cl E/WMAL ME19..........183 H1
The Goldings RHAM ME8.............96 F6
Golding St WCHPL E1...............24 D2
Goldsel Rd SWLY BR8...............88 D1
Goldsmid Rd TON TN9.............240 F2
Goldsmith St WOOL/PLUM SE18.......27 M8
Goldsmith GRAYS RM17..............32 A9
Goldsmith Ct TENT TN30...........301 J6
Goldsmith Rd PECK SE15............40 G2
 RHAM ME8.........................97 H9
Goldsmiths Whf GRAYS RM17 *.......48 E1
Goldstone Dro RCANTE CT3.........170 F4
Goldstone Wk WALD ME5............125 M4
Gold St GVE DA12..................92 F7
Goldsworth Dr STRD ME2............72 A6
Goldsworthy Gdns
 BERM/RHTH SE16...................24 F7
Goldthorne Cl
 MAID/BEAR ME14...................13 K4
Goldups La FAV ME15..............193 L2
Goldwell Cl RASHE TN25...........306 B1
Goldwell La RASHE TN25...........306 B1
 RASHW TN26......................251 K7
Coldwell Rd THHTH CR7.............82 C8
Goldwing Cl CAN/RD E16............26 B2
Golf Cl STRHM/NOR SW16............33 L3
Golf Course Rd
 CDW/CHF RM16.....................33 L3
Golf Ct DEAL CT14 *..............203 H9
Golf Links Av GVW DA11............69 M4
Golford Rd CRBK TN17.............298 C2
Golf Rd BMLY BR1..................63 J8
 DEAL CT14.......................203 H9
Golf Road Pl DEAL CT14...........233 H1
Gomm Rd BERM/RHTH SE16............24 F6
Gomshall Av WLGTN SM6.............82 D9
Gonson St DEPT SE8................25 L9
Conville Rd THHTH CR7.............82 E7
Gooch Cl MAIDW ME16..............155 J4
Goodall Cl RHAM ME8...............97 H4
Goodban Sq RCANTE CT3............200 E1
Goodbury Rd BGR/WK TN15..........119 N7
Goodcheap La KEN/WIL TN24........253 N6
Goodfellow Wy DVE/WH CT16.........8 C2
Goodhart Wy WWKM BR4..............85 H3
Goodhew Rd SNWD SE25.............83 M3
Godley Stock Rd EDEN TN8.........175 C6
Goodman's Stile WCHPL E1..........24 D2
Goodman's Yd WCHPL E1.............24 C3
Goodmead Rd ORP BR6...............87 J2
Goodnestone Hl RCANTE CT3........199 N4
Goodnestone Rd RCANTE CT3........199 L1
 SIT ME10........................130 A2
Goodrich Rd EDUL SE22.............40 F7
Goods Hl TENT TN30..............300 E7
Goods Station Rd RTW TN1.........267 J6
Goodtrees La EDEN TN8............267 J6
Goodway Gdns POP/IOD E14..........25 N2
Goodwin Av WSTB CT5..............105 N4
Goodwin Cl BERM/RHTH SE16.........24 C6
 EDEN TN8........................206 C6
Goodwin Dr MAID/BEAR ME14........155 N4
 SCUP DA14........................64 F1
Goodwin Pk MARG CT9.............112 E8
Goodwin Rd CROY/NA CRO...........82 G9
 HOO/HM ME5.......................
 RAM CT11........................142 G7
Goodwood Cl WOOL/PLUM SE18........27 L6
Goosander Wy WOOL/PLUM SE18.......27 L6
Goose Cl WALD ME5.................95 M7
Goosefields FAV ME15............133 N4
Goose Green Cl
 STMC/STPC BR5....................64 C8
Gooseneck La HDCN TN27...........247 M4
Gophir La CANST EC4R..............24 A3
Gordon Av ORP BR6.................77 J3
 SIT ME10........................130 B1
 TIL RM18.........................44 C8
Gordon Crs CROY/NA CRO...........83 K5
Gordon Gv CMBW SE5................40 B5
Gordon Pl GVE DA12...............49 N7
Gordon Pl WOOL/PLUM SE18.........111 M4
Gordon Prom East GVE DA12........49 P7
Gordon Rd BECK BR3...............61 M9
 BELV DA17........................29 J4
 BFN/LL DA15......................44 A6
 CANT CT1..........................4 C6

CDW/CHF RM16......................32 F5
 DART DA1.........................46 D8
 FAV ME13........................133 H5
 FOLK CT20.......................310 A5
 GILL ME7.........................96 B1
 HB CT6..........................107 L2
 HOO/HM ME5.......................73 K2
 MARG CT9........................112 F2
 PECK SE15........................41 H5
 SEV TN13........................148 E6
 SEV TN13.........................
 STH/RUST TN4....................270 F1
 STRD ME2.........................72 A7
 WSTB CT5........................105 L7
Gordon Sq BRCH CT7...............110 C6
Gordon Wy BMLY BR1...............63 H8
Gordons Wy OXTED RH8............174 C4
Gordon Ter LYDD TN29 *...........342 B7
 ROCH ME1.........................19 F7
Gordon Wy BMLY BR1...............62 E7
Gore Court Rd
 MAID/SHEP ME15..................186 C6
 SIT ME10........................129 M3
Gore End Cl BRCH CT7.............110 C6
Gore Green Rd HOO/HM ME5..........51 M9
 HOO/HM ME5.......................51 M9
Gore La CRBK TN17................274 D5
 RASHW TN26......................279 J6
 SWCH CT13.......................201 H8
Gore Ms CANT CT1...................5 J1
Gore Rd RDART DA2.................67 H6
Goretop La DEAL CT14.............202 B5
Gorham Cl SNOD ME6...............66 D2
Gorham Dr MAID/SHEP ME15.........186 C2
 TON TN9.........................241 H1
Goring St HDTCH EC3A..............24 B2
Gorman Rd WOOL/PLUM SE18..........26 C7
Gorrell Rd WSTB CT5.............105 M6
Gorringe Av EYN DA4..............51 K6
Gorringe Park Av MTCM CR4........125 K1
Gorse Av RDART DA2................67 H6
Gorse Crs DIT/AY ME20...........154 C4
Gorse La RCANTW CT4.............107 P4
Gorse Rd CROY/NA CRO.............83 P1
 STMC/STPC BR5....................87 P6
Gorse Wy HART DA3.................91 J2
Gorse Wood Rd HART DA3............91 K1
Gorst Rd GILL ME7................
Goschen Rd DVW CT17.............291 J7
Gosfield Rd HB CT6..............107 M2
Gosling Wy BRXN/ST SW9............40 A2
Gosport Wy PECK SE15.............40 E1
Gossage Rd WOOL/PLUM SE18.........27 L8
Gosselin St WSTB CT5............105 M6
Goss Hall La RCANTE CT3..........171 H9
Goss Hl SWLY BR8.................66 C5
Gosshill Rd CHST BR7.............63 L8
Gossington Cl CHST BR7...........63 M3
Gossington St SE DEPT SE8.........25 H9
Goston Gdns THHTH CR7............60 A3
Coteley Mere KEN/WIL TN24........252 F2
Gothic Cl DART DA1...............66 D2
 DEAL CT14.......................232 C8
Goudhurst Cl CANTW/ST CT2........136 F9
 MAIDW ME16.......................12 C4
Goudhurst Rd BMLY BR1.............62 C4
 CRBK TN17.......................275 N4
 CRBK TN17.......................276 A8
 RAM ME8..........................96 E1
 STPH/PW TN12....................244 C4
 STPH/PW TN12....................274 A5
Gouge Av GVW DA11................49 J9
Gough Rd FOLK CT20..............310 B8
Goulding Gdns THHTH CR7..........60 B2
Gould Rd WALD ME5...............125 N2
Goulston St WCHPL E1.............24 C2
Gourney Gv CDW/CHF RM16...........32 B2
Gourock Rd ELTH/MOT SE9...........43 L6
Gover HI WBY/YAL ME18...........181 N5
Gowers La CDW/CHF RM16............32 C5
Gower's Wk WCHPL E1..............24 D2
Gowland Pl BECK BR3..............61 M8
Gowlett Rd PECK SE15.............40 G4
Gowlland Cl CROY/NA CRO..........83 M4
Grace Av BRXN/ST SW9.............40 A4
 MAIDW ME15......................155 J6
Gracechurch St BANK EC3V.........24 A3
Grace Cl ELTH/MOT SE9............43 H5
Grace Hl FOLK CT20..............10 E3
Grace Meadow DVE/WH CT16..........8 C9
Grace Rd CROY/NA CRO.............83 H5
 IOS ME12.........................57 J7
Graces Aly WCHPL E1..............24 D3
Graces Ms CMBW SE5..............40 E3
Grace's Rd CMBW SE5.............40 E3
Grace Taylor Ms
 FOLKN C13 *.....................310 L4
Gracious La SEV TN13............178 F6
Gracious Lane Br
 BGR/WK TN15.....................149 M1
Gracious Lane End RSEV TN14......178 E6
The Gradient SYD SE26............60 C3
Graduate Pl STHWK SE1............24 A6
Grafton Av ROCH ME1..............95 H6
Grafton Gn HB CT6...............107 H3
Grafton Rd BRDST CT10...........143 K5
 CROY/NA CRO......................83 H5
 SIT ME10........................129 N1
Graham Cl CROY/NA CRO............84 D6
Graham Rd BXLYHN DA7.............45 H5
 BFN/LL DA15 *....................44 D7
 MAID/BEAR ME14..................155 M6
 OXTED RH8.......................174 B4
Grainey Rd RSIT ME9.............127 P1
Grain Rd HOO/HM ME5..............
 HOO/HM ME8.......................73 K4
 RHAM ME8........................126 F2
Grampian Cl ORP BR6..............86 G3

RTWE/PEM TN2.....................23 K1
Grampian Wy MAID/SHEP ME15.......186 D2
Grampion Cl KEN/WIL TN24.........252 F5
Gramsci Wy CAT SE6...............61 P2
Granada St MAID/SHEP ME15.........13 F5
Granary STPH/PW TN12............243 J5
Granary Ct MAID/BEAR ME14........156 B7
 RHAM ME8.........................97 J5
Granary Court Rd
 WOOL/PLUM SE18...................27 H8
Granby Rd ELTH/MOT SE9...........43 K3
 GVW DA11.........................49 H7
 WOOL/PLUM SE18...................27 J6
Grand Depot Rd
 WOOL/PLUM SE18...................27 H8
Grand Dr HB CT6.................107 H2
Grand Pde NROM TN28.............337 K9
Grandshore La CRBK TN17..........276 D3
Grandsire Gdns HOO/HM ME3........73 L1
Grand View Av
 BH/WHM TN16.....................145 M2
Grange Av SNWD SE25..............60 B8
Grangecliffe Gdns SNWD SE25......60 B8
Grange Cl BFN/LL DA15............64 C2
 BH/WHM TN16.....................176 E2
 E/WMAL ME19.....................183 J1
 EDEN TN8........................206 D9
Grange Ct GDST RH9..............204 B5
 WLGTN SM6 *......................82 A7
Grange Crs RDART DA2.............47 H7
 TENT TN30.......................301 H4
 THMD SE28........................28 B4
Grange Dr CHST BR7...............63 J5
 ORP BR6.........................117 K3
Grange Gdns SNWD SE25............60 E8
 STH/RUST TN4....................270 A4
Grange Hl RDV CT15..............181 H5
 SNWD SE25........................60 E8
 WALD ME5..........................7 G7
Grangehill Pl ELTH/MOT SE9.......43 K4
Grangehill Rd ELTH/MOT SE9.......43 K3
Grangemill Rd CAT SE6............61 N1
Grangemill Wy CAT SE6............61 N1
Grange Park Rd THHTH CR7.........60 D9
Grange Rd BGR/WK TN15...........151 M5
 BRDST CT10......................113 C7
 DEAL CT14.......................232 G4
 FOLK CT20.......................310 B5
 HART DA3.........................91 L4
 MAID/BEAR ME14..................155 M6
 ORP BR6.........................117 H2
 HB CT6..........................107 N2
 HYTHE CT21......................308 C3
 ORP BR6..........................86 C6
 RAM CT11........................142 E6
 SEV TN13.........................20 C7
 SNWD SE25........................60 D9
 SOCK/AV RM15.....................30 F4
 STH/RUST TN4....................270 A4
 STHWK SE1........................23 P4
 STHWK SE1........................24 A4
 TENT TN30.......................300 C4
The Grange BGR/WK TN15...........120 C3
 CROY/NA CRO......................84 C4
 E/WMAL ME19.....................183 P5
 GVE DA12.........................67 K7
 RDV CT15........................229 N9
 STHWK SE1........................24 C6
 WSTB CT5........................105 H8
Grange Wk STHWK SE1..............24 C6
Grange Walk Ms STHWK SE1.........24 C6
Grange Wy BRDST CT10............143 L2
 ERITH DA8........................46 B1
 HART DA3.........................91 J3
 ROCH ME1.........................95 H1
Grangeways Cl GVW DA11...........69 K5
Grangewood BXLY DA5..............45 H9
Grangewood Av CDW/CHF RM16.......32 F6
Grangewood La BECK BR3...........61 M5
Grange Wk STHWK SE1..............24 C6
Granite St WOOL/PLUM SE18.........27 M8
Grant Cl BRDST CT10.............113 K7
Grant Dr MAID/SHEP ME15..........186 A5
Grantham Av DEAL CT14...........232 F4
Grantham Wy CDW/CHF RM16.........32 B4
Grantley Ct ASH TN23............282 D1
Granton Rd SCUP DA14............64 D4
 HOO/HM ME3.......................72 D4
Grants Hl CRBK TN17.............299 H9
Grasdene Rd WLGTN SM6............
Grant Rd CROY/NA CRO.............83 L7
 WLGTN SM6........................82 A4
Granville Av BRXN/ST SW9.........40 A5
 BRDST CT10......................143 N1
Granville Cl CROY/NA CRO.........83 M4
Granville Dr HYTHE CT21.........308 C8
Granville Gv LEW SE13............42 A4
Granville Marina Ct
 RAM CT11 *.......................17 J3
Granville Ms SCUP DA14...........64 C4
Granville Pde FOLK CT20.........310 D8
Granville Pk LEW SE13............42 A3
Granville Pl IOS ME12............57 L6
Granville Rd BH/WHM TN16........176 C2
 BRDST CT10......................143 M7
 DEAL CT14.......................233 H7
 GILL ME7.........................96 B1
 GVW DA11.........................49 H8
 HYTHE CT21......................308 C8
 MAID/BEAR ME14..................155 M6
 OXTED RH8.......................174 B4
 RDV CT15........................292 C1
 RTW TN1.........................267 J4
 SCUP DA14........................64 C3
 SEV TN13.........................20 D7

WELL DA16........................44 E4
Granville Rd East FOLK CT20.....310 C8
Granville Sq PECK SE15 *.........40 E1
Granville St DEAL CT14..........233 J4
Grapple Rd MAID/BEAR ME14........155 M5
Grasdene Rd
 WOOL/PLUM SE18...................44 C1
Grasmere Av ORP BR6..............86 C7
 ORP BR6..........................
Grasmere Gdns FOLKN CT19........310 E4
 ORP BR6..........................86 C7
Grasmere Gv STRD ME2............72 C5
Grasmere Rd BMLY BR1.............62 D7
 BXLYHN DA7.......................45 L2
 KEN/WIL TN24....................252 F5
 ORP BR6..........................
 SNWD SE25........................83 N3
 WSTB CT5........................105 P6
Grasmere St SNWD SE25...........199 J9
Grasshaven Wy THMD SE28..........27 N4
Grassington Rd SCUP DA14.........64 C5
Grasslands RMAID ME17...........187 H7
Grassmere DIT/AY ME20...........153 M3
 LYDD TN29.......................337 K2
Grassmount FSTH SE23.............61 H1
Grassway WLGTN SM6..............82 B8
Grassy Gld GILL ME7.............96 E8
Grassy La SEV TN13...............20 E7
Grately Wy PECK SE15 *...........40 E1
Gravel Castle Rd RCANTW CT4......228 C6
Gravel Hl BXLYHS DA6.............45 K6
 CROY/NA CRO......................84 B4
 FAV ME13........................191 H3
Gravel Hill Cl BXLY DA5..........45 K7
Gravel La RDV CT15..............312 A2
 WCHPL E1.........................24 C2
Gravelly Bottom Rd
 RMAID ME17......................187 L9
Gravelly Fld ASH TN23...........251 P9
Gravelly Ways
 STPH/PW TN12....................213 K6
Gravel Pit Wy ORP BR6............87 H6
Gravel Rd EYN DA4................67 H6
 HAYES BR2........................85 P6
Gravel Wk ASH TN23................2 C2
 CANT CT1..........................4 E5
Gravesend Cl CHST BR7............63 N2
Graveney Cl HOO/HM ME3...........52 C9
Graveney Gv PGE/AN SE20..........61 J6
Graveney Rd FAV ME15............133 J6
 MAID/SHEP ME15..................121 L9
Gravesend Rd BGR/WK TN15........121 J2
 GVE DA12.........................70 G3
 GVE DA12.........................71 H3
Gray Cl RFOLK CT18..............288 F7
Grayland Ct BMLY BR1.............63 H7
Graylands GRAYS RM17 *...........33 H4
Graylen Cl DEAL CT14............233 H2
Graylings Ct SIT ME10...........129 K3
The Graylings ROCH ME1...........94 G3
Grayne Av HOO/HM ME3.............56 D3
Grays End Cl CDW/CHF RM16........32 B6
Grays Farm Rd STMC/STPC BR5......64 D7
Grayshott Cl SIT ME10...........129 N2
Grays Rd BH/WHM TN16............146 C6
Graystone Rd WSTB CT5...........105 P3
Grays Wy CANT CT1...............166 A6
Grazeley Cl BXLYHS DA6...........45 L6
Great Bounds Dr
 STH/RUST TN4....................240 B6
Great Brooms Rd
 STH/RUST TN4....................240 E9
Great Brownings SYD SE26.........61 K6
Great Conduit St
 HYTHE CT21 *....................309 H5
Great Courtlands RRTW TN3........269 M5
Great Cross Av GNWCH SE10........42 C1
Great Dover St STHWK SE1.........24 A5
Great Elms EFON TN11............211 P1
Great Elms Rd HAYES BR2..........85 M1
Greatfield Cl LEW SE13...........41 N5
Great Footway RRTW TN3..........269 L4
Great Gatton Cl CROY/NA CRO......84 D4
Great Hall Ar RTW TN1 *..........22 D5
Great Harry Dr ELTH/MOT SE9......43 K5
Great House Ct EGRIN RH19 *......265 J8
Great Lines GILL ME7.............6 E2
Great Maze Pond STHWK SE1........24 A5
Greatness La RSEV TN14..........149 H6
Greatness Rd RSEV TN14..........149 H6
Greatorex St WCHPL E1............24 D1
Great Queen St DART DA1..........46 F7
Great St Helen's HDTCH EC3A......24 A2
Great South Av CHAT ME4..........95 M5
Great Spilmans EDUL SE22.........40 E6
Great Stour Pl
 CANTW/ST CT2 *....................4 D2
Great Swan Aly LOTH EC2R.........24 A2
Great Thrift STMC/STPC BR5.......86 C1
Great Till Cl RSEV TN14.........148 D1
Great Tower St MON EC3R..........24 B3
Great Winchester St OBST EC2N....24 A2
Greatwood CHST BR7..............63 J5
Greavney Ms ASH TN23 *...........54 C4
Grebe Cl HYTHE CT21.............308 B7
Grebe Crs HYTHE CT21............308 B7
Grebe Crest WTHK RM20............31 K7
Grecian Rd NRWD SE19............60 B5
Grecian St MAID/BEAR ME14........13 G1
Greenacre RCANTW CT4............228 A3
Greenacre Cl SWLY BR8............88 D1
 WALD ME5.........................95 M4
Greenacre Dr DEAL CT14..........233 H8
Greenacres PI WLGTN SM6..........82 A4
 OXTED RH8........................
Green Acres CROY/NA CRO..........83 L7
 RDV CT15........................260 E1
 SCUP DA14........................64 D3
Greenacres ELTH/MOT SE9..........43 L7
 OXTED RH8.......................175 H5
Greenacres Cl ORP BR6............86 D8

Greenacre Sq
BERM/RHTH SE16 * 24 C5
Greenbank *KEN/WIL* TN24 .....252 C3
WALD ME5 ....95 N6
Green Bank *WAP* E1W 95 H5
Greenbanks *DART* DA1 ....66 E1
RFOLK CT18 ....287 H2
Greenbay Rd *CHARL* SE7 ....43 H1
Greenborough Cl
MAID/SHEP ME15 ....186 B5
Green Chain Wk *BECK* BR3 ....62 A6
CHST SE7 ....43 K9
ELTH/MOT SE9 ....43M6
SYD SE26 ....61 K5
THMD SE28 ....28 C4
Green Cl *HAYES* BR2 ....62 C9
RFOLK CT18 ....288 E8
ROCH ME1 ....95 J4
Green Cloth Ms *CANT* CT1 ....5 H1
Green Ct *FOLKN* CT19 ....311 H4
RCANTW CT4 ....197 M2
Green Court Av *CROY/NA* CRO .83 N6
Green Court Gdns
CROY/NA CRO 83 N6
Greencourt Rd
STMC/STPC BR5 ....86 F2
Green Court Rd *SWLY* BR8 ......88 C5
Greencroft *ASH* TN23 ....282 A2
Green Dl *EDUL* SE22 ....40 E6
Greendale Wk *GVW* DA11 ....69 J2
Green Dell *CHR* DA11 ....69 J2
Green Dragon Yd *WCHPL* E1 ..24 D1
Green Farm Cl *ORP* BR6 ....86 D9
Green Farm La *GVE* DA12 ....70 G2
Greenfell Man *DEPT* SE8 * 25 J8
Greenfield *EDEN* TN8 ....206 E9
Greenfield Cl *DIT/AY* ME20 ....124 F7
THRUST TN14 ....269 P5
Greenfield Dr *BMLY* BR1 ....62 G8
Greenfield Gdns
STMC/STPC BR5 ....86 E6
Greenfield Rd *FOLKN* CT19 ....311 H4
LINE ME7 ....73 K9
MSTR CT12 ....143 H2
RDART DA2 ....65 M4
WCHPL E1 ....24 D2
Greenfields *MAID/SHEP* ME15 .186 B5
Greenfields Cl *HOO/HM* ME3 ...72 D4
Greenfinches *GILL* ME7 ....96 C8
HART DA3 ....68 F9
Greenfrith Dr *TONN* TN10 .....210 E3
Green Gdns *ORP* BR6 ....86 D9
Greenhaven Dr *THMD* SE28 .....28 A2
Green Hedges *TENT* TN30 .....301 J7
Green Hedges Av *EGRIN* RH19 .264 C6
Green Hedges Cl *EGRIN* RH19 .264 C6
Green Hl *MAID/SHEP* ME15 .....186 E2
ORP BR6 ....115 P6
WOOL/PLUM SE18 ....26 C8
Greenhill Cl *MSTR* CT12 ....141 J5
Greenhill Gdns *HB* CT6 ....107 J3
MSTR CT12 ....141 J5
Green Hill La *RMAID* ME17 .....218 E2
Greenhill La *HDCN* TN27 ....249M2
WARL CR6 ....144 B2
Greenhill Rd *GVW* DA11 ....69 K1
HB CT6 ....107 J3
RSEV TN14 ....119 H9
Green Hills *RCANTW* CT4 ....228 B6
Greenhithe *MAID/SHEP* ME15 ..12 E7
Greenhithe Cl *ELTH/MOT* SE9 ..44 A6
**Greenhill STPH/PW* TN12 ....246 B4
Green Holm Rd *ELTH/MOT* SE9 .43M6
Green House La *CANTW/ST* CT2 ..4 B1
Green Hundred Rd *PECK* SE15 ..24 D9
Greenhurst La *OXTED* RH8 .....175 K8
Greenhurst Rd *WNWD* SE27 ....60 A4
Greening St *ABYW* SE2 ....28 B7
Greenland Ms *DEPT* SE8 ....24 G8
Greenland Quay
BERM/RHTH SE16 ....24 G7
Greenlands *BGR/WK* TN15 .....151 L5
Green Lands *GVE* DA12 ....92 C2
Greenland Wy *CROY/NA* CRO 82 C4
Green La *ASH* TN23 ....282 B3
BRDST CT10 ....113 K8
CDW/CHF RM16 ....32 D1
CRBK TN17 ....299M5
DEAL CT14 ....232 G8
DVE/WH CT16 ....290 F2
DVE/WH CT16 ....291 J5
E/WMAL ME19 ....122 B8
EDEN TN8 ....207 K5
ELTH/MOT SE9 ....43 L9
FOLKN CT19 ....311 H4
HDCN TN27 ....249 H8
HOO/HM ME3 ....52 B2
HOO/HM ME3 ....56 D2
HYTHE CT21 ....308 F5
LINE ME7 ....234 F6
MARG CT9 ....113 K4
MEO DA13 ....92 C4
PGE/AN SE20 ....61 K6
RASHE TN25 ....192 D9
RASHW TN26 ....279 N6
RCANTE CT3 ....200 C7
RCANTW CT4 ....194 D1
RDV CT15 ....260 E1
RDV CT15 ....262 E7
RDV CT15 ....289 N1
RFOLK CT18 ....258 C8
RFOLK CT18 ....289 L9
RMAID ME17 ....185 P8
RMAID ME17 ....187 N8
RMAID ME17 ....216 C5
RMAID ME17 ....216 G1
RSIT ME9 ....128 A4
RSIT ME9 ....130 A6
STPH/PW TN12 ....214 D9
STPH/PW TN12 ....243 J4
THHTH CR7 ....60 B7
WSTB CT5 ....105 L6

Green Lane Av *HYTHE* CT21 ....308 E5
Greenlane Wd *CRBK* TN17 ....60 C8
The Green La *RTON* TN11 ....209 L9
Greenlaw St *WOOL/PLUM* SE18 .27 H6
Green Leaf Av *WLGTN* SM6 ....82 C8
Greenleaf Cl
BRXS/STRHM SW2 * 40 A8
Greenleas *RTWE/PEM* TN2 ....271M2
Green Leas *WSTB* CT5 ....106 C5
Greenleigh Av *STMC/STPC* BR5 ..87 J1
Greenly Wy *NROM* TN28 ....337 H7
Greenmead Cl *SNWD* SE25 .....83M2
Green Mdw *LYDD* TN29 ....327 H4
Greenoak Rk *BH/WHM* TN16 ..145 M3
Green Porch Cl *SIT* ME10 ....99 P7
Green Rd *BRCH* CT7 ....110 C5
STPH/PW TN12 ....273 P5
Greensand Rd
MAID/SHEP ME15 ....186 D1
Green Sands
MAID/BEAR ME14 ....125 P5
Greensand Wy *EDEN* TN8 ....176 D7
GDST RH9 ....204 A1
HDCN TN27 ....210 E8
MAID/SHEP ME15 ....184 D9
OXTED RH8 ....175 H2
RASHW TN26 ....302 C5
MAID ME17 ....215 P1
RMAID ME17 ....218 F1
RSEV TN14 ....178 C8
RTON TN11 ....181 J6
SEV TN13 ....21 C5
WBY/YAL ME18 ....183 H8
Greens End *WOOL/PLUM* SE18 .27 H4
Greenside *BXLY* DA5 ....44 G3
MAID/SHEP ME15 ....13 H6
RASHW TN26 ....279M9
SWLY BR8 ....65 M8
Greenside Cl *CAT* SE6 ....62 B1
Greenside Rd *CROY/NA* CRO 82 C5
Greensland Wy *ASH* TN23 .....282 A4
RASHW TN26 ....251 M3
Greensleeves Wy
E/WMAL ME19 ....153 K9
Greensole La *MSTR* CT12 ....142 D4
Green St *GILL* ME7 ....7 H2
Greenstede Av *EGRIN* RH19 ...265 F3
Green Street Green Rd
DART DA1 ....46 G9
RDART DA2 ....67 J2
Greenstreet Hl *NWCR* SE14 * 41 K4
The Green *BGR/WK* TN15 * 120 C2
BH/WHM TN16 * 147 K9
BH/WHM TN16 ....176 E2
BXLYHN DA7 ....45 J2
CANTW/ST CT2 ....135 P7
CANTW/ST CT2 ....165 M3
CDW/CHF RM16 ....33 H1
CROY/NA CRO 114 C5
CTHM CR5 ....118 A8
HAYES BR2 ....85 K4
HYTHE CT21 ....308 C5
LYDD TN29 ....326 C2
MSTR CT12 ....142 C5
ORP BR6 * 117 K4
RAIN RM13 ....30 B1
RASHE TN25 ....223 P8
RCANTE CT3 ....168 C9
RCANTE CT3 ....169M2
RCANTW CT4 ....165 L9
RCANTW CT4 ....229 H5
RDART DA2 ....67 H1
RRTW TN5 ....269 K5
RSIT ME9 * 98 C3
RTON TN11 ....209 L9
SCUP DA14 ....64 C6
SEV TN13 ....149 J7
STMC/STPC BR5 ....64 D6
WELL DA16 ....44 A5
Greentrees Av *TONN* TN10 .....211 J5
Green V *BXLYHS* DA6 ....44 F6
Greenvale Gdns *RHAM* ME8 .....96 E4
Greenvale Rd *ELTH/MOT* SE9 ...43 K5
Greenview Av *BECK* BR3 ....84 B5
Green View Av *RTON* TN11 ....209M9
Greenview Crs *RTON* TN11 .....210 B6
Green Wk *DART* DA1 ....45 P5
STHWK SE1 * 24 B6
Green Wy *ELTH/MOT* SE9 ....43 H6
HART DA3 ....91 H2
HAYES BR2 ....85 P3
LYDD TN29 ....342 B7
MAIDW ME16 ....154 C9
RTWE/PEM TN2 ....241 H9
Greenway *BH/WHM* TN16 ....145M5
CHST BR7 ....63 L4
CRBK TN17 ....297 N3
FAV ME15 ....132 E5
WALD ME5 ....95 J8
WLGTN SM6 ....82 B8
Greenway Court Rd
RMAID ME17 ....187 P1
Greenway Gdns *CROY/NA* CRO .84 C7
Greenway La *RMAID* ME17 .....108 B8
Greenways *BECK* BR3 ....61 N8
HART DA3 ....69 H9
MAID/BEAR ME14 ....156 C7
RSIT ME9 * 98 C3
SIT ME10 ....130 A2
The Greenways
STPH/PW TN12 ....242 C4
The Greenway *OXTED* RH8 .....175 K9
Greenwich Church St
GNWCH SE10 * 25M9
Greenwich Cl *MAIDW* ME16 ....155 J8
WALD ME5 ....95 J8
Greenwich Crs *EHAM* E6 ....26 F1
Greenwich Foot Tnl
GNWCH SE10 ....25 M8
Greenwich Hts
WOOL/PLUM SE18 * 43 J1
Greenwich High Rd
GNWCH SE10 ....41 P1
Greenwich Park St
GNWCH SE10 * 25 N9

Greenwich Quay *DEPT* SE8 ......25 L9
Greenwich South St
GNWCH SE10 ....41 P2
Greenwich Vw *POP/IOD* E14 ....25M4
Greenwood Cl *BFN/LL* DA15 ...144 C1
STMC/STPC BR5 ....86 F5
Greenwood Rd *BXLY* DA5 ....65 M3
CROY/NA CRO 82 G4
Greenwood Wy *SEV* TN13 ....20 B3
Greggs Wood Rd
RTWE/PEM TN2 ....271 H2
Gregor Ms *BKHTH/KID* SE3 .....42 E1
Gregory Cl *RHAM* ME8 ....127 H1
Gregory Crs *ELTH/MOT* SE9 .....43 M6
Grenaby Av *CROY/NA* CRO 83 J4
Grenaby Rd *CROY/NA* CRO 83 J4
Grenada Rd *CHARL* SE7 ....42 C1
Grenade St *POP/IOD* E14 ....25 J5
Grenadier *RTON* TN11 * 180 B8
Grenadier Cl *RHAM* ME8 ....97 L4
Grenard Cl *PECK* SE15 * 40 C1
Grenham Bay Av *BRCH* CT7 ....110 F6
Grenham Rd *BRCH* CT7 ....110 F5
Grenville Cl *MEO* DA13 ....92 B6
Grenville Gdns *BRCH* CT7 ....110 F5
Grenville Rd *CDW/CHF* RM16 .....31 L8
CROY/NA CRO 114 F4
Grenville Wy *BRDST* CT10 ......113 K9
Gresham Av *HART* DA3 ....91 J2
MARG CT9 ....111 P4
WARL CR6 ....144 B3
Gresham Rd *BECK* BR3 ....61 L8
BRXN/ST SW9 ....40 A4
EDEN E16 ....26 C2
OXTED RH8 ....175 J5
RMAID ME17 ....185 J8
*SWD SE25 * 83M1
Greshams *EDEN* TN8 ....206 B8
Greville Av *SAND/SEL* CR2 .....114 A4
Greybury La *EDEN* TN8 ....236 C6
Greycot Rd *BECK* BR3 ....61 N4
Grey Eagle St *WCHPL* E1 ....24 C1
Greyfriars Cl *MAID* ME14 ....16 B9
Greyhound La *CDW/CHF* RM16 ..33 H5
Greyhound Wy *DART* DA1 ....45 N6
Greyladies Gdns
GNWCH SE10 * 42 A3
Greys Park Cl *HAYES* BR2 ....85M9
Greystead Rd *FSTH* SE23 ....41 J8
Greystone Pk *RSEV* TN14 ....177M1
Greystones Rd *CMBW* SE15 ....149 K2
Greystones Rd
MAID/BEAR ME14 ....125 K9
MSTR CT12 ....142 C7
Grey Wethers
MAID/BEAR ME14 * 16 B3
Grey Willow Gdns *ASH* TN23 ..252 A9
Gribble Bridge La *HDCN* TN27 .300 C2
Grice Av *BH/WHM* TN16 ....115 L7
Grice Cl *RFOLK* CT18 ....288 C3
Grierson Rd *FSTH* SE23 ....41 L7
Grieves Rd *GVW* DA11 ....69 K2
Griffin Cl *GILL* ME7 ....139 J9
Griffin Manor Wy *THMD* SE28 ...27 L6
Griffin Rd *WOOL/PLUM* SE18 ....27 L8
The Griffins *CDW/CHF* RM16 ....32 C5
Griffin St *DEAL* CT14 ....233 J2
Griffin Wk *GRH* DA9 ....47 M6
Grifon Cl *CDW/CHF* RM16 ....31 M6
Grifon Rd *CDW/CHF* RM16 ....31 M6
Griggs La *HDCN* TN27 ....247 P5
Grigg's Pl *STHWK* SE1 * 24 B6
Griggs Wy *BGR/WK* TN15 ....151 K5
Grimsby Gv *CAN/RD* E16 ....27 J5
Grimsel Pth *CMBW* SE5 ....40 B1
Grimshill Ct *CANTW/ST* CT2 * ..136 B9
Grimshill Rd *WSTB* CT5 ....105 L6
Grimston Av *FOLK* CT20 ....10 A5
Grimston Gdns *FOLK* CT20 ....10 A5
Grimthorpe Av *WSTB* CT5 ....105 K7
Grindall Av *MAIDW* ME14 ....83M7
Grindal Cl *CROY/NA* CRO * 83 J5
Grindley Gdns *CROY/NA* CRO * ..83 L3
Grinling Pl *DEPT* SE8 ....25 K9
Grinsell Hl *MSTR* CT12 ....141M6
Grinstead La *EGRIN* RH19 ....25 H8
Grisbrook Farm Cl *LYDD* TN29 ..342 C6
Grizedale Cl *ROCH* ME1 ....95 J6
Grocers' Hall Ct *LOTH* EC2R 24 A2
Gromefield *RRTW* TN5 ....269 H9
Groombridge Cl *WELL* DA16 ......73M9
Groombridge Hl *RRTW* TN5 ......269 H6
Groombridge Rd *RRTW* TN5 .....268 F8
Groombridge Sq
MAID/SHEP ME15 * 186 C5
Groom Cl *HAYES* BR2 ....85 L1
Groom Wy *RMAID* ME17 ....189M6
Grosmont Rd
WOOL/PLUM SE18 ....27 N8
Grummant Rd *PECK* SE15 ....40 F2
Grummock Av *RAM* CT11 ....142 C5
Grundy's Hl *RAM* CT11 * 17 F4
Grundy St *POP/IOD* E14 ....25 L2
Guardian Av *CDW/CHF* RM16 ....31 N5
Guardian Ct *RHAM* ME8 ....96 F5
Gubyon Av *HNHL* SE24 ....40 C6
Guernsey Cl *HNHL* SE24 ....40 C6
Guernsey Wy *KEN/WIL* TN24 ...252 F2
Guestwick *TONN* TN10 ....211 J5
Guibal Rd *LEE/GVN* SE12 ....63 L1
Guildables La *OXTED* RH8 ....205 P1
Guildcount La *SWCH* CT13 ......201 N1
Guildford Av *WGOS* CT8 ....111 L5
Guildford Gdns *STRD* ME2 ....7 J1
Guildford La *KEN/WIL* TN24 .....252 F2
Guildford Rd *CANT* CT1 ....72 E1
Guildford Lawn *RAM* CT11 ....17 F4
CROY/NA CRO 83 J3
EHAM E6 ....26 F2

WSTB CT5 ....105 L7
Grosvenor Sd *HART* DA3 * 68 C9
Grosvenor Ter *CMBW* SE5 ....40 C1
Grosvenor Wk *RTW* TN1 ....22 D2
Grosvenor Wharf Rd
POP/IOD E14 ....25 N7
Grote's Buildings
BKHTH/KID SE3 ....42 C3
Grote's Pl *BKHTH/KID* SE3 ....42 C3
Grotto Common *MARG* CT9 ....15 J4
Grotto Hl *MARG* CT9 ....15 J4
Grotto Rd *MARG* CT9 ....15 J4
Grove Av *IOS* ME12 ....80 E5
RTW TN1 ....22 D6
Grovebury Cl *ERITH* DA8 ....29 J9
Grovebury Rd *THMD* SE28 ....28 A5
Grove Cl *FAV* ME13 ....132 C7
FSTH SE23 ....61 M2
HAYES BR2 ....85 K6
RTON TN11 ....182 D8
Grove Ferry Hl *RCANTE* CT3 ....139 H6
Grove Ferry Rd *RCANTE* CT3 ....139 J6
Grove Gdns *MARG* CT9 ....14 B7
Grove Green La
MAID/BEAR ME14 ....156 B7
Grove Green Rd
MAID/BEAR ME14 ....156 C7
Grove Hill *RDART* DA2 ....46 F4
Grove Hill Gdns *RTW* TN1 ....22 E7
Grove Hill Rd *CMBW* SE5 ....40 E4
RTW TN1 ....22 E5
Groveherst Av *SIT* ME10 ....99 N6
Grovehurst La
STPH/PW TN12 ....274 B3
Grovehurst Rd *RSIT* ME9 ....99 M3
Groveland Rd *BECK* BR3 ....61 M9
Grovelands *RMAID* ME17 ....189 M6
Grovelands Cl *CMBW* SE5 ....40 E3
Grovelands Rd
STMC/STPC BR5 ....64 C6
Grove La *CMBW* SE5 ....40 E4
LYDD TN29 ....334 E2
MAID/SHEP ME15 ....214 C3
RYE TN31 ....332 F9
Grove Market Pl
ELTH/MOT SE9 * 43 K7
Grove Pk *CMBW* SE5 ....40 E3
Grove Park Av *SIT* ME10 ....99 H9
Grove Park Rd *ELTH/MOT* SE9 ...64 B3
Grove Pl *FAV* ME13 ....132 C7
Grove Rd *BELV* DA17 ....28 E9
BGR/WK TN15 ....151 M5
BH/WHM TN16 ....145M5
BXLYHN DA7 ....45 L5
CHAT ME4 ....95 N4
DEAL CT14 ....233 J6
EDEN TN8 ....238 C8
FAV ME13 ....163 K8
FOLK CT20 ....11 G3
GILL ME7 ....73 N9
GRAYS RM17 ....32 D7
GVW DA11 ....48 C8
LING RH7 ....235 H4
MAID/SHEP ME15 ....185 P5
RAM CT11 ....16 D4
RCANTE CT3 ....139 J9
RCANTE CT3 ....168 F6
RSEV TN14 ....149 H6
SLH/COR SS17 ....34 C1
STRD ME2 ....72 B7
STRD ME2 ....95 J9
STRD ME7 ....82 F1
THHTH CR7 ....82 B9
Grover St *RTW* TN1 ....4 C7
The Grove *BH/WHM* TN16 ....145 N3
BXLYHS DA6 ....44 F5
DEAL CT14 ....233 H3
DVE/WH CT16 ....291 K6
GVW DA12 ....69 N8
HB CT6 ....107 H4
KEN/WIL TN24 ....253 H3
MAID/BEAR ME14 ....156 D9
RCANTW CT4 ....228 C6
RTWE/PEM TN2 ....241 N9
RYE TN31 ....338 F6
SCUP DA14 ....64 C4
SLH/COR SS17 * 34 C1
SWCM DA10 ....48 C6
SWLY BR8 ....65 P9
WGOS CT8 ....111 L5
WWKM BR4 ....84 B6
Grove V *CHST* BR7 ....63 L5
EDUL SE22 ....40 E5
Groveway *IOS* ME12 ....80 D5
Grovewood Dr
MAID/BEAR ME14 ....156 A8
Grub St *OXTED* RH8 ....175M5

RTW TN1 ....22 E5
Guildhall Buildings
CITYW EC2V 24 A2
Guildhall St *CANT* CT1 ....4 E4
Guildhall St North *FOLKN* CT19 .10 E3
Guild Rd *CHARL* SE7 ....42 B2
ERITH DA8 ....30 C3
Guilford Av *DVE/WH* CT16 ......261 H6
Guilford Rd *SWCH* CT13 ....202 E2
Guillat Av *RSIT* ME9 * 129 L7
Guilton *RCANTE* CT3 ....200 C1
Guinness Dr *HOO/HM* ME3 ....72 E5
Guinness Ct *CROY/NA* CRO * 83 L6
STHWK SE1 * 24 B5
Guinness Sq *STHWK* SE1 ....24 B5
Guildeford La *RYE* TN31 ....340 A1
Guildeford Rd *RYE* TN31 ....339 H6
Gulands *RMAID* ME17 ....187 H7
Gulland Rd *BFN/LL* DA15 ....63 P1
Gulliver St *BERM/RHTH* SE16 ....25 J6
Gumley Rd *WTHK* RM20 ....31 N9
Gumping Rd *STMC/STPC* BR5 ....86 D6
Gun Back La *STPH/PW* TN12 ....273 P5
Gundulph Rd *CHAT* ME4 ....62 C9
HAYES BR2 ....62 C9
Gundulph Sq *ROCH* ME1 ....19 F4
Gunfleet Ct *CHAT* ME4 * 50 A8
Gun Hl *TIL* RM18 ....12 C1
Gunlands *STPH/PW* TN12 ....273 P2
Gun La *STRD* ME2 ....18 C1
Gunnell Cl *SNWD* SE25 ....83 L5
SYD SE26 * 60 G5
Gunning La *WOOL/PLUM* SE18 ...27 H8
Gunning Rd *GRAYS* RM17 ....32 C6
Gunning St *WOOL/PLUM* SE18 ...27M7
Gunnis Cl *RHAM* ME8 ....126 F1
Gunn Rd *SWCM* DA10 ....48 C7
Gun Pit Rd *LING* RH7 ....234 F5
Gun St *WCHPL* E1 ....24 C1
Gunthorpe St *WCHPL* E1 ....24 C1
Gun Tower Ms *ROCH* ME1 ....94 G2
Gunwhale Cl *BERM/RHTH* SE16 ..24 G7
Gunyard Ms
WOOL/PLUM SE18 * 43 J1
Gurdon Rd *CHARL* SE7 ....26 B8
Gurling Rd *RDV* CT15 ....262 E7
Gurney Crs *CROY/NA* CRO 82 E5
Gushmere *FAV* ME13 ....163 M5
Guston Rd *MAID/BEAR* ME14 ....13 K2
Guthrie Gdns *DVE/WH* CT17 * ..290 F4
Guy Barnett Gv
BKHTH/KID SE3 ....42 E4
Guy Cl *BRDST* CT10 ....113 N6
Guy Rd *CROY/NA* CRO * 82 D7
Guysclift Rd *LEW* SE13 ....62 A6
Guy St *STHWK* SE1 ....24 A5
Gwillim Cl *BFN/LL* DA15 ....44 C7
Gwydor Rd *BECK* BR3 ....84 A1
Gwydyr Rd *HAYES* BR2 ....62 D9
Gwynne Av *CROY/NA* CRO 82 G4
Gwynne Gdns *EGRIN* RH19 ....264 F6
Gwynn Rd *GVW* DA11 ....68 C3
Gwyn Rd *MSTR* CT12 ....143 H2
Gybbon Rt *STPH/PW* TN12 ....246 B6
Gybbons Rd *CRBK* TN17 ....319M5
Gylcote Cl *CMBW* SE5 ....40 D5
Gypsy Wy *HOO/HM* ME3 ....53 L5

Habington Cl *CMBW* SE5 * 40 D1
Habitat Cl *PECK* SE15 ....41 L5
Hackenden Cl *EGRIN* RH19 ......265 H5
Hackenden La *EGRIN* RH19 ......265 J4
Hackfield *ASH* TN23 ....252 C8
Hackington Cl *CANTW/ST* CT2 ..136 D9
Hackington Crs *BECK* BR3 ....61 N5
Hackington Rd
CANTW/ST CT2 ....136 C4
Hackington Ter
CANTW/ST CT2 ....166 D2
Hacklinge Hl *DEAL* CT14 ....202 A8
Hackney Rd *MAIDW* ME14 ....185 H1
Hadden Rd *THMD* SE28 ....28 C6
Haddington Rd *BMLY* BR1 ....62 B2
Haddon Gv *BFN/LL* DA15 ....44 C8
Haddon Rd *STMC/STPC* BR5 ......87 K2
Haddo St *GNWCH* SE10 ....25 L9
Hadleigh Cl *GILL* ME7 ....73 P6
Hadleigh Gdns *HB* CT6 ....107 N1
Hadley Cl *MEO* DA13 ....92 C6
Hadley Rd *BELV* DA17 ....28 E7
MTCM CR4 ....82 C1
Hadlow Castle *RTON* TN11 * 171 P2
Hadlow Dr *MARG* CT9 ....113 K3
Hadlow Pk *RTON* TN11 ....211 P1
Hadlow Rd *MAID/BEAR* ME14 ....13 K2
SCUP DA14 ....64 C3
TON TN9 ....210 C7
TONN TN10 ....211 L5
TONN TN10 ....211 L5
WELL DA16 ....44 C1
Hadlow Rd East *TONN* TN10 ....211 L6
Hadlow Stair Rd *TONN* TN10 ...211 J6
Hadlow Rd *MAID/BEAR* ME14 ....69 J6
Hadrian Gdns *ASH* TN23 ....282 D8
Hadrian St *GNWCH* SE10 ....25 P6
Haffenden Cl *STPH/PW* TN12 ...245 J3
Haffenden Rd *TENT* TN30 ....301 H6
Hafton Rd *CAT* SE6 ....62 C9
Ha-Ha Rd *WOOL/PLUM* SE18 ....43 H2
Haig Av *CHAT* ME4 ....95M4
GILL ME7 ....96 B2
ROCH ME1 ....95 J5
Haig Gdns *GVE* DA12 ....49 N8
Haig Rd *BH/WHM* TN16 ....116 H6
CDW/CHF RM16 ....33 H6
Haileybury Rd *ORP* BR6 ....87 H8
Hailey Rd *ERITH* DA18 ....28 F5
Hailstone Cl *RTON* TN11 ....211 P2
Haimo Rd *ELTH/MOT* SE9 ....43 H6

Hainault St *ELTH/MOT* SE9 ......43 M9
Haine Rd *MSTR* CT12 ....142 E5
Hainford Cl *BROCKY* SE4 ....41 K5
Hainthorpe Rd *WNWD* SE27 ......60 D2
Hainton Cl *RYHPL* E1 ....24 E2
Halcot Av *BXLYHS* DA6 ....45 K6
Halcrow St *WCHPL* E1 ....24 E1
Haldane Gdns *GVW* DA11 ....48 C9
Haldane Rd *THMD* SE28 ....28 C3
Halden Cl *MAID/SHEP* ME15 .....186 C5
Halden La *CRBK* TN17 ....299 N5
Hale Cl *ORP* BR6 ....86 D8
Hale Ct *STPH/PW* TN12 ....213 H3
Hale House
WOOL/PLUM SE18 * 43 J1
Hale La *RSEV* TN14 ....148 E2
Hale Oak Rd *EDEN* TN8 ....208 D6
RSEV TN14 ....208 F1
Hale Rd *HOO/HM* ME3 ....52 C9
Hales Cl *TENT* TN30 ....301 J7
Hales Dr *CANTW/ST* CT2 ....166 E1
Hale St *POP/IOD* E14 ....129 L4
STPH/PW TN12 ....213 H3
Halesworth Rd *LEW* SE13 ....44 P4
Haleys Pl *ROCH* ME1 ....124 F5
Halfmile Ride *MARG* CT9 ....112 D7
Half Moon La *HNHL* SE24 ....40 D7
RTON TN11 ....210 A4
Halfmoon Pas *WCHPL* E1 ....24 C2
Half Moon Wy *HOO/HM* ME3 .....53 M5
Halfpence La *GVE* DA12 ....70 D9
Halfpenny Cl *MAIDW* ME16 ......184 F1
Halfway Cl *PUR* RM19 ....30 D7
Halfway Rd *IOS* ME12 ....57 M8
Half Way St *BFN/LL* DA15 ....44 A9
Half Yoke *MAIDW* ME16 * 184 C3
Halifax St *SYD* SE26 ....61 H2
Halifield Dr *BELV* DA17 ....28 D6
Hallam Cl *CHST* BR7 ....63 K4
Hall Av *KEN/WIL* TN24 ....283 J2
SOCK/AV RM15 ....10 B4
Hall Cl *SIT* ME10 ....99 M8
Hall Crs *DEAL* CT14 ....232 E4
SOCK/AV RM15 ....30 F5
Hallcroft Ct *RAM* CT11 ....16 B3
Hall Dr *SYD* SE26 ....5 H1
Hallett Wk *CANT* CT1 * 5 H1
Halley St *POP/IOD* E14 ....25 H1
Hall Hl *BGR/WK* TN15 ....149 N8
OXTED RH8 ....174 C8
Halliday Ct *HYTHE* CT21 * 308 F5
Halliday Dr *DEAL* CT14 ....233 H6
Hallowell Av *CROY/NA* CR0 ....82 D8
Hall Pk *DART* DA1 ....46 F5
DIT/AY ME20 ....154 E5
Hall Rd *DART* DA1 ....46 C9
HOO/HM ME3 ....54 A2
ROCH ME1 ....124 B2
SOCK/AV RM15 ....30 F5
Hall Wy *DART* DA1 ....125 P2
Hallsfield Rd *WALD* ME5 ....61 J3
Hall's Hole Rd *RTWE/PEM* TN2 ..35 K5
Hallsland Wy *OXTED* RH8 ....175 J9
Hallsville Rd *CAN/RD* E16 ....26 A2
Hall Ter *SOCK/AV* RM15 ....30 G5
The Hall *BKHTH/KID* SE3 ....63 H1
Hall Vw *ELTH/MOT* SE9 ....63 H7
Hallwards *STPH/PW* TN12 ....246 B7
Hallwood Cl *RHAM* ME8 ....96 G9
Hallywell Crs *EHAM* E6 ....26 G1
Halons Rd *ELTH/MOT* SE9 ....43 L8
Halpin Pl *WALW* SE17 * 19 H7
Halsbrook Rd *BKHTH/KID* SE3 ...42 G4
Halsford La *EGRIN* RH19 ....264 E6
Halsford Park Rd *EGRIN* RH19 ...264 E6
Halsmere Rd *CMBW* SE5 ....40 B2
Halstatt Rd *DEAL* CT14 ....232 F6
Halstead Cl *CANTW/ST* CT2 * .....
CROY/NA CR0 ....83 H7
Halstead Gdns *MARG* CT9 ....113 L3
Halstead La *RSEV* TN14 ....117 M9
Halstead Rd *MAID/SHEP* ME15 ..185 N6
Halstow Rd *GNWCH* SE10 ....50 B8
Halstow Wy *ASH* TN23 ....252 C9
Halt Dr *TIL* RM18 ....33 P7
Halton Rd *CDW/CHF* RM16 ....33 J6
Halt Robin La *BELV* DA17 ....29 J5
The Halt *RCANTW* CT4 * 105 N7
WSTB CT5 ....105 N7
Hambledon *WALW* SE17 * ....24 M
Hambledon Cl *MAIDW* ME16 .....154 C3
Hambledon Gdns *SNWD* SE25 ...60 F9
Hambledon Pl *DUL* SE21 ....40 F9
Hambledown Rd
ELTH/MOT SE9 * 43 P8
Hamble La *SOCK/AV* RM15 ....31 J1
Hamble Rd *TONN* TN10 ....210 E5
Hambro Av *HAYES* BR2 ....83 J6
Hambrook Cl *RCANTW* CT4 ....194 C5
Hambrook Rd *SNWD* SE25 ....61 H9
Hambrook Wk *SIT* ME10 ....99 N6
The Hamele *CANTW/ST* CT2 ...137 L8
Hamelin Rd *GILL* ME7 ....96 C6
Hamerton Rd *GVW* DA11 ....48 F6
Hamfield Cl *OXTED* RH8 ....174 F3
Hamilton Cl *BERM/RHTH* SE16 ...19 P5
MSTR CT12 ....142 F3
NROM TN28 ....337 K8
Hamilton Crs *SIT* ME10 ....129 K2
Hamilton Rd *BFN/LL* DA15 ....64 C3
BXLYHN DA7 ....45 G9
DEAL CT14 ....232 C3
DIT/AY ME20 ....291 H7
GILL ME7 ....73 K8
KEN/WIL TN24 ....282 C2
LYDD TN29 ....342 B6

WNWD SE27 ....60 D5
WSTB CT5 ....105 L5
Hamilton Sq *STHWK* SE1 * 24 A5
Hamilton St *DEPT* SE8 ....25 K9
Ham La *GILL* ME7 ....126 D2
RMAID ME17 ....189 K6
Hamlea Cl *BKHTH/KID* SE3 ....42 E6
Hamlet Cl *RUH* SE15 ....60 F6
Hamlet Rd *NRWD* SE19 ....60 F6
The Hamlet *CMBW* SE5 ....40 E4
Hamlet Wy *STHWK* SE1 ....24 A5
Hamlin Rd *SEV* TN13 ....148 D6
Hamlyn Gdns *MAID/SHEP* ME15 .60 E2
Hammelton Rd *BMLY* BR1 ....63 P7
Hammett St *TWRH* EC3 * 24 D3
Ham Mill La *LYDD* TN29 ....323 P7
Hammond Cl *RDV* CT15 ....229 P1
Hammonds *HAWK* TN18 ....317 J4
Hammond's Rd *FOLK* CT20 ....310 B6
Hammonds Sq *SNOD* ME6 ....123 P5
Hamond Hl *CHAT* ME4 ....6 A4
Hampden Av *BECK* BR3 ....61 L8
Hampden La *ASH* TN23 * 282 D1
Hampden Ms *ASH* TN23 * 282 D2
Hampden Rd *ASH* TN23 ....282 D2
BECK BR3 ....61 L8
GRAYS RM17 ....32 C8
Hampshire Cl *WALD* ME5 ....95 P7
Hampshire Dr *WALD* ME5 ....26 E6
Hampshire Drive Rd
MAID/SHEP ME15 ....185 P3
Hampshire Rd *CANT* CT1 ....167 J5
Hampson Wy
MAID/BEAR ME14 ....156 D8
Hampstead St *THMD* SE28 ....28 A4
Hampstead La
WBY/YAL ME15 * 213 K1
Hampton Cl *HB* CT6 ....106 F3
WALD ME5 ....95 M9
Hampton Crs *GVE* DA12 ....70 J1
Hampton Gdns *HB* CT6 ....106 F3
Hampton La *RASHE* TN25 ....254 C7
Hampton Pier Av *HB* CT6 ....106 G2
Hampton Rd *CROY/NA* CR0 ....83 H5
MAID/BEAR ME14 ....156 D1
Hampton Rd *RTON* TN11 ....181 J6
Hampton V *HYTHE* CT21 ....309 M5
Hampton Wy *EGRIN* RH19 ....265 J9
Ham River Hl *HOO/HM* ME3 ....72 A1
Ham Rd *FAV* ME15 ....132 F4
Ham Shades Cl *DART* DA1 ....64 P2
Ham Shades La *WSTB* CT5 ....105 P5
Hamstreet Rd *RASHW* TN26 .....304 B3
Ham Vw *CROY/NA* CR0 ....84 B3
Hamwick Gn *WALD* ME5 ....125 P4
Hanameel St *CAN/RD* E16 ....26 C4
Hanbury Cl *WBY/YAL* ME15 * 183 M4
Hanbury Dr *BH/WHM* TN16 ....115 L7
Hanbury St *WCHPL* E1 ....24 D1
Hancock Cl *STRD* ME2 ....72 B6
Hancock Rd *NRWD* SE19 ....60 D5
Hancocks *HDCN* TN27 ....274 B5
Hancocks Fld *DEAL* CT14 ....232 F4
Handcroft Rd *CROY/NA* CR0 ......82 C5
Handel Crs *TIL* RM18 ....49 L1
Handel Rd *LEW* SE13 ....44 G9
Handforth Rd *BRXN/ST* SW9 .....40 A1
Hanford Rd *SOCK/AV* RM15 ....30 F4
Hang Grove Hl *ORP* BR6 ....116 C7
Hangman's La *DEAL* CT14 .....262 C5
RDV CT15 ....291 P7
Hankey Pl *STHWK* SE1 ....24 A5
Hanley Pl *BECK* BR3 ....61 N6
Hanmer Wy *STHWK* SE1 * 24 D7
Hannah Cl *BECK* BR3 ....61 P9
Hannah Mary Wy *STHWK* SE1 * .24 D7
Hannen Rd *WNWD* SE27 * 60 B2
Hannibal Rd *WCHPL* E1 ....24 F1
Hannibal Wy *CROY/NA* CR0 ....82 E9
Hanover Av *RMAID* ME17 * 185 H8
RTW TN1 ....22 D3
Hanover Sq *FOLK* CT20 ....107 L1
Hanover St *CROY/NA* CR0 ....82 C7
FOLK CT20 ....107 L1
Hanover Wy *BXLYHN* DA7 ....44 P2
Hansler Rd *EDUL* SE22 ....40 F6
Hanslett's La *FAV* ME13 ....161 P1
Hansol Rd *BXLYHS* DA6 ....44 G6
Hansom Ter *BMLY* BR1 * 62 F7
Hanson Cl *BECK* BR3 * 61 P5
Hanway *RHAM* ME8 ....96 D4
Harbex Cl *BXLY* DA5 ....45 K8
Harbinger Rd *POP/IOD* E14 ....25 L7
Harbledown Gdns *MARG* CT9 ....113 K2
Harbledown Pl
STMC/STPC BR5 * 87 K1
Harbord Cl *CMBW* SE5 ....40 D3
Harborough Av *BFN/LL* DA15 ....44 A8
Harbour Approach Rd
FOLK CT20 ....11 G5
Harbourland Cl
MAID/BEAR ME14 ....155 N4
Harbourne La *RASHE* TN26 ....301 M3
Harbour Pde *RAM* CT11 ....17 H4
Harbour Rd *CMBW* SE5 ....40 C4
RYE TN31 ....338 F8
Harbour St *BRDST* CT10 ....113 N9
FOLK CT20 ....11 G4
RAM CT11 ....17 J3
WSTB CT5 ....105 L4
The Harbour *RMAID* ME17 ....217 H5
Harbour View Rd *DVW* CT17 .....291 J7
Harbour Wy *FOLK* CT20 ....11 G4

Harcourt Av *BFN/LL* DA15 ....44 E7
WLGTN SM6 ....82 A8
Harcourt Dr *CANTW/ST* CT2 ....4 A1
HB CT6 ....106 C2
Harcourt Fld *WLGTN* SM6 ....82 A8
Harcourt Gdns *RHAM* ME8 ....127 H1
Harcourt Rd *BROCKY* SE4 ....41 M5
BXLYHS DA6 ....45 H8
FOLKN CT19 ....310 C4
THHTH CR7 ....82 A8
WLGTN SM6 ....82 A8
Harcourt Wy *GDST* RH9 ....204 B4
Hardcastle Cl *SNWD* SE25 ....83 M3
Hardcastle Cl *WWKM* BR4 ....84 E8
Hardel Wk *BRXS/STRHM* SW2 ...40 A8
Harden Rd *GVW* DA11 ....69 K1
LYDD TN29 ....342 C5
Hardens Manorway
WOOL/PLUM SE18 ....26 E6
Harders Rd *PECK* SE15 ....41 J4
Hardess St *HNHL* SE24 ....40 C4
Hardie Cl *E/WMAL* ME19 * 153 N5
Harding Cl *CROY/NA* CR0 ....83 J4
Harding Cl *ST-RH/RUST* TN4 .....240 D6
Hardinge Cl *RHAM* ME8 ....126 F1
Hardinge Rd *KEN/WIL* TN24 .....2 E2
Hardinge St *WCHPL* E1 ....24 F2
Harding Rd *BXLYHN* DA7 ....45 J6
Harding Rd *KEN/WIL* TN24 ....2 E2
Hardings La *PGE/AN* SE20 ....61 K5
Hardman Rd *CHAT* SE7 ....26 C8
Hardres Court Rd
RCANTW CT4 ....196 F5
RCANTW CT4 ....226 E4
Hardres Rd *RAM* CT11 ....17 G2
Hardres St *RAM* CT11 ....17 G3
Hardres Ter *STMC/STPC* BR5 * ...82 F1
Hards Town *CHAT* ME4 ....6 E5
Hardwick Crs *DART* DA1 ....47 H7
Hardwicke Rd *DVW* CT17 ....291 J9
RTON TN11 ....210 B4
Hardwick Rd *WALL* ME19 ....152 A5
Hardy Av *CAN/RD* E16 ....26 B9
GVW DA11 ....69 J1
Hardy Cl *BERM/RHTH* SE16 ......19 M2
CANTW/ST CT2 ....166 B5
KEN/WIL TN24 ....283 K1
Hardy Cv *DART* DA1 ....46 C5
Hardy Rd *BKHTH/KID* SE3 ....42 G4
NROM TN28 ....343 J1
RDV CT15 ....262 D8
Hardy St *MAID/BEAR* ME14 ......13 F1
Harebell Cl *IOS* ME12 * 78 A3
MAID/BEAR ME14 ....156 B7
Harebell Dr *EHAM* E6 ....27 H1
Hare & Billet Rd
BKHTH/KID SE3 ....42 B2
Harebrook *RAM* CT11 ....17 H1
Haredale Cl *ROCH* ME1 * 95 J7
Haredale Rd *HNHL* SE24 ....40 C5
Haredon Cl *FSTH* SE23 ....41 J8
Harefield Ms *BROCKY* SE4 ....41 M4
Harefield Rd *BROCKY* SE4 ....41 M4
SCUP DA14 ....65 J3
Hare La *LING* RH7 ....234 A4
Hares Bank *CROY/NA* CR0 ....114 G4
Harescroft *RTWE/PEM* TN2 ......270 C9
Hareson Rd *EGRIN* RH19 ....265 L7
Hare Ter *WTHM* RM20 * 31 N8
Harfield Gdns *CMBW* SE5 * 40 E4
Harfst Wy *SWLY* BR8 ....65 H4
Hargate La *RTWE/PEM* TN2 ......270 C9
Hargood Rd *BKHTH/KID* SE3 .....42 G2
Harkness Dr *CANTW/ST* CT2 .....4 A1
CROY/NA CR0 ....83 L7
Harland Rd *LEE/GVPK* SE12 .....42 E9
Harlands Gv *ORP* BR6 ....86 F8
Harland Wy *ST-RH/RUST* TN4 ...240 C6
Harlech Cl *STRD* ME2 ....71 P6
Harlescott Rd *PECK* SE15 ....41 K5
Harleyford Rd *BMLY* BR1 ....62 F7
Harley Gdns *ORP* BR6 ....86 F8
Harlinger St *WOOL/PLUM* SE18 ..26 D4
Harlington Rd *BXLYHN* DA7 ......44 G4
Harman Av *GVW* DA11 ....69 M4
HYTHE CT21 ....307 N4
Harman Cl *STHWK* SE1 * 24 D8
Harmans Dr *EGRIN* RH19 ....265 L7
Harmans Md *EGRIN* RH19 ....265 K7
Harmer Rd *SWCM* DA10 ....48 D7
Harmer St *GVE* DA12 ....49 H7
Harmony Cl *WLGTN* SM6 ....82 E6
Harmony St *ST/RUST* TN4 ....270 A4
Harness Rd *WOOL/PLUM* SE18 ..62 E8
Harmsworth Gdns
BRDST CT10 ....113 M8
Harness Rd *THMD* SE28 ....27 P5
Harnet St *SWCH* CT13 ....201 N1
Harnetts Cl *SWLY* BR8 * 28 E8
Harold Av *BELV* DA17 ....28 F6
GILL ME7 ....96 B2
WGOS CT8 ....111 M5
Harold Ct *FAV* ME15 ....152 F7
Harold Est *STHWK* SE1 * 24 B8
Harold Rd *BRCH* CT7 ....110 E5
CDW/CHF RM16 ....33 K8
MARG CT9 ....112 G3
NRWD SE19 ....60 D6
RDART DA1 ....130 A1
SIT ME10 ....130 A1
STRD ME2 ....94 A3
Harold's Rd *DVE/WH* CT16 .....9 F7
Harold St *DVE/WH* CT16 ....8 E2
OBOR ME11 ....77 J3
Harp Cross La *MON* EC3R 24 B3
Harpenden Rd *WNWD* SE27 .....60 B1
Harper Cl *CDW/CHF* RM16 ....31 M8
Harper Rd *EHAM* E6 ....26 G2
Harp Farm Rd
MAID/BEAR ME14 ....125 P6

Harple La *MAID/BEAR* ME14 .....156 C3
Harps Av *IOS* ME12 ....7B E1
Harpswood La *HYTHE* CT21 ......308 F4
Harptree Dr *WALD* ME5 ....95 J9
Harradden Rd *BKHTH/KID* SE3 ...42 C2
Harrap Cha *GRAYS* RM17 ....32 AB
Harrier Dr *SIT* ME10 ....129 P5
Harrier Ms *THMD* SE28 ....27 L6
Harrier Wy *EHAM* E6 ....26 C1
Harries Rd *RTWE/PEM* TN2 ....30 D8
Harriet Cl *BRXS/STRHM* SW2 ....40 A8
Harriet Gdns *CROY/NA* CR0 ......83 M1
Harringe La *RASHE* TN25 ....307 J2
Harrington Cl *CROY/NA* CR0 .....82 A6
Harrington Rd *SNWD* SE25 ....83 M1
Harrington Wy
WOOL/PLUM SE18 ....26 E6
Harriott Cl *FOLKN* CT19 ....310 E4
Harriott Cl *GNWCH* SE10 ....26 A7
Harris Cl *GVW* DA11 ....69 J2
Harris Ct *GILL* ME7 ....96 C4
Harrison Dr *HOO/HM* ME3 ....53 L4
RMAID ME17 * 188 F5
Harrison Rd *BGR/WK* TN15 ......151 J5
RAM CT11 ....16 D5
Harrison's Ri *CROY/NA* CR0 .....82 B4
Harrison Whf *PUR* RM19 ....30 D8
Harrison Ter *FAV* ME13 * 132 E3
Harrison Wy *SEV* TN13 ....148 F7
Harris Rd *BXLYHN* DA7 ....44 G2
IOS ME12 ....57 L6
Harris's Aly *RCANTE* CT3 ....169 K9
Harris St *CMBW* SE5 ....40 D1
Harrowby Gdns *GVW* DA11 ....69 M4
Harrow Ct *RSIT* ME9 ....127 N5
Harrow Dene *BRDST* CT10 ....113 K8
Harrow Rd *ORP* BR6 ....87 J8
WARL CR6 ....144 C1
Harrow La *POP/IOD* E14 ....25 M3
Harrow Manor Wy *THMD* SE28 ..27 J4
Harrow Pl *WCHPL* E1 ....24 D2
Harrow Rd *GILL* ME7 ....96 C8
RSEV TN14 ....114 C9
WARL CR6 ....144 C1
Harrow Wy *ASH* TN23 ....282 B3
MAID/BEAR ME14 ....156 H7
Harriets Cnr *WSTB* CT5 ....25 N3
Harry Pry *ST-RH/RUST* TN4 ......253 H5
Harrys Rd *RSIT* ME9 ....131 H2
Harry Wells Rd *HB* CT6 ....106 C3
Hart Cnr *WTHK* RM20 * 31 N8
Hart Dyke Rd *STMC/STPC* BR5 ..87 K6
SWLY BR8 ....65 K9
Hartfield Cl *TONN* TN10 ....211 H5
Hartfield Crs *WWKM* BR4 ....85 K7
Hartfield Gv *PGE/AN* SE20 ....61 H7
Hartfield Pl *GVW* DA11 ....48 F6
Hartfield Rd *EDEN* TN8 ....237 H5
WWKM BR4 ....85 K8
Hartford Rd *BXLY* DA5 ....45 L6
Hart Hl *HDCN* TN27 ....190 C8
Harting Rd *ELTH/MOT* SE9 ....63 J3
Hartington Rd *ORP* BR6 ....86 D9
Hartington St *CHAT* ME4 ....6 D6
Hartlake Rd *RTON* TN11 ....241 M1
Hartlands Cl *BXLY* DA5 ....45 H7
Hartland Wy *CROY/NA* CR0 ......84 B6
Hartley Bottom Rd *HART* DA3 ...91 L5
Hartley Cl *BMLY* BR1 ....65 H3
MAID/SHEP ME15 ....186 C5
Hartley Court Gdns
CRBK TN17 ....297 L4
Hartley Hl *HART* DA3 ....91 K5
Hartley Ms *RHAM* ME8 ....96 D4
Hartley Rd *CROY/NA* CR0 ....82 C7
CRBK TN17 ....297 M5
CROY/NA CR0 ....83 H4
HART DA3 ....91 J8
WELL DA16 ....44 E1
Hartlip Cl *IOS* ME12 ....57 K9
Hartlip Hl *RSIT* ME9 ....97 P7
Hartmann Rd *CAN/RD* E16 ....26 F7
Hartnokes *HAWK* TN18 ....317 J4
Hartnup St *MAIDW* ME16 ....185 H1
Harton Cl *BMLY* BR1 ....63 H7
Harton St *DEPT* SE8 ....41 N2
Hartpiece Cl *RHAM* ME8 ....97 J4
Hartscroft *CROY/NA* CR0 ....114 B5
Hartsdown Pk *MARG* CT9 ....14 C6
Hart Shaw *HART* DA3 ....91 K8
Hartshill Rd *GVW* DA11 ....69 K1
Hartsland Rd *SEV* TN13 ....149 H8
Hart's La *GDST* RH9 ....204 A3
NWCR SE14 ....41 L1
Hartslock Dr *ABYW* SE2 ....28 C5
Hartsmead Rd *ELTH/MOT* SE9 ...63 K1
Hart St *MAIDW* ME16 ....26 D8
MON EC3R 24 B3
Hartville Rd *WOOL/PLUM* SE18 ..27 M7
Harty Av *RHAM* ME8 ....126 E2
Harty Cl *CDW/CHF* RM16 ....32 C4
Harty Ferry Rd *IOS* ME12 ....79 P6
Harty Ferry Vw *WSTB* CT5 ....105 K8
Harty Ter *IOS* ME12 * 58 E3
Harvel Av *STRD* ME2 ....71 N8
Harvel Cl *CHST* BR7 ....64 C9
Harvel Crs *ABYW* SE2 ....28 C8
Harvel La *MEO* DA13 ....121 N6
Harvel Rd *MEO* DA13 ....121 D2
Harvel St *MEO* DA13 ....122 D2
Harvest Bank Rd *WWKM* BR4 ....85 K7
Harvesters Cl *RHAM* ME8 ....97 H8
Harvesters Wy
MAID/BEAR ME14 ....156 A8
Harvest Hl *EGRIN* RH19 ....265 H6
Harvest Rdg *E/WMAL* ME19 ......153 L2
Harvest Rd *TONN* TN10 ....210 C4
Harvest Wy *ASH* TN23 ....282 A1
RFOLK CT18 ....307 J8
SWLY BR8 ....88 B4

Harvey CDW/CHF RM16 ....32 C5
Harvey Av DEAL CT14 ....233 H6
Harvey Dr SIT ME10 ....129 P3
WSTB CT5 ....106 A5
Harvey Gdns CHARL SE7 ....26 A8
Harvey Pl N FOLK CT20 ....11 G3
Harvey Rd CMBW SE5 ....60 D2
KEN/WIL TN24 ....253 J7
RHAM ME8 ....97 H6
Harvey St FOLK CT20 ....11 G3
Harville Rd RASHE TN25 ....223 M8
Harvill Rd SCUP DA14 ....64 B7
Harwich St WSTB CT5 ....105 L6
Harwick Dr NROM TN28 ....337 H5
Harwood Av BMLY BR1 ....62 F8
Harwood Rd RHAM ME8 ....97 L5
Harwoods Cl EGRIN RH19 ....265 J9
Harwood's La EGRIN RH19 ....265 J9
Hasborough Rd FOLKN CT19 ......11 K2
Hascombe Ter DEAL CT14 * 40 D5
Haseley End FSTH SE23 * 41 J8
Haslam Av SUTN SM3 ....65 N8
Haslam Cl RCANTW CT4 * 54 G3
Hasted Cl ERH DA9 ....48 A7
Hasted Rd CHARL SE7 ....42 C9
HOO/HM ME3 ....72 A5
RSIT ME9 ....98 C7
Hasteds RMAID ME17 * 187 M1
Haste Hill Cl
MAID/SHEP ME15 ....185 M8
Haste Hill Rd
MAID/SHEP ME15 ....185 M8
Hastings Av MARG CT9 ....112 F4
Hastings Cl PECK SE15 * 40 C1
WTHK RM20 ....31 P9
Hastings Pl SWCH CT13 ....201 N2
Hastings Rd CROY/NA CR0 ....83 L5
HAWK TN18 ....317 H7
HAWK TN18 ....319 J8
HAYES BR2 ....85 P5
MAID/SHEP ME15 ....15 H6
RTWE/PEM TN2 ....271 N2
STPH/PW TN12 ....272 A3
Hastings St WOOL/PLUM SE18 ...27 K6
Hatcham Park Ms NWCR SE14 ....24 B5
Hatcham Park Rd NWCR SE14 * ..41 L2
Hatcham Rd PECK SE15 ....24 B5
Hatcher's Ms STHWK SE1 ....24 B5
Hatches La RTON TN11 ....212 E4
Hatchet Rd RMAID ME17 * 189 K6
Hatch St FAV ME13 ....132 F6
Hatcliffe Cl BKHTH/KID SE3 ....42 G4
Hatcliffe St GNWCH SE10 ....26 A8
Hatfeild Cl BKHTH/KID SE3 * 42 E1
Hatfeild Rd CDW/CHF RM16 ....31 N8
MARG CT9 ....16 D3
RAM CT11 ....16 D3
Hatham Green La
BGR/WK TN15 ....120 G4
Hathaway Cl HAYES BR2 ....86 A5
Hathaway Ct RMAID ME1 ....18 E6
Hathaway Rd CROY/NA CR0 ....82 C7
GRAYS RM17 ....32 C7
Hatherall Rd MAID/BEAR ME14 ...13 J1
Hatherley Crs SCUP DA14 ....64 C2
Hatherley Rd SCUP DA14 ....64 C3
Hathern Gdns ELTH/MOT SE9 ....63 L3
Hathorne Cl PECK SE15 ....41 H5
Hathway St PECK SE15 ....41 L5
Hatmill La STPH/PW TN12 ....273 H1
Hatstone St
BERM/RHTH SE16 ....19 P5
Hattersfield Cl BELV DA17 ....28 E7
Hatton Cl CDW/CHF RM16 ....31 N6
GVW DA11 ....69 J2
WOOL/PLUM SE18 ....63 P1
Hatton Rd CROY/NA CR0 ....82 B5
WALD ME5 ....125 P2
Havannah St POP/IOD E14 ....25 K5
Havelock Rd BELV DA17 ....29 J6
CROY/NA CR0 ....83 L6
DART DA1 ....63 L1
DEAL CT14 ....233 H6
GVW DA11 ....69 J2
HAYES BR2 ....85 M1
TON TN9 ....210 E7
Havelock St GILL ME7 * 1 G4
Havelock Wk FSTH SE23 ....41 J9
Haven Cl ELTH/MOT SE9 ....63 K7
MEO DA13 ....121 K7
ROCH ME1 ....94 E6
SCUP DA14 ....64 E5
SWLY BR8 ....88 B3
Haven Dr HB CT6 ....108 C4
Havengore Av GVE DA12 ....50 A8
Haven Hl BGR/WK TN15 ....121 K1
Haven Rd FOLKN CT19 ....32 D5
Havens Ms BOW E3 ....25 J1
Haven St HOO/HM ME3 ....72 C2
The Haven DEAL CT14 * 263 J2
GRAYS RM17 ....30 B7
HYTHE CT21 ....308 B7
Hawkenbury Rd KEN/WIL TN24 ...2 F6
Haven Wy CHAT ME4 ....73 H6
Havering Cl RTWE/PEM TN2 ......271 J2
Havering St WCHPL E1 ....25 H2
Haverthwaite Rd ORP BR6 ....86 E1
Havil St CMBW SE5 ....40 E3
Havisham Cl ROCH ME1 * 95 J3

Havisham Pl NRWD SE19 .....60 B5
Havisham Rd CDW/CHF DA12 .....50 C9
Hawarden Gv HNHL SE24 .....60 B8
Hawarden Pl RCANTE CT5 * 169 K9
Hawbeck Rd RHAM ME8 .....126 F2
Hawden Cl RTON TN11 .....210 C6
Hawden La RTON TN11 .....210 C7
Hawden Rd TON TN9 .....210 E8
Hawe Cl CANTW/ST CT2 .....136 F9
Hawe Farm Wy HB CT6 .....107 N4
Hawe La CANTW/ST CT2 .....137 M6
Hawes Av RAM CT11 .....142 G5
Hawes La WWKM BR4 .....84 F5
Hawfield Bank ORP BR6 .....87 L7
Hawgood St BOW E3 .....25 K1
Hawk Cnr WTHK RM20 .....31 N8
Hawkenbury Cl
    RTWE/PEM TN2 .....23 J7
Hawkenbury Md
    RTWE/PEM TN2 .....270 G7
Hawkenbury Ri HOO/HM ME3 .....21 R8
Hawkenbury Rd
    RTWE/PEM TN2 .....271 H7
    STPH/PW TN12 .....246 F3
Hawkenbury Vls
    STPH/PW TN12 * 246 F3
Hawke Pl BERM/RHTH SE16 * 24 C5
Hawke Rd NRWD SE19 .....60 D5
Hawkesbury St DVW CT17 .....313 L1
Hawkes Cl CANTW/ST CT2 .....136 F9
Hawkesfield Rd FSTH SE23 .....61 L1
Hawkes Pl SEV TN13 .....20 D7
Hawkes Rd DIT/AY ME20 .....124 E8
Hawkhurst Cl BRCH CT7 .....111 J5
Hawkhurst Rd
    BUR/ETCH TN19 .....316 A4
    HAWK TN18 .....297 L8
    RHAM ME8 .....96 D3
Hawkhurst Wy BRDST CT10 .....143 M2
    WWKM BR4 .....84 B1
Hawkins Av GVE DA12 .....69 N3
Hawkins Cl CHAT ME4 .....6 D1
    SIT ME10 .....99 M8
Hawkins Dr CDW/CHF RM16 .....33 P4
Hawkins Rd FOLKN CT19 .....310 A5
Hawkins Ter CHARL SE7 .....66 C4
Hawkins Wy CAT SE6 .....61 N4
Hawkley Gdns WNWD SE27 .....60 B1
Hawkridge Dr GRAYS RM17 .....32 E8
Hawksbrook La BECK BR3 .....94 F5
Hawksdown DEAL CT14 .....232 C9
Hawks Hill La RSIT ME9 .....129 K9
Hawkshill Rd DEAL CT14 .....233 H9
Hawkslade Rd PECK SE15 .....41 K6
Hawk's La CANT 4 D4
Hawks Ms GNWCH SE10 * 42 A1
Hawksmoor Cl EHAM E6 .....26 F7
    WOOL/PLUM SE18 .....27 M8
Hawksmoor Ms WCHPL E1 .....24 E5
Hawkstone Est
    BERM/RHTH SE16 .....24 F7
Hawkstone Rd
    BERM/RHTH SE16 .....24 F7
Hawks Wy ASH TN23 .....282 B1
Hawkwood MAIDW ME16 .....154 C7
Hawkwood Cl ROCH ME1 .....19 J6
Hawkwood La CHST BR7 .....63 N7
Hawkwood Rd DART DA1 .....66 E1
Hawley Sq MARG CT9 .....15 H5
Hawley St MARG CT9 .....15 H5
Hawley Ter RDART DA2 * 66 G3
Hawser Rd ROCH ME1 .....95 H5
Hawstead La ORP BR6 .....87 N9
Hawstead Rd LEW SE13 .....41 P9
Hawthorn RASHW TN26 .....322 F6
Hawthorn Av CANTW/ST CT2 .....166 F2
    IOS ME12 .....57 J8
    THHTH CR7 .....60 C7
Hawthorn Cl DVW CT17 .....290 F5
    EDEN TN8 .....206 C8
    GVE DA12 .....69 M3
    HYTHE CT21 * 308 D7
    LYDD TN29 .....357 L2
    RAM CT11 .....143 K3
    STMC/STPC BR5 .....86 E5
Hawthorn Cnr HB CT6 .....108 D7
Hawthornden Cl
    E/WMAL ME19 .....153 K9
Hawthornden La HAYES BR2 * 85 J6
Hawthornden Rd HAYES BR2 .....85 K6
Hawthorn Dr WWKM BR4 .....85 H6
Hawthorne Av
    BH/WHM TN16 .....115 N9
    RHAM ME8 .....96 F4
Hawthorne Cl BMLY BR1 .....63 K9
    RDV CT15 .....260 E1
Hawthorne Rd BMLY BR1 .....63 K9
Hawthorn Gv PGE/AN SE20 .....61 J9
Hawthorn La SEV TN13 .....148 E7
Hawthorn Pl ERITH DA8 .....29 H8
Hawthorn Rd ASH TN23 .....282 E4
    BXLYHS DA6 .....45 H5
    DART DA1 .....66 D1
    SIT ME10 .....129 M1
    STRD ME2 .....18 A3
Hawthorns HART DA3 .....91 N4
    WALD ME5 * 125 L4
The Hawthorns BRDST CT10 .....113 H9
    DIT/AY ME20 .....154 D3
    OXTED RH8 .....175 K9
Hawthorn Ter BFN/LL DA15 .....44 B7
Hawthorn Wy
    RTWE/PEM TN2 .....241 H9
    TONN TN10 .....210 F3
Haxted Rd BMLY BR1 .....62 F7
Hay Currie St POP/IOD E14 .....25 L2
Hayday Rd CAN/RD E16 .....26 E1
Haydens Cl STMC/STPC BR5 .....87 K4
Haydens Ms TON TN9 .....210 F7
The Haydens TON TN9 .....210 F7

Haydon Cl MAIDW ME16 .....154 G8
Haydon St TWRH EC3N 24 C3
Haydon Wk TWRH EC3N 24 C2
Hayes Cha WWKM BR4 .....84 G3
Hayes Cl HAYES BR2 .....85 N6
    HOO/HM ME3 .....71 L4
    WTHK RM20 .....31 M9
Hayesden La RRTW TN3 .....239 M5
Hayesford Park Dr HAYES BR2 * 85 J2
Hayes Gdns HAYES BR2 .....85 N6
Hayes Gv EDUL SE22 .....40 F4
Hayes Hi HAYES BR2 .....85 H5
Hayes Hill Rd HAYES BR2 .....85 J5
Hayes La BECK BR3 .....62 B9
    HAYES BR2 .....85 N6
    RSIT ME9 .....128 A7
Hayes Mead Rd HAYES BR2 .....85 H5
Hayes Plat RYE TN31 .....330 B8
Hayes Rd HAYES BR2 .....85 K1
    RDART DA2 .....67 J2
Hayes St HAYES BR2 .....85 L5
Hayes Ter CDW DA12 * 70 G4
Hayes Wd HAYES BR2 .....84 F1
Hayes Wood Av HAYES BR2 .....85 L5
Hayfield E/WMAL ME19 .....153 L2
Hayfield Rd STMC/STPC BR5 .....87 H2
Hayfields WALD ME5 .....126 A3
Hay Hi SWCH CT13 .....201 L8
Hay La DEAL CT14 .....201 M8
Hayle TIL RM18 .....34 B6
Hayle Mill Rd
    MAID/SHEP ME15 .....185 L3
Hayle Pl MAID/SHEP ME15 * 185 L3
Hayle Rd MAID/SHEP ME15 .....13 F7
Hayley Cl STRD ME2 .....94 B4
Haymakers La ASH TN23 .....252 A9
Haymans Hi STPH/PW TN12 .....274 A1
Hayman Wk DIT/AY ME20 * 124 E7
Haymen St CHAT ME4 .....6 A7
Haymerle Rd STHWK SE1 * 24 B8
Hayne Rd BECK BR3 .....61 M8
Haynes Cl BRCH/KID SE3 .....42 C4
Haynes La NRWD SE19 .....60 E5
Haynes Rd GVW DA11 .....69 K2
Hay Pl SWLY BR8 * 88 B3
Hayrick Cl MAID/BEAR ME14 .....156 B7
Haysel SIT ME10 .....129 P5
Hays La STHWK SE1 * 24 B4
Haysleigh Gdns PGE/AN SE20 .....60 E2
Hays Rd SNOD ME6 .....116 C5
Hayton Rd RASHE TN25 .....285 P7
Haywain Cl ASH TN23 .....282 B5
    MAID/BEAR ME14 .....156 C8
    STPH/PW TN12 .....243 H4
Hayward Cl DART DA1 .....45 M9
Hayward Gdns
    DEAL CT14 .....232 F5
    KEN/WIL TN24 .....255 K9
Hayward Dr DART DA1 * 66 F2
Haywardens LING RH7 .....234 G4
Hayward's Cl NROM TN28 .....336 G7
Hayward's Hi FAV ME13 .....161 P8
Haywood Pl CDW/CHF RM16 * 33 K5
Haywood Ri ORP BR6 .....86 F9
Haywood Rd HAYES BR2 .....85 N1
Hazebrouck Rd FAV ME13 .....132 D6
Hazel Av HOO/HM ME3 .....75 L4
    MAIDW ME16 .....155 H7
Hazelbank RRTW TN3 .....269 L5
Hazelbank Rd CAT SE6 .....62 B1
Hazel Cl CROY/NA CR0 .....84 A4
    MTCM CR4 .....44 A2
    RDV CT15 .....260 D1
Hazelden Cl BGR/WK TN15 .....120 D5
Hazeldene Rd WELL DA16 .....44 E3
Hazeldon Rd BROCKY SE4 .....41 L6
Hazeldown Cl CDW CT17 .....290 F5
Hazel Dr ERITH DA8 .....48 A5
Hazel End SWLY BR8 .....88 D2
Hazel Gdns CDW/CHF RM16 .....32 F6
Hazel Gv ORP BR6 .....86 C6
    SYD SE26 .....61 K3
    WALD ME5 .....95 N6
Hazel Hts RASHE TN25 .....252 B4
Hazelhurst BECK BR3 .....62 B7
Hazel Wk HAYES BR2 .....86 B3
Hazel Wy STHWK SE1 * 24 C7
Hazel Wood Rd TIL RM18 .....33 P7
Hazelwood Cl
    RTWE/PEM TN2 .....240 G9
Hazelwood Dr OXTED RH8 .....154 C8
Hazelwood Hts OXTED RH8 .....175 K7
Hazelwood Meadow
    SWCH CT13 .....201 N3
Hazelwood Rd OXTED RH8 .....175 L8
    RSEV TN14 .....116 E6
Hazeldean Rd HAYES BR2 .....85 N1
Hazelmere Rd GILL ME7 * 96 D1
    HB CT6 .....108 A5
Hazelmere Rd WSTB CT5 .....105 H7
Hazling Dane RDV CT15 .....260 A3
Hazy Hill Cl CROY/NA CR0 .....83 J6
Head Hi FAV ME13 .....133 N7
Head Hill Rd FAV ME13 .....133 N5
Headingley Rd MAIDW ME16 .....154 G6
Headland Wy LING RH7 .....234 F5

Headley Av WLGTN SM6 .....82 E9
Headley Dr CROY/NA CR0 .....114 F2
The Head Race MAIDW ME16 .....185 J1
Head St WCHPL E1 .....24 G2
Heaf Gdns DIT/AY ME20 * 154 E5
Heald St NWCR SE14 .....41 M2
Healy Dr ORP BR6 .....86 G8
Heansill La HAWK TN18 .....316 G6
Heard Wy SIT ME10 .....100 A9
Hearn's Buildings WALW SE17 * 24 A7
Hearns Rd STMC/STPC BR5 .....87 K1
Hearns Rd STMC/STPC BR5 .....87 K1
Heartenoak Rd HAWK TN18 .....317 J2
Heart In Hand Rd HB CT6 .....108 C8
Hearts Delight La
    RCANTE CT3 .....169 L5
Hearts Delight Rd RSIT ME9 .....129 J4
Heath Av BXLYHN DA7 .....28 C3
Heath Cl CANTW/ST CT2 .....137 L6
    STMC/STPC BR5 .....87 K3
    SWLY BR8 .....88 E5
Heathclose Av DART DA1 .....46 B8
Heathclose Rd DART DA1 .....46 A9
Heathcote Cl DIT/AY ME20 .....154 E2
Heathcote Dr EGRIN RH19 .....264 E6
Heathdene Dr BELV DA17 .....28 G3
Heathedge SYD SE26 * 61 H1
Heathend Rd BXLY DA5 .....45 N9
Heatherbank CHST BR7 .....63 L6
    ELTH/MOT SE9 .....43 K5
Heather Bank STPH/PW TN12 .....243 J5
Heatherbank Cl DART DA1 .....45 N7
Heather Cl EHAM E6 .....27 H2
    LEW SE13 .....42 B8
    MARG CT9 .....112 B5
    MAID/SHEP ME15 .....185 N1
    TENT TN30 .....301 J4
Heather Dr DART DA1 .....46 A8
    SWLY BR8 .....88 A7
Heather Rd LEE/GVPK SE12 .....62 E1
Heatherside Rd SCUP DA14 .....64 E2
The Heathers CRBK TN17 .....297 M4
Heather Wk TONN TN10 .....210 E4
Heatherway LING RH7 .....234 G5
Heather Wy SAND/SEL CR2 .....114 A3
Heatherwood Cl RMAID ME17 .....187 P9
Heathfield CHST BR7 .....63 N5
    RMAID ME17 .....187 H7
Heathfield Av DVE/WH CT16 .....291 N7
    MAID/BEAR ME14 .....155 P5
Heathfield Cl CAN/RD E16 .....26 E1
    HAYES BR2 .....85 M9
    MAID/BEAR ME14 .....155 N5
    WALD ME5 .....95 N7
Heathfield Gdns
    CROY/NA CR0 * 83 H8
Heathfield La CHST BR7 .....63 N5
Heathfield Rd BMLY BR1 .....62 D6
    BXLYHS DA6 .....45 H5
    CROY/NA CR0 .....83 H8
    HAYES BR2 .....85 M9
    KEN/WIL TN24 .....3 C1
    MAID/BEAR ME14 .....155 N5
    WALD ME5 .....95 N7
Heathfield Ter SWLY BR8 * 4 C6
    WOOL/PLUM SE18 .....27 M9
Heathfield V SAND/SEL CR2 .....114 A3
Heathfield Wy RCANTW CT4 .....228 C6
Heath Gdns DART DA1 * 46 C9
    PGE/AN SE20 .....60 F1
Heathlands Rd DART DA1 .....46 B8
Heath La BKHTH/KID SE3 .....42 B3
    DART DA1 .....46 C9
Heathlee Rd BKHTH/KID SE3 .....42 D5
    DART DA1 .....46 C9
Heathley End CHST BR7 .....63 N5
Heathorn St MAID/BEAR ME14 .....13 H2
Heath Park Dr BMLY BR1 .....63 J9
Heath Ri HAYES BR2 .....85 K3
Heath Rd BXLY DA5 .....45 L9
    CDW/CHF RM16 .....33 K5
    DART DA1 .....45 P7
    MAID/SHEP ME16 .....184 D7
    MAIDW ME16 .....154 E9
    RMAID ME17 .....187 H7
    THHTH CR7 .....60 D7
Heathside RASHW TN26 .....322 E5
Heath Side CHST BR7 .....86 D5
Heathside Av BXLYHN DA7 .....44 C3
    RSIT ME9 .....148 B9
Heath St DART DA1 .....46 D8
The Heath E/WMAL ME19 .....153 M7
Heathview Av DART DA1 .....45 N7
Heathview Crs DART DA1 .....46 A8
Heath View Dr ABYW SE2 .....28 C9
Heath View Gdns
    RASHW TN26 .....322 E5
Heath View Rd
    CDW/CHF RM16 .....32 D5
Heathview Rd THHTH CR7 .....82 E1
Heath Vls WOOL/PLUM SE18 * 27 N8
Heathway BKHTH/KID SE3 .....42 E1
    CROY/NA CR0 .....83 J1
Heath Wy ERITH DA8 .....45 L2
Heathwood Dr RAM CT11 .....143 K5
Heathwood Gdns CHARL SE7 .....26 F7
    SWLY BR8 .....65 J8
Heathwood Pde SWLY BR8 * 65 J8
Heathwood Wk BXLY DA5 .....45 N9
Heaton Rd CANT CT1 .....166 D6
    PECK SE15 .....41 H4
Heavenham Rd BGR/WK TN15 .....149 N2
Heaverine Cl WOOL/PLUM SE18 .....27 L8
Heavitree Rd
    WOOL/PLUM SE18 .....27 M8
Heber Rd EDUL SE22 .....40 F4
Heckford St WAP E1W 24 G4
Hectorage Rd TON TN9 .....210 F7
Hectors La EGRIN RH19 .....265 M9
Hector St WOOL/PLUM SE18 .....27 P8
Hedgecourt Pl EGRIN RH19 .....264 B4
Hedge Place Rd GRH DA9 .....47 M7

Hedgerows ASH TN23 .....282 A1
The Hedgerows GVW DA11 .....69 J7
The Hedgerow
    MAID/BEAR ME14 .....156 B7
The Hedges MAID/BEAR ME14 .....155 M5
Hedgley St LEE/GVPK SE12 .....42 D6
Hedingham Rd
    CDW/CHF RM16 .....31 M8
Hedley Av WHM RM20 .....31 M9
Hedley St MAID/BEAR ME14 .....13 G3
Heeley Cl RSIT ME9 .....129 L7
Heel La CANTW/ST CT2 .....137 H5
Heel Rd FAV ME13 .....191 N4
Heighton Gdns CROY/NA CR0 .....82 G9
The Heights BECK BR3 * 62 A6
    CHARL SE7 .....26 D8
    SEV TN13 * 148 D7
    WSTB CT5 .....105 K7
Helder Gv LEE/GVPK SE12 .....42 D8
Helding Cl HB CT6 .....107 N4
Helena Av MARG CT9 .....112 D5
Helena Corniche FOLK CT20 .....309 P4
Helena Rd RFOLK CT18 .....311 M1
Helena Sq BERM/RHTH SE16 .....25 H5
Helen Cl DART DA1 .....46 B8
Helen Keller Cl TONN TN10 .....210 C6
Helen La WOOL/PLUM SE18 * 27 J7
Helen Thompson Cl RSIT ME9 .....99 M2
Heligan Cl ORP BR6 .....86 G8
Helleborine GRAYS RM17 .....32 M2
Hellings St WAP E1W * 24 D4
Hellyar Ct ROCH ME1 * 19 G7
Helmdon Cl PECK SE15 * 127 H2
Helsinki Sq BERM/RHTH SE16 .....25 J6
Helvellyn Av RAM CT11 .....142 G5
Helvetia St CAT SE6 .....61 L6
Hemley Rd CDW/CHF RM16 .....33 L2
Hemmings Cl SCUP DA14 .....64 D1
Hempstead La RSIT ME9 .....130 D2
Hempstead Rd GILL ME7 .....96 D8
    GILL ME7 .....126 C2
Hempstead Valley Dr GILL ME7 .....96 D8
Hempsted St ASH TN23 * 2 D4
Hemp Wk WALW SE17 * 24 A7
Hemsted Rd ERITH DA8 .....45 N1
Hemsley Cl MAID/BEAR ME14 .....156 D7
Henderson Dr DART DA1 .....46 C5
Henderson Rd BH/WHM TN16 .....115 M6
    CROY/NA CR0 .....83 J3
Hendley Dr CRBK TN17 .....297 P2
Hendre Rd STHWK SE1 .....24 C8
Hendy Rd SNOD ME6 .....124 A5
Heneage Crs CROY/NA CR0 .....114 F4
Heneage La HDTCH EC3A 24 B2
Heneage St WCHPL E1 * 24 C1
Henfield Cl BXLY DA5 .....45 J7
Hengest Av DEAL CT14 .....233 J2
Hengist Ct MAID/BEAR ME14 * 13 C4
Hengist Rd BRCH CT7 .....110 D6
    ERITH DA6 .....45 L1
    LEE/GVPK SE12 .....42 E8
    WGOS CT8 .....111 L5
Hengist Wy HAYES BR2 .....84 C1
Hengrave Rd FSTH SE23 .....41 J8
Hengrove Ct BXLY DA5 .....45 J8
Henham Gdns STPH/PW TN12 .....213 H4
Henhurst Rd MEO DA13 .....69 P8
Heniker La RMAID ME17 .....217 J5
Henley Cl BERM/RHTH SE16 * 24 F6
    RHAM ME8 .....96 G6
    RTWE/PEM TN2 .....271 J8
    RYE TN31 .....338 D6
    WALD ME5 .....95 M8
Henley Deane GVW DA11 .....69 J3
Henley Dr BERM/RHTH SE16 .....24 C7
Henley Flds MAID/BEAR ME14 .....156 B8
    TENT TN30 .....301 J5
Henley Mdw TENT TN30 .....301 H5
Henley Rd CAN/RD E16 .....27 H4
    STPH/PW TN12 .....243 H2
Henry Addington Cl EHAM E6 .....27 J1
Henry Cooper Wy
    ELTH/MOT SE9 .....63 H2
Henryson Rd BROCKY SE4 .....41 N6
Henry St BMLY BR1 .....62 F7
    CHAT ME4 .....7 F7
    GRAYS RM17 .....32 D9
    RHAM ME8 .....96 G5
Hensford Gdns SYD SE26 .....61 H3
Henshaw St WALW SE17 .....24 A7
Hensil La HAWK TN18 .....316 G6
Henslowe Rd EDUL SE22 .....40 G3
Henson Cl ORP BR6 .....86 C6
Henville Rd BMLY BR1 .....62 E4
Henwick Rd ELTH/MOT SE9 .....43 H4
Henwood Cl KEN/WIL TN24 .....3 G3
Henwood Green Rd
    RTWE/PEM TN2 .....271 N1
Henwoods Crs
    RTWE/PEM TN2 .....271 N2
Henwoods Mt
    RTWE/PEM TN2 .....271 P2
Hepburn Cl CDW/CHF RM16 .....31 N7
Hepburn Gdns HAYES BR2 .....85 J5
Herald Gdns WLGTN SM6 .....82 A7
Herbert Pl WOOL/PLUM SE18 .....27 P9
Herbert Rd BXLYHN DA7 .....44 C2
    CHAT ME4 .....6 D7
    HAYES BR2 .....85 N2
    KEN/WIL TN24 .....282 C2
    RAM CT11 .....143 H6
    RHAM ME8 .....97 H6
    SWCM DA10 .....68 G5
    SWLY BR8 .....88 D4
    WOOL/PLUM SE18 .....43 M1

Hereford Cl KEN/WIL TN24 .....252 F2
Hereford Gdns BRCH CT7 .....110 G6
Hereford Rd NWCR SE14 * 41 M1
Hereford Retreat PECK SE15 * 40 C1
Hereford Rd
    MAID/SHEP ME15 .....185 P4
Hereson Rd BRCH CT7 .....17 H1
Hereward Av BRCH CT7 .....110 E5
Herga Hyll CDW/CHF RM16 .....33 H1
Heritage Cl WSTB CT5 .....105 H8
Heritage Dr GILL ME7 .....96 C5
Heritage Gdns DVE/WH CT16 .....8 E2
Heritage Hl HAYES BR2 .....85 M9
Heritage Rd FOLK CT20 .....310 A5
    WALD ME5 .....95 M8
Herman Ter CHAT ME4 .....6 D6
Hermitage Cl HYTHE CT21 .....308 C5
Hermitage Ct MAIDW ME16 .....154 E7
Hermitage Gdns CROY/NA CR0 .....60 C6
Hermitage La CROY/NA CR0 .....83 L4
    DIT/AY ME20 .....154 E5
    EGRIN RH19 .....265 J8
    MAID/BEAR ME14 .....156 E1
    RMAID ME17 .....216 B4
Hermitage Rd EGRIN RH19 .....264 C5
    HOO/HM ME3 .....71 L4
    NRWD SE19 .....60 B5
The Hermitage FSTH SE23 .....41 J9
    LEW SE13 * 42 A5
Hermitage Wall WAP E1W 24 D4
Hermit Rd CAN/RD E16 .....26 D2
Herne Av HB CT6 .....107 M2
Herne Bay Rd RCANTE CT3 .....137 K4
    WSTB CT5 .....106 B3
Herne Dr HB CT6 .....107 H4
Herne Hl HNHL SE24 .....40 C6
Herne Hill Rd HNHL SE24 .....40 D2
Herne Pl HNHL SE24 .....40 B7
Herne Rd RHAM ME8 .....96 E6
Herne St HB CT6 .....107 M5
Herneville Gdns HB CT6 .....107 N2
Heron Cl HAYES BR2 .....85 M1
    RSIT ME9 .....96 C6
Heron Crs SCUP DA14 .....64 A3
Herondale SAND/SEL CR2 .....114 A3
Heronden Rd
    MAID/SHEP ME15 .....186 C5
    SWCH CT13 .....200 F9
Heron Dr SIT ME10 .....78 B2
Heron Forstal Av RFOLK CT18 .....288 C9
Herongate Rd SWLY BR8 .....65 N5
Heron Hi BELV DA17 .....28 C1
Heron Hill La MEO DA13 .....122 A1
Heron Pl ORP BR6 .....265 J8
Heron Quays POP/IOD E14 .....25 K4
Heron Rd CROY/NA CR0 * 153 N3
    DIT/AY ME20 .....153 N5
    HNHL SE24 .....40 D1
Heron's Brook RASHE TN25 .....253 H5
Herons Cl RCANTW CT4 .....194 D3
Heron's Wy HYTHE CT21 .....308 B7
    RTWE/PEM TN2 .....241 P9
Heronsgate Dr EGRIN RH19 .....265 J8
Heron Wk ASH TN23 .....252 B9
Heron Wy HOO/HM ME3 .....54 C4
    WALD ME5 .....95 M8
    WTHK RM20 .....31 L8
Herrington Rd CHARL SE7 .....26 C6
Herschel Rd BRCH CT7 .....110 G5
    FSTH SE23 .....41 K8
Herschell Rd East DEAL CT14 .....233 H6
Herschell Sq DEAL CT14 .....233 H6
Hertford Pl RAM CT11 * 17 F5
Hertford Rd MARG CT9 .....112 C5
Hertford St RAM CT11 .....16 E5
Herts Crs MAID/SHEP ME15 .....185 L8
Hertsmere Rd POP/IOD E14 .....25 K4
Herying Cl STRD ME2 .....124 A5
Hesiers Hi WARL CR6 .....145 H2
Hesiers Rd WARL CR6 .....145 H1
Hesketh Av RDART DA2 .....47 H9
Heskett Pk RTWE/PEM TN2 .....271 P2
Hesperus Crs POP/IOD E14 .....25 L7
Hessel St WCHPL E1 .....24 E2
Hesterman Wy CROY/NA CR0 .....82 D5
Hestia Wy ASH TN23 .....282 B3
Heston St DEPT SE8 .....41 M2
Hevelius Cl GNWCH SE10 .....26 A8
Hever Av BGR/WK TN15 .....120 D5
Hever Court Rd GVE DA12 .....69 N5
Hever Gdns BMLY BR1 .....63 L8
    STRD ME2 .....94 E1
Heversham BXLYHN DA7 .....44 G8
    SIT ME10 .....129 K2
Hever Rd BGR/WK TN15 .....120 B2
    EDEN TN8 .....237 H2
Heversham Rd BXLYHN DA7 .....45 J3
Hever Wood Rd
    BGR/WK TN15 .....120 B2
Hewett Pl SWLY BR8 .....88 C1
Hewett Cl CROY/NA CR0 .....84 C7
    GILL ME7 .....73 M9
    MAIDW ME16 .....155 J5
Hewitt Av DVE/WH CT16 .....8 C1
Hewitts Pl KEN/WIL TN24 .....253 J8
Hewitts Rd ORP BR6 .....117 N2
Hexal Rd CAT SE6 .....62 C2
Hexham Rd WNWD SE27 .....60 C8
Hextable Cl ASH TN23 .....282 C2
    RHAM ME8 .....155 H5
Heyford Ct RFOLK CT18 .....288 E8
Hibbs Cl SWLY BR8 .....65 H8
Hibernia Dr GVE DA12 .....13 G5
Hibernia St RAM CT11 .....17 G3
Hichisson Rd PECK SE15 .....41 J6
Hickin Cl CHATN 25 M6
Hickin St POP/IOD E14 .....25 M6
Hickman Cl CAN/RD E16 .....26 E1

Hickory Dell GILL ME7 ....96 D9
Hicks Forstal Rd RCANTE CT3 ...137 L1
Hicks St DEPT SE8 ....25 H8
Hidden Meadow FAV ME13 * ...132 F6
Higham Cl MAID/SHEP ME15 ...185 J1
Higham Gdns TONN TN10.....211 J5
Higham La RCANTW CT4 ....197 N5
  RTON TN31 ....211 H1
  RYE TN31 ....329 P7
Higham Rd HOO/HM ME3 .....52 A4
  HOO/HM ME3 ....72 D4
Higham School Rd
  TONN TN10 ....211 H4
Higham Vw MAID/SHEP ME14 ...125 K9
High Ash La TIL RM18.........33 P6
High Bank ROCH ME1 ....95 J4
High Banks MAID/SHEP ME15 ...185 L6
Highbanks Cl WELL DA16 ....44 C1
Highbarrow Rd CROY/NA CR0 ...83 J5
High Beeches ORP BR6.........117 H1
  RTWE/PEM TN2 ....270 G2
  SCUP DA14 ....26 B7
Highberry E/WMAL ME19 ......153 M2
Highbourne Pk RMAID ME17...190 B6
Highbrook Rd BKHTH/KID SE5 ...43 H4
High Broom Crs WWKM BR4 ...84 E4
High Brooms Rd
  STH/RUST TN4 ....240 F9
Highbury Av THHTH CR7 ....60 A8
Highbury Cl WWKM BR4 ....84 E6
Highbury Gdns MSTR CT12 * ...142 G2
High Bury La TENT TN30 ......301 H8
Highclere St SYD SE26 ....41 L5
Highcombe CHARL SE7 ....26 C9
Highcombe Cl ELTH/MOT SE9 ...43 H9
High Cross Rd BGR/WK TN15 ...180 E2
Highcross Rd MEO DA13 ....68 B5
Highdaun Dr
  STRHM/NOR SW16 ....82 L1
High Dewar Rd RHAM ME8 .....97 K6
High Dr CTHM CR3..........144 C7
High Elms RHAM ME8 ....97 H4
High Elms Rd ORP BR6 ....116 D5
Highfield Av ERITH DA8 ....28 G9
  ORP BR6 ....116 C1
Highfield Cl CANTW/ST CT2 ...166 A1
  HAWK TN18 ....317 J5
  HYTHE CT21 ....308 F5
  LEW SE13 ....42 B7
  MSTR CT12 ....142 C1
  RHAM ME8 ....96 D7
  RTWE/PEM TN2 ....271 G2
Highfield Dr HAYES BR2 ....85 H1
  WWKM BR4 ....84 E7
Highfield Gdns
  CDW/CHF RM16 ....32 E5
  MARG CT9 ....14 C7
Highfield Hl NRWD SE19 ....60 D6
Highfield La KEN/WIL TN24 ...283 M2
Highfield Rd BGR/WK TN15 ...149 K1
  BH/WHM TN16 ....145 M2
  BMLY BR1 ....86 A1
  BXLYHS DA6 ....45 M8
  DART DA1 ....46 D8
  EGRIN RH19 ....264 C5
  IOS ME12 ....77 N1
  KEN/WIL TN24 ....253 K9
  MSTR CT12 ....142 G1
  RHAM ME8 ....96 D7
  STH/RUST TN4 ....240 F9
  STMC/STPC BR5 ....64 B9
Highfield Rd North DART DA1...46 D7
Highfield Rd South DART DA1...46 D8
Highfields Av HB CT6 ....107 P2
Highfields Rd EDEN TN8.........206 D5
Highfields La EDEN TN8.........206 D5
Highfields Vw HB CT6 ....107 M7
High Firs SWLY BR8 ....88 D1
Highgate Hl HAWK TN18........317 H5
Highgate Rd WSTB CT5.......106 A5
High Gv BMLY BR1..........62 C7
  WOOL/PLUM SE18..........43 P7
Highgrove RTWE/PEM TN2 ...270 D8
Highgrove Cl CHST BR7 ....63 J7
Highgrove Rd WALD ME5......95 M9
High Halden Rd HDCN TN27...278 B7
High House La CDW/CHF RM16...33 L6
  RTON TN11 ....211 L1
Highland Cl FOLK CT20.......310 C2
Highland Cft BECK BR3.........61 P4
Highland Rd BMLY BR1.........62 D7
  BXLY DA6 ....45 J6
  MAID/SHEP ME15 ....186 B4
  NRWD SE19 ....60 D6
  RCANTW CT4 ....195 K2
  RSEV TN14 ....118 A5
Highlands Cl STRD ME2 ....71 M9
Highlands Crs LYDD TN29....337 M1
Highlands Hl SWLY BR8 ....66 A8
Highlands Pk BGR/WK TN15 ...149 K6
Highlands Rd STMC/STPC BR5 ...87 J4
Highland Ter LEW SE13 * 41 P4
High La CTHM CR3 ....144 A6
High Level Dr SYD SE26 ....60 C3
High Limes NRWD SE19 * 60 E5
Highmead WOOL/PLUM SE18 ...44 B1
High Md WWKM BR4 ....84 A6
High Meadow RYE TN31......329 P6
High Meads Rd CAN/RD E16 ...26 E2
High Minnis RCANTW CT4.....256 E2
Highmore Rd BKHTH/KID SE5 ...42 C1
High Oak Hl RSIT ME9 ....98 F6
High Pk RYE TN31 ....329 P6
High Point ELTH/MOT SE9 .....63 M2
High Rdg CRBK TN17 ....274 C9
Highridge GILL ME7 ....96 C5
  HYTHE CT21 ....309 M4
Highridge Cl
  MAID/BEAR ME14 ....156 C7
High Rd CDW/CHF RM16 ....31 P4
  CDW/CHF RM16 ....32 G1
  RDART DA2 ....66 C2
High Rocks La RRTW TN3 ....269 P7
Highshore Rd PECK SE15 ....40 G3
High Snoad Wd RASHE TN25 ...192 D9

Highstead Crs ERITH DA8.........45 N2
Highsted Rd RSIT ME9 ....129 H6
High St ASH TN23 ....2 E3
  BECK BR3 ....61 M6
  BGR/WK TN15 ....149 L6
  BGR/WK TN15 ....149 M2
  BGR/WK TN15 ....151 J5
  BGR/WK TN15 ....151 K1
  BH/WHM TN16 ....147 K9
  BH/WHM TN16 ....176 D5
  BMLY BR1 ....62 E9
  BRDST CT10 ....113 K8
  CANT CT1 ....4 E4
  CANTW/ST CT2 ....137 M9
  CHAT ME4 ....6 D5
  CRBK TN17 ....274 D8
  CRBK TN17 ....297 P3
  CRBK TN17 ....319 M3
  CROY/NA CR0 ....2 D5
  DART DA1 ....46 E7
  DEAL CT14 ....233 J5
  DIT/AY ME20 ....154 E1
  DVE/WH CT16 ....8 B2
  DVE/WH CT16 ....290 E2
  E/WMAL ME19 ....153 P6
  EDEN TN8 ....206 D9
  EDEN TN8 ....267 H5
  EGRIN RH19 ....265 J8
  EYN DA4 ....89 K6
  GILL ME7 ....7 J2
  GRAYS RM17 ....32 B9
  GRH DA9 ....47 P5
  GVE DA12 ....49 M7
  GVW DA11 ....48 D1
  HAWK TN18 ....316 C4
  HB CT6 ....107 L1
  HDCN TN27 ....277 M4
  HDCN TN27 ....249 H8
  HDCN TN27 ....278 A7
  HOO/HM ME3 ....54 G4
  HOO/HM ME3 ....72 D4
  HYTHE CT21 ....309 H5
  IOS ME12 ....57 K5
  IOS ME12 ....78 C1
  IOS ME12 ....79 K4
  LING RH7 ....234 G5
  LYDD TN29 ....326 G7
  LYDD TN29 ....334 E5
  LYDD TN29 ....334 A7
  MAID/BEAR ME14 ....12 E5
  MARG CT9 ....15 G4
  MARG CT9 ....112 A7
  MSTR CT12 ....141 K6
  MSTR CT12 ....142 B4
  NROM TN28 ....336 C7
  ORP BR6 ....86 D9
  ORP BR6 ....87 J4
  ORP BR6 ....116 B5
  OXTED RH8 ....174 G6
  OXTED RH8 ....175 L4
  PGE/AN SE20 ....61 J6
  PUR RM19 ....30 C8
  QBOR ME11 ....77 H2
  RAM CT11 ....16 D2
  RASHE TN25 ....223 P8
  RCANTE CT5 ....168 C8
  RCANTE CT5 ....169 K9
  RCANTW CT4 ....197 L1
  RCANTW CT4 ....257 L4
  RDART DA2 ....67 P2
  RDV CT15 ....292 E1
  RFOLK CT18 ....286 G2
  RHAM ME8 ....97 J6
  RMAID ME17 ....189 J7
  RMAID ME17 ....217 H5
  ROCH ME1 ....19 F4
  ROCH ME1 ....124 B1
  RRTW TN3 ....295 H3
  RSEV TN14 ....118 E4
  RSEV TN14 ....148 F1
  RSIT ME9 ....98 C8
  RTON TN11 ....209 K9
  RTON TN11 ....211 P2
  RTW TN1 ....22 D6
  RTWE/PEM TN2 ....271 M2
  RYE TN31 ....338 F7
  SCUP DA14 ....64 C3
  SEV TN13 ....21 G4
  SEV TN13 ....148 B7
  SIT ME10 ....99 M8
  SNOD ME6 ....125 P5
  SNWD SE25 ....83 L1
  SOCK/AV RM15 ....50 F4
  STH/RUST TN4 ....239 P6
  STMC/STPC BR5 ....87 K1
  STPH/PW TN12 ....243 J9
  STPH/PW TN12 ....245 J8
  STPH/PW TN12 ....246 C6
  STRD ME2 ....18 C1
  STRD ME2 ....93 P9
  SWCH CT13 ....201 J8
  SWCH CT13 ....201 P1
  SWCM DA10 ....48 D6
  SWLY BR8 ....65 N9
  TENT TN30 ....301 H8
  THHTH CR7 ....83 H7
  TON TN9 ....210 F9
  WADH TN5 ....314 E5
  WADH TN5 ....213 N1
  WBY/YAL ME18 ....213 N1
  WSTB CT5 ....105 L4
  WWKM BR4 ....84 E5
Highstreet Rd FAV ME13 ....134 D3
High Street St Lawrence
  RAM CT11 ....16 A3
The High St HDCN TN27.......221 H5
High Tor Cl BMLY BR1 ....62 F6
High Trees BRXS/STRHM SW2...40 A9
  CROY/NA CR0 ....84 B5
High Trees Cl KEN/WIL TN24...253 K8
High Vw HOO/HM ME3...........71 J3
Highview MEO DA13 ....122 C5
High View Av GRAYS RM17......32 D8

WLGTN SM6 ....82 E9
Highview Cl FAV ME13 ....164 C1
High View Cl NRWD SE19 ....60 F8
Highview Dr WALD ME5 ....95 P8
High View Gdns GRAYS RM17...32 D8
Highview Rd NRWD SE19 ....60 E5
Highview Rd IOS ME12 ....148 C3
  SCUP DA14 ....64 C3
Highview Ter DART DA1 * 86 D7
The Highway ORP BR6 ....87 J9
  WAP E1W 24 D6
High Weald Landscape Trail
  EGRIN RH19 ....264 C9
High Weald Wk RRTW TN3....269 H9
  RRTW TN5 ....269 N1
  RTON TN11 ....241 M6
  RTWE/PEM TN2 ....240 G8
  RTWE/PEM TN2 ....271 H7
  STH/RUST TN4 ....22 A7
  TON TN9 ....241 H2
Highwood Cl ORP BR6.........86 D6
Highwood Dr ORP BR6.........86 D6
Highwoods Cl HOO/HM ME3 ...71 K3
High Woods La
  BRXN/ST SW9 ....40 B3
Hilary Cl BXLYHN DA7 ....45 K2
  HB CT6 ....107 P2
Hilary Gdns ROCH ME1 ....94 E4
Hilbert Cl RTWE/PEM TN2 ....23 H1
Hilbert Rd RTWE/PEM TN2 ...270 F3
Hilborough Wy ORP BR6 ....86 E9
Hilda Lockert Wk
  BRXN/ST SW9 ....40 B3
Hilda May Av SWLY BR8 ....65 N9
Hilda Rd CHAT ME4 ....6 D7
  IOS ME12 ....57 N1
Hilda Ter BRXN/ST SW9 * 40 A3
Hilda Vale Rd ORP BR6 ....86 B8
Hilden Av RTON TN11 ....210 C6
Hildenborough Crs
  MAIDW ME16 ....154 C5
Hildenborough Gdns
  BMLY BR1 ....62 C5
Hildenborough Rd
  RTON TN11 ....180 C7
  RTON TN11 ....209 M7
Hilden Dr ERITH DA8 ....46 B1
Hildenlea Pl HAYES BR2 ....62 C8
Hildenley Park RTON TN11 ...210 C6
Hilders Cl EDEN TN8 ....206 C6
Hildersham Cl BRDST CT10 ...113 K7
Hildersham La EDEN TN8 ....206 A6
Hilary Av GVW DA11 ....69 J2
Hilary Cl EGRIN RH19 ....265 H5
Hilary Rd MAID/BEAR ME14 ...155 M5
Hilda Av RDV CT15 ....229 P9
Hillbeck Cl PECK SE15 ....41 J1
Hillborough Dr HB CT6 ....108 C4
Hillborough Gv WALD ME5 ...125 M2
Hill Brow BMLY BR1 ....63 H1
  DART DA1 ....45 P7
  MAID/BEAR ME14 ....156 C7
  SIT ME10 ....99 N9
Hillbrow Av CANTW/ST CT2 ...137 L6
  HB CT6 ....107 N4
Hillbrow Dr IOS ME12 ....69 N5
Hillbrow La ASH TN23 ....252 C8
Hillcrest Av ASH TN23 ....2 A6
  BMLY BR1 ....62 C6
  MAID/SHEP ME15 ....186 A4
Hillcrest Cl BECK BR3 ....84 C3
  KEN/WIL TN24 ....253 H5
  SYD SE26 ....60 C3
Hillcrest Dr GRH DA9 ....47 N6
  RTWE/PEM TN2 ....270 C1
Hillcrest Gdns DEAL CT14 ....232 F7
  RAM CT11 ....16 A4
Hillcrest Rd BH/WHM TN16 ...145 N1
  BMLY BR1 ....62 E3
  CHAT ME4 ....95 L4
  DART DA1 ....45 N8
  DEAL CT14 ....263 H4
  EDEN TN8 ....206 C6
  HYTHE CT21 ....308 G4
  ORP BR6 ....87 J2
  RCANTE CT3 ....168 B8
Hillcrest Vw BECK BR3 ....84 C3
Hillcroft Rd EHAM E6 ....27 P1
  HB CT6 ....107 N3
Hilden Shaw
  MAID/SHEP ME15 ....185 M3
Hilldown Rd HAYES BR2 ....85 H5
Hill Dr SWCH CT13 ....201 J7
Hilldrop Rd BMLY BR1 ....62 F5
Hill End ORP BR6 ....86 D6
  WOOL/PLUM SE18 ....43 J2
Hillery Cl WALW SE17 ....18 D7
Hillfield Rd SEV TN13 ....148 D5
Hillgarth STH/RUST TN4 .....240 D7
Hill Green Rd RSIT ME9 ....127 M5
Hill House Dr CDW/CHF RM16 ...33 J8
  MSTR CT12 ....141 K5

Hill House Rd RDART DA2.........47 J8
Hilliard's Ct WAP E1W * 24 F4
Hillier Gdns CROY/NA CR0 ....82 F9
Hillier's La CROY/NA CR0 .....82 D7
Hillingdale BH/WHM TN16 ...145 L3
Hillingdon Av SEV TN13 .....149 H6
Hillingdon Ri SEV TN13 .....149 J7
Hillingdon Rd BXLYHN DA7 ...45 L4
  WDTK RM20 ....69 H1
Hill La RFOLK CT18 ....287 N7
Hillman Av HB CT6.........106 F2
Hillmead Dr BRXN/ST SW9 ...40 B5
Hillmore Gv SYD SE26 ....61 K4
Hill Pk KEN/WIL TN24 ....283 M1
Hillreach WOOL/PLUM SE18 ...26 C8
Hill Ri RDART DA2 ....67 K4
Hill Rd DART DA1 ....46 E7
  FOLKN CT19 ....311 H3
  ROCH ME1 ....94 D9
Hillsboro Rd EDUL SE22 ....40 E6
Hillsgrove Cl WELL DA16 .....44 E1
Hill Shaw HART DA3 ....94 C1
Hillshaw Crs STRD ME2 ....94 C1
Hillside EYN DA4 ....89 K6
  GRAYS RM17 ....32 E7
  RDART DA2 ....67 L4
  RDART DA2 ....67 N2
Hillside Av CANTW/ST CT2 ...166 B5
  GVE DA12 ....69 P1
  OBOR ME11 ....77 H4
  STRD ME2 ....72 B7
Hillside Ct EGRIN RH19 ....265 H5
Hillside Cl STRD ME2 * 18 E1
  SWLY BR8 ....89 H3
  WBY/YAL ME18 ....183 M4
Hillside Gdns
  BRXS/STRHM SW2 * 60 A1
Hillside La HAYES BR2 ....85 H7
Hillside Rd BGR/WK TN15 ...149 L2
  BH/WHM TN16 ....145 P4
  CHAT ME4 ....6 B4
  CROY/NA CR0 ....82 C9
  DART DA1 ....46 B8
  DVW CT17 ....291 H5
  FAV ME13 ....191 K5
  HAYES BR2 ....58 B9
  SEV TN13 ....149 J8
  WSTB CT5 ....105 P5
Hillside Ter FAV ME13 * 132 F6
  GVE DA12 * 49 M9
The Hillside ORP BR6.........117 J3
Hillside Vw BMLY BR1 ....119 N6
Hills Pl STRD ME2 * 93 M9
Hill's Ter CHAT ME4 * 6 D5
The Hill CRBK TN17 ....298 A5
  GVW DA11 ....48 C7
  HDCN TN27 ....221 H2
  RCANTE CT3 ....168 B8
Hill Top CRBK TN17 ....275 K8
Hilltop MAID/SHEP ME15 .....184 C8
  TON TN9 ....240 E2
  WSTB CT5 * 105 L7
Hilltop Dr RYE TN31 ....338 E5
Hilltop Gdns DART DA1 ....86 F6
  ORP BR6 ....86 F6
Hilltop Rd IOS ME12 ....78 A2
  STRD ME2 ....72 C6
  WTHK RM20 ....69 J1
Hilltop Wk CTHM CR5 ....144 B5
Hill Vw KEN/WIL TN24 ....151 K5
  KEN/WIL TN24 ....283 M1
Hill View Cl BGR/WK TN15 ...151 K5
Hillview Crs ORP BR6 ....86 F5
Hill View Rd HART DA3 ....94 B5
  WELL DA16 ....95 K9
Hill View Rd CANTW/ST CT2 ...166 B2
  WSTB CT5 ....105 L6
Hillworth BECK BR3 * 61 P8
Hillworth Rd
  BRXS/STRHM SW2 ....40 A2
Hillyard St BRXN/ST SW9 .....40 A3
Hillyfield Cl STRD ME2 ....71 P6
Hillyfields ASH TN23 ....2 A6
Hilly Flds BROCKY SE4 * 41 N5
Hilly Fields Crs BROCKY SE4 ...41 N5
Hilton Cl FAV ME13 ....132 C7
Hilton Dr SIT ME10 ....99 J8
Hilton Rd ASH TN23 ....252 C7
  HOO/HM ME3 ....53 B9
Hinchliffe Wy MARG CT9 .....113 J5
Hinckley Rd EDUL SE22 ....40 C5
Hind Cl LYDD TN29 ....326 C6
Hind Crs ERITH DA8 ....45 L1
Hinde Cl SIT ME10 ....99 J8
Hindhead Wy POP/IOD E14 ...25 K2
Hindmans Rd EDUL SE22 .....40 E6
Hindmarsh Cl WCHPL E1 * ...24 C7
Hindsley's Pl FSTH SE23 .....41 J3
Hines Ter WALD ME5 * 95 P5
Hinksden Rd CRBK TN17 ....317 P5
Hinksey Pth ABYW SE2 ....28 C5
Hinstock Rd
  WOOL/PLUM SE18 ....43 J9
Hinton Cl ELTH/MOT SE9 .....43 J9
Hinton Crs GILL ME7 ....96 E5
Hinton Rd BRXN/ST SW9 .....40 A4
Hinxhill Rd KEN/WIL TN24 ...253 M9
Hirst Cl DVE/WH CT16 ....291 J3
Hitchen Hatch La SEV TN13 ...148 A8
Hither Chantlers RRTW TN3...269 M5

Hither Farm Rd
  BKHTH/KID SE3 ....42 G4
Hither Rd RCANTE CT3 ....220 D3
Hither Green La LEW SE13 ....42 A6
Hitherwood Dr DUL SE21 .....60 F3
Hive La GVW DA11 ....48 F7
Hoaden Rw RCANTW CT3 * ...170 A2
Hoades Wood Rd
  CANTW/ST CT2 ....137 M6
Hoads Wood Gdns
  RASHE TN25 ....252 B5
Hoath Cl GILL ME7 ....96 D5
Hoath La RHAM ME8 ....96 D7
Hoath Meadow
  STPH/PW TN12 * 273 P2
Hoath Rd RCANTE CT3 ....137 N6
Hoath Wy RHAM ME8 ....96 D6
Hobart Crs DVE/WH CT16 .....291 J5
Hobart Gdns SIT ME10 ....129 K1
  THHTH CR7 ....60 D7
Hobart Rd MSTR CT12 ....142 F3
  TIL RM18 ....33 L3
Hobbs La RYE TN31 ....331 J7
Hobbs Rd WNWD SE27 ....60 C3
Hobday St POP/IOD E14 ....25 L2
Hoblands End CHST BR7 ....64 A5
Hockenden La SWLY BR8 ....65 J7
Hockeredge Gdns WGOS CT8 ...111 N5
Hockers La MAID/BEAR ME14...156 C4
Hockers La MAID/BEAR ME14...156 C5
Hoddesdon Rd BELV DA17 .....28 F8
Hodgkins Cl CDW/CHF RM16...33 N8
Hodgkins Cl THMD SE28 ....28 C3
Hodgson Crs SNOD ME6 .....123 P5
Hodgson Rd WSTB CT5 ....104 F7
Hodister Cl CMBW SE5 ....40 C1
Hodsoll St BGR/WK TN15 ...121 N5
Hodson Crs STMC/STPC BR5 ...87 L3
Hogarth Cl CAN/RD E16 ....26 E1
  HB CT6 ....108 B5
Hogarth Crs CROY/NA CR0 ....83 H4
Hogarth Rd CDW/CHF RM16...32 G1
Hogben La RMAID ME17 .....188 G1
Hogben Cl RFOLK CT18 ....286 C5
Hogbrook Hill La RDV CT15 ...289 N5
Hogg La CDW/CHF RM16 ....32 B2
  RCANTW CT4 ....196 D9
Hog Gn RCANTW CT4 ....257 L5
Hog Hl MAID/BEAR ME14 ....156 A4
Hog Hole La RRTW TN3.......294 F5
Hognore La BGR/WK TN15 ...121 N7
Hogshaugh Pas WAP E1W * ...24 D5
Hogtrough La OXTED RH8 ....174 E4
Hogtrough La OXTED RH8 ....174 E4
Holbeach Gdns BFN/LL DA15...44 E7
Holbeach Rd CAT SE6 ....41 N8
Holbeam Wy ASH TN23 ....2 B5
Holbeck Rw PECK SE15 ....40 G11
Holborn La CHAT ME4 * 6 D5
Holborn Rd PLSTW E15 ....27 H5
Holbrook Cl HB CT6 ....107 N6
Holbrook Dr MSTR CT12 ....142 D2
Holbrook La CHST BR7 ....63 P6
Holbrook Wy HAYES BR2 .....85 H3
Holburne Cl BKHTH/KID SE3 ...42 G2
Holburne Gdns BKHTH/KID SE3...43 H2
Holburne Rd BKHTH/KID SE3...42 G2
Holcombe Cl RCANTW CT4 ...176 E2
Holcombe Hl ROCH ME1 ....95 H3
Holcote Cl BELV DA17 ....28 D6
Holdenby Rd BROCKY SE4 .....41 L6
Holden Cnr STH/RUST TN4 ...240 B8
Holden Vw KEN/WIL TN24 ....282 B2
Holden Park Rd
  STH/RUST TN4 ....240 C9
Holden Rd STH/RUST TN4 ...240 C8
Holder Cl WALD ME5 ....95 P8
Holdernesse Wy WNWD SE27...60 B4
Holding St RHAM ME8 ....97 H3
Hole La EDEN TN8 ....206 A4
Holford Cl WALD ME5 ....95 L2
Holford St TON TN9 ....210 E9
Holgate St CHARL SE7 ....26 E6
Holland Cl BRDST CT10 ....113 M5
  HAYES BR2 ....85 J6
  IOS ME12 ....57 K7
Holland Crs OXTED RH8 .....175 K9
Holland Gv BRXN/ST SW9 ....40 A3
Holland La OXTED RH8 ....175 K9
Holland Rd MAID/BEAR ME14...13 G3
  OXTED RH8 ....175 K9
  SNWD SE25 ....83 M2
  WBY/YAL ME18 ....125 K1
Hollands Av FOLKN CT19 ....311 J4
Hollands Cl GVE DA12 ....70 C4
Holland Wy BRXN/ST SW9 ....265 K4
Holland Wy HAYES BR2.........85 J6
Hollicondane Rd RAM CT11...17 F1
Hollies Av BFN/LL DA15 .....243 N1
Hollies Cl STRHM/NOR SW16...60 A5
The Hollies GVE DA12 ....69 P5
  HART DA3 ....68 G9
Hollingbourne Av BXLYHN DA7...45 H2
Hollingbourne Hl
  RMAID ME17 ....158 A8
Hollingbourne Rd HNHL SE24...60 A2
  EHAM E6 ....96 F3
Hollington Pl KEN/WIL TN24 ...2 D2
Hollingworth Rd
  MAID/SHEP ME15 ....186 C6
  STMC/STPC BR5 ....86 C4
Hollingworth Wy
  BH/WHM TN16 ....176 E2
Hollis Pl GRAYS RM17 ....32 B6
Hollman Gdns
  STRHM/NOR SW16 ....61 N2
Hollowfield Av GRAYS RM17...32 E5
Hollow La CANT CT1 ....166 D7
  LING RH7 ....235 L9

Hydes Orch HDCN TN27 247 P4
Hyde St DEPT SE8 25 K9
The Hyde RCANTW CT4 195 K1
Hyde V GNWCH SE10 42 A1
Hylton St WOOL/PLUM SE18 27 N7
Hyndewood FSTH SE23 61 K2
Hyndman St PECK SE15 24 E9
Hyperion Dr STRD ME2 71 P6
Hyson Rd BERM/RHTH SE16 24 E8
Hythe Av BXLYHN DA7 44 G1
Hythe Cl FOLK CT20 310 C6
STH/RUST TN4 240 D8
STMC/STPC BR5 87 K1
Hythe Pl SWCH CT13 201 P2
Hythe Rd HYTHE CT21 308 B3
KEN/WIL TN24 3 H4
LYDD TN29 326 G6
RASHE TN25 284 C4
SIT ME10 99 L9
THHTH CR7 60 D8
Hythe St DART DA1 46 E7

I

Ian's Wk HYTHE CT21 309 M4
Ibbotson Av CAN/RD E16 26 A2
Iberian Av WLGTN SM6 82 C8
Ibis Cl WSTB CT5 105 J8
Icehouse Wd OXTED RH8 175 J7
Ickleton Rd ELTH/MOT SE9 63 J3
Ida St POP/IOD E14 25 M2
Ide Hill Rd RSEV TN14 177 N8
Iden Cl HAYES BR2 62 C9
Iden Crs STPH/PW TN12 246 B7
Iden La HDCN TN27 220 A6
Iden Rd RYE TN31 338 E2
STRD ME2 72 C6
Idenwood Cl RHAM ME8 96 G8
Idleigh Court Rd HART DA3 91 L6
Idmiston Rd WNWD SE27 60 C2
Idol La MON EC3R 24 B3
Idonia St DEPT SE8 41 M1
Iffin La RCANTW CT4 196 D1
Ifield Cl MAID/SHEP ME15 186 C3
Ifield Wy GVE DA12 69 P5
Ightham By-Pass
BGR/WK TN15 150 F6
Ightham Rd ERITH DA8 45 J1
RTON TN11 180 F8
Ildersly Gv DUL SE21 60 D1
Ilderton Rd BERM/RHTH SE16 24 F9
Ilex Rd FOLKN CT19 310 C5
Ilex Wy STRHM/NOR SW16 60 A4
Ilfracombe Rd BMLY BR1 62 D2
Ilkley Cl NRWD SE19 * 60 D5
Ilkley Rd CAN/RD E16 26 D1
Illustrious Cl WALD ME5 95 M9
Imberhorne La EGRIN RH19 264 D9
Imberhorne Wy EGRIN RH19 264 E5
Imbert Cl NROM TN28 337 H7
Impala Gdns STH/RUST TN4 270 E2
Imperial Av IOS ME12 58 D9
Imperial Dr GVE DA12 70 B4
IOS ME12 80 C3
Imperial Pl CHST BR7 63 L7
Imperial Rd GILL ME7 7 H7
Imperial Wy ASH TN23 281 P1
CHST BR7 63 N2
Impton La WALD ME5 125 L5
Inca Dr ELTH/MOT SE9 43 M8
Ince Rd CANTW/ST CT2 137 L6
Inchmery Rd CAT SE6 61 P1
Inchwood CROY/NA CR0 84 E8
Independents Rd
BKHTH/KID SE3 42 D4
Indescon Ct POP/IOD E14 25 L5
India St TWRH EC3N 24 C2
Indigo Ms POP/IOD E14 * 25 M3
Indus Rd CHARL SE7 42 G1
Infant House
WOOL/PLUM SE18 * 43 J1
Ingatestone Rd SNWD SE25 83 N2
Ingham Cl SAND/SEL CR2 114 A3
Ingleborough La
BGR/WK TN15 151 N4
Ingleborough St BRXN/ST SW9 40 A3
Ingleby Rd CDW/CHF RM16 33 J6
Ingleby Wy CHST BR7 63 L4
Ingle Cl BRCH CT7 111 J6
Ingleden Cl SIT ME10 99 N6
Ingleden Park Rd TENT TN30 301 J6
Ingledew Rd
WOOL/PLUM SE18 27 L8
Inglefield Sq WAP E1W * 24 E4
Inglemere Rd FSTH SE23 61 K2
Ingle Rd CHAT ME4 95 L4
Ingleside Cl BECK BR3 61 N6
Ingleside Gv BKHTH/KID SE3 26 A9
Ingles La FOLK CT20 10 E4
Ingles Rd FOLK CT20 10 C5
Ingleton Av WELL DA16 44 C6
Ingleton St BRXN/ST SW9 40 A3
Inglewood CROY/NA CR0 114 B3
SWLY BR8 * 65 N8
Inglewood Cl POP/IOD E14 25 K7
Inglewood Copse BMLY BR1 63 J8
Inglewood Rd BXLYHN DA7 45 M5
Inglis Rd CROY/NA CR0 83 L5
Inglis St CMBW SE5 40 B2
Ingoldsby Rd BRCH CT7 110 E6
CANT CT1 166 C6
FOLKN CT19 311 H4
GVE DA12 50 A9
Ingram Rd DART DA1 46 E9
GILL ME7 96 B1
GRAYS RM17 32 D7
THHTH CR7 60 C7
Ingress Park Av GRH DA9 48 A6
Ingress Ter MEO DA13 * 68 D3
Inigo Jones Rd CHARL SE7 43 H1
Inner Lines GILL ME7 72 G9
Innes St PECK SE15 40 E1
Innes Yd CROY/NA CR0 83 H7
Institute Rd CHAT ME4 6 E5
FAV ME13 132 G6
Instone Rd DART DA1 46 D8
Inverary Ct RAM CT11 * 143 K3
Inverine Rd CHARL SE7 26 C8
Invermore Pl
WOOL/PLUM SE18 27 K7
Inverness Ter BRDST CT10 143 M1
Inverton Rd PECK SE15 41 K5
Invicta Cl CHST BR7 63 L4
Invicta Ct SIT ME10 99 N7
Invicta Pde SCUP DA14 * 64 D3
Invicta Rd BKHTH/KID SE3 42 E1
FOLKN CT19 310 G4
IOS ME12 57 L6
MARG CT9 112 G5
RDART DA2 47 H7
WSTB CT5 105 N5
Inville Rd WALW SE17 24 A8
Inwood Cl CROY/NA CR0 84 B6
Iona Cl CAT SE6 41 N8
WALD ME5 126 A4
Iona Rd MAID/SHEP ME15 185 M4
Ionia Wk GVE DA12 70 B2
Irchester St RAM CT11 17 H3
Irchester Vls RAM CT11 * 17 H3
Ireland Cl EHAM E6 26 G1
Irene Rd ORP BR6 86 G4
Ireton Pl GRAYS RM17 32 B7
Iris Av BXLY DA5 44 G7
Iris Cl CROY/NA CR0 84 A5
EHAM E6 26 F1
WALD ME5 125 M5
Iris Crs BXLYHN DA7 28 E9
Iron Bar La CANT CT1 5 F5
Iron Mill La DART DA1 45 P5
Iron Mill Pl DART DA1 45 P5
Ironmonger La LOTH EC2R 24 A2
Ironside Cl BERM/RHTH SE16 24 G5
WALD ME5 95 M6
Ironstones RRTW TN3 269 N5
Irvine Dr MARG CT9 113 H5
Irvine Gdns SOCK/AV RM15 31 J2
Irvine Rd HOO/HM ME3 71 K4
Irvine Wy ORP BR6 86 G4
Irving Wy SWLY BR8 65 M8
Irwell Est BERM/RHTH SE16 * 24 F5
Irwin Av WOOL/PLUM SE18 44 A1
Isabella Dr ORP BR6 86 D8
Isambard Ms POP/IOD E14 25 M6
Isambard Pl BERM/RHTH SE16 24 F4
Isis Cl HYTHE CT21 307 P4
Island Rd BERM/RHTH SE16 24 G7
CANTW/ST CT2 137 M7
RCANTE CT3 138 B9
Island Rw POP/IOD E14 25 J2
Island Wall WSTB CT5 105 K5
Island Wy East CHAT ME4 73 H6
Island Wy West CHAT ME4 73 H5
Isla Rd WOOL/PLUM SE18 27 K9
Islay Whf POP/IOD E14 * 25 M1
Islehurst Cl CHST BR7 63 L7
Islingham Farm Rd
HOO/HM ME3 72 C4
Ismays Rd BGR/WK TN15 180 E1
Istead Ri MEO DA13 69 K6
Itchingwood Common Rd
OXTED RH8 175 M9
Ivanhoe Rd CMBW SE5 40 F4
HB CT6 107 M2
WGOS CT8 111 M4
Ivedon Rd WELL DA16 44 E3
Ivens Wy RMAID ME17 188 E5
Iverhurst Cl BXLYHS DA6 44 F6
Iversgate Cl RHAM ME8 97 J4
Ivers Wy CROY/NA CR0 114 E2
Ives Rd CAN/RD E16 25 P1
TON TN9 210 C9
Ivor Gv ELTH/MOT SE9 43 M9
Ivory Cl FAV ME13 132 D4
Ivorydown BMLY BR1 62 E3
Ivy Bower Cl GRH DA9 47 P6
Ivychurch Cl PGE/AN SE20 61 H6
Ivychurch Gdns MARG CT9 113 K3
Ivy Church La STHWK SE1 * 24 C8
Ivychurch Rd LYDD TN29 335 J3
Ivy Cl DART DA1 46 G7
GVE DA12 69 N3
RFOLK CT18 287 H5
RMAID ME17 187 N9
Ivy Cottage Hl MSTR CT12 141 M5
Ivy Ct CANTW/ST CT2 136 D7
STHWK SE1 * 24 D8
Ivydale Rd BROCKY SE4 41 K4
Ivy House La SEV TN13 148 C2
Ivy House Rd WSTB CT5 105 N5
Ivy La CANT CT1 5 G5
RAM CT11 16 E5
RSEV TN14 147 M1
Ivymount Rd WNWD SE27 60 A2
Ivy Pl CANT CT1 4 C7
ROCH ME1 * 94 F4
Ivy Rd BROCKY SE4 41 M5
CAN/RD E16 26 B2
Ivy St RHAM ME8 97 J6
Ivy Wy FOLKN CT19 311 H4
Izane Rd BXLYHS DA6 45 H5

J

Jaarlen Rd LYDD TN29 342 A6
Jacinth Dr SIT ME10 99 K8
Jackass La GDST RH9 174 C7
HAYES BR2 115 L1
Jack Bailey Rw FAV ME13 * 134 B7
Jack Evans Ct SOCK/AV RM15 31 K2
Jacklin Cl WALD ME5 125 L2
Jackson Av ROCH ME1 95 K6
Jackson Cl GRH DA9 47 M6
RHAM ME8 96 F5
Jackson Rd CANT CT1 4 B6
HAYES BR2 85 P6
Jacksons La TENT TN30 301 H8
Jackson's Pl CROY/NA CR0 83 J5
Jackson St WOOL/PLUM SE18 27 H9
Jackson's Wy CROY/NA CR0 84 D7
Jacob Cl MARG CT9 112 D6
Jacob's La HOO/HM ME3 73 P1
Jacob St STHWK SE1 24 C5
Jacob Yd FAV ME13 * 132 G6
Jade Cl CAN/RD E16 26 E2
SIT ME10 99 K7
Jaffray Rd HAYES BR2 85 N1
Jaggard Wy STPH/PW TN12 246 B6
Jagger Cl RDART DA2 47 J8
Jago Cl WOOL/PLUM SE18 27 K9
Jago Wk CMBW SE5 40 D1
Jail La BH/WHM TN16 115 N9
Jamaica Rd STHWK SE1 24 C5
THHTH CR7 82 G3
Jamaica St WCHPL E1 24 F1
Jamaica Ter
MAID/BEAR ME14 155 M5
James Allchin Gdns
KEN/WIL TN24 253 J5
James Av BGR/WK TN15 * 120 B2
James Cl RCANTE CT3 170 E9
RFOLK CT18 286 G1
James Hall Gdns DEAL CT14 233 H6
James Haney Dr
KEN/WIL TN24 253 J4
James Joyes Wk HNHL SE24 * 40 B5
James Rd DART DA1 46 A8
STRD ME2 94 A4
James St ASH TN23 2 B3
CHAT ME4 6 C5
FOLKN CT19 11 F1
GILL ME7 7 J1
IOS ME12 57 M6
MAID/BEAR ME14 13 F2
RAM CT11 16 E5
ROCH ME1 19 G7
Jamestown Wy POP/IOD E14 25 N3
James Watt Wy ERITH DA8 29 L9
James Whatman Ct
MAID/SHEP ME15 * 13 K6
James Whatman Wy
MAID/BEAR ME14 12 D2
Jamuna Cl POP/IOD E14 25 H1
Jane St WCHPL E1 24 E2
Janet St POP/IOD E14 25 K6
Janeway Pl BERM/RHTH SE16 24 E5
Janeway St BERM/RHTH SE16 24 D5
Japonica Cl WALD ME5 125 P3
Jardine Rd WAP E1W 24 G3
Jarman's Fld RASHE TN25 224 A8
Jarrett Av STRD ME2 72 D5
Jarrett Cl BRXS/STRHM SW2 40 B9
Jarretts Cl RYE TN31 338 F7
Jarrow Rd BERM/RHTH SE16 24 F7
Jarvis Dr KEN/WIL TN24 283 K1
Jarvis La CRBK TN17 274 F7
Jarvis Pl TENT TN30 301 J4
Jarvis Rd EDUL SE22 40 E5
Jarvist Pl DEAL CT14 263 J2
Jasmine Cl E/WMAL ME19 153 N4
HAYES BR2 86 C6
RCANTW CT4 195 L2
Jasmine Ct LEE/GVPK SE12 42 E7
Jasmine Gdns CROY/NA CR0 84 E7
Jasmine Gv PGE/AN SE20 61 H7
Jasmine Pl RCANTE CT3 * 169 K8
Jasmine Rd E/WMAL ME19 153 N4
Jasmine Vls STPH/PW TN12 * 245 H4
Jason Cl CDW/CHF RM16 33 M2
Jason Wk ELTH/MOT SE9 63 L3
Jasper Av ROCH ME1 95 H4
Jasper Rd CAN/RD E16 26 E2
NRWD SE19 60 F5
Javelin Rd E/WMAL ME19 152 G9
Jay Gdns CHST BR7 63 K3
Jayne Wk WSTB CT5 105 J8
Jefferson Cl ASH TN23 252 C8
Jefferson Dr RHAM ME8 96 F5
Jefferson Rd IOS ME12 57 M7
Jefferstone Gdns
LYDD TN29 337 K1
Jefferstone La LYDD TN29 337 H2
Jeffery St GILL ME7 7 H1
Jeffrey Cl STPH/PW TN12 246 B5
Jeffrey St MAID/BEAR ME14 13 G3
Jeken Rd ELTH/MOT SE9 42 G5
Jelf Rd BRXS/STRHM SW2 40 A6
Jellicoe Av GVE DA12 69 N2
Jellicoe Cl KEN/WIL TN24 283 K1
Jemmett La RASHE TN25 283 N4
Jenkins' Dl CHAT ME4 6 C7
Jenkins Dr MAID/SHEP ME15 186 B6
Jenner Cl SCUP DA14 64 C3
Jenner Rd ROCH ME1 95 H2
Jenners Cl LING RH7 234 G5
Jenner's Wy LYDD TN29 337 K2
Jenner Wy DIT/AY ME20 124 E7
Jennett Rd CROY/NA CR0 82 F7
Jennifer Ct HOO/HM ME3 * 73 L2
Jennifer Gdns MARG CT9 113 H5
Jennifer Rd BMLY BR1 62 D2
Jenningham Dr
CDW/CHF RM16 32 B4
Jennings Rd EDUL SE22 40 F7
Jenningtree Rd ERITH DA8 46 B1
Jenningtree Wy BELV DA17 29 H5
Jenny La LING RH7 234 F5
Jenson Wy NRWD SE19 60 F6
Jenton Av BXLYHN DA7 44 G2
Jephson St CMBW SE5 40 D2
Jeremiah St POP/IOD E14 25 L2
Jerningham Rd NWCR SE14 41 L3
Jerome Rd DIT/AY ME20 123 N9
Jerome St WCHPL E1 24 C1
Jerrard St LEW SE13 41 P4
Jersey Cl RASHE TN25 252 F1
Jersey Dr STMC/STPC BR5 86 E3
Jersey La RCANTW CT4 196 B5
Jersey Rd CAN/RD E16 26 D1
STRD ME2 72 A7
Jerviston Gdns
STRHM/NOR SW16 60 A5
Jervois House
WOOL/PLUM SE18 * 43 J1
Jeskyns Rd MEO DA13 69 P8
Jesmond Rd CDW/CHF RM16 32 E4
CROY/NA CR0 83 L4
Jesmond St FOLKN CT19 10 E2
Jessamine Pl RDART DA2 47 J8
Jessamine Ter SWLY BR8 * 65 L7
Jesse's Hl RCANTW CT4 227 M1
Jessett Cl ERITH DA8 29 J7
Jessica Ms CANT CT1 5 H2
SIT ME10 99 M7
Jesson Cl LYDD TN29 337 M1
Jessops Wy MTCM CR4 82 B3
Jessup Cl WOOL/PLUM SE18 27 K7
Jesuit Cl CANTW/ST CT2 136 F9
Jetty Rd HOO/HM ME3 54 B9
IOS ME12 57 H5
IOS ME12 80 C4
Jetty Wk GRAYS RM17 32 B9
Jevington Wy LEE/GVPK SE12 42 F9
Jewell Gv STPH/PW TN12 245 J4
Jewels Hl WARL CR6 115 K6
Jewry La CANT CT1 4 E4
Jewry St TWRH EC3N 24 C2
Jews Wk SYD SE26 61 H3
Jeyes Rd GILL ME7 7 H5
Jezreels Rd GILL ME7 7 K7
Jim Bradley Cl
WOOL/PLUM SE18 27 H7
Jiniwin Rd ROCH ME1 95 J7
Joan Crs ELTH/MOT SE9 43 H8
Jocelyn St PECK SE15 40 G2
Jockey La CRBK TN17 298 A2
Jodane Rd DEPT SE8 25 J7
Jodrell Wy WTHK RM20 31 J8
Johannesburg Rd
DVE/WH CT16 291 K3
John Badger Cl
KEN/WIL TN24 253 H4
John Dutton Wy
KEN/WIL TN24 * 253 H5
John Felton Rd
BERM/RHTH SE16 * 24 D5
John Fisher St WCHPL E1 24 D3
John Hall Cl FAV ME13 132 E3
John Harrison Wy
BERM/RHTH SE16 24 G6
GNWCH SE10 26 A6
John Maurice Cl STHWK SE1 24 A7
John McKenna Wk
BERM/RHTH SE16 * 24 D6
John Newington Cl
KEN/WIL TN24 253 H4
John Penn St LEW SE13 41 P2
John Rennie Wk WAP E1W 24 E3
John Roll Wy
BERM/RHTH SE16 24 D6
John Ruskin St CMBW SE5 40 B1
Johns Cl HART DA3 91 J2
Johnsdale OXTED RH8 175 J5
John's Gn SWCH CT13 201 M4
John Silkin La DEPT SE8 24 G8
Johnson Av GILL ME7 73 J8
Johnson Cl GVW DA11 69 H2
KEN/WIL TN24 283 K1
Johnson Ct FAV ME13 132 E4
Johnson Rd CROY/NA CR0 83 J4
HAYES BR2 85 N2
SIT ME10 129 L1
Johnsons Av RSEV TN14 118 A4
Johnson St WCHPL E1 24 F2
Johnsons Wy GRH DA9 48 A7
Johnsons Whf GRH DA9 * 47 N5
Johnson Wy IOS ME12 58 A9
Johns Pl WCHPL E1 24 E2
John's Rd BH/WHM TN16 145 N5
MEO DA13 92 A2
John's Ter CROY/NA CR0 83 K5
John St BRDST CT10 * 113 N9
GRAYS RM17 32 D9
MAID/BEAR ME14 155 M6
ROCH ME1 19 G7
SNWD SE25 83 M1
STH/RUST TN4 270 D3
John Tapping Cl DEAL CT14 232 G8
John William Cl WTHK RM20 31 N8
John Williams Cl NWCR SE14 24 G9
John Wilson St
WOOL/PLUM SE18 27 H7
John Wooley Cl LEW SE13 * 42 C5
Joiners Arms Yd CMBW SE5 * 40 D2
Joiners Ct CHAT ME4 95 N4
Joiner St STHWK SE1 * 24 A4
Jointon Rd FOLK CT20 10 B5
Jonson Cl MTCM CR4 82 A1
Jordan Cl MAID/SHEP ME15 186 B6
The Jordans EGRIN RH19 265 H8
Joseph Hardcastle Cl
NWCR SE14 41 K1
Joseph St BOW E3 25 J1
Joshua St POP/IOD E14 25 M2
Josling Cl GRAYS RM17 32 A9
Joslin Rd PUR RM19 30 F8
Joss Gap Rd BRDST CT10 113 N4
Jowett St PECK SE15 40 F1
Joyce Cl CRBK TN17 297 P3
Joyce Green La DART DA1 46 D2
Joyden's Wood Rd BXLY DA5 65 M3
Joyes Cl DVE/WH CT16 261 H9
FOLKN CT19 311 H4
Joyes Rd DVE/WH CT16 261 H9
FOLKN CT19 311 H4
Joy La WSTB CT5 105 H7
Joy Rd GVE DA12 49 N9
Joy Wd RMAID ME17 186 A6
Jubilee Cl GRH DA9 47 M7
HYTHE CT21 308 C7
Jubilee Crs BGR/WK TN15 150 F6
GVE DA12 70 A1
QBOR ME11 77 H2
Jubilee Fld TENT TN30 332 B1
Jubilee Ri BGR/WK TN15 149 L6
Jubilee Rd DEAL CT14 202 A7
ORP BR6 117 P1
RCANTE CT3 168 C8
SWCH CT13 201 N2
WTHK RM20 31 L9
Jubilee St SIT ME10 99 M9
WCHPL E1 24 F2
Jubilee Ter GILL ME7 73 J9
The Jubilee GNWCH SE10 * 41 P1
Jubilee Wy DVE/WH CT16 291 P5
SCUP DA14 64 C1
Jubilee Wy (Elevated Rd)
DVE/WH CT16 9 J2
Judd Rd FAV ME13 132 D6
TON TN9 240 E2
Jude St CAN/RD E16 26 A2
Judeth Gdns GVE DA12 70 A4
Judges Ter EGRIN RH19 265 H8
Judkins Cl WALD ME5 95 P8
Juglans Rd ORP BR6 87 H5
Julian Pl POP/IOD E14 25 L8
Julian Rd FOLKN CT19 10 B3
ORP BR6 117 H1
Julians Cl SEV TN13 20 C7
Julians Wy SEV TN13 20 C7
Julian Tayler Pth FSTH SE23 * 61 H1
Julie Cl BRDST CT10 113 M7
Julien Pl KEN/WIL TN24 253 K9
Juliette Wy PUR RM19 30 C5
Junction Ap LEW SE13 42 A4
Junction Rd DART DA1 46 D7
GILL ME7 96 A2
RBTBR TN32 328 B3
Juniper Cl ASH TN23 252 B7
BH/WHM TN16 145 P2
CANT CT1 166 F6
MAIDW ME16 154 G6
RTWE/PEM TN2 240 G8
WALD ME5 125 M1
Juniper La EHAM E6 26 F1
Juniper St WCHPL E1 * 24 F3
Juno Wy NWCR SE14 24 G9
Jupiter La ASH TN23 282 B3
Jurgens Rd PUR RM19 * 30 F7
Jury's Gap Rd LYDD TN29 341 P7
LYDD TN29 344 G1
Jury St GVE DA12 49 M7
Jutland Cl HOO/HM ME3 55 H1
Jutland Rd CAT SE6 42 A8

K

Kake St RCANTW CT4 225 M3
Kale Rd ERITHM DA18 28 C5
Kangley Bridge Rd SYD SE26 61 M4
Karen Ct BMLY BR1 62 D7
ELTH/MOT SE9 42 G6
Karloff Wy HOO/HM ME3 72 B5
Kashgar Rd WOOL/PLUM SE18 27 N8
Kashmir Rd CHARL SE7 43 H1
Katharine St CROY/NA CR0 83 H7
Katherine Cl BERM/RHTH SE16 24 G4
Katherine Ct WALD ME5 125 N3
Katherine Gdns ELTH/MOT SE9 43 H5
Katherine Rd EDEN TN8 236 D1
Kay St WELL DA16 44 D2
Kearsney Abbey Vls
DVE/WH CT16 * 290 E3
Keary Rd SWCM DA10 48 D8
Keat Farm Cl HB CT6 108 C5
Keating Cl ROCH ME1 94 F3
Keats Av CAN/RD E16 26 C4
Keats Cl STHWK SE1 * 24 C7
Keats Gdns TIL RM18 49 M3
Keats Pl EGRIN RH19 264 G7
Keats Rd BELV DA17 29 H6
DIT/AY ME20 153 N1
WELL DA16 44 A2
Keats Wy CROY/NA CR0 83 P3
Kechill Gdns HAYES BR2 85 K4
Keddow's Cl HYTHE CT21 308 C7
Kedleston Dr STMC/STPC BR5 86 G3
Keeble Cl WOOL/PLUM SE18 * 27 J9
Keedonwood Rd BMLY BR1 62 D4
Keefe Cl WALD ME5 125 J4
Keel Cl BERM/RHTH SE16 24 G4
Keeley Ms GILL ME7 * 96 B3
Keeley Rd CROY/NA CR0 83 H6
Keel Gdns STH/RUST TN4 240 B9
Keeling Rd ELTH/MOT SE9 43 H6
Keemor Cl WOOL/PLUM SE18 * 43 L1
Keen's Rd CROY/NA CR0 83 H8
Keeper's Hl RCANTW CT4 198 A5
The Keep BKHTH/KID SE3 42 E3
Keesey St WALW SE17 24 A9
Keetons Rd BERM/RHTH SE16 24 E6
Keightley Dr ELTH/MOT SE9 43 N9
Keith Av EYN DA4 67 H5
MSTR CT12 142 F4
Keith Park Crs BH/WHM TN16 115 M6
Kelbrook Rd BKHTH/KID SE3 43 J3
Kelchers La RTON TN11 212 A5
Kellaway Rd BKHTH/KID SE3 42 G3
WALD ME5 125 M3
Kellerton Rd LEW SE13 42 C6
Kellett Rd BRXS/STRHM SW2 40 A5
Kelling Gdns CROY/NA CR0 82 G4
Kellner Rd THMD SE28 27 N6
Kelly Av PECK SE15 40 F2
Kelly Dr GILL ME7 73 J8
Kelmore Gv EDUL SE22 40 G5
Kelsall Cl BKHTH/KID SE3 42 F3
Kelsey La BECK BR3 61 N9
Kelsey Park Av BECK BR3 61 P9
Kelsey Park Rd BECK BR3 61 N8
Kelsey Rd STMC/STPC BR5 64 D8
Kelsey Sq BECK BR3 61 N8
Kelsey Wy BECK BR3 61 N9
Kelso Dr GVE DA12 70 B3
Kelvedon Rd DEAL CT14 233 H7
Kelvin Cl TONN TN10 210 G3
Kelvin Gdns CROY/NA CR0 82 D4

Kelvin Gv SYD SE26 ....61 H2
Kelvington Ct CROY/NA CR0 ....84 B4
Kelvington Rd PECK SE15 ....41 K6
Kelvin Pde ORP BR6 ....86 F5
Kelvin Rd TIL RM18 ....49 L3
  WELL DA16 ....48 A4
Kemble Cl RTWE/PEM TN2 ....271 H1
Kemble Dr HAYES BR2 ....85 F7
Kemble Rd CROY/NA CR0 ....83 H1
  FSTH SE23 ....81 K9
Kembleside Rd
  BH/WHM TN16 ....145 M5
Kemerton Rd BECK BR3 ....61 P8
  CMBW SE5 ....40 C4
  CROY/NA CR0 ....83 L4
Kemnal Rd CHST BR7 ....63 N5
Kemp Cl WALD ME5 ....125 K1
Kemps Pl RASHE TN25 * 223 P8
Kemp Gdns CROY/NA CR0 ....83 H3
Kemp Rd WSTB CT5 ....106 B4
Kemps Dr POP/IOD E14 ....42 C6
Kempthorne Rd DEPT SE8 ....25 H7
Kempt St WOOL/PLUM SE18 ....27 H9
Kempton Cl ERITH DA8 ....29 H9
  WALD ME5 ....125 P2
Kempton Wk CROY/NA CR0 ....84 B3
Kempt St WOOL/PLUM SE18 ....27 H9
Kemsdale Rd FAV ME13 ....134 A7
Kemsing Cl BXLY DA5 ....44 G8
  THHTH CR7 * 83 H1
Kemsing Gdns CANTW/ST CT2 .....136 C9
Kemsing Rd BGR/WK TN15 ....150 E2
  LEW SE13 ....26 B8
Kemsley Cl GRH DA9 ....47 P7
  CVW DA11 ....69 K3
Kemsley Rd BH/WHM TN16 ....145 N4
Kemsley Street Rd
  MAIDW/BEAR ME14 ....126 F4
Kenardington Rd
  RASHW TN26 ....322 E4
Kenbrook Rd KEN/WIL TN24 ....252 F2
Kenbury St CMBW SE5 ....40 C3
Kendal Cl CMBW SE5 ....40 B1
  RAIN CT11 * 142 G6
Kendal Dr TON TN9 ....210 F8
Kendale CDW/CHF RM16 ....33 J6
Kendal Av BECK BR3 ....61 L8
  E/WMAL ME19 ....153 K9
Kendall Rd BECK BR3 ....61 L8
  WOOL/PLUM SE18 ....47 K4
Kendal Meadow WSTB CT5 ....106 C5
Kendal Pk STH/RUST TN4 ....270 B3
Kendal Rd BRDST CT10...................113 M8
Kendal Wy RHAM ME8 ....96 G6
Kender St NWCR SE14 ....41 J1
Kenfield Rd RCANTW CT4 ....195 P5
Kenilworth Cl RDV CT15 ....292 F1
Kenilworth Ct SIT ME10 ....99 K9
Kenilworth Dr RHAM ME8 ....96 G8
Kenilworth Gdns
  WOOL/PLUM SE18 ....43 M3
Kenilworth Rd PGE/AN SE20 ....61 K7
  STMC/STPC BR5 ....86 D5
Kenley Cl BXLY DA5 ....45 J8
  CHST BR7 ....64 A9
Kenley Gdns THHTH CR7 ....82 C1
Kenmare Rd THHTH CR7 ....82 F3
Kenmere Rd WELL DA16 ....48 D4
Kennard Cl ROCH ME1 ....94 E4
Kennard St CAN/RD E16 ....98 F9
Kenneys Av CHAT ME4 ....95 L4
Kennedy Cl FAV ME13 ....132 C4
  STMC/STPC BR5 ....86 E5
Kennedy Gdns SEVT TN13 ....149 H8
Kennedy Rd BARK IG11 ....79 H6
Kennedy Wk WALW SE17 * 24 A7
Kennel Barn Rd RSIT ME9 ....128 D8
Kennel Hl RDV CT15 ....260 F2
Kennelling Rd FAV ME13 ....191 J7
Kennel Wood Crs
  CROY/NA CR0 ....114 G5
Kennet Sq MTCM CR4 ....60 A4
  TONN TN10 ....210 F5
Kennet St WAP E1W 24 A1
Kennet Dr DEAL CT14 ....232 F7
Kennett La RASHE TN25 ....285 P7
Kenning St BERM/RHTH SE16 ....24 F5
Kennington Cl
  MAID/SHEP ME15 ....186 C3
  RHAM ME8 ....96 E2
Kennington Pk KEN/WIL TN24 ....252 C7
Kennington Rd
  KEN/WIL TN24 ....253 K7
Kensington Ct CANT CT1 ....167 H4
  IOS ME12 ....78 B1
  KEN/WIL TN24 ....2 C2
  MAID/SHEP ME15 ....185 P2
  SIT ME10 ....129 L2
  WELL DA16 ....48 A6
Kent Cl BGR/WK TN15 * 120 B2
  ORP BR6 ....116 F1
  ROCH ME1 ....95 H6
  STPH/PW TN12 ....243 H5
  STRHM/NOR SW16 ....82 D7
Kent Gdns BRCH CT7 ....110 G6
Kent Gate Wy CROY/NA CR0 ....114 C1
Kent Hatch Rd OXTED RH8 ....175 M6
Kent House La BECK BR3 ....61 L5
Kent House Rd BECK BR3 ....61 L6
Kentish Gdns RTWE/PEM TN2 ......270 B8
Kentish Rd BELV DA17 ....28 F7
Kentish Wy BMLY BR1 ....62 F8
Kentlea Rd THMD SE28 ....27 M5
Kentmere Av RAM CT11 ....142 E5
Kentmere Rd
  WOOL/PLUM SE18 ....43 M3
Kenton Gdns MSTR CT12 ....141 J6
Kent Pl WALD ME5 ....17 H4
Kent Rd DART DA1 ....46 E7
  FOLKN CT19 ....310 B4
  GRAYS RM17 ....50 B4

CVW DA11 ....49 L9
HART DA3 ....68 B8
IOS ME12 ....57 K7
MARG CT9 ....112 G5
SNOD ME6 ....123 P7
STH/RUST TN4 ....270 D2
STMC/STPC BR5 ....87 J3
STRD ME2 ....93 P8
WWKM BR4 ....48 A4
Kent St WBY/YAL ME18....................182 F1
  WSTB CT5 ....105 L6
Kent Ter HOO/HM ME3 * 51 M9
  MEO DA13 * 92 E7
  RAM CT11 ....17 H4
  RHAM ME8 ....97 M4
Kent Vw SOCK/AV RM15 ....30 F5
Kent View Dr IOS ME12 ....79 K6
Kentwell Cl BROCKY SE4 * 41 L5
Kenward Ct RTON TN11 ....211 P2
Kenward Rd ELTH/MOT SE9 ....42 G6
  MAIDW ME14 ....155 H7
  WBY/YAL ME18 ....185 H8
Kenwood Av SART DA3 ....68 G9
  WALD ME5 ....125 M1
Kenwood Dr BECK BR3 ....62 A9
Kenwyn Rd DART DA1 ....46 B6
Kenya Rd CHARL SE7 ....43 H1
Kenya Ter MAID/BEAR ME14 ....155 M5
Kerbey St POP/IOD E14 ....25 L2
Kerfield Crs CMBW SE5 ....40 D2
Kerfield Pl CMBW SE5 ....40 D2
Kerry Av PUR RM19 ....30 C5
Kerry Ct CAN/RD E16 ....26 D3
Kerry Hill Wy
  MAID/BEAR ME14 ....155 K6
Kerry Pth NWCR SE14 * 25 J9
Kerry Rd CDW/CHF RM16 ....32 E4
  NWCR SE14 * 25 J9
Kershaw Cl CDW/CHF RM16............31 M6
Kerton Rd LYDD TN29 ....347 K1
Kesteven Cl STRD ME2 ....93 P9
Keston Av HAYES BR2 ....85 M9
  KCHT RM20 * 13 H9
Keston Cl WELL DA16 ....44 E1
Keston Ct RHAM ME8 * 96 D4
Keston Gdns HAYES BR2 ....85 M8
Keston Park Cl HAYES BR2 ....86 A8
Keston Rd PECK SE15 ....40 G4
  THHTH CR7 ....82 B1
Kestrel Av EHAM E6 ....26 F1
  HNHL SE24 ....40 B6
Kestrel Cl SIT ME10 ....129 P3
Kestrel Ct NWCR SE14 * 41 J9
Kestrel Rd WALD ME5 ....125 P3
Kestrel Wy CROY/NA CR0 ....114 G3
Keswick Cl TON TN9 ....210 F8
Keswick Dr MAIDW ME16 ....155 K8
Keswick Rd BXLYHN DA7 ....45 J3
  ORP BR6 ....86 G5
  SIT ME10 ....130 B2
  WWKM BR4 ....85 H6
Ketridge La WBY/YAL ME18.............183 L1
Kettle Cl RFOLK CT18 ....288 E7
Kettle Hl FAV ME13 ....161 L8
Kettle Rd FAV ME13 ....161 K7
Kettle La MAID/SHEP ME15 ....184 D4
Kettlewell Ct SWLY BR8 ....65 P8
Kevin Dr RAM CT11 ....142 G6
Kevington Cl STMC/STPC BR5 ....86 C1
Kevington Dr CHST BR7 ....64 C6
Kewlands MAID/BEAR ME14 ....155 P6
Keycol Hl RSIT ME9 ....128 F9
Keyes Av CHAT ME4 ....95 L4
Keyes Pl TON TN9 ....240 C2
Keyes Pl FOLKN CT19 ....311 H4
Keyes Rd DART DA1 ....46 G5
Keymer Cl BH/WHM TN16 ....145 M1
Keynsham Gdns
  ELTH/MOT SE9 ....43 J6
Keynsham Rd ELTH/MOT SE9 ....43 H6
Keyse Rd STHWK SE1 ....24 C6
The Keys RFOLK CT18 ....288 F7
Keys Sq SIT ME10 ....99 H9
Keyworth Cl STPH/PW TN12 ....242 C3
Keyworth Ms CANT CT1 * 5 H1
Kezia St DEPT SE8 ....25 H8
Khartoum Pl CVE DA12 ....49 N7
Khartoum Rd CHAT ME4 ....6 D1
Khartoum Sq DVE/WH CT16 ....291 H1
Khyber Rd GILL ME7 ....73 H8
Kibbles La STH/RUST TN4 ....240 B9
Kidbrooke Gdns
  BKHTH/KID SE3 ....42 A3
Kidbrooke Gv BKHTH/KID SE3 ....42 A2
Kidbrooke La ELTH/MOT SE9 ....43 J5
Kidbrooke Park Cl
  BKHTH/KID SE3 ....42 B2
Kidbrooke Park Rd
  ELTH/MOT SE9 ....42 F6
Kidbrooke Wy BKHTH/KID SE3 ....42 F5
Kidderminster Pl
  CROY/NA CR0 ....82 C5
Kidderminster Rd
  CROY/NA CR0 ....82 C5
Kidd Pl CHARL SE7 ....44 A6
Kilbride Ct BRDST CT10 * 143 L3
Kildare Rd CAN/RD E16 ....26 B1
Kilgour Rd FSTH SE23 ....41 L7
Kilburns Mill Cl WLGTN SM6 ....82 A6
Kilearn Rd CAT SE6 ....42 D1
Killewarren Wy
  STMC/STPC BR5 ....87 K4
Killick Cl SEV TN13 ....148 D6
Killick Rd HOO/HM ME3 ....73 K2
Killip Ct CAN/RD E16 ....26 C1
Kilmarlin Av
  STRHM/NOR SW16 ....60 A9
Kilmorie Rd FSTH SE23 ....42 A1
Kiln Barn Rd DIT/AY ME20 ....154 B4
Kilnbridge Ct
  MAID/SHEP ME15 ....184 G4
Kiln Cl RASHE TN25 ....222 E1
  SIT ME10 ....129 P2
Kilndown GVE DA12 ....69 N5
Kilndown Cl ASH TN23 ....282 B2
  MAIDW ME14 ....155 H5

Kilndown Gdns
  CANTW/ST CT2 ....136 F9
  MARG CT9 ....113 K3
Kiln Dr RYE TN31 ....338 E4
Kilner St POP/IOD E14 ....25 K1
Kiln Fld TENT TN30 ....301 K8
Kiln La MAIDW TN26 ....280 E4
  RTON TN11 ....235 K9
Kiln Rd RASHE TN25 ....306 A3
Kilnspray Br RSIT ME9 ....77 J8
Kilnstow RSEV TN14 ....117 N7
Kimball Pl ELTH/MOT SE9 ....42 C5
Kimberley Av PECK SE15 ....41 K4
Kimberley Cl DVE/WH CT16 ....291 K4
Kimberley Dr SCUP DA14 ....64 F1
Kimberley Gv WSTB CT5 ....104 G8
Kimberley Rd BECK BR3 ....61 K8
  CROY/NA CR0 ....7 K6
  GILL ME7 ....7 K6
  MSTR CT12 ....142 D7
Kimbolton Cl LEE/GVPK SE12 ....42 D7
Kimmeridge Rd ELTH/MOT SE9 ......63 J3
Kimpton Rd CMBW SE5 ....40 E2
Kinburn St BERM/RHTH SE16 * 24 H1
Kincaid Rd PECK SE15 ....41 H1
Kincraig Dr SEV TN13 ....148 F6
Kinder Cl THMD SE28 ....28 B3
Kindersley Cl EGRIN RH19 ....265 L8
Kinfauns Rd BRXS/STRHM SW2 .....60 A1
King Alfred Av CAT SE6 ....42 A6
King Arthur Cl PECK SE15 ....41 J1
King Arthur Dr MSTR CT12 ....142 L6
King Arthur's Dr STRD ME2 ....72 A6
King Charles Ter WAP E1W * 24 E3
Kingcup Cl CROY/NA CR0 ....84 A5
King David La WCHPL E1 ....24 F3
King Edward Av BRDST CT10 ....113 M9
  DART DA1 ....46 D7
  HB CT6 ....107 N2
King Edward Dr
  CDW/CHF RM16 ....32 F6
King Edward Rd BRCH CT7 ....95 L4
  CHAT ME4 ....95 L4
  DEAL CT14 ....233 H1
  GILL ME7 ....7 J6
  GRH DA9 ....47 N6
  MAID/SHEP ME15 ....185 L1
  RAM CT11 ....16 B4
  ROCH ME1 ....19 F6
King Edward's Rd
  SLH/COR SS17 ....34 C1
King Edward St WSTB CT5 ....105 L8
Kingfield St POP/IOD E14 ....25 M7
Kingfisher Cl HYTHE CT21 ....289 K4
Kingfisher Cl KEN/WIL TN24 ....283 K1
  MARG CT9 ....112 A5
  RSIT ME9 ....99 M2
  STMC/STPC BR5 ....87 L1
  THMD SE28 ....28 B3
  WSTB CT5 ....105 K7
Kingfisher Ct HB CT6 ....107 J3
Kingfisher Dr GRH DA9 ....47 N6
  WALD ME5 ....95 P7
Kingfisher Gdns
  SAND/SEL CR2 ....114 A4
Kingfisher Ri EGRIN RH19 ....265 J8
Kingfisher Rd DIT/AY ME20 ....153 N2
Kingfisher St EHAM E6 ....26 F1
Kingfisher Wlk WBRDST CT10 * 113 L8
Kingfisher Wy CROY/NA CR0 ....84 A2
King Gdns CROY/NA CR0 ....82 A8
King Garth Ms FSTH SE23 ....61 J1
King George Av CAN/RD E16 ....125 K1
King George St GNWCH SE10 ....42 A1
King George VI Av TIL RM18 ....34 A7
King George VI Av TIL RM18 ....34 A7
King Harolds Wy BXLYHN DA7 ....44 F1
King Henry Ms ORP BR6 ....86 G9
King Henry's Dr
  CROY/NA CR0 ....114 F3
King Henry Ter WAP E1W * 24 E3
King Hl E/WMAL ME19 ....153 H8
King John St WCHPL E1 ....24 C1
King John's Wk ELTH/MOT SE9 ....43 J8
Kinglake Est WALW SE17 * 24 B8
Kinglake St WALW SE17 * 24 B8
King Lear's Wy DVW CT17 * 313 J1
King & Queen Cl
  ELTH/MOT SE9 ....63 J3
King & Queen Wharf
  BERM/RHTH SE16 * 24 G4
Kings Acre MAID/SHEP ME15 ....186 D2
Kingsand Rd LEE/GVPK SE12 ....62 E1
King's Arms Yd LOTH EC2R 24 A2
King's Av RAIN TN30 ....2 A3
  BMLY BR1 ....62 E1
  BRCH CT7 ....110 E5
  BRDST CT10 ....113 N8
  MSTR CT12 ....142 G3
  ROCH ME1 ....19 K1
  RYE TN31 ....338 G6
  SWCH CT13 ....202 E5
  WSTB CT5 ....105 M5
King's Bastion GILL ME7 ....6 E3
Kingsbridge Cl POP/IOD E14 ....25 K7
Kings Cha KEN/WIL TN24 ....253 K7
Kings Cl DART DA1 ....46 B6
  DEAL CT14 ....263 H3
Kings Copse EGRIN RH19 * 265 J8
Kingscote Rd CROY/NA CR0 ....83 N4
Kingscote St BLKFR EC4V * 24 H3
Kingsdale Rd PGE/AN SE20 ....61 K7
  WOOL/PLUM SE18 ....27 N9
Kingsdon Sq NRWD SE19 ....60 D4
King St CANT CT1 ....7 J3
  CANTW/ST CT2 ....137 L9
  CHAT ME4 ....6 D4
  DEAL CT14 ....233 J5
  DVE/WH CT16 ....8 D4

GVE DA12 ....50 B9
MARG CT9 .... 12 B4
WSTB CT5 ....105 N4
Kingsdown Hl DEAL CT14 ....263 H4
Kingsdown Pk DEAL CT14 * 263 J3
  WSTB CT5 ....105 N4
Kingsdown Rd DEAL CT14 ....233 J7
  RDV CT15 ....262 E9
  RSIT ME9 ....160 B1
Kings Dr GVE DA12 ....69 M2
Kingsferry Br RSIT ME9 ....77 J8
Kingsfield Rd HB CT6 ....107 K8
Kingsfield Ter DART DA1 * 46 D7
Kingsford St KEN/WIL TN24 ....283 N2
Kingsford Ter ASH TN23 * 282 D2
Kingsgate Av BRDST CT10 ....113 L4
Kingsgate Bay Rd
  BRDST CT10 ....113 M3
Kingsgate Cl BXLYHN DA7 ....44 C2
  MAIDW ME16 ....155 H8
  STMC/STPC BR5 ....64 B7
Kingsgate Gdns CANT CT1 * 136 E4
Kingsgate Rd KEN/WIL TN24 ....252 C4
Kingsgate Rd KEN/WIL TN24 ....252 C4
Kingslawn Cl FSTH SE23 ....61 H1
Kings Head Aly JOS ME12 * 42 A4
Kings Head Rd BECK BR5 ....61 K6
King's Highway
  WOOL/PLUM SE18...........................27 N9
Kings Hill Av E/WMAL ME19 ....153 H8
Kingshill Dr HOO/HM ME3 ....73 L1
Kingsholm Gdns
  ELTH/MOT SE9 ....43 H5
Kingshurst Rd LEE/GVPK SE12 ....42 E8
Kingsland La TENT TN30 ....320 D9
Kingsland Gdns ELTH/MOT SE9 ......43 J8
Kings Keep HAYES BR2 * 62 C9
Kingsland Gdns DEAL CT14 ....232 D5
Kingsland Hollow LYDD TN29 ....337 M1
Kingsland La RASHW TN26 ....219 M9
  RASHE TN25 ....252 C2
Kings La STPH/PW TN12 ....244 B2
Kingsleigh Wk HAYES BR2 ....85 J1
Kingsley Cl DART DA1 ....46 G6
Kingsley Ms CHST BR7 ....63 M5
  WAP E1W * 24 E3
Kingsley Rd CROY/NA CR0 ....82 F5
  MAID/SHEP ME15 ....13 G6
  ORP BR6 ....116 G1
  WALD ME5 ....125 P5
Kingsley Wk CDW/CHF RM16 ....33 H7
Kings Orch ELTH/MOT SE9 ....43 J7
Kingsley Wood Dr
  ELTH/MOT SE9 ....63 K2
Kingslyn Crs NRWD SE19 ....60 E7
Kingsman Dr CDW/CHF RM16 ....32 F4
Kingsman St
  WOOL/PLUM SE18 ....26 C7
Kingsmarsh La LYDD TN29 ....336 B9
Kingsmead BH/WHM TN16 ....145 N1
  FOLKN CT19 ....310 E4
Kingsmead Ct
  CANTW/ST CT2 * 166 F2
Kings Meadow KEN/WIL TN24 ....255 H2
Kingsmead Pk
  BRXS/STRHM SW2 ....60 A1
Kings Ms CANT CT1 * 5 F2
  RAM CT11 * 16 D4
Kings Mill Ct SIT ME10 ....99 M9
Kingsnorth Gdns FOLK CT20 ....10 B4
Kingsnorth Rd ASH TN25 ....282 D2
  FAV ME13 ....132 F7
  RHAM ME8 ....96 F2
Kingsoak Ms WALD ME5 ....125 L1
Kings Orch ELTH/MOT SE9 ....43 J7
  ROCH ME1 ....19 G5
Kings Pde ASH TN23 * 282 C2
King's Pk CANT CT1 ....5 J3
Kings Reach
  MAID/SHEP ME15 ....186 A3
Kingsridge Gdns DART DA1 ....46 E6
Kings Rd BH/WHM TN16 ....145 M2
  BRCH CT7 ....111 H7
  DVW CT17 ....291 H6
  FAV ME13 ....132 F6
  FOLK CT20 ....310 A5
  IOS ME12 ....58 D9
  ORP BR6 ....86 G8
  RAM CT11 ....16 D1
  RCANTE CT3 ....229 J1
  SNWD SE25 ....60 F7
  TON TN9 ....240 F2
  WALD ME5 ....96 A5
Kings Ropewalk DVW CT17 ....313 J1
Kings Rw MAID/SHEP ME15 * 185 M2
Kings Standing Wy
  RTWE/PEM TN2 ....241 J7
King Stairs Cl
  BERM/RHTH SE16 ....24 E5
Kingsthorpe Rd SYD SE26 ....61 K3
Kings Toll Rd RTWE/PEM TN2 ....272 B2
Kingston Av MARG CT9 ....112 A5
Kingston Cl DVW CT17 ....290 C4
  HB CT6 ....108 B5
  MSTR CT12 ....142 C3
Kingston Ct CVW DA11 ....48 F7
Kingston Crs BECK BR3 ....61 M7
  WALD ME5 ....125 N1
Kingston Dr
  MAID/SHEP ME15 ....185 M3
Kingston Gdns CROY/NA CR0 ....82 E8
Kingston Rw PGE/AN SE20 ....61 K7
Kingston Sq NRWD SE19 ....60 D4
King St CANT CT1 ....137 L9
  CANTW/ST CT2 ....137 L9
  CHAT ME4 ....6 D4
  DEAL CT14 ....233 J5
  DVE/WH CT16 ....8 D4

E/WMAL ME19 ....153 J4
GILL ME7 ....7 J2
GVE DA12 ....49 M7
IOS ME12 ....57 J6
LYDD TN29 ....334 C9
MAID/BEAR ME14 ....13 G4
MARG CT9 ....15 G5
RAM CT11 ....19 C7
ROCH ME1 ....19 C7
SIT ME10 ....99 M9
SWCH CT13 ....201 P1
Kings Wk MAID/BEAR ME14 ....13 H5
Kings Wy CROY/NA CR0 ....82 E9
Kingsway GILL ME7 ....96 E5
  LYDD TN29 ....327 J4
  STMC/STPC BR5 ....86 E2
  WSTB CT5 ....18 E2
Kingswear Gdns STRD ME2 ....8 E2
Kingswood KEN/WIL TN24 ....252 C4
Kingswood Av BELV DA17 ....28 E7
  CHAT ME4 ....95 K4
  HAYES BR2 ....83 P9
  SWLY BR8 ....88 E1
  THHTH CR7 ....82 E7
Kingswood Cl DART DA1 ....46 C5
  ORP BR6 ....86 E4
  RTWE/PEM TN2 ....270 H2
Kingswood Ct LEW SE13 * 23 H4
Kingswood Dr NRWD SE19 ....60 E3
Kingswood Pl LEW SE13 ....42 C5
Kingswood Rd GILL ME7 ....7 K1
  HAYES BR2 ....62 C9
  SEV TN13 ....148 D6
Kingswood Vls DVW CT17 * 291 H5
Kingswood Wy
  SAND/SEL CR2 ....114 A6
  WLGTN SM6 ....82 D9
Kingsworth Cl BECK BR3 ....84 B2
King William La CNWCH SE10 ....25 P3
King William Rd GILL ME7 ....96 E5
King William St SNWK SE1 * 24 A4
King William Wk GNWCH SE10 ....25 M9
Kinlet Rd WOOL/PLUM SE18 ....43 N1
Kinnaird Av BMLY BR1 ....62 D5
Kinnaird Cl BMLY BR1 ....62 D5
Kinnibrugh Dr LING RH7 ....235 K8
Kinnings Rw TON TN9 ....210 F8
Kinross Cl WALD ME5 ....95 N7
Kinsale Rd PECK SE15 ....40 G4
Kinveachy Gdns CHARL SE7 ....26 F8
Kinver Rd SYD SE26 ....61 L3
Kipling Av TIL RM18 ....49 M2
Kipling Ct STHWK SE1 * 24 A5
Kipling Dr DIT/AY ME20 ....123 N9
Kipling Rd ASH TN23 ....2 C5
  BXLYHN DA7 ....44 G2
  DART DA1 ....46 G2
Kipling St STHWK SE1 * 24 A5
Kipling Wy EGRIN RH19 ....264 F7
Kipping Cl RFOLK CT18 ....288 D8
Kippington Cl SEV TN13 ....20 B1
Kippington Dr ELTH/MOT SE9 ....63 H3
Kippington Rd SEV TN13 ....20 C2
Kirby Cl CRBK TN17 ....298 A3
Kirby Est BERM/RHTH SE16 * 24 E6
Kirby Gv STHWK SE1 * 24 B3
Kirkdale LEW SE13 ....42 C5
  RDART DA2 ....47 J8
Kirby's La CANTW/ST CT2 ....4 D3
Kirkdale MAID/SHEP ME15 ....185 L6
Kirkdale Cnr SYD SE26 * 61 J3
Kirkdale Rd MAID/SHEP ME15 ....185 L5
  RTW TN1 ....23 F2
Kirkham Rd EHAM E6 ....26 F2
Kirkham St
  WOOL/PLUM SE18 ....27 M9
Kirkins Cl STPH/PW TN12 ....273 H7
Kirkland Cl BFN/LL DA15 ....44 A7
Kirkland Ter BECK BR3 ....61 N5
Kirk La HOO/HM ME3 * 52 D7
  WOOL/PLUM SE18 ....27 K9
Kirkstead Rd THHTH CR7 * 2 D2
Kirkmichael Rd POP/IOD E14 ....25 M2
Kirkside Rd BKHTH/KID SE3 ....26 B2
Kirkstone Av RAM CT11 ....142 C5
Kirkstone Wy BMLY BR1 ....62 C6
Kirkwood Rd PECK SE15 ....41 H3
Kirtley Rd SYD SE26 ....61 L3
Kirton Cl RFOLK CT18 ....288 C8
Kirwyn Wy CMBW SE5 ....40 C1
Kitchener Av CHAT ME4 ....95 L5
  GVE DA12 ....69 M3
Kitchener Cl RCANTW CT4 ....228 B6
Kitchener Rd DVW CT17 ....291 H6
  HOO/HM ME3 ....72 F3
  STRD ME2 ....72 A7
  THHTH CR7 .... 2 D2
Kitchener Sq FOLKN CT19 ....311 H5
Kitchenour La RYE TN31 ....331 K8
Kite Farm WSTB CT5 ....106 C3
Kite La STPH/PW TN12 ....273 H2
Kitewell La LYDD TN29 ....342 D1
Kither Rd ASH TN23 ....282 D1
Kit Hl FAV ME13 ....163 N4
Kit Hill Av WALD ME5 ....125 K2
Kitley Gdns NRWD SE19 ....60 F7
Kitsbridge La RASHW TN26 ....324 C2
Kitson Rd CMBW SE5 ....40 E2
  CROY/NA CR0 ....83 H9
Kittiwake Cl HB CT6 ....108 C6
Kittiwake Cl
  SAND/SEL CR2 ....114 B4
Kitto Rd NWCR SE14 ....41 K3
Knapdale Cl FSTH SE23 ....61 H1
Knaphill Rd CAT SE6 ....61 N1
Knapmill Wy CAT SE6 ....61 N1
Knatchbull Rd CMBW SE5 ....40 C2
Knatchbull Wy RASHE TN25 ....284 F3
Knatts La BGR/WK TN15 ....120 B5
Knatts Valley Rd EYN DA4 ....119 P1
Knaves Acre HDCN TN27 ....247 N4

Kna - Law 381

Knave Wood Rd
BGR/WK TN15 149 K2
Knee Hl ABYW SE2 28 B8
Knee Hill Crs ABYW SE2 28 B7
Kneller Rd BROCKY SE4 41 L5
Knight Av CANTW/ST CT2 166 B4
GILL ME7 73 K9
Knighten St WAP E1W 24 E4
Knighthead Point
POP/IOD E14 * 25 K5
Knighton Park Rd SYD SE26 61 K4
Knighton Rd RSEV TN14 148 E2
Knightrider Ct
MAID/SHEP ME15 13 F6
Knightrider St
MAID/SHEP ME15 13 F6
SWCH CT13 201 P2
Knight Rd STRD ME2 18 B5
TONN TN10 211 H4
Knight's Av BRDST CT10 113 N7
Knightsbridge Cl
STH/RUST TN4 22 A1
Knights Cl HOO/HM ME3 73 L2
RTWE/PEM TN2 271 N1
Knights Cft HART DA3 91 J8
Knightsfield Rd SIT ME10 99 L7
Knight's Hl WNWD SE27 60 B4
Knight's Hill Sq WNWD SE27 60 B3
Knights Manor Wy DART DA1 46 F7
Knights Pk RTWE/PEM TN2 241 J8
Knights Pl RTWE/PEM TN2 * 271 N1
Knights Rdg ORP BR6 87 J9
RTWE/PEM TN2 271 N1
Knights Rd CAN/RD E16 26 B4
DVE/WH CT16 9 F2
HOO/HM ME3 73 K1
Knights Templars DVW CT17 8 B6
Knights Wy DVE/WH CT16 291 H4
HDCN TN27 247 N4
RTWE/PEM TN2 241 J9
Knockhall Cha GRH DA9 48 A6
Knockhall Rd GRH DA9 48 A7
Knock Hl TENT TN30 333 K3
Knockholt Rd ELTH/MOT SE9 43 H6
MARG CT9 113 K2
RSEV TN14 117 N8
Knock Mill La BGR/WK TN15 120 D7
Knock Rd ASH TN23 282 D1
Knockwood Rd TENT TN30 301 K6
Knold Pk MARG CT9 112 D5
Knole Cl CROY/NA CR0 * 83 P3
Knole Gv EGRIN RH19 264 F5
Knole La BGR/WK TN15 21 H5
Knole Rd DART DA1 46 A8
SEV TN13 149 J8
WALD ME5 125 P3
The Knole ELTH/MOT SE9 63 L3
FAV ME13 132 E6
MEO DA13 69 J6
Knole Wy BGR/WK TN15 21 G3
Knoll Hl RASHE TN25 306 D4
Knoll La ASH TN23 282 B1
Knoll Pl DEAL CT14 233 H8
Knoll Ri ORP BR6 86 G5
Knoll Rd BXLY DA5 45 J8
SCUP DA14 64 D4
The Knoll BECK BR3 61 P7
HAYES BR2 85 K6
Knoll Wy IOS ME12 80 B3
Knolly's Cl STRHM/NOR SW16 60 A2
Knolly's Rd STRHM/NOR SW16 60 A2
Knott Ct MAID/BEAR ME14 155 M6
Knott Crs KEN/WIL TN24 283 K1
Knott's La CANT CT1 5 F3
RDV CT15 292 E1
Knotts Pl SEV TN13 20 D2
Knowle Av BXLYHN DA7 44 G1
Knowle Cl BRXN/ST SW9 40 A4
RRTW TN3 269 K5
Knowle La STPH/PW TN12 243 K5
Knowle Rd HAYES BR2 85 P6
MAID/BEAR ME14 155 M6
ROCH ME1 124 B1
STPH/PW TN12 243 L7
Knowler Wy HB CT6 107 P1
Knowles Gdns HDCN TN27 247 N4
Knowles Hill Crs LEW SE13 42 B6
Knowlton Gdns MAIDW ME16 184 G1
Knowlton Gn HAYES BR2 85 J2
Knowlton Wk CANT CT1 5 H2
Knowsley Wy RTON TN11 210 A4
Knoyle St NWCR SE14 25 H9
Kohima Pl DVE/WH CT16 291 N5
Koonowla Cl BH/WHM TN16 115 N9
Kossuth St GNWCH SE10 25 P8
Kydbrook Cl STMC/STPC BR5 86 D4
Kyetop Wk RHAM ME8 96 G8
Kymbeline Ct DEAL CT14 232 G5
Kynaston Av THHTH CR7 83 H2
Kynaston Crs THHTH CR7 83 H2
Kynaston Rd BMLY BR1 62 E4
STMC/STPC BR5 87 J4
THHTH CR7 83 H2

L

La Belle Alliance Sq RAM CT11 17 H3
Labour-in-Vain Rd
BGR/WK TN15 120 G7
Laburnum Av DART DA1 46 C9
SWCH CT13 201 N2
SWLY BR8 65 M9
Laburnum Ct DVE/WH CT16 290 F3
Laburnum Dr DIT/AY ME20 153 P2
Laburnum Gdns CROY/NA CR0 84 A4
Laburnum Gv GVW DA11 49 H8
Laburnum La CANTW/ST CT2 137 N6
Laburnum Pl ELTH/MOT SE9 * 43 L6
SIT ME10 129 M1
Laburnum Rd STRD ME2 94 D1
Laburnum Wy HAYES BR2 86 C4
Labworth Cl IOS ME12 77 N1
Lacebark Cl BFN/LL DA15 44 B8
Lacey Cl RMAID ME17 187 H7
Laceys La RMAID ME17 215 H3
Lackington St LVPST EC2M 24 A1
Lacock Gdns
MAID/SHEP ME15 185 M2
Lacon Rd EDUL SE22 40 G5
Lacton Oast KEN/WIL TN24 253 L9
Lacton Wy KEN/WIL TN24 253 K9
Lacy Cl MAIDW ME16 155 J5
Ladas Rd WNWD SE27 60 C4
Ladbroke Hurst LING RH7 235 K8
Ladbrooke Crs SCUP DA14 64 F2
Ladbrook Rd SNWD SE25 60 D9
Ladds La SNOD ME6 123 P3
Ladds Wy SWLY BR8 88 C1
Lade Fort Crs LYDD TN29 343 K6
Ladham Rd CRBK TN17 274 F6
Ladyclose Av HOO/HM ME3 52 A9
Ladycroft Gdns ORP BR6 86 D9
Ladycroft Rd LEW SE13 41 P4
Ladycroft Wy ORP BR6 86 D9
Ladyfields GVW DA11 69 K3
HB CT6 108 A8
WALD ME5 126 A3
Ladyfields Cl RSIT ME9 98 G9
Lady Garne Rd RDV CT15 312 A1
Ladygrove CROY/NA CR0 114 B3
Ladymount WLGTN SM6 82 C8
Lady Oak La CRBK TN17 296 B8
Lady's Gift Rd STH/RUST TN4 240 B9
Ladyship Ter EDUL SE22 * 41 H8
Ladysmith Gv WSTB CT5 104 G8
Ladysmith Rd ELTH/MOT SE9 43 L7
WSTB CT5 105 J9
Ladywell DVE/WH CT16 8 C2
Ladywell Rd LEW SE13 41 N6
Ladywood Av STMC/STPC BR5 86 F2
Ladywood Rd CANTW/ST CT2 137 L6
RDART DA2 67 L4
STRD ME2 94 A4
Lady Wootton's Gn CANT CT1 5 G4
Lafone St STHWK SE1 24 C5
Lagado Ms BERM/RHTH SE16 24 G4
Lagham Ct GDST RH9 * 204 B5
Lagham Pk GDST RH9 204 B4
Lagham Rd GDST RH9 204 B5
Lagonda Wy DART DA1 46 C5
Lagoon Rd STMC/STPC BR5 87 J2
Lagos Av MSTR CT12 142 F3
Lairdale Cl DUL SE21 40 C9
Laird Av CDW/CHF RM16 32 E5
Lake Av BMLY BR1 62 E5
Lakedale Rd WOOL/PLUM SE18 27 M8
Lake Dr HOO/HM ME3 71 L1
Lake Gdns WLGTN SM6 82 A7
Lakehall Gdns THHTH CR7 82 G2
Lakehall Rd THHTH CR7 82 G2
Lakelands MAID/SHEP ME15 185 M4
RMAID ME17 188 F5
Lakemead ASH TN23 252 B9
Lake Ri WTHK RM20 31 K7
Lake Rd CROY/NA CR0 84 C6
DIT/AY ME20 154 D4
STH/RUST TN4 270 B4
Laker Rd ROCH ME1 95 H8
Lakeside ASH TN23 * 252 B8
BECK BR3 61 P9
RTWE/PEM TN2 271 H2
SNOD ME6 123 N7
WLGTN SM6 82 A8
Lakeside Av THMD SE28 27 P4
Lakeside Cl BFN/LL DA15 44 E6
EDEN TN8 207 N6
SNWD SE25 60 G8
Lakeside Dr HAYES BR2 85 P7
Lakes Rd HAYES BR2 85 M9
Lakeswood Rd
STMC/STPC BR5 86 C3
Lakeview Cl SNOD ME6 123 P7
Lake View Rd EGRIN RH19 265 J3
SEV TN13 148 F8
Lakeview Rd WELL DA16 44 D5
WNWD SE27 60 A4
Lakewood Dr RHAM ME8 96 F8
Laking Av BRDST CT10 113 M6
Laleham Gdns MARG CT9 112 G3
Laleham Rd CAT SE6 42 A8
MARG CT9 112 G4
Laleham Wk MARG CT9 112 G4
Lambarde Av ELTH/MOT SE9 63 L3
Lambarde Cl STRD ME2 * 123 P1
Lambarde Dr SEV TN13 148 F8
Lambarde Rd SEV TN13 148 F7
Lambardes HART DA3 91 J7
Lambardes Cl ORP BR6 117 K5
Lamb Cl TIL RM18 49 N3
Lambden Rd HDCN TN27 250 A3
Lamberhurst By RRTW TN3 295 K3
Lamberhurst Cl
STMC/STPC BR5 87 L5
Lamberhurst Gn RHAM ME8 96 E4
Lamberhurst Rd
STPH/PW TN12 273 K7
STPH/PW TN12 273 P2
WNWD SE27 60 A3
Lamberhurst Wy MARG CT9 113 L2
Lambersart Cl
RTWE/PEM TN2 240 G9
Lambert Cl BH/WHM TN16 145 N1
Lambert Ms SNOD ME6 123 P5
Lambert Rd CAN/RD E16 26 C2
Lambert's Pl CROY/NA CR0 83 J5
STPH/PW TN12 274 A3
Lamberts Rd RTWE/PEM TN2 240 G9
Lambert's Yd TON TN9 210 E9
Lambeth Cl WALD ME5 125 N1
Lambeth Rd CANT CT1 137 H9
CROY/NA CR0 82 F5
Lambeth Wk PECK SE15 40 F3
Lambfrith Gv GILL ME7 126 E2
Lambourn Cl EGRIN RH19 265 H5
Lambourne Dr E/WMAL ME19 182 G1
Lambourne Gv
BERM/RHTH SE16 24 G7
Lambourne Pl BKHTH/KID SE3 42 F2
RHAM ME8 97 K4
Lambourne Rd
MAID/SHEP ME15 186 C1
Lambourne Wk CANT CT1 5 K5
Lambourn Wy
RTWE/PEM TN2 270 G7
WALD ME5 125 P3
Lambs Bank TON TN9 240 E2
Lambscroft Av ELTH/MOT SE9 62 G2
Lambsfrith Gv GILL ME7 126 E2
Lamb's La South RAIN RM13 29 P1
Lamb's Pas STLK EC1Y 24 A1
Lamb St WCHPL E1 24 C1
Lamb's Wk WSTB CT5 105 K8
Lambton Rd DVW CT17 291 H6
Lamb Wk STHWK SE1 24 B5
Lamerock Rd BMLY BR1 62 D3
Lamerton St DEPT SE8 25 K9
Laming Rd BRCH CT7 111 J7
Lammas Dr SIT ME10 99 M8
Lammas Ga FAV ME13 132 G5
Lamorbey Cl BFN/LL DA15 64 B1
Lamorbey Pk BFN/LL DA15 * 44 D9
Lamorna Av GVE DA12 69 P2
Lamorna Cl ORP BR6 87 H4
Lampington Rw RRTW TN3 269 K5
Lamplighters Cl DART DA1 46 F7
GILL ME7 126 C1
Lampmead Rd LEW SE13 42 C6
Lamport Cl WOOL/PLUM SE18 26 G7
Lamson Rd RAIN RM13 29 L1
Lanbury Rd PECK SE15 41 K5
Lancashire Rd
MAID/SHEP ME15 186 B4
Lancaster Av MTCM CR4 82 D2
RFOLK CT18 311 L1
WNWD SE27 60 B1
Lancaster Cl HAYES BR2 85 J1
MSTR CT12 142 G3
RASHW TN26 304 D7
Lancaster Ct RHAM ME8 96 F7
Lancaster Dr EGRIN RH19 265 K5
POP/IOD E14 25 M4
Lancaster Gdns BRCH CT7 110 G7
HB CT6 108 A5
Lancaster House
WOOL/PLUM SE18 * 43 J1
Lancaster Rd DVW CT17 8 C3
SNWD SE25 60 G9
WTHK RM20 31 N7
Lancaster Wy E/WMAL ME19 152 G9
Lance Cl SIT ME10 99 N6
Lancelot Av STRD ME2 71 N8
Lancelot Cl DEAL CT14 232 F7
STRD ME2 71 N9
Lancelot Rd WELL DA16 44 C5
Lances Cl MEO DA13 92 B4
Lancet La MAID/SHEP ME15 185 L5
Lancey Cl CHARL SE7 26 E7
Lanchester Cl HB CT6 106 F3
Lanchester Wy NWCR SE14 41 J2
Lancing Rd CROY/NA CR0 82 E3
ORP BR6 87 J6
Landale Gdns DART DA1 46 C9
Landau Ter HAYES BR2 85 P7
Landau Wy ERITH DA8 30 A8
Landbury Wk RASHE TN25 252 C5
Landcroft Rd EDUL SE22 40 F7
Landells Rd EDUL SE22 40 F7
Lander Rd GRAYS RM17 32 E8
Landgate RYE TN31 338 F6
Landmann Wy NWCR SE14 24 G9
Landon Rd HB CT6 107 P1
Landons Cl POP/IOD E14 25 M4
Landor Ct GILL ME7 126 D2
Landrail Rd RSIT ME9 98 C3
Landseer Av GVW DA11 69 H2
Landseer Cl TONN TN10 211 H4
Landstead Rd
WOOL/PLUM SE18 43 P1
Landway BGR/WK TN15 149 L5
Land Wy HOO/HM ME3 71 M2
The Landway BGR/WK TN15 149 M2
BGR/WK TN15 151 J5
MAID/BEAR ME14 156 D9
STMC/STPC BR5 64 E9
Lane Av GRH DA9 48 A7
Lane End BXLYHN DA7 45 K4
HB CT6 107 J1
Lanercost Rd
BRXS/STRHM SW2 60 A1
Lanes Av GVW DA11 69 K2
Laneside CHST BR7 63 M4
The Lanes MSTR CT12 141 L6
The Lane BKHTH/KID SE3 42 E4
RDV CT15 291 N1
RRTW TN3 269 H3
Lanfranc Gdns CANTW/ST CT2 166 B3
Lanfranc Rd DEAL CT14 233 H1
Langafel Cl HART DA3 68 C8
Langbrook Rd BKHTH/KID SE3 43 H4
Lang Ct WSTB CT5 106 B3
Langdale ASH TN23 252 B9
Langdale Av RAM CT11 142 F5
Langdale Cl ORP BR6 86 C7
RHAM ME8 96 G5
Langdale Crs BXLYHN DA7 45 J2
Langdale Ri MAIDW ME16 155 H7
Langdale Rd GNWCH SE10 42 A1
THHTH CR7 82 F1
Langdale St WCHPL E1 * 24 E2
Langdon Av RCANTE CT3 200 F1
Langdon Cl RDV CT15 292 E1
Langdon House
WOOL/PLUM SE18 * 43 J1
Langdon Rd FOLKN CT19 310 A4
HAYES BR2 62 F9
Langdon Shaw SCUP DA14 64 B4
Langdon Wy STHWK SE1 24 D7
Langford Gn CMBW SE5 40 E4
Langford Pl SCUP DA14 64 C2
Langham Cl MARG CT9 112 A4
Langham Gv MAIDW ME16 155 H8
Langham Park Pl HAYES BR2 85 J1
Langholm Rd ASH TN23 282 D1
RRTW TN3 269 L5
Langhorne Gdns FOLK CT20 10 D6
Langland Gdns CROY/NA CR0 84 C6
Langlands Dr RDART DA2 67 L4
Langley Ct BECK BR3 * 84 E1
Langley Gdns MARG CT9 113 K2
STMC/STPC BR5 86 C3
Langley Rd BECK BR3 84 A1
SAND/SEL CR2 114 A3
SIT ME10 99 N8
WELL DA16 28 B9
Langley Wy WWKM BR4 84 G5
Langley Wd BECK BR3 * 85 H2
Langmead St WNWD SE27 60 B3
Langney Dr ASH TN23 282 A2
Langport Rd NROM TN28 337 H7
Langridge Dr EGRIN RH19 265 H8
Langsmead LING RH7 234 B1
Langston Hughes Cl
HNHL SE24 * 40 B5
Langthorn Ct LOTH EC2R 24 A2
Langthorne Crs GRAYS RM17 32 D7
Langton Cl MAID/BEAR ME14 13 K3
Langton La CANT CT1 166 F8
Langton Ri FSTH SE23 41 H8
Langton Rd BRXN/ST SW9 40 B1
RRTW TN3 269 L5
STH/RUST TN4 269 P5
Langton Wy BKHTH/KID SE3 42 E2
CDW/CHF RM16 33 K7
CROY/NA CR0 83 K8
Langworth Cl RDART DA2 66 D2
Lanier Rd LEW SE13 42 A7
Lankester Parker Rd
ROCH ME1 95 H8
Lankton Cl BECK BR3 62 A7
Lannoy Rd ELTH/MOT SE9 43 N9
Lanrick Rd POP/IOD E14 25 N2
Lanridge Rd ABYW SE2 28 C6
Lansbury Crs DART DA1 46 G6
Lansbury Gdns POP/IOD E14 * 25 N2
Lansdowne Av BXLYHN DA7 44 E1
MAID/SHEP ME15 185 P5
ORP BR6 86 C5
Lansdowne Hl WNWD SE27 60 B2
Lansdowne La CHARL SE7 26 E8
Lansdowne Ms CHARL SE7 26 E8
Lansdowne Pl NRWD SE19 60 F6
STHWK SE1 24 A6
Lansdowne Rd BMLY BR1 62 E6
CHAT ME4 95 K4
CROY/NA CR0 83 J6
RTW TN1 23 G3
SEV TN13 149 J8
TON TN9 210 E8
Lansdowne Sq GVW DA11 49 K7
RTW TN1 23 F3
Lansdowne Wood Cl
WNWD SE27 60 B2
Lansdown Pl GVW DA11 49 K9
Lansdown Rd CANT CT1 5 F7
SCUP DA14 64 D2
SIT ME10 130 B1
TIL RM18 49 K3
Lanterns Ct POP/IOD E14 25 K6
Lanthorne Ct BRDST CT10 * 113 N7
Lanthorne Ms RTW TN1 22 E1
RTW TN1 22 E4
Lanthorne Rd BRDST CT10 113 M6
Lanvanor Rd PECK SE15 41 J3
Lapins La E/WMAL ME19 182 G1
Lapis Cl GVE DA12 50 D9
La Providence ROCH ME1 19 G5
Lapse Wood Wk FSTH SE23 41 H9
Lapwing Cl CROY/NA CR0 114 B4
ERITH DA8 * 46 B1
IOS ME12 78 C2
Lapwing Dr ASH TN23 282 G6
RSIT ME9 98 C3
Lapwing Rd HOO/HM ME3 56 D3
Lapwings HART DA3 68 F9
Lapworth Cl ORP BR6 87 K6
Lara Cl LEW SE13 42 A7
Larch Cl BRDST CT10 113 J9
DEPT SE8 25 J9
DIT/AY ME20 154 A2
WARL CR6 144 B4
Larch Crs HOO/HM ME3 73 L4
TONN TN10 210 F4
Larchcroft WALD ME5 125 M1
Larch Dene ORP BR6 86 B6
The Larches EGRIN RH19 265 K4
FAV ME13 132 D5
HOO/HM ME3 71 L4
WSTB CT5 105 K6
Larch Gv BFN/LL DA15 44 B9
STPH/PW TN12 242 G3
Larch Rd DART DA1 46 D9
RDV CT15 230 C8
Larch Ter IOS ME12 * 57 J8
Larch Tree Wy CROY/NA CR0 84 D7
Larch Wk KEN/WIL TN24 252 F3
Larch Wy HAYES BR2 86 B4
Larch Wood Cl WALD ME5 126 A4
Larchwood Rd ELTH/MOT SE9 63 M1
Larcombe Cl CROY/NA CR0 83 L8
Larissa St WALW SE17 * 24 A8
Larkbere Rd SYD SE26 61 L3
Larkey Vw RCANTW CT4 195 M2
Larkfield STPH/PW TN12 242 B2
Larkfield Av GILL ME7 96 B2
SIT ME10 99 M8
Larkfield Cl DIT/AY ME20 153 P3
Larkfield Rd DIT/AY ME20 153 P3
SCUP DA14 64 B2
SEV TN13 148 B8
Larkfields GVW DA11 69 J2
Larkhill Ter
WOOL/PLUM SE18 * 43 L1
Larkin Cl STRD ME2 72 B5
Larking Dr MAIDW ME16 155 J5
Larkscliff Ct BRCH CT7 * 110 E5
Larks Fld HART DA3 91 J1
Larksfield Rd FAV ME13 132 F4
Larkspur Cl E/WMAL ME19 153 P3
ORP BR6 87 K6
Larkspur Rd E/WMAL ME19 153 N3
WALD ME5 125 K1
Larkstore Pk
STPH/PW TN12 * 246 B4
Larkswood Cl ERITH DA8 46 A2
Larkwell La HART DA3 91 J1
Larner Rd ERITH DA8 45 N1
Lascelles Rd DVW CT17 291 H9
Laser Quay STRD ME2 19 K3
Lassa Rd ELTH/MOT SE9 43 J6
Lassell St GNWCH SE10 25 N8
La-Tene DEAL CT14 232 G7
Latham Cl BH/WHM TN16 145 M1
EHAM E6 26 F2
RDART DA2 67 L1
Latham Rd BXLYHS DA6 45 J6
Latham's Wy CROY/NA CR0 82 E5
Latimer Cl HB CT6 106 G4
Latimer Pl GILL ME7 73 J8
Latimer Rd CROY/NA CR0 * 82 G7
Latona Dr GVE DA12 70 B4
Latona Rd PECK SE15 24 D9
La Tourne Gdns ORP BR6 86 D7
Latymers RTON TN11 238 G5
Laud St CROY/NA CR0 83 H7
Launcelot Rd BMLY BR1 62 E3
Launch St POP/IOD E14 25 M6
Launder's La RAIN RM13 30 B1
Laundry Rd MSTR CT12 141 L5
Laura Dr SWLY BR8 66 A6
Laura Pl ROCH ME1 94 E4
Laureate Cl MARG CT9 112 G3
Laurel Av GVE DA12 69 N1
LYDD TN29 337 L2
Laurel Bank STH/RUST TN4 240 E9
Laurel Cl DART DA1 46 C9
FOLK CT20 310 B5
SCUP DA14 64 C2
Laurel Crs CROY/NA CR0 84 D7
Laurel Dene EGRIN RH19 265 J7
Laurel Dr OXTED RH8 175 J7
Laurel Gv PGE/AN SE20 61 H6
RMAID ME17 187 N9
SYD SE26 61 K4
Laurel Pl FAV ME13 * 134 A8
Laurel Rd GILL ME7 73 J8
RTWE/PEM TN2 270 G1
The Laurels CMBW SE5 * 40 B1
HART DA3 68 G9
MAIDW ME16 185 H1
RDART DA2 * 66 C2
Laurel Vls STPH/PW TN12 * 245 H4
Laurel Wy RCANTW CT4 195 M2
Laurence Pountney Hl
CANST EC4R 24 A3
Laureston Pl DVE/WH CT16 8 E2
Laurie Gray Av WALD ME5 125 J4
Laurie Gv NWCR SE14 41 L2
Laurier Rd CROY/NA CR0 83 L4
Lauriston Cl RAM CT11 142 F7
Lauriston Mt BRDST CT10 113 M8
Lausanne Rd MARG CT9 15 H5
PECK SE15 41 J2
Lausanne Ter MARG CT9 * 15 H5
Lavenda Cl GILL ME7 126 D1
Lavender Cl E/WMAL ME19 153 N4
HAYES BR2 85 P3
MARG CT9 112 B5
Lavender Ct SIT ME10 129 P2
Lavender Gdns WADH TN5 315 J5
Lavender Hl SWLY BR8 65 M9
TON TN9 240 F1
Lavender La MSTR CT12 142 B7
Lavender Ms CANT CT1 4 C5
Lavender Rd BERM/RHTH SE16 25 H4
CROY/NA CR0 82 E3
E/WMAL ME19 153 N4
Lavenders Rd E/WMAL ME19 153 K5
Lavender Wy CROY/NA CR0 84 A3
Lavengro Rd WNWD SE27 60 C1
Lavernock Rd BXLYHN DA7 45 J3
Laverstoke Rd MAIDW ME16 155 H4
Lavidge Rd ELTH/MOT SE9 63 J1
Lavington Rd CROY/NA CR0 82 E7
Lavinia Rd DART DA1 46 F7
Lawdon Gdns CROY/NA CR0 82 G8
Lawford Gdns DART DA1 46 C6
Lawless St POP/IOD E14 * 25 L3
Lawley Cl MSTR CT12 143 H3
Lawn Cl BMLY BR1 62 F6
CHAT ME4 95 N4
SWLY BR8 65 L8
TENT TN30 300 G8
Lawn House Cl POP/IOD E14 25 M5
Lawn Pk SEV TN13 178 G3
Lawn Rd BECK BR3 61 N6
BRDST CT10 113 M9
DEAL CT14 233 H8
GVW DA11 48 G7
TON TN9 240 E1
Lawns Crs GRAYS RM17 32 E9
Lawns Pl GRAYS RM17 * 32 E9
The Lawns BKHTH/KID SE3 * 42 D4
NRWD SE19 60 D7
SCUP DA14 64 D3
STPH/PW TN12 243 J9
Lawn Ter BKHTH/KID SE3 42 D4
Lawn Vls RAM CT11 * 17 F4
Lawrance Sq GVW DA11 * 69 K2
Lawrence Cl FOLKN CT19 310 C5
MAID/SHEP ME15 185 M4
Lawrence Ct FOLKN CT19 11 H1
Lawrence Dr GVE DA12 93 H1
Lawrence Gdns HB CT6 107 P2
TIL RM18 49 M1
Lawrence Hill Gdns DART DA1 46 C7
Lawrence Hill Rd DART DA1 46 C7
Lawrence Rd ERITH DA8 45 K1
SNWD SE25 83 L1
TONN TN10 211 H4
WWKM BR4 85 K8
Lawrence St CAN/RD E16 26 A1
GILL ME7 7 H3

Lawrie Park Av SYD SE26 .....61 H4
Lawrie Park Crs SYD SE26 ....61 H4
Lawrie Park Gdns SYD SE26...61 H4
Lawrie Park Rd SYD SE26......61 H4
Laws Cl THHTH CR7............83 J1
Lawson La RASHE TN25.......283 M9
Lawson Cl CAN/RD E16........26 C2
Lawson Cl GILL ME7 * 73 M9
Lawson Gdns DART DA1.......46 A5
Lawson Rd DART DA1..........46 D5
Law St STHWK SE1............24 SA
Laxey Rd ORP BR6...........116 C1
The Laxey MAID/SHEP ME15 ..185 K2
Laxley Cl CMBW SE5..........40 B1
Laxton Cl MAID/SHEP ME15...156 C9
Laxton Dr RMAID ME17.......216 D1
Laxton Gdns STPH/PW TN12...242 F2
Laxton Wy CANT CT1..........43 K6
   FAV ME13.................133 H8
   SIT ME10..................99 L8
   WSTB CT5.................106 B5
Layard Rd BERM/RHTH SE16...24 F2
   THHTH CR7................60 D8
Layard Sq BERM/RHTH SE16...24 E7
Layfield Rd GILL ME7.........73 M8
Layhams Rd HAYES BR2......115 K2
   WWKM BR4................98 E1
Laytam Cl STRD CT10.........113 J8
Laymarsh Cl BELV DA17......216 C3
Layton Crs CROY/NA CR0......82 F9
Layzell Wk ELTH/MOT SE9.....43 H9
Lea Av RYE TN31............338 D6
Lea Cl HYTHE CT21..........308 C5
Leacon Rd ASH TN23...........2 A5
Leacroft EGRIN..............264 C6
Leadenhall Market BANK EC3V..24 B2
Leadenhall St BANK EC3V.....24 B2
Leadenhall St BANK EC3V.....24 B2
Leaf Gv STRHM/NOR SW16.....60 B5
Leafield RASHE TN25........285 L7
Leafield Cl STRHM/NOR SW16 ..60 B5
Leafield La SCUP DA14.......45 L1
Leafy Gld RHAM ME8..........96 E8
Leafy Gv HAYES BR2..........98 A5
Leafy La MEO DA13..........122 B1
Leafy Oak Rd LEE/GVPK SE12 ..62 C3
Leafy Wy CROY/NA CR0.........3 L6
Leahurst Rd LEW SE13........42 C7
Lealands Av RTON TN11......209 M9
Lealands Cl RRTW TN3.......269 H9
Leaman Cl RHAM ME3.........53 M3
Leamington Av BMLY BR1.....62 C4
   ORP BR6...................86 F8
Leamington Cl BMLY BR1......62 C5
Leamouth Rd EHAM E6........26 F2
   POP/IOD E14..............25 N2
Leander Dr GVE DA12.........70 B3
Leander Rd ROCH ME1........95 H7
   THHTH CR7................82 L1
Lea Rd BECK BR3.............61 N8
   CDW/CHF RM16.............33 H8
   SEV TN13................179 H3
Learoyd Gdns EHAM E6........27 H3
Learoyd Rd RAINH TN28.....336 G8
Leasam La RYE TN31.........338 D5
Leas Dl ELTH/MOT SE9........63 J2
Leas Gn BRDST TN10.........113 J9
   CHST BR7.................64 B5
Leas La WARL CR6...........144 A3
Leas Rd DEAL CT14..........232 G4
   WARL CR6................144 A3
The Leas DEAL CT14.........263 J5
   FAV ME13................132 E5
   FOLK CT20................10 C7
   IOS ME12.................14 B2
   WADH TN5................294 B9
   WSTB CT5................106 C5
Leasway CDW/CHF RM16.......32 L8
Leatherbottle Gn
   ERITHM DA18..............28 E6
Leather Cl EDEN TN8........236 D1
Leathermarket Ct STHWK SE1...24 A5
Leathermarket St STHWK SE1...24 C5
Leather Rd BERM/RHTH SE16...24 C5
Leather St WAP E1W..........24 G3
Leathwell Rd DEPT SE8.......41 J5
Leatt Cl BRDST CT10.........113 L9
Lea V DART DA1.............45 M5
Leaveland Cl ASH TN23......282 C2
   BECK BR3.................84 D1
Leaves Green Crs HAYES BR2 ..115 M5
Leaves Green Rd HAYES BR2 ..115 N5
Lebanon Gdns RHM/NM16.....145 N2
Lebanon Rd CROY/NA CR0.....83 K5
Lebrun Sq BKHTH/KID SE3.....42 F5
Leckwith Av ABYW SE2........28 D9
Lecomfield Cl TON TN9......240 C2
Leda Rd WOOL/PLUM SE18....26 D6
Ledbury Rd CROY/NA CR0.....83 H8
Ledbury St PECK SE15........40 C1
Ledgers Rd WARL CR6.......144 D1
Ledrington Rd NRWD SE19....61 N9
Leechcroft Av BFN/LL DA15...44 H6
   SWLY BR8.................65 P9
Lee Church St LEW SE13......42 C5
Lee Cl ORP BR6.............87 L6
Leeds House RTON TN11 *....211 P2
Leeds Rd RMAID ME17.......187 H8
Leeds Sq RHAM ME8..........96 E5
Lee Gn STMC/STPC BR5.......64 F4
Lee Green HOO/HM ME3.......72 D3
Lee High Rd LEW SE13........42 E5
Lee Pk BKHTH/KID SE3........42 C9
Lee Rd BKHTH/KID SE3........42 D4
   SNOD ME6................125 P5
The Lees RASHE TN25........284 E3
Lees Court Rd FAV ME13.....162 F6
Leeson Rd BRXN/ST SW9......40 L4
Leesons Hl CHST BR7.........64 A9
Leesons Wy STMC/STPC BR5...64 A8
Lees Rd KEN/WIL TN24.......253 K8
   RASHE TN25..............284 F1
   WBY/YAL ME18............213 M5
The Lees CROY/NA CR0........84 C6
   HB CT6..................107 P1

Leet Cl GILL ME7............73 L9
   IOS ME12.................79 H2
Lee Ter BKHTH/KID SE3.......42 C4
Leeward Rd ROCH ME1........95 H5
Leeway DEPT SE8............41 L4
Leewood Cl LEE/GVPK SE12 *...42 D7
Leewood Pk SWLY BR8........66 B8
Legatt Rd ELTH/MOT SE9......43 H6
Legge La E/WMAL ME19......123 L6
Legge St LEW SE13...........42 A6
Leggatt La RRTW TN3........269 K3
Leghorn Rd WOOL/PLUM SE18 ..27 L8
Leicester Av MARG CT9......113 H5
Leicester Dr RTWE/PEM TN2...270 C8
Leicester Gdns IOS ME12......80 B4
Leicester Rd CROY/NA CR0....83 K4
   MAID/SHEP ME15..........186 A4
   TIL RM18.................52 B9
Leigham V STRHM/NOR SW16...60 A2
Leigham Av MAID/SHEP ME15...185 N5
Leigh Cl IOS ME12...........77 P2
Leigh Crs CROY/NA CR0......114 E2
Leigh Pl RDART DA2 *.........66 G4
   WELL DA16................44 C3
Leigh Place La GDST RH9.....174 A8
Leigh Rd GVW DA11..........69 M1
   MSTR CT12................72 C4
   RTON TN11...............142 E3
   RTON TN11...............210 A8
Leigh Ter STMC/STPC BR5 *....64 E2
Leighton Cl STH/RUST TN4....270 D1
Leighton Gdns TIL RM18.......49 L1
Leighton Rd DVE/WH CT16....291 K6
Leighton St CROY/NA CR0.....82 G5
Leighville Dr HB CT6........107 J2
Leila Parnell Pl CHARL SE7....26 D9
Leith Hl STMC/STPC BR5......64 C7
Leith Park Rd GVW DA11......49 K9
Leivers Rd DEAL CT14........232 F6
Leman St WCHPL E1..........24 C2
Le May Av LEE/GVPK SE12.....62 F2
Lennon Av CANT CT1.........43 M6
Lemomwell Dr ELTH/MOT SE9 ..43 M6
Lenacre Av DVE/WH CT16.....260 C6
Lenacre La DVE/WH CT16.....260 C6
Lenacre St RASHE TN25......222 B7
Lenanton Rd BGR/WK TN15...151 J6
Lendrin Cl GILL ME7 *.........72 B8
Leneda Rd RTWE/PEM TN2....270 B8
Leney Rd WBY/YAL ME18......183 M4
Lenfield Av MAID/BEAR ME14...13 J4
The Length BRCH CT7........140 A2
Lenham Cl BRDST CT10.......143 M2
Lenham Forstal Rd
   RMAID ME17..............219 P1
Lenham Gdns MARG CT9......112 A5
Lenham Heath Rd
   RMAID ME17..............189 J8
   HDCN TN27...............247 N3
   LEW SE13.................42 D5
Lenham Rd BXLYHN DA7.......28 E9
   HDCN TN27...............247 N3
   LEW SE13.................42 D5
   MRST TN14................88 A7
   THHTH CR7...............187 H8
Lenmore Av GRAYS RM17.....32 D6
Lennard Av WWKM BR4.......85 H6
Lennard Cl WWKM BR4.......85 H6
Lennard Rd CROY/NA CR0.....83 H5
   FOLK CT20................11 H3
   HAYES BR2................86 A5
   SEV TN13................148 D5
   SYD SE26.................61 J5
Lennard Rw SOCK/AV RM15...30 G4
Lennard Ter SYD SE26 *......61 K5
Lennox Av GVW DA11.........49 L7
Lennox Gdns CROY/NA CR0....82 G8
Lennox Rd GVW DA11.........49 L8
Lennox Rd East GVW DA11....49 L8
Lenor Cl BXLYHS DA6........44 G5
Lensbury Wy ABYW SE2.......28 C6
Lenside Dr MAID/SHEP ME15...186 D1
Lenthall Av GRAYS RM17......32 B5
Lenthorp Rd GNWCH SE10....26 A8
Lentmead Rd BMLY BR1.......62 D2
Lenton St WOOL/PLUM SE18...27 L7
Leof Crs CAT SE6............61 P4
Leonard Av RSEV TN14......118 G9
   SWCM DA10...............48 C8
Leonard Cl MAIDW ME16.....154 G6
Leonard Pl HAYES BR2 *......85 P7
Leonard Rd CHAT ME4........64 A6
   LYDD TN29...............343 K5
Leonard's Av RAM CT11......143 K3
Leonard St CAN/RD E16......26 F4
Leopold Cl PECK SE15........40 G1
Leopold Rd RAM CT11.......143 K4
   RAM CT11.................17 H4
Leo St PECK SE15............41 H1
Leros Barracks CANT CT1 *...166 G2
Le Roux Cl RFCLK CT18......288 C8
Leroy St STHWK SE1 *........24 D7
Lerryn Gdns BRDST CT10.....113 L5
Lescombe Cl FSTH SE23.......61 L2
Lescombe Rd FSTH SE23......61 L2
Lesley Av CANT CT1.........166 F6
Lesley Cl BXLY DA5..........45 L8
   MEO DA13.................69 K7
   SWLY BR8.................65 M9
Lesley Pl MAIDW ME16.......12 C3
Leslie Av MARG CT9........112 A6
Leslie Crs TENT TN30......301 J5
Leslie Gv CROY/NA CR0......83 K5
Leslie Grove Pl CROY/NA CR0 *..83 K5
Leslie Park Rd CROY/NA CR0...83 K5
Leslie Rd BRCH CT7.........111 H5
   CAN/RD E16...............26 C2
   GILL ME7.................73 H6
Leslie Smith Dr FAV ME13...132 F6
Lesney Pk ERITH DA8.........29 J9
Lesney Park Rd ERITH DA8....29 J9
Lessing St FSTH SE23........41 L8
Lessness Av BXLYHN DA7.....44 F1
Less-ness Pk BELV DA17.....28 E8

Lested La RMAID ME17.......186 E9
Lester Rd CHAT ME4..........6 C6
Lestock Cl SNWD SE25.......60 D9
Letchworth Av CHAT ME4.....95 L5
Letchworth Cl HAYES BR2.....85 K2
Letchworth Dr HAYES BR2.....85 K2
Le Temple Rd STPH/PW TN12...243 J2
Letter Box La SEV TN13......179 H5
Levendale Rd FSTH SE23.....61 L1
Leven Rd POP/IOD E14.......25 N1
Leveret Cl CROY/NA CR0.....114 G5
Leverholme Gdns
   ELTH/MOT SE9.............63 J3
Lever Sq CDW/CHF RM16......33 H7
Leveson Rd CDW/CHF RM16....33 J6
Levett Cl HOO/HM ME3.......56 D2
Levetts La RBTBR TN14.....328 E4
Leviathan Wy CHAT ME4.......6 C7
Lewd La HDCN TN27........249 H5
Lewes Cl GRAYS RM17........32 B9
Lewes Rd BMLY BR1..........63 H8
   EGRIN RH19..............265 K8
Lewing Cl ORP BR6..........86 F9
Lewin Rd BXLYHS DA6........44 G5
   RHAM ME8.................96 E4
Lewis Cl FAV ME15..........132 D6
Lewis Ct ASH TN23 *........282 C1
Lewis Court Dr RMAID ME17..185 N6
Lewis Cl HAYES BR2.........112 G2
Lewis Gv LEW SE13..........42 A5
Lewisham High St LEW SE13...41 P7
Lewisham Hl LEW SE13.......41 P7
Lewisham Pk LEW SE13.......41 P9
Lewisham Rd DVW CT17......290 F4
   LEW SE13.................42 A3
Lewisham Wy BROCKY SE4....41 M3
Lewis Ms SNOD ME6.........123 N7
Lewis Rd MEO DA13..........69 K7
   SCUP DA14................64 C1
   WELL DA16................44 E4
Lewson Street Rd RSIT ME9...131 K5
Lexden Rd MTCM CR4........82 C1
Leybank RTON TN11........210 B6
Leybourne Cl HAYES BR2.....85 K2
   WALD ME5................125 M3
Leybourne Dell CRBK TN17...299 P9
Leybourne Dr MARG CT9.....112 A5
Leybourne Rd STRD ME2......72 P7
Leybourne Wy DIT/AY ME20...123 N9
Leyburne Rd BRDST CT10.....143 N2
Leyburn Gdns CROY/NA CR0...83 K6
Leyburn House
   WOOL/PLUM SE18 *.........43 J1
Leycroft Cl CANTW/ST CT2...166 D1
Leycroft Gdns ERITH DA8.....46 B2
Leydenhatch La SWLY BR8....65 M7
Leyden St WCHPL E1.........24 C1
Leyes Rd CAN/RD E16........26 E5
Leyhill Cl SWLY BR8.........88 D2
Leyland Rd LEE/GVPK SE12....42 D6
Leylang Rd NWCR SE14.......41 K1
Leysdown Av BXLYHN DA7.....45 L5
Leysdown Rd ELTH/MOT SE9....63 J1
   IOS ME12.................79 L4
Leyton Av GILL ME7.........96 B5
Leyton Cross Rd RDART DA2...66 F5
Leywood Rd MED DA13.......122 E2
Lezayre Rd ORP BR6.........116 C1
Liardet St NWCR SE14.......25 H4
Libya Ter MAID/BEAR ME14...155 M5
Lichfield Av CANT CT1......166 G6
Lichfield Wy SAND/SEL CR2...114 A4
Lidcote Gdns BRXN/ST SW9 *...40 B5
Liddon Rd BMLY BR1.........62 C9
Lidgate Rd PECK SE15.......40 F1
Lidsing Rd MAID/BEAR ME14...125 P9
Lidwells La CRBK TN17......274 C7
Liege Ct SIT ME10..........99 N5
Liffler Rd WOOL/PLUM SE18...27 M9
Lighterman's Rd POP/IOD E14...25 N5
Lighthouse Rd RDV CT15....292 E5
Lilac Cl RDART DA2 *........71 N9
Lilac Gdns CROY/NA CR0.....84 F1
   RHAM ME8 *...............65 M9

Lilac Gn E/WMAL ME19......153 P4
Lilac Pl MEO DA13..........92 C4
Lilac Rd STRD ME2..........94 D1
Lilah Ms HAYES BR2.........85 P5
Lila Pl SWLY BR8...........66 C6
Lilburne Gdns ELTH/MOT SE9..43 J6
Lilburne Rd ELTH/MOT SE9....43 J6
Lilian Barker Cl LEE/GVPK SE12 ..42 B4
Lilechurch Rd HOO/HM ME3...55 P9
Lilley Cl WAP E1W...........24 D4
Lillian Rd RAM CT11.........17 H1
Lillian Vls STPH/PW TN12 *...245 H4
Lilleburn E/WMAL ME19......153 L2
Lillie Rd BH/WHM TN16......145 N3
Limden Cl WADH TN5........314 D6
Lime Av GVW DA11..........49 H8
Lime Cl ASH TN23..........252 C6
   BMLY BR1.................85 P1
   STPH/PW TN12.............22 C3
   IOS ME12.................80 C6
   SIT ME10.................99 P7
   WARL CR6................144 B4
Lime Ct RHAM ME8..........126 F2
Lime Crs E/WMAL ME19......153 P5
Lime Gv BFN/LL DA15........44 B7
   HDCN TN27...............278 E9
   IOS ME12.................92 C6
   ORP BR6..................86 C6
   SIT ME10................129 P1
   WARL CR6................144 B4
Limefield Cl
   MAID/SHEP ME15..........186 A4
Lime Kiln Dr CHARL SE7......26 C9
Lime Kiln Rd DEAL CT14.......4 D1
Limekiln Rbt DVW CT17........8 B7
Lime Pit La RSEV TN14......148 B2
Lime Rd SWLY BR8..........65 M9
Limes Av CROY/NA CR0.......82 C7
   PGE/AN SE20..............61 H6
Limes Cl TENT TN30.......301 K6
Limesford Rd PECK SE15.....41 K5
Limes Gv HAWK TN18.......317 H1
   LEW SE13.................42 A5
Limes Pl CROY/NA CR0 *.....132 C6
Limes Rd BECK BR3..........84 C2
   CROY/NA CR0..............83 J3
   DVE/WH CT16.............291 K6
   FOLK CT19...............310 C5
Limes Rw ORP BR6..........116 A6
The Limes ASH TN23........282 D3
   CMBW SE5.................40 E4
   EDEN TN8................206 D9
   EGRIN RH19..............264 D3
   EYN DA4..................68 D2
   PUR RH19.................30 D6
Limestone Wk ABYW SE2......28 C5
Lime St FENCHST EC3M.......24 B2
Lime Street Pas BANK EC3V *..24 B2
Limes Wk PECK SE15.........41 J5
Lime Tree Av CROY/NA CR0...210 F8
Limetree Cl WALD ME5.......95 N7
Lime Tree Gv CROY/NA CR0....84 C7
Lime Trees STPH/PW TN12...246 B5
Lime Tree Ter CAT SE6 *.....41 N9
Lime Tree Wk SEV TN13......21 F4
   WWKM BR4.................85 J8
Limewood Cl BECK BR3.......84 F2
Limewood Rd ERITH DA8......45 L1
Limpsfield Av THHTH CR7.....59 P5
Limpsfield Wk WARL CR6.....144 B3
Linacre Cl PECK SE15........41 H4
The Linces DVE/WH CT16....291 J3
Linchmere Rd LEE/GVPK SE12...42 D8
Lincoln Av CANT CT1 *........5 J7
Lincoln Cl ERITH DA8........45 P3
Lincoln Gdns BRCH CT7......110 G6
Lincoln Green Rd
   STMC/STPC BR5............86 G2
Lincoln Rd ERITH DA8........45 P3
   MAID/SHEP ME15..........185 N5
   MTCM CR4.................82 D2
   SCUP DA14................64 D4
   SNWD SE25................61 H9
Lincolns Md LING ME9.......234 F6
Lincoln Rd BMLY BR1........62 E2
Lincon Rd GILL ME7.........73 K8
Lindal Rd BROCKY SE4.......41 M6
Linden Av BRDST CT10......113 N8
   DART DA1.................46 C9
   EGRIN RH19..............264 D3
   HB CT6..................107 K2
   THHTH CR7................82 G1
   WSTB CT5................105 N6
Linden Cha SEV TN13 *......22 B7
Linden Chase Rd SEV TN13...148 C7
Linden Cl ORP BR6..........30 F9
   RTWE/PEM TN2............22 B7
   SIT ME10................129 L2
Linden Crs ASH TN23.......243 H5
   WGOS CT8................106 A6
Linden Crs FOLK CT19......310 E4
Linden Dr IOS ME12.........57 H9
Lindenfield CHST BR7........63 M8
Linden Gdns RTWE/PEM TN2...270 C7
Linden Gv CANTW/ST CT2......4 C5
   PECK SE15................41 J3
   SYD SE26.................61 J5
Linden Leas WWKM BR4.......84 G6
Linden Park Rd
   RTWE/PEM TN2............270 C7
Linden Rd GILL ME7.........96 B1
   KEN/WIL TN24..............3 G4
   RCANTW CT4..............195 M2
   RMAID ME17..............185 H7
   WGOS CT8................111 N5
Linden Sq SEV TN13........148 C7
The Lindens CROY/NA CR0....114 F1
   DIT/AY ME20.............154 D3
Lindenthorpe Rd BRDST CT10 ..113 L7
Lindfield Rd CROY/NA CR0....83 L3
   ELTH/MOT SE9.............43 K6
Lindisfarne Cl GVE DA12.....70 D5
Lindisfarne Gdns MAIDW ME16 ..12 C7
Lindley Est PECK SE15.......40 G1
Lindley St WCHPL E1........24 F1
Lindridge Cl HB CT6........107 M6
Lindridge La STPH/PW TN12...245 P4
Lindsell St GNWCH SE10.....42 A2
Lindsey Cl BMLY BR1........63 H9
   MTCM CR4................82 D1
Lind St DEPT SE8...........41 P5
Lindway WNWD SE27.........60 E6
Lineacre Cl RHAM ME8.......96 C8
Lines Ter CHAT ME4..........6 C4
Linford Rd CDW/CHF RM16....33 K8
Lingards Rd LEW SE13.......42 A5
Lingey Cl BFN/LL DA15.......64 B1
Lingfield Av RDART DA2......47 H8
Lingfield Common Rd
   LING RH45...............234 F4
Lingfield Crs ELTH/MOT SE9...43 P5
Lingfield Rd BGR/WK TN15...151 K5
   EDEN TN8................206 F9
   EGRIN RH19..............264 C3
   GVE DA12................69 M1
Lingley Dr STRD ME2........72 C5
Ling Rd CAN/RD E16.........26 E1
Linington Rd BRCH CT7......111 H6
Link Fld HAYES BR2.........85 K3
Link Hill La HDCN TN27....219 K8
Link La CANT CT1............5 F5
Link Rd CANTW/ST CT2......136 C7

Links Ct DEAL CT14 *.......203 H9
Links Crs LYDD TN29.......337 M1
Linksfield Rd WGOS CT8.....111 H5
Links Gdns STRHM/NOR SW16 ...60 A6
Links Rd BECK BR3 *........233 H1
   WWKM BR4.................84 F5
The Links E/WMAL ME19.....152 F2
   WALD ME5................125 N6
Links Vw DART DA1..........46 C9
Links View Rd CROY/NA CR0...84 D7
Links Wy BECK BR3..........84 B5
   LYDD TN29 *.............325 N6
   NROM TN28...............337 J7
Linksway FOLKN CT19.......310 D4
Linksway Cl FOLKN CT19....310 E4
Links Yd WCHPL E1.........24 C1
The Link RYE TN31.........338 D7
Linkway DIT/AY ME20.......154 B3
   RTWE/PEM TN2............241 H9
Linkway CRO................99 L2
Linley Cl TN RM18..........50 F1
Linley Rd BRDST CT10......113 K8
Linnell Rd CMBW SE5........40 E5
Linnet Av STPH/PW TN12....243 H4
   WSTB CT5................105 J8
Linnet Cl SAND/SEL CR2....114 A4
   THMD SE28...............28 D7
Linnet Wy PUR RH19........30 E8
Linsey St BERM/RHTH SE16...24 D7
Linslade Rd ORP BR6........117 H1
Linton Cl CHARL SE7 ....26 D8
   RSIT ME9.................99 H2
Linton Dann Cl HOO/HM ME3...73 K1
Linton Crs EHAM E6.........26 F2
Linton Gld CROY/NA CR0.....114 B4
Linton Gore RMAID ME17....185 H6
Linton Gv WNWD SE27.......60 F1
Linton Hl RMAID ME17......215 K2
Linton Rd MAID/SHEP ME15...185 L8
Linwood Av RSIT ME9.......82 M7
Linwood Cl CMBW SE5.......40 F3
Lion Cl BROCKY SE4.........41 N7
Lion Rd BXLYHS DA6........44 G5
Lionel Gdns ELTH/MOT SE9...43 H6
Lionel Rd ELTH/MOT SE9.....43 H6
   TON TN9.................240 D1
Lion Fld FAV ME13.........132 D6
Lion Rd BXLYHS DA6........44 G5
   CROY/NA CR0..............83 H2
   EHAM E6..................26 G1
Lions Cl ELTH/MOT SE9......62 G2
Lion's Rd NROM TN28.......336 F7
Lion Wk RCANTE CT3 *......200 E1
Lion Yd FAV ME13..........132 D7
Liphook Crs FSTH SE23......41 J8
Liphook Wy MAIDW ME16....155 H4
Lipscombe Rd
   RTWE/PEM TN2............270 C2
Liptraps La RTWE/PEM TN2...270 C1
Lipwell Hl HOO/HM ME3......53 H4
Lisford St PECK SE15........40 F2
Liskeard Gdns BKHTH/KID SE3...42 E2
Lisle Cl GVE DA12..........70 D1
Lisle Pl GRAYS RM17........32 B6
Lismore Cl MAID/SHEP ME15...185 M4
Lismore Rd HB CT6.........108 A5
   WSTB CT5................106 A6
Liss Rd SWCH CT13.........201 H3
Lister Cl DEAL CT14........233 H4
   DVW CT17................291 J6
   E/WMAL ME19.............153 N4
Lister Rd MARG CT9........112 F5
   TIL RM18.................49 L3
Lister Wy FOLK CT20 *......10 F7
Listmas Rd CHAT ME4.........7 F7
Listowel Cl BRXN/ST SW9...40 C6
The List RCANTE CT3.......168 F6
Little Acre BECK BR3.......61 N9
Little Av RDEAL CT14.......236 C4
Little Aurels FSTH SE23.....61 H3
Little Birches BFN/LL DA15...64 A1
Little Bornes DUL SE21.....60 F5
Little Boundes Cl
   STH/RUST TN4............240 B6
Littlebourne Av RHAM ME8...96 E2
Littlebourne Rd
   MAID/BEAR ME14..........155 N2
   RCANTE CT3..............167 K4
Littlebrook Cl ASH TN23......2 A1
   CROY/NA CR0..............84 A3
Littlebrook Manor Wy
   DART DA1.................46 G6
Little Brook Rd ASH TN23.....2 A1
Little Brownings FSTH SE23...61 H1
Little Browns La EDEN TN8...205 P6
Little Buckland Av
   MAIDW ME16...............12 A1
Little Chequers RASHE TN25 ..223 P8
Little Copse Rd RCANTW CT4 ..195 M2
Little Ct WWKM BR4.........85 H6
Littlecourt Rd SEV TN13.....20 D1
   MEO DA13.................69 J6
Littledale ABYW SE2........27 P9
Little Fld STPH/PW TN12....246 B5
Littlefield Rd RHAM ME8.....97 L4
Little Flds RTON TN11 *.....211 P2
Little Footway RRTW TN3....269 L5
The Glovers SIT ME10 *......129 N2
Little Harts Heath
   STPH/PW TN12............275 L1
Little Heath Rd BXLYHN DA7 ....45 H2
Little John Av WALD ME5....125 L3
Littlejohn Rd STMC/STPC BR5 ..87 H3
Little Julians HI SEV TN13...178 F3
Little King St EGRIN RH19...265 H1
Little London Ct STHWK SE1 *...24 D5
Little Lullenden LING RH7...234 G4
Little Mallett RRTW TN3....269 L5
Little Market Rw
   E/WMAL ME19.............153 M2
Little Md FOLKN CT19......310 D4

Little Meadow CANTW/ST CT2...165 M3
Littlemede ELTH/MOT SE9 ....63 L2
Littlemore Rd ABYW SE2 .....27 P5
Little Mount Sion RTW TN1 ...22 D6
Little Oakham Ct
  HOO/HM ME3.............54 G4
Little Orch RMAID/BEAR ME17 ...185 J8
Little Oxley DIT/AY ME20 ....153 M2
Little Paddocks WSTB CT5 ...106 C7
Little Queen St DART DA1 ....46 F8
Little Redlands BMLY BR1 ....63 J8
Little Robhurst RASHW TN26...279 L9
Littlestone Cl BECK BR3 .....61 N5
Littlestone Rd NROM TN28 ....337 J7
Little Thrift STMC/STPC BR5 ...86 D1
Little Tilden Gill TENT TN30 ...301 K8
Little Walton SWCH CT13 .....201 K7
Littlewood LEW SE13 ....42 A6
Little Wd SEV TN13 ....149 H7
Little Wood Cl STMC/STPC ME5...64 C7
Liverpool Gv WALW SE17 .....24 A8
Liverpool Lawn RAM CT11 .....17 F5
Liverpool Rd CAN/RD E16 ....25 P7
  DEAL CT14 ....233 H9
  THHTH CR7 ....60 C9
Liverpool St LVPST EC2M 24 B1
Livesey Cl WOOL/PLUM SE18...27 K6
Livesey Pl PECK SE15 ....23 J8
Livesey St WBY/YAL ME18 ....183 N1
Livingstone Buildings
  GILL ME7 ....96 A1
Livingstone Circ GILL ME7....96 A1
Livingstone Cl LYDD TN29 ....327 M2
Livingstone Gdns GVE DA12 ...69 P4
Livingstone Rd BRDST CT10 ...113 K7
  GILL ME7 ....69 P4
  GVE DA12 ....69 P4
  THHTH CR7 ....60 B9
Lizban St BKHTH/KID SE3 .....42 F1
Llanover Rd WOOL/PLUM SE18...43 L1
Llewellyn St BERM/RHTH SE16...24 D5
Lloyd Park Av CROY/NA CRO...83 L8
Lloyd Rd BRDST CT10 ....113 M8
Lloyd's Av TWRH EC3N 24 B2
Lloyds Gn TENT TN30 ....332 A1
Lloyd's Pl BKHTH/KID SE3 *...42 C3
Lloyds Wy BECK BR3 ....84 B2
Lloyd Vls BROCKY SE4 ....41 N3
Loampit Hl LEW SE13 ....41 N3
Loampits Cl TON TN9 ....210 C7
Loampit V LEW SE13 ....41 P4
Lobelia Cl GILL ME7 ....96 B1
Locarno Av RHAM ME8 ....96 D4
Lochaber Rd LEW SE13........42 C5
Lochat Rd HOO/HM ME3 ....72 E1
Lochmere Cl ERITH DA8 ......28 C9
Lochnagar St POP/IOD E14 ...25 M1
Lock Cha LEW SE13 ....42 C4
Lockesley Dr STMC/STPC BR5 ...86 G3
Lockham Farm Av
  MAID/SHEP ME15 ....186 A6
Lockholt Cl ASH TN23 ....252 B6
Lockington Gv ROCH ME1 .....19 F6
Lock La MAIDW ME16 ....155 J3
Lockmead Rd LEW SE13 ....42 A4
Lockside TON TN9 ....210 F8
Locksley Cl MAIDS ME15 .....125 K3
Locksley Est POP/IOD E14 ...25 J2
Locksley St POP/IOD E14 ....25 J1
Locks Meadow LING RH7 ......235 K8
Lock St GILL ME7 ....7 H2
Lockswood MAIDW ME16 ....155 J5
Locks Yd BGR/WK TN15 * 21 J4
Lockwood Cl SYD SE26 ....61 K3
Lockwood Sq
  BERM/RHTH SE16 ....24 E6
Lockyer Est STHWK SE1 * 24 A5
Lockyer Pl BH/WHM TN16 * ...176 E2
Lockyer Rd PUR RM19 ....30 F8
Lockyers Hl MEO DA13 ....92 F9
Lockyer St STHWK SE1 ....24 A5
Loddington La RMAID ME17 ...215 M3
Loder Cl RMAID ME17 ....189 J6
Loder St PECK SE15 ....41 J1
Lodge Av CROY/NA CRO 62 E7
  DART DA1 ....67 C2
Lodge Cl EGRIN RH19 ....264 F7
  ORP BR6 ....87 J5
  WBY/YAL ME18 ....183 L3
Lodge Ct GVE DA12 ....70 G5
Lodge Crs ORP BR6 ....87 J5
Lodge Field Rd WSTB CT5 ....106 C5
Lodge Gdns BECK BR5 ....84 C2
  RMAID ME17 ....218 A4
Lodge Hl HOO/HM ME3 ....72 F1
  WELL DA16 ....44 B3
Lodge Hill La HOO/HM ME3 ...52 F8
Lodge La BH/WHM TN16 ......176 D5
  BXLY DA5 ....44 F7
  CDW/CHF RM16 ....32 C6
  CROY/NA CRO 114 C2
  GVE DA12 ....93 J1
  RTW TN9 ....269 M9
Lodge Oak La TON TN9 ....240 C1
Lodge Rd BMLY BR1 ....62 G6
  CROY/NA CRO 49 P6
  MAID/BEAR ME14 ....156 A7
  STPH/PW TN12 ....246 B4
  TON TN9 ....210 E8
  WLGTN SM6 ....82 A9
Lodge Wk WARL CR6 ....144 D1
Lodge Wood Dr RASHE TN25...252 C6
Lodore St POP/IOD E14 ......25 M2
Loewen Rd CDW/CHF RM16....33 H6
Loftie St BERM/RHTH SE16 ...24 D5
Logs Hl CHST BR7 ....63 J7
Logs Hill Cl CHST BR7 ......63 J7
Lolesworth Cl WCHPL E1 .....24 C2
Loman Pth SOCK/AV RM15....31 J2
Lomas Cl CROY/NA CRO 114 F2
Lomas La HAWK TN18 ....318 G9
Lomas Rd SIT ME10 ....130 C1
Lombard St BANK EC3V 24 A2
  EYN DA4 ....89 P1

MARG CT9....................15 G3
Lombard Wall CHARL SE7 .....26 A6
Lombardy Cl GILL ME7 ....96 B6
Lombardy Dr
  MAID/BEAR ME14 ....155 P7
Lomond Gdns SAND/SEL CR2 ...114 B2
Lomond Gv CMBW SE5 ....40 D1
Loncroft Rd CMBW SE5 ....24 B9
London Br CANST EC4R 24 A3
London Bridge St STHWK SE1 ...24 A4
London Bridge Wk
  STHWK SE1 * 24 A4
Londonderry Pde ERITH DA8 *...45 M1
London La BMLY BR1 ....62 D1
  CRBK TN17 ....276 D6
London Loop CROY/NA CRO....84 A7
  SAND/SEL CR2 ....114 A3
London Rd BGR/WK TN15 .....120 E4
  BGR/WK TN15 ....151 M1
  BH/WHM TN16 ....146 D8
  BMLY BR1 ....62 D6
  CANTW/ST CT2..............4 A3
  CROY/NA CRO 82 C5
  DART DA1 ....252 G4
  DEAL CT14 ....233 K6
  DIT/AY ME20 ....154 A3
  DVW CT17 ....291 J5
  EGRIN RH19 ....264 G6
  E/WMAL ME19 ....152 D5
  E/WMAL ME19 ....153 N3
  EYN DA4 ....89 J3
  FAV ME13 ....132 E7
  FAV ME15 ....164 G2
  FSTH SE23 ....41 J9
  GRAYS RM17 ....32 B9
  GVW DA11 ....45 J4
  HYTHE CT21 ....308 E4
  MAIDW ME16 ....12 A5
  PUR RM19 ....30 D6
  RAM CT11 ....16 A5
  RDART DA2 ....47 J8
  RDV CT15 ....290 C1
  RHAM ME8 ....97 M7
  RSEV TN14 ....117 N3
  RSIT ME9 ....98 A7
  RTON TN11 ....209 M2
  RTON TN11 ....210 D7
  SEV TN13 ....20 E2
  SIT ME10 ....99 K9
  SOCK/AV RM15 ....30 C4
  STH/RUST TN4 ....22 C4
  STH/RUST TN4 ....240 C5
  STRD ME2 ....65 L8
  SWLY BR8 ....82 F5
  THHTH CR7 ....82 F5
  TIL RM18 ....49 M5
  TONN TN10 ....210 E7
  WADH TN5 ....315 P3
  WLGTN SM6 ....82 A8
  WTHK RM20 ....31 N9
London Rd Purfleet PUR RM19...30 E9
London Rd (River)
  DVE/WH CT16 ....290 F3
London Rd Rocky Hl
  MAIDW ME16 ....12 C5
London Rd Temple Ewell
  DVE/WH CT16 ....290 D2
London Rd West Thurrock
  WTHK RM20 ....31 J9
London St FENCHST EC3M 24 B3
  FOLK CT20 ....11 G3
London Wall LVPST EC2M......24 A1
London Wall Buildings
  LVPST EC2M * 24 A1
Lone Barn Rd RMAID ME17 ...190 A5
Lonefield RASHW TN26 ....281 N7
Lonewood Wy RTON TN11 .....182 A9
Long Acre STMC/STPC BR5 ...87 L6
Longacre WSTB CT5 ....106 C5
Long Acre Cl CANTW/ST CT2 ...282 A1
Longacre Rd ASH TN23 ....282 A1
Longage Hl RCANTW CT4 .....256 F7
Long Barn Rd RSEV TN14 ....178 D9
The Long Barrow
  KEN/WIL TN24 ....283 H3
Long Beech ASH TN25 ....252 B8
Longbridge KEN/WIL TN24 ...253 L8
Longbridge Wy LEW SE13 ....42 A6
Longbrook St LEE/GVPK SE12...125 L3
Longbury Dr STMC/STPC BR5...64 D9
Long Catlis Rd RHAM ME8 ...126 G1
Long Ct PUR RM19 ....30 D7
Longcroft ELTH/MOT SE9......63 L2
Longdown Rd HAYES BR2 .....85 P9
Longdown Rd CAT SE6 ....51 P4
Long Dr SWCH CT13 ....201 K9
Longfellow Rd GILL ME7......7 H7
Longfellow Wy STHWK SE1 ...24 C7
Longfield BMLY BR1 ....62 D7
  TENT TN30 ....301 H8
Longfield Av HART DA5 ......68 G8
  HOO/HM ME3 ....53 L4
Longfield Cl WSTB CT5 ......106 A2
Longfield Crs SYD SE26......61 J2
Longfield Est STHWK SE1 * ...24 C7
Longfield Pl
  MAID/SHEP ME15 ....185 N3
Longfield Rd DVW CT17 ......291 J9
  MEO DA13 ....91 P2
  RTWE/PEM TN2 ....241 J8
Longfields Dr
  MAID/BEAR ME14 ....156 D7
Longford Cl RHAM ME8 ....97 M3
Longford Ter FOLK CT20 .....10 E5
Longford Rd FOLK CT20.......10 L6
Longham Copse
  MAID/SHEP ME15 ....186 C2
Longheath Gdns
  CROY/NA CRO 83 P2
Long Hi CTHM CR3 ....144 B6
  RCANTW CT4 ....194 D1

Longhill Av GILL ME7 ....7 F6
Longhill Rd CAT SE6 ....51 B1
Longhouse Rd CDW/CHF RM16...53 J6
Longhurst Dr WALD ME5 .....125 L3
Longhurst Rd CROY/NA CRO...83 N3
  LEW SE13 ....42 C6
Longlands Park Crs
  BFN/LL DA15 ....64 A2
Longlands Rd BFN/LL DA15...64 A2
Long La BXLYHN DA7 ....44 G1
  CDW/CHF RM16 ....32 C5
  CROY/NA CRO 83 P5
  RDV CT15 ....259 N7
  RMAID ME17 ....216 A5
  STHWK SE1 ....24 A5
Longleat La ABYW SE2 ......28 B9
Long Length ASH TN23 ......282 A5
Longley Rd CROY/NA CRO 82 G4
  RHAM ME8 ....97 J5
  ROCH ME1 ....95 H3
Longley St STHWK SE1 ......24 D8
Long Market CANT CT1 ......5 H4
Long Mark Rd CAN/RD E16...26 E2
Longmarsh Vw EYN DA4 ......67 H7
Longmead CHST BR7 ....63 L8
Longmead Cl HB CT6 ....107 H5
Longmead Dr SCUP DA14 ....64 F1
Longmeade CAT SE6 ....50 B9
Longmeadow SEV TN13 ......148 C6
Long Meadow Cl BECK BR3...84 F4
Longmeadow Rd BFN/LL DA15...44 A9
Long Meadow Wy
  CANTW/ST CT2 ....136 E9
Long Meads RRTW TN3 ......269 N5
Long Mead Wy TONN TN10...210 E5
Longmete Rd RCANTE CT3....169 N3
Long Mill La BGR/WK TN15...181 K2
Longparish Cl MAIDS ME15 ...79 J6
Longparish Cl
  MAID/SHEP ME15 ....186 C4
Long Pond Rd BKHTH/KID SE3...42 B3
Longport CANT CT1 ....5 H5
Long Reach Cl WSTB CT5 ....105 K8
Longreach Rd ERITH DA8 ....46 B1
Long Rede La MAIDW ME16...154 D9
Longridge SIT ME10 ....130 A3
Longridge Vls
  STPH/PW TN12 * 245 K6
Long Rock WSTB CT5 ....106 B3
Longsfield RASHE TN26 .....306 B1
Longshaw Rd
  MAID/SHEP ME15 ....186 C7
Longshore DEPT SE8 ....25 J7
Longstall Wy RSIT ME9 .....131 M5
Longtail Ri HB CT6 ....107 K4
Longton Av SYD SE26 ....60 C3
Longton Gv SYD SE26 ......61 H5
Longtye Dr WSTB CT5 ......106 B7
Longview Wy
  RTWE/PEM TN2 ....240 D9
Longwalk MEO DA13 ....69 J7
Long Wk STHWK SE1 ....24 B6
Longwood WALD ME5 ....125 N5
Longworth Cl THMD SE28....28 C2
Lonsdale Av MARG CT9 .....113 H2
Lonsdale Cl ELTH/MOT SE9...63 J8
Lonsdale Crs RDART DA2 ....67 J1
Lonsdale Dr RHAM ME8 .....97 H8
Lonsdale Gdns RTW TN1....22 D4
  STRHM/NOR SW16 ....60 B7
Lonsdale Rd BXLYHN DA7....45 H3
  SNWD SE25 ....83 N1
Lookers La HYTHE CT21 .....308 C6
Loop Court Ms SWCH CT15...201 N1
Loop Rd CHST BR7 ....63 N5
Loop St SWCH CT13 ....201 N1
Loose Down Rd FAV ME13 ...192 B4
Loose Rd MAID/SHEP ME15...185 M6
Lord Chatham's Ride
  RSEV TN14 ....147 L2
Lord Holland La
  BRXN/ST SW9 * 40 A3
Lordine La RBTBR TN32 .....329 J9
Lords Cl DUL SE21 ....60 C1
  RSIT ME9 ....130 D3
Lordship La EDUL SE22 .....40 F7
Lord St CAN/RD E16 ....26 C2
  GVE DA12 ....49 M8
Lordswood Cl RDART DA2 ....67 L3
Lords Wood Cl WALD ME5 ...125 N4
Lords Wood La WALD ME5....95 N9
Lord Warden Av DEAL CT14...233 J7
Lord Warden Sq DVW CT17 *..313 L1
Lord Warwick St
  WOOL/PLUM SE18 ....26 G6
Lorimar Ct SIT ME10 ....99 K7
Lorina Rd MSTR CT12 ....143 L4
Lorn Ct BRXN/ST SW9 ......40 A3
Lorne Av CROY/NA CRO 84 A6
Lorne Gdns CROY/NA CRO....84 A6
Lorne Rd DVE/WH CT16 .....291 J6
  RAM CT11 ....16 C4
Lorton Cl GVE DA12 ....70 A1
Lossenham La HAWK TN18...330 C2
Lothbury LOTH EC2R 24 A2
Lothian Rd BRXN/ST SW9....40 B2
Lotus Rd BH/WHM TN16 .....146 A3
Loudon Av ASH TN25 ....252 B6
Loudon Wy ASH TN23 ....252 B6
Loughborough Pk
  BRXN/ST SW9 ....40 B3
Loughborough Rd
  BRXN/ST SW9 ....40 B3
Louisa St WCHPL E1 ....24 F2
Louis Cl CHST BR7 ....63 K3
Louise Bennett Cl HNHL SE24 *..40 B5
Louisville Av GILL ME7 .....96 A2
Louvain Rd RDART DA2 .....67 H2
Lovage Ap EHAM E6 ....26 F1
Lovat La MON EC3R 24 A3
Lovegrove St STHWK SE1....24 D8
Lovegrove Wk POP/IOD E14...25 N4
Lovelace Av HAYES BR2......86 B5
Lovelace Cl BGR/WK TN15...120 B1

RHAM ME8....................96 C9
Lovelace Ct RASHW TN26 ....280 B5
Lovelace Gn ELTH/MOT SE9 ...43 K4
Lovelace Rd DUL SE21 ....60 C1
Love La BXLY DA5 ....45 J7
  CANT CT1 ....5 G5
  FAV ME15 ....123 G9
  HDCN TN27 ....248 B4
  IOS ME12 ....58 D9
  MARG CT9 ....15 G3
  RCANTE CT3 ....199 H5
  ROCH ME1 ....19 F5
  RYE TN31 ....338 E6
  SNWD SE25 ....61 H9
  SOCK/AV RM15 ....30 C5
  TIL RM18 ....34 J8
  WBY/YAL ME18 ....183 J9
  WOOL/PLUM SE18 ....27 H7
  WOOL/PLUM SE18 ....44 C3
Love Wk CMBW SE5 ....40 D3
Lovibonds Av ORP BR6 ....86 C7
Low Cl GRH DA9 ....45 N8
Lowdells Cl EGRIN RH19 .....264 F4
Lowdells Dr EGRIN RH19 .....264 F6
Lowdells La EGRIN RH19 .....264 F5
Lowden Rd HNHL SE24 ....40 B5
Lowe Av CAN/RD E16 ....26 B1
Lowell St POP/IOD E14 ......25 H2
Lower Addiscombe Rd
  CROY/NA CRO 83 J5
Lower Bell La DIT/AY ME20 ...154 A2
Lower Blackhouse Hl
  HYTHE CT21 ....309 J5
Lower Bloors La RHAM ME8 ...97 H4
Lower Boxley Rd
  MAID/BEAR ME14 ....12 C2
Lower Bridge St CANT CT1 ...5 F5
Lower Camden CHST BR7 .....63 K7
Lower Chantry La CANT CT1 ...5 G6
Lower Church St
  CROY/NA CRO 82 G6
Lower Coombe St
  CROY/NA CRO 83 H8
Lower Crs SLH/COR SS17 ....33 P6
Lower Cft SWLY BR8 ....88 E1
Lower Dene EGRIN RH19 .....265 K7
Lower Denmark Rd ASH TN23...2 E7
Lower Emsden Rd
  RCANTW CT4 ....164 D8
Lower Fant Rd MAIDW ME16 ...11 J5
Lower Farm Rd RMAID ME17...215 N4
Lower Gravel Rd HAYES BR2...85 P5
Lower Gn RTON TN11 ....209 L9
Lower Green Rd RRTW TN3 ...269 P2
Lower Hartlip Rd RSIT ME9...127 N1
Lower Haysden La TON TN9...209 N9
Lower Hazelhurst WADH TN5...314 F3
Lower Herne Rd HB CT6 .....107 K6
Lower Higham Rd GVE DA12...50 B9
Lower Lea Crossing
  POP/IOD E14 ....25 P3
Lower Lees Rd RCANTW CT4...194 E1
Lower Mere EGRIN RH19 .....265 J8
Lower Mill La DEAL CT14 ....233 H4
Lower Northdown Av
  MARG CT9 ....112 C3
Lower Norton La RSIT ME9 ...131 M5
Lower Park Rd BELV DA17 ....28 F6
Lower Platts WADH TN5 ......315 J5
Lower Rainham Rd GILL ME7 ...97 L5
  RHAM ME8 ....97 L5
Lower Range Rd GVE DA12 ...50 A8
Lower Rd BELV DA17 ....28 G6
  BERM/RHTH SE16 ....290 C2
  DVE/WH CT16 ....132 D6
  FAV ME13 ....70 C1
  GVE DA12 ....71 K1
  HARH RM3 ....48 E5
  MAID/SHEP ME15 ....184 C4
  RASHW TN26 ....302 G6
  RCANTE CT3 ....200 B4
  RMAID ME17 ....217 H3
  RSEV TN14 ....150 E2
  RSIT ME9 ....131 J3
  STMC/STPC BR5 ....87 J5
  SWLY BR8 ....66 B6
  TENT TN30 ....321 N8
  TIL RM18 ....49 L5
Lower Rochester Rd
  HOO/HM ME3 ....71 M1
Lower Sandgate Rd
  FOLK CT20 ....10 D7
Lower Sands LYDD TN29 .....327 J4
Lower Santon La RCANTE CT3...169 N1
Lower Stone St
  MAID/SHEP ME15 ....13 F5
Lower St DEAL CT14 ....233 J4
  MAID ME15 ....187 K4
  RTON TN11 ....209 M5
  SWCH CT13 ....201 J8
Lower Thames St MON EC3R...24 A3
Lower Tovil MAID/SHEP ME15...185 K1
Lower Twydall La GILL ME7 ...96 F2
Lower Vicarage Rd
  KEN/WIL TN24 ....252 F2
Lower Wall Rd HYTHE CT21...307 L8
  RASHE TN25 ....306 D8
Lower Warren Rd WALD ME5...125 K7
Lower Woodlands Rd
  GILL ME7 ....73 M9
Lowfield Rd IOS ME12 ....77 N1
Lowfield St DART DA1 ....46 E8
Lowlands Rd SOCK/AV RM15...30 F4
Low Meadow STRD ME2.......93 P9

Lowood St WCHPL E1 ....24 E3
The Lowry TON TN9 ....240 E1
Lowslip Hl RDV CT15 ....312 A1
Low Street La TIL RM18 .....33 N8
Lowther Cl FSTH SE23 ....41 L8
Lowther Rd DVW CT17 ....291 J7
  RDV CT15 ....310 A9
Loxford Ldg FOLK CT20 * 310 A9
Loxley Cl SYD SE26 ....61 K4
Loxton Rd FSTH SE23 ....41 K9
Loxwood Cl ORP BR6 ....261 J9
  STMC/STPC BR5 ....64 D6
Lubbock Cl MAID/SHEP ME15...186 B6
Lubbock Rd CHST BR7 ....63 K6
Lubbock St NWCR SE14 ......41 J1
Lucas Cl EGRIN RH19 * 265 J7
Lucas Crs CRH DA9 ....47 P6
Lucas Rd GRAYS RM17 ....32 B6
  PGE/AN SE20 ....61 J5
  SNOD ME6 ....123 M6
Lucas St DEPT SE8 ....41 N3
Lucerne Gv WSTB CT5 ....104 C8
Lucerne La RDV CT15 ....22 B6
Lucerne Rd ORP BR6 ....86 G5
  THHTH CR7 ....82 G2
Lucerne St MAID/BEAR ME14...13 G3
Lucy Av FOLKN CT19 ....310 D4
Lucy's Hl HYTHE CT21 ....308 B5
Luddenham Cl ASH TN23 .....282 C2
  MAID/BEAR ME14 ....155 P6
Luddesdon Rd ERITH DA8 ....45 J1
Ludford Cl CROY/NA CRO 93 J4
Ludgate Hl STP EC4M 24 A1
Ludham Cl THMD SE28 ......28 B2
Ludlow Cl HAYES BR2 ....62 E9
Ludlow Pl GRAYS RM17 ......32 C6
Luffield Rd ABYW SE2 ....28 A6
Luffman Rd LEE/GVPK SE12...51 L3
Lugard Rd PECK SE15 ....41 H3
Lughorse La WBY/YAL ME18...183 P9
Lukes Cl DVW CT17 ....291 P9
Lukin St WCHPL E1 ....24 F3
Lullarook Cl BH/WHM TN16...145 M1
Lullingstone Av SWLY BR8 ...65 P6
Lullingstone Cl GILL ME7 ...126 E2
  STMC/STPC BR5 ....64 D6
Lullingstone Crs
  STMC/STPC BR5 ....64 C6
Lullingstone La EYN DA4 ....89 H7
  LEW SE13 ....42 B7
Lullington Garth BMLY BR1...62 C6
Lullington Rd PGE/AN SE20 ...60 G1
  WSTB CT5 ....106 A4
Lulworth Cl SLH/COR SS17 ...34 A1
Lulworth Rd ELTH/MOT SE9...63 J1
  PECK SE15 * 41 H3
  WELL DA16 ....44 B3
Lumley Cl BELV DA17 ....28 F9
Lumsden Ter CHAT ME4 ......6 A6
Lunar Cl BH/WHM TN16 ......145 N1
Luna Rd THHTH CR7 ....60 C9
Lunedale Rd RDART DA2 .....47 J3
Lunghurst Rd CTHM CR3 .....144 D6
Lunham Rd NRWD SE19 ......60 E6
Lunsford La DIT/AY ME20 ....123 N6
Lupin Cl BRXS/STRHM SW2 ...60 B1
  CROY/NA CRO 84 A5
Lupton Cl LEE/GVPK SE12 ...62 F3
Lurkins Ri CRBK TN17 ....274 C9
Lushington Rd CAT SE6 .....51 P4
  MAID/BEAR ME14 ....155 K5
Lusted Hall La
  BH/WHM TN16 ....145 M5
Luton Av BRDST CT10 ....143 L1
Luton Cl BRDST CT10 ....143 L1
Luton High St WALD ME5 ....95 P4
Luton Rd CHAT ME5 ....6 D2
  CHAT ME4 ....7 H6
  FAV ME13 ....133 H6
  SCUP DA14 ....64 L2
Lutwyche Rd FSTH SE23 .....61 M1
Luxfield Rd ELTH/MOT SE9 ...43 J4
Luxford St BERM/RHTH SE16...24 E8
Luxmore St BROCKY SE4 .....41 M2
Luxon Rd MEO DA13 ....122 F1
Luxted Rd ORP BR6 ....116 B6
Lyall Av DUL SE21 ....60 E3
Lyall Wy RHAM ME8 ....126 C1
Lychfield Dr STRD ME2 ......72 A6
Lych Gate Rd ORP BR6 ......87 H5
Lyconby Gdns CROY/NA CRO...84 C6
Lydbrook Cl SIT ME10 ....129 K1
Lydd Cl BFN/LL DA15 ....64 A2
Lydden Hl RDV CT15 ....259 N5
Lydd Rd BXLYHN DA7 ....45 H1
  RYE TN31 ....344 A1
  WALD ME5 ....95 N3
Lydd Town Crossing
  LYDD TN29 ....342 D4
Lydia Cl DEAL CT14 ....236 C3
Lydia Rd ERITH DA8 ....29 L9
Lydos Cl LYDD TN29 ....343 K7
Lydstep Rd CHST BR7 ....63 L5
Lyell Cl HYTHE CT21 ....308 F6
Lyell St BRCH CT7 ....110 C6

Lyford St WOOL/PLUM SE18 26 F7
Lyle Cl STRD ME2 72 B7
Lyle Ct MAIDW ME16 155 H7
Lyle Pk SEV TN13 148 G8
Lymden La WADH TN5 314 E7
Lyme Farm Rd LEE/GVPK SE12 42 E5
Lymer Av NRWD SE19 60 F4
Lyme Rd WELL DA16 44 D2
Lyminge Cl RHAM ME8 96 F4
SCUP DA14 64 B3
Lyminge Wy MARG CT9 113 H4
Lymington Ct
MAID/SHEP ME15 186 C7
Lymington Rd WGOS CT8 111 L6
Lympne Hl HYTHE CT21 307 P5
Lympstone Gdns PECK SE15 40 G1
Lyncourt BKHTH/KID SE3 * 42 B3
Lyndale Cl BKHTH/KID SE3 26 A9
Lynden Wy SWLY BR8 65 L9
Lyndhurst Av MARG CT9 112 G3
RHAM ME8 96 F7
Lyndhurst Cl BXLYHN DA7 45 K4
CANTW/ST CT2 166 D1
CROY/NA CR0 83 L7
ORP BR6 86 C8
Lyndhurst Dr SEV TN13 148 D9
Lyndhurst Farm Cl EGRIN RH19 264 A4
Lyndhurst Gv CMBW SE5 40 E3
SIT ME10 129 M3
Lyndhurst Leys HAYES BR2 * 62 B8
Lyndhurst Prior SNWD SE25 * 60 E9
Lyndhurst Rd BRDST CT10 113 M8
BXLYHN DA7 45 K4
DVW CT17 290 F5
LYDD TN29 326 G6
MAID/SHEP ME15 185 P3
RAM CT11 17 J2
THHTH CR7 82 F1
Lyndhurst Sq PECK SE15 40 F2
Lyndhurst Wy MEO DA13 69 J7
PECK SE15 40 F2
Lyndon Av BFN/LL DA15 44 B6
Lyndon Rd BELV DA17 28 F7
Lyndon Wy RFOLK CT18 287 H1
Lynette Av STRD ME2 72 A6
Lyngate Ct MARG CT9 113 J3
Lyngs Cl WBY/YAL ME18 213 N2
Lynmead Cl EDEN TN8 206 C6
Lynmere Rd WELL DA16 44 D3
Lynmouth Dr IOS ME12 58 C9
Lynmouth Ri STMC/STPC BR5 87 J1
Lynne Cl ORP BR6 116 G1
Lynors Av STRD ME2 72 A5
Lynstead Cl BMLY BR1 62 G8
Lynsted Cl ASH TN23 282 C2
BXLYHS DA6 45 K6
Lynsted Ct BECK BR3 61 L8
Lynsted Gdns ELTH/MOT SE9 43 H5
Lynsted La RSIT ME9 130 G6
Lynsted Rd IOS ME12 57 N9
RHAM ME8 96 E3
Lynton Av STMC/STPC BR5 87 J1
Lynton Cl EGRIN RH19 265 K6
Lynton Dr WALD ME5 125 N2
Lynton Est STHWK SE1 * 24 D7
Lynton Pde MARG CT9 * 112 F3
Lynton Park Av EGRIN RH19 265 K6
Lynton Rd CROY/NA CR0 82 F3
GVW DA11 49 L9
HYTHE CT21 309 H6
STHWK SE1 24 C7
Lynton Rd South GVW DA11 49 L9
Lynwood FOLKN CT19 10 C1
Lynwood Gdns CROY/NA CR0 82 E8
Lynwood Gv ORP BR6 86 F4
Lyons Crs TON TN9 210 F8
Lyoth Rd STMC/STPC BR5 86 D6
Lypeatt Ct CANTW/ST CT2 * 136 B9
Lyric Ms SYD SE26 61 J3
Lysander Cl BRDST CT10 143 H1
RCANTW CT4 198 B3
Lysander Rd E/WMAL ME19 152 G9
Lysander Wk RFOLK CT18 288 D8
Lysander Wy ORP BR6 86 D7
Lytchet Rd BMLY BR1 62 E6
Lytcott Gv EDUL SE22 40 F6
Lytham Av HB CT6 107 J5
Lytham Cl THMD SE28 28 D2
Lytham St WALW SE17 24 A8
Lytton Gdns WLGTN SM6 82 C8
Lytton Rd CDW/CHF RM16 33 H7
Lyveden Rd BKHTH/KID SE3 42 F1

M

Mabel Rd SWLY BR8 66 A5
Maberley Crs NRWD SE19 60 G6
Maberley Rd BECK BR3 61 K9
NRWD SE19 60 F7
Mabledon Av KEN/WIL TN24 3 H5
Mabledon Cl NROM TN28 336 G7
Mabledon Rd TON TN9 240 D1
Macarthur Ter CHARL SE7 * 26 E9
Macaulay Cl DIT/AY ME20 123 P9
Macbean St WOOL/PLUM SE18 27 H6
Macclesfield Rd SNWD SE25 83 N2
Macdonald Pde WSTB CT5 105 H7
Macdonald Rd DVW CT17 291 H6
GILL ME7 * 73 K9
Mace Cl WAP E1W 24 E4
Mace La ASH TN23 3 G3
RSEV TN14 116 E7
Macgregor Rd CAN/RD E16 26 D1
Machell Rd PECK SE15 41 J4
Mackenders Cl DIT/AY ME20 124 E7
Mackenders La DIT/AY ME20 124 F7
Mackenzie Dr FOLK CT20 310 B6
Mackenzie Rd BECK BR3 61 L7
Mackenzie Ter
DVE/WH CT16 * 291 J4
Mackenzie Wy GVE DA12 69 P5
Mackerel Hl RYE TN31 331 L8
Mackie Rd BRXS/STRHM SW2 40 A8
Mackintosh Cl HOO/HM ME3 53 M5
Macklands Wy RHAM ME8 97 K4
Macks Rd BERM/RHTH SE16 24 D7
Maclean Rd FSTH SE23 41 L7
Maclean Ter GVE DA12 * 70 B1
Macleod Cl GRAYS RM17 32 E7
Macleod House
WOOL/PLUM SE18 * 43 J1
Macoma Rd WOOL/PLUM SE18 27 L9
Macoma Ter
WOOL/PLUM SE18 27 L9
Maconochies Rd
POP/IOD E14 * 25 L8
Macquarie Wy POP/IOD E14 25 L7
Madan Cl BH/WHM TN16 176 F1
Madan Rd BH/WHM TN16 176 E1
Mada Rd ORP BR6 86 C7
Madden Av WALD ME5 95 K9
Madden Cl SWCM DA10 48 C7
Maddocks Cl SCUP DA14 64 F5
Madeira Av BMLY BR1 62 C7
Madeira Pk RTW TN1 22 D7
Madeira Rd MARG CT9 15 K4
NROM TN28 337 K7
Madeira Wk RAM CT11 17 G4
Madeline Rd PGE/AN SE20 60 G6
Madginford Cl
MAID/SHEP ME15 186 D1
Madginford Rd
MAID/SHEP ME15 186 C1
Madison Crs WELL DA16 44 E1
Madison Gdns BXLYHN DA7 44 E1
Madison Wy SEV TN13 148 E8
Madron St STHWK SE1 24 B8
Maesmaur Rd BH/WHM TN16 145 N6
Mafeking Rd WALD ME5 125 L2
Magazine Rd KEN/WIL TN24 2 D2
Magdala Rd BRDST CT10 113 K7
DVW CT17 291 J6
Magdalen Cl GILL ME7 126 D1
Magdalen Ct BRDST CT10 113 M8
CANT CT1 5 G7
Magdalen St STHWK SE1 24 B4
Magdelan Gv ORP BR6 87 J8
Magness Rd DEAL CT14 232 F7
Magnet Rd WTHK RM20 31 M9
Magnolia Av MARG CT9 113 J3
RHAM ME8 96 E9
Magnolia Dr BH/WHM TN16 145 N1
RCANTW CT4 195 N2
Magpie Cl DIT/AY ME20 153 P3
Magpie Ct IOS ME12 78 A1
Magpie Hall Cl HAYES BR2 85 P3
Magpie Hall La HAYES BR2 85 P4
Magpie Hall Rd CHAT ME4 95 L6
RASHW TN26 282 A6
Magpie La MAID/BEAR ME14 127 J4
RCANTW CT4 256 G6
Magpie Pl NWCR SE14 * 25 H9
Magri Wk WCHPL E1 24 F1
Maguire St STHWK SE1 24 C5
Magwitch Cl ROCH ME1 94 G2
Mahogany Cl
BERM/RHTH SE16 25 H4
Maida Rd BELV DA17 28 F6
CHAT ME4 95 N4
Maida Vale Rd DART DA1 46 A7
Maiden Erlegh Av BXLY DA5 44 G9
Maiden La CANT CT1 166 C6
DART DA1 46 A5
Maidenstone Hl GNWCH SE10 42 A2
Maidstone Rd ASH TN23 2 B2
BGR/WK TN15 149 N7
CHAT ME4 6 B5
CHAT ME4 95 K6
GILL ME7 126 E3
HDCN TN27 217 K9
HDCN TN27 220 E1
RHAM ME8 126 F2
RMAID ME17 187 H9
RMAID ME17 189 K6
ROCH ME1 94 G7
RSIT ME9 128 C4
RTON TN11 211 P2
RTWE/PEM TN2 241 M9
SCUP DA14 64 F5
SEV TN13 148 D7
SIT ME10 99 H8
STPH/PW TN12 213 H2
STPH/PW TN12 215 L9
STPH/PW TN12 242 G3
STPH/PW TN12 245 K2
SWLY BR8 65 K7
WBY/YAL ME18 183 J9
The Mailyns RHAM ME8 96 F7
Main Barracks
WOOL/PLUM SE18 * 26 G8
Maine Cl DVE/WH CT16 291 J4
Main Ga TIL RM18 * 49 K3
Main Gate Rd CHAT ME4 72 F8
Mainridge Rd CHST BR7 63 L3
Main Rd BFN/LL DA15 64 A2
BH/WHM TN16 145 N1
EDEN TN8 206 C5
EYN DA4 67 H5
EYN DA4 89 K3
HART DA3 91 M1
HOO/HM ME3 54 B9
HOO/HM ME3 72 F3
IOS ME12 57 J5
ORP BR6 * 117 K3
QBOR ME11 77 J2
RDART DA2 68 A7
RSEV TN14 147 H3
RSEV TN14 147 M9
STMC/STPC BR5 64 E7
SWLY BR8 65 P7
SWLY BR8 88 B3
Main Road Gorse Hl EYN DA4 89 N5
Main St CHAT ME4 73 H5
RYE TN31 330 A7
RYE TN31 332 E9
RYE TN31 338 A3
RYE TN31 338 E1
Maismore St PECK SE15 24 D9
Maison Dieu Rd DVE/WH CT16 8 C2
Maitland Cl GNWCH SE10 41 P1
Maitland Ct FAV ME13 132 E4
Maitland Rd SYD SE26 61 K5
Majendie Rd
WOOL/PLUM SE18 27 L8
Major Cl BRXN/ST SW9 40 B4
WSTB CT5 105 J8
Major Rd BERM/RHTH SE16 * 24 D6
Makenade Av FAV ME13 132 G8
Malabar St POP/IOD E14 25 K5
Malam Gdns POP/IOD E14 25 L3
Malan Cl BH/WHM TN16 145 P2
Malcolm Cl PGE/AN SE20 * 61 J6
Malcolm Rd PGE/AN SE20 61 J6
SNWD SE25 83 M3
Malcolm Sargent Rd
ASH TN23 282 E2
Malden Av SNWD SE25 83 N1
Malden Dr MAID/BEAR ME14 155 L4
Maldon Cl CMBW SE5 * 40 E4
Maldon Rd WLGTN SM6 82 A9
Maley Av WNWD SE27 60 B1
Malfort Rd CMBW SE5 40 E4
Malham Dr MARG CT9 112 F4
Malham Rd FSTH SE23 41 K9
Mallams Ms BRXN/ST SW9 40 A4
Mallard Cl DART DA1 46 F6
HB CT6 107 K4
Mallard Ct IOS ME12 78 A1
Mallard Pl EGRIN RH19 265 J8
Mallard Rd SAND/SEL CR2 114 A4
Mallards KEN/WIL TN24 282 G1
Mallards Wy
MAID/SHEP ME15 186 D1
Mallard Wk CROY/NA CR0 84 A2
Mallard Wy HOO/HM ME3 54 F4
Mallet Rd LEW SE13 42 B7
Malling Ct CROY/NA CR0 * 83 P3
Mallingdene Cl HOO/HM ME3 52 B8
Malling Rd SNOD ME6 123 N7
WBY/YAL ME18 182 F2
WBY/YAL ME18 183 N2
Mallings La MAID/BEAR ME14 156 F8
Malling Ter MAIDW ME16 155 H8
Malling Wy HAYES BR2 85 J4
Mallinson Rd CROY/NA CR0 82 C7
Mallory Cl BECK BR3 61 L8
BROCKY SE4 41 L5
MSTR CT12 143 H2
Mallow Cl CROY/NA CR0 84 A5
GVW DA11 69 J3
Mallow Ct GRAYS RM17 32 E9
The Mall DVE/WH CT16 * 8 B2
FAV ME13 132 F7
GILL ME7 * 7 H1
Mallys Pl EYN DA4 67 J7
Malmains Cl BECK BR3 84 G2
Malmains Rd DVW CT17 291 H8
Malmains Wy BECK BR3 84 F1
Malmaynes Hall Rd
HOO/HM ME3 54 A5
Malmeady Ct DEAL CT14 * 232 F8
Malmesbury Rd CAN/RD E16 25 P1
Malmesbury Ter CAN/RD E16 26 A1
Malpas Rd BROCKY SE4 41 M3
CDW/CHF RM16 33 K6
Malta Av WALD ME5 95 M7
Malta Rd TIL RM18 49 K3
Malta Ter MAID/BEAR ME14 155 M5
Maltby Cl ORP BR6 87 H5
Maltby St STHWK SE1 24 C6
Malthouse Cl RMAID ME17 189 L6
Malthouse Hl HYTHE CT21 308 G5
MAID/SHEP ME15 185 L7
Malthouse La GVE DA12 70 G4
RASHW TN26 304 A7
Malt House La TENT TN30 301 H8
Malthouse Rd BGR/WK TN15 121 J3
CANTW/ST CT2 4 E1
Maltings Cl RTON TN11 211 P2
Malting's Pl STHWK SE1 24 B5
The Maltings CANT CT1 * 5 G5
DEAL CT14 232 G9
MAID/BEAR ME14 156 B7
ORP BR6 86 G5
OXTED RH8 175 J7
RCANTE CT3 168 C9
RHAM ME8 97 K6
RMAID ME17 185 N7
RTON TN11 * 211 P2
SNWD SE25 * 60 E9
Malt Ms ROCH ME1 19 F5
Malton Ms WOOL/PLUM SE18 27 M9
Malton St WOOL/PLUM SE18 27 M9
Malton Wy RTWE/PEM TN2 271 J2
Malt St STHWK SE1 24 D9
Malus Cl WALD ME5 125 M4
Malvern Av BXLYHN DA7 44 G1
Malvern Meadow
DVE/WH CT16 290 F2
Malvern Pk HB CT6 108 A6
Malvern Rd DVE/WH CT16 290 F2
DVW CT17 8 A4
GILL ME7 96 B4
GRAYS RM17 32 F7
KEN/WIL TN24 252 E5
ORP BR6 87 J8
THHTH CR7 82 F1
Malvina Av GVE DA12 69 M1
Malyons Rd LEW SE13 41 P6
SWLY BR8 65 P6
Malyons Ter LEW SE13 41 P6
Mamignot Cl
MAID/BEAR ME14 156 C7
Managers St POP/IOD E14 * 25 M4
Manaton Cl PECK SE15 41 H4
Manchester Cl WALD ME5 95 P8
Manchester Gv POP/IOD E14 25 M8
Manchester Rd POP/IOD E14 25 M8
THHTH CR7 60 C9
Manciple Cl CANTW/ST CT2 166 B5
Manciple St STHWK SE1 24 A5
Mandarin La HB CT6 107 K4
Mandela Rd CAN/RD E16 26 B2
Mandela St BRXN/ST SW9 40 A1
Mandela Wy STHWK SE1 24 C7
Mandeville Rd CANTW/ST CT2 4 C1
Mangers La DVE/WH CT16 291 H5
Mangers Pl DVE/WH CT16 291 H4
Mangold Wy ERITHM DA18 28 C6
Mangravet Av
MAID/SHEP ME15 185 P4
Manilla St POP/IOD E14 25 K5
Manister Rd ABYW SE2 27 P6
Manley Cl DVE/WH CT16 261 H9
Mann Cl CROY/NA CR0 83 H7
Mannering Cl DVW CT17 290 G4
Manning Cl EGRIN RH19 264 G6
Manning Rd STMC/STPC BR5 87 L2
Manning St SOCK/AV RM15 30 F4
Manningtree St WCHPL E1 24 D2
Mannock Rd DART DA1 46 F4
Manns Hl RCANTW CT4 226 F4
Mann Sq TON TN9 240 G2
Manor Av BROCKY SE4 41 M3
DEAL CT14 232 G5
Manorbrook BKHTH/KID SE3 42 E5
Manor Cl CANT CT1 166 B7
DART DA1 45 M5
DEAL CT14 232 F5
GDST RH9 204 C5
GVE DA12 70 D1
HB CT6 108 C4
MAID/BEAR ME14 156 E9
QBOR ME11 77 H4
RDART DA2 66 A2
SOCK/AV RM15 30 F4
STH/RUST TN4 270 B4
THMD SE28 28 B2
WARL CR6 144 B2
Manor Ct MAID/BEAR ME14 156 E9
MEO DA13 92 E2
Manordene Rd THMD SE28 28 B2
Manor Dr BRCH CT7 110 G7
HART DA3 91 K3
Manor Est BERM/RHTH SE16 24 E7
Manor Farm Cl HYTHE CT21 307 N3
Manor Farm Rd
STRHM/NOR SW16 60 A8
Manorfield ASH TN23 252 B9
Manor Fld GVE DA12 70 G4
Manorfields Cl CHST BR7 64 B9
Manor Forstal HART DA3 91 J7
Manor Gdns WALD ME5 125 L1
Manor Gv BECK BR3 61 P8
PECK SE15 24 F9
SIT ME10 129 M2
TONN TN10 210 F7
Manor House Dr ASH TN23 282 F4
MAIDW ME16 155 J9
Manor House Gdns EDEN TN8 206 D9
Manor La HART DA3 90 F4
LEW SE13 42 C6
ROCH ME1 94 E3
Manor Lane Ter LEW SE13 42 C5
Manor Lea Rd BRCH CT7 140 A3
Manor Leaze RASHE TN25 284 G3
Manor Ms DEAL CT14 262 E3
Manor Mt FSTH SE23 41 J9
Manor Pk CHST BR7 63 P8
LEW SE13 42 B6
STH/RUST TN4 270 B5
Manor Park Cl WWKM BR4 84 E5
Manor Park Rd CHST BR7 63 N7
WWKM BR4 84 E5
Manor Pl CHST BR7 63 P8
Manor Pound La RASHE TN25 284 F1
Manor Ri DVW CT17 291 H9
MAID/BEAR ME14 156 E9
Manor Rd BECK BR3 61 N8
BFN/LL DA15 64 B2
BGR/WK TN15 120 C5
BH/WHM TN16 145 P5
BRCH CT7 140 A3
BXLY DA5 45 K9
CAN/RD E16 25 P1
CHAT ME4 6 B4
DART DA1 45 N5
DEAL CT14 232 F5
DVW CT17 291 H9
EDEN TN8 206 C9
EGRIN RH19 264 F6
ERITH DA8 29 L9
FOLK CT20 10 D4
GRAYS RM17 32 D9
GVE DA12 * 49 M7
HART DA3 91 M2
HB CT6 108 C4
LYDD TN29 342 B7
MEO DA13 92 D2
QBOR ME11 77 H4
RSEV TN14 147 L9
RSIT ME9 159 N3
SNWD SE25 83 M1
STH/RUST TN4 240 B8
STH/RUST TN4 269 P4
SWCM DA10 48 C8
TIL RM18 49 L3
WLGTN SM6 82 A8
WSTB CT5 105 P3
WTHK RM20 31 M9
WWKM BR4 84 E6
Manor Rd North WLGTN SM6 82 A8
Manor Rw TENT TN30 * 301 H8
Manor St GILL ME7 72 G9
Manor Vw HART DA3 * 91 K3
Manor Wy ASH TN23 2 A1
BECK BR3 61 N9
BKHTH/KID SE3 42 E5
BXLY DA5 45 J9
BXLYHN DA7 45 M4
GRAYS RM17 48 G1
HAYES BR2 85 P3
IOS ME12 80 A1
IOS ME12 80 E5
STMC/STPC BR5 86 D1
SWCM DA10 48 C5
The Manor Wy WLGTN SM6 82 A8
Manse Fld RASHE TN25 284 E3
Mansel Dr ROCH ME1 94 F4
Mansell La RDV CT15 258 E9
Mansell St WCHPL E1 24 C3
Mansergh Cl
WOOL/PLUM SE18 43 J1
Manse Wy SWLY BR8 88 F1
Mansfield Cl STMC/STPC BR5 87 L4
Mansfield Rd SWLY BR8 65 N5
Mansfield Wk MAIDW ME16 185 J1
Mansion Gdns DVE/WH CT16 291 H3
Mansion House Cl
HDCN TN27 278 A6
Mansion House Pl
MANHO EC4N 24 A2
Mansion Rw GILL ME7 72 G9
Manstead Gdns RAIN RM13 29 N2
Manston Cl PGE/AN SE20 61 J7
Manston Court Rd MARG CT9 112 D9
MSTR CT12 142 B4
Manston Rd MARG CT9 112 C7
MSTR CT12 141 M2
MSTR CT12 142 A2
Manthorpe Rd
WOOL/PLUM SE18 27 K8
Mantle Rd BROCKY SE4 41 L4
Mantles Hl DEAL CT14 232 C8
Manton Rd ABYW SE2 27 P7
The Manwarings
STPH/PW TN12 273 P2
Manwood Av CANTW/ST CT2 166 E1
Manwood Cl SIT ME10 129 N3
Manwood Rd BROCKY SE4 41 M7
SWCH CT13 201 P2
Manwood St CAN/RD E16 26 G4
Maple Av GILL ME7 96 B1
MAIDW ME16 155 H6
Maple Cl ASH TN23 252 A7
CANTW/ST CT2 165 P2
DIT/AY ME20 153 P2
MARG CT9 113 K4
STMC/STPC BR5 86 E2
SWLY BR8 65 N8
Maple Ct RCANTE CT3 138 B8
Maple Crs BFN/LL DA15 44 C7
Maplecroft Cl EHAM E6 26 E2
Mapledale Av CROY/NA CR0 83 N7
Maple Dr EGRIN RH19 265 K7
LYDD TN29 337 L2
Maple Gdns RCANTE CT3 138 B9
Maple Leaf Dr BFN/LL DA15 44 B9
Maple Leaf Sq
BERM/RHTH SE16 * 24 G5
Maple Rd DART DA1 46 C9
GRAYS RM17 32 D9
GVE DA12 69 N3
HOO/HM ME3 73 L4
PGE/AN SE20 61 J6
STRD ME2 71 P9
Maplescombe La EYN DA4 89 M7
Maplesden STPH/PW TN12 * 245 J4
Maplesden Cl MAIDW ME16 154 E9
Maples Pl WCHPL E1 * 24 E1
The Maples BRDST CT10 113 H9
HART DA3 68 F9
IOS ME12 78 B1
Maple St IOS ME12 57 L7
Maplethorpe Rd THHTH CR7 82 F1
Mapleton Cl HAYES BR2 85 K2
Mapleton Rd BH/WHM TN16 176 F6
EDEN TN8 207 H2
Maple Tree Pl BKHTH/KID SE3 43 J2
Maplin Rd CAN/RD E16 26 B2
Maplins Cl RHAM ME8 * 97 J5
Mara Ct CHAT ME4 * 95 L5
Maran Wy ERITHM DA18 28 C6
Marathon Paddock GILL ME7 96 A2
Marathon Wy THMD SE28 27 N5
Marble Quay WAP E1W * 24 C4
Marbrook Ct LEE/GVPK SE12 62 G2
Marcella Rd BRXN/ST SW9 40 A3
Marcellina Wy ORP BR6 86 F7
Marcet Rd DART DA1 46 C6
Marchants STPH/PW TN12 * 242 E9
Marchant St NWCR SE14 25 H9
Marchwood Cl CMBW SE5 40 E1
Marcia Rd STHWK SE1 24 B7
Marconi Rd GVW DA11 69 H2
Marconi Wy ROCH ME1 95 J7
Marcus Garvey Ms EDUL SE22 41 H7
Marcus Garvey Wy
BRXN/ST SW9 40 A5
Marcus Rd DART DA1 46 A8
Mardale Cl RHAM ME8 97 K5
Mardell Rd CROY/NA CR0 84 A2
Marden Av HAYES BR2 85 K3
MSTR CT12 16 A1
Marden Crs BXLY DA5 45 L6
CROY/NA CR0 82 E3
Marden Rd CROY/NA CR0 82 E3
STPH/PW TN12 245 M4
STRD ME2 72 C6
Marden Sq BERM/RHTH SE16 24 E6
Mardol Rd KEN/WIL TN24 252 F4
Mardyke Vw SOCK/AV RM15 * 31 H6
Marechal Niel Av BFN/LL DA15 63 P2
Marechal Niel Pde
BFN/LL DA15 * 63 P2
Maresfield CROY/NA CR0 83 K7
Maresfield Cl DVE/WH CT16 291 J5
Margaret Gardner Dr
ELTH/MOT SE9 63 K1
Margaret Rd BXLY DA5 44 F7
Margarets Rd RDV CT15 262 F6
Margaret St FOLK CT20 11 G4
Margate Cl GILL ME7 73 L9
Margate Hl BRCH CT7 141 J1
Margate Rd BRDST CT10 112 G9
HB CT6 107 N3
HB CT6 108 B8
Margetts La ROCH ME1 124 C4
Margetts Pl STRD ME2 72 C4
Maria Cl BERM/RHTH SE16 24 D7
Marian Av IOS ME12 58 A9
Marian Cl CDW/CHF RM16 31 P4

Marian Sq STPH/PW TN12 ....246 C5
Maria Ter WCHPL E1 ....24 G1
Marie Curie CMBW SE5 * 40 E2
Marie Manor Wy RDART DA2 * 67 J2
Marigold St BERM/RHTH SE16...24 E5
Marigold Wy CROY/NA CR0 ....84 A5
Marilyn Crs BRCH CT7 ....111 J6
Marina Ct DEAL CT14 * 233 J1
Marina Dr DART DA1 ....46 G9
  GVW DA11 ....49 K8
  IOS ME12 ....58 A9
  WELL DA16 ....44 A3
Marina Esp RAM CT11 ....17 J3
Marina Rd RAM CT11 ....17 J3
The Marina DEAL CT14 ....233 J1
Marina Av RDART DA2 ....327 K5
Marine Ct PUR RM19 ....30 C7
Marine Crs FOLK CT20 ....11 F6
  WSTB CT5 ....106 B3
Marine Dr BRDST CT10 ....113 M2
  HOO/HM ME3 ....73 L4
  MARG CT9 ....15 F4
  WOOL/PLUM SE18 ....26 G7
Marine Gap WSTB CT5 ....105 K5
Marine Gdns MARG CT9 ....15 H2
Marine Pde DVE/WH CT16 ....8 E5
  FOLK CT20 ....11 G5
  IOS ME12 ....57 M6
  NROM TN28 ....337 K8
  WSTB CT5 ....105 N3
Marine Parade Ms FOLK CT20 ....11 G5
Marine PI IOS ME12 * 57 M6
Marine Rd DEAL CT14 ....233 J5
Mariners Lea BRDST CT10 ....113 J9
The Mariners ROCH ME1 * 18 E7
Mariners Wy GVW DA11 ....49 J8
Marine St BERM/RHTH SE16 ....24 D6
Marine Ter FOLK CT20 ....11 G5
  MARG CT9 ....14 E5
Marine Vw CHAT ME4 ....73 H6
Marine Walk St HYTHE CT21 *....309 H5
Marion Cl WALD ME5 ....125 M3
Marion Crs MAID/SHEP ME15...185 N2
  STMC/STPC BR5 ....87 J2
Marion Rd CROY/NA CR0 ....83 H2
Marischal Rd LEW SE13 ....42 B4
Marisco Cl CDW/CHF RM16......33 J7
Maritime Av HB CT6 ....107 P2
Maritime Ga GVW DA11 ....49 J8
  STRD ME2 ....47 P6
Maritime Quay POP/IOD E14 ....25 K8
Maritime Wy CHAT ME4 ....72 C3
Marjan Cl DVW CT17 ....291 H6
Mark Av RAM CT11 ....142 G7
Mark Cl BXLYHN DA7 ....44 G2
  HAYES BR2 ....221 M5
Market Buildings
  MAID/BEAR ME14 ....12 E4
Market La HYTHE CT21 * 309 H5
Market Meadow
  STMC/STPC BR5 ....87 K1
Market Pde BMLY BR1 * 62 E7
  SCUP DA14 * 64 C3
  SNWD SE25 * 83 M1
Market PI BERM/RHTH SE16 * 24 D7
  BXLYHN DA7 ....45 J5
  DART DA1 ....46 E8
  HDCN TN27 ....221 H5
  MARG CT9 ....15 G3
  RCANTE CT3 ....229 J1
  TIL RM18 * 49 L3
Market Rd RYE TN31 ....338 E7
Market Sq BH/WHM TN16 ....176 D3
  BMLY BR1 ....62 E8
  RTW TN1 ....22 E5
Market St DART DA1 ....46 E8
  DEAL CT14 ....233 J5
  FAV ME15 ....12 B1
  HB CT6 ....107 L1
  MARG CT9 ....15 G3
  RTWE/PEM TN2 * 22 C6
  RYE TN31 ....338 F7
  STPH/PW TN12 ....246 C4
  SWCH CT13 ....201 P1
  WOOL/PLUM SE18 ....27 H7
Market Vw RCANTE CT3 ....229 J1
Market Wy BH/WHM TN16 ....176 D3
Marker Yard Ms STHWK SE1 ....24 C8
Markfield CROY/NA CR0 ....114 C5
Markland Rd DVW CT17 ....291 H8
  RDV CT15 ....290 C8
Mark La GVE DA12 ....50 A8
  MON EC3R 14 A8
Marks Rd WARL CR6 ....144 B3
Marks Sq GVW DA11 ....69 K5
Markstone Ter ORP BR6 * 87 H4
Mark St CHAT ME4 ....95 M4
Mark Wy SWLY BR8 ....88 F2
Markwell Cl SYD SE26 ....86 H1
Marlborough Cl BRDST CT10...141 K1
  CDW/CHF RM16 ....32 D5
  NROM TN28 ....337 J6
  ORP BR6 ....86 C4
  STH/RUST TN4 ....22 A1
Marlborough Crs SEV TN13 ....20 A1
Marlborough Gv STHWK SE1 ....24 D8
Marlborough La CHARL SE7 ....26 D9
Marlborough Pde
  MAIDW ME16 * 184 E1
Marlborough Park Av
  BFN/LL DA15 ....44 C9
Marlborough Rd
  BXLYHN DA7 ....44 F4
  DART DA1 ....46 C7
  DEAL CT14 ....232 F7
  DVW CT17 ....290 G8
  GILL ME7 ....7 G5
  HAYES BR2 ....85 M1
  MARG CT9 ....15 G7
  RAM CT11 ....16 E4
  WOOL/PLUM SE18 ....27 J6
  WSTB CT5 ....105 L9

Marlborough Wy
  KEN/WIL TN24 ....253 J2
Marie Place Rd
  STPH/PW TN12 ....275 K4
Marler Rd FOLK CT19 ....310 B5
  FSTH SE23 ....41 M9
Marley Av BXLYHN DA7 ....28 C9
Marley Ct CANTW/ST CT2 *....136 B9
Marley La DEAL CT14 ....231 P2
  HDCN TN27 ....248 D5
  RCANTE CT3 ....138 C4
  RCANTW CT4 ....137 K1
Marley Rd BERM/RHTH SE16 * 24 G7
  HOO/HM ME3 ....73 K1
  RMAID ME17 ....288 C5
  RYE TN31 ....338 D6
Marley Wy ROCH ME1 ....95 H4
Marlhurst EDEN TN8 ....206 C6
Marlings Cl CHST BR7 ....86 F1
Marlings Park Av CHST BR7 ....86 F1
Marling Wy GVE DA12 ....70 A4
Marlow Av PUR RM19 ....30 D7
Marlow Cl PGE/AN SE20 ....61 H9
  WSTB CT5 ....106 A5
Marlow Copse WALD ME5 ....125 L4
Marlowe Av CANT CT1 ....4 E6
Marlowe Ct CHST BR7 ....63 P5
Marlowe Rd ASH TN23 ....2 C3
  DIT/AY ME20 ....153 N1
  DVE/WH CT16 ....291 J4
  MARG CT9 ....112 C5
The Marlowes DART DA1 ....45 M5
Marlowe Wy CROY/NA CR0 ....82 D6
Marlow Mdw CANTW/ST CT2...137 L8
Marlow Rd PGE/AN SE20 ....61 H9
Marlow Wy BERM/RHTH SE16...24 G5
Marlpit Cl EDEN TN8 ....206 D6
  EGRIN RH19 ....265 H5
Marlton St GNWCH SE10 ....26 A8
Marlwood Cl BFN/LL DA15 ....64 A1
Marmadon Rd
  WOOL/PLUM SE18 ....27 N7
Marmont Rd PECK SE15 ....40 G2
Marmora Rd EDUL SE22 ....41 J2
Marne Av WELL DA16 ....44 C4
Marnock Rd BROCKY SE4 ....41 M6
Marram Rd POP/IOD E14 ....25 H1
Maroons Wy CAT SE6 ....61 N4
Marquis Dr GILL ME7 ....126 C2
Marrabon Cl BFN/LL DA15 ....64 A1
Marr Cl IOS ME12 ....57 P9
Marriott Rd DART DA1 ....46 G8
Marryat Cl BFN/LL DA15 ....142 C1
Marsala Rd LEW SE13 ....42 G5
Marsden Rd PECK SE15 ....40 F4
Marsden Wy ORP BR6 ....86 C8
Marshall Crs BRDST CT10 ....113 K9
  OBGR ME11 * 77 H4
Marshall Gdns RTON TN11 ....221 F7
Marshall Rd RHAM ME8 ....96 F5
Marshalls Gv WOOL/PLUM SE18 ...26 F7
Marshalls Land TENT TN30...301 H4
Marsham Cl CHST BR7 * 63 M4
Marsham Crs RMAID ME17...216 E1
Marsham St MAID/BEAR ME14 ...13 G4
Marsham Wy STRD ME2 ....93 P9
Marshborough Rd
  SWCH CT13 ....201 H3
Marshbrook Cl BKHTH/KID SE3 ...43 H4
Marsh Crs HOO/HM ME3 ....53 L4
  NROM TN28 ....336 C2
Marsh Farm Rd MSTR CT12 ....141 J9
Marshfield St POP/IOD E14 ...25M6
Marshfoot Rd GRAYS RM17 ....32 C8
Marsh Green Rd EDEN TN8 ...236 C5
Marshlands LYDD TN29 ....326 F6
Marshlands Cl LYDD TN29 ....326 F6
Marshland Vw HOO/HM ME3 ....54 G5
Marsh La DEAL CT14 ....232 F5
  HOO/HM ME3 ....54 F3
  RSIT ME9 ....131 L1
Marsh Quarter La HAWK TN18...329 K1
Marsh Ri SIT ME10 ....99 P5
Marsh Rd RASHW TN26 ....304 D9
Marsh St DART DA1 ....46 G4
  POP/IOD E14 * 25 L7
  STRD ME2 ....18 E1
Marsh Ter STMC/STPC BR5 * 87 L1
Marsh Vw CRBK CT3 ....64 A2
  HYTHE CT21 ....308 B7
Marsh Wall POP/IOD E14 ....25 K5
Marsh Wy DAGW RM9 ....29 J2
  DIT/AY ME20 ....123 P9
Marshwood Cl CANT CT1 ....167 H1
Marston Cl RSIT ME9 ....97 H4
Marston Cl WALD ME5 ....125 K2
Marston Dr MAID/BEAR ME14 ....13 J5
  WARL CR6 ....144 B5
Marston Wy NRWD SE19 ....90 B6
Martello Cl RYE TN31 ....338 E8
Martello Dr HYTHE CT21 ....308 D6
Martello Rd FOLK CT20 ....11 H2
Martello Ter FOLK CT20 ....310 C8
Martell Rd DUL SE21 ....60 D2
Marten Rd FOLK CT20 ....10 A4
Martens Av BXLYHN DA7 ....45 L5
Martens Cl BXLYHN DA7 ....45 L5
Martha Cl FOLKN CT19 ....310 E4
Martham St THMD SE28 ....28 C5
Martha St WCHPL E1 ....24 F2
Martin Bowes Rd
  ELTH/MOT SE9 ....43 K4
Martin Cl SAND/SEL CR2...114 A5
Martin Ct GILL ME7 ....126 D2
Martin Crs CROY/NA CR0 ....82 F5
Martindale Av CAN/RD E16 ....26 B3
  ORP BR6 * 87 H9
Martindale Cl CANT CT1 * 4 E7
Martin Dale Crs RDV CT15 ....262 B6
Martin Dene BXLYHS DA6 ....45 H6
Martindown Rd WSTB CT5 ....105 K7
Martineau St WCHPL E1 ....24 F2
Martin Hardie Wy TONN TN10...211 H5

Martin La CANST EC4R 24 A3
Martin Ri BXLYHS DA6 ....45 H6
Martin Rd RDART DA2 ....66 C2
  SOCK/AV RM15 ....30 C4
  STRD ME2 ....7 L1
Martin Cl HOO/HM ME3 ....71 M1
  MSTR CT12 ....143 H2
Martins Av LEE/GVPK SE12 ....62 G9
  TENT TN30 ....301 K7
  WWKM BR4 ....84 C6
Martin La STPH/PW TN12 ....182 F9
Martin Sq DIT/AY ME20 ....153 P5
Martin's Av HAYES BR2 ....62 C8
Martin's Shaw SEV TN13 ....148 B7
The Martins RASHW TN26 ....279 F7
  SYD SE26 ....61 H4
Martin St THMD SE28 ....27 M4
Martin's Vw HYTHE CT21 ....308 C7
Marton Cl CAT SE6 ....61 N2
Martyns Pl EGRIN RH19 ....265 K8
Martyrs' Field Rd CANT CT1 ......4 C7
Marvels Cl LEE/GVPK SE12 ....62 F1
Marvels La LEE/GVPK SE12 ....62 F1
Marwell BH/WHM TN16 ....176 C2
Marwell Cl WWKM BR4 ....85 J6
Marwood Cl WELL DA16 ....44 D4
Mary Ann Buildings DEPT SE8...25 N3
Marybank WOOL/PLUM SE18 ....26 C7
Mary Datchelor Cl CMBW SE5 ...40 D2
Mary Day's CRBK TN17 ....274 D9
Mary Dukes Pl
  MAID/SHEP ME15 * 13 H6
Mary Green Wk CANT CT1 ......5 H1
Maryfield Cl BXLY DA5 ....65 N2
Maryland Ct RHAM ME8 ....97 H9
Maryland Dr MAIDW ME16 ....184 E1
Maryland Gv CANT CT1 ....167 H6
Maryland Rd RTWE/PEM TN2...270 C7
  THHTH CR7 ....60 B7
Mary Last Cl SNOD ME6 ....123M6
Mary Lawrenson Pl
  BKHTH/KID SE3 ....42 D1
Maryon Gv WOOL/PLUM SE18 ...26 F7
Maryon Rd CHARL SE7 ....26 F7
Mary Rd DEAL CT14 ....232 F6
Mary Rose Cl CDW/CHF RM16 ...31M7
  DART DA1 ....47 J9
Mary Stamford Gn RYE TN31...339 K9
Mary St CAN/RD E16 ....26 A1
Mascall's Court La
  STPH/PW TN12 ....243 J5
Mascall's Court Rd
  STPH/PW TN12 ....243 J5
Mascalls Pk STPH/PW TN12...242 G4
Mascalls Rd CHARL SE7 ....26 D9
Masefield Cl ERITH DA8 ....45 P2
Masefield Dr HOO/HM ME3 ....52 B8
Masefield Rd DART DA1 ....45 L9
  GVW DA11 ....69 H2
Masefield Vw ORP BR6 ....86 C6
Masefield Wy TON TN9 ....240 C1
Mask Cl BRXS/STRHM SW2 *.....40 A9
Mason Cl BERM/RHTH SE16 ....24 D8
  BXLYHN DA7 ....45 K4
  EGRIN RH19 ....265 H6
Mason Rd RYE TN31 ....338 D7
Mason's Av CITYW EC2V 24 A2
  CROY/NA CR0 ....83 H7
Masons Hi HAYES BR2 ....62 E9
  WOOL/PLUM SE18 ....27 J7
Mason's Ri BRDST CT10 ....113M8
Masons Rd DVW CT17 ....291 H6
Masons Wk SEV TN13 * 24 A7
Massinger St STHWK SE1 ....24 B7
Master Cl OXTED RH8 ....175 H5
Master Gunners Pl
  WOOL/PLUM SE18 ....43 J2
Masters Dr BERM/RHTH SE16...24 E8
Masters La E/WMAL ME19 ....123 J8
Master's St WCHPL E1 ....24 G1
Masthead Cl GRH DA9 ....47 J5
Masthouse Ter POP/IOD E14...25 K7
Mast House Ter POP/IOD E14 *...25 K7
Mastmaker Rd POP/IOD E14.....25 K5
Matchless Dr
  WOOL/PLUM SE18 ....43 L1
Matfield Cl HAYES BR2 ....85 K2
Matfield Crs MAID/BEAR ME14 ...13 K2
Matfield Rd BELV DA17 ....28 F9
Matfield Gdns GVE DA12 ....40 F5
Matilda Cl GILL ME7 ....96 E6
  NRWD SE19 ....59 N9
Matlock St WCHPL E1 ....25 H2
Matterdale Gdns
  MAID/BEAR ME14 ....184 D1
Matthew Cl MTCM CR4 ....82 C2
Matthews Cl DEAL CT14 ....233 H5
Matthew's Gdns
  CROY/NA CR0 ....114 C5
Matthews La RTON TN11 ....182 A5
Matthew's Pl DVW CT17 ....16 A8
Matthews Rd HB CT6 ....107 H4
Mattingly Wy PECK SE15 ....40 F1
Mattinson Pl HEST ME9 ....158 C5
Matts Hill Rd RSIT ME9 ....127 H3
Maud Cashmore Wy
  WOOL/PLUM SE18 ....26 G6
Maude Rd CMBW SE5 ....40 E3
  SWLY BR8 ....66 A5
Maudslay Rd ELTH/MOT SE9 ...43 K4
Maud St CAN/RD E16 ....26 A1
Maugham Ct WSTB CT5 ....105 L8
Maunder Cl CDW/CHF RM16 ...31 N7
Maunders Cl WALD ME5 ....125 L1
Maunsell Rd KEN/WIL TN24...282 C1
Mauritius Rd GNWCH SE10 ....25 P7
Mavelstone Rd BMLY BR1 ....62 H5
Mawbey Pl STHWK SE1 ....24 C8
Mawbey Rd STHWK SE1 ....24 C8
Maxey Rd WOOL/PLUM SE18 ...27 K7
Maximfeldt Rd ERITH DA8 ....29 K8
Maximilian Dr STRD ME2 ....124 A1

Maxim Rd DART DA1 ....45 N6
  ERITH DA8 ....29 K8
Maxine Gdns BRDST CT10 ....113 L8
Maxted Rd PECK SE15 ....40 F4
Maxton Cl MAID/BEAR ME14...156 C7
Maxton Rd DVW CT17 ....291 H9
Maxwell Cl CROY/NA CR0 ....82 D5
Maxwell Dr MAIDW ME16 ....154 C6
Maxwell Gdns ORP BR6 ....86 C7
Maxwell Rd ASH TN23 * 233 H5
  WELL DA16 ....44 C5
Maya Cl PECK SE15 ....41 H3
Mayall Rd BRXN/ST SW9 ....40 B6
May Av GVW DA11 ....49 H8
  STMC/STPC BR5 ....87 J2
Maybourne Ct RYE TN31 *......61 H5
Maybury Av RDART DA2 ....47 H9
Maybury Cl STMC/STPC BR5 ....64 E9
Maycroft Av GRAYS RM17 ....32 E8
Maycroft Gdns GRAYS RM17...32 E8
Mayday Gdns BKHTH/KID SE3 ...43 J5
Mayday Rd THHTH CR7 ....82 C5
Maydowns Rd WSTB CT5 ....106 A4
Mayerne Rd ELTH/MOT SE9 ...43 H6
Mayers Rd DEAL CT14 ....232 F8
Mayes Cl SWLY BR8 ....88 F1
  WARL CR6 ....144 A3
Mayeswood Rd
  LEE/GVPK SE12 ....62 C3
Mayfair STRD ME2 ....72 C7
Mayfair Av BXLYHN DA7 ....44 F2
  MAID/SHEP ME15 ....185M5
Mayfair Cl BECK BR3 ....61 K9
Mayfair Rd DART DA1 ....46 C6
Mayfield BXLYHN DA7 ....45 H4
  LING RH7 ....235 K8
  SWCM DA10 ....48 C7
Mayfield Av DVE/WH CT16 ....291 J5
  ORP BR6 ....86 C5
Mayfield Cl PGE/AN SE20 *......61 H7
  RHAM ME8 ....97 H4
  WALD ME5 ....125M4
Mayfield Crs THHTH CR7 ....82 E1
Mayfield Gdns THHTH CR7 ....82 E1
Mayfield Rd BELV DA17 ....29 H7
  BMLY BR1 ....85 P2
  DVE/WH CT16 ....261 H9
  GVW DA11 ....49 K9
  RFOLK CT18 ....287 H2
  STH/RUST TN4 ....22 B5
  WALD ME5 ....95 L9
Maynards Quay WAP E1W * 24 F3
Maynard's La STPH/PW TN12...242 F8
May Pl STPH/PW TN12 * 245 L5
Mayplace Av BXLYHN DA7 ....45 K4
Mayplace La
  WOOL/PLUM SE18 ....27 J9
Mayplace Rd BXLYHN DA7 ....45 L4
Mayplace Rd East
  BXLYHN DA7 ....45 L4
Mayplace Rd West
  BXLYHN DA7 ....45 J4
Maypole Crs ERITH DA8 ....30 A9
Maypole La CRBK TN17 ....274 D8
Maypole Rd EGRIN RH19 ....264 C6
  GVE DA12 * 50 B9
  ORP BR6 ....117 N1
May Rd GILL ME7 * 7 G4
  RDART DA2 ....66 F5
  ROCH ME1 ....95 J3
May's Buildings Ms
  GNWCH SE10 ....42 B1
May's Hill Rd HAYES BR2 ....62 C8
Mays Rd RDART DA2 ....16 C4
May St HB CT6 ....108 C6
  SNOD ME6 ....124 A5
  STRD ME2 ....94 A4
May Ter GILL ME7 ....72 C9
Mayton Cl CANTW/ST CT2...136 C4
Maytree Wk
  BRXS/STRHM SW2 ....60 A1
Mayville Rd BRDST CT10 ....113 K7
Mayweed Av WALD ME5 ....125 K1
Maywood Cl BECK BR3 * 61 P6
Maze Hl BKHTH/KID SE3 ....42 D1
  GNWCH SE10 ....25 P9
McAlpine Crs
  MAID/SHEP ME15 ....185 L8
McAuley Cl ELTH/MOT SE9 ....43 L6

McCabe Cl STPH/PW TN12 ....246 B7
McCall Crs CHARL SE7 ....26 F8
McCarthy Av CANTW/ST CT2...137 L6
McClean Wk IOS ME12 * 79 H7
McCudden Rd DART DA1 * 47 J9
McCudden Row GILL ME7 * 72 C9
McDermott Rd BGR/WK TN15...151 J5
  PECK SE15 ....40 G4
McDowall Cl CAN/RD E16 ....26 B1
Mcindoe Rd EGRIN RH19 ....264 C6
Mciver Cl ECRIN RH19 ....264 C4
McKenzie Cl DIT/AY ME20 ....154 E4
McKenzie Rd WALD ME5 ....125M2
McKerrell Rd PECK SE15 ....40 G2
McKillop Wy SCUP DA14 ....64 E6
McKinlay Ct BRCH CT7 ....110 E5
McLeod Rd ABYW SE2 ....28 B7
McMillan Cl GVE DA12 ....69 N3
McMillan St DEPT SE8 ....25 K9
McNeil Rd CMBW SE5 ....40 E3
Mead Cl CDW/CHF RM16 ....31M8
  SEV TN13 ....88 F2
Mead Crs DART DA1 ....46 D9
Meades Cl LING RH7 ....235 K8
  STPH/PW TN12 ....244 C5
The Meades LING RH7 ....235 L8
The Meade RFOLK CT18 ....288 C8
Meadfield Rd MEO DA13 ....92 B6
Meadow Av CROY/NA CR0 ....83 K1
Meadowbank BKHTH/KID SE3 ...42 D4
Meadow Bank E/WMAL ME19...153 K4
  RTON TN11 ....209 L9
Meadow Bank Cl
  BGR/WK TN15 ....120 C3
Meadowbank Rd CHAT ME4 ......6 E5
Meadowbrook FOLK CT20 ....310 B7
  OXTED RH8 ....174 F6
Meadowbrook Cl
  FOLK CT20 * 310 B7
Meadowbrook Ct
  KEN/WIL TN24 ....252 G3
Meadowbrook Rd
  KEN/WIL TN24 ....252 G3
Meadow Cl BXLYHS DA6 ....45 H6
  CAT SE6 ....61 N4
  CHST BR7 ....107 P2
  RCANTW CT4 ....194 F3
  RCANTW CT4 ....197 M2
  RFOLK CT18 ....288 E8
  RSIT ME9 ....98 F3
  SEV TN13 ....148 F8
  SLH/COR SS17 ....33 P6
  STRD ME2 ....123M1
  WALD ME5 ....95 L9
Meadow Ct BGR/WK TN15...151 J1
  MARG CT9 ....112 C4
  RASHE TN25 ....308 A1
  RHAM ME8 ....96 E3
Meadowcourt Rd
  BKHTH/KID SE3 ....42 D5
Meadow Crs STRD ME2 ....123M1
Meadow Cft BMLY BR1 ....63 K9
Meadowcroft Cl EGRIN RH19...264 F5
Meadowcroft
  MAID/BEAR ME14 ....156 B8
Meadowdown Cl THMD SE28...27 M3
Meadow Dr GV RASHE TN25...285 L8
Meadow Hill Rd RTW TN1 ....22 E6
Meadowlands CANT CT1 * 4 A1
  OXTED RH8 ....205 K1
Meadow La EDEN TN8 ....206 C6
  LEE/GVPK SE12 ....62 C2
  MEO DA13 ....122 A4
Meadow Ri RSIT ME9 ....99 L2
Meadow Rd ASH TN23 ....252 D5
  CANTW/ST CT2 ....137 L7
  CANTW/ST CT2 ....166 B2
  CDW/CHF RM16 ....32 D4
  GVW DA11 ....48 G9
  HAYES BR2 ....62 C7
  RRTW TN3 ....268 C9
  RTW TN1 ....22 D2
  STH/RUST TN4 ....269 P4
  TON TN9 ....240 D1
Meadowside DART DA1 ....46 B9
  ELTH/MOT SE9 ....42 G5
The Meadows HB CT6 ....107 N4
  RTWE/PEM TN2 ....241 N9
Meadow Vw BFN/LL DA15 ....44 D7
  HOO/HM ME3 * 53 F8
  RASHW TN26 ....251 L3
  RSIT ME9 * 98 C3
  SWLY BR8 * 88 C3
  WALD ME5 ....95 L9
Meadowview Rd BXLY DA5 ....44 G7
  CAT SE6 ....61 N3
Meadow Vw Rd RDV CT15...229 P9
  RMAID ME17 ....185 N8
  THHTH CR7 ....82 G2

Milne Rd KEN/WIL TN24 ....253 J9
Milner Rd GILL ME7 ....73 K8
RDV CT15 ....230 C8
THHTH CR7 ....60 C9
WSTB CT5 ....105 H8
Milners RMAID ME17 * 187 J5
Milo Rd EDUL SE22 ....40 F7
Milroy Av GVW DA11 ....69 J1
Milstead Cl IOS ME12 ....57 K8
MAID/BEAR ME14 ....13 K3
Milsted Rd RHAM ME8 ....96 F4
Milton Av CROY/NA CRO 83 J4
GVE DA12 ....49 P9
HNHL ME3 ....52 B8
MARG CT9 ....15 J6
RSEV TN14 ....118 A4
Milton Cl CANT CT1 ....167 H6
DVE/WH CT16 ....291 J3
STHWK SE1 ....24 C7
Milton Crs EGRIN RH19 ....264 F7
Milton Ct BARB EC2Y 24 A1
Milton Court Rd NWCR SE14 ....25 H9
Milton Dr RTWE/PEM TN2 ....270 C1
Milton Gdns FOLK TN18 ....49 M2
TON TN9 ....240 C2
Milton Hall Rd GVE DA12 ....49 P9
Milton La E/WMAL ME19 ....153 J9
Milton Pl GVE DA12 ....49 N7
Milton Rd ASH TN23 ....2 C5
BELV DA17 ....28 F7
CANT CT1 ....166 F6
CROY/NA CRO 83 J4
DVE/WH CT16 ....291 J5
GILL ME7 ....96 C1
GRAYS RM17 ....32 C7
GVE DA12 ....49 M7
HNHL SE24 ....40 B6
SEV TN15 ....148 D6
SWCM DA10 ....48 C7
WELL DA16 ....44 B2
Milton Sq MARG CT9 ....15 H6
Milton St BARB EC2Y 24 A1
MAIDW ME16 ....185 H1
SWCM DA10 ....48 C7
Milverton Wy ELTH/MOT SE9 ....63 K1
Milward St WCHPL E1 ....24 E1
Mimms Ter STPH/PW TN12 * 245 H2
Mimosa Cl ORP BR6 ....87 K7
Minard Rd CAT SE6 ....42 C9
Mina Rd WALW SE17 ....24 B8
Mincers Cl WALD ME5 ....125 P3
Mincing La MON EC3R 24 E5
Minden Rd PGE/AN SE20 ....61 H7
Mindleheim Av EGRIN RH19 ....265 L6
Mineral St WOOL/PLUM SE18 ....27 M7
Minerva Av DVW CT17 ....13 G4
Minerva Cl DVE/WH CT16 ....291 K5
SCUP DA14 ....64 A3
Minerva Rd STRD ME2 ....72 A7
Minet Rd CMBW SE5 ....40 B3
Ming St POP/IOD E14 ....25 K3
Ministry Wy ELTH/MOT SE9 ....63 K1
Minnis La RDV CT15 ....290 C6
Minnis Ter DVW CT17 * 291 H5
Minnis Wy DEAL CT14 ....202 A3
Minnow Wk WALW SE17 ....24 B7
Minor Canon Rw ROCH ME1 ....19 F5
Minories TWRH EC3N 24 C3
Minshull Pl BECK BR3 * 61 N6
Minster Cl BRDST CT10 ....143 M2
Minster Ct FENCHST EC3M 24 B3
Minster Dr CROY/NA CRO 83 K8
HB CT6 ....107 J2
IOS ME12 ....5B B8
Minster Rd BMLY BR1 ....62 F6
BRCH CT7 ....141 J2
FAV ME13 * 133 H6
IOS ME12 ....77 P1
RAM CT11 ....16 A6
RHAM ME8 ....96 F3
WGOS CT8 ....111 N6
Mintching Wood La RSIT ME9 ....150 F1
Minter Av RFOLK CT18 ....288 C5
Minter Cl RFOLK CT18 ....288 C5
Minterne Av SIT ME10 ....129 K3
Minters Orch BGR/WK TN15 ....151 L5
Mint Rd WLGTN SM6 ....62 A2
The Mint CANTW/ST CT2 * 166 B3
RYE TN31 ....338 F7
Mint Wk CROY/NA CRO 83 H7
WARL CR6 ....144 A2
The Mint Yd CANT CT1 * 5 J4
Miranda Cl WCHPL E1 ....24 F1
Miranda Ct IOS ME12 ....57 K7
Mirfield St CHARL SE7 ....26 E6
Miriam Rd WOOL/PLUM SE18 ....27 MB
Miskin Rd DART DA1 ....46 C8
RMAID ME17 ....73 K2
Miskin Wy GVE DA12 ....69 P5
Misling La RCANTW CT4 ....256 B3
Mission Pl PECK SE15 ....40 C2
Mistletoe Cl CROY/NA CRO 84 A5
Mitali Pas WCHPL E1 ....24 D2
Mitcham Rd CROY/NA CRO 82 D5
LYDD TN29 ....326 C6
Mitchell Av CHAT ME4 ....95 L4
GVW DA11 ....69 H1
RFOLK CT18 ....288 E7
Mitchell Cl ABYW SE2 ....28 D8
BELV DA17 ....29 H6
DART DA1 ....66 E1
RMAID ME17 ....189 K6
Mitchell Rd E/WMAL ME19 ....182 G1
ORP BR6 ....86 G8
Mitchell Wy BMLY BR1 ....61 N2
Mitchell Wy RBR/ST TN15 * 62 F7
Mitchem Cl BGR/WK TN15 ....120 B2
Mitre Cl HAYES BR2 ....62 D8
Mitre Ct TN9 ....210 F8
Mitre Rd ROCH ME1 ....19 G3
Mitre Sq HDTCH EC3A 24 B2
Mitre St HDTCH EC3A 24 B2
The Mitre POP/IOD E14 ....25 J3

Moat Cl ORP BR6 ....116 C1
Moat Cl ELTH/MOT SE9 * 43 K7
Moat Cft WELL DA16 ....44 E4
Moat Farm RTWE/PEM TN2 ....270 D9
Moat Farm Cl FOLKN CT19 ....310 F4
Moat Farm Rd FOLKN CT19 ....310 F4
HOO/HM ME3 ....54 A2
Moatfield Meadow ASH TN23 ....282 E4
Moat La CANTW/ST CT2 ....136 A9
CANTW/ST CT2 ....267 L1
EDEN TN8 ....267 L1
ERITH DA8 ....46 A2
RCANTE CT3 ....200 E1
Moat Rd EGRIN RH19 ....265 H6
HDCN TN27 ....247 L4
Moat Sole SWCH CT13 ....201 N1
The Moat HDCN TN27 ....221 H3
Moat Wy OBOR ME11 ....77 J2
Mockbeggar La CRBK TN17 ....299 M3
Mockbeggar Rd WLSD SE 299 M3
Mockett Dr BRDST CT10 ....113 L6
Mock La ASH TN23 ....281 N2
Model Farm Cl ELTH/MOT SE9 ....63 J2
Moiety Rd POP/IOD E14 ....25 H9
Moira Rd ELTH/MOT SE9 ....43 K5
Molash Rd STMC/STPC BR5 ....87 L1
Molehill Rd WSTB CT5 ....106 C7
Molescroft Cl WALD ME5 ....63 N2
Molescroft Wy TON TN9 ....240 C2
Moles Md EDEN TN8 ....206 D8
Molesworth St LEW SE13 ....42 A4
Molineux Rd MSTR CT12 ....141 J6
Molland Cl RCANTE CT3 ....170 D9
Molland La RCANTE CT3 ....170 D9
Molland Lea RCANTE CT3 ....170 D9
Mollison Rd GVE DA12 ....70 A4
Molloy Rd RASHW TN26 ....281 N7
Molyneux Park Gdns
STH/RUST TN4 ....22 B3
Monarch Cl TIL RM18 ....49 M1
WALD ME5 ....95 M8
WWKM BR4 ....64 C7
Monarch Dr CAN/RD E16 ....26 E1
Monarch Ms WNWD SE27 ....60 A4
Monarch Rd BELV DA17 ....28 F6
Mona Rd PECK SE15 ....41 J5
Monastery Av DVE/WH CT16 ....8 D1
Monastery St CANT CT1 ....5 C5
Mona St CAN/RD E16 ....26 A1
Monckton's Av
MAID/BEAR ME14 ....155 K5
Monckton's Dr
MAID/BEAR ME14 ....155 K5
Monckton's La
MAID/BEAR ME14 ....155 K8
Moncrief Rd CMBW SE5 ....40 D5
Moncrieff St PECK SE15 ....40 D5
Moncrif Cl MAID/BEAR ME14 ....156 E8
Mongeham Church Cl
DEAL CT14 ....232 C5
Mongeham Rd DEAL CT14 ....232 C7
Monica Cl FAV ME13 ....133 H6
Monins Rd DVW CT17 ....291 J8
Monivea Rd BECK BR3 ....61 M6
Monkdown MAID/SHEP ME15 ....186 D5
Monk Dr CAN/RD E16 ....26 A4
Monkery La RASHE TN25 ....191 P9
Monks Cl ABYW SE2 ....28 C7
CANTW/ST CT2 ....166 F2
FAV ME13 ....132 E5
Monkshill Rd FAV ME13 ....134 B5
Monks La OXTED RH8 ....205 N4
WADH TN5 ....294 C8
Monks Orch DART DA1 ....66 C1
Monks Orchard Rd BECK BR3 ....84 D5
Monk St WOOL/PLUM SE18 ....27 H7
Monks Wk HDCN TN27 ....271 P5
DVE/WH CT16 ....291 H4
RYE TN31 ....330 A5
Monk Ter FSTH SE23 ....61 M1
Monkton Court La RDV CT15 ....260 E1
Monkton Gdns MARG CT9 ....113 K2
Monkton Pl RAM CT11 ....16 E5
Monkton Rd BGR/WK TN15 ....151 J5
WELL DA16 ....44 E5
Monkton St CANT CT1 ....140 D5
Monkwood Cl ROCH ME1 ....94 G6
Monmouth Cl MTCM CR4 ....82 D1
RHAM ME8 ....96 E4
WELL DA16 ....44 C5
Monnow Rd SOCK/AV RM15 ....30 F3
STHWK SE1 ....24 D8
Mons Ct SIT ME10 ....99 N5
Monson Rd NWCR SE14 ....25 H9
RTW TN1 ....22 E3
Monson Wy RTW TN1 ....22 E3
Mons Wy HAYES BR2 ....85 P3
Montacute Gdns
RTWE/PEM TN2 ....22 B7
Montacute Rd CAT SE6 ....41 N8
CROY/NA CRO 114 C5
RTWE/PEM TN2 ....270 D7
Montague Av BROCKY SE4 ....41 M5
STHWK SE1 ....24 A4
SWLY BR8 ....88 E1
Montague Cl IOS ME12 ....57 K7
STHWK SE1 ....24 A3
Montague Pl SWLY BR8 * 88 E1
Montague Rd CROY/NA CRO 82 G5
RAM CT11 ....17 G1
Montague Sq NWCR SE14 ....41 J1
Montague Ter HAYES BR2 * 85 K1
Montagu Gdns WLGTN SM6 ....82 B8
Montana Gdns CAT SE6 ....61 M4
Montbelle Rd ELTH/MOT SE9 ....63 M2
Montbretia Cl STMC/STPC BR5 ....87 K1
Montcalm Cl HAYES BR2 ....85 K5
Montcalm Rd CHARL SE7 ....43 H1
Montcalm Ter
DVE/WH CT16 * 291 J4

Monteagle Wy PECK SE15 ....41 H4
Montefiore Av RAM CT11 ....143 L3
Montefiore Cottages
....17 H1
Monteith Cl RRTW TN5 ....269 M5
Montem Rd FSTH SE23 ....41 M8
Monterey Cl BXLY DA5 ....65 L1
Montesquieu Ter
CAN/RD E16 * 26 A2
Montfort Cl ASH TN23 ....282 C1
CANTW/ST CT2 ....136 F9
Montfort Dr E/WMAL ME19 ....183 H1
Montfort Rd BGR/WK TN15 ....149 K2
STRD ME2 ....18 C1
WALD ME5 ....125 K8
Montgomerie Ms FSTH SE23 ....41 J8
Montgomery Av WALD ME5 ....85 P2
Montgomery Cl BFN/LL DA15 ....44 A6
MTCM CR4 * 82 D1
Montgomery Rd EYN DA4 ....67 K7
GILL ME7 ....7 H6
STH/RUST TN4 ....270 E1
Montgomery Wy FOLKN CT19 ....310 C5
Monthorpe Rd WCHPL E1 ....24 D1
Montpelier Av BXLY DA5 ....44 F8
WSTB CT5 ....105 L8
Montpelier Ga MAIDW ME16 * 154 F2
Montpelier Pl WCHPL E1 ....24 F2
Montpelier Rd PECK SE15 ....41 H2
Montpelier Rw BKHTH/KID SE3 ....42 D5
Montpelier V BKHTH/KID SE3 * 42 D3
Montrave Rd PGE/AN SE20 ....61 J5
Montreal Cl DVE/WH CT16 ....291 J4
Montreal Rd SEV TN13 ....148 D8
TIL RM18 ....49 L5
Montrose Av BFN/LL DA15 ....44 C8
WALD ME5 ....96 B4
WELL DA16 ....43 P4
Montrose Cl WELL DA16 ....44 B4
Montrose Wy FSTH SE25 ....41 K9
Mont St Aignan Wy
EDEN TN8 ....206 D9
Montserrat Cl NRWD SE19 ....60 D4
Monument St MON EC3R 24 A3
Monynton Wy KEN/WIL TN24 ....283 J3
Monypenny CRBK TN17 ....319 L5
Monypenny Cl RTON TN11 ....211 N2
Monza St WAP E1W 24 F3
Moodkee St BERM/RHTH SE16 ....24 F6
Moon Cl LEE/GVPK SE12 * 42 E5
Moon Hl RDV CT15 ....259 P1
Moon's La EGRIN RH19 ....265 N1
Moonstone Dr WALD ME5 ....125 N3
Moorcroft Gdns HAYES BR2 ....85 P2
Morden La RTON TN11 ....208 F9
Moordown WOOL/PLUM SE18 ....43 M2
Moore Av TIL RM18 ....49 P8
WTHK RM20 ....31 P8
Moore Cl LYDD TN29 ....335 H2
Mooreland Rd BMLY BR1 ....62 D6
Moore Rd NRWD SE19 ....60 C5
SWCM DA10 ....48 C7
Moore St STRD ME2 ....72 A7
Moorfield CANTW/ST CT2 ....136 E9
Moorfield Rd ORP BR6 ....87 H4
Moorfields LVPST EC2M 24 A1
Moorfields Highwalk
BARB EC2Y * 24 A1
Moorgate LOTH EC2R 24 A2
Moorgate Pl LOTH EC2R 24 A2
Moorhead Wy BKHTH/KID SE3 ....42 F5
Moorhen Cl ERITH DA8 ....46 B1
Moor Hl HAWK TN18 ....317 H6
Moorhouse Rd OXTED RH8 ....176 H4
Mooring Rd ROCH ME1 ....95 J5
The Moorings
EGRIN RH19 ....264 D5
MAID/SHEP ME15 * 13 F5
RSIT ME9 ....101 K8
Moorland Rd BRXN/ST SW9 ....40 B5
RDV CT15 ....259 N1
Moor La BARB EC2Y 24 A1
LYDD TN29 ....335 L2
RASHW TN26 ....302 E8
Moor Park Cl RHAM ME8 ....97 K6
Moor Pl EGRIN RH19 ....264 C6
LVPST EC2M * 24 A1
The Moor Rd RSEV TN14 ....148 C5
Moorside Rd BMLY BR1 ....62 C3
Moorstock La RASHE TN25 ....285 K6
Moor St RHAM ME8 ....97 L6
The Moor HAWK TN18 ....317 H6
Moorwell Dr RDV CT15 ....259 M1
Morant Rd CDW/CHF RH6 ....33 J6
Morants Court Rd RSEV TN14 ....148 B3
Morant St POP/IOD E14 ....25 K3
Moray Av BRCH CT7 ....110 C5
Mordaunt Av WGOS CT8 ....111 M5
Morden Hl LEW SE13 ....42 A3
Morden La LEW SE13 ....42 A3
Morden Rd BKHTH/KID SE3 ....42 E3
Morden Road Ms
BKHTH/KID SE3 ....42 E3
Morden St LEW SE13 ....41 P7
Morden Wharf Rd
GNWCH SE10 ....25 P6
Mordred Rd CAT SE6 ....62 C1
Morecambe Cl POP/IOD E14 ....25 L8
Morecambe St POP/IOD E14 ....26 A2
More Cl CAN/RD E16 ....26 A2
Morehall Av FOLKN CT19 ....310 C5
Morelands Av CDW/CHF RH16 ....32 D5
Morel Ct SEV TN15 ....148 D2
Morello Cl ASHF TN23 * 191 H3
SWLY BR8 ....68 G9
More London Pl STHWK SE1 * 24 B4
More London Riverside
STHWK SE1 ....24 B4
Moremead Rd CAT SE6 ....61 M3
Morement Rd HOO/HM ME3 ....71 J1
Morena St CAT SE6 ....41 P8
Moreton Ct DART DA1 ....45 N4
Moreton Rd SAND/SEL CR2 ....83 J9
Moreton Ter RASHW TN26 * 281 M7

RTW TN1 ....22 E5
Mountfield Ter CAT SE6 ....42 B8
Mountfield Wy
STMC/STPC BR5 ....87 K1
WGOS CT8 ....111 L7
Mount Gdns SYD SE26 ....61 H2
Mount Green Av MSTR CT12 ....142 C7
Mount Harry Rd SEV TN13 ....147 N6
Mounthurst Rd HAYES BR2 ....85 K4
Mountjoy Cl THMD SE28 ....28 A5
Mount La MAID/BEAR ME14 ....156 E8
RSIT ME9 ....127 M2
Mount Lodge Ter ROCH ME1 * 94 C5
Mount Pleasant
BH/WHM TN16 ....145 N2
CHAT ME4 ....135 P7
CHAT ME4 ....7 F6
DIT/AY ME20 ....154 F1
DVW CT17 * 7 F6
RTON TN11 ....210 A4
STPH/PW TN12 ....242 G3
TENT TN30 ....301 K7
WNWD SE27 ....60 C3
Mount Pleasant Av RTW TN1 ....22 C4
Mountpleasant Cl
RFOLK CT18 ....287 H1
Mount Pleasant Dr
MAID/BEAR ME14 ....156 D7
Mount Pleasant La
RRTW TN5 ....294 G1
Mount Pleasant Pl
WOOL/PLUM SE18 ....27 L7
Mount Pleasant Rd DART DA1 ....46 F7
FOLK CT20 ....13 F5
LEW SE13 ....42 A7
LING RH7 ....234 F5
RSEV TN14 ....178 G9
RTW TN1 ....22 D3
Mount Ri FSTH SE23 ....61 J1
Mount Rd BXLYHS DA6 ....44 C6
CANT CT1 ....167 H6
CHAT ME4 ....45 P7
DART DA1 ....45 P7
DVW CT17 ....313 H1
NRWD SE19 * 60 C1
ROCH ME1 ....94 F4
Mounts Cl DEAL CT14 ....232 F4
Mountsfield Cl MAIDW ME16 ....12 A2
Mount Sion CRBK TN17 ....298 D8
Mount Sion RTW TN1 ....22 D6
Mounts La CRBK TN17 ....319 N4
Mounts Pond Rd
BKHTH/KID SE3 ....42 B3
Mounts Rd GRH DA9 ....47 P7
Mount St HYTHE CT21 ....309 H5
Mounts Vw RASHE TN25 ....252 C5
Mount Ter WCHPL E1 ....24 E1
The Mount BMLY BR1 ....63 J7
BXLYHS DA6 ....45 K6
CBE 6 C6
FAV ME13 * 132 E7
STH/RUST TN4 * 239 P6
Mountview RSIT ME9 ....129 J3
Mount View Ct CHAT ME4 * 6 C6
Mount View Rd HB CT6 ....107 M4
Mount Vw ORP BR6 ....86 B8
Mount Vls WNWD SE27 ....60 B2
Mowbray Rd NRWD SE19 ....60 F7
Mowll St BRXN/ST SW9 ....40 A1
Moyes Cl MSTR CT12 ....142 C7
Moyle Cl RHAM ME8 ....96 E4
Moyle Ct HYTHE CT21 ....309 H6
Moys Cl CROY/NA CRO 82 D3
Mozart Ct CHAT ME4 ....6 A6
Muckingford Rd TIL RM18 ....33 N7
Mucking Wharf Rd
SLH/COR SS17 ....34 B2
Muggeridge Cl SAND/SEL CR2 ....83 J9
Muirfield Cl
BERM/RHTH SE16 * 24 E8
Muirfield Crs POP/IOD E14 ....25 L6
Muirkirk Rd CAT SE6 ....42 A9
Muir Rd MAID/BEAR ME14 ....13 F7
RAM CT11 ....143 L3
Muir St CAN/RD E16 ....26 C4
Mulberry Cl GILL ME7 ....126 D1
MEO DA13 ....92 C3
RAM CT11 ....17 H1
RTWE/PEM TN2 ....240 C8
Mulberry Dr CANT CT1 ....4 C5
HYTHE CT21 ....309 J4
Mulberry Dr PUR RM19 ....30 C7
Mulberry Fld SWCH CT13 ....201 N1
Mulberry Hl RCANTW CT4 ....194 E2
Mulberry La CROY/NA CRO 83 L5
Mulberry Ms NWCR SE14 ....41 M2
Mulberry Pl ELTH/MOT SE9 ....43 H5
Mulberry Rd ASH TN23 ....252 A6
RAM 66 J5
Mulberry St WCHPL E1 ....24 D2
Mulberry W BELV DA17 ....29 H5
Mulberry Wy CROY/NA CRO 83 L5
Mulgrave Rd CROY/NA CRO 83 J7
WCHPL E1 * 26 C7
Mulkern Rd ARCH N19 ....32 F9
Mullein Ct GRAYS RM17 ....32 C3
Mullet Rd BGR/WK TN15 ....120 B1
Mulvaney Wy STHWK SE1 ....24 A5
Mumford Mills GNWCH SE10 ....41 P2
Mumford Rd HNHL SE24 ....40 B6
Muncies Ms CAT SE6 ....62 A1
Mundania Rd EDUL SE22 ....41 H7
Munday Bois Rd HDCN TN27 ....219 M9
Munford Dr SWCM DA10 ....48 D8
Mungo Park Rd GVE DA12 ....69 P4
Munnery Wy ORP BR6 ....86 B7
Munn Rd STMC/STPC BR5 ....87 K4
Munns La RSIT ME9 ....97 P8
Munsgore La RSIT ME9 ....128 F3
Munton Rd WALW SE17 ....24 A7
Murchison Av BXLY DA5 ....45 H1
Murdock Ct CAN/RD E16 ....26 D5
Murdock St PECK SE15 ....24 E9
Murillo Rd LEW SE13 ....42 B3
Murrain Dr MAID/SHEP ME15 ....186 D2
Murray Av BMLY BR1 ....62 F9

Murray House
WOOL/PLUM SE18 * 43 J1
Murray Rd STMC/STPC BR5 64 D9
STRD ME2 72 C7
Murray Sq CAN/RD E16 26 B2
Murston Rd SIT ME10 130 A2
Murthwaite Ct IOS ME12 78 A2
Murton-Neale Cl HAWK TN18 317 J4
Murton Pl FAV ME13 133 P4
Musbury St WCHPL E1 24 F2
Muscatel Pl CMBW SE5 40 E2
Muschamp Rd PECK SE15 40 F4
Muscovy Rd RASHE TN25 252 E1
Muscovy St TWRH EC3N 24 B3
Muscovy Wy HB CT6 107 K3
Musgrave Av EGRIN RH19 265 H9
Musgrave Cl MSTR CT12 141 N2
Musgrave Rd SIT ME10 99 N8
Musgrove ASH TN23 2 B7
Musgrove Rd NWCR SE14 41 K2
Musket La RMAID ME17 187 L1
Mussenden La EYN DA4 90 A3
Mustang Rd E/WMAL ME19 152 G9
Mustards Rd IOS ME12 80 B5
Mutrix Gdns MARG CT9 111 P4
Mutrix Rd MARG CT9 112 A5
Mutton Hl LING RH7 265 K1
Mutton La FAV ME13 132 D8
Myatt Rd BRXN/ST SW9 40 B2
Mycenae Rd BKHTH/KID SE3 26 B9
Myers La NWCR SE14 24 G9
Mylis Cl SYD SE26 61 H3
Mymms Cl WSTB CT5 106 B6
Mynn Crs MAID/BEAR ME14 156 D8
Myra St ABYW SE2 27 P8
Myrdle St WCHPL E1 24 D1
Myron Pl LEW SE13 42 A4
Myrtle Aly WOOL/PLUM SE18 27 H6
Myrtle Cl ERITH DA8 45 N1
Myrtle Crs WALD ME5 95 L9
Myrtledene Rd ABYW SE2 27 P8
Myrtle Gn ASH TN23 252 A5
Myrtle Gv ASH TN23 * 252 B9
SOCK/AV RM15 30 F5
Myrtle Pl RDART DA2 47 K9
Myrtle Rd CROY/NA CR0 84 D7
DART DA1 66 D1
FOLKN CT19 11 H1
The Myrtles IOS ME12 * 77 P2
Myrtle Vls NROM TN28 * 336 F7
STPH/PW TN12 * 245 H4
Mystole La RCANTW CT4 195 K3
Mystole Rd RCANTW CT4 195 H3
Myton Rd DUL SE21 60 D2

N

Nackington Rd RCANTW CT4 196 F2
Nadine St CHARL SE7 26 D8
Nags Head La ROCH ME1 19 J7
WELL DA16 44 D4
Nailbourne Cl RCANTW CT4 228 A3
Naildown Cl HYTHE CT21 309 M4
Naildown Rd HYTHE CT21 309 M4
Nairn Ct TIL RM18 * 49 K3
Nairne Cl RASHW TN26 281 M8
Nairne Gv EDUL SE22 40 D6
Nairn St POP/IOD E14 25 M1
Namton Dr STRHM/NOR SW16 82 E1
Namur Pl RDV CT15 291 N4
Nankin St POP/IOD E14 25 K2
Nansen Rd GVE DA12 69 P3
Napchester Rd DVE/WH CT16 261 H8
Napier Av POP/IOD E14 25 K8
Napier Barracks FOLK CT20 * 309 P3
Napier Cl DEPT SE8 41 M1
SIT ME10 129 K1
Napier Ct LEE/GVPK SE12 62 F1
Napier Gdns HYTHE CT21 309 H6
Napier Rd BELV DA17 28 E7
BRDST CT10 113 K7
DVE/WH CT16 291 J4
GILL ME7 7 K6
GVW DA11 49 K9
HAYES BR2 62 F9
RTWE/PEM TN2 23 J7
SNWD SE25 83 N1
Napier Ter IOS ME12 * 57 M6
Napleton Rd FAV ME13 132 F6
RAM CT11 16 B4
Napoleon Dr STPH/PW TN12 245 J4
Napwood Cl RHAM ME8 96 G8
Nare Rd SOCK/AV RM15 30 F3
Nares Rd RHAM ME8 126 G1
Nargate St RCANTE CT3 168 D8
Narrabeen Rd FOLKN CT19 310 B5
Narrow Boat Cl THMD SE28 27 L5
Narrowbush La LYDD TN29 335 H6
Narrow St POP/IOD E14 25 H3
Narrow Wy HAYES BR2 85 P3
Naseby Av FOLK CT20 310 A6
Naseby Rd NRWD SE19 60 D5
Nash Bank MEO DA13 69 K8
Nash Cl WALD ME5 125 P3
Nash Court Gdns MARG CT9 112 D5
Nash Court Rd MARG CT9 112 E5
Nash Cft MEO DA13 69 J3
Nashenden Farm La
ROCH ME1 94 E5
Nashenden La ROCH ME1 94 E4
Nash Gdns BRDST CT10 113 N9
Nash Gn BMLY BR1 62 E6
Nash Hl RFOLK CT18 287 H2
Nash La HAYES BR2 115 K1
MARG CT9 112 E6
Nash Rd BROCKY SE4 41 L5
MARG CT9 112 D5
RCANTE CT3 169 M5
Nash St MEO DA13 69 L8
Nasmyth Rd BRCH CT7 111 H5
Natal Rd CHAT ME4 95 M4
DVE/WH CT16 291 K3
THHTH CR7 60 D9
Nathaniel Cl WCHPL E1 24 C1
Nathan Wy THMD SE28 27 N6
National Ter
BERM/RHTH SE16 * 24 E5
Nativity Cl SIT ME10 129 M1
Nat's La RASHE TN25 254 B4
Nautilus Cl IOS ME12 78 A1
Nautilus Dr IOS ME12 78 A2
Naval Rw POP/IOD E14 25 M3
Naylands MARG CT9 14 D6
Naylor Rd PECK SE15 41 H1
Nazareth Cl PECK SE15 41 H3
Neale Cl EGRIN RH19 264 E5
Neale St CHAT ME4 95 L4
Neal Rd BGR/WK TN15 120 B1
Neal's Place Rd
CANTW/ST CT2 166 B2
Neal Ter FSTH SE23 * 41 K9
Neame Rd BRCH CT7 111 H6
Neason Wy FOLKN CT19 11 J1
Neate St CMBW SE5 24 B9
Neath Ct MAID/SHEP ME15 * 186 B3
Neatscourt Rd EHAM E6 26 E1
Neb La OXTED RH8 174 F7
Nebraska St STHWK SE1 24 A5
Neckinger STHWK SE1 24 C6
Neckinger Est
BERM/RHTH SE16 24 C6
Neckinger St STHWK SE1 24 C5
Nectarine Wy LEW SE13 41 P3
Needleman St
BERM/RHTH SE16 24 G5
Neills Rd RRTW TN3 294 E5
Nelgarde Rd CAT SE6 41 N8
Nelldale Rd BERM/RHTH SE16 24 E7
Nellington Rd RRTW TN3 269 N4
Nello James Gdns WNWD SE27 60 D3
Nelson Av IOS ME12 78 D1
TON TN9 210 D9
Nelson Cl BH/WHM TN16 145 P2
CROY/NA CR0 82 G5
IOS ME12 57 J8
KEN/WIL TN24 253 L9
Nelson Ct BRCH CT7 110 F5
Nelson Crs RAM CT11 17 F5
Nelson Mandela Rd
BKHTH/KID SE3 42 G4
Nelson Park Rd RDV CT15 262 E7
Nelson Pl BRDST CT10 113 N8
SCUP DA14 64 C3
Nelson Rd BELV DA17 28 E8
CDW/CHF RM16 33 L2
DART DA1 46 C7
GILL ME7 7 K4
GNWCH SE10 25 M9
GVW DA11 69 K1
HAYES BR2 85 M1
ROCH ME1 124 B1
RTWE/PEM TN2 23 J7
SCUP DA14 64 C3
WSTB CT5 105 K5
Nelson St CAN/RD E16 26 A3
DEAL CT14 233 J2
FAV ME13 132 F7
WCHPL E1 24 E2
Nelson Ter DVE/WH CT16 291 J4
WALD ME5 95 P5
Nepicar La BGR/WK TN15 121 M9
Neptune Cl STRD ME2 72 E8
Neptune Gap WSTB CT5 * 105 L4
Neptune St BERM/RHTH SE16 24 F6
Neptune Ter RSIT ME9 * 98 D3
Neptune Wy STRD ME2 72 E9
Nesbit Cl BKHTH/KID SE3 42 C4
Nesbit Rd ELTH/MOT SE9 43 H5
LYDD TN29 337 L1
Nesbitt Sq NRWD SE19 * 60 E6
Nesham St WAP E1W 24 D4
Ness Rd ERITH DA8 30 A9
LYDD TN29 342 B6
Ness St BERM/RHTH SE16 24 D6
The Ness CANT CT1 166 F7
Nestor Ct WBY/YAL ME18 183 P3
Nethan Dr SOCK/AV RM15 30 F3
Nether Av NROM TN28 337 J8
Netherby Rd FSTH SE23 41 J8
Nethercourt Farm Rd
RAM CT11 142 G6
Nethercourt Gdns RAM CT11 142 G6
Nethercourt Hl RAM CT11 142 G6
Nethergong Hl RCANTE CT3 138 G5
Netherhale Farm Rd
BRCH CT7 110 G9
Nethern Court Rd CTHM CR3 144 D8
Nethersole Cl CANTW/ST CT2 136 F9
Nethersole Rd RCANTW CT4 229 H5
Netley Cl CROY/NA CR0 114 F2
MAID/BEAR ME14 156 A6
Nettlefield KEN/WIL TN24 253 H4
Nettlefold Pl WNWD SE27 60 B2
Nettlepole La HDCN TN27 220 D9
Nettlestead Cl BECK BR3 61 M6
Nettlestead La
WBY/YAL ME18 183 H5
Nettleton Rd NWCR SE14 41 K2
Neuchatel Rd CAT SE6 61 M1
Nevada St GNWCH SE10 42 A1
Nevell Rd CDW/CHF RM16 33 J6
Nevill Ct E/WMAL ME19 153 K3
STH/RUST TN4 270 A6
Neville Cl BFN/LL DA15 64 B3
MAID/BEAR ME14 155 N4
PECK SE15 40 G1
Neville Pl MEO DA13 * 92 B2
Neville Rd CHAT ME4 95 K4
CROY/NA CR0 83 J4
Nevill Gdns DEAL CT14 232 G8
Nevill Ga RTWE/PEM TN2 270 E7
Nevill Pk STH/RUST TN4 270 B4
Nevill Pl SNOD ME6 123 P6
Nevill Rdg STH/RUST TN4 270 A5
Nevill Rd SNOD ME6 123 P6
Nevill St RTW TN1 22 C7
RTWE/PEM TN2 270 D7
Nevill Ter RTWE/PEM TN2 22 B7
New Acres Rd THMD SE28 27 M5
Newark Knok EHAM E6 27 H2
Newark St WCHPL E1 24 E1
Newark Yd STRD ME2 18 D1
Newbarn La RSEV TN14 146 E1
New Barn Rd MEO DA13 68 G4
RMAID ME17 217 H8
SWLY BR8 65 N7
New Barns Av MTCM CR4 82 C1
New Barns Rd
MAID/BEAR ME14 155 M4
Newbery Rd ERITH DA8 45 P2
Newbridge Av SIT ME10 99 M7
New Broad St LVPST EC2M 24 A1
Newburgh Rd GRAYS RM17 32 E8
Newbury Av MAIDW ME16 155 J6
Newbury Cl BRCH CT7 111 J7
FOLK CT20 310 A6
HOO/HM ME3 52 B8
Newbury La WADH TN5 294 D7
Newbury Rd HAYES BR2 62 E9
New Butt La DEPT SE8 * 41 N1
Newby Pl POP/IOD E14 25 M3
Newcastle Hl RAM CT11 17 G3
Newchapel Rd LING RH7 234 D7
Newchurch La LYDD TN29 324 E8
New Church Rd CMBW SE5 40 D1
Newchurch Rd MAID/SHEP
ME15 185 M2
Newcomen Rd IOS ME12 57 L6
STH/RUST TN4 270 D3
Newcomen St STHWK SE1 24 A5
New Concordia Whf
STHWK SE1 * 24 C5
New Covenant Pl ROCH ME1 19 J7
New Crane Pl WAP E1W * 24 F4
New Cross Rd NWCR SE14 41 M1
New Cross St MARG CT9 15 G4
New Cut CHAT ME4 6 A4
MAID/SHEP ME15 185 J4
New Cut Rd FAV ME13 164 B8
MAID/BEAR ME14 156 A8
Newdigate
STRHM/NOR SW16 * 60 A3
New Dover Rd CANT CT1 5 H6
RFOLK CT18 311 L2
Newell St POP/IOD E14 25 J3
Newenden Cl ASH TN23 282 C2
MAID/BEAR ME14 155 P6
Newenden Rd STRD ME2 72 C5
New England Rd
STH/RUST TN4 270 D1
New Farm Av HAYES BR2 85 K1
New Farthingdale LING RH7 235 K9
New Ferry Ap
WOOL/PLUM SE18 27 H6
New Forest La RCANTW CT4 164 B8
New Gardens Rd RSIT ME9 131 H3
Newgate CROY/NA CR0 83 H5
Newgate Gap MARG CT9 112 F2
Newgate Lower Prom
MARG CT9 15 K2
Newgate Prom MARG CT9 15 K2
New Goulston St WCHPL E1 24 C2
New Green Pl
BRXS/STRHM SW2 40 A8
NRWD SE19 60 E5
Newhache LING RH7 235 K8
New Haine Rd MSTR CT12 112 F9
New Hall Cl LYDD TN29 326 G6
New Hall Farm La
HOO/HM ME3 54 F2
Newham's Rw STHWK SE1 24 B5
Newham Wy CAN/RD E16 26 A1
Newhaven Gdns
ELTH/MOT SE9 43 H5
Newhaven La CAN/RD E16 26 B1
Newhaven Rd SNWD SE25 83 J2
New House Cl CANT CT1 166 C8
New House La GVW DA11 69 K2
RCANTW CT4 196 B1
Newhouse La FAV ME13 162 F5
HDCN TN27 247 L5
New House Ter EDEN TN8 * 206 D8
New Hythe La DIT/AY ME20 153 P2
Newick Cl BXLY DA5 45 K7
Newing Cl RCANTE CT3 168 B8
Newing Gn BMLY BR1 63 H6
Newington Rd MSTR CT12 142 G2
RAM CT11 16 B2
RFOLK CT18 287 M8
Newington Wk
MAID/BEAR ME14 * 155 P6
Newitt Rd HOO/HM ME3 73 K2
New Kent Rd STHWK SE1 24 A7
New King St DEPT SE8 25 K9
Newland Green La
HDCN TN27 249 L1
Newland Rd IOS ME12 57 H9
Newlands ASH TN23 282 A2
DVE/WH CT16 291 J1
RRTW TN3 269 M4
Newlands Av SIT ME10 129 J1
Newlands Crs EGRIN RH19 264 G6
Newlands Dr DEAL CT14 232 G9
Newlands Farm Rd
HOO/HM ME3 53 P3
Newlands La MEO DA13 122 A4
MSTR CT12 143 J2
Newlands Pk SYD SE26 61 J5
Newlands Quay WAP E1W 24 F3
Newlands Ri STH/RUST TN4 270 D2
Newlands Rd HDCN TN27 220 E5
MSTR CT12 143 J3
STH/RUST TN4 270 E2
Newland St CAN/RD E16 26 F4
Newlands Wy STH/RUST TN4 270 D1
Newlands Wd CROY/NA CR0 114 C3
Newlands Woods
CROY/NA CR0 * 114 C3
New La LYDD TN29 342 B6
Newling Cl EHAM E6 26 G2
New Lodge Dr OXTED RH8 175 J4
New London St MON EC3R * 24 B3
New Lydd Rd RYE TN31 339 N9
New Lydenburg St CHARL SE7 26 D6
Newlyn Cl ORP BR6 86 G8
Newlyn Dr STPH/PW TN12 246 C4
Newlyn Rd WELL DA16 44 B3
Newlyn's Meadow RDV CT15 289 N3
Newman Dr SIT ME10 99 N6
Newman Rd BMLY BR1 62 E7
CROY/NA CR0 82 E4
RCANTE CT3 229 H1
Newmans Cl BRDST CT10 113 M7
Newmarsh Rd THMD SE28 27 N4
New Mill Rd STMC/STPC BR5 64 E7
Newnham Cl RHAM ME8 96 F4
THHTH CR7 60 C8
Newnham La FAV ME13 161 K5
Newnham Pl CDW/CHF RM16 33 H7
Newnhams Cl BMLY BR1 63 K9
Newnham St CHAT ME4 7 F6
New Place Gdns LING RH7 235 H5
New Place Sq
BERM/RHTH SE16 * 24 E6
New Pond Rd CRBK TN17 298 F9
Newport Av POP/IOD E14 25 N3
Newports SWLY BR8 88 C4
New Pound La
WBY/YAL ME18 182 D1
Newquay Rd CAT SE6 61 P1
New Rectory La ASH TN23 282 E4
New Rents ASH TN23 2 C3
New Rd ABYW SE2 28 C7
CANTW/ST CT2 136 E2
CANTW/ST CT2 165 K1
CANTW/ST CT2 165 P1
CHAT ME4 6 B5
CRBK TN17 297 N3
DIT/AY ME20 153 P3
EYN DA4 67 J8
GDST RH9 204 D3
GRAYS RM17 32 C9
GVW DA11 49 M7
HDCN TN27 219 P8
HDCN TN27 247 N4
HOO/HM ME3 52 A4
HYTHE CT21 308 G3
IOS ME12 57 J8
IOS ME12 78 C1
MEO DA13 92 A2
ORP BR6 87 H4
OXTED RH8 175 L6
RAIN RM13 30 C4
RCANTW CT4 257 L5
RDV CT15 260 D1
RMAID ME17 186 F6
ROCH ME1 19 J7
ROCH ME1 124 E5
RSEV TN14 147 L9
RTON TN11 238 F8
RYE TN31 338 G6
STPH/PW TN12 243 H3
SWLY BR8 65 P6
WCHPL E1 24 E1
WELL DA16 44 D3
New Road Av CHAT ME4 6 A4
New Road Hl HAYES BR2 115 P3
RASHE TN25 306 A3
New Romney Pl SWCH CT13 * 201 N2
New Ruttington La CANT CT1 5 G2
New Stairs CHAT ME4 6 B1
Newstead Av ORP BR6 86 E7
Newstead Rd LEE/GVPK SE12 42 D8
New St BGR/WK TN15 121 N1
BH/WHM TN16 176 D3
CANT CT1 4 C7
CANTW/ST CT2 4 B2
CHAT ME4 6 A6
DEAL CT14 233 J2
DVE/WH CT16 8 D4
FOLK CT20 11 F3
IOS ME12 57 K7
KEN/WIL TN24 2 C2
LVPST EC2M 24 B1
LYDD TN29 342 B6
MARG CT9 15 G4
RCANTE CT3 200 F1
SWCH CT13 201 P2
New Street Hl BMLY BR1 62 F4
New Street Rd MEO DA13 91 M7
New Swan Yd GVE DA12 * 49 M7
Newton Abbot Rd GVW DA11 69 K1
Newton Av TONN TN10 210 G3
Newton Cl MAIDW ME16 12 B7
WALD ME5 125 P3
Newton Gdns STPH/PW TN12 242 G2
Newton Pl POP/IOD E14 25 K7
Newton Rd FAV ME13 132 G6
RTW TN1 22 D3
TIL RM18 49 L3
WELL DA16 44 C4
WSTB CT5 106 A4
Newton's Ct GRH DA9 47 K5
Newton Ter HAYES BR2 85 N3
Newton Willows RRTW TN3 269 H9
New Tower Buildings
WAP E1W * 24 E4
New Town Gn KEN/WIL TN24 252 G9
Newtown Rd ASH TN23 3 F6
New Town Rd KEN/WIL TN24 282 G1
New Town St CANT CT1 5 G1
RCANTW CT4 165 K7
New Union Cl POP/IOD E14 25 M6
New Union St BARB EC2Y 24 A1
New Wharf Rd TON TN9 210 E8
New Years La RSEV TN14 146 G1
Nicholas Cl MAIDW ME16 154 F9
Nicholas Dr MSTR CT12 142 C7
Nicholas La MANHO EC4N 24 A3
Nicholas Rd CROY/NA CR0 82 D8
RASHE TN25 252 D2
Nichol La BMLY BR1 62 E6
Nicholls Av BRDST CT10 143 L2
Nicholson House
WOOL/PLUM SE18 * 43 J1
Nicholson Rd CROY/NA CR0 83 L5
Nickelby Cl THMD SE28 28 B2
Nicklaus Dr WALD ME5 125 L2
Nickle Bank RCANTW CT4 * 165 H8
Nickleby Cl ROCH ME1 95 H4
Nickleby Rd GVE DA12 50 C9
Nickle Ga RCANTW CT4 * 165 H9
Nickley Wood Rd
RASHW TN26 303 N1
Nicolson Rd STMC/STPC BR5 87 K4
Niederwald Rd SYD SE26 61 L3
Nigel Rd PECK SE15 40 G4
Nigeria Rd CHARL SE7 42 G1
Nightingale Av HYTHE CT21 308 C7
WSTB CT5 105 J8
Nightingale Cl BH/WHM TN16 115 M9
DIT/AY ME20 153 N2
EGRIN RH19 264 G9
GVW DA11 69 J3
KEN/WIL TN24 283 K1
RCANTW CT4 165 K6
RHAM ME8 97 H8
Nightingale Cnr
STMC/STPC BR5 * 87 L1
Nightingale Ct STRD ME2 * 71 L9
Nightingale Gv LEW SE13 42 B6
Nightingale La BMLY BR1 62 G8
RDV CT15 229 M3
RSEV TN14 178 A6
Nightingale Pl MARG CT9 15 K4
WOOL/PLUM SE18 27 H9
Nightingale Rd BGR/WK TN15 149 J2
DVE/WH CT16 291 K5
FAV ME13 132 F6
HB CT6 107 K7
SAND/SEL CR2 114 A5
STMC/STPC BR5 86 D3
The Nightingales CRBK TN17 277 J8
Nightingale V
WOOL/PLUM SE18 27 H9
Nightingale Wy EHAM E6 26 F1
SWLY BR8 65 N9
Nile Rd GILL ME7 7 J4
Nile Ter PECK SE15 24 C8
Nina Vls STPH/PW TN12 * 245 H4
Nine Acres KEN/WIL TN24 252 F4
Nine Acres Rd STRD ME2 93 P3
Nine Ash La FAV ME13 163 M1
Nine Elms Gv GVW DA11 49 L8
Ninehams Rd BH/WHM TN16 145 N6
Nineteenth Rd MTCM CR4 82 D1
Nineveh La HAWK TN18 298 B9
Ninhams Wd ORP BR6 86 B8
Ninn La ASH TN23 251 M7
Nisbett Wk SCUP DA14 64 C3
Nithdale Rd WOOL/PLUM SE18 43 M1
Niven Cl HOO/HM ME3 72 C4
Nixon Av MSTR CT12 143 H3
Nizels La RTON TN11 209 L1
No1 St WOOL/PLUM SE18 27 J6
No2 St WOOL/PLUM SE18 27 J6
Noah's Ark BGR/WK TN15 149 N3
Noah's Ark Rd DVW CT17 291 H7
Noahs Ark Ter DVW CT17 291 J7
Noakes Meadow ASH TN23 252 C9
Nobel Cl RSIT ME9 131 H3
Nobel Ct FAV ME13 132 E6
Noble Ct MARG CT9 * 111 P5
Noble Gdns MARG CT9 111 P5
Noble Tree Rd RTON TN11 209 N4
Nonsuch Cl CANT CT1 167 H4
The Nook WBY/YAL ME18 183 N9
Norah La HOO/HM ME3 71 K3
Norbiton Rd POP/IOD E14 25 J2
Norbury Cl STRHM/NOR SW16 60 A7
Norbury Crs
STRHM/NOR SW16 60 A8
Norbury Hl STRHM/NOR SW16 60 A6
Norbury Rd THHTH CR7 60 C8
Norcroft Gdns EDUL SE22 40 G8
Nordenfeldt Rd ERITH DA8 29 J8
Nore Cl GILL ME7 96 B5
IOS ME12 57 L7
Noreen Av IOS ME12 78 A1
Norfield Rd RDART DA2 65 L3
Norfolk Cl DART DA1 46 G7
WALD ME5 125 P2
Norfolk Crs BFN/LL DA15 44 A8
Norfolk Dr ASH TN23 2 A4
Norfolk Gdns BXLYHN DA7 45 H2
Norfolk Pl CDW/CHF RM16 31 M8
WELL DA16 44 C3
Norfolk Rd CANT CT1 166 D6
GVE DA12 49 P8
MAID/SHEP ME15 185 P3
MARG CT9 112 G3
RTW TN1 22 E6
THHTH CR7 60 C9
TON TN9 210 D9
Norfolk Sq MSTR CT12 * 142 G2
Norfolk St WSTB CT5 105 L6
Norheads La BH/WHM TN16 145 K3
Norhyrst Av SNWD SE25 60 F9
Norlands Crs CHST BR7 63 M7
Norlands Ga CHST BR7 * 63 M7
Norman Cl MAID/BEAR ME14 155 N6
ORP BR6 86 D7
RHAM ME8 126 E1
RSEV TN14 149 J2
STRD ME2 18 A7
Normandy Cl EGRIN RH19 * 265 J8
SYD SE26 61 L2
Normandy Rd BRXN/ST SW9 40 A2
Normandy Ter CAN/RD E16 26 C2
Normandy Wy ERITH DA8 45 N2
Normanhurst Av WELL DA16 44 F2
Normanhurst Rd
BGR/WK TN15 151 K5
STMC/STPC BR5 64 D8
Norman Pde SCUP DA14 * 64 G2
Norman Ri CRBK TN17 298 A3
Norman Rd ASH TN23 282 F1
BELV DA17 28 G5
BRDST CT10 113 K7
CANT CT1 4 E7
DART DA1 46 E9
E/WMAL ME19 153 H3

FAV ME13 ....132 F6
GNWCH SE10 ....41 P1
MARG CT9 ....111 N4
RAM CT11 ....16 A5
ROC CT15 ....292 C1
RTW TN1 ....23 F2
SNOD ME6 ....125 P7
THHTH CR7 ....82 G2
WSTB CT5 ....105 L8
Normans Cl DVW DA11 ....49 L8
Normans La EDEN TN8 ....235 P1
Norman St DVW CT17 ....8 C3
RSEV TN14 ....177 M6
Normanton Cl STRHM/NOR SW16 ....60 A4
Norreys Rd RHAM ME8 ....97 H7
Norrie Rd BRCH CT7 ....110 C7
Norrington Md FOLKN CT19 ....310 D4
Norrington Rd CROY/NA CRO 83 M6
North Ash Rd HART DA3 ....91 J7
North Av RAM CT11 ....16 E4
North Bank Ct STRD ME2 ....18 A5
North Barrack Rd DEAL CT14 ....233 J5
Northbourne HAYES BR2 ....85 K4
North Bourne Rd DVW CT17 ....291 J7
Northbourne Rd DEAL CT14 ....231 M6
RHAM ME8 ....96 C2
Northbourne Wy MARG CT9 ....113 K4
Northbrooke KEN/WIL TN24 ....2 E1
Northbrooke La KEN/WIL TN24 ....2 E1
Northbrook Rd CROY/NA CRO 83 J2
LEW SE13 ....42 E6
Northcliffe Gdns BRDST CT10 ....113 M6
North Cl BXLYHS DA6 ....41 H5
FOLK CT20 ....310 A7
North Colonnade
POP/IOD E14 ....25 L4
Northcote Rd CROY/NA CRO 83 J3
DEAL CT14 ....233 J4
DEAL CT14 ....263 J4
GVW DA11 ....49 K9
SCUP DA14 ....64 A3
STRD ME2 ....18 B2
TON TN9 ....210 E9
North Ct MAID/SHEP ME15 * 185 M2
North Court Cl RCANTE CT3 ....169 K8
North Court La DEAL CT14 ....231 H5
North Cray Rd BXLY DA5 ....65 J1
SCUP DA14 ....64 G5
North Crs RMAID ME17 ....185 J1
North Cross Rd EDUL SE22 ....40 F6
North Dane Wy WALD ME5 ....95 P9
Northdown KEN/WIL TN24 ....252 F5
RSIT ME9 ....160 E5
North Down STPH/PW TN12 ....246 B5
Northdown Ar MARG CT9 * 112 G3
Northdown Av MARG CT9 ....112 G3
Northdown Cl
MAID/BEAR ME14 ....155 N5
STPH/PW TN12 ....242 C3
Northdown HI BRDST CT10 ....113 J6
Northdown Pde MARG CT9 * 112 G3
Northdown Park Rd
MARG CT9 ....112 G4
Northdown Rd BGR/WK TN15 ....149 K2
BRDST CT10 ....113 K6
GDST RH9 ....174 D1
HART DA3 ....68 C8
MARG CT9 ....113 J4
WELL DA16 ....44 D5
North Downs Cl RDON WLCT4 ....194 C1
Northdowns Cl RDV CT15 ....261 J2
North Downs Crs
CROY/NA CRO 114 E4
North Downs Rd
CROY/NA CRO 114 E4
North Downs Wy
BGR/WK TN15 ....121 H9
CANT CT1 ....5 J6
CANTW/ST CT2 ....165 P4
CVE DA12 ....49 M8
DVE/WH CT16 ....291 L5
DVW CT17 ....313 H2
GDST RH9 ....174 C4
HYTHE CT21 ....286 C4
MAID/BEAR ME14 ....126 B9
MAID/BEAR ME14 ....155 L8
OXTED RH8 ....145 K8
RASHE TN25 ....221 N4
RASHE TN25 ....222 E6
RASHE TN25 ....254 E1
RASHE TN25 ....255 K6
RCANTW CT4 ....197 N2
RCANTW CT4 ....223 N1
RCANTW CT4 ....228 D3
RCANTW CT4 ....229 K6
RDV CT15 ....311 M2
RFOLK CT18 ....311 M2
RMAID ME17 ....157 N6
RMAID ME17 ....189 L4
SEV TN13 ....148 C3
STRD ME2 ....93 N5
North Downs Wy & Saxon
Shore Wy FOLKN CT19 ....310 E2
Northdown Ter EGRIN RH19 * 264 C5
Northdown Vw RMAID ME17 ....188 C5
Northdown Vw MARG CT9 ....113 H4
North Dr BECK BR3 ....84 E1
North Eastling Rd RSIT ME9 ....161 K3
North End CROY/NA CRO 83 H6
EGRIN RH19 * 264 E5
North End La ORP BR6 ....116 C3
Northend Rd ERITH DA8 ....45 P2
Northern By-Pass HDCN TN27 ....221 H2
Northey St POP/IOD E14 ....25 H3

North Farm La
RTWE/PEM TN2 ....240 C9
North Farm Rd
RTWE/PEM TN2 ....270 F1
Northfield HART DA5 ....68 D9
Northfield Av STMC/STPC BR5 ....87 K3
Northfield Cl BMLY BR1 ....63 J7
Northfields GRAYS RM17 ....32 C7
MAIDW ME16 ....184 E1
RTW TN3 ....239 M9
Northfleet Cl
MAID/SHEP ME15 * 155 P7
North Folly Rd
MAID/SHEP ME15 ....184 E8
North Foreland Av
BRDST CT10 ....113 N6
North Foreland Rd
BRDST CT10 ....113 N6
North Frith RTON TN11 * 211 J1
Northgate CANT CT1 ....19 G4
Northgate Borough CANT CT1 ....5 G2
Northgrove Rd HAWK TN18 ....317 H4
North Hill Rd HAWK TN18 ....316 E5
North Holmes Rd CANT CT1 ....5 H5
North Kent Av GVW DA11 ....48 C7
Northlands HYTHE CT21 * 309 H5
Northlands Av ORP BR6 ....68 F8
Northlands St CMBW SE5 ....40 C5
North La CANTW/ST CT2 ....4 D3
FAV ME15 ....132 F6
FAV ME15 ....164 A4
Northleigh Cl
MAID/SHEP ME15 ....185 M5
North Lockside CHAT ME4 * 33 J5
North Lyminge La
RFOLK CT18 ....287 H1
North Meadow
E/WMAL ME19 ....152 E5
North Military Rd DVW CT17 ....8 B5
Northolme Cl
CDW/CHF RM16 * 32 D6
Northolme Ri ORP BR6 ....86 F6
Northover BMLY BR1 ....62 D5
North Pk ELTH/MOT SE9 ....43 K7
North Pasley Rd CHAT ME4 ....73 H8
North Peckham Est PECK SE15 ....40 F1
North Pends KEN/WIL TN24 ....253 H3
North Pole La HAYES BR2 ....115 K1
North Pole Rd
WBY/YAL ME18 ....184 A1
North Pondside CHAT ME4 * 72 G7
North Pondside CHAT ME4 ....72 G7
Northridge RYE TN31 ....329 P7
North Riding HART DA3 ....69 H9
North Rd BELV DA17 ....28 C6
BMLY BR1 ....62 F7
CHAT ME4 ....72 G7
CRBK TN17 ....274 D7
DART DA1 ....45 J7
DEAL CT14 ....263 J2
DVW CT17 ....8 A3
FOLK CT20 ....309 P5
FOLK CT20 ....310 B7
HOO/HM ME3 ....52 B2
HYTHE CT21 ....309 H5
MSTR CT12 ....171 P2
PUR RM19 ....30 F7
QBOR ME11 ....77 H2
SWCH CT13 ....202 F2
WOOL/PLUM SE18 ....27 M7
WWKM BR4 ....84 E5
North Rd West HYTHE CT21 ....308 F4
North Salts RYE TN31 ....338 F6
North Several
BKHTH/KID SE3 * 42 B3
Northside Rd BMLY BR1 ....62 E7
Northside The CHAT ME4 * 73 J7
Northstead Rd
BRXS/STRHM SW2 ....60 A1
North St BMLY BR1 ....62 E7
BXLYHN DA7 ....45 J8
DART DA1 ....46 C8
DEAL CT14 ....233 J2
DVW CT17 ....291 J8
EDEN TN8 ....267 H2
FOLKN CT19 ....49 M8
HB CT6 ....107 L1
HDCN TN27 ....247 M4
HDCN TN27 ....278 B6
KEN/WIL TN24 ....2 E2
MAIDW ME16 ....184 A4
NROM TN28 ....336 F7
RMAID ME17 ....217 H5
RTWE/PEM TN2 ....99 M7
SIT ME10 ....51 H3
STRD ME2 ....18 D1
North Tenter St WCHPL E1 ....24 C2
North Trench TONN TN10 * 210 F4
Northumberland Aly TWRH EC3N 24 B2
Northumberland Av
KEN/WIL TN24 ....252 C4
MARG CT9 ....113 H4
RHAM ME8 ....97 H5
WELL DA16 ....44 A5
Northumberland Cl ERITH DA8 ....45 L1
Northumberland Ct
MAID/SHEP ME15 * 186 A4
Northumberland Gdns
BMLY BR1 ....86 B1
MTCM CR4 ....82 D2
Northumberland Pk
ERITH DA8 ....45 L1
Northumberland Rd EHAM E6 ....26 F2
MEO DA13 ....69 K6
SLH/COR SS17 ....33 N5
Northumberland Wy
ERITH DA8 ....45 L2
Northumbria St POP/IOD E14 ....25 K2
North Vw MAID/SHEP ME15 ....185 N2
RCANTE CT3 ....138 C8

RRTW TN3 * 239 M9
Northview SWLY BR8 ....65 N8
North View Av TIL RM18 ....49 L2
North View Rd SEV TN13 ....149 H6
North Wk CROY/NA CRO 83 L6
Northwall Ms DEAL CT14 ....233 H2
Northwall Quay DVW CT17 ....8 D7
North Wall Rd DEAL CT14 ....233 H2
North Wy DEAL CT14 ....231 P2
MAID/BEAR ME14 ....155 N5
Northway WLGTN SM6 ....82 B8
Northway Rd CMBW SE5 ....40 C4
CROY/NA CRO 83 L5
Northwood CDW/CHF RM16 ....33 J5
Northwood Av HOO/HM ME3 ....53 L4
Northwood Dr SIT ME10 ....129 N4
Northwood Pl ERITH DA18 ....28 E6
Northwood Rd BRDST CT10 ....143 H1
FSTH SE23 ....41 M9
THHTH CR7 ....60 C8
TONN TN10 ....210 E4
WSTB CT5 ....105 M4
Nortons Cl TENT TN30 ....300 F2
Nortons Wy STPH/PW TN12 ....242 B2
Norval Rd BRXN/ST SW9 * 40 A3
Norview Rd WSTB CT5 ....105 J7
Norway Dro RDV CT15 ....262 F7
Norway Rd GNWCH SE10 ....25 H6
Norway Pl POP/IOD E14 ....25 J3
Norway St GNWCH SE10 ....25 L9
Norwich Cl MAID/BEAR ME14 * 155 L5
Norwich Av TONN TN10 ....210 C5
Norwich Cl STRD ME2 ....71 M9
Norwich Pl BXLYHS DA6 ....45 J5
Norwich Rd THHTH CR7 ....60 C9
Norwood Cl HOO/HM ME3 ....52 E4
Norwood Gdns ASH TN23 ....2 C3
Norwood High St WNWD SE27 ....60 C3
Norwood La LYDD TN29 ....335 N7
MEO DA13 ....92 C2
Norwood Park Rd WNWD SE27 ....60 C4
Norwood Rd IOS ME12 ....58 C9
Norwood Rd HNHL SE24 ....40 A9
Norwood St ASH TN23 ....2 C3
Notley St CANT CT1 ....5 G2
CMBW SE5 ....40 D1
Notley Ter CANT CT1 * 5 C2
Notson Rd SNWD SE25 ....83 N1
Nottidge Rd STH/RUST TN4 ....270 A7
Nottingham Av CAN/RD E16 ....26 D1
MAID/SHEP ME15 ....186 A5
Nottingham Rd BRCH CT7 ....110 C8
SAND/SEL CR2 ....83 H9
Nouds La RSIT ME9 ....131 J5
Nouds Rd RSIT ME9 ....131 J5
Novar Cl ORP BR6 ....86 G4
Nova Rd CROY/NA CRO 82 G5
Novar Rd ELTH/MOT SE9 ....43 N9
The Nower RSEV TN14 ....146 C5
RSEV TN14 ....147 L1
Nubia Wy BMLY BR1 ....62 C3
Nuding Cl LEW SE13 ....41 M9
Nuffield Rd SWLY BR8 ....66 A5
Nugent Rd SNWD SE25 ....60 F9
Nunappleton Wy OXTED RH8 ....175 M8
Nunhead Gv PECK SE15 ....41 H4
Nunhead La PECK SE15 ....41 H4
Nunnery Flds CANT CT1 ....166 F6
Nunnery La RTON TN11 ....233 J4
Nunnery Rd CANT CT1 ....166 E5
Nunnington Cl ELTH/MOT SE9 ....63 J2
Nunns Wy GRAYS RM17 ....32 C7
Nursery Av BXLYHN DA7 ....45 H4
CROY/NA CRO 86 A6
MAID/BEAR ME14 ....156 E9
MAIDW ME16 ....154 G6
Nursery Cl BROCKY SE4 ....41 M3
CROY/NA CRO 86 A6
IOS ME12 ....57 M7
ORP BR6 ....88 G4
RAM CT11 ....16 B2
RDART DA2 ....47 J8
RFOLK CT18 ....288 C5
SEV TN13 ....149 H7
SWLY BR8 ....66 A5
TONN TN10 ....211 H6
WADH TN5 ....315 M3
WSTB CT5 ....105 P5
Nursery Est HB CT6 * 107 H5
Nursery Flds BRCH CT7 ....141 J1
HYTHE CT21 ....308 E5
Nursery Gdns CHST BR7 ....63 M5
HOO/HM ME3 ....73 L2
MARG CT9 ....113 K4
Nurserylands HB CT6 ....107 L5
Nursery La DVE/WH CT16 ....260 G9
FAV ME13 ....162 F7
RFOLK CT18 ....288 D5
Nursery Pl SEV TN13 ....148 C2
Nursery Rd DIT/AY ME20 ....154 B3
MEO DA13 ....92 B2
RHAM ME8 ....96 G6
STH/RUST TN4 ....240 E9
STPH/PW TN12 ....242 G1
THHTH CR7 ....83 J1
Nursery Rw WALW SE17 ....24 A7
The Nursery ERITH DA8 ....45 J6
Nursery Wk CANTW/ST CT2 ....4 C1
Nursery Wy OXTED RH8 * 175 N5
Nurstead Av HART DA3 ....68 F9
Nurstead Church La
MEO DA13 ....92 B1
Nurstead La HART DA3 ....91 N1
Nurstead Rd ERITH DA8 ....45 J1
Nutberry Av CDW/CHF RM16 ....32 B5

Nutberry Cl CDW/CHF RM16 ....32 B5
RSIT ME9 ....131 J3
Nutbrook St PECK SE15 ....40 F3
Nutcroft Rd PECK SE15 ....41 H1
Nutfield Cl WALD ME5 ....95 N6
Nutfield Rd EDUL SE22 ....40 F6
THHTH CR7 ....82 G1
Nutfields BGR/WK TN15 ....130 G6
Nutfield Wy ORP BR6 ....86 B6
Nuthatch HART DA3 ....68 F9
Nuthatch Gdns THMD SE28 ....27 L5
Nutley Cl KEN/WIL TN24 ....252 C8
RYE TN31 ....338 D6
SWLY BR8 ....65 P7
Nutmead Cl BXLY DA5 ....45 L9
Nutmeg La POP/IOD E14 ....25 N2
Nut Tree Cl ORP BR6 ....87 L7
Nutts Av IOS ME12 ....80 E5
Nut St PECK SE15 ....40 F1
Nutwood Cl
MAID/BEAR ME14 ....156 B8
Nuxley Rd BELV DA17 ....28 E9
Nyanza St WOOL/PLUM SE18 ....27 L9
Nynehead St NWCR SE14 ....41 L1
Nyon Gv FSTH SE23 ....61 M1

Oakapple La MAIDW ME16 ....154 F9
Oak Av CROY/NA CRO 84 D6
GILL ME7 ....73 L9
HDCN TN27 ....278 F9
IOS ME12 ....78 E1
RDV CT15 ....260 C5
SEV TN13 ....178 G4
Oakbank CROY/NA CRO 114 F1
Oakbank Gv HNHL SE24 ....40 C5
Oakbrook Cl BMLY BR1 ....62 E6
Oak Bungalows LYDD TN29 * 342 B6
Oak Caer RASHE TN25 ....306 A3
Oak Cl DART DA1 ....45 N5
HOO/HM ME3 ....73 L4
Oak Cottage Cl CAT SE6 ....42 C9
Oak Crs CAN/RD E16 ....25 P1
Oak Cft EGRIN RH19 ....265 K8
Oakcroft Rd LEW SE13 ....42 B3
Oakdale La EDEN TN8 ....176 D9
Oakdale Rd HB CT6 ....107 K2
PECK SE15 ....41 J4
STH/RUST TN4 ....22 A2
Oakdene Av CHST BR7 ....63 L4
ERITH DA8 ....45 L1
Oakdene Rd MSTR CT12 ....143 H3
SEV TN13 ....148 F7
STMC/STPC BR5 ....87 H3
Oak Dr DIT/AY ME20 ....153 P2
HOO/HM ME3 ....71 K4
LYDD TN29 ....337 L2
RFOLK CT18 ....288 E7
Oak End Cl STH/RUST TN4 ....240 D7
Oakenden La EDEN TN8 ....238 A9
Oakenpole ASH TN25 ....252 B8
Oak Farm Gdns HDCN TN27 ....247 N3
Oak Farm La BGR/WK TN15 ....121 P4
Oakfield CRBK TN17 ....319 N5
HAWK TN18 ....317 H4
Oakfield Ct MSTR CT12 * 142 G4
Oakfield Court Rd
RTWE/PEM TN2 ....23 F5
Oakfield Gdns BECK BR3 ....84 D3
Oakfield La HAYES BR2 ....85 M8
RDART DA2 ....66 D1
Oakfield Park Rd DART DA1 ....66 D1
Oakfield Pl DART DA1 ....66 C1
Oakfield Rd CROY/NA CRO 83 H5
EDEN TN8 ....206 C6
KEN/WIL TN24 ....252 G5
PGE/AN SE20 ....61 H7
STPH/PW TN12 ....242 E9
Oakfields SEV TN13 ....21 F6
SIT ME10 ....129 K2
Oakfield Wy EGRIN RH19 ....265 J5
The Oakfield RYE TN31 ....338 E4
Oak Gdns CROY/NA CRO 84 D6
Oak Gv RDV CT15 ....230 C7
WWKM BR4 ....84 B6
Oak Grove Rd PGE/AN SE20 ....61 J7
Oakham Cl CAT SE6 ....61 M1
Oakham Dr HAYES BR2 ....85 K1
Oak HI SWCH CT13 ....201 J4
Oakhill Rd BECK BR3 ....84 G2
ORP BR6 ....86 G6
PUR RM19 ....30 E8
Oak Hill Rd SEV TN13 ....35 J6
Oakhouse Rd BXLYHS DA6 ....45 J6
Oakhurst Av BXLYHN DA7 ....44 G1
Oakhurst Cl CHST BR7 ....63 K7
WALD ME5 ....125 L2
Oakhurst Gdns BXLYHN DA7 ....44 G1
Oakhurst Rd BXLYHN DA7 ....45 L5
Oaklands ASH TN25 ....252 C8
GDST RH9 ....204 B5
RASHE TN25 ....283 P4
Oaklands Av BFN/LL DA15 ....44 B8
BRDST CT10 ....113 K8
THHTH CR7 ....82 F1
WWKM BR4 ....84 E7
Oaklands Cl BGR/WK TN15 ....120 B1
BXLYHS DA6 ....45 H6
STMC/STPC BR5 ....86 F3
Oaklands Dr SOCK/AV RM15 ....31 M1
Oaklands La BH/WHM TN16 ....115 H9
Oaklands Rd BMLY BR1 ....62 G9
BXLYHS DA6 ....45 H5
GVW DA11 ....49 K9
HAWK TN18 ....317 H5
RDART DA2 ....47 H9

Oaklands Wy CANTW/ST CT2 ....137 N6
RTON TN11 ....210 C6
Oak La HDCN TN27 ....247 N4
IOS ME12 ....78 E2
LYDD TN29 ....342 A6
POP/IOD E14 ....25 J3
RSIT ME9 ....97 N5
SEV TN13 ....21 F6
Oakea Rd STPH/PW TN12 ....242 G5
Oakleigh Cl SWLY BR8 ....65 N9
WALD ME5 ....125 K3
Oakleigh Ct OXTED RH8 * 175 H5
STPH/PW TN12 ....273 N2
Oakleigh Gdns ORP BR6 ....86 F8
Oakleigh La RCANTW CT4 ....167 N7
Oakleigh Park Av CHST BR7 ....63 L8
Oakley Av CROY/NA CRO 82 D8
Oakley Cl EGRIN RH19 ....265 J9
WTHK SH20 ....31 M9
Oakley Dr BFN/LL DA15 ....43 P9
HAYES BR2 ....85 P7
LEW SE13 ....42 B7
Oakley Pk BFN/LL DA15 ....44 E8
Oakley Pl STHWK SE1 ....24 C8
Oakley Rd HAYES BR2 ....85 P7
SNWD SE25 ....83 N2
Oak Lodge Dr WWKM BR4 ....84 E4
Oak Lodge La BH/WHM TN16 ....176 E1
Oak Lodge Rd NROM TN28 * 336 C6
Oakmead MEO DA13 ....210 F4
TONN TN10 ....210 F4
Oakmead Av HAYES BR2 ....85 K3
Oakmead Rd CROY/NA CRO 82 C5
Oakmere Rd ABYW SE2 ....27 P9
Oakmore Gdns
STMC/STPC BR5 * 87 K1
Oakridge BRDST CT10 ....113 M4
Oak Rdg RASHE TN25 ....305 J7
Oakridge Rd BMLY BR1 ....62 C3
Oak Rd BH/WHM TN16 ....176 E5
ERITH DA8 ....45 L1
ERITH DA8 ....46 A2
GRAYS RM17 ....32 D9
CRH DA9 ....47 L7
GVE DA12 ....49 N2
HOO/HM ME3 ....73 L4
ORP BR6 ....117 H2
RTWE/PEM TN2 ....270 C1
SIT ME10 ....100 B9
STPH/PW TN12 ....242 C2
STRD ME2 ....93 N5
Oaks Av HB CT6 ....107 J4
NRWD SE19 ....60 E4
Oaks Dene WALD ME5 ....125 L4
Oaksford Av SYD SE26 ....61 H2
Oaks Forstal HAWK TN18 ....318 C9
Oakshade Rd BMLY BR1 ....62 B3
Oakshaw OXTED RH8 ....174 C3
Oakside Rd RCANTE CT3 ....229 H1
Oaks La CROY/NA CRO 83 P7
Oaks Pk CANTW/ST CT2 ....166 A4
Oaks Rd CROY/NA CRO 83 N9
FOLK CT20 ....310 A5
TENT TN30 ....301 J8
The Oaks BRCH CT7 ....140 A2
BRDST CT10 ....113 L6
DIT/AY ME20 ....154 C5
EGRIN RH19 ....265 K8
HAYES BR2 ....86 B5
RCANTE CT3 ....138 C8
RDART DA2 ....47 H7
SWLY BR8 ....65 N8
WOOL/PLUM SE18 ....27 K8
Oak St DEAL CT14 ....233 J6
Oaks Vw HYTHE CT21 ....308 B7
Oak Ter WALD ME5 ....125 M3
Oak Tree Av CRH DA9 ....47 M8
MAID/SHEP ME15 ....185 P4
Oak Tree Cl EGRIN RH19 * 264 F5
RTW TN1 ....270 D7
STPH/PW TN12 ....245 J4
Oak Tree Gdns BMLY BR1 ....62 F4
Oak Tree Gv MARG CT9 ....111 P5
Oak Tree Rd ASH TN23 ....252 C9
Oakum Ct CHAT ME4 ....95 N4
Oakvale Cl DVW CT17 ....206 C8
Oakview Gv CROY/NA CRO 84 D5
Oakview Rd CAT SE6 ....61 N4
Oak Wk HYTHE CT21 ....309 H5
Oak Warren SEV TN13 ....178 F5
Oak Wy CROY/NA CRO 84 A3
Oakway CDW/CHF RM16 ....32 B8
HAYES BR2 ....62 B8
Oakway Cl BXLY DA5 ....44 G7
Oakways ELTH/MOT SE9 ....43 M7
Oakwood MARG CT9 * 113 H5
Oakwood Av BECK BR3 ....84 B6
Oakwood Cl CHST BR7 ....63 K5
DART DA1 ....47 H9
LEW SE13 ....42 B7
Oakwood Ct MAIDW ME16 ....12 A6
Oakwood Dr BXLYHN DA7 ....45 L5
NRWD SE19 ....60 C9
WSTB CT5 ....105 P5
Oakwood Gdns ORP BR6 ....86 D6
Oakwood Ms WSTB CT5 * 105 L7
Oakwood Pk MAID/BEAR ME14 * 155 H4
Oakwood Pl CROY/NA CRO 82 F3
Oakwood Ri HART DA3 ....68 F9
RTWE/PEM TN2 ....271 H1
Oakwood Rd CANTW/ST CT2 ....137 M6
CROY/NA CRO 82 F5
MAIDW ME16 ....155 H9
ORP BR6 ....86 D6
Oakwood Ter SEV TN13 * 130 B1
Oakwood Vls RAM CT11 * 143 K3
Oare Rd FAV ME15 ....152 E4
Oast Cl RTWE/PEM TN2 ....270 C1
Oast Rd OXTED RH8 ....175 L3
SIT ME10 ....129 M3
WBY/YAL ME18 ....213 N1
Oast House Dr RYE TN31 ....338 C8

Oasthouse Fld LYDD TN29 ....335 N1
Oast House Wy
STMC/STPC BR5...............87 J1
Oast La FAV ME13 ....192 B5
Oast Rd OXTED RH8...............210 D6
The Oast CANT CT1 * 166 C6
Oastview RHAM ME8................97 K6
Oast Vw STPH/PW TN12 ....273 P2
Oaten Hill CANT CT1 ....5 F6
Oaten Hill Pl CANT CT1 ....5 F6
Oates CI HAYES BR2.................62 B9
Oatfield CI CRBK TN17............297 P2
Oatfield Dr CRBK TN17............297 P2
Oatfield Rd ORP BR6.................86 C5
The Oaze WSTB CT5................105 K8
Oban Rd SNWD SE25.................83 J1
Oban St POP/IOD E14..............25 N2
Oborne CI HNHL SE24................40 B6
Occupation La
WOOL/PLUM SE18.............43 M2
Ocean CI BRCH CT7..................111 J5
Ocean Rd WCHPL E1................24 C1
Ocean Ter IOS ME12..................58 D9
Ocean Vw BRDST CT10............143 M5
Ocelot Ct WALD ME5..................7 G7
Ockham Dr STMC/STPC BR5.....64 C6
Ockley La HAWK TN18.............317 J2
Ockley Rd CROY/NA CRO..........82 E4
HAWK TN18.......................317 J4
Ockman La RYE TN51 * 338 F7
Octagon Ar LVPST EC2M...........24 B1
Octavia Ct WALD ME5...............125 N2
Octavian Dr HYTHE CT21..........307 P4
Octavius St DEPT SE8................41 N1
Odeon Pde ELTH/MOT SE9 * 43 J5
Odessa St BERM/RHTH SE16 .....25 J6
Odiham Dr MAIDW ME16..........155 H5
Odo Rd DVW CT17....................291 J7
Offenham Rd ELTH/MOT SE9 ....63 K3
Offen's Dr STPH/PW TN12 ....246 B6
Offham Rd E/WMAL ME19.........159 H5
Officers Ter CHAT ME4...............72 F8
Offley CI MARG CT9.................113 H4
Offley Rd BRXN/ST SW9.............40 A1
Ogilby St WOOL/PLUM SE18......26 C7
Oglander Rd PECK SE15.............40 F5
Okehampton Cl
KEN/WIL TN24...................253 J7
Okehampton Crs WELL DA16.....44 D2
Olantigh Rd RASHE TN25.........224 A6
Olave Rd MARG CT9.................112 C4
Old Ash CI KEN/WIL TN24 ....252 F4
Old Ashford Rd HDCN TN27 ....221 H5
RMAID ME17......................189 M6
Old Badgins Rd FAV ME13........162 D6
The Old Bailey RMAID ME17....188 F5
Old Bakery CI LYDD TN29 ....337 L1
Old Bakery Ms FAV ME15 *.......164 A1
Old Barn CI BGR/WK TN15......149 M2
GILL ME7............................96 C8
TON TN9...........................240 C1
Old Barn Rd E/WMAL ME19....153 L2
Old Barn Wy BXLYHN DA7........45 M5
Old Bexley La BXLY DA5.............65 N1
Old Billet La IOS ME12................79 J1
Old Boundary Rd MARG CT9....111 N4
Old Bridge Rd WSTB CT5..........105 M5
Old Broad St LVPST EC2M..........24 B2
Old Bromley Rd BMLY BR1........62 B4
Oldbury CI STMC/STPC BR5........87 L1
Oldbury La BGR/WK TN15 ....150 E7
Oldbury Vis BGR/WK TN15 * 150 E7
The Old Carriageway
GILL ME7............................126 C2
SEV TN13...........................148 B8
Old Castle St WCHPL E1............24 C1
Old Chapel Rd SWLY BR8...........88 B4
Old Charlton Rd
DVE/WH CT16...................291 J6
Old Chatham Rd DIT/AY ME20...125 J7
MAID/BEAR ME14.............124 E5
Old Church La WBY/YAL ME18..182 F7
Old Church Rd RCANTW CT4....195 M2
ROCH ME1........................124 C4
RTWE/PEM TN2................241 N8
WBY/YAL ME18................182 E6
WCHPL E1 *.......................24 C2
Old Coach Rd BGR/WK TN15 ...241 H8
Old Court Hl RDV CT15.............199 L9
The Old Courthouse
CHAT ME4 *..........................6 B4
Old Convent EGRIN RH19 * 265 H6
The Old Ctyd BMLY BR1............62 F7
Old Crossing Rd MARG CT9 .....112 A4
Old Dairy Cl HART DA3...............1 J3
Old Dartford Rd EYN DA4............89 L5
Old Dover Rd BKHTH/KID SE3 ....42 A6
CANT CT1..............................5 F6
RFOLK CT18.......................311 M2
Old Downs HART DA3................91 H2
Old Dr MAID/SHEP ME15..........185 L5
Old Farleigh Rd
SAND/SEL CR2..................114 A6
Old Farm Av BFN/LL DA15.........43 P9
Old Farm Gdns SWLY BR8..........65 P9
Old Farm Rd BRCH CT7............110 E6
Old Farm Rd East BFN/LL DA15..44 C1
Old Farm Rd West
BFN/LL DA15......................64 B1
Old Ferry Rd RSIT ME9...............76 C9
Oldfield CI BMLY BR1.................86 A1
MAID/SHEP ME15.............186 B2
RHAM ME8........................106 A6
Oldfield Dr ROCH ME1...............94 B9
Oldfield Gv DEPT SE8................24 C7
Oldfield Rd BMLY BR1................86 A1
BXLYHN DA7.......................45 J8
Old Folk WSTB CT5..................106 B6
Old Folkestone Rd DVW CT17....315 H2
Old Forge La RSIT ME9.............128 A9
Old Forge Wy SCUP DA14..........64 D3
Old Garden Ct RCANTW CT4....195 M2

Old Gardens Cl
RTWE/PEM TN2.................270 E8
The Old Gdn SEV TN13............148 C8
Old Gate Rd FAV ME13.............132 E6
Old George Ct HOO/HM ME3 *....72 F5
Old Green Rd MARG CT9..........113 H4
Old Hadlow Rd TONN TN10.....211 H6
Old Hall Dr MSTR CT12 ....142 B7
Old Ham La RMAID ME17.........189 J7
Oldhawe HI HB CT6.................138 A1
The Old High St FOLK CT20.......11 F4
Old HI CHST BR7........................63 L7
ORP BR6............................116 F1
Old Hockley Rd FAV ME13........191 P9
Old Homesdale Rd HAYES BR2....85 M1
Old Hook Rd IOS ME12..............78 F6
Oldhouse La LYDD TN29..........334 F4
Old House La RRTW TN3...........269 J5
Old House Rd MEO ME15 *.......127 P3
Old Jamaica Rd STHWK SE1.......24 D6
Old James St PECK SE15...........41 H4
Old Jewry LOTH EC2R.................24 A2
Old Kent Rd STHWK SE1.............24 B8
STPH/PW TN12.................242 G3
Old Kingsdown Cl
BRDST CT10 *....................143 K1
Old Lain RMAID ME17..............188 C5
Old La BGR/WK TN15..............150 E8
BH/WHM TN16...................145 N6
OXTED RH8........................175 J6
Old Lenham Rd RSIT ME9.........159 P9
Old London Rd BGR/WK TN15 ..121 J9
HYTHE CT21.......................308 D5
RSEV TN14..........................117 M9
TONW TN10.......................210 F7
Old Loose HI
MAID/SHEP ME15.............185 L7
Old Maidstone Rd SCUP DA14...65 H6
Old Manor Wy BXLYHN DA7......45 M5
ELTH/MOT SE9...................63 K4
Old Mill CI EYN DA4..................89 K5
Old Mill La DIT/AY ME20..........155 H1
Old Mill Rd RMAID ME17.........187 J3
WOOL/PLUM SE18.............27 L9
The Old MI RSIT ME9 *..............130 D1
Old Montague St WCHPL E1......24 D2
Old Orch ASH TN23..................252 A9
HAWK TN18........................318 B9
Old Orchard La
E/WMAL ME19...................153 L3
The Old Orch RHAM ME8............97 J6
Old Otford Rd RSEV TN14..........148 C3
Old Palace STPH/PW TN12 * 243 J9
Old Palace Rd CROY/NA CRO ...83 H7
Old Park Av CANT CT1..............167 H2
Old Park CI DVE/WH CT16........291 H3
Old Park HI DVE/WH CT16........291 H3
Old Park Rd ABYW SE2...............27 P8
DVE/WH CT16...................291 J5
Old Pattens La ROCH ME1........156 E9
Old Perry St CHST BR7................64 A6
Old Pond Rd ASH TN23............252 C8
Old Post Office La
BKHTH/KID SE3..................42 F4
Old Rectory Cl RASHE TN25 ....283 P4
RFOLK CT18.......................288 E6
Old Regent Dr CRBK TN17........319 L3
Old Rd BRCH CT7...................139 M3
CHAT ME4.............................6 B5
DART DA1..........................45 M5
EGRIN RH19......................265 J8
LEW SE13............................42 C5
RCANTW CT4....................257 L5
STPH/PW TN12.................212 G4
WBY/YAL ME18................183 J4
Old Rd East GVE DA12...............49 P9
Old Rd West GVW DA11............49 K9
Old Roman Rd RDV CT15.........262 B7
Old Ruttington La CANT CT1 ......5 G3
Old School CI BECK BR3.............61 K8
CANTW/ST CT2.................137 L7
RMAID ME17.....................189 L7
Old School Gdns MARG CT9.....115 K7
Old School La E/WMAL ME19...122 C9
Old School Ms FOLK CT20 *.....310 C8
Old School PI CROY/NA CRO......82 F8
RCANTW CT4....................195 K1
Old School Yd BRDST CT10 *....113 K8
Old Soar Rd BGR/WK TN15......181 L5
Oldstairs Rd DEAL CT14...........263 J4
Oldstead Rd BMLY BR1..............62 B5
Old Surrenden Manor Rd
RASHW TN26.....................280 C2
Old Tannery Cl KENT TN30 *....300 G8
Old Terry's Lodge Rd
BGR/WK TN15...................150 C1
Old Tovil Rd
MAID/SHEP ME15.............185 L1
Old Town CROY/NA CRO...........82 C7
Old Trafford CI MAIDW ME16...154 C6
Old Tramyard
WOOL/PLUM SE18.............27 M7
Old Tree La RMAID ME17.........185 P9
Old Tree Rd RCANTE CT3.........138 B3
Old Tye Av BH/WHM TN16......145 P1
Old Valley Rd RCANTW CT4....228 C7
Old Vicarage Gdn
CANTW/ST CT2.................137 L7
Old Vicarage Gdns
RASHE TN25......................223 P8
The Old Vicarage
SWCH CT13 *.....................201 K3
The Old Wk RSEV TN14............148 C2
Old Wardsdown WADH TN5.....315 M5
Old Watling St STRD ME2...........71 K7
Old Wy RASHW TN26...............322 F7

Old Woolwich Rd GNWCH SE10...25 N9
The Old Yews HART DA3............68 F9
Oleander CI ORP BR6.................86 F9
O'leary Sq WCHPL E1................24 F1
Olive Gv RAM CT11 *.................17 H2
Olive Rd PLSTW/IOD E14...........25 N4
Oliver CI CHAT ME4....................95 N4
WTHK RM20........................47 M1
Oliver Crs EYN DA4....................89 L3
Oliver Gdns EHAM E6.................26 F1
Oliver Gv SNWD SE25................83 L1
Oliver Ms PECK SE15..................40 G5
Oliver Rd DART DA1...................46 D9
Oliver Rd STPH/PW TN12 ....246 B6
SWLY BR8............................65 M9
WTHK RM20........................47 N1
Oliver Twist CI RHAM ME8...........18 D7
Olivine CI SIT ME10....................99 K7
Olliffe CI WALD ME5.................125 M5
Olliffe Gv POP/IOD E14..............25 M6
Olmar St STHWK SE1.................24 D9
Olron Crs BXLYHS DA6...............44 F6
Olven Rd WOOL/PLUM SE18......43 N1
Olyffe Av WELL DA16................44 C3
Olyffe Dr BECK BR3...................62 A7
Omega St NWCR SE14...............41 M2
Omer Av MARG CT9.................113 H3
Ommaney Rd NWCR SE14.........41 K2
Onega Ga BERM/RHTH SE16......25 M2
One Tree CI FSTH SE23...............41 J7
Onslow Crs CHST BR7................63 M7
Onslow Dr SCUP DA14...............64 F2
Onslow Rd CROY/NA CRO..........82 F4
ROCH ME1...........................95 J3
Ontario Wy POP/IOD E14...........25 K3
Opal CI CAN/RD E16...................26 E2
Openshaw Rd ABYW SE2............28 A8
Ophir Ter PECK SE15..................40 G2
Oppenheim Rd LEW SE13............42 A5
Optima Pk DART DA1 *................46 A4
Orache Dr MAID/BEAR ME14....156 D1
Orange Court La ORP BR6........116 B3
Orange Dr BERM/RHTH SE16.....24 F6
Orangery La ELTH/MOT SE9.......43 K6
Orange St CANT CT1 *.................4 E4
WAP E1W............................24 D4
Orange Ter ROCH ME1...............19 H6
Orbital One DART DA1 *.............67 H1
Orbit Cl WALD ME5...................125 M5
Orb St WALW SE17.....................24 A8
Orchard Av BELV DA17................28 E9
CROY/NA CRO.....................84 B6
DART DA1...........................46 B8
DEAL CT14.........................232 C4
DIT/AY ME20.....................156 D3
GVW DA11..........................69 M4
MEO ME15............................92 A2
MSTR CT12.........................142 G1
RASHE TN25......................283 P5
RCANTE CT3......................168 C9
RMAID ME17.....................185 H8
RSEV TN14........................149 H6
RTWE/PEM TN2................270 G1
STPH/PW TN12.................273 N2
WSTB CT5..........................105 N3
Orchard Ct WLGTN SM6 *.........82 A9
Orchard Crs STPH/PW TN12.....273 P2
Orchard Dr BKHTH/KID SE3 .....42 C3
DVW CT17.........................290 F4
EDEN TN8..........................206 C8
GRAYS RM17.......................32 B5
Orchard Fld HYTHE CT21 *.......286 D6
RASHW TN26.....................280 C4
Orchard Gdns MARG CT9..........111 P4
Orchard Ga HDCN TN27..........247 N4
Orchard Gn ORP BR6.................86 F6
Orchard Gv CROY/NA CRO.........84 B6
DIT/AY ME20.....................154 A2
IOS ME12.............................78 C1
ORP BR6..............................86 C6
PGE/AN SE20.......................60 G6
Orchard Hts RASHE TN25.........252 F4
Orchard hl DART DA1.................45 N6
LEW SE13............................41 P5
Orchard La BRCH CT7..............140 A3
KEN/WIL TN24...................253 J3
RASHE TN25......................192 E9
Orchard Lea MEO DA13 *...........68 G5
Orchard Ms DEAL CT14 *...........233 J4
Orchard Pl FAV ME13................132 G6
MAIDW ME16.......................12 C6
POP/IOD E14.......................25 P3
SIT ME10...........................129 P2
STMC/STPC BR5 *................64 C6
Orchard Ri CROY/NA CRO..........84 B5
RRTW TN3.........................268 C9
Orchard Ri East BFN/LL DA15 ....44 A6
Orchard Ri West BFN/LL DA15 ...44 A6
Orchard Rd BELV DA17..............28 F4
BMLY BR1............................62 G7
GVW DA11...........................68 C1
HB CT6..............................107 J3
LYDD TN29........................337 M1
MAID/BEAR ME14.............156 D9
MARG CT9..........................111 P5
ORP BR6..............................86 C9
ORP BR6............................117 K3
RSEV TN14........................148 E1

SCUP DA14..........................64 A3
SEV TN13...........................148 D7
SOCK/AV RM15...................33 N5
STPH/PW TN12.................211 H4
SWCH CT13........................201 J7
SWCM DA10.........................48 C6
TENT TN30........................301 H4
WELL DA16..........................44 D4
Ospringe Rd MAID/SHEP ME15.132 E7
Ospringe St FAV ME13..............132 E7
Ossory Rd STHWK SE1...............24 D9
Osterberg Rd DART DA1.............46 F5
Osterley Gdns THHTH CR7..........60 C8
Ostlers Ct HOO/HM ME3 *..........71 L3
SNOD ME6.........................123 P5
Ostlers La BRCH CT7................139 N3
Oswald Rd DVW CT17..............291 J5
Oswald St DVW CT17...............291 J5
Osward CROY/NA CR0.............114 C4
Oswyth Rd CMBW SE5................40 E3
Otford CI BMLY BR1...................63 L9
BXLY DA5 *..........................65 J7
PGE/AN SE20.......................61 J7
Otford Crs BROCKY SE4..............41 M7
Otford La RSEV TN14................117 N7
Otford Rd RSEV TN14...............148 C3
Otham CI CANTW/ST CT2........136 F9
Otham La MAID/SHEP ME15....186 F1
Otham St MAID/SHEP ME15....186 A6
Otley Rd CAN/RD E16.................26 D2
Otlinge Rd STMC/STPC BR5......87 L1
Ottawa Crs DVE/WH CT16........291 K4
Ottawa Rd TIL RM18....................49 L5
Otterbourne Pl
EGRIN RH19 *....................264 D7
MAID/SHEP ME15.............186 A3
Otterbourne Rd CROY/NA CR0 ..83 H6
Otterden CI ASH TN23..............282 C2
ORP BR6..............................86 F8
Otterden Rd FAV ME13.............191 H1
Otterden St CAT SE6..................61 N3
Otterham Quay La RHAM ME8....97 L6
Otteridge Rd
MAID/BEAR ME14.............156 D9
Otterpool La RASHE TN25.........307 M2
Otters CI STMC/STPC BR5..........87 L1
Otto CI SYD SE26.......................61 H2
Otway St CHAT ME4.....................6 D7
Otway Ter CHAT ME4..................6 E6
Oulton CI THMD SE28..................28 B2
Out Elmstead La
RCANTW CT4....................228 B4
Outfall Av LYDD TN29..............347 K5
Outram Rd CROY/NA CR0..........83 L6
Outwich St HDTCH EC3A............24 B2
Oval Gdns GRAYS RM17.............32 D6
Oval Rd CROY/NA CR0...............83 J6
The Oval BFN/LL DA15................44 A8
HART DA3............................68 G3
LYDD TN29........................327 H5
Ovenden Rd STHWK TN14........147 L5
Overbrae BECK BR3....................61 N5
Over Barn Rd BECK BR3..............61 N7
Overbury Crs CROY/NA CR0.....114 F4
Overcliffe GVW DA11...................49 L7
Overcliff Rd GRAYS RM17...........32 E8
LEW SE13............................41 N4
Overcourt CI BFN/LL DA15.........44 D7
Overdale RSEV TN14.................178 G9
Overdown Rd CAT SE6................61 N3
Overhill Rd EDUL SE22................40 G8
Overhill Wy BECK BR3.................84 C2
Overland La RCANTE CT3..........170 B8
Overmead ELTH/MOT SE9..........43 P8
SWLY BR8............................88 B2
Over Minnis HART DA3................91 J7
Overstand CI BECK BR3................84 D2
Overstone Gdns CROY/NA CR0 ..84 C4
Overton Rd ABYW SE2................28 B6
BRXN/ST SW9.......................40 A5
Overton Shaw EGRIN RH19 .....265 H5
Overton's Yd CROY/NA CR0........83 H7
Overy Liberty DART DA1..............46 E8
Overy St DART DA1.....................46 E8
Ovett CI NRWD SE19..................60 E5
Ovex CI POP/IOD E14.................25 N3
Owen CI CROY/NA CR0..............83 J3
E/WMAL ME19....................153 N4
THMD SE28..........................28 B4
Owenite St ABYW SE2.................28 A7
Owen CI HYTHE CT21..............309 M4
Owen Sq DEAL CT14..................232 C7
Owens Wy FSTH SE23.................41 L8
GILL ME7.............................73 N9
Owen Wk PGE/AN SE20.............60 C6
Owgan CI CMBW SE5.................40 D7
Owletts CI MAID/SHEP ME15....186 A5
Owl's Hatch Rd HB CT6.............106 C5
Ownsted HI CROY/NA CR0.......114 C8
Oxenden Crs RCANTE CT3........169 K8
Oxenden Park Dr HB CT6..........107 K2
Oxenden Rd FOLK CT20...........310 B7
Oxenden Wy RCANTW CT4.......228 C6
Oxenford St PECK SE15...............40 F4
Oxenhill Rd BGR/WK TN15........116 A2
Oxenhoath Rd RTON TN11.......181 M7
Oxen Lease ASH TN23..............252 B9
Oxenturn Rd RASHE TN25.........253 P2
Oxestalls Rd DEPT SE8...............25 H8
Oxford Av CDW/CHF RH16.........33 H7
Oxford CI DART DA1....................67 H3
Oxford Ct MANHO EC4N............24 A3
Oxford Ms BXLY DA5...................45 J9
Oxford Rd CANT CT1 *.................4 E7
GILL ME7.............................96 A3
MAID/BEAR ME14.............186 A2
NRWD SE19.........................60 D3
SCUP DA14..........................64 C4
SLH/COR SS17......................34 A1
WLGTN SM6 *.......................82 D3
Oxford St MARG CT9..................15 H6
SNOD ME6.........................123 P5
WSTB CT5..........................105 L5
Oxford Ter FOLK CT20................10 C5
Oxhawth Crs HAYES BR2............86 C1
Ox La TENT TN30......................301 J5
Ox Lea RRTW TN3....................269 M5
Oxleas EHAM E6..........................27 J2
Oxleas CI WELL DA16.................43 P3
Oxley CI STHWK SE1...................24 C8

Oxley Shaw La
E/WMAL ME19 ....153 M2
Oxney Cl BRCH CT7 ....110 G6
Oxonian St EDUL SE22 ....40 F5
Oxted Rd CDST RH9 ....174 C7
Oyster Catchers Cl
CAN/RD E16 ....26 C2
Oyster Cl HB CT6 ....106 G3
SIT ME10 * 99 M8
Oyster Creek RYE TN31 ....339 J9
Oyster Rw WCHPL E1 ....24 F2
The Oysters WSTB CT5 * 105 M4
Ozolins Wy CAN/RD E16 ....26 A2

P

Pace Pl WCHPL E1 ....24 E2
Pacific Cl SWCM DA10 ....48 C6
Pacific Rd CAN/RD E16 ....26 D2
Packer Pl WALD ME5 ....95 M6
Packer's La RAM CT11 ....17 G5
Packham Rd GVW DA11 ....69 K2
Packhorse Rd SEV TN15 ....148 B8
Packmores Rd CAN/RD ME9 ....43 P6
Padbrook Cl OXTED RH8 ....175 K5
Padbrook La RCANTE CT3 ....169 N3
Paddlesworth Rd SNOD ME16 ...123 K4
Paddock Cl BGR/WK TN15 ....151 M6
BKHTH/KID SE3 ....42 E4
CDW/CHF RM16 ....33 J1
EDEN TN8 ....232 E4
EYN DA4 ....67 J7
FOLK CT20 ....310 C6
LING RH7 ....234 F5
LYDD TN29 ....342 A6
ORP BR6 ....86 C8
OXTED RH8 ....175 J7
RRTW TN5 ....268 G3
SYD SE26 ....61 K3
Paddock Gdns EGRIN RH19 ....265 H9
NRWD SE19 ....60 C4
Paddock Rd BRCH CT7 ....111 H6
BXLYHS DA6 ....44 G5
Paddocks Cl STMC/STPC BR5 ...87 L6
The Paddocks ASH TN23 ....251 P8
BRDST CT10 ....11 L1
CDW/CHF RM16 ....33 H1
EDEN TN8 ....267 J1
GILL ME7 ....96 D9
HB CT6 ....108 C5
MARC CT9 ....113 H8
SEV TN13 ....21 J1
The Paddock BH/WHM TN16 ...176 D2
CANT CT1 ....5 J5
CHAT ME4 ....8 D2
DVE/WH CT16 ....8 B2
MEO DA13 ....122 A6
RCANTE CT3 * 169 K8
RRTW TN3 ....268 E3
RTON TN11 ....211 P1
RYE TN31 ....330 K6
SIT ME10 * 129 L3
Paddock Vw WSTB CT5 ....105 L7
Paddock Wy CHST BR7 ....63 P6
OXTED RH8 ....175 J7
Padfield Rd CMBW SE5 ....40 C4
Padgate Hl MAID/SHEP ME15 ...13 C5
Padsole La MAID/SHEP ME15 ...13 G5
Padstow Cl ORP BR6 ....86 G8
Padua Rd PGE/AN SE20 ....61 J7
Padwell La ASH TN23 ....251 P9
Paffard Cl CANTW/ST CT2 ....137 L7
Pageant Cl TIL RM18 ....49 N2
Pageant Crs BERM/RHTH SE16 ..25 J4
Pageant Wk CROY/NA CR0 ....83 K7
Page Cl RDART DA2 ....68 A2
Page Crs CROY/NA CR0 ....82 C9
ERITH DA8 ....48 D6
Page Heath La BMLY BR1 ....63 H9
Page Heath Vls BMLY BR1 ....63 H9
Pagehurst Rd CROY/NA CR0 ....83 M4
STPH/PW TN12 ....245 P6
Paget Cl PFOLK CT18 ....310 C5
Page Rd RFOLK CT18 ....288 C9
Page's Wk STHWK SE1 ....24 B7
Paget Gdns CHST BR7 ....63 M7
Paget Ri WOOL/PLUM SE18 ....43 L1
Paget Rw GILL ME7 ....7 H2
Paget St FSBYE EC1V 6 C8
Paget Ter WOOL/PLUM SE18 ....27 J9
Pagette Wy GRAYS RM17 ....32 B3
Pagitt St CHAT ME4 ....95 K4
Pagnell St NWCR SE14 ....41 M1
Pagoda Gdns BKHTH/KID SE3 ...42 B5
Paiges Farm Cl RSEV TN14 ......179 H9
Paine Av LYDD TN29 ....342 B6
Painesfield La LYDD TN29 ......326 C2
Pains Hl OXTED RH8 ....175 M8
Painters Ash La GVW DA11 ....69 H7
Painter's Forstal Rd
FAV ME13 ....162 B1
Palace Cl MAID/SHEP ME15 ....13 F5
Palace Cl WSTB CT5 ....106 A4
Palace Gn CROY/NA CR0 ....114 C2
Palace Gv BMLY BR1 ....62 F7
NRWD SE19 ....60 D5
Palace Rd BH/WHM TN16 ....146 B6
BMLY BR1 ....62 F7
NRWD SE19 ....60 F6
Palace Sq NRWD SE19 ....60 F6
Palace Vw BMLY BR1 ....62 F9
CROY/NA CR0 ....84 C8
LEE/GVPK SE12 ....62 E1
Palewell Cl STMC/STPC BR5 ....64 D8
Palins Wy CDW/CHF RM16 ....32 B4
Pallant Wy ORP BR6 ....86 C8
Pallet Wy WOOL/PLUM SE18 ....43 J2
Palliser Dr RAIN RM13 ....29 M1
Palmar Crs BXLYHN DA7 ....45 J4

Palmar Rd BXLYHN DA7 ....45 J3
MAIDW ME16 ....155 J6
Palmarsh Rd STMC/STPC BR5 ..87 L1
Palm Av SCUP DA14 ....64 F5
Palm Bay Av MARC CT9 ....113 H2
Palm Bay Gdns MARC CT9 ....113 H2
Palmbeach Av HYTHE CT21 ....308 C7
Palmarsh Rd BXLYHN DA7 ....44 F4
Palmer Av GVE DA12 ....69 P5
Palmer Cl HB CT6 ....107 N6
WWKM BR4 ....84 G6
Palmer Crs MARC CT9 ....113 H5
Palmer Rd RCANTE CT3 ....169 K8
Palmer's Av GRAYS RM17 ....32 D8
Palmers Brook RTON TN11 ....182 A9
Palmers Cross Hl
CANTW/ST CT2 ....165 P3
Palmer Dr GRAYS RM17 ....32 D7
Palmers Green La
STPH/PW TN12 ....243 L8
Palmers Orch RSEV TN14 ....118 C5
Palmerston Av BRDST CT10 ....141 M4
DEAL CT14 ....233 H6
Palmerston Crs
WOOL/PLUM SE18 ....27 K9
Palmerston Gdns WTHK RM20 ..31 N8
Palmerston Rd CHAT ME4 ....95 L5
CROY/NA CR0 ....83 J2
ORP BR6 ....86 D8
WTHK RM20 ....31 N8
Palmerston St FOLKN CT19 ....10 E2
Palmers Yd HDCN TN27 ....247 P4
Palmeston Rd
DVE/WH CT16 * 261 H9
Palm Tree Cl RDV CT15 ....260 E1
Palm Tree Wy RFOLK CT18 ....286 C1
Palting Wy FOLK CT20 ....10 B5
Panfield Rd ABYW SE2 ....27 P6
Pankhurst Av CAN/RD E16 ....26 C4
Pankhurst Rd HOO/MM ME3 ....73 K1
Panmure Rd SYD SE26 ....61 H2
Pannell Cl EGRIN RH19 ....264 G7
Pannell Dr RFOLK CT18 ....288 C9
Pannell Rd HOO/MM ME3 ....56 C2
Pantenyu La RSIT ME9 ....130 D3
Panter's SWLY SE8 ....85 P6
Pantheon Gdns ASH TN23 ....282 C3
Pantiles STH/RUST TN4 ....22 C6
The Pantiles BMLY BR1 ....63 J9
BXLYHN DA7 ....45 J3
RTWE/PEM TN2 ....22 C7
Panton Cl CROY/NA CR0 ....82 D3
WALD ME5 ....125 P1
Paper La KEN/WIL TN24 ....283 J2
Papillons Wk BKHTH/KID SE3 ...42 E3
Pappion Gv WALD ME5 ....125 K3
Papworth Cl FOLKN CT19 ....310 D4
Papworth Wy
BRXS/STRHM SW2 ....40 A8
Parade CANT CT1 ....5 F5
Parade Ms BRXS/STRHM SW2 ...60 B1
Parade Rd FOLK CT20 ....310 B8
The Parade BH/WHM TN16 * ...145 M6
BRCH CT7 ....110 D6
BROCKY SE4 * 41 N3
CROY/NA CR0 * 82 C9
CROY/NA CR0 * 82 E9
DART DA1 * 45 P6
EDUL SE22 * 40 E4
EGRIN RH19 * 264 E5
FOLK CT20 ....11 G4
GVE DA12 * 69 P1
HART DA3 * 91 H2
KEN/WIL TN24 ....283 J5
MARC CT9 * 92 B4
NROM TN28 ....343 K4
PGE/AN SE20 * 61 J7
RAM CT11 * 17 G3
SIT ME10 * 129 N3
SOCK/AV RM15 * 30 F5
STRD SW10 * 48 D6
SYD SE26 * 61 H5

ORP BR6 ....87 H7
OBOR ME11 ....77 K3
RMAID ME17 ....185 K9
RTON TN11 ....210 C5
SIT ME10 ....129 M3
WSTB CT5 ....105 N3
WWKM BR4 ....31 K9
WWKM BR4 ....84 F6
Park Av Ingress GRH DA9 ....48 A5
Park Barn Rd RMAID ME17 ....187 L6
Park Cha BRDST CT10 ....143 K2
Park Cl MARC CT9 * 113 J3
OXTED RH8 ....175 J4
RFOLK CT18 ....288 D8
STH/RUST TN4 ....270 B6
Park Corner Rd MEO DA13 ....68 E2
Park Ct DUL SE21 * 60 D2
SYD SE26 * 61 H5
ERITH DA8 ....48 C8
Park Crs CHAT ME4 ....95 L6
ERITH DA8 ....48 C8
Park Crescent Rd MARC CT9 ...15 K6
Parkcroft Rd LEE/GVPK SE12 ...42 D8
Parkdale Rd WOOL/PLUM SE18..27 M8
Park Dr CHARL SE7 ....26 F9
HART DA3 ....68 C9
RASHW TN26 ....251 M3
SIT ME10 ....129 L4
Park End BMLY BR1 ....62 D7
Park Ter TIL RM18 ....49 N2
Parker Cl CAN/RD E16 ....26 F4
RHAM ME8 ....97 H9
Parker Pl RFOLK CT18 ....288 F7
Parker Rd CROY/NA CR0 ....83 H8
GRAYS RM17 ....32 A3
Parkers Rw STHWK SE1 * 24 C5
Parker St CAN/RD E16 ....26 F4
Parker Ter ORP BR6 * 87 H5
Park Farm Cl CANTW/ST CT2...136 D7
FOLKN CT19 ....310 C5
RASHW TN26 ....281 M7
Park Farm Rd BMLY BR1 ....63 H7
E/WMAL ME19 ....122 F6
FOLKN CT19 ....310 D5
Parkfield BGR/WK TN15 ....149 L8
Parkfield Rd FOLKN CT19 ....10 D2
NWCR SE14 ....41 M2
RHAM ME8 ....97 J4
Parkfields CROY/NA CR0 ....84 C5
STRD ME2 ....71 L8
Parkfield Wy HAYES BR2 ....86 A3
Park Gdns ERITH DA8 ....29 J7
Parkgate BKHTH/KID SE3 ....42 D4
Park Ga BRDST CT10 ....143 L2
Park Gv BXLYHN DA7 ....45 L5
Park Hall Rd DUL SE21 ....60 D7
Park Hl BMLY BR1 ....85 P1
FSTH SE23 ....61 H1
Park Hill Rd CROY/NA CR0 ....83 L7
CROY/NA CR0 ....83 K6
HAYES BR2 ....62 C8
Parkhill Rd BFN/LL DA15 ....64 A2
BXLY DA5 ....45 H8
Park House Gdns
STH/RUST TN4 ....240 D8
Parkhouse St CMBW SE5 ....40 D7
Parkhurst Gdns BXLY DA5 ....45 J8
Parkhurst Rd BXLY DA5 ....45 J8
Parkland Ct SEV TN15 ....179 H5
Parkland Ct BRDST CT10 ....113 L7
Parklands OXTED RH8 ....175 H7
Park La BGR/WK TN15 ....149 M5
BRCH CT7 ....111 H7
CROY/NA CR0 ....83 J7
HAWK TN18 ....297 J8
LING RH7 ....235 H4
MAID/BEAR ME14 ....155 L5
MARC CT9 ....15 K5
RASHW TN26 ....281 H1
RCANTW CT4 ....197 N6
RCANTW CT4 ....257 L4
RMAID ME17 ....186 A9
SEV TN13 ....21 G1
SOCK/AV RM15 ....30 C4
SWLY BR8 ....66 C8

NROM TN28 ....337 K8
OXTED RH8 ....175 J4
OBOR ME11 ....77 H2
RAM CT11 ....16 C2
RCANTE CT3 ....169 N1
RTON TN11 ....181 M6
SIT ME10 ....129 M3
SNWD SE25 ....83 K1
STH/RUST TN4 ....240 D7
STH/RUST TN4 ....270 C5
STMC/STPC BR5 ....87 K5
SWCM DA10 ....48 C7
SWCM DA10 ....48 C7
SWLY BR8 ....88 E1
WARL CR6 ....115 H8
WBY/YAL ME18 ....182 C6
WLGTN SM6 ....82 A6
Park Rd North KEN/WIL TN24 ...2 D2
Parkside BECK BR3 * 61 P8
BKHTH/KID SE3 * 42 D1
CDW/CHF RM16 ....32 B4
DVE/WH CT16 * 233 H5
EGRIN RH19 ....264 F7
HOO/MM ME3 ....52 B9
RSEV TN14 ....117 M7
SCUP DA14 ....64 D1
Parkside Av BMLY BR1 ....85 P1
BXLYHN DA7 ....45 M3
TIL RM18 ....49 M5
Parkside Cl PGE/AN SE20 ....61 J6
Parkside Cross BXLYHN DA7 ...45 N3
Parkside Ms ANG EA6 ....144 D1
Parkside Pl ERITH DA8 * 48 B5
Parkside Pl CANT CT1 ....167 J1
Parkside Rd BELV DA17 ....28 C7
Parkside Ter ORP BR6 * 87 H5
Parkstone Rd PECK SE15 ....40 J3
Park St ASH TN23 ....2 E5
CROY/NA CR0 ....83 H7
DEAL CT14 ....233 J5
DVE/WH CT16 ....8 C2
LYDD TN29 ....342 A6
RTWE/PEM TN2 ....22 C7
Park Ter CRH DA9 ....48 A6
RSEV TN14 ....147 L9
The Park DUL SE14 ....64 B4
DVE/WH CT16 ....8 C2
EGRIN RH19 ....265 H8
Park V CEN/WIL TN24 ....252 C3
ELTH/MOT SE9 ....43 M9
WELL DA16 ....44 F4
Park Vis RTON TN11 * 212 A1
SWCH CT13 * 201 K8
Park Vis CNWCH SE10 ....25 N9
Park Wy BXLY DA5 ....65 P2
MAID/SHEP ME15 ....185 N3
RMAID ME17 ....185 H8
Parkway CDW/CHF RM16 ....33 H1
CROY/NA CR0 ....114 F3
ERITHM DA18 ....28 F1
TONN TN10 ....210 C5
The Parkway BRCH CT7 ....111 J6
RYE TN31 ....332 E9
Park Wood Cl ASH TN23 ....282 E3
Parkwood Rd BRDST CT10 ....143 K2
RTWE/PEM TN2 ....270 F2
Park Wood La STPH/PW TN12 ..246 F7
Parkwood Rd BH/WHM TN16 ...45 H8
BXLY DA5 ....45 K6
Park Wood Rd CANTW/ST CT2..136 C3
Parliament Ct WCHPL E1 * 24 B2
Parnell Cl CDW/CHF RM16 ....31 M8
Parnham St POP/IOD E14 * 25 H2
Paroma Rd BELV DA17 ....28 F6
Parr Av GILL ME7 ....73 K3
Parr Cl CDW/CHF RM16 ....31 M8
Parrock Av GVE DA12 ....69 N9
Parrock Rd GVE DA12 ....69 N8
Parrock St GVE DA12 ....49 M8
Parrs Heath Ms ROCH ME1 * ...19 L3
Parry Av EHAM E6 ....26 C2
Parry Pl WOOL/PLUM SE18 ....27 J7
Parry Rd SNWD SE25 ....60 E9
Parsonage Cha IOS ME12 * 77 P2
Parsonage Ct STH/RUST TN4 ..269 N3
WARL CR6 ....101 H4
Parsonage Fields MSTR CT12 ..140 D5
Parsonage La EYN DA4 ....67 H5
RRTW TN5 ....295 J1
RSIT ME9 ....130 D3
SCUP DA14 ....65 H5
STRD ME2 ....72 C7

Pascoe Rd LEW SE13 ....42 B6
Pasley Rd GILL ME7 ....72 G5
Pasley Rd East CHAT ME4 ....72 G8
The Passage MARC CT9 * 15 J2
Passey Pl ELTH/MOT SE9 ....43 K7
Passfield Dr POP/IOD E14 ....25 L1
Pastens Rd OXTED RH8 ....175 M7
Pastime Cl SIT ME10 ....99 M6
Paston Cl WLGTN SM6 ....82 B7
Paston Crs LEE/GVPK SE12 .....42 F8
Pasture Rd CAT SE6 ....42 C9
The Pasture KEN/WIL TN24 .....252 C5
RFOLK CT18 ....288 E8
The Patch SEV TN13 ....148 D7
Patchways LYDD TN29 ....325 L3
Patmos Rd BRXN/ST SW9 ....40 B1
Patricia Cl WELL DA16 ....44 D1
Patricia Wy BRDST CT10 ....143 J1
Patrixbourne Av RHAM ME8 ....96 F4
Patrixbourne Rd RCANTW CT4..197 N1
Patrol Pl CAT SE6 ....41 P7
Pattenden Gdns
STPH/PW TN12 ....213 H3
Pattenden La STPH/PW TN12 ...244 C1
Pattens Cl CHAT ME4 ....95 K6
Pattens La CHAT ME4 ....41 M9
Patterdale Cl BMLY BR1 ....62 C5
Patterdale Rd PECK SE15 ....41 J1
RDART DA2 ....47 J9
Patterson Cl DEAL CT14 ....232 F5
Patterson Rd NRWD SE19 ....60 F2
Pattina Wk BERM/RHTH SE16 ..25 H4
Paulet Rd CMBW SE5 ....40 B3
Paul Gdns CROY/NA CR0 ....83 L6
Paulinus Cl STMC/STPC BR5 ...64 E8
Paul Julius Cl POP/IOD E14 .....25 N1
Pauls Md LING RH7 ....235 H4
Paul's Pl DVE/WH CT16 ....8 B1
The Pavement TENT TN30 ....301 H4
WNWD SE27 * 60 C5
Pavilion Cl DEAL CT14 ....233 H1
Pavilion Dr SIT ME10 ....99 L5
Pavilion La WBY/YAL ME18 .....193 H3
Pavilion Meadow DVW CT17 ....290 E3
Pavilion Rd FOLKN CT19 ....10 E2
Pavilion Wy EGRIN RH19 ....265 H8
Pawleyne Cl PGE/AN SE20 ....61 J6
Pawson's Rd CROY/NA CR0 .....83 H5
Paxton Av RFOLK CT18 ....288 C9
Paxton Ct FSTH SE23 * 60 E3
Paxton Rd BMLY BR1 ....62 E6
FSTH SE23 ....61 L2
Payden St RSIT ME9 ....190 B1
Payers Pk FOLK CT20 ....11 F4
Paynell Ct BKHTH/KID SE3 .....42 C4
Paynesfield Rd
BH/WHM TN16 ....145 N4
Payne's La MAID/SHEP ME15 ..185 M4
Payne St DEPT SE8 ....25 J9
Pays La RASHE TN25 ....222 A1
Pay St RFOLK CT18 ....288 C5
Payton Cl MARC CT9 ....112 E7
Peabody Cl CROY/NA CR0 ....5 J2
Peabody Cl CROY/NA CR0 ....83 P5
GNWCH SE10 * 41 P2
Peabody Est CMBW SE5 * 40 D2
HNHL SE24 * 40 F4
WALW SE17 * 24 A7
Peabody Hl DUL SE21 ....60 B9
Peace Cl SNWD SE25 ....83 K1
Peace Gv WOOL/PLUM SE18 ...27 H9
Peace Rd POP/IOD E14 * 69 J2
Peachum Rd BKHTH/KID SE3 ...26 A9
Peacock Gdns CROY/NA CR0 ...114 B4
Peacock Ms MAIDW ME16 * 12 D5
Peacock Ri WALD ME5 ....125 M1
Peacock St GVE DA12 ....49 N8
Peafield Wood Rd
RCANTW CT4 ....227 K6
Peak Dr SWCH CT13 ....201 J7
Peak Hill SYD SE26 ....61 J3
Peak Hill Av SYD SE26 ....61 J3
Peak Hill Gdns SYD SE26 ....61 J3
The Peak SYD SE26 ....61 J3
Peal Cl HOO/MM ME3 ....73 L2
Peall Rd CROY/NA CR0 ....82 E5
Pean Court Rd WSTB CT5 ....135 L2
Pean Hl WSTB CT5 ....135 L2
Pearcefield Av FSTH SE23 ....41 J9
Pear Cl NWCR SE14 ....41 L1
Pearsewood Rd ERITH DA8 .....45 P2
Pearfield Rd FSTH SE23 ....61 L2
Pearl Cl EHAM E6 ....27 H2
Pearl St WAP E1W 24 E4
Pearl Wy E/WMAL ME19 ....153 K9
Pearman Cl RHAM ME8 ....97 K5
Pearse Pl RRTW TN5 ....295 H2
Pearse St PECK SE15 ....24 B9
Pearson's Av NWCR SE14 * 41 N2
Pearsons Green Rd
STPH/PW TN12 ....243 K4
Pearson's Rd NWCR SE14 ....41 N2
Pearson's Wy BSLDS CT10 ....113 K6
Pear Tree Av DIT/AY ME20 .....154 B4
Pear Tree Cl BRDST CT10 ....113 H9
CRBK TN17 * 298 A4
ERITH DA8 ....45 M2
SWLY BR8 ....65 M8
Peartree Cl HAYES BR2 ....86 B7
Pear Tree La GILL ME7 ....96 B7
LYDD TN29 ....327 H5
MAID/SHEP ME15 ....185 N5
Peartree La STRD ME2 ....71 J5
WAP E1W * 24 F3
Peartree Rd HOO/MM ME3 .....71 K4
Peartree Rd FOLK CT6 ....107 P5
Peartree Wy GNWCH SE10 .....26 E7
Peasley La CRBK TN17 ....296 C5
Peatfield Cl BFN/LL DA15 ....64 A2
Peat Wy HOO/MM ME3 ....55 H1
Peckarmans Wd SYD SE26 .....60 G2
Peckford Pl BRXN/ST SW9 ....40 A3

Peckham CI *STRD* ME2 ....72 C7
Peckham Gv *PECK* SE15 ....40 E1
Peckham High St *PECK* SE15 ....40 G2
Peckham Hill St *PECK* SE15 ......40 G1
Peckham Hurst Rd
  WBY/YAL ME18 ....181 P4
Peckham Park Rd *PECK* SE15 ....40 E2
Peckham Rd *CMBW* SE5 ....40 E2
Pennine Rye *EDUL* SE22 ....40 G5
Pecks Yd *WCHPL* E1 * 24 C1
Pedding HI *RCANTE* CT3 ....200 B1
Pedding La *RCANTE* CT3 ....200 A1
Peel Dr *ORP* BR6 ....86 D8
Peel St *MAID/BEAR* ME14 ....13 F1
Peers La *RMAID* ME17 ....215 P5
Pegasus CI *CAT* SE6 ....69 N2
Pegasus Wy *EGRIN* RH19 ....265 K5
Pegden *RCANTW* CT4 * 257 L4
Peggotty CI *HOO/HM* ME3 ....71 K4
Pegley Gdns *LEE/GVPK* SE12 ....62 E1
Pegwell Av *RAM* CT11 ....142 F7
Pegwell Rd *RAM* CT11 ....142 F7
Pegwell CI *RAM* CT11 ....142 G7
Pegwell St *WOOL/PLUM* SE18 ....26 E6
Pekin St *POP/IOD* E14 ....25 K2
Pelham CI *RHAM* ME8 ....69 J2
Pelham Gdns *FOLK* CT20 ....310 D7
Pelham Rd *BXLYHN* DA7 ....45 J4
  GVW DA11 ....49 K8
  PGE/AN SE20 ....61 J8
Pelham Rd South *GVW* DA11 .....49 K9
Pelican CI *STRD* ME2 ....71 L9
Pelinore Rd *CAT* SE6 ....62 C1
Pellatt Rd *EDUL* SE22 ....40 F6
Pell CI *WADH* TN5 ....294 B9
Pellings CI *HAYES* BR2 ....62 C9
Pelling St *POP/IOD* E14 ....25 J2
Pellipar Rd *WOOL/PLUM* SE18 ...26 E8
Pells La *BGR/WK* TN15 ....120 D5
Pelton Rd *GNWCH* SE10 ....65 N9
Pelwood Rd *RYE* TN15 ....344 B1
Pemberton Gdns *SWLY* BR8 ......65 N9
Pemberton Rd *KEN/WIL* TN24 .....3 G4
Pemberton Sq *STRD* ME2 ....72 C7
Pemberton Rd *CTPH/PW* TN12 ..242 B2
Pembroke *CHART* ME4 ....72 C7
Pembroke Av *MARC* CT9 ....112 A4
Pembroke Gdns *RHAM* ME8 .....127 H1
Pembroke Ms *NROM* TN28 ......337 H5
  SEV TN13 * 21 L5
Pembroke Pde *ERITH* DA8 ....29 H8
Pembroke PI *EYN* DA4 ....79 J7
Pembroke Rd *BMLY* BR1 ....62 C8
  CHART ME4 * 72 C7
  EHAM E6 ....26 C1
  ERITH DA8 ....29 H8
  RMAID ME17 ....185 H8
  SEV TN13 ....21 F3
  SNWD SE25 ....38 F5
  TON TN9 ....210 D9
Pembury CI *BRXN/ST* SW9 ....40 A2
Pembury CI *HAYES* BR2 ....62 A5
Pembury Crs *SCUP* DA14 ....65 M1
Pembury Crs *SIT* ME10 ....271 N1
Pembury Gdns *MAIDW* ME16, ...12 A6
Pembury Gra *RTWE/PEM* TN2 ..271 K2
Pembury Gv *TON* TN9 ....241 N5
Pembury Hall Rd
  RTWE/PEM TN2 ....241 M6
Pembury PI *RASHE* TN25 ....252 C5
Pembury Rd *BXLYHN* DA7 ....44 D1
  RTON TN11 ....241 K6
  RTWE/PEM TN2 ....23 H3
  SNWD SE25 ....83 M1
  TON TN9 ....240 E1
Pembury St *SIT* ME10 ....129 M1
Pembury Wks *RTON* TN11 ....241 L7
Pembury Rd *RHAM* ME8 ....97 H4
Pemdevon Rd *CROY/NA* CR0 ......7 N1
Penang St *WAP* E1W 24 E4
Penarth St *PECK* SE15 ....40 G3
Penberth Rd *CAT* SE6 ....62 A1
Pencester Ct *DVE/WH* CT16 * 8 E3
Pencester Rd *DVE/WH* CT16 ....8 D3
Pencraig Wy *PECK* SE15 * 24 E9
Pencroft Dr *DART* DA1 ....46 C8
Penda Rd *ERITH* DA8 ....45 K1
Pendennis Rd *ORP* BR6 ....87 K6
  SEV TN13 ....148 G8
Penderel Ms *TENT* TN30 ....301 J7
Penderry Rd *CAT* SE6 ....62 B1
Pendlebury House
  WOOL/PLUM SE18 * 43 J1
Pendragon Rd *BMLY* BR1 ....62 A2
Pendrell Rd *BROCKY* SE4 ....41 L4
Pendrell St *WOOL/PLUM* SE18 ...27 J3
Penenden *HART* DA3 ....91 J6
Penenden Heath Rd
  MAID/BEAR ME14 ....155 N5
Penenden St *MAID/BEAR* ME14 ..13 F1
Penerley Rd *CAT* SE6 ....41 P9
  RAIN RM13 ....29 N1
Penfield La *RSIT* ME9 ....129 P9
Penfold CI *CROY/NA* CR0 ....82 F7
  MAID/SHEP ME15 ....186 B5
  WALD ME5 ....95 N7
Penfold Gdns *RDV* CT15 ....229 N9
Penfold HI *RMAID* ME17 ....187 L3
Penfold Rd *FOLKN* CT19 ....11 J2
Penfolds CI *TONN* TN10 ....210 F5
Penford Gdns *ELTH/MOT* SE9 ....43 H5
Penford St *CMBW* SE5 ....40 B3
Pengarth Rd *BXLY* DA5 ....44 F6
Penge La *PGE/AN* SE20 ....61 J6
Penge Rd *SNWD* SE25 ....61 N6
Penguin CI *STRD* ME2 ....71 M9
Penhale CI *ORP* BR6 ....87 H8
Penhall Rd *CHARL* SE7 ....26 E7
Penhall Rd *BXLY* DA5 ....44 E8
Penhurst St *MAID/BEAR* ME14 ..156 C7
Peninsular Park Rd *CHARL* SE7 ...26 B8
Penlee CI *EDEN* TN8 ....206 D8

Penmon Rd *ABYW* SE2 ....27 P6
Pennack Rd *PECK* SE15 ....24 C9
Pennant Rd *ROCH* ME1 ....95 H7
Penn Ct *SIT* ME10 ....130 A5
Pennethorne Rd *PECK* SE15 ......41 H1
Penney CI *DART* DA1 ....46 D8
Penn Gdns *CHST* BR7 ....63 M8
Pennine Wk *RTWE/PEM* TN2 .....23 J1
Pennine Wy *BXLYHN* DA7 ....45 J1
  GVW DA11 ....69 J2
  KEN/WIL TN24 ....252 E5
  MAID/SHEP ME15 ....186 D2
Pennington CI *CANTW/ST* CT2 ..137 P6
Pennington Mnr
  STH/RUST TN4 * 240 C7
Pennington PI *STH/RUST* TN4 ..240 E7
Pennington Rd
  STH/RUST TN4 ....240 D7
Pennington St *WAP* E1W 24 D4
Pennington Wy
  LEE/GVPK SE12 ....62 F1
Penn La *BXLY* DA5 ....44 F7
  RSEV TN14 ....177 M5
Penns Rd *RTWE/PEM* TN2 ....271 M2
Penny Cress Gdns
  MAIDW ME16 ....155 H9
Penny Cress Rd *IOS* ME12 ....78 A3
Pennycroft *SAND/SEL* CR2 ......114 B5
Pennyfields *CRBK* TN17 ....298 A3
  POP/IOD E14 ....25 K3
Penny Pot La *RCANTW* CT4 .....195 K5
  RCANTW CT4 ....225 J1
Pennyroyal Av *EHAM* E6 ....26 H2
Penpool La *WELL* DA16 ....44 D4
Penrith CI *BECK* BR3 ....61 P1
Penrith PI *STRHM/NOR* SW16 ....60 D1
Penrith Rd *THHTH* CR7 ....60 C8
Penry St *STHWK* SE1 * 24 B7
Penshurst Av *BFN/LL* DA15 ....44 C7
Penshurst Gdns *MARG* CT9 .....113 L5
  HART DA3 ....69 H8
  RHAM ME8 ....96 C4
Penshurst Gn *HAYES* BR2 ....85 J2
Penshurst Ri *FAW* ME13 ....132 E5
Penshurst Rd *BXLYHN* DA7 ....45 H2
  RAM CT11 ....17 J2
  RTON TN11 ....238 F5
  RTON TN11 ....239 J7
  THHTH CR7 ....60 B3
Penshurst Wy *STMC/STPC* BR5 ..87 K1
The Penstocks *MAIDW* ME16 ....185 J1
The Pentagon *CHAT* ME4 * 5 H7
Pentridge St *PECK* SE15 ....40 F1
Pentstemon Dr *SWCM* DA10 ......48 C6
Pent Vale *FOLKN* CT19 ....310 D5
Penventon Ct *TIL* RM18 * 49 L3
Pen Wy *TONN* TN10 ....211 H5
Pepingstraw Cl
  E/WMAL ME19 * 152 E5
Pepper CI *EHAM* E6 ....26 C1
Pepper HI *GVW* DA11 ....68 C2
Peppermead Sq *LEW* SE13 * 41 N6
Peppermint Ct *CROY/NA* CR0 .....82 D4
Pepys St *POP/IOD* E14 ....25 L6
Pepys Av *IOS* ME12 ....57 K6
Pepys CI *GVW* DA11 ....69 H2
  TIL RM18 ....49 N2
Pepys Est *DEPT* SE8 ....25 J9
Pepys Park Est *DEPT* SE8 ....25 J7
Pepys Ri *ORP* BR6 ....86 G5
Pepys St *NWCR* SE14 ....41 K3
Pepys Wy *STRD* ME2 ....71 P7
Perch La *RRTW* TN3 ....272 E7
Percival Rd *ORP* BR6 ....86 C6
Percival Ter *DVW* CT17 ....291 J9
Percy Av *BRDST* CT10 ....113 L4
Percy Rd *BXLYHN* DA7 ....45 G5
  CAN/RD E16 ....25 P1
  MARG CT9 ....15 K3
  PGE/AN SE20 ....61 K7
  RAM CT11 ....16 E1
  SNWD SE25 ....83 L2
Percy St *GRAYS* RM17 ....32 D9
Percy Ter *STH/RUST* TN4 ....270 D2
Peregrine CI *HYTHE* CT21 ....308 C7
Peregrine Dr *SIT* ME10 ....44 B2
Peregrine Gdns *CROY/NA* CR0 ...64 B5
Peregrine Rd *E/WMAL* ME19 ....183 H1
Peri Ct *CANT* CT1 ....166 D6
Peridot St *EHAM* E6 ....26 F1
Perie Rw *WELL* DA16 * 72 G9
Perifield *DUL* SE21 ....40 C9
Perimeter Rd *DArT*/AV ME20 ...154 J1
Periton Rd *ELTH/MOT* SE9 ....43 H5
Periwinkle CI *SIT* ME10 ....99 H9
Perkins Av *MARG* CT9 ....112 C5
Perkins Ct *SIT* ME10 ....99 H9
Perkins CI *GRH* DA9 ....47 M6
Perkins Rd *BKHTH/KID* SE3 ....42 C3
Perpins Rd *ELTH/MOT* SE9 ....44 F4
Perran Ct *HART* DA3 ....91 J1
Perran Rd *BRXS/STRHM* SW2 ....60 B1
Perries Md *FOLKN* CT19 ....310 D4
Perryfield St *MAID/BEAR* ME14 ..12 E1
Perry Av *EGRIN* RH19 ....265 N5
Perry Gv *DART* DA1 ....46 G5
Perry Hall CI *ORP* BR6 ....87 H4
Perry Hall Rd *ORP* BR6 ....86 G5
Perry HI *CAT* SE6 ....61 M1
Perry Mnr *CHST* BR7 ....52 C7
Perry Rd *BERM/RHTH* SE16 ......24 H6
Perry Ri *FSTH* SE23 ....61 L2
Perry St *CHAT* ME4 ....169 M5
Perrys La *ORP* BR6 ....117 J7
Perrys St *CHAT* ME4 ....64 B5
  CHST BR7 ....45 N4
  DART DA1 ....49 J9

MAID/BEAR* ME14 ....12 E1
Perry V *FSTH* SE23 ....61 K1
Perry Wy *SOCK/AV* RM15 ....30 F5
Persant Rd *CAT* SE6 ....62 C2
Perseverance PI
  BRXN/ST SW9 * 40 A1
Perth Gdns *SIT* ME10 ....129 K1
Perth Rd *BECK* BR3 ....62 A8
Pested Bars Rd *RMAID* ME17 ...185 P6
Pested La *RASHE* TN25 ....192 E8
Petchart CI *CHST* BR7 ....94 B3
Peter Av *OXTED* RH8 ....174 G5
Peterboat CI *GNWCH* SE10 ....25 P7
Peters CI *WELL* DA16 ....44 A3
Petersfield *RTWE/PEM* TN2 ......271 P1
Petersfield Dr *MEO* DA13 ....122 A4
Petersham CI *STMC/STPC* BR5 ..64 B8
Petersham Gdns
  STMC/STPC BR5 * 64 C8
Petersham Ter *CROY/NA* CR0 * ..82 D7
Peterstone Rd *ABYW* SE2 ....28 A5
Peter St *DEAL* CT14 ....233 J2
  DVE/WH CT16 ....8 D4
Peterwood Wy *CROY/NA* CR0 ....82 E6
Petfield CI *IOS* ME12 ....78 C1
Petham Gn *MAID/SHEP* ME8 .....96 F4
Peto St North *CAN/RD* E16 ....26 A2
Petrel CI HB CT6 ....108 C6
Petrel Wy *RFOLK* CT18 ....290 A5
Petro St South *CAN/RD* E16 ......26 A4
Petta La *RCANTE* CT3 ....169 K7
Pett Bottom Rd *RCANTW* CT4 ..197 H9
  RCANTW CT4 ....227 H2
Petten CI *STMC/STPC* BR5 ....87 L5
Pettenden Dr *SIT* ME10 ....90 N6
Petten Gv *STMC/STPC* BR5 ....87 K5
Petteridge La *CTPH/PW* TN12 ..272 F2
Pettfield Hill Rd *FAV* ME13 ....191 N2
Petticoat La *CDW/CHF* RM16 ...187 M8
Petticoat Sq *WCHPL* E1 ....24 C2
Petticoat Tower *WCHPL* E1 * 24 C2
Pettits Rw *FAV* ME13 * 132 E6
Pettman CI *HB CT6 ....107 L3
Pettman Crs *THMD* SE28 ....27 L7
Pettman Ms *WSTB* CT5 * 105 K4
Pett's Crs *MSTR* CT12 ....141 J7
Pett St *WOOL/PLUM* SE18 ....26 F7
Petts Wood Rd
  STMC/STPC BR5 ....86 C2
Petty Wales *MON* EC3R 24 B5
Petworth Rd *BXLYHS* DA6 ....45 J6
Peverel Dr *MAID/BEAR* ME14 ...156 C7
Peverell Rd *DVE/WH* CT16 ....291 J2
Pewter Ct *CANT* CT1 * 4 A4
Peyton PI *GNWCH* SE10 ....42 A1
Pharos Dr *DVE/WH* CT16 ....8 E1
Pheasant CI *CAN/RD* E16 ....26 C2
Pheasant La
  MAID/SHEP ME15 ....185 N4
Pheasant Rd *CHAT* ME4 * 95 P4
Pheasants' Hall Rd
  RCANTW CT4 ....197 L8
Phelps CI *BGR/WK* TN15 ....120 B1
Phelp St *MALW* SE17 ....24 A9
Philchurch PI *WCHPL* E1 ....24 D2
Philimore CI *WOOL/PLUM* SE18 ..27 M8
Philip Corby CI *MARG* CT9 ....112 G3
Philip Gdns *CROY/NA* CR0 ....64 C6
Philippa Gdns *ELTH/MOT* SE9 ...43 H5
Philip Rd *PECK* SE15 ....40 G4
Philip Sydney Rd *WTHK* RM20 ...31 H8
Phillip Av *SWLY* BR8 ....88 C1
Philippa Ct *SIT* ME10 ....99 H47
Phillip Rd *FOLKN* CT19 ....310 B5
Phillips Ct *DART* DA1 ....46 B7
Phillips Ct *RHAM* ME8 ....96 E4
Phillips Rd *BRCH* CT7 ....111 H7
Philpot La *FENCHC* EC3M 24 B5
Philpots La *RTON* TN11 ....209 K4
Philpott St *WCHPL* E1 * 24 E2
Phineas Pett Rd
  ELTH/MOT SE9 ....43 J4
Phoebeth Rd *LEW* SE13 ....41 N6
Phoenix Ct *WWKM* BR4 ....64 B6
Phoenix Ct *POP/IOD* E14 ....25 K7
Phoenix Dr *HAYES* BR2 ....85 N8
  WBY/YAL ME18 ....183 M5
Phoenix Pk
  MAID/SHEP ME15 * 186 C7
Phoenix PI *DART* DA1 ....46 D8
Phoenix Rd *PGE/AN* SE20 ....61 J5
  WALD ME5 ....125 N3
Phoenix Wharf Rd *STHWK* SE1 ..24 C3
Picardy Manorway *BELV* DA17 ...28 G6
Picardy Rd *BELV* DA17 ....28 G6
Picardy St *BELV* DA17 ....28 F6
Pickelden La *RCANTW* CT4 ......194 G5
Pickering Gdns *SNWD* SE25 ....83 L3
Pickering St
  MAID/SHEP ME15 ....185 M5
Pickford CI *BXLYHN* DA7 ....44 G5
Pickforde La *WADH* TN5 ....315 J5
Pickford La *BXLYHN* DA7 ....44 G4
Pickhurst Gn *HAYES* BR2 ....85 J4
Pickhurst Md *HAYES* BR2 ....85 J3
Pickhurst Pk *HAYES* BR2 ....84 G5
Pickhurst Ri *WWKM* BR4 ....84 G5
Pickle's Wy *HOO/HM* ME3 ....52 A2
Pickneybush La *LYDD* TN29 .....325 M8
Pickwick Crs *ROCH* ME1 ....95 H4
Pickwick Gdns *GVW* DA11 ....69 H2
Pickwick Rd *DUL* SE21 ....40 D8
Picton Rd *RAM* CT11 ....16 C4
Picton St *CMBW* SE5 ....40 C2
Piedmont Rd
  WOOL/PLUM SE18 ....27 L8
Pie Factory Rd *RDV* CT15 ....229 P5

Pier Approach Rd *GILL* ME7 ....73 K8
Pier Av *HB CT6 ....107 K2
  WSTB CT5 ....105 P5
Pierce Mill La *RTON* TN11 ....212 C5
Pier Head *WAP* E1W * 24 E4
Piermont PI *BMLY* BR1 ....63 H8
Piermont Rd *EDUL* SE22 ....41 H6
Pierpoint Rd *WSTB* CT5 ....105 L7
Pierremont Av *BRDST* CT10 .....113 K9
Pierremont Rd *CAN/RD* E16 ......26 G5
  CHAT ME4 ....29 K9
  DART DA8 ....29 K9
  GRH DA9 ....47 P5
  SIT ME10 ....49 K7
The Pier *DVE/WH* CT16 ....260 G8
Pier Wy *WOOL/PLUM* SE18 ....27 L6
Pigdown La *EDEN* TN8 ....237 L5
Pigeon La *HB CT6 ....107M4
Piggs Cnr *GRAYS* RM17 * 32 D6
Pigott St *POP/IOD* E14 ....25 K2
Pigsdean Rd *MEO* DA15 ....93 J4
Pike CI *BMLY* BR1 ....62 F4
  FOLKN CT19 ....10 C3
Pikefish La *STPH/PW* TN12 ......213M9
Pike Rd *RDV* CT15 ....230 F7
Pikes La *CTPH/PW* TN12 ....246 B6
Pikey La *E/WMAL* ME19 ....153 L7
Pilckem CI *CANT* CT1 ....167 J3
Pile La *STPH/PW* TN12 ....246 D5
Pilgrimage St *STHWK* SE1 ....24 A5
Pilgrims La *CDW/CHF* RM16 ....145M9
  OXTED RH8 ....145M9
  RCANTW CT4 ....194 F2
  WSTB CT5 ....135 J1
Pilgrims Lakes *RMAID* ME17 ....188 F4
Pilgrims Ms *POP/IOD* E14 ....25 N3
Pilgrims Rd *CANT* CT1 ....93 N8
  SWCM DA10 ....48 C5
Pilgrims Vw *GRH* DA9 ....48 A7
  MAID/BEAR ME14 ....156 B2
Pilgrims' Wy *BGR/WK* TN15 .....121 J9
Pilgrims Wy East *RSEV* TN14 ...149 H1
Pilgrims Wy West *RSEV* TN14 ..148 E1
Pilkington Rd *ORP* BR6 ....86 D7
  PECK SE15 ....41 H5
Pillar Box La *RTON* TN11 ....181 M6
Pillar Box Rd *BGR/WK* TN15 ....150 B7
Pilot CI *DEPT* SE8 ....25 J9
Pilot Rd *ROCH* ME1 ....95 H6
Pilots Av *DEAL* CT14 ....232 F5
Pilot's Farm Rd *RCANTW* CT4 ..196 F7
Pilots Pk *GVE* DA12 ....49 N7
Pimpernel CI
  MAID/BEAR ME14 ....156 E8
Pimpernel Wy
  MAID/BEAR ME14 ....125 K1
Pinchbeck Rd *ORP* BR6 ....116 C1
Pinchin & Johnsons Yd
  WCHPL E1 * 24 D3
Pinchin St *WCHPL* E1 ....24 D3
Pincott PI *BROCKY* SE4 ....41 K4
Pincott Rd *BXLYHS* DA6 ....45 J6
Pincroft Wd *HART* DA3 ....91 H6
Pindar St *SDTCH* EC2A 24 B1
Pine Av *GVE* DA12 ....49 P9
  WWKM BR4 ....84 C5
Pine CI *IOS* ME12 ....57 K6
  SWLY BR8 ....88 E1
Pine Coombe *CROY/NA* CR0 ......84 A8
Pinecrest Gdns *ORP* BR6 ....86 C8
Pinecroft *WELL* DA16 ....44 C1
Pinefield CI *POP/IOD* E14 * 25 K7
Pine Gld *ORP* BR6 ....86 A8
Pine Gv *EDEN* TN8 ....206 C8
  EGRIN RH19 ....264 E5
  GILL ME7 ....96 D9
Pineham Rd *RDV* CT15 ....199 L6
Pinehurst *RSEV* TN14 ....149 K6
Pinelands CI *BKHTH/KID* SE3 * ..42 D1
Pineneedle La *HB CT6 ....148 G8
Pine PI *MAID/SHEP* ME15 ....185 K2
Pine Rdg *TONN* TN10 ....211 H6
Pine Ri *MEO* DA13 ....92 B5
Pine Rd *STRD* ME2 ....18 A4
Pinesfield La *E/WMAL* ME19 ....122 C7
Pineside Rd *RCANTE* CT3 ....168 B8
Pines Rd *BMLY* BR1 ....63 J8
The Pines *BRDST* CT10 ....116 H6
  CDW/CHF RM16 ....32 C4
  NRWD SE19 * 60 B5
Pine Tree Av *CANTW/ST* CT2 ......4 B1
Pine Tree CI *BGR/WK* TN15 ......180 C7
Pine Vw *BGR/WK* TN15 ....151 M5
Pine Wk *HB CT6 ....108 B5
Pine Wy *FOLKN* CT19 ....310 A4

Pine Way CI *EGRIN* RH19 ....265 H9
Pinewood Av *BFN/LL* DA15 ....44 A9
  SEV TN15 ....149 J6
Pinewood CI *CROY/NA* CR0 ......84 B7
  MSTR CT12 ....143 H5
  ORP BR6 ....86 E5
  STPH/PW TN12 ....242 G3
  TIL RM18 ....34 A4
Pinewood Dr
  MAID/BEAR ME14 ....126 A5
  ORP BR6 ....86 F9
Pinewood Gdns
  STH/RUST TN4 ....240 D8
Pinewood PI *BXLY* DA5 ....65 N1
Pinewood Rd *ABYW* SE2 ....28 E5
  HAYES BR2 ....85 K1
  RTWE/PEM TN2 ....270 C3
Pin HI *CANT* CT1 * 4 D6
Pinkham *STPH/PW* TN12 ....213 H5
Pinks HI *SWLY* BR8 ....88 D2
Pinnacle HI *BXLYHN* DA7 ....45 K5
Pinnacle HI North *BXLYHN* DA7 ..45 K5
The Pinnacles *CHAT* ME4 ....73 J6
Pinnell Rd *ELTH/MOT* SE9 ....43 H5
Pinners HI *RDV* CT15 ....199M9
Pinners La *RDV* CT15 ....229M1
Pinnock La *STPH/PW* TN12 ......246 B8
Pinnock's Av *GVW* DA11 ....49M9
Pintail CI *EHAM* E6 ....26 F1
  HOO/HM ME3 ....52 B2
Pintail Wy *HB CT6 ....107 P4
Pinton HI *WADH* TN5 ....314 F3
Pinto Wy *BKHTH/KID* SE3 ....42 F5
Pioneer Rd *DVE/WH* CT16 ....299M4
  SIT ME10 ....40 G2
Pioneer St *PECK* SE15 ....40 F1
Pioneer Wy *SWLY* BR8 ....65 N9
Pipers Gdns *CROY/NA* CR0 ....84 B4
Piper's Green Rd
  BH/WHM TN16 ....177 H4
Pipers La BH/WHM* TN16 ....177 H4
Pippin Av *RCANTW* CT4 ....197 N3
Pippin CI *CROY/NA* CR0 ....84 C9
  RMAID ME17 ....184 C9
Pippin Cft *GILL* ME7 ....99 J8
Pippin Rd *STPH/PW* TN12 ....212 C4
The Pippins *MEO* DA13 ....92 B3
Pippin Wy *E/WMAL* ME19 ....183 H1
Piquet Rd *PGE/AN* SE20 ....61 K9
Pirbright CI *MAID* ME5 ....126 A5
Pirbright Crs *CROY/NA* CR0 ......114 F1
Pirie St *CAN/RD* E16 ....26 C4
Pirrip CI *GVE* DA12 ....50 B9
Pitchfont La *OXTED* RH8 ....175 K2
Pitfield *HART* DA3 ....91 H6
Pitfield Crs *THMD* SE28 ....27 P4
Pitfield Dr *MEO* DA13 ....92 A7
Pitfold Rd *LEE/GVPK* SE12 ....42 E8
Pitlake *CROY/NA* CR0 ....82 G6
Pit La *EDEN* TN8 ....206 C9
Pitman St *CMBW* SE5 ....40 C1
Pitsea PI *WCHPL* E1 * 24 G2
Pitsea St *WCHPL* E1 ....24 G2
Pitstock Rd *RSIT* ME9 ....130 A9
Pittlesden *TENT* TN30 ....301 H8
Pittlesden PI *TENT* TN30 * 301 H8
Pitt Rd *MAIDW* ME16 ....184 C2
  ORP BR6 ....86 D8
  RMAID ME17 ....187 K3
  THHTH CR7 ....83 H2
Pittville Gdns *SNWD* SE25 ....60 C9
Pivington La *HDCN* TN27 ....220 A8
Pixley St *POP/IOD* E14 ....25 J2
Pixot HI *STPH/PW* TN12 ....243 J8
Pix's La *CRBK* TN17 ....319M3
Pixton Wy *CROY/NA* CR0 ....114 C2
Pixwell La *DEAL* CT14 ....232 C6
Pizien Well Rd
  WBY/YAL ME18 ....183 H5
Place Farm Av *ORP* BR6 ....86 C5
Place La *RASHM* TN26 ....252 G5
  RSIT ME9 ....97 N9
The Place *RCANTW* CT4 ....229 J5
Plain Rd *FOLK* CT20 ....310 D7
  RASHE TN25 ....284 C4
  STPH/PW TN12 ....243 J2
Plains Av *MAID/SHEP* ME15 .....185 N2
Plains of Waterloo *RAM* CT11 ....17 C3
Plaistow La *BMLY* BR1 ....62 F6
Plaistow Sq
  MAID/BEAR ME14 * 155 P6
Plaistow St *LING* RH7 ....234 F5
Plane Av *GVW* DA11 ....49 H8
Plane St *SYD* SE26 ....61 H2
Plane Wk *TONN* TN10 ....210 F3
Plantation CI *GRH* DA9 ....47M7
  RASHW TN26 ....251M2
Plantation La *FENCHST* EC3M 24 B3
  MAID/BEAR ME14 ....156 D8
  WARL CR6 ....104 C4
Plantation Rd *ERITH* DA8 ....46 A2
  FAV ME13 ....132 F7
  GILL ME7 ....73 N9
  SWLY BR8 ....66 A6
  WSTB CT5 ....106 C4
The Plantation *BKHTH/KID* SE3 ..42 A3
Plassy Rd *CAT* SE6 ....41 P8
Platt Common *BGR/WK* TN15 ...151M5
The Platters *RHAM* ME8 ....96 F6
The Plat *EDEN* TN8 ....206 E9
  RYE TN31 ....344 F3
Platt House La *BGR/WK* TN15 ..121M7
Platt Mill Ter *BGR/WK* TN15 * ..151M5
The Platt *LING* RH7 ....234 F5
  RMAID ME17 ....217 H3
Plawsfield Rd *BECK* BR3 ....61 L1
Plaxdale Green Rd
  BGR/WK TN15 ....120 G6
Plaxtol CI *BMLY* BR1 ....62 G7

Plaxtol La BGR/WK TN15 ....180 F3
Plaxtol Rd ERITH DA8 ....45 J1
Playden La RYE TN31 ....338 E1
Playfield Crs EDUL SE22 ....40 B6
Playgreen Wy CAT SE6 ....61 N5
Playground Cl BECK BR3 ....61 K8
Playing Flds SWCH CT13 * 201 M3
Playstool Cl RSIT ME9 ....98 C8
Playstool Rd RSIT ME9 ....98 B8
Peasance Rd STMC/STPC BR5 ....64 D8
Pleasance Rd Central
  LYDD TN29 ....343 L9
Pleasance Rd North
  LYDD TN29 ....343 K7
Pleasance Rd South
  LYDD TN29 ....347 L1
Pleasant Gv CROY/NA CRO 84 C7
Pleasant Valley La
  MAID/SHEP ME15 ....184 G7
Pleasant Vw ERITH DA8 ....29 K8
  ORP BR6 ....86 D9
Pleasent Pl IOS ME12 ....77 N1
Pleasure House La
  RMAID ME17 ....217 K2
Plevna St POP/IOD E14 ....25 M6
Pleydell Av NRWD SE19 ....60 E6
Plevdell Gdns FOLK CT20 ....10 C6
  NRWD SE19 * 60 F5
Plimsoll Av FOLKN CT19 ....310 G3
Plimsoll Cl POP/IOD E14 ....25 L2
Plomley Cl RHAM ME8 ....126 G1
Plough Cl HB CT6 ....108 A8
Plough Hl BGR/WK TN15 ....151 J8
  RDV CT15 ....312 C2
Plough La CROY/NA CRO 82 D8
  EDUL SE22 ....40 F7
  WSTB CT5 ....106 C3
Plough Lane Cl WLGTN SM6 ......82 C9
Ploughmans Wy RHAM ME8 ......97 M8
  WALD ME5 ....125 M4
Plough Rd IOS ME12 ....78 G2
  LINC RH7 ....235 K7
  ORP BR6 ....86 D9
Plough St WCHPL E1 * 24 C2
Plough Wy BERM/RHTH SE16 ....24 A2
  IOS ME12 ....78 A2
Plover Cl DIT/AY ME20 ....153 N2
  IOS ME12 ....78 A2
Plover Rd HB CT6 ....108 C5
  WALD ME5 ....126 A4
Plover Wy BERM/RHTH SE16 .....25 H6
Plowenders Cl E/WMAL ME19 ...152 E1
Pluckley Cl RHAM ME8 ....96 F3
Pluckley Gdns MARG CT9 ....113 K3
Pluckley Rd HDCN TN27 ....220 G5
  HDCN TN27 ....249 J7
  RASHW TN26 ....250 F4
Plug La MED DA13 ....92 E9
Plumbers Rw WCHPL E1 ....24 D1
Plumbridge St GNWCH SE10 * ...42 A2
Plumford Rd FAV ME13 ....162 D2
Plum La WOOL/PLUM SE18 ....43 M1
Plumpton Wk CANT CT1 ....5 H2
Plumpudding La FAV ME13 ....134 E5
Plumstead Common Rd
  WOOL/PLUM SE18 ....27 K9
Plumstead High St
  WOOL/PLUM SE18 ....27 L7
Plumstead Rd
  WOOL/PLUM SE18 ....27 J6
Plumstone Rd BRCH CT7 ....141 H2
Plum Tree Gdns RASHW TN26 ...302 G6
Plumtree Gv GILL ME7 ....73 J7
Plum Tree La RSIT ME9 ....127 L5
Plumtree Rd HDCN TN27 ....247 K1
Plumtrees MAIDW ME16 ....184 F1
Plurenden Rd RASHW TN26 ......280 D9
Plymouth Dr BGR/WK TN15 ......21 G2
Plymouth Pk BGR/WK TN15 ......21 H2
Plymouth Rd BMLY BR1 ....61 F7
  CAN/RD E16 ....26 B1
  CDW/CHF RM16 ....31 M8
Plymouth Whf POP/IOD E14 ......25 N7
Plympton Cl BELV DA17 ....28 G5
Plymstock Rd WELL DA16 ....44 E1
Poachers Cl WALD ME5 ....95 P9
Pochard Crs HB CT6 ....107 K3
Pocket Hl SEV TN13 ....178 F4
Podkin Wd WALD ME5 ....125 L5
Poets Cnr MARG CT9 ....15 J6
Poets Wk DEAL CT14 ....232 C8
Point Cl GNWCH SE10 ....42 A2
Point Rd RTON TN11 * 181 J6
Pointer Cl THMD SE28 ....28 C2
Pointers Cl POP/IOD E14 ....25 L8
Polebrook Rd GNWCH SE10 ......42 A2
Polebrook Rd BKHTH/KID SE3 ...42 C4
Polecroft La CAT SE6 ....61 M1
Polesden Rd RTWE/PEM TN2 .....23 J7
Polesteeple Hl
  BH/WHM TN16 ....145 N2
The Poles RSIT ME9 ....97 P2
Polhill RSEV TN14 ....118 B9
Polhill Dr WALD ME5 ....125 L3
Police Station Rd
  E/WMAL ME19 ....153 K4
Poll Cl ASH TN23 ....252 C9
  CAN/RD E16 ....26 B5
Pollard Pl STPH/PW CT5 * 105 K8
Pollards Oak Crs OXTED RH8 ....175 K8
Pollards Oak Rd OXTED RH8 .....175 K8
Pollards Wd Rd OXTED RH8 ......175 K6
Pollards Wood Rd
  OXTED RH8 ....175 L7
Polley Cl RTWE/PEM TN2 ....271 N1
Pollyhaugh EYN DA4 ....89 K7
Polo Wy SIT ME10 ....106 B5
Polperro Cl ORP BR6 ....86 C5
Polsted Rd CAT SE6 ....41 M8
Polthorne Gv
  WOOL/PLUM SE18 ....27 K7
Polytechnic St
  WOOL/PLUM SE18 ....27 H7
Pomell Wy WCHPL E1 ....24 C2

Pomeroy St NWCR SE14 ....41 J1
Pomfret Houses
  RCANTW CT4 * 195 L2
Pomfret Rd CMBW SE5 ....40 B4
  RCANTW CT4 ....195 L2
Pommeus La DEAL CT14 ....262 C1
Poncia Rd ASH TN23 ....282 D1
Pond Cl BKHTH/KID SE3 ....42 E5
Pond Cottage La BECK BR3 ......84 D5
Pond Dr SIT ME10 ....129 P3
Pond Farm Rd RMAID ME17 .....157 N3
  RSIT ME9 ....128 C4
Pondfield La GVE DA12 ....70 G6
Pondfield Rd HAYES BR2 ....85 H5
  ORP BR6 ....86 C7
Pond Hl HOO/HM ME3 ....52 E2
  RCANTE CT15 ....198 G6
Pond Hill Rd FOLK CT20 ....309 P2
Poona Rd RTW TN1 ....23 F6
Poorhole La DART DA1 ....112 F8
Pootings Rd EDEN TN8 ....206 E2
Poot La RSIT ME9 ....75 J9
Pope Dr STPH/PW TN12 ....246 B5
Pope House La TENT TN30 ......301 J3
Pope Rd HAYES BR2 ....85 N2
Popes Gv CROY/NA CRO 84 C7
Popes La CANTW/ST CT2 ....137 K6
  OXTED RH8 ....205 J2
Popjak Rd RSIT ME9 * 129 L7
Poplar Av GVE DA12 ....69 N5
  ORP BR6 ....86 C6
Poplar Bath St POP/IOD E14 .....25 L5
Poplar Cl ASH TN23 ....84 D5
  HOO/HM ME3 ....73 L4
  STRD ME2 ....94 E1
Poplar Dr HB CT6 ....107 H4
  RDV CT15 ....230 C7
Poplar Gv MAIDW ME16 ....155 H7
Poplar High St POP/IOD E14 .....25 M3
Poplar La LYDD TN29 ....342 C5
Poplar Mt BELV DA17 ....28 G7
Poplar Pl THMD SE28 ....28 B5
Poplar Rd BRDST CT10 ....113 K7
  HNHL SE24 ....40 C5
  RAM CT11 ....16 D3
  STRD ME2 ....94 D1
  TENT TN30 ....332 A2
Poplars Cl HART DA3 ....91 J1
The Poplars ASH TN25 * 282 D1
  RCANTE CT3 ....138 C8
Poplar Wk CROY/NA CRO 83 H6
  HNHL SE24 ....40 C5
  MED DA13 ....92 C3
Poplicans Rd STRD ME2 ....94 A3
Poppy Cl BELV DA17 ....28 H7
  GILL ME7 ....96 B1
  HAYES BR2 ....85 N9
  MAIDW ME16 ....12 A7
Poppy La CROY/NA CRO 83 P4
Poppy Meadow
  STPH/PW TN12 ....243 H4
Popsal La RCANTE CT3 ....199 L1
Porchester Cl HART DA3 ....91 J1
  MAID/SHEP ME15 ....185 M5
Porchester Md BECK BR3 ....61 P5
Porchfield Cl GVE DA12 ....69 N1
Porcupine Cl ELTH/MOT SE9 .....63 J1
Porlock St STHWK SE1 ....24 A5
Porrington Cl CHST BR7 ....63 K7
Portal Cl WNWD SE27 ....60 A2
Port Av GRH DA9 ....47 P7
Portbury Cl PECK SE15 ....40 C5
Portchester Cl CMBW SE5 ....40 C5
Port Cl MAID/BEAR ME14 ....156 C7
Porte Cl IOS ME12 ....78 A1
Porter Cl IOS ME12 ....78 A1
  WTHK RM20 ....31 M9
Porter La EHAM E6 ....24 F1
Porters Cl STPH/PW TN12 ....272 C2
Porter's La FAV ME13 ....162 E2
Porters Wk RMAID ME17 ....187 H7
  WAP E1W * 24 E5
Porthcawe Rd SYD SE26 ....61 L3
Port Hl ORP BR6 ....117 J6
Porthkerry Av WELL DA16 ....44 C5
Portland Av BFN/LL DA15 ....44 C7
  GVE DA12 ....69 M1
  SIT ME10 ....130 B1
Portland Cl HYTHE CT21 ....308 G5
  KEN/WIL TN24 ....252 E2
Portland Cr RAM CT11 ....17 C2
Portland Crs ELTH/MOT SE9 .....63 J1
Portland Pl HART DA3 * 96 P5
  SNOD 123 P5
Portland Malthouse
  FAV ME13 * 132 C7
Portland Rd BMLY BR1 ....62 C3
  EGRIN RH19 ....265 H8
  ELTH/MOT SE9 ....63 J1
  GILL ME7 ....73 L9
  GVW DA11 ....49 M9
  HYTHE CT21 ....308 C5
  ROCH ME1 ....124 B1

SNWD SE25 ....83 N1
Portland Sq WAP E1W 24 E4
Portland St CHAT ME4 ....95 N4
  WALW SE17 ....23 G8
Portlight Pl WSTB CT5 ....105 H8
Portman Cl BXLY DA5 ....45 N9
  BXLYHN DA7 ....44 F4
Portman Pk TON TN9 ....210 F7
Portmeadow Wk ABYW SE2 ......28 C5
Portree Ms GILL ME7 * 96 A3
Portree St POP/IOD E14 ....25 N2
Port Ri CHAT ME4 ....A6
Portsdown Cl MAIDW ME16 .....184 G1
Portsea Rd TIL RM18 ....49 N2
Portsmouth Cl STRD ME2 ....94 C1
Portsoken St WCHPL E1 ....24 C3
Port Victoria Rd HOO/HM ME3 ...56 B5
Portway WSTB CT5 ....105 K6
Portway Gdns
  WOOL/PLUM SE18 ....43 H2
Portway Rd HOO/HM ME3 ....52 B8
Post Barn Rd CHAT ME4 ....95 L4
Postern La TON TN9 ....210 C8
Postling ASH TN23 ....252 B8
Postling Rd FOLKN CT19 ....310 B4
Postmill Cl CROY/NA CRO 83 D7
Postmill Dr MAID/SHEP ME15 ...141 P8
Post Office Rd HAWK TN18 ......317 H4
Post Office Sq RTW TN1 * 22 D5
Potash La BGR/WK TN15 ....151 M6
Potier St STHWK SE1 ....24 A6
Pot Kiln La RASHW TN26 ....279 M4
Potten Street Rd BRCH CT7 .....109 N7
Potters Cl CROY/NA CRO 84 B5
  RASHE TN25 ....23 H2
Potters Flds STHWK SE1 * 24 B4
Potter's La HAWK TN18 ....297 M9
Potter St SWCH CT13 ....201 P1
Pottery Rd BXLY DA5 ....45 N9
  HOO/HM ME3 ....73 K2
Pottery St BERM/RHTH SE16 * ...24 E5
Pottingfield Rd RYE TN31 ....338 C6
Poulders Rd SWCH CT13 ....201 L2
Poulters Wd HAYES BR2 ....85 N9
Poulton Cl DVW CT17 ....290 C7
Poulton La RCANTW/ST CT3 ....200 D1
Poultry CITYW EC2V 41 G1
Pound Bank Cl BGR/WK TN15 ...120 C3
Pound Cl ORP BR6 ....86 E6
Pound Ct ASH TN23 ....282 D5
Pound Court Dr ORP BR6 ....86 E6
Poundfield Rd HAWK TN18 ......318 D9
Poundhurst Rd RASHW TN26 ....304 E5
Pound La ASH TN23 ....282 C4
  CANTW/ST CT2 ....4 D3
  RASHE TN25 ....284 C5
  RCANTW CT4 ....193 J7
  RCANTW CT4 ....257 L5
  RSEV TN14 ....117 L9
  SEV TN13 ....21 G1
Pound Park Rd CHARL SE7 ......42 D4
Pound Pl ELTH/MOT SE9 ....43 L7
Pound Rd STPH/PW TN12 ....212 F4
Poundsbridge Hl RRTW TN3 ......J4
Poundsbridge La RTON TN11 ....239 J6
Pounsley Rd SEV TN13 ....148 D6
Pout Rd SNOD ME6 ....123 N6
Poverest Rd STMC/STPC BR5 ....86 A1
Povey Av STRD ME2 ....72 C5
Powdermill Cl
  RTWE/PEM TN2 ....240 F9
Powder Mill La DART DA1 ....66 C1
  RTON TN11 ....209 N8
  STH/RUST TN4 ....270 E1
Powell Av RDART DA2 ....67 L1
Powell Cl DIT/AY ME20 ....154 E1
Powerscroft Rd SCUP DA14 .....64 E5
Power Station Rd IOS ME12 .....59 N9
Powis St WOOL/PLUM SE18 .....27 H6
Powlett Rd STRD ME2 ....72 C6
Powster Rd BMLY BR1 ....62 F4
Powys Cl BXLYHN DA7 ....28 C9
Poynder Rd TIL RM18 ....49 M2
Poynings Cl ORP BR6 ....87 K6
Poyntell Crs CHST BR7 ....63 P7
Poyntell Rd STPH/PW TN12 ....246 C5
Pragnell Rd LEE/GVPK SE12 .....62 F1
Prall's La STPH/PW TN12 ....242 F7
Pratling St DIT/AY ME20 ....154 C1
The Precincts CANT CT1 ....5 F3
  ROCH ME1 ....19 J5
Premier Av CDW/CHF RM16 .....32 D5
Premiere Pl POP/IOD E14 ....25 K3
Premier Pl DART DA1 ....154 D1
Prendergast Rd
  ELTH/MOT SE9 ....42 C4
Prentis Cl SIT ME10 ....99 K9
Prentis Quay SIT ME10 ....99 N9
Prentiss Ct CHARL SE7 ....26 E7
Prescot St WCHPL E1 ....24 C3
Prescott Av STMC/STPC BR5 ....86 C3
Prescott Cl RDV CT15 ....291 M2
Presidents Dr WAP E1W 24 E7
Prestage Wy POP/IOD E14 ......25 M5
Prestbury Sq ELTH/MOT SE9 ....63 K5
Prestedge Av RAM CT11 ....143 K2
Prestley Dr TONN TN10 ....210 C3
Preston Av FAV ME13 ....133 H8
  GILL ME7 ....96 B5
Preston Cl STHWK SE1 ....24 B7
Preston Dr BXLYHN DA7 ....44 F2
Preston Gv FAV ME13 ....132 F7
Preston Hall Gdns IOS ME12 ....80 B3
Preston Hl RCANTE CT3 ....169 L7
Preston La FAV ME13 ....132 F7
  RCANTE CT3 ....169 L4
Preston Malthouse
  FAV ME13 * 132 C7
Preston Pde WSTB CT5 ....104 C7
Preston Pk FAV ME13 ....132 C7
Preston Pl FAV ME13 * 132 C7
Preston Rd GVW DA11 ....49 J9
  MSTR CT12 ....142 C1
  NRWD SE19 ....60 B5
  RCANTE CT3 ....139 M9

RCANTE CT3 ....169 L4
  POP/IOD E14 ....25 M4
Preston St FAV ME13 ....132 C7
Prestwood Cl
  WOOL/PLUM SE18 ....44 C1
Prestwood Gdns
  CROY/NA CRO 83 H4
Pretoria Pde LEW SE13 * 41 N3
Pretoria Rd CANT CT1 ....5 J4
  CHAT ME4 ....7 K6
  GILL ME7 ....7 K6
Prettymans La EDEN TN8 ....206 C6
Price's Av MARG CT9 ....112 F5
  RAM CT11 ....16 B4
Prickley Wd HAYES BR2 ....85 J5
Priddy's Yd CROY/NA CRO * 83 H6
Pridham Rd THHTH CR7 ....83 J1
Pridmore Rd SNOD ME6 ....123 N5
Priest Av CANTW/ST CT2 ....166 B4
Priestfield Rd FSTH SE23 ....61 L2
Priest Flds HB CT6 ....108 C5
Priestfields ROCH ME1 ....124 D6
Priest Hl OXTED RH8 ....175 L5
Priestlands Park Rd
  BFN/LL DA15 ....64 B2
Priestley Dr DIT/AY ME20 ....123 N9
Priest Wk WSTB CT5 ....106 A5
Priestwood Rd MEO DA13 ......122 C1
Prima Rd BRXN/ST SW9 ....40 A1
Primmett Cl BXLYHN DA7 ....120 B1
Primrose Av RHAM ME8 ....96 E9
Primrose Cl CAT SE6 ....95 K7
  DIT/AY ME20 ....82 A5
Primrose Dr RCANTW CT4 ....155 N5
Primrose La CROY/NA CRO 83 P5
  RSIT ME9 ....129 H7
Primrose Rd DVW CT17 ....291 H6
  STRD ME2 ....92 C2
Primrose Wk NWCR SE14 ....41 L1
  STPH/PW TN12 ....243 H4
Primrose Wy MSTR CT12 ....142 B7
  WSTB CT5 ....106 B5
Prince Andrew Rd
  BRDST CT10 ....113 K6
Prince Arthur Rd ME7 ....73 H9
Prince Charles Av EYN DA4 ......67 K8
  IOS ME12 ....80 A5
  SIT ME10 ....130 A5
  WALD ME5 ....125 N1
Prince Charles Rd
  BKHTH/KID SE3 ....42 D2
  BRDST CT10 ....113 J6
Prince Charles Wy WLGTN SM6 ...82 A7
Prince Consort Dr CHST BR7 ....63 P7
Prince Edward Prom
  RAM 16 B7
Prince Henry Rd CHARL SE7 .....43 H1
Prince Imperial Rd CHST BR7 ...63 M6
Prince John Rd
  ELTH/MOT SE9 ....43 J6
Princelet St WCHPL E1 ....24 C1
Prince of Orange La
  GNWCH SE10 * 42 A1
Prince of Wales Pier DVW CT17 ...9 F7
Prince of Wales Rd
  BKHTH/KID SE3 ....42 D2
  CAN/RD E16 ....26 D2
Prince of Wales Rbt DVW CT17 ...8 C6
Prince of Wales
  Ter DEAL CT14 ....233 J4
Prince Philip Av
  CDW/CHF RM16 ....32 B4
Prince Regent La
  CAN/RD E16 ....26 D2
Prince Rd SNWD SE25 ....83 K2
Prince Rupert Rd
  ELTH/MOT SE9 ....43 K5
Princes Av IOS ME12 ....58 D9
  RDART DA2 ....142 C3
  RDART DA2 ....67 J4
  STMC/STPC BR5 ....86 F2
  WALD ME5 ....125 M1
Princes Cl BRCH CT7 ....110 E6
  SCUP DA14 ....65 K6
Princes Crs MARG CT9 ....15 H5
Princes Dr SWCH CT13 ....202 F1
Prince's Gdns HAYES BR2 ....113 H5
Prince's Pde HYTHE CT21 ......309 L5
Prince's Pln HAYES BR2 ....85 P4
Princes Rd IL LEW SE13 ....42 A3
Princes Riverside Rd
  BERM/RHTH SE16 ....24 G4
Princes Rd DART DA1 ....46 B8
  GVE DA12 ....69 N3
  PGE/AN SE20 ....61 K5
  RAM CT11 ....16 D1
  RDART DA2 ....47 J9
  SWLY BR8 ....86 B9
Princess Alice Wy THMD SE28 ...27 L5
Princess Anne Rd
  CROY/NA CRO 113 K6
Princess Cl WSTB CT5 ....106 B3
Princesses Pde DART DA1 * 45 P6
Princess Margaret Av
  MARG CT9 ....113 J3
  TIL RM18 ....142 F3
Princess Margaret Rd
  TIL RM18 ....34 A7
Princess Mary Av CHAT ME4 ....78 H8
Princess Pde ORP BR6 ....86 D7
Princess St BXLYHN DA7 ....45 H4
  FOLKN CT19 ....11 G1

Princes St DEAL CT14 ....233 J2
  DVW CT17 ....8 D4
  GVE DA12 ....49 M7
  MAID/BEAR ME14 ....13 G5
  MARG CT9 ....15 G4
  RAM CT11 ....17 F4
  ROCH ME1 ....95 H5
Princes Ter RTWE/PEM TN2 * ...308 E6
Prince St DEPT SE8 ....25 J5
Princes Vw DART DA1 ....46 C9
Princes Wy CANTW/ST CT2 ....4 A3
  CROY/NA CRO 82 E9
  MAID/BEAR ME14 ....156 D3
  WWKM BR4 ....85 J8
Princethorpe Rd SYD SE26 ......61 K3
Prince William Ct DEAL CT14 * ...233 J2
Prinys Dr RHAM ME8 ....126 F1
Priolo Rd CHARL SE7 ....26 D8
Prior Cl GRAYS RM17 ....32 A7
Prioress Rd DVW CT17 * 166 C4
  WNWD SE27 ....60 B2
Prioress St STHWK SE1 ....24 B6
Prior Rd LYDD TN29 ....343 J5
Priorsdean Rd MAID/BEAR ME16 ...184 D2
Priorsford Av
  STMC/STPC BR5 ....87 H1
Prior St GNWCH SE10 ....42 A1
Priory Av STMC/STPC BR5 ....86 E3
Priory Cl BECK BR3 ....63 K7
  BMLY BR1 ....63 K7
  DART DA1 ....46 C6
  MAID/SHEP ME15 ....336 E7
  NROM TN28 ....336 E7
Priory Dr ABYW SE2 ....28 C8
Priory Flds EYN DA4 ....89 L6
Priory Gdns CANT CT1 ....166 F6
  DART DA1 ....11 F5
  FOLK CT20 ....11 F5
  SNWD SE25 ....83 L1
Priory Ga MAID/BEAR ME14 ....13 F5
Priory Gate Rd DVW CT17 ....8 B3
Priory Gv DIT/AY ME20 ....154 C5
  DVW CT17 ....8 B3
  TON TN9 ....240 E1
Priory Hl DART DA1 ....46 D7
  DVW CT17 ....8 A3
Priory La EYN DA4 ....89 L5
  RASHE TN25 ....285 K4
Priory Leas ELTH/MOT SE9 * 43 J9
Priory of St Jacob CANT CT1 ....166 C6
Priory Pk BKHTH/KID SE3 ....42 D4
Priory Rd CROY/NA CRO 82 F4
  DART DA1 ....46 C5
  DVE/WH CT16 ....8 C3
  FAV ME13 ....132 E5
  MAID/SHEP ME15 ....13 F6
  RAM CT11 ....16 E5
  RASHE TN25 ....305 M1
  RHAM ME8 ....96 D4
  STRD ME2 ....18 B5
  TON TN9 ....240 F1
Priory Rw FAV ME13 ....132 C7
Priory Station Approach Rd
  DVW CT17 ....8 B3
Priory St DVE/WH CT16 ....8 C3
  TON TN9 ....240 E1
The Priory BKHTH/KID SE3 ......42 D4
  CROY/NA CRO * 82 F7
  ORP BR6 ....87 J4
Priory Wk TON TN9 ....240 E1
Pristling La STPH/PW TN12 .....245 N9
Pritchard Dr POP/IOD E14 ......288 D8
Priter Rd BERM/RHTH SE16 * ...24 D5
Probert Rd BRXS/STRHM SW2 ...40 A6
Probyn Rd BRXS/STRHM SW2 ....60 B1
Proctor Wk RFOLK CT18 ....288 C8
The Progress Est
  MAID/SHEP ME15 * 186 D7
Progress Wy CROY/NA CRO 82 E6
The Promenade IOS ME12 ....80 E5
Prospect Av STRD ME2 ....72 B7
Prospect Cl BELV DA17 ....28 F7
  SYD SE26 ....61 H3
  WGOS CT8 ....111 M6
Prospect Gdns MSTR CT12 ......141 J3
Prospect Gv GVE DA12 ....49 P8
Prospect Ms HYTHE CT21 * 309 H5
Prospect Pl BRCH CT7 ....109 P9
  BRDST CT10 ....113 N9
  CANT CT1 * 5 E7
  DART DA1 ....46 E7
  DVW CT17 ....291 J6
  GRAYS RM17 ....32 B9
  GVE DA12 ....49 P8
  HAYES BR2 ....62 F9
  MAIDW ME16 ....12 B7
  RAM CT11 ....16 E4
  WAP E1W * 24 F4
Prospect Rd BRCH CT7 ....110 C6
  BRDST CT10 ....113 N9
  FOLK CT20 ....310 A8
  HYTHE CT21 ....309 H5
  MSTR CT12 ....141 J6
  RTWE/PEM TN2 ....23 J5
  SEV TN13 ....149 H8
  STH/RUST TN4 ....240 C5
Prospect Rw CHAT ME4 ....6 D1
Prospect St BERM/RHTH SE16 ...24 E5
Prospect Ter WOOL/PLUM SE18 ...27 F5
Prospect Wy RASHE TN25 ......284 F2
Provender La HYTHE CT21 ......131 L7
Provender Wk FAV ME13 * 132 C5
Provender Wy
  MAID/BEAR ME14 ....156 A3
Providence Sq STHWK SE1 * 24 D5

Providence St ASH TN23 ......252 F9
GRH DA9 ......47 N6
Provincial Ter PGE/AN SE20 * 61 K6
Prusom St WAP E1W 24 C4
Puckle La CANT CT1 ......166 F6
Puddingcake La CRBK TN17 ......320 A1
Pudding La MAID/BEAR ME14 ......12 E4
MON EC5R 24 A5
RCANTE CT3 ......200 E1
Pudding Rd RHAM ME8 ......97 J6
Puddledock La
BH/WHM TN16 ......177 H8
RDART DA2 ......65 N4
Puffin Cl CROY/NA CR0 ......84 A2
Puffin Rd CT6 ......108 B6
HOO/HM ME3 ......5 L3
Pullman Ct MSTR CT12 ......143 H3
Pullman Ms LEE/GVPK SE12 ......62 F2
Pullman Pl ELTH/MOT SE9 ......43 J6
Puma Ct WCHPL E1 ......24 C1
Pump Cl E/WMAL ME19 ......153 L3
Pump House La MAID/BEAR ME14 ......24 D8
Pump House Ms WCHPL E1 * 24 D8
Pump La ABYV CT2 ......24 D1
NWCR SE14 ......41 J1
RHAM ME8 ......96 C3
Punch Crt HART DA3 ......91 H7
Purbeck Rd CHAT ME4 ......95 K4
Purbrook Est STHWK SE1 * 24 B5
Purbrook La RASHW TN26 ......281 K1
Purdake Ms LEW SE13 * 42 B4
Purfleet By-Pass PUR RM19 ......30 F8
Purfleet Deep Whf
PUR RM19 ......30 F9
Purfleet Rd SOCK/AV RM15 ......30 E4
Purland Rd THMD SE28 ......27 N5
Purley Wy CROY/NA CR0 ......82 C5
Purneys Rd ELTH/MOT SE9 ......43 H5
Purrett Rd WOOL/PLUM SE18 ......27 N8
Purser Wy GILL ME7 ......73 J8
Puttenden Rd RTON TN11 ......181 J9
Puttney Dr SIT ME10 ......99 P6
Pye Alley La WSTB CT5 ......135 K2
Pymers Md DUL SE21 ......40 C9
Pym Pl GRAYS RM17 ......32 B7
Pyott Ms CANT CT1 ......5 H2
Pyrmont Gv WNWD SE27 ......60 B2
Pyrus Cl WALD 125 M5
Pyson's Rd MSTR CT12 ......143 H2
Pytchley Crs NRWD SE19 ......60 C5
Pytchley Rd EDUL SE22 ......40 E4

Quadrangle Cl STHWK SE1 * 24 B7
The Quadrangle HNHL SE24 * 40 C6
Quadrant Rd THHTH CR7 ......82 G1
The Quadrant BXLYHN DA7 ......30 D7
PUR RM19 ......30 F7
Quaggy Wk BKHTH/KID SE3 ......42 E5
Quail Gdns CROY/NA CR0 ......114 B4
Quaker Cl SEV TN13 ......148 J8
Quaker Dr CRBK TN17 ......298 A1
Quaker La CRBK TN17 ......298 A1
Quakers Ct HART DA3 ......68 D9
Quaker's Hall La SEV TN13 ......148 H7
Quantock Cl RTWE/PEM TN2 ......23 K1
Quantock Dr BFN/LL TN4 ......
Quantock Gdns MSTR CT12 ......142 C1
Quantock Ms PECK SE15 ......40 G3
Quantock Rd BXLYHN DA7 ......45 N5
The Quarries RMAID ME17 ......185 P7
Quarrington La RASHE TN25 ......254 A9
Quarry Bank TON TN9 ......240 D2
Quarry Cl OXTED RH8 ......175 H6
Quarry HI BGR/WK ME7 ......149 J8
GRAYS RM17 ......32 B8
Quarry Hill Rd BGR/WK ME7 ......149 J8
TON TN9 ......240 E1
Quarry Ms PUR RM19 ......30 D7
Quarry Ri EGRIN RH19 ......265 K5
TON TN9 ......240 D2
Quarry Rd HYTHE CT21 ......308 C4
MAID/SHEP ME15 ......185 M1
OXTED RH8 ......175 H6
RTW TN1 ......23 F1
Quarry Sq MAID/BEAR ME14 ......13 F2
Quarry Vw ASH TN23 ......282 A1
E/WMAL ME19 ......152 D5
Quarry Wk HYTHE CT21 ......
Quarry Wy WTHK RM20 ......31 J9
Quarry Wd RASHE TN25 ......306 B1
Quay House POP/IOD E14 ......25 K5
Quay La GRH DA9 ......47 P5
SWCH CT13 ......73 H7
Quayside CHAT ME4 ......73 H7
Quebec Av BH/WHM TN16 ......176 E2
Quebec Rd TIL RM18 ......49 L3
Quebec Sq BH/WHM TN16 ......176 E2
Quebec Wy DVE/WH CT16 ......291 J4
Quebec Wy BERM/RHTH SE16 ......24 C5
Queen Adelaide Rd
PGE/AN SE20 ......61 J5
Queen Anne Av BXLYHN DA7 ......44 F4
Queen Anne Rd
MAID/BEAR ME14 ......13 H4
Queen Anne Ter WAP E1W * 24 E5
Queen Bertha Rd RAM CT11 ......16 B5
Queen Bertha's Av
MANHG CT6 ......94 C2
Queenborough Dr IOS ME12 ......58 B9
Queenborough Gdns
CHST BR7 ......45 L4
Queenborough Rd IOS ME12 ......77 L1
Queendown Av RHAM ME8 ......96 G9
Queendown Rd BRCH CT7 ......111 N9

Queen Elizabeth Av
MARG CT9 ......113 J4
TIL RM18 ......34 B7
Queen Elizabeth II Br
WTHK RM20 ......47 L3
Queen Elizabeth Rd
DVE/WH CT16 ......9 C3
Queen Elizabeth's Dr
CROY/NA CR0 ......114 C4
Queen Elizabeth Sq
MAID/SHEP ME15 ......186 A5
Queen Elizabeth St
STHWK SE1 ......24 C5
Queen Elizabeth's Wk
WLGTN SM6 ......82 C8
Queen Mary Av TIL RM18 ......34 B7
Queen Mary Rd NRWD SE19 ......60 B5
The Queen Mother Ct
ROCH ME1 ......94 G2
Queen's Av BRCH CT7 ......110 E6
BRDST CT10 ......113 N7
CANT/W/ST CT2 ......
FOLK CT20 ......290 G8
HB CT6 ......108 A5
MAIDW ME16 ......12 A2
MARG CT9 ......15 G6
MSTR CT12 ......142 G3
SNOD ME6 ......123 P5
Queensbridge Dr HB CT6 ......107 H1
Queen's Cl WLGTN SM6 ......82 A9
Queens Cl HAWK TN18 ......317 J4
KEN/WIL TN24 ......2 E2
MARG CT9 ......112 F2
Queenscroft Rd
ELTH/MOT SE9 ......43 H6
Queensdown Rd DEAL CT14 ......263 H4
Queen's Farm Rd CVE DA12 ......149 H5
Queen's Gdns DVE/WH CT16 ......8 D5
HB CT6 ......107 L1
RDART DA2 ......47 H9
STH/RUST TN4 ......22 C6
Queens Garth FSTH SE23 * 61 J1
Queens Gate Gdns CHST BR7 ......63 P7
Queen's Gate Rd RAM CT11 ......16 C2
Queens House MAIDW ME16 ......154 F9
Queen's Mead Rd HAYES BR2 ......62 D8
Queens Ms DEAL CT14 ......233 J5
FOLK CT20 * 310 A8
Queens Pde FAV ME13 * 132 G6
MARG CT9 ......112 F2
Queen's Ri BDEAL CT14 ......262 E5
Queen's Rd BECK BR3 ......61 L8
BMLY BR1 ......62 E8
BRDST CT10 ......113 N9
CHST BR7 ......63 M5
CROY/NA CR0 ......82 G3
EGRIN RH19 ......265 J8
ERITH DA8 ......29 K9
FAV ME13 ......132 E6
GILL ME7 ......7 J3
CVE DA12 ......69 N2
HAWK TN18 ......317 J4
IOS ME12 ......2 E2
KEN/WIL TN24 ......253 K8
LYDD TN29 ......342 B6
NROM TN28 ......337 H7
PECK SE15 ......41 J2
RAM CT11 ......17 J2
RCANTE CT3 ......170 E9
RCANTE CT3 ......229 J1
SNOD ME6 ......123 P5
STH/RUST TN4 ......270 E2
WALD ME5 ......96 A5
WELL DA16 ......44 D3
WGOS CT8 ......111 N5
WLGTN SM6 ......82 A9
Queens Rd Upper
KEN/WIL TN24 ......2 D1
Queens Rw WALW SE17 ......24 H8
Queensthorpe Ms SYD SE26 * 61 K3
Queensthorpe Rd SYD SE26 ......61 K5
Queen St ASH TN23 ......2 D4
BXLYHN DA7 ......45 H4
CHAT ME4 ......6 D4
CROY/NA CR0 ......85 H9
DEAL CT14 ......233 J5
DVE/WH CT16 ......8 D4
E/WMAL ME19 ......153 H9
ERITH DA8 ......29 K9
FOLK CT20 ......11 G3
GVE DA12 ......49 M7
HAWK TN18 ......318 C9
HB CT6 ......107 L1
MARG CT9 ......15 F5
RAM CT11 ......17 F5
ROCH ME1 ......19 G7
STPH/PW TN12 ......243 K4
Queen's Wy IOS ME12 ......57 J8
MAID/BEAR ME14 ......156 C3
Queensway EGRIN RH19 ......265 H7
HOO/HM ME3 ......38 E8
LYDD TN29 ......327 H4
STMC/STPC BR5 ......86 E2
WWKM BR4 ......85 K8
Queenswood Av THHTH CR7 ......82 F2
WLGTN SM6 ......82 C8
Queenswood Rd
BFN/LL DA15 ......44 B7
DIT/AY ME20 ......125 J6
FSTH SE23 ......61 L2
Queen Victoria Rw
DVE/WH CT16 * 8 C3
Queen Victoria St
MANHG CT6 ......24 A2
Queen Victoria Ter WAP E1W * 24 E5
Quentin Pl LEW SE13 ......42 C4
Quentin Rd BKHTH/KID SE3 ......42 C4
Quentins Dr BH/WHM TN16 * 146 C1
Quentins Wk
BH/WHM TN16 * 146 C1

Quernmore Cl BMLY BR1 ......62 E5
Quernmore Rd BMLY BR1 ......62 E5
Quern Rd DEAL CT14 ......232 F7
Querns Pl CANT CT1 ......5 J4
Querns Rd CANT CT1 ......5 J4
The Quern MAID/SHEP ME15 ......185 K2
Quested Rd FOLKN CT19 ......310 D5
Quested Wy RMAID ME17 ......188 D1
Questor DART DA1 * 66 F1
Quetta Rd MSTR CT12 ......142 E3
Quex Rd WGOS CT8 ......111 N5
Quex View Rd BRCH CT7 ......111 H8
Quickbourne La RYE TN31 ......330 B6
Quickrells Av HOO/HM ME3 ......52 B3
Quickstep Cl SIT ME10 ......99 N6
Quickthorn Crs WALD ME5 ......95 K9
Quiet Nook HAYES BR2 ......85 N7
Quilter Rd STMC/STPC BR5 ......87 K5
Quilter St WOOL/PLUM SE18 ......27 N8
Quince Orch RASHW TN26 ......304 D7
Quince Rd LEW SE13 ......41 P3
Quincewood Gdns
TONN TN10 ......210 E3
Quinion Cl MAID ME5 ......125 L5
Quinnell St RHAM ME8 ......97 H5
Quixley St POP/IOD E14 ......25 N5
Quixote Crs STRD ME2 ......72 B6
Quorn Rd EDUL SE22 ......40 E5

R

Rabbit Hole RCANTW CT4 ......228 D7
Rabbits Rd RYE TN31 ......67 M8
Rablus Pl EYN DA4 * 89 L3
Raby St POP/IOD E14 ......25 H2
Racecourse Rd LING RH7 ......235 J6
Racefield Cl CVE DA12 ......70 G5
Rackham Cl WELL DA16 ......44 D3
Radcliffe Rd CROY/NA CR0 ......83 L6
STHWK SE1 ......24 B6
Radfall Ride WSTB CT5 ......106 B9
Radfall Rd WSTB CT5 ......106 B8
Radfield Wy ELTH/MOT SE9 ......43 P8
Radford Rd LEW SE13 ......42 F5
Radland Rd CAN/RD E16 ......26 D2
Radleigh Gdns CHAT ME4 ......95 K5
Radlet Av SYD SE26 ......61 H2
Radley Cl BRDST CT10 ......113 M7
Radley Cr BERM/RHTH SE16 ......24 G5
Radley Ter CAN/RD E16 ......26 A1
Radnor Av WELL DA16 ......44 D6
Radnor Bridge Rd FOLK CT20 ......11 G5
Radnor Cliff FOLK CT20 ......11 G6
Radnor Cliff Crs FOLK CT20 ......310 C8
Radnor Cl CHST BR7 ......64 A5
HB CT6 ......107 N5
MTCM CR4 ......61 H9
Radnor Crs WOOL/PLUM SE18 ......44 C1
Radnor Park Av FOLKN CT19 ......10 D2
Radnor Park Crs FOLKN CT19 ......10 D2
Radnor Park Gdns FOLKN CT19 ......10 D2
Radnor Park Rd FOLKN CT19 ......10 D3
Radnor Pk West FOLKN CT19 ......10 D3
Radnor Rd PECK SE15 ......41 J2
Radnor St FOLKN CT19 ......11 H4
Radnor Wk CROY/NA CR0 ......84 B4
Raeburn Av DART DA1 ......46 B6
Raeburn Cl TONN TN10 ......211 H4
Raeburn Rd BFN/LL DA15 ......44 A7
Rafford Wy BMLY BR1 ......62 G8
Raggatt Pl MAID/SHEP ME15 ......185 N1
Ragge Wy BGR/WK TN15 ......149 L5
Ragglesworth CHST BR7 ......63 L7
Rag Hill Rd BH/WHM TN16 ......145 N6
Raglan Ct CROY/NA CR0 ......82 G9
Raglan Rd BELV DA17 ......28 F6
HAYES BR2 ......85 M1
WOOL/PLUM SE18 ......27 K8
Ragstone Ct DIT/AY ME20 ......154 B4
Ragstone Hollow
RASHE TN25 ......306 B1
Ragstone Rd
MAID/SHEP ME15 ......186 D2
Railton Rd HNHL SE24 ......40 A6
Railway Ap EGRIN RH19 ......264 C7
Railway Ar BRXN/ST SW9 ......40 A5
Railway Ar BERM/RHTH SE16 ......24 F7
Railway HI RCANTW CT4 ......228 D3
Railway Pl BELV DA17 ......28 F6
Railway Ri EDUL SE22 ......40 D5
Railway St CHAT ME4 ......6 B5
GILL ME7 ......7 J3
GVW DA11 ......48 E6
Railway Ter BH/WHM TN16 ......176 E1
LEW SE13 ......41 P6
MARG CT9 ......14 G6
OBOR ME11 ......77 J2
Rainbow Av POP/IOD E14 ......25 L8
Rainbow La SH/COR SS17 ......34 F1
Rainbow Rd CDW/CHF RM16 ......31 N7
MAID/SHEP ME15 ......185 M2
Rainham Rd GILL ME7 ......7 H7
Rainham Vls STPH/PW TN12 ......214 F6
Rainsborough Av DEPT SE8 ......25 H7
Rainton Rd CHARL SE7 ......26 B6
Raleana Rd POP/IOD E14 ......25 M4
Raleigh Av WLGTN SM6 ......82 C8
Raleigh Cl ERITH DA8 ......29 L9
Raleigh Ct BECK BR3 ......61 M1

Raleigh Ms ORP BR6 ......86 G9
Raleigh Rd PGE/AN SE20 ......61 K6
Raleigh Wy IOS ME12 ......57 N1
Ralph Perring Ct BECK BR3 ......84 D1
Ramac Wy CHARL SE7 ......26 C7
Ramillies Cl WALD ME5 ......95 M9
Ramillies Rd BFN/LL DA15 ......44 D7
Ram La RASHW TN26 ......251 H1
Rammell Ms CHART SE17 ......298 A3
Ramones Ter MTCM CR4 * 82 B1
Rampart St WCHPL E1 ......24 E2
Rampion Cl MAID/BEAR ME14 ......156 D7
Ramsden Cl STMC/STPC BR5 ......87 K5
Ramsden La CRBK TN17 * 318 F2
Ramsden Rd ERITH DA8 ......45 M1
ORP BR6 ......87 J4
Ramsey Cl CANTW/ST CT2 ......4 B2
Ramsey Rd THHTH CR7 ......82 E8
Ramsgate Rd BRDST CT10 ......143 L2
MARG CT9 ......15 H7
SWCH CT13 ......171 P4
Ramslye Rd STH/RUST TN4 ......270 A4
Ramstone Cl RASHE TN25 ......284 F5
Ramus Wood Av ORP BR6 ......86 F9
Rancliffe Gdns ELTH/MOT SE9 ......43 J5
Rancorn Rd MARG CT9 ......14 B6
Randall Cl ERITH DA8 ......29 H9
Randall Gdns GVW DA11 ......49 K8
Randall Pl GNWCH SE10 ......42 A2
Randall Rd CHAT ME4 ......95 K5
Randall St MAID/BEAR ME14 ......12 E1
Randisbourne Gdns CAT SE6 * 61 P2
Randlesdown Rd CAT SE6 ......61 N3
Randle Wy ASH TN23 ......282 A5
Randolph Ap CAN/RD E16 ......26 D2
Randolph Cl BXLYHN DA7 ......45 L4
ORP BR6 ......166 F6
Randolph Gdns
KEN/WIL TN24 ......253 H4
Randolph La RYE TN31 ......338 D1
Randolph Rd DVW CT17 ......291 H6
GILL ME7 ......7 J3
HAYES BR2 ......86 A3
Randolph Sq MARG CT9 * 15 J5
Ranelagh Gdns GVW DA11 ......49 K8
Ranelagh Gv CAT SE6 ......113 K8
Ranelagh Rd DEAL CT14 ......233 J4
IOS ME12 ......57 J6
Rangefield Rd BMLY BR1 ......62 G8
Range Rd GVE DA12 ......49 P8
HYTHE CT21 ......308 C7
IOS ME12 ......79 K6
Rangeworth Pl BFN/LL DA15 ......64 B2
Rangoon St TWRH EC3N * 24 C2
Rankine Rd RTWE/PEM TN2 ......270 C1
Ranleigh Gdns BXLYHN DA7 ......45 H1
Ranmore Av CROY/NA CR0 ......84 A1
Ranmore Pth STMC/STPC BR5 ......87 H1
Ranscombe Cl STRD ME2 * 72 A2
Ransom Rd CHARL SE7 * 26 D8
Ranters La CRBK TN17 ......295 P5
Ranworth Cl ERITH DA8 ......45 N3
Raphael Av TIL RM18 ......49 L2
Raphael Dr SIT ME10 ......99 N2
Rapier Cl PUR RM19 ......30 E8
Rashleigh Wy EYN DA4 ......89 P1
Raspberry Hill La RSLP ME9 ......76 E9
Ratcliffe Cl LEE/GVPK SE12 ......42 E8
Ratcliffe Cross St WCHPL E1 * 24 C2
Ratcliffe Hwy HOO/HM ME3 ......51 H2
Ratcliffe La POP/IOD E14 ......25 H2
Rathbone Sq CROY/NA CR0 * 83 H8
Rathbone St CAN/RD E16 ......26 A1
Rathfern Rd CAT SE6 ......61 M9
Rathgar Rd BRXN/ST SW9 ......40 B4
Rathmore Rd CHARL SE7 ......26 C6
GVW DA11 ......49 L8
Ratling Rd RCANTE CT3 ......199 K9
Rattington St RCANTW CT4 ......195 L1
Rattray Rd BRXS/STRHM SW2 ......40 A5
Raul Rd PECK SE15 ......41 J2
Ravel Gdns SOCK/AV RM15 ......30 F2
Ravel Rd SOCK/AV RM15 ......30 G2
Raven Cl DIT/AY ME20 ......153 P5
Ravenbourne Av BECK BR3 ......61 N9
Ravenbourne Pk BROCKY SE4 ......41 N9
Raven Rw WCHPL E1 ......24 E1
Ravensbourne Park Crs
CAT SE6 ......41 M8
Ravensbourne Pl DEPT SE8 ......41 P5
Ravensbourne Rd BMLY BR1 ......62 E9
CAT SE6 ......41 M8
DART DA1 ......46 A4
Ravensbury Rd
STMC/STPC BR5 ......86 G1
Ravenscar Rd BMLY BR1 ......62 C3
Ravens Cl HAYES BR2 ......62 D8
Ravenscourt Rd
CANTW/ST CT2 ......166 A1
DEAL CT14 ......233 H4
STMC/STPC BR5 ......64 G9
Ravenscroft Cl CAN/RD E16 ......26 B1
Ravenscroft Rd BECK BR3 ......61 J8
CAN/RD E16 ......26 B1
Ravens Dane Cl
MAID/SHEP ME15 ......186 D2
Ravenshill CHST BR7 ......63 M7
Ravensmead Rd HAYES BR2 ......62 B6
Ravens Ms BKHTH/KID SE3 * 42 E6
Ravens Wy LEE/GVPK SE12 ......42 E6
Ravenswood BXLY DA5 ......45 M6
Ravenswood Av
RTWE/PEM TN2 ......270 F2
STRD ME2 ......72 B7
WWKM BR4 ......84 F5
Ravenswood Crs WWKM BR4 ......84 F5
Ravenswood Rd CROY/NA CR0 ......82 G7
Ravensworth Rd
ELTH/MOT SE9 ......63 K5
WOOL/PLUM SE18 ......35 J5
Ravine Gv WOOL/PLUM SE18 ......27 M9

Rawdon Rd MAID/SHEP ME15 ......13 G7
RAM CT11 ......16 A5
Rawlings Cl BECK BR3 ......84 F2
ORP BR6 ......86 G9
Rawling St RSIT ME9 ......129 N9
Rawlins Cl SAND/SEL CR2 ......114 C2
Rawson Cl CDW/CHF RM16 ......31 M8
Rawsthorne Cl CAN/RD E16 ......26 C4
Ray Bell Ct BROCKY SE4 * 41 M5
Rayfield Cl HAYES BR2 ......85 P3
Rayfield Ct SNOD ME6 ......123 P4
Rayford Av LEE/GVPK SE12 ......42 D8
Rayford Cl DART DA1 ......46 C6
Rayham Rd WSTB CT5 ......105 P6
Rayford St THHTH CR7 ......82 F2
Rayleas Cl WOOL/PLUM SE18 ......43 M2
Rayleigh Cl MAID ME16 ......155 J5
Rayleigh Rd CAN/RD E16 ......26 C4
Raymead Av THHTH CR7 ......82 F2
Raymere Gdns
WOOL/PLUM SE18 ......43 P1
Raymer Rd MAID/BEAR ME14 ......155 N6
Raymond Av CANT CT1 ......5 G7
Raymond Cl SYD SE26 ......61 K5
Raymond Fuller Wy
KEN/WIL TN24 ......253 H5
Raymond Rd BECK BR3 ......84 B1
Raymoor Av LYDD TN29 ......337 M1
Raymouth Rd
BERM/RHTH SE16 ......24 E7
Rayners HI RMAID ME17 ......190 A1
Rays HI EYN DA4 ......89 P1
Rays Rd WWKM BR4 ......84 F4
Reach Cl RDV CT15 ......292 E2
Reachfields HYTHE CT21 ......308 F6
Reach Rd HYTHE CT21 ......307 L5
RDV CT15 ......292 E2
Reader's Bridge Rd
TENT TN30 ......300 C3
Readers La RYE TN31 ......332 C8
Reading Cl DEAL CT14 ......232 G8
Reading Rd DVW CT17 ......290 G8
Reading St BRDST CT10 ......113 L5
TENT TN30 ......321 M3
Reading Street Rd
BRDST CT10 ......113 K5
Readscroft Rd RHAM ME8 ......96 G9
Reardon Pth WAP E1W * 24 D4
Reardon St WAP E1W 24 E4
The Rear STH/RUST TN4 * 22 C6
Reaston St NWCR SE14 ......41 J1
Recce La RFOLK CT18 ......258 D9
Record St PECK SE15 ......24 G9
Recreation Av SNOD ME6 ......123 P5
Recreation Cl
MAID/BEAR ME14 ......13 H1
Recreation Ground Rd
TENT TN30 ......301 J8
Recreation Rd HAYES BR2 ......62 D8
SYD SE26 ......61 K3
Recreation Wy SIT ME10 ......99 N5
Rectory Cl DART DA1 ......45 N5
RASHW TN26 ......302 F5
ROCH ME1 ......94 B9
SCUP DA14 ......64 D3
SNOD ME6 ......123 P5
Rectory Dr STH/RUST TN4 ......239 P6
Rectory Field Crs CHARL SE7 ......42 C1
Rectory Flds CRBK TN17 ......298 F4
Rectory Gdns BECK BR3 * 61 N7
CHST BR7 ......63 N7
WSTB CT5 ......106 C4
Rectory Gra ROCH ME1 ......95 H4
Rectory Gv CROY/NA CR0 ......82 G5
Rectory La BGR/WK TN15 ......150 F7
BH/WHM TN16 ......145 P8
BH/WHM TN16 ......147 K9
HYTHE CT21 ......308 C3
MAIDW ME16 ......12 A2
RCANTW CT4 ......228 D5
RFOLK CT18 ......287 H2
RMAID ME17 ......188 F6
RMAID ME17 ......216 F4
RYE TN31 ......330 E8
RYE TN31 ......338 E4
SCUP DA14 ......64 D5
SEV TN13 ......21 G5
WLGTN SM6 ......82 B8
Rectory La North
E/WMAL ME19 ......153 L2
Rectory La South
E/WMAL ME19 ......153 M2
Rectory Meadow MEO DA13 ......68 E5
Rectory Park Rd
STPH/PW TN12 ......273 P6
Rectory Pl CHST BR7 ......63 N7
WOOL/PLUM SE18 ......27 H7
Rectory Rd BECK BR3 ......61 N7
BGR/WK TN15 ......111 M9
BRDST CT10 ......113 N8
CDW/CHF RM16 ......33 J1
DEAL CT14 ......232 E5
GRAYS RM17 ......32 E6
HAYES BR2 ......115 N2
HOO/HM ME3 ......52 A6
LYDD TN29 ......325 P9
SIT ME10 ......130 A2
SWCM DA10 ......48 C8
TIL RM18 ......33 L1
Rectory Sq WCHPL E1 ......24 G1
Rectory Wy KEN/WIL TN24 ......252 F4
Reculver Av BRCH CT7 ......111 M7
Reculver Cl HB CT6 ......108 C4
Reculver Dr HB CT6 ......108 B3
Reculver La HB CT6 ......108 D5
Reculver Rd
BERM/RHTH SE16 ......24 G7
HB CT6 ......107 P2
Reculvers Rd WGOS CT8 ......111 N6
Redan Pl IOS ME12 ......57 M6
Redan Ter CMBW SE5 ......40 B5
Redbank E/WMAL ME19 ......153 M2

Red Barracks Rd
  WOOL/PLUM SE18.....................26 J7
Redberry Gv *SYD* SE26.....................61 J2
Redberry Rd *ASH* TN23.....................282 E3
Redbourne Dr *THMD* SE28.....................28 C2
Redbridge Cl *WALD* ME5 *.....................95 N5
Redbridge Gdns *CMBW* SE5.....................40 E1
Redbrook St *RASHW* TN26.....................280 B9
Redbrooks Wy *HYTHE* CT21.....................308 E4
Redcar St *CMBW* SE5 *.....................40 C1
Redcastle Cl *WCHPL* E1.....................24 F5
Red Cedars Rd *ORP* BR6.....................86 F4
Redcliffe La
  MAID/BEAR ME14.....................155 N5
Redcot La *RCANTE* CT4.....................137 N6
Redding Cl *RDART* DA2.....................67 L1
Reddins Rd *BECK* BR3.....................40 G1
Reddons Rd *BECK* BR3.....................61 L6
Reddy Rd *ERITH* DA8.....................29 L9
Rede Court Rd *STRD* ME2.....................71 N7
Rede Wood Rd *MAIDW* ME16.....................154 D9
Redfern Av *GILL* ME7.....................96 B9
Redfern Rd *CAT* SE6.....................42 A8
Redford Av *THHTH* CR7.....................82 E1
Redgarth Ct *EGRIN* RH19.....................264 E5
Redgate Dr *HAYES* BR2.....................85 L6
Redgrave Ct *SNWD* SE25.....................83 L5
Red HI *CHST* BR7.....................63 L4
  WBY/YAL ME18.....................183 M5
Redhill Rd *BGR/WK* TN15.....................91 H8
  WGOS CT8.....................111 L5
Redhill Wd *HART* DA3.....................91 K8
Red House Gdns
  WBY/YAL ME18.....................183 L4
Red House La *RCANTW* CT4.....................196 D3
Redhouse La *BH/WHM* TN16.....................145 M6
Red House Rd *CROY/NA* CRO.....................22 C3
Redhouse Wall *DEAL* CT14.....................202 G9
Redland Shaw *ROCH* ME1.....................95 K5
Redlands Rd *SEV* TN15.....................20 B2
Red La *OXTED* RH8.....................175 L9
  OXTED RH8.....................205 L3
Redleaf Cl *BELV* DA17.....................28 F9
  RTWE/PEM TN2.....................270 C2
Red Lion Ct *STRM/STPC* BR5.....................87 K3
  WALW SE17.....................24 A9
Red Lion La *WOOL/PLUM* SE18.....................43 L2
Red Lion Pl
  WOOL/PLUM SE18 *.....................43 L7
Red Lodge Crs *BXLY* DA5.....................65 M2
Red Lodge Rd *BXLY* DA5.....................65 M2
  WWKM BR4.....................84 F5
Redmans La *SEV* TN14.....................118 E1
Redman's Rd *WCHPL* E1.....................24 F1
Redmead La *WAP* E1W.....................24 D4
Redmill Cl *FOLK* CT20.....................310 B6
Red Oak Cl *ORP* BR6.....................86 C7
Redoubt Wy *LYDD* TN29.....................327 L2
Redpoll Wk *STPH/PW* TN12.....................243 H4
Redpoll Wy *ERITHM* DA18.....................28 C6
Red Post HI *HNHL* SE24.....................40 D6
Redriff Rd *BERM/RHTH* SE16.....................25 H6
Redroofs Cl *BECK* BR3.....................51 N1
Redsells Cl *MAID/SHEP* ME15.....................186 D2
Redshank Rd *CHAT* ME4.....................72 C6
Redstart Cl *CROY/NA* CRO.....................114 G4
  EHAM E6.....................26 F1
  NWCR SE14 *.....................41 L1
Red St *MEO* CT15.....................68 F5
Redsull Av *DEAL* CT14.....................232 F6
Red Tree Orch *ASH* TN23.....................282 B1
Redvers Rd *CHAT* ME4.....................95 M4
  WALW CR6.....................144 A3
Redwall La *MAIDE* ME17.....................214 C3
Redwell Gv *E/WMAL* ME19.....................183 K1
Redwell Rd *BGR/WK* TN15.....................150 E8
Redwing Cl *SAND/SEL* CR2.....................114 A5
Redwing Ct *ORP* BR6.....................87 H4
Redwing Ms *CMBW* SE5.....................40 C7
Redwing Rd *WALD* ME5.....................95 N8
Redwings La *RTWE/PEM* TN2.....................241 N7
Redwood Cl *BERM/RHTH* SE16.....................25 H4
  BFN/LL DA15.....................44 C9
  CANTW/ST CT2.....................
  WALD ME5.....................125 N3
Redwood Pk *BRXN* TN11.....................242 B4
Redyear Ct *KEN/WIL* TN24 *.....................253 K8
Reed Av *CANT* CT1.....................167 H2
  ORP BR6.....................86 F7
Reed Cl *BCAN/RD* E16.....................26 B1
  LEE/GVPK SE12.....................42 G8
Reed Crs *ASH* TN23.....................282 F5
Reedham Crs *HOO/HM* ME3.....................52 C9
Reedham St *PECK* SE15 *.....................40 C3
Reedland Crs *FAV* ME13.....................132 F5
Reedmace Cl *ASH* TN23.....................282 F5
Reeds Cl *HB* CT6.....................107 N2
Reeds La *RTON* TN11.....................181 H6
Reed St *HOO/HM* ME3.....................52 B2
Rees Gdns *CROY/NA* CRO.....................83 L3
Reeves Cl *STPH/PW* TN12.....................246 H5
Reeves Cnr *CROY/NA* CRO.....................82 G6
Reeves Ct *DIT/AY* ME20.....................153 P9
Reeves Crs *SWLY* BR8.....................65 M9
Reeves Rd *WOOL/PLUM* SE18.....................27 J9
Reeves Ter *WALD* ME5.....................315 J5
Reeves Wy *WSTB* CT5.....................106 B5
Reform Rd *CHAT* ME4.....................7 F7
Regal Cl *WCHPL* E1.....................24 D1
Regal Crs *WLGTN* SM6.....................62 A7
Regal Dr *EGRIN* RH19.....................265 J8
  RHAM ME8.....................126 F2
Regency Ct *SIT* ME10.....................129 L1
Regency Ms *BECK* BR3.....................62 A7
Regency Pl *CANT* CT1.....................5 J1
Regency Rd *CROY/NA* CRO.....................84 B5
Regency Wy *BXLYHN* DA7.....................44 F4
Regeneration
  BERM/RHTH SE16 *.....................24 C7
Regent Cl *CDW/CHF* RM16.....................32 D5
Regent Dr *MAID/SHEP* ME15.....................185 M3
Regent Pl *RTWE/PEM* TN2 *.....................23 J4

Regent Rd *GILL* ME7.....................7 G4
  HNHL SE24.....................40 B7
Regents Ct *ASH* TN23.....................2 C3
Regents Dr *HAYES* BR2.....................85 N9
Regents Pl *ASH* TN23.....................2 C3
Regent Sq *CRBK* TN17.....................319 L5
  WSTB CT5.....................105 L4
Regent Wy *E/WMAL* ME19.....................153 K9
Reginald Av *STRD* ME2.....................94 B3
Reginald Rd *DEPT* SE8.....................41 L6
  MAIDW ME16.....................12 C7
Reginald Sq *DEPT* SE8.....................41 N1
Regina Rd *SNWD* SE25.....................60 C9
Regis Crs *SIT* ME10.....................99 N7
Reidhaven Rd
  WOOL/PLUM SE18.....................27 M7
Reigate Rd *BMLY* BR1.....................62 E1
Reigate Wy *WLGTN* SM6.....................82 D9
Reinden Gv *MAID/SHEP* ME15.....................186 C2
Relf Rd *PECK* SE15.....................40 C4
Reliance Ar *BRXN/ST* SW9 *.....................40 A5
Rembrandt Cl *POP/IOD* E14.....................25 N6
  TONN TN10.....................211 H4
Rembrandt Dr *GVW* DA11.....................69 H2
Rembrandt Rd *LEW* SE13.....................42 G5
Remington Rd *EHAM* E6.....................26 C4
Remus Cl *ASH* TN23.....................282 C4
Rendezvous St *FOLK* CT20.....................15 C3
The Rendezvous *MARC* CT9.....................15 G3
Rendle Cl *CROY/NA* CRO.....................83 L2
Renforth St *BERM/RHTH* SE16.....................24 F7
Renfrew Cl *EHAM* E6.....................26 E7
Rennell St *LEW* SE13.....................42 A4
Rennets Cl *ELTH/MOT* SE9.....................43 P6
Rennets Wood Rd
  ELTH/MOT SE9.....................43 P6
Rennie Est *BERM/RHTH* SE16.....................24 E7
Renown Cl *CROY/NA* CRO.....................82 G5
Renown Rd *WALD* ME5.....................125 P5
Renshaw Cl *BELV* DA17.....................28 E9
Rentain Rd *RCANTW* CT4.....................195 L1
Renton Dr *STRM/STPC* BR5 *.....................87 L4
Rephidim St *STHWK* SE1.....................24 B6
Repository Rd
  WOOL/PLUM SE18.....................26 C9
Repton Cl *BRDST* CT10.....................113 L7
Repton Ct *BECK* BR3.....................51 P7
Repton Manor Rd *ASH* TN23.....................2 A1
Repton Rd *ORP* BR6.....................87 H8
Repton St *POP/IOD* E14.....................25 P2
Repton Wy *WALD* ME5.....................125 L1
Reservoir Av *LGHD* TN29.....................347 L5
Reservoir Cl *GRH* DA9.....................68 D7
  THHTH CR7.....................60 D9
Reservoir Rd *BROCKY* SE4.....................41 L1
  WSTB CT5.....................105 M4
Resolution Cl *WALD* ME5.....................95 M3
Resolution Wy *DEPT* SE8.....................41 L6
Resteil Cl *BXHTH/KID* SE3.....................25 P9
Rest Harrow *FAV* ME13.....................162 F7
Restharrow Rd
  MAID/BEAR ME14.....................156 B8
Restmore Wy *CHAT* ME4.....................75 J3
Restmore Cl *HOO/HM* ME3.....................52 A4
Restons Crs *ELTH/MOT* SE9.....................43 P7
Reston Wy *CAN/RD* E16.....................26 E3
The Retreat *BRCH* CT7.....................111 J5
  GRAYS RM17.....................32 C9
  MSTR CT12.....................142 G4
  ORP BR6.....................117 J1
  SEV TN13 *.....................21 G2
  THHTH CR7.....................60 C3
Rettendon Dr *SIT* ME10.....................99 N6
Reunion Rw *WAP* E1W *.....................24 E3
Reveley Sq *BERM/RHTH* SE16.....................25 H5
Revell Ri *WOOL/PLUM* SE18.....................27 N9
Revelon Rd *BROCKY* SE4.....................41 L5
Revenge Rd
  MAID/BEAR ME14.....................125 P5
Reventlow Rd *ELTH/MOT* SE9.....................43 N9
Reverdy Rd *STHWK* SE1.....................24 D7
Reynard Cl *BMLY* BR1.....................63 K9
Reynard Pl *NRWD* SE19.....................60 F6
Reynard Pl *NWCR* SE14 *.....................25 P5
Reynolds Cl *HB* CT6.....................107 N2
  TONN TN10.....................211 H4
Reynolds Flds *HOO/HM* ME3.....................71 L1
Reynolds La *RCANTE* CT3.....................108 F7
  STH/RUST TN4.....................
Reynolds Rd *CROY/NA* CRO.....................83 K8
Rhee Wall *RASHW* TN26.....................322 F7
Rheims Ct *CANTW/ST* CT2.....................166 C5
Rheims Wy *CANTW/ST* CT2.....................4 A5
Rhodaus Cl *CANT* CT1.....................4 E6
Rhodaus Town *CANT* CT1.....................4 E6
Rhodes Gdns *BRDST* CT10.....................113 L7
Rhode St *CHAT* ME4.....................75 J4
Rhodeswell Rd *BOW* E3.....................25 H1
Rhodewood Cl
  MAID/SHEP ME15.....................186 D2
Rhododendron Av *MEO* DA13.....................112 D2
Ribblesdale Rd *RDART* DA2.....................47 J9
Ribbon Dance Ms *CMBW* SE5.....................40 D7
Ribston Cl *HAYES* BR2.....................86 A5
Ribston Gdns *STPH/PW* TN12.....................242 F7
Ricardo St *POP/IOD* E14.....................25 L2
Rice Pde *STRM/STPC* BR5 *.....................86 E2
Rices Hl *EGRIN* RH19.....................265 H7
Richard Cl *WOOL/PLUM* SE18.....................26 F7
Richard House Dr *CAN/RD* E16.....................26 E2
Richard's Cl *RTON* TN11.....................208 E8
Richardson Cl *GRH* DA9.....................474 M6
Richardson Rd *STH/RUST* TN4.....................270 C2
Richardson Wy *MSTR* CT12.....................142 B6
Richard St *CHAT* ME4.....................6 H5
  WCHPL E1.....................24 F2
Richard Watts Ct *CHAT* ME4 *.....................6 B3
Richborough Cl
  STMC/STPC BR5.....................87 L1
Richborough Dr *STRD* ME2.....................72 A6
Richborough Rd *SWCH* CT13.....................171 M6

WGOS CT8.....................111 N6
Richborough Wy *ASH* TN23.....................282 B5
Richdore Rd *RCANTW* CT4.....................225 K3
Richmer Rd *ERITH* DA8.....................46 A1
Richmond Av *MARG* CT9.....................112 C4
Richmond Cl *BH/WHM* TN16.....................145 L4
  STRD ME2.....................94 B3
  WALD ME5.....................125 N1
Richmond Dr *HB* CT6.....................108 B6
  NROM TN28.....................337 H5
  SIT ME10.....................99 M7
Richmond Gdns
  CANTW/ST CT2.....................166 B2
Richmond Gn *CROY/NA* CRO.....................82 G7
Richmond Meech Dr
  MAID/BEAR ME14.....................253 H5
Richmond Pl *RTWE/PEM* TN2.....................270 E8
  WOOL/PLUM SE18.....................27 K7
Richmond Rd *CROY/NA* CRO.....................82 D7
  GILL ME7.....................73 J9
  GRAYS RM17.....................32 D9
  RAM CT11.....................16 D4
  THHTH CR7.....................60 C3
  WSTB CT5.....................106 A5
Richmond St *FOLKN* CT19.....................310 A5
  HB CT6.....................107 L1
  IOS ME12.....................57 M6
Richmond Wy
  EGRIN RH19.....................265 J8
  MAID/SHEP ME15.....................185 M5
Richmount Gdns
  BKHTH/KID SE3.....................42 E4
Rich St *POP/IOD* E14.....................25 J3
Rickard Cl *BRXS/STRHM* SW2.....................40 A9
Ricketts Hill Rd
  BH/WHM TN16.....................145 N3
Riddlesdale Av *STH/RUST* TN4.....................270 D7
Riddons Rd *LEE/GVPK* SE12.....................42 G4
Rideout St *WOOL/PLUM* SE18.....................26 C7
Rider Cl *BFN/LL* DA15.....................44 A7
Ridge Av *DART* DA1.....................45 P7
Ridgebrook Rd *BKHTH/KID* SE3.....................42 G5
Ridge Cl *THMD* SE28.....................28 F3
Ridgecroft Cl *BXLY* DA5.....................45 L9
Ridgelands *RTW* TN1.....................239 P5
Ridge La *MEO* DA13.....................122 B2
Ridgemount Av *CROY/NA* CRO.....................84 A6
The Ridge *BXLY* DA5.....................45 H8
  CTHM CR3.....................175 H1
  KEN/WIL TN24.....................253 H4
  ORP BR6.....................86 E6
Ridge Wy *DART* DA1.....................45 P7
  EDEN TN8.....................206 D6
Ridgeway Av *GVE* DA12.....................69 M2
  GRAYS RM17.....................32 E9
  HAYES BR2.....................85 K6
  HYTHE CT21.....................307 P4
  RDART DA2.....................67 L4
  RTWE/PEM TN2.....................270 E8
  WSTB CT5.....................106 B5
Ridgeway Cliff *HB* CT6.....................107 H1
Ridgeway Crs *ORP* BR6.....................86 F7
  TONN TN10.....................210 G6
Ridgeway Crescent Gdns
  ORP BR6.....................86 F6
Ridgeway Dr *BMLY* BR1.....................42 C9
The Ridgeway
  STH/RUST TN4.....................240 E8
Ridgeway East *BFN/LL* DA15.....................44 B6
The Ridgeway *BRDST* CT10.....................143 K1
  CHAT ME4.....................95 K7
  CROY/NA CRO.....................82 E7
  DVW CT17.....................290 F5
  FAV ME13.....................164 B1
  GILL ME7 *.....................73 J3
  GVE DA12.....................70 G6
  MARC CT9.....................113 G4
  RASHE TN25.....................284 C3
  TONN TN10.....................210 G6
Ridgeway Wk *HB* CT6.....................107 M7
Ridgeway West *BFN/LL* DA15.....................44 A6
Ridgewell Cl *SYD* SE26.....................61 M3
Ridgewood *HART* DA3.....................68 G8
Ridgway *MAIDW* ME16.....................184 C1
Ridgway Rd *BRXN/ST* SW9.....................40 B8
Ridgwell Rd *CAN/RD* E16.....................26 D1
Ridham Av *SIT* ME10.....................99 P5
Riding Gate Rbt *CANT* CT1.....................4 A6
Riding Hl *KEN/WIL* TN24.....................252 F5
Riding La *RTON* TN11.....................180 B8
  RTON TN11.....................210 A3
Riding Pk *RTON* TN11.....................210 A3
The Ridings *BH/WHM* TN16.....................145 P2
  CANT CT1.....................5 H2
  MARC CT9.....................113 K2
  RTWE/PEM TN2.....................271 J2
  STPH/PW TN12.....................243 H2
  WSTB CT5.....................106 C5
Ridlands Gv *OXTED* RH8.....................175 P6
Ridlands La *OXTED* RH8.....................175 P6
Ridlands Ri *OXTED* RH8.....................175 P6
Ridley Cl *HB* CT6.....................107 M6
Ridley Rd *HAYES* BR2.....................62 D9
  ROCH ME1.....................78 F1
  WELL DA16.....................44 D2
Ridsdale Rd *PGE/AN* SE20.....................61 H7
Riefield Rd *ELTH/MOT* SE9.....................43 N5
Rifle St *POP/IOD* E14.....................25 L1
Rigby Gdns *CDW/CHF* RM16.....................33 J7
Rigden Rd *ASH* TN23.....................282 E1
Rigden St *POP/IOD* E14.....................25 L2
Rigshill Rd *FAV* ME13.....................190 C6
Riley Rd *STHWK* SE1.....................24 C6
Riley Rd *EHAM* E6.....................26 D1
Rill Wk *EGRIN* RH19.....................265 L7
Ring Cl *BMLY* BR1.....................62 E3
Ringden Av *STPH/PW* TN12.....................242 F4
Ringer's Rd *BMLY* BR1.....................62 E3
Ringlestone Crs
  MAID/BEAR ME14.....................155 L4
Ringlestone Rd *RMAID* ME17.....................158 C5

Ringlet Cl *CAN/RD* E16.....................26 C1
Ringlet Rd *CHAT* ME4.....................73 H5
Ringmer Wy *BMLY* BR1.....................86 A2
Ringmore Ri *FSTH* SE23.....................41 H8
Ringold Av *MSTR* CT12.....................142 F4
Ringshall Rd *CHST* BR7.....................64 C9
Ringsle Rd *RTON* TN11.....................209 M6
Ringside *EDEN* TN8.....................206 C7
Ringstead Rd *CAT* SE6.....................41 L6
Ring Wall *DEAL* CT14.....................202 D8
Ringwold Cl *BECK* BR3.....................61 L6
Ringwood Av *CROY/NA* CRO.....................82 D4
  ORP BR6.....................117 K4
Ringwood Cl *CANTW/ST* CT2.....................166 D1
  RHAM ME8.....................96 C7
Ringwood Rd
  MAID/SHEP ME15.....................185 P3
Ringwould Rd *DEAL* CT14.....................262 G3
  RDV CT15.....................262 C4
Ripley Cl *BMLY* BR1.....................86 A2
  CROY/NA CRO.....................114 F1
Ripley Rd *BELV* DA17.....................28 J8
  CAN/RD E16.....................26 D2
  KEN/WIL TN24.....................253 K9
Ripon Cl *RHAM* ME8.....................96 C3
Ripon Rd *WOOL/PLUM* SE18.....................27 J9
Rippersley Rd *WELL* DA16.....................44 C2
Ripple Rd *DEAL* CT14.....................262 D2
Rippolson Rd
  WOOL/PLUM SE18.....................27 N8
Risborough Barracks
  FOLK CT20.....................310 A6
Risborough La *FOLK* CT20.....................310 A6
Risborough Wy *FOLK* CT20.....................310 B5
Risden La *HAWK* TN18.....................317 L1
Risdon Cl *CANTW/ST* CT2.....................137 L7
Risdon St *BERM/RHTH* SE16.....................24 F6
Risedale Rd *BXLYHN* DA7.....................45 K4
Riseldine Rd *FSTH* SE23.....................41 L7
The Rise *ASH* TN23.....................282 B1
  BXLY DA5.....................44 E8
  DART DA1.....................45 L5
  DEAL CT14.....................265 H5
  EGRIN RH19.....................265 J8
  GILL ME7.....................126 D2
  GVE DA12.....................70 A3
  IOS ME12.....................57 L1
  RDV CT15.....................292 C1
  ROCH ME1.....................95 J3
  RSIT ME9.....................129 J3
  SEV TN13.....................179 H4
Rising Rd *ASH* TN23.....................2 A6
Ritchie Rd *CROY/NA* CRO.....................83 H8
Ritch Rd *SNOD* ME6.....................123 M5
Ritter St *WOOL/PLUM* SE18.....................27 H9
Rivendell Cl *HOO/HM* ME3.....................56 D3
River Bank Cl
  MAID/SHEP ME15.....................13 H5
Riverbank Rd *BMLY* BR1.....................62 F8
River Barge Cl *POP/IOD* E14.....................25 M5
River Cl *MAID/SHEP* ME15.....................184 C4
  RAIN RM13.....................29 N1
River Ct *RCANTW* CT4.....................165 L9
River Dr *DVW* CT17.....................290 G4
Riverdale Est *TON* TN9 *.....................240 G1
Riverdale Rd *BXLY* DA5.....................45 H8
  CANT CT1.....................166 C1
  ERITH DA8.....................28 G8
  WOOL/PLUM SE18.....................27 N8
River Gdns *CROY/NA* CRO *.....................290 C5
  WEST.....................71 N8
River Grove Pk *BECK* BR3.....................61 M7
Riverhead Cl *MAIDW* ME16.....................155 J6
  MARG CT9.....................112 G4
Riverhill *CROY/NA* CRO.....................85 P9
Riverhill *SEV* TN13.....................179 K7
River Lawn Rd *TON* TN9.....................210 F9
Rivermead *CHAT* ME4.....................73 J5
River Meadow *DVW* CT17.....................290 G4
River Pde *SEV* TN13 *.....................148 D7
Riverpark Gdns *HAYES* BR2.....................62 B6
River Park Vw *ORP* BR6.....................87 J1
Rivers Cl *WBY/YAL* ME18.....................183 M4
Rivers Ct *MSTR* CT12 *.....................141 K7
Riversdale *GVW* DA11.....................69 J1
Riversdale Rd *ASH* TN23.....................282 C5
  MSTR CT12.....................142 F5
River Side *DART* DA1.....................45 N6
Riverside *CHARL* SE7.....................6 B3
  CHAT ME4.....................290 D2
  DVE/WH CT16.....................290 D2
  EDEN TN8.....................206 D6
  EYN DA4.....................89 J6
Riverside Cl *STMC/STPC* BR5.....................282 D5
  RCANTW CT4.....................197 M2
  STMC/STPC BR5.....................64 E8
Riverside Est *SND* ME3 *.....................72 E9
Riverside Ms *CROY/NA* CRO *.....................82 D7
  RCANTW CT4.....................197 M2
Riverside Rd *MSTR* CT12.....................171 P2
  SCUP DA14.....................64 D2
Riverside Wy *DART* DA1.....................46 E6
Rivers Rd *RSIT* ME9.....................131 J3
River St *DVW* CT17.....................290 F4
  GILL ME7.....................72 G9
Riverview *ASH* TN23.....................252 E8
River Vw *CANTW/ST* CT2.....................137 L6
  CDW/CHF RM16.....................33 M8
  GILL ME7.....................96 C6
  MAID/SHEP ME15.....................185 L1
  OBOR ME11.....................77 H4
Riverview Pk *CAT* SE6.....................61 N1
Riverview Rd *GRH* DA9 *.....................47 N9
Riverview Ter *TUR PUR* RM19 *.....................30 E8
River Wk *DIT/AY* ME20.....................153 L8
  GNWCH SE10.....................26 A5
River WHf *BELV* DA17 *.....................29 J5
Riverwood La *CHST* BR7.....................63 P8
Riviera *FOLK* CT20.....................310 C8
The Riviera *FOLK* CT20.....................310 C8
Roach St *STRD* ME2.....................18 C2
Road of Remembrance
  FOLK CT20.....................11 F5

Roan Ct *STRD* ME2 *.....................71 P7
Roan St *GNWCH* SE10.....................25 M9
Robert Keen Cl *PECK* SE15.....................40 G2
Robert Lowe Cl *NWCR* SE14.....................41 K1
Roberton Dr *BMLY* BR1.....................62 G8
Roberts Cl *ELTH/MOT* SE9.....................43 P9
  SIT ME10.....................99 L7
  STMC/STPC BR5.....................87 K2
  THHTH CR7.....................60 D9
Roberts House
  MAIDW ME16.....................154 D9
Roberts Orchard Rd
  MAIDW ME14.....................154 D9
Robert Sq *LEW* SE13.....................42 A5
Roberts Rd *BELV* DA17.....................28 F8
  NROM TN28.....................343 K3
  NROM TN28.....................123 N5
  SNOD ME6.....................123 N5
  WSTB CT5.....................104 G8
Robert St *CROY/NA* CRO.....................83 H7
  LEW SE13.....................233 J2
  WOOL/PLUM SE18.....................27 L8
Robeson St *BOW* E3.....................25 J3
Robina Cl *BXLYHS* DA6.....................44 F5
Robin Cl *EGRIN* RH19.....................265 H6
Robin Hill Dr *CHST* BR7.....................63 J5
Robin Hood Cl *MTCM* CR4.....................82 B5
Robin Hood Gdns
  POP/IOD E14 *.....................25 M3
Robin Hood Gn
  STMC/STPC BR5.....................87 H2
Robin Hood La *BXLYHS* DA6.....................44 F5
  LYDD TN29.....................342 B7
  POP/IOD E14.....................25 M3
  WALD ME5.....................125 J4
Robin Hood La (Upper)
  WALD ME5.....................125 K4
Robinia Av *GVW* DA11.....................49 H8
Robinia Cl *PGE/AN* SE20.....................60 C7
Robins Av *RMAID* ME17.....................189 K7
Robin's Cl *HYTHE* CT21.....................308 D7
  RMAID ME17.....................189 K7
Robins Gv *WWKM* BR4.....................85 K7
Robson Cl *EHAM* E6.....................26 F2
Robson Dr *DIT/AY* ME20.....................154 C2
  HOO/HM ME3.....................56 A1
Robson Rd *WNWD* SE27.....................60 B2
Robus Cl *RFOLK* CT18.....................287 H1
Robyns Cft *GVW* DA11.....................69 J2
Robyns Wy *EDEN* TN8.....................236 E1
Rocastle Rd *BROCKY* SE4.....................41 L6
Rocfort Rd *SNOD* ME6.....................123 P5
Rochdale Rd *ABYW* SE2.....................28 A8
  RTW TN1.....................270 F2
Rochdale Wy *DEPT* SE8.....................41 N1
Rochester Av *BMLY* BR1.....................62 F8
  CANT CT1.....................5 J7
  ROCH ME1.....................95 H2
Rochester Br *ROCH* ME1.....................19 F3
Rochester Cl *BFN/LL* DA15.....................44 D7
Rochester Ct *STRD* ME2.....................72 E7
Rochester Crs *HOO/HM* ME3.....................35 K1
Rochester Dr *BXLY* DA5.....................45 H3
Rochester Gdns *CROY/NA* CRO.....................83 K7
Rochester Ga *ROCH* ME1 *.....................19 H6
Rochester Rd *DART* DA1.....................46 G8
  DIT/AY ME20.....................154 F1
  GVE DA12.....................70 D1
  ROCH ME1.....................124 D2
  STRD ME2.....................94 C3
  TONN TN10.....................210 G6
  WALD ME5.....................125 H1
Rochester St *CHAT* ME4.....................95 K4
Rochester Wk *STHWK* SE1 *.....................24 A2
Rochester Wy *BKHTH/KID* SE3.....................42 F2
  DART DA1.....................45 N8
  ELTH/MOT SE9.....................43 K4
Rochester Way Relief Rd
  ELTH/MOT SE9.....................43 J6
Rochford Wy *CROY/NA* CRO.....................82 D3
Rock Av *GILL* ME7.....................7 J2
Rockbourne Rd *FSTH* SE23.....................41 K9
Rock Channel *RYE* TN31.....................338 F7
Rockdale Gdns *SEV* TN13 *.....................21 L4
Rockdale Pleasance
  SEV TN13 *.....................21 G4
Rockdale Rd *SEV* TN13.....................21 F5
Rockell's Pl *EDUL* SE22.....................41 H7
Rockfield Cl *OXTED* RH8.....................175 J7
Rockfield Rd *OXTED* RH8.....................175 J6
Rock Grove Wy
  BERM/RHTH SE16.....................24 D7
Rockhampton Rd
  STRHM/NOR SW16.....................60 A3
Rock Hl *ORP* BR6.....................118 A1
  SYD SE26.....................60 F3
Rock Hill Rd *HDCN* TN27.....................219 M8
Rockingham Pl *HB* CT6.....................107 N4
Rockmount Rd *NRWD* SE19.....................60 D5
  WOOL/PLUM SE18.....................27 N8
Rock Rd *BGR/WK* TN15.....................151 J5
  MAID/BEAR ME14.....................155 M5
  SIT ME10.....................129 M1
Rocks Cl *E/WMAL* ME19.....................153 H6
Rocks Hl *CRBK* TN17.....................276 C7
The Rocks Rd *E/WMAL* ME19.....................153 P6
Rockstone Wy *MSTR* CT12.....................142 E3
Rockwell Gdns *NRWD* SE19.....................60 E3
Rocky Bourne Rd
  RASHE TN25.....................305 N2
Rocky Hill Ter *MAID/BEAR* ME14 *.....................12 C5
Rocombe Crs *FSTH* SE23.....................41 J8
Rocque La *BKHTH/KID* SE3.....................42 D4
Roden Gdns *CROY/NA* CRO.....................83 K3
Rodeo Cl *ERITH* DA8.....................46 C2
Roding Ms *WAP* E1W.....................24 D4
Roding Rd *EHAM* E6.....................27 J2
Rodmell Rd *RTWE/PEM* TN2.....................22 D7
Rodmer Cl *IOS* ME12.....................58 C8
Rodmersham Gn *RSIT* ME9.....................131 M8
  SIT ME10.....................131 N8
Rodney Av *TONN* TN10.....................211 H6

Ryarsh La E/WMAL ME19 ....153 J5
Ryarsh Pk E/WMAL ME19 * 152 G6
Ryarsh Rd E/WMAL ME19..........123 J1
Rycaut Cl MAIDW ME16...........12 B6
Rycaut Cl RHAM ME8.............126 C2
Rycroft La RSEV TN14...........178 D6
Rycuff Sq BKHTH/KID SE3........42 D5
Rydal Av RAM CT11..............142 F5
Rydal Cl STH/RUST TN4..........270 B3
Rydal Dr BXLYHN DA7............45 J2
    STH/RUST TN4...............270 E3
    WWKM BR4...................85 H6
Rydal Mt HAYES BR2 *...........85 J1
Ryde Cl WALD ME5...............95 N6
Ryde Dr SLH/COR SS17...........34 B1
Ryder Dr BERM/RHTH SE16........24 E8
Ryders RRTW TN5................269 M5
Ryder's Av WGOS CT8............111 L5
Ryde St CANTW/ST CT2...........4 B3
Rye Cl BXLY DA5................45 *7
Ryecotes Md DUL SE21...........40 C9
Rye Crs STMC/STPC BR5..........87 L5
Ryecroft GVE DA12..............70 A4
    HART DA3...................91 N1
Ryecroft Rd LEW SE13...........42 A6
    RSEV TN14..................148 F2
    STMC/STPC BR5..............86 E3
    STRHM/NOR SW16.............60 A5
Ryedale EDUL SE22..............41 H7
Ryedale Ct SEV TN15...........148 D6
Ryefield Rd NRWD SE19..........60 C5
Ryegrass Cl WALD ME5...........95 M9
Rye Hill Pk PECK SE15..........41 J5
Ryelands Crs LEE/GVPK SE12....42 G7
Rye La PECK SE15...............40 C2
    RSEV TN14..................148 E4
Rye Rd HAWK TN18...............317 K5
    LYDD TN29..................334 E5
    PECK SE15..................41 K5
    RYE TN31...................338 C2
    TENT TN30..................332 D2
Rye Wk HB CT6..................107 P4
Rykhill CDW/CHF RM16...........33 J6
Ryland Pl FOLK CT20............11 H3
Rylands Rd KEN/WIL TN24.......252 C5
Rymer Rd CROY/NA CRO...........83 K4
Rymers Cl RTWE/PEM TN2........270 C1
Rymer St HNHL SE24.............40 B7
Rymill St CAN/RD E16...........27 H4
Rype Cl LYDD TN29.............342 B7
Rysted La BH/WHM TN16.........176 D2
Ryswick Ms NROM TN28..........337 H5

S

Sabbarton St CAN/RD E16........26 A2
Sabina Rd CDW/CHF RM16.........33 K7
Sacketts Hl BRDST CT10........112 C7
Sackville Av HAYES BR2.........85 K5
Sackville Cl EGRIN RH19.......264 F5
    RASHW TN26.................251 M2
    SEV TN15...................148 G7
Sackville Ct EGRIN RH19 *....265 J8
Sackville La EGRIN RH19.......264 E5
Saddington St GVE DA12........49 M8
Saddlers Cl MAID/BEAR ME14...156 D7
Saddlers Hl RCANTE CT3.......199 N5
Saddlers Ms WSTB CT5..........106 C5
Saddler's Pk EYN DA4..........89 J7
Saddler's Wall La LYDD TN29..334 C4
Saddlers Wy ASH TN23.........282 E4
Saddleton Gv WSTB CT5.........105 L6
Saddleton Rd WSTB CT5.........105 L6
Sadlers Cl WALD ME5...........125 J3
Saffron Av POP/IOD E14........25 N3
Saffron Cl CROY/NA CRO........82 D5
Saffron Rd CDW/CHF RM16.......31 M7
Saffron's Pl FOLK CT20........11 G4
Saffron Wy SIT ME10...........99 N7
Sage Cl EHAM E6...............26 C1
Sage Rd ROCH ME1..............94 F3
Sage St WCHPL E1..............24 F3
Saigasso Cl CAN/RD E16........26 D2
Sailmakers Ct CHAT ME4........95 N4
Sainsbury Rd NRWD SE19........60 E4
St Agnes Gdns IOS ME12........57 L7
St Agnes Rd EGRIN RH19.......265 H6
St Aidan's Rd EDUL SE22.......41 H7
St Albans Cl GILL ME7.........73 L8
    GVE DA12...................69 P2
St Alban's Gdns GVE DA12......49 N7
St Alban's Rd DART DA1........46 F7
    RCANTE CT3.................138 B8
    STRD ME2...................71 J9
St Alfege Rd CHARL SE7........26 E9
St Alphege Cl WSTB CT5.......105 J7
St Alphege St WSTB CT5.......105 L5
St Alphege La CANT CT1........4 E3
St Alphege Rd DVE/WH CT16....291 K6
St Ambrose Gn RASHE TN25.....223 P8
St Amunds Cl CAT SE6..........61 N3
St Andrew Rd GILL ME7.........73 K8
St Andrews
    BERM/RHTH SE16 *...........24 E8
    CANT CT1...................4 C6
    FOLKN CT19.................310 E4
    HB CT6.....................107 L2
    MAIDW ME16.................184 F1
    MARG CT9...................112 C6
    STPH/PW TN12...............243 H3
    WSTB CT5...................105 M7
St Andrews Ct STH/RUST TN4...240 D8
St Andrews Dr ORP BR6.........87 J3
St Andrews Gdns DVW CT17 *...291 J7
St Andrew's Pk
    MAIDW ME16 *...............154 F9

St Andrews Park Rd
    STH/RUST TN4...............240 D8
St Andrew's Rd CROY/NA CRO....83 H8
    DEAL CT14..................233 H5
    GVE DA12 *.................49 M8
    MAIDW ME16.................184 F1
    NROM TN28..................337 J7
    RAM CT11...................143 L4
    STPH/PW TN12...............243 H5
    TIL RM18...................49 J5
St Andrews Wy DEAL CT14......231 H6
    OXTED RH8..................175 P7
St Annes Cl CDW/CHF RM16 *....32 C4
St Anne's Cl MAIDW ME16.......12 C4
St Anne's Dr HB CT6...........107 J3
St Anne's Gdns MARG CT9......112 E4
St Anne's Pas POP/IOD E14 *...25 J2
St Anne's Rd ASH TN25........282 C1
    WSTB CT5...................105 L5
St Anne's Rw POP/IOD E14......25 J2
St Anne St POP/IOD E14........25 J2
St Ann's Green La
    STPH/PW TN12...............245 L1
St Ann's Rd FAV ME13.........132 E7
    LYDD TN29..................326 F7
St Anns Wy BH/WHM TN16 *.....146 E4
St Anthony's La WAP E1W *.....24 D4
St Anthony's Ct HAYES BR2.....86 B5
St Anthony's Wy MARG CT9.....113 H4
St Arvans Cl CROY/NA CRO......83 K7
St Asaph Rd BROCKY SE4........41 K4
St Aubyns Cl ORP BR6..........86 C7
St Aubyns Gdns ORP BR6........86 C6
St Aubyn's Rd NRWD SE19.......60 F5
St Audrey Av BXLYHN DA7.......45 J3
St Augustine Rd
    CDW/CHF RM16...............33 J7
    MARG CT9...................
St Augustine's Crs WSTB CT5..106 C3
St Augustine's Pk RAM CT11...15 C5
St Augustine's Rd BELV DA17..28 E7
    CANT CT1...................5 H6
    DEAL CT14..................232 E5
    RAM CT11...................16 D6
St Austell Rd BKHTH/KID SE3..42 A3
St Barnabas Cl BECK BR3.......62 A8
    GILL ME7...................96 A3
    MAIDW ME16.................155 H4
    RTW TN1 *..................23 F1
St Bartholomew's Cl
    SYD SE26...................61 J5
St Bartholomew's La
    ROCH ME1...................19 K7
St Bartholomew's Ter
    ROCH ME1...................19 K7
St Bart's DVW CT17 *..........8 A2
St Bart's Rd SWCH CT13.......201 M2
St Benedict Rd SNOD ME6......123 M5
St Benedict's Av GVE DA12....70 A2
St Benedict's Lawn
    RAM CT11 *.................16 D6
St Benet's Rd GDST RH9.......111 M6
St Benets Wy TENT TN30.......301 J1
St Benjamins Dr ORP BR6......117 K5
St Bernards CROY/NA CRO.......83 K7
St Bernards Cl WNWD SE27......60 D3
St Bernards Rd TOWN TN10.....210 F4
St Blaise Av BMLY BR1.........62 F8
St Botolph Rd GVE DA11.......69 H2
St Botolph's Av SEV TN13......20 D1
St Botolph's Cl SEV TN13......20 E1
St Botolph St HDTCH EC3A.....24 C2
St Breiades Ct EDEN TN8......206 B7
St Brides Cl ERITHM DA18.....28 C5
St Catherines Cl RAM CT11 *..143 L3
St Catherine's Dr FAV ME13...132 C7
    NWCR SE14..................41 K3
St Catherine's Gv MSTR CT12..142 C3
St Cecilia Rd CDW/CHF RM16...33 J7
St Chad's Dr GVE DA12.........70 A2
St Chad's Rd TWRH EC3N........24 C2
St Christopher Cl MARG CT9...113 J5
St Christophers LING RH7 *...234 C5
St Christophers Gn
    BRDST CT10 *...............113 L8
St Christopher's Ms
    WLGTN SM6..................82 B9
St Clair Cl OXTED RH8........174 F6
St Clair's Rd CROY/NA CRO.....83 K6
St Clare Rd DEAL CT14........233 H8
St Clare St TWRH EC3N.........24 C2
St Clements Av WTHK RM20......31 K9
St Clements Cl GVW DA11 *.....69 K2
    IOS ME12...................80 B5
St Clements Ct BRDST CT10 *..113 K8
    PUR RM19...................30 D7
St Clements Rd IOS ME12 *....80 C4
    ORP BR6....................111 M4
    WTHK RM20..................48 J1
St Clements Yd EDUL SE22 *...40 F6
St Clere Hill Rd BGR/WK TN15.120 C6
St Cloud Rd WNWD SE27.........60 C3
St Columba's Cl GVE DA12.....70 A2
St Cosmus Cl RASHE TN25......222 E1
St Crispin's Rd WGOS CT8.....111 M5
St Davids Av DVW CT17........313 H2
St Davids Cl
    BERM/RHTH SE16 *...........42 E8
    BRCH CT7...................111 J5
    WSTB CT5...................105 M7
    WWKM BR4...................84 E4
St David's Crs GVE DA12.......69 P3
St David's Rd DEAL CT14......233 H3
    MAIDW ME16.................38 E9
    RAM CT11...................143 L5
    STH/RUST TN4...............270 E2
    SWLY BR8...................65 P5
St Davids Sq POP/IOD E14......25 L8
St Denis Rd WNWD SE27.........60 D3
St Denys Rd RFOLK CT18.......288 E7
St Donatt's Rd NWCR SE14.....41 M2
St Dunstan's Cl CANTW/ST CT2..4 B2

St Dunstan's Dr GVE DA12......70 A2
St Dunstan's Hl MON EC3R *...24 B3
St Dunstan's La MON EC3R.....24 B3
St Dunstan's Rd MARG CT9....112 F3
    SNWD SE25..................83 L1
St Dunstan's Rbt
    CANTW/ST CT2...............4 B2
St Dunstan's Ter CANTW/ST CT2..4 A2
St Eanswythe Wy FOLK CT20....11 F4
St Edith's Rd BGR/WK TN15...149 M5
St Edmunds Cl ABYW SE2.......28 C5
St Edmunds Rd CANT CT1........4 D5
    DART DA1...................46 F5
    DEAL CT14..................232 D5
St Edwards Cl CROY/NA CRO...114 C5
    EGRIN RH19.................264 F7
St Elmos Rd BERM/RHTH SE16...25 H5
St Faith's La
    MAID/BEAR ME14.............156 E8
St Faith's Rd HNHL SE24......40 B9
St Faith's St MAID/BEAR ME14.12 E4
St Fidelis' Rd ERITH DA8.....29 J7
St Filians Rd CAT SE6........42 A9
St Francis Av GVE DA12........70 A3
St Francis Cl DEAL CT14......232 D5
    MAID/BEAR ME14.............155 N6
    MARG CT9...................113 J5
    ORP BR6....................86 F3
    STRD ME2...................71 N9
St Francis Rd EDUL SE22......40 E5
    FOLKN CT19.................310 C5
    MEO DA15...................122 C2
St Francis Wy CDW/CHF RM16...33 K7
St George's Av GRAYS RM17.....32 D7
    GVW DA11...................57 K8
    IOS ME12...................80 C5
St Georges Centre CANT CT1 *..5 G5
St Georges Cl THMD SE28......28 C1
    WSTB CT5...................105 M7
St George's Ct BGR/WK TN15..151 J1
    DVW CT17 *.................291 H5
    GVE DA12...................69 P5
St Georges La CANT CT1........4 E5
    MON EC3R *.................24 A5
St George's Lees SWCH CT13..201 P2
St Georges Ms
    BERM/RHTH SE16.............25 J7
    TON TN9 *..................240 F1
St Georges Pde CAT SE6 *.....61 M1
St George's Pk
    RTWE/PEM TN2...............270 C8
St George's Pl CANT CT1.......5 F5
    HYTHE CT21.................308 C7
    IOS ME12...................57 P3
    SWCH CT13..................202 A2
St George's Rd BECK BR3.......61 P7
    BMLY BR1...................63 K8
    BRDST CT10.................113 M8
    DEAL CT14..................233 J3
    FOLK CT20..................310 C5
    GILL ME7...................73 J3
    RAM CT11...................143 L4
    SCUP DA14..................64 F5
    SEV TN13...................148 G7
    STMC/STPC BR5..............86 E5
    WELL DA16..................44 D4
St George's Rd West BMLY BR1.63 J8
St George's Rbt CANT CT1......5 F5
St Georges Sq GVW DA11 *.....49 M7
    MAIDW ME16.................12 A6
St George's Ter CANT CT1......4 E4
    PECK SE15..................40 C1
St Georges Wy CROY/NA CRO....83 H6
St George's Wy PECK SE15.....24 B9
St German's Pl BKHTH/KID SE3.42 E3
St German's Rd FSTH SE23.....41 L9
St Giles Cl CDW/CHF RM16......33 H1
    ORP BR6....................86 E9
St Giles Rd CMBW SE5.........40 E2
    DVW CT17 *.................313 J1
St Giles Wk DVW CT17.........313 J1
St Gothard Rd WNWD SE27......60 D3
St Gregory's CANT CT1 *.......5 F5
St Gregory's Cl DEAL CT14...232 E5
St Gregory's Crs GVE DA12....70 A2
St Gregory's Rd CANT CT1......5 H3
St Helena Rd
    BERM/RHTH SE16.............24 C7
St Helens Cnr
    MAID/SHEP ME15 *...........184 D3
St Helens La
    MAID/SHEP ME15.............184 D3
St Helen's Pl ERITH DA8......28 C5
St Helen's Pl OBST EC2N......24 B2
St Helens Rd ERITH DA18......28 C5
    HOO/HM ME3.................73 N2
    IOS ME12...................57 M7
St Helier's Cl MAIDW ME16...184 D1
St Hilda Rd FOLKN CT19.......310 B5
St Hildas BGR/WK TN15........181 J5
St Hilda's Rd HYTHE CT21....308 C6
St Hilda's Wy GVE DA12.......70 A2
St Hugh's Rd PGE/AN SE20.....60 F8
St Hugh Ter RFOLK CT18 *....288 C6
St Jacob's Pl CANT CT1 *.....166 C6
St James' Av BRDST CT10.....113 K8
    MSTR CT12..................142 C3
St James Cl IOS ME12.........80 B5
St James' Gdns WSTB CT5.....105 M7
St James La DVE/WH CT16.......8 E4
    RDART DA2..................47 L8
St James Ms POP/IOD E14......25 N4
St James Oaks GVW DA11 *.....49 L8
St James' Pk RTW TN1.........23 F5
St James' Park Rd MARG CT9..111 P5
St James Pl DART DA1.........46 D8
St James Rd DEAL CT14.......233 H5
St James's Av BECK BR3........61 L9
St James's NWCR SE14.........41 L2

    GVW DA11...................49 L8
St James's Cl
    WOOL/PLUM SE18.............27 K9
St James's Crs BRXN/ST SW9..40 A4
St James Sq HART DA3 *.......68 C9
St James's Rd
    BERM/RHTH SE16.............24 D6
    CROY/NA CRO................83 H6
    EGRIN RH19.................264 C7
    GVW DA11...................49 L8
    SEV TN13...................148 G7
St James's St GVW DA11.......49 L7
St James's Ter BRCH CT7.....111 J5
St James St DVE/WH CT16......8 E4
St James Ter BRCH CT7.......111 J5
    ORP BR6 *..................117 K5
St James Wy BXLY DA5.........45 J8
St Jean's Rd WGOS CT8........64 C4
St John's Av MSTR CT12.......142 F5
St ME10......................130 A2
St John's Church Rd
    FOLKN CT19.................10 D2
St Johns Cl BH/WHM TN16 *...146 C1
    HOO/HM ME3.................71 L4
    RFOLK CT18.................288 D5
St Johns Ct GDST RH9 *.......204 C5
    KEN/WIL TN24 *.............283 K2
St John's Crs BRXN/ST SW9...40 A4
    CANTW/ST CT2...............136 C6
St Johns Est STHWK SE1 *.....24 C5
St John's Hl SEV TN13........149 H8
St John's La ASH TN23........2 E4
    CANT CT1...................91 J3
    HART DA3...................
St John's Meadow LING RH7...234 A1
St Johns Pde SCUP DA14 *.....64 D3
St John's Pk BKHTH/KID SE3...42 E1
St John's Rd CAN/RD E16......26 B2
    CDW/CHF RM16...............33 J8
    CROY/NA CRO................82 C7
    DVW CT17 *.................
    ERITH DA8..................29 J8
    FAV ME13...................132 G6
    GILL ME7...................73 K1
    HYTHE CT21.................308 F4
    MARG CT9...................15 H5
    NROM TN28..................336 F7
    PGE/AN SE20................60 F8
    RDART DA2..................47 J8
    RDV CT15...................230 C7
    SCUP DA14..................64 D3
    STH/RUST TN4...............270 D1
    STMC/STPC BR5..............86 E5
    WELL DA16..................44 D4
    WSTB CT5...................106 C5
St John's St FOLK CT20.......11 F3
    MARG CT9...................15 H5
St John's Ter
    WOOL/PLUM SE18.............27 K9
St John's V DEPT SE8.........41 N3
St John's Wy EDEN TN8........206 C7
    ROCH ME1...................288 C5
St Josephs Cl ORP BR6........86 G5
St Joseph's V BKHTH/KID SE3..42 C4
St Julian's Cl
    STRHM/NOR SW16 *...........60 A3
St Julian's Farm Rd
    WNWD SE27..................60 A3
St Julien Av CANT CT1........167 J3
St Justin Cl STMC/STPC BR5...88 E1
St Katharine's Wy TWRH EC3N..24 C4
St Katherine Rd IOS ME12.....57 N9
St Katherine's La SNOD ME6...123 N6
St Katherines Rd
    ERITHM DA18................28 C5
St Keverne Rd ELTH/MOT SE9...63 J5
St Kilda Rd ORP BR6..........86 G5
St Kitts Ter NRWD SE19.......60 D3
St Laurence Av DART DA1......46 D8
St Laurence Cl RSIT ME9......130 C3
St Lawrence Av RAM CT11......16 A7
    STH/RUST TN4...............240 A6
St Lawrence Cl CANT CT1......166 G6
St Lawrence Forstal
    CANT CT1...................166 G6
St Lawrence Rd POP/IOD E14...25 M4
St Lawrence Ter
    DVE/WH CT16 *..............291 J4
St Lawrence Wy
    BRXN/ST SW9................40 A3
St Leonards Av CHAT ME4......95 L4
St Leonards Cl GRAYS RM17....32 A9
    WELL DA16..................44 D4
St Leonards Rd BR BR6........86 F8
St Leonard's Rd CROY/NA CRO..82 C7
    DEAL CT14..................232 D5
    HYTHE CT21.................308 G6
    MAIDW ME16.................155 H4
    POP/IOD E14................25 M4
St Leonard's St
    E/WMAL ME19................153 J5
St Louis Gv HB CT6...........107 P3
St Louis Rd WNWD SE27........60 C3
St Lukes Av MAID/BEAR ME14...13 H5
    RAM CT11...................
    WGOS CT8...................111 M5
St Lukes Cl RDART DA2........67 L4
    SNWD SE25..................83 M8
    SWCH CT13..................201 N1
St Lukes Rd MAID/BEAR ME14...13 H2
    RAM CT11...................17 G1

STH/RUST TN4.................270 E2
St Luke's Sq CAN/RD E16......26 A2
St Luke's Wk RFOLK CT18.....288 C8
St Magnus Cl BRCH CT7........111 H5
St Margarets
    STPH/PW TN12 *.............273 P2
St Margarets Av BFN/LL DA15..63 P2
    BH/WHM TN16 *..............146 C1
    EGRIN RH19.................265 H2
    SLH/COR SS17...............34 B1
St Margarets Banks
    ROCH ME1...................19 J7
St Margarets Cl MAIDW ME16...184 C1
    ORP BR6....................87 J8
    RDART DA2..................67 K1
    WSTB CT5...................105 H8
St Margaret's Ct
    HOO/HM ME3.................53 L5
St Margaret's Crs GVE DA12...70 A2
St Margaret's Dr DEAL CT14...232 G9
    RHAM ME8...................96 P9
St Margaret's Gv
    WOOL/PLUM SE18.............27 K9
St Margaret's Ms ROCH ME1....19 F5
St Margarets Rd BRCH CT7.....141 N1
    BROCKY SE4.................41 M5
    EGRIN RH19.................265 J5
    EYN DA4....................67 L6
    RDV CT15...................230 C7
    WGOS CT8...................111 M6
St Margaret's Ter
    ROCH ME1 *.................4 E5
St Margarets Ter RYE TN31....338 E7
    WOOL/PLUM SE18.............27 K8
St Mark's Av GVW DA11........49 J8
St Mark's Cl FOLK CT20.......310 A6
    WSTB CT5...................105 M6
St Marks Ct DIT/AY ME20 *....124 E7
St Marks Houses GILL ME7 *...62 F9
St Mark's Rd HAYES BR2.......62 D9
    RTWE/PEM TN2...............270 C9
    SNWD SE25..................83 M1
St Mark St WCHPL E1..........24 C2
St Martins Av CANT CT1.......5 J4
St Martins Cl CANT CT1.......5 J4
    DVW CT17...................313 J1
    ERITHM DA18................28 C5
    MAID/BEAR ME14.............156 D5
St Martins Dr EYN DA4........89 J7
St Martins Gdns CDW/CHF RM16 *.33 J7
St Martin's Hl CANT CT1......5 J5
St Martin's La BECK BR3......84 E2
St Martins Meadow
    BH/WHM TN16................147 K8
St Martin's Pl CANT CT1......5 J4
St Martin's Rd CANT CT1......5 H4
    DART DA1...................46 F7
    DEAL CT14..................232 E5
    FOLK CT20..................310 A5
    NROM TN28..................336 D7
    RDV CT15...................291 M3
St Martin's Ter CANT CT1.....5 J4
St Martin's Vw HB CT6........107 M6
St Mary At Hl MON EC3R.......24 B3
St Mary Axe HDTCH EC3A.......24 B2
St Marychurch St
    BERM/RHTH SE16.............24 E5
St Mary Graces Ct
    TWRH EC3N..................24 C3
St Mary Newington Cl
    WALW SE17 *................24 B8
St Mary's SWCH CT13..........201 N1
St Mary's Av HAYES BR2.......62 C9
    MARG CT9...................113 J4
St Mary's Church Rd
    RSEV TN14..................177 M1
St Mary's Cl BGR/WK TN15.....151 M5
    GRAYS RM17.................32 E9
    GVE DA12...................69 N1
    OXTED RH8..................175 H5
    RASHW TN26.................304 D7
    RDV CT15...................287 J5
    STMC/STPC BR5..............64 D8
    SWCH CT13..................201 J4
    SWCH CT13..................201 J8
    WBY/YAL ME18...............213 M6
St Mary's Ct BH/WHM TN16.....176 D2
    CANT CT1 *.................4 D5
    E/WMAL ME19 *..............153 J4
St Mary's Dr SEV TN13........148 D8
St Marys Gdns
    BERM/RHTH SE16 *...........24 C5
St Mary's Gdns CHAT ME4......73 H8
    LYDD TN29..................326 E9
St Mary's Gn BH/WHM TN16.....145 M3
    KEN/WIL TN24...............282 ...
St Mary's Gv BH/WHM TN16.....145 M3
    WADH TN5...................315 H5
St Mary's Meadow
    RCANTE CT3.................169 K8
St Marys Ms KEN/WIL TN24.....253 J9
St Marys Pl RCANTE CT3 *.....24 D2
St Mary's Pth WCHPL E1 *.....24 D2
St Marys Pl RCANTE CT3.......169 K8
St Mary's Rd BGR/WK TN15.....151 K2
    BRDST CT10 *...............113 N9
    BXLY DA5...................45 J3
    CDW/CHF RM16...............33 J7
    DEAL CT14..................233 H8
    FAV ME13...................
    GILL ME7...................73 J9
    GRH DA9....................47 L6
    HYTHE CT21.................308 A6
    MSTR CT12..................141 J6
    NROM TN28..................336 G5
    PECK SE15..................41 J3
    RCANTW CT4.................167 N9
    SNWD SE25..................60 G9
    STRD ME2...................18 D1

SWLY BR8 ....88 C1
TON TN9 ....240 E2
St Marys Rw IOS ME12 * 78 A1
St Mary's St CANT CT1 ....4 D5
St Mary St WOOL/PLUM SE18 ...26 D7
St Mary's Vw RSIT ME9 ....98 D8
St Marys Wy HART DA3 ....68 C9
St Matthews Wy
   HOO/HM ME3 ....38 E9
St Matthew's Wy
   HOO/HM ME3 ....38 E9
St Meddens CHST BR7 ....63 P6
St Mellion Cl THMD SE28 ....69 L6
St Merryn Cl WOOL/PLUM SE18 ...43 P1
St Michael's Aly BANK EC3V * 24 A2
St Michaels Av MARC CT9 ....113 J5
St Michaels Cl BMLY BR1 ....26 E1
   CAN/RD E16 ....26 E1
   CANTW/ST CT2 ....165 P3
   CHAT ME4 ....6 B7
   DIT/AY ME20 ....155 H1
   ERITH DA18 * 28 C5
   SOCK/AV RM15 ....30 F3
St Michaels Ct RTON TN11 * 210 B3
   STRD ME2 * 4 C7
St Michael's Pl CANTW/ST CT2 ...157 L6
St Michaels Ri WELL DA16 * 44 D2
St Michael's Rd
   CANTW/ST CT2 ....166 D2
   CDW/CHF RM16 ....33 J8
   CROY/NA CR0 ....83 J9
   EGRIN RH19 ....265 H6
   MAIDW ME16 ....12 A6
   STH/RUST TN4 ....270 E1
   WELL DA16 ....44 D4
St Michael's St FOLK CT20 ....11 G3
St Michaels Ter TENT TN30 * 301 H4
St Michael's Wk RFOLK CT18 ....288 C8
St Mildred's Av BRCH CT7 ....110 F6
   BRDST CT10 ....113 M9
   RAM CT11 ....16 B5
St Mildred's Cl TENT TN30 ....301 H8
St Mildreds Ct DEAL CT14 ....233 H8
   LOTH EC2R * 24 A2
St Mildreds Gdns WGOS CT8 * ..111 N4
St Mildreds Pl CANT CT1 ....4 C7
St Mildreds Rd CAT SE6 ....42 C8
   MARG CT9 ....112 F3
   MSTR CT12 ....141 J7
   RAM CT11 ....16 B5
   WGOS CT8 ....111 M4
St Monicas Rd DEAL CT14 ....263 J2
St Nicholas Cl CANTW/ST CT2 ...137 L6
   DEAL CT14 ....232 E5
St Nicholas Dr SEV TN13 ....21 C5
St Nicholas Gdns STRD ME2 .....71 P7
St Nicholas Rd CANT CT1 ....166 B6
   FAV ME13 ....132 D6
   HYTHE CT21 ....308 C5
   NROM TN28 ....337 J7
   WOOL/PLUM SE18 ....27 N8
St Nicholas St DEPT SE8 ....41 M2
St Nicolas La CHST BR7 ....63 J7
St Norbert Rd BROCKY SE4 ....41 L5
St Olaves Est STHWK SE1 * 24 B5
St Oswald's Rd
   STRHM/NOR SW16 ....60 D7
St Patrick's Cl DEAL CT14 ....233 H3
   WSTB CT5 ....105 M7
St Patrick's Gdns GVE DA12 ....69 P3
St Patrick's Rd DEAL CT14 ....233 H2
   DVW CT17 ....315 H2
   RAM CT11 ....143 L4
St Paul's Av
   BERM/RHTH SE16 * 24 G4
   FAV ME13 ....132 D6
St Paul's Cl CHARL SE7 ....26 E8
   SOCK/AV RM15 ....30 F3
   STRD ME2 * 94 C1
   SWCM DA10 ....48 C8
   TONN TN10 ....22 A5
St Paul's Cray Rd CHST BR7 ....63 P7
St Pauls Crs FAV ME13 ....164 B1
St Paul's Pl SOCK/AV RM15 ....30 F3
St Paul's Rd ERITH DA8 ....45 L1
   FAV ME13 ....164 B1
   MARG CT9 ....15 K3
   THHTH CR7 ....60 C9
St Paul's Sq SIT ME10 ....99 M9
St Pauls Ter CANT CT1 * 5 C5
St Paul's Wy FOLK CT20 ....310 B2
   POP/IOD E14 ....25 J1
St Paul's Wood Hl
   STMC/STPC BR5 ....64 A8
St Peters Av BH/WHM TN16 * ...146 C1
St Peters Cl CHST BR7 ....63 P6
   DIT/AY ME20 ....154 A5
   IOS ME12 ....77 L1
   SWCM DA10 ....48 D8
St Peter's Ct BRDST CT10 ....113 L8
   FAV ME13 ....132 D6
   LEE/GVPK SE12 * 43 J7
St Peter's Footpath MARG CT9 ...15 K7
St Peters Gdns WNWD SE27 ....60 A2
St Peter's Gv CANT CT1 ....4 D4
St Peter's La CANT CT1 ....4 D3
St Peter's Park Rd
   BRDST CT10 ....113 L8
St Peters Pth ROCH ME1 * 19 G6
St Peter's Rd BRDST CT10 ....113 K8
   CDW/CHF RM16 ....33 J7
   CROY/NA CR0 ....3 J8
   DIT/AY ME20 ....154 A3
   FAV ME13 ....15 H7
   MARG CT9 ....15 L4
   WSTB CT5 ....105 L4
St Peter's Rbt CANTW/ST CT2 ......4 D4
St Peters Rw RRTW TN3 ....268 C3
St Peter's St CANT CT1 ....4 D4

MAIDW ME16 ....12 D5
RTWE/PEM TN2 ....23 H5
SAND/SEL CR2 ....83 J9
SWCH CT13 * 201 P1
St Peter St MAIDW ME16 ....12 D5
   ROCH ME1 ....19 H7
St Philip's Av
   MAID/SHEP ME15 ....13 H7
St Pier's La LING RH7 ....233 J6
St Quentin Rd WELL DA16 ....44 B4
St Radigund's Pl CANT CT1 * 5 F2
St Radigund's Rd CHST CT17 ....291 H6
St Radigunds St CANT CT1 ....5 D3
St Richard's Rd DEAL CT14 ....232 E7
St Ronan's Ct
   MAID/SHEP ME15 * 185 P4
St Saviour's Cl FAV ME13 ....185 H4
   FOLKN CT19 ....310 C4
St Saviours Est STHWK SE1 * 24 C6
St Saviour's Rd CROY/NA CR0 .....83 H5
   MAID/SHEP ME15 ....186 A5
Saints Cl WNWD SE27 ....60 B1
St Stephen's Cl CANTW/ST CT2 ....4 E1
St Stephen's Ct CANTW/ST CT2 ....4 E1
   CDST RH9 ....204 B5
   RTW TN1 * 23 F1
St Stephen's Crs THHTH CR7 ......60 A9
St Stephen's Flds
   CANTW/ST CT2 * 4 E2
St Stephen's Gn
   CANTW/ST CT2 ....166 E1
St Stephen's Gv LEW SE13 ....42 A4
St Stephen's Hl
   CANTW/ST CT2 ....136 D9
St Stephen's Rd
   CANTW/ST CT2 * 4 E2
St Stephen's Sq
   MAID/SHEP ME15 ....185 K1
St Stephen's St TON TN9 ....240 E1
St Stephen's Wk ASH TN23 ....282 D2
St Stephens Wy FOLK CT20 ......310 C7
St Stephons Ct RTW TN1 * 23 F1
Saint's Wk CDW/CHF RM16 ....33 K7
St Swithin's La MANHO EC4N 24 A5
St Swithin's Rd WSTB CT5 ....106 A4
St Swithun's Cl EGRIN RH19 * ...265 J7
St Swithun's Rd LEW SE13 * 42 B6
St Teresa Wk CDW/CHF RM16 ....33 J7
St Theresa's Cl KEN/WIL TN24 ......2 C2
St Thomas Cl BXLY DA5 ....45 J8
St Thomas' Dr STMC/STPC BR5 ...86 D5
St Thomas Hl CANTW/ST CT2 ....166 B1
St Thomas Rd BELV DA17 ....29 H5
   CAN/RD E16 ....26 B2
   DART DA1 * 49 J9
St Thomas's Av GVW DA11 ....69 M1
St Thomas's Pl GRAYS RM17 ......32 C9
St Thomas St STHWK SE1 ....24 B6
St Thomas Well GVE DA12 * 70 C7
St Vincent Cl WNWD SE27 ....60 B2
St Vincent Rd RDV CT15 ....262 D9
St Vincents Av DART DA1 ....46 C6
St Vincent's Cl RCANTE CT3 ....168 C8
   WSTB CT5 ....105 M7
St Vincents La E/WMAL ME19 ...152 C2
St Vincents Rd DART DA1 ....46 C7
St Welcume's Wy
   RMAID ME17 ....188 F5
St Werburgh Crs
   HOO/HM ME3 ....73 K2
St William's Wy ROCH ME1 ....95 J3
St Winifred Rd FOLKN CT19 ......310 C5
St Winifred's Rd
   BH/WHM TN16 ....146 A3
Saladin Dr PUR RM19 ....30 D7
Salamons Wy RAIN RM13 ....29 K2
Salbris Cl LYDD TN29 ....327 H6
Salcot Crs CROY/NA CR0 ....114 F4
Salcote Rd GVE DA12 ....70 A4
Salcott Rd CROY/NA CR0 ....82 D7
Salehurst Rd BROCKY SE4 ....41 M7
Salem Pl CROY/NA CR0 ....83 H7
   GVW DA11 ....69 L1
Salen St MAID/SHEP ME15 ....13 C7
Salhouse Cl THMD SE28 ....28 E2
Salisbury Av BRDST CT10 ....143 L2
   RAM CT11 ....17 H1
   RHAM ME8 ....96 G6
   SWLY BR8 ....83 J8
Salisbury Cl SIT ME10 ....130 B1
   TONN TN10 ....210 G5
   WALW SE17 ....24 A7
Salisbury Pl BRXN/ST SW9 ....45 J3
Salisbury Rd BXLY DA5 ....45 J9
   CANTW/ST CT2 ....166 D2
   CHAT ME4 ....6 E6
   CROY/NA CR0 ....83 M3
   DEAL CT14 ....232 G7
   DVE/WH CT16 ....8 E1
   DVE/WH CT16 ....8 E1
   FOLKN CT19 ....310 B4
   GRAYS RM17 ....33 J9
   GVW DA11 ....49 K9
   HAYES BR2 ....85 P2
   HB CT6 ....107 N1
   MAID/BEAR ME14 ....13 C1
   RDART DA2 ....67 J8
   RDV CT15 ....292 G1
   RRTW TN3 ....269 L5
   STH/RUST TN4 ....270 C4
   TONN TN10 ....210 G6
   WSTB CT5 ....105 L6
Salisbury Ter PECK SE15 ....41 J4
Salisbury Vls NROM TN28 * 336 F7
Salix Rd MAID/SHEP ME15 ....32 E9
Sallows Shaw MEO DA13 ....92 D7
Sally Port GILL ME7 ....72 C9
Sally Port Gdns GILL ME7 * 6 E1
Salmestone Ri MARG CT9 ....112 D5
Salmestone Rd MARG CT9 ....112 D5
Salmon Crs IOS ME12 ....77 H1
Salmon La POP/IOD E14 ....25 H2
Salmon Rd BELV DA17 ....28 E4

DART DA1 ....46 F4
Salmon St POP/IOD E14 * 25 J2
Salomons Rd PLSTW E13 ....26 D1
Saltash Rd WELL DA16 ....44 C4
Saltbox Hl BH/WHM TN16 ....115 L7
Saltcote Cl DART DA1 ....45 N7
Saltcote St RYE TN31 ....338 F4
Salter Rd BERM/RHTH SE16 ....24 G1
Saltford Cl ERITH DA8 ....46 B5
Salthouse Cl LYDD TN29 ....334 E5
Saltings Rd SNOD ME6 ....123 P6
The Saltings NROM TN28 ....337 K8
   WSTB CT5 ....105 L4
Salt La HOO/HM ME3 ....55 M1
Saltoun Rd BRXS/STRHM SW2 ...40 A5
Salt's Av MAID/SHEP ME15 ....185 L8
Salts Cl WSTB CT5 ....105 L3
Salt's Dr BRDST CT10 ....113 K8
Saltwell St POP/IOD E14 ....25 K3
Saltwood Cl ORP BR6 ....87 K8
Saltwood Gdns MARG CT9 ....113 K3
Saltwood Rd MAID/SHEP ME15 ..185 M7
Saltwood Rd
   MAID/SHEP ME15 ....185 L2
Samara Cl WALD ME5 ....185 L2
Sam Bartram Cl CHARL SE7 ....26 D8
Samian Crs FOLKN CT19 ....309 P1
Samos Rd PGE/AN SE20 ....61 H8
Samphire Cl
   MAID/BEAR ME14 ....156 B8
Samphire Ct DVE/WH CT16 ....8 E2
   GRAYS RM17 ....32 F9
Samphire Wy CHAT ME4 ....72 C6
Sampson Cl BELV DA17 ....28 C8
Sampson St WAP E1W * 24 D4
Samuel Cl NWCR SE14 ....24 G9
   WOOL/PLUM SE18 ....26 F7
Samuel Ms LYDD TN29 ....342 C5
Samuel St PECK SE15 ....40 F1
   WOOL/PLUM SE18 ....26 F7
Sancroft Av CANTW/ST CT2 ....166 B3
Sanctuary Cl BRDST CT10 ....143 L2
   DART DA1 ....67 J5
   DVW CT17 ....290 E3
Sanctuary Rd RHAM ME8 ....96 D5
The Sanctuary BXLY DA5 ....44 F7
Sandbach Pl
   WOOL/PLUM SE18 ....27 K8
Sandbanks Hl RDART DA2 ....68 A5
Sandbanks Rd FAV ME13 ....133 L3
Sandbourne Dr
   MAID/BEAR ME14 ....155 L3
Sandbourne Rd BROCKY SE4 ......41 L3
Sandcliff Rd ERITH DA8 ....29 J7
Sand End WSTB CT5 * 105 N3
Sanderling Wy GRH DA9 ....47 N6
   RSIT ME9 ....99 L2
Sandersons Av RSEV TN14 ....117 P4
Sanderson Wy TON TN9 ....211 H9
Sanderstead Rd
   STMC/STPC BR5 ....87 J3
Sandfield Gdns THHTH CR7 ....60 B9
Sandfield Pl THHTH CR7 * 60 C9
Sandfield Rd RTON TN11 ....268 E1
   THHTH CR7 ....60 B9
Sandford Rd BXLYHS DA6 ....44 G5
   HAYES BR2 ....85 K1
Sandford Rw WALW SE17 ....24 A8
Sandgate Cl RHAM ME8 ....127 J1
Sandgate Cl FOLK CT20 ....310 C8
Sandgate Rd FOLK CT20 ....10 B6
   WELL DA16 ....44 E1
Sandgate St PECK SE15 ....24 F8
Sandhawes Hl EGRIN RH19 ....265 K4
Sandhill La HOO/HM ME3 ....71 M1
Sandhills WLGTN SM6 ....82 C8
Sandhurst Av
   RTWE/PEM TN2 ....271 P2
Sandhurst Cl CANTW/ST CT2 .....136 F9
   RHAM ME8 ....96 B3
   RTWE/PEM TN2 ....270 F1
Sandhurst La CRBK TN17 ....319 J4
Sandhurst Pde CAT SE6 * 42 A9
Sandhurst Pk
   RTWE/PEM TN2 ....270 G2
Sandhurst Rd BFN/LL DA15 ....64 B2
   BXLY DA5 ....44 F6
   CAT SE6 ....42 B9
   ORP BR6 ....87 N3
   RTWE/PEM TN2 ....270 C1
   TIL RM18 ....49 L3
Sandiland Crs HAYES BR2 ....85 J6
Sandilands CROY/NA CR0 ....83 M7
   KEN/WIL TN24 ....3 J5
   SEV TN13 ....148 C7
Sandison St PECK SE15 ....40 F3
Sand La CRBK TN17 ....277 H4
Sandle's Rd BRCH CT7 ....110 C6
Sandlewood Dr BRCH CT7 ....140 A3
Sandling La MAID/BEAR ME14 ....155 J4
Sandling Pl
   MAID/BEAR ME14 * 155 L4
Sandling Ri ELTH/MOT SE9 ....63 L2
Sandling Rd HYTHE CT21 * 308 E1
   MAID/BEAR ME14 ....155 L4
The Sandlings HYTHE CT21 * 308 B7
Sandling Wy PECK SE15 * 40 F1
Sandown Cl DEAL CT14 ....203 J9
   RTWE/PEM TN2 ....271 J2
Sandown Dr HB CT6 ....107 J2
   RHAM ME8 ....96 G7

Sandown Gv RTWE/PEM TN2 ....271 J2
Sandown Lees SWCH CT13 ....202 B2
Sandown Pk RTWE/PEM TN2 .....271 J3
Sandown Rd CDW/CHF RM16 ....33 H1
   DEAL CT14 ....203 J9
   E/WMAL ME19 ....153 J4
   GVE DA12 ....69 N5
   SNWD SE25 ....83 N2
Sandpiper Cl BERM/RHTH SE16 ...25 J5
   GRH DA9 ....47 N6
Sandpiper Dr ERITH DA8 ....46 B1
Sandpiper Rd RFOLK CT18 ....288 D9
   SAND/SEL CR2 ....114 A5
   WALD ME5 ....125 J8
Sandpit Rd RSIT ME9 ....105 J8
Sandpit Hl RCANTE CT3 ....138 F4
Sandpit Rd BMLY BR1 ....62 C4
   DART DA1 ....46 C5
Sandpits Rd CROY/NA CR0 ....84 A8
Sandringham Ct
   E/WMAL ME19 ....183 H2
Sandringham Dr BXLY DA5 ....65 N1
   WELL DA16 ....44 A4
Sandringham Rd BMLY BR1 ....62 D4
   CROY/NA CR0 ....83 H2
   RHAM ME8 ....127 H1
Sand Rd RRTW TN3 ....269 M8
Sandrock Rd LEW SE13 ....41 N4
   RTWE/PEM TN2 ....23 H2
Sandstone Dr SIT ME10 ....99 M6
Sandstone La ERITH DA16 ....26 D8
Sandstone Rd
   MAID/BEAR ME14 ....125 P5
Sandtoft Rd CHARL SE7 ....26 C9
Sandway Rd RMAID ME17 ....188 G7
   STMC/STPC BR5 ....87 K1
Sandwich Cl FOLK CT20 ....310 C6
Sandwich Rd DVE/WH CT16 ......261 H9
   MSTR CT12 ....142 A9
   RCANTE CT3 ....201 G1
   RDV CT15 ....229 P1
   RDV CT15 ....260 D1
   SWCH CT13 ....201 L7
Sandwood Rd BRDST CT10 ....143 L3
Sandy Bank Rd GVE DA12 ....49 M9
Sandy Bury ORP BR6 ....86 E7
Sandycroft ABYW SE2 ....27 P9
Sandycroft Rd STRD ME2 ....71 P6
Sandy Dell GILL ME7 ....126 D2
Sandy Hill Av
   WOOL/PLUM SE18 ....27 J8
Sandy Hill Rd
   WOOL/PLUM SE18 ....27 J8
Sandyhurst La RASHE TN25 ....252 B3
Sandy La BGR/WK TN15 ....152 A3
   BGR/WK TN15 ....180 E1
   BH/WHM TN16 ....176 E1
   CDW/CHF RM16 ....33 J8
   EGRIN RH19 ....265 H7
   E/WMAL ME19 ....153 H3
   HYTHE CT21 ....309 N4
   KEN/WIL TN24 ....255 L8
   MAID/BEAR ME14 ....155 P5
   MAID/BEAR ME14 ....155 P5
   OXTED RH8 ....174 F5
   OXTED RH8 ....175 L3
   RASHW TN26 ....281 J1
   RDART DA2 ....67 H8
   SEV TN13 ....148 D6
   SNOD ME6 ....123 M7
   SOCK/AV RM15 ....30 D3
   STMC/STPC BR5 ....64 F6
   WTHK RM20 ....31 J9
Sandy La North WLGTN SM6 ....82 D7
Sandy Mt MAID/BEAR ME14 ......156 E7
Sandy Ridge BRCH CT7 ....111 K5
Sandy Rdg BGR/WK TN15 ....151 K5
   CHST BR7 ....63 J3
Sandy's Rw WCHPL E1 ....24 B1
Sandy Wy CROY/NA CR0 ....84 C7
San Feliu Ct EGRIN RH19 ....265 L6
Sanford St NWCR SE14 ....25 H9
Sanger Ct GVE DA12 ....15 F7
Sangro Pl CANT CT1 ....167 J3
San Juan Dr CDW/CHF RM16 .....31 M8
San Marcos Dr CDW/CHF RM16 ..31 M8
Sanspareil Av IOS ME12 ....77 P1
Santiago Wy WTHK RM20 ....31 N9
Santon La RCANTE CT3 ....139 N9
Sapho Pk GVE DA12 ....70 B3
Saphora Cl ORP BR6 ....86 E9
Sapphire Cl SIT ME10 ....99 K7
Sapphire Rd DEPT SE8 ....25 M9
Saracen Cl CROY/NA CR0 ....83 J3
Saracen Flds WALD ME5 ....125 N5
Saracens St POP/IOD E14 ....25 J2
Sara Crs GRH DA9 ....47 N5
Sara Pk GVE DA12 ....70 A3
Sark Cl LYDD TN29 ....326 G6
Sarre Pl SWCH CT13 ....201 N2
Sarsen Hts WALD ME5 ....125 L4
Sarsens Cl CHAT ME4 ....72 B9
Sartor Rd PECK SE15 ....41 K3
Sassoon Cl DIT/AY ME20 ....123 P9
Satanita Cl CAN/RD E16 ....26 E1
Satis Av RSIT ME9 ....99 M7
Saturn La RFOLK CT18 ....289 N9
Satmore La RFOLK CT18 ....289 M9
Saunders Cl GVW DA11 ....69 J1
   POP/IOD E14 ....25 J3

Saunders La RCANTE CT3 ....200 G1
Saunders Ness Rd
   POP/IOD E14 ....25 N7
Saunders Rd STH/RUST TN4 ....270 B8
   WOOL/PLUM SE18 ....27 N8
Saunders Wy DART DA1 ....66 F1
   RYE TN31 ....344 B1
   THMD SE28 ....28 A3
Savage Gdns EHAM E6 ....25 L2
Savanah Cl PECK SE15 ....40 F1
Save Rd MAID ME5 ....125 N2
Savemake Dr HB CT6 ....107 N4
Savile Gdns CROY/NA CR0 ....83 L6
Saville Rd CAN/RD E16 ....26 F4
Saville Rw HAYES BR2 ....85 J5
Savoy Rd DART DA1 ....46 C5
Saw Lodge Fld ASH TN23 ....282 F4
Sawpit Rd RSIT ME9 ....159 P4
Sawyers Ct CHAT ME4 ....95 N4
Saxby's La LING RH7 ....234 G5
Saxbys Rd BGR/WK TN15 ....150 A3
Saxby Wd RTON TN11 ....209 L9
Saxon Av FAV ME13 ....132 C1
Saxon Cl E/WMAL ME19 ....182 C1
   GVW DA11 ....68 C2
   HYTHE CT21 ....309 K5
   RSEV TN14 ....148 E2
   STRD ME2 ....71 P6
Saxon Hl BH/WHM TN16 * 176 E1
Saxon Pl RTW DA4 ....89 P2
   STRD ME2 ....18 A6
Saxon Rd BMLY BR1 ....62 D6
   CROY/NA CR0 ....83 J7
   FAV ME13 ....132 C1
   RAM CT11 ....16 D6
   RCANTW CT4 ....197 M2
   RDART DA2 ....66 E3
   WGOS CT8 ....111 N4
Saxon Shore Wy DEAL CT14 ......233 J1
   DVE/WH CT16 ....8 E5
   FAV ME13 ....133 J4
   GVE DA12 ....49 N7
   HB CT6 ....108 C2
   HOO/HM ME3 ....51 J5
   HYTHE CT21 ....307 K6
   RASHW TN26 ....306 E6
   RASHW TN26 ....304 E6
   RASHW TN26 ....322 C4
   RASHW TN26 ....323 L1
   RCANTE CT3 ....108 F7
   RCANTE CT3 ....135 G5
   RCANTE CT3 ....170 G5
   RCANTE CT3 ....171 H1
   RDV CT15 ....292 F3
   RFOLK CT18 ....287 H4
   ROCH ME1 ....19 G4
   RSIT ME9 ....158 D1
   RSIT ME9 ....100 A1
   RYE TN31 ....333 J8
   RYE TN31 ....339 H4
   STRD ME2 ....72 E7
   SWCH CT13 ....171 M7
   WSTB CT5 ....106 A3
Saxon St DVW CT17 ....106 A3
Saxon Wk RSIT ME9 ....99 L2
Saxton Cl LEW SE13 ....42 B4
Saxton St GILL ME7 ....73 J9
Saxville Rd STMC/STPC BR5 ....64 D9
Sayer Cl GRH DA9 ....47 N6
Sayer Rd HDCN TN27 ....221 H2
The Sayers EGRIN RH19 ....264 F7
Sayers La TENT TN30 ....301 H8
Sayes Court Rd
   STMC/STPC BR5 ....64 C9
Sayes Court St DEPT SE8 ....25 J8
Scabhardour Rd RSEV TN14 ....179 H9
Scadbury Gdns
   STMC/STPC BR5 ....64 C8
Scads Hill Cl ORP BR6 ....86 G5
Scandrett St WAP E1W * 24 E4
Scanlons Bridge Rd
   HYTHE CT21 ....308 F5
Scarborough Cl
   BH/WHM TN16 ....145 M3
Scarborough Dr IOS ME12 ....58 C8
Scarborough St WCHPL E1 ....24 C2
Scarbrook Rd CROY/NA CR0 ....83 H7
Scarlet Cl STMC/STPC BR5 ....87 K1
Scarlet St CAT SE6 ....62 G2
Scarsbrook Rd BKHTH/KID SE3 ...43 H4
Scawen Rd DEPT SE8 ....25 H8
Sceales Dr MSTR CT12 ....142 C6
Sceptre Wy WSTB CT5 ....105 J7
Scholars Rd BAL SW12 ....59 L8
Scholey Cl STRD ME2 ....124 A1
School Ap BGR/WK TN15 ....151 J5
School Av GILL ME7 ....96 B2
School Cl DART DA1 ....45 J5
   MEO DA13 ....92 D4
The School Cl WGOS CT8 ....111 M4
School Fld EDEN TN8 ....206 D8
Schoolfield Rd WTHK RM20 ....31 K9
School Hl RCANTW CT4 ....194 C4
   RRTW TN3 ....295 J1
School House La
   STPH/PW TN12 ....274 C1
Schoolhouse La WAP E1W * 24 C3
School Houses
   CDW/CHF RM16 * 33 H1
School La BGR/WK TN15 ....125 C8
   BGR/WK TN15 ....149 L6
   CANT CT1 ....135 P6
   CDW/CHF RM16 ....33 H1
   E/WMAL ME19 ....122 B8
   EYN DA4 ....90 C5
   FAV ME13 ....191 J5
   HB CT6 ....107 M6
   HOO/HM ME3 ....71 L1

MAID/SHEP ME15 ....186 B2
MEO DA13 ....122 B3
RAM CT11 ....17 F3
RCANTE CT5 ....138 D7
RCANTE CT5 ....139 D7
RCANTE CT5 ....168 F8
RCANTE CT5 ....169 K9
RCANTE CT5 ....199 M5
RCANTE CT5 ....200 B4
RCANTW CT4 ....161 N8
RCANTW CT4 ....196 C6
RDART DA12 ....68 A2
RFOLK CT18 ....287 M9
RMAID ME17 ....188 C9
RMAID ME17 ....217 H3
ROCH ME1 ....94 C9
RSIT ME9 ....98 C4
RSIT ME9 ....98 C7
RSIT ME9 ....99 K3
RSIT ME9 ....128 C2
RSIT ME9 ....130 C5
RTON TN11 ....181 H5
RTON TN31 ....211 P2
RYE TN31 ....338 F3
SWLY BR8 ....66 B6
WELL DA16 ....4 D4
School Ter HAWK TN18 ....317 H4
School Rd RTWE/PEM TN2 ....270 C7
School Rd CHST BR7 ....63 N7
DEAL CT14 ....230 G5
DEAL CT14 ....231 H6
FAV ME13 ....132 E7
GVE DA12 ....69 N2
HDCN TN27 ....221 H2
HYTHE CT21 ....308 G3
RASHW TN26 ....251 M2
RASHW TN26 ....280 C4
RASHW TN26 ....322 D5
RCANTE CT5 ....170 D9
RFOLK CT18 ....288 B5
SIT ME10 ....130 A2
SWCH CT13 ....201 N1
Schooner Ct POP/IOD E14 ....25 N6
Schooner Ct GRH DA9 ....47 J5
Schreiber Ms GILL ME7 * 96 A1
Scimitar Cl GILL ME7 ....96 B4
Scocles Rd IOS ME12 ....78 C2
Scoles Crs BRXS/STRHM SW2 ....40 A9
Scoones Cl RSIT ME9 ....130 D3
Scords La BH/WHM TN16 ....177 K8
Scotby Av WALD ME5 ....125 N1
Scotchmen Cl IOS ME12 ....57 N9
Scotia Rd BRXS/STRHM SW2 ....40 A8
Scotland La GVE DA12 ....70 CB
Scotney Cl ORP BR6 ....86 B8
Scotsdale Cl CHST BR7 ....201 N4
Scotsdale Rd LEE/GVPK SE12 ....42 F6
Scotshall La WARL CR6 ....114 F9
Scott's La RASHE TN25 ....255 L9
Scott Av RHAM ME8 ....97 K6
Scott Cl DIT/AY ME20 ....154 B4
Scott Crs ERITH DA8 ....45 P2
Scott Lidgett Crs
  BERM/RHTH SE16 ....24 D5
Scotton St RASHE TN25 ....224 A8
Scott Rd CDW/CHF RM16 ....33 H7
  GVE DA12 ....69 P4
  TON TN30 ....240 C1
Scotts Acre RYE TN31 ....339 P9
Scotts Av HAYES BR2 ....62 B8
Scotts La BR2 ....62 B9
Scotts Pas WOOL/PLUM SE18 * 27 J7
Scotts Rd BMLY BR1 ....62 E5
Scotts Ter CHAT ME4 ....6 B7
Scott St MAID/SHEP ME15 ....12 E1
Scotts Wy RTWE/PEM TN2 ....270 B8
  SEV TN13 ....148 D7
Scoulding Rd CAN/RD E16 ....26 A2
Scouler St POP/IOD E14 ....25 N5
Scragged Oak Rd
  MAID/BEAR ME14 ....126 E4
  MAID/BEAR ME14 ....156 E2
  MAID/BEAR ME14 ....157 M4
Scrapsgate Rd IOS ME12 ....58 A9
Scraps Hl RSIT ME9 ....130 D1
Scratchers La EYN DA4 ....90 A7
Scratton Flds GVE DA12 ....92 E2
Scrooby St CAT SE6 ....41 P7
Scudders Hl HART DA3 ....90 F5
Scutari Rd EDUL SE22 ....41 H6
Scylla Rd PECK SE15 ....51 H4
Sea Ap IOS ME12 ....80 B3
Seaborough Rd
  CDW/CHF RM16 ....33 K6
Seabourne Wy LYDD TN29 ....326 F7
Seabrook Ct HYTHE CT21 ....309 N4
Seabrook Dr WWKM BR4 ....85 H6
Seabrook Gdns HYTHE CT21 ....309 M5
Seabrook Rd RTON TN11 ....210 D7
Seabrook V HYTHE CT21 ....309 N3
Seacourt Rd ABYW SE2 ....28 C5
Seacroft Rd BRDST CT10 ....143 M5
Seadown Cl HYTHE CT21 ....309 N3
Seafield Rd BRDST CT10 ....113 J9
  CANTW CT2 ....18 H3
  WSTB CT5 ....106 A3
Seaford Ct ROCH ME1 * 18 E7
Seager Av FAV ME13 ....132 E4
Seager Buildings DEPT SE8 * 41 N2
Seager Pl BOW E3 ....25 J1
Seager Rd IOS ME12 ....57 N6
Seagrave Cl WCHPL E1 ....24 C1
Seagrave Crs FOLKN CT19 ....11 J3
Seagull La CAN/RD E16 ....26 B3
Sealand Ct ROCH ME1 * 18 E6
Seal Dr BGR/WK TN15 ....149 L6
Seal Hollow Rd SEV TN13 ....21 J1
Seally Rd GRAYS RM17 ....32 B8
Seal Rd SEV TN13 ....149 J6
Seamark Cl MSTR CT12 ....140 E6
Seamark Rd MSTR CT12 ....140 E4

Seapoint Rd BRDST CT10 ....143 N1
Searles Dr EHAM E6 ....27 J1
Searles St STHWK SE1 ....24 A7
Sea Rd BRCH CT7 ....111 J5
  DEAL CT14 ....263 H2
  HYTHE CT21 ....309 M5
  RYE TN31 ....344 A1
Sears St CMBW SE5 ....40 D1
Seasalter Beach WSTB CT5 ....105 H7
Seasalter Cl IOS ME12 ....80 C3
Seasalter Cross WSTB CT5 ....104 F8
Seasalter La WSTB CT5 ....134 G1
Seasalter Rd FAV ME13 ....133 P5
Seaside Av IOS ME12 ....58 C8
Sea St HB CT6 ....106 G3
  RCANTE CT5 ....292 F1
Seathorpe Av IOS ME12 ....58 C9
Seaton Av HYTHE CT21 ....308 G4
Seaton Rd DART DA1 ....46 A8
  GILL ME7 ....96 E5
  RCANTE CT5 ....168 F6
  WELL DA16 ....4 C6
Seaview HOO/HM ME3 ....56 D3
Sea View Av BRCH CT7 ....110 F5
Seaview Av IOS ME12 ....80 F6
Sea View Cl RFOLK CT18 ....311 L2
Sea View Gdns IOS ME12 ....80 C4
Sea View Hts BRCH CT7 ....110 E5
Seaview Hts LYDD TN29 * 336 A4
Sea View Rd BRCH CT7 ....110 F5
  BRDST CT10 ....113 M7
  HB CT6 ....107 J1
  MSTR CT12 ....142 C6
  RDV CT15 ....292 E3
Seaview Rd GILL ME7 ....7 J4
  NROM TN28 ....343 J3
Sea View Sq HB CT6 * 107 L1
Seaview Ter FOLK CT20 * 310 A8
  MARG CT9 ....14 C5
Seaview Ter OBOR ME11 * 77 J2
  RSIT ME9 ....98 C5
  RYE TN31 * 338 F7
Seaview Vis BRDST CT10 * 113 L4
Seaville Dr HB CT6 ....108 B5
Sea Wall LYDD TN29 ....327 H6
  WSTB CT5 ....105 L4
Seaway Crs LYDD TN29 ....337 L1
Seaway Gdns LYDD TN29 ....337 M1
Seaway Rd LYDD TN29 ....337 M1
Second Av BRDST CT10 ....113 M3
  GILL ME7 ....96 B3
  IOS ME12 ....57 K7
  IOS ME12 ....79 M2
  MARG CT9 ....112 C2
  OBOR ME11 ....77 H4
  RYE TN31 ....344 A1
  WALD ME5 ....95 P5
  WTHK RM20 ....31 K3
Secretan Rd ROCH ME1 ....94 G5
Sedan Wy WALW SE17 ....24 B8
Sedcombe Cl SCUP DA14 ....42 F6
Sedgebrook Rd
  BKHTH/KID SE3 ....43 H3
Sedge Crs WALD ME5 ....125 K1
Sedgehill Rd CAT SE6 ....61 N4
Sedgemere Rd ABYW SE2 ....28 B6
Sedgeway CAT SE6 ....42 D9
Sedgewood Cl HAYES BR2 ....61 P8
Sedgmoor Pl CMBW SE5 ....40 E1
Sedley MEO DA13 ....68 E4
Sedley Cl DIT/AY ME20 ....154 D2
  HOO/HM ME3 ....52 C9
  RHAM ME8 ....95 P6
Seeley Dr DUL SE21 ....61 H1
Seething La MON EC3R 24 B4
Seeton Cl PECK SE15 ....40 C8
Sefton Cl STMC/STPC BR5 ....86 G1
Sefton Rd CROY/NA CRO 83 M5
  ORP BR6 ....86 G1
Segrave Rd FOLKN CT19 ....11 J5
Selah Dr SWLY BR8 ....65 L7
Selby Cl CHST BR7 ....107 P2
Selbourne Av BXLY DA5 ....44 C9
Selborne Rd CMBW SE5 ....85 K7
  CROY/NA CRO 3 J6
  MARG CT9 ....112 C5
Selbourne Cl HART DA3 ....69 H9
Selbourne Rd GILL ME7 ....73 K8
Selbourne Wk
  MAID/SHEP ME15 ....186 C5
Selby Cl CHST BR7 ....107 P2
Selby Rd MAID/SHEP ME15 ....186 C5
  PGE/AN SE20 ....60 GB
  PLSTW E13 ....26 C1
Selbys LING W1 ....235 H4
Selden Rd PECK SE15 ....51 K1
Selhurst New Rd SNWD SE25 ....83 K3
Selhurst Rd CROY/NA CRO 83 K3
  SNWD SE25 ....83 K3
Selkirk Dr ERITH DA8 ....45 N2
Selkirk Rd DVW/CHT CT16 ....291 J4
Sellindge Cl BECK BR3 ....61 N9
Selling Ct FAV ME13 ....163 M6
Selling Rd FAV ME13 ....133 H8
  RCANTW CT4 ....164 C9
Selwyn Crs WELL DA16 ....44 D5
Selwyn Dr BRDST CT10 ....113 K3
Selwyn Rd TIL RM18 ....49 K3
Semaphore Rd BRCH CT7 ....110 G5
Semper Rd CDW/CHF RM16 ....33 K5
Semple Cl MSTR CT12 ....141 K5

Senacre La MAID/SHEP ME15 ....186 B5
Senacre Sq MAID/SHEP ME15 ....186 B5
Senate St PECK SE15 ....41 J3
Seneca Rd THHTH CR7 ....83 H1
Sene Pk HYTHE CT21 ....309 J4
Senlac Cl RAM CT11 ....142 C6
Senlac Pl RRTW TN3 * 269 M9
Senlac Rd LEE/GVPK SE12 ....42 F9
Senrab St WCHPL E1 ....24 G2
Sequoia Gdns ORP BR6 ....86 C1
Serenaders Rd BRXN/ST SW9 ....40 A3
Serene Ct BRDST CT10 ....113 N9
Sermon Dr SWLY BR8 ....65 J9
Serpentine Rd SEV TN13 ....149 H8
Serviden Dr BMLY BR1 ....63 H7
Sessions House Sq
  MAID/BEAR ME14 ....12 E2
Setchell Rd STHWK SE1 ....24 C7
Setchell Wy STHWK SE1 ....24 C7
Setford Rd WALD ME5 ....95 P8
Setterfield House
  HYTHE CT21 * 309 J5
Setterfield Rd MARG CT9 ....15 H7
Settington Av WALD ME5 ....95 P5
Settles St WCHPL E1 ....24 D2
Sevastopol Pl CANT CT1 ....167 J3
Sevenacre Rd FAV ME13 ....132 F4
Seven Acres SWLY BR8 ....88 C3
Seven Mile La BGR/WK TN15 ....152 A4
  RTON TN11 * 211 J4
Sevenoaks By-Pass SEV TN13 ....178 D2
Sevenoaks Rd BGR/WK TN15 ....150 D8
  BROCKY SE4 ....41 M7
  ORP BR6 ....116 C3
  RSEV TN14 ....117 N3
  RSEV TN14 ....148 C1
Sevenoaks Wy
  STMC/STPC BR5 ....64 E9
Seven Stars Yd WCHPL E1 * 24 E9
Seven Stones Dr BRDST CT10 ....143 M5
Severn Tc RM18 ....32 A4
Severnake Cl POP/IOD E14 ....25 P2
Severn Cl TONN TN10 ....210 F5
Severn Rd SOCK/AV RM15 ....54 N4
  WALD ME5 ....95 P9
Sevington La KEN/WIL TN24 ....253 J9
Sevington Pk
  MAID/SHEP ME15 ....185 L5
Seward Rd BECK BR3 ....61 K8
Sewell Cl BRCH CT7 ....111 H7
  CDW/CHF RM16 ....31 M8
Sewell Rd ABYW SE2 ....27 H6
  THMD SE28 ....27 H6
Sexburga Dr IOS ME12 ....58 B8
Sextant Av POP/IOD E14 ....25 N2
Sextant Pk STRD ME2 * 19 K3
Sextant Rd TIL RM18 ....49 K3
Seymour Av WALD ME5 ....111 N4
  WSTB CT5 ....105 M5
Seymour Cl HB CT6 ....107 N5
Seymour Dr HAYES BR2 ....86 A5
Seymour Gdns BROCKY SE4 ....41 K4
Seymour Pl CANT CT1 ....167 J2
  SNWD SE25 ....83 P3
Seymour Rd CDW/CHF RM16 ....31 M6
  GVW DA11 ....49 K9
  RDV CT15 ....262 E8
  RHAM ME8 ....95 P6
  TIL RM18 ....49 K3
  WALD ME5 ....7 F6
Seymour St WOOL/PLUM SE18 ....27 K7
Seymour Ter PGE/AN SE20 ....61 H7
Seymour Vis PGE/AN SE20 ....61 H7
Seymour Wk SWCM DA10 ....48 C3
Seyssel St POP/IOD E14 ....25 M7
Shacklands Rd RSEV TN14 ....118 F5
Shackleton Cl FSTH SE23 ....61 H1
  WALD ME5 ....95 K8
The Shades STRD ME2 ....71 K3
Shadoxhurst Rd RASHW TN26 ....303 H5
Shad Thames STHWK SE1 ....24 D5
Shadwell Gdns WCHPL E1 * 24 F3
Shadwell Pierhead WAP E1W * 24 F5
Shaftesbury Av FOLKN CT19 ....310 B4
Shaftesbury Ct E/WMAL ME19 ....153 N3
Shaftesbury Dr MAIDW ME16 ....155 K8
Shaftesbury La DART DA1 ....47 H5
Shaftesbury Rd BECK BR3 ....61 M8
  CANTW/ST CT2 ....166 D1
  FSTH SE23 ....61 H1
  STH/RUST TN4 ....270 D2
  WSTB CT5 ....105 L5
Shaftsbury St HART TN11 ....17 H3
Shah Pl RAM CT11 ....16 E3
Shakespeare Av TIL RM18 ....49 M3
Shakespeare Farm Rd
  HOO/HM ME3 ....54 D1
Shakespeare Rd BRCH CT7 ....111 H5
  BXLYHN DA7 ....44 D2
  DART DA1 ....46 C5
  DVW CT17 ....291 J9
  HB CT6 ....7 J6
  HNHL SE24 ....40 G5
  MARG CT9 ....15 H6
  SIT ME10 ....50 E2
  TON TN9 ....210 C5
Shakespeare Ter FOLK CT20 ....10 C5
Shalford Cl ORP BR6 ....86 C7
Shalloak Rd CANTW/ST CT2 ....137 J8
Shallons Rd ELTH/MOT SE9 ....65 H5
Shallows Rd BRDST CT10 ....113 H7
Shalmsford Rd RCANTW CT4 ....195 G2
Shalmsford St RCANTW CT4 ....195 H1
The Shambles SEV TN13 ....148 C1
Shamrock Av WSTB CT5 ....105 J7
Shamrock Rd CROY/NA CRO 82 E3
Shandon Ct RTWE/PEM TN2 ....270 C7
Shand St STHWK SE1 ....24 C5
Shandy Wy WCHPL E1 ....24 C1
Shanklin Cl WALD ME5 ....95 P8
Shannon Wy BECK BR3 ....61 P5
  SOCK/AV RM15 ....54 G1
Shapland Cl HB CT6 ....107 P3

Shardcroft Av HNHL SE24 ....40 B6
Shardeloes Rd BROCKY SE4 ....41 M3
Shard's Sq PECK SE15 ....24 D9
Share & Coulter Rd WSTB CT5 ....106 C5
Sharfleet Dr STRD ME2 ....71 K8
Sharland Cl THHTH CR7 ....82 F3
Sharland Rd GVE DA12 ....69 N1
Sharman Ct SCUP DA14 ....64 C3
Sharnal St HOO/HM ME3 ....123 H6
Sharnal St HOO/HM ME3 ....53 N7
Sharon Crs WALD ME5 ....125 L1
Sharp's Fld HDCN TN27 ....247 P4
Sharps Gn GILL ME7 ....96 C1
Sharp Wy DART DA1 ....46 D4
Sharratt St PECK SE15 ....51 K1
Sharsted Hl RSIT ME9 ....161 H4
Sharsted Wy GILL ME7 ....126 D2
  MAID/BEAR ME14 * 156 E7
Shawbrooke Rd ELTH/MOT SE9 ....43 H5
Shawbury Rd EDUL SE22 ....40 F6
Shaw Cl HOO/HM ME3 ....52 B9
  MAID/BEAR ME14 * 155 P5
  THMD SE28 ....28 A4
Shaw Crs POP/IOD E14 ....25 H2
  TIL RM18 ....49 M2
Shaw Cross KEN/WIL TN24 ....252 G4
Shawdon Av DART DA1 ....202 F5
Shawfield Pk BMLY BR1 ....63 K2
Shaw Rd BH/WHM TN16 ....145 M5
  BMLY BR1 ....62 D2
  EDUL SE22 ....40 E5
Shaw's Cottages FSTH SE23 ....61 L2
Shawstead Rd WALD ME5 ....95 P7
Shaws Wy ROCH ME1 ....93 M7
The Shaw CHST BR7 ....63 N6
  RTWE/PEM TN2 ....23 H7
Shaxton Crs CROY/NA CRO 114 B5
Sheafe Dr CRBK TN17 ....297 P2
Sheal's Crs MAID/SHEP ME15 ....185 M1
Shearers Cl MAID/BEAR ME14 ....156 B8
Shearman Rd BKHTH/KID SE3 ....42 G1
Shearwater HART DA3 ....68 F9
  MAIDW ME16 ....154 C7
Shearwater Av WSTB CT5 ....105 H7
Shearwater Ct IOS ME12 ....57 K8
Shear Wy LYDD TN29 ....326 C1
Shearway Rd FOLKN CT19 ....310 C4
Sheenewood SYD SE26 ....60 F1
Sheen Rd STMC/STPC BR5 ....86 C1
Sheen Wy WLGTN SM6 ....82 E9
Sheepbarn La WARL CR6 ....115 K6
Sheepcote La ASH TN23 ....282 F4
Sheephurst La
  STPH/PW TN12 ....244 C4
Sheepstreet La WADH TN5 ....314 F9
Sheerness Docks IOS ME12 * 57 K6
Sheerstone RSIT ME9 ....99 L3
Sheerwater Rd CAN/RD E16 ....26 E1
  RCANTE CT5 ....169 N3
Sheerways FAV ME13 ....132 D2
Sheet Glass Rd OBOR ME11 ....77 J4
Sheet Hl BGR/WK TN15 ....180 C2
Sheffield Gdns CDEAL CT14 ....233 H5
Sheffield Rd STN/RUST TN4 ....240 C7
The Sheilings BGR/WK TN15 ....149 L5
Shelbury Cl SCUP DA14 ....64 C2
Shelbury Rd EDUL SE22 ....41 H6
Shelden Dr RHAM ME8 ....97 J6
Sheldon Cl LEE/GVPK SE12 ....61 H7
  PGE/AN SE20 ....61 H7
  RCANTE CT5 ....199 J3
Sheldon Rd BXLYHN DA7 ....45 H2
Sheldon St CROY/NA CRO 83 H7
Sheldon Wy DIT/AY ME20 ....153 P1
Sheldrake Cl CAN/RD E16 ....26 C4
Sheldwich Ter HAYES BR2 * 85 P5
Shelford Rd NRWD SE19 ....60 E6
Shelibank La RDART DA2 ....67 P4
Shell Ct HB CT6 ....7 J6
Shelley Av CANT CT1 ....167 H2
Shelley Cl BGR/WK TN15 ....86 F7
Shelley Dr WELL DA16 ....43 P8
Shelley Pl TIL RM18 ....49 M2
Shelley Rd EGRIN RH19 ....264 C1
  WMERE ME16 ....185 H1
Shelleys La RSEV TN14 ....147 H1
Shellons St FOLK CT20 ....11 F6
Shelmerdine Cl BOW E3 ....25 N1
Shelton Cl TONN TN10 ....210 F5
Shelton La RCANTW CT4 ....258 F1
Shenden Cl SEV TN13 ....179 H4
Shenden Wy SEV TN13 ....179 H4
Shenley Av MAID/BEAR ME14 ....155 J2
Shenley Pk HDCN TN27 * 247 P7
Shenley Rd CMBW SE5 ....40 E2
Shepherd Cl ASH TN23 ....282 E5
Shepherd Dr KEN/WIL TN24 ....283 K1
Shepherds Cl ORP BR6 ....86 C7
Shepherd's Close Rd
  RCANTW CT4 ....198 B6
Shepherdsgate CANTW/ST CT2 ....4 D2
Shepherds Ga GILL ME7 ....96 C9
Shepherdsgate Dr HB CT6 ....107 M6
Shepherdsgrove La
  EGRIN RH19 ....266 A3
Shepherds La DART DA1 ....46 A9
Shepherds Leas ELTH/MOT SE9 ....43 H5
Shepherd St GVW DA11 ....49 H8
Shepherds Wk HYTHE CT21 ....308 D7

RTWE/PEM TN2 ....23 J5
  WSTB CT5 ....106 B6
Shepherds Wy HOO/HM ME3 ....54 C4
  RMAID ME17 ....187 H7
  SAND/SEL CR2 ....114 A2
  WSTB CT5 ....106 B6
Shepherdswell Rd RDV CT15 ....260 A1
Sheppard Dr BERM/RHTH SE16 ....24 E8
Shepperton Cl MAID/SHEP ME15 ....125 P1
Shepperton Rd STMC/STPC BR5 ....86 B5
  ERITH DA8 ....46 B1
Sheppey Cl BRCH CT7 ....110 G6
  ERITH DA8 ....46 B1
Sheppey Crs IOS ME12 * 57 M9
Sheppey Rd MAID/SHEP ME15 ....185 L4
Sheppey St IOS ME12 ....57 J6
Sheppey Vw WSTB CT5 ....105 K3
Sheppey Wy RSIT ME9 ....77 J8
Sheppey Pl GVE DA12 ....49 M8
Sheppey Wy KEN/WIL TN24 ....253 H4
Shepway Cl FOLKN CT19 ....10 C3
Shepway Ct MAID/SHEP ME15 * 185 P3
Sherard Rd ELTH/MOT SE9 ....43 J3
Sheraton Cl WALD ME5 ....125 L4
Sherborne Cl RTWE/PEM TN2 ....23 K7
Sherborne Crs BGR/WK TN15 ....149 M2
Sherborne La MANHO EC4N 24 A3
Sherborne Rd RCANTE CT5 ....169 N4
Sherbourne Cl BGR/WK TN15 ....120 B1
Sherbourne Dr MAIDW ME16 ....184 G1
  STRD ME2 ....72 A6
Sheridance Cl BXLYHN DA7 ....45 J5
Sherenden La STPH/PW TN12 ....245 H9
Sherenden Rd RTON TN11 ....241 N2
Sherfield Rd GRAYS RM17 ....32 C3
Sheridan Cl EGRIN RH19 ....264 F7
  MAID/BEAR ME14 ....155 K4
  WALD ME5 ....125 L4
Sheridan Ct DART DA1 ....46 C5
Sheridan Rd BELV DA17 ....28 F7
  BXLYHN DA7 ....44 C4
  DVE/WH CT16 ....291 J4
Sheridan St WCHPL E1 ....24 E2
Sheriff Dr WALD ME5 ....125 M3
Sheringham La MAIDW ME16 ....155 J5
Sheringham Rd PGE/AN SE20 ....61 H9
Sherington Rd CHARL SE7 ....26 C9
Sherlies Av ORP BR6 ....86 F6
Sherman Cl GILL ME7 ....96 E5
Sherman Rd BMLY BR1 ....62 E7
Sherndon La EDEN TN8 ....236 C7
Sherndds MAID/SHEP ME15 ....185 N4
Sheron Cl DEAL CT14 ....232 F4
Sherriffs Court La MSTR CT12 ....140 C6
Sherway Cl HDCN TN27 ....247 P4
Sherway Rd HDCN TN27 ....248 E2
Sherwin Rd NWCR SE14 ....41 K2
Sherwood CDW/CHF RM16 ....35 H7
Sherwood Av WALD ME5 ....125 M3
Sherwood Cl BXLY DA5 ....44 E7
  FAV ME13 ....132 E5
  HB CT6 ....107 M4
  KEN/WIL TN24 ....252 G2
  WSTB CT5 ....105 K8
Sherwood Ct WGOS CT8 * 111 M4
Sherwood Gdns POP/IOD E14 ....25 K7
  RAM CT11 ....143 K3
  STHWK SE1 ....24 D8
Sherwood Pk RTWE/PEM TN2 ....271 H3
  WWKM BR4 ....84 F6
Sherwood Park Av BFN/LL DA15 ....44 CB
Sherwood Park Rd MTCM CR4 ....82 B1
Sherwood Rd RRTW TN3 ....269 K5
  BRCH CT7 ....110 G6
  CROY/NA CRO 83 N4
  WELL DA16 ....44 A3
Sherwoods WALD ME5 ....125 J4
Sherwood Wy RTWE/PEM TN2 ....270 C2
  WWKM BR4 ....84 F6
Shieldhall St ABYW SE2 ....28 B7
Shifford Pth FSTH SE23 ....61 K2
Shillingheld Cl MAID/BEAR ME14 ....156 C7
Shimmin Rd RSIT ME9 * 129 L7
Shingle Barn La WBY/VAL ME18 ....184 A1
Shinglewell Rd ERITH DA8 ....45 J1
Shinners Cl SNWD SE25 ....83 M2
Shipbourne Rd RTON TN11 ....180 C9
  TON TN10 ....210 F7
Ship Cl LYDD TN29 ....326 C6
Ship Field Cl BH/WHM TN16 ....145 N6
Ship Hl BH/WHM TN16 ....145 N6
Ship La ROCH ME1 ....19 K7
  SOCK/AV RM15 ....30 C5
  SWLY BR8 ....66 D7
Shipley Hills Rd MEO DA13 ....92 G5
Shipley Mill Cl ASH TN23 ....282 F4
Shipman Rd CAN/RD E16 ....26 E2
  FSTH SE23 ....61 K1
Shipmans Wy DVE/WH CT16 ....291 H4
Ship & Mermaid Rw STHWK SE1 ....24 A5
Ship St DEPT SE8 ....41 N2
  FOLKN CT19 ....265 H8
Ship Tavern Pas BANK EC3V 24 B3
Shipwright Rd BERM/RHTH SE16 ....25 H5
Shipwrights Av CHAT ME4 ....95 M4
Shipwrights Wy STHWK SE1 ....24 D8
The Shipyard FAV ME13 ....132 C4
Shirburn Cl FSTH SE23 ....41 J8
Shirburt St POP/IOD E14 ....25 K3

Shirebrook Rd BKHTH/KID SE3 .....43 H3
Shirehall Rd DART DA2 .....66 D4
Shire La FAV ME13 .....191 H5
The Shires STPH/PW TN12 .....243 H2
Shires Wk EDEN TN8 .....206 C7
Shireway CI FOLKN CT19 .....310 D4
Shirley Av BXLY DA5 .....44 F8
   CROY/NA CR0 .....83 P5
Shirley CI DART DA1 .....46 C5
   GVE DA12 .....70 D1
Shirley Crs BECK BR3 .....84 B1
Shirley Gdns STH/RUST TN4 .....269 P4
Shirley Gv STH/RUST TN4 .....269 P5
   STH/RUST TN4 .....270 A3
Shirley Hills Rd CROY/NA CR0 .....84 A9
Shirley Oaks Rd CROY/NA CR0 .....84 A9
Shirley Park Rd CROY/NA CR0 .....83 N5
Shirley Rd BFN/LL DA15 .....64 A2
   CROY/NA CR0 .....83 N5
Shirley Rw SNWD SE25 * 60 G8
Shirley St CAN/RD E16 .....26 A2
Shirley Wy CROY/NA CR0 .....84 C7
   MAID/SHEP ME15 .....156 D9
Shoebury Ter IOS ME12 * 78 G2
Sholden Bank DEAL CT14 .....268 A5
Sholden Gdns STMC/STPC BR5 .....87 K2
Sholden New Rd DEAL CT14 .....232 E4
Sholden Rd STRD ME2 .....72 C6
Shooter's HI DVW CT17 .....8 A1
   RDV CT15 .....230 D9
   WOOL/PLUM SE18 .....43 K2
Shooters Hill Rd
   BKHTH/KID SE3 .....42 C2
   WOOL/PLUM SE18 .....43 J2
Shore CI BRCH CT7 * 110 E5
   HB CT6 .....106 G3
Shoreditch High St
   LVPST EC2M 24 B1
Shorefields RHAM ME8 .....97 K4
Shoregate La RSIT ME9 .....75 K9
Shoreham La ORP BR6 .....117 P1
   RSEV TN14 .....117 P6
   SEV TN13 .....148 E8
   TENT TN30 .....301 H4
Shoreham PI RSEV TN14 .....118 F6
Shoreham Rd RSEV TN14 .....118 C8
   STMC/STPC BR5 .....64 D7
Shoreham Wy HAYES BR2 .....85 K3
Shorehill La BGR/WK TN15 .....119 M9
The Shore GVW DA11 .....48 C6
Shorland Ct ROCH ME1 * 7 L1
Shorncliffe Crs FOLK CT20 .....310 B6
Shorncliffe Rd FOLK CT20 .....10 C4
   FOLK CT20 .....310 C6
   STHWK SE1 .....24 C8
Shorndean St CAT SE6 .....42 A9
Shorne CI BFN/LL DA15 .....44 D7
   STMC/STPC BR5 .....87 L1
Shornefield CI BMLY BR1 .....63 L9
Shorne Ifield Rd GVE DA12 .....70 D5
Shorter St WCHPL E1 .....24 C4
Shortlands CI DART DA1 .....28 E6
Shortlands Gdns HAYES BR2 .....62 C8
Shortlands Gv HAYES BR2 .....62 B9
Shortlands Rd HAYES BR2 .....62 B9
   SIT ME10 .....129 P1
Short La LYDD TN29 .....323 M8
   OXTED RH8 .....175 L8
   RDV CT15 .....289 N3
Short's Prospect IOS ME12 * 79 H7
Shorts Reach ROCH ME1 * 18 E6
Short St CHAT ME4 .....6 C5
   IOS ME12 .....57 K6
   RCANTE CT5 .....230 D1
   SWCH CT13 .....201 P1
Shorts Wy ROCH ME1 * 94 F4
Shortway ELTH/MOT SE9 .....43 J4
Shottenden Rd BRCH CT7 * 111 L9
Shottenden La RCANTW CT4 .....193 J5
Shottenden Rd FAV ME13 .....192 F4
   GILL ME7 .....73 K8
Shottery CI ELTH/MOT SE9 .....63 J2
Shoulder of Mutton Aly
   POP/IOD E14 .....25 K4
Shovelstrode La EGRIN RH19 .....265 N3
Showfields Rd
   RTWE/PEM TN2 .....270 D7
Shrapnel CI WOOL/PLUM SE18 .....43 P9
Shrapnel Rd ELTH/MOT SE9 .....43 K4
Shrewsbury La
   WOOL/PLUM SE18 .....43 M2
Shrewsbury Rd BECK BR3 .....61 L9
Shrimpton CI RCANTW CT4 .....164 C9
Shroffold Rd BMLY BR1 .....62 C3
Shropshire Ct MTCM CR4 .....82 D1
Shropshire Ter
   MAID/SHEP ME15 .....186 B4
Shrubbery Rd EYN DA4 .....67 K7
   GVE DA12 .....49 M9
The Shrubbery DEAL CT14 .....233 H8
   RCANTW CT4 * 228 C5
Shrubcote TENT TN30 .....301 K8
Shrub Hill Rd WSTB CT5 .....106 C7
Shrublands Av CROY/NA CR0 .....64 A8
Shrublands CI SYD SE26 .....61 J2
Shrublands Dr
   RTWE/PEM TN2 * 23 H2
Shrub La WADH TN5 .....314 F9
Shrubsall CI ELTH/MOT SE9 .....43 J9
Shrubsole Av IOS ME12 .....57 L7
Shrubsole Dr
   MAID/BEAR ME14 .....155 K1
Shuart La BRCH CT7 .....110 A9
Shurland Av IOS ME12 .....78 B1
   IOS ME12 .....80 F6
   SIT ME10 .....128 C2
Shurland Gdns PECK SE15 * 40 F1
Shurlock Av SWLY BR8 .....69 H5
Shurlock Dr ORP BR6 .....86 D8
Shuttle CI BFN/LL DA15 .....44 B8

Shuttlemead BXLY DA5 .....45 H8
Shuttle Rd BRDST CT10 .....113 N9
   DART DA1 .....46 A4
Shuttlesfield La RCANTW CT4 .....257 J8
Sibert's CI RDV CT15 .....260 A3
Sibley CI BXLYHS DA6 .....64 G3
Sibthorpe Rd LEE/GVPK SE12 .....42 A5
Sidcup By-Pass Rd SCUP DA14 .....64 A3
Sidcup HI SCUP DA14 .....64 H4
Sidcup Hill Gdns SCUP DA14 * 64 E4
Sidcup PI SCUP DA14 .....64 G4
Sidcup Rd ELTH/MOT SE9 .....43 J9
   LEE/GVPK SE12 .....42 F6
Siddons Rd CROY/NA CR0 .....82 F7
   FSTH SE23 .....61 L1
Sidewood Rd ELTH/MOT SE9 .....43 P9
The Sidings MEO DA13 * 92 B2
   RFOLK CT18 .....287 H1
Sidmouth Rd PECK SE15 .....40 F2
   STMC/STPC BR5 .....87 J2
   WELL DA16 .....44 E1
Sidney CI RTWE/PEM TN2 .....270 B8
Sidney Gdns RSEV TN14 .....149 H1
Sidney Rd BECK BR3 .....61 L8
   GILL ME7 .....73 J8
Sidney Sq WCHPL E1 * 24 F1
Sidney St FOLKN CT19 .....11 G1
   MAIDW ME16 .....185 H1
Siebert Rd BKHTH/KID SE3 .....26 B9
Siemens Rd WOOL/PLUM SE18 .....26 E6
Sienna Ct RHAM ME8 * 126 C1
Signal Ct LING RH7 .....235 H4
Siggon Fld RTON TN11 * 212 B5
Silchester Ct
   MAID/BEAR ME14 .....155 P5
Silecroft Ct ASH TN25 * 252 B8
Silecroft Rd BXLYHN DA7 .....45 J2
Silk CI LEE/GVPK SE12 .....42 E6
Silkham Rd OXTED RH8 .....174 C3
Silk Mills CI RSEV TN14 .....149 H6
Silk Mills Pth LEW SE13 .....42 A4
Silver Av BRCH CT7 .....111 J7
Silver Bank WALD ME5 .....95 M8
Silver Birch Av MEO DA13 .....122 A4
Silver Birch CI CAT SE6 .....61 M7
   RDART DA2 .....67 J9
   THMD SE28 .....27 P4
Silver Birches
   STH/RUST TN4 * 240 E9
   WALD ME5 .....125 M2
Silver Birch Gv WALD TN23 .....282 E4
Silver CI NWCR SE14 * 41 L1
   STH/RUST TN4 .....240 E8
Silverdale HART DA3 .....91 J1
   MAIDW ME16 .....184 E1
Silverdale Av IOS ME12 .....78 A1
Silverdale Dr ELTH/MOT SE9 .....63 J1
   HB CT6 .....108 A8
   RHAM ME8 .....97 H7
Silverdale Gv SIT ME10 .....129 K2
Silverdale La HAWK TN18 .....328 C1
   STH/RUST TN4 .....270 E2
Silverdale Rd BXLYHN DA7 .....45 P1
   RAM CT11 .....142 F7
   STH/RUST TN4 .....270 E2
   STMC/STPC BR5 .....64 C9
Silver HI CHAT ME4 .....6 C6
   ROCH ME1 .....94 E4
Silver Hill Gdns CHAT ME4 .....6 C6
   KEN/WIL TN24 .....253 K8
Silver Hill Rd KEN/WIL TN24 .....253 K8
Silverhurst Dr TONN TN10 .....210 F4
Silverlands Rd RFOLK CT18 .....286 C1
Silver La WWKM BR4 .....84 C6
Silverleigh Rd THHTH CR7 .....82 E1
Silverlocke Rd GRAYS RM17 .....32 E9
Silvermere Rd LEW SE13 .....42 A9
Silvermere Rw SNWD SE25 * 60 G8
Silver Rd GVE DA12 .....70 A1
Silverspot CI RHAM ME8 .....97 J7
Silver Spring CI ERITH DA8 .....45 J7
Silversted La BH/WHM TN16 .....146 F5
The Silvers BRDST CT10 .....113 H9
Silver St DEAL CT14 .....233 J2
   FOLKN CT19 .....12 D1
Silvertown Wy CAN/RD E16 .....26 A3
Silver Tree WALD ME5 .....125 J4
Silver Wk BERM/RHTH SE16 .....25 N1
Silverweed Rd WALD ME5 .....95 L9
Silverwood CI BECK BR3 .....61 N6
   CDW/CHF RH6 .....316 G3
   CROY/NA CR0 .....114 C5
Silvester Rd EDUL SE22 .....40 F6
Silwood Estate Regeneration
   Area DEPT SE8 .....24 G8
Silwood St BERM/RHTH SE16 .....24 G8
Simcoe Ter DVE/WH CT16 * 291 J4
Simmonds La
   MAID/SHEP ME15 .....186 E5
Simmonds Rd CANT CT1 .....4 B7
Simmons PI CDW/CHF RH16 .....32 B4
Simmons Rd WOOL/PLUM SE18 .....28 F3
Simms Rd STHWK SE1 * 24 D7
Simnel Rd LEE/GVPK SE12 .....42 F6
Simon Av MARG 113 J5
Simone CI BMLY BR1 .....63 H3
Simone Weil Av
   KEN/WIL TN24 .....252 E5
Simon's Av ASH TN23 .....282 C1
Simpson Rd SIT ME10 .....99 K9
   SNOD ME6 .....125 P7
Simpsons Rd HAYES BR2 .....62 E9
   POP/IOD E14 .....25 M4
Sinclair CI RHAM ME8 .....97 H9
Sinclair Wy RDART DA2 .....67 K3
Singapore Dr DVE/WH CT16 * 291 H1
Singledge Av DVE/WH CT16 .....291 H1
Singles Cross RSEV TN14 * 117 L9
Single's Cross La RSEV TN14 .....117 K9
Single St BH/WHM TN16 .....116 C9

Singleton CI CROY/NA CR0 .....83 H4
   MSTR CT12 .....141 J6
Singleton HI ASH TN23 .....252 A9
Singleton Rd ASH TN23 .....251 P8
Singlewell Rd GVW DA11 .....69 M2
Sion HI RAM CT11 .....17 K5
Sion Houses RTW TN1 * 22 D6
Sion Wk RTW TN1 * 22 D6
Sirdar Strd GVE DA12 .....70 B4
Sir David's Pk STH/RUST TN4 .....240 D8
Sir Evelyn Rd ROCH ME1 .....94 C6
Sir John Hawkins Wy CHAT ME4 .....6 B4
Sir John Kirk CI CMBW SE5 .....40 C1
Sir John Moore Av
   HYTHE CT21 .....308 F5
Sir John Moore Barracks
   FOLK CT20 * 310 A7
Sir Thomas Longley Rd
   STRD ME2 .....19 K3
Sise La MANHO EC4N * 24 A2
Siskin CI ERITH DA8 .....45 P6
Siskin Gdns STPH/PW TN12 .....243 H4
Sissinghurst La HDCN TN27 .....276 G8
Sissinghurst Dr MAIDW ME16 .....154 G8
Sissinghurst Rd CRBK TN17 .....276 C8
   CROY/NA CR0 .....83 N5
   HDCN TN27 .....277 L6
Sister Mabels Wy PECK SE15 .....40 C1
Sisulu PI BRXN/ST SW9 .....40 A4
Sittingbourne Rd
   MAID/BEAR ME14 .....13 H4
Siward Rd HAYES BR2 .....62 F9
Six Bells La SEV TN13 .....21 G5
Six Bells Ms RYE TN31 .....330 E8
Six Fields Pth TENT TN30 .....301 H8
Six Penny CI EDEN TN8 .....266 D2
Sixth Av IOS ME12 .....79 N2
Skeete Rd RFOLK CT18 .....288 B8
Skeet Hill La STMC/STPC BR5 .....87 N6
Skeffington St
   WOOL/PLUM SE18 .....27 K6
Skene CI RHAM ME8 .....97 K5
Sketchley Gdns
   BERM/RHTH SE16 .....24 G8
Skevnes Rd EDEN TN8 .....206 C9
Skibbs La ORP BR6 .....87 M7
Skid Hill La WARL CR6 .....115 J9
Skiffington CI
   BRXS/STRHM SW2 .....40 A9
Skinner Gdns CRBK TN17 .....276 D8
Skinner Rd LYDD TN29 .....342 B7
Skinners CI DIT/AY ME20 .....124 F7
Skinners La EDEN TN8 .....206 E8
Skinner St CHAT ME4 .....6 C6
   GILL ME7 .....7 H2
Skinner's Wy RMAID ME17 .....187 H7
Skinner's Ey EYN DA4 .....67 L6
Skippers CI GRH DA9 .....47 P6
Skye CI MAID/SHEP ME15 .....185 M4
Skylark Wy ASH TN23 .....282 C6
Sladebrook Rd BKHTH/KID SE3 .....43 H4
Slade CI WALD ME5 .....125 N5
Sladedale Rd
   WOOL/PLUM SE18 .....27 M8
Slade Gdns ERITH DA8 .....45 P7
Slade Green Rd ERITH DA8 .....45 P7
Slade Rd RMAID ME17 .....190 C3
Slades CI WSTB CT5 .....106 B6
Slades Dr CHST BR7 .....63 N3
The Slade RRTW TN3 .....295 H4
   TON TN9 .....210 E8
Slaggrove PI LEW SE13 .....41 N6
Slaithwaite Rd LEW SE13 .....42 A1
Slaney Rd STPH/PW TN12 .....246 C5
Slatin Rd STRD ME2 .....72 A7
Sleepers Stile Rd WADH TN5 .....294 C6
Sleigh Rd CANTW/ST CT2 .....137 L7
Slicketts HI CHAT ME4 * 6 D5
Slines New Rd CTHM CR3 .....144 A5
Slines Oak Rd CTHM CR5 .....144 A4
Slip La RDV CT15 .....288 M2
Slip Mill Rd HAWK TN18 .....316 C2
Slippers PI BERM/RHTH SE16 .....24 E6
Slip Rd CHAT ME4 .....72 C7
The Slip BH/WHM TN16 .....176 D2
Sloane Gdns ORP BR6 .....86 D1
Sloane Sq HART DA3 * 68 C9
Sloane Wk CROY/NA CR0 .....84 C3
Slocum CI THMD SE28 .....28 B5
Sloe La BRDST CT10 .....112 C7
Slough Rd RSIT ME9 .....129 P9
Sly St WCHPL E1 * 24 E2
Small Bridge Rd
   STPH/PW TN12 .....274 A6
Small Grains HART DA3 .....90 E7
Small Hythe CI
   MAID/SHEP ME15 .....186 E1
Smallhythe Rd TENT TN30 .....300 D8
Small Profits WBY/YAL ME18 .....183 P7
Smarden CI BELV DA17 .....28 F8
Smarden Rd HDCN TN27 .....247 P5
   HDCN TN27 .....278 B4
Smarts HI RTON TN11 .....238 F8
Smarts Rd GVE DA12 .....69M2
Smeaton St WAP E1W 24 E4
Smeeth La ASH TN25 .....130 A1
Smeetham Gdns STRD ME2 .....72 B6
Smiles PI LEW SE13 .....42 A5
Smith CI BERM/RHTH SE16 .....25 N1
Smithers CI RTON TN11 .....211 P1
Smithers La STPH/PW TN12 .....213 H3
Smithfield Rd HOO/HM ME3 .....56 E3
Smithies Rd ABYW SE2 .....28 B3
Smith Rd WALD ME5 .....125 N2
Smith's HI MAID/SHEP ME15 .....184 B7
Smiths La EDEN TN8 .....176 D9
Smith St RTON TN11 .....238 F3
Smith St STPD ME2 .....18 E3
Smithy Dr ASH TN25 .....282 F4
Smithy St WCHPL E1 .....24 F1

Smolletts EGRIN RH19 .....264 F8
Smugglers Leap MSTR CT12 * 141 K4
Smugglers Ms HAWK TN18 .....317 G5
Smugglers Wy BRCH CT7 .....111 H5
Smugglers Wharf GPA DA9 .....47 P6
Smyrks Rd WALW SE17 .....24 B8
Smythe Rd EYN DA4 .....66 G7
Smythe St POP/IOD E14 .....25 L3
Snag La RSEV TN14 .....116 G5
Snakes HI RCANTE CT3 .....199 K2
Snargate La LYDD TN29 .....323 M9
Snargate St DVW CT17 .....8 C6
Snatts HI OXTED RH8 .....175 J5
Snell Gdns HB CT6 .....106 C4
Snelling Av GVW DA11 .....69 K1
Snipe CI ERITH DA8 .....46 B1
   RASHE TN25 .....252 F2
   RTWE/PEM TN2 .....241 P9
Snoad La STPH/PW TN12 .....245M9
Snodhurst Av WALD ME5 .....95 K9
Snodland Rd E/WMAL ME19 .....123 K7
Snoggers HI FAV ME13 .....164 B5
Snoll Hatch Rd
   STPH/PW TN12 .....212 C5
Snowball Rd ASH TN23 .....282 C4
Snowdon Av MAID/BEAR ME14 .....13 J5
Snowdon CI FOLKN CT19 .....310 F5
Snowdon CI WALD ME5 .....95 N7
Snowdon Pde
   MAID/BEAR ME14 * 13 K5
Snowdown CI PGE/AN SE20 .....61 J7
Snowdown Rd FOLKN CT19 .....310 F5
Snowfields STHWK SE1 .....24 A5
Snugharne La HDCN TN27 .....248 D9
Soames St PECK SE15 .....40 F4
Sobraon Wy CANT CT1 .....167 J5
Solander Gdns WCHPL E1 * 24 E3
Solar Ct RAM CT11 * 16 A7
Solefields Rd SEV TN13 .....178 C4
Soleoak Dr SEV TN13 .....21 F7
Soleshill Rd RCANTW CT4 .....193M2
Sole St MEO DA13 .....92 E2
Solomon Rd RHAM ME8 .....97 J8
Solomon's La PECK SE15 .....41 H5
Solomon's Pas PECK SE15 .....41 H5
Solway TIL RM18 .....34 B6
Solway Rd EDUL SE22 .....40 G3
Somerden Rd STMC/STPC BR5 .....87 L4
Somerfield CI MAIDW ME16 * 12 A1
Somerfield La MAIDW ME16 .....12 A1
Somerfield Rd MAIDW ME16 .....12 A4
Somerfield St
   BERM/RHTH SE16 .....25 H5
Somerhill Av BFN/LL DA15 .....44 C6
Somerhill Rd TON TN9 .....240 D1
   WELL DA16 .....44 E3
Somerleyton Rd BRXN/ST SW9 .....40 A5
Somerset Av WELL DA16 .....44 B6
Somerset Barracks
   FOLK CT20 * 310 A7
Somerset CI SIT ME10 .....129 K1
   WALD ME5 .....95 P6
   WSTB CT5 .....105 J7
Somerset Ct MSTR CT12 * 142 G2
Somerset Gdns LEW SE13 .....41 P7
Somerset Rd CANT CT1 .....167 H4
   DART DA1 .....46 B7
   DEAL CT14 .....232 G6
   FOLKN CT19 .....310 B5
   MAID/SHEP ME15 .....185 L3
   ORP BR6 .....87 H4
   SLH/COR SS17 .....33 P5
   STH/RUST TN4 .....270 D2
Somerset St Little
   TWRH EC3N * 24 C2
Somerset Vis RRTW TN3 * 269 H9
Somersham Rd BXLYHN DA7 .....44 G5
Somerton Rd PECK SE15 .....41 H5
Somertrees Av LEE/GVPK SE12 .....62 F1
Somerville Gdns
   STH/RUST TN4 .....22 B8
Somerville Rd DART DA1 .....46 F7
   PGE/AN SE20 .....61 K6
Somme Ct CANT CT1 .....167 J3
Somner CI CANTW/ST CT2 .....4 A2
Somner Wk MAID/SHEP ME15 .....186 C5
Sondes CI HB CT6 .....107 M4
Sondes Rd DEAL CT14 .....233 J4
Sondes St WALW SE17 .....24 A9
Songhurst CI CROY/NA CR0 .....82 E5
Sonora Wy SRTFD E15 * 41 K9
Soper CI FSTH SE23 .....61 K1
Soper's La HAWK TN18 .....316 F2
Sophia CI CAN/RD E16 .....26 C2
Sophia Sq BERM/RHTH SE16 .....25 H5
Sophia St STPH/PW TN12 .....272 D3
Sophurst Wt
   STPH/PW TN12 * 272 E3
Sopwith CI BH/WHM TN16 .....145 N1
Sorrel Bank CROY/NA CR0 .....114 B4
Sorrell CI RDV CT15 .....228 H4
Sorrel Gdns EHAM E6 .....26 H8
Sorrel La POP/IOD E14 .....25 N2
Sorrell CI BRXN/ST SW9 .....40 A3
Sorrell Rd WALD ME5 .....125 L1
Sortit Wy GVW DA11 .....69 K1
Sortmill Rd SNOD ME6 .....124 A6
Sotherton Rd KEN/WIL TN24 .....283 H1
Souberg CI DEAL CT14 .....233 H1
Sounds Ldg SWLY BR8 .....88 B3
Southall CI MSTR CT12 .....141 K5
Southall PI STHWK SE1 .....24 A5
Southampton Gdns
   MTCM CR4 .....82 D2
Southampton Ms CAN/RD E16 .....26 B5
Southampton Wy CMBW SE5 .....40 D1
South Ash Rd BGR/WK TN15 .....121 H1
South Av RDV CT15 .....229 K3
   RHAM ME8 .....96 D4
   SIT ME10 .....129 P2
South Bank BH/WHM TN16 .....176 E2
   HOO/HM ME3 .....52 B6
   RMAID ME17 .....217 H3
   RHAM ME8 .....246 B7
South Barham Rd
   RCANTW CT4 .....228 B8
Southborough Rd HAYES BR2 .....85 P2
Southborough Rd BMLY BR1 .....63 J9
Southbourne ASH TN23 .....282 B3
   HAYES BR2 .....85 K4
Southbourne Gdns
   LEE/GVPK SE12 .....42 F6
Southbourne Gv WALD ME5 .....125M1
Southbourne La FOLKN CT19 .....11 H5
Southbridge PI CROY/NA CR0 .....83 H8
Southbridge Rd CROY/NA CR0 .....83 H8
Southbrook Rd LEW SE13 .....42 C7
South Bush La RHAM ME8 .....97 L8
South Canterbury Rd
   CANT CT1 .....166 F6
South Cliff Pde BRDST CT10 .....143M5
South CI BXLYHS DA6 .....44 F5
   CANT CT1 .....5 F4
The South Colonnade
   POP/IOD E14 .....25 K4
Southcote Rd SNWD SE25 .....83 N2
South Court Rd RCANTE CT3 .....169 K9
South Crs CAN/RD E16 .....25 N1
   RMAID ME17 .....185 H6
Southcroft Av WELL DA16 .....44 A4
   WWKM BR4 .....84 B1
Southcroft Rd ORP BR6 .....86 F7
South Croxted Rd DUL SE21 .....60 D2
Southdene RSEV TN14 .....117 N7
Southdown Rd CTHM CR3 .....144 C7
South Dr ORP BR6 .....77 H1
South Eastern Rd RAM CT11 .....16 C4
   STRD ME2 .....18 E1
South Eden Park Rd BECK BR3 .....84 E1
South End CROY/NA CR0 .....83 H9
Southend CI ELTH/MOT SE9 .....43M7
Southend La CAT SE6 .....61 N5
Southend Rd BECK BR3 .....61 N9
   GRAYS RM17 .....32 D7
Southern Av SNWD SE25 .....60 F9
Southernden Rd HDCN TN27 .....218 D9
Southerngate Wy NWCR SE14 .....41 L1
Southern Wy FOLK CT20 .....88 C1
Southernwood Ri FOLK CT20 .....310 C7
Southey St PGE/AN SE20 .....61 K6
Southey Wy TIL RM18 .....49M2
Southey Wy DIT/AY ME20 .....123 N3
Southfield Rd CHST BR7 .....64 B9
   STH/RUST TN4 .....270 D2
Southfields ROCH ME1 .....94 G3
   RRTW TN3 .....269M1
   WADH TN5 .....294 A9
Southfield Shaw MEO DA13 .....122 C4
Southfields Rd BGR/WK TN15 .....120 C2
   CTHM CR5 .....144 E8
   GDST RH9 .....174 E1
Southfleet Av GVW DA11 .....240 E9
Southfleet Av HART DA3 .....68 F8
Southfleet Rd GVW DA11 .....49 K9
   ORP BR6 .....86 F7
   RDART DA2 .....67 J5
   SWAM DA10 .....49 P8
South Ga CAN RM19 .....50 F7
Southgate Rd TENT TN30 .....301 K8
South Gipsy Rd WELL DA16 .....44 F4
South Green La RSIT ME9 .....128 A6
South Hall CI EYN DA4 .....66 G7
South Hall Dr RAIN RM13 .....29 N1
South HI CHST BR7 .....63 K5
South Hill Rd GVE DA12 .....49M9
   HAYES BR2 .....85 K4
Southholme CI NRWD SE19 .....60 E3
Southhill Rd CHAT ME4 .....6 B7
   CHST BR7 .....63 J6
South Kent Av GVW DA11 .....48 C7
Southland Rd
   WOOL/PLUM SE18 .....44 B1
Southlands EGRIN RH19 .....265 H9
Southlands Av ORP BR6 .....86 F8
Southlands Gv BMLY BR1 .....63 J9
Southlands La OXTED RH8 .....204 E1
Southlands Rd HAYES BR2 .....85 N1
Southland Ter PUR RM19 * 50 E8
South La ASH TN23 .....282 D5
Southlees La RSIT ME9 .....158 A2
South Lodge Av MTCM CR4 .....82 D1
Southmead CI DEAL CT14 * 233 H1
South Military Rd DVW CT17 .....313 K1
South Molton Rd CAN/RD E16 .....26 B2
South Motto ASH TN23 .....282 C5
South Norwood HI SNWD SE25 .....60 E8
Southold Ri ELTH/MOT SE9 .....63 J1
Southover BMLY BR1 .....62 E4
South Pk SEV TN13 .....20 E4
South Park Crs CAT SE6 .....42 C9
South Park Rd
   MAID/SHEP ME15 .....185 N2
South PI SDTCH EC2A 24 A1
South Place Ms LVPST EC2M * 24 A1
South Pondside Rd CHAT ME4 * 72 C7
Southport Rd
   WOOL/PLUM SE18 .....27 L7
South Rd DEAL CT14 .....263 J3
   DVW CT17 .....291 J7
   ERITH DA8 .....29 J1
   FAV ME13 .....132 E6
   GILL ME7 .....72 C8

HB CT6 .....107 M1
HYTHE CT21 .....309 H6
SOCK/AV RM15.....31 M3
STPH/PW TN12.....245 K3
SWCH CT13.....171 P3
South Rw BKHTH/KID SE3.....42 E5
Southsea Av IOS ME12.....58 B7
Southsea Dr HB CT6.....107 J2
South Sea St
  BERM/RHTH SE16 .....25 J6
Southspring ELTH/MOT SE9 .....43 P8
South Stour Av ASH TN23.....2 E7
South St BMLY BR1.....62 E8
  CANT CT1.....167 H1
  DEAL CT14.....233 J4
  FAV ME15.....163 N5
  GVE DA12.....49 M8
  LYDD TN29.....342 B6
  MAIDW ME16.....184 D5
  MEO DA13.....92 A8
  OBOR ME17.....77 H2
  WSTB CT5.....105 P6
South Street Rd RSIT ME9.....127 M6
South Tenter St WCHPL E1.....24 C3
South Ter EYN DA4 *.....89 L4
South Trench TONN TN10 *.....210 F5
South Undercliff RYE TN31.....338 F7
South V NRWD SE19.....60 E5
Southvale Rd BKHTH/KID SE3.....42 C3
South Vw BMLY BR1.....62 G8
  CDW/CHF RM16.....33 J1
Southview SWLY BR8.....88 E1
South View Av TIL RM18.....49 L2
South View Cl BXLY DA5.....45 H7
South View Cl SWLY BR8.....88 E1
  IOS ME12 *.....60 C6
South View Gdns IOS ME12.....57 L8
South View Hts WTHK RM20 *.....31 M9
Southview Rd BMLY BR1.....62 B3
  CTHM CR3.....144 E9
South View Rd RDART DA2.....66 D7
  STH/RUST TN4.....240 E9
  WADH TN5.....294 A9
  WSTB CT5.....105 L8
  WTHK RM20.....31 M9
Southviews SAND/SEL CR2.....114 A5
South Wk WAWH BR4.....85 K1
South Wall DEAL CT14.....232 G2
Southwall Rd DEAL CT14.....232 G3
Southwark Park Est
  BERM/RHTH SE16 *.....24 E7
Southwark Park Rd
  BERM/RHTH SE16.....24 C7
Southwark Pl BMLY BR1.....63 K9
Southwark Rd STRD ME2.....71 M9
Southwater Cl BECK BR3.....61 P6
South Wy CROY/NA CR0.....82 E9
  RAM CT11.....31 H6
Southway HAYES BR2.....85 K4
  WLGTN SM6.....82 B8
Southways RMAID ME17.....216 G3
Southwell Cl CDW/CHF RM16.....31 M8
Southwell Gdns IOS ME12.....40 C4
  STRD ME2.....82 F5
  STRD ME2 .....71 L9
South Wharf Rd GRAYS RM17.....32 A9
Southwick Cl EGRIN RH19.....264 C6
Southwold Pl WGOS CT8.....111 L6
Southwold Rd BXLY DA5.....45 K7
Southwood MAIDW ME16.....184 E1
Southwood Av
  STH/RUST TN4.....270 D2
Southwood Cl BMLY BR1.....86 A1
Southwood Gdns RAM CT11.....16 B4
Southwood Hls RAM CT11.....16 B4
Southwood Rd ELTH/MOT SE9.....63 M1
  RAM CT11.....16 B4
  STH/RUST TN4.....269 N3
  THMD SE28.....28 A2
  WSTB CT5.....105 A4
Southy Ms CAN/RD E16.....26 B4
Sovereign Bvd GILL ME7.....96 B4
Sovereign Cl WAP E1W.....24 E5
Sovereign Crs
  BERM/RHTH SE16.....25 H3
Sovereigns Wy
  STPH/PW TN12.....244 G3
Sovereign Wy TON TN9.....210 F9
Sowell St BRDST CT10.....113 L8
Sowerby Cl ELTH/MOT SE9.....43 K6
Spa Cl NRWD SE19.....60 E5
Spade La RSIT ME9.....97 M8
Spa Hi THHTH CR7.....60 D7
Spanton Crs HYTHE CT21.....308 F4
Spar CT11.....212 A1
Sparepenny La EYN DA4.....89 K4
Sparkeswood Av CRBK TN17.....319 L2
Sparke Ter CAN/RD E16 *.....26 A2
Sparks Cl HAYES BR2.....85 L1
Spa Rd BERM/RHTH SE16.....24 C6
Sparrow Castle MARG CT9.....15 H6
Sparrow Dr STMC/STPC BR5.....86 C5
Sparrows La ELTH/MOT SE9.....43 N9
Sparta St GNWCH SE10.....42 A2
Speakers Ct CROY/NA CR0 *.....83 J5
Spearhead Rd
  MAID/BEAR ME14.....155 L5
Spearman St
  WOOL/PLUM SE18 *.....27 H9
Spectrum Pl WALW SE17 *.....24 A8
Speedgate Hl HART DA3.....90 D6
Speedwell Av WALD ME5.....125 L1
Speedwell Cl GILL ME7.....96 B1
  MAID/BEAR ME14.....156 B8
Speedwell Rd WSTB CT5.....105 J8
Speedwell St DEPT SE8.....41 N1
Spekehill ELTH/MOT SE9.....63 K2
Speke Rd BRDST CT10.....113 K7
  THHTH CR7.....60 D7
Spekes Rd GILL ME7.....96 D8
Spelders Hl RASHE TN25.....254 B5
Speldhurst Cl ASH TN23.....282 B3
  HAYES BR2.....85 J2
Speldhurst Hl MAIDW ME16.....155 J8
Speldhurst Gdns MARG CT9.....113 L2

Speldhurst Hl RRTW TN5.....239 N9
Speldhurst Rd RRTW TN5.....269 L3
  STH/RUST TN4.....240 C7
Spelman St WCHPL E1.....24 D1
Spelmonden Rd
  STPH/PW TN12.....273 N4
Spence Cl BERM/RHTH SE16.....25 J5
  RFOLK CT18.....288 D8
Spencer Cl ORP BR6.....86 F6
  WALD ME5.....95 M9
Spencer Ct FOLK CT20 *.....309 D5
Spencer Ms RTW TN1 *.....22 D5
Spencer Pl CROY/NA CR0.....83 J4
Spencer Rd BMLY BR1.....62 D6
  BRCH CT7.....111 H5
  SAND/SEL CR2.....83 K9
Spencer Sq RAM CT11.....16 E5
Spencer St GVW DA11.....49 L8
  RAM CT11.....16 B4
Spencer Wk TIL RM18.....49 L3
Spencer Wy
  MAID/SHEP ME15.....186 B4
Spenlow Dr WALD ME5.....125 M4
Spenny La STPH/PW TN12.....244 B5
Spenser Ms DUL SE21.....40 D9
Spenser St HB CT6.....107 L2
  HNHL SE24.....40 B6
Speranza St WOOL/PLUM SE18.....27 N8
Spert St POP/IOD E14.....25 H3
Speyside TONN TN10.....210 E5
Spey St POP/IOD E14.....25 M1
Spicer Cl CHDW SE1.....40 B3
Spicers Homes SIT ME10 *.....129 N2
Spices Yd CROY/NA CR0.....83 H8
Spielman Rd DART DA1.....46 F5
Spillett Cl FAV ME15.....132 E6
The Spillway
  MAID/SHEP ME15.....185 J1
Spindle Cl WOOL/PLUM SE18.....26 F6
Spindle Gld MAID/BEAR ME14.....155 P7
Spindle La RSIT ME9.....128 B1
Spindlewood Ail MAID ME25 *.....125 N2
Spindlewood End ASH TN23.....252 A5
Spindlewood Gdns
  CROY/NA CR0.....83 J8
Spindrift Av POP/IOD E14.....25 L7
Spinel Cl WOOL/PLUM SE18.....27 N8
Spinnaker Ct ROCH ME1 *.....95 H5
Spinners Cl HDCN TN27.....278 A6
Spinney La BCK BECK.....84 E1
Spinney Gdns NRWD SE19.....60 F4
Spinney La RCANTE CT3.....229 J2
Spinney Oak BMLY BR1.....63 J8
The Spinneys BMLY BR1.....63 J8
The Spinnie ASH TN23.....252 B6
  DVW CT17.....290 F5
  MAID/SHEP ME15.....185 N1
  MARG CT9.....113 K4
  SCUP DA14.....64 B5
  SWLY BR8.....65 N8
  TON TN9.....240 D2
  WALD ME5.....125 N4
Spinney Wy RSEV TN14.....116 E5
Spire Av WSTB CT5.....105 N6
Spire Cl GVE DA12.....49 M9
The Spires CANTW/ST CT2 *.....4 D1
  DART DA1.....66 D1
  STRD ME2.....71 J9
Spirit Quay WAP E1W.....24 D4
Spitalfield La NROM TN28.....336 F7
Spital Sq WCHPL E1.....24 B1
Spital St DART DA1.....46 D7
Spital Yd WCHPL E1 *.....24 B1
Spitfire Cl WALD ME5.....95 N8
Spitfire House
  WOOL/PLUM SE18 *.....43 J1
Spitfire Rd E/WMAL ME19.....152 G9
Spitfire Wy RFOLK CT18.....288 D8
Spital La RCANTW CT4.....226 E5
Spode La EDEN TN8.....237 H5
Sponden La HAWK TN18.....317 P6
Spongs La CRBK TN17.....320 C7
Spooner Wk WLGTN SM6.....82 C9
Sportsbank St CAT SE6.....42 A8
Sportsfield MAID/BEAR ME14.....13 J2
Sportsman's Cottages
  E/WMAL ME19.....153 J7
Spot La MAID/SHEP ME15.....186 D1
Spout Hi CROY/NA CR0.....36 D8
Spout La EDEN TN8.....206 D1
The Spout
  STPH/PW TN12.....273 J3
Spratling La MSTR CT12.....142 E3
Spratling St MSTR CT12.....142 E3
Spray Hi RRTW TN5.....295 J5
The Sprig WOOL/PLUM SE18.....27 J7
The Sprig MAID/BEAR ME14.....156 D8
Springall St DEPT SE8.....41 H1
Springbank Rd LEW SE13.....42 C7
Springbourne CE BECK BR3.....62 A7
Springcroft HART DA3.....91 K5
Spring Cross HART DA3.....91 K4
Springett Cl DIT/AY ME20.....124 E7
Springett Wy LYDD TN29.....324 C9
Springfarm Rd LYDD TN29.....324 C9
Springfield EGRIN RH19.....264 C4
Springfield Av
  MAID/BEAR ME14.....155 K6
  SWLY BR8.....88 E1
  TENT TN30.....301 J5
Springfield Cl RAM CT11.....143 K2
Springfield Gdns BMLY BR1.....86 A1
  WWKM BR4.....84 E6
Springfield Gv CHARL SE7.....26 D9
Springfield Pl RRTW TN5 *.....269 H9
Springfield Ri SYD SE26.....61 H5
Springfield Rd BMLY BR1.....86 A1
  BXLYHN DA7.....45 K4
  CDW/CHF RM16.....32 F5
  DIT/AY ME20.....123 N9
  DVE/WH CT16 *.....291 J5
  EDEN TN8.....206 D9
  GILL ME7.....73 L9

MARG CT9.....113 K2
RRTW TN5.....269 H9
SIT ME10.....99 L9
STH/RUST TN4.....240 C8
SYD SE26.....61 H5
THHTH CR7.....60 C7
WELL DA16.....44 D4
WLGTN SM6.....82 A9
Springfields WADH TN5.....315 J5
Springfield Ter CHAT ME4 *.....6 B5
Springfield Wy HYTHE CT21.....309 H4
STMC/STPC BR5.....64 C9
Spring Gdns BH/WHM TN16.....145 M3
  ORP BR6.....117 J1
  STH/RUST TN4 *.....269 N4
  WLGTN SM6.....82 B9
Spring Gv GVE DA12.....49 M9
Springhead RTWE/PEM TN2.....270 C3
Spring Head Rd
  RTWE/PEM TN2.....271 N2
Springhead Rd ERITH DA8.....29 L9
  FAV ME15.....132 F4
  GVW DA11.....48 C9
Spring Hi RTON TN11.....268 F2
  RYE TN31.....330 A6
  SEV TN13.....61 J5
Spring Hollow LYDD TN29.....337 M1
Springholm Cl BH/WHM TN16.....145 M3
Springhurst Cl CROY/NA CR0.....84 C8
Spring La BGR/WK TN15.....150 E7
  CANT CT1.....5 J5
  CANTW/ST CT2.....137 M9
  HYTHE CT21.....309 M1
  OXTED RH8.....174 C7
  SNWD SE25.....83 N3
  STH/RUST TN4.....240 A6
Spring Park Av CROY/NA CR0.....84 A4
Springpark Dr BECK BR3.....62 A9
Spring Park Rd CROY/NA CR0.....84 A4
Springrice Rd LEW SE13.....42 A7
Spring Shaw Rd
  STMC/STPC BR5.....64 C7
Spring Ter FOLK CT20 *.....11 F4
Spring Tide Cl PECK SE15 *.....25 H6
Spring V BXLYHN DA7.....45 K5
  GEN DA9.....48 A9
  MAIDW ME16.....184 B5
Springvale RHAM ME8.....96 F8
  RSIT ME9.....99 L2
Spring Vale Cl SWLY BR8.....65 P6
Springvale Cl CROY/NA CR0 *.....68 G1
Spring V North DART DA1.....46 G8
Spring V South DART DA1.....46 G8
Spring Wk WCHPL E1.....105 P7
Springwater Cl
  WOOL/PLUM SE18 *.....43 J2
Spring Wy EGRIN RH19.....265 K4
Springwell Rd
  STRHM/NOR SW16.....60 D3
  TON TN9.....240 E1
Springwood Cl ASH TN23.....252 B6
Springwood Rd MAIDW ME16.....154 F9
Sprotlands Av KEN/WIL TN24.....253 J9
Sprotshill Cl SIT ME10.....99 M8
Spruce Cl DIT/AY ME20.....153 P2
Sprucedale Cl SWLY BR8.....65 N6
Sprucedale Gdns
  CROY/NA CR0.....84 A8
Spruce Rd BH/WHM TN16.....145 N1
Sprules Rd BROCKY SE4.....41 L3
Spurgeon Av NRWD SE19.....60 D7
Spurgeon Rd NRWD SE19.....60 D6
Spurgeon St STHWK SE1.....24 A6
Spurling Rd EDUL SE22 *.....40 F5
Spurrell Av RDART DA2.....65 M3
Spur Rd ORP BR6.....87 H6
Spurway MAID/BEAR ME14.....156 D8
Spurwing Cl HAM BR2.....85 K5
Square Hill Rd
  MAID/SHEP ME15.....13 H6
The Square BH/WHM TN16.....145 M5
  LING RH7.....234 F5
  MAID/SHEP ME15 *.....214 C5
  RCANTE CT3 *.....169 K9
  RCANTW CT4.....257 L5
  RMAID ME17 *.....187 J6
  RMAID ME17 *.....187 J6
  RTON TN11.....211 P2
  SEV TN15.....148 C7
  SWLY BR8 *.....65 M9

Stadium Wy DART DA1.....45 N7
  SIT ME10.....100 B8
Stadler Cl MAIDW ME16.....155 J5
Staffa Rd MAID/BEAR ME14.....185 M4
Staffhurst Wood Rd
  OXTED RH8.....205 M4
Stafford Cl ASH TN23.....252 C7
  CDW/CHF RM16.....31 M7
  GRH DA9.....48 D5
  SLH/COR SS17.....33 P6
Stafford Gdns CROY/NA CR0.....82 E9
Stafford Rd CROY/NA CR0.....82 F8
  RTWE/PEM TN2.....271 H4
  SCUP DA14.....64 A3
  WLGTN SM6.....82 D6
Staffordshire St PECK SE15.....40 G2
  RAM CT11.....17 J3
Stafford St GILL ME7.....7 H5
Stafford Wy SEV TN15.....179 H5
Stag Rd RTWE/PEM TN2.....240 C8
  WALD ME5.....95 N9
Stagshaw Cl
  MAID/SHEP ME15.....185 M1
Stainer Rd TONN TN10.....211 J4
Staines Dr STHWK SE1 *.....24 A4
Staines Ct MAID/BEAR ME14.....13 G3
Stainsby Ct CHST BR7.....63 P7
Stainsby Pl POP/IOD E14 *.....25 K2
Stainsby Rd POP/IOD E14.....25 K2
Stairfoot La MAIDW ME16.....184 B5
StairFoot La SEV TN13.....148 B7
Stair Rd TONN TN11.....211 J6
Stake La STRD ME2.....93 P8
Staley St BGR/WK TN15.....121 K4
Stalham ct GILL ME7 *.....126 L1
Stalham St BERM/RHTH SE16.....24 F6
Stalin Av WALD ME5.....125 L1
Stalisfield Rd FAV ME13.....191 J2
Stambourne Wy NRWD SE19.....60 E6
  WWKM BR4.....84 E2
Stamford Dr HAYES BR2.....85 J1
The Stampers MAIDW ME16.....185 J1
Stanam Rd RTWE/PEM TN2.....271 P3
Stanbridge Rd EDEN TN8.....206 C8
Stanbrook Rd ABYW SE2.....28 D6
  GVW DA11.....49 K9
Stanbury Crs FOLK CT19.....311 J3
Stanbury Pl PECK SE15.....41 H2
Stancomb Av RAM CT11.....16 C6
Standard Rd BELV DA17.....29 J5
  BXLYHS DA6.....44 G5
  ORP BR6.....116 B4
Standen Cl EGRIN RH19.....264 D5
  RHAM ME8.....127 H1
Standen La RFOLK CT18.....288 D7
Standen St CRBK TN17.....318 D4
Standen St CRBK TN17 *.....270 D5
Stane Wy WOOL/PLUM SE18.....43 H1
Stanford Dr MAIDW ME16.....155 J5
Stanford Gdns SOCK/AV RM15.....31 H4
Stanford La RTON TN11.....210 B1
Stanford-le-Hope By-Pass
  CDW/CHF RM16.....33 K2
Stanford Pl STHWK SE1 *.....24 B7
Stanford Rd CDW/CHF RM16.....32 F5
  CDW/CHF RM16.....33 M1
Stanfords Pl LING RH7.....234 G6
Stanford Wy STRD ME2.....94 B4
Stangate Rd E/WMAL ME19.....123 J9
  STRD ME2.....71 L8
Stanger Rd SNWD SE25.....83 M1
Stangrove Rd EDEN TN8.....206 D9
Stanham Pl DART DA1.....46 A5
Stanham Rd DART DA1.....46 C5
Stanhope Av HAYES BR2.....85 K5
Stanhope Gv BECK BR3.....84 C2
Stanhope Rd ASH TN23.....282 B1
  BFN/LL DA15.....64 C5
  BXLYHN DA7.....43 G3
  DEAL CT14.....233 J5
  DVE/WH CT16.....291 K5
  RTW TN1.....270 F5
  STRD ME2.....18 C1
  SWCM DA10.....48 D2
Stanhopes OXTED RH8.....175 L4
Stan La WBY/YAL ME18.....182 A4
Stanley Av BECK BR3.....62 A9
  IOS ME12.....40 C4

Stannet Wy WLGTN SM6.....82 B8
Stansfeld Av RFOLK CT18.....288 D8
Stansfeld Rd CAN/RD E16.....26 E2
Stanstead Cl HAYES BR2.....85 L5
Stanstead Ga CAT SE6.....41 M9
Stansted Crs BXLY DA5.....44 F9
Stansted Cl MAIDW ME16.....155 H5
Stansted Rd MSTR CT12.....120 E4
Stanswood Gdns CMBW SE5.....40 E1
Stanton Cl STMC/STPC BR5.....87 K4
Stanton Rd CROY/NA CR0.....83 H4
  PECK SE15 *.....40 G2
Stanton Wy SYD SE26.....61 M3
Stanworth St STHWK SE1.....24 C5
Staple Cl BXLY DA5.....65 M2
  SIT ME10.....99 M8
Staple Dr STPH/PW TN12.....246 C6
Stapleford Ct SEV TN13.....148 E8
Staplehurst Av BRDST CT10.....143 M2
Staplehurst Gdns MARG CT9.....113 K2
  LEW SE13.....42 K6
  RHAM ME8.....96 E5
  STPH/PW TN12.....215 N7
  STPH/PW TN12.....246 C7
Staple Rd RCANTE CT3.....199 N1
Staplers Ct MAID/BEAR ME14.....155 N4
Staples Ct BERM/RHTH SE16.....25 J4
Staple St STHWK SE1.....24 A5
Staplestreet Rd FAV ME13.....134 A8
Stapleton Gdns CROY/NA CR0.....82 F9
Stapleton Rd BXLYHN DA7.....45 H1
  ORP BR6.....87 H3
Stapley Rd BELV DA17.....28 F8
Starbeck Cl ELTH/MOT SE9.....43 L8
Starboard Av GRH DA9.....47 P7
Starboard Wy POP/IOD E14.....25 K6
Starborough Rd EDEN TN8.....235 P5
Star Hi DART DA1.....19 H7
  ROCH ME1.....19 H7
Star Hill Rd RSEV TN14.....147 N1
  RSEV TN14.....148 B3
Star La FOLKN CT19.....310 A4
  GILL ME7.....7 J4
  MARG CT9.....112 F8
  STMC/STPC BR5.....87 L1
Starle Cl CANT CT1.....5 H1
Starling Cl HART DA3.....68 F9
Starling Rd CROY/NA CR0.....84 E1
Star Mill Ct WALD ME5 *.....96 A4
Star Mill La WALD ME5.....96 A4
Star Pl WAP E1W.....24 C5
Star Rd KEN/WIL TN24.....3 H4
  WALD ME5.....96 A4
Starts Hill Av ORP BR6.....86 C9
Starts Hill Rd ORP BR6.....86 C9
Starveacre La RSEV TN14.....129 K3
State Farm Av ORP BR6.....86 C8
Station Ap BECK BR3.....61 N1
  BGR/WK TN15.....151 J5
  BKHTH/KID SE3.....42 F4
  BRCH CT7.....110 D6
  BXLYHN DA7.....44 G3
  BXLYHN DA7.....45 J3
  CAT SE6.....61 M4
  CHST BR7.....63 J5
  CROY/NA CR0 *.....83 J6
  DART DA1.....46 E7
  E/WMAL ME19 *.....118 D9
  EDEN TN8.....206 D9
  HAYES BR2.....85 K5
  MAIDW ME16.....12 D6
  MSTR CT12.....141 K7
  NROM TN28.....337 H7
  ORP BR6.....87 H6
  ORP BR6.....87 J9
  OXTED RH8.....175 H5
  RCANTE CT3.....199 H6
  RDV CT15.....262 B6
  RTW TN14.....149 H1
  RTW TN1.....22 C3
  RYE TN31.....338 E6
  STMC/STPC BR5.....87 J1
  STPH/PW TN12.....243 H2
  STPH/PW TN12.....246 B4
  SYD SE26.....61 M3
  SWLY BR8.....88 D1
  WELL DA16.....44 C3
Station Approach Rd
  RAM CT11.....16 D1
Station Buildings HAYES BR2 *.....85 K5
Station Ct BGR/WK TN15.....151 J5
Station Crs BKHTH/KID SE3.....26 B8
Station Dr DEAL CT14.....232 F8
Station Est BECK BR3.....84 A1
Station Hl HAYES BR2.....85 K6
  HYTHE CT21.....208 E9
Station Pde BECK BR3 *.....84 A1
  BMLY BR1 *.....62 E7
  BXLYHN DA7.....44 G3
  SEV TN15.....20 D1
Station Pas PECK SE15.....41 J2
Station Ri WNWD SE27.....42 E4
Station Rd ASH TN23.....2 E1
  BELV DA17.....29 J9
  BFN/LL DA15.....64 C1
  BGR/WK TN15.....151 J5
  BH/WHM TN16.....147 J8
  BMLY BR1.....62 E7
  BRCH CT7.....110 C6
  CRBK TN17.....278 F9
  CROY/NA CR0.....83 J6
  CTHM CR3.....144 B7
  DART DA1.....46 E7
  DEAL CT14.....232 F8
  DIT/AY ME20.....154 B3
  DIT/AY ME20.....154 E2
  EDEN TN8.....206 C2
  EDEN TN8.....206 D7
  EGRIN RH19.....264 C7
  EYN DA4.....67 H8

EYN DA4 ......89 J7
FOLKN CT19 ......310 C5
CDST RH9 ......204 B5
GRH DA3 ......47 N6
GVW DA11 ......49 P5
HART DA3 ......68 C9
HAYES BR2 ......62 C8
HB CT6 ......107 K3
HDCN TN27 ......221 H5
HDCN TN27 ......242 N4
HDCN TN27 ......250 B5
HOO/HM ME3 ......52 A5
HYTHE CT21 ......309 J5
LEW SE13 ......42 A4
LING RH7 ......235 H4
LYDD TN29 ......326 F7
LYDD TN29 ......342 C5
MAID/BEAR ME14 ......12 E3
MAID/BEAR ME15 ......184 F4
MARC CT9 ......14 D5
MEO DA13 ......68 A1
MEO DA15 ......92 B2
MSTR CT12 ......141 K7
NROM TN28 ......336 G7
NRWD SE19 ......60 C5
ORP BR6 ......86 G6
PGE/AN SE20 ......61 J5
RASHE TN25 ......284 C5
RCANTE CT5 ......199 H6
RCANTW CT4 ......165 L9
RCANTW CT4 ......167 N8
RCANTW CT4 ......129 L2
RDV CT15 ......229 N9
RDV CT15 ......262 C8
RFOLK CT18 ......287 H2
RMAID ME8 ......97 K4
RMAID ME17 ......269 H9
RRTW TN3 ......269 H9
RSEV TN14 ......117 N5
RSEV TN14 ......118 F5
RSIT ME9 ......148 C1
RSIT ME9 ......98 C8
RSIT ME9 ......131 H5
RYE TN31 ......330 B4
SCUP DA14 ......64 C2
SEV TN13 ......148 D5
SNWD SE25 ......5 L1
STMC/STPC BR5 ......87 K1
STPH/PW TN12 ......242 G2
STPH/PW TN12 ......246 C4
STRD ME2 ......18 E2
STRD ME2 ......94 B4
SWLY BR8 ......58 D1
TENT TN30 ......301 H8
TIL RM18 ......50 D1
WADH TN5 ......314 C9
WBY/VAL ME18 ......183 K9
WGOS CT8 ......111 N4
WSTB CT5 ......105 M4
WWKM BR4 ......84 F5
Station Rd East CANT CT1 ......4 D6
  OXTED RH8 ......175 H5
Station Rd North BELV DA17 ......28 G6
Station Rd West CANTW/ST CC2 ......4 D3
  OXTED RH8 ......175 H5
Station Sq STMC/STPC BR5 ......86 D2
Station Ter SIT ME10 ......129 N1
Station Yd CMBW SE5 ......40 C2
Staunton St DEPT SE8 ......25 J9
Staveley CI PECK SE15 ......41 L2
Stave Yard Rd
  BERM/RHTH SE16 ......25 H4
Steadman CI HOO/HM ME3 ......71 L2
Stead St WALW SE17 ......24 A7
Stebondale St POP/IOD E14 ......25 M8
Stede HI RMAID ME17 ......188 G3
Stedly SCUP DA14 * 64 C3
Stedman CI BXLY DA5 ......65 N2
Steeds CI ASH TN23 ......282 D6
Steeds La RASHW TN26 ......282 D7
Steele Av GRH DA9 ......47 N6
Steele's La MEO DA13 ......92 A8
Steele St STRD ME2 ......72 A7
Steellands Ri WADH TN5 ......315 J5
Steel's La WCHPL E1 ......24 C2
Steelyard Pas CANST EC4R 24 A1
Steep CI ORP BR6 ......116 C1
Steep HI CROY/NA CRO 83 K8
Steeple Heights Dr
  BH/WHM TN16 ......145 N2
Steerforth CI ROCH ME1 ......95 H4
Steers PI RTON TN11 ......181 P9
Steers Wy BERM/RHTH SE16 ......25 H5
Stella CI STPH/PW TN12 ......245 J4
Stelling Rd ERITH DA8 ......48 C1
Stembridge Rd PGE/AN SE20 ......61 H8
Stembrook DVE/WH CT16 ......8 D3
Stempe CI RFOLK CT18 ......288 E9
Stenning Av TIL RM18 ......34 A7
The Stennings EGRIN RH19 ......264 F5
Stephen CI BRDST CT10 ......113 M9
  ORP BR6 ......86 G7
Stephen Rd BXLYHN DA7 ......45 L4
Stephens CI FAV ME13 ......132 E5
  MARC CT9 ......112 A6
  RAM CT11 ......16 C1
Stephenson Av TIL RM18 ......49 L2
Stephenson Rd
  CANTW/ST CC2 ......166 E1
Stephenson St CAN/RD E16 ......26 D5
Stephen's Rd STH/RUST TN4 ......270 D2
Stepney Cswy WCHPL E1 ......24 C2
Stepneyford La CRBK TN17 ......299 M6
Stepney Gn WCHPL E1 ......24 C1
Stepney High St WCHPL E1 ......24 C1
Steps Hill Rd RSIT ME9 ......127 N7
Step Style SIT ME10 ......130 A3
Sterling Av MAIDW ME16 ......155 H7
Sterling CI BRDST CT10 ......113 K8
Sterling Gdns NWCR SE14 ......25 H9
Sterling Rd OBOR ME1 ......77 J2
  SIT ME10 ......129 L4
Sterndale Rd DART DA1 ......46 F8
Sternhall La PECK SE15 ......40 G4

Sterry St STHWK SE1 ......24 A5
Steucers La FSTH SE23 ......41 L9
Steve Biko La CAT SE6 ......61 N1
Stevedale Rd WELL DA16 ......44 E5
Stevedore St WAP E1W 24 E4
Stevens Ct RAM CT11 * 142 C7
Stevens CI BECK BR3 ......61 N5
  BXLY DA5 ......65 M5
  HDCN TN27 ......219 N7
  RDART DA2 ......67 L4
  SNOD ME6 ......123 P5
Stevenson CI ERITH DA8 ......46 B1
  MAID/SHEP ME15 ......12 E7
Stevenson Crs
  BERM/RHTH SE16 ......24 D8
Stevenson Wy DIT/AY ME20 ......123 N9
Stevens Rd DIT/AY ME20 ......124 E7
Stevens St STHWK SE1 ......24 B6
Stewart CI WCHPL E1 ......24 B1
Stewart Rd RTWE/PEM TN2 ......270 F1
Stewart St POP/IOD E14 ......25 M5
Steyning Gv ELTH/MOT SE9 ......63 K3
Steynton Av BXLY DA5 ......64 G1
Stickens La E/WMAL ME19 ......153 M6
Stickfast La RMAID ME17 ......217 N6
  RSIT ME9 ......99 H5
Stickland Rd BELV DA17 ......28 F7
Stifford Clays Rd
  CDW/CHF RM16 ......32 A4
Stifford HI CDW/CHF RM16 ......31 N4
Stifford Rd SOCK/AV RN15 ......31 J5
Stilebridge La STPH/PW TN12 ......215 K7
Stiles CI ERITH DA8 ......28 G8
  FOLKN CT19 ......310 D4
  HAYES BR2 ......86 A3
  IOS ME12 ......78 A1
Still La STH/RUST TN4 ......240 C7
Stillness Rd FSTH SE23 ......41 L7
Stillwater Ms CHAT ME4 ......73 H5
Stirling CI RHAM ME8 ......127 H1
  ROCH ME1 ......94 F4
  SCUP DA14 ......64 E3
Stirling Dr ORP BR6 ......87 J9
Stirling Rd E/WMAL ME19 ......152 C9
  RDV CT15 ......265 L5
  MSTR CT12 ......142 F2
Stirling Rd KEN/WIL TN24 ......282 C1
Stisted Wy HDCN TN27 ......219 N7
Stockbury Dr MAIDW ME16 ......155 J5
Stockbury Gdns MARC CT9 ......113 K5
Stockbury Rd CROY/NA CRO 83 P5
Stockdale Gdns DEAL CT14 ......233 H5
Stockenbury STPH/PW TN12 ......212 G4
Stockers Brow RSIT ME9 ......129 P6
Stocker's HI FAV ME13 ......133 P9
Stockett La RMAID ME17 ......185 H8
Stock HI BH/WHM TN16 ......145 N1
Stockholm Rd
  BERM/RHTH SE16 ......24 F8
Stockholm Wy WAP E1W * 24 D4
Stockland Green Rd
  BH/WHM TN16 ......129 P4
Stock La RASHE TN25 ......284 B5
  RDART DA2 ......67 J6
Stocks Green Rd RTON TN11 ......209 P5
Stocks PI POP/IOD E14 ......25 J3
Stocks Rd TENT TN30 ......333 L3
Stockton CI MAID/BEAR ME14 ......155 N4
Stockwell Rd BMLY BR1 ......62 F8
Stockwell Park Wy
Stockwell St GNWCH SE10 ......25 M9
Stodart Rd PGE/AN SE20 ......61 J7
Stoddards La RYE TN31 ......330 D8
Stoddart CI FOLKN CT19 ......310 B5
Stodmarsh Rd RCANTE CT3 ......167 L3
Stofield Gdns ELTH/MOT SE9 ......63 H3
Stoke Rd HOO/HM ME3 ......53 P2
  HOO/HM ME3 ......54 C3
  HOO/HM ME3 ......73 N1
Stokes Rd CROY/NA CRO 84 A5
Stombers La RFOLK CT18 ......288 F6
Stonar CI RAM CT11 ......143 K3
  SWCH CT13 ......201 P1
Stoneacre Ct
  MAID/SHEP ME15 * 185 M2
Stoneacre La
  MAID/SHEP ME15 ......186 A4
Stone Barn Av BRCH CT7 ......111 H7
Stonebridge RASHE TN25 ......254 B4
Stone Br TENT TN30 ......333 L5
Stonebridge Green Rd
  HDCN TN27 ......219 P6
Stonebridge Rd CVW DA11 ......48 C5
Stonebridge Vls
  NROM TN28 * 336 F6
Stonebridge Wy FAV ME13 ......132 C6
Stonechat Sq EHAM E6 ......26 F1
Stone Court La
  RTWE/PEM TN2 ......241 P9
Stonecroft MEO DA13 ......122 B5
Stonecroft Rd ERITH DA8 ......45 L1
Stonecroft Wy CROY/NA CRO 82 D4
Stonecrop CI CHAT ME4 ......73 J6
Stonecross Lea MALL ME5 ......95 N5
Stone Cross Lees SWCH CT13 ......201 N3
Stonedane CI FAV ME13 ......132 F5
Stonefield CI BXLYHN DA7 ......45 J4
Stonefield Wy CHARL SE7 ......43 H1
Stone Gdns BRDST CT10 ......113 N8
Stonegate RASHE TN25 ......223 P8
Stonegate CI FAV ME13 ......64 E9
Stonegate Rd WADH TN5 ......314 A5
Stonehall Rd RDV CT15 ......260 A8
Stoneheap Rd RDV CT15 ......231 M8
Stone HI RASHE TN25 ......285 H6
Stone Hill Rd HDCN TN27 ......219 N8
Stonehills Ct DUL SE21 ......60 E2
Stonehill Woods Pk
  RDART DA2 * 65 K5

Stonehorse La HOO/HM ME3 ......72 A4
Stone House Ct HDTCH EC3A 24 A2
Stonehouse La ORP BR6 ......117 L3
  PUR RM19 ......31 H8
Stone House Ms
  BRDST CT10 * 113 N7
Stonehouse Rd ORP BR6 ......117 L4
Stoneings La RSEV TN14 ......146 C3
Stoneleigh CI EGRIN RH19 ......265 J6
Stoneleigh Park Av
  CROY/NA CRO 84 A5
Stoneleigh Rd OXTED RH8 ......175 P6
Stoneness Rd WTHK RM20 ......31 L9
Stone Park Av BECK BR3 ......84 D1
Stone Pit La HAWK TN18 ......318 B9
Stone Place Rd GRH DA9 ......47 L6
Stone Rd BRDST CT10 ......113 N8
  HAYES BR2 ......85 J2
Stone Rw RRTW TN3 ......268 G3
Stones Cross Rd SWLY BR8 ......88 B2
Stonestile Farm Rd
  HDCN TN27 ......190 F8
Stone Stile La RCANTW CT4 ......193 N2
Stonestile Rd HDCN TN27 ......247 K2
Stone St CRBK TN17 ......298 A2
  FAV ME13 ......132 F6
  GVE DA12 ......49 H7
  HYTHE CT21 ......307 P5
  RASHE TN25 ......308 A2
  RCANTW CT4 ......196 C9
  TONN TN 23 F2
Stone Street Rd
  BGR/WK TN15 ......149 P9
Stoneswood Rd OXTED RH8 ......175 L7
Stonewall EHAM E6 ......27 H1
Stonewall Park Rd RRTW TN3 ......269 L5
Stonewood RDART DA2 ......68 A2
Stonewood CI
  STH/RUST TN4 * 240 D9
Stoney Aly WOOL/PLUM SE18 ......43 L3
Stoneyard La POP/IOD E14 ......25 L3
Stoney Bank GILL ME7 ......96 C5
Stoneycroft CI LEE/GVPK SE12 ......42 D8
Stoney La HDTCH EC3A 24 B2
  NRWD SE19 ......60 F5
Stoney Rd FAV ME13 ......164 C1
Stoney St STHWK SE1 ......24 A4
Stony Cnr HART DA3 ......91 P1
Stony La ROCH ME1 ......94 G8
Stopes St PECK SE15 ......40 F1
Stopford Rd GILL ME7 ......7 J6
Store Rd CAN/RD E16 ......27 H5
Storers Quay POP/IOD E14 ......25 N7
Stories Ms CMBW SE5 * 40 E5
Stories Rd CMBW SE5 ......40 E4
Storks Rd BERM/RHTH SE16 ......24 D6
Stormaway Strd GVE DA12 ......70 B3
Storrington Rd CROY/NA CRO 83 K5
Storway Ct STRD 18 C5
Stour CI ASH TN23 ......252 B8
  HAYES BR2 ......85 M8
Stour Crs CANT CT1 ......167 J1
Stour Ct SWCH CT13 ......201 N1
Stourfields KEN/WIL TN24 ......252 C5
Stourmouth Rd RCANTE CT3 ......169 M1
Stour Rd CDW/CHF RM16 ......33 L7
  DART DA1 ......46 A4
  RCANTW CT4 ......195 L1
Stour Valley CI RCANTE CT3 ......138 C6
Stour Valley Wy ASH TN23 ......251 P6
  CANTW/ST CC2 ......4 A5
  HDCN TN27 ......220 E8
  KEN/WIL TN24 ......253 J7
  RCANTE CT3 ......168 D3
  RCANTW CT4 ......194 C3
  RCANTW CT4 ......224 E2
  RMAID ME17 ......189 M8
  SWCH CT13 ......202 A1
Stour Valley Wy RCANTE CT3 ......139 N7
Stowage DEPT SE8 ......25 L9
The Stowage DEPT SE8 ......25 K9
Stowell Av CROY/NA CRO 114 C4
Stowe Rd ORP BR6 ......87 J8
Stowting HI RASHE TN25 ......255 P8
Stowting Rd ORP BR6 ......86 F8
Stradella Rd HNHL SE24 ......40 C7
Strafford St POP/IOD E14 ......25 K5
Straight La LYDD TN29 ......334 F5
Straightsmouth GNWCH SE10 ......25 L9
Strait Rd EHAM E6 ......26 E3
Strakers HI RDV CT15 ......231 L9
Straker's Rd EDUL SE22 ......41 H5
Strand RYE TN31 ......330 E8
Strand Approach Rd GILL ME7 ......73 L8
Strand CI MEO DA13 ......92 B4
Strandfield CI
  WOOL/PLUM SE18 ......27 M8
Strand St SWCH CT13 ......171 N9
The Strand DEAL CT14 ......233 J4
Stranger's CI CANT CT1 ......166 B6
Stranger's La CANT CT1 ......166 B6
Strangford PI HB CT6 ......107 N5
Strangford Rd WSTB CT5 ......105 N4
Stratford Av RHAM ME8 ......96 C6
Stratford Dr
  MAID/SHEP ME15 ......186 A5
Stratford House Av BMLY BR1 ......63 J9
Stratford La RHAM ME8 ......96 B6
Stratford Rd E/WMAL ME19 ......153 H4
  THHTH CR7 ......82 F1
Stratford St RTW TN1 ......270 F3
Strathaven Rd LEE/GVPK SE12 ......42 F7
Stratheden Rd BKHTH/KID SE3 ......42 A3
Strathmore HI RHAM ME8 ......54 B7
Strathmore Rd CROY/NA CRO 83 H4
Strathnairn St STHWK SE1 ......24 D7
Strathyre Av
  STRHM/NOR SW16 ......60 A9
Stratton CI BXLYHN DA7 ......45 J3
Strattondale St POP/IOD E14 ......25 M6

Stratton Rd BXLYHN DA7 ......44 G4
Stratton Ter BH/WHM TN16 ......176 D5
Strawberry CI RRTW TN3 ......270 B8
Strawberry Flds RYE TN31 ......329 P6
  SWLY BR8 ......65 N8
Strawberry V TON TN9 ......240 F1
Straw Mill HI
  MAID/SHEP ME15 ......185 K2
Streamdale ABYW SE2 ......28 A9
Stream La HAWK TN18 ......317 H7
Streamline Ms EDUL SE22 ......41 H9
Stream Pk EGRIN RH19 ......264 D5
Stream Pit La HAWK TN18 ......318 B9
Streamside DIT/AY ME20 ......154 A3
Stream Side TON TN10 ......210 C3
Streamside CI HAYES BR2 ......85 K1
The Stream DIT/AY ME20 ......154 A3
Stream Wk WSTB CT5 ......105 L4
Stream Wy BELV DA17 ......28 F9
Streetfield EDEN TN8 ......206 D3
Streete Court Rd WGOS CT8 ......111 N5
Street End Rd WALB TN16 ......153 E5
Streeters La WLGTN SM6 ......82 C7
Streetfield HB CT6 ......107 N6
  RMAID ME17 ......218 A5
Streetfield Ms BKHTH/KID SE3 ......42 A3
Streetfield Rd RHAM ME8 ......96 C5
The Street ASH TN23 ......251 P9
  BGR/WK TN15 ......91 H9
  BGR/WK TN15 ......150 C6
  BGR/WK TN15 ......181 J4
  BRCH CT7 ......111 H2
  BRCH CT7 ......141 J1
  CRBK TN17 ......276 D8
  CRBK TN17 ......277 H2
  DEAL CT14 ......201 P6
  DEAL CT14 ......231 H8
  DEAL CT14 ......232 A1
  DEAL CT14 ......232 E4
  E/WMAL ME19 ......122 B8
  E/WMAL ME19 ......122 C9
  EYN DA4 ......89 N7
  FAV ME13 ......132 E3
  FAV ME13 ......161 K6
  FAV ME13 ......164 B1
  GILL ME7 ......126 E4
  GVE DA12 ......70 B9
  GVE DA12 ......70 C4
  HDCN TN27 ......219 N7
  HDCN TN27 ......250 C2
  HOO/HM ME3 ......53 L5
  HOO/HM ME3 ......56 B1
  HYTHE CT21 ......306 C5
  KEN/WIL TN24 ......253 H6
  KEN/WIL TN24 ......253 L9
  MAID/BEAR ME14 ......155 P1
  MAID/BEAR ME14 ......156 F8
  MEO DA13 ......92 B5
  RASHE TN25 ......254 D3
  RASHE TN25 ......255 H3
  RASHE TN25 ......255 K9
  RASHW TN26 ......251 M2
  RASHW TN26 ......280 C3
  RASHW TN26 ......281 M8
  RASHW TN26 ......304 D8
  RCANTE CT5 ......139 P8
  RCANTE CT3 ......168 F7
  RCANTW CT4 ......169 M1
  RCANTW CT4 ......198 C2
  RCANTW CT4 ......199 N5
  RCANTW CT4 ......200 E1
  RCANTW CT4 ......200 E4
  RCANTW CT4 ......167 N9
  RCANTW CT4 ......194 C3
  RCANTW CT4 ......196 A8
  RCANTW CT4 ......197 N5
  RCANTW CT4 ......197 P9
  RDART DA2 ......224 C1
  RDV CT15 ......226 F5
  RDV CT15 ......228 C6
  RDV CT15 ......228 G5
  RDV CT15 ......229 N5
  RDV CT15 ......260 D1
  RDV CT15 ......261 P7
  RDV CT15 ......262 A5
  RFOLK CT18 ......312 A1
  RFOLK CT18 ......287 M9
  RFOLK CT18 ......288 E7
  RMAID ME17 ......218 A3
  RSIT ME9 ......97 P2
  RSIT ME9 ......98 E1
  RSIT ME9 ......99 M2
  RSIT ME9 ......127 N1
  RSIT ME9 ......127 P5
  RSIT ME9 ......128 G3
  RSIT ME9 ......130 F7
  RSIT ME9 ......158 C3
  RSIT ME9 ......160 D5
  STRD ME2 ......93 M9
  SWCH CT13 ......171 M9
  TENT TN30 ......332 A3
  TENT TN30 ......333 J1
  WBY/YAL ME18 ......182 E3
  WBY/YAL ME18 ......183 P4
Strettit Gdns STPH/PW TN12 ......212 C5
Stretton Rd CROY/NA CRO 83 J4
Strickland Av DART DA1 ......46 F5
Strickland St DEPT SE8 ......41 N3
Strickland Wy ORP BR6 ......86 G8
Stringer Dr BRCH CT7 ......111 H7
Strode Crs IOS ME12 ......57 L6
Strode Park Rd HB CT6 ......107 N4
Strond Green Gdns
  CROY/NA CRO 83 P4
Strond Green Wy
  CROY/NA CRO 83 P4
Strond St DVW CT17 ......8 C6

Strongbow Crs ELTH/MOT SE9 ......43 K6
Strongbow Rd ELTH/MOT SE9 ......43 K6
Stroud Green Wy
  CROY/NA CRO 83 N4
Strouds Rd SNWD SE25 ......83 M3
Strover St GILL ME7 ......73 J8
Strumer Ct E/WMAL ME19 ......183 H1
Struttons Av DVW DA11 ......69 K1
Strype St WCHPL E1 ......24 C1
Stuart CI MAID/BEAR ME14 ......13 K1
  RTWE/PEM TN2 ......270 C8
  SWLY BR8 ......65 P6
Stuart Ct DVW CT17 * 8 B7
Stuart Crs CROY/NA CRO 84 C7
Stuart Evans CI WALL DA16 ......44 E4
Stuart Mantle Wy ERITH DA8 ......45 M1
Stuart Rd FOLKN CT19 ......11 H1
  GILL ME7 ......96 A3
  GRAYS RM17 ......32 C8
  GVW DA11 ......49 L7
  PECK SE15 ......41 J4
  THHTH CR7 ......83 H1
  WELL DA16 ......44 D2
Stuart Wy EGRIN RH19 ......265 J8
Stubbs Dr BERM/RHTH SE16 ......24 E8
Stubbs HI ORP BR6 ......117 K7
Stubpond La LING RH7 ......264 A1
Studfall CI HYTHE CT21 ......308 C7
Studholme St PECK SE15 ......41 H1
Studland CI KEN/WIL TN24 ......252 G5
Studland CI BFN/LL DA15 ......64 B2
Studland Rd SYD SE26 ......61 K4
Studley Ct DEAL CT14 ......64 D4
Studley Crs HART DA3 ......68 G8
Stumble La ASH TN23 ......282 E7
Stumps Hill La BECK BR3 ......61 N5
Stuppington Ct Farm
  CANT CT1 ......166 D8
Stuppington La CANT CT1 ......166 D8
Sturdee Av GILL ME7 ......96 B2
Sturdy Rd PECK SE15 ......41 H5
Sturges Fld CHST BR7 ......309 J5
Sturges Rd KEN/WIL TN24 ......2 D2
Sturla Rd CHAT ME4 ......95 M4
Sturry Court Ms
  CANTW/ST CC2 ......137 L7
Sturry HI CANTW/ST CC2 ......137 L7
Sturry Rd CANT CT1 ......5 H1
  CANT CT1 ......5 H1
Sturry Wy RHAM ME8 ......96 F4
Statfield St WCHPL E1 ......24 D2
Styants Bottom Rd
  BGR/WK TN15 ......150 C7
Styles CI EDEN TN8 ......207 J5
Styles CI RHAM ME8 ......127 H1
Styles Gdns BRXN/ST SW9 ......40 C3
Styles La MAID/BEAR ME14 ......155 P1
Styles Wy BECK BR3 ......84 F1
Sudbury EHAM E6 ......27 H2
Sudbury Crs BMLY BR1 ......62 E4
Sudbury Gdns CROY/NA CRO 83 K8
Sudbury PI WGOS CT8 ......111 L6
Suffield CI SAND/SEL CR2 ......114 A6
Suffield Rd PGE/AN SE20 ......61 J8
Suffolk Av RHAM ME8 ......97 J5
  WGOS CT8 ......111 L6
Suffolk Dr ASH TN23 ......2 A4
Suffolk La CANST EC4R 24 A5
Suffolk Rd CANT CT1 ......167 J4
  DART DA1 ......46 E7
  GVE DA12 ......49 H2
  MAID/SHEP ME15 ......186 A3
  SCUP DA14 ......64 E5
  SNWD SE25 ......82 E1
Suffolk St WSTB CT5 ......105 L6
Suffolk Wy BGR/WK TN15 ......21 C3
Sugar Loaf Wk FOLKN CT19 ......310 C6
Sullivan Av CAN/RD E16 ......26 E1
Sullivan CI DART DA1 ......46 E7
Sullivan Rd TIL RM18 ......49 L2
  TONN TN10 ......211 H5
Sultan Rd WALD ME5 ......125 P5
Sultan St BECK BR3 ......61 K8
  CMBW SE5 ......40 C1
Summer CI HYTHE CT21 ......308 C5
  TENT TN30 ......301 K6
Summercourt Rd WCHPL E1 ......24 F2
Summerfield Av STH/RUST TN4 ......240 C8
Summerfield St
  LEE/GVPK SE12 ......42 D8
Summer HI CANTW/ST CC2 ......166 B9
  CHST BR7 ......63 H6
Summerhill HDCN TN27 ......247 K3
Summerhill Av STH/RUST TN4 ......240 C8
Summerhill CI ORP BR6 ......86 F8
Summerhill Pk
  KEN/WIL TN24 ......283 M1
Summerhill Rd DART DA1 ......46 D8
  STPH/PW TN12 ......245 N1
Summerhouse Dr RDART DA2 ......65 M4
Summer La CANTW/ST CC2 ......136 D7
Summer Leeze KEN/WIL TN24 ......253 H9
Summer Leeze Gdns
  KEN/WIL TN24 ......253 H9
Summer Rd BRCH CT7 ......109 P9
Summerton Wy THMD SE28 ......28 C3
Summervale Rd
  STH/RUST TN4 ......270 A7
Summerville Av IOS ME12 ......77 P2
Summit Wy NRWD SE19 ......60 E6
Sumner Av PECK SE15 ......40 F2
Sumner CI ORP BR6 ......86 D8
Sumner Gdns CROY/NA CRO 82 F5
  PECK SE15 ......24 C9
  PECK SE15 ......40 F2
Sumner Rd South
  CROY/NA CRO 82 F5
Sumpter Wy FAV ME13 ......132 D6
Sunbeam Av HB CT6 ......106 E2

Sunburst Cl STPH/PW TN12 .....245 J4
Sunbury St WOOL/PLUM SE18....26 C6
Sun Ct ERITH DA8.........45 P3
Suncroft Pl SYD SE26 ....61 J2
Sunderland Cl ROCH ME1.......97 K5
Sunderland Dr RHAM ME8......97 K6
Sunderland Mt FSTH SE23 *....61 K1
Sunderland Rd FSTH SE23....41 K9
Sundew Gv RAM CT11.......17 F1
Sundial Av SNWD SE25.......60 F8
Sundorne Rd CHARL SE7......26 C8
Sundridge Av BMLY BR1......63 H7
  WELL DA16.........43 P3
Sundridge Cl CANTW/ST CT2 ..136 F9
  DART DA1.........46 G7
Sundridge Dr WALD ME5......125 M1
Sundridge Hl RSEV TN14......147 K3
  STRD ME2.........94 B4
Sundridge La RSEV TN14......147 J2
Sundridge Pde BMLY BR1 *....62 F6
Sundridge Rd CROY/NA CR0....83 L5
  RSEV TN14.........147 P5
  RSEV TN14.........148 A3
Sunfields Pl BKHTH/KID SE3....42 F1
Sunhill Pl RTWE/PEM TN2 *....271 M2
Sun In Sands Rbt
  BKHTH/KID SE3.........42 F1
Sunken Rd CROY/NA CR0......83 P9
Sunland Av BXLYHS DA6......44 C5
Sun La BKHTH/KID SE3.......42 F1
  GVE DA12.........69 N1
  HYTHE CT21.........309 H5
Sunningdale Av FOLKN CT19...310 D4
Sunningdale Cl
  BERM/RHTH SE16 *.........24 E8
  RHAM ME8.........96 C8
  THMD SE28.........28 D2
Sunningdale Dr RHAM ME8.....96 C8
Sunningdale Rd HAYES BR2....85 P1
Sunningdale Vk HB CT6.......107 J5
Sunninghill GVW DA11.......69 J1
Sunninghill Rd LEW SE13......41 P3
Sunningvale Av
  BH/WHM TN16.........115 M9
Sunningvale Cl
  BH/WHM TN16.........145 N1
Sunny Bank HYTHE CT21......308 C5
  SIT ME10.........100 A9
  SNWD SE25.........83 M1
Sunnybank RDV CT15 *.......144 B2
Sunnybank RDV CT15........230 C9
Sunnycroft Rd SNWD SE25....60 D9
Sunnydale ORP BR6.......86 B6
Sunnydale Rd LEE/GVPK SE12..42 F6
Sunnydene St SYD SE26......61 L5
Sunnyfields Cl RHAM ME8.....97 H6
Sunnyfields Dr IOS ME12.....77 L1
Sunnyhill Rd HB CT6.......106 C3
Sunnymead CANTW/ST CT2 ...136 C6
Sunnymead RRTW TN3 *......339 M9
Sunnyside DEAL CT14.......41 M8
Sunny Side MEO DA13 *......92 B7
Sunnyside Av IOS ME12.......78 A1
Sunnyside Cl DEAL CT14......232 C8
Sunnyside Gdns SWCT13 .....200 M2
Sunnyside Rd FOLK CT20.....309 P4
  FOLK CT20.........310 A8
  STH/RUST TN4.........269 P4
Sun Pas BERM/RHTH SE16....24 D6
Sun Pier CHAT ME4 *.......6 A4
Sun Rd CANT MS........40 C5
  HAYES BR2.........85 P5
  WSTB CT5.........105 J7
Sun Rd SWCM DA10........48 D7
Sunset Cl ERITH DA8.......45 P3
  ME10 CT.........79 M1
  WSTB CT5.........105 K8
Sunset Gdns NRWD SE19.....60 E8
Sunset Rd CMBW SE5.......40 C5
  THMD SE28.........27 P5
Sun St CANT CT1.......4 E4
  SDTCH EC2A.........7 J2
Sun Ter MAID ME15.......125 N1
Sun Valley Wy RDV CT15.....230 D9
Super Abbey Est
  DIT/AY ME20 *.........154 G2
Superior Dr ORP BR6.......116 C1
Surf Crs IOS ME12.......79 M1
Surlingham Cl THMD SE28 ...28 C5
Surrenden Rd FOLKN CT19...310 C5
  STPH/PW TN12.........246 B6
Surrey Canal Rd
  BERM/RHTH SE16.........24 F9
Surrey Cl BGR/WK TN15 *....120 B2
  RTWE/PEM TN2.........270 C8
Surrey Gdns BRCH CT7.......110 C6
Surrey Gv WALW SE17.......24 B8
Surrey Ms WNWD SE27......60 E3
Surrey Quays Rd
  BERM/RHTH SE16.........24 F6
Surrey Rd CANT CT1.......167 J5
  MAID/SHEP ME15.........186 A3
  MARG CT9.........112 C2
  PECK SE15.........42 A4
  WWKM BR4.........84 E5
Surrey Sq WALW SE17.......24 B8
Surrey St CROY/NA CR0......83 H7
Surrey Ter WALW SE17.......24 B8
Surrey Water Rd
  BERM/RHTH SE16.........24 G4
Surridge Gdns NRWD SE19...60 D5
Surtees Cl KEN/WIL TN24 ...283 H2
Susannah St POP/IOD E14....25 L2
Susan Rd BKHTH/KID SE3.....63 J7
Susan Wd RASHW TN26......302 C5
Susan Wd CHST BR7.......63 J7
Sussex Av CANT CT1.......167 J5
  KEN/WIL TN24.........2 C2
  MARG CT9.........15 J7
Sussex Border Pth
  EDEN TN8.........236 D9
  EGRIN RH19.........264 A9

EGRIN RH19.........265 K7
HAWK TN18.........317 J8
RRTW TN3.........268 C4
TENT TN30.........332 B6
WADH TN5.........315 L2
Sussex Cl BGR/WK TN15 *....120 B2
  HB CT6.........106 C2
  RTWE/PEM TN2.........270 F7
Sussex Dr WALD ME5.......125 M1
Sussex Gdns BRCH CT7......110 C6
  HB CT6.........106 C2
  WGOS CT8 *.........111 N4
Sussex Man WGOS CT8 *....111 N4
Sussex Ms RTWE/PEM TN2 ...22 C7
Sussex Rd DART DA1.......46 G8
  ERITH DA8.........45 K1
  FOLKN CT19.........10 L2
  MAID/SHEP ME15.........186 A2
  MTCM CR4 *.........82 D2
  NROM TN28.........336 F7
  SCUP DA14.........64 D4
  STMC/STPC BR5.........87 K3
  TON TN9.........240 D1
  WWKM BR4.........84 E5
Sussex St WALW SE17.......24 B8
Sussex Ter PGE/AN SE20 *....61 J6
  PUR RM19.........30 E8
Sussex Wk CANT CT1.......167 J5
Sutcliffe Rd WELL DA16......44 E3
  WOOL/PLUM SE18.........27 M9
Sutherland Av BH/WHM TN16..145 N2
  STMC/STPC BR5.........86 C3
  WELL DA16.........43 P5
Sutherland Cl GVE DA12......70 D1
  HYTHE CT21.........308 F5
Sutherland Dr BRCH CT7......111 J6
Sutherland Rd BELV DA17....28 F6
  CROY/NA CR0.........82 F4
  DEAL CT14.........233 H5
  RTW TN1.........22 E6
Sutlej Rd CHARL SE7.......42 G1
Sutton Baron Rd RSIT ME9 ..128 C5
Sutton Cl BECK BR3.......61 P7
  FOLKN CT19.........310 D4
  RHAM ME8.........97 K6
Sutton Ct STPH/PW TN12 ...245 H4
Sutton Copse RTWE/PEM TN2 ..245 J4
Sutton Gdns CROY/NA CR0 ...83 L2
Sutton La DEAL CT14.......232 B9
Sutton Rd MAID/SHEP ME15..185 N3
  RCANTE CT3.........138 B6
  RMAID ME17.........186 F7
The Suttons RYE TN31......344 A2
Sutton St MAID/BEAR ME14..156 G9
  WCHPL E1.........24 F2
Sutton Valence HI
Swadelands Cl RMAID ME17..189 K6
Swaffield Rd SEV TN13.......149 H7
Swain Cl STRD ME2.......71 P7
Swain Rd RHAM ME8.......96 E8
  TENT TN30.........301 J4
  THHTH CR7.........83 H2
Swaisland Rd DART DA1......45 P2
Swaislands Dr DART DA1.....45 P6
Swale Av IOS ME12.......57 K7
  OBOR ME11.........77 H4
Swale Rd (Due to open 2006)
  RSIT ME9.........77 J7
Swalecliffe Av HB CT6.......106 C2
Swalecliffe Court Dr
  WSTB CT5.........106 A4
Swalecliffe Rd WSTB CT5....106 A4
Swale Cl SOCK/AV RM15......30 C2
Swaledale Rd RDART DA2 ...47 J9
Swale Heritage Trail
  FAV ME13.........132 D2
  SIT ME10.........110 D1
Swale Rd DART DA1.......46 A4
  STRD ME2.........71 L8
Swallands Rd CAT SE6......61 N2
Swallow Av WSTB CT5.......105 J7
Swallow Cl BXLYHN DA7.....45 N2
  CDW/CHF RM16.........31 N7
  CRH DA3.........47 M6
  MARG CT9.........112 B5
  NWCR SE14.........41 J2
Swallow Ct HB CT6 *.......107 L7
Swallowdale SAND/SEL CR2 ..114 A5
Swallow Dr RTWE/PEM TN2 ...271 J2
Swallowfield KEN/WIL TN24 ..283 H1
  LING RH7.........235 K7
Swallowfield Rd CHARL SE7...26 C8
Swallow Rd DIT/AY ME20....95 M9
Swallows Cl WALD ME5......26 F1
Swallowtail Cl STMC/STPC BR5..87 L1
Swamp Rd LYDD TN29.......335 P9
Swan Cl CROY/NA CR0 *....83 K2
  SIT ME10.........130 A1
  STMC/STPC BR5.........64 C9
Swan Cottages TENT TN30 ...332 A2
Swanfield Rd WSTB CT5......105 L6
Swan Gn RASH TN25.......285 K7
Swanland Dr TON TN9......240 D6
Swan La CANST EC4R.......24 A3
  CRBK TN17.........274 E5
  DART DA1.........46 D6
  RASHE TN25.........285 M6
Swanley La SWLY BR8.......65 P9
Swanley Rd WELL DA16......44 E2
Swanley Village Rd SWLY BR8...66 B7
Swan Md STHWK SE1.......24 B6
Swan Rd FOLKN CT19.......210 G8
Swann Wy RFOLK CT18.....288 D6
Swan Pas WCHPL E1.......26 F1
Swan Rdg EDEN TN8.......206 E6
Swan Rd BERM/RHTH SE16...24 F5
  RASHE TN25.........285 M6
Swanscombe St DART DA10...48 D7
Swanstree Av SIT ME10.....130 A3
Swan St E/WMAL ME19.....153 K4

TENT TN50.........331 N2
Swanton La RCANTE CT3 ...167 P3
  RDV CT15.........259 M7
Swanton Rd ERITH DA8......45 J1
  WBY/VA ME18.........182 B4
Swanzy Rd RSEV TN14.......149 H5
Sward Rd STMC/STPC BR5 ...87 H3
Swarling Hill Rd RCANTW CT4 ..196 D5
Swattenden La CRBK TN17 ...297 N5
Swaylands Rd BELV DA17 *...28 F6
Swaynesland Rd OXTED RH8..206 A1
Swaynes Wy SWCM DA10...201 J8
Swedenbourg Gdns WCHPL E1..24 D3
Sweden Ga BERM/RHTH SE16...25 H7
Sweechbridge Rd HB CT6....108 F2
Sweechgate CANTW/ST CT2 ..137 K6
Sweeney Crs STHWK SE1.....24 C5
Sweeps Hill Cl
  RTWE/PEM TN2.........271 N1
Sweeps La STMC/STPC BR5 ...87 K5
Sweet Bay Crs ASH TN23....252 A6
Sweetbriar La DVE/WH CT16...230 C7
Sweetings La RRTW TN3....294 E6
Sweetlove Pl RCANTE CT3 ...169 K8
Sweetlands La E/WMAL ME19..159 F8
Sweyne Rd SWCM DA10......48 C7
Sweyn Pl BKHTH/KID SE3.....42 E3
Sweyn Rd MARG CT9.......112 F2
Swievelands Rd
  BH/WHM TN16.........145 L4
Swift Cl WALD ME5.......95 N8
Swift Pl STRD ME2 *.......95 N9
Swift Wy WALD ME5 *......28 A3
Swiftsden Wy HAYES BR2.....62 C5
Swiftsure Rd CDW/CHF RM16..31 M7
Swifts vw CRBK TN17.......298 A1
Swiller's La GVE DA12.......70 C4
Swinburne Av BRDST CT10 ...143 M1
Swinburne Gv CROY/NA CR0...83 P3
Swinburne Gdns TIL RM18....49 M5
Swinford Gdns BRXN/ST SW9 ...40 B4
  MARG CT9.........113 H5
Swingate Av HOO/HM ME3 ...52 B3
Swingate Cl WALD ME5......125 M5
Swingate La WOOL/PLUM SE18..44 A1
Swinton Av HOO/HM ME3 ...72 F2
Swires Shaw HAYES BR2 ...85 N8
Swissland Hl EGRIN RH19....265 H2
Swiss Wy FOLKN CT19.......311 K4
Switch House Av LYDD TN29...37 J5
Switland Gdns
  ELTH/MOT SE9.........63 K3
Sybil Phoenix Cl DEPT SE8...24 A8
Sycamore Av BFN/LL DA15 ...44 B7
  GVE DA12.........49 P8
  HB CT6.........107 P1
  HYTHE CT21.........308 D6
  LYDD TN29.........342 C5
  SAND/SEL CR2.........83 X9
  TIL RM18.........49 M5
Sycamore Crs MAIDW ME16..155 H7
Sycamore Dr DIT/AY ME20....154 D3
  EGRIN RH19.........265 K7
  SWLY BR8.........65 N9
Sycamore Gdns LYDD TN29...242 C4
  STPH/PW TN12.........242 G4
Sycamore Gra CAT SE6......143 L5
  PGE/AN SE20.........60 C7
Sycamore Ms CAT SE6 *.....29 J8
Sycamore Rd DART DA1 *...45 J8
  STRD ME2.........94 A7
The Sycamores RCANTE CT3..138 B9
Sychem La RTON TN11......242 B4
Sychem Pl STPH/PW TN12 ...242 B2
Sydcot Dr DEAL CT14.......233 H1
Sydcote DUL SE21 *.......60 C1
Sydenham Av FSTH SE23 *...61 H4
  SYD SE26.........60 G2
Sydenham Pk SYD SE26.....61 J2
Sydenham Park Rd FSTH SE23..61 J2
Sydenham Ri FSTH SE23.....61 H1
Sydenham Rd CROY/NA CR0...83 J5
  DEAL CT14.........233 J2
  SYD SE26.........61 K4
Sydenham Station Ap
  SYD SE26.........61 J3
Sydmons Ct FSTH SE23 *....41 P9
Sydney Av SIT ME10.......129 K1
Sydney Cooper Cl
  CANTW/ST CT2.........166 A2
Sydney Rd ABYW SE2.......28 C6
  BXLYHS DA6.........44 F5
  CHAT ME4.........6 D7
  DEAL CT14.........232 F6
  RAM CT11.........17 H2
  SCUP DA14.........64 A3
  TIL RM18.........49 N5
  WSTB CT5.........105 M6
Sydney St ASH TN23.......252 F9
Sylewood Cl ROCH ME1.....94 G6
Sylvan Cl CDW/CHF RM16....31 P7
  OXTED RH8.........206 D9
  SAND/SEL CR2.........83 L9
Sylvan Gv PECK SE15.......41 J5
Sylvan Gld WALD ME5.......125 M5
Sylvan Ms GRH DA3 *.......47 P5
Sylvan Rd NRWD SE19.......60 F5
  RHAM ME8.........96 F6
Sylvan Ter PECK SE15 *.....41 H1
Sylvan Wy WWKM BR4......85 H8
Silverdale Rd CROY/NA CR0...82 C7
Sylvester Av CHST BR7.....62 G4
Sylvestre Cl STRD ME2.....123 P1
Symmonds Dr SIT ME10.....99 P9
Symonds Cl BGR/WK TN15...90 B8
Symonds La WBY/VAL ME18..213 M3
Symonds Rd HOO/HM ME3 ...52 A5
Symons Av CHAT ME4......95 L4

T

Tabard Garden Est STHWK SE1..24 A5
Tabard St STHWK SE1.......24 A5
Tabret Cl KEN/WIL TN24....252 C3
Tabrums Wy MS BROCKY SE4
Taburn Gn WALD ME5.......125 N1
Taddington Wood La
  WALD ME5.........125 K3
Taddy Gdns MARG CT19......113 H5
Tadworth Rd CROY/NA CR0 ...252 G4
Taeping St POP/IOD E14......25 L7
Tailiour Cl SIT ME10.......99 N7
Tainter Rd RTON TN11......211 N1
Tainters Hl EDEN TN8 *......237 L3
Tait Rd CROY/NA CR0.......83 K4
Talavera Rd CANT CT1.......167 H5
Talbot Av HB CT6.......106 C3
Talbot Ct BANK EC3V *......24 A3
Talbot Pl BKHTH/KID SE3....42 E5
Talbot Rd EDUL SE22......40 E5
  HAWK TN18.........317 H6
  LING RH7.........234 C6
  MAIDW ME16.........155 H6
  MARG CT9.........112 G3
  THHTH CR7.........83 M5
Talbot Yd STHWK SE1 *......24 A4
Talcott Pth
  BRXS/STRHM SW2 *.........40 A9
Talfourd Pl PECK SE15......40 F2
Talfourd Rd PECK SE15......40 F2
Talisman Sq SYD SE26......60 G3
Tall Elms Cl HAYES BR2.....85 J2
Tallents Cl EYN DA4.......67 H6
Tallis Cl CAN/RD E16.......26 C2
Tallis Gv CHARL SE7.......26 C9
Tall Trees EGRIN RH19 *.....265 J8
Tall Trees Cl RMAID ME17...187 N9
Tally Ho Rd RASHW TN26....281 N7
Tally Rd OXTED RH8.......175 P7
Talmage Cl FSTH SE23......41 P9
Talma Rd BRXS/STRHM SW2 ...40 A5
Talus Cl PUR RM19.......30 G7
Tamar Dr SOCK/AV RM15....30 F2
Tamarind Cl GILL ME7......126 D1
Tamarind Yd WAP E1W *....24 D4
Tamar Rd TONN TN10......210 E5
Tamar St WOOL/PLUM SE18...27 P7
Tame La LYDD TN29.......306 G8
Tamesis Strd GVE DA12.....70 B4
Tameis Rd RASHE TN25....255 J4
Tams Gdns SE6 CT1 *......61 H1
Tamworth Pk MTCM CR4.....82 A1
Tamworth Pl CROY/NA CR0 *..83 H6
Tamworth Rd CROY/NA CR0...86 E5
Tandridge Dr ORP BR6......86 C5
Tandridgehill La GDST RH9 ..234 D3
Tandridge La LING RH7.....234 C1
  OXTED RH8.........174 D9
Tandridge Rd WARL CR6.....144 A4
Tanfield Rd CROY/NA CR0....175 P7
Tangier Cl DVE/WH CT16....291 M4
Tangleberry La BMLY BR1 *...86 A1
Tangle Oak EGRIN RH19.....264 B4
Tanglewood Cl CROY/NA CR0...83 P7
  RHAM ME8.........96 C1
Tangmere Cl GILL ME7......96 F1
Tanhouse Rd OXTED RH8 ...174 G8
Tanker Hi RHAM ME8......96 G8
Tankerton Circ WSTB CT5....105 N5
Tankerton Rd WSTB CT5.....105 M3
Tankerton Ter CROY/NA CR0 *...82 E4
Tank Farm St LYDD TN29....347 L5
Tank Hill Rd PUR RM19.....30 D7
Tank La PUR RM19.......30 D7
Tanner's Hl DEPT SE8.......41 N2
  HYTHE CT21.........309 H3
Tanner's Hill Gdns
  HYTHE CT21.........309 H3
Tanners Md EDEN TN8......206 D9
Tanners Ms DEPT SE8......41 M2
Tanner St STHWK SE1.......132 F6
Tannery Cl CROY/NA CR0.....84 A2
Tannery La ASH TN23.......201 N1
  SWCH CT13.........201 N1
  TON TN9.........210 F9
Tappen Rd TON TN9.......210 F9
Tapestry Cl BELV DA17......28 E3
Tappen Dr CRBK TN17......273 H5
Tappesfield Rd PECK SE15...41 L4
Tara Ter BROCKY SE4 *......41 L4
Tarbert Rd EDUL SE22......40 F5
Tarbert Wk WCHPL E1 *....24 E3
Target Firs DVE/WH CT16....290 E2
Tarleton Gdns FSTH SE23....41 H9
Tarling Rd CAN/RD E16.....26 C2
Tarling St WCHPL E1.......24 E2
Tarnwood Pk ELTH/MOT SE9 ..43 K9
Tarragon Cl NWCR SE14....41 L1
Tarragon Gv SYD SE26.....61 K5
Tarragon Rd MAIDW ME16 ...154 F9
Tarriff Crs DEPT SE8.......25 J9
Tarry La DEPT SE8 *.......41 J1
Tarves Wy GNWCH SE10....41 P1
Tasker Cl MAID/SHEP ME15 ...158 H9
Tasker Rd CDW/CHF RM16 ...33 J6
Tassell Cl E/WMAL ME19....153 P3

Taswell Cl DVE/WH CT16......8 E2
Taswell Rd RHAM ME8......97 K5
Taswell St DVE/WH CT16......8 E2
Tate Rd CAN/RD E16.......26 G4
Tates Av HART TN18.......317 J5
Tates Orch HART.........91 J5
Tatler Cl WALD ME5.......126 A3
Tatnell Rd FSTH SE23.......41 L7
Tatsfield La BH/WHM TN16...146 A6
Tattersall Cl ELTH/MOT SE9 ...43 J6
Tattlebury La CRBK TN17....274 E8
Tattlebury Rd HDCN TN27...247 L2
Tatum St WALW SE17.......24 B7
Taunton Cl BXLYHN DA7....45 M4
  MAID/SHEP ME15.........186 C5
Taunton Rd GVW DA11......48 E6
  LEW SE13.........42 C6
Taunton V GVE DA12.......42 C6
Taveners Rd RHAM ME8......96 G7
Tavern Cl BDR ME6.......151 J5
Tavistock Cl RHAM ME8......97 H7
  SIT ME10.........129 L1
  WALD ME5.........125 L4
Tavistock Crs MTCM CR4....83 J4
Tavistock Gv CROY/NA CR0...83 J5
Tavistock Rd CROY/NA CR0...83 J5
  HAYES BR2.........85 K1
  RAM CT11.........143 K3
  WELL DA16.........44 E2
Tawy Br ABYW SE2.......28 B5
Tawney Rd THMD SE28.....28 A3
Tawny Wy BERM/RHTH SE16...24 G7
Tayburn Cl POP/IOD E14.....25 M2
Tay Cl WALD ME5.......95 N8
Tay Flats STPH/PW TN12 *...246 G2
Taylor Cl DEPT SE8.......25 J9
  ORP BR6.........86 G8
  RMAID ME17.........188 E5
Taylor Rd FOLK CT19......310 B5
  LYDD TN29.........343 K6
  MSTR CT12.........141 J6
  SNOD ME6.........123 N6
  WLGTN SM6.........82 A9
Taylor Rw RDART DA2......66 C2
Taylor's Buildings
  WOOL/PLUM SE18.........27 J7
Taylors Cl LYDD TN29......337 L2
  SCUP DA14.........64 B3
Taylors Hi RCANTW CT4.....122 A7
Taylors La E/WMAL ME19....172 A7
  HOO/HM ME3.........71 K7
  LYDD TN29.........337 L2
  STRD ME2.........18 E2
Taylor St SEV TN13.......61 H3
Taylors Pas ASH TN23......240 C9
Taylor St STH/RUST TN4....240 C9
Taylors Yd RASHE TN25....223 P8
Taymount Ri FSTH SE23.....61 J1
Taywood Cl KEN/WIL TN24 ..253 J8
Tea Garden La RRTW TN3...269 P6
Teal Cl BERM/RHTH SE16....26 E1
  HOO/HM ME3 *.........56 D3
  SAND/SEL CR2.........114 A5
Teal Av STMC/STPC BR5....87 L1
Teal Dr HB CT6.......107 K4
Teal Wy RSIT ME9.......99 M3
Teapot La DIT/AY ME20....154 D3
Teasaucer Hl
  MAID/SHEP ME15.........185 L3
Teasel Cl CROY/NA CR0......84 A5
  MAID/BEAR ME14.........156 C8
Teasel Crs THMD SE28......27 M4
Teasel Rd MAID ME15.......125 L1
Tebbs Wy BGR/WK TN15....150 F9
Tedders Leas Rd RFOLK CT18 ..287 J4
Tedder Av WALD ME5......95 M7
Tedder Rd SAND/SEL CR2...114 A2
  STH/RUST TN4.........270 E1
Teddington Cl CANT CT1......5 H1
Teelin Cl LYDD TN29.......337 L1
Teesdale Gdns SNWD SE25...60 D8
Teesdale Rd RDART DA2....47 J9
Teevan Cl CROY/NA CR0....83 M4
Teevan Rd CROY/NA CR0....83 M4
Teignmouth Rd WELL DA16...44 E4
Teise Cl RTWE/PEM TN2....23 H7
Telegraph Hl HAM/HW ME3 ...71 L5
Telegraph Pl POP/IOD E14...25 L7
Telford Rd NRWD SE19.....60 F5
Telford St FOLKN CT19......310 B5
Telford Rd CHST BR7.......63 J1
Telfords Yd WAP E1W *....24 D3
Telham Rd MAI MSTR CT12..16 A1
Tell Gv EDUL SE22.......40 E5
Tellson Av WOOL/PLUM SE18 ...43 H2
Telston Cl BGR/WK TN15...148 E2
Telston La RSEV TN14.......148 E2
Temeraire Hts FOLK CT20...309 P4
Temeraire Pl
  BERM/RHTH SE16.........24 E5
Templar Dr GVW DA11......48 E6
Templar Rd E/WMAL ME19 ...152 C9
Templar St CMBW SE5.....40 B3
Temple Av CROY/NA CR0....85 J2
Temple Boat Yd STRD ME2 *...18 C4
Temple Cl ASH TN23.......282 C5
  DVE/WH CT16.........8 E1
  FSTH SE23.........61 J1
Temple Ct STRD ME2 *.....27 K6
Temple Gdns SIT ME10....130 A2
  STRD ME2.........18 A4
Temple Hl DART DA1.......46 F6
Temple Hill Sq DART DA1....46 F5
Temple Ms CANT CT1.......4 B3
Templer Av CDW/CHF RM16...33 H7
Templer Wy ASH TN23.....282 B5
Temple Rd CANTW/ST CT2 ...4 A1
  CROY/NA CR0.........83 J8

Temple Side DVE/WH CT16 290 E2
Templeton Cl THHTH CR7 60 D7
Temple Wy DEAL CT14 201 P6
E/WMAL ME19 153 N4
Ten Acre Wy RHAM ME8 97 L5
Tenby Rd WELL DA16 44 F2
Tenchley's La OXTED RH8 175 N7
Tench St WAP E1W * 24 E4
Tenda Rd BERM/RHTH SE16 24 E7
Tennants Rw TIL RM18 * 49 J3
Tennison Rd SNWD SE25 83 L1
Tennis St STHWK SE1 24 A5
Tennyson Av CANT CT1 167 J1
GRAYS RM17 32 C6
HOO/HM ME3 52 B9
Tennyson Cl WELL DA16 44 A2
Tennyson Gdns RCANTE CT3 199 J9
Tennyson Pl FOLKN CT19 311 H4
Tennyson Ri EGRIN RH19 264 F7
Tennyson Rd ASH TN23 282 D2
DART DA1 46 G6
GILL ME7 7 H6
PGE/AN SE20 61 K6
Tennyson Wk GVW DA11 69 H2
TIL RM18 49 M3
Ten Perch Rd CANT CT1 166 C6
Tensing Av GVW DA11 * 69 J2
Tenterden Cl ELTH/MOT SE9 63 K3
Tenterden Dr CANTW/ST CT2 136 E9
Tenterden Gdns CROY/NA CR0 83 M4
Tenterden Rd CRBK TN17 319 M2
CROY/NA CR0 83 M4
HDCN TN27 278 B8
HDCN TN27 300 A4
TENT TN30 322 B5
WALD ME5 * 95 N9
Tenterden Wy MARG CT9 * 113 H4
Tenter Gnd WCHPL E1 * 24 C1
Tent Peg La STMC/STPC BR5 86 D2
Teredo St LEW SE13 41 P3
Terence Cl CHAT ME4 95 M4
GVE DA12 70 B1
Terlingham La RFOLK CT18 310 D1
Terminus Dr HB CT6 108 A5
Terminus Rd MAIDW ME16 184 F1
Tern Crs STRD ME2 71 L9
Terrace Rd MAIDW ME16 12 C5
RDV CT15 230 C8
SIT ME10 130 A2
The Terraces RDART DA2 47 J8
Terrace St GVE DA12 49 M7
The Terrace CANTW/ST CT2 166 E1
DEPT SE8 * 25 J7
FAV ME13 * 132 D6
FSTH SE23 * 41 L8
GVE DA12 49 N7
GVE DA12 * 70 B9
RDV CT15 229 N9
ROCH ME1 19 G6
RTON TN11 * 211 P2
SEV TN13 148 C7
Terry's Lodge Rd
BGR/WK TN15 120 F8
Terry Wk DIT/AY ME20 153 M2
Testers Cl OXTED RH8 175 L7
Teston La MAID/SHEP ME15 184 B4
Teston Rd E/WMAL ME19 152 C4
E/WMAL ME19 183 M1
Tetty Wy HAYES BR2 62 E8
Teviot Av SOCK/AV RM15 30 F2
Teviot Cl WELL DA16 44 D2
Teviot St POP/IOD E14 25 M1
Tewkesbury Av FSTH SE23 41 H9
Tewson Rd WOOL/PLUM SE18 27 M8
Teynham Cl MARG CT9 113 L3
Teynham Dr WSTB CT5 105 N4
Teynham Gn HAYES BR2 85 K2
RHAM ME8 96 D2
Teynham Rd WSTB CT5 105 M5
Teynham St RSIT ME9 131 L1
Thackeray Av TIL RM18 49 M2
Thackeray Rd DIT/AY ME20 153 N1
Thakeham Cl SYD SE26 61 H4
Thalia Cl GNWCH SE10 25 N9
Thame Rd BERM/RHTH SE16 24 G5
Thames Av HOO/HM ME3 53 L4
IOS ME12 57 K7
RHAM ME8 97 H6
Thamesbank Pl THMD SE28 28 B2
Thames Cir POP/IOD E14 25 K7
Thames Cl RAIN RM13 29 N2
Thames Dr CDW/CHF RM16 33 H8
Thames Ga DART DA1 46 G6
Thamesmere Dr THMD SE28 27 P3
Thames Pth BERM/RHTH SE16 25 J6
Thames Rd CAN/RD E16 26 E4
DART DA1 46 A4
TONN TN10 210 F5
Thames St GNWCH SE10 25 M9
Thames Vw GRAYS RM17 33 H8
HOO/HM ME3 52 C9
Thames Wy GVW DA11 48 E7
GVW DA11 49 J8
Thamley PUR RM19 30 D7
Thanescroft Gdns
CROY/NA CR0 83 K7
Thanet Coastal Pth BRCH CT7 110 F5
BRDST CT10 113 N4
MARG CT9 14 A5
MSTR CT12 142 B9
Thanet Dr HAYES BR2 85 N7
Thanet Gdns FOLKN CT19 11 J1
Thanet Pl CROY/NA CR0 83 H8
Thanet Place Gdns
BRDST CT10 113 N7
Thanet Rd BRDST CT10 113 N9
BXLY DA5 45 J8
ERITH DA8 45 N1
MARG CT9 15 J5
RAM CT11 17 H1
WGOS CT8 111 L4
Thanet Ter RASHW TN26 * 251 M3
Thanet Vw RDV CT15 * 230 C9
Thanet Wy FAV ME13 133 M8
FAV ME13 134 F3
HB CT6 107 J3
HB CT6 108 B7
WSTB CT5 105 J9
Thanington Rd CANT CT1 166 B6
Tharp Rd WLGTN SM6 82 C9
Thatch Barn Rd HDCN TN27 247 N3
Thatcher Rd STPH/PW TN12 246 B5
Thatchers La HOO/HM ME3 52 B3
The Thatchers MAIDW ME16 * 154 G7
Thaxted Rd ELTH/MOT SE9 63 N1
Thayers Farm Rd BECK BR3 61 L7
Theatre St HYTHE CT21 309 H5
The Courtyard HAYES BR2 115 P1
Thelma Cl GVE DA12 70 B4
Theobald Rd CROY/NA CR0 82 G6
Theobalds HAWK TN18 317 H4
Theobalds Av GRAYS RM17 32 D8
Theobald St STHWK SE1 24 A6
Theodore Cl RTWE/PEM TN2 271 H1
Theodore Pl GILL ME7 7 H2
Theodore Rd LEW SE13 42 B7
The Queens Wk STHWK SE1 24 B4
Therapia La CROY/NA CR0 82 D4
Therapia Rd EDUL SE22 41 J7
Theresa Rd HYTHE CT21 308 G6
Thermopylae Ga POP/IOD E14 25 L7
Thesiger Rd PGE/AN SE20 61 K6
Thicket Gv PGE/AN SE20 60 G6
Thicket Rd PGE/AN SE20 61 H6
Thicket Ter PGE/AN SE20 * 60 G6
Third Av CHAT ME4 95 P5
GILL ME7 96 B3
GVW DA11 * 49 K9
IOS ME12 79 N1
MARG CT9 112 G2
WTHK RM20 31 K9
Third St RRTW TN3 269 L5
Thirlemere Cl MAIDW ME16 155 J4
Thirlmere KEN/WIL TN24 252 F3
Thirlmere Av RAM CT11 142 F5
Thirlmere Cl GILL ME7 96 D1
STRD ME2 72 C6
Thirlmere Gdns RCANTE CT3 199 J9
Thirlmere Ri BMLY BR1 62 D5
Thirlmere Rd BXLYHN DA7 45 L3
STH/RUST TN4 270 A3
Thirsk Rd SNWD SE25 83 J1
Thirza Rd DART DA1 46 F7
Thisilefield Cl BXLY DA5 44 F9
Thistlebank WALD ME5 125 M2
Thistlebrook ABYW SE2 28 B6
Thistledown
MAID/BEAR ME14 156 C8
STPH/PW TN12 * 242 E7
Thistledown Cl GILL ME7 126 D1
Thistle Dr WSTB CT5 105 J9
Thistle Hill Wy IOS ME12 78 B2
Thistlemead CHST BR7 63 M8
Thistle Rd GVE DA12 50 A8
Thistlewood Crs
CROY/NA CR0 114 G6
Thomas Bata Av TIL RM18 34 A7
Thomas Cribb Ms EHAM E6 26 G2
Thomas Dean Rd SYD SE26 * 61 M3
Thomas Dinwiddy Rd
LEE/GVPK SE12 62 F1
Thomas Dr GVE DA12 69 P1
Thomas' La CAT SE6 41 P8
Thomas More St WAP E1W * 24 D3
Thomas North Ter
CAN/RD E16 * 26 A1
Thomas Rd FAV ME13 132 F6
POP/IOD E14 25 J2
SIT ME10 130 A1
Thomas St ROCH ME1 95 H3
STH/RUST TN4 270 D3
WOOL/PLUM SE18 27 H7
Thompson Cl DEAL CT14 232 G9
FOLKN CT19 310 E4
RHAM ME8 97 K6
Thompson Rd EDUL SE22 40 F7
Thompson's Av CMBW SE5 * 40 C1
Thomson Cl SNOD ME6 123 P4
Thomson Crs CROY/NA CR0 82 F5
Thomson Rd KEN/WIL TN24 252 E4
Thong La BGR/WK TN15 151 H7
GVE DA12 70 C1
Thorburn Sq STHWK SE1 24 D7
Thorley Rd CDW/CHF RM16 32 B4
Thornbridge Rd DEAL CT14 232 F6
Thorn Cl HAYES BR2 86 B3
WALD ME5 125 J4
Thorncombe Rd EDUL SE22 40 E6
Thorndale Cl WALD ME5 95 J9
Thornden Cl HB CT6 106 F4
Thornden Ct CANTW/ST CT2 * 136 B9
Thornden La CRBK TN17 319 N6
Thornden Wood Rd
CANTW/ST CT2 136 D3
Thorndike Cl CHAT ME4 * 95 L6
Thorndike Rd LYDD TN29 326 G2
Thorndon Cl STMC/STPC BR5 64 B8
Thorndon Rd STMC/STPC BR5 64 B8
Thorne Cl CAN/RD E16 26 B2
ERITH DA8 28 G9
Thorne Hl MSTR CT12 141 N5
Thorneloe Gdns CROY/NA CR0 82 G9
Thorne Rd MSTR CT12 141 J6
Thorne's Cl BECK BR3 62 A9
The Thorn Est HDCN TN27 250 A3
Thornet Wood Rd BMLY BR1 63 L9
Thorneycroft Rd FAV ME13 191 J5
Thornfield Gdns
RTWE/PEM TN2 271 J3
Thornford Rd LEW SE13 42 A6
Thorn Gdns RAM CT11 143 K3
Thornham Rd RHAM ME8 96 F3
Thornham St GNWCH SE10 25 L9
Thornhill Av WOOL/PLUM SE18 44 A1
Thornhill Pl MAID/BEAR ME14 13 F1
Thornhill Rd CROY/NA CR0 83 H4
Thorn Hill Rd IOS ME12 80 B2
Thorn La RCANTW CT4 226 B8
Thornlaw Rd WNWD SE27 60 A3
Thornlea ASH TN23 252 B7
Thorn Rd STPH/PW TN12 245 L6
Thornsbeach Rd CAT SE6 42 A9
Thornsett Pl PGE/AN SE20 61 H8
Thornsett Rd PGE/AN SE20 61 H8
Thornsett Ter PGE/AN SE20 * 61 H8
Thorn's Meadow
BH/WHM TN16 147 K8
Thornton Av CROY/NA CR0 82 E3
Thornton Cl KEN/WIL TN24 253 K8
Thornton Dene BECK BR3 61 N8
Thornton La DEAL CT14 230 E3
SWCH CT13 201 H9
Thornton Rd BELV DA17 * 28 G7
BMLY BR1 62 E4
THHTH CR7 82 F2
Thornton Rw THHTH CR7 82 F2
Thornton St BRXN/ST SW9 40 A3
Thorntree Rd CHARL SE7 26 E8
Thornville St DEPT SE8 41 N2
Thornwood Rd LEW SE13 42 C6
Thorold Cl SAND/SEL CR2 114 A4
Thorold Rd CHAT ME4 7 F6
Thorpe Av TONN TN10 210 F5
Thorpe Cl CROY/NA CR0 114 F5
ORP BR6 86 F6
SYD SE26 * 61 K3
Thorpe Wk RHAM ME8 126 F2
Thorpewood Av SYD SE26 61 H1
Thorsden Wy NRWD SE19 * 60 E4
Thrale Wy RHAM ME8 127 H1
Thrawl St WCHPL E1 24 C1
Thread La FAV ME13 134 C8
Threadneedle St LOTH EC2R 24 A2
Three Acres Site
FOLKN CT19 * 310 E3
Three Colt St POP/IOD E14 * 25 J3
Three Corners BXLYHN DA7 45 K3
Three Elm La TONN TN10 211 L4
Three Gates Rd HART DA3 90 D4
Three King's Yd SWCH CT13 * 201 P1
Three Leg Cross Rd
WADH TN5 315 H3
Three Oak La STHWK SE1 24 C5
Threshers Dr
MAID/BEAR ME14 156 A7
Threshers Fld EDEN TN8 * 237 P3
Thriffwood FSTH SE23 61 J2
Thrift La BH/WHM TN16 * 146 F2
The Thrift RDART DA2 68 A2
Throckmorton Rd CAN/RD E16 26 C2
Throgmorton Av OBST EC2N 24 A2
Throgmorton St OBST EC2N 24 A2
Throwley Cl ABYW SE2 28 B6
Throwley Dr HB CT6 107 H2
Throwley Rd FAV ME13 162 B9
Thrupp Paddock BRDST CT10 113 M4
Thrush Cl WALD ME5 95 N7
Thruxted La RCANTW CT4 195 H2
Thundersland Rd HB CT6 107 N2
Thurbarn Rd CAT SE6 61 P4
Thurland Rd BERM/RHTH SE16 24 D6
Thurlby Rd WNWD SE27 60 A3
Thurlestone Ct
MAID/BEAR ME14 * 12 E1
Thurlestone Rd WNWD SE27 60 A2
Thurloe Wk GRAYS RM17 32 B6
Thurlow Av HB CT6 107 P1
Thurlow Hl DUL SE21 40 C9
Thurlow Park Rd DUL SE21 60 B1
Thurlow St WALW SE17 24 B8
Thurlow Wk WALW SE17 24 B8
Thurrock Park Wy
GRAYS RM17 49 H1
Thursland Rd SCUP DA14 64 G4
Thursley Crs CROY/NA CR0 114 G2
Thursley Rd ELTH/MOT SE9 63 K2
Thurston Dr STRD ME2 71 M8
Thurston Pk WSTB CT5 105 M5
Thurston Rd DEPT SE8 41 P3
Thwaite Cl ERITH DA8 29 H9
Thyer Cl ORP BR6 86 D8
Thyssel La RYE TN31 330 A7
Tibbenham Pl CAT SE6 61 N1
Tibbs Court La
STPH/PW TN12 272 G1
Ticehurst Cl STMC/STPC BR5 64 C6
Ticehurst Rd FSTH SE23 61 L1
Tichborne Cl MAIDW ME16 155 H6
Tickford Cl ABYW SE2 28 B5
Tickham La RSIT ME9 160 G1
Ticknars La LYDD TN29 335 H5
Tidal Basin Rd CAN/RD E16 26 A3
Tidenham Gdns CROY/NA CR0 83 K7
Tideswell Rd CROY/NA CR0 84 D7
The Tideway ROCH ME1 95 H6
Tidey St BOW E3 25 K1
Tidford Rd WELL DA16 44 B3
Tiepigs La WWKM BR4 85 H6
Tiger La HAYES BR2 85 L1
Tilbrook Rd BKHTH/KID SE3 42 G4
Tilbury Cl PECK SE15 40 F1
STMC/STPC BR5 64 D8
Tilbury Rd RHAM ME8 97 K4
Tilden Cl RASHW TN26 279 L9
Tilden Gill Rd TENT TN30 301 K8
Tilden La STPH/PW TN12 245 H1
Tilden Rd HDCN TN27 217 P8
Tilebarn Cnr TONN TN10 211 H6
Tile Farm Rd ORP BR6 86 E7
Tile Flds RMAID ME17 187 N1
Tile Kiln Hl CANTW/ST CT2 135 P8
Tile Kiln La BXLY DA5 65 N2
FOLKN CT19 310 C4
Tile Kiln Rd KEN/WIL TN24 252 F2
Tile Lodge Rd HDCN TN27 220 C3
Tilford Av CROY/NA CR0 114 F2
Tilghman Wy SNOD ME6 124 A4
Tillard Cl RCANTW CT4 196 A8
Till Av EYN DA4 89 L4
Tiller Rd POP/IOD E14 25 K6
Tillery La LYDD TN29 334 F6
Tillingbourne Gn
STMC/STPC BR5 87 H2
Tillingham Av RYE TN31 338 E7
Tillmans BGR/WK TN15 151 K5
Tillman St WCHPL E1 24 E2
Tilmans Md EYN DA4 89 L4
Tilsden La CRBK TN17 298 B4
Tilson Cl CMBW SE5 40 E1
Tilton Rd BGR/WK TN15 151 H5
Tilt Yard Ap ELTH/MOT SE9 43 K7
Timber Bank MEO DA13 122 A5
Timberbank WALD ME5 95 M8
Timber Cl CHST BR7 63 L8
Timbercroft La
WOOL/PLUM SE18 27 M9
Timberland Cl PECK SE15 * 40 G1
Timberland Rd WCHPL E1 * 24 E2
Timber Pond Rd
BERM/RHTH SE16 24 G5
Timbertop Rd BH/WHM TN16 145 M3
Timber Tops WALD ME5 126 A5
Timms Cl BMLY BR1 86 A1
Timothy Cl BXLYHS DA6 44 G6
Timothy Rd POP/IOD E14 25 J1
Timperley Cl DEAL CT14 * 232 G3
Tina Gdns BRDST CT10 113 M7
Tinbridge Oast FAV ME13 * 133 K8
Tindal St BRXN/ST SW9 40 B2
Tinker Pot La BGR/WK TN15 119 P8
Tinkerpot Ri BGR/WK TN15 119 P8
Tinkers La WADH TN5 315 H3
Tinsley Cl SNWD SE25 61 H9
Tinsley Rd WCHPL E1 24 F1
Tintagel Crs EDUL SE22 40 F5
Tintagel Gdns STRD ME2 18 A2
Tintagel Rd STMC/STPC BR5 87 K6
Tintern Rd MAIDW ME16 155 H5
Tinto Rd CAN/RD E16 26 B1
Tipton Dr CROY/NA CR0 83 K8
Tirrell Rd CROY/NA CR0 83 H3
Tisdall Pl WALW SE17 24 A7
Titan Rd GRAYS RM17 32 B8
Titchfield Rd
MAID/SHEP ME15 186 C5
Tithe Barn La ASH TN23 252 A9
Tithe Orch EGRIN RH19 264 B4
Titmuss Av THMD SE28 28 A3
Titsey Hl WARL CR6 145 J9
Titsey Rd OXTED RH8 175 L3
Tiverton Cl CROY/NA CR0 83 L4
Tiverton Dr ELTH/MOT SE9 43 N9
Tivoli Brooks MARG CT9 15 G7
Tivoli Gdns WOOL/PLUM SE18 26 F7
Tivoli Park Av MARG CT9 14 E7
MARG CT9 112 D5
Tivoli Rd MARG CT9 15 G7
WNWD SE27 60 C4
Tobago St POP/IOD E14 25 K5
Tobruk Wy WALD ME5 95 L8
Toby Gdns RTON TN11 211 P2
Toby Rd LYDD TN29 343 K6
Todd Crs SIT ME10 99 P6
Toddington Crs WALD ME5 125 J4
Toft Av GRAYS RM17 32 E7
Tokenhouse Yd LOTH EC2R 24 A2
Toledo Paddock GILL ME7 96 A1
Tolgate La STRD ME2 18 D2
Tolgate Wy MAID/BEAR ME14 155 K1
Tolhurst La WADH TN5 314 E5
Tolhurst Rd STPH/PW TN12 242 B2
Tollemache Cl MSTR CT12 141 N2
Toll Ga DEAL CT14 232 F5
Tollgate Cl WSTB CT5 105 K6
Tollgate Dr DUL SE21 60 E1
Tollgate Ms BGR/WK TN15 151 K5
Tollgate Pl HDCN TN27 247 P4
Tollgate Rd EHAM E6 26 F1
RDART DA2 47 K8
Toll La HDCN TN27 221 K3
Tolsey Md BGR/WK TN15 151 K4
Tolsford Cl FOLKN CT19 310 A5
RFOLK CT18 287 H5
Tom Cribb Rd
WOOL/PLUM SE18 27 K6
Tom Jenkinson Rd
CAN/RD E16 26 B4
Tom Joyce Cl SNOD ME6 123 N6
Tomlin Cl SNOD ME6 123 P5
STPH/PW TN12 246 B5
Tomlin Dr MARG CT9 113 H6
Tomlin's Ter POP/IOD E14 25 H2
Tom Smith Cl GNWCH SE10 25 P9
Tonbridge By-Pass
RSEV TN14 179 K9
RTON TN11 209 M2
Tonbridge Chambers
TON TN9 * 240 E1
Tonbridge Rd BGR/WK TN15 180 F1
MAIDW ME16 154 G9
RTON TN11 210 A4
RTON TN11 211 L3
RTON TN11 212 C5
RTWE/PEM TN2 241 K9
SEV TN13 21 G7
WBY/YAL ME18 182 F3
WBY/YAL ME18 183 P4
Tonford La CANT CT1 166 A6
CANTW/ST CT2 165 N5
Tonge Rd SIT ME10 130 B1
Tong La STPH/PW TN12 273 J5
Tong Rd STPH/PW TN12 273 J3
Tongswood Dr HAWK TN18 317 L5
Tontine St FOLK CT20 11 F4
Tookey Rd NROM TN28 336 G8
Tooley St GVW DA11 49 H8
STHWK SE1 24 A4
Tootswood Rd HAYES BR2 85 H2
Topcliffe Dr ORP BR6 86 E8
Top Dartford Rd SWLY BR8 66 A5
Toplands Av SOCK/AV RM15 30 E4
Topley Dr HOO/HM ME3 53 L5
Topley St ELTH/MOT SE9 42 G5
Topmast Point POP/IOD E14 * 25 K5
Top Pk BECK BR3 85 H2
Top Rd TENT TN30 333 H2
Torbay Rd STPH/PW TN12 213 J5
Torcross Dr FSTH SE23 61 J1
Tor Gv THMD SE28 27 M4
Tormore Ms DEAL CT14 232 F5
Tormore Pk DEAL CT14 232 F5
Tormount Rd
WOOL/PLUM SE18 27 M9
Toronto Cl DVE/WH CT16 291 J4
Toronto Rd GILL ME7 96 B2
TIL RM18 49 L3
Torrens Wk GVE DA12 70 A4
Torrey Dr BRXN/ST SW9 40 A3
Torridge Gdns PECK SE15 41 J5
Torridge Rd THHTH CR7 82 G2
Torridon Rd CAT SE6 42 B9
Torrington Cl WBY/YAL ME18 182 E3
Torrington Pl ASH TN23 * 252 E9
WAP E1W 24 D4
Torrington Rd ASH TN23 252 F9
Torrington Sq CROY/NA CR0 * 83 J4
Tor Rd WELL DA16 44 E2
Torr Rd PGE/AN SE20 61 K6
Torver Wy ORP BR6 86 E7
Tothill St MSTR CT12 141 K5
Totnes Rd WELL DA16 44 D1
Tottan Ter WCHPL E1 * 24 G2
Totton Rd THHTH CR7 60 A9
Toulon St CMBW SE5 40 C1
Tourmaline Dr SIT ME10 99 K8
Tournay Cl ASH TN23 252 C9
Tourney Cl HYTHE CT21 307 N4
Tourney Rd LYDD TN29 342 A7
Tourtel Rd CANT CT1 5 G2
Toussaint Wk
BERM/RHTH SE16 24 D6
Tovey Sq GILL ME7 73 M9
Tovil Cl PGE/AN SE20 60 G8
Tovil Gn MAID/SHEP ME15 185 K1
Tovil Hl MAID/SHEP ME15 185 K2
Tovil Rd MAID/SHEP ME15 185 L1
Tower Br TWRH EC3N 24 C4
Tower Bridge Rd STHWK SE1 24 B6
Tower Buildings WAP E1W * 24 E4
Tower Cl EGRIN RH19 264 G6
GVE DA12 70 A4
ORP BR6 86 G6
PGE/AN SE20 61 H6
Tower Cft EYN DA4 89 K6
Tower Ct EGRIN RH19 * 265 H6
Tower Est LYDD TN29 327 J4
Tower Gdns HYTHE CT21 309 H6
MAID/BEAR ME14 156 E9
Tower Hamlets Rd DVW CT17 8 A2
Tower Hamlets St DVW CT17 * 291 K7
Tower Hl DVW CT17 8 A3
E/WMAL ME19 152 E5
MON EC3R 24 B3
WSTB CT5 105 M3
Tower Hill Ter MON EC3R * 24 B3
Tower La MAID/BEAR ME14 156 D8
Tower Mill Rd PECK SE15 40 E1
Tower Park Rd DART DA1 45 P6
Tower Pl MON EC3R 24 B3
Tower Rd BELV DA17 29 H7
BXLYHN DA7 45 K5
DART DA1 46 C8
ORP BR6 86 G6
WSTB CT5 105 M4
Towers Rd GRAYS RM17 32 D8
Tower St DVW CT17 8 A3
RYE TN31 338 F6
Towers Vw KEN/WIL TN24 252 F2
Towers Wd EYN DA4 67 K7
Tower Vw CROY/NA CR0 84 B5
E/WMAL ME19 153 J9
Tower Wy CANT CT1 * 4 D4
Tower Whf GVW DA11 * 48 F5
Town Acres TON TN9 210 F6
Towncourt Crs
STMC/STPC BR5 86 D2
Towncourt La STMC/STPC BR5 86 E3
Townfield Cnr GVE DA12 49 N9
Towngate Wood Pk
TONN TN10 * 210 G3
Town Hl E/WMAL ME19 153 K3
LING RH7 235 H5
RRTW TN3 295 H3
Town Hill Cl E/WMAL ME19 153 K3
Townland Cl HDCN TN27 278 B7
Town La RCANTW CT4 165 K6
Townley Rd BXLYHS DA6 45 J5
EDUL SE22 40 E6
Townley St RAM CT11 16 E5
WALW SE17 24 A8
Town Rd HOO/HM ME3 72 A1
RCANTW CT4 196 A7
Townsend Farm Rd
RDV CT15 292 E1
Townsend Rd SNOD ME6 123 M4
WOOL/PLUM SE18 27 J6
Townsend Sq WALW SE17 24 A7
Townsend Ter DVW CT17 * 313 J1
Townshend Cl SCUP DA14 64 D5
Townshend Rd CHST BR7 63 M4
Town Square Crs GRH DA9 47 M8
Town Wk FOLK CT20 10 E5
Townwall St DVE/WH CT16 8 E4
Towpath Wy CROY/NA CR0 83 L3
Towton Rd WNWD SE27 60 C1
Toynbec Cl CHST BR7 63 M3
Toynbee St WCHPL E1 24 C1
Toy's Hl BH/WHM TN16 177 K7
EDEN TN8 207 K3
The Tracies RSIT ME9 98 D8
Trader Rd EHAM E6 27 J2
Tradescant Dr MEO DA13 92 C3
Tradewinds WSTB CT5 105 J8
Trafalgar Av PECK SE15 24 C9
Trafalgar Gdns WCHPL E1 24 G1
Trafalgar Gv GNWCH SE10 25 N9
Trafalgar Ms RAM CT11 * 16 E5
Trafalgar Rd BRCH CT7 141 N1
DART DA1 66 E1
GNWCH SE10 25 P8
GVW DA11 49 L8
ROCH ME1 124 B1
Trafalgar St GILL ME7 7 H3
WALW SE17 24 A8
Trafalgar Wy CROY/NA CR0 82 E6

POP/IOD E14 ....25 M4
Trafford Rd THHTH CR7 ....82 E2
The Tram Rd FOLK CT20 ....11 H4
Tramways CHAT ME4 ....95 P4
Tranquil Ri ERITH DA8 ....29 K8
Tranquil V BKHTH/KID SE5 ....42 D3
Transfesa Rd LYDD TN29 ....347 K5
Transmere Rd STMC/STPC BR5 ...86 D5
Transom Sq POP/IOD E14 ....25 L8
Tranton Rd BERM/RHTH SE16 ....24 E6
Trapfield CI MAID/BEAR ME14 ..156 F8
Trapfield La
    MAID/BEAR ME14 ....156 F8
Trapham Rd MAIDW ME16 ....155 J7
Travers Gdns RSIT ME9 ....128 G8
Travers Rd CT14 ....232 F4
Travertine Rd WALD ME5 ....125 N4
Treasury Vw RCANTE CT3 ....168 F8
Trebble Rd SWCM DA10 ....48 C7
Treblico CI RTWE/PEM TN2 ......270 C1
Tredegar Rd RDART DA2 ....66 A2
Tredown Rd SYD SE26 ....61 J4
Tredwell CI HAYES BR2 ....85 N1
Tredwell Rd WNWD SE27 ....60 B3
Treebourne Rd
    BH/WHM TN16 ....145 M2
Tree La BGR/WK TN15 ....181 H5
Tree Rd CT14 ....21 J3
Treetops BGR/WK TN15 ....149 M2
    GDST RH9 ....204 B4
    GVE DA12 ....69 H4
    TON TN9 ....240 C2
Treetops CI ABYW SE2 ....28 D8
Tree View CI NRWD SE19 ....82 B2
Treevaill Gdns BMLY BR1 ....62 F3
Tregony Rd ORP BR6 ....86 C8
Treherne Ct BRXN/ST SW9 * 40 B2
Trelawn Crs WALD ME5 ....125 N3
Trelawn Rd BRXS/STRHM SW2 ...40 A6
Trellyn CI MAIDW ME16 ....154 C5
Treloar Gdns NRWD SE19 ....60 D5
Tremaine CI BROCKY SE4 ....41 N3
Tremaine Rd PGE/AN SE20 ....61 H8
Trenchard CI KEN/WIL TN24 .....253 J9
Trenchard St GNWCH SE10 ....25 N8
Trench Rd TONN TN10 ....210 E4
Trenear CI ORP BR6 ....87 H8
Trenholme Rd PGE/AN SE20 ......61 H6
Trenholme Ter PGE/AN SE20 .....61 H6
Trent TIL RM18 ....34 B7
Trentham Dr STMC/STPC BR5 ....87 H1
Trenton CI MAIDW ME16 ....154 C5
Trent Rd WALD ME5 ....95 N9
Tresco CI BMLY BR1 ....62 C5
Tresco Rd PECK SE15 ....41 H5
Tressillian Crs BROCKY SE4 ....41 N4
Tressillian Rd BROCKY SE4 ....41 N4
Trevale Rd ROCH ME1 ....94 C5
Trevarno Ter
    MAID/SHEP ME15 * 185 K1
Trevelyan CI DART DA1 ....86 A9
Trevereux HI OXTED RH8 ....176 B8
Trevino Dr WALD ME5 ....125 L5
Treviso Rd FSTH SE23 ....61 K1
Trevithick Dr DART DA1 ....46 F5
Trevithick St DEPT SE8 ....25 K4
Trevor Dr MAIDW ME16 ....154 C7
Trewin CI DIT/AY ME20 ....154 C2
Trewsbury Rd SYD SE26 ....61 K4
The Triangle BFN/LL DA15 * 44 C8
Tribune Ct IOS ME12 ....57 K8
Tribune Dr SIT ME10 ....59 N8
Trident Cl STRD ME2 ....19 K2
Trident St BERM/RHTH SE16 .....24 G7
Triggs Rw RSIT ME9 * 131 J3
Trilby Rd FSTH SE23 ....61 K1
Trilby Wy WSTB CT5 ....105 J8
Trim St NWCR SE14 ....25 J9
Trimworth Rd FOLKN CT19 .....310 C5
Trinidad St POP/IOD E14 ....25 L3
Trinity Buoy Whf
    POP/IOD E14 * 25 N1
Trinity CI HAYES BR2 ....85 P5
    LEW SE13 ....42 B5
    RTWE/PEM TN2 ....23 J3
Trinity Ct ELTH/MOT SE9 ....43 M7
Trinity Dr FOLK CT20 ....10 B6
Trinity Gdns CAN/RD E16 ....26 A1
    DART DA1 ....46 D7
    FOLK CT20 ....10 C6
Trinity Gn WCHPL E1 * 24 F1
Trinity Gv GNWCH SE10 ....42 A2
Trinity Ms PGE/AN SE20 * 61 J7
Trinity Pk BXLYHS DA6 ....45 H5
    DEAL CT14 ....232 F5
    RAM CT11 ....17 H2
Trinity Ri BRXS/STRHM SW2 .....40 B8
Trinity Rd FOLK CT20 ....10 E5
    GILL ME7 ....13 J2
    GVE DA12 ....49 N8
    IOS ME12 ....57 L6
    RASHE TN25 ....252 E3
    SIT ME10 ....99 N7
Trinity Sq BRDST CT10 ....113 L6
    MARG CT9 ....15 H3
    MON EC3M 24 B3
Trinity St CAN/RD E16 ....26 A1
Trinity Wl MARG CT9 ....15 H3
Tristan Gdns STH/RUST TN4 ....269 H4
Tristan Sq BKHTH/KID SE3 ....44 A7
Tristram Rd BMLY BR1 ....61 D5
Tritton Av CROY/NA CRO 82 D8
Tritton CI KEN/WIL TN24 ....253 J2
Tritton Flds KEN/WIL TN24 .....253 H2
Tritton Gdns LYDD TN29 ....347 M8
Tritton La NROM TN28 ....336 G7
Tritton Rd WNWD SE27 ....60 D2
Triumph CI CDW/CHF RM16 ......31 M7
Triumph Rd EHAM E6 ....26 C2
Trivett CI DTCH ME9 ....67 P2
Trojan Wy CROY/NA CRO 82 E7
Trolling Down HI RDART DA2 ....67 H1
Troodos HI MAID/BEAR ME14 ..155 L4

Troon CI BERM/RHTH SE16 * 24 E8
Troon St WCHPL E1 ....25 H2
Trosley Av GVW DA11 ....69 M1
Trosley Rd BELV DA17 ....28 F9
Trossachs Rd EDUL SE22 ....40 E6
Trothy Rd STHWK SE1 * 24 D7
Trottiscliffe Rd
    E/WMAL ME19 ....152 D1
Trotts La BH/WHM TN16 ....176 D5
Trotwood CI WALD ME5 ....125 L4
Troubridge CI KEN/WIL TN24 ..283 K1
Troughton Ms MARG CT9 ....14 B6
Troughton Rd CHARL SE7 ....26 C8
Troutbeck Rd NWCR SE14 ....41 J2
Troy La EDEN TN8 ....206 A6
Troy Rd NRWD SE19 ....60 D5
Troys Md RMAID ME17 ....187 N1
Troy Town PECK SE15 ....40 G4
Troy Town La RASHE TN25 ......254 C5
Trubridge Rd HOO/HM ME3 ....73 K7
Trueman CI CANTW/ST CT2 ....135 P6
Trundley's Rd DEPT SE8 ....24 F6
Trundley's Ter DEPT SE8 ....24 G7
Truro Cl RHAM ME8 ....96 G5
Truro Rd GVE DA12 ....69 P2
    RAM CT11 ....17 H5
Truro Wk TONN TN10 ....210 G5
Trusedale Rd EHAM E6 ....26 G2
Truslove Rd WNWD SE27 ....60 A4
Trycewell La BGR/WK TN15 ......150 G6
Tuam Rd WOOL/PLUM SE18 ......27 L9
Tubbenden CI ORP BR6 ....86 F6
Tubbenden Dr ORP BR6 ....86 E8
Tubbenden La ORP BR6 ....86 E8
Tubbenden La South ORP BR6 ...86 E8
Tubs HI SEV TN13 * 20 D1
Tubs Hill Pde SEV TN13 * 20 D1
Tudeley La KEN/WIL TN24 ....240 G2
    TON TN9 ....241 H2
Tudeley Rd TON TN9 ....241 H2
Tudor Av LYDD TN29 ....327 H5
    MAID/BEAR ME14 ....155 N6
Tudor Byway KEN/WIL TN24 ...252 G5
Tudor CI BRCH CT7 ....111 J5
    CHST BR7 ....65 K7
    DART DA1 ....46 B7
    EGRIN RH19 ....264 E1
    GVW DA11 ....49 J9
Tudor Crs RSEV TN14 ....149 N1
Tudor Dr RAM CT11 ....149 H1
Tudor End KEN/WIL TN24 ....252 G4
Tudor Gdns WWKM BR4 ....84 F7
Tudor Gv HOO/HM ME3 ....72 F3
    RHAM ME8 ....97 H5
Tudor Pde ELTH/MOT SE9 * 43 J5
Tudor PI NRWD SE19 * 62 F6
Tudor Rd BECK BR3 ....62 A9
    CANT CT1 ....6 D3
    FOLKN CT19 ....310 A5
    KEN/WIL TN24 ....252 G4
    NRWD SE19 ....62 F6
    RAM CT11 ....83 N2
Tudor Wy STMC/STPC BR5 ....86 C9
Tudway Rd BKHTH/KID SE3 ......42 C5
Tufa CI WALD ME5 ....125 N4
Tufnail Rd DART DA1 ....46 F4
Tufton Rd KEN/WIL TN24 ....252 G4
    RHAM ME8 ....97 J5
Tufton St ASH TN23 ....3 D4
    MAID/BEAR ME14 ....13 G4
Tugboat St THMD SE28 ....27 M5
Tugela Rd CROY/NA CRO 83 J3
Tugela St CAT SE6 ....61 M1
Tugmutton CI ORP BR6 ....86 C8
Tuilp CI CROY/NA CRO 84 A5
    EHAM E6 ....26 F1
Tulip Tree CI TON TN9 ....240 D1
Tulse CI BECK BR3 ....62 A9
Tulse HI BRXS/STRHM SW2 ....40 A9
Tulsemere Rd WNWD SE27 ....60 C1
Tumblefield Rd
    BGR/WK TN15 ....121 J6
Tumblers HI RMAID ME17 ....217 J3
Tummons Gdns SNWD SE25 ....60 E8
Tunbury Av WALD ME5 ....125 L4
Tunbury Av South WALD ME5 ..125 L4
Tunis Ct CANT CT1 ....167 J3
Tunis Rw BRDST CT10 ....113 N8
Tunley Gn POP/IOD E14 ....25 J1
Tunnan Leys EHAM E6 ....26 B5
Tunnel Av GNWCH SE10 ....25 N5
Tunnel Rd BERM/RHTH SE16 ....24 F5
    RTW TN1 ....22 E2
Tunstall CI ORP BR6 ....86 F8
Tunstall Rd CANTW/ST CT2 ....136 F9
    CROY/NA CRO 63 J9
    RSIT ME9 ....129 K5
Turnstock Wy BELV DA17 ....28 D6
Tupman CI ROCH ME1 ....18 D7
Tuppy St WOOL/PLUM SE18 ......27 K6
Turgis CI RMAID ME17 ....168 F7
Turketel Rd FOLK CT20 ....310 D6
Turkey Oak CI NRWD SE19 ....60 E7
Turks Hall PI STRD ME2 * 93 M9
Turmine CI IOS ME12 ....78 A2
Turnagain La CANT CT1 ....4 E4
Turnberry CI
    BERM/RHTH SE16 * 24 E8
Turnberry Wy ORP BR6 ....86 E5
Turnbull Rd RDART DA2 ....47 L8
Turnbury CI THMD SE28 ....28 C2
Turnden Gdns MARG CT9 ....113 K8
Turner Av CRBK TN17 ....297 M4
Turner Av CRBK TN17 ....298 A4
Turner CI CMBW SE5 ....40 B2
    SIT ME10 ....99 P7
Turner Ct CMBW SE5 * 40 B2
Turner Rd BH/WHM TN16 ....115 M6
    RDART DA2 ....67 P2

TONN TN10 ....211 H5
Turners Av TENT TN30 ....301 J7
Turners Gdns SEV TN15 ....179 H4
Turners Green La WADH TN5 ...294 A9
Turners Green Rd WADH TN5 ...294 A8
Turner's Hill Rd EGRIN RH19 ...264 F9
Turners Meadow Wy
    BECK BR3 ....61 M7
Turner's Oak Shaw HART DA3 ...91 H6
Turners PI EYN DA4 * 57 J7
Turner's Rd POP/IOD E14 ....25 J1
Turner St CAN/RD E16 ....26 A2
    HOO/HM ME3 ....73 K2
    RAM CT11 ....17 G3
    WCHPL E1 ....24 E1
Turners Wy CROY/NA CRO 82 F6
Turney Rd DUL SE21 ....40 C8
Turnham Rd BROCKY SE4 ....41 L6
Turnpike CI DEPT SE8 ....41 M1
Turnpike Dr
    HYTHE CT21 ....308 F5
Turnpike Dr ORP BR6 ....117 K3
Turnpike Hill HYTHE CT21 ....308 F4
Turnpike La CDW/CHF RM16 .....33 L8
Turnpike La HAYES BR2 ....85 P3
Turnpike La HAYES BR2 ....85 P2
Turnstone HART DA3 ....68 D3
Turnstone CI RSIT ME9 ....99 M2
    SAND/SEL CR2 ....114 B4
Turnstone Rd WALD ME5 ....125 P3
The Turnstones GVE DA12 ....69 P1
Turo Av CDW/CHF RM16 ....32 D5
Turpin CI WAP E1W 24 G3
Turpington CI HAYES BR2 ....85 P5
Turpington La HAYES BR2 ....85 P2
Turpin La ERITH DA8 ....29 M9
Tuscan Dr WALD ME5 ....125 P4
Tuscan Rd WOOL/PLUM SE18 ....27 L8
Tuskar St GNWCH SE10 ....25 P8
Tutsham Wy STPH/PW TN12 ....242 C3
Tuxford Rd STH/RUST TN4 ....269 N5
Tweed TIL RM18 ....34 B7
Tweed Rd TONN TN10 ....210 F5
Tweed Ter HYTHE CT21 * 308 F6
Tweedy Rd BMLY BR1 ....62 E7
Twelve Acres KEN/WIL TN24 ...253 H9
Twickenham CI CROY/NA CRO 82 E7
Twigg CI ERITH DA8 ....45 N1
Twine Ct WCHPL E1 ....24 G2
The Twins STPH/PW TN12 * 246 G8
Twin Tumps Wy THMD SE28 .....27 P3
Twisden Rd E/WMAL ME19 ......153 N4
Twisleton Ct DART DA1 ....46 D7
Twiss Av HYTHE CT21 ....309 J5
Twiss Gv HYTHE CT21 ....309 J5
Twiss Rd HYTHE CT21 ....309 J5
The Twitten LING RH7 * 234 C5
Twitton Mdw RSEV TN14 ....148 D1
Two Oaks HOO/HM ME3 ....71 P2
Twydall Gn RHAM ME8 ....96 E3
Twydall La RHAM ME8 ....96 F4
Twyford CI RHAM ME8 ....97 K4
Twyford Ct MAID/BEAR ME14 ..156 A6
Twyford Rd RTON TN11 ....211 J7
Twyhurst Ct EGRIN RH19 ....264 C5
Twyne CI CANTW/ST CT2 ....137 M7
Tydeman Rd
    MAID/SHEP ME15 ....186 C1
Tye La ORP BR6 ....86 A8
Tyers Est STHWK SE1 * 24 B5
Tyers Ga STHWK SE1 * 24 B5
Tyeshurst CI ABYW SE2 ....28 D8
Tyland La MAID/BEAR ME14 ....155 L1
Tyler CI CANTW/ST CT2 ....166 E1
    E/WMAL ME19 ....153 N4
Tyler Dr RHAM ME8 ....97 K4
Tyler Hill Rd CANTW/ST CT2 ...135 P7
Tylers Green Rd SWLY BR8 ....88 B3
Tyler St GNWCH SE10 ....25 P8
Tyler Wy WSTB CT5 ....106 C3
Tylney Av NRWD SE19 ....60 F4
Tylney Rd BMLY BR1 ....63 H8
    FSTH SE23 ....61 K1
Tyndall CI WELL DA16 ....44 B4
Tyndall Rd WELL DA16 ....44 B4
Tyne CI WALD ME5 ....95 N9
Tynedale CI RDART DA2 ....47 K9
Tyne Gdns SOCK/AV RM15 ....30 F3
Tynemouth CI EHAM E6 ....27 J2
Tynemouth Rd
    WOOL/PLUM SE18 ....27 M8
Tyne Rd TONN TN10 ....210 E5
Tyne St WCHPL E1 ....24 C2
Typhoon Rd E/WMAL ME19 .....152 G9
Tyron Wy SCUP DA14 ....64 A3
Tyrrell Av WELL DA16 ....44 C6
Tyrrell Rd EDUL SE22 ....40 C5
Tyrrells Hall CI GRAYS RM17 .....32 E9
Tyrwhitt Rd LEW SE13 ....41 N4
Tysoe Ct IOS ME12 ....77 P2
Tyson Av MARG CT9 ....111 P4
Tyson Gdns FSTH SE23 * 41 J8
Tyson Rd FOLKN CT19 ....311 H4
    FSTH SE23 ....41 J8

Ullswater Rd WNWD SE27 ....60 B2
Ulstan CI CTHM CR3 ....144 D8
Ulster Rd MARG CT9 ....112 E5
Ulundi Rd BKHTH/KID SE3 ....43 N1
Ulverscroft Rd EDUL SE22 ....40 G6
Umberston St WCHPL E1 * 24 D2
Undercliff FOLK CT20 ....310 B8
Undercliffe Rd LEW SE13 ....41 L8
Underdown Av CHAT ME4 ....95 L5
Underdown La HB CT6 ....107 L4
Underdown Rd WALT CT17 ....291 J8
    HB CT6 ....107 L2
Underhill Rd EDUL SE22 ....40 E6
    FOLK CT20 ....309 N2
Underlyn La STPH/PW TN12 ....245 H1
Underriver House Rd
    RTON TN11 ....179 P6
Undershaft HDTCH EC3A 24 B2
Undershaw Rd BMLY BR1 ....62 C2
Underwood CROY/NA CRO 114 F1
    RFOLK CT18 ....288 E6
Underwood CI CANT CT1 ....166 F7
    CHAT ME4 ....95 L9
The Underwood
    ELTH/MOT SE9 ....63 K1
Undine CI POP/IOD E14 ....25 L7
Unicorn Wk GRH DA9 ....47 M6
Union Crs MARG CT9 ....15 H4
Union Pk MAID/SHEP ME15 * ...186 C7
Union CI WAP E1W * 24 F3
    CHAT ME4 ....5 G2
    DVW CT17 ....11 J2
    FAV ME13 ....132 F6
    IOS ME12 ....57 J6
    MAID/BEAR ME14 ....13 F4
    RAM CT11 ....17 G5
    ROCH ME1 ....19 H1
    WADH TN5 ....315 M5
Union Quay DVW CT17 ....3 J4
Union Rd CROY/NA CRO 83 H4
    DEAL CT14 ....233 J5
    HAYES BR2 ....85 N2
    IOS ME12 ....58 D9
    RAM CT11 ....145 L4
    RCANTW CT4 ....197 L2
Union Sq RTWE/PEM TN2 * 22 C7
Union St CANT CT1 ....5 G4
    CHAT ME4 ....5 G4
    DVW CT17 ....11 J2
    FAV ME13 ....132 F6
    IOS ME12 ....57 J6
    MAID/BEAR ME14 ....13 F4
    RAM CT11 ....17 G5
    ROCH ME1 ....19 H1
    WADH TN5 ....315 M5
Unity CI CROY/NA CRO 87 K7
    WNWD SE27 ....60 C4
Unity PI RAM CT11 ....17 H2
Unity Wy IOS ME12 ....58 D9
    SIT ME10 ....129 M2
Unity Wy WOOL/PLUM SE18 ....26 D8
University Gdns BXLY DA5 ....45 H8
University St CANTW/ST CT2 ...166 C1
University Wy DART DA1 ....47 J4
    EYN DA4 ....89 J9
Unwin CI DIT/AY ME20 ....154 F1
    PECK SE15 ....24 D9
Upchat Rd HOO/HM ME3 ....72 A7
Upchurch Wk MARG CT9 ....113 K5
Updale Rd SCUP DA14 ....64 B3
Updown Wy RCANTW CT4 ....195 N2
Upfield CROY/NA CRO 83 N6
Uphill RFOLK CT18 ....288 E6
Upland Rd BXLYHN DA7 ....45 H4
    CTHM CR5 ....145 L4
    EDUL SE22 ....40 G6
    SAND/SEL CR2 ....83 J9
Uplands BECK BR3 ....61 N8
    CANTW/ST CT2 ....136 E9
Uplands CI STPD ME2 ....71 M9
Uplands Rd ORP BR6 ....87 J5
Uplands Wy IOS ME12 ....77 L2
    SEV TN15 ....148 E8
Uplees Rd FAV ME13 ....102 C8
Upnor Rd STRD ME2 ....72 D7
Upnor Wy WALW SE17 ....24 B3
Upper Abbey Rd BELV DA17 ....28 E7
Upper Approach Rd
    BRDST CT10 ....143 M1
Upper Austin Lodge Rd
    EYN DA4 ....89 J9
Upper Bank St POP/IOD E14 .....25 L4
Upper Barn HI
    MAID/SHEP ME15 ....184 D8
Upper Beulah HI NRWD SE19 .....60 F7
Upper Brents FAV ME13 ....132 C5
Upper Bridge St CANT CT1 ....5 F6
    RASHE TN25 ....224 A8
Upper Britton PI GILL ME7 ....7 G3
Upper Brockley Rd
    BROCKY SE4 ....41 M2
Upper Bush Rd STRD ME2 ....93 N4
Upper Chantry La CANT CT1 ....5 G8
Upper Court Rd CTHM CR3 ......144 D8
Upper Cumberland Wk
    RTW TN1 ....23 J5
Upper Dame Rd MARG CT9 ......112 F4
Upper Dr BH/WHM TN16 ....145 M3
Upper Dumpton Park Rd
    RAM CT11 ....17 J1
Upper Dunstan Rd
    STH/RUST TN4 ....270 E2
Upper Elmers End Rd
    BECK BR3 ....84 B1
Upper Fant Rd MAIDW ME16 ...185 H1
Upper Field Rd SIT ME10 ....100 A9
Upper Gore La SWCH CT13 * 201 H8
Upper Green Rd RTON TN11 ....180 H5
Upper Grosvenor Rd RTW TN1 ..22 D2
Upper Gv SNWD SE25 ....15 H4
Upper Grove Rd BELV DA17 ....28 E7
Upper Haysden La
    STH/RUST TN4 ....240 A3
Upper Holly Hill Rd
    BELV DA17 ....28 G8

Upper Hunton HI
    MAID/SHEP ME15 ....184 H5
Upper Luton Rd WALD ME5 ....7 H7
Upper Malthouse HI
    HYTHE CT21 ....308 G5
Upper MI WBY/YAL ME18 ....183 L5
Upper Nellington RRTW TN3 ....269 N4
Upper North St POP/IOD E14 ....25 L2
Upper Park Rd BELV DA17 ....28 F7
    BMLY BR1 ....62 F7
Upper Profit RRTW TN5 ....269 M5
Upper Rd DVE/WH CT16 ....291 P6
    MAID/SHEP ME15 ....13 J7
    WLGTN SM6 ....16 F3
Upper St Ann's Rd FAV ME13 ...132 E7
Upper Sheridan Rd BELV DA17 ...28 F7
Upper Shirley Rd
    CROY/NA CRO 83 P7
Upper Spring La
    BGR/WK TN15 ....150 E7
Upper Stephens RRTW TN3 .....269 M5
Upper Stone St
    MAID/SHEP ME15 ....13 G6
Upper Strand St SWCH CT13 ....201 P1
Upper St DEAL CT14 ....231 H6
    DEAL CT14 ....263 J5
Upper Tile Kiln La
    RMAID ME17 ....157 P9
    RMAID ME17 ....187 J6
    STH/RUST TN4 ....22 A4
Upperton Rd SCUP DA14 ....64 B4
Upper Vicarage Rd
    KEN/WIL TN24 ....252 G2
Upstall St CMBW SE5 ....40 B2
Upton CI BXLY DA5 ....45 H7
    FOLKN CT19 ....310 D4
Upton Quarry RRTW TN5 ....269 L5
Upton Rd BRDST CT10 ....113 L8
    BXLYHS DA6 ....45 H5
    THHTH CR7 ....60 D8
    WOOL/PLUM SE18 ....27 K9
Upton Rd South BXLY DA5 ....45 H7
Uptons HDCN TN27 ....247 M5
Upwood Rd LEE/GVPK SE12 ......42 E7
Uridge Crs TONN TN10 ....210 F6
Uridge Rd TONN TN10 ....210 F6
Urlwin Wk BRXN/ST SW9 ....40 A2
Urquhart CI WALD ME5 ....95 M9
Ursuline Dr WOOS CT5 ....111 K8
Usborne CI STPH/PW TN12 ......266 C6
Usk Rd SOCK/AV RM15 ....30 F2
Uvedale CI CROY/NA CRO 114 G5
Uvedale Crs CROY/NA CRO 114 G5
Uvedale Rd OXTED RH8 ....175 J5

V

Valance Vw CRBK TN17 * 277 H1
Valan Leas HAYES BR2 ....62 C9
Vale Av RTW TN1 ....22 C5
    STH/RUST TN4 ....240 C8
Valebrook CI FOLK CT20 ....309 P2
Vale CI ORP BR6 ....86 B8
Vale Dr WALD ME5 ....95 J9
Vale End EDUL SE22 ....40 F5
Valence Rd ERITH DA8 ....45 M1
Valenciennes Rd SIT ME10 ......129 M2
Valentia Dr BRXN/ST SW9 * 40 A5
Valentine Av BXLY DA5 ....64 C1
Valentine CI GILL ME7 ....96 D5
Valentine Rd
    MAID/SHEP ME15 ....186 B4
Valentyne CI CROY/NA CRO 115 H5
Valerie CI PI RAM CT11 ....14 E4
Valerian CI WALD ME5 ....125 K1
Vale Ri TON TN9 ....210 C9
Vale Rd BMLY BR1 ....63 L8
    BRDST CT10 ....113 L9
    DART DA1 ....48 B9
    GVW DA11 ....49 J9
    HAWK TN18 ....317 H5
    MAID/SHEP ME15 ....185 K7
    RAM CT11 ....16 C4
    RDV CT15 ....262 A1
    STH/RUST TN4 ....22 C5
    TON TN9 ....210 D9
    WSTB CT5 ....105 L6
Vale Sq RAM CT11 ....16 B4
Valeswood Rd BMLY BR1 ....62 D4
The Vale BRDST CT10 ....113 M9
    CROY/NA CRO 84 A6
Valetta Wy ROCH ME1 ....18 E7
Valewood Rd DVW CT17 ....291 J8
    RCANTE CT3 ....229 H1
Valiant Rd WALD ME5 ....125 P3
Valiant Wy EHAM E6 ....26 C1
Valkyrie Av WSTB CT5 ....105 J6
The Vallance RSIT ME9 ....150 F7
Valley CI DART DA1 ....69 P3
    MAID/SHEP ME15 ....185 L5
    RTON TN11 ....182 A9
Valley Dr DVW CT17 ....21 F4
Valley Forge CI TONN TN10 ......211 J6
Valley Gdns GRH DA9 ....47 P7
Valley Gv CHARL SE7 ....26 D8
Valley La BGR/WK TN15 ....121 M5
    MEO CM15 ....122 D3
Valley Rd BGR/WK TN15 ....149 H3
    BMLY BR1 ....62 D4
Valley Rd CANT CT1 ....166 D6
    DART DA1 ....45 P7
    DVW CT17 ....290 F4
    ERITH DA8 ....29 H7
    FOLK CT20 ....310 D7
    GILL ME7 ....90 E6
    HART DA3 ....90 E6
    HAYES BR2 ....84 C2
    MARG CT9 ....112 D9
    RCANTW CT4 ....228 B4

STH/RUST TN4 ....270 A4
STMC/STPC BR5.................64 D7
The Valley RMAID ME17 ....185 J8
Valley Vw BH/WHM TN16......145 M3
GRH DA9.........................47 P7
RDV CT15 * 230 D9
STH/RUST TN4 ....64 D7
Valley View Rd ROCH ME1 .....94 G5
Valley View Ter EYN DA4 * 99 N5
Valley Wk CROY/NA CRO.......80 A5
HYTHE CT21....................309 N4
Valliers Wood Rd BFN/LL DA15...43 P9
Valmar Rd CMBW SE5...........40 C2
Vambery Rd
WOOL/PLUM SE18.............27 K9
Vanbrugh Flds BKHTH/KID SE3.42 E1
Vanbrugh Hl GNWCH SE10......25 P8
Vanbrugh Park Rd
BKHTH/KID SE3................42 D1
Vanbrugh Park Rd West
BKHTH/KID SE3................42 D1
Vanbrugh Ter BKHTH/KID SE3..42 D2
Vanburgh Cl CAN/RD E16.......26 E6
CANT CT1........................88 F5
Vancouver Cl ORP BR6..........87 H8
Vancouver Dr RHAM ME8.......96 E2
Vancouver Rd FSTH SE23.......61 L1
Vandome Cl CAN/RD E16........26 C2
Vandyke Cross ELTH/MOT SE9..43 J6
Vanessa Cl BELV DA17..........28 F8
Vanessa Wk GVE DA12..........70 B4
Vanessa Wy BXLY DA5..........65 M2
Vange Cottage Ms
ROCH ME1 * 18 E7
Vange Ms ROCH ME1 * 18 E7
Vanguard Cl CAN/RD E16.......26 B1
CROY/NA CRO...................82 C5
THHTH CR7......................82 C1
Vanguard St DEPT SE8..........41 N2
Vanguard Wy CROY/NA CRO...83 L8
EDEN TN8........................266 A3
EDEN TN8........................235 P3
EGRIN RH19......................266 A3
LING RH7.........................236 B9
OXTED RH8.......................175 K2
STRD ME2........................92 C7
WARL CR6........................114 C7
Vanity La RMAID ME17..........215 J2
Vanity Rd IOS ME12.............80 D6
Vanoc Gdns BMLY BR1..........62 E5
Vanquisher Wk GVE DA12.......70 E2
Vansittart St NWCR SE14........41 L1
Varcoe Rd BERM/RHTH SE16...24 E8
Varden St WCHPL E1.............24 E2
Varley Rd CAN/RD E16...........26 E6
Varne Pl FOLKN CT19............11 K5
Varne Rd FOLKN CT19...........11 K5
Varnes St DIT/AY ME20.........39 M3
Vassall Rd BRXN/ST SW9.......40 A1
Vauban Est
BERM/RHTH SE16 * 24 C6
Vaudan St BERM/RHTH SE16...25 J5
Vaughan Av TONN TN10........211 H4
Vaughan Dr SIT ME10...........99 N6
Vaughan Rd BERM/RHTH SE16..40 C3
WELL DA16.......................45 N1
Vaughan Wy WAP E1W..........24 C7
Vaughan Williams Cl DEPT SE8..41 N1
Vauxhall Av CANT CT1..........167 H1
HB CT6............................106 F3
Vauxhall Bri GVW DA11..........49 K8
Vauxhall Crs CANT CT1.........167 H1
SNOD ME6........................123 N7
Vauxhall Gdns TON TN9........240 F2
Vauxhall Industrial Rd
CANT CT1........................137 H9
Vauxhall La RTON TN11.........240 G3
STH/RUST TN4 ....240 C6
Vauxhall Pl DART DA1...........137 H9
Vauxhall Rd CANTW/ST CT2...137 H9
Vectis Dr SIT ME10..............99 N6
Veda Rd LEW SE13..............41 N5
Veles Rd SNOD ME6............123 N5
Venetian Rd CMBW SE5.........40 C3
Venette Cl RAIN RM13..........29 N1
Venner Rd SYD SE26............61 J5
Venners Cl BXLYHN DA7.......45 N3
Ventnor Cl WALD ME5...........95 P6
Ventnor Rd NWCR SE14.........41 K1
Venture Cl BXLY DA5............44 G8
LYDD TN29......................327 H5
Venue St POP/IOD E14.........25 L1
Venus Rd WOOL/PLUM SE18...28 C6
Verbania Wy EGRIN RH19......265 L7
Verbena Cl SOCK/AV RM15.....31 M2
Verdant La BMLY BR1............62 C3
CAT SE6..........................42 C9
Verdayne Av CROY/NA CRO....84 A5
Verdun Rd WOOL/PLUM SE18..29 P9
Vereth Rd RAM CT11............16 D5
Vermont Rd NRWD SE19........60 D5
STH/RUST TN4 ....269 P4
Verney Rd BERM/RHTH SE16..24 E8
Verney Wy BERM/RHTH SE16..24 E8
Vernham Rd
WOOL/PLUM SE18.............27 K9
Vernon Cl BGR/WK TN15......120 C3
STMC/STPC BR5.................64 D9
Vernon Pl CANT CT1..............5 F6
DEAL CT14.......................233 J1
Vernon Rd RTW TN1............270 F2
SWD DA10........................48 D7
Veroan Rd BXLYHN DA7........46 A4
Verona Gdns GVE DA12.........70 A3
Versailles Rd PGE/AN SE20....60 D6
Veryan Cl STMC/STPC BR5.....87 K1
Vesper Ct HDCN TN27.........249 H8
Vesta Rd BROCKY SE4..........41 L5
Vestey Ct WGOS CT8...........111 M4
Vestris Rd FSTH SE23...........61 K1
Vestry Rd CMBW SE5............40 E2
RSEV TN14......................148 G3

Vevey St FSTH SE23.............61 M1
Vexil Cl PUR RM19...............30 C7
Viaduct Cl MSTR CT12..........143 H4
Viaduct St EYN DA4 * 67 J8
RASHW TN26 * 304 C8
The Viaduct DVW CT17.........313 L1
Vian St LEW SE13................41 P4
Via Romana GVE DA12...........50 D9
Viburnum Cl RAIN RM13........252 B7
Vicarage Cl DIT/AY ME20.......154 E1
ERITH DA8........................29 H9
HOO/HM ME3.....................54 E5
LING RH7.........................234 G5
STRD ME2........................93 P9
Vicarage Ct BECK BR3...........61 L9
Vicarage Cs MARG CT9 *.......15 H7
Vicarage Dr BECK BR3...........61 N7
GVW DA11........................48 G7
Vicarage Gdn MSTR CT12......140 D5
Vicarage Gdns RCANTE CT3...169 K9
Vicarage Gv CMBW SE5.........40 D2
Vicarage Hl BH/WHM TN16....176 E2
RCANTW CT4 * 195 P7
Vicarage La ASH TN23............2 E4
DEAL CT14.......................231 H6
DEAL CT14.......................233 H8
FAV ME13........................132 D8
FAV ME13........................163 M6
GVE DA12........................70 C1
HDCN TN27......................220 B5
HOO/HM ME3....................73 M4
MAID/SHEP ME15..............184 C4
RCANTW CT4 * 257 L5
RDV CT15........................229 M1
RDV CT15........................292 E1
RSIT ME9.........................98 D5
SWCH CT13 * 201 N1
Vicarage Pk WOOL/PLUM SE18..27 K8
Vicarage Pl MARG CT9...........15 G6
Vicarage Rd BXLY DA5..........45 K9
CROY/NA CRO...................82 F7
FOLK CT20......................310 C8
GILL ME7...........................7 G3
IOS ME12..........................58 D9
LING RH7.........................234 G5
LYDD TN29......................341 M5
STH/RUST TN4 ....240 C7
STRD ME2........................93 M9
WBY/VAL ME18.................213 P1
WOOL/PLUM SE18.............27 K8
Vicarage Sq GRAYS RM17......32 B9
Vicarage St BRDST CT10......113 J8
FAV ME13........................132 C5
Vicars Hl LEW SE13...............41 P5
Vicars Oak Rd NRWD SE19.....60 E5
Vicary Wy MAIDW ME16.......155 J7
Vickers Cl RFOLK CT18........288 D8
Vickers Rd ERITH DA8...........29 J8
Victor Av MARG CT9.............113 J5
Victoria Av BRDST CT10.......113 K5
CDW/CHF RM16..................32 D5
HYTHE CT21....................308 C5
MARG CT9........................112 C4
RDV CT15........................292 C1
WGOS CT8......................111 N6
Victoria Cl CDW/CHF RM16....32 D5
RMAID ME17....................218 F3
WALD ME5.......................125 J3
Victoria Cl HYTHE CT21 *.....309 H6
MAIDW ME16 * 12 C6
Victoria Crs ASH TN23...........2 D6
DVW CT17........................313 K6
NRWD SE19......................60 E5
Victoria Dock Rd CAN/RD E16..26 B3
Victoria Dr E/WMAL SW20....182 G1
EYN DA4..........................67 K8
HB CT6...........................107 H1
Victoria Gdns BH/WHM TN16..115 M9
Victoria Gv FOLK CT20.........310 E9
HYTHE CT21....................309 N5
Victoria Ms DEAL CT14 *......233 H5
Victoria Pde RAM CT11..........16 B2
RAM CT11........................16 B2
Victoria Pk DEAL CT14 *.......233 H4
DVE/WH CT16 * 5 F4
HB CT6...........................107 L1
Victoria Pl FAV ME13...........132 F6
HYTHE CT21 * 308 C5
Victoria Rd ASH TN23............2 D6
BFN/LL DA15.....................64 B2
BRDST CT10.....................113 K7
BXLYHS DA6......................45 J6
CANT CT1..........................4 C7
DART DA1........................46 D6
DEAL CT14.......................233 J4
DEAL CT14.......................263 H4
ERITH DA8......................236 D1
ERITH DA8.......................29 K9
FOLKN CT19......................10 D3
GVW DA11........................49 K9
HAYES BR2.......................85 N2
HYTHE CT21 * 309 H6
MARG CT9........................15 H6
NROM TN28.....................337 K9
RAM CT11........................17 H2
RFOLK CT18.....................311 L1
RTON TN11......................212 A4
RTW TN1..........................12 C2
SEV TN13........................21 F5
SIT ME10........................129 L1
STH/RUST TN4 ....240 B8
WALD ME5.......................125 K5
Victoria Rd West NROM TN28..337 J8
Victoria Row CANT CT1..........5 E4
Victoria St BELV DA17...........28 E8
DIT/AY ME20...................124 E7
DVW CT17......................291 J6
GILL ME7...........................7 K1
HB CT6...........................107 J2
MAIDW ME16 * 12 C6
NROM TN28.....................336 F7
ROCH ME1........................19 G6

Victoria Ter IOS ME12 *..........18 E1
ROCH ME1........................94 F4
Victoria Vs RTW TN1 * 25 F5
Victoria Works
STMC/STPC BR5.................86 E2
Victoria Wy CHARL SE7.........26 C8
EGRIN RH19.....................265 J9
Victoria Yd WCHPL E1 *.........24 D2
Victor Rd POG/AN SE20..........61 K6
Victory Cl CDW/CHF RM16.....31 M7
Victory Pk STRD ME2 * 19 K2
Victory Pl NRWD SE19..........60 E5
Victory Rd RDV CT15...........262 E7
Victory St IOS ME12 * 57 K6
Victory Wy BERM/RHTH SE16..25 K5
GRH DA9.........................47 J5
Vidgeon Av HOO/HM ME3.....73 K1
Vidler Cl BH/WHM TN16......145 M1
Vierfield Rd BFN/LL DA15......44 E9
Viewland Rd
WOOL/PLUM SE18.............27 N8
Viewlands Av BH/WHM TN16..146 F5
View Rd HOO/HM ME3...........52 B9
View Ter LING RH7..............235 K3
The View ABYW SE2.............28 D8
Vigerons Wy CDW/CHF RM16..33 J7
Vigilant Cl SYD SE26............60 G3
Vigilant Wy GVE DA12..........70 B4
Vigo Hl E/WMAL ME19..........121 P7
Vigo Rd BGR/WK TN15.........121 H6
Viking Cl BRCH CT7.............110 E5
STRD ME2........................18 A7
Viking Gdns EHAM E6...........26 F1
Viking Rd GVW DA11............68 C2
Viking Wy BELV DA17...........29 H6
BH/WHM TN16...................90 B9
Villa Cl GVE DA12................70 D1
Villacourt Rd
WOOL/PLUM SE18.............44 C1
Village Green Av
BH/WHM TN16..................145 P2
Village Green Rd DART DA1...46 A5
Village Green Wy
BH/WHM TN16..................145 P2
Village CharL SE7................26 B9
The Village Wy BECK BR3......61 N9
HNHL SE24......................40 D7
RASHW TN26...................304 D8
Villa Rd BRXN/ST SW9..........40 A4
HOO/HM ME3....................71 K4
Villas Rd WOOL/PLUM SE18...27 K7
Villa St WALW SE17.............24 A8
Villiers Rd BECK BR3............61 K8
CANT CT1........................167 J3
Vincennes Est WNWD SE27...60 D5
Vincent Cl BFN/LL DA15........44 A9
BRDST CT10.....................143 H1
FOLK CT20......................310 B7
HAYES BR2.......................85 L1
Vincent Gdns IOS ME12.........57 L7
Vincent Pl NR KEN/WIL TN24..253 J5
Vincent Rd CROY/NA CRO.....125 H6
DIT/AY ME20...................125 H6
MARG CT9........................112 B9
RDV CT15........................181 M3
WOOL/PLUM SE18 * 27 J7
Vincents Cl BERM/RHTH SE16..25 K5
Vincent Sq BH/WHM TN16....115 M7
Vincent St CAN/RD E16.........26 B1
Vine Av SEV TN13................21 F1
Vine Cl RAM CT11...............143 K2
Vine Ct WCHPL E1................24 D2
Vine Court Rd SEV TN13........21 G1
Vinegar St WAP E1W.............24 E4
Vinegar Yd STHWK SE1.........24 B5
Vine Lands LYDD TN29.........342 A6
Vine La STHWK SE1 * 24 B4
The Vineries CAT SE6 * 41 N9
GILL ME7..........................96 B1
Vine Rd ORP BR6...............116 C1
Vines La ROCH ME1.............19 F5
RTON TN11......................209 P1
Vine St TWRH EC3N............24 C5
Vine Street Crs TWRH EC3N *..24 C5
The Vine SEV TN13...............21 G1
Vine Wk STPH/PW TN12.......246 B6
Vineyard Cl CAT SE6.............41 N9
Vineyard Crs EHAM ME8.......41 N9
Vineyard Park Rd FSTH SE23..41 K9
Vineyard La WADH TN5.........314 F4
Viney Bank CROY/NA CRO....114 C3
Viney Rd LEW SE13..............41 P4
Viney's Gdns TENT TN30.......301 K6
Vining St BRXN/ST SW9.........40 A5
Voyagers Cl THMD SE28.......133 N4
Vinson Cl ORP BR6...............78 D3
Vinten Ct HB CT6................107 N6
Vinters Pk
MAID/BEAR ME14 * 156 A1
Vinters Rd MAID/BEAR ME14..13 J4
Vintners Wy
MAID/BEAR ME14..............156 B8
Viola Av ABYW SE2..............28 A7
Violet Av MSTR CT12...........143 H2
Violet Cl DEPT SE8...............25 J9
WALD ME5.......................125 L5
Violet Gdns CROY/NA CRO.....82 G9
Violet La CROY/NA CRO.........82 G9
Virginia Rd GILL ME7............73 J8
THHTH CR7......................60 A9
WSTB CT5........................105 P6
Virginia St WAP E1W............24 D3
Viscount Dr EHAM E6...........26 C1
The Vista ELTH/MOT SE9.......43 J8
Vivian Sq PECK SE15............41 H4
Vixen Cl WALD ME5..............95 P8
Vlissingen Dr DEAL CT14......233 H1
Voce Rd WOOL/PLUM SE18....45 P1
Volante Dr SIT ME10.............99 M7
Volante Wy GVE DA12...........70 A3
Volta Wy CROY/NA CRO.........82 E5
Voluntaries Cl EHAM E6.........26 F1
Vulcan Cl EHAM E6...............27 H2
WALD ME5.......................95 N7
WSTB CT5.......................105 K7

Vulcan Rd BROCKY SE4.........41 M3
Vulcan Ter BROCKY SE4........41 M3
Vulcan Wy CROY/NA CRO.....115 H4
The Vyne BXLYHN DA7..........45 K4
Wacher Cl CANTW/ST CT2....166 E2
Wadard Ter SWLY BR8 * 89 H2
Wadding St WALW SE17.........24 A7
Waddington Dr RFOLK CT18..288 D8
Waddington Wy NRWD SE19..60 C7
Waddon Cl CROY/NA CRO......82 F7
Waddon Court Rd
CROY/NA CRO...................82 F8
Waddon New Rd
CROY/NA CRO...................82 E8
Waddon Park Av
CROY/NA CRO...................82 F7
Waddon Rd CROY/NA CRO....82 F7
Wade Av STMC/STPC BR5.....87 L1
Wade House STHWK SE1 *.....24 D5
Wades Cl LYDD TN29...........325 P9
Wade's Pl POP/IOD E14.........25 L3
Wadeville Cl BELV DA17.........28 F8
Wadham Pl SIT ME10...........130 A3
Wadham Rd PUT/ROE SW15..61 H8
Wadlands Brook Rd
EGRIN RH19.....................264 G3
Wadlands Rd HOO/HM ME3...52 B5
Wagg Cl EGRIN RH19..........265 K9
Waghorn Rd SNOD ME6.......125 P5
Waghorn St PECK SE15.........95 N4
PECK SE15.......................40 G4
Wagner St PECK SE15...........41 J1
Wagoners Ct
MAID/BEAR ME14 * 156 B8
Wagon La STPH/PW TN12....213 K9
Wagtail Gdns SAND/SEL CR2..114 A4
Wagtail Wk BECK BR3...........84 F2
Wagtail Wy STMC/STPC BR5..87 K1
Waid Cl DART DA1................46 F7
Wainscott Rd STRD ME2.........72 D5
Wainscott Wk STRD ME2.......72 D4
Wakeley Rd RHAM ME8.........97 L5
Wakeling St WCHPL E1 * 25 H2
Wakely Cl BH/WHM TN16.....145 M3
Wakerly Cl EHAM E6.............26 G2
Wakley St FSBYE EC1V..........23 M3
Walberton St KEN/WIL TN24..252 C9
Walbrook MANHO EC4N........24 A3
Walburgh St WCHPL E1..........24 E2
Walcheren Cl DEAL CT14......233 H1
Walcot Sq LBTH SE11............23 P7
Waldeck Gv WNWD SE27......60 B2
Waldeck Rd DART DA1...........46 F7
Waldegrave Rd BMLY BR1......85 P2
NRWD SE19......................60 F6
Waldegrove CROY/NA CRO....83 L7
Walden Av CHST BR7............63 L3
Walden Cl BELV DA17...........28 E8
Walden Gdns THHTH CR7......82 E1
Waldenhurst Rd
STMC/STPC BR5.................87 L4
Walden Pde CHST BR7 * 63 K5
Walden Rd CHST BR7...........63 K5
Waldens Cl STMC/STPC BR5..87 L4
Waldenshaw Rd FSTH SE23...41 J9
Waldens Rd STMC/STPC BR5..87 M3
The Waldens RMAID ME17....187 P9
Waldenstein Wk WCHPL E1 *..24 E2
Waldershare Av SWCH CT13..202 F3
Waldershare La RDV CT15....261 M6
Waldershare Rd RDV CT15....261 H3
Waldersiade Rd CHAT ME4....95 L7
Waldersiade Woods
WALD ME5.......................125 J2
Waldon Til RM18..................34 A7
Waldo Rd BMLY BR1.............62 C9
Waldram Crs FSTH SE23........41 J9
Waldram Park Rd FSTH SE23..41 K9
Waldrist Wy ERITH DA18.......28 G5
Waldron Dr MAID/SHEP ME15..185 L5
Waldron Gdns HAYES BR2.....62 B9
Waldronhyrst CROY/NA CRO..82 G8
Waldron Rd BRDST CT10......143 N2
Waldron Wk BRDST CT10 *...143 N2
OXTED RH8......................175 J7
Waldstock Rd THMD SE28.....27 P3
Walerand Rd LEW SE13.........42 A3
Wales Cl PECK SE15.............41 H1
Waley St WCHPL E1 * 24 C1
Walkden Rd CHST BR7..........63 J5
Walker Cl DART DA1...............45 P4
Walker House HNHL SE24 *....40 B5
Walkerscroft Md CAT SE6......61 P1
DUL SE21 * 40 C9
Walkhurst Rd CRBK TN17.....276 E5
Walkley Rd DART DA1............46 B6
The Walk OXTED RH8...........174 D9
Wallace Cl RTWE/PEM TN2...270 D8
THMD SE28......................28 C3
Wallace Gdns SWCM DA10....48 C2
Wallace Ms FOLK CT19.........310 G4
Wallace Rd GRAYS RM17.......32 B7
ROCH ME1........................95 K6
Wallace Wy BRDST CT10......113 K9
Wallbridge La RHAM ME8.......97 N5
Wallbutton Rd BROCKY SE4...41 L5
Wall Cl HOO/HM ME3............53 K9
Waller Hl CRBK TN17...........276 E5
Waller Rd LYDD TN29...........343 K5
Wallers Av HB CT6...............107 H1
Wallers RRTW TN5 * 269 M1
Wallers Rd FAV ME13...........132 D6
Wallis Av MAID/SHEP ME15..186 B6

Wallis Cl RDART DA2............66 A2
Wallis Pk GVW DA11.............48 F6
Wallis Cl KEN/WIL TN24.........3 H3
The Wall SIT ME10...............99 M9
Wallwood Rd RAM CT11........17 J1
Wallwood St POP/IOD E14....25 J1
Walmer Castle Rd DEAL CT14.233 H8
Walmer Cl ORP BR6..............86 E8
Walmer Crs DEAL CT14 * 232 G8
Walmer Gdns DEAL CT14.....232 F7
MSTR CT12......................142 B7
SIT ME10.........................99 L9
Walmer Rd WSTB CT5.........105 M6
Walmers Av HOO/HM ME3.....71 J3
Walmer Ter WOOL/PLUM SE18..71 J3
Walmer Wy DEAL CT14.........232 F7
FOLK CT20......................310 C6
Walmsley Rd BRDST CT10....113 L8
Walner Gdns NROM TN28.....336 C6
Walner La NROM TN28.........336 C6
Walnut Cl DEPT SE8..............25 J9
KEN/WIL TN24.................252 C3
STPH/PW TN12.................243 H3
WALD ME5.......................95 N6
Walnut Hill Rd MEO DA13.......69 K6
Walnuts Rd ORP BR6............87 H5
Walnut Tree Av DART DA1.......66 C1
MAID/SHEP ME15..............185 M6
Walnut Tree Cl CHST BR7......63 N7
Walnut Tree La
CANT/ST CT2...................137 P6
MAID/SHEP ME15..............185 M6
Walnut Tree Rd ERITH DA8...309 H5
Walnut Tree Rd ERITH DA8....29 K8
GNWCH SE10 * 25 P8
Walnut Wy BERM/RHTH SE16..25 J8
Walnut Tree Wy MEO DA13....92 B5
Walnut Wy RTWE/PEM TN2...240 C9
Walpole Cl E/WMAL ME19....153 H3
CRAYS RM17....................32 D7
Walpole Rd CROY/NA CRO.....83 J6
HAYES BR2.......................85 N2
Walsby Dr SIT ME10.............99 M9
Walsham Cl THMD SE28........28 C3
Walsham Rd NWCR SE14.......41 K3
WALD ME5.......................125 J4
Walsh Crs CROY/NA CRO......115 H6
Walsingham Cl RHAM ME8....126 C2
Walsingham Pk CHST BR7.....63 P8
Walsingham Rd
CROY/NA CRO..................114 F4
STMC/STPC BR5.................64 D7
Walter Burke Av ROCH ME1 * ..94 B9
Walter's Farm Rd TON TN9...210 F9
Walters Green Rd RTON TN11..268 D2
Walters Rd HOO/HM ME3......73 L1
SNWD SE25 *....................83 K1
Walters Wy FSTH SE23..........41 K6
Walters Yd BMLY BR1............62 E8
Walter Ter WCHPL E1............24 G2
Waltham Cl DART DA1............46 A7
KEN/WIL TN24.................253 J7
MARG CT9........................15 H1
STMC/STPC BR5.................87 L5
Waltham Rd RCANTW CT4....225 N1
RHAM ME8........................96 E8
Walton Gdns FOLKN CT19....310 C4
Walton Gn CROY/NA CRO....114 C4
Walton Manor Cl FOLKN CT19..310 C3
Walton Rd FOLKN CT19.........10 E1
SCUP DA14.......................64 D2
TONN DA14......................211 J4
Walton's Hall Rd
SLH/COR SS17..................33 P5
The Wattons FOLKN CT19....310 F3
Walton Wy MTCM CR4..........80 F1
Walt Whitman Cl HNHL SE24 *..40 B5
Walwyn Av BMLY BR1............63 H9
Wandale La HDCN TN27........219 J9
Wandle Bank CROY/NA CRO...82 D7
Wandle Court Gdns
CROY/NA CRO...................82 D7
Wandle Rd WLCTN SM6.........82 A6
Wandle Side WLCTN SM6......82 A7
Wanless Rd HNHL SE24.........40 C5
Wanley Rd CMBW SE5..........40 D5
Wansbury Wy SWLY BR8........88 F2
Wanstead Cl BMLY BR1.........62 G8
Wanstead Rd BMLY BR1........62 G8
Wansunt Rd BXLY DA5..........45 L9
Wantage Rd LEE/GVPK SE12..42 G6
Wantsum Cl HB CT6............108 C5
Wantsume Lees SWCH CT13..171 M9
Wantsum Wk BRCH CT7........110 D6
BRCH CT7.......................109 P6
HB CT6...........................108 D5
Wantsum Wy BRCH CT7......109 P8
Wapping Dock St WAP E1W....24 E4
Wapping High St WAP E1W....24 D4
Wapping La WAP E1W............24 E3
Wapping Wall WAP E1W.........24 E3
Warbank Cr CROY/NA CRO...115 H4
Warbank Crs CROY/NA CRO..115 H4
Warberry Park Gdns
STH/RUST TN4 ....270 B4
Warblers Cl STRD ME2...........18 C1
Warburton Cl EGRIN RH19....265 K7
Wardalls Gv NWCR SE14 * 41 J1
Ward Av GRAYS RM17...........32 C7
Ward Cl ERITH DA8...............29 J9
SAND/SEL CR2 *................83 K9
Warden Bay Rd IOS ME12......80 C4
Warden Cl MAIDW ME16......155 H8
Warden House Ms DEAL CT14..233 F7
Warden Mill Cl
WBY/VAL ME18.................183 L4
Warden Point
WY WSTB CT5 * 105 K8
Warden Rd IOS ME12.............79 J3
ROCH ME1........................95 H3

Warden Ter WBY/YAL ME18 * ...183 L5
Warden View Gdns IOS ME12 ....80 A6
Wardes WBY/YAL ME18 * ...183 N9
Wardour Cl BRDST CT10 ...113 N9
Wardsbrook Rd WADH TN5 ...315 H7
Wards Hill Rd IOS ME12 ...58 E8
Ward's La WADH TN5 ...314 C3
Wardwell La RSIT ME9 ...98 D4
Warehorne Rd RASHW TN26 ...304 C8
Warepoint Dr THMD SE28 ...27 L5
Ware St MAID/BEAR ME14 ...156 C7
Warham Rd RSEV TN14 ...148 C1
    SAND/SEL CR2 ...83 H9
Warham St CMBW SE5 ...40 B1
Waring Cl ORP BR6 ...116 C1
Waring Dr ORP BR6 ...116 C1
Waring Rd SCUP DA14 ...64 E5
Waring St WNWD SE27 ...60 C3
Warland Rd BGR/WK TN15 ...120 C5
    WOOL/PLUM SE18 ...48 F5
Warlingham Cl RHAM ME8 ...97 K5
Warlingham Rd THHTH CR7 ...82 C1
Warmington Rd HNHL SE24 ...40 C7
Warminster Rd SNWD SE25 ...60 G8
Warminster Sq SNWD SE25 ...60 G8
Warmlake Rd RMAID ME17 ...216 E1
Warndon St BERM/RHTH SE16 ...24 F7
Warne Pl BFN/LL DA15 ...44 D7
Warner Rd BMLY BR1 ...62 D6
    CMBW SE5 ...40 C2
Warner St CHAT ME4 ...6 C7
Warner Ter POP/IOD E14 * ...25 K1
Warnett Ct SNOD ME6 * ...123 P4
Warnford Gdns
    MAID/SHEP ME15 ...185 M3
Warnford Rd ORP BR6 ...86 G9
Warre Av RAM CT11 ...16 B6
Warren Av BMLY BR1 ...62 C6
    ORP BR6 ...86 G9
    SAND/SEL CR2 ...114 A2
Warren Cl BXLYHS DA6 ...45 J6
    EGRIN RH19 ...264 B5
    FOLKN CT19 ...11 K1
    SIT ME10 ...130 A3
Warren Ct BGR/WK TN15 ...21 G3
    CHARL SE7 ...26 D8
Warren Dr BRDST CT10 ...113 K8
    ORP BR6 ...87 J9
The Warren Dr WGOS CT8 ...111 L6
Warren Gdns ORP BR6 ...87 H9
Warren Hts RASHW TN26 * ...284 F3
Warren La CDW/CHF RM16 ...31 N7
    KEN/WIL TN24 ...252 D5
    OXTED RH8 ...261 N5
    RDV CT15 ...259 N6
    RSIT ME9 ...127 M2
    WOOL/PLUM SE18 ...27 J6
Warren Pk WARL CR6 ...144 A3
Warren Rd BXLYHS DA6 ...45 J6
    CROY/NA CR0 ...83 K5
    DART DA1 ...66 E2
    FOLKN CT19 ...11 J2
    HAYES BR2 ...85 J6
    MEO DA13 ...68 F4
    MEO DA15 ...93 K3
    NROM TN28 ...337 J7
    ORP BR6 ...86 G9
    SCUP DA14 ...64 E3
    WALD ME5 ...125 J5
The Warrens HART DA3 ...91 J5
Warren St RMAID ME17 ...190 C5
Warren Ter CDW/CHF RM16 * ...31 N5
The Warren GVE DA12 ...69 P5
    RASHE TN25 ...288 F4
    RTON TN11 ...238 F5
    SLH/COR SS17 * ...34 D2
    WADH TN5 ...315 J5
    WSTB CT5 ...105 K8
Warren Vw GVE DA12 ...70 C5
    RASHE TN25 ...252 C5
Warren Wy FOLKN CT19 ...11 J2
Warren Wood Cl HAYES BR2 ...85 K6
Warren Wood Rd ROCH ME1 ...95 J7
Warrington Pl POP/IOD E14 * ...25 M4
Warrington Rd CROY/NA CR0 ...82 C7
    STPH/PW TN12 ...242 C3
Warrior Av GVE DA12 ...69 N5
Warspite Rd WOOL/PLUM SE18 ...26 F6
Warten Rd RAM CT11 ...143 L5
Warwall EHAM E6 ...27 J2
Warwick Cl BXLY DA5 ...45 H8
    ORP BR6 ...87 H7
Warwick Crs ROCH ME1 ...94 E4
    SIT ME10 ...99 K9
Warwick Dr RAM CT11 ...142 C7
Warwick Gdns MEO DA13 ...92 B6
    THHTH CR7 * ...82 F5
Warwick Pk RTW TN1 ...22 D7
Warwick Pl GVW DA11 ...48 F6
    MAIDW ME16 ...12 B6
Warwick Rd CANT CT1 ...167 M4
    DEAL CT14 ...233 J7
    KEN/WIL TN24 ...253 H5
    MARG CT9 ...112 G5
    PGE/AN SE20 ...61 H9
    RTW TN1 ...22 D7
    SCUP DA14 ...64 D4
    THHTH CR7 ...60 A9
    WELL DA16 ...44 E4
    WSTB CT5 ...105 L4
Warwickshire Pth DEPT SE8 ...41 M1
Warwick Ter
    WOOL/PLUM SE18 ...27 L9
Warwick Wy DART DA1 ...66 E1
Washford Farm Rd ASH TN23 ...282 B3
Washington Cl DVE/WH CT16 ...291 J4
Washington La LYDD TN29 ...335 J6
Washneys Rd ORP BR6 ...117 H7
Washpond La WARL CR6 ...144 F3
Wassall La CRBK TN17 ...319 L3
Wass Dro RCANTE CT3 ...170 C4
Wastdale Rd FSTH SE23 ...41 K9
Watchbell La RYE TN31 ...338 F7
Watchbell St RYE TN31 ...338 F7

Watchester Av RAM CT11 ...16 C6
Watchester La MSTR CT12 ...141 J7
Watchmans Ter WALD ME5 ...95 P4
Watcombe Rd DEAL CT14 ...233 N2
Waterbank Rd CAT SE6 ...61 P2
Waterbrook Av
    KEN/WIL TN24 ...283 K4
Watercress Dr RSEV TN14 ...149 H5
Watercress La KEN/WIL TN23 ...252 B9
Watercroft Rd RSEV TN14 ...117 N4
Waterdale Rd ABYW SE2 ...27 P9
Waterdales GVW DA11 ...49 H9
Waterditch La RMAID ME17 ...190 C5
Waterdown Rd
    STH/RUST TN4 ...270 A7
Waterfall Rd RASHW TN26 ...251 M3
Water Farm RCANTW CT4 ...257 L5
Waterfield RTWE/PEM TN2 ...270 D9
Waterfield Cl BELV DA17 * ...28 F6
    THMD SE28 ...28 A4
Waterfield Gdns SNWD SE25 ...83 K1
Waterfront WTHK RM20 * ...31 M1
Watergate St DEPT SE8 ...25 K9
Waterham Rd FAV ME13 ...134 D4
Waterhead Cl ERITH DA8 ...45 N1
Wateringbury Cl
    STMC/STPC BR5 ...64 D9
Wateringbury Rd
    E/WMAL ME19 ...153 N9
Waterlakes EDEN TN8 ...236 D1
Water La CANT CT1 * ...4 D4
    CANTW/ST CT2 ...137 L8
    E/WMAL ME19 ...153 K4
    EDEN TN8 ...235 N2
    FAV ME13 ...132 B9
    GDST RH9 ...204 A5
    HAWK TN18 ...297 M8
    HDCN TN27 ...247 K5
    HDCN TN27 ...248 F7
    MAID/BEAR ME14 ...157 H7
    MAID/SHEP ME15 ...13 F5
    MAID/SHEP ME15 ...214 C4
    NWCR SE14 ...41 J1
    OXTED RH8 ...175 K2
    PUR RM19 ...30 D7
    RMAID ME17 ...188 A8
    RSEV TN14 ...118 E6
    SCUP DA14 ...65 H2
Waterloo Crs DVE/WH CT16 ...8 E5
    FOLK CT20 ...310 A6
    GILL ME7 ...7 H4
    SIT ME10 ...99 J9
    TON TN9 ...240 E1
    WSTB CT5 ...105 L4
Waterloo St GVE DA12 ...49 N8
    MAID/SHEP ME15 ...13 G7
Waterloo Ter IOS ME12 * ...78 C2
Waterlow Rd
    MAID/BEAR ME14 ...13 G1
    MEO DA13 ...122 B6
Waterman's La
    STPH/PW TN12 ...243 J6
Watersend DVE/WH CT16 ...290 D2
Waterside DART DA1 ...45 N6
    EGRIN RH19 ...265 L7
    GILL ME7 ...96 C8
    MAID/BEAR ME14 ...12 C3
Waterside Av BECK BR3 ...84 E2
Waterside Cl BERM/RHTH SE16 ...24 D5
    FAV ME13 ...132 C5
Waterside Ga DIT/AY ME20 * ...153 M2
    LEW SE13 * ...42 B5
    STRD ME2 ...72 E9
Waterside Ms WGOS CT8 ...111 N4
Waterside Rd GILL ME7 ...96 E2
Waters Edge
    MAID/SHEP ME15 ...185 M1
Waterson Rd CDW/CHF RM16 ...33 J7
Waters Pl GILL ME7 ...96 D8
Waters Rd CAT SE6 ...62 C2
Waterstone Pl FAV ME13 * ...132 C2
Water St DEAL CT14 ...233 J2
Waterton Av GVE DA12 ...50 A8
Water Tower Hl CROY/NA CR0 ...83 J8
Waterworks Cottages
    RSEV TN14 ...149 H5
Waterworks Hl RDV CT15 ...262 A5
Waterworks La RDV CT15 ...262 A5
Watery La BGR/WK TN15 ...150 A5
    RCANTW CT4 ...196 B6
    SCUP DA14 ...64 D5
Watford Rd CAN/RD E16 ...26 E1
Watkin Rd FOLKN CT19 ...10 D1
Watkins Cl STPH/PW TN12 ...246 B4
Watkins Wy RASHE TN25 * ...65 M1
Watling Av WALD ME5 ...96 A4
Watling Pl SIT ME10 ...129 P2
Watlings Cl CROY/NA CR0 ...84 B3
Watling St BXLYHS DA6 ...45 L6
    CANT CT1 * ...4 E5
    DART DA1 ...47 H8
    GVE DA12 ...70 E7
    GVW DA11 ...69 M4
    MEO DA13 ...68 C2
    PECK SE15 ...24 B9
    STRD ME2 ...18 A1
    WALD ME5 ...96 A4
Watlington Gv SYD SE26 ...61 L4
Watney Market WCHPL E1 ...24 C2
Watneys Rd MTCM CR4 ...32 C2
Watney St WCHPL E1 ...24 C2
Watson Av WALD ME5 ...95 J9
Watson Cl WTHK RM20 ...47 N2
Watsons Cl RASHE TN25 ...252 F1
Watsons Hl SIT ME10 ...99 M9
Watson's St DEPT SE8 ...41 N1
Watts Av ROCH ME1 ...19 F7
Watts Cl SNOD ME6 ...124 A5
Watts Crs PUR RM19 ...30 F7
Watt's Cross Rd RTON TN11 ...209 N3
Watts Gv BOW E3 ...25 K1
Watt's La CHST BR7 ...63 M9
Watt's St CHAT ME4 ...6 A6
    WAP E1W ...24 E3
Wat Tyler Rd BKHTH/KID SE3 ...42 A3
Wauchope Rd WSTB CT5 ...104 C8
Wavell Dr BFN/LL DA15 ...44 A7
Wavell Rd SYD SE26 ...60 P3
Waveney Av PECK SE15 ...41 H5
Waveney Cl WAP E1W ...24 D4
Waveney Rd TONN TN10 ...210 E5
Waverley Av IOS ME12 ...58 B9
Waverley Cl HAYES BR2 ...85 N2
    RMAID ME17 ...185 M9
    WALD ME5 ...126 A3
Waverley Crs
    WOOL/PLUM SE18 ...27 L9
Waverley Dr RTWE/PEM TN2 ...271 J2
Waverley Gdns
    CDW/CHF RM16 ...32 B5
    EHAM E6 ...26 F1
Waverley Rd MARG CT9 ...14 B7
    SNWD SE25 ...83 N1
    WOOL/PLUM SE18 ...27 K8
Wayborough Hl MSTR CT12 ...141 L4
Wayfaring Gn GRAYS RM17 ...32 A8
Wayfield Rd WALD ME5 ...95 L7
Way Hl MSTR CT12 ...141 M5
Waylands SWLY BR8 ...65 N3
Waylands Cl RSEV TN14 ...117 M3
Waylett Pl WNWD SE27 ...60 B2
Wayne Cl BRDST CT10 ...113 K8
    ORP BR6 ...86 C7
Waynflete Av CROY/NA CR0 ...2 C4
Wayside CROY/NA CR0 * ...114 C1
    TENT TN30 ...301 J5
Wayside Av TENT TN30 ...301 J4
Wayside Cl EDEN TN8 ...206 E7
Wayside Gv CHST BR7 ...63 L3
Wayside Wy DART DA1 ...47 H8
Weald Cl BERM/RHTH SE16 ...24 E8
    HAYES BR2 ...85 P6
    MAID/SHEP ME15 ...185 P5
    MEO DA13 ...69 J6
    RSEV TN14 ...178 C9
    SIT ME10 ...129 L3
Wealden Av TENT TN30 ...301 J5
Wealden Cl RTON TN11 ...210 B5
Wealden Ct WALD ME5 * ...7 J2
Walden Forest Pk HB CT6 * ...137 K1
Wealden Wy DIT/AY ME20 ...153 M2
Wealdhurst Pk BRDST CT10 ...113 J8
Weald Rd SEV TN13 ...178 C4
The Weald CHST BR7 ...63 K5
    EGRIN RH19 ...265 J5
    KEN/WIL TN24 ...253 H5
Weald Vw STPH/PW TN12 ...243 L8
    WADH TN5 ...294 A9
Weald View Rd TON TN9 ...240 E2
Wealdway BGR/WK TN15 ...151 N6
    E/WMAL ME19 ...152 B2
    MEO DA13 ...69 M5
    RTON TN11 ...269 K2
    RTON TN11 ...211 P7
    STPH/PW TN12 ...182 E9
    TON TN9 ...210 F9
Wear Bay Crs FOLKN CT19 ...11 J5
Wear Bay Rd FOLKN CT19 ...11 J3
Weardale Av RDART DA2 ...67 J1
Weardale Rd LEW SE13 ...42 D7
Weare Rd STH/RUST TN4 ...240 F9
Wearside Rd LEW SE13 ...41 P5
Weatherall Cl FAV ME13 ...164 C2
Weatherly Cl ROCH ME1 ...19 C7
Weatherly Dr BRDST CT10 ...113 L2
Weaver Cl EHAM E6 ...27 J3
Weavering Cl STAPL SE2 ...72 E5
Weavering St
    MAID/BEAR ME14 ...156 C7
Weavers Cl GVW DA11 ...49 L9
    STPH/PW TN12 ...242 B4
Weavers La RSEV TN14 ...149 H6
    STHWK SE1 ...24 B6
The Weavers HDCN TN27 ...278 A7
    MAIDW ME16 ...154 G8
Weavers Wy ASH TN23 ...282 B1
    DVE/WH CT16 ...291 H4
Weaver Wk WNWD SE27 ...60 B3
Webb Cl FOLKN CT19 ...310 D4
    HOO/HM ME3 ...35 K1
Webber Cl ERITH DA8 ...46 B1
Webb Rd BKHTH/KID SE3 ...26 A8
Webbs Meadow BGR/WK TN15 ...21 C4
Webb St STHWK SE1 ...24 B6
Webster Rd BERM/RHTH SE16 ...24 D6
    RHAM ME8 ...97 J5
Webster Wy RFOLK CT18 ...288 E8
Weddington La RCANTE CT3 ...170 F9
Wedgewood Cl MAIDW ME16 ...154 C7
Wedgewood Dr WALD ME5 ...95 M7

Wedgwoods BH/WHM TN16 * ...145 M6
Wedgwood Wy NRWD SE19 ...60 C6
Weeds Wood Rd WALD ME5 ...125 L1
Weekes Ct OBOR ME11 * ...57 J2
Weekes La HDCN TN27 ...278 E5
Week St MAID/BEAR ME14 ...12 E5
Weigall Pl RAM CT11 ...16 B5
Weigall Rd LEE/GVPK SE12 ...42 F5
Weighton Rd PGE/AN SE20 ...61 H8
Weird Wd HART DA3 ...68 G9
Weir Rd BXLY DA5 ...45 K8
Welbeck Av BFN/LL DA15 ...44 C6
    BMLY BR1 ...62 E5
    HAYES BR2 ...85 L6
Welbeck Cl STPH/PW TN12 ...246 C5
Wellan Cl BFN/LL DA15 ...44 D6
Weller Av ROCH ME1 ...95 J4
Weller Pl ORP BR6 * ...116 B5
Wellers Cl BH/WHM TN16 ...176 D3
Wellesley Cl BRDST CT10 ...143 K1
Wellesley Ct DEAL CT14 ...26 D8
    CHARL SE7 * ...26 D8
    WGOS CT8 ...111 M6
Wellesley Court Rd
    CROY/NA CR0 ...83 J6
Wellesley Rd CROY/NA CR0 ...2 E5
    CROY/NA CR0 ...83 H5
    CROY/NA CR0 ...83 H5
    DVE/WH CT16 ...8 E4
    IOS ME12 ...57 M7
    MARG CT9 ...3 J2
    WGOS CT8 ...111 M6
Wellesley St WCHPL E1 ...24 C1
Wellesley Vls KEN/WIL TN24 * ...3 J2
Wellfield EGRIN RH19 ...265 M9
Wellfield Rd HART DA3 ...91 J1
Wellfield Rd FOLK CT20 ...310 D6
Wellfield St HNHL SE24 ...40 F2
Well Hall Pde ELTH/MOT SE9 ...43 K5
Well Hall Rd ELTH/MOT SE9 ...43 K5
Well Hl ORP BR6 ...86 G7
Well Hill La ORP BR6 ...118 A2
Wellhouse Rd BECK BR3 ...84 C3
Wellhurst Cl ORP BR6 ...116 C2
Welling High St WELL DA16 ...44 D4
Welling Rd CDW/CHF RM16 ...33 M2
Wellington Av BFN/LL DA15 ...44 C7
Wellington Ct NWCR SE14 ...41 J1
    WGOS CT8 * ...111 M4
Wellington Cottages
    HAWK TN18 ...316 C2
Wellington Crs RAM CT11 ...17 H4
Wellington Gdns CHARL SE7 ...26 D8
    MARG CT9 * ...15 J3
Wellington Gv GNWCH SE10 ...42 A1
Wellingtonia Wy EDEN TN8 ...206 D8
Wellington Ms HYTHE CT21 ...309 M5
Wellington Pde BFN/LL DA15 * ...44 C6
    DEAL CT14 ...263 K2
Wellington Pl FOLK CT20 ...310 A8
    MAID/BEAR ME14 ...12 E1
Wellington Rd BELV DA17 ...28 E8
    BXLY DA5 ...44 F7
    CROY/NA CR0 ...82 G4
    DART DA1 ...66 E6
    DEAL CT14 ...233 J4
    DVE/WH CT16 ...290 E2
    FOLK CT20 ...310 A6
    GILL ME7 ...7 J8
    HAYES BR2 ...85 L1
    SIT ME10 ...99 J9
    STMC/STPC BR5 ...64 A5
    TIL RM18 ...49 L3
    WGOS CT8 ...111 M6
Wellington St GVE DA12 ...49 N8
    WOOL/PLUM SE18 ...27 H2
    WSTB CT5 ...105 L4
Wellington Ter FOLK CT20 * ...310 A8
    WAP E1W * ...24 E3
Wellington Town Rd
    EGRIN RH19 ...264 C5
Wellington Wy
    E/WMAL ME19 ...152 G9
Wellis Gdns MARG CT9 ...43 P4
Wellis La CANTW/ST CT2 ...31 P4
    CDW/CHF RM16 ...33 J8
    FAV ME13 ...161 N1
    RDV CT15 ...258 E3
Wellmeade Dr SEV TN15 ...178 G5
Wellmeadow Rd LEW SE13 ...42 C7
Well Penn Rd HO/HM ME3 ...52 E4
Well Rd MAID/BEAR ME14 ...13 F7
    OBOR ME11 ...57 M6
    RFOLK CT18 ...287 H7
    TENT TN30 ...301 H7
Wells Av CANT CT1 ...5 J7
Wells Cl BH/WHM TN16 ...176 D3
    NROM TN28 ...337 H7
    RTW TN1 ...22 C4
    SAND/SEL CR2 ...83 K9
    TENT TN30 ...301 H7
    TON TN9 ...210 C6
Wells Lea EGRIN RH19 ...264 C5
Wells Meadow EGRIN RH19 ...264 C5
Wellsmoor Gdns BMLY BR1 ...63 J5
Wells Park Rd SYD SE26 ...60 G2
Wells Rd BMLY BR1 ...64 A1
    HAYES BR2 ...85 P4
Wells Rd BMLY BR1 ...63 P1
    FOLKN CT19 ...310 B5
    STRD ME2 ...94 C1

Well St E/WMAL ME19 ...153 M6
    WMAL ME19 ...185 K7
Wells Wy CMBW SE5 ...24 E3
    FAV ME15 ...132 E4
Well Winch Rd SIT ME10 ...99 L9
Welsdene Rd MARG CT9 ...112 A5
Welsford St STHWK SE1 ...24 D8
Welson Rd FOLK CT20 ...310 C2
Welton Cl TON TN9 ...240 C2
Welton Rd WOOL/PLUM SE18 ...44 A1
Wembury Pk LING RH7 ...234 B9
Wemmick Cl ROCH ME1 ...95 J7
Wemyss Rd BKHTH/KID SE3 ...42 C5
Wenerss Wy CANT CT1 ...167 H4
Wenderton La RCANTE CT3 ...169 K5
Wendover Cl STRD ME2 ...94 A9
Wendover Rd ELTH/MOT SE9 ...43 H4
    HAYES BR2 ...85 L1
Wendover Wy ORP BR6 ...87 K5
    WELL DA16 ...44 C6
Wenham's La LYDD TN29 ...335 M3
Wennington Rd RAIN RM13 ...29 N1
Wensley Cl ELTH/MOT SE9 ...43 K7
Wentland Cl CAT SE6 ...62 B1
Wentland Rd CAT SE6 ...62 B1
Wents Wd MAID/BEAR ME14 ...156 C7
Wentworth Av MARG CT9 ...111 P4
Wentworth Cl GVW DA11 ...69 L4
    HAYES BR2 ...85 F9
    ORP BR6 ...86 F9
    RFOLK CT18 ...287 H2
    THMD SE28 ...28 C2
Wentworth Crs PECK SE15 ...40 G1
Wentworth Dr DART DA1 ...46 A8
    HOO/HM ME3 ...52 B8
    MSTR CT12 ...142 F3
    RHAM ME8 ...97 J9
    SIT ME10 ...99 K9
Wentworth Gdns HB CT6 ...107 J4
Wentworth Pl CDW/CHF RM16 ...32 E6
Wentworth Rd CROY/NA CR0 ...82 F4
Wentworth St WCHPL E1 ...24 C2
Wenvoe Av BXLYHN DA7 ...45 K3
Wernbrook St
    WOOL/PLUM SE18 ...27 K9
Wemdee Rd SNWD SE25 ...83 M1
Wesley Av CAN/RD E16 ...26 B4
Wesley Cl MAIDW ME16 ...154 E9
    STMC/STPC BR5 ...64 A5
Wesley Ter RFOLK CT18 ...287 H1
Wessex Ct BECK BR3 * ...61 L7
Wessex Dr ERITH DA8 ...45 N3
Wessex Wk BXLY DA5 ...65 M1
Wesson Md CMBW SE5 * ...40 C1
West Ap STMC/STPC BR5 ...63 L3
West Arbour St WCHPL E1 ...24 G2
West Av WLGTN SM6 ...82 D9
Westbere La CANTW/ST CT2 ...137 N7
Westbourne ASH TN23 ...282 A2
Westbourne Dr FSTH SE23 ...41 K9
Westbourne Rd BXLYHN DA7 ...24 C4
    CROY/NA CR0 ...83 L3
    SYD SE26 ...61 K5
Westbrook St SIT ME10 ...99 M9
Westbrook
    MAID/SHEP ME15 ...185 L6
Westbrook Av MARG CT9 ...111 P6
Westbrook Cottages
    MARG CT9 ...14 C6
Westbrooke Dr STMC/STPC BR5 * ...87 L5
Westbrooke Cl CHAT ME4 ...95 M4
Westbrooke Crs WELL DA16 ...44 E4
Westbrooke Rd BFN/LL DA15 ...63 P1
    WELL DA16 ...44 E4
Westbrook Gdns MARG CT9 ...14 B6
Westbrook La HB CT6 ...106 D6
Westbrook Rd BKHTH/KID SE3 ...42 F2
    MARG CT9 ...60 D7
Westbrook Ter
    RTWE/PEM TN2 ...270 G7
Westbury Crs DVW CT17 ...291 H9
Westbury Rd BMLY BR1 ...63 H7
    CROY/NA CR0 ...83 J5
    DVW CT17 ...291 J9
    PGE/AN SE20 ...61 K7
    WGOS CT8 ...111 N5
Westbury Ter BH/WHM TN16 ...176 C6
West Cliff WSTB CT5 ...105 K6
West Cliff Av RAM CT11 ...17 F5
West Cliff Dr HB CT6 ...106 C2
Westcliff Dr IOS ME12 ...58 D9
West Cliff Gdns FOLK CT20 ...11 F5
    HB CT6 ...106 C3
Westcliff Gdns MARG CT9 ...14 C6
West Cliff Ms BRDST CT10 ...143 N1
West Cliff Prom RAM CT11 ...16 C7
West Cliff Rd BRDST CT10 ...143 M1
    RAM CT11 ...16 C5
Westcliff Rd MARG CT9 ...14 B6
Westcliff Terrace Man
    RAM CT11 ...16 A6
Westcombe Av CROY/NA CR0 ...82 D3
Westcombe Hl BKHTH/KID SE3 ...26 B8
Westcombe Park Rd
    BKHTH/KID SE3 ...25 P9
West Common Rd HAYES BR2 ...85 K6
Westcott Av GVW DA11 ...69 L2
Westcott Cl BMLY BR1 ...64 A5
    CROY/NA CR0 ...114 C3
Westcott House
    POP/IOD E14 * ...25 K3
West Ct MAID/SHEP ME15 * ...185 M2
Westcourt La RCANTW CT4 ...229 J7
Westcourt Pde GVE DA12 ...70 E2
Westcourt St GILL ME7 ...72 F9
West Crescent Rd GVE DA12 ...49 M7
West Cross TENT TN50 ...300 G8
West Cross Ms TENT TN30 * ...300 G8
Westdale Rd
    WOOL/PLUM SE18 ...27 K9
Westdean Av LEE/GVPK SE12 ...42 F9
Westdean Cl DVW CT17 ...290 F5

Westdown Rd CAT SE6 .....41 N8
West Dr RMAID ME17 .....217 L3
  WALD ME5 .....95 J9
West Dumpton La RAM CT11 ...143 K2
Wested La SWLY BR8 .....88 F4
West End BGR/WK TN15 .....149 L2
  BH/WHM TN16 .....177 J1
Westerdale Rd GNWCH SE10 ...26 B8
Westergate Rd ABYW SE2 .....28 D9
  STRD ME2 .....71 H6
Westerham Cl CANTW/ST CT2 ..136 F9
  MARG CT9 .....113 K4
  RHAM ME8 .....96 E2
Westerham Dr BFN/LL DA15 ....44 E7
Westerham Hl BH/WHM TN16...146 C7
Westerham Rd
  BH/WHM TN16 .....177 N1
  HAYES BR2 .....115 N1
  OXTED RH8 .....175 K5
  RSEV TN14 .....147 P8
  SEV TN13 .....148 B8
  SIT ME10 .....90 C3
Westerhill Rd RMAID ME17 .....215 H1
Westerhout Cl DEAL CT14 .....233 H1
Westerley Crs SYD SE26 * 41 N4
Western Av RASH TN23 .....2 B3
  CHAT ME4 .....72 G7
  HAWK TN18 .....317 H4
  HB CT6 .....107 J2
  IOS ME12 .....57 M9
  RCANTW CT4 .....197 L2
  WTHK RM20 * 31 J7
Western Cl DVW CT17 .....8 A7
Western Cross Cl GRH DA9 .....48 A7
Western Docks DVW CT17 * 318 L1
Western Esp BRDST CT10 .....143 N2
  HB CT6 .....107 H1
Western Gdns KEN/WIL TN24 ..253 H9
Western Gtwy CAN/RD E16 .....26 B3
Western Link FAV ME13 .....132 D5
Western Rd BGR/WK TN15 ....155 J1
  BRXN/ST SW9 .....40 A4
  DEAL CT14 .....233 H3
  HAWK TN18 .....317 H4
  MAIDW ME16 .....155 H5
  MARG CT9 .....113 H5
  RTW TN1 .....270 F5
  STH/RUST TN4 .....240 CB
  WADH TN5 .....294 A9
Western Undercliff RAM CT11 ...16 B7
Western Wy THMD SE28 .....27 N5
Westferry Circ POP/IOD E14 ....25 K4
Westferry Rd POP/IOD E14 .....25 K3
  SEV TN13 .....149 H7
Westfield CANTW/ST CT2 .....135 P7
Westfield Cl DVE DA12 .....246 D3
Westfield La RFOLK CT18 .....287 J5
Westfield Rd BECK BR3 .....61 MB
  BRCH CT7 .....110 G6
  BXLYHN DA7 .....45 L4
  CRO RM20 .....82 G6
  MARG CT9 .....112 A5
Westfields HDCN TN27 .....250 C1
Westfield Sole Rd
  MAID/BEAR ME14 .....126 A5
Westfield St WOOL/PLUM SE18...26 E6
Westfield Ter CRBK TN17 .....297 L6
Westfield VIs
  STPH/PW TN12 * 244 G4
West Gdns WAP E1W* 24 E3
Westgate Av BRCH CT7 .....111 P9
Westgate Bay Av WGOS CT8 ....111 L4
Westgate Cl CANTW/ST CT2 ...166 B3
Westgate Court Av
  CANTW/ST CT2 .....166 C3
Westgate Gv CANTW/ST CT2 ....4 C5
Westgate Hall Rd CANT CT1 * 4 C4
Westgate Rd BECK BR3 .....62 A7
  DART DA1 .....46 D7
  FAV ME13 .....133 H6
  SNWD SE25 .....83 N1
Westgate Ter WSTB CT5 .....105 L4
West Gn SIT ME10 .....99 N5
West Gv GNWCH SE10 .....42 A3
Westgrove La GNWCH SE10 ....42 A2
West Hallowes ELTH/MOT SE9 ..43 H9
Westharold SWLY BR8 .....65 M9
West Heath Cl DART DA1 * 45 H7
West Heath La SEV TN13 .....178 C4
West Heath Rd BXLYHN DA7 ....28 C8
  DART DA1 .....45 P7
West Hill DART DA1 .....46 D7
  EGRIN RH19 .....264 G8
  EGRIN RH19 .....265 H2
  ORP BR6 .....116 A6
  OXTED RH8 .....174 G6
West Hill Bank OXTED RH8....174 G6
Westhill Cl LGVE DA12 .....49 M9
West Hill Dr DART DA1 .....46 C7
West Hill Rd DART DA1 .....46 C7
West Hill Rd HB CT6 .....107 H1
West Holme ERITH DA8 .....29 J7
Westholme ORP BR6 .....86 F4
Westhorne Av ELTH/MOT SE9...43 H2
Westhurst Dr CHST BR7 .....63 M4
West Hythe Rd HYTHE CT21 ...307 P7
West India Av POP/IOD E14......25 K4
West India Dock Rd
  POP/IOD E14 .....25 J2
West Kent Av LGVE DA11 ....48 C7
Westland Dr HAYES BR2 .....85 J6
Westlands Av SIT ME10 .....129 J1
Westlands Rd HB CT6 .....106 G3
West Ln SWLY BR8 .....88 D3
Westlea Rd WOT/HER KT12 ...56 A2
Westmead Gdns FOLK CT20 ...310 A8
West Lea DEAL CT14 .....233 H2
West Leigh EGRIN RH19 .....265 J9

Westleigh Dr BMLY BR1 .....63 J8
Westleigh Rd WGOS CT8 .....111 L5
Westmarsh Cl
  MAID/SHEP ME15 .....186 C4
Westmarsh Dr MARG CT9 .....113 K3
Westmarsh Dro RCANTE CT3...170 B3
Westmead DIT/AY ME20 .....186 B5
Westmeads Rd WSTB CT5 .....105 M4
West Ml GVW DA11 .....49 K7
West Mill Rd DIT/AY ME20 .....124 B9
Westminster Av THHTH CR7 ....60 B8
Westminster Rd CANT CT1 .....137 H9
Westminster Wk
  MSTR CT12 * 143 H5
Westmont Cl BECK BR3 .....62 A6
Westmoors ASH TN23 .....282 A2
Westmoor St CHARL SE7 .....26 E7
Westmoreland Av WELL DA16...44 A8
Westmoreland Dr RSIT ME9 .....98 C5
Westmoreland Pl HAYES BR2 * ..62 E9
Westmoreland Rd HAYES BR2...85 H2
  WALW SE17 .....24 A9
Westmoreland Ter
  PGE/AN SE20 * 60 E1
Westmoreland Rd BH/WHM TN16 ..145 M6
Westmorland Cl
  MAID/SHEP ME15 .....186 B4
Westmorland Rd
  MAID/SHEP ME15 .....186 B4
Westmorland Wy MTCM CR4 ...82 C1
West Motney Wy RHAM ME8 ....97 K3
Westmount Av CHAT ME4 .....6 B5
Westmount Rd ELTH/MOT SE9...43 K4
West Norman Rd DVE/WH CT16 ..9 P7
West Oak BECK BR5 .....62 B7
Weston Av WTHK RM20 .....31 J8
Weston Gv BMLY BR1 .....62 D7
Weston Rd BMLY BR1 .....62 D7
  STRD ME2 .....71 H5
Weston St STHWK SE1 .....24 A6
Westonville Av MARG CT9 .....112 A4
Westover Gdns BRDST CT10 ...113 K6
Westover Rd BRDST CT10 .....113 K6
Westow Hl NRWD SE19 .....60 E5
Westow St NRWD SE19 .....60 E5
West Pde HYTHE CT21 .....308 G7
West Pk ELTH/MOT SE9 .....43 M1
West Park Av MARG CT9 .....113 J4
  STH/RUST TN4 .....240 DB
West Park Rd
  MAID/SHEP ME15 .....185 N1
West Parkside GNWCH SE10 ....25 P5
  WARL CR6 .....114 D9
West Pas IOS ME12 * 57 J6
West Pl LYDD TN29 .....334 E5
Westport St WCHPL E1 .....24 G2
Westree Cl MAIDW ME16 .....12 C6
Westree Rd MAIDW ME16 .....12 C6
West Rdg SIT ME10 .....129 L3
Weston Ton TN9 .....240 D2
West Rd CRBK TN17 .....274 DB
  CRBK TN17 .....295 N4
  FOLK CT20 .....309 P3
  GILL ME7 .....72 GB
  MSTR CT12 .....171 P3
West Shaw HART DA3 .....68 BB
West Side RDV CT15 .....261 P7
West St ASH TN25 .....2 C4
  BGR/WK TN15 .....151 J1
  BMLY BR1 .....62 E7
  BXLYHN DA7 .....45 H5
  CRO/NA CR0 .....83 H8
  DEAL CT14 .....233 H2
  DVW CT17 .....8 A6
  E/WMAL ME19 .....153 J4
  EGRIN RH19 .....265 HB
  ERITH DA8 .....29 J7
  FAV ME13 .....132 B9
  GILL ME7 .....7 K1
  GRAYS RM17 .....32 B9
  GVW DA11 .....49 M7
  IOS ME12 .....57 J5
  LING RH7 .....299 K7
  MAID/SHEP ME15 .....214 L1
  NROM TN28 .....336 F7
  OBOR ME11 .....77 H2
  RASHW TN26 .....251 K2
  RMAID ME17 .....188 D5
  RMAID ME17 .....189 M3
  RYE TN31 .....338 F7
  SIT ME10 .....129 M1
  STRD ME2 .....72 B9
West Street Pl CROY/NA CR0 * ..83 H8
West Tenter St WCHPL E1 .....24 E2
West Ter BFN/LL DA15 * 44 A9
  FOLK CT20 .....10 E5
West Thurrock Wy
  WTHK RM20 .....31 L8
West Undercliff RYE TN31 .....338 D7
Westview CHAT ME4 .....73 H5
West Vw HDCN TN27 * 247 L2
West View Cl HB CT6 .....107 H4
West View Gdns EGRIN RH19 ...265 HB
West View Rd DART DA1 .....46 F7
  SWLY BR8 .....88 C3
West Wk MAIDW ME16 .....154 C9
West Wy CROY/NA CR0 .....84 B6
  STMC/STPC BR5 .....86 E2
  WWKM BR4 .....84 G3
Westway RMAID ME17 .....185 HB
  RTWE/PEM TN2 .....271 H4
West Way Gdns CROY/NA CR0 ...84 A6
Westways BH/WHM TN16 .....176 D2
  EDEN TN8 .....206 DB
Westwell Cl STMC/STPC BR5 ....87 L5
Westwell Ct TENT TN30 .....300 C8
Westwell La RASHE TN25 .....221 MB
  RASHE TN25 .....252 B3
Westwood Av NRWD SE19 .....60 C7
Westwood Cl BMLY BR1 .....63 H9
Westwood La WELL DA16 .....44 C5
Westwood Pk FSTH SE23 .....41 H8
Westwood Pl PAV ME13 .....132 GB
  SYD SE26 * 60 G4

West Wood Rd RSIT ME9 .....127 L6
Westwood Rd BRDST CT10 .....112 C9
  CAN/RD E16 .....26 C4
  MAID/SHEP ME15 .....185 M4
  MEO DA13 .....68 C4
  STH/RUST TN4 .....269 N5
  STPH/PW TN12 .....212 F4
West Woodside BXLY DA5 .....44 C9
Westwood Wy SEV TN13 .....148 C7
Wetheral Dr MAID/BEAR ME14 ..155 N1
Weybridge Cl MAID ME15 .....125 P1
Weybridge Ct STHWK SE1 * 24 E8
Weybridge Rd THHTH CR7 .....82 F1
Weyburn Dr MSTR CT12 .....142 C3
Wey Cl WALD ME5 .....95 P9
Weyhill Cl MAID/BEAR ME14 ...155 P6
Weyhill Rd WCHPL E1 * 24 D2
Weyman Rd BKHTH/KID SE3 ...42 G7
Weymouth Cl EHAM E6 .....27 J2
  FOLKN CT19 .....310 A5
Weymouth Rd FOLKN CT19 ....310 A5
  FOLKN CT19 * 310 A4
Wey St RASHW TN26 .....324 D3
Wharfedale Gdns
  STRHM/NOR SW16 .....82 E1
Wharfedale Rd MARG CT9 .....15 K6
  RDART DA2 .....49 J9
Wharf La HOO/HM ME3 .....52 B2
Wharf Rd GILL ME7 * 75 J8
  GRAYS RM17 .....32 A9
  GVE DA12 .....50 A7
  MAID/SHEP ME15 .....105 K1
  SLH/COR SS17 .....34 D2
Wharfside Cl ERITH DA8 .....29 LB
Wharfside Rd CAN/RD E16 .....26 F1
The Wharf GRH DA9 * 25 P1
Wharncliffe Gdns SNWD SE25 ...60 E8
Wharncliffe Rd SNWD SE25....60 DB
Wharton Gdns KEN/WIL TN24 ....3 K7
Wharton Rd BMLY BR1 .....62 F7
Whatley Rd EDUL SE22 .....40 F6
  PGE/AN SE20 .....61 K6
Whatman Cr
  MAID/BEAR ME14 .....155 P6
Whatman Rd FSTH SE23 .....41 K8
Whatmer Cl CANTW/ST CT2 ...137M7
Wheatcroft Cl SIT ME10 .....130 A1
Wheatcroft Gv RHAM ME8 .....97 J7
Wheatear Wy WALD ME5 .....95 N7
Wheatfield Cl MAIDW ME16 .....155M4
Wheatfield Cl CRBK TN17 .....297 P2
Wheatfield Dr CRBK TN17 .....297 N5
Wheatfield Lea CRBK TN17 .....297 P2
Wheatfields
  MAID/BEAR ME14 .....156 A8
  WALD ME5 .....126 A3
Wheathill Wy CRBK TN17 .....297 P2
Wheathill Rd PGE/AN SE20 .....61 HB
Wheatley Cl CRO DA9 .....47 N6
Wheatley Rd MSTR CT12 .....143 H5
  WSTB CT5 .....105 M4
Wheatsheaf Cl FAV ME13 .....164 B1
  MAID/SHEP ME15 .....186 B2
Wheat Sheaf Cl POP/IOD E14 ....25 P1
Wheatsheaf Gdns IOS ME12 * ...57 J7
Wheatsheaf HI RSEV TN14 .....117 N3
  RSEV TN14 .....177 N7
Wheatsheaf La RDV CT15 .....262 A6
Wheatsheaf Wy TONN TN10 ...210 C8
Wheeler Av OXTED RH8 .....174 G5
Wheeler La WCHPL E1 * 24 C1
Wheeler Pl HAYES BR2 .....85 L1
Wheeler's La RMAID ME17 .....215 J2
Wheelers Wy EGRIN RH19 ....264 B5
Wheelock Cl ERITH DA8 .....45 K1
The Wheelwrights
  RHAM ME8 * 98 E3
Wheelwrights Wy
  SWCH CT13 * .....201 JB
Whelan Wy WLGTN SM6 .....82 C7
Wheler Ct FAV ME13 .....132 D6
Wheler Rd HDCN TN27 .....221 H2
Whetsted Rd STPH/PW TN12 ...242 E1
Whetstone Rd BKHTH/KID SE3 ..42 G3
Whidborne Cl DEPT SE8 .....41 N3
Whiffen's Av CHAT ME4 .....6 D3
Whiffen's Av West CHAT ME4 * ...6 D3
Whiffin Wk E/WMAL ME19 .....154 A3
Whimbrel Cl ERITH DA8 .....45 K1
Whimbrel Gn DIT/AY ME20 ...153 N2
The Whimbrels CHAT ME4 * 73 H6
Whinchat Rd THMD SE28 .....27 L6
Whinfell Wy GVE DA12 .....50 E4
Whinless Rd DVW CT17 .....291 H7
Whinyates Rd ELTH/MOT SE9 ...43 J4
Whippendell Cl
  STMC/STPC BR5 .....64 D7
Whistler Rd TONN TN10 .....210 G3
Whiston Av RASHW TN26 .....280 B4
Whitbread Rd BROCKY SE4 .....41 L5
Whitburn Rd LEW SE13 .....41 P6
Whitby Cl BH/WHM TN16 .....145 L4
  GRH DA9 .....47 N6
Whitby Ter DVE/WH CT16 * 291 J4
Whitcher Cl NWCR SE14 .....25 H9
Whitchurch Cl MAIDW ME16 ...12 B4
Whitcombe Cl WALD ME5 .....125 P3
White Acre Dr DEAL CT14 .....232 G9
Whiteacre La RCANTW CT4 .....225 L6
White Av GVW DA11 .....49 N9
Whitebeam Av HAYES BR2 .....86 B4
Whitebeam Cl ASH TN23 .....252 A5
  BGR/WK TN15 .....149M2

Whitebeam Dr RMAID ME17 ...184 G8
White Bear Pas
  STH/RUST TN4 * 22 D6
Whiteline Gdns
  STPH/PW TN12 .....213 H4
Whitebread La RYE TN31 .....330 C5
Whitechapel High St
  WCHPL E1 .....24 C2
Whitechapel Rd WCHPL E1 .....24 C2
White Church La WCHPL E1 .....24 D2
White Cliffs Country Trail
  RDV CT15 .....261 N2
  SWCH CT13 .....201 L9
Whitecliff Wy FOLKN CT19 .....11 K1
White Cottage Rd
  TONN TN10 .....210 F4
Whitecroft SWLY BR8 .....65 NB
Whitecroft Cl BECK BR3 .....84 C1
Whitecroft Wy BECK BR3 .....84 G1
Whitefield Cl STMC/STPC BR5....64 F1
Whitefield Rd STH/RUST TN4 ...270 D2
Whitefoot La CAT SE6 .....62 A2
Whitefoot Ter BMLY BR1 .....62 D2
White Friars SEV TN13 .....178 F3
Whitefriars SWCH CT13 .....201 N1
Whitefriars Meadow
  SWCH CT13 * 201 P2
Whitefriars St CANT CT1 .....5 F5
Whitegate Cl STH/RUST TN4 ...240 C9
Whitegates Av BGR/WK TN15 ..120 B1
Whitehall LYDD TN29 .....334 E5
Whitehall Bridge Rd
  CANTW/ST CT2 .....4 B3
Whitehall Cl CANTW/ST CT2 .....4 A4
Whitehall Dr RMAID ME17 .....187 N9
Whitehall Gdns CANTW/ST CT2...4 C4
Whitehall La ERITH DA8 .....45 P3
  GRAYS RM17 .....32 D9
Whitehall Pde EGRIN RH19 ....265 JB
Whitehall Pl CAR SM5 .....82 AB
Whitehall Rd CANTW/ST CT2 ....5 D7
  GRAYS RM17 .....32 D7
  HAYES BR2 .....85 N2
  MAID/BEAR ME14 .....157 K6
  SIT ME10 .....129 H1
  THHTH CR7 .....82 F2
Whitehall Wy RASHE TN25 .....285 L7
White Hart Cl SEV TN13 .....179 H4
White Hart Pde SEV TN13 * 148 D7
The White Hart Pde
  SEV TN13 * 148 D7
White Hart Rd ORP BR6 .....87 H4
  WOOL/PLUM SE18 .....27 M7
White Hart Wd SEV TN13 .....179 H5
White Hart Yd GVE DA12 * 49 M7
  STHWK SE1 .....24 A4
Whitehaven Cl HAYES BR2 .....85 K1
Whitehead Cl RDART DA2 .....66 C2
Whiteheads La
  MAID/BEAR ME14 .....156 EB
White Hl RASHE TN25 .....223 J2
White Hill Cl RCANTW CT4 .....196 F5
Whitehill La GVE DA12 .....69 P2
Whitehill Pde GVE DA12 .....69 N2
White Hill Rd
  MAID/BEAR ME14 .....126 G4
Whitehill Rd DART DA1 .....46 A6
  GVE DA12 .....69 N1
  MEO DA13 .....68 B6
White Horse Av HCHST BR7 ....63 L3
  RFOLK CT18 .....288 F9
Whitehorse Hl WALD ME5 * 7 J4
White Horse La CANT CT1 * 4 E4
Whitehorse La SNWD SE25.....83 K1
White Horse Rd CRO/NA CR0 ...83 K1
Whitehouse Dro RCANTE CT3...171 L4
White House Rd RSEV TN14 ...178 G6
White Kennett St WCHPL E1 ...24 C2
Whitelake Rd THMD SE28 .....210 F5
Whiteleaves Ri STRD ME2 .....94 A4
Whiteley Rd NRWD SE19 .....60 D4
White Lion Ct BANK EC3V * 24 A2
Whitelocks Cl RCANTW CT4 ...228 A5
White Ldg NRWD SE19 .....60 B6
White Lodge Cl SEV TN13 .....148 G8
White Marsh Ct WSTB CT5 * 105 M4
Whitenbrook HYTHE CT21 .....309 N4
Whiteness Dro RCANTE CT3....113 M4
Whiteoak Rd TON TN9 * 240 E2
White Oak Cl DEAL CT14 .....62 AB
White Oak Gdns BFN/LL DA15...44 B8
White Oak Sq SWLY BR8 * 88 E3
White Post Hl EYN DA4 .....89 M4
White Post La MEO DA13 .....92 C1
Whitepost La PECK SE15 * 41 J1
White Post Rd PECK SE15 .....24 D1
White Rd CHAT ME4 * 6 D5
White Rock Pl MAIDW ME16 ...12 C6
Whites Grounds STHWK SE9 ....24 B5
Whites Grounds Est
  STHWK SE1 * 24 B5
Whites HI DEAL CT14 .....231 H7
White's La HAWK TN18 .....317 K4
Whites Meadow BMLY BR1 * ...86 B1
White's Rw WCHPL E1 .....24 C1
Whitethorn Gdns
  CROY/NA CR0 .....83 N6
Whitewall Rd STRD ME2 .....19 J1

Whitewall Wy STRD ME2 .....19 J1
White Rd Av OBOR ME11 .....77 H1
Whitewebbs Wy
  STMC/STPC BR5 .....64 B7
Whitewood Cottages
  BH/WHM TN16 .....145 M5
White Wood Rd SWCH CT13 ...201 J9
Whitfield Av ASH TN23 .....252 E9
Whitfield Av BRDST CT10 .....113 K6
  DVE/WH CT16 .....291 H1
Whitfield HI DVE/WH CT16.....290 C3
Whitfield Rd BXLYHN DA7 .....45 H1
  GNWCH SE10 .....42 B2
White San SAND/SEL CR2 .....83 H9
Whitgift St CROY/NA CR0 .....83 J5
Whiting Crs FAV ME13 .....132 C5
Whitings Wy EHAM E6 .....27 H1
Whitmore Av CDW/CHF RM16 ...32 C3
Whitmore Cl CDW/CHF RM16 ...33 M2
Whitmore Rd BECK BR3 .....61 N8
Whitmore St MAIDW ME16 .....185 H1
Whitney Wk SCUP DA14 .....64 G5
Whitstable Cl BECK BR3 .....61 M7
Whitstable Pl CROY/NA CR0 ...83 H8
Whitstable Rd CANTW/ST CT2 ....1 A1
  FAV ME13 .....133 H6
  HB CT6 .....106 F3
Whitstone La BECK BR3 .....84 E2
Whittell Gdns SYD SE26 .....61 J2
Whittington Av BANK EC3V 24 A2
Whittington Ter RDV CT15 * ...259 N1
Whitworth Rd SNWD SE25 .....60 E9
  WOOL/PLUM SE18 .....43 L1
Whyborne Crest
  RTWE/PEM TN2 .....270 G7
Whyman Av CHAT ME4 .....95 M5
Whytecliffs BRDST CT10 .....143M2
Wichling Cl CANTW/ST CT2 ...166 F1
  STMC/STPC BR5 .....87 L5
Wickenden Crs KEN/WIL TN24...253 K9
Wickenden Rd SEV TN13 .....149 H7
Wicken La HDCN TN27 .....221 K5
Wickens Meadow
  RSEV TN14 * 148 L4
Wickers Oake NRWD SE19 * ...60 F3
Wicker St WCHPL E1 * 24 D2
The Wickets KEN/WIL TN24 * ..283 J1
The Wicket CROY/NA CR0 .....84 D6
Wickham Av CROY/NA CR0 .....84 B6
  RAM CT11 .....143 M4
Wickham Cha WWKM BR4 .....84 G4
Wickham Cl RSIT ME9 .....98 CB
  WCHPL E1 * 24 F1
Wickham Ct WWKM BR4 * .....84 GB
Wickham Court La
  RCANTE CT3 .....168 E5
Wickham Court Rd
  WWKM BR4 * 84 F6
Wickham Crs WWKM BR4 .....84 F6
Wickham Fld RSEV TN14 * 148 E1
Wickham Gdns BROCKY SE4 ...41 M4
  STH/RUST TN4 .....270 A3
Wickham La ABYW SE2 * 28 E6
  WELL DA16 .....28 E6
Wickham Rd BECK BR3 .....61 P9
  BROCKY SE4 .....41 M4
  CDW/CHF RM16 .....33 K5
  CROY/NA CR0 .....83 P6
  GRH DA9 * 47 N6
  White St ROCH ME1 * 95 J3
Wickhams Wy HART DA3 .....91 J2
Wickham Ter BGR/WK TN15 ....77 H2
Wickham Wy BECK BR3 .....84 F1
Wickhurst Rd RSEV TN14 .....178 EB
Wick La RCANTW CT4 .....228 G2
Wicks Cl ELTH/MOT SE9 .....63 H5
Wicksteed Cl BXLY DA5 .....65 M2
Wickwood St CMBW SE5 .....40 B3
Widbury RTW TN1 .....269 L5
Widbury Cl RTW TN1 .....269 L5
Widdecombe Rd ELTH/MOT SE9 ...63 J4
Widegate St WCHPL E1 .....24 B1
Widgeon Cl CAN/RD E16 .....26 C2
Widgeon Rd ERITH DA8 .....46 B1
  STRD ME2 .....71M9
Widgeon Wk RFOLK CT18 .....288 E9
Widmore Lodge Rd BMLY BR1 ...63 HB
Widmore Rd BMLY BR1 .....62 GB
Widred Rd DVW CT17 .....8 A2
Wierton Hl RMAID ME17 .....216 A5
Wierton La RMAID ME17 .....186 B9
Wierton Rd RMAID ME17 .....216 B1
Wife of Bath Hl
  CANTW/ST CT2 .....166 B4
Wigmore La RDV CT15 .....230 EB
Wigmore Rd RHAM ME8 .....96 E9
Wigmore Wy RDV CT15 .....230 D9
Wigwam Paddocks
  BRCH CT7 .....111 H5
Wihtred Rd RSIT ME9 .....130 C3
Wilberforce Rd FOLK CT20 .....187 JB
  RMAID ME17 * .....185 JB
Wilberforce Wy GVE DA12 .....69 P4
Wilbrough Rd BRCH CT7 .....111 H6
Wilcox Cl RCANTE CT3 .....228 G2
Wilde Cl TIL RM18 .....49 N3
Wilderness Av
  BGR/WK TN15 .....149 L7
Wilderwick Rd EGRIN RH19 ...265 K1
Wilderness Gdns RYE TN31 ...329 P6
Wilderness Hl MARG CT9 .....15 K4
Wilderness Rd EGRIN RH19 ...265 K1
Wilderness Rd CHST BR7 .....63 M6
  OXTED RH8 .....175 H6
Wilde Rd ERITH DA8 .....45 L1
Wilderwick Rd EGRIN RH19 ...265 K1
Wildfell Rd CAT SE6 .....41 PB
Wild Goose Dr PECK SE15 .....41 J2
Wildish Rd FAV ME13 .....132 D5

Wildman Cl RHAM ME8...............126 G2
Wild's Rents STHWK SE1...............24 B6
Wildwood Cl LEE/GVPK SE12....42 D8
Wildwood Gld GILL ME7...............187 P9
Wiles Av NROM TN28...............336 C7
Wilfred Av RAIN RM13...............29 M1
Wilfred Rd RAM CT11...............16 C2
Wilfred St GVE DA12...............49 M7
Wilgate Green Rd FAV ME13...162 B5
Wilkes Rd BRDST CT10...............143 K1
Wilkes St WCHPL E1...............24 C1
Wilkie Rd BRCH CT7...............111 H5
Wilkinson Dr DEAL CT14...............253 J6
Wilkinson Gdns NRWD SE19...60 E7
Wilkinson Rd CAN/RD E16...26 C2
Wilks Av DART DA1...............66 F1
Wilks Cl RHAM ME8...............97 L4
Wilks Gdns CROY/NA CRO...84 B5
Will Adams Wy RHAM ME8...96 C5
Will Crooks Gdns
 ELTH/MOT SE9...............43 H5
Willement Rd FAV ME15...132 E6
Willenhall Rd
 WOOL/PLUM SE18...............27 J8
Willersley Av BFN/LL DA15...84 B7
 ORP BR6...............86 E7
Willersley Cl BFN/LL DA15...84 A7
Willesborough Ct...............253 K8
Willesborough Rd
 KEN/WIL TN24...............253 J4
Willesley Gdns CRBK TN17...298 A1
Willett Cl STMC/STPC BR5...82 F2
Willett Hl THHTH CR7...............82 C7
Willetts Hl MSTR CT12...............140 E5
Willetts La RRTW TN3...............268 B4
Willett Wy STMC/STPC BR5...86 E2
William Av FOLKN CT19...............10 A1
 MARG CT9...............113 H5
William Barefoot Dr
 ELTH/MOT SE9...............63 L1
William Booth Rd
 PGE/AN SE20...............60 G7
William Cl LEW SE13...............42 A4
William Ellis Wy
 BERM/RHTH SE16 *...............24 D6
William Gibbs Ct FAV ME13 *...132 C2
William Hall Ter FAV ME13 *...132 D7
William Judge Cl TENT TN30...301 L8
William Luck Cl
 STPH/PW TN12...............212 F4
William Margrie Cl PECK SE15 *...40 C3
William Petty Wy
 STMC/STPC BR5...............87 K5
William Pitt Av DEAL CT14...232 G3
William Rd HYTHE CT21...309 J5
William Rigby Dr ASH ME12...52 N9
William Rd ASH TN23...............252 E9
 STRD ME3...............94 B4
Williamson Rd GNWCH SE10...26 A8
William Rd LYDD TN29...343 K6
William Sq BERM/RHTH SE16...25 H4
William St FAV ME13 *...............132 C6
 GRAYS RM17...............32 D9
 GVE DA12...............49 M8
 HB CT6...............107 L1
 RHAM ME8...............97 H4
 SIT ME10...............129 M2
 STH/RUST TN4...............270 D3
Willicombe Pk RTWE/PEM TN2...23 K2
Williams Av ASH TN23...............282 B5
Willington Dr DEAL CT14...233 H7
Willington Pl DEAL CT14...............233 H7
Willington Rd DVE/WH CT16...291 H2
Willington Gn
 MAID/SHEP ME15...............186 B4
Willington St
 MAID/SHEP ME15...............156 C9
 MAID/SHEP ME15...............186 B5
Willis Ct IOS ME12...............77 P2
Willis La RASHW TN26...325 J1
Willis Rd CROY/NA CRO...83 H4
 ERITH DA8...............49 J2
Willop Wy LYDD TN29...327 K3
Willoughby Av CROY/NA CRO...82 E8
Willoughby Wy CHARL SE7...26 C7
Willow Av BFN/LL DA15...44 C7
 BRDST CT10...............113 J9
 FAV ME13...............132 D6
 HOO/HM ME3 *...............73 L4
 SWLY BR8...............88 E1
Willowbank Cl LYDD TN29...337 M1
Willowbrook Est PECK SE15 *...40 F1
Willowbrook Rd PECK SE15...24 C9
Willowby Gdns RHAM ME8...127 H1
Willow Farm Wy HB CT6...107 P4
Willowfields Cl
 WOOL/PLUM SE18...............27 M8
Willow Gdns HOO/HM ME3 *...73 K2
Willow Gv CHST BR7...............63 L5
Willowherb Cl CHAT ME4...73 J6
Willow Industries
 MAID/BEAR ME14 *...............155 L1
Willow La STPH/PW TN12...243 L4
 WOOL/PLUM SE18...............26 C7
Willow Lea EGRIN RH19...265 J8
Willow Md EGRIN RH19...265 J8
Willowmead DIT/AY ME20...153 M2
Willow Mt CROY/NA CRO...83 K8

Willow Pk RSEV TN14...............148 E2
Willow Ri HDCN TN27...............47 H9
Willow Rd DART DA1...............46 C9
 DEAL CT14...............232 B6
 DIT/AY ME20...............153 N1
 ERITH DA8...............46 A2
 STRD ME3...............71 N9
 WSTB CT5...............105 K9
Willows Ct CANTW/ST CT2 *...136 B9
Willowside SNOD ME6...............125 P4
The Willows BECK BR5 *...............61 N7
 BGR/WK TN15 *...............150 C6
 CANTW/ST CT2 *...............137 M9
 GRAYS RM17...............32 C9
 HB CT6 *...............107 J2
 HOO/HM ME3 *...............56 D2
 RASHW TN26...............281 L7
 RHAM ME8...............97 H4
 RSIT ME9...............98 C8
 WALD ME5 *...............125 L4
Willow Ter EYN DA4 *...............89 K6
 PGE/AN SE20 *...............61 H7
Willow Tree Cl HB CT6...............108 A5
 KEN/WIL TN24...............253 J8
Willow Tree Rd
 RTWE/PEM TN2...............270 B7
Willow Tree Wk BMLY BR1...62 F7
Willowtree Wy
 STRHM/NOR SW16...............60 A7
Willow V CHST BR7...............63 L5
Willow Wk DART DA1 *...............46 E6
 MEO DA13...............122 A2
 ORP BR6...............86 C7
 RTWE/PEM TN2...............241 H9
 STHWK SE1 *...............24 J7
Willow Wy HDCN TN27...............278 E9
 MAID/SHEP ME15...............13 J7
 MARG CT9...............112 B5
 SYD SE26...............61 H2
 WSTB CT5...............106 B6
Willow Waye RDV CT15...260 E1
Willow Wents WBY/YAL TN15...182 D2
Willow Wood Crs SNWD SE25...83 K5
Willow Wood Rd MEO DA13...122 A5
Willsham Rd FSTH SE23...28 A8
Wilman St NWCR SE14...41 J2
Wilson's Rd RAM CT11...............16 C5
Wilman Rd STH/RUST TN4...270 D3
Wilmar Gdns WWKM BR4...84 E5
Wilmington Av ORP BR6...87 K6
Wilmington Court Rd
 RDART DA5...............66 A2
Wilmington Wy RHAM ME8...96 E4
Wilmot Cl PECK SE15 *...............40 C1
Wilmot Rd DART DA1...............46 A8
Wilmott Pl SWCH CT13...............201 J8
Wilmount St
 WOOL/PLUM SE18...............27 J7
Wilson Av DEAL CT14...............232 E6
 ROCH ME1...............95 J5
Wilson Cl KEN/WIL TN24...253 L8
 MAID/SHEP ME15...............186 B4
 RTON TN11...............210 B5
 SAND/SEL CR2...............83 J9
 SLH/COR SS17...............34 B1
Wilson Gv BERM/RHTH SE16...24 E5
Wilson La EYN DA4...............67 M8
Wilson Rd CMBW SE5...............40 D2
 TONN TN10...............211 H5
Wilsons La MAID/SHEP ME15...184 F7
Wilson's Pl POP/IOD E14...25 J2
Wilson St LVPST EC2M...............24 A1
Wilsons Wy MEO DA13...............122 A2
Wiltie Gdns FOLKN CT19...............10 D3
Wilton Cl DEAL CT14...............232 G4
Wilton Dr DIT/AY ME20...............154 A4
Wilton Rd ABYW SE2...............28 B6
 FOLKN CT19...............10 A2
 MSTR CT12...............142 E5
Wilton Ter SIT ME10 *...............99 J9
Wiltshire Cl RDART DA2...............47 K8
 WALD ME5...............95 P6
Wiltshire Rd BRXN/ST SW9...40 A4
 ORP BR6...............86 D1
 THHTH CR7...............60 A9
Wiltshire Wy
 MAID/SHEP ME15...............186 B3
 RTWE/PEM TN2...............270 C1
Wimborne Cl STMC/STPC BR5...64 B9
Wimborne Cl LEE/GVPK SE12...42 D6
Wimborne Pl MSTR CT12...142 G4
Wimborne Wy BECK BR3...61 K9
Wimbourne Dr RHAM ME8...96 G8
Wimpole St HAYES BR2...............85 M1
Wimshurst Cl CROY/NA CRO...82 D5
Winans Wk BRXN/ST SW9...40 A3
Winant Wy DVE/WH CT16...291 J4
Winch Cl CRBK TN17...............298 C4
Winchcomb Gdns
 ELTH/MOT SE9...............43 J4
Wincheap CANT CT1...............166 D6
Wincheap Rbt CANT CT1...4 C6
Winchelsea Av BXLYHN DA7...45 H1
Winchelsea Cl DVW CT17 *...8 A4
Winchelsea Rd DVW CT17...291 J8
 RYE TN31...............338 E7
 WALD ME5...............95 N9
Winchelsea St DVW CT17...291 J8
Winchelsea Ter DVW CT17...291 J8
Winchester Av MSTR CT12...125 L1
Winchester Cl HAYES BR2...84 A9
Winchester Crs GVE DA12...69 P2
Winchester Gdns CANT CT1...166 F6
Winchester Gv WALD TN15...20 E1
Winchester Ms DEAL CT14...232 G6
Winchester Pk HAYES BR2...84 A9
Winchester Pl
 MAID/BEAR ME14 *...............13 G2
Winchester Rd BXLYHN DA7...44 F8

Winchester Sq STHWK SE1...24 A4
Winchester St STHWK SE1...24 A4
Winchester Wy RHAM ME8...97 K6
Winchfield Rd SYD SE26...61 L4
Winch's Garth STPH/PW TN12...246 C4
Wincliff Rd TON TN9...............240 E1
Wincrofts Dr ELTH/MOT SE9...60 C7
Windall Cl NRWD SE19...............60 C7
Windermere Av RAM CT11...142 F5
Windermere Cl DART DA1...46 B9
 ORP BR6...............86 C7
Windermere Dr RHAM ME8...96 C7
Windermere Gdns
 RCANTE CT5...............199 J9
Windermere Gv SIT ME10...129 L2
Windermere Rd BXLYHN DA7...45 J5
 CROY/NA CRO...............83 L5
 WWKM BR4...............85 H6
Winfield Cl SYD SE26...............61 K3
Windham Av CROY/NA CRO...114 C4
Wind Hl HDCN TN27...............220 D3
Windle Cl NRWD SE19...............70 A3
Winding Hl FAV ME15...............163 H5
Windlass Pl DEPT SE8...............25 H7
Windley Cl FSTH SE23...............61 J1
Windmill Cl
 BERM/RHTH SE16 *...............24 D7
 CANT CT1...............5 K4
 KEN/WIL TN24...............253 K8
 LEW SE13 *...............42 A3
 RCANTW CT4...............197 M2
 STRD ME2...............72 E6
Windmill Cr RMAID ME17...185 N8
Windmill Dr HAYES BR2...85 M8
Windmill Gv CROY/NA CRO...83 H4
Windmill Hts
 MAID/BEAR ME14...............156 E8
Windmill Hl BGR/WK TN15...151 P5
 RMAID ME17...............218 C2
 STPH/PW TN12...............243 J8
Windmill La BGR/WK TN15...151 P4
 EGRIN RH19...............264 C5
 FAV ME13...............132 E4
 WADH TN5...............294 D7
Windmill La East
 E/WMAL ME19...............153 J6
Windmill La West
 E/WMAL ME19...............153 J6
Windmill Pde RAM CT11 *...16 C5
Windmill Rd BGR/WK TN15...151 N5
Windmill Pl RAM CT11 *...16 D5
Windmill Quay Rd IOS ME12...78 D6
Windmill Ri IOS ME12...............78 E1
Windmill Rd CANT CT1...167 H4
 CROY/NA CRO...............83 H4
 GILL ME7...............7 H6
 HB CT6...............107 M4
 MTCM CR4...............60 A6
 SEV TN15...............178 D6
 SIT ME10...............99 L8
 WSTB CT5...............105 L7
Windmill St GVE DA12...............49 M8
 HYTHE CT21...............308 C6
 RTWE/PEM TN2...............23 H5
 STRD ME2...............72 C5
Windmill Vw MARG CT9 *...112 F5
Windmill Wk MSTR CT12...142 G3
Windrose Cl
 BERM/RHTH SE16...............24 C5
Windrush La FSTH SE23...............61 K2
Windsor Av CDW/CHF RM16...32 C5
 CHAT ME4...............95 L4
 MARG CT9...............112 C3
Windsor Cl BRDST CT10...113 K8
 CHST BR7...............63 M4
 MAID/BEAR ME14...............13 J1
 WNWD SE27...............61 L9
Windsor Ct MARG CT9 *...112 C4
Windsor Dr DART DA1...............46 A7
 ORP BR6...............117 H1
 SIT ME10...............129 L3
Windsor Gdns CROY/NA CRO...82 D7
 HB CT6...............106 C3
 IOS ME12...............80 E4
Windsor Gv WNWD SE27...............60 C3
Windsor Ms CAT SE6...............42 A9
 NROM TN28...............337 H5
Windsor Pl EGRIN RH19...............265 K8
Windsor Rd BXLYHS DA6...44 G5
 CANT CT1...............166 E7
 GILL ME7...............7 J4
 GVE DA12...............69 M3
 MSTR CT12...............142 C5
 THHTH CR7...............60 B8
Windsor Wk CMBW SE5...............40 E5
Windspoint Dr PECK SE15 *...24 D9
Windward Rd ROCH ME1...............95 H5
Windy Rdg BMLY BR1...............62 F3
Windyridge GILL ME7...............96 B5
Wine Cl IAP E1W...............24 E3
Winehouse La RFOLK CT18...289 M9
Winfield La BGR/WK TN15...181 H1
Winford Ms ROCH ME1...............95 H2
Winforton St GNWCH SE10...42 A2
Winfrieds Cl CRBK TN17 *...319 L3
Wingate Crs CROY/NA CRO...82 C3
Wingate Rd FOLKN CT19...310 C4
 SCUP DA14...............64 E4
Wingfield GRAYS RM17...............32 A8
Wingfield Ms PECK SE15 *...40 G7
Wingfield Rd PECK SE15 *...49 M8
Wingfield St PECK SE15 *...40 F7
Wingham Cl
 MAID/SHEP ME15...............186 C4
 RHAM ME8...............96 C4
Wingham Rd RCANTE CT3...168 F8
Wingham Well La
 RCANTE CT3...............198 C1
Wingmore Rd HNHL SE24...40 C4
Wing Rd IOS ME12...............80 F6

Wingrove Dr
 MAID/BEAR ME14...............156 E7
 STRD ME2...............19 G1
Wingrove Hl DVW CT17...............156 E7
Wingrove Rd CAT SE6...............62 C1
Wings Ct BRDST CT10...............113 N8
Winifred Rd COB DA12...............143 H2
Winifred Rd DART DA1...............29 K8
Winifred Rd CROY/NA CRO...156 C9
Winnifred St CAN/RD E16...26 C4
Winlaton Rd BMLY BR1...............62 B3
Winn Common Rd
 WOOL/PLUM SE18...............27 M9
Winnipeg Dr DVE/WH CT16...291 J4
Winnipeg Dr ORP BR6...............116 C1
Winn Rd LEE/GVPK SE12...42 E9
Winser Rd CRBK TN17...............319 N5
Winsford Rd CAT SE6...............61 N2
Winsor Ter EHAM E6...............27 J1
Winstanley Crs RAM CT11...143 J4
Winstanley Rd IOS ME12...57 L6
Winston Av E/WMAL ME19...153 J9
Winston Cl CANT CT1...............167 H5
 GRH DA9...............29 M7
Winston Ct BRCH CT7...............111 H5
Winston Dr STRD ME2...............72 C6
Winstone Scott Av RRTW TN3...269 K4
Winston Gdns HB CT6...............108 A6
Winterage La RFOLK CT18...288 C5
Winterborne Av ORP BR6...86 E7
Winterbourne Rd SE6...41 M9
Winterbrook Rd HNHL SE24...40 E2
Winter Dr RFOLK CT18...............288 C7
Winterfield La E/WMAL ME19...153 M4
Wintergreen Cl CHAT ME4...73 J6
Winterstoke Crs RAM CT11...17 K1
Winterstoke Rd CAT SE6...41 M9
Winterstoke Wy RAM CT11...17 H1
Winthorpe St WCHPL E1...............24 E1
Winthrop St WCHPL E1...............24 E1
Winton Rd ORP BR6...............86 C8
Winton Wy LYDD TN29...............326 E9
Wireless Rd BH/WHM TN16...115 N9
Wire Mill La LING RH7...............234 B9
The Wirrals MAID ME5...............125 M1
Wirral Wood Cl CHST BR7...63 L5
Wisbeach Rd CROY/NA CRO...83 J2
Wiseacre RRTW TN3...............295 H4
Wise's La BGR/WK TN15...121 H5
Wise's Wy RAM CT11 *...............17 J5
Wishart Rd BKHTH/KID SE3...43 K1
The Wish RASHW TN26...303 L9
Wish Ward RYE TN31...............338 E7
Wisley Rd STMC/STPC BR5...64 C6
Wistaria Cl ORP BR6...............86 C6
Wisteria Gdns SWLY BR8...65 M8
Wisteria Rd LEW SE13...............42 B5
Witches La SEV TN15...............148 C8
Witham Rd PGE/AN SE20...61 J9
Witherby Cl SAND/SEL CR2...83 K9
Witham St SWRD SE1...............18 A2
Withens Cl STMC/STPC BR5...87 K1
Witherton Wy ELTH/MOT SE9...43 J9
Witham Rd RRTW TN3...............269 H9
Witley Crs CROY/NA CRO...114 F1
Witney Pth FSTH SE23...............61 K2
Wittersham Cl WALD ME5...95 N9
Wittersham La RYE TN31...332 E8
Wittersham Rd BMLY BR1...62 D4
 CRBK TN17...............331 J1
 TENT TN30...............320 D9
 TENT TN30...............332 E2
Wivenhoe Ash TN23...............282 B5
Wivenhoe Cl PECK SE15...40 G4
 RHAM ME8...............97 K4
Wiverton Rd SYD SE26...61 J5
Woburn Rd CROY/NA CRO...83 H5
Wodeham Gdns WCHPL E1...24 D1
Wodehouse Av PECK SE15...40 F2
Wodehouse Cl DIT/AY ME20...123 N9
Wodehouse Rd DART DA1...46 D5
Wokindon Rd
 CDW/CHF RM16...............33 J6
Wolds Dr ORP BR6...............86 B8
The Wold CHAT CR3...............144 D7
Wolfe Cl HAYES BR2...............85 K3
Wolfe Crs CHARL SE7...............26 C5
Wolfe Rd MADW ME16...184 C1
Wolfe Ter HAYES BR2...............291 H4
Wolfington Rd WNWD SE27...60 B5
Wolfram Cl LEW SE13...............42 C6
Wolfs Rd OXTED RH8...............175 K2
Wolfs Wd OXTED RH8...............175 K8
Wollaston Cl RHAM ME8...126 C2
Wollaston Rd DEAL CT14...233 J5
Wolseley Av HB CT6...............24 A1
Wolseley Rd KEN/WIL TN24...270 F1
Wolseley St STH/RUST TN4...270 F1
Wolsey Cl ELTH/MOT SE9 *...43 K7
Wolsey Crs CROY/NA CRO...114 D5
Wolsey Ms ORP BR6...............86 G9
Wolsey St WCHPL E1...............24 E1
Wolsey Ct DART DA1...............46 B5
Wolvercote Rd ABYW SE2...28 C5
Wombwell Gdns GVW DA11...69 J1
Wood Av FOLKN CT19...............310 C4
Woodbank Rd BMLY BR1...62 A7
Woodbastwick Rd SYD SE26...61 K5
Woodberry Dr SIT ME10...130 A2
Woodberry Gv BXLY DA5...65 M2
Woodbine Rd PGE/AN SE20...61 H1
Woodbine Rd BFN/LL DA15...44 A9
Woodbridge Dr
 MAID/SHEP ME15...............185 K2
Woodbrook HDCN TN27...221 J3
Woodbrook Rd ABYW SE2...27 P9

Woodbury Cl EGRIN RH19...265 L8
Woodbury Cl BH/WHM TN16...146 A5
 CROY/NA CRO...............84 C5
 EGRIN RH19...............265 L8
 STH/RUST TN4...............270 D5
Woodbury Gdns BMLY BR1...62 F2
Woodbury La TENT TN30...301 H8
Woodbury Park Gdns
 STH/RUST TN4...............270 E3
Woodbury Park Rd
 STH/RUST TN4...............22 D1
Woodbury Rd HAWK TN18...317 J3
 WALD ME5...............125 K4
Woodchurch Cl BFN/LL DA15...63 P2
 WALD ME5...............95 N9
Woodchurch Crs RHAM ME8...96 F4
Woodchurch Dr BMLY BR1...63 H6
Woodchurch Rd BRCH CT7...141 N1
 RASHW TN26...............281 L8
 RASHW TN26...............322 E2
 TENT TN30...............301 K7
Wood Cl BXLY DA5...............65 N2
 DIT/AY ME20...............154 D4
Woodclyffe Dr CHST BR7...63 L8
Woodcock Gdns RFOLK CT18...288 C8
Woodcock HI LING RH7...............264 C2
Woodcock La CRBK TN17...318 D3
 RMAID ME17...............218 F4
Woodcocks CAN/RD E16...27 H5
 HDCN TN27...............247 N4
Woodcombe Crs FSTH SE23...41 J9
Woodcote Cl WSTB CT5...............106 C5
Woodcote Dr ORP BR6...............86 E4
Woodcote Rd WNWD SE27 *...60 B4
Wood Cottage La
 FOLKN CT19...............310 A4
Woodcourt Cl SIT ME10...129 M3
Woodcroft ELTH/MOT SE9...43 J2
Woodcroft Ms DEPT SE8...25 H7
Woodcroft Rd THHTH CR7...82 C2
Woodcut HI MAID/BEAR ME14...155 M4
Woodcutters Av
 STMC/STPC BR5...............32 D5
Wood Dene PECK SE15 *...41 H2
Wood Dr CHST BR7...............63 H5
 SEV TN13...............20 B5
Wooden Bridge Ter
 WNWD SE27 *...............60 B2
Woodend NRWD SE19...............60 B2
Wood End SWLY BR8...............88 B1
Wooderson Cl SNWD SE25...83 K1
Woodfall Dr DART DA1...45 P5
Woodfarrs CMBW SE5...............60 G3
Woodfield Av FOLKN CT19...310 B4
 GVW DA11...............49 M9
 RTON TN11...............210 B5
Woodfield Rd TON TN9...240 B4
Woodfields SEV TN13...............148 C8
Woodford Av RAM CT11...143 J3
Woodford Ct BRCH CT7...............111 H6
Woodford Gv E/WMAL ME19...153 H3
Woodford Rd MADW ME16...184 C1
Woodgate Cl FAV ME13...132 F5
Woodgate La RSIT ME9...............128 D3
Woodgate Rd E/WMAL ME19...122 E9
Woodgate Wy TON TN9...240 G2
Woodget Cl EHAM E6...............26 F2
Woodhall Dr DUL SE21...............60 F2
Woodhall Dr DUL SE21...............60 F2
Woodhall Ter OBOR ME11 *...77 J2
Woodham Rd CAT SE6...............62 A2
Woodhatch Cl EHAM E6...26 F1
Woodhead Dr ORP BR6...............86 F7
Wood HI CANTW/ST CT2...136 D7
Woodhill WOOL/PLUM SE18...26 F7
Woodhill Crs CANTW/ST CT2...271 M2
Woodhouse Cl EDUL SE22...40 G5
Woodhurst WALD ME5...............125 J1
Woodhurst Av
 STMC/STPC BR5...............86 D3
Woodhurst Cl CHST BR7...94 A4
Woodhurst La OXTED RH8...175 H7
Woodhurst Pk OXTED RH8...175 H6
Woodhurst Rd ABYW SE2...27 P8
Woodington Cl
 ELTH/MOT SE9...............43 L7
Woodknoll Dr CHST BR7...63 K7
Woodland Av BRCH CT7...............111 H7
 HART DA3...............91 J2
 RCANTE CT3...............229 H1
Woodland Cl DVW CT17...290 F5
 E/WMAL ME19...............153 H4
 HART DA3...............91 J3
 NRWD SE19...............60 E5
 STH/RUST TN4...............270 E1
Woodland Ct OXTED RH8...174 C4
Woodland Crs GNWCH SE10...26 E6
Woodland Dr TENT TN30...206 E7
 IOS ME12...............58 B9
Woodland Gv GNWCH SE10...25 P8
Woodland HI NRWD SE19...60 E5
Woodland Ri BGR/WK TN15...149 L7
 HYTHE CT21...............175 H6
 OXTED RH8...............175 H6
Woodland Rd HB CT6...............106 G4
 NRWD SE19...............60 E4
 RFOLK CT18...............286 E1
 STH/RUST TN4...............270 E1
Woodlands CANTW/ST CT2...135 N6
 FAV ME13...............134 D6
 RMAID ME17...............184 G8
 RTWE/PEM TN2...............272 A1
 TENT TN30...............322 C2
Woodlands Av BFN/LL DA15...44 A9
 SNOD ME6...............123 N5
Woodlands Cl BMLY BR1...63 K8
 CDW/CHF RM16...............32 F6

MAID/BEAR ME14 ....155 N5
SWLY BR8 ....65 P8
WBY/YAL ME18 ....183 P5
Woodlands Ct
STH/RUST TN4 * 240 D7
Woodlands Dr GDST RH9 ....204 B4
HYTHE CT21 ....309 M3
Woodlands La GVE DA12 ....70 F6
Woodlands Pde
DIT/AY ME20 * 154 C4
Woodlands Pk BXLY DA5 ......65 M3
Woodlands Park Rd
BKHTH/KID ME14 ....25 P9
Woodlands Ri SWLY BR8 ....65 P8
Woodlands Rd BMLY BR1 ....68 K3
BXLYHN DA7 ....44 G4
DIT/AY ME20 ....154 B3
EGRIN RH19 ....265 K4
GILL ME7 ....96 C4
KEN/WIL TN24 ....253 J7
ORP BR6 ....117 H1
RCANTE CT3 ....198 E7
SIT ME10 * 130 A2
TON TN9 ....240 D5
Woodlands St LEW SE13 ....42 B8
Woodlands Ter GILL ME7 * 96 C3
SWLY BR8 * 88 B5
The Woodlands CMBW SE5 * ..40 B1
LEW SE13 ....42 B8
NRWD SE19 ....60 D6
ORP BR6 ....117 J1
Woodland Ter CHARL SE7 ......26 F7
Woodland Vw TENT TN30 ....332 B1
Woodland Wy ABYW SE2 ....28 B1
BRDST CT10 ....113 M4
CANTW/ST CT2 ....136 C9
CROY/NA CRO 84 D5
GRH DA9 ....47 N6
LYDD TN29 ....327 L2
MAID/BEAR ME14 ....155 N5
STH/RUST TN4 ....240 A6
STMC/STPC BR5 ....86 C1
SWCH CT13 ....201 K4
WWKM BR4 ....84 F7
Wood La ASH TN23 ....282 G5
CRBK TN17 ....299 M4
RDART DA2 ....67 M2
Woodlark Rd CHAT ME4 ....73 H6
Woodlea DIT/AY ME20 ....153 M2
HART DA3 ....68 G9
KEN/WIL TN24 ....3 F1
Woodlea Dr HAYES BR2 ....85 H2
Woodleas MAIDW ME16 ....184 E1
Woodley Rd ORP BR6 ....87 K6
Wood Lodge Gdns BMLY BR1 ..63 J6
Wood Lodge Gra SEV TN13 * .149 H7
Wood Lodge La WWKM BR4 ....84 F7
Woodman Av WSTB CT5 ....106 C4
Woodman St ELTH/MOT SE9 ..43 K8
Woodmere Av CROY/NA CRO ..84 A4
Woodmere CI CROY/NA CRO ...84 A4
Woodmere Gdns
CROY/NA CRO 84 A4
Woodmere Wy BECK BR3 ......84 G2
Woodmount SWLY BR8 ....88 A4
Woodnesborough La
SWCH CT13 ....201 J7
Woodnesborough Rd
SWCH CT13 ....201 M2
Woodpecker Dr RSIT ME9 * 99 M2
Woodpecker Gld RHAM ME8 ...96 F8
Woodpecker Ms LEW SE13 .....42 B5
Woodpecker Mt
CROY/NA CRO 114 B3
Woodpecker Rd DIT/AY ME20 .153 N5
THMD SE28 ....28 B3
Woodquest Av HNHL SE24 ......40 B6
Wood Ride STMC/STPC BR5 ....86 F1
Wood Rd BH/WHM TN16 ....145 M3
HYTHE CT21 ....308 G5
Woodrow WOOL/PLUM SE18 ..26 H7
Woodrow Cha HB CT6 ....107 M5
Woodruff CI RHAM ME8 ....97 N2
Woodrush PI NWCR SE14 ....41 L1
Woodrush PI CHAT ME4 ....73 H6
Woodseer St WCHPL E1 ....24 C1
Woodsgate Wy
RTWE/PEM TN2 ....271 L2
Woods Hl RCANTW CT4 ....225 K5
Woodside ASH TN23 ....282 A2
FAV ME13 ....164 C2
MEO DA13 ....122 A5
ORP BR6 ....87 H9
RHAM ME8 ....96 F8
Woodside Av CHST BR7 ....63 N4
SNWD SE25 ....83 N3
Woodside CI BXLYHN DA7 ......45 H5
DVE/WH CT16 ....290 F3
RTWE/PEM TN2 ....271 P2
Woodside Court Rd
CROY/NA CRO 83 M4
Woodside Crs BFN/LL DA15 ....64 A2
Woodside Dr RDART DA2 ....65 N3
Woodside Gdns SIT ME10 .....129 L3
Woodside Gn CROY/NA CRO ...83 M4
Woodside La BXLY DA5 ....44 F7
Woodside Pde
BFN/LL DA15 * 64 A2

Woodside Pk SNWD SE25 ....83 M3
Woodside Rd BFN/LL DA15 .....64 A2
BMLY BR1 ....85 P2
BXLYHN DA7 ....45 H5
CANTW/ST CT2 ....137 L6
MAID/SHEP ME15 ....185 P4
RSEV TN14 ....147 L9
RTWE/PEM TN2 ....271 P2
SEV TN13 ....148 G8
SNWD SE25 ....83 M3
STH/RUST TN4 ....270 A4
TON TN9 ....240 E2
Woods Ley RCANTE CT3 ....170 E9
Wood's PI DART CT11 ....291 J5
STHWK SE1 ....24 B6
Wood's End EGRIN RH19 ....41 H2
Woodstock EGRIN RH19 ....264 F6
Woodstock CI BXLY DA5 ....45 H9
Woodstock Gdns BECK BR3 ...61 P7
Woodstock Rd CROY/NA CRO ..84 C6
DEAL CT14 ....233 H5
SIT ME10 ....129 M4
STRD ME2 ....18 A2
Woodstock St CAN/RD E16 .....26 A2
Woodstock Ter POP/IOD E14 ...25 L3
Woodstock Wy
KEN/WIL TN24 ....252 F5
Wood St CAN/RD E16 ....26 C3
EGRIN RH19 ....264 C7
GILL ME7 ....72 C9
GRAYS RM17 ....32 D2
IOS ME12 ....57 L6
RSIT ME9 ....130 E5
RTW TN1 ....23 F2
STRD ME2 ....94 A4
SWLY BR8 ....66 C7
Woodsyre SYD SE26 ....60 F3
Wood V FSTH SE23 ....41 H9
Woodvale Av SNWD SE25........60 F9
Wood View CI BGR/WK TN15 .120 B2
Woodview CI ORP BR6 ....86 D6
Woodview Crs RTON TN11 .....210 B5
Woodview Ri STRD ME2 ....71 P6
Woodview Rd SWLY BR8 ....65 L8
Woodville CANTW/ST CT2 * ...105 N6
Woodville CI CANT CT1 ....166 C6
LEE/GVPK SE12 ....42 E6
Woodville Gv WELL DA16 * 44 C4
Woodville PI GVE DA12 ....49 M8
Woodville Rd
MAID/SHEP ME15 * 185 M1
MSTR CT12 ....142 G3
THHTH CR7 ....60 D9
Woodville St
WOOL/PLUM SE18 ....26 F7
Woodward CI GRAYS RM17 .....32 C7
Woodward Rd EDUL SE22 ....40 E7
Woodward Hts GRAYS RM17 ...32 C7
Woodward Ter GRH DA9 ....47 L7
Wood Wy ORP BR6 ....86 B6
Wood Whf GNWCH SE10 ....25 L9
Woodyard La DUL SE21 ....40 E8
The Woodyard DEAL CT14 * ...233 J5
Woodyates Rd
LEE/GVPK SE12 ....42 E7
Woolacombe Rd
BKHTH/KID SE3 ....43 L1
Woolaston Cl
MAID/SHEP ME15 ....185 L2
Woolbrook CI RHAM ME8 ....97 L4
Woolbrook Dr DART DA1 ....45 N7
Woolcomber St DVE/WH CT16 ..8 E3
Wooldeys Rd RHAM ME8 ....97 J4
Wooler St WALW SE17 ....24 A8
Woolett Rd SIT ME10 ....99 J9
Woolf CI THMD SE28 ....28 A4
Woollett CI DART DA1 ....46 A5
Woollett St MAID/BEAR ME14 ..13 F5
Woolley Cl STH/RUST TN4 ....240 C8
Woolley Rd MAID/SHEP ME15 .186 C3
STH/RUST TN4 ....240 C8
Woolmer Dr KEN/WIL TN24 ....240 C8
Woolmore St POP/IOD E14 .....25 M5
Woolpack HI RASHE TN25 ......284 E3
Woolreeds Rd ASH TN23 ....282 D1
Woolstapers Wy
BERM/RHTH SE16 ....24 D6
Woolstone Rd FSTH SE23 ....61 L1
Woolwich Church St
CHARL SE7 ....26 E7
Woolwich CI WALD ME5 ....95 M7
Woolwich Common
WOOL/PLUM SE18 ....27 H9
Woolwich Foot Tnl
CAN/RD E16 ....27 H5
Woolwich High St
WOOL/PLUM SE18 ....27 H6
Woolwich Manor Wy
CAN/RD E16 ....27 J5
Woolwich Manorway
CAN/RD E16 ....27 J3
Woolwich New Rd
WOOL/PLUM SE18 ....27 H9
Woolwich Rd ABYW SE2 ....28 D9
BXLYHN DA7 ....45 J4

GNWCH SE10 ....26 B8
Wooster Gdns POP/IOD E14 ...25 N2
Wootton La RCANTW CT4 ....258 F5
Wopsle CI ROCH ME1 ....95 J7
Worbeck Rd PGE/AN SE20 ......60 B2
Worcester Av E/WMAL ME19 ..183 H1
Worcester CI CROY/NA CRO 84 C6
FAV ME13 ....133 H8
GRH DA9 ....48 B3
IOS ME12 ....78 C1
MEO DA13 ....69 K6
STRD ME2 ....71 N7
Worcester Dr SIT ME10 ....99 L8
Worcester Gdns
MAID/SHEP ME15 ....186 A4
Wordsworth CI TIL RM18 ....49 N3
WALD ME5 ....95 P7
Wordsworth Gdns
RCANTE CT3 ....199 J9
Wordsworth Ri EGRIN RH19 ...264 F7
Wordsworth Rd
MAID/BEAR ME14 ....155 N5
PGE/AN SE20 ....61 K6
STHWK SE1 ....24 C8
WELL DA16 ....44 A2
Wordsworth Wy DART DA1 ....123 P9
Worgan St BERM/RHTH SE16 ..24 C6
Workhouse La
MAID/BEAR ME14 ....185 H7
Workhouse Rd
E/WMAL ME19 ....122 F9
FAV ME13 ....192 B1
RMAID ME17 ....128 C3
World's End RSIT ME9 ....131 K6
World's End La ORP BR6 ....117 H2
Worleys Dr ORP BR6 ....86 B8
Worlingham Rd EDUL SE22 ......40 E7
Wormdale Hi RSIT ME9 ....128 C2
Wormdale Rd RSIT ME9 ....128 B1
Wormwood St OBST EC2N 24 B2
Worsfold Ct
MAID/SHEP ME15 * 185 M2
Worships HI SEV TN13 ....148 D8
Worsley Bridge Rd CAT SE6 ....61 M4
Worsted La EGRIN RH19 ....265 L9
Worth CI ORP BR6 ....86 F3
Worth Gv WALW SE17 * 24 A8
Worthing Rd WTHK RM20 ....31 P9
Worthing St DVE/WH CT16 ....8 C5
Worthington St DVE/WH CT16 ..8 C3
Worth La FOLK CT20 ....310 B8
Wortley Rd CROY/NA CRO 82 F4
Wotton CI MAID/SHEP ME15 ..186 B6
Wotton Rd ASH TN23 ....282 E2
ROCH ME1 ....94 B8
WTHK RM20 ....31 P9
Wouldham Ter
STMC/STPC BR5 * 64 D9
Wraightsfield Av LYDD TN29 ..327 H6
Wraik HI WSTB CT5 ....135 J1
Wrangleden Cl
MAID/SHEP ME15 ....186 B6
Wrangleden Rd
MAID/SHEP ME15 ....186 A6
Wrangling La MEO DA13 ....122 C2
Wreight Ct FAV ME13 ....132 E4
Wrekin Rd WOOL/PLUM SE18 ..43 N1
Wren CI CAN/RD E16 ....26 A2
DIT/AY ME20 ....153 N5
SAND/SEL CR2 ....114 A4
STMC/STPC BR5 ....64 F9
Wren Ms SEV TN13 * 42 C5
Wren Rd CMBW SE5 ....40 D7
SCUP DA14 ....64 E2
Wrens CI CRST ME3 ....94 B9
Wrens Cft GVW DA11 ....69 J5
Wrens Cross
MAID/SHEP ME15 * 13 F6
Wrens Rd RSIT ME9 ....128 C7
Wrentham Av WLSDN NW10 ...106 C4
Wrenthorpe Rd BMLY BR1 ....62 C1
Wren Wk TIL RM18 ....49 M1
Wren Wy WALD ME5 ....95 N8
Wricklemarsh Rd
BKHTH/KID SE3 ....43 L1
Wrigglesworth St NWCR SE14 ..41 K1
Wright CI LEW SE13 ....42 B5
RHAM ME8 ....96 F4
Wrights CI TENT TN30 ....301 H7
Wrights Rd SNWD SE25 ....60 E9
Wright's Rw CAR SM5 ....82 A8
Wright's Wy IOS ME12 ....79 J7
Wrotham Hill Rd
BGR/WK TN15 ....121 J7
Wrotham Rd BGR/WK TN15 ...151 J5
BRDST CT10 ....113 N9
MEO DA13 ....121 P5
WELL DA16 ....44 C2
Wrotham Water La
E/WMAL ME19 ....121 N9
Wrotham Water Rd
E/WMAL ME19 ....121 N9
Wrottesley Rd
WOOL/PLUM SE18 ....27 K9
Wroxham Rd THMD SE28 ....28 C3

Wroxton Rd PECK SE15 ....41 H3
Wulfere Wy STRD ME2 ....72 E4
Wulfred Wy BGR/WK TN15 ....149 N3
Wyatt CI BGR/WK TN15 ....151 J5
Wyatt Pt STRD ME2 ....19 B2
Wyatt Rd DART DA1 ....45 P4
Wyatt St MAID/BEAR ME14 .....13 G4
Wybourne La HOO/HM ME3 .....53 J5
Wych Elm Wy HYTHE CT21 ....308 D6
Wycherley CI BKHTH/KID SE3 ..42 D1
Wycherley Crs DVE/WH CT16 .291 J1
Wychwood Av THHTH CR7 ....60 B9
Wycliffe CI WELL DA16 ....44 B2
Wycliffe Rw GVW DA11 ....49 K9
Wydenhurst Rd CROY/NA CRO ..83 M4
Wydeville Manor Rd
LEE/GVPK SE12 ....62 F3
Wye Cl ORP BR6 ....86 G4
Wye Gdns MARG CT9 ....159 J1
Wye Rd BGR/WK TN15 ....151 K4
GVE DA12 ....69 P1
RASHE TN25 ....223 J8
TONN TN10 ....210 F5
Wyham CI GVE DA12 ....70 A5
OBOR ME11 ....177 M7
Wykeham Gv RMAID ME17 .....187 K4
Wykeham Rd SIT ME10 ....130 A1
Wykeham St STRD ME2 ....72 B7
Wyke Manor Rd
MAID/BEAR ME14 ....13 F4
Wyles Rd CHAT ME4 ....95 K4
Wyles St GILL ME7 ....75 J8
Wyleu St FSTH SE23 ....41 L8
Wylie Rd HOO/HM ME3 ....75 L1
Wynan Rd POP/IOD E14 ....25 L8
Wyncham Av BFN/LL DA15 ....44 B9
Wyncote Wy SAND/SEL CR2 ...114 A3
Wyncroft CI BMLY BR1 ....63 K9
Wyndcliff Rd CHARL SE7 ....26 C9
Wyndham Av MARG CT9 ....112 G3
RTON TN11 ....209 L9
Wyndham CI ORP BR6 ....86 D5
RTON TN11 ....209 L9
Wyndham Est CMBW SE5 ....40 C1
Wyndham Rd CHAT ME4 ....95 H4
CMBW SE5 ....40 C1
DVW CT17 ....291 J7
Wyndham Wy RASHE TN25 ....252 C5
The Wynd HDCN TN27 ....221 J1
Wyndham Ms BERM/RHTH SE16 ..24 E2
Wyndyat Rd FSTH SE23 ....61 K2
Wynell Rd FSTH SE23 ....61 K2
Wyness CT STRD ME2 * 72 B7
Wynford Gv STMC/STPC BR5 ...64 D9
Wynford PI BELV DA17 ....28 F8
Wynford Wy ELTH/MOT SE9 ....43 H5
Wynne Rd BRXN/ST SW9 ....40 A5
Wynn Rd WSTB CT5 ....105 P5
Wynn's Av BFN/LL DA15 ....44 C4
Wynnstow Pk OXTED RH8 .....175 J7
Wynton Gdns SNWD SE25 ....83 K2
The Wytchlings
RMAID ME17 ....187 N3
Wytherling Cl
MAID/BEAR ME14 ....156 C9
Wythes CI BMLY BR1 ....63 K8
Wythes Rd CAN/RD E16 ....26 F2
Wythfield Rd ELTH/MOT SE9 ....43 K7
Wyvern CI DART DA1 ....46 C8
ORP BR6 ....87 J7
SNOD ME6 ....99 M7
Wyvern Wy KEN/WIL TN24 ....3 J2
Wyvill CI RHAM ME8 ....97 H9
Wyvis St POP/IOD E14 ....25 L1

Y

Yabsley St POP/IOD E14............25 M4
Yalding CI STRD ME2 ....72 B6
Yalding Gv STMC/STPC BR5 ....87 L2
Yalding Hl WBY/YAL ME18 .....183 P8
Yalding Rd BERM/RHTH SE16 ..24 D6
Yantlet Dr STRD ME2 ....71 L8
Yardhurst Gdns MARG CT9 ....113 L2
Yardley CI TON TN9 ....210 C7
Yardley Park Rd TON TN9 ......210 F7
The Yard RCANTW CT4 ....228 C5
Yarnton Wy ABYW SE2 ....28 B5
Yarrow Av BRDST CT10 ....143 M1
Yarrow CI MAID/BEAR ME14 ..156 C7
Yarrow Crs EHAM E6 ....25 P1
Yarrow Rd WALD ME5 ....125 K1
Yateley St WOOL/PLUM SE18 ..26 E6
Yates CI RYE TN31 ....344 B1
Yaugher La RSIT ME9 ....127 L2
Yeates Dr SIT ME10 ....99 P6
Yeats CI LEW SE13 * 42 A6
Yelsted La MAID/BEAR ME14 ..126 A6
RSIT ME9 ....127 K4
Yelsted Rd RSIT ME9 ....127 K6
Yeoman CI EHAM E6 ....27 J5
Yeoman Dr GILL ME7 ....96 F8
Yeoman Gdns KEN/WIL TN24 .255 K8
STPH/PW TN12 ....242 F3

Yeoman La MAID/BEAR ME14 .156 E9
Yeoman Pk MAID/SHEP ME15 .186 D1
Yeoman's Mdw SEV TN13 ....20 C5
Yeoman St BERM/RHTH SE16 ..25 M4
Yeoman Wy MAID/SHEP ME15 .186 E1
Yeo St BOW E3 ....25 L1
Yeovil CI ORP BR6 ....86 F6
Yester Dr CHST BR7 ....63 J6
Yester Pk CHST BR7 ....63 K6
Yester Rd CHST BR7 ....63 J6
Yewele CI OBOR ME11 ....77 J2
Yew CI ASH TN23 ....252 B7
Yewdale CI BMLY BR1 ....62 C5
Yew La EGRIN RH19 ....264 E5
Yew Rd HOO/HM ME3 ....75 L4
The Yews GVE DA12 ....69 P1
Yew Tree CI BRDST CT10 ....113 J9
DEAL CT14 * 232 F5
DIT/AY ME20 ....154 D3
HART DA3 ....69 H8
RASHE TN25 ....286 A7
SEV TN13 ....148 C8
WALD ME5 ....126 A4
YALE ME13 ....44 C2
Yew Tree Gdns BRCH CT7 ......111 H6
CANTW/ST CT2 * 137 M9
Yew Tree Green Rd
STPH/PW TN12 ....243 F3
Yew Tree Ms DEAL CT14 ....232 F6
Yewtree Rd BECK BR3 ....61 H9
Yew Tree Rd LYDD TN29 ....337 L1
STH/RUST TN4 ....240 D9
Yoakes La LYDD TN29 ....335 P3
Yoakley Sq MARG CT9 ....112 G5
Yoke CI STRD ME2 * 72 B7
Yokosuka Wy GILL ME7 ....96 F6
Yolande Gdns ELTH/MOT SE9 ..43 J6
Yopps Gn BGR/WK TN15 ....181 H2
York & Albany CI DEAL CT14 ..232 G8
York Av BFN/LL DA15 ....64 A1
EGRIN RH19 ....265 K8
GILL ME7 ....7 G4
WALD ME5 ....125 K2
York CI CMBW SE5 * 40 C3
EHAM E6 ....27 K5
York Rd PECK SE15 ....41 J2
York HI STRHM/NOR SW16 ......60 B2
WALD ME5 ....95 P4
Yorkland Av WELL DA16 ....44 B5
York Ms FOLKN CT19 * 310 E4
York Pde TONN TN10 ....210 F4
York Ri ORP BR6 ....86 F5
York Rd BH/WHM TN16 ....145 L4
CANT 4 C7
CROY/NA CRO 82 H4
DART DA1 ....46 C4
DEAL CT14 ....233 J6
GVE DA12 ....69 N2
CVW DA11 ....49 H8
HB CT6 ....107 J1
KEN/WIL TN24 ....255 H6
MAID/SHEP ME15 ....185 P2
ROCH ME1 ....95 H3
RTW TN1 ....22 C5
SAND/SEL CR2 ....114 A4
TONN TN10 ....210 G5
Yorkshire Rd MTCM CR4 ....82 D2
POP/IOD E14 ....25 H2
York Sq POP/IOD E14 * 25 H2
York St BRDST CT10 ....113 N9
DVE/WH CT16 ....8 D4
RAM CT11 ....5 G6
York Street Rbt DVW CT17 ....8 D5
York Ter BRCH CT7 ....111 J6
ERITH DA8 ....45 L2
Young CI DEAL CT14 ....232 G3
Young Rd CAN/RD E16 ....26 D2
Young's PI ROY CT15 ....312 A1
Ypres Ct CANT 167 J3
Ypres Dr SIT ME10 ....99 N5

Z

Zambra Wy BGR/WK TN15 .....149 L5
Zampa Rd BERM/RHTH SE16 ...24 F8
Zangwill Rd BKHTH/KID SE3 ....43 N2
Zarena Ct FOLK CT20 * 310 C8
Zealand Rd CANT CT1 ....166 E6
Zelah Rd STMC/STPC BR5 ....87 J4
Zenoria St EDUL SE22 ....40 F5
Zermatt Rd THHTH CR7 ....60 B4
Zetland Av GILL ME7 ....83 H4
Zetland Dr STMC/STPC BR5 .....64 C9
Zillah Gdns RHAM ME8 ....96 E8
Zion PI GVW DA11 ....49 M8
MARG CT9 ....15 J3
THHTH CR7 ....83 J1
Zion Rd THHTH CR7 ....83 J1

AAIS
 DART DA1 ...46 E8
The Abbey Clinic
 BELV DA17 ...28 E8
Abbey Court School
 STRD ME2 ...71 P7
Abbey Primary School
 ABYW SE2 ...28 B6
Abbey (rems of)
 ABYW SE2 ...28 A9
The Abbey School
 FAV ME15 ...132 F8
Abbey Trading Estate
 SYD SE26 ...61 L4
Abbey Wood School
 ABYW SE2 ...27 P6
ABC Cinema
 CAT SE6 ...41 P9
 GVE DA12 ...49 M7
Aberdeen Wharf
 WAP E1W ...24 E4
The Academy at Peckham
 PECK SE15 ...40 F2
Acorn Business Centre
 MAIDW ME16 ...185 H1
Acorn Industrial Park
 DART DA1 ...45 P9
Acorn Trading Centre
 WTHK RM20 ...31 P9
Acumen (Anglo School)
 NRWD SE19 ...60 E7
Adamsrill Primary School
 FSTH SE23 ...61 L2
Addey & Stanhope School
 NWCR SE14 ...41 M2
Addington Business Centre
 CROY/NA CRO ...115 H4
The Addington Golf Club
 CROY/NA CRO ...114 C3
Addington High School
 CROY/NA CRO ...115 H6
Addington Palace Golf Club
 CROY/NA CRO ...114 B1
Addiscombe CC
 CROY/NA CRO ...83 M7
Adisham CE Primary School
 RCANTE CT3 ...199 C7
Admiral Hyson Industrial Estate
 BERM/RHTH SE16 ...24 E7
Adult Education Centre
 CANT CT1 ...4 E2
 DART DA1 ...46 FB
 GILL ME7 ...7 L5
 MARC CT9 ...15 G5
 POP/IOD E14 ...25 M6
 ROCH ME1 ...19 H5
 TON TN9 ...210 E9
Agora Shopping Centre
 PECK SE15 ...40 C3
Airport Industrial Estate
 BH/WHM TN16 ...115 N9
Albany Centre & Theatre
 DEPT SE8 ...41 M1
Albany Clinic
 BFN/LL DA15 ...64 C3
Albion Health Centre
 WCHPL E1 ...24 E1
Albion J & I School
 BERM/RHTH SE16 ...24 F5
Albion Street Health Centre
 BERM/RHTH SE16 ...24 F5
Albright Industrial Estate
 RAIN RM13 ...29 L1
Alderwood Primary School
 ELTH/MOT SE9 ...43 P7
Aldington Primary School
 RASHE TN25 ...306 B2
Alexander McLeod
 Primary School *ABYW SE2* ...28 A8
Alexandra Hospital
 WALD ME5 ...125 L5
Alexandra Infant School
 PGE/AN SE20 ...61 K6
Alexandra Junior School
 SYD SE26 ...61 K5
Alfred Salter Primary School
 BERM/RHTH SE16 ...24 C5
Alleyns School
 EDUL SE22 ...40 E6
Allhallows Primary School
 HOO/HM ME3 ...38 FB
Allington Primary School
 MAIDW ME16 ...154 G5
All Saints CE Junior School
 NRWD SE19 ...60 E7
All Saints CE Primary School
 BKHTH/KID SE3 ...42 C3
 CHAT ME4 ...6 E7
 MAIDP SHEP ME15 ...13 F6
All Saints Industrial Estate
 MARC CT9 ...15 F6
All Souls CE Primary School
 FOLKN CT19 ...310 B5
Alma Primary School
 BERM/RHTH SE16 ...24 D7
Alpine Business Centre
 EHAM E6 ...27 H1
Alscot Road Industrial Estate
 STHWK SE1 ...24 C7
Amherst School
 SEV TN13 ...148 D8
Anchorage Point
 Industrial Estate *CHARL SE7* ...26 C6
Anchor Bay Industrial Estate
 ERITH DA8 ...45 P1
Anchor Business Park
 SIT ME10 ...100 A8
Anchorians All Weather
 Sports Club *RHAM ME8* ...97 J5
Andrew Sketchley Theatre
 WCHPL E1 ...24 D1
Anerley School
 PGE/AN SE20 ...60 G7

Angel Centre
 DART DA1 ...46 E7
Angel Indoor Bowling
 TON TN9 ...210 F9
Angel Leisure Centre
 TON TN9 ...210 F9
Angel Walk Shopping
 Precinct *TON TN9* ...210 E9
Angerstein Business Park
 GNWCH SE10 ...26 B7
Angiesea Centre
 GVW DA11 ...49 M7
Angley School
 CRBK TN17 ...297 N2
Anthony Roper Primary School
 EYN DA4 ...89 K6
Apiary Business Park
 RMAID ME17 ...186 G9
Applegarth Primary School
 CROY/NA CRO ...114 C1
Aquarius Golf Club
 PECK SE15 ...41 J6
The Archbishop Lanfranc
 School *CROY/NA CRO* ...82 D3
Archbishop Michael Ramsey
 School *CMBW SE5* ...40 B1
Archbishop's Palace
 MAIDW ME16 ...12 C6
The Archbishops School
 CANTW/ST CT2 ...166 D1
Archbishop Tenisons
 CE School *CROY/NA CRO* ...83 L7
Archcliffe Fort
 DVW CT17 ...313 L1
Arches Court School
 DVE/WH CT16 ...291 J2
Arden Business Park
 STRD ME2 ...19 K1
Arden Junior School
 GILL ME7 ...73 K9
Arden Theatre
 FAV ME15 ...132 F6
Arena Essex
 WTHK RM20 ...31 K5
Argent Business Park
 QBOR ME11 ...77 J5
Argyle Shopping Centre
 RAM CT11 ...17 F4
Arklow Trading Centre
 NWCR SE14 ...25 H9
Arlington Square Shopping
 Centre *MARC CT9* ...14 E5
Arnhem Wharf Primary School
 POP/IOD E14 ...25 J6
Arnolds Business Park
 STPH/PW TN12 ...213 H5
Arts Centre
 BMLY BR1 ...63 H7
 GVE DA12 ...49 M7
Art School
 BECK BR3 ...84 B2
Ashburton Community School
 CROY/NA CRO ...83 N4
Ashburton Primary School
 CROY/NA CRO ...83 N3
Ashfield Farm
 RCANTW CT4 ...226 D8
Ashford Borough Museum
 ASH TN23 ...2 D4
Ashford Business Park
 KEN/WIL TN24 ...283 K2
Ashford Civic Centre
 ASH TN23 ...3 F5
Ashford College
 ASH TN23 ...2 D4
Ashford Golf Club
 RASHE TN25 ...252 C2
Ashford International Hotel
 KEN/WIL TN24 ...252 E5
Ashford Market
 KEN/WIL TN24 ...283 J2
Ashford School
 ASH TN23 ...3 F5
Ashford South CP School
 ASH TN23 ...2 A7
Ashford Town FC
 RASHW TN26 ...282 C8
Ashgrove Trading Estate
 BMLY BR1 ...62 B5
Ashleigh Commercial Estate
 CHARL SE7 ...26 D7
Ashmead Primary School
 DEPT SE8 ...41 N3
Assembly Hall Theatre
 RTW TN1 ...22 E4
Associated Newspapers
 BERM/RHTH SE16 ...24 G6
Astor College for the Arts
 DVW CT17 ...291 J7
The Astor of Hever
 Community School
 MAIDW ME16 ...155 H9
Astor Theatre
 DEAL CT14 ...233 H5
Athelney Primary School
 CAT SE6 ...61 N2
The Atman Clinic
 STH/RUST TN4 ...270 D2
Austin Lodge Golf Club
 EYN DA4 ...119 K3
Aveley FC
 SOCK/AV RM15 ...30 F3
Aveley Primary School
 SOCK/AV RM15 ...31 H4
Aveley School (School House)
 SOCK/AV RM15 ...31 H4
The Aveley School
 SOCK/AV RM15 ...30 G3
Avenue Theatre
 SIT ME10 ...129 N2
Avicenna Medical Centre
 E/WMAL ME19 ...153 M2

Axton Chase School
 HART DA3 ...68 D9
Aycliffe County
 Primary School *DVW CT17* ...313 H2
Aylesford Cemetery
 DIT/AY ME20 ...154 C2
Aylesford Primary School
 DIT/AY ME20 ...154 C3
Aylesford Priory
 DIT/AY ME20 ...154 C2
Aylesford School
 DIT/AY ME20 ...154 C3
Aylesham Cemetery
 RCANTW CT4 ...228 E4
The Aylesham Centre
 PECK SE15 ...40 C2
Aylesham Health Centre
 RCANTE CT3 ...229 H1
Aylesham Industrial Estate
 RCANTE CT3 ...229 H2
Aylesham Primary School
 RCANTE CT3 ...229 H1
Aylwin Secondary School
 BERM/RHTH SE16 ...24 C7
Babington House School
 BECK BR3 ...63 K5
Bacons College
 BERM/RHTH SE16 ...24 C5
Bat Apple Theatre Company
 RTW TN1 ...23 G2
Baldwins Hill Primary School
 EGRIN RH19 ...264 F5
Balfour Infant School
 CHAT ME4 ...95 K5
Balfour Junior School
 CHAT ME4 ...95 K4
Balfour Medical Centre
 GRAYS RM17 ...32 D7
Balgowan Primary School
 BECK BR3 ...61 L8
Ballard Business Park
 STRD ME2 ...18 A6
 STRD ME2 ...94 E1
Balmoral Clinic
 GILL ME7 ...7 J2
Balmoral Trading
 BARK IG11 ...27 N1
Bandon Hill Cemetery
 WLGTN SM6 ...82 C9
Bank of England (& Museum)
 LOTH EC2R ...24 A2
Bannockburn Primary School
 WOOL/PLUM SE18 ...27 N7
Bapchild & Tonge CE
 Aided School *SIT ME10* ...130 C2
Barham CE Primary School
 RCANTW CT4 ...228 B5
Barham Crematorium
 RCANTW CT4 ...228 F7
Baring Primary School
 LEE/GVPK SE12 ...42 E8
Baring Road Medical Centre
 LEE/GVPK SE12 ...62 E1
Barkantine Clinic
 POP/IOD E14 ...25 K5
Barming Primary School
 MAIDW ME16 ...184 E1
Barnehurst Primary School
 BXLYHN DA7 ...45 L2
Barnehurst Public Pay &
 Play Golf Club
 BXLYHN DA7 ...45 M4
Barnes Cray Primary School
 DART DA1 ...46 A5
Barnsole Infant School
 GILL ME7 ...96 B2
Barnsole Junior School
 GILL ME7 ...96 B2
Barrington Primary School
 BXLYHN DA7 ...44 F3
Barrow Grove Junior School
 SIT ME10 ...129 L1
The Barry Clinic
 STH/RUST TN4 ...270 D2
Barton Business Park
 CANT CT1 ...167 J5
Barton Court Grammar School
 CANT CT1 ...5 H5
Barton Junior School
 DVE/WH CT16 ...291 K5
Baston School
 HAYES BR2 ...85 L6
Bata Medical Centre
 TIL RM18 ...34 B7
Bath Factory Estate
 HNHL SE24 ...40 C7
Bayham Abbey
 RRTW TN5 ...294 B1
The Bay Museum
 RDV CT15 ...292 C2
BBC Radio Kent
 CHAT ME4 ...6 A3
Beacon Hill Industrial Estate
 PUR WM13 ...30 E7
Bean Primary School
 RDART DA2 ...68 A2
Bearsted Golf Club
 MAID/BEAR ME14 ...156 E7
Bearsted Green Business
 Centre *MAID/BEAR ME14* ...156 F7
Bearsted Vineyard
 MAID/SHEP ME15 ...187 H1
Beauherne Community
 School *CANTW/ST CT2* ...166 C4
Beaver Industrial Estate
 ASH TN23 ...282 C1
Beaverwood School for Girls
 CHST BR7 ...64 A5
Beckenham Business Centre
 BECK BR3 ...61 L5
Beckenham Crematorium
 SNWD SE25 ...61 J9
Beckenham CC
 BECK BR3 ...61 P6

Beckenham Hospital
 BECK BR3 ...61 M8
Beckenham Leisure Centre
 BECK BR3 ...61 L7
Beckenham Place Park
 Golf Course *BECK BR3* ...61 P5
Beckenham RFC
 BECK BR3 ...84 B1
Beckenham Town FC
 BECK BR3 ...84 D2
Becket Sports Centre
 DART DA1 ...46 C7
Beckley CE Primary School
 RYE TN31 ...330 F9
Beckmead School
 BECK SE15 ...40 G4
Beckton Special School
 CAN/RD E16 ...26 L1
Beddington Infants School
 WLGTN SM6 ...82 B7
Beddington Medical Centre
 CROY/NA CRO ...82 D8
Beddington Park Primary
 School *CROY/NA CRO* ...82 C7
Beddington Trading Estate
 CROY/NA CRO ...82 D5
Bedensfield Clinic
 SCUP DA14 ...64 G4
Bedgebury Junior School
 CRBK TN17 ...296 D6
Bedington Infant School
 WLGTN SM6 ...82 B8
Bedonwell Clinic
 ABYW SE2 ...28 D9
Bedonwell Medical Centre
 BELV DA17 ...28 E8
Bedonwell Primary School
 BELV DA17 ...28 D9
Beechcroft Farm Industrial
 Estate *BGR/WK TN15* ...90 C7
Beechings Way Industrial
 Centre *RHAM ME8* ...96 C2
Beechwood School Sacred
 Heart *RTWE/PEM TN2* ...271 H4
Belhus Golf Club & Leisure
 Centre *SOCK/AV RM15* ...31 H2
Bellamy's Wharf
 BERM/RHTH SE16 ...24 C4
Bellenden Primary School
 PECK SE15 ...40 G4
Bellenden Road Business
 Centre *PECK SE15* ...40 F3
Bellenden Road Retail Park
 PECK SE15 ...40 F2
Bellingham Trading Estate
 CAT SE6 ...61 P2
Bell Shopping Centre
 SIT ME10 ...129 N1
Bell Wood Community Junior
 School *MAID/SHEP ME15* ...186 B6
Bell Wood Infant School
 MAID/SHEP ME15 ...186 B6
Belmont
 FAV ME13 ...162 A7
Belmont Farm Business
 Centre *RASHW TN26* ...250 F8
Belmont Primary School
 BXLYHN DA7 ...45 J1
Belvedere Industrial Estate
 BELV DA17 ...29 J4
Belvedere Link Business Park
 BELV DA17 ...29 H6
Belvedere Primary School
 BELV DA17 ...28 G7
Benedict House Preparatory
 School *BFN/LL DA15* ...64 B3
Benenden CE Primary School
 CRBK TN17 ...298 C9
Benenden Hospital
 CRBK TN17 ...299 M4
Benenden School
 CRBK TN17 ...298 F7
Benham Business Park
 RASHE TN25 ...307 N1
Bennett Memorial Diocesan
 CE School *STH/RUST TN4* ...270 B2
Bensham Manor School
 THHTH CR7 ...83 H2
Benson Primary School
 CROY/NA CRO ...84 B7
Bentley Street Industrial Estate
 GVE DA12 ...49 N7
Bermondsey Trading Estate
 BERM/RHTH SE16 ...24 F7
Bessemer Grange J & I School
 EDUL SE22 ...40 E5
Bessemer Park Industrial Estate
 BRXN/ST SW9 ...40 B5
Bethany School
 CRBK TN17 ...274 G3
Bethersden Business Centre
 RASHW TN26 ...280 B7
Bethersden Primary School
 RASHW TN26 ...280 C5
Bethlem Royal Hospital
 BECK BR3 ...84 D4
Beths Grammar School
 for Boys *BXLY DA5* ...45 J7
Beulah Infant School
 THHTH CR7 ...60 C8
Bexley College
 ERITH DA8 ...29 H7
Bexley CC
 BXLY DA5 ...45 J9
Bexley Grammar School
 WELL DA16 ...44 D5
Bexleyheath Centre
 BXLYHN DA6 ...44 G5
Bexleyheath Golf Club
 BXLYHS DA6 ...44 G4
Bexleyheath Marriott Hotel
 BXLYHS DA6 ...45 K5
Bexleyheath School
 BXLYHN DA7 ...45 H4

Bexley Hospital
 BXLY DA5 ...65 N1
Bexley RFC
 BXLY DA5 ...45 J8
Bickley Park CC
 BMLY BR1 ...63 J8
Bickley Park Preparatory
 School *BMLY BR1* ...63 H9
Bickley Park School
 BMLY BR1 ...63 J8
Bidborough CE Primary
 School *STH/RUST TN4* ...239 P6
Biddenden Vinyards &
 Cider Works *HDCN TN27* ...300 C2
Biggin Hill Airport
 BH/WHM TN16 ...115 M6
Biggin Hill Business Park
 BH/WHM TN16 ...115 N9
Biggin Hill Primary School
 BH/WHM TN16 ...145 P1
Bigland Green Primary School
 WCHPL E1 ...24 E2
Billingsgate Fish Market
 POP/IOD E14 ...25 L4
Birches Industrial Estate
 EGRIN RH19 ...264 D5
Birchington Primary School
 BRCH CT7 ...111 H7
Birchington & Westgate
 Health Clinic *BRCH CT7* ...111 H5
Birchmere Business Park
 THMD SE28 ...27 N5
Birchwood Park Golf Club
 RDART DA2 ...65 L6
Birchwood Primary School
 SWLY BR8 ...65 M7
Bird College
 SCUP DA14 ...64 C2
Birkbeck Primary School
 SCUP DA14 ...64 D2
Bishop Challoner RC School
 WCHPL E1 ...24 F5
Bishop Challoner Girls School
 WCHPL E1 ...24 D3
Bishop Challoner School
 HAYES BR2 ...62 B8
Bishop John Robinson CE
 Primary School *THMD SE28* ...28 B3
Bishop Justus CE (Secondary)
 School *HAYES BR2* ...85 P4
Bishops Down Primary School
 STH/RUST TN4 ...270 B3
Blackfen School for Girls
 BFN/LL DA15 ...44 D7
Blackheath Bluecoat CE School
 BKHTH/KID SE3 ...42 F1
Blackheath Business Estate
 GNWCH SE10 ...42 A2
The Blackheath Clinic
 BKHTH/KID SE3 ...42 E5
Blackheath High School GDST
 BKHTH/KID SE3 ...42 D3
Blackheath High Senior School
 BKHTH/KID SE3 ...42 E1
Blackheath Hospital
 BKHTH/KID SE3 ...42 D4
Blackheath Preparatory School
 BKHTH/KID SE3 ...42 E2
Blackheath RFC
 (the Rectory Field)
 BKHTH/KID SE3 ...42 F1
Blacklands County Junior
 School *E/WMAL ME19* ...153 N5
Black Lion Leisure Centre
 GILL ME7 ...73 H9
Blackshots Leisure Centre
 CDW/CHF RM16 ...32 G5
Blackthorn Medical Centre
 MAIDW ME16 ...154 F9
Blackwall Trading Estate
 POP/IOD E14 ...25 N1
Blackwell Primary School
 EGRIN RH19 ...265 H5
The Blazing Donkey Country
 Hotel & Inn *DEAL CT14* ...201 L8
Bleak House Dickens Maritime &
 Smuggling
 BRDST CT10 ...113 P3
Blean CP School
 CANTW/ST CT2 ...136 M9
Blenheim Primary School
 ORP BR6 ...87 L6
Blenheim Shopping Centre
 PGE/AN SE20 ...61 J6
Bleriot Memorial
 DVE/WH CT16 ...9 G1
Blessed John Roche Catholic
 School *POP/IOD E14* ...25 K2
Bligu Business Centre
 RASHE TN25 ...283 J9
Blubery House Cranbrook
 School *CRBK TN17* ...298 A2
Blue Chalet Industrial Park
 BGR/WK TN15 ...120 C3
Blue Gate Fields Primary
 School *WCHPL E1* ...24 F3
Bluewater Shopping Centre
 GRH DA9 ...47 N8
Blyth's Wharf
 POP/IOD E14 ...25 H3
Bobbing Primary School
 RSIT ME9 ...99 J7
The Bob Hope Theatre
 ELTH/MOT SE9 ...43 K7
Bodiam Castle (NT)
 RBTBR TN32 ...328 G5
Bodiam CE Primary School
 RBTBR TN32 ...328 E5
Bodiam Manor School
 RBTBR TN32 ...328 F5
Bonnygate Primary School
 SOCK/AV RM15 ...31 L1
Bonus Pastor School
 BMLY BR1 ...62 C3

Borden CE Primary School RSIT ME9 ...128 G2
Borden Grammar School SIT ME10 ...129 M2
Borough Cemetery RTWE/PEM TN2 ...270 F8
Borough Green Primary School BGR/WK TN15 ...151 K5
Borstal Manor Junior School ROCH ME1 ...94 E4
Bough Beech Sailing Club EDEN TN8 ...208 A6
Boughton Golf Club FAV ME15 ...163 N1
Boughton Monchelsea Primary School RMAID ME17 185 N9
Boughton Under Blean Primary School FAV ME13 ...164 A1
Bourne Road Industrial Park DART DA1 ...45 M6
Bower Grove School MAIDW ME16 ...184 C1
The Bower Mount Clinic MAIDW ME16 ...12 A5
Bowes Industrial Centre MEO DA13 ...92 A8
Bowling Alley
BERM/RHTH SE16 ...24 C6
BXLYHS DA6 ...45 H5
EGRIN RH19 ...265 H7
EHAM E6 ...27 H1
LEW SE13 ...42 A4
MAID/BEAR ME14 ...13 G4
MARG CT9 ...15 H4
MARG CT9 ...15 K2
ORP BR6 ...87 H5
WSTB CT5 ...105 L3
Bowling Centre
ASH TN23 ...3 F4
CHAT ME4 ...6 C4
The Bow Window Inn Hotel RCANTE CT5 ...168 C8
Boxgrove Primary School ABYW SE2 ...28 B6
Boxmend Industrial Estate RMAID ME17 ...186 C8
Boyd Business Centre STRD ME2 ...19 J1
Brabourne CE Primary School RASHE TN25 ...255 H9
Bradbourne School RSEV TN14 ...148 F6
Bradfields School WALD ME5 ...95 M8
Bradstow School BRDST CT10 ...143 M1
Brady Primary School RAIN RM13 ...29 P1
Brady Recreation Centre WCHPL E1 ...24 D1
Brampton Primary School BXLYHN DA7 ...44 F5
Branbridges Industrial Estate STPH/PW TN12 ...213 H5
Brands Hatch Motor Racing Circuit HART DA3 ...90 B8
Brandshatch Place Hotel BGR/WK TN15 ...90 D8
Brattle Farm Museum STPH/PW TN12 ...246 A8
Breaside Preparatory School BMLY BR1 ...62 C7
Breaside Pre Prep School BMLY BR1 ...62 E6
Bredgar CE Primary School RSIT ME9 ...129 H8
Bredhurst CE Primary School GILL ME7 ...126 E4
Bredlinghurst School PECK SE15 ...41 J1
Brenchley & Matfield CE Primary School STPH/PW TN12 ...243 H9
Brenley Corner FAV ME13 ...133 M9
Brent Knoll School FSTH SE23 ...61 K2
The Brent Primary School RDART DA2 ...47 J8
Brenzett Aeronautical Museum LYDD TN29 ...335 J2
Brenzett District CE Primary School LYDD TN29 ...335 H3
Brian Johnston Centre BGR/WK TN15 ...149 L7
Briary Primary School HB CT6 ...107 H4
Brick Lane Music Hall CAN/RD E16 ...26 E4
Bricklehurst Manor Preparatory School WADH TN5 ...314 C2
Brickmakers Industrial Estate SIT ME10 ...100 A8
Bridge Country Leisure Club WSTB CT5 ...104 F8
Bridge Industrial Centre MAIDW ME16 ...185 K1
The Bridge Leisure Centre SYD SE26 ...61 M4
Bridge & Patrixbourne CE Primary School RCANTW CT4 ...197 M1
Bridge Place Country Club RCANTW CT4 ...197 M3
Bridge Road Business Centre ASH TN23 ...252 C7
Bridge View Industrial Estate OBOR ME11 ...77 J5
WTHK RM20 ...31 K9
Bridgewood Manor Hotel WALD ME5 ...125 J2
Brigstock Medical Centre THHTH CR7 ...82 G2

Brindishe Primary School LEE/GVPK SE12 ...42 D6
Britannia Village Primary School CAN/RD E16 ...26 C4
The British School DEAL CT14 ...233 J2
Brit School for Performing Arts SNWD SE25 ...83 J3
Brittania Business Park DIT/AY ME20 ...154 D4
Brixton Academy BRXN/ST SW9 ...40 A4
Brixton Recreation Centre BRXN/ST SW9 ...40 A4
Broadgate Ice Arena (Ice Rink) LVPST EC2M ...24 A1
Broad Hembury Holiday Park RASHW TN26 ...282 E7
Broadlands Industrial Estate CANTW/ST CT2 ...135 N6
Broadmead Primary School CROY/NA CR0 ...83 J3
Broad Oak Industrial Estate CANTW/ST CT2 ...166 C1
Broadstairs CC BRDST CT10 ...143 K2
Broadstairs Health Centre BRDST CT10 ...113 M9
Broadstairs Youth & Leisure Centre BRDST CT10 ...113 N8
Broadwater Down Primary School RTWE/PEM TN2 ...270 C7
Broadway Shopping Centre BXLYHS DA6 ...45 H5
MAIDW ME16 ...12 D5
Broadway Square Shopping Centre BXLYHN DA7 ...45 J5
Brockhill Country Park HYTHE CT21 ...308 E3
Brockhill Park School (Lower) HYTHE CT21 ...308 F4
Brockhill Park School (Upper) HYTHE CT21 ...308 F3
Brocklebank Industrial Estate GNWCH SE10 ...26 B7
Brockley Cross Business Centre BROCKY SE4 ...41 L4
Brockley Primary School BROCKY SE4 ...41 M6
Brockwell Lido HNHL SE24 ...40 B7
Broke Hill Golf Club RSEV TN14 ...117 N3
Bromley Cemetery BMLY BR1 ...62 D6
Bromley College of Further & Higher Education BMLY BR1 ...62 E7
HAYES BR2 ...85 N3
Bromley County Court BMLY BR1 ...62 E7
Bromley Court Hotel BMLY BR1 ...62 C5
Bromley FC HAYES BR2 ...85 L2
Bromley Golf Club HAYES BR2 ...85 P4
Bromley High School GDST BMLY BR1 ...86 B1
Bromley Hospitals NHS Trust ORP BR6 ...86 G8
Bromley Industrial Centre BMLY BR1 ...63 H9
Bromley Mall Indoor Market BMLY BR1 ...62 E8
Bromley Museum ORP BR6 ...87 J4
Bromley Road Infant School BECK BR3 ...61 P7
Bromley Road Retail Park CAT SE6 ...61 P1
Bromley Tennis Centre ORP BR6 ...86 E7
Brompton Medical Centre GILL ME7 ...72 C9
Brompton Westbrook Primary School GILL ME7 ...6 E3
Bromstone CP School BRDST CT10 ...113 J9
Bronte School GVW DA11 ...48 L8
Brook Community Primary School RASHE TN25 ...254 B5
Brooke House School for the Deaf MARG CT9 ...14 A6
Brookfield Industrial Estate ASH TN23 ...252 C7
Brookfield Infant School DIT/AY ME20 ...153 P2
Brookfield Junior School DIT/AY ME20 ...153 N2
Brook Industrial Park STMC/STPC BR5 ...87 K1
Brookland CE Primary School LYDD TN29 ...334 C5
Brooklands Primary School BKHTH/KID SE3 ...42 E4
Brookmarsh Trading Estate DEPT SE8 ...41 P1
Brookmead Industrial Estate MTCM CR4 ...82 B5
The Brook Theatre CHAT ME4 ...6 C3
Broome Park Golf Club RCANTW CT4 ...228 E9
Broomhill Bank School RTW TN3 ...269 P2
Broomhill Lodge Hotel RYE TN31 ...338 D2
Broomsleigh Business Park CAT SE6 ...61 M4
Brothwick Wharf DEPT SE8 ...25 K8

Brunel Engine House BERM/RHTH SE16 ...24 F5
Brunswick Centre Industrial Estate ASH TN23 ...252 C7
Brunswick House Clinic MAIDW ME16 ...12 B3
Brunswick House Primary School MAIDW ME16 ...12 B3
Brunswick Park Primary School CMBW SE5 ...40 D1
Bryony School RHAM ME8 ...96 F7
Bryony School (Upper) RHAM ME8 ...97 J9
Buckland Hospital DVW CT17 ...291 H6
Bullers Wood School CHST BR7 ...63 K7
Burgess Business Park CMBW SE5 ...40 D1
Burnham Trading Estate DART DA1 ...46 D5
Burnhill Business Centre BECK BR3 ...61 N7
Burnt Ash Infant School BMLY BR1 ...62 E4
Burnt Ash School BMLY BR1 ...62 D4
Burnt Oak Junior School BFN/LL DA15 ...44 C9
Burrswood Medical Centre RRTW TN3 ...268 F8
Bursted Wood Primary School BXLYHN DA7 ...45 K3
Burwood School ORP BR6 ...87 L6
The Business Academy Bexley ERITHM DA18 ...28 D5
The Butterfly Centre RDV CT15 ...288 E1
Butterfly Sports Club ELTH/MOT SE9 ...43 M7
Buzzard Creek Industrial Estate BARK IG11 ...27 N1
Bygrove (JM) School BARK IG11 ...25 L2
Byron School GILL ME7 ...7 J6
Bysing Wood CP School FAV ME13 ...132 D5
Cabot Place POP/IOD E14 ...25 K4
Cage Green Primary School TONN TN10 ...210 C5
The Caldecott Community Care for Children RASHE TN25 ...284 B2
Callis Grange Nursery & Infant School BRDST CT10 ...113 L6
Calverton Primary School CAN/RD E16 ...26 E2
Camber Sands Holiday Park RYE TN31 ...344 A1
Camberwell Business Centre CMBW SE5 ...40 D1
Camberwell College of Arts CMBW SE5 ...40 E2
Camberwell Leisure Centre CMBW SE5 ...40 D2
Camberwell New Cemetery FSTH SE23 ...41 K7
Camberwell Trading Estate CMBW SE5 ...40 B3
Camden Centre RTW TN1 ...22 E2
Camden House Clinic BKHTH/KID SE3 ...42 C3
Camelot Primary School PECK SE15 ...41 H1
Camer Park Country Park MEO DA13 ...92 D4
Campanile Hotel CRH DA9 ...47 K4
Camping & Caravanning Club Site FOLKN CT19 ...311 K4
Canada Place POP/IOD E14 ...25 L4
Canada Square POP/IOD E14 ...25 L4
Canada Water Retail Park BERM/RHTH SE16 ...24 G6
Canada Wharf Museum BERM/RHTH SE16 ...25 J4
Canal Industrial Park GVE DA12 ...49 P7
Canary Riverside POP/IOD E14 ...25 J4
Canary Wharf Pier POP/IOD E14 ...25 J4
Canary Wharf Tower POP/IOD E14 ...25 K4
Cannock House School ORP BR6 ...87 N9
Cannon Wharf Business Centre DEPT SE8 ...25 H7
Canterbury Bowling Club CANT CT1 ...4 E7
Canterbury Cathedral CANT CT1 ...5 F4
Canterbury Christ Church College CANT CT1 ...5 G4
CANTW/ST CT2 ...4 E5
RCANTE CT3 ...167 L3
Canterbury Christ Church University College MARG CT9 ...15 J4
Canterbury City FC & Greyhound Racing (Kingsmead Stadium) CANTW/ST CT2 ...166 F2
Canterbury City Retail Park CANT CT1 ...137 J9
Canterbury Environment Centre CANT CT1 ...4 E4

Canterbury Golf Club CANT CT1 ...167 K4
Canterbury Health Centre CANT CT1 ...5 F6
The Canterbury High School CANTW/ST CT2 ...4 A4
Canterbury Indoor Market CANT CT1 ...4 D3
Canterbury Industrial Estate NWCR SE14 ...24 G9
Canterbury Industrial Park RCANTE CT3 ...138 D9
Canterbury Pilgrims Hospital CANT CT1 ...4 D4
Canterbury Road Health Centre MARG CT9 ...14 C5
Canterbury Road Primary School SIT ME10 ...130 A2
Canterbury & St Augustines Magistrates Court CANT CT1 ...5 G4
Canterbury Tales CANT CT1 ...4 E4
Cantium Retail Park STHWK SE1 ...24 D9
Capel-le-Ferne Primary School RFOLK CT18 ...289 M9
Capel Primary School RTON TN11 ...242 A2
Capital Industrial Estate BELV DA17 ...28 G7
BELV DA17 ...29 H4
Capital Wharf WAP E1W ...24 D4
Capstone Farm Country Park GILL ME7 ...96 A7
Cardwell Primary School WOOL/PLUM SE18 ...26 G7
Carew Manor School WLGTN SM6 ...82 C7
Cartwright & Kelsey Primary School RCANTE CT3 ...170 D9
Cascades Leisure Centre GVE DA12 ...70 C3
Casino ROCH ME1 ...19 H5
Castilion Primary School THMD SE28 ...28 B2
Castle CANT CT1 ...4 D6
Castlecares Industrial Park SIT ME10 ...100 A8
Castle Bank CRBK TN17 ...276 C2
Castle Clinic DVE/WH CT16 ...8 E3
Castlecombe Primary School ELTH/MOT SE9 ...63 J4
Castle Community School DEAL CT14 ...233 H5
Castle Hill Primary School CROY/NA CR0 ...114 F1
Castle Remains RMAID ME17 ...217 H3
Castle Road Business Precinct SIT ME10 ...100 A9
Castle Road Industrial Estate SIT ME10 ...130 A1
Castle View Business Centre ROCH ME1 ...19 H5
Catford Cricket & Sports Club CAT SE6 ...41 P9
Catford Cyphers CC CAT SE6 ...61 M1
Catford Girls School CAT SE6 ...62 B2
Catford Trading Estate CAT SE6 ...61 P1
Catford Wanderers Sports Club CAT SE6 ...62 A3
Cathedral Gateway CANT CT1 ...4 E4
Cator Park School for Girls BECK BR3 ...61 L6
Cayley Primary School POP/IOD E14 ...25 H1
Cecil Road Primary School GVW DA11 ...49 K9
The Cedars School ROCH ME1 ...95 H2
Central Business Park STRD ME2 ...19 K2
Centrale Shopping Centre CROY/NA CR0 ...83 H6
Central Hall Theatre & Cinema CHAT ME4 ...6 C4
Central Park Arena DART DA1 ...46 E9
Chadwell St Mary Primary School CDW/CHF RM16 ...33 N7
Chaffinch Business Park BECK BR3 ...61 K9
Chafford School RAIN RM13 ...29 P1
Chaffords Sports Complex RAIN RM13 ...29 P1
Chalkin Business Park RTWE/PEM TN2 ...241 N9
Challock CP School RASHE TN25 ...222 E1
Chambers Wharf BERM/RHTH SE16 ...24 D5
The Channel School FOLKN CT19 ...310 F4
Channel Tunnel Exhibition Centre (summer only) RFOLK CT18 ...287 N8
Channel Tunnel Passenger Terminal RFOLK CT18 ...287 N8
Chantry Primary School GVE DA12 ...49 N8
Chapter School STRD ME2 ...71 M8
Charing CE Primary School HDCN TN27 ...221 H3

Charles Darwin School BH/WHM TN16 ...116 A9
Charles Dickens Centre & Eastgate House ROCH ME1 ...19 H5
The Charles Dickens High School BRDST CT10 ...113 K9
Charles Edward Brook School CMBW SE5 ...40 B2
Charles Edward Brook Upper School CMBW SE5 ...40 B2
Charlotte Turner Primary School DEPT SE8 ...25 K9
Charlton Athletic FC (The Valley) CHARL SE7 ...26 D8
Charlton CE Primary School DVE/WH CT16 ...291 K5
Charlton Health & Fitness Centre CHARL SE7 ...26 D8
Charlton House CHARL SE7 ...26 E9
Charlton Manor Junior School CHARL SE7 ...43 H1
Charlton RFC ELTH/MOT SE9 ...43 M8
Charlton School CHARL SE7 ...26 F9
Charlton Shopping Centre DVE/WH CT16 ...8 B2
Charlwoods Industrial Estate EGRIN RH19 ...265 H5
The Charter School EDUL SE22 ...40 D6
Chartham CP School RCANTW CT4 ...195 G2
Chartham Park Golf Club EGRIN RH19 ...264 F2
Chart Hills Golf Club HDCN TN27 ...278 B2
Chart Sutton Business Estate RMAID ME17 ...186 E9
Chartwell Business Centre BMLY BR1 ...63 H9
Chatham Dockyard (World Naval Base) GILL ME7 ...72 F8
Chatham Girls Grammar School MAID ME5 ...96 A4
Chatham Grammar Boys School CHAT ME4 ...95 L5
Chatham House Grammar School RAM CT11 ...17 F2
Chatham South School CHAT ME4 ...95 K6
Chatsworth Infant School BFN/LL DA15 ...44 C9
Chaucer Business Park BGR/WK TN15 ...150 A4
WSTB CT5 ...105 P5
Chaucer College Canterbury CANTW/ST CT2 ...166 C1
Chaucer Hospital CANT CT1 ...166 F8
The Chaucer Hotel CANT CT1 ...5 F5
Chaucer Technology School CANT CT1 ...167 H5
Chelsfield Lakes Golf Centre ORP BR6 ...117 M2
Chelsfield Park Hospital ORP BR6 ...87 N9
Chelsfield Primary School ORP BR6 ...87 M9
Chequers Shopping Centre MAID/BEAR ME14 ...13 F5
Cheriton Primary School FOLK CT20 ...309 P1
Cherry Garden Pier BERM/RHTH SE16 ...24 E5
Cherry Garden School BERM/RHTH SE16 ...24 D7
Cherry Lodge Golf Club BH/WHM TN16 ...146 B2
Cherry Orchard Primary School CHARL SE7 ...42 G1
Chestfield CC WSTB CT5 ...106 A6
Chestfield Medical Centre WSTB CT5 ...106 C6
Chestfield (Whitstable) Golf Club WSTB CT5 ...106 C6
Chevening Cross RSEV TN14 ...147 P5
Chevening Primary School RSEV TN14 ...148 A7
Cheverne Middle School IOS ME12 ...57 N6
Chiddingstone Castle EDEN TN8 ...238 A2
Chiddingstone CE Primary School EDEN TN8 ...238 B2
Childeric Primary School NWCR SE14 ...41 L1
Chilham St Marys CE Primary School RCANTW CT4 ...194 C3
Chilston Park RMAID ME17 ...219 K1
Chilston Park Hotel RMAID ME17 ...219 L1
Chilton CP School RAM CT11 ...142 F6
Chiltonian Industrial Estate LEE/GVPK SE12 ...42 D7
Chimnocks Wharf POP/IOD E14 ...25 H3
Chislehurst Caves CHST BR7 ...63 L7
Chislehurst Cemetery CHST BR7 ...64 A4
Chislehurst Golf Club CHST BR7 ...63 M6
Chislehurst Natural Health Centre CHST BR7 ...63 M5
Chislehurst & Sidcup GRM School BFN/LL DA15 ...64 D1
Chislet CE Primary School RCANTE CT3 ...138 F4

Chrisp Street Health Centre *POP/IOD* E14 .....25 L2
Christchurch CE Junior School *RAM* CT11 .....16 C5
Christ Church Centre *RTW* TN1 .....22 D5
Christ Church CE Primary School *BRXN/ST* SW9 .....40 A2
FOLK CT19 .....10 D3
FSTH SE23 .....61 K1
WOOL/PLUM SE18 .....43 L2
Christ Church High School *BECK* BR3 .....282 C3
Christ Church Primary School *ERITH* DA8 .....29 J9
Christian Meeting Hall *BECK* BR3 .....61 N7
Christine King 6th Form College *LEW* SE13 .....42 B4
Chrysolite Primary School *STHWK* SE1 .....24 A6
Chunnel Industrial Estate *ASH* TN23 .....2 D6
Church Down Adult School *LEE/GVPK* SE12 .....62 E1
Churchfield School *WOOL/PLUM* SE18 .....27 N7
Churchfields Primary School *BECK* BR3 .....61 K9
Churchill Business Park *BH/WHM* TN16 .....176 E2
Churchill CE Primary School *BH/WHM* TN16 .....176 D1
Churchill Clinic *WALD* ME5 .....95 M7
The Churchill Hotel *DVW* E8 .....E5
Churchill House School *RAM* CT11 .....16 E6
The Churchill School *RFOLK* CT15 .....288 D8
Churchill Theatre *HAYES* BR2 .....8 C7
Church Road Business Centre *SIT* ME10 .....100 B8
Church Stairs *WAP* E1W 24 E5
Church Trading Estate *ERITH* DA8 .....46 A1
Cinema 3 *CANTW/ST* CT2 .....136 D9
Cineworld Cinema *BXLYHS* DA6 .....45 K5
City Banking College *STHWK* SE1 .....24 A5
City Business Centre *BERM/RHTH* SE16 .....24 F5
City Business Park *CANT* CT1 .....167 H1
The City of London Academy *EDUL* SE22 .....40 G6
STHWK SE1 .....24 D8
City of London College *WCHPL* E1 .....24 D2
City of London Polytechnic Sports Ground *ELTH/MOT* SE9 .....62 C1
City Wall *ROCH* ME1 .....19 F4
Civic Centre & Bromley Palace *BMLY* BR1 .....62 F8
Civic Centre & Woodville Halls *GVW* DA11 .....49 M8
Civil Service Sports Ground *ELTH/MOT* SE9 .....42 G7
Clanricarde Medical Centre *RTW* TN1 .....22 D4
Claredon Hotel *BKHTH/KID* SE3 .....42 D3
Clare House *E/WMAL* ME19 .....153 N4
Clare House Primary School *BECK* BR3 .....62 A8
Claremont Primary School *RTW* TN1 .....23 F6
Clarendon House Grammar School *RAM* CT11 .....16 E4
Clarendon & Westbury Community Centre *DVW* CT17 .....291 J8
Clearways Industrial Estate *BGR/WK* TN15 .....120 B2
Cleeve Park School *SCUP* DA14 .....64 E2
Cliffe Woods County Primary School *HOO/HM* ME3 .....52 C8
Clifton Hotel *FOLK* CT20 .....10 C6
Cliftonville CP School *MARG* CT9 .....112 C3
Cliftonville Theatre *MARG* CT9 .....15 K2
Clouster's Green *WAP* E1W 24 D4
CM Booth Collection of Historic Vehicles *CRBK* TN17 .....319 L3
Coalhouse Fort *TIL* RM18 .....50 C2
Cobbs Wood Industrial Estate *ASH* TN23 .....2 B4
Cobham Primary School *OVE* DA12 .....70 C9
Cobourg Primary School *CMBW* SE5 .....24 C8
Cobtree Manor Park Golf Club *MAID/BEAR* ME14 .....155 J1
Cobtree Medical Centre *RMAID* ME17 .....217 H2
Coldecott School *RASHE* TN25 .....284 C5
Coldharbour Industrial Estate *CMBW* SE5 .....40 C3
Coldharbour Leisure Centre *ELTH/MOT* SE9 .....63 K1

Coldharbour Sports Ground *ELTH/MOT* SE9 .....63 L1
Colebrook Industrial Estate *RTWE/PEM* TN2 .....241 H8
Colfes Preparatory School *LEE/GVPK* SE12 .....42 F7
The College of St Barnabas *LING* RH7 .....235 H9
College Square Shopping Centre *MARG* CT9 .....15 H4
Colliers Green CE Primary School *CRBK* TN17 .....275 L6
Collingwood Industrial Estate *RMAID* ME17 .....187 H9
Collingwood Preparatory School *WLGTN* SM6 .....82 A9
Coloma Convent Girls School *CROY/NA* CR0 .....84 A7
Colyers Lane Medical Centre *ERITH* DA8 .....45 M2
Colyers Primary School *ERITH* DA8 .....45 M2
Combe Bank Senior School *DEN* DA4 .....147 M8
Comber Grove Primary School *CMBW* SE5 .....40 C1
Comelle House Trading Estate *DEPT* SE8 .....25 H8
Comfort Inn *RAM* CT11 .....17 J2
The Commodore Catamaran Yacht Club *IOS* ME12 .....57 P6
Community Arts Centre *CNWCH* SE10 .....41 P1
Community Centre (Island History Trust) *POP/IOD* E14 .....25 M7
Community College & School *CNWCH* SE10 .....42 A1
Community Education Centre & Library *RYE* TN31 .....338 F7
Community Support Centre *DVW* CT17 .....291 J6
Compass Centre *CHAT* ME4 .....73 H7
Complementary Health Centre *LEW* SE13 .....42 C7
Concorde Business Park *BH/WHM* TN16 .....115 N9
Coney Hill School *HAYES* BR2 .....85 J6
Connaught Barracks (MOD) *DVE/WH* CT16 .....291 M5
Connections Business Park *RSEV* TN14 .....148 G5
Conquest Industrial Estate *PECK* SE15 .....41 H4
Consort Clinic *PECK* SE15 .....41 H4
Convent Preparatory School *GVE* DA12 .....69 N1
Conway Medical Centre *WOOL/PLUM* SE18 .....27 L8
Conway Primary School *WOOL/PLUM* SE18 .....27 M7
Coopers Lane Primary School *LEE/GVPK* SE12 .....62 E1
Coopers Technology College *CHST* BR7 .....63 N7
Cooting Road Industrial Estate *RCANTE* CT3 .....228 C2
Corinthian Sports Club *HART* DA3 .....90 C3
Corn Exchange *ROCH* ME1 .....19 G4
Cornwallis School *MAID/SHEP* ME15 .....185 L8
Cossington House Surgery *CANT* CT1 .....5 G7
Cottage Industrial Estate *DIT/AY* ME20 .....154 G2
County Court *CHAT* ME4 .....6 A3
The County Hotel *CANT* CT1 .....4 E4
County Primary Infant School *RHAM* ME8 .....97 H6
County Square Shopping Centre *ASH* TN23 .....2 D3
County Primary School *CROY/NA* CR0 .....114 C4
Coward Industrial Estate *CDW/CHF* RM16 .....33 J8
Cowgate Cemetery *DVW* CT17 .....8 C4
Coxheath Primary School *RMAID* ME17 .....185 H8
Crabble Corn Mill *DVW* CT17 .....290 G4
Cranbrook CE Primary School *CRBK* TN17 .....298 A1
Cranbrook Clinic *CRBK* TN17 .....298 A2
Cranbrook RFC *CRBK* TN17 .....298 A1
Cranbrook School *CRBK* TN17 .....298 A2
Crawford Primary School *CMBW* SE5 .....40 C2
Crayfield Industrial Park *STMC/STPC* BR5 .....64 E8
Crayfields Business Park *STMC/STPC* BR5 .....64 E7
STMC/STPC BR5 .....87 K2
Crayford Commercial Centre *DART* DA1 .....45 N6
Crayford Industrial Estate *DART* DA1 .....45 P6
Crayford Leisure Centre & Greyhound Stadium *DART* DA1 .....45 N7
Crayford Medical Centre *DART* DA1 .....45 P6
Craylands Primary School *SWCM* DA10 .....48 B6

Crayside Industrial Estate *DART* DA1 .....46 A4
Cray Valley Golf Club *STMC/STPC* BR5 .....64 C7
Creek Road Health Centre *DEPT* SE8 .....25 L9
Creek Road Industrial Estate *DEPT* SE8 .....25 L9
Crest Industrial Estate *STPH/PW* TN12 .....245 H3
Criton Industrial Estate *CDW/CHF* RM16 .....33M2
Crockenhill Primary School *SWLY* BR8 .....88 B3
Crockham Hill CE Primary School *EDEN* TN8 .....176 D9
Crofton Leisure Centre *BROCKY* SE4 .....41 N7
Crofton School *BROCKY* SE4 .....41 N7
Crook Log Primary School *BXLYHS* DA6 .....44 F5
Crook Log Sports Centre *WELL* DA16 .....44 F4
Crossways Academy Sixth Form *BROCKY* SE4 .....41 L3
Crowden House Cranbrook School *CRBK* TN17 .....298 B2
Crown Court Clinic *ROCH* ME1 .....19 H6
Crown Lane Primary School *WNWD* SE27 .....60 C3
Crown Woods School *ELTH/MOT* SE9 .....43 N6
Croydon Cemetery *THHTH* CR7 .....82 E2
Croydon Clocktower Cinema *CROY/NA* CR0 .....2 A6
Croydon College *CROY/NA* CR0 .....83 J6
Croydon Fairfield Halls Cinema *CROY/NA* CR0 .....83 J7
Croydon FC *SNWD* SE25 .....83 P2
Croydon Indoor Bowling Club *SAND/SEL* CR2 .....83 P9
Croydon Road Industrial Estate *BECK* BR3 .....83 P1
Croydon Sports Arena *SNWD* SE25 .....83 P2
Cryalls Business Estate *SIT* ME10 .....129 K1
Crystal Palace FC (Selhurst Park) *SNWD* SE25 .....83 K1
Crystal Palace Museum *NRWD* SE19 .....60 F5
Cuaco Sports Ground *BECK* BR3 .....61 N5
Cubitt Town Primary School *POP/IOD* E14 .....25 M6
Cudham CE Primary School *BH/WHM* TN16 .....146 B1
Culloden Primary School *POP/IOD* E14 .....25 N2
Culverstone Green Primary School *MEO* DA13 .....121 P2
Cumberland Comprehensive School *CAN/RD* E16 .....26 A1
Cutty Sark Clipper Ship *GNWCH* SE10 .....25 L9
Cuxton Industrial Estate *STRD* ME2 .....94 B4
Cygnet Clinic Beckton *EHAM* E6 .....27 J1
Cygnet Leisure Centre *GVW* DA11 .....49 J9
Cypress Infant School *SNWD* SE25 .....60 E8
Cypress Junior School *SNWD* SE25 .....60 E8
Cyprus College of Art *WNWD* SE27 .....60 B3
Cyril Jackson Primary School *POP/IOD* E14 .....25 J3
D2 Trading Estate *SIT* ME10 .....100 A8
Daily Telegraph *POP/IOD* E14 .....25 K6
Dajen Business Park *SWLY* BR8 .....95 P5
Dale Hill Hotel & Golf Club *WADH* TN5 .....315 K5
Dalmain Primary School *FSTH* SE23 .....41 L9
Dame Janet Community Junior School *MSTR* CT12 .....142 G2
Dame Janet Infant School *MSTR* CT12 .....142 G2
Dame Sybil Thorndike Health Centre *ROCH* ME1 .....95 H2
Damilola Taylor Centre *PECK* SE15 .....40 F1
The Dane Court Grammar School *BRDST* CT10 .....113 J9
Danecourt School (Special School) *GILL* ME7 .....96 C4
Dane John Mound & Monument *CANT* CT1 .....4 D6
Danley Middle School *IOS* ME12 .....57 N9
Danson Primary School *WELL* DA16 .....45 J3
Danson Watersports Centre *BXLYHS* DA6 .....44 E6
Darenth Primary School *RDART* DA2 .....67 M5
Darenth Valley Golf Club *RSEV* TN14 .....118 F6
Darent Industrial Park *ERITH* DA8 .....30 A8
Darent Valley Hospital *RDART* DA2 .....47 K9

Darrick Wood Primary School *ORP* BR6 .....86 C8
Darrick Wood School *ORP* BR6 .....86 C7
Darrick Wood Sports Centre *ORP* BR6 .....86 D7
Darrick Wood Swimming Pool *ORP* BR6 .....86 C8
Dartford County Court *DART* DA1 .....46 E7
Dartford FC *EYN* DA4 .....66 G7
RDART DA2 .....47 H9
Dartford Golf Club *DART* DA1 .....66 B1
Dartford Grammar School for Boys *DART* DA1 .....46 C7
Dartford Grammar School for Girls *DART* DA1 .....46 C8
Dartford Hospital School *HART* DA3 .....91 J9
Dartford Magistrates Court *DART* DA1 .....46 E8
Dartford Museum & Library *DART* DA1 .....46 E8
Dartford Natural Health Centre *DART* DA1 .....46 E8
Dartford Technology College *DART* DA1 .....46 C8
Dartford Tunnel *WTHK* RM20 .....47 K2
Dartford West Health Centre *DART* DA1 .....46 C8
Darwin Leisure Centre *BH/WHM* TN16 .....146 A1
David Livingstone Primary *THHTH* CR7 .....60 C7
David Lloyd Health Club *MAIDW* ME16 .....12 E6
David Lloyd Tennis Centre *DART* DA1 .....64 E4
David Salomon's House *RRTW* TN3 .....240 A9
Davidson J & I School *CROY/NA* CR0 .....83 L4
Davington Primary School *FAV* ME13 .....132 E5
Days Lane Primary School *BFN/LL* DA15 .....44 B7
Deacon Industrial Estate *DIT/AY* ME20 .....154 F2
Deacon Trading Estate *STRD* ME2 .....18 C3
Deacon Trading Estate *TON* TN9 .....210 G9
Deal Castle *DEAL* CT14 .....233 J4
Deal Rowing Club *DEAL* CT14 .....233 J4
Deal Squash Racket Club *DEAL* CT14 .....233 J1
Deal Town FS & S Club *DEAL* CT14 .....232 G5
Deal Victoria & Barnes CC *DEAL* CT14 .....232 G7
Deal & Walmer Community Health Clinic *DEAL* CT14 .....232 G4
Deangate Ridge Athletics Stadium *HOO/HM* ME3 .....53 J8
Deangate Ridge Golf Club *HOO/HM* ME3 .....53 J9
Deansfield Primary School *ELTH/MOT* SE9 .....43 L4
Deanwood Primary Education Technology School *RHAM* ME8 .....126 G1
De Bradelei Wharf Shopping Centre *DVW* CT17 .....8 D5
Delce Junior School *ROCH* ME1 .....95 H4
Delta Wharf *GNWCH* SE10 .....25 N5
Denehoim Primary School *CDW/CHF* RM16 .....32 D5
Denture Clinic *SWCH* CT13 .....201 P2
Denvale Trade Centre *STMC/STPC* BR5 .....87 J2
Denver Industrial Estate *RAIN* RM13 .....29 L1
Deptford Business Centre *DEPT* SE8 .....24 G8
Deptford Green School *DEPT* SE8 .....41 M1
Deptford Park Business Centre *DEPT* SE8 .....25 H8
Deptford Park Primary School *DEPT* SE8 .....25 H8
Deptford Trading Estate *DEPT* SE8 .....25 H8
Discovery Business Park *BERM/RHTH* SE16 .....24 G3
Design Museum *STHWK* SE1 .....24 C5
Detling CE Primary School *MAID/BEAR* ME14 .....156 D3
De Vere Village Hotel *MAIDW* ME16 .....155 K3
Dickens House Museum *BRDST* CT10 .....113 N9
Diggerland *STRD* ME2 .....94 E2
Dilkes Primary School *SOCK/AV* RM15 .....31 J2
Diocesan & Payne Smith CE Primary School *CANT* CT1 .....5 F3
Discovery School *E/WMAL* ME19 .....153 L9
Ditton CE Junior School *DIT/AY* ME20 .....154 B3
Ditton Infant School *DIT/AY* ME20 .....154 B3
Docklands Medical Centre *POP/IOD* E14 .....25 K7

Docklands Sailing Centre *POP/IOD* E14 .....25 K6
Docklands Sailing & Watersports Centre *POP/IOD* E14 .....25 J6
Dockley Road Industrial Estate *BERM/RHTH* SE16 .....24 C6
Dockmaster's House *POP/IOD* E14 .....25 K3
Dockyard Industrial Estate *WOOL/PLUM* SE18 .....26 F6
Doddington Place *RSIT* ME9 .....160 F4
Doddington Primary School *RSIT* ME9 .....160 G5
Dog Kennel Hill Primary School *CMBW* SE5 .....40 E4
Dolphin Sailing Barge Museum *SIT* ME10 .....99 P9
Dome *CNWCH* SE10 .....25 P4
Dominican Priory *CANT* CT1 .....4 E3
Dominoes Health Centre *GRAYS* RM17 .....32 B9
Donnington Manor Hotel *SEV* TN13 .....148 C3
Dormansland Primary School *LING* RH7 .....235 L8
Dorset Road Industrial Estate *IOS* ME12 .....57 J8
Dorset Road Infant School *ELTH/MOT* SE9 .....63 J1
Dorton College of Further Education *BGR/WK* TN15 .....149 K7
Dorton House School *BGR/WK* TN15 .....149 L7
The Dover Business Centre *DVW* CT17 .....8 A5
Dover Castle & Secret War Time Tunnels *DVE/WH* CT16 .....9 G3
Dover College *DVW* CT17 .....8 B5
Dover Cruise Liner Terminal 1 *DVW* CT17 .....313M1
Dover Cruise Liner Terminal 2 *DVW* CT17 .....313M2
Dover Grammar School for Boys *DVW* CT17 .....291 H7
Dover Grammar School for Girls *DVE/WH* CT16 .....291 L6
Dover Harbour Board Offices *DVW* CT17 .....8 D3
Dover Health Centre *DVE/WH* CT16 .....8 D2
Dover Leisure Centre *DVE/WH* CT16 .....9 F3
Dover Museum *DVE/WH* CT16 .....8 D4
Dover Road Primary School *GVW* DA11 .....49 J9
Dover Water Sports Centre *DVW* CT17 .....8 E7
Downderry Primary School *BMLY* BR1 .....62 C5
Downe Primary School *ORP* BR6 .....116 B5
Downham Health Centre *BMLY* BR1 .....62 C5
Down House-Home of Charles Darwin *ORP* BR6 .....116 A6
The Downs CE Primary School *DEAL* CT14 .....232 C7
Downsview Infant School *KEN/WIL* TN24 .....253 H2
Downsview Primary School *NRWD* SE19 .....60 C6
SWLY BR8 .....66 C3
Downs Way County Primary School *OXTED* RH8 .....175 H3
Drapers Mill Primary School *MARG* CT9 .....112 C5
Dreamland Amusement Park *MARG* CT9 .....15 F5
Dreamland Cinema/Bingo *MARG* CT9 .....15 F5
Drew Primary School *CAN/RD* E16 .....26 F4
The Drop Redoubt *DVW* CT17 .....8 C5
Druidstone Park & Art Park *CANTW/ST* CT2 .....135 N5
Duke of Clarence Trading Estate *IOS* ME12 .....57 J5
Duke of York School *RDV* CT15 .....291 N5
Dukes Head Hotel *CAR* SM5 .....82 A8
Dulverton Primary School *BFN/LL* DA15 .....63 P1
Dulwich College *DUL* SE21 .....40 E9
Dulwich College Preparatory School *DUL* SE21 .....60 E2
Dulwich College Track *DUL* SE21 .....40 E8
Dulwich Hamlet FC *EDUL* SE22 .....40 E6
Dulwich Hamlet Junior School *DUL* SE21 .....40 D7
Dulwich Hospital *EDUL* SE22 .....40 E5
Dulwich Leisure Centre *EDUL* SE22 .....40 G5
Dulwich Medical Centre *EDUL* SE22 .....40 G6
Dulwich Picture Gallery *DUL* SE21 .....40 E7
Dulwich Preparatory School *DUL* SE21 .....40 D5
Dulwich & Sydenham Hill Golf Club *DUL* SE21 .....60 G1
Dulwich Village CE Infant School *DUL* SE21 .....40 E7

Dunbar Wharf
POP/IOD E14 ....25 J5
Dundee Wharf
POP/IOD E14 ....25 J5
Dungeness Power Station
LYDD TN29 ....347 K5
Dungeness Power Stations'
Visitor Centre *LYDD* TN29 ....347 J4
Dunkerleys Hotel &
Restaurant *DEAL* CT14 ....233 J3
Dunkirk CP School
FAV ME13 ....164 E1
Dunn Street Farm
RASHE TN25 ....222 B5
Dunton Green Primary School
SEV TN13 ....148 D5
Duppas Junior School
CROY/NA CR0 ....82 C9
Durand Primary School
BRXN/ST SW9 ....40 A2
Durands Wharf
BERM/RHTH SE16 ....25 J3
Dymchurch Martello Tower
LYDD TN29 ....326 C6
Dymchurch Primary School
LYDD TN29 ....326 F6
Eaglesfield School
WOOL/PLUM SE18 ....43 L2
Ealdham Primary School
ELTH/MOT SE9 ....42 C5
East Beckton District Centre
EHAM E6 ....26 C2
East Borough Primary School
MAID/BEAR ME14 ....13 J3
Eastchurch CE Primary School
IOS ME12 ....79 L3
Eastcote Primary School
ELTH/MOT SE9 ....43 P4
East Court
EGRIN RH19 ....265 J6
East Court School
RAM CT11 ....17 K2
East Farleigh Primary School
MAID/SHEP ME15 ....184 F5
East Greenwich Christ Church
CE Primary School
GNWCH SE10 ....25 P7
East Grinstead Health Clinic
EGRIN RH19 ....265 H6
East Kent Business Centre
DVE/WH CT16 ....8 E5
East Kent Light Railway
RDV CT15 ....260 B1
East Kent Retail Park
BRDST CT10 ....112 G8
Eastling Primary School
FAV ME13 ....161 K7
East London RFC
EHAM E6 ....26 C1
Eastmead Trading Estate
ASH TN23 ....2 E7
East Peckham Primary
School *STPH/PW* TN12 ......212 C3
Eastry Medical Surgery
SWCH CT13 ....201 J8
Eastry Primary School
SWCH CT13 ....201 J8
East Stour Primary School
KEN/WIL TN24 ....282 G2
East Thamesmead Business
Park *ERITHM* DA18 ....28 E5
East Tilbury Junior &
Infants Schools
TIL RM18 ....34 B8
Eastwell Manor Hotel
RASHE TN25 ....222 G6
East Wickham Primary School
WELL DA16 ....44 B2
Ebbsfleet Industrial Estate
GVW DA11 ....48 E6
Ebury Hotel
CANT CT1 ....5 J7
Ecclesbourne Primary School
THHTH CR7 ....83 H2
Edenbridge District War
Memorial Hospital
EDEN TN8 ....236 D2
Edenbridge Golf & Tennis Centre
EDEN TN8 ....206 B8
Edenbridge Leisure Centre
EDEN TN8 ....206 D8
The Edenbridge Medical Centre
EDEN TN8 ....206 D8
Edenbridge Primary School
EDEN TN8 ....206 D9
Eden Business Centre
ASH TN23 ....2 E7
Edenham High School
CROY/NA CR0 ....84 B4
Edgebury Primary School
CHST BR7 ....63 N3
Edmund Waller Primary School
NWCR SE14 ....41 K3
Efira Road Retail Park
BRXS/STRHM SW2 ....40 A6
Egerton CE Primary School
HDCN TN27 ....219 M7
Eglinton Junior School
WOOL/PLUM SE18 ....27 H9
Eglinton Primary School
WOOL/PLUM SE18 ....43 L1
Elaine Primary School
STRD ME2 ....71 N8
Elbourne Trading Estate
BELV DA17 ....28 C6
Elfrida Primary School
CAT SE6 ....61 P3
Elham CE Primary School
RCANTW CT4 ....257 L5
Eliot Bank Primary School
FSTH SE23 ....61 H1
Elizabeth Trading Estate
NWCR SE14 ....24 C9

Ellen Wilkinson Primary School
EHAM E6 ....26 E1
Ellingham Industrial Centre
ASH TN23 ....282 D3
Ellington High School
RAM CT11 ....16 B2
Ellington School For Girls
RAM CT11 ....16 B2
Elliot Park School
IOS ME12 ....58 B9
Elm Court Industrial Estate
GILL ME7 ....126 B2
Elm Court School
WNWD SE27 ....60 B1
Elmcourt School
CROY/NA CR0 ....83 J8
The Elms Medical Centre
HOO/HM ME3 ....73 K2
Elmwood Primary School
CROY/NA CR0 ....82 G4
Elm Wood Primary School
WNWD SE27 ....60 D2
Eltham Bus Station
ELTH/MOT SE9 ....43 K6
Eltham Cemetery
ELTH/MOT SE9 ....43 N5
Eltham CE Primary School
ELTH/MOT SE9 ....43 H9
Eltham College Junior School
ELTH/MOT SE9 ....43 H9
Eltham College Senior School
ELTH/MOT SE9 ....63 H1
Eltham Crematorium
ELTH/MOT SE9 ....43 P5
Eltham Green School
ELTH/MOT SE9 ....43 H7
Eltham Health Clinic
ELTH/MOT SE9 ....43 L7
Eltham Health & Fitness Centre
ELTH/MOT SE9 ....43 L7
Eltham Hill Tech College
ELTH/MOT SE9 ....43 J7
Eltham Palace (remains)
ELTH/MOT SE9 ....43 J8
Eltham Pools
ELTH/MOT SE9 ....43 J6
Eltham Warren Golf Club
ELTH/MOT SE9 ....43M6
Emery Theatre
POP/IOD E14 ....25 L2
Empire Cinema
SWCH CT13 ....201 N1
English Martyrs RC Primary
School *STRD* ME2 ....72 B7
Ennersdale Primary School
LEW SE13 ....42 B6
Enterprise Business Centre
DVE/WH CT16 ....291 H1
Enterprise Business Estate
DVE/WH CT16 ....19 K2
Enterprise Business Park
POP/IOD E14 ....25 L5
Enterprise Industrial Estate
BERM/RHTH SE16 ....24 F8
Eric Liddell Sports Centre
ELTH/MOT SE9 ....63 H1
Erith Cemetery
ERITH DA8 ....28 G9
Erith & District Hospital
ERITH DA8 ....29 J9
Erith Health Centre
ERITH DA8 ....29 K9
Erith Library & Museum
ERITH DA8 ....29 K8
Erith Playhouse
ERITH DA8 ....29 L8
Erith School
ERITH DA8 ....45 L1
Erith School Community
Sports Centre *ERITH* DA8 .....45 L1
Erith Small Business Centre
ERITH DA8 ....29 K9
Erith Sports Centre
ERITH DA8 ....29 K9
Erith Stadium
ERITH DA8 ....29 K9
Estcots County Primary
School *EGRIN* RH19 ....265 K7
Etchinghill Golf Club
RFOLK CT18 ....287 J4
Ethelbert Road Infant School
FOLKN CT19 ....132 E7
Eureka Leisure Park
ASH TN23 ....2 D3
The Eurogate Business Park
ASH TN23 ....2 D3
Eurolink Business Centre
BRXS/STRHM SW2 ....40 A5
Eurolink Industrial Centre
SIT ME10 ....129 P1
Eurolink Industrial Estate
SIT ME10 ....100 A9
Europa Trading Estate
ERITH DA8 ....29 J8
WTHK RM20 ....31 N8
European School of Osteopathy
MAID/BEAR ME14 ....155 P1
Evegate Business Centre
RASHE TN25 ....284 C6
Eveline Lowe Primary School
STHWK SE1 ....24 D8
Eversley Medical Centre
THHTH CR7 ....82 F3
ExCeL Exhibition Centre
CAN/RD E16 ....26 C3
Express by Holiday Inn
CAN/RD E16 ....25 P2
CANTW/ST CT2 ....165 K2
CROY/NA CR0 ....85 H6
DART DA1 ....47 H5
GNWCH SE10 ....26 A6

Eynsford Castle
EYN DA4 ....89 K6
Eynsford CC
EYN DA4 ....89 K6
Eythorne Elvington
Primary School *RDV* CT15 ....230 D9
Faircharm Trading Estate
DEPT SE8 ....41 P1
Fairchildes Primary School
CROY/NA CR0 ....115 H6
Fairfax Business Centre
MAID/SHEP ME15 ....186 C1
Fairfield Pool & Leisure Centre
DART DA1 ....46 E8
Fairlawn Primary School
FSTH SE23 ....61 J1
Fairview Community
Junior School *RHAM* ME8 ......96 F9
Fairview Industrial Centre
DAGW RM9 ....29 J2
Fairview Industrial Estate
OXTED RH8 ....174 G6
OXTED RH8 ....175 K9
Fairview Industrial Park
RASHW TN26 ....304 G8
Fairwood Industrial Park
ASH TN23 ....2 A4
The Falstaff Hotel
CANTW/ST CT2 ....4 D5
The Family Medical Centre
WALD ME5 ....125 P3
Fan Museum
GNWCH SE10 ....42 A1
Farleigh Court Golf Club
WARL CR6 ....114 D6
Farleigh Primary School
WARL CR6 ....144 A2
Farleigh Rovers FC
WARL CR6 ....144 C1
Farleigh Trading Estate
MAID/SHEP ME15 ....185 K2
Farnborough Primary School
ORP BR6 ....86 E9
Farningham Woods
(Nature Reserve) *SWLY* BR8 ....89 J1
Farrington & Stratford
House School *CHST* BR7 ....63 P6
Faversham Cottage Hospital
FAV ME13 ....132 F6
Faversham Golf Club
FAV ME13 ....162 B6
Faversham Industrial Estate
FAV ME13 ....133 J6
Faversham Town FC
FAV ME13 ....132 G8
Fawkham CE Primary School
HART DA3 ....90 D5
Fawkham Manor Hospital
HART DA3 ....90 F5
The Fayreness Hotel
BRDST CT10 ....113M3
Featherby Infant School
RHAM ME8 ....96 D3
Featherby Junior School
RHAM ME8 ....96 D3
Felbridge Primary School
EGRIN RH19 ....264 C4
Fenstanton J & I School
BRXS/STRHM SW2 ....40 A9
The Ferry Inn
IOS ME12 ....102 F6
Ferry Lane Industrial Estate
RAIN RM13 ....29M1
Financial Times
POP/IOD E14 ....25M2
Finchcocks
CRBK TN17 ....295 P2
Firepower (Museum of
Artillery) *WOOL/PLUM* SE18 ...27 J6
Fisher Athletic FC
BERM/RHTH SE16 ....24 C4
Flagship Brewery
CHAT ME4 ....72 F8
Flamstead House Museum
GNWCH SE10 ....42 B1
Flaxman Sports Centre
CMBW SE5 ....40 C3
Fleetdown J & I School
DART DA1 ....67 J1
Fleetway Sports Club
GVE DA12 ....49 N9
Fleur de Lis Heritage Centre
FAV ME13 ....132 F6
Flicks Cinema
DEAL CT14 ....233 J3
Folkestone CC
FOLKN CT19 ....10 A2
Folkestone Invicta FC
FOLKN CT19 ....310 D5
Folkestone Race Course
RASHE TN25 ....307 P1
Folkestone Rowing Club
FOLK CT20 ....310 B8
Folkestone RFC
RFOLK CT18 ....309 K1
The Folkestone School
for Girls *FOLK* CT20 ....310 C7
Folkestone Sports Centre
& Ski Slope *FOLKN* CT19 ....10 B1
Folkestone Yacht & Motor
Boat Club *FOLKN* CT19 ....11 H4
Follys End Christian
High School *SNWD* SE25 .....83 K3
Fondu Sports Club
PUR RM19 ....30 F7
Fordcombe CE Primary
School *RRTW* TN3 ....268 G3
Fordgate Business Park
BELV DA17 ....29 H5
The Foreland School
BRDST CT10 ....113M7
Forestdale Primary School
CROY/NA CR0 ....114 B3

Forest Hill Business Centre
FSTH SE23 ....61 J1
Forest Hill Industrial Estate
FSTH SE23 ....61 J1
Forest Hill School
FSTH SE23 ....61 K2
Forest Hills Pools
FSTH SE23 ....61 J1
Forge Close Clinic
HAYES BR2 ....85 K5
The Former Health Centre
CHARL SE7 ....26 E7
Forster Park Primary School
CAT SE6 ....62 C2
Fort Amherst Heritage Park &
Caverns
CHAT ME4 ....6 C2
Fort Luton Museum
CHAT ME4 ....95M5
Fort Pitt Grammar School
ROCH ME1 ....95 K2
Fossdene Primary School
CHARL SE7 ....26 C8
Fosse Bank New School
RTON TN11 ....210 B3
Fosters Primary School
WELL DA16 ....44 E3
Four Elms Primary School
EDEN TN8 ....207 J5
Four Seasons Hotel
POP/IOD E14 ....25 J4
Foxfield Primary School
WOOL/PLUM SE18 ....27 K8
Fox's Cross
WSTB CT5 ....135 J2
Franklin Industrial Estate
PGE/AN SE20 ....61 J7
The Frank Walters Business
Park *BRDST* CT10 ....113 J9
The Freda Gardham
Community School
RYE TN31 ....338 G6
Free Trade Wharf
WAP E1W 24 C3
Freight Services Centre
DVE/WH CT16 ....9 J3
Fremlin Walk Shopping Centre
MAID/BEAR ME14 ....12 E4
French Hospital
RYE TN31 ....331 N9
Frewen College
RYE TN31 ....330 B8
Friars School
ASH TN23 ....251 N9
The Friends of Canterbury
Cathedral *CANT* CT1 ....5 F3
Frittenden CE Primary School
CRBK TN17 ....277 H2
Fulston Manor School
SIT ME10 ....129 N3
Furley Park Primary School
ASH TN23 ....282 F6
Furness School
SWLY BR8 ....65 P5
Furness Swanley FC
SWLY BR8 ....88 C2
Gads Hill School
STRD ME2 ....71 L5
Galley Hill Industrial Estate
SWCM DA10 ....48 C6
Galleywall Primary School
BERM/RHTH SE16 ....24 E7
Gallions Mount Primary School
WOOL/PLUM SE18 ....27 N8
Gallions Primary School
EHAM E6 ....27 J2
Gallions Reach Shopping Park
EHAM E6 ....27 J1
Gaphouse School
BRDST CT10 ....143M2
Gardener Industrial Estate
BECK BR3 ....61 L4
The Garden of England
Crematorium *RSIT* ME9 ....99 K5
Garlinge Infant School
MARG CT9 ....112 B5
Garrison Cricket Ground
Pavilion *GILL* ME7 ....7 F2
Garrison Sports Stadium
GILL ME7 ....72 G9
Gate House Wood Touring
Park *BGR/WK* TN15 ....151 P5
Gateway Business Centre
BECK BR3 ....61 L5
WOOL/PLUM SE18 ....27 K6
Gateway Community
College North
CDW/CHF RM16 ....32 G5
Gaza Trading Estate
RTON TN11 ....209 J3
Gemini Business Estate
NWCR SE14 ....24 G8
Geoffrey Whitworth Theatre
DART DA1 ....46 A5
George Green School
POP/IOD E14 ....25M8
The George Hotel
CRBK TN17 ....298 A2
RYE TN31 ....338 F7
George Spurgen Comm
Primary School *FOLKN* CT19 ...311 H4
Georges Turles House Clinic
CANTW/ST CT2 ....4 A3
Giffin Business Centre
DEPT SE8 ....41 N1
Gilbert Scott Primary School
SAND/SEL CR2 ....114 B2
The Gillingham College
GILL ME7 ....96 C2
Gillingham FC (Priestfield
Stadium) *GILL* ME7 ....96 B1

Gillingham Golf Club
GILL ME7 ....96 B4
Gillingham Ice Bowl
GILL ME7 ....96 D5
Gillingham Library & Arts
Centre *GILL* ME7 ....7 G1
Gillingham Medical Centre
GILL ME7 ....96 C2
The Glade Business Centre
WTHK RM20 ....31 J8
The Glades Shopping Centre
BMLY BR1 ....62 E8
Glebe School
WWKM BR4 ....84 G5
Glencoe Junior School
CHAT ME4 ....95M4
Globe Industrial Estate
GRAYS RM17 ....32 C9
Globe Wharf
BERM/RHTH SE16 ....24 G3
Globe Works Industrial Estate
GRAYS RM17 ....32 D8
Gloucester Primary School
PECK SE15 ....40 E1
Goacher's Brewery
MAID/SHEP ME15 ....185 K2
Godden Green Clinic
BGR/WK TN15 ....179 N1
Godinton House
ASH TN23 ....251 P5
Godinton Primary School
ASH TN23 ....252 N1
Godinton Way Industrial Estate
ASH TN23 ....2 C4
Goldsmiths College
LEW SE13 ....25 K9
LEW SE13 ....42 C5
NWCR SE14 ....41M2
Goldsmiths College Sports
Ground *SCUP* DA14 ....65 H2
Goldsmith University of
London *NWCR* SE14 ....41M2
Goldwyn Community Special
School *ASH* TN23 ....251 N5
Gonville Primary School
THHTH CR7 ....82 E2
Goodnestone CE Primary
School *RCANTE* CT3 ....199M5
Goodnestone Park Gardens
RCANTE CT3 ....199 L6
Goodrich J & I School
EDUL SE22 ....40 G7
Good Shepherd RC Primary
School *BMLY* BR1 ....62 D3
CROY/NA CR0 ....114 E2
Goose Green Primary School
EDUL SE22 ....40 F5
Goose Green Trading Estate
EDUL SE22 ....40 F5
Gordonbrock Primary School
BROCKY SE4 ....41 N6
Gordon Primary School
ELTH/MOT SE9 ....43 K5
STRD ME2 ....72 A7
Gore Court CC
SIT ME10 ....99 J9
Goudhurst & Kilndown CE
Primary School *CRBK* TN17 ...274 E8
Grace School
FOLK CT20 ....11 F4
Grain Power Station
HOO/HM ME3 ....56 D5
Granby Sports Club
ELTH/MOT SE9 ....63 J4
Grand Shaft (Lower Entrance)
DVW CT17 ....8 C5
Grand Shaft (Upper Entrance)
DVW CT17 ....8 B6
The Grange Medical Centre
RAM CT11 ....16 D5
Grange Moor Hotel
MAIDW ME16 ....12 A7
Grange Park College
E/WMAL ME19 ....153 K2
The Granville School
SEV TN13 ....148 F8
Granville Theatre & Cinema
RAM CT11 ....17 J3
Gravel Hill Primary School
BXLYHS DA6 ....45 K6
Graveney CP School
FAV ME13 ....133 N4
Gravesend County Court
GVW DA11 ....49M7
Gravesend CC
GVE DA12 ....49 L8
Gravesend Grammar School
GVE DA12 ....49 P8
Gravesend Grammar School
for Girls *GVW* DA11 ....49 L9
Gravesend Museum
GVE DA12 ....49M7
Gravesend & Northfleet FC
GVW DA11 ....48 E6
Gravesend & North Kent
Hospital *GVW* DA11 ....49 L7
Gravesend Rowing Club
GVE DA12 ....49 N7
Gravesend Yacht Club
GVE DA12 ....49 P7
Grays Athletic FC
GRAYS RM17 ....32 C9
Grays Business Centre
GRAYS RM17 ....32 D6
Grays Convent School
GRAYS RM17 ....32 C8
Grays County Court
GRAYS RM17 ....32 B9
Grays Farm Primary School
STMC/STPC BR5 ....64 D7

Grays Health Centre
GRAYS RM17 ....32 B8
The Grays School
GRAYS RM17 ....32 C6
Great Chart CC
ASH TN23 ....251 P8
Great Chart Primary School
ASH TN23 ....252 A9
Great Comp Garden
BGR/WK TN15 ....151 P6
Great Dixter
RYE TN31 ....329 P6
Great Hall Arcade
RTW TN1 ....22 D5
Great Hollanden Business
Centre *RTON* TN11 ....179 P9
Great Jubilee Wharf
WAP E1W 24 F4
Greatness Park Cemetery
RSEV TN14 ....149 J6
Greatstone Primary School
NROM TN28 ....343 J2
Greenacre School
WALD ME5 ....95 L9
Greenacres Primary School
ELTH/MOT SE9 ....63 L1
Greenfields School
HDCN TN27 ....300 E1
Greenhithe Health Clinic
GRH DA9 ....47 P6
Greenland Pier
BERM/RHTH SE16 ....25 J6
Green Lane Business Park
ELTH/MOT SE9 ....63 L1
Greenshields Industrial Estate
CAN/RD E16 ....26 B4
Greenslade Primary School
WOOL/PLUM SE18 ....27 L9
Green Street Green Primary
School *ORP* BR6 ....116 C1
Greenvale Infant School
CHAT ME4 ....95 M4
Greenvale Primary School
SAND/SEL CR2 ....114 A5
Greenvale School
FSTH SE23 ....61 L2
Greenwich Centre
Business Park *DEPT* SE8 ....41 P1
Greenwich Cinema
GNWCH SE10 ....42 A1
Greenwich College
GNWCH SE10 ....42 A1
Greenwich Community College
WOOL/PLUM SE18 ....27 J7
WOOL/PLUM SE18 ....27 J7
Greenwich Industrial Estate
CHARL SE7 ....26 C7
GNWCH SE10 ....41 P1
Greenwich Natural
Health Centre *GNWCH* SE10 ....42 A1
Greenwich Pier
GNWCH SE10 ....25 M8
Greenwich Theatre &
Art Gallery *GNWCH* SE10 ....42 B1
Griffen Manor School
WOOL/PLUM SE18 ....44 A2
Grinling Gibbons Primary School
DEPT SE8 ....25 J9
Groombridge Place Gardens &
Enchanted Forest
RRTW TN5 ....269 H8
Grosvenor Casino
RAM CT11 ....17 H4
Grosvenor Medical Centre
RTW TN1 ....22 D2
Grove Bowls Club
RTW TN1 ....22 E5
Grove Dairy Farm
Business Centre *RSIT* ME9 ....99 H8
Grove Ferry Boat Club
RCANTE CT3 ....139 J6
Grove Medical Centre
DEPT SE8 ....25 H7
Grove Park CP School
SIT ME10 ....99 J8
Guardian Industrial Estate
STPH/PW TN12 ....245 H2
Guardian Newspapers
POP/IOD E14 ....25 L5
Gueldar Rose Medical Centre
STPH/PW TN12 ....246 C5
Guildhall Museum
ROCH ME1 ....19 G4
Guildhall University
WCLPL E1 ....24 D2
Gulbenkian Theatre
CANTW/ST CT2 ....136 C9
Guru Nanak Sports Club
GVE DA12 ....49 N8
Guston CE Primary School
DVE/WH CT16 ....291 M4
Guys Hospital
STHWK SE1 ....24 A4
Gypsy Moth IV
GNWCH SE10 ....25 M9
Haberdashers Askes Hatcham
College
NWCR SE14 ....41 K3
Hadlow College
CANT CT1 ....5 J5
Hadlow College of Agriculture
& Horticulture *RTON* TN11 ....211 N2
Hadlow School
RTON TN11 ....211 P2
Hailey Road Business Park
ERITHM DA18 ....28 F5
Haimo Primary School
ELTH/MOT SE9 ....43 H6
Haine Hospital
MSTR CT12 ....112 F9
Haine Industrial Estate
MSTR CT12 ....142 E3
Halfway Houses Primary
School *IOS* ME12 ....77 M1

Halley Primary School
POP/IOD E14 ....25 H1
Halling Primary School
STRD ME2 ....124 A2
Hall Place
BXLY DA5 ....45 L7
Hallsville Primary School
CAN/RD E16 ....26 B2
Halsford Park Primary School
EGRIN RH19 ....264 E6
Halstead Place School
RSEV TN14 ....117 M6
Halstead Primary School
RSEV TN14 ....117 N6
Halstow Primary School
GNWCH SE10 ....26 A8
Hamilton House Hotel
GNWCH SE10 ....42 B2
Hamilton Road Industrial Estate
WNWD SE27 ....60 D3
Hamlet International Industrial
Estate
ERITH DA8 ....29 J8
Hammerwood Park
EGRIN RH19 ....266 D6
Hammonds Corner
LYDD TN29 ....336 D7
Hampton Pier Yacht Club
HB CT6 ....106 G1
Hampton Primary School
HB CT6 ....107 H3
Hampton Road Industrial Park
CROY/NA CRO 83 H5
Ham Street Primary School
RASHW TN26 ....304 C7
Harbinger Primary School
POP/IOD E14 ....25 K7
Harbour School
RDV CT15 ....290 F8
Harcourt CP School
FOLKN CT19 ....310 B4
Harden Road Industrial Estate
LYDD TN29 ....342 C5
Harenc School
SCUP DA14 ....64 E4
Harrietsham CE Primary
School *RMAID* ME17 ....188 F5
Harris City Technology College
NRWD SE19 ....60 F7
Harry Gosling Primary School
WCHPL E1 ....24 D2
Hartley Primary School
HART DA3 ....91 H2
Hartsdown Leisure Centre
MARG CT9 ....14 D7
Hart Street Business Centre
MAIDW ME16 ....12 D6
Harvey Clinic
FOLK CT20 ....10 D4
The Harvey Grammar School
for Boys *FOLKN* CT19 ....310 D5
Haseltine Primary School
CAT SE6 ....61 M3
Haslemere Industrial Estate
MAID/SHEP ME15 ....186 C6
Hatcham Mews Business
Centre *NWCR* SE14 ....41 K1
Hawes Down Clinic
WWKM BR4 ....84 C6
Hawes Down Primary School
WWKM BR4 ....84 C5
Hawkhurst CE Primary School
HAWK TN18 ....317 H6
HAWK TN18 ....317 J4
Hawkhurst Cottage Hospital
HAWK TN18 ....316 F4
Hawkhurst Golf Club
HAWK TN18 ....317 H4
Hawkhurst Squash Club
HAWK TN18 ....316 G4
Hawkinge Crematorium
RFOLK CT18 ....288 C7
Hawkinge Health Centre
RFOLK CT18 ....288 E8
Hawkins Clinic
DEAL CT14 ....233 H3
Hawksmoor Primary School
THMD SE28 ....28 A5
Hawkwell Business Centre
RTWE/PEM TN2 ....242 A7
Hawley Health Centre
MARG CT9 ....15 G5
Hawthorn Farm Caravan Park
RDV CT15 ....262 A7
Hayesbrook School
TON TN9 ....240 D1
Hayes Grove Priory Hospital
ORP BR6 ....85 K6
Hayes Primary School
HAYES BR2 ....85 L5
Hayes School
HAYES BR2 ....85 L6
Hayes Tennis Club
HAYES BR2 ....85 L5
Haymerle School
PECK SE15 ....24 D9
Haysden Country Park
TON TN9 ....240 A1
Hays Galleria
STHWK SE1 ....24 B4
Hazelwood School
OXTED RH8 ....175 K7
Hazlitt Theatre
MAID/BEAR ME14 ....13 F4
Headcorn CC
HDCN TN27 ....247 P3
Headcorn Primary School
HDCN TN27 ....247 M3
Heath Farm School
HDCN TN27 ....220 C3
Heathfield College
HAYES BR2 ....115 M1
Heath House Preparatory
School *BKHTH/KID* SE3 ....42 D3

Heavers Farm Primary School
SNWD SE25 ....83 L2
Heber Primary School
EDUL SE22 ....40 F7
Heckford Street Business
Centre *WAP* E1W 24 C3
Hedgend Industrial Estate
BRCH CT7 ....140 A1
Helen Allson School
MED DA15 ....92 B4
Hempstead House Country
Hotel *RSIT* ME9 ....130 D3
Hempstead Infant School
GILL ME7 ....96 D9
Hempstead Junior School
GILL ME7 ....96 D9
Hempstead Valley Shopping
Centre *GILL* ME7 ....126 D1
Henderson Business Park
STRD ME2 ....19 J2
Henwick Primary School
ELTH/MOT SE9 ....43 H4
Henwood Business Centre
KEN/WIL TN24 ....3 H3
Henwood Industrial Estate
KEN/WIL TN24 ....3 H1
The Hereson School
BRDST CT10 ....143 M1
Heritage Centre &
Town Model *RYE* TN31 ....338 E7
Hermitage Primary School
WAP E1W 24 D4
Herne Bay FC
HB CT6 ....107 L3
Herne Bay Golf Club
HB CT6 ....107 L4
Herne Bay High School
HB CT6 ....107 J3
Herne Bay Museum Centre
HB CT6 ....107 L1
Herne Bay School
HB CT6 ....107 L2
Herne Bay West Industrial
Estate *HB* CT6 ....107 H3
Herne CE Junior School
HB CT6 ....107 M5
Herne Hill School
HNHL SE24 ....60 D1
Herne Hill Stadium
(Cycle Centre) *DUL* SE21 ....40 D7
Herne Infant School
HB CT6 ....107 N6
Hernhill CE Primary School
FAV ME13 ....134 B7
Heronsgate Primary School
THMD SE28 ....27 L6
Herringham Primary School
CDW/CHF RM16 ....33 J6
Hersden Community Primary
School *RCANTE* CT3 ....138 B8
Hever Castle and Gardens
EDEN TN8 ....237 L2
Hever Castle Golf Club
EDEN TN8 ....207 L3
Hever CE Primary School
EDEN TN8 ....237 L3
Hextable Primary School
SWLY BR8 ....65 P5
Higgs Industrial Estate
BRXN/ST SW9 ....40 B4
Higham Primary School
HOO/HM ME3 ....71 L2
High Elms Country Park
ORP BR6 ....116 D2
High Elms Golf Club
ORP BR6 ....116 D2
Highfield Business Centre
RTON TN11 ....4 B7
Highfield Industrial Estate
FOLKN CT19 ....11 H1
Highfield Infant School
HAYES BR2 ....85 H1
Highfield Junior School
HAYES BR2 ....85 H1
High Firs Primary School
SWLY BR8 ....88 E1
High Halden CE Primary
School *RASHW* TN26 ....279 M9
High Halstow Primary School
HOO/HM ME3 ....53 K5
Highshore School
PECK SE15 ....40 F2
Highsted Grammar School
for Girls *SIT* ME10 ....129 N3
Highview Primary School
WLGTN SM6 ....82 D9
The Highway Primary School
ORP BR6 ....87 K9
The Highway Trading Centre
WCHPL E1 ....24 C3
Highworth Grammar School
for Girls *KEN/WIL* TN24 ....2 B1
Hildenborough CE Primary
School *RTON* TN11 ....209 P4
Hilden Grange School
RTON TN11 ....210 E6
Hilden Oaks School
TONN TN10 ....210 E6
Hillborough Business Centre
HB CT6 ....108 C6
Hill Mead Infant School
BRXN/ST SW9 ....40 B5
Hillmead Primary School
BRXN/ST SW9 ....40 B5
Hill School
BH/WHM TN16 ....146 C8
Hills Grove Primary School
WELL DA16 ....44 L1
Hillside Industrial Estate
FOLK CT20 ....310 D7
Hillside Primary School
STMC/STPC BR5 ....87 K4
Hilltop Primary School
STRD ME2 ....72 C6

Hillview School for Girls
TON TN9 ....240 G1
Hilly Fields Medical Centre
BROCKY SE4 ....41 N6
Hilton Business Centre
ASH TN23 ....282 C2
Hilton Docklands Pier
BERM/RHTH SE16 ....25 J4
Historical Society Museum
CHAT ME4 ....6 B2
The Historic Dockyard Chatham
GILL ME7 ....72 F7
Hitherfield Primary School
STRHM/NOR SW16 ....60 A1
Hither Green Cemetery
CAT SE6 ....62 D1
Hither Green Primary School
LEW SE13 ....62 D1
HM Prison Belmarsh
THMD SE28 ....27 M6
HM Prison Canterbury
CANT CT1 ....5 H4
HM Prison Elmley
IOS ME12 ....79 K8
HM Prison Maidstone
MAID/BEAR ME14 ....12 C2
HM Prison Rochester
ROCH ME1 ....94 G6
HM Prison Standford Hill
IOS ME12 ....79 H7
HM Prison Swaleside
IOS ME12 ....79 K7
HMS Belfast
STHWK SE1 ....24 B4
HM Young Offender
Institution *DVW* CT17 ....291 J9
Hoath CP School
RCANTE CT3 ....138 B4
Hobbs Industrial Estate
RMAID ME17 ....264 A1
Hoebrook Primary School
CAT SE6 ....41 N8
Holborn College
WOOL/PLUM SE18 ....26 E7
Holbury Centre
ERITH DA8 ....46 A1
Holiday Inn
BGR/WK TN15 ....151 P3
BXLY DA5 ....45 K7
KEN/WIL TN24 ....252 C5
WALD ME5 ....95 J9
Hollingbourne Primary School
RMAID ME17 ....187 P1
Hollydale Primary School
PECK SE15 ....41 J3
Holmesdale Community
School Technology College
SNOD ME6 ....123 P6
Holmewood House School
RRTW TN3 ....269 M6
Holos Clinic
SWCH CT13 ....201 P1
Hoitye Golf Club
EDEN TN8 ....266 G5
Holy Cross RC Primary School
CAT SE6 ....41 N8
SOCK/AV RM15 ....31 L3
Holy Family RC Primary School
BKHTH/KID SE3 ....42 F5
POP/IOD E14 ....25 K3
The Holy Family RC Primary
School *RMAID* ME17 ....186 B7
Holy Innocents C Primary
School *ORP* BR6 ....86 C7
Holy Trinity CE Junior School
WLGTN SM6 ....82 B8
Holy Trinity CE Primary School
DART DA1 ....46 C6
FSTH SE23 ....61 J1
GVE DA12 ....49 N8
Holy Trinity College
BMLY BR1 ....62 C7
Holy Trinity Foyer
MAID/BEAR ME14 ....13 G4
Holy Trinity Lamorbey CE
Primary School
BFN/LL DA15 ....44 C9
Holy Trinity & St Johns CE
Primary School *MARG* CT9 ....15 H5
Holywell Primary School
RSIT ME9 ....97 P3
Homefarm Estate
DIT/ASY ME20 ....154 E3
Homeopathic Hospital
RTW TN1 ....22 C4
Homewood School
TENT TN30 ....301 J6
Honeycrest Industrial Park
STPH/PW TN12 ....246 B4
Honiton House School
MARG CT9 ....112 F2
Honor Oak Crematorium
FSTH SE23 ....41 K6
Honor Oak Gallery
FSTH SE23 ....41 K7
Honor Oak Health Centre
BROCKY SE4 ....41 L5
Hook Lane Primary School
WELL DA16 ....44 C4
Hoo St Werburgh Primary
School *HOO/HM* ME3 ....73 K2
The Hope Anchor Hotel
RYE TN31 ....338 E7
Hopewell School
ASH TN23 ....282 B1
Hop Farm & Country Park
STPH/PW TN12 ....213 H6
Horizon Industrial Estate
PECK SE15 ....24 D9
The Horniman Museum &
Gardens *FSTH* SE23 ....41 H9

Horniman Primary School
FSTH SE23 ....41 H9
Horn Park Primary School
LEE/GVPK SE12 ....42 F8
Horn Stairs
BERM/RHTH SE16 ....25 J4
Horsmonden Primary School
STPH/PW TN12 ....273 P2
Horsted Primary School
WALD ME5 ....95 J9
Horsted Retail Park
WALD ME5 ....95 J8
Horton Kirby CE Primary School
EYN DA4 ....67 J9
Horton Kirby Trading Estate
EYN DA4 ....67 J8
Hospital Barn Farm
MAID/SHEP ME15 ....184 E7
Hotel du Vin & Bistro
RTW TN1 ....22 E4
Hotel Ibis
GNWCH SE10 ....25 M9
POP/IOD E14 ....25 M3
WTHK RM20 ....31 J9
Hochfield Village Primary
School *RASHW* TN26 ....251 L2
Hoverspeed Terminal
DVW CT17 ....8 E7
Howard Primary School
CROY/NA CRO 83 H9
Howard School
RHAM ME8 ....96 G6
Howland Quay
BERM/RHTH SE16 ....24 G6
Howletts Wild Animal Park
RCANTW CT4 ....167 P6
HSBC Sports Club
BECK BR3 ....61 L5
HSBC Tower
POP/IOD E14 ....25 L4
Hubbard School
EGRIN RH19 ....265 P1
Hugh Christie Technology
College *TONN* TN10 ....210 G4
Hull Park Sports Club
DEAL CT14 ....232 E3
Hundred of Hoo School
HOO/HM ME3 ....73 J2
Hunton CE Primary School
MAID/SHEP ME15 ....214 C3
Huntsman Sports Club
BKHTH/KID SE3 ....42 E5
Hurst Green School
OXTED RH8 ....175 K8
Hurstmere School
BFN/LL DA15 ....44 D9
Hurst Primary School
BXLY DA5 ....44 F9
Hythe Community Clinic
HYTHE CT21 ....309 H5
Hythe Community School
HYTHE CT21 ....308 G5
Hythe CC
HYTHE CT21 ....309 H5
Hythe Imperial Golf Club
HYTHE CT21 ....309 K5
The Hythe Imperial Hotel
HYTHE CT21 ....309 J6
Hythe Ranges
HYTHE CT21 ....308 D8
Hythe St Leonard CE Junior
School *HYTHE* CT21 ....308 G5
Hythe & Saltwood Sailing Club
HYTHE CT21 ....309 H6
Hythe Swimming Pool
HYTHE CT21 ....309 J6
Ichthus Primary School
CMBW SE5 ....40 E1
Ide Hill CE Aided Primary
School *RSEV* TN14 ....177 M7
Iden Croft Herbs
STPH/PW TN12 ....246 D7
Ifield School
GVE DA12 ....69 N4
Ightham Primary School
BGR/WK TN15 ....150 E7
IKEA Store
CROY/NA CRO 82 E5
WTHK RM20 ....31 L8
Ilderton Primary School
BERM/RHTH SE16 ....24 F9
Imberhorne Business Centre
EGRIN RH19 ....264 E5
Imberhorne School
EGRIN RH19 ....264 E6
The Imber Sports Centre
EGRIN RH19 ....264 C5
Imperial College at Wye
RASHE TN25 ....223 P8
Imperial Oyster Cinema
WSTB CT5 ....105 K4
Imperial Retail Park
GVW DA11 ....49 L7
Indoor Bowls & Sports Centre
CHAT ME4 ....6 B2
Independent Business Park
EGRIN RH19 ....264 D5
Information Communications
& Technology Centre
Canterbury College
CANT CT1 ....5 G6
Innkeeper's Lodge *BECK* BR3 ....84 D3
MAID/BEAR ME14 ....12 C2
RCANTW CT4 ....167 J8
STH/RUST TN4 ....240 C7
Invicta Grammar School for
Girls *MAID/BEAR* ME14 ....13 K4
Invicta Primary School
BKHTH/KID SE3 ....26 B9
Invicta Sports Club
DART DA1 ....46 D6
IORA Independent School
BRXN/ST SW9 ....40 A4

Island Clinic *POP/IOD* E14 .....25 M5
Isle of Sheppey Cemetery *IOS* ME12 .....57 M9
Istead Rise Primary School *MEO* DA13 .....69 J7
Ivydale Primary School *BROCKY* SE4 .....41 K5
Ivydene Industrial Estate *EGRIN* RH19 .....265 N9
Iwade Primary School *RSIT* ME9 .....99 L2
James Allens Preparatory Girls School *EDUL* SE22 .....40 D6
James Dixon Primary School *PGE/AN* SE20 .....60 G7
James Wolfe Primary School *GNWCH* SE10 .....41 P1
Jamiatul Ummah School *WCHPL* E1 .....24 E2
Jempsons Trading Estate *RYE* TN31 .....338 E7
Jenner Health Centre *FSTH* SE23 .....41 L9
Jessop Primary School *HNHL* SE24 .....40 B5
Jewish Community Theatre *CMBW* SE5 .....40 D4
John Ball Primary School *BKHTH/KID* SE3 .....42 C3
John Dixon Clinic *BERM/RHTH* SE16 .....24 E6
John Donne Primary School *PECK* SE15 .....41 H2
John Goodhew Medical Centre *SIT* ME10 .....99 M5
John Mayne CE Primary School *HDCN* TN27 .....278 A7
John Orwell Sports Centre *WAP* E1W 24 D4
John Roan Lower School *BKHTH/KID* SE3 .....42 D1
John Roan School *BKHTH/KID* SE3 .....42 C1
John Ruskin College *SAND/SEL* CR2 .....114 B2
John Stainer Primary School *BROCKY* SE4 .....41 L4
John Wilson Business Park *WSTB* CT5 .....106 A5
Joseph Conrad's Grave *CANTW/ST* CT2 .....166 C3
Joseph Wilson Industrial Estate *WSTB* CT5 .....105 N7
Joydens Wood Infant School *RDART* DA2 .....65 N3
Joydens Wood Junior School *BXLY* DA5 .....65 N3
Joy Lane Autism Unit *WSTB* CT5 .....105 K7
Jubilee Corner *RMAID* ME17 .....217 P7
Jubilee Country Park *HAYES* BR2 .....86 C1
Jubilee Hall *CANT* CT1 .....4 B7
Jubilee Primary School *BRXS/STRHM* SW2 .....40 A7
THMD SE28 .....28 B3
The Judd School *TON* TN9 .....240 D1
Julians Primary School *STRHM/NOR* SW16 .....60 A3
The Julie Rose Stadium *KEN/WIL* TN24 .....253 J5
Junior Kings School *CANTW/ST* CT2 .....137 K8
Juno Way Industrial Estate *NWCR* SE14 .....24 G9
Jury's Inn Hotel *CROY/NA* CR0 .....83 H6
Kangley Business Centre *SYD* SE26 .....61 M4
Kavanagh Cinema *HB* CT6 .....107 L1
Kearsney Abbey *DVE/WH* CT16 .....290 E3
Keen Students Supplementary School *WCHPL* E1 .....24 D1
Keir Hardie Primary School *CAN/RD* E16 .....26 B1
Kelsey Park School *BECK* BR3 .....61 N9
Kemnal Technology College *STMC/STPC* BR5 .....64 D6
Kemsing Primary School *BGR/WK* TN15 .....149 N2
Kenden Business Park *STRD* ME2 .....72 D7
Kender Primary School *NWCR* SE14 .....41 J2
Kengate Industrial Estate *HYTHE* CT21 .....308 E6
Kennington CE Junior School *KEN/WIL* TN24 .....252 G2
Kennington CC *KEN/WIL* TN24 .....252 G2
Kenningtons Primary School *SOCK/AV* RM15 .....30 F2
Kensington Avenue Primary School *THHTH* CR7 .....60 A7
Kent Battle of Britain Museum *RFOLK* CT18 .....288 C8
Kent & Canterbury Hospital *CANT* CT1 .....166 F7
Kent CCC (St Lawrence Ground) *CANT* CT1 .....166 G6
Kent College *CANTW/ST* CT2 .....166 B1
Kent College J & I School *CANTW/ST* CT2 .....165 P3
Kent College School *RTWE/PEM* TN2 .....241 N6

Kent County Crematorium *HDCN* TN27 .....221 J5
Kent County Opthalmic & Aural Hospital *MAID/BEAR* ME14 .....13 F3
Kent County Showground *MAID/BEAR* ME14 .....156 F2
Kent & East Sussex Railway *HAWK* TN18 .....330 G1
RBTBR TN32 .....328 G6
RYE TN31 .....330 A4
Kent & East Sussex Steam Railway *TENT* TN30 .....320 B3
Kent & Sussex Crematorium *RTWE/PEM* TN2 .....270 E8
Kent & Sussex Hospital *STH/RUST* TN4 .....22 C2
Kestner Industrial Estate *GRH* DA9 .....47 N5
Keston CE Primary School *HAYES* BR2 .....85 N9
Keynes College *CANTW/ST* CT2 .....136 C9
Kidbrooke Park Primary School *BKHTH/KID* SE3 .....42 G3
Kidbrooke School *BKHTH/KID* SE3 .....43 H3
Kilmorie Primary School *FSTH* SE23 .....61 L1
The King Ethelbert School *BRCH* CT7 .....111 K6
Kingfisher Community Primary School *WALD* ME5 .....95 N7
The Kingfisher Medical Centre *DEPT* SE8 .....25 J9
King & Queen Wharf *WAP* E1W 24 G3
King's College Hospital *CMBW* SE5 .....40 C4
Kings College London *CMBW* SE5 .....40 D5
Kings College School of Medicine & Dentistry *CMBW* SE5 .....40 C4
DUL SE21 .....40 D7
Kingsdale School *DUL* SE21 .....60 E2
Kingsdown & Ringwould CE Primary School *DEAL* CT14 .....263 H5
Kings Farm Infant School *GVE* DA12 .....69 N4
GVE DA12 .....70 C3
Kings Hill Business Park *E/WMAL* ME19 .....153 H8
Kings Hill Golf Club *E/WMAL* ME19 .....183 J1
Kings Hill Primary School *E/WMAL* ME19 .....153 H9
Kingsley Primary School *CROY/NA* CR0 .....82 E5
Kingsmead County Primary School *CANT* CT1 .....5 F2
Kingsmead Leisure Centre *CANTW/ST* CT2 .....5 F2
Kings North CE Primary School *ASH* TN23 .....282 E5
Kingsnorth Industrial Estate *ASH* TN23 .....282 E2
HOO/HM ME3 .....74 B1
Kingsnorth Power Station *HOO/HM* ME3 .....74 B2
Kings Preparatory School *ROCH* ME1 .....19 F6
Kings Road Clinic *WALD* ME5 .....96 A5
Kings School *ROCH* ME1 .....19 F5
Kings School of English *BECK* BR3 .....61 M8
Kings School Recreation Centre *CANTW/ST* CT2 .....4 E1
The Kings School *CANT* CT1 .....5 F3
Kings Stairs *BERM/RHTH* SE16 .....24 E5
Kingstanding Business Park *RTON* TN11 .....241 J7
Kingswood Primary School *RMAID* ME17 .....187 P9
WNWD SE27 .....60 D3
Kitchener Barracks *CHAT* ME4 .....6 C1
Kit's Coty House *DIT/AY* ME20 .....125 H7
Klondyke Industrial Estate *QBOR* ME11 .....77 H3
Knightsmead Special School *SOCK/AV* RM15 .....31 J3
Knights Park Industrial Estate *STRD* ME2 .....18 B4
Knights Templar Church (Ruins) *DVW* CT17 .....8 A7
Knockhall Community Primary School *GRH* DA9 .....48 A6

Knole Park Golf Club *BGR/WK* TN15 .....21 J1
Kobi Nazrul Primary School *WCHPL* E1 .....24 D2
KP Estate *RAIN* RM13 .....29 K3
Laban Centre *DEPT* SE8 .....41 P1
Laddingford Farm Industrial Estate *WBY/YKL* ME18 .....213 L6
Lady Boswells CE Primary School *TUN* TN15 .....21 H5
Ladycross Business Park *EGRIN* RH19 .....265 M1
Lady Joanna Thornhill (End) Primary School *RASHE* TN25 .....223 P8
Ladywell Arena *LEW* SE13 .....41 P7
Ladywell Cemetery *BROCKY* SE4 .....41 M6
Ladywell Leisure Centre *LEW* SE13 .....42 A6
Laker Industrial Estate *BECK* BR3 .....61 M4
Lakeside Retail Park *WTHK* RM20 .....31 K7
Lakeside Shopping Centre *WTHK* RM20 .....31 L6
Laleham School *MARC* CT9 .....112 C3
Lamberhurst CE Primary School *RRTW* TN3 .....295 J1
Lamberhurst Golf Club *RRTW* TN3 .....295 J1
Lamb House *RYE* TN31 .....338 F7
Lambs Court *POP/IOD* E14 .....25 H3
Lamont Business Centre *CROY/NA* CR0 .....82 D4
Lamorbey Swimming Centre *BFN/LL* DA15 .....64 C1
Langafel CE Primary School *HART* DA3 .....68 E9
Langbourne Primary School *DUL* SE21 .....60 E2
Langdon Cliffs Visitor Centre & Viewpoint (NT) *DVE/WH* CT16 .....291 P6
Langdon Park School *POP/IOD* E14 .....25 L2
Langdon Primary School *RDV* CT15 .....261 P7
Langley Park Girls School & Sports Centre *BECK* BR3 .....84 E2
Langley Park Golf Club *BECK* BR3 .....84 G3
Langley Park School for Boys *BECK* BR3 .....84 E3
Langton Green CP School *RRTW* TN3 .....269 K4
Lansbury Lawrence Primary School *POP/IOD* E14 .....25 L2
Lansdowne Primary School *SIT* ME10 .....130 B2
TIL RM18 .....49 K3
Lansdowne Road Clinic *RTW* TN1 .....23 F3
Larkfield Leisure Centre *DIT/AY* ME20 .....153 P1
Larkfield Priory Hotel *DIT/AY* ME20 .....153 N3
Larkfield Trading Estate *DIT/AY* ME20 .....124 A8
Larkins Brewery *EDEN* TN8 .....238 D2
Lashenden (Headcorn) Airfield *HDCN* TN27 .....248 B7
Lathe Barn *LYDD* TN29 .....327 H1
Launcelot Primary School *BMLY* BR1 .....62 E3
Lawn Primary School *GVW* DA11 .....48 G7
Lawrence Trading Estate *GNWCH* SE10 .....25 P7
MADW/MEI ME15 ..
Lawrence Trading Estate *GNWCH* SE10 .....25 P7
MADW/MEI ME15 .....32 D7
Lawrence Wharf *BERM/RHTH* SE16 .....25 J4
Leathermarket Gardens *STHWK* SE1 .....24 A5
Leathersellers Sports Ground *ELTH/MOT* SE9 .....42 G8
Leeds & Broomfield CE Primary School *RMAID* ME17 .....187 K4
Leeds Castle *RMAID* ME17 .....187 N4
Leeds Castle Golf Club *RMAID* ME17 .....187 N3
Lee Manor Primary School *LEW* SE13 .....42 C7
Leeside Court *BERM/RHTH* SE16 .....24 G4
Leesons Primary School *STMC/STPC* BR5 .....64 C9
The Leigh City Technology College (East Campus) *DART* DA1 .....47 H9
The Leigh City Technology College *DART* DA1 .....46 G9
The Leigh City Technology College (West Campus) *DART* DA1 .....46 G9
Leigh Green Industrial Estate *TENT* TN30 .....301 M9
Leigh House Clinic *CANTW/ST* CT2 .....4 C2
Leigh Primary School *RTON* TN11 .....209 L9
Leopold Street Clinic *BOW* E3 .....25 J1

Lesnes Abbey *ABYW* SE2 .....28 C7
Lessness Heath Primary School *BELV* DA17 .....28 F8
Lewisham Bridge Primary School *LEW* SE13 .....41 P4
Lewisham Business Centre *NWCR* SE14 .....24 G9
Lewisham Centre *LEW* SE13 .....42 A4
Lewisham College *DEPT* SE8 .....41 N2
Lewisham Crematorium *CAT* SE6 .....62 D1
Lewisham Police Station *LEW* SE13 .....42 A5
Leybourne Business Centre *E/WMAL* ME19 .....153 M2
Leybourne SS Primary School *E/WMAL* ME19 .....153 M2
Leyton Cross *DART* DA1 .....66 A1
Liberty Square *POP/IOD* E14 .....25 J4
Lime Tree Restaurant & Hotel *RMAID* ME17 .....189 C6
Limpsfield CE Infant School *OXTED* RH8 .....175 L5
Limpsfield Chart Golf Club *OXTED* RH8 .....175 N5
Limpsfield Grange School *OXTED* RH8 .....175 K3
Limpsfield Lawn Tennis Club *OXTED* RH8 .....175 K4
Linden Grove CP School *ASH* TN23 .....282 D2
Lingfield Notre Dame School *LING* RH7 .....235 J6
Lingfield Park Racecourse *LING* RH7 .....235 J7
Lingfield Primary School *LING* RH7 .....234 G5
Lingfield Squash & Leisure Club *LING* RH7 .....235 J6
The Link Day Primary School *CROY/NA* CR0 .....82 D8
The Link Secondary School *CROY/NA* CR0 .....82 E8
Linton Mead Primary School *THMD* SE28 .....28 A3
Liongate Clinic *STH/RUST* TN4 .....270 D3
Little Acorns School *RASHW* TN26 .....301 H2
Littlebourne CE Primary School *RCANTE* CT3 .....168 C8
Littlebrook Business Centre *DART* DA1 .....47 J4
Little Danson Welfare Clinic *WELL* DA16 .....44 C5
Little Hickmotts School *STPH/PW* TN12 .....245 N1
Little Satmar Holiday Park *RFOLK* CT18 .....289 M9
Littlestone Golf Club *NROM* TN28 .....337 K7
Little Switzerland Camping & Caravan Site *FOLKN* CT19 .....311 K3
Little Theatre *FOLK* CT20 .....310 B8
Little Thurrock Primary School *GRAYS* RM17 .....32 E6
Livesey Museum for Children *PECK* SE15 .....24 E9
Livingstone Hospital *DART* DA1 .....46 F8
Lloyds *BANK* EC3V 24 B2
CHAT ME4 .....6 B1
Lloyds Register CC *DUL* SE21 .....40 D9
Loampit Business Centre *STRD* ME2 .....72 D7
Lock Meadow Leisure Complex *MAIDW* ME16 .....12 E6
Lock Meadow Market *MAIDW* ME16 .....12 E7
Locks View Court *POP/IOD* E14 .....25 H3
Lombard Business Park *CROY/NA* CR0 .....82 E4
Lombard Trading Estate *CHARL* SE7 .....26 C7
London Arena *POP/IOD* E14 .....25 L6
London Beach Hotel & Golf Club *TENT* TN30 .....301 H3
London Bridge City Pier *STHWK* SE1 .....24 B4
London City Airport *CAN/RD* E16 .....26 F4
London Dungeon *STHWK* SE1 .....24 A4
London Golf Club *BGR/WK* TN15 .....120 F2
London Guildhall University Sports Ground *LEE/GVPK* SE12 .....62 G1
London House School *WGOS* CT8 .....111 M4
The London Industrial Estate *EHAM* E6 .....27 H1
London Industrial Park *EHAM* E6 .....27 J1
London International Cruise Terminal *TIL* RM18 .....49 L5
London Islamic School/Madrasah *WCHPL* E1 .....24 E2
London Ladies & Girls FC *CAT* SE6 .....61 P4

London Lane Clinic *BMLY* BR1 .....62 D6
London Living Theatre *SYD* SE26 .....61 K3
London Road Medical Centre *THHTH* CR7 .....82 F3
London Road Trading Estate *SIT* ME10 .....129 L1
London Temple Visitors Centre *LING* RH7 .....234 B8
London Transport Bus Depot *BXLYHN* DA7 .....45 K4
Longlands Primary School *BFN/LL* DA15 .....64 A2
Long Lane AFC *BKHTH/KID* SE3 .....42 G3
Long Mead Primary School *RTON* TN11 .....210 E5
Longport Police Station *RFOLK* CT18 .....287 N9
Loose Infant School *MAID/SHEP* ME15 .....185 M6
Loose Junior School *MAID/SHEP* ME15 .....185 M5
Lordswood Health Centre *WALD* ME5 .....125 P4
Lordswood Industrial Estate *WALD* ME5 .....125 P4
Lordswood Leisure Centre *WALD* ME5 .....125 P2
Lorimar Business Centre *RAIN* RM15 .....29 K2
Loughborough Primary School *CMBW* SE5 .....40 B3
Lovell's Wharf *GNWCH* SE10 .....25 N8
Lower Halstow School *RSIT* ME9 .....98 C4
Lower Sydenham Industrial Estate *CAT* SE6 .....61 M4
Lowfield Medical Centre *DART* DA1 .....46 E8
Lucas Vale Primary School *DEPT* SE8 .....41 N2
Luddenham Primary School *FAV* ME13 .....132 B4
Lullingstone Castle *EYN* DA4 .....89 H9
Lullingstone Park Golf Club *ORP* BR6 .....88 C8
Lullingstone Roman Villa *EYN* DA4 .....88 G7
Lunsford Primary School *DIT/AY* ME20 .....153 P2
Lutemer House Business Centre *POP/IOD* E14 .....25 L4
Luton Infant School *CHAT* ME4 .....95 P4
Luton Junior School *WALD* ME5 .....95 P4
Luton Medical Centre *WALD* ME5 .....95 P5
Lydd-Ashford Airport *LYDD* TN29 .....342 F5
Lydd Camp *LYDD* TN29 .....342 A7
Lydd County Primary School *LYDD* TN29 .....342 B6
Lydden CP School *RDV* CT15 .....260 A8
Lydden International Motor Racing Circuit *RCANTW* CT4 .....259 J3
Lydd Golf Club *LYDD* TN29 .....342 D3
Lydd Town Museum *LYDD* TN29 .....342 A6
Lyminge CE Primary School *RFOLK* CT18 .....287 H1
Lympne CE Primary School *HYTHE* CT21 .....307 P4
Lympne Industrial Estate *HYTHE* CT21 .....307 M4
Lyndean Industrial Estate *ABYW* SE2 .....28 B6
Lyndhurst Primary School *CMBW* SE5 .....40 D5
Lynsted & Norton Primary School *RSIT* ME9 .....130 F6
Mace Industrial Estate *HYTHE* CT21 .....3 F2
Magdinford Park Infant School *MAID/SHEP* ME15 .....186 C1
Magdinford Park Junior School *MAID/SHEP* ME15 .....186 D1
Madni Girls School *WCHPL* E1 .....24 E2
Magnet Estate *CDW/CHF* RM16 .....31 M8
Mahatma Gandhi Industrial Estate *BRXN/ST* SW9 .....40 B4
Maidstone General Hospital *MAIDW* ME16 .....154 F8
Maidstone Grammar School *MAID/SHEP* ME15 .....185 N1
Maidstone Grammar School for Girls *MAIDW* ME16 .....12 C2
Maidstone Industrial Centre *MAIDW* ME16 .....12 D3
Maidstone Lawn Tennis Club *MAIDW* ME16 .....155 H7
Maidstone Leisure Centre *MAID/SHEP* ME15 .....185 P1
Maidstone Museum & Bentlif Art Gallery *MAID/BEAR* ME14 .....12 E3
Maison Dieu House *DVE/WH* CT16 .....8 C2
Malcolm Primary School *PGE/AN* SE20 .....61 J6
Malham Road Industrial Estate *FSTH* SE23 .....41 K9
The Malling School *E/WMAL* ME19 .....153 N5

Malory School
BMLY BR1 ....62 E3
Manford Industrial Estate
ERITH DA8 ....29 N9
Manor Brook Medical Centre
BKHTH/KID SE3 ....42 F3
Manor Clinic
FOLK CT20 ....10 D5
Manorfield Primary School
POP/IOD E14 ....25 L1
Manor Hotel
GVE DA12 ....69 P5
Manor Oak Primary School
STMC/STPC BR5 ....87 L2
Manor Park Country Park
E/WMAL ME19 ....153 J6
Manor Way Business Centre
DAGW RM9 ....29 J1
Manor Way Industrial Estate
GRAYS RM17 ....48 C1
Manston Caravan & Camping
Park *MSTR* CT12 ....142 C2
Manzoori Clinic
SWLY BR8 ....65 P6
Maple House Independent
Montessori
THHTH CR7 ....83 H1
Maple House School
THHTH CR7 ....60 C9
Maplesden Noakes School
MAIDW ME16 ....12 B1
Marden Medical Centre
STPH/PW TN12 ....245 H3
Marden Primary School
STPH/PW TN12 ....244 G4
Margate Business Centre
MARC CT9 ....15 G4
Margate Caves
MARC CT9 ....15 H5
Margate FC
MARC CT9 ....14 E7
Margate Lawn Tennis Club
MARC CT9 ....112 C5
Margate Museum
MARC CT9 ....15 G3
Marina Office
DVW CT17 ....8 D7
Marine Road Clinic
DEAL CT14 ....233 J4
Marion Richardson Primary
School *WCHPL* E1 ....24 G2
Marion Vian Primary School
BECK BR3 ....84 A2
Maritime Industrial Estate
CHARL SE7 ....26 C7
Maritime Museum
GNWCH SE10 ....25 P7
RAM CT11 ....17 H5
Marlborough CC
DUL SE21 ....40 G9
Marlborough House School
HAWK TN18 ....316 C4
Marlborough Park School
BFN/LL DA15 ....44 C9
Marlborough Road Industrial
Estate *DEAL* CT14 ....232 E7
Marle Place
STPH/PW TN12 ....273 K4
Marlowe Arcade Shopping
Centre *CANT* CT1 ....4 E5
Marlowe Business Centre
NWCR SE14 ....41 L1
Marlowe Park Medical Centre
CANT CT1 ....94 C1
Marlowe Theatre
CANT CT1 ....4 E3
Marriott Tudor Park Hotel &
Country Club
MAIDE/BEAR ME14 ....156 G9
Marsh Mill Industrial Estate
FOLKN CT19 ....11 J1
Marvels Lane Primary School
LEE/GVPK SE12 ....62 G3
Mary Bax's Stone
DEAL CT14 ....202 F5
Mascalls School
STPH/PW TN12 ....243 H5
Masonic Library & Museum
CMTW 4 D4
Matrix Business Centre
DART DA1 ....46 E6
Maudlin's Green
WAP E1W 24 C4
The Maudsley Hospital
CMBW SE5 ....40 D3
Maunsbney Primary School
WALD ME15 ....95 M9
May Avenue Industrial Estate
GVW DA11 ....49 K9
Maybrook Industrial Estate
HART DA3 ....91 J5
Mayday University Hospital
THHTH CR7 ....82 C3
Mayflower Primary School
POP/IOD E14 ....25 K2
Mayplace Primary School
BXLYHN DA7 ....45 M5
Maypole Primary School
BXLY DA5 ....65 N1
McArthur Glen Designer
Outlet *ASH* TN23 ....282 F1
MDO Majidiah (UK)
WCHPL E1 ....24 E3
Meadowgate School
BROCKY SE4 ....41 K4
Meadowside Leisure Centre
BKHTH/KID SE3 ....42 G5
The Meadow Special School
STMC/STPC BR5 ....64 C8
Meadows School
STH/RUST TN4 ....240 C6
Meadow View Industrial
Estate *RASHW* TN26 ....304 F8

Mead Road Infant School
CHST BR7 ....63 N5
The Mead School
RTWE/PEM TN2 ....270 D7
The Meads Primary School
EGRIN RH19 ....265 H9
Medway City Estate
STRD ME2 ....19 K3
Medway Civic Centre
STRD ME2 ....18 C2
Medway Community College
CHAT ME4 ....95 M5
Medway Crematorium
WALD ME5 ....125 K4
Medway Heritage Centre
CHAT ME4 ....6 B2
Medway Little Theatre
ROCH ME1 ....19 H6
Medway Maritime Hospital
GILL ME7 ....7 G5
Medway RFC
ROCH ME1 ....94 G4
Medway Secure Training
Centre *ROCH* ME1 ....94 G7
Medway Towns Rowing Club
ROCH ME1 ....94 F3
Medway Trading Estate
MAIDW ME16 ....12 D7
Medway Valley Leisure Park
STRD ME2 ....94 D3
Medway Yacht Club
HOO/HM ME3 ....73 H4
Melbourne CP School
DVE/WH CT16 ....291 K9
Mellish Industrial Estate
WOOL/PLUM SE18 ....26 E6
Memorial Hospital
WOOL/PLUM SE18 ....43 L3
Meopham CP School
MEO DA13 ....92 B4
Meopham Medical Centre
MEO DA13 ....92 B6
Meopham School
MEO DA13 ....92 B6
Mereworth Community
School *WRTY/YAL* ME18 ....182 D3
Meridian Locality Mental Health
Centre
CHARL SE7 ....26 D9
Meridian Primary School
GNWCH SE10 ....25 N8
Meridian Sports Club
CHARL SE7 ....43 J1
Meridian Trading Estate
CHARL SE7 ....26 C7
Merlin Primary School
BMLY BR1 ....62 E2
Mermaid Inn Hotel
RYE TN31 ....338 E7
Mersham Primary School
RASHE TN25 ....283 P5
Merton Court Preparatory
School *SCUP* DA14 ....64 E3
Metro Business Centre
SYD SE26 ....61 M5
Metropolitan Police Hayes
Sports Club *HAYES* BR2 ....85 J6
Michael Faraday Primary
School *WALW* SE17 ....24 A4
Middle Park Primary School
ELTH/MOT SE9 ....43 H8
Middlesex Hospital Sports
Ground *CHST* BR7 ....64 B4
Midfield Primary School
CHST BR7 ....64 C6
Mid Kent Business Park
SNOD ME6 ....124 A5
Mid Kent College of FE
CHAT ME4 ....95 J8
Mid Kent College of Higher &
Further Education
ROCH ME1 ....95 J3
Mid Kent Golf Club
GVW DA11 ....69 M2
Mid Kent Shopping Centre
MAIDW ME16 ....155 H5
Mierscourt Primary School
RHAM ME8 ....97 J7
The Mildmay Hotel
DVW CT17 ....8 A4
Mile End & Bow Business
Centre *WCHPL* E1 ....24 E1
Mile End Stadium
BOW E3 ....25 H1
Milesham Industrial Estate
PUR RH19 ....30 D6
Milestone School
HART DA3 ....91 J5
Mile Town Industrial Park
IOS ME12 ....57 J7
Military Barracks
WOOL/PLUM SE18 ....27 H8
Millennium Balloon
STHWK SE1 ....24 B4
Millennium Harbour
Development *POP/IOD* E14 .....25 J5
The Millennium Primary School
GNWCH SE10 ....26 A6
Millennium Quay
DEPT SE8 ....25 L9
Millennium Wharf Development
POP/IOD E14 ....25 N6
Mill Hall Business Estate
DIT/AY ME20 ....154 C2
Mill Lane Trading Estate
CROY/NA CR0 ....82 E7
Millside Industrial Estate
DART DA1 ....46 D5
Millwall FC (The New Den)
BERM/RHTH SE16 ....24 F1
Milstead & Frinsted CE
Primary School
RSIT ME9 ....159 M3

Milton Court Primary School
SIT ME10 ....99 M8
Milton Road Business Park
GVE DA12 ....49 N8
Minnis Bay Sailing Club
BRCH CT7 ....110 D6
Minster Abbey
MSTR ME12 ....58 D9
MSTR CT12 ....141 K7
Minster Abbey Gatehouse
Museum *IOS* ME12 ....58 D9
Minster CE Primary School
MSTR CT12 ....141 J7
Minster College
IOS ME12 ....77 P1
Minster In Sheppey Primary
School *IOS* ME12 ....78 C1
Minster & Rayment Rural
Life Museum *MSTR* CT12 ......141 K6
Minster-Thanet Cemetery
MSTR CT12 ....141 J4
Mint Business Park
CAN/RD E16 ....26 B1
Minterne Junior School
WOOL/PLUM SE18 ....129 L3
Minters Industrial Estate
DEAL CT14 ....232 D5
Mitcham Road Crematorium
THHTH CR7 ....82 D2
Moatbridge School
ELTH/MOT SE9 ....43 H7
Moatlands Golf Club
STPH/PW TN12 ....243 H6
Model Village
HART DA3 ....16 E7
Mongeham Primary School
DEAL CT14 ....232 E5
Monks Hill Sports Centre
SAND/SEL CR2 ....114 A2
Monks Orchard Primary School
CROY/NA CR0 ....84 A2
Monson Primary School
NWCR SE14 ....41 K1
Montbelle School
ELTH/MOT SE9 ....63 M3
Montbelle Primary School
ELTH/MOT SE9 ....63 M2
Montgomery Grant
Maintained School
RCANTE CT3 ....137 P5
Montpelier Business Park
ASH TN23 ....252 C8
Moor House School
OXTED RH8 ....175 J3
Morden College Homes
BKHTH/KID SE3 ....42 E3
Morden Mount Primary School
LEW SE13 ....41 P5
Morehall Primary School
FOLKN CT19 ....310 C5
More Park RC Primary School
E/WMAL ME19 ....153 L4
Moreton Industrial Estate
SWLY BR8 ....88 C1
Morley Business Centre
TON TN9 ....210 C9
Mote CC
MAID/SHEP ME15 ....13 J7
Mote Park Sailing Club
MAID/SHEP ME15 ....156 B9
Motor Museum
RAM CT11 ....16 E6
Motorway Industrial Estate
DIT/AY ME20 ....155 H2
Mottingham Community
Health Clinic *ELTH/MOT* SE9 ...63 J3
Mottingham Primary School
ELTH/MOT SE9 ....63 K2
Mudchute City Farm
POP/IOD E14 ....25 M7
Mulberry Business Centre
BERM/RHTH SE16 ....24 C5
Mulberry School for Girls
WCHPL E1 ....24 E2
Mulgrave Primary School
WOOL/PLUM SE18 ....27 H7
Mundella Primary School
FOLKN CT19 ....10 E1
Munroe Centre
STHWK SE1 ....24 A4
Murray Business Centre
STMC/STPC BR5 ....64 D9
Murston Infant School
SIT ME10 ....130 A1
Murston Junior School
SIT ME10 ....100 A9
Museum in Docklands
POP/IOD E14 ....25 K3
Museum of Canterbury with
Rupert Bear *CANT* CT1 ....4 D4
Museum of Kent Life
MAIDW ME16 ....155 J5
The Museum
CRBK TN17 ....298 A2
Music School
MAID/SHEP ME15 ....12 E6
TON TN9 ....240 E1
Myatt Garden Primary School
BROCKY SE4 ....41 M3
Myatts Field Clinic
BRXN/ST SW9 ....40 B2
Napier Road Secondary School
GILL ME7 ....7 K4
The National Centre for Young
People with Epilepsy
LING RH7 ....235 K5
National Maritime Museum
GNWCH SE10 ....25 N9
National Nature Reserve
RASHW TN26 ....304 E7
National Pinetum & Garden
CRBK TN17 ....296 C7

National Sports Centre
NRWD SE19 ....60 C5
Nature Reserve
CROY/NA CR0 ....114 B5
FAV ME15 ....102 E8
FAV ME15 ....162 C1
FAV ME13 ....163 N8
FOLKN CT19 ....311 K3
HB CT6 ....107 N9
HOO/HM ME3 ....53 L3
IOS ME12 ....101 K2
IOS ME12 ....103 N2
LYDD TN29 ....346 G2
MSTR CT12 ....140 D4
MSTR CT12 ....142 B9
RASHE TN25 ....254 E2
RASHW TN26 ....251 L1
RCANTW CT4 ....226 A6
WADH TN5 ....124 B4
WADH TN5 ....314 F2
Natwest Sports Club
BECK BR3 ....61 M5
Negus 6th Form Centre
WOOL/PLUM SE18 ....27 L3
Nelson Dock Museum
BERM/RHTH SE16 ....25 J4
Neptune Industrial Estate
STRD ME2 ....72 E8
Nevill Golf Club
RTWE/PEM TN2 ....270 C9
New Addington Pools &
Fitness Centre
CROY/NA CR0 ....114 F4
New Ash Green Primary School
HART DA3 ....91 J6
New Atlas Wharf Development
POP/IOD E14 ....25 J6
New Beacon School
SEV TN13 ....178 E5
New Caledonian Wharf
BERM/RHTH SE16 ....25 J6
New Century Cinema
SIT ME10 ....129 P1
New Crane Wharf
WAP E1W 24 F4
New Cross Sports Arena
NWCR SE14 ....41 L1
Newham Leisure Centre
PLSTW E13 ....26 D1
New Hythe Business Park
DIT/AY ME20 ....124 B8
Newington CE Primary School
RSIT ME9 ....98 C7
Newington Industrial Estate
RSIT ME9 ....98 A8
Newington Infant School
MSTR CT12 ....142 F4
Newington Junior Foundation
School
MSTR CT12 ....142 F4
Newlands Primary School
RAM CT11 ....143 K3
New Life School
EGRIN RH19 ....264 C6
New Road Business Estate
DIT/AY ME20 ....154 A4
New Road Industrial Estate
IOS ME12 ....57 J7
New Road Trading Estate
CHAT ME4 ....6 D6
New Royal
FAV ME13 ....132 C5
The New School at West
Heath *SEV* TN13 ....178 C5
News International
WAP E1W 24 C3
Newstead Wood School
for Girls *ORP* BR6 ....86 E7
New Woodlands School
BMLY BR1 ....62 C3
SYD SE26 ....61 H2
Nightingale Primary School
WOOL/PLUM SE18 ....27 J9
Ninnacres School
WOOL/PLUM SE18 ....27 L8
Nizels Golf & Leisure Club
RTON TN11 ....209 K1
The Noble Clinic
STPH/PW TN12 ....243 J9
Nonington CE Primary School
RDV CT15 ....229 M1
Normandy Primary School
ERITH DA8 ....45 M2
Norman Park Athletics Track
HAYES BR2 ....85 L3
North Borough Junior School
MAID/BEAR ME14 ....155 L5
Northbourne CE Primary
School *DEAL* CT14 ....231 M4
Northbourne Court
DEAL CT14 ....231 P4
Northbourne Park
Preparatory School
DEAL CT14 ....231 K3
Northbrook CE School
LEW SE13 ....42 C6
North Clinic
BMLY BR1 ....62 E7
North Croydon Medical Centre
THHTH CR7 ....82 C3
North of School
MARG CT9 ....113 H4
Northdown Industrial Estate
BRDST CT10 ....113 K7
North Downs Business Park
RSEV TN14 ....148 D1
North Downs Golf Club
CDST RH9 ....174 D1
Northend Primary School
ERITH DA8 ....45 P2
North End Trading Estate
ERITH DA8 ....45 N1
North Farm Industrial Estate
RTWE/PEM TN2 ....241 H8

Northfleet Cemetery
CVW DA11 ....48 G9
Northfleet Industrial Estate
CVW DA11 ....48 D5
Northfleet School for Girls
GVW DA11 ....69 H1
Northfleet Technology College
GVW DA11 ....49 H9
North Foreland Golf Club
BRDST CT10 ....113 M5
Northgate Clinic
CANT CT1 ....5 G2
Northiam CE Primary School
RYE TN31 ....330 A8
North Kent Magistrates Court
CHAT ME4 ....6 C3
The North School
KEN/WIL TN24 ....3 H5
Northumberland Heath
Medical Centre *ERITH* DA8 ....45 M1
Northumberland Heath
Primary School *ERITH* DA8 .....45 K1
North West Kent College
DART DA1 ....66 C1
GVE DA12 ....50 B9
Northwood Primary School
ERITHM DA18 ....28 D6
The Norton Knatchbull School
KEN/WIL TN24 ....3 J1
Norwood Heights Shopping
Centre*NRWD* SE19 ....60 C5
Norwood School
WNWD SE27 ....60 C4
Notre Dame RC Primary School
WOOL/PLUM SE18 ....27 J9
Nugent Industrial Park
STMC/STPC BR5 ....87 K1
Nunnery Fields Hospital
CANT CT1 ....166 E6
Nuralite Industrial Estate
DUL SE21 ....51 J8
Oakfield Preparatory School
DUL SE21 ....60 D1
Oakfield Primary School
DART DA1 ....66 D1
Oakfield Road Industrial
Estate *PGE/AN* SE20 ....61 H6
Oakland Primary School
BH/WHM TN16 ....145 M1
Oaklands Primary School
WALD ME15 ....125 L1
Oakley School
RTWE/PEM TN2 ....271 K3
TONN TN10 ....210 E5
Oak Lodge JMI School
WWKM BR4 ....84 E4
The Oaks Infant School
SIT ME10 ....129 L3
Oak Tree County Primary
School *ASH* TN23 ....252 C9
Oak Trees Community
School *MAID/SHEP* ME15 ......186 A4
Oakwood Hospital
MAIDW ME16 ....154 G8
Oakwood Park
Grammar School
MAIDW ME16 ....155 H9
Oakwood Trading Estate
BRDST CT10 ....113 J6
The Oast Golf Club
RSIT ME9 ....100 D9
Oasthouse Theatre
RHAM ME8 ....97 J6
Oastpark Golf Club
SNOD ME6 ....123 M7
Occupational Health Centre
CROY/NA CR0 ....83 J7
Ockendon School
SOCK/AV RM15 ....31 K1
Odeon Cinema
BECK BR3 ....61 N8
CANT CT1 ....5 F5
ELTH/MOT SE9 ....43 J5
HAYES BR2 ....62 E8
MAIDW ME16 ....12 E6
RTWE/PEM TN2 ....241 J9
Offham CC
E/WMAL ME19 ....152 E5
Offham Primary School
E/WMAL ME19 ....152 L4
Old Beckenhamian RFC
WWKM BR4 ....84 C7
Old Bellgate Wharf
Development *POP/IOD* E14 .....25 J6
Old Bexley Business Park
BXLY DA5 ....45 K8
Old Bexley CE Primary School
BXLY DA5 ....45 H9
Oldborough Manor
Community School
MAID/SHEP ME15 ....185 N4
Old Brocklians Sports Ground
ELTH/MOT SE9 ....42 C7
Old Bromlians CC
HAYES BR2 ....85 J2
Old Cemetery
EDUL SE22 ....41 H7
Old Colfeian Sports Club
LEE/GVPK SE12 ....62 E6
Old Elthamians Sports Club
CHST BR7 ....64 C5
The Old Guild Theatre
GVW DA11 ....49 H9
Old Hospital
RCANTW CT4 ....257 L4
Old Jamaica Business Estate
STHWK SE1 ....24 C6
Old Judd RFC
TON TN9 ....210 E8
Old Lighthouse
LYDD TN29 ....347 M5
The Old Oast Business Centre
DIT/AY ME20 ....154 F2

Old Palace School
CROY/NA CR0 ....82 G7
The Old Priory School
RAM CT11 ....16 D5
Old Railway Works (Industrial
Estate) *KEN/WIL* TN24 ......252 G9
Old Royal Naval College
CNWCH SE10 ....25 N8
Old Royal Observatory
Greenwich *CNWCH* SE10 ......42 B1
Old St James' Church (ruins)
DVE/WH CT16 ....9 F3
Old Spitalfields Market Hall
WCHPL E1 ....24 B1
Old Station Museum
CAN/RD E16 ....27 H5
Old Sun Wharf
POP/IOD E14 ....25 H3
Old Timber Yard Industrial
Estate *MSTR* CT12 ....142 E4
Old Wilsonians Sports Club
WWKM BR4 ....85 H5
Oliver Goldsmith Primary
School *CMBW* SE5 ....40 F2
OM Medical Centre
IOS ME12 ....57 L6
The Open University
EGRIN RH19 ....265 H7
Orbital Park
KEN/WIL TN24 ....283 J2
Orchard Business Centre
MAIDW ME16 ....155 H4
RTWE/PEM TN2 ....240 C9
SYD SE26 ....61 M4
TON TN9 ....240 C1
Orchard Industrial Estate
MAID/SHEP ME15 ....186 C8
Orchard Medical Centre
RMAID ME19 ....185 H9
Orchard Place Business Centre
E/WMAL ME19 ....152 B6
Orchard Primary School
SCUP DA14 ....64 D4
Orchard School
CANT CT1 ....166 E6
Orchard Shopping Centre
DART DA1 ....46 E7
The Orchard Theatre
DART DA1 ....46 E7
Orchard Way Primary School
CROY/NA CR0 ....84 B4
Orion Business Centre
BERM/RHTH SE16 ....24 G8
Orpington College of FE
ORP BR6 ....87 H5
The Orpington Halls
ORP BR6 ....87 H6
Orpington Mental Health
Centre *ORP* BR6 ....86 C7
Orpington Retail Park
CDW/CHF RM16 ....87 K1
Orsett CE Primary School
CDW/CHF RM16 ....33 H1
Orsett Golf Club
CDW/CHF RM16 ....33 M5
Orsett Heath School
CDW/CHF RM16 ....33 N1
Orsett Industrial Estate
CDW/CHF RM16 ....33 N1
Osmani Primary School
WCHPL E1 ....24 D1
Ospringe CE Primary School
FAV ME13 ....132 D7
Otford Primary School
RSEV TN14 ....148 F1
Our Lady of Grace RC
Primary School *CHARL* SE7 ...26 C9
Our Lady of Hartley RC
Primary School *HART* DA3 ....91 J2
Our Lady of Lourdes RC
Primary School *LEW* SE13 ....42 B4
Our Lady of the Rosary RC
School *BFN/LL* DA15 ....44 A7
Our Lady RC Primary School
POP/IOD E14 ....25 J2
Our Lady & St Philip Neri
Infant School *FSTH* SE23 .....61 K2
Our Lady & St Phillip Neri
Junior School *SYD* SE26 ......61 L3
Our Ladys Catholic Primary
School *DART* DA1 ....46 D7
Oval Primary School
CROY/NA CR0 ....83 K5
Owletts (NT)
CDW DA12 ....70 B9
Owl House
RRTW TN3 ....272 F9
Oxted Health Centre
OXTED RH8 ....175 J5
Oxted & Limpsfield Hospital
OXTED RH8 ....174 C4
Oxted School
OXTED RH8 ....175 J4
Paddock Wood Business
Centre *STPH/PW* TN12 ....243 H2
Paddock Wood Primary
School *STPH/PW* TN12 ....243 H3
Painters Ash Primary School
GVW DA11 ....69 H2
Painters Farm Caravan &
Camping Site *FAV* ME15 ....162 A1
Palace Industrial Estate
MAID/SHEP ME15 ....186 C7
Palace Wood Junior School
MAIDW ME16 ....155 H6
Palmarsh Primary School
HYTHE CT21 ....308 C7
Palm Bay County Primary
School *MARG* CT9 ....113 J2
Palmer's College
GRAYS RM17 ....32 C7
The Pantiles Shopping Arcade
RTWE/PEM TN2 ....22 C7

Parchmore Medical Centre
THHTH CR7 ....60 C9
Parish CE Primary School
BMLY BR1 ....62 E6
Parish Church CE Primary
School *CROY/NA* CR0 ....82 C7
Parker Industrial Centre
RDART DA2 ....47 J8
Park Farm Industrial Estate
FOLKN CT19 ....310 E3
Park Farm Recreation Centre
ASH TN23 ....282 D4
Park Farm Retail Park
FOLKN CT19 ....310 E3
Park Hall Trading Estate
WNWD SE27 ....60 C2
Park Hill Junior School
CROY/NA CR0 ....83 J7
Park House RFC
HAYES BR2 ....85 M6
Park Mall Shopping Centre
ASH TN23 ....2 D5
Park Medical Centre
BERM/RHTH SE16 ....24 C7
Park Mews Small Business
Centre *HNHL* SE24 ....40 C7
Park Road Industrial Estate
SWLY BR8 ....65 P9
Parkside Business Estate
DEPT SE8 ....25 J9
Parkside Community Primary
School *CANT* CT1 ....167 J2
Parkway Primary School
ERITHM DA18 ....28 D6
Park Way Primary School
MAID/SHEP ME15 ....185 N2
Park Wood Golf Club
BH/WHM TN16 ....145 P7
Parkwood Hall School
SWLY BR8 ....66 B9
Parkwood Industrial Estate
MAID/SHEP ME15 ....186 D7
Parkwood Primary School
RHAM ME8 ....97 H9
Pashley Manor & Gardens
BUR/ETCH TN19 ....315 M7
Passenger Terminal Building
DVE/WH CT16 ....9 J3
Passport Language Schools
BMLY BR1 ....62 F7
The Pavilion Leisure Centre
BMLY BR1 ....62 E8
The Pavilion Shopping Centre
TON TN9 ....210 E9
Paxton Primary School
NRWD SE19 ....60 F5
Peall Road Industrial Estate
CROY/NA CR0 ....82 E5
Peckham Park Primary School
PECK SE15 ....40 C1
Peckham Pulse Healthy Living
Centre *PECK* SE15 ....40 C1
Peckham Rye Primary School
PECK SE15 ....41 H4
Pedham Place Industrial
Estate *SWLY* BR8 ....88 F2
The Peel Trading Centre
TON TN9 ....210 F8
Pelham Primary School
BXLYHN DA7 ....45 J1
Pembroke Lodge Museum &
Art Gallery *BRCH* CT7 ....110 C6
Pembury Hospital
RTWE/PEM TN2 ....241 K9
Pembury Primary School
RTWE/PEM TN2 ....241 N9
Pencester Surgery
DVE/WH CT16 ....8 D3
Pendragon Secondary School
BMLY BR1 ....62 E2
Pennypot Industrial Estate
HYTHE CT21 ....308 E6
Penshurst CE Primary School
RTON TN11 ....238 F5
Penshurst Place & Gardens
RTON TN11 ....238 G5
Pentagon Shopping Centre
CHAT ME4 ....6 C4
Pent Valley Technology
College *FOLKN* CT19 ....310 C4
Perry Court Rudolf Steiner
School *RCANTW* CT4 ....195 M4
Perry Hall Primary School
ORP BR6 ....86 C3
Perrymount Primary School
FSTH SE23 ....61 K1
Peter Hills School
BERM/RHTH SE16 ....24 C4
Petham CP School
RCANTW CT4 ....196 B8
Pharos
DVE/WH CT16 ....9 G2
Phoenix Business Centre
POP/IOD E14 ....25 K1
Phoenix Community Primary
School *KEN/WIL* TN24 ....252 C4
Phoenix Industrial Estate
STRD ME2 ....19 H1
Phoenix Leisure Centre
CAT SE6 ....41 P8
Pickford Lane Medical Centre
BXLYHN DA7 ....44 G2
Pickhurst Infant School
HAYES BR2 ....85 H3
Pickhurst Junior School
HAYES BR2 ....85 J3
Pier Pavilion Sports Centre
HB CT6 ....107 K1
Pier Road Industrial Estate
GILL ME7 ....73 K3
Pilgrims Way CP School
CANT CT1 ....5 K7

Pilgrims Way J & I School
PECK SE15 ....24 F9
Pilton CE School
CROY/NA CR0 ....82 G6
Pine Lodge Touring Park
MAID/SHEP ME15 ....187 J1
The Pines Garden
RDV CT15 ....292 F2
Pioneer Business Park
MSTR CT12 ....143 H4
Pioneers Industrial Park
CROY/NA CR0 ....82 D5
Platt CE Primary School
BGR/WK TN15 ....151 M5
Platt Industrial Estate
BGR/WK TN15 ....151 M4
Plaxtol Primary School
BGR/WK TN15 ....181 H4
Playhouse Theatre
WSTB CT5 ....105 L5
Plaza Cinema
OXTED RH8 ....175 H5
Pluckley CE Primary School
HDCN TN27 ....250 C2
Plumcroft Primary School
WOOL/PLUM SE18 ....27 K9
Plumstead Leisure Centre
WOOL/PLUM SE18 ....27 N8
Plumstead Manor School
WOOL/PLUM SE18 ....27 L8
The Pointer School
BKHTH/KID SE3 ....42 E2
Polo Farm Sports Club
RCANTE CT3 ....167 L4
Poplar Business Park
POP/IOD E14 ....25 M3
Portal House School
RDV CT15 ....292 F1
Portland Medical Centre
SNWD SE25 ....83 N2
Port Lympne Wild Animal
Park, Mansion & Garden
HYTHE CT21 ....307 K5
Port Richborough Business
Park *SWCH* CT13 ....171 P5
P&O Stena Line
DVW CT17 ....313 K1
Postley Industrial Centre
MAID/SHEP ME15 ....185 M2
Poulton Business Park
DVW CT17 ....290 C6
Poultwood Public Golf Club
RTON TN11 ....211 J1
Pound Park Nursery School
CHARL SE7 ....26 E8
Poverest Primary School
STMC/STPC BR5 ....87 H2
Powell-Cotton Museum,
Quex House & Gardens
BRCH CT7 ....111 J8
The Powell School
DVE/WH CT16 ....291 J5
Power Industrial Estate
ERITH DA8 ....45 P2
Pratts Bottom Primary
School *ORP* BR6 ....117 K5
Premier Business Park
CHAT ME4 ....95 N5
Premier Cinema
PECK SE15 ....40 G3
Premier Lodge
DVE/WH CT16 ....9 F4
CDW DA12 ....69 N5
PUR RM19 ....31 H7
TON TN9 ....240 G2
WBY/YAL ME18 ....183 M3
Prendergast School
BROCKY SE4 ....41 N5
Preston Hall Hospital
DIT/AY ME20 ....154 E3
Preston Primary School
RCANTE CT3 ....169 M2
PR for Schools
SYD SE26 ....61 J2
Princes Court Business Centre
WAP E1W 24 E3
Princes Golf Club
SWCH CT13 ....172 E8
Princes Park Medical Centre
WALD ME5 ....95 N8
Princess Christian's Hospital
RTON TN11 ....180 B9
The Princess Royal University
Hospital
ORP BR6 ....86 B7
Priory Fields School
DVW CT17 ....291 J7
Priory Hill
IOS ME12 ....80 F6
Priory House School
CAT SE6 ....41 P9
Priory Infant School
RAM CT11 ....16 E3
Priory Leisure Centre
STMC/STPC BR5 ....87 K5
Priory School
STMC/STPC BR5 ....87 K5
Priory Shopping Centre
DART DA1 ....46 D7
Priory Special School
SNWD SE25 ....83 L1
The Priory
ORP BR6 ....86 B6
Progress Business Park
CROY/NA CR0 ....82 E6
Prospect of Whitby
WAP E1W 24 F4
Pump House
BERM/RHTH SE16 ....25 H4
Pumping Station Museum
CHAT ME4 ....6 C4
Purfleet Industrial Park
PUR RM19 ....30 C4

Purfleet Primary School
PUR RM19 ....30 D7
Pursuit Centre
WAP E1W 24 F3
Pysons Road Industrial Estate
MAID/SHEP ME15 ....143 H1
Quarry Hill Infant School
GRAYS RM17 ....32 C8
Quarry Hill Junior School
GRAYS RM17 ....32 C8
Quarry Wood Industrial Estate
DIT/AY ME20 ....154 C2
DIT/AY ME20 ....154 D5
Quebec House
BH/WHM TN16 ....176 E2
Quebec Industrial Estate
BERM/RHTH SE16 ....25 H5
Queenborough Business Centre
QBOR ME11 ....77 J4
Queenborough First School
QBOR ME11 ....77 K2
Queenborough Yacht Club
RSIT ME9 ....56 G2
Queen Elizabeth Hospital
CHARL SE7 ....26 C9
Queen Elizabeths Grammar
School *FAV* ME13 ....132 C5
Queen Elizabeth the Queen
Mothers Hospital
MARG CT9 ....112 F5
Queen Marys Hospital
SCUP DA14 ....64 C4
Queens Hall & Winter Gardens
MARG CT9 ....15 H2
The Queens House
GNWCH SE10 ....25 N9
Queen's Road Cemetery
CROY/NA CR0 ....83 H3
Queens Road Practice
NWCR SE14 ....41 K2
Queen Victoria Cottage
Hospital *RTON* TN11 ....240 F3
Queen Victoria Hospital
EGRIN RH19 ....265 J5
Queen Victoria Memorial
Hospital *HB* CT6 ....107 N2
Quex Caravan Park
WGOS CT8 ....111 M7
RAF Manston History Museum
MSTR CT12 ....141 P2
Raglan Primary School
BMLY BR1 ....85 M1
Railton Road Clinic
BRXN/ST SW9 ....40 B6
Railway Street Industrial Estate
GILL ME7 ....73 K9
Rainbow Quay
BERM/RHTH SE16 ....25 H6
Rainham Mark Grammar
School *RHAM* ME8 ....96 G4
Rainham School for Girls
RHAM ME8 ....96 F6
Rainham Shopping Centre
RHAM ME8 ....97 J5
Ramac Industrial Estate
CHARL SE7 ....26 B8
Ramada Hotel
DVE/WH CT16 ....290 G1
Ramsgate Athletic & FC
RAM CT11 ....16 A4
Ramsgate Boat Club
RAM CT11 ....16 E4
Ramsgate Brewery
RAM CT11 ....17 H4
Ramsgate Holy Trinity
Primary School
RAM CT11 ....143 M3
Ramsgate New Port
Ferry Terminal *RAM* CT11 ...16 E7
The Ramsgate School
MSTR CT12 ....142 F2
Ramsgate Sports Centre
RAM CT11 ....16 D3
Ramsgate Swimming Pool
RAM CT11 ....16 B1
Rangefield Primary School
BMLY BR1 ....62 C4
Range Road Industrial Estate
HYTHE CT21 ....308 F6
Rathfern Primary School
CAT SE6 ....41 M9
Ravensbourne College of
Design & Communication
CHST BR7 ....63 L4
The Ravensbourne School
HAYES BR2 ....85 L1
Ravensquay Business Centre
STMC/STPC BR5 ....87 J2
Ravens Wood School
HAYES BR2 ....85 N7
Raynehurst Junior School
GVW DA12 ....70 B2
Rectory Business Centre
SCUP DA14 ....64 D3
Rectory Paddock School
STMC/STPC BR5 ....64 E8
Reculver Country Park
HB CT6 ....108 F4
Reculver Primary CE Primary
School *HB* CT6 ....108 D6
Reculver Towers & Roman Fort
HB CT6 ....108 F3
Red Gates School
CROY/NA CR0 ....82 F9
Redhill Junior School
CHST BR7 ....63 M4
Redlands Primary School
WCHPL E1 ....24 F1
Redriff Primary School
BERM/RHTH SE16 ....25 H5
Regent Fitzroy
MARG CT9 ....113 J4

Regional Sports Centre
TIL RM18 ....49 M3
Regis Business Park
IOS ME12 ....57 J7
Regis Industrial Estate
IOS ME12 ....57 J7
Regis Manor Comm.
Primary School
SIT ME10 ....99 M7
Remains of St Mary's Church
RDV CT15 ....108 G3
Research Development &
Business Centre
CANTW/ST CT2 ....136 B9
Restoration House
ROCH ME1 ....19 G6
Richborough Business Park
SWCH CT13 ....171 P8
Richborough Castle
SWCH CT13 ....171 M6
Rich Industrial Estate
PECK SE15 ....24 E9
STHWK SE1 ....24 B6
Richmond First School
IOS ME12 ....57 M7
Richmond Infant School
GILL ME7 ....73 J9
The Ridge Golf Club
RMAID ME17 ....217 L1
Ridge View School
TONN TN10 ....210 C4
Riding School
E/WMAL ME19 ....154 A8
The Ripple School
DEAL CT14 ....232 B9
Ripple Vale School
DEAL CT14 ....232 D9
Ritzy Cinema
BRXN/ST SW9 ....40 A5
River Court School
RCANTW CT4 ....195 L1
River CP School
DVW CT17 ....290 F4
Riverside Business Centre
TON TN9 ....210 C9
Riverside Business Park
KEN/WIL TN24 ....3 G5
Riverside Country Park
GILL ME7 ....96 G1
Riverside Golf Club
THMD SE28 ....28 D2
Riverside Industrial Estate
CANT CT1 ....166 C2
DART DA1 ....46 E6
HYTHE CT21 ....308 A6
Riverside Primary School
BERM/RHTH SE16 ....24 D5
Riverside Retail Park
CANT CT1 ....166 C6
RSEV TN14 ....149 H4
Riverside School
ASH TN23 ....252 C8
Riverside Swimming Centre
ERITH DA8 ....29 K8
Riverston School
LEE/GVPK SE12 ....42 E6
The River Surgery
DVE/WH CT16 ....290 F3
Riverview Clinic
GVE DA12 ....70 B4
Riverview Primary School
GVE DA12 ....70 A3
Robert Browning Primary
School *WALW* SE17 ....24 A8
The Robert Napier School
GILL ME7 ....96 B5
Rochester Airport
ROCH ME1 ....95 H7
Rochester Airport Industrial
Estate *ROCH* ME1 ....95 H8
Rochester Castle
ROCH ME1 ....19 F4
Rochester Cathedral
ROCH ME1 ....19 F5
Rochester & Cobham Park
Golf Club *GVE* DA12 ....70 F9
Rochester Grammar School
for Girls *ROCH* ME1 ....95 H4
Rochester Health Centre
ROCH ME1 ....95 J3
Rockliffe Manor Primary
School *WOOL/PLUM* SE18 .....27 N9
Rockmount Primary School
NRWD SE19 ....60 C5
Rodmersham Primary School
RSIT ME9 ....130 A6
Rodmersham Squash Club
RSIT ME9 ....129 P7
Rolvenden Primary School
CRBK TN17 ....319 L5
Roman Industrial Estate
CROY/NA CR0 ....83 K4
Roman Museum
CANT CT1 ....5 F4
Roman Painted House
DVE/WH CT16 ....8 D4
Romney Hythe & Dymchurch
Railway
LYDD TN29 ....326 E8
LYDD TN29 ....327 J3
LYDD TN29 ....347 M2
NROM TN28 ....333 J2
Romney Warren Golf Club
NROM TN28 ....337 K7
Roper House School for
the Deaf *CANTW/ST* CT2 ....4 C2
Ropery Business Park
CHARL SE7 ....26 D7
Rope Walk Shopping Centre
RYE TN31 ....338 E6
Roseacre Junior School
MAID/BEAR ME14 ....156 D8

Rose Bruford College
  BFN/LL DA15 .... 44 D9
  DEPT SE8 .... 25 L9
Rose & Crown Hotel
  TON TN9 .... 210 F8
Rose Hill School
  STH/RUST TN4 .... 270 B3
Rosemead Preparatory School
  DUL SE21 .... 60 C1
Rosendale Primary School
  DUL SE21 .... 40 C8
Rose Street School
  IOS ME12 .... 57 K6
Rosetta Primary School
  CAN/RD E16 .... 26 C1
Rosherville CE Primary School
  GVW DA11 .... 49 J7
Rotherhithe Civic Centre
  BERM/RHTH SE16 .... 24 F5
Rotherhithe Primary School
  BERM/RHTH SE16 .... 24 F7
Rowhill Grange Hotel & Spa
  RDART DA2 .... 66 A4
Rowhill School
  RDART DA2 .... 66 C5
Royal Albion Hotel
  BRDST CT10 .... 113 N9
Royal Arsenal
  WOOL/PLUM SE18 .... 27 J6
Royal Blackheath Golf Club
  ELTH/MOT SE9 .... 43 K8
Royal Cinque Ports Golf Club
  DEAL CT14 .... 203 H9
Royal Cinque Ports Yacht Club
  DVE/WH CT16 .... 8 E5
The Royal Dock Community
  School *CAN/RD* E16 .... 26 D2
Royal Docks Medical Centre
  EHAM E6 .... 27 H2
Royal Engineers Museum
  GILL ME7 .... 72 C9
Royal Mint Court
  TWRH EC3N 24 C3
Royal Museum & Art Gallery
  with Buffs Museum
  CANT CT1 .... 4 E4
Royal National Theatre
  CMBW SE5 .... 40 A1
Royal Observatory Greenwich
  GNWCH SE10 .... 25 N9
Royal Park Primary School
  SCUP DA14 .... 64 C2
Royal St Georges Golf Club
  SWCH CT13 .... 202 C1
Royal School for Deaf Children
  WGOS CT8 .... 111 M4
The Royal School for
  Deaf Children *MARG* CT9 .... 15 J5
Royal Star Arcade
  MAID/BEAR ME14 .... 12 E4
Royal Temple Yacht Club
  RAM CT11 .... 17 F5
Royal Terrace Pier
  GVE DA12 .... 49 N6
Royal Tunbridge Wells
  Business Park
  RTWE/PEM TN2 .... 240 G8
Royal Victoria Docks
  Watersport Centre
  CAN/RD E16 .... 26 B3
Royal Victoria Hospital
  FOLKN CT19 .... 10 C2
Royal Victoria Place
  Shopping Centre
  RTW TN1 .... 22 E2
Royston Primary School
  BECK BR3 .... 61 K7
RSPB
  IOS ME12 .... 77 M9
RSPB Nature Reserve
  LYDD TN29 .... 342 E7
RSPB Reserve
  LYDD TN29 .... 342 C9
RSPB Site
  HOO/HM ME3 .... 74 B7
  RTON TN11 .... 241 L5
Rural Heritage Centre
  RCANTW CT4 .... 257 M3
Rushey Green Primary School
  CAT SE6 .... 41 P9
Ruskin House School
  HNHL SE24 .... 40 C6
Russell Hotel
  MAID/BEAR ME14 .... 155 N5
  RTW TN1 .... 22 D3
Rusthall Medical Centre
  STH/RUST TN4 .... 269 N4
Ruxley Corner Industrial
  Estate *SCUP* DA14 .... 64 F5
Ruxley Park Golf Centre
  STMC/STPC BR5 .... 64 F7
Ryarsh CP School
  E/WMAL ME19 .... 123 H9
Rye Art Gallery
  RYE TN31 .... 338 F6
Rye Castle Museum
  RYE TN31 .... 338 F7
Rye Community Clinic
  RYE TN31 .... 338 E6
Rye Football & CC
  RYE TN31 .... 338 F6
Rye Golf Club
  RYE TN31 .... 339 L9
Rye Harbour Sailing Club
  RYE TN31 .... 339 K9
Rye Industrial Estate
  RYE TN31 .... 338 G8
Ryelands Primary School
  SNWD SE25 .... 83 N2
Rye Lodge Hotel
  RYE TN31 .... 338 F7

Rye Sports Centre
  RYE TN31 .... 338 E6
Sackville Community College
  EGRIN RH19 .... 265 K7
Sackville School
  RTON TN11 .... 209 P4
Sacred Heart RC School
  CMBW SE5 .... 40 C2
Safari Cinema
  CROY/NA CRO 82 C5
Sai Medical Centre
  POP/IOD E14 .... 25 M4
St Albans Road Infant School
  DART DA1 .... 46 F7
St Alfege with St Peter CE
  Primary School
  GNWCH SE10 .... 25 M9
St Andrews CE School
  CROY/NA CRO 82 G8
St Andrews Medical Centre
  STH/RUST TN4 .... 240 D8
St Andrews School
  ROCH ME1 .... 19 F6
St Anne's Trading Estate
  POP/IOD E14 .... 25 J2
St Anselms RC Primary School
  DART DA1 .... 46 G6
St Anselms RC School
  CANT CT1 .... 167 H7
St Anthonys CE Primary School
  EDUL SE22 .... 40 F7
  PGE/AN SE20 .... 61 H7
St Anthonys School
  MARG CT9 .... 113 H4
St Augustine of Canterbury
  RC Primary School
  RHAM ME8 .... 126 C2
St Augustine's Abbey
  CANT CT1 .... 5 H4
St Augustines Abbey
  RAM CT11 .... 16 D6
St Augustines Business Park
  HB CT6 .... 106 E3
St Augustines Catholic
  Primary School
  HYTHE CT21 .... 309 K5
St Augustines College
  WGOS CT8 .... 111 M5
St Augustines Cross
  MSTR CT12 .... 142 B7
St Augustine's Golf Club
  MSTR CT12 .... 142 A7
St Augustines Primary School
  BELV DA17 .... 28 E6
St Augustines RC Primary
  School *CAT* SE6 .... 61 P4
  STH/RUST TN4 .... 270 D1
St Barnabas CE Primary School
  RTW TN1 .... 270 E3
St Bartholomews CE Primary
  School *SYD* SE26 .... 61 J5
St Bartholomews Hospital
  ROCH ME1 .... 19 K7
  SWLY BR8 .... 65 P9
St Bartholomews RC Primary
  School *SWLY* BR8 .... 65 N9
St Bartholomews School
  SIT ME10 .... 99 N7
St Barts and the Royal London
  Hospital
  WCHPL E1 .... 24 E1
St Barts Hospital Sports
  Ground *CHST* BR7 .... 63 P5
St Benedicts School
  WALD ME5 .... 125 P3
St Botolphs CE Primary School
  GVW DA11 .... 49 H8
St Catherines RC Girls School
  BXLYHS DA6 .... 45 K6
St Chads RC Primary School
  SNWD SE25 .... 83 K2
St Christophers School
  BECK BR3 .... 62 A8
  CANT CT1 .... 166 C6
St Cleres Hall Golf Club
  SLH/COR SS17 .... 34 A1
St Cleres School
  SLH/COR SS17 .... 34 B1
St Columbas RC Boys School
  BXLYHS DA6 .... 45 K6
St Crispins CP School
  WGOS CT8 .... 111 M6
St Cyprians Greek Orthodox
  Primary School
  THHTH CR7 .... 60 C8
St Davids College
  WWKM BR4 .... 84 E4
St Dunstans College
  CAT SE6 .... 41 M9
St Eanswythe CE Primary
  School *FOLK* CT20 .... 11 F5
St Edmunds Catholic School
  DVE/WH CT16 .... 291 K5
St Edmunds Junior School
  CANTW/ST CT2 .... 166 B1
St Edmunds RC Primary School
  POP/IOD E14 .... 25 K7
St Edmunds School
  CANTW/ST CT2 .... 166 B1
St Edwards RC Primary School
  IOS ME12 .... 57 K6
St Ethelberts Catholic Primary
  School
  RAM CT11 .... 17 C1
St Faiths Adult Education
  Centre *MAID/BEAR* ME14 ... 12 E4
St Faiths at Ash School
  RCANTE CT3 .... 200 D1
St Fidelis Catholic Primary
  School *ERITH* DA8 .... 29 H9
St Francesca Cabrini Primary
  School *FSTH* SE23 .... 41 J7

St Francis Catholic Primary
  School *MAID/BEAR* ME14 ... 13 F3
St Francis RC Primary School
  PECK SE15 .... 24 D9
St George's Business Centre
  ASH TN23 .... 252 B7
St Georges Business Park
  SIT ME10 .... 130 A1
St Georges CE High School
  BRDST CT10 .... 113 H8
St Georges CE Middle School
  IOS ME12 .... 78 E1
St Georges Centre
  GVW DA11 .... 49 M7
St Georges CE Primary School
  BGR/WK TN15 .... 151 J1
  BMLY BR1 .... 62 C8
  PECK SE15 .... 40 E1
St Georges CE School
  GVW DA11 .... 69 L1
St Gregorys Catholic
  Comprehensive School
  STH/RUST TN4 .... 270 C1
St Gregory's Cemetery
  CANT CT1 .... 5 H3
St Gregory's Centre
  CANT CT1 .... 5 G4
St Gregorys College
  WGOS CT8 .... 111 M3
St Gregorys RC Primary School
  MARG CT9 .... 112 D6
St Helens CE Primary School
  HOO/HM ME3 .... 52 B3
St Helens RC Primary School
  BXTN/ST SW9 .... 40 A4
St Hilarys School
  SEV TN13 .... 148 G7
St James CE J & I School
  BERM/RHTH SE16 .... 24 D6
St James CE Primary School
  HOO/HM ME3 .... 42 B2
  NWCR SE14 .... 41 L2
St James Infant School
  E/WMAL ME19 .... 153 N4
St James Medical Centre
  CROY/NA CRO 83 J4
St James RC Primary School
  HAYES BR2 .... 86 C2
St James's J & I School
  DVW CT17 .... 23 G3
St James the Great RC Primary
  School *PECK* SE15 .... 40 F2
  THHTH CR7 .... 60 B8
St Joachims RC Primary School
  CAN/RD E16 .... 27 K5
St John Business Centre
  MARG CT9 .... 15 H6
St John Fisher Catholic School
  CHAT ME4 .... 95 L4
St John Fisher RC
  Comprehensive School
  ROCH ME1 .... 95 K3
St John Fisher RC Primary
  School *ERITHM* DA18 .... 28 D6
St Johns Angell Town CE
  Primary School
  BRXN/ST SW9 .... 40 B3
St Johns CE Infant School
  CHAT ME4 .... 6 A6
St John's Cemetery
  MARG CT9 .... 112 D6
St Johns CE Primary School
  CROY/NA CRO 84 A7
  MAID/BEAR ME14 .... 156 A6
  PGE/AN SE20 .... 61 J6
  STH/RUST TN4 .... 270 E1
St Johns Infant School
  STH/RUST TN4 .... 270 D3
St Johns RC Comprehensive
  School *GVE* DA12 .... 49 P9
St Johns RC Primary School
  BERM/RHTH SE16 .... 25 H5
  GVE DA12 .... 49 P9
St Johns & St Clements CE
  J & I School *PECK* SE15 ..... 40 C4
St John the Baptist CE
  Primary School *CAT* SE6 .... 62 A3
St John the Divine CE
  Primary School *CMBW* SE5 ... 40 B1
St Josephs Academic RC
  School *BKHTH/KID* SE3 ...... 42 C4
St Joseph's Annexe
  ABYW SE2 .... 28 B9
St Josephs Catholic
  Infant School *NRWD* SE19 ... 60 C5
St Josephs Catholic Primary
  School *BMLY* BR1 .... 62 C6
St Josephs College
  STRHM/NOR SW16 .... 60 C5
St Josephs RC Junior School
  CMBW SE5 .... 40 C1
  NRWD SE19 .... 60 C5
St Josephs RC Primary School
  BERM/RHTH SE16 .... 24 F6
  DART DA1 .... 45 M5
  DEPT SE8 .... 41 N1
  GNWCH SE10 .... 25 P8
  RCANTE CT3 .... 229 J1
  STHWK SE1 .... 24 D5
St Josephs RC School
  GVW DA11 .... 49 H8
St Josephs School
  BRDST CT10 .... 113 L8
St Judes CE Primary School
  HNHL SE24 .... 40 B7
St Katharines Knockholt CE
  Primary School *RSEV* TN14 ... 147 J2
St Katherines School
  SNOD ME6 .... 123 N6
St Lawrence CE Primary
  School *BGR/WK* TN15 ...... 150 B9
St Lawrence College
  RAM CT11 .... 143 J4

St Lawrence Industrial Estate
  RAM CT11 .... 16 A1
St Leonard's Tower (remains)
  E/WMAL ME19 .... 153 H6
St Lukes CE Infant School
  CAN/RD E16 .... 270 F1
St Lukes CE Primary School
  CAN/RD E16 .... 26 A2
  POP/IOD E14 .... 25 N7
  WNWD SE27 .... 60 C4
St Luke's Health Centre
  CAN/RD E16 .... 26 A2
St Margaret Clitherow Primary
  School
  TONN TN10 .... 210 E4
St Margaret Clitherow RC
  Primary School *THMD* SE28 ... 28 A4
St Margaret Lee CE Primary
  School *LEW* SE13 .... 42 F4
St Margarets at Cliffe
  Primary School *RDV* CT15 ... 292 F1
St Margarets at Troy Town
  Primary School *ROCH* ME1 ... 19 F7
St Margarets CE Primary School
  WOOL/PLUM SE18 .... 27 K9
St Margarets Collier Street CE
  Primary School
  STPH/PW TN12 .... 214 C9
St Margaret's Infant School
  RHAM ME8 .... 97 H6
St Margarets Old School
  BGR/WK TN15 .... 179 N6
St Marks CE Primary School
  DIT/AY ME20 .... 124 E7
  HAYES BR2 .... 62 E9
  SNWD SE25 .... 83 M1
  STH/RUST TN4 .... 270 A7
St Marks Industrial Estate
  CAN/RD E16 .... 26 E4
St Martin in the Fields High
  School *BRXS/STRHM* SW2 ... 40 B7
St Martins CE Primary School
  FOLK CT20 .... 309 N2
St Martins Hospital
  CANT CT1 .... 167 J4
St Martins School
  DVW CT17 .... 291 H4
St Mary CE Primary School
  FOLKN CT19 .... 11 K1
St Mary Magdalene CE Primary
  School *WOOL/PLUM* SE18 ... 26 C7
St Mary Magdalene Peckham
  CE Primary School
  PECK SE15 .... 41 H3
St Mary Magdalen's Primary
  School *BROCKY* SE4 .... 41 L5
St Mary of Charity CE Primary
  School *FAV* ME13 .... 132 C6
St Marys Abbey
  E/WMAL ME19 .... 153 K4
St Mary & St Joseph Catholic
  School *SCUP* DA14 .... 64 B4
St Mary & St Michael RC Primary
  School *WCHPL* E1 .... 24 F2
St Marys Catholic Primary School
  GILL ME7 .... 73 K9
  WSTB CT5 .... 105 M3
St Marys CE Junior School
  OXTED RH8 .... 175 N4
St Marys CE Primary School
  ASH TN23 .... 2 B2
  DVE/WH CT16 .... 8 E2
  EGRIN RH19 .... 264 G6
  LEW SE13 .... 41 P6
  SWLY BR8 .... 88 D1
St Mary's Church
  DVE/WH CT16 .... 9 G2
St Marys High School
  CROY/NA CRO 83 H5
St Marys Island CE (Aided)
  Primary School
  CHAT ME4 .... 73 H5
St Marys Medical Centre
  STRD ME2 .... 72 B7
St Marys Primary School
  STRD ME2 .... 72 B7
St Marys RC J & I School
  CROY/NA CRO 83 J5
St Marys RC Primary School
  BECK BR3 .... 62 A6
  DEAL CT14 .... 232 E6
  ELTH/MOT SE9 .... 43 L6
  TIL RM18 .... 49 K5
St Marys Westbrook
  FOLK CT20 .... 310 D6
St Matthews CE Infant School
  ROCH ME1 .... 94 F4
St Matthews Primary School
  STH/RUST TN4 .... 240 E9
St Michaels CE Junior School
  MAIDW ME16 .... 12 B7
St Michaels CE Primary School
  RYE TN31 .... 338 E6
  TENT TN30 .... 301 J4
St Michaels CE Aided Primary
  School Hall *WELL* DA16 ...... 44 E2
St Michaels RC Primary School
  CHAT ME4 .... 6 B6
St Michaels RC Secondary
  School *BERM/RHTH* SE16 ... 24 D5
St Michaels Sydenham CE
  Primary School *SYD* SE26 ... 61 L3
St Mildreds Infant School
  BRCH CT7 .... 113 L9
St Nicholas at Wade Camping
  Site *BRCH* CT7 .... 109 P8
St Nicholas at Wade CE
  Primary School *BRCH* CT7 ... 109 P8
St Nicholas CE Infant School
  STRD ME2 .... 18 B1

St Nicholas' Cemetery
  ROCH ME1 .... 95 H3
St Nicholas CE Primary School
  NROM TN28 .... 336 F6
St Nicholas Court
  BRCH CT7 .... 109 N8
St Nicholas School
  CHST BR7 .... 63 N6
St Nicholas Special School
  CANT CT1 .... 166 E6
St Olaves Grammar School
  ORP BR6 .... 87 J7
St Olaves Preparatory School
  ELTH/MOT SE9 .... 63 M1
St Patricks Infants School
  WAP E1W 24 E4
St Patricks RC Primary School
  WOOL/PLUM SE18 .... 27 L7
St Paulinus CE Primary School
  DART DA1 .... 45 N5
St Pauls CE Infant School
  RRTW TN3 .... 269 N4
St Pauls CE Primary School
  SWLY BR8 .... 66 B7
  WCHPL E1 .... 24 D3
St Pauls CE Junior School
  STH/RUST TN4 .... 269 N4
St Pauls Cray CE Primary
  School *STMC/STPC* BR5 ...... 64 E9
St Pauls Cray Health Clinic
  STMC/STPC BR5 .... 64 C8
St Pauls Infant School
  MAID/BEAR ME14 .... 155 M5
St Pauls with St Lukes CE
  Primary School *BOW* E3 ...... 25 J1
St Peter Chanel RC Primary
  School *SCUP* DA14 .... 64 B4
St Peter & Paul RC Primary
  School *CHST* BR7 .... 64 A8
St Peters Catholic Primary
  School *EGRIN* RH19 .... 264 F6
St Peters CE Infants School
  STH/RUST TN4 .... 240 C9
St Peters CE Junior School
  BRDST CT10 .... 113 L6
St Peters CE Primary School
  DIT/AY ME20 .... 154 E1
  FOLKN CT19 .... 11 H4
  GDST RH9 .... 174 D9
  RTWE/PEM TN2 .... 23 G5
  WALW SE17 .... 24 A8
  WMAL E14 .... 24 F4
St Peters Infant School
  ROCH ME1 .... 95 H3
St Peters Methodist Primary
  School *CANT* CT1 .... 4 D4
St Peters RC Primary School
  SIT ME10 .... 129 L2
  WOOL/PLUM SE18 .... 27 J8
St Peters School of English
  CANT CT1 .... 4 E3
St Philip Howard Catholic
  Primary School *HB* CT6 .... 107 K1
St Phillips Infant School
  SYD SE26 .... 61 H5
St Philomenas RC Primary
  School *STMC/STPC* BR5 ...... 87 K4
St Piers Further Education
  College (NCYPE) *LING* RH7 ... 235 K6
St Piers School (NCYPE)
  LING RH7 .... 235 K5
St Radigund's Abbey
  RDV CT15 .... 290 C7
St Radigunds Comm Primary
  School *DVW* CT17 .... 291 H6
St Richards RC Primary School
  DVE/WH CT16 .... 291 L6
St Ronans School
  HAWK TN18 .... 317 M4
St Saviours CE Primary School
  BECK BR3 .... 40 C4
  POP/IOD E14 .... 25 L1
St Saviours RC Primary School
  LEW SE13 .... 42 A5
St Saviours School
  WGOS CT8 .... 111 M5
St Simon of England RC
  Primary School *ASH* TN23 ... 252 D9
St Simon Stock RC School
  MAIDW ME16 .... 155 H8
St Stephens CE Infant School
  MAID/SHEP ME15 .... 185 K1
St Stephens CE Primary School
  DEPT SE8 .... 41 N3
  GDST RH9 .... 204 C4
St Stephens Junior School
  CANTW/ST CT2 .... 166 E1
St Stephens Primary School
  TON TN9 .... 240 G1
St Stephens RC Primary School
  WELL DA16 .... 44 C4
St Teresas RC Primary School
  KEN/WIL TN24 .... 252 D5
St Thomas a' Becket RC
  Primary School *ABYW* SE2 ... 27 P6
St Thomas Becket RC Primary
  School *SNWD* SE25 .... 83 M3
St Thomas' Hall
  CANT CT1 .... 5 F4
St Thomas More RC Primary
  School *BXLYHN* DA7 .... 45 H3
  ELTH/MOT SE9 .... 43 J4
  WALD ME5 .... 125 M1
St Thomas More RC School
  ELTH/MOT SE9 .... 43 L7
St Thomas of Canterbury RC
  Primary School *GRAYS* RM17 ... 32 C7
  RHAM ME8 .... 96 E4
St Thomas Primary School
  SEV TN13 .... 20 E4

St Thomas RC Primary School
CANT CT1 ....5 C3
St Thomas School
SIT ME10 ....130 B3
St Thomas the Apostle College
PECK SE15 ....41 J2
St Ursulas Convent School
CNWCH SE10 ....42 B1
St Vincents Catholic Primary
School *ELTH/MOT* SE9 ....63 J3
St Werburgh CP Junior School
HOO/HM ME3 ....73 J2
St Werburgh Medical Centre
HOO/HM ME3 ....73 L1
St William of Perth RC Primary
School
ROCH ME1 ....94 G4
St William of York Primary
School *FSTH* SE23 ....41 L9
St Winifreds Catholic Junior
School *LEE/GVPK* SE12 ....42 D7
St Winifreds RC Infant School
LEW SE13 ....42 C6
Salmestone Grange
MARG CT9 ....112 D5
Salmestone Primary School
MARG CT9 ....112 D5
Saltwood CE Primary School
HYTHE CT21 ....308 G3
Samphire Hoe Country Park
RDV CT15 ....312 E3
Samuel Jones Industrial Estate
PECK SE15 ....40 E1
Sandgate Primary School
FOLK CT20 ....310 C7
Sandgate Trading Estate
BERM/RHTH SE16 ....24 EB
Sandhurst CP School
HAWK TN18 ....318 C9
Sandhurst Primary School
CAT SE6 ....42 C8
Sandling Primary School
MAID/BEAR ME14 ....155 N4
Sandown Clinic
DEAL CT14 ....233 J1
Sandown Primary School
DEAL CT14 ....233 H2
Sandwich Industrial Estate
SWCH CT15 ....201 P1
Sandwich Infant School
SWCH CT13 ....201 N1
Sandwich Junior School
SWCH CT15 ....201 N1
Sandwich Lawn Tennis Club
SWCH CT15 ....202 A1
Sandwich Leisure Park
SWCH CT15 ....201 M1
Sandwich Sailing & Motor
Boat Club *SWCH* CT13 ....201 M3
Sandwich Sports &
Leisure Centre *SWCH* CT13 ...201 N3
Sandwich Technology School
SWCH CT13 ....201 N3
Saxon Way Primary School
GILL ME7 ....73 K9
Sayer Clinic
CROY/NA CRO ....82 EB
Schooling Licensed
Conveyancers *GRAYS* RM17 ....32 C8
School of Health
RDART DA2 ....47 H7
Scotney Castle Garden (NT)
RRTW TN3 ....295 L4
Scotts Park Primary School
BMLY BR1 ....62 G7
Scott Wilkie Primary School
CAN/RD E16 ....26 D2
Seabrook CE Primary School
HYTHE CT21 ....309 N5
Seasalter Sailing Club
WSTB CT5 ....104 C7
Sea Street Industrial Estate
HB CT6 ....107 H3
Seaview Caravan Park
HB CT6 ....106 D2
Sedgehill School
CAT SE6 ....42 A7
Sedleys CE Primary School
MEO DA13 ....68 E4
Selhurst High School for Boys
SNWD SE25 ....83 J3
The Selhurst Medical Centre
SNWD SE25 ....83 K3
Sellindge Primary School
RASHE TN25 ....285 K7
Sellindge Sports Club
RASHE TN25 ....285 L7
Selling CE Primary School
FAV ME13 ....163 L6
Selsdon High School
SAND/SEL CR2 ....114 A2
Selsted CE Primary School
RDV CT15 ....258 F7
Senacre Technology College
MAID/SHEP ME15 ....186 A5
Senacre Wood Primary School
MAID/SHEP ME15 ....186 B4
SENCO
STRD ME2 ....94 A4
Sene Valley Golf Club
HYTHE CT21 ....309 K3
Seven Islands Leisure Centre
BERM/RHTH SE16 ....24 F6
Seven Mills Primary School
POP/IOD E14 ....25 K5
Sevenoaks Business Centre
RSEV TN14 ....149 H6
Sevenoaks CC
SEV TN13 ....21 C2
Sevenoaks Hospital
SEV TN13 ....149 H6
Sevenoaks Library, Museum &
Art Gallery
BGR/WK TN15 ....21 G3

Sevenoaks Primary School
SEV TN15 ....148 G7
Sevenoaks RFC
BGR/WK TN15 ....21 H3
Sevenoaks School
BGR/WK TN15 ....21 H6
Sevenoaks School Track
BGR/WK TN15 ....21 H6
Sevenoaks Swimming Centre
BGR/WK TN15 ....21 H3
Sevenoaks Way Industrial
Estate *STMC/STPC* BR5 ....64 E9
Shadwell Dock Stairs
WAP E1W 24 G3
Shahjalal Medical Centre
WCHPL E1 ....24 D2
Shakespeare Business Centre
BRXN/ST SW9 ....40 B4
Shamel Business Centre
STRD ME2 ....19 G1
Shapla J & I School
WCHPL E1 ....24 D3
Shatterlocks Infant School
DVW CT17 ....291 J5
Shawcroft School
STMC/STPC BR5 ....87 M2
Shaw Primary School
SOCK/AV RM15 ....31 L2
Shears Green Primary School
GVW DA11 ....69 K2
Shearway Business Park
FOLKN CT19 ....310 C3
Sheerness Clinic
IOS ME12 ....57 L7
Sheerness Golf Club
IOS ME12 ....57 P9
Sheldon Business Centre
STRD ME2 ....72 D7
Sheldwich CP School
FAV ME15 ....162 F6
Shell & Dunkirk Memorials
DVW CT17 ....8 E5
Shenstone School
DART DA1 ....45 M6
Shepherd Neame Brewery
FAV ME15 ....132 F5
Shepherds Community School
BROCKY SE4 ....41 M4
Sheppey College
IOS ME12 ....57 K5
Sheppey Community Hospital
IOS ME12 ....78 A2
Sheppey Little Theatre
IOS ME12 ....57 M6
Sheppey RFC
IOS ME12 ....58 A9
Sheppey Yacht Club
IOS ME12 ....57 N6
Shepway Cross
HYTHE CT21 ....307 P5
Shepway Infant School
MAID/SHEP ME15 ....186 B3
Shepway Junior School
MAID/SHEP ME15 ....186 B3
Sherdale Business Centre
STRD ME2 ....18 B4
Sherington Primary School
CHARL SE7 ....26 C9
Sherwin Knight Primary
School *STRD* ME2 ....71 N9
Sherwood Park Infant
School *RTWE/PEM* TN2 ......270 G2
Sherwood Park Primary
School *BFN/LL* DA15 ....44 D7
RTWE/PEM TN2 ....270 G2
Sherwood Park School
WLGTN SM6 ....82 C7
Sherwood School
MTCM CR4 ....82 B1
Shipbourne Primary School
RTON TN11 ....180 F6
Shirley Clinic
CROY/NA CRO 83 P5
Shirley High School
CROY/NA CRO 84 A7
Shirley Oaks Hospital
CROY/NA CRO 83 P4
Shirley Park Golf Club
CROY/NA CRO 83 N6
Shirley Wanderers RFC
WWKM BR4 ....84 F8
Shiva Medical Clinic
IOS ME12 ....78 B1
Sholden CE Primary School
DEAL CT14 ....232 D4
Shooters Hill Golf Club
WOOL/PLUM SE18 ....43 N2
Shooters Hill Post 16 Campus
WOOL/PLUM SE18 ....43 L1
The Shopping Centre
MARG CT9 ....15 G4
Shoreham County Primary
School *RSEV* TN14 ....118 E5
Shorncliffe Military Cemetery
HYTHE CT21 ....309 P4
Shorne CE Primary School
GVE DA12 ....70 G4
Shorncliffe Industrial Estate
FOLK CT20 ....310 A7
Shorne Wood Country Park
GVE DA12 ....70 E7
Showcase Bluewater Cinema
GRH DA9 ....47 M9
Sibertswold Primary School
RDV CT15 ....259 P1
Sibton Park (School)
KFOLK CT18 ....256 G9
Sidcup Cemetery
BXLY DA5 ....64 F1
Sidcup Golf Club
BFN/LL DA15 ....64 C1
Sidcup Health Centre
SCUP DA14 ....64 C2

Sidcup Sports Club
SCUP DA14 ....64 B3
Sidney Cooper Gallery
CANT CT1 ....4 D3
Silver Screen Cinema
DVE/WH CT16 ....8 E3
FOLK CT20 ....11 F5
Simon Langton Grammar
School For Boys
CANT CT1 ....166 F8
Simon Langton Grammar
School for Girls
CANT CT1 ....166 G7
Simpsons Industrial Estate
RYE TN31 ....339 H9
Singleton Medical Centre
ASH TN25 ....252 A9
Singlewell Primary School
GVE DA12 ....69 P5
Sir Francis Drake Primary
School *DEPT* SE8 ....25 H8
Sir John Cass Foundation/
Redcoat School *WCHPL* E1 ...24 G1
Sir Joseph Williams Maths
School *ROCH* ME1 ....94 G5
Sir Roger Manwoods School
SWCH CT15 ....201 P2
Sir William Burrough Primary
School *POP/IOD* E14 ....25 H2
The Sir William Nottidge
Technology School
WSTB CT5 ....105 N6
Sissinghurst CE Primary
School *CRBK* TN17 ....276 D8
Site of Greenwich Hospital
CNWCH SE10 ....26 A8
Sittingbourne Adult
Education Centre *SIT* ME10 ...129 J4
Sittingbourne Industrial Park
SIT ME10 ....99 K9
SIT ME10 ....99 N9
Sittingbourne & Kemsley
Light Railway *SIT* ME10 ......100 A6
Sittingbourne Memorial
Hospital *SIT* ME10 ....129 N2
Sittingbourne & Milton Regis
Golf Club *RSIT* ME9 ....128 C2
Sittingbourne Retail Park
SIT ME10 ....99 M6
Sittingbourne Sports Centre
SIT ME10 ....129 P2
Six Bridges Trading Estate
STHWK SE1 ....24 D8
The Skinners Company
School *STH/RUST* TN4 ....270 D2
Skinner Street Primary School
GILL ME7 ....7 H1
Ski Slope
STMC/STPC BR5 ....64 F7
Slade Green FC
ERITH DA8 ....46 B2
Slade Green Primary School
ERITH DA8 ....46 A1
Slade Green School
TON TN9 ....210 E8
Sloane Hospital
BECK BR3 ....62 B7
Smallhythe Place (NT)
TENT TN30 ....320 G5
Smarden Business Estate
HDCN TN27 ....278 E1
Smarden Primary School
HDCN TN27 ....249 H7
Smeeth CP School
RASHE TN25 ....284 E3
Smiths Court Hotel
MARG CT9 ....112 G2
Smithy Street School
WCHPL E1 ....24 F1
Snodland CE Primary School
SNOD ME6 ....123 N5
Snodland Clinic
SNOD ME6 ....123 P5
Sodefield School
SEV TN13 ....179 H3
The Somerfield Hospital
MAIDW ME16 ....12 A3
Somers Heath Primary School
SOCK/AV RM15 ....31 K3
South Avenue Infant School
SIT ME10 ....129 P2
South Aylesford Retail Park
DIT/AY ME20 ....154 D4
Southborough Cemetery
STH/RUST TN4 ....240 A7
Southborough Primary School
HAYES BR2 ....86 B2
South Borough Primary
School *MAID/SHEP* ME15 ...185 M1
South Croydon Sports Club
SAND/SEL CR2 ....83 K9
Southfields School
GVE DA12 ....69 N4
South Kent College *ASH* TN25 ....2 E5
ASH TN23 ....282 C2
DVE/WH CT16 ....8 E4
FOLK CT20 ....10 B4
South Kent Hospital
FOLK CT20 ....310 B6
Southlake Primary School
ABYW SE2 ....28 C5
Southlands School
NROM TN28 ....337 H7
South Lewisham Health
Centre *CAT* SE6 ....62 A3
South London Gallery
CMBW SE5 ....40 E2
South London Tamil School
CROY/NA CRO 83 H4
South London Theatre
WNWD SE27 ....60 C2
South Norwood Country Park
SNWD SE25 ....83 P1

South Norwood Hill Medical
Centre *SNWD* SE25 ....60 E8
South Norwood Medical
Centre *SNWD* SE25 ....83 K1
South Norwood Pools &
Fitness Centre *SNWD* SE25 ...83 M2
South Norwood Sports Centre
SNWD SE25 ....83 M2
South of England Rare Breeds Centre
RASHW TN26 ....303 J6
South Park Hotel
SAND/SEL CR2 ....83 K8
South Quay Plaza
POP/IOD E14 ....25 L5
South Rise Primary School
WOOL/PLUM SE18 ....27 L8
Southwall Industrial Estate
DEAL CT14 ....232 G2
Southwark Cathedral
STHWK SE1 ....24 A4
Southwark College
BERM/RHTH SE16 ....24 E6
CMBW SE5 ....40 E1
Southwark Park Primary
School *BERM/RHTH* SE16 .....24 E6
Southwark Park Sports Centre
BERM/RHTH SE16 ....24 F7
Southwark Sports Ground
DUL SE21 ....40 F9
The Space Arts Centre Cinema
BERM/RHTH SE16 ....25 J7
The Spa Hotel
STH/RUST TN4 ....270 B5
Spa Industrial Park
RTWE/PEM TN2 ....241 H9
Spa Valley Railway
RRTW TN3 ....269 K8
Spectrum Business Centre
STRD ME2 ....72 E7
Spectrum Business Estate
MAID/SHEP ME15 ....186 C7
Speldhurst CE Primary School
RRTW TN3 ....269 M1
Spinnens Acre County Junior
School *MAID* ME5 ....126 A4
Spitalfields Market Hall
WCHPL E1 ....24 C1
Splashworld Swimming Centre
WELL DA16 ....44 F5
Spotlites Theatre Company
CHAT ME4 ....6 E5
Springfield Christian School
CAT SE6 ....61 M2
Springfield Industrial Estate
HAWK TN18 ....317 H5
Spring Grove School
RASHE TN25 ....223 M8
Spring Park Primary School
CROY/NA CRO 84 D7
Springvale Retail Park
STMC/STPC BR5 ....64 E9
STMC/STPC BR5 ....87 L2
Squerryes Court Manor House
& Gardens *BH/WHM* TN16 ...176 D4
Stade Court Hotel
HYTHE CT21 ....309 H6
Stafford Cross Business Park
CROY/NA CRO 82 E9
Stafford House Tutorial
College *CANT* CT1 ....166 G6
Stag Theatre
SEV TN13 ....21 F4
Stalham Business Centre
OBOR ME11 ....77 J4
Standard Industrial Estate
CAN/RD E16 ....26 E5
Stanhope CP School
ASH TN23 ....282 D3
Stanhope Industrial Park
SLH/COR SS17 ....34 E2
Stanley Technical High School
SNWD SE25 ....60 F9
Stansted CE Primary School
BGR/WK TN15 ....121 J4
Stanton Square Industrial
Estate *CAT* SE6 ....61 M3
Staplehurst Primary School
STPH/PW TN12 ....246 B6
Starborough Castle
EDEN TN8 ....236 A4
Star Business Centre
DAGW RM9 ....29 J1
Steam Tug 'Cervia'
RAM CT11 ....17 G5
Stebon Primary School
POP/IOD E14 ....25 J1
Stella Maris Catholic Primary
School *FOLKN* CT19 ....10 C1
Stelling Minnis CE Primary
School *RCANTW* CT4 ....226 E4
Stephen Hawking School
POP/IOD E14 ....25 H2
Stepney Day Hospital
WCHPL E1 ....24 F2
Stepney Greencoat CE Primary
School *POP/IOD* E14 ....25 J2
Stepney Green School
WCHPL E1 ....24 G1
Stewart Fleming Primary
School *PGE/AN* SE20 ....61 J9
Stifford Clays Health Centre
CDW/CHF RM16 ....32 C4
Stifford Clays Primary School
CDW/CHF RM16 ....32 C4
Stifford Primary School
GRAYS RM17 ....31 P8
Stillness Primary School
BROCKY SE4 ....41 L7
Stirling Way Industrial Estates
CROY/NA CRO 82 D1
Stocks Green Primary School
RTON TN11 ....210 B6
Stodmarsh National Nature
Reserve *RCANTE* CT3 ....168 E1

Stoke Community School
HOO/HM ME3 ....54 C3
Stone Bay School
BRDST CT10 ....113 N7
Stone Chapel
FAV ME13 ....132 B6
Stonegate CE Primary School
WADH TN5 ....314 D9
Stone House Hospital
RDART DA2 ....47 J7
Stone Lake Retail Park
CHARL SE7 ....26 D7
Storey Primary School
CAN/RD E16 ....27 H4
Stour Leisure Centre
KEN/WIL TN24 ....3 F5
Stour Retail Park
CANT CT1 ....167 J1
Stour Valley Industrial Estate
RCANTW CT4 ....165 M8
Stowting CE Primary School
RASHE TN25 ....256 A9
Streatham & Croydon RFC
THHTH CR7 ....82 F2
Streete Court School
GDST RH9 ....174 B6
Strood Cemetery
STRD ME2 ....18 A4
Strood Retail Park
STRD ME2 ....18 D2
Strood Swimming Pool
STRD ME2 ....18 A1
Strood Yacht Club
STRD ME2 ....18 C4
Sturry CE Primary School
CANTW/ST CT2 ....137 M6
Stutfall Castle
HYTHE CT21 ....307 M6
Summerlands Special School
HDCN TN27 ....221 J6
Sundridge & Brasted CE
Primary School *RSEV* TN14 ...177 M1
Sundridge Park Golf Club
BMLY BR1 ....62 G5
Surex Swimming Pools
BH/WHM TN16 ....115 N9
Surrey Docks Farm
BERM/RHTH SE16 ....25 J5
Surrey Docks Health Centre
BERM/RHTH SE16 ....25 H5
Surrey Docks Watersports
Centre *BERM/RHTH* SE16 .....25 H6
Surrey Quays Leisure Park
BERM/RHTH SE16 ....24 G6
Surrey Quays Shopping Centre
BERM/RHTH SE16 ....24 G6
Surrey Square J & I School
WALW SE17 ....24 A8
Sussex Road Primary School
TON TN9 ....240 D1
Sutcliffe Park Athletics Track
ELTH/MOT SE9 ....42 F6
Sutton at Hone CE Primary
School *EYN* DA4 ....66 G6
Sutton Valence Preparatory
School *RMAID* ME17 ....216 F2
Sutton Valence Primary
School *RMAID* ME17 ....217 H3
Sutton Valence School
RMAID ME17 ....216 G3
Swadelands Specialist School
RMAID ME17 ....189 K6
Swalecliffe Primary School
WSTB CT5 ....106 A4
The Swan Brewery
WBY/YAL ME18 ....182 B5
Swan Business Park
DART DA1 ....46 D5
Swanley School
SWLY BR8 ....65 M9
Swanscombe Business Centre
SWCM DA10 ....48 C6
Swan Valley Community
Woods *SWCM* DA10 ....48 D8
Sweetwoods Park Golf Club
EDEN TN8 ....267 H4
The Sweyne Junior School
SWCM DA10 ....48 D8
Swingate Infant School
DVE/WH CT16 ....125 P4
Sydenham Girls School
SYD SE26 ....61 H2
Sydenham High School Junior
Department *SYD* SE26 ....61 H3
Sydenham High School
(Secondary) *SYD* SE26 ....61 H2
Sydenham High School Sports
Ground *BECK* BR3 ....61 N4
Taberner House
CROY/NA CRO 83 H7
TA Centre
DVW CT17 ....291 K6
Tait Road Industrial Estate
CROY/NA CRO 83 J4
Tandridge Golf Club
OXTED RH8 ....174 F7
Tanmanry Trading Estate
TON TN9 ....210 F9
Target Business Centre
MAID/SHEP ME15 ....186 C7
Tatsfield Primary School
BH/WHM TN16 ....145 N6
Tavy Clinic
ABYW SE2 ....28 B5
TCA Leisure Centre
TIL RM18 ....49 L3
Teardrop Industrial Estate
SWLY BR8 ....89 H2
Technical Procurement
Sports Club *RASHE* TN25 ....252 E1
Temple Ewell CE Primary
School *DVE/WH* CT16 ....290 E1
Temple Hill Primary School
DART DA1 ....46 G6

Temple Mill Primary School
STRD ME2 ....72 B5
Temple of Bacchus
CMBW SE5 ....40 C3
Temple School
STRD ME2 ....72 B6
Tennis Club
GILL ME7 ....9 E6
Tenterden CE Junior School
TENT TN30 ....301 J8
Tenterden Golf Club
TENT TN30 ....301 L6
Tenterden Infant School
TENT TN30 ....301 H8
Tenterden Leisure Centre
TENT TN30 ....301 J8
Tenterden Vineyard Park
TENT TN30 ....320 G5
Terence Macklin Gallery
WSTB CT5 ....105 L4
Teynham Medical Centre
RSIT ME9 ....131 H3
Teynham Parochial CE
Primary School *RSIT* ME9 ...131 H3
Thames Barrier
CAN/RD E16 ....26 E5
Thames Barrier Information &
Learning Centre
WOOL/PLUM SE18 ....26 E6
Thameside Industrial Estate
CAN/RD E16 ....26 E4
Thameside Primary School
GRAYS RM17 ....32 D9
Thameside Theatre
GRAYS RM17 ....32 B8
Thames Industrial Park
TIL RM18 ....34 B7
Thamesmead Leisure Centre
THMD SE28 ....27 P5
Thamesmead Shopping Centre
THMD SE28 ....27 P5
Thamesview Business Centre
RAIN RM13 ....29 K1
Thames View Primary School
RHAM ME8 ....96 C4
Thamesview School
GVE DA12 ....70 B2
Thanet Business Centre
MARC CT9 ....15 J4
Thanet College
MARG CT9 ....15 G4
Thanet Crematorium
MARC CT9 ....112 D6
Thanet Reach Business Park
BRDST CT10 ....113 H9
Thanet Technical College
BRDST CT10 ....143 M1
Thanet Wanderers RUFC
BRDST CT10 ....113 L7
Thanington (Canterbury)
School of Music
CANTW/ST CT2 ....166 A6
Theatre Centre
BECK BR3 ....61 P8
Theatre Royal
MARC CT9 ....15 H4
Theodore McLeary
Primary School *EDUL* SE22 ....40 F5
Therapia Trading Estate
CROY/NA CR0 ....82 C4
Thistlebrook Industrial Estate
ABYW SE2 ....28 B6
The Thomas Aveling School
ROCH ME1 ....95 H6
Thomas Francis Academy
BRXN/ST SW9 ....40 B5
Thomas Peacocke Community
College *RYE* TN31 ....338 E6
Thomas Road Industrial Estate
POP/IOD E14 ....25 K1
Thomas Tallis School
BKHTH/KID SE3 ....42 F4
Thornhills Medical Centre
DIT/AY ME20 ....153 P3
Thornlea Health Centre
RDV CT15 ....229 P9
Thornton Heath Health Centre
THHTH CR7 ....83 H1
Thornton Heath Pools &
Fitness Centre *THHTH* CR7 .....83 H1
Thornton Road Industrial Estate
CROY/NA CR0 ....82 D3
Thorntree Primary School
CHARL SE7 ....26 E8
Thurlow Park School
WNWD SE27 ....60 B1
Thurrock Athletics Stadium
CDW/CHF RM16 ....32 E5
Thurrock & Basildon College
CDW/CHF RM16 ....32 G7
Thurrock Business Centre
WTHK RM20 ....31 J9
Thurston Industrial Estate
LEW SE13 ....41 P4
Ticehurst CE Primary School
WADH TN5 ....315 H6
Tidemill Primary School
DEPT SE8 ....41 N1
Tilbury Fort
TIL RM18 ....49 N5
Tilbury/Gravesend Passenger
Ferry *TIL* RM18 ....49 M5
Tilbury Manor Infant School
TIL RM18 ....49 M1
Tilbury Manor Junior School
TIL RM18 ....49 M1
Tiller Centre (Swimming Baths)
POP/IOD E14 ....25 K6
Tiller Leisure Centre
POP/IOD E14 ....25 K6
Tilling Green Infant School
RYE TN31 ....338 D7
Timbercroft Primary School
WOOL/PLUM SE18 ....44 A1

Titan Industrial Estate
GRAYS RM17 ....32 B7
Tivoli Industrial Estate
MARC CT9 ....15 F6
Tobacco Dock
WAP E1W 24 E3
Tollgate Primary School
WAP E1W 83 P5
Tomas Seth Business Park
QBOR ME11 ....77 J3
Tom Thumb Theatre
MARC CT9 ....112 G2
Tonbridge Castle
TON TN9 ....210 E8
Tonbridge Cemetery
TONN TN10 ....210 F5
Tonbridge FC (Longmead
Stadium) *RTON* TN11 ....210 E5
Tonbridge Grammar School
for Girls *TON* TN9 ....240 F2
Tonbridge Market
TON TN9 ....210 E8
Tonbridge Oast Theatre
RTON TN11 ....210 C6
Tonbridge RFC
TON TN9 ....210 E7
Tonbridge School
TONN TN10 ....210 E7
Tonbridge School Athletics
Track *TONN* TN10 ....210 E7
Tonbridge Swimming Pool
TON TN9 ....210 E8
Tonbridge Town Sailing Club
RTON TN11 ....239 P1
Torridon Primary School
CAT SE6 ....62 B1
Tovil Green Business Park
MAID/SHEP ME15 ....185 K2
The Tower Bridge Exhibition
STHWK SE1 ....24 C4
Tower Bridge Primary School
STHWK SE1 ....24 C5
Tower Bridge Wharf
WAP E1W 24 D4
Tower Hamlets College
POP/IOD E14 ....25 L3
WCHPL E1 ....24 F1
Tower Industrial Estate
BGR/WK TN15 ....120 G8
SNWD SE25 ....83 M1
Tower Medical Centre
WCHPL E1 ....24 D2
Tower of London
TWRH EC3N 24 C3
Tower Retail Park
DART DA1 ....45 P6
The Towers School
KEN/WIL TN24 ....252 C1
Tower Stairs
MON EC3R 24 B5
Townley Grammar School
for Girls *BXLYHS* DA6 ....45 H7
Town Medical Centre
SEV TN13 ....21 F4
Toy & Model Museum
RRTW TN3 ....273 K9
Tramshed Theatre
WOOL/PLUM SE'18 ....27 J7
Travel Inn
BGR/WK TN15 ....151 P4
CAN/RD E16 ....26 E5
CDW/CHF RM16 ....31 M6
EGKN RH19 ....264 D4
E/WMAL ME19 ....153 M1
FOLKN CT19 ....310 D4
GILL ME7 ....96 C4
GVW DA11 ....49 L7
GVW DA11 ....13 L6
KEN/WIL TN24 ....283 J3
MAID/BEAR ME14 ....157 K9
MAIDW ME16 ....154 C5
MAIDW ME16 ....155 J3
OXTED RH8 ....175 P2
RDR RM19 ....30 C8
RAIN RM13 ....30 C2
RASHE TN25 ....221 M8
RDV CT15 ....291 N5
RDV CT15 ....312 D2
SAND/SEL CR2 ....83 M9
SIT ME10 ....99 J8
WSTB CT5 ....105 K8
Travelodge
FAV ME15 ....164 G2
GRH DA9 ....47 L6
KEN/WIL TN24 ....252 F4
MSTR CT12 ....112 F9
POP/IOD E14 ....25 N2
WSTB CT5 ....134 F3
WTHK RM20 ....31 J6
Treetops Special School
GRAYS RM17 ....32 C7
Trefoil Montessori School
of Arts *LING* RH7 ....234 A1
Trenchwood Medical Centre
TONN TN10 ....210 F5
Trinity Business Centre
BERM/RHTH SE16 ....25 J3
Trinity College Centre
PECK SE15 ....40 E1
Trinity College of Music
GNWCH SE10 ....25 M9
Trinity Hospital
GNWCH SE10 ....25 N8
Trinity School
CROY/NA CR0 ....83 P6
Trinity School Belvedere
BELV DA17 ....29 H7
Trinity Theatre & Arts Centre
RTW TN1 ....22 D3
Trinity Trading Estate
SIT ME10 ....99 N8
Tripcock Point Development
Site *THMD* SE28 ....27 N3
Trosley Country Park
MEO DA13 ....122 B6

Trottiscliffe CE Primary School
E/WMAL ME19 ....122 B8
Tudor Court Primary School
CDW/CHF RM16 ....32 A5
Tudor House
MARC CT9 ....15 H3
Tuke School
PECK SE15 ....41 H2
Tunbridge Wells Borderers
Sports Club
RTWE/PEM TN2 ....270 D9
Tunbridge Wells Girls Grammar
School *STH/RUST* TN4 ....270 C2
Tunbridge Wells Golf Club
STH/RUST TN4 ....270 B5
Tunbridge Wells Grammar
School *STH/RUST* TN4 ....240 D9
Tunbridge Wells High School
RTWE/PEM TN2 ....271 H2
Tunbridge Wells Hockey Club
RTW TN1 ....270 E7
Tunbridge Wells Independent
Hospital *RRTW* TN3 ....268 G5
Tunbridge Wells Museum &
Art Gallery *RTW* TN1 ....22 D3
Tunbridge Wells Nuffield
Hospital *RTWE/PEM* TN2 ....23 J4
Tunbridge Wells Sports
Centre *STH/RUST* TN4 ....270 D1
Tunbury Primary School
WALD ME5 ....125 L4
Tunnel Avenue Trading Estate
GNWCH SE10 ....25 N5
Tunnel Industrial Estate
WTHK RM20 ....31 J7
Tunstall CE Primary School
RSIT ME9 ....129 K5
Turney School
DUL SE21 ....40 C8
Turnham Primary School
BROCKY SE4 ....41 L5
Twenty Twenty Industrial
Estate *MAIDW* ME16 ....155 H4
Two Chimneys Caravan Park
BRCH CT7 ....111 L8
Twydall Health & Welfare Clinic
RHAM ME8 ....96 E3
Twydall Infant School
RHAM ME8 ....96 E4
Twydall Junior School
RHAM ME8 ....96 E4
Tyrwhitt Drake Museum of
Carriages *MAID/SHEP* ME15 ...13 F6
UCI Cinema
BERM/RHTH SE16 ....24 C6
WTHK RM20 ....31 J7
UCI Filmworks Cinema
GNWCH SE10 ....26 A7
UGC Cinema
STRD SE2 ....94 D3
Ulcombe CE Primary School
RMAID ME17 ....218 A4
Underling Industrial Estate
STPH/PW TN12 ....215 L8
Unicorn Primary School
BECK BR3 ....84 E2
Union Mill
CRBK TN17 ....298 A3
University Hospital Lewisham
LEW SE13 ....41 N3
University of East London
EHAM E6 ....27 H3
University of Greenwich
DART DA1 ....66 F1
E/WMAL ME19 ....153 H8
ELTH/MOT SE9 ....43 P7
GNWCH SE10 ....25 N8
WOOL/PLUM SE18 ....27 H6
University of Greenwich at
Medway *CHAT* ME4 ....73 H7
University of Greenwich
(Mansion Site)
ELTH/MOT SE9 ....43 N7
University of Greenwich
Sports Ground
ELTH/MOT SE9 ....43 J5
ELTH/MOT SE9 ....43 N8
University of Kent at
Canterbury *CANTW/ST* CT2 ...136 C8
University of Kent Canterbury
CANTW/ST CT2 ....136 C9
University of London
NWCR SE14 ....41 L2
Upbury Arts College
GILL ME7 ....7 F4
Upchurch River Valley
Golf Club *RHAM* ME8 ....97 N4
Upland Primary School
BXLYHN DA7 ....45 H4
Upnor Castle
STRD ME2 ....72 F5
Upper Brents Industrial Estate
FAV ME15 ....132 G4
Upton Day Hospital
BXLYHS DA6 ....44 G5
Upton Junior School
BRDST CT10 ....113 L9
Upton Primary School
BXLY DA5 ....44 G6
Upton Road School
BXLYHS DA6 ....44 G6
Ursuline College & St Angela's
School *WGOS* CT8 ....111 L5
The Vale Medical Centre
FSTH SE23 ....61 L1
Vale School
BH/WHM TN16 ....176 G2
Vale View Community School
DVW CT17 ....291 J8
Valley Park Community School
MID/BEAR ME14 ....155 P8
Valley Primary School
HAYES BR2 ....62 D8
Valmar Trading Estate
CMBW SE5 ....40 C2

Vauxhall Road Industrial
Estate *DART* CT1 ....137 H9
Vestry Industrial Estate
RSEV TN14 ....148 G4
VI Components Industrial Park
ERITH DA8 ....29 K8
Victoria Business Centre
WELL DA16 ....44 C3
Victoria Hospital
DEAL CT14 ....232 G4
Victoria Hotel
CANTW/ST CT2 ....166 C3
Victoria Industrial Park
DART DA1 ....46 D6
Victoria Road Primary School
ASH TN23 ....2 C5
Victoria Wharf
POP/IOD E14 ....25 H3
Victoria Wharf Industrial
Estate *DEPT* SE8 ....25 J8
Vigo RFC
MEO DA13 ....122 D4
Vigo Village School
MEO DA13 ....122 B5
Viking Ship 'Hugin'
MSTR CT12 ....142 D7
The Vine Medical Centre
WELL DA16 ....155 J9
Vintners Park Crematorium
MAID/BEAR ME14 ....156 A6
VIP Trading Estate
CHARL SE7 ....26 D7
Virgo Fidelis Convent Schools
NRWD SE19 ....60 C5
Voyager Business Estate
BERM/RHTH SE16 ....24 D6
VUE Cinema
CROY/NA CR0 ....82 E6
WTHK RM20 ....31 K6
Vulcan Business Centre
CROY/NA CR0 ....115 H3
Waddon Clinic
CROY/NA CR0 ....82 F9
Waddon Infant School
CROY/NA CR0 ....82 F9
Wainscott Primary School
STRD ME2 ....72 D5
Wakeley Junior School
RHAM ME8 ....97 K5
Walderslade Medical Centre
WALD ME5 ....95 M8
Walderslade Primary School
WALD ME5 ....125 M2
Waldo Industrial Estate
BMLY BR1 ....62 G9
The Wallace Centre
DEPT SE8 ....25 J3
Wallett's Court Country
House Hotel *RDV* CT15 ....292 C1
Wallington County Grammar
School *WLCTN* SM6 ....82 A7
Walmer Castle & Gardens
DEAL CT14 ....233 J8
Walmer & Kingsdown Golf
Club *DEAL* CT14 ....263 J4
Walmer Lawn Tennis &
Croquet Club *DEAL* CT14 ....233 J7
Walnut Leisure Centre
ORP BR6 ....87 H5
Walnuts Shopping Centre
ORP BR6 ....87 H5
Walworth Lower School
WALW SE17 ....24 A8
Walworth Upper School
WALW SE17 ....24 B8
Wapping Sports Centre
WAP E1W 24 E4
Wapping Wharf
WAP E1W 24 F4
Warden House Primary School
DEAL CT14 ....232 N4
Wardens Medical Centre
TON TN9 ....210 F8
Warehouse Theatre
CROY/NA CR0 ....83 J6
Warlingham Park School
WARL CR6 ....144 D1
Warlingham Sports Club
WARL CR6 ....144 A2
Warmlake Business Estate
RMAID ME17 ....217 H1
Warren Primary School
CDW/CHF RM16 ....31 M6
Warren Retail Park
KEN/WIL TN24 ....252 E5
Warren Road Primary School
ORP BR6 ....86 G8
Warren Wood CP School
ROCH ME1 ....95 H6
Warsop Trading Estate
EDEN TN8 ....236 E1
Warwick Leadlay Gallery
GNWCH SE10 ....25 M9
Waterfront Leisure Centre
WOOL/PLUM SE18 ....27 H6
Watergate School
CAT SE6 ....61 P4
LEW SE13 ....41 P5
Watermill Museum
EDEN TN8 ....235 N1
Watling Street Surgery
CANT CT1 ....4 D5
Watts Charity Almshouses
ROCH ME1 ....13 H3
Wavelengths Leisure Pool &
Library *DEPT* SE8 ....41 N1
Waverley Lower Secondary
School *EDUL* SE22 ....41 H6
Waverley School
PECK SE15 ....41 J6
Wayfield County Primary
School *WALD* ME5 ....95 M4
Weald Community Primary
School *RSEV* TN14 ....178 G9

Weald of Kent Golf Club
HDCN TN27 ....217 K9
The Weald of Kent Grammar
School *TON* TN9 ....240 G2
Weald Sports Centre
CRBK TN17 ....297 P1
Wellesley House School
BRDST CT10 ....143 L1
The Welling Clinic
WELL DA16 ....44 C5
Welling Medical Centre
WELL DA16 ....44 B5
Welling School
WELL DA16 ....44 D2
Welling United FC
WELL DA16 ....44 E4
Wennington Hall Farm
Business Centre *RAIN* RM13 ...30 B2
The Wernher Collection at
Ranger's House
GNWCH SE10 ....42 B2
Wesley Sports Centre
FAV ME15 ....132 G7
West Beckton Health Centre
CAN/RD E16 ....26 D1
West Borough CP School
MAIDW ME16 ....154 G9
West Borough Sports Centre
MAIDW ME16 ....155 H9
Westbrooke School
WELL DA16 ....44 F4
Westcourt Primary School
GVE DA12 ....70 A1
Westerham Golf Club
BH/WHM TN16 ....176 G2
Westfield Business Centre
STRD ME2 ....19 E1
Westgate Archway & Museum
CANTW/ST CT2 ....4 D3
Westgate & Birchington
Golf Club *WGOS* CT8 ....111 L5
Westgate College Rnid
WGOS CT8 ....111 J9
Westgate Hall
CANTW/ST CT2 ....4 D3
Westgate Pavilion & Theatre
WGOS CT8 ....111 M3
Westgate Primary School
DART DA1 ....46 D8
West Gate Towers
CANT CT1 ....4 E3
West Hill Primary School
DART DA1 ....46 C7
West India Pier
POP/IOD E14 ....25 J5
West India Shopping Centre
POP/IOD E14 ....25 K4
West Kent College
TON TN9 ....240 D1
West Kent College of
Further Education
STH/RUST TN4 ....270 D1
West Kent Golf Club
ORP BR6 ....115 P6
West Kingsdown Industrial
Estate *BGR/WK* TN15 ....120 B3
West Kingsdown Medical
Centre *BGR/WK* TN15 ....120 C3
Westlands School
SIT ME10 ....129 J1
West Lane Trading Estate
SIT ME10 ....99 P9
West Lodge Preparatory
School *BFN/LL* DA15 ....64 B2
West Malling CE Primary
School *E/WMAL* ME19 ....153 J4
West Malling Golf Club
E/WMAL ME19 ....152 D2
West Malling Industrial Park
E/WMAL ME19 ....152 F2
Westmeads Community Infant
School *WSTB* CT5 ....105 L5
Westminster Industrial Estate
WOOL/PLUM SE18 ....26 E6
West Minster Primary School
IOS ME12 ....57 J8
Westmount Centre
DVW CT17 ....8 A4
West Norwood Clinic
WNWD SE27 ....60 C1
West Norwood Crematorium
WNWD SE27 ....60 C2
West Thamesmead Business
Park *THMD* SE28 ....27 N6
West Thornton Primary School
CROY/NA CR0 ....82 E4
West Thurrock Primary School
WTHK RM20 ....31 K9
West View Hospital
TENT TN30 ....300 F9
West Wickham Swimming
Baths *WWKM* BR4 ....84 F5
Westwood College
WELL DA16 ....43 P5
Westwood Industrial Estate
MARC CT9 ....112 F7
Westwood Language College
for Girls *NRWD* SE19 ....60 C6
Westwood Primary School
WELL DA16 ....44 A5
Whaddon House Clinic
CMBW SE5 ....40 E4
Wheelbarrow Park Estate
PADD W2 / *HDCN* TN27 ....244 G2
White Cliffs Business Park
DVE/WH CT16 ....291 H1
White Cliffs Experience
DVE/WH CT16 ....8 D4
Whitefriars
CANT CT1 ....4 E5
Whitehall Industrial Estate
MSTR CT12 ....143 H5
Whitehill Infant School
GVE DA12 ....69 N2

Whitehorse Manor Primary
School *THHTH* CR7 ....83 J1
Whitehouse Surgery
DVW CT17 ....8 A4
The Whitemill Museum
SWCH CT13 ....171 M9
White Oak Primary School
SWLY BR8 ....65 N8
Whitfield CP School
DVE/WH CT16 ....261 H9
Whitfield Surgery
DVE/WH CT16 ....261 H9
Whitgift Almshouses
CROY/NA CR0 ....83 H6
Whitgift School
SAND/SEL CR2 ....83 H9
Whitgift Shopping Centre
CROY/NA CR0 ....83 H6
Whitstable County Junior
School *WSTB* CT5 ....105 L5
Whitstable Health Centre
WSTB CT5 ....105 L5
Whitstable Museum & Gallery
WSTB CT5 ....105 L5
Whitstable RFC
WSTB CT5 ....106 B4
Whitstable St Alphege CE
Primary & Infants School
WSTB CT5 ....105 L5
Whitstable & Seasalter CE
Junior School *WSTB* CT5 ....105 M4
Whitstable & Seasalter Golf
Club *WSTB* CT5 ....105 K5
Whitstable & Tankerton
Hospital *WSTB* CT5 ....105 P4
Whitstable Yacht Club
WSTB CT5 ....105 L4
Wickhambreaux CE Primary
School *RCANTE* CT3 ....168 F6
Wickham Court School
WWKM BR4 ....84 C8
Wickham Theatre
WWKM BR4 ....84 C7

Widmore Centre
BMLY BR1 ....62 G8
Wildernesse Golf Club
BGR/WK TN15 ....149 M7
Wildernesse School
BGR/WK TN15 ....149 K6
Wildernesse Sports Centre
BGR/WK TN15 ....149 K6
Wildwood Wildlife Park
HB CT6 ....137 K1
Willesborough Health Centre
KEN/WIL TN24 ....283 J1
Willesborough Industrial Park
KEN/WIL TN24 ....253 K8
Willesborough Primary School
KEN/WIL TN24 ....253 K9
William Edwards School
CDW/CHF RM16 ....32 D3
William Harvey Hospital
KEN/WIL TN24 ....253 M8
Willow Bank Industrial Estate
RSIT ME9 ....76 C9
Willow Business Park
SYD SE26 ....61 J2
Willowfield School
HNHL SE24 ....40 C5
The Willows Clinic
CHST BR7 ....63 L5
Wilmington Boys Grammar
School *RDART* DA2 ....66 B2
Wilmington Grammar School
for Girls *RDART* DA2 ....66 B1
Wilmington Hall School
RDART DA2 ....66 A2
Wilmington Primary School
RDART DA2 ....66 B2
Winchcombe Business Centre
PECK SE15 ....24 B9
Wincheap Industrial Estate
CANT CT1 ....4 B7
Wincheap Park & Ride
CANT CT1 ....166 B6

Wincheap Primary School
CANT CT1 ....166 D6
Windmill Business Centre
MEO DA13 ....92 A7
Windmill Trading Estate
MTCM CR4 ....82 B2
Windrush Primary School
THMD SE28 ....28 A4
Wingfield Primary School
BKHTH/KID SE3 ....42 E4
Wingham Bird Park
RCANTE CT3 ....169 M7
Wingham Business Centre
RCANTE CT3 ....169 L9
Wingham Industrial Estate
RCANTE CT3 ....199 L1
Wingham Primary School
RCANTE CT3 ....169 K9
Winsor Primary School
EHAM E6 ....27 H2
Winston Churchill's Britain at
War Experience
STHWK SE1 ....24 B4
Winterbourne Infant School
THHTH CR7 ....82 F1
Wittersham CE Primary
School *TENT* TN50 ....332 A3
Woldingham Golf Club
WARL CR6 ....144 A5
Woldingham School
GDST RH9 ....174 B1
Wolsey Junior School
CROY/NA CR0 ....114 G2
Woodacre Special School
SOCK/AV RM15 ....31 J1
Woodbrook School
BECK BR3 ....61 M7
Woodchurch CE Primary
School *RASHW* TN26 ....302 F4
Woodfalls Business Centre
WBY/YAL ME18 ....213 L4
Woodhill Primary School
CHARL SE7 ....26 F7

Woodlands Health Centre
STPH/PW TN12 ....242 G2
Woodlands Manor Golf Club
BGR/WK TN15 ....120 A8
Woodlands Medical Centre
LEW SE13 ....42 B7
Woodlands Park
HDCN TN27 ....278 E9
Woodlands Primary School
GILL ME7 ....96 C2
TONN TN10 ....211 H4
Woodlands Road Cemetery
GILL ME7 ....96 C1
Woodlea Primary School
CTHM CR3 ....144 C7
Woodside Health Centre
SNWD SE25 ....83 N2
Woodside Infants School
CROY/NA CR0 ....83 M4
Woodside Primary School
CDW/CHF RM16 ....32 G6
Woodside School
BELV DA17 ....28 G7
Wood Wharf
POP/IOD E14 ....25 L4
Wood Wharf Business Park
POP/IOD E14 ....25 M5
Woolmans Wood Caravan
Park *WALD* ME5 ....125 H1
Woolmore Primary School
POP/IOD E14 ....25 M3
Woolpack Corner
HDCN TN27 ....278 B9
Woolwich Cemetery
WOOL/PLUM SE18 ....44 B1
Woolwich County Court
WOOL/PLUM SE18 ....27 H6
Woolwich Crown Court
THMD SE28 ....27 M5
Woolwich Polytechnic School
THMD SE28 ....27 P4
World End
TIL RM18 ....49 M5

Worsley Bridge Junior School
BECK BR3 ....61 N6
Worth CP School
DEAL CT14 ....202 A5
Wotton Trading Estate
ASH TN23 ....282 E2
Wrencote
CROY/NA CR0 ....83 H7
Wren Industrial Estate
MAID/SHEP ME15 ....186 C7
Wrotham Heath Golf Club
BGR/WK TN15 ....152 A5
Wrotham Road Health Clinic
GVW DA11 ....49 M9
Wrotham Road Primary School
GVW DA11 ....49 M8
Wrotham Secondary School
BGR/WK TN15 ....151 K3
Wyborne Primary School
ELTH/MOT SE9 ....43 M9
Wye Business Park
RASHE TN25 ....223 P7
Wye Crown
RASHE TN25 ....224 D8
The Wyvern School
KEN/WIL TN24 ....253 J8
Yalding Organic Gardens
WBY/YAL ME18 ....213 N3
Yalding St Peter & St Paul
WBY/YAL ME18 ....213 P1
Yew Tree Industrial Estate
DIT/AY ME20 ....154 C2
Yew Tree Park
RCANTW CT4 ....196 C9
York Road Junior School &
Language Unit
DART DA1 ....46 F8
Ypres Tower
RYE TN31 ....338 F7
Zobel College
SEV TN13 ....21 F2

Acknowledgements

The Post Office is a registered trademark of Post Office Ltd. in the UK and other countries.

Schools address data provided by Education Direct.

Petrol station information supplied by Johnsons

One-way street data provided by © Tele Atlas N.V. *Tele Atlas* ◄

Garden centre information provided by

Garden Centre Association  Britains best garden centres

Wyevale Garden Centres

The boundary of the London congestion charging zone supplied by
Transport for London

The statement on the front cover of this atlas is sourced, selected and quoted
from a reader comment and feedback form received in 2004.

Notes

Notes

Notes